THE DIARY OF
ELIHU HUBBARD SMITH
1771-1798

Memoirs of the

AMERICAN PHILOSOPHICAL SOCIETY

Held at Philadelphia

For Promoting Useful Knowledge

VOLUME 95

Elihu Hubbard Smith by James Sharples or Ellen Wallace Sharples.
Courtesy of Yale University Art Gallery.

THE DIARY OF

ELIHU HUBBARD SMITH

(1771-1798)

Edited by

JAMES E. CRONIN
Wesleyan University

AMERICAN PHILOSOPHICAL SOCIETY
INDEPENDENCE SQUARE · PHILADELPHIA
1973

Copyright © 1973 by the American Philosophical Society

Library of Congress Catalog
Card Number 72-83462

International Standard Book Number 0-87169-095-0

To

Elizabeth, Phoebe, and Timothy

Acknowledgments

My prolonged connection with this "Diary" of Elihu Hubbard Smith goes back thirty years during the course of which a number of individuals to whom I am much indebted have died. These include Professor Stanley T. Williams, who told me of the existence of the "Diary" and who was my adviser for my Yale doctoral dissertation, a biography of Smith; Miss Frances G. Colt, a collateral descendant of Smith who owned the manuscript, permitted me to keep it for years, and originally gave me permission to publish it; and Carl Rollins, printer for the Yale University Press, who supplied me with the typescript for much of the "Diary."

To Miss Elizabeth Thomson, Research Associate at the Yale Medical Library and to Whitfield J. Bell, Jr., Librarian of the American Philosophical Society, I owe lasting gratitude for their advice, their interest in the Smith manuscript and their assistance in finding a publisher for it. I am indebted to Yale University Librarian Rutherford D. Rogers and Stanley D. Truelson of the Medical Library for permission to publish the manuscript which Yale now holds.

For their courteous help, I wish to thank the librarians and staffs of the Yale, Harvard, Wesleyan, and University of Pennsylvania libraries, the New York, Boston, Philadelphia, and Litchfield public libraries, the Morgan Library, the Library of Congress, the Surgeon General's Library, the Library Company of Philadelphia, and the Historical Societies of Litchfield, Fairfield, Connecticut, New York, and Pennsylvania. I would like to note especially the generous assistance of the staff of the Yale Medical Library, and Miss Polly Pierce, Curator of the Historical Room, Stockbridge Library.

A substantial grant-in-aid and a three-month leave from Wesleyan did much to speed my editorial efforts at a critical time.

To friends at Wesleyan I am grateful, particularly to University Archivist John W. Spaeth, Jr., Professors Arthur R. Schultz, and Arthur R. Upgren, Jr., for advice, to Mrs. Louise B. Smith, Mrs. Adair W. Bather and Mrs. Laura C. Calhoun of my office for skillful and gracious assistance. Finally, to my wife Elizabeth whose connection with the "Diary" is as old as mine, my deepest gratitude for her help.

I am, of course, solely responsible for any errors of fact or aberrations of interpretation to be found here.

J.E.C.

June, 1971

Contents

	PAGE
A Glossary of Names Frequently Mentioned in the Diary	xi
Introduction	1
Notes from Recollections of My Life from My Birth till the Age of Eleven	17
Reuben Hitchcock	36
Thomas O'Hara Croswell	40
The "Diary"	43
Notebook No. 1: September-October, 1795	43
Notebook No. 2: October, 1795-March, 1796	77
Notebook No. 3: March-July, 1796	144
Notebook No. 4: August-November, 1796	196
Notebook No. 5: November, 1796-September, 1797	254
Notebook No. 6: September, 1797-September, 1798	360
Genealogy	465
Index	469

A Glossary of
Names Frequently Mentioned in the Diary

Only a few of the individuals mentioned by Smith are listed here. Some names were omitted because they are fully identified in the text, others because they are of no importance or so well known that they need no gloss.

Adams, Charles—Harvard 1789, M.A. also 1789. New York attorney, notary public, son of President John Adams. Through him Smith met and dined with the President.

Alsop, Richard—sometime businessman, minor poet, dilettante, son of a wealthy shipowner and merchant. Associated with Smith and others in the writing of *The Echo* and other pieces.

Barlow, Joel—Yale 1778, a soldier, lawyer, Connecticut Wit, author of *The Columbiad*. He spent most of his middle years abroad. He represented America at various times, as consul to Algiers and as minister to France. Although his politics were far more liberal than Smith's by the 1790's, they remained friendly.

Barton, Benjamin Smith, M.D.—professor of botany at the University of Pennsylvania. Like many doctors of the time, he published on a wide variety of subjects.

Beers, Isaac—famous New Haven bookseller.

Bird, John—Yale 1786. Childhood associate of Smith who became a brilliant and eccentric lawyer in Troy, New York, member of Congress (1799-1801), again elected to fill a vacancy in 1803.

Bringhurst, Joseph—friend of Smith from his Philadelphia days; with C. B. Brown he founded the "*Belles Lettres* Club," a typical eighteenth-century literary society. It later became "The Society for the Attainment of Useful Knowledge."

Brown, Charles Brockden—first professional American novelist, his works noted for their psychological motivation. Of his novels, see *Arthur Mervyn* (1799) for a picture of a yellow-fever epidemic of the sort which Smith also describes. This Diary is the source of much of our knowledge of his nature and disposition.

Catlin, Lynde—Yale 1786. Childhood associate of Smith, protégé of John Jacob Astor, cashier of the New York Branch Bank of the United States and, from 1820 until his death in 1833, president of the Merchant's Bank.

Champion, The Rev. Judah—pastor of Congregational Church, Litchfield, 1753-1810. A chaplain in the Revolution, Champion is well spoken of except in Smith's vitriolic account.

Cogswell, Mason Fitch—Yale 1780. Brilliant surgeon, famous humanitarian, better than average versifier, associated with Smith and others in the writing of *The Echo* and other pieces. Credited with being first American doctor to remove a cataract successfully, the first to tie the carotid artery, a principal in the establishment of the Deaf and Dumb Asylum in Hartford, the first in America, one of the founders of the Connecticut Retreat for the Insane.

Collier, Thomas—publisher and printer of the *Litchfield Monitor*, 1784-1807.

Cope, Thomas Pym—Philadelphian, friend of Smith. As owner of a line of packet ships he became one of the wealthiest men of his day.

Dennie, Joseph—Harvard 1790, a lawyer who much preferred journalism. The moving force in a group of young writers in New Hampshire similar to the earlier Wits in Connecticut. As editor of *The Farmer's Weekly Museum* in Walpole Dennie, always on the lookout for writers, found Smith and tried to enlist him as a contributor.

Dingley, Amasa—native of Marshfield, Massachusetts, Harvard 1785, a New York physician. Smith did not like him.

Dunlap, William—early in his career a student of Benjamin West in London. Portrait painter, art historian, biographer, publisher, theater manager and producer; first professional American dramatist, he wrote or adapted more than sixty plays.

Dwight, Theodore—attorney, politician, minor poet, younger brother to Timothy Dwight and a lesser light. Lifetime friend, and associate of Smith and others in the writing of *The Echo* and other pieces. Served as Federalist representative from Connecticut in the Ninth Congress, December, 1806-March, 1807. Founded the *New York Daily Advertiser ca.* 1817.

Dwight, Timothy—one of the most famous divines and teachers of his century, grandson of Jonathan Edwards, Connecticut Wit, head of the Academy at Greenfield Hill (thought by many to be better than Yale), president of Yale.

Fenno, John—Federalist, editor of the *Gazette of the United States,* who was aided by prominent Federalists, especially Hamilton. He engaged in controversy with Benjamin Bache's paper, the *Aurora* and Philip Freneau's *National Gazette.*

Gahn, Henry—Swedish chemist who introduced Smith to the Venetian physician and diplomat, Dr. Scandella. Smith died of yellow fever while unsuccessfully attempting to save Scandella from the same disease.

Genet, Citizen—turbulent, troublesome central figure in an intrigue apparently designed to involve the United States in France's quarrel with England.

Godwin, William—radical political philosopher, source of occasional inspiration for Wordsworth, Coleridge, and Southey. Smith and his friends knew almost by heart his most famous book, *Inquiry Concerning Political Justice and its Influence on General Virtue and Happiness* (1793).

Hillhouse (probably James)—Yale 1773. United States representative and senator. Another brother William was a New Haven lawyer. The poet, James Hillhouse (1789-1841), was the senator's son.

Hitchcock, Reuben—Yale (Berkeley Scholar) 1786. Smith's long-suffering roommate who became a minister and died young.

Hopkins, Lemuel—physician, one of the original Connecticut Wits with Timothy Dwight, Trumbull, Barlow, and Humphreys. A half-brother to Samuel's father.

Hopkins, Samuel M.—Yale 1791. An attorney.

Jay, John—Chief Justice of the United States Supreme Court, governor of New York. In 1794 he represented the United States in London to arrange with Lord Grenville for settlement of dangerous problems arising from various debt questions and British occupations of the Northwest Posts.

Johnson, H.—friend of Smith, businessman.

Johnson, Seth—friend of Smith, businessman.

Johnson, William—Yale 1788, M.A. 1792; L.L.D. Hamilton 1819 and Princeton 1820. Died 1848. Brother to two above, Smith's roommate, an attorney, who later, as a reporter of the Supreme Court and of the Court of Chancery, was to acquire a massive legal reputation. A long-time associate of Chancellor James Kent who dedicated his *Commentaries* to him.

Johnson, William—a physician, almost certainly not an M.D., not related to Smith's roommate. He was a poet and translator of considerable ability who died young.

Kent, James—Yale 1781. When Smith knew him, a struggling young lawyer, often lastingly horrified by Smith's heresies. A failure as a professor of law (Columbia College, 1793-1798), Kent became judge of the New York Supreme Court and chancellor of the New York Court of Chancery, the first American judge to achieve an international reputation through his *Commentaries.*

Lewis, Daniel L.—Yale 1788. Lawyer, state's attorney for Connecticut.

Lovegrove (Mr. and Mrs.)—an English couple, he, according to Smith, a lout, she a sentimental, discontented lady ideally suited to attract an inexperienced young man. She had some pretentions to intellectualism, knew Hannah More and had a friend, Miss Norton, who was an acquaintance "of a promising young genius . . . whose name is Coldridge [*sic*] & who is soon to publish a volume of poems."

Miller, Edward, M.D.—with Dr. Samuel Mitchill and Smith he founded the *Medical Repository* in 1797. (Another younger Dr. Miller deserted New York and left his practice, such as it was, to Smith, in 1793.)

Mitchill, Samuel L., M.D.—prominent New York doctor; joint editor of the *Medical Repository.*

Mumford, Thomas—Yale 1790. An attorney, husband of Smith's sister Mary.

GLOSSARY OF NAMES

Pierce—a Litchfield family. Sally, Smith's schoolmate and friend, opened her own school in her dining room with one pupil in 1792, later highly successful. She prepared Henry Ward Beecher for college. Her brother Timothy after six months of instruction under Smith in New York went home to practice medicine.

Reeve, Tapping—Connecticut attorney, head of a law school in Litchfield, perhaps the most famous of its time. Married to Aaron Burr's sister. Noah Webster attended this school.

Rush, Benjamin, M.D.—responsible to a notable degree for reputation which Philadelphia gained as the medical center of the nation, delegate from Pennsylvania to the Continental Congress, a signer of the Declaration of Independence (immediately after Franklin), Surgeon General of the Armies of the Middle States. A man of extraordinary ability, a perfectionist; his friends while excellent were not numerous.

Sheldon, Daniel, M.D.—in whose tiny medical school in Litchfield (six pupils) Smith studied. A frail-looking little man, he took from two to four drachms of opium daily for forty years but in his old age freed himself of the habit "without detriment" by gradually reducing his dose. He prescribed substantial doses of opium for his patients but also recommended a careful diet and horseback riding. His reputation as "a skillful physician, diligent and observing" is not substantiated in Smith's remarks.

Stiles, Ezra—president of Yale, considered by many to be dangerously tolerant of liberal ideas to which he had been addicted himself in his youth.

Strong, Jedidiah—one of Litchfield's most important citizens, a judge who fell spectacularly apart through drink.

Strong, Idea—long-suffering daughter of Jedidiah Strong.

Tracy, Uriah—Yale 1778. Prominent Federalist lawyer and politician, representative and senator from Connecticut, confidante of Hamilton and Adams.

Tracy, Mrs. Uriah (Susan Bull)—one of Smith's first teachers who retained her beauty. She fascinated Smith all of his life.

Turner, George—a New York resident who became judge of the North Western territory.

Watson, James—Yale 1776, a lawyer who practiced in Connecticut and moved to New York in 1786. He served as U.S. senator for two years to fill a vacancy. Smith knew him as a member of the Board of Governors of New York Hospital.

Webster, Noah—Yale 1778, his connections with Smith, thirteen years his junior, were numerous. He was Smith's music teacher in Litchfield. After moving to New York, Webster published the daily *Minerva* and the weekly *Herald*. An authority on the fever himself, recognized as such even by Benjamin Rush who at first opposed him, he valued Smith's studies and published his essay on yellow fever in 1796. He visited Smith frequently, sought his advice on manuscripts, and in 1795 tried to interest Smith in becoming his partner. The abilities, interests and enthusiasms of the two young men were strikingly similar.

Wolcott, Frederic—childhood associate of Smith who, overshadowed by his famous brother and father, had a long but not distinguished political career.

Woolsey, William—he and his brothers welcomed Smith to their homes in New York. William became one of New York's most successful businessmen, president of a bank, a railroad, an insurance company and Bible society, and father of one of Yale's greatest presidents, Theodore Dwight Woolsey.

THE DIARY OF
ELIHU HUBBARD SMITH

To those into whose hands my papers may come, when I cease to exist, they will be valuable: for my connections in many instances, have been with those, who either have been, or promise to be, in some good measure, distinguished actors in the scene around me.

If my present resolution hold, this plan will not be limited to those who merit to be called my friends; but will be extended to a variety of characters—perhaps more interesting, on some accounts to the Historian and Philosopher.

Elihu Hubbard Smith

Introduction

THE TEXT

What remains of Elihu Hubbard Smith's manuscript diary, which he variously entitled "Diary," "Journal," and "Memoirs," is a set of six hard-cover notebooks, varying slightly in size, but approximately five inches by seven inches. The earliest is marked "Vol. III." The first daily entry is for Friday, September 4, 1795. The final entry in the last notebook, three-hundred-fifty thousand words later, is for September 15, 1798, four days before his death.

The missing volumes, I and II, were probably destroyed by Smith himself after he had copied from them sections which he considered worth saving: these include a full-blown, overwritten "Introduction" to "Vol. I" and some of the autobiographical account of his early years. If the style of the "Introduction" is an indication of that for the remainder of "Vol. I" he showed good taste in destroying it. He remarks that "Vol. II" was mostly concerned with "Miss E.A.K." (otherwise unidentified) and that it was full of "querulous repining." By October 6, 1796, he could note coolly that he had met her again, that she was married "and carried the evidence with her." In a copy of a letter to Theodore Dwight, dated June 5, 1796, which appears in the "Diary," Smith wrote: "About two years since, I commenced a diary, a journal. . . . I have continued this journal ever since." This would date the beginning of the lost section approximately June, 1794, nine months after Smith arrived in New York.

The manuscript volumes are as follows:

Notebook #1: "The Diary of E. H. Smith, Vol. III" (September, 1795-October, 1795).

Notebook #2: "The Diary of E. H. Smith, Vol. IV" (October, 1795-December, 1795). "The Diary of E. H. Smith, Vol. V" (January, 1796-March, 1796).

Notebook #3: "The Journal of E. H. Smith, New Series, Vol. I" (March, 1796-July, 1796).

Notebook #4: "The Journal of E. H. Smith, New Series, Vol. II" (August, 1796-November, 1796).

Notebook #5: "Memoirs: or Notices concerning the Life, Studies, Opinions, and Friends, of E. H. Smith, Vol. I" (November, 1796-September, 1797).

Notebook #6: "Memoirs: or Notices concerning the Life, Studies, Opinions, and Friends, of E. H. Smith, Vol. II" (September, 1797-September, 1798).

Smith experimented continually with the diary form, as the changing titles indicate, and no two volumes are alike. Some abound in weekly or monthly summaries, with long adjurations to himself to live better, to tend to his profession, to discover ways to make enough money to get out of debt; others contain first drafts or copies of most, if not all, of the letters he wrote during various periods, over one hundred eighty in all. Occasionally he interspersed his daily entries with medical or literary essays. As he became somewhat more successful, or perhaps simply more involved in New York life, the letters in the "Diary" become more numerous but shorter. After February, 1798, except for copying his family letters, he almost abandoned the habit.

During the last months of his life his style became terse and choppy, abounding in sentence fragments and devoid of any attempts at grace. Although the "Diary" never sinks to the level of William Dunlap's ungrammatical semi-shorthand or Noah Webster's unrivaled terseness, it moves in that direction. Even the handwriting, so exquisitely fine and regular in the beginning, degenerates to a scrawl difficult to decipher.

Almost all of the "Diary," as such, is reprinted here, that is, his daily entries, introductions and summaries for each month, and his letters, most of which he copied. Smith's indexes for each volume are omitted. Other omitted material falls principally into four categories: his letters to William Buel on the fever, which were published by Noah Webster; essays, short articles or medical notes, most of which appeared in *The Medical Repository*; occasional notes on books which he read, or fragments of his attempts at translating short sections of various French works; an incomplete "Utopia." Such deletions, except for the indexes, are identified and noted in the text where they occur.

Some liberty has been taken in the arrangement of textual material in order to approximate the form it would have had if the lost volumes had been preserved and also to present an almost complete chronological account of his life. For example, the section entitled "Notes from recollection of my life, from my birth till the age of eleven" has been set at the beginning although this section is found in the final quarter of the manuscript. Such rearrangements have been indicated in each instance.

In transcription, the original punctuation, spelling and misspelling (including his almost invariable misspelling of Litchfield) have been maintained with two general exceptions: dashes have been omitted when they followed or preceded periods or other marks in such a way as to constitute double punctuation; Smith's use of superior letters in abbreviations, such as W^m, rec^d, Septr has been abandoned and replaced by Wm., recd., Septr. to simplify the typography. As a matter of common sense, the infrequent misspellings resulting from haste, such as "th" for "the" and "an" for "and" have been repaired without comment. When he deleted words and inserted others only his final judgment is printed.

EDITING

In the footnotes, biographical commonplace information of the "Dictionary of Biography" sort is generally based on one or more of the following sources: Franklin

B. Dexter, *Yale Biographies and Annuals* (New York, 1911); *Biographical Directory of the American Congress, 1774-1927* (U.S. Government Printing Office, 1928); *The Dictionary of American Biography* (American Council of Learned Societies, New York, 1928). Frequent debt to these sources is hereby acknowledged but not hereafter cited.

It was the intention of the editor to identify each book or play that Smith actually read, each play that he saw (the date given is that of first performance), and each incident or individual of consequence. Inevitably, some major figure will have been overlooked, but this is probably better than giving a degree of literary immortality to every sufferer from a cold in the head who came to Smith for relief, or any casual stroller who passed him on the street.

HISTORY OF THE MANUSCRIPT

After Smith's death the manuscript was passed down from generation to generation in the Smith family to Miss Frances G. Colt of Pittsfield, Massachusetts, who willed it to the Yale Medical Library. Much of the time from 1941 to 1950 the manuscript was in the possession of this editor. It served as the chief source for his unpublished Yale doctoral dissertation, *The Life of Elihu Hubbard Smith* (1946). Smith's letters to Brown which he copied into the "Diary" are quoted from in Harry R. Warfel's *Charles Brockden Brown* (Univ. of Florida Press, Gainesville, 1949); the manuscript is also used as the source for two brief articles and a note by this editor: "Elihu Hubbard Smith and the New York Friendly Club, 1795-1798," *Publications of the Modern Language Association,* 64, No. 3, Part 1 (June, 1949): pp. 471-479; "Elihu Hubbard Smith and the New York Theatre (1793-1798)," *New York History* 31 (1949): pp. 136-148; "John Adams on the History of the American Revolution," *Pennsylvania Magazine of History and Biography* 73 (January, 1949): pp. 92-93.

BIOGRAPHICAL NOTE

YALE AND GREENFIELD HILL
1782-1786, 1787

When Smith entered Yale he was a chubby boy four feet tall and eleven years old. Although four of his classmates were fourteen, the average age of the class was seventeen. Aside from an occasional acrid sentence of recollection in his "Diary," including his tribute to Reuben Hitchcock, we know almost nothing of his experiences there beyond the fact that he despised some of the tutors and had a low opinion of many of his associates; however, what we know of the climate of the place and the troubled waters into which he was tossed makes plain some of the elements of his experience.

The school was overcrowded with 218 students, according to President Ezra Stiles "the greatest number ever together at once in an American College."[1] The following year the enrollment increased to 270, possibly a result of efforts of young men to evade the draft.[2] Facilities were inadequate: a dormitory-recitation hall, a chapel and dining hall. Because the dormitory accommodated only 100, the majority of students roomed off campus, a situation which caused severe disciplinary problems. The construction of the dining hall, which replaced Old College Hall, was delayed and Smith's class could not enter until the building was completed late in the fall. Because classrooms were inadequate, classes were frequently held in the rooms of poor students who rented the space. College standards had fallen so low that as Jeremiah Mason, Smith's roommate in his junior year, wrote in his *Memoir,* students usually graduated knowing approximately as much as they were supposed to know when they were admitted.[3]

Violence was not uncommon; riots, although less frequent than they had been in the administrations of presidents Dagget and Clap, occurred now and then. Tutors' windows were smashed and their lives, seriously or half-jokingly, threatened. The greatest unrest was, however, intellectual. President Stiles himself, who had been infected with unbelief in his early years, was suspected of being too sympathetic to such thinking in his maturity.[4] He, nevertheless, struggled hard against deism and free thought that was everywhere in the college and widespread in the state. Students were given Locke to read and Locke was then "refuted." What happened to Smith and to many of his classmates was that Locke remained in their minds; the refutations were forgotten. Smith entered Yale a Christian and departed with his faith deeply disturbed.

The curriculum offered almost no options. Most of the work in the freshman year was in "Tongues and Logic." During the second year rhetoric, geometry, and geography were the principal subjects. The study of languages was continued "in some measure" during the second and third years. Juniors studied natural philosophy, astronomy, and mathematics. The senior year was given over almost entirely to subjects designed to pre-

---

[1] *The Literary Diary of Ezra Stiles, President of Yale College,* ed. Franklin B. Dexter (New York, 1901) **3**: p. 48.
[2] Franklin B. Dexter, *Sketch of the History of Yale University* (New York, 1887), p. 43. In 1777 the enrollment was 132; in 1783, 270; but in 1787, 139.
[3] *Memoir, Autobiography and Correspondence of Jeremiah Mason,* ed. G. J. Clark: Preface by G. S. Hilliard (Kansas City, Missouri, 1917); for this and other pertinent comments see pp. 8, 10, 11. Mason, whom Dexter calls "probably the ablest lawyer that ever practised in New England," studied law in New Haven before moving to Vermont and then New Hampshire where for several years he was attorney general. He was also U.S. senator from New Hampshire, 1813-1817; state House, 1820, 1821, 1824, and president of the Portsmouth branch of the U.S. Bank, 1825-1829. He did not mention Smith in his *Memoir* but he called on him occasionally in New York.
[4] Abiel Holmes, *The Life of Ezra Stiles, D.D., LL.D.* (Boston, 1798), p. 42.

INTRODUCTION

pare students for the ministry: metaphysics and ethics on weekdays, divinity and ethics on Saturdays. During all four years students were required to read a selection of religious works. It was provided that on Tuesdays and Fridays "Every undergraduate in his turn shall declaim in English, Latin, Greek or Hebrew tongue, and in no other without special permission from the president."[5]

These requirements are impressive but Jeremiah Mason wrote that Stiles insisted that the class of 1788 study Hebrew, but he added: "We learned the alphabet, and worried through two or three Psalms, after a fashion; with most of us it was a mere pretense."[6]

Some twenty years earlier John Trumbull and Timothy Dwight as undergraduates had rebelled against the sterility of the curriculum and later, as tutors, had joined with Joseph Howe to liberalize it. Their efforts, however, were directed mainly toward unofficial rather than formal changes such as gathering students together in the evening for literary discussions and assisting them in the practice of oratory and histrionics.[7]

One of the most important elements in Smith's education was extracurricular. While he was an undergraduate two literary societies were particularly active, the Linonian society, of which his father had been a member, and a younger organization called the Brothers in Unity which was open to freshmen. Smith and most of his Litchfield associates joined the latter group, probably in their first year. A study of the membership list of the Brothers in Unity shows that to an almost overwhelming degree the Yale men with whom Smith associated or was intimate with after graduation were members of this group. The list includes Uriah Tracy, Noah Webster, Ichabod Wetmore, and Oliver Wolcott from the class of 1778; Mason F. Cogswell and Thomas Lord, 1780; William Pitt Beers and Decius Wadsworth, 1785; Lynde Catlin, Thomas Gold, Reuben Hitchcock, William Leffingwell, and William Miller (Smith's class) 1786; Daniel Lewis, Joseph Strong, and William Johnson, 1788. In New York it was William Johnson who became his roommate and closest friend, and when his favorite sister Mary was married it was to Thomas Mumford (Yale 1790), a Brother in Unity. On the other hand, he had almost nothing to do with Linonians, except for James Kent. His intimacy with his Brothers lasted until his death.

Although the Brothers had been organized by David Humphreys in 1768 primarily as a debating club, it soon became a full-fledged literary, dramatic, and fraternal organization. It brought Smith into close contact for four years with a select group who loved literature and good conversation and were keenly interested in frequent presentation of scenes and sections of plays.[8] Smith does not mention participating as an actor; surprisingly enough we learn from the "Diary" that his roommate, Reuben Hitchcock, acted even though he was deep in preparation for the ministry.[9]

The Brothers had a private library of several hundred books which helped make less onerous than it might have been the college law that made books from the college library available only to the "President, Fellows, Tutors, Masters and Bachelors residing at College, and the two senior classes." The Brothers' library had a heterogeneous collection of novels, books of travel, and works of the major poets. Later, and probably in Smith's day, there was a noticeable lack of the great Elizabethan, Jacobean, and Caroline poets[10] which may partially explain why Smith in all his life, although he wrote great quantities of verse, never really understood what lyrical poetry was.

To some extent, probably because he was simply too young to be "taken along," he appears to have been exempted from sexual excesses, violence, and the extremes of misconduct, but staying out of trouble must have been particularly difficult at times, especially near the end of his senior year when he was in the midst of disorder. About April 18 Stiles began to examine the classes in order of their rank. He had decided to make another effort to raise college standards. The examinations were so difficult that the seniors rioted. The riots continued sporadically until May 1 when the civil authorities were called in. Even then the disturbance was not entirely quelled. Stiles himself does not appear to have been in danger; the students concentrated their attack on the tutors, many of whom had their windows broken. Stile wrote: "The Dread of Examina. & Fear of havg. a Degree depend on Merit has produced a Commotion and Convulsion in Coll. & the following Martyrdoms to the cause of poor Scholarship." He listed a number of students who were dismissed, rusticated, or persuaded that they should leave Yale. Order was re-

---

[5] *The Laws of Yale College*, pp. 5 ff. Each student, on admission, purchased a copy of the *Laws* which then became his receipt. It is obvious that the college had a large supply. Smith's class apparently used an edition printed in 1774; a copy published in that year, now in the Yale Memorabilia Room, is signed for 1783. This fact helps to explain a number of discrepancies between the *Laws* and the practices of 1783.

[6] *Memoir*, p. 11.

[7] For a discussion of the influence of these three men on the Yale curriculum see Alexander Cowie, *John Trumbull, Connecticut Wit* (Chapel Hill, Univ. of North Carolina Press, 1936), pp. 43, 73 *passim*.

[8] *A Catalogue of Members of the Society of Brothers in Unity, Yale College, 1841* (New Haven, 1841), p. 2; *Catalogue of the Society of Brothers in Unity* (New Haven, 1854), pp. 2, 19 ff., 26, 29.

[9] The *Laws* specifically forbade "acting in a comedy or tragedy" (fine, 3 shillings) "or being present at a comedy or tragedy." That the law was a dead letter is clear since Stiles notes the formation of a third society whose principal purpose was the presentation of full-length plays. *Literary Diary* 3: p. 14.

[10] *Catalogue of Books in the Brothers and Linonian Libraries* (New Haven, 1808), pp. 11 ff. This was the earliest extant catalog found; the presumption is that the general nature of the collection was unchanged.

stored.[11] There is no evidence that Smith had any part in the activities. On September 13, 1786, he was graduated with his class, the youngest man to be graduated from Yale up to his time.[12]

To his father he was now a problem child, a Yale B.A. just turned fifteen, too young to study for the law or to begin medical training, with not enough Latin even to write a prescription, in no way equipped to be much of anything. Most disturbing of all, he was obviously a confirmed unbeliever. Reuben Smith's solution was unorthodox, perhaps unique: he sent Elihu to a preparatory school. His choice was a school which was soon to be known as one of the finest in America: the great Timothy Dwight's Academy at Greenfield Hill in Fairfield, Connecticut. Dwight was a man of high intelligence, massive learning, and great energy with an enduring compassion and liking for young people. At the time, although he was only thirty-four, his reputation for piety was already great in Connecticut. Probably this reason more than any other, persuaded Reuben Smith to send his son here rather than to one of the half dozen or more other academies that had been established in Connecticut during the preceding six years.

Dwight's academy was only three years old. It consisted of one large room thirty-four feet long by twenty-two feet wide. Along the north and south walls were fastened boards at desk height and under each was a smaller shelf to hold books and slates. Pupils sat along the benches made of slabs of wood with the bark still on the under side. To recite it was necessary for the student to turn about and face the master. At the east end were a few prized seats and desks in front of them so that the wall served as a back rest.

Accounts differ regarding the average enrollment during the twelve years in which Dwight conducted the Academy. It apparently was seldom less than forty or more than sixty, and it was popular almost from its inception. Students came from New England and the Middle Atlantic States, from the South and even from foreign countries.

With a student body so diverse, all of them crammed into one room, and without professional assistance of any kind, Dwight accomplished extraordinary things. One of his devices, not an invention of his own, seems to have been his practice of having older students help to teach the younger ones. In this process, of course, the "teacher" teaches himself and often learns much more than he would as a student. Dwight also put into practice his own theories of education that were unusual for the eighteenth century but surprisingly similar to those of Johann Pestalozzi. He believed that gentleness would accomplish more than brutality, that a quiet talk with a student was more effective than a public reprimand, and that a regular course of exercise was important for all of his students. A radical departure in pedagogy was his practice of admitting girls to the study of subjects of college grade.[13] Students were boarded at houses near the academy. Smith mentions in the "Diary" that he lived with Dr. David Rogers, a prominent Fairfield County physician.[14]

Somewhere in these early years Elihu learned English grammar and the skills for sophisticated composition; it is more likely that these came to him at Greenfield Hill rather than at Yale. More important was the influence that Dr. Dwight exercised on his mind, a point to which Smith repeatedly testifies in the "Diary." Certainly from about this time Smith shared with Dwight the conviction that it was the duty of an intelligent man to interest himself in everything concerned with the betterment of the human race. He also began to emulate Dr. Dwight the poet. The teacher somehow found time almost every day to compose a few verses and he liked to have his students do the same. It is probable that, as stated in Smith's obituary in the *Medical Repository*, he composed a large amount of verse at this time. If so, most of it has been lost except for five sonnets, which may have been written at this time but were not published until he was a medical student in Philadelphia during the winter of 1790-1791. Miss Bailey[15] has suggested that some stanzas of a juvenile sort, "Lines addressed to a Lady, on his embarking to pay a Visit to a Friend," which appeared in the *American Magazine* for June, 1788, following a poem by Dr. Dwight, may be his work. This hypothesis can be neither substantiated nor denied. The lines have the invulnerable anonymity of so many thousands of mediocre eighteenth-century verses whose only virtue is that they scan. The sonnets are another matter: if they were composed at this time, as the evidence would indicate, they are among the first known to have been written in America and, as pioneer work, deserve some consideration. A discussion of their merits and the question of authorship will appear later in these pages.

According to Smith's own account he returned to Christianity during this year—although not for long. More enduring was the improvement of himself as a

---

[11] Stiles, *Literary Diary*, **3**: p. 227n. See also Mason, *Memoir*, p. 11.

[12] According to Dexter (*Sketch of the History of Yale*, p. 100) the youngest man ever to be graduated from Yale was Charles Chauncey, fifteen years and twenty-six days of age when he received his degree in 1792; Smith was fifteen years and nine days old.

[13] For a fuller description of Dwight's academy and comments on its nature and development see Charles E. Cunningham, *Timothy Dwight, 1752-1817* (New York, 1942), pp. 106 ff. For a contemporary account see Musings of Memory, manuscript, Fairfield Historical Society, p. 3 (this is a copy of the original by K. P. Perry in 1880). For illustration of the jealous eye that President Stiles kept on Timothy Dwight see Stiles, *Literary Diary* **3**: p. 247. Dwight (1752-1817; Yale 1769) conducted his academy from 1783 to 1795 then became president of Yale, a position he retained with great honor until his death.

[14] Dr. Rogers may have served as a surgeon in the Revolution. See *History and Genealogy of the Families of Old Fairfield*, comp. & ed. Donald L. Jacobus (New Haven, 1930-1934).

[15] Marcia Edgerton Bailey, *A Lesser Hartford Wit, Dr. Elihu Hubbard Smith, 1771-1798*, Univ. of Maine Studies, 2 ser., No. 11 (Orono, Maine, Univ. Press, 1928), p. 32.

person which he attributed to Dwight's benevolent efforts: he felt that he left Greenfield Hill almost completely changed from the cynical, ignorant boy who had been graduated from Yale a year earlier, and to his death, although he and Dwight agreed in few things except their shared curiosity and humanity, he revered the great man.

LITCHFIELD
September, 1787–September, 1790

From Greenfield Hill, Smith returned to his father's house to become what he called "a kind of apprentice" in the family apothecary shop. At the same time he became for three years one of the six boys whom Dr. Sheldon had as medical students. It was an unfortunate arrangement. Sheldon was kindly but extremely informal and offered no systematic instruction. He had studied under Dr. Bird and had begun practicing in Litchfield in 1784. He is described as a small, frail man, "disposed to consumption," who was expected to die young. About this time, and for forty years thereafter, he took from two to four drachmas of opium a day and then in two years "without detriment" gradually reduced his intake until he was free of the habit. He had a reputation as an excellent physician but it is difficult to believe that he always knew where he was and what he was doing.[16]

Smith's friend, Mason Fitch Cogswell, in a poem dated January, 1788, and probably sent in a letter, describes the young man this way:

> No folly lures his feet from virtue's way,
> No gay delusion leads his feet astray,
> But every eye with rapture sees the youth
> Opposing vice, and zealous for the truth.[17]

The final line was peculiarly apt. One of those who found it true was Jedidiah Strong whose name is still plain on a milestone beside the Litchfield Library near which his home once stood.

Strong was born in Litchfield in 1738, son of one of the first settlers of the town, a Yale graduate, lawyer, state representative for Litchfield for about twenty years, member of the Continental Congress, Judge of the County Court for eleven years, delegate to the State Convention which ratified the Constitution of the United States, town clerk for sixteen years, selectman for thirteen years, constable, juror, surveyor and all-around first citizen. A widower, he married his second wife, Susannah Wyllys, in 1788 and almost immediately his character deteriorated. He became the town drunk, mistreated his daughter, Idea, and grossly abused his wife. Within a year she successfully petitioned the general court for a divorce. A letter signed "Nestor" appeared in the Monitor for April 20, 1790, in which the writer objected to certain unnamed men who had grown old in office and who were no longer worthy of their positions because of their intemperance, paralytic debility, etc. Strong was clearly indicated as the object of the attack. The Litchfield Monitor for July 26, 1790, carried the full story. On September 27 another letter to the paper presented a résumé of the situation. That Elihu Smith had something to do with Strong's public disgrace is certain. He himself states in the "Diary" that he incited others to strip Strong of his offices.[18] Although neither of the letters can be positively identified, the style of the September 27 communication suggests that it is his. Interestingly enough, whatever he did had no effect on his lifelong friendship with Idea. So much for zeal.

Nothing in the imperfect files for the Litchfield Monitor for the years 1787-1791 carries Smith's name. The custom of the time was anonymity, a pseudonym from the classics or a nickname; Smith was "Ella," probably what his friends called him instead of Elihu. There was, however, a noticeable increase in original literary contributions to the Monitor while he was in Litchfield. The supposition that some of the pieces were his is strengthened by a letter that Smith wrote to Cogswell from Philadelphia on January 2, 1791:

I have some further directions to give you—about an old Affair—which flourished little while I was present—& in my absence seems almost dead. A Journeyman of Mr. Collier of Litchfield—who is now here—informs me that the "Third Address" has never been published. He tells me farther—that the "Flowers" are sent home. From this I conclude that Mr. Collier does not intend to print them. You know what a disappointment this will be to me.[19]

It seems likely that either the first or the second "Address" is the "Address to Liberty" which appeared in the Monitor for February 9, 1790. A few lines will show the spirit of the piece:

Fair daughter of Heaven: delight of the skies,
Our glory and patron, dear Liberty rise!
(Thou good universal! thou sweetner of gall!
Elixir of life; benefactor of all!)
The spirit of freedom, on all to bestow,
In church and in state, on the high and the low.
Extend thy dominion, to humanize th' east,
Whose princes are daemons, whose subjects but beasts. . . .

A number of other pieces of verse and prose may be attributed to him with varying degrees of probability but need not be dwelt on here.[20] A fragment from his

---

[16] G. W. Russell, "Early Medicine and Early Medical Men in Connecticut," *Proc. Conn. Med. Soc.* (1892), pp. 123-124.

[17] The poem is dated January, 1788. On the reverse side it is addressed to the care of Elihu H. Smith. It is filed with a collection of nineteen letters to Mason Fitch Cogswell, written between February 12, 1790, and August 8, 1798, in the Correspondence and Papers of Dr. Mason Fitch Cogswell (originals or copies of many of the letters appear in the "Diary").

[18] For the story of the fall of Judge Strong see Payne K. Kilbourne, *A Biographical History of the County of Litchfield, Connecticut* (New York, 1851), pp. 193-195. See also Smith, "Diary," entry for November 8, 1795.

[19] Cogswell Papers.

[20] These include some earlier contribution. See "A Rural Ode," *Monitor*, June 4, 1787, which, from certain stylistic

weather journal kept from May, 1789, to February, 1792, and a letter to Cogswell are all that remain to be considered in this period. The weather journal's chief value lies in the further evidence it supplies regarding Smith's methodical habits and his enduring interest in atmospheric phenomena.[21] The letter is the first that Smith wrote to Cogswell although the contents indicate that they had known one another for some time and also that they had a mutual friend in Timothy Dwight. An excerpt will serve to show something of Smith's control of a competent prose style at the age of eighteen:

Litchfield Febry. 12. 1790

My dear Mason,

I shall write to you with all the familiarity of a friendship of ten thousand years establishment. I do not recollect whether I mention'd to you, while I was in Hartford, that I expected you to write frequently and lengthily to me; but whether that were the case or not, I certainly did expect it. From the commencement of such an intercourse as I hope ours will be; that of unreservedness & friendship; frequent communication becomes a duty, & it ought to be a pleasure. We have been long acquainted with each other, by the mutual happiness of friends, & since personality is added to the other qualifications of the acquaintance, have no good reason for continuing in any way estranged to each other. To dismiss this business of exordium—for which I feel myself very miserably calculated—I have open'd a door to the most intimate communications—& all that is wanting on your part, is the excercise of that polite & friendly attention & openness, with which you used me while at Hartford, and for which I feel to you great obligations. To be short—for what significance belongs there to circumlocutions in friendship? I shall write often to you—unreservedly, friendly and unceremoniously—I shall expect the same from you. You are sufficiently well acquainted with me to calculate upon the degree of satisfaction derivable from the communication—& to take a great deal to myself—use me according to that calculation. If you over-rate my powers, I shall be the gainer; and if you do not, I shall yet gain more pleasure from your correspondence, than from that of many of my friends who profess to think well of me—i.e. if you write at all.[22]

PHILADELPHIA
1790-1791

When Smith left home to study at the College of Philadelphia he found himself part of a huge migration. In the summer of 1790 Congress, then in session in New York, passed a bill providing that the capitol of the nation should be on a site on the Potomac, but providing also that for ten years Philadelphia should be the seat of government. At the end of the summer there was an exodus from New York of government officials and their families, clerks, lawyers, politicians, and the army of hangers-on. Highways and waterways to Philadelphia were so crowded with human beings and freight that one observer compared it to Broadway on May 1, the metropolitan moving day.

The effect on the economy of Philadelphia was inevitable and instantaneous. Houses for sale or rent, even rooms, were hard to find. The smallest house brought three hundred dollars a year. At a time when working men received a dollar a day and board, board for a gentleman was from eight to twelve dollars a week, "without wine, fire or candles," as one newcomer complained.

Smith rented a room from a John Riley, one of several of that name in the city; then, since his classes did not begin until November, he had time to savor his first acquaintance with the most cosmopolitan city in the Union. He almost certainly called on Oliver Wolcott, Jr., son of his father's old friend in Litchfield. No doubt he also explored Philadelphia's library of over twelve thousand volumes and read the *Gazette of the United States,* edited by John Fenno, printer to the Senate of the United States, and its Republican rival, the *Aurora,* edited by Benjamin Franklin Bache. This was also the most probable time for his composing his "Ode Written on Leaving the Place of My Nativity," one of his better efforts at verse which, however, did not appear in the *Gazette* until June, 1791. At some time in the interim he registered for Dr. Rush's class by paying the fee of twenty-four dollars and receiving the usual identification pass; he also, presumably at this time, learned a system of shorthand which may have been the one that the young writer Charles Brockden Brown invented.

Dr. Rush was undoubtedly well known to him by reputation. Among all the great men in Philadelphia, he was one of the most prominent. To a notable degree he was responsible for the reputation which Philadelphia gained and kept as the medical center of the nation. His interests were by no means confined to medicine. He was intensely, almost ferociously, concerned with nearly every aspect of society. As a young man he had taken his preliminary training at the College of New Jersey (Princeton), and the College of Philadelphia. He completed his preparation at the University of Edinburgh and then spent a year or more "walking the hospital," in this case St. Thomas's Hospital, London. During the Revolution he rose rapidly in national importance as a delegate from Pennsylvania to the Continental Congress, a signer of the Declaration of Independence (immediately after Franklin), and as Physician General of the army hospitals of the Middle States. Because of his strong convictions, not only on medicine but on slavery, capital punishment, criminology, and whatever, he

---

peculiarities, appears to be his. Even more likely is a respectable piece of literary criticism, *Monitor,* September 8, 1788, over the signature "L." A possibility is "The Punishment of Avarice; An Oriental Dialogue," *Monitor,* March 23, 1789, a playlet, immaturely philosophical, stiff, and artificial. Almost certain attribution can be made for a poem, *Monitor,* April 30, 1790, which was reprinted in the *Gazette of the United States* for June 22, 1791, while Smith was in Philadelphia. In each instance the lines were entitled, "A Fragment"; in the *Monitor* the lines are anonymous whereas in Philadelphia they are signed "Ella."

[21] A copy of the fragment of the weather journal is to be found in a letter from E. Champion Bacon to E. C. Herrick among the Herrick Papers, Yale Univ. Library.

[22] Cogswell Papers. It seems clear that this was the first letter that Smith wrote to Cogswell. It by no means nullifies the assertion that two years earlier Cogswell had written verses to Smith, for their acquaintance could well have begun in 1787.

made many enemies and his friends, while strong, were not numerous. He was certainly the best-known if not the best-liked doctor in America.

At this time Rush was lecturing at the revitalized College of Philadelphia, not the University of Pennsylvania.[23] The competition from the medical school at the University would account for the few students who elected Rush's course of lectures in 1790 as compared with the number usually registered. In Smith's class there were forty-five men; the following year the enrollment jumped to seventy-two. In the 1790 class were young men from eight states and Jamaica, with students from Pennsylvania and the South in the majority. Connecticut was represented by James Wells, Edward Tudor, Apollos King, and Smith. Joseph Strong, Smith's friend and Yale classmate, attended Rush's lectures during the following year but may have been already in Philadelphia studying with other doctors.[24]

With a new acquaintance, Robert Johnson of Pennsylvania, Smith arranged some sort of division of labor. Smith took shorthand notes; Johnson's contribution is unknown, nor does the "Diary" contain any mention of him. From their notebook[25] it is evident that Rush's course covered with some thoroughness the common diseases of man. After the early lectures on the "Nature of the Blood" and "Animal Pathology," students learned the symptoms and recommended cures for cholera morbus, dysentery, fevers, smallpox, erysipelas, ophthalmia, nervous diseases, and gout. As might be expected from Rush's preoccupation with fevers, yellow fever in particular, that subject received the most intensive treatment. No evidence indicates that the lectures were accompanied by laboratory demonstrations or clinical work. It was not that such procedure was unknown so much as that it was reserved for special students, of whom Rush customarily had five or six. This group of privileged individuals lived with the doctor and worked at his free clinic and dispensary. The fee was large, 100 pounds, cash, to keep the number small.[26]

On the lighter side, the lectures contained occasional humor, for example, the doctor's remarks on love:

It is the excess of this passion which constitutes disease. The symptoms are a virtual silence concerning, or a constant talking of the person beloved. A love of solitude. If a woman keeps her eyes always on a man when he is in her company, or else avoids fixing them on him—in either case it is a sign she loves him—Love, when it is successful polishes men, but makes women appear awkward.

Love affects both sexes & all ages. The remote causes are idleness & the reading of Novels & Romances. The proximate cause is too much action in the Brain, & vessels of the heart.—Cure—Matrimony.

Then Dr. Rush goes on to treat in the same agreeable manner of Grief—Anger—Fear; Lust & Dreaming. But as they are not of primary importance I omit them. They are curious to the philos. *enquirer*.

In addition to his emphasis on disease and his rare forays into humor Rush stressed the necessity for a student's acquiring a familiarity with modern languages; Smith worked hard almost daily at this for the rest of his life. Although German bested him he read French easily but spoke it badly. Rush also lectured on the importance of a thorough knowledge of climatic conditions of many countries with special emphasis on the locality in which the physician expected to practise. He spoke of the advisability of learning extempore speaking and was emphatic in his advice to his students on the necessity for acquiring a clear hand:

The writing of a fair and legible hand should be considered as part, not only of the learning but of the morality of a physician.

Not only did Smith follow Rush's advice as dutifully and persistently as though the great man were looking over his shoulder, but he also adopted his active interest in the manumission of slaves and humanitarian activities of all kinds, his idealistic approach to medicine and his habit of publishing in many fields. Even his handwriting improved markedly after 1790. To a degree, of course, Rush was simply reinforcing the teachings of the great Timothy Dwight.

The lectures ended on February 7, 1791. So far as we know, although it is stated in his obituary that he studied in Philadelphia "with Dr. Rush and others," this was the limit of his formal training. He by no means exhausted the offerings of the available schools. After 1789 no bachelor's degree was awarded for medicine in Philadelphia, but even for this Smith would

---

[23] Nathan G. Goodman, *Benjamin Rush, Physician and Citizen, 1746-1813* (Philadelphia, 1934), pp. 97, 128 *passim*. Goodman gives an excellent account of the tangled skein of relationships between the College of Philadelphia, the legislature, and the University of Pennsylvania, matters of no great importance here; sufficient is the fact that in the autumn of 1791 the two schools were merged and Rush was elected professor of the institutes of medicine and clinical medicine.

[24] In one of the uncataloged ledgers of Benjamin Rush at the Library Company of Philadelphia, is a list entitled "Catalogue of the Students who have Attended my Lectures," the names are grouped by years and by states.

[25] That Charles Brockden Brown invented a shorthand system is to be found in David Lee Clark, *Charles Brockden Brown: Pioneer Voice of America* (Durham, N.C., Duke Univ. Press, 1952), p. 17. In September, 1792, while he was on a visit to New York, Smith made a longhand copy of the notes and added an introduction in which he gave the above information. Both shorthand and longhand original versions of the notes have disappeared; however, some time after 1798, Dr. Benjamin F. Thompson of Setauket, Long Island, found the longhand version in the possession of the son of one of Smith's friends. Dr. Thompson made a copy which he sent to J. Hulse of Baltimore in June, 1820. This copy is now in the Army Medical Library in Washington, D.C., where it was miscataloged under the name of "Elisha H. Smith." The title of the extant copy is: "A Course of Lectures on the Theory and Practice of Medicine. By Benjamin Rush M.D. Professor in the University of Pennsylvania from November 1790 to February '91." Smith, in the Introduction to his notes speaks of Rush as a professor at the University of Pennsylvania, which he was when Smith transcribed his notes. In the Introduction he writes, "The work now stands as a monument to the joint labors of my fellow student Robert Johnson and myself...."

[26] Logan Papers, VIII, iii, Historical Society of Pennsylvania.

have been ineligible since he was under the minimum age of twenty-one and had not taken the extensive list of required courses. Moreover, he did not serve as an interne at the Pennsylvania Hospital, nor had he written the required thesis. The minimum age for an M.D. was twenty-four; Smith was twenty. When, in the "Diary," he deplores his lack of training he is not indulging in hypercritical self-deprecation. It is true that he used the lancet frequently for phlebotomy but his customary reaction to watching an operation, even eight years later, was to get sick. We read of his accompanying a friend hoping to watch the birth of a baby; he had never observed such an occurrence. Almost all references to him label him "Doctor." Strictly speaking, he was never a doctor.

For the next four or five months he remained in Philadelphia trying to become a writer. This does not mean that he had changed his mind about his profession; it is simply another instance of his determination to be both literary man and physician.

Characteristically, he had swiftly developed an active social life. Equally characteristic was his choice of people who were already important or who would in a few years attain prominence. At some time during his stay he met Charles Brockden Brown—probably quite early if it was indeed Brown's shorthand system which he used in taking his medical notes. Later to become America's first professional novelist, Brown was wasting his time in a not too enthusiastic attempt to become a lawyer at the office of Alexander Wilcocks. Smith met and associated with John Fenno, editor of the *Gazette*. His interest in writing brought him into contact with William Rogers, D.D., who, by 1793, was Professor of English and Belles Lettres at the University of Pennsylvania, and also with Joseph Bringhurst, Jr., a young Quaker who may have been studying medicine at the time.[27] He came to know numerous Philadelphia doctors, most of whom were members of the College of Philadelphia faculty and later of the faculty at the University of Pennsylvania; these included Wistar, Griffiths, Barton, and Jackson.

A few of his new friends were in business rather than medicine or literature, men such as Thomas Pym Cope who was later to own a line of packet ships and become one of the richest men in America; Samuel Coates, the philanthropist, one of whose major interests was the Philadelphia Hospital; and William Eddy, a wealthy insurance man active in prison reform.

His first major literary effort, in March, 1791, was the composition or completion of the short first version of *Edwin and Angelina* as a two-act prose drama rather than as an opera in verse which it later became. He may have begun the work as early as 1787 in Greenfield Hill although that is unlikely.

On February 23, 1791, the *Gazette of the United States* carried the first of a series of poems by "Ella," "Birtha," and "Henry." In thirty-two issues of the paper there were thirty-five poems by these three contributors. It was a kind of literary correspondence similar to Captain Robert Merry's Della Cruscan correspondence with Mrs. Hanna Cowley which began in the London *World* in June, 1787. This literary framework or unifying device was common in the eighteenth century although, as Miss Bailey has said, the American group included relatively more sonnets than the others. "Ella" wrote twenty-one poems: nine sonnets, nine odes, two "fragments" and one longer piece in four-line stanzas entitled "Laura and Mary." "Birtha" wrote nine poems (possibly ten if the unsigned poem dated April 16 be attributed to him). "Henry" wrote four. "Ella" is Smith,[28] "Birtha" and "Henry" have been conjectured to be variously Cogswell, Brown, Joseph Bringhurst, and Theodore Dwight. Nobody knows.

On merit alone the poetical correspondence deserves little attention; the sonnets have a certain historical importance as pioneer American efforts. Credit for writing the first American sonnet is usually given to Colonel David Humphreys who composed the lines "Addressed to my Friends at Yale College," perhaps as early as 1776 although it was not published until 1804. Probably the first sonnet written and published in America was in Italian and appeared in the *Columbia Magazine* for June, 1787. Davidson in his study of American sonnets finds ninety-one called "original" by their authors, which appeared in the most important magazines and newspapers between 1786 and 1800. In this group the

---

[27] Joseph Bringhurst, Jr. remains a shadowy figure. The most likely candidate as far as age, occupation, and avocation are concerned is Joseph, son of John, son of James. The fact that he was called "Junior" although his Christian name was not the same as his father's is not significant. In the eighteenth century a man was sometimes called "Junior" to distinguish him from an uncle or an older cousin of the same name. Another Joseph, of the same family (craftsmen, coachmakers, and hardware merchants in Philadelphia) was not born until 1774, which would make him even more precocious than Smith. A Joseph Bringhurst is listed in the *Philadelphia Directory* for 1791 (but not thereafter) as a "gentleman" living at 114 S. Front Street. See Josiah Granville Leach, *History of the Bringhurst Family with Notes on the Clarkson, De Peyster and Boude Families* (printed for private circulation, Philadelphia, Lippincott Co., 1901), pp. 32, 39, 41 (A copy of this rare book is in Univ. of Penna. Lib.).

[28] That Smith is "Ella" is scarcely a matter for dispute. He used "Ella" as a second signature in a letter to Cogswell from Philadelphia, March 28, 1791; Cogswell Papers. He also referred to a poetical correspondence. As mentioned earlier, the poem, "A Fragment," which appeared in the *Gazette of the United States,* June 22, 1791, signed "Ella," had previously been printed anonymously in the Litchfield *Monitor,* April 30, 1790. In *American Poems, Selected an Original* (Litchfield, 1793), edited by Smith, are verses addressed to "Ella"; a note written in the Woolsey family copy of the book (p. 292) ascribes the poem to Joseph Bringhurst, Jr. Mrs. Annie Russell Marble, in *Heralds of American Literature* (Chicago & London, 1907), p. 77, mentions that Philip Freneau and his wife carried on a poetical correspondence under the names of "Ella" and "Birtha." This hypothesis that Freneau and his wife had anything to do with the Philadelphia series does not hold up under investigation. For the refutation, too long to be given here, see James E. Cronin, "The Life of Elihu Hubbard Smith" (Ph.D. dissertation, 1946, unpublished, Yale University Library), pp. 134-135.

sonnets signed "Ella" are among the first. If they were really "Sonnets by a youth not seventeen years of age" as they were signed in the *American Museum or Universal Magazine* when they were reprinted in 1791 they must have been written in 1787 or earlier, probably at Greenfield Hill. It seems highly unlikely that they attained their printed form so early.[29] Smith shared with his contemporaries difficulties with the sonnet form which now strike us as strange. Usually the sonnets of the time were obvious attempts to imitate the efforts of William Lisle Bowles or Charlotte Smith. Both the Petrarchan and Shakespearean forms were attempted. Would-be poets found the latter somewhat easier to handle, but many of the surviving sonnets are strange mixtures of both. Smith is not unusual, therefore, in using his own variant to honor John Trumbull who in 1790 did a portrait of Washington for the city of Philadelphia. It appeared in the *Gazette* for June 11, 1791:

Sonnet IX
TO MR. JOHN TRUMBULL
Trumbull! to thee, with hesitating hand,
  I wake the tremulously-breathing lyre;
  Fearful that Age, altho the Muse inspire,
Should weep that Modesty had lost command.

Tis not, alone, that energy divine
  Lives o'er the canvas, as the pencil moves;
  That tint perfects the exquisite design,
  And *life* is present; that my soul approves:

But that the Spirit brooding o'er the immense
  Of unknown Beauty, to existence gave
  The *plan,* where Wisdom, Liberty, and Sense,
  The high-soul'd Patriot, and the Warrior brave,
Live with the appropriate character of face
  In all the pencil's manners-painting grace.[30]

Readers avid to savor further efforts by the author will find some fourteen sonnets in the "Diary," written by him between July 18, 1796, and September 11, 1797. One of the characteristics, not only of Smith's sonnets but scores and hundreds of others written by contemporaries of much greater reputation than his, was what must be called a fundamental misconception regarding poetry. Smith's own revealing comments are scattered throughout the "Diary" but are to be found particularly in his entries for July 25, 1797, and September 11, 1797.

---

[29] For discussions of early American sonnets see L. G. Sterner, "The Sonnet in American Literature" (Ph.D. dissertation, Univ. of Penna., 1930), pp. x-xi; H. Carter Davidson, "The Sonnet in Seven Early American Magazines and Newspapers," *Amer. Literature* 4 (May, 1932): pp. 181-185; Raymond D. Havens, *The Influence of Milton on English Poetry* (Cambridge, Harvard Univ. Press, 1922), pp. 485 ff., 524 ff.

[30] The John Trumbull (1756-1843; Harvard 1773) referred to here was the son of Jonathan Trumbull, Revolutionary governor of Connecticut. He served briefly but with distinction in the Continental Army before becoming a pupil of the painter, Benjamin West, in London. Thereafter he became with Gilbert Stuart one of the most famous American painters of his age. He was a first-cousin-once-removed to John Trumbull (1750 o.s.-1831), lawyer and poet, one of the older Connecticut Wits.

In discussing his verse there is danger of sliding into condescension. He was never trying to adumbrate Shakespeare. When he felt that his sister would profit from cold baths or early rising he wrote her a sonnet to make his point. He was using sonnets to serve purposes no longer expected of them.

About June, 1790, he left Philadelphia, his apprenticeship in literature and medicine now finished. His character had assumed the shape it was to retain for the remaining seven years of his life. In his formative period, between the ages of fifteen and twenty, he had as his teachers two major figures of the century, Timothy Dwight and Benjamin Rush. Both men were essentially builders of character. Both saw the world as far from perfect, but both felt certain that they not only should but could do something to change it. Smith attempted to follow where they led. He had their honesty and rigid self-discipline; he tried hard to have their humaneness. What he lacked was their almost inhuman vitality. He tried, not always successfully, to make up for this lack by a massive effort of the will.

THE CONNECTICUT WITS, WETHERSFIELD AND HARTFORD 1791-1793

Back home in Litchfield, Smith found the prospects dull. There was little of the excitement of the metropolis and most of his friends were elsewhere. He could anticipate a certain amount of security as heir to his father's thriving drug business and extensive practice, but it also meant replacing his friend, the unfortunate Thomas O'Hara Croswell who was his father's assistant. Most important, he could not be his own man: living at home meant either regular attendance at Sunday services or serious disagreement with his father. He strongly disliked religion (which in Litchfield was the Congregational church) and he loathed the Reverend Judah Champion, his old teacher.

A few months after his return he moved to Wethersfield, Connecticut, three miles outside of Hartford. It was a farming community of about two thousand chiefly given to raising onions. He swiftly discovered that Wethersfield had all the doctors it needed and at no time in slightly more than a year and a half there was he able to support himself. Perhaps it was not entirely the number of other doctors; he was never able to make a living through his practice.

He enjoyed himself in what was to be his usual fashion, treating a few patients, making friends, writing, and conversing. For most of his stay his host was John Williams, Yale 1781, the son of the local sheriff. Williams was wealthy, charming, restless, unhappy, and lazy. He tried, mostly because of Smith's constant prodding, to interest himself in a variety of things; eventually, to Smith's disgust, he settled on religion and philosophy. He had talents of a sort, enough to win for himself an honorary M.A. from Harvard, but little ability to think for himself. He leaned heavily on Smith, as the "Diary" will show. Eventually this became an annoyance, but for the time they were good companions.

On November 3, 1791, an amateur group in town presented *The Gamester* and *The Belle's Stratagem*. Elihu read the prefatory address written by Cogswell.[31] On the more serious side he interested himself in the formation of a state medical society. As early as 1652 licenses to practice medicine were granted in Connecticut but, since the license was not required, many doctors did not bother to obtain one. Several times various groups of reputable physicians attempted to form medical societies. What they wanted was the power to regulate and control both doctors and the practice of medicine in their own localities. One of the earliest of such societies was founded in Litchfield in 1779; one of the largest was the Medical Society of New Haven County, established in 1784. None of these societies was especially strong or particularly effective: they could specify qualifications for membership, but they could not require reputable physicians to join, nor could they control quacks, of whom there were hundreds. It was the quacks who did their utmost to prevent the formation of a state society the first move of which, they knew, would be to disqualify them. Surprisingly enough, however, the unqualified practitioners were supported by many conservative doctors who feared that a medical society would use its great power selfishly and evolve into a tightly controlled irresponsible monopoly. Repeatedly this collection of strange bedfellows lobbied successfully to prevent the legislature's granting a charter for a state society. At last, in April, 1792, at the request of the Medical Society of New Haven County, the physicians and surgeons of Hartford County met to appoint delegates for a state convention in Hartford. The convention, convened in May, managed to secure permission from the legislature to form the Connecticut State Medical Society. It was thereupon established. In the list of forty-seven doctors who were charter members, Smith's name did not appear. Not until the Hartford County Medical Society was organized late in September, did he take any part in the affair as clerk of the meeting.[32] Miss Bailey is in error in assuming that references to the formation of a medical society found in Smith's letters to Cogswell in 1793 had anything to do with either the county or state societies since both had been functioning for at least a year. He was probably thinking of an eclectic medical group or, more likely, a national society. This would have been typical of him; his mind continually reached out beyond the parochial limitations of the minds of most men of his time. Precisely this kind of "big" thinking resulted in his being the central force in publishing *American Poems* and in the establishment of the first national medical magazine, *The Medical Repository*—and this while he quite literally had not one dollar in his pocket.

In the midst of his concern for medical things, between September 10 and September 25, he visited New York, perhaps to assess the possibilities of moving there. While in the city he spent part of his time transcribing his shorthand notes of Dr. Rush's lectures.

Meanwhile, perhaps as early as the first or second month of 1792, he had been in close association with a rather amorphous group known as the "Hartford Wits," or the "Connecticut Wits." Although the members constituted a kind of school of American letters they were actually two groups. Timothy Dwight, John Trumbull, Joel Barlow, David Humphreys, and Lemuel Hopkins were the original Wits who, in addition to their individual works, combined to produce the *Anarchiad*. By 1792, however, Dwight was teaching at Greenfield Hill, Barlow and Humphreys were in Europe, and Trumbull had worked so hard as a state legislator trying to secure an enlargement of funds for Yale that he had a nervous breakdown. Of the original group only Hopkins, so far as we know, took part in writing the *Echo*. Smith, of course, knew Dwight; Barlow and Humphreys he may never have seen; Trumbull he met at least once. His relationship with these men was that of editor and biographer.[33] It was mainly a younger group with whom Smith collaborated. Cogswell, mentioned earlier, and Hopkins were Hartford doctors. Theodore Dwight, Timothy's younger brother, was a lawyer, vehement Federalist, a director of the Connecticut Bible Society, intensely interested in politics. Despite Smith's remark in the "Diary" that "My friend Theodore Dwight is distinguished for his love of everything, which promotes conviviality & merriment," Theodore comes down to us as a morose and wearily argumentative individual preoccupied with saving his soul in public. Richard Alsop of Middletown was a wealthy young sometime businessman and sometime scholar-poet.[34] Hopkins practiced medicine in Hartford for many years and retained a strong almost youthful interest in literature.

When one considers the prevalence of literary clubs in the eighteenth century it is easy to believe that these writers may have had some such organization and that it may have been a continuation of the "club of wits" to which Barlow and his friends had belonged a decade

---

[31] Cogswell Papers.

[32] For accounts of efforts to form a state medical society see Charles J. Bartlett, "Medical Licensure in Connecticut," *The Heritage of Connecticut Medicine*, ed. Herbert Thoms (New Haven, Connecticut, 1942); Creighton Barker, "The Origins of the Connecticut State Medical Society," *ibid.*; A. M. Wainwright, *The Medical History of Hartford County*, from *The Memorial History of Hartford County*, Connecticut, by permission of the publishers (bound separately, n.d.); Herbert Thoms, "Elihu Hubbard Smith, Physician, Editor, 'Connecticut Wit,'" *Bull. Soc. Medical History of Chicago* 3 (1923-1925): pp. 471-473; see also Smith's letter to Cogswell, dated Litchfield, August 21, 1793, in which he speaks of the "Med: Co. Meeting of Hartd. Coy." of which he was clerk. He also writes here of his membership in the State Medical Society (Cogswell Papers).

[33] Smith published biographical and critical sketches of all five which appeared in the *Monthly Magazine and British Register* for July, August, September, October, and November, 1798. *American Poems*, of course, contains numerous selections from their writings.

[34] See *Richard Alsop, A Hartford Wit* (Middletown, Conn., Mattabesett Press, 1939).

earlier. It was not however, as has been so frequently stated, the Friendly Club, a New York group to which Smith later belonged.[35]

The most important historical contribution of the group was *The Echo,* the first column of which appeared in the *American Mercury* for August 8, 1791. Subsequent numbers appeared at irregular intervals in the same paper until August, 1795. After that date they were printed in the *Courant,* perhaps, as Leon Howard suggests in *The Connecticut Wits*[36] because of the increasing discomfort of the liberal *Mercury* in sponsoring a column which became more and more Federalist in tone.

The Echo eventually "petered out" rather than ended. The original plan, if there was one, was gradually abandoned to be replaced by miscellaneous satires and occasional poems on almost anything.

Smith may have been part of the collaboration from the beginning. Surviving letters and handwritten notes in books show him to have written, or to have had a part in the composition of at least two and perhaps three pieces of the *Echo* type, only one of which eventually appeared as an *Echo*. In *The Echo With Other Poems*[37] the twelfth number of the *Echo* has a footnote on the Princess de Lambelle attributing authorship of the lines describing her to someone unnamed but so identified that it can be no other than Smith. His authorship of another poem is vouched for in a copy once owned by John Trumbull. Now in the Connecticut Historical Society, the page reads: "Extracts from Democracy, and Epic Poem, by Aquiline Nimblechops. . . ." The name "Dr. Elihu Smith" is written immediately beneath the title in Trumbull's hand. The introduction to the poem states that the first canto was printed in New York in March, 1794, and excited much attention. A second canto was written but not printed because of the "timidity of the booksellers." At the time of the riot which was the subject of the satire Smith had been living in New York for six months. A letter from Alsop to Cogswell dated January 16, 1793,[38] makes clear that Cogswell and Smith wrote the piece which Alsop has edited and somewhat modified.

Smith's lines, identified from Alsop's letter read:

> We urge illustrious Adams on to fate;
> Condemn his principles, his book detest,
> Misquote his sentiments, his conduct wrest,
> Charge him with loving what ourselves we love,
> Charge him with hate of what we disapprove,
> And load with vilest terms of reprobation
> The very phantom of our own creation.

He may have had a share with Cogswell in *Echo* number ten, but it is a matter of the mildest kind of historical importance.

Even a casual reading of the *Echo* would impress one with the essentially narrow partisanship of the younger Hartford Wits. Their adherence to the Federalist party was much more than a political loyalty; it was the union of a class, one might even say a caste, whose tenets were based on Congregationalism, superior education, property, and conservatism: a mixture of tangibles and intangibles which produced remarkably concrete results. The religious elements of the mixture had undergone a transformation by the end of the last decade of the eighteenth century. Many of the brilliant men who were young in those years no longer felt it necessary to attend services or even to believe in the doctrines of the church but, in a way almost impossible to explain, and which, perhaps can be understood only by those who have lived long in New England, the Congregational church, denied and often scorned, still guided the actions of its wandering children.

Successful as the *Echo* was in terms of approbation from Federalist readers it added nothing to Smith's income. His uneasiness was probably one reason for his aforementioned trip to New York in the spring of 1793. There he had met Dr. Miller to whose New York practice he succeeded six months later. Whatever the weighed value of the various factors of his situation he moved back to Litchfield from Wethersfield.

Home again he worked swiftly to complete a major project, the editing and publishing of an anthology of American poetry, *American Poems, Selected and Original,* Vol. I. Charles Brockden Brown, who had fled Philadelphia to avoid the terrible epidemic of yellow fever which ravaged the city in the summer of 1793, was his guest and it has been said that Brown had a hand in the editing. This could be true but has not been established. Smith's credit for the major part of the work is beyond question. It is also certain that others assisted with the editing,[39] the most likely candidates being the younger Wits. Cogswell, at least, lent substantial aid in the form of money to help defray printing costs not immediately covered by subscriptions. Smith felt obliged to keep him informed of every stage of the publication and called upon him without apology to assist in distributing the book and collecting money. The part Cogswell may have played in preparing Volume I is further indicated by numerous "Diary" references to the cooperation Smith expected from him in compiling the second volume, which never appeared.

American Poems, printed by Thomas Collier in Litchfield, 1793, is generally considered to be our first an-

---

[35] This fact is clear from Smith's "Diary" and other evidence to be cited later in the text.

[36] (Univ. of Chicago Press, 1943), p. 201.

[37] Published as "Printed at the Porcupine Press by Pasquin Petronius" (New York, 1807). Alsop was an editor; Isaac Riley was the printer. The press got its name from the drawing of a porcupine with the legend, *Noli me tangere,* which appeared with the *Echoes*.

[38] MS letter Alsop to Cogswell in Trumbull's copy of *The Echo With Other Poems,* Conn. Hist. Soc.

[39] Smith's major responsibility for the work is clear from his letters to Cogswell dated June 21, 1793, and thereafter (Cogswell Papers). That others were also helping is clear from the letters, from the Postscript (in the front of the book) in *American Poems* which refers to "the editors," and the note heading the list of subscribers at the back of the book. A facsimile reproduction with an introduction by William K. Bottorff is now available, *Scholars' Facsimiles & Reprints* (Gainesville, Fla., 1966).

thology of American verse.⁴⁰ Even the most thoroughly grounded scholars of the period might have some difficulty in naming a single poem contained in it. The anthologists have avoided it. It has survived more as a literary marker than as a classic, as a courageous adventure in editing and publishing.

That the volume did not contain poems that had attained and still retain some critical approval was deliberate if somewhat unfortunate. A section from the "Preface" reads:

The publishers have observed it to be a matter of much regret, among persons of reading and taste, that the frail security of an obscure newspaper, was the only one they had for some of the handsomest specimens of American poetry.

The editors believed that they were surrounded by literary wealth from which it was necessary to choose some of the brightest gems. It was not that they were semi-literate provincials: all of them had read Shakespeare and Milton and venerated them. But in the same afternoon that they read *Lycidas* they could read Mrs. Sarah Wentworth Morton's *Ouabi* and give it equal praise.

The volume came off the press in July. Then came the tedious and unrewarding business of distributing the volumes to subscribers, often by hand or messenger, and the placing of some copies in bookstores in the larger towns. Collier was one of the legion of eighteenth-century printers with more courage than business sense. In this instance he seems eventually to have received most or all of the money due to him, but it took years.

Once this project was under way, Smith left for New York where he arrived on the afternoon of September 5, 1793. This move was the result of a sudden decision made no earlier, his letters indicate, than August. Behind him he left his books scattered among friends around Connecticut. He also left without waiting to secure letters of recommendation or a certificate from Dr. Fish certifying that he was a member of the Medical Society of the State of Connecticut. He wrote to Cogswell shortly before leaving Litchfield asking him to send these letters and papers after him as soon as possible. He was particularly anxious to have letters from Dr. Hopkins to his friends in New York. Miss Bailey is in error in saying that he carried these papers to New York with him. For some reason they never arrived.

NEW YORK
1793-1795

New York, to Smith, was a friendly place from the beginning. He settled immediately into a social group many of whose members were probably acquaintances of some duration and all of whom became his staunch friends for the remainder of his life. For a time he lived with William Woolsey at 2 Golden Hill Street, but his first address was 5 Golden Hill Street, also the address of Thomas Mumford his future brother-in-law who was practicing law in the city. George Muirson Woolsey, brother of William and also a storekeeper lived nearby. William Dunlap lived not far away.⁴¹ There were numerous others with whom he was already at least casually acquainted.

About two weeks after his arrival he was given an oral examination to determine his fitness to practice in New York. The imposing examining committee was composed of the mayor, Richard Varick; three doctors: Bard, Rogers and Mitchill; and two judges: Hobart and Lansing.⁴² It lasted for about half an hour. The

---

⁴⁰ The right of the volume to this designation depends, to some extent, on a definition of terms. *A Collection of Poems by Several Hands* (Boston, 1744) was largely the work of the Reverend Mather Byles. It is possible that Joseph Green and the Reverend John Adams also contributed poems, some of which were tributes to Byles's genius. It is not an anthology in the usual sense of the word. A volume of congratulatory poems in Greek, Latin, and English was published by the faculty of Harvard on the accession of George III: *Pietas et Gratulatio Collegii Cantabrigiensis Apud Nov-Anglos* (Boston, 1761). James Rivington of New York made an attempt to publish a colonial anthology in 1773, but he was interrupted by the Revolution. See R. W. Griswold, *The Poets and Poetry of America* (Philadelphia, 1855), p. 4. Mathew Carey published an anthology containing selections from the works of both English and American authors: *Beauties of Poetry, British and American* (Philadelphia, 1791). In the year following the appearance of *American Poems*, J. Carey published an anthology so like it in material and arrangement that at first glance it would seem to be no more than a second edition. See *The Columbia Muse* (New York, 1794).

⁴¹ This was a tight little group. William Woolsey, who was twenty-seven in 1793, was at the beginning of a successful career. He became president of a fire insurance company, a bank, a railroad, and a Bible society, as well as the father of Theodore Dwight Woolsey, president of Yale (1844-1871). George Muirson also became prosperous but not quite so spectacularly. Dunlap, who was twenty-seven, had during the previous year inherited from his father a looking-glass and china store which served to keep him financially sound, although he was far more interested in portrait painting and playwriting. He was to become a kind of one-man American dramatic movement. Dunlap was married to Elizabeth, sister of the Woolseys. Timothy Dwight was married to Elizabeth's half-sister. And William Woolsey was married to Timothy Dwight's sister. It seems probable that their acquaintance with Smith began during the year which he spent at Greenfield Hill. Thomas Mumford married Mary Smith on January 29, 1795.

⁴² Richard Varick was mayor of New York from 1789 to 1800. Bard was either Dr. John Bard (1716-1799) or his equally famous son, Samuel (1742-1821). John was a pioneer in sanitation in New York, the first American surgeon to take part in a systematic dissection for the purpose of instruction, and the first president of the Medical Society of the State of New York. Samuel, who studied in Edinburgh and London, was a specialist in internal medicine and midwifery. He was connected with the Columbia medical school (formerly King's College) for forty years, for the last twenty as dean of the faculty. Despite his specialty, midwifery, and his political affiliations (Tory), he was personal physician to George Washington while the federal government was in New York. John R. B. Rogers is mentioned (in the obituary of his son, J. Kearney Rogers) as a doctor who attained high eminence in his profession about the year 1800 (New York *Intelligencer*, November 15, 1851); he was on the staff of the New York Hospital with Smith. From another source: he was a graduate of Edinburgh, a practitioner of

doctors asked most of the questions and the others were apparently satisfied of his character as the doctors were of his knowledge. He passed.[43] At almost the same time, a Dr. Miller[44] became ill and retired leaving orders that his patients were to be referred to Smith. Miller had enjoyed a good practice. One might assume therefore that Smith started in high gear and went on from there to earn his living for the first time. In fact he did nothing of the kind. The practice dwindled. Smith after recovering from an attack of influenza applied himself to study and observed:

> Every day, & every book I read, more & more, shews me my deficiency, & tho I hardly hope for the character of a great physician, & certainly never can deserve it, I am determined not to fail in endeavoring after juster claims to it, than most of those who obtain, & think they deserve it.[45]

Characteristically, he also continued his literary work. He began to revise his play, *Edwin and Angelina*, which he had found among his papers when he was packing to leave Litchfield. To this two-act prose drama he added a few new scenes and submitted it to the managers of the Old American Company in December. The managers, after the fashion of theatrical entrepreneurs, tucked it away and forgot it. His revived interest in playwriting may have owed its inspiration to William Dunlap, also a friend of the Woolseys, with whom he began an almost daily association. Dunlap was finishing his tragedy, *Fountainville Abbey*, and reading selections to his friends. He records the coincidence of his play and Smith's being accepted at the same time.[46]

A few days earlier, on the thirteenth of November, Noah Webster, Smith's old music teacher, reappeared in New York.[47] He had been practicing law in Hartford and was full of plans for his newspapers. With his usual great energy he went to work. On December 9 he published the first number of the *Minerva* which appeared daily thereafter at four o'clock in the afternoon. He also published the *Herald,* a weekly paper.[48] Webster's appearance, too, was the beginning of an association that lasted until Smith's death. The "Diary" will record the many great projects which they discussed and some of which they carried out. They shared almost identical interests in the future of American publishing, literature, scholarship, education, medicine, and science in general.

On November 19, 1793, at a quarterly meeting of the Manumission Society, Smith was proposed for membership at the same time as George Muirson Woolsey and the Reverend Samuel Miller. Many of his friends were already members, including William Woolsey, Dr. James Cogswell, William Johnson, William Dunlap, and Thomas Mumford. At the next quarterly meeting the candidates were admitted to membership. At the same time Noah Webster's name was presented and he was admitted in May.[49] Webster had long been actively concerned with the problem of slavery but Smith had not, even though meetings of those who were united in their opposition to slavery occurred regularly at Yale commencements when he was an undergraduate. If he had cared to do so, he could have joined the Connecticut Manumission Society to which Webster, Theodore Dwight, and Lemuel Hopkins[50] belonged. Like the Philadelphia society, the New York branch was started by Quakers, but from the beginning it included a number of learned and intelligent men of other sects or no sect at all; indeed, it was precisely among those whose tendencies were deistic or even agnostic that the real enthusiasm for societies of this nature was to be found in the last decade of the eighteenth century in America. The Manumission Society in New York when it was organized chose John Jay as president and Alexander Hamilton as secretary. By 1794 neither of these gentlemen attended the meetings with any regularity.

---

eminence, particularly skilled in obstetrics: see an uncataloged collection of newspaper items on medical men (Toner Collection at the Library of Congress). Samuel Latham Mitchill (1764-1831), a doctor, editor, United States senator and representative, studied under Dr. Samuel Bard, and completed his training in Edinburgh. On his return he studied law and entered politics. In addition he held several professorships at Columbia in chemistry, agriculture, and botany. With Edward Miller and Smith he founded *The Medical Repository* in 1797 and was its principal editor for twenty-three years. Judge John Sloss Hobart (1738-1805; Yale 1757) was a justice of the Supreme Court of New York 1777-1798. Judge John Lansing (1754- ?) served six terms in the New York Assembly, was a member of Congress under the Articles of Confederation, mayor of Albany 1786-1790, a judge of the Supreme Court of New York 1790-1801. In 1828 he disappeared while on his way to mail a letter.

[43] Smith described the examination briefly in a letter to Cogswell dated October 12, 1793 (Cogswell Papers).

[44] Not to be confused with Edward Miller mentioned above. No further information available.

[45] The October 12, 1793, letter to Cogswell.

[46] William Dunlap, *A History of the American Theatre* (New York, 1832), p. 136.

[47] Webster (1758-1843; Yale 1778). In "Notes from recollection of my life . . ." Smith says that Webster taught him psalmody in 1779 when he was eight. Alain White, *Brief History of Litchfield* (Litchfield Tercentenary Committee, 1935), p. 12, writes that Webster arrived in Litchfield in 1780. Smith is unreliable on dates in his childhood.

[48] *Notes on the Life of Noah Webster,* compiler Emily E. Ford, ed. Emily Ford Skeel (New York, 1912) **1**: p. 445. Webster's diary is included in this work.

[49] Miller, two years older than Smith, was a Presbyterian minister who came to New York from Dover, Maryland, in 1793. In 1813 he became professor of ecclesiastical history in the Theological Seminary at Princeton. Despite his profession he became a frequent visitor of Smith with whom he enjoyed long arguments. He was a brother of Smith's associate Dr. Edward Miller who came to New York in 1796. James Cogswell was the older brother of Mason Fitch Cogswell. William Johnson, Yale, 1788, an attorney, shortly after this time became Smith's roommate and closest friend. For the above proceedings see Minutes from the Society for the Manumission of Slaves, VI (January, 1785-November, 1797), New-York Historical Society.

[50] Webster was interested in manumission and was in communication with Dr. Rush on the subject as early as 1789; Ford, *Life of Noah Webster* **1**: pp. 274, 344. For Dwight's membership see a copy of his report for May 9, 1793, as secretary of the society (Baldwin Collection, Yale Univ. Library); Hopkins's name appears in a list of members of the society made by Webster; Ford, *Life of Noah Webster* **2**: append. 21, pp. 480-481.

The chief activity of the Manumission Society was the maintenance of a school for the children of slaves. In May, 1794, Smith was elected a trustee of the school, an office he filled efficiently until May, 1797. In November, 1794, he was elected secretary *pro tem* to fill a vacancy left by the departure of Thomas Mumford for Onondago County. At the same meeting Thomas Eddy, the philanthropist and occasional associate of Smith, was proposed. At the next annual meeting Smith was appointed secretary for the following year and the minutes for that time are in his hand. In May, 1794, James Kent, Yale, 1781, the young lawyer who had arrived in New York from Poughkeepsie was proposed as a member. Kent was to become one of the first American judges, if not the first, to earn an international reputation. He became an associate and rather horrified admirer of Smith whom, half a century later he was to characterize: "Smith was brilliant. . . . He was a wit and a fine scholar, but a terrible Freethinker."[51] The relationship is recorded in the Diary but never explained. The two men met frequently and had scores of long, serious conversations, some of which must have touched on religion. Yet if Smith had ever been brought before Kent for his freethinking, Kent almost certainly would have sent him to prison as he did at least one other man.

On January 5, 1794, the Board of Managers of the City Dispensary elected Smith to membership for a year. His services were gratuitous, but it gave him experience that he needed. At about the same time he began to live at 2 Golden Hill Street which, despite its name, was in one of the poorer sections of the city.

He continued his efforts to bring together enough material for a second volume of *American Poems*; in particular he wanted to print several poems by Cogswell and agreed to Cogswell's insistence that they be published anonymously.

Early in February, 1794, he found money enough for a trip to Philadelphia to visit his old friends, including Charles Brockden Brown and Dr. Rush. Two months later he sent Rush a long letter from New York in which he enclosed an abstract of a case of hemophilia which had occurred in Litchfield shortly after his father had settled there and mentioned a patient of his own whom he had recently treated successfully for this disease using common salt for a remedy. His success he ascribed to information that Rush had given him. He then continued a discussion of philosophy which he had begun with the doctor in Philadelphia. He explained that he had come on a translation of Sallust by a "very learned man, of the name of Taylor." After giving a brief sketch of the author he enclosed an extract of several hundred words on the subject of evil as Sallust understood it. Sallust denied that evil could have any substance and was, therefore, no more than an absence of good, as darkness is no more than an absence of light. Since Smith presented the extract with no other comment than that he supposed Rush to be glad to have it, it may be suggested that Smith agreed with the conclusion.[52]

Despite his activity, his growing circle of friends and his gradual acclimatization, Smith emerged from the winter of 1794 in a thoroughly unhappy state of mind. Even the acceptance of his play in June by John Hodgkinson brought no change in his mood. He was in love. The "Diary" will show that he was for much of his life more or less in love with Mrs. Tracy, wife of Senator Uriah Tracy, but this love in 1794 was a much deeper, more corrosive thing. All that is known of her is that her initials were E.A.K. and that she would have nothing whatever to do with him. However, not all of his gloom was caused by Miss E.A.K.; Reuben Hitchcock, his best friend, died in July, 1794.

Perhaps in an effort to analyze himself—something he frequently tried—he began in July, 1794, to write a history of his life. At about the same time, and quite likely in the same volume, he started a journal that he would keep with scarcely a break until he died. It included a résumé of his life which began with his birth and continued through his first term at Yale. About seventeen months later, Smith happened upon his "Introduction" while he was leafing through the first volume of the "Diary" with the thought of destroying it. Although he thoroughly disapproved of both the spirit and tone of the "Introduction," which he described as "querulous repining" he copied it entire.

The following month he began to make notes on his paternal ancestors. These he later copied into his extant "Diary." It appears never to have occurred to him to make a similar record of his mother's ancestry. In addition he wrote an essay, "On the Evils of Fear"; both this essay and the genealogical record survive. For some reason when he came to copy his account of his life he left off at the point where he passed his entrance examination to Yale. At about this time, he visited Amboy, New Jersey, for the first of many times, a summer resort for most of his friends but particularly Dunlap who had a farmhouse there. At this time, too, or early in 1795, Dunlap painted his portrait.[53]

It is almost certain that, on the anniversary of his

---

[51] Photostat of a letter from James Kent to his son, April 15, 1847; Kent Papers, Library of Congress. In this letter Kent's memory had obviously failed him; he makes many incorrect statements including his statement that he met Smith in 1799. Smith was already dead.

[52] Manuscript Correspondence of Dr. Benjamin Rush, **16**: MS 1, Library Company of Philadelphia. Thomas Taylor (1758-1835) translated and published in whole or in part the works of Aristotle, Plato, Proclus, Plotinus, Pausanias, Porphyry, and Ocellus Lucanus. Smith had apparently been reading *On the Gods and the World; and the Pythagoric Sentences of Demophilus, Translated from the Greek; and five Hymns by Proclus, in the original Greek, with a poetical Version. To which are added five Hymns by the Translator* (London, 1793). The translation is attributed to Taylor. Smith copied Chapter 12 almost verbatim omitting only one line in which Sallust used adultery as an illustration.

[53] William Dunlap, *History of the Rise and Progress of the Arts of Design in the United States* (New York, 1834) **1**: p. 268.

arrival in New York, Smith made up his accounts financial and spiritual as he did annually thereafter. On the credit side were the many friendships he had made, the fact that his play had been accepted, if not produced, and that he had faithfully continued his reading in medicine. On the debit side was the fact that despite the gift of a thriving medical practice he had been unable to earn more than one-sixth of the amount of money he needed for his austere existence.

A list of his closest friends in the city may be found in the roster of the Friendly Club. The club, about which an astonishing amount has been written, most of it false, was almost certainly founded between September, 1793, and September, 1794.[54] It has been suggested that it was an extension or revival of the short-lived Philological Club founded by Noah Webster in 1788, of which both Dunlap or Samuel Mitchill were members.[55] If so, it is strange that neither Webster nor Mitchill were members of the newer organization in 1795. Smith gives the roster among the earliest pages of the extant portion of the "Diary." Two other lists are furnished by Dunlap, in his *Life of Brown* and in his *History of the American Theatre*. These lists agree neither with each other nor with Smith's nor, indeed, with a partial list furnished by a member, Chancellor Kent, over fifty years later. One of the reasons could be that after Smith's early death the membership changed, but this would not account for Dunlap's mentioning Richard Alsop, Mason Fitch Cogswell, and Theodore Dwight as original members. Some of them were guests but they were not, with the possible exception of Brown, part of the first group. Smith, on questions of this sort, is almost always meticulously accurate.[56]

In the city during this period there were clubs without number. Of these, the best known were the Union Society, the Uranian, the Athenian-Horanian, the Belles Lettres, the Debating Society, the Philological Society, the Calliopean, and the Literary Club (perhaps another name for the Horanian), the Ermenian, the Information, the Union, and the Anacreontic.[57]

This fondness for clubs might be flippantly explained by saying that people of that time had an unquenchable desire to hear themselves talk. It was more than that. A vast interest in intellectual progress was astir. Intelligent people believed in magnificent ideas (two of our greatest documents witness it). There was a feeling that an enormous amount of improvement was to be gained by prolonged discussion of ideas which we now have either ceased to believe or which we can no longer hope to see realized. There was a great interest in Man, the sort of fellow he was, whether he could be improved or could improve himself until he became perfect; most people rather thought he could be if he were given a reasonable amount of time, say a hundred years. The hope was naïve, but we need to remember that it was there if we hope to understand Smith and his associates.

Little that was not to be virtually duplicated in his "Diary" happened to Smith in the early months of 1795. He received a letter from Cogswell accompanying a package of manuscripts addressed to the poet, William Cowper, which Smith was asked to put aboard ship for England. Several months later he still had the manuscript because opportunity had been lacking to send it by the most direct route. And, as he ungraciously pointed out to Cogswell, any other way of sending it would have "cost ten times its value in postage." Moreover, said Smith, there was a report that Mr. Cowper was insane and confined in a mad-house. He decided, however, to dispatch the manuscripts because "if *he* can not receive pleasure from them, somebody else may; and they will not be lost. The reputation of the author may be farther extended thereby, than if they should only reach him to whom they are directed." We know no more of the package and it adds little to our knowledge of Cowper to speculate much on the hypothesis that some of his sad days may have been spent gloomily leafing the pages of a minor Connecticut Wit.

Smith's letters in the summer of 1795 show him to have been working vigorously for the Manumission Society, trying hard to gather enough material for volume two of *American Poems,* revising his play into a three-act opera and becoming associated with the newly founded Humane Society instituted in 1794, among the trustees of which were Dunlap and DeWitt Clinton. It was a curious society having as its immediate purpose "rescuscitation [*sic*], or revival from apparent death." It was also designed "for general improvement in the medical profession. . . ." It did not attract strong support. Smith's "Diary" records at least three instances, before he lost patience with it, when he attended meetings which were dismissed for lack of a quorum.

This brings us, then, to the "Diary" itself. From the first entry, dated September 4, 1795, to the final entry, New York, September 15, 1798, four days before he died of yellow fever, he wrote almost half a million words. This, to be sure, included some earlier writing that he copied. The total manuscript constitutes a document of considerable value as social history. To the casual reader it will appear that Smith reported virtually everything that he said, thought, or did, sometimes in almost too much detail. In fact, the "Diary" is a self-conscious literary effort by an unusually intelligent man. He intended it as a first draft of his autobiography. To a degree, therefore, he was writing for

---

[54] Smith, who arrived in New York in September, 1793, calls himself an "original member." It is plain from his "Diary" entry for September 6, 1795, that the club was at least a year old.

[55] Allen Walker Read, "The Philological Society of New York, 1788," *American Speech* 9 (April, 1934): pp. 131, 135; Dunlap, *Rise and Progress of the Arts and Design* 1: p. 267.

[56] See Dunlap, *Life of Brown* 1: p. 57; *History of the American Theatre*, p. 114; Kent in the previously mentioned letter to his son, April 5, 1847. For an examination of the subject see James E. Cronin, "Elihu Hubbard Smith and the New York Friendly Club, 1795-1798," *Publ. Modern Lang. Assoc.* 64, No. 3, Part I (June 1949): pp. 471-479.

[57] For other New York clubs at the end of the eighteenth century see A. W. Read, "The Philological Society of New York," previously cited, pp. 131-136; Eleanor Bryce Scott, "Early Literary Clubs in New York City," *Amer. Literature* 5 (March, 1933): pp. 3-16.

our eyes. There are, however, some things he chooses not to tell us; references to his sex life, for example, when he makes them at all, are cryptic and tangential. Other matters of no great importance, are sometimes left obscure; his trip to New Jersey to swear to the fact that he knew a certain person, unnamed, had been given the power of attorney, or the fact that he and his roommate were reading Morse's *Geography* because they were court-appointed referees in a lawsuit. Another characteristic of the "Diary" is that it is no textbook-type summary of the major events of the time; one would scarcely know from the "Diary" that there ever was such a thing as the French Revolution. He was notably selective in the things that interested him and that he chose to discuss. Few men today would note in their diaries that they had dined with a president of the United States and fail to add even a word of comment, but the lack of such a word by Smith is itself a comment, on him, and on the president. Nevertheless, the major interest in the "Diary" lies, of course, in his observations on society, politics, medicine, literature and the personalities of the time. He went to school to Timothy Dwight and Benjamin Rush. He debated with Hamilton, dined with Adams, collaborated with Webster, edited the works of Charles Brockden Brown and William Dunlap, and was casually acquainted with an astonishing number of senators, governors, college presidents, judges, inventors, millionaires, and poets. He himself was one of the pioneers of our literary history, although he died at the age of twenty-seven.

Notes from Recollections of My Life from My Birth till the Age of Eleven

This account of what it was to be a child in late eighteenth century New England is unique in its fullness and vividness of detail. Nowhere else in our records of this period do we have so precise a statement of what constituted preparation for college and the way in which the entrance examinations were conducted. Smith compiled these notes in 1797 with the addition of some material that he had written several years earlier. He later felt that he had been unduly critical of some of the individuals whose portraits he etches in acid here.

I was born on the morning of the fourth of September 1771, a healthy and vigorous infant. From this moment, I know nothing of myself till I was near two years old, except from information, that I was very fat & very ruddy, & much addicted to crying, or as the good women say *"a tewsome baby."*

It is curious to trace the progress of memory in children, from its origin to its maturity. In few respects, perhaps, do individuals more differ from each other than in the period at which commence the operations of this faculty. It is not my purpose to examine the subject philosophically in this place, & least of all at this time; I will only remark that I have been the more minute on the infancy of my life, as it is a somewhat singular display of early retentiveness of memory, than from any value I set upon the anecdotes recorded.

The knowledge which a child obtains of his parents is, I believe, too gradual to allow of any precise mental impression, from whence to date the recollection of them: I mean when he is constantly under their care. At least, this is my case. For some reason, which I do not now remember, a lady in the neighborhood, who had a daughter of my age, exchanged children with my mother, for a short time. This was before either of us were weaned. One of the first persons of whom I have any remembrance is this little girl. Of her sister, who was a year or two older, my memory is about as early and entire. We three were play-mates. Next to them, I best remember a young woman, with whose mother I was put to be weaned. It will at once appear that the exchange & the weaning are facts learnt from others. The first event whose date I can any wise ascertain is my having gone to school, one afternoon, with the two little girls above mentioned. I recollect the position which I occupied in the room; and, from circumstances, conclude this must have been before I was two years old. The School-Master, & my little companions are all dead; I went without the privity of my parents; & of consequence am I unable to determine this point satisfactorily. I recollect nothing of the birth or early infancy of my eldest sister; tho' she was not born till the twenty ninth of the October subsequent to my being two years old. This sister was named Mary Sheldon, in remembrance of the friend of my parents; as I was Elihu Hubbard, from my mother's eldest brother, with whom she lived previous to his death; which happened, from pulmonary consumption, the August preceeding her marriage. I believe I was about two years & a half old when I had a severe illness. Many circumstances are vividly imprest on my mind. Conversing with my parents on the subject a few years since, I was able to bring to their recollection several things, which they had forgotten, & at first were persuaded had not been, till I convinced them, by a comparison with other events which they admitted to be true. I mention this, to shew that my memory of this sickness does not depend on after information from others. In one particular, only, were my parents able to correct me. The disease, they tell me, was the Croup, Rattles, or Hives (Cynanche Trachealis)[1] as it is variously denominated. They gave me no aid in fixing the exact date. I well recollect the room in which I lay, the part of it, the kind of bed, & could at this time dispose of the principal articles of furniture in the order they were then arranged. But I have no remembrance of either of my parents; nor of the physician who, I have since been told, consulted with my father. I have, however, a vivid idea of a sister of my father's—my aunt Azubah, who was then there; & I had an indistinct notion of a sister of my mother's being with me also; but in this circumstance I was wrong: as my parents have lately assured me she was not then at Lichfield. The countenance of my aunt Azubah is particularly striking; & I suspect that, even at the period here spoken of, she wore spectacles. Indeed, I have no recollection of her without. This, however, may be the effect of frequent subsequent impressions; for I can not affirm that she wore them so early. If she did, it may be one cause of my particular remembrance of her. Be this as it may, a fact still more powerfully fixed in my memory, is, that I had two Blisters—one on each leg. I have since learned that they were blisters,[2] for at that time, I was wholly ignorant

---

[1] "Croup," frequently fatal to children, was an inflammatory disease of the larynx or trachea. "Rattles," no longer in common use, was apparently jargon for the same disease. "Hives," at the time, in addition to its usual meaning, could also mean an inflammation of the throat.

[2] Smith, as a physician, also raised blisters on his patients in an attempt to cure a variety of diseases. In April, 1796, he used

of the true cause of my painful sensations. They had been put on while I was asleep, & weakened me by the pain they occasioned—as I suppose. My notion was that Eunice & Mary Adams, my little play-fellows, had drawn off the under sheet from the featherbed, & forced the end of the feathers thro' the ticking, so as to prick me. It is possible that I had dreamt this. My exclamation, on awakening, as has been often reported to me, was that the girls had "put prickers in my bed." These circumstances are as fresh in my memory as yesterday's transactions.

It was after this, I believe, tho' I know not how long, that I went to School to a Mr. Swift[3]—since a clergyman, and settled at Williams Town in Massachusetts, or Bennington in Vermont. The only circumstance by which I remember having been under the instruction of this gentleman, is the following. I went to school early one morning. Whether in Spring or Autumn, I am uncertain. The weather was so cool as to require the use of fires. I found no person had yet arrived at the house; & the coals were yet covered up. Shortly after, Mr. Swift came. He seated himself before the fire, on the hearth; raked open the coals; took me on his knees & carest me. He afterwards unbuttoned one of the knees of his breeches, & put up his stocking, & I well remember that his garter was gaily particolored. To these caresses & this fine garter I am probably indebted for my remembrance of Mr. Swift; of whom my memory bears no other traces. This another instance of my early & retentive memory—for no person beside myself could have known the fact, except Mr. Swift who, probably never thought of it again. My parents (in a conversation with them—some time ago, since I lived in New York) supposed that I never went to School, to Mr. Swift. But Mr. J. Morris happening to be present, we were able to ascertain the time exactly; which perfectly corresponded with my conviction. My father thought that Mr. Swift was after Mr. Morris; but this was contrary to my recollection, & contrary to fact. My present belief is that Mr. S. left Lichfield the spring of 1775.

It must have been, I think, the succeeding summer that I went to school to Miss Susan Bull—now Mrs. Tracy:[4] but of this I have not the faintest recollection: a circumstance the more extraordinary, as I was a particular favorite, often admitted to sit on her lap, receive her caresses; & she uncommonly beautiful & engaging. Nor is it less remarkable that I should have no recollection of her voice—a voice wonderful in sweetness & delicacy, of that peculiar frame that it reaches irresistably to the inmost recesses of sensibility, & moves it in uniform. I was passionately sensible to music from my earliest moments: Of all other instruments the voice most enchanted me: Where may I find, even now, when half their powers of expression are lost, tones so simply, so irresistibly winning as those of Mrs. Tracy: how then is it possible that I should have no remembrance of her, tho' she so often lulled me to sleep, or incited me to joy, by the music of her song.

It was in the autumn of 1775 that I was under the instruction of Mr. James Morris—who afterwards married a sister of my mother. This autumn also, Octr. 19th, 1775, my second sister—Abigail—was born. I have no recollection of her as an infant but on one single occasion. I remember having once seen my mother dress her. The circumstances are fresh in my mind.

Since having fixed the date of my pupilship under Mr. Morris, I have seen & asked him, & find my memory correct. The exact date is somewhere among my diurnal memoranda. He remained in the School till the succeeding Spring or Summer, & then went into the American Army, with an Ensign's commission. Under his care I, who had almost forgotten my letters, in the short space of six months, learned to read, with fluency, in the Bible—then the highest school-book in the New England common schools. I also learnt many things by rote; & remember to have spoken in public, at a quarterly exhibition of our school, a little poem of Dr. Watts, beginning—I think—for I have scarcely looked at it since—

"How doth the little busy Bee."[5]

The mention of this Poem reminds me of one of the best beloved friends of my infant years—Mr. Sheldon, the father of Miss Mary Sheldon. He was, at that time, the most respectable man in the County, a Judge of their Court, one of the State Senators, & much beloved. I was to him as a grandson, & he delighted to confer on me many little favors. On the occasion of this exhibition, when he learnt that I was to speak in public for the first time, he made me repeat the Poem, from a chair in his house, before delivering it in school, & compliment me with a sixteenth of a dollar—a prodigious reward, as I then thought. Before this time, I not only recollect this gentleman, but the several members of his house, an apprentice & woman who lived with my parents, & several of the neighbours & their children.

Before having determined the exact date of Mr. Morris's residence at Lichfield, I was in some doubt whether it was in the autumn & winter of 1775-76, or in the spring & summer of 1776. What occasioned my difficulty was the uncertainty I found myself in, as to the date of my visit to Middletown. I am inclined to think, however, (for even now I am uninformed) that it was

---

a blister in an attempt to cure a child of pneumonia but the child died.

[3] Possibly Seth Swift (Yale 1774). Born in Kent, Litchfield County, he was ordained pastor of the Congregational Church in Williamstown, Massachusetts, in 1779 and remained there until his death in 1807.

[4] Mrs. Tracy was the daughter of Isaac Bull of Litchfield. Smith carried his emotional attachment to her into his maturity, as will be seen hereafter. His letters to her, copies of which appear in the "Diary," contain some references designed to be obscure to anyone but her, but one of his chief interests appears in his persistent but ultimately unsuccessful efforts to convert her to free thinking. She outlived him by almost half a century, dying in Hartford, Connecticut, in 1843 at the age of eighty-four.

[5] *Divine Songs for Children*, xx, "Against Idleness and Mischief."

the winter preceeding my entrance into my fourth year—i.e. the winter of 1774-75: And from this circumstance. When I went to Middletown, I wore petticoats; & when I returned, I was in breeches. This is only of consequence as it serves to give date to my memory. I believe I [was] carried to my maternal Grandparents'—in Middletown, in a sleigh, & left there. I remember my father's carrying me home, on a pillow before him, on horseback, in April:—after sheep-shearing. My mother's sister—my aunt Phebe—had made me a suit of cloaths, of some red stuff or other—& I went home much elated, & not expecting to be known in my new habiliments.

Many circumstances of my residence at my Grandfather's are still present to me. He was a tall, handsome, dark-complexioned man: by occupation a shoe-maker. He likewise possessed a fine & pretty large farm. He often gave me butter-nuts & hickory nuts, which he kept in a small chamber over his shop, to which he mounted by a ladder on the outside; bringing down his leathern apron full, to crack on his lap-stone with the broad-headed hammer. He was a man above men in general in his situation of life, even in New-England, both in respect to his talents & attainments, & was much respected. He died while I was quite young, of the Pleurisy. My grandmother, who is yet alive, & near a hundred, I do not distinctly recollect at this period. She is now, & has been for many years, superannuated: not utterly imbecile in mind or body, but wanting the quick conceptions & steady reason of younger days. Piety & benevolence, the perusal of the Scriptures, & the distribution of comfortable things to the poor, nearly divide her waking hours. Nor did I ever see a person so ready to resign all personal accomodations, to oblige others—especially the poor, and this altogether without ostentation. If you tell her that, at her age, she ought to allow herself more indulgence than formerly—that her food, her apparel &c. should be more generous & costly, she replies "he that giveth to the poor lendeth to the Lord"[6]—or by some other quotation from Scripture, & is content. There is in this some superstition perhaps, but I am sure no hypocrisy. She may teaze you sometimes as her exhortations to religion, but you must be deeply imprest with a sense of her sincerity & amiableness. For many years, she could only see by the help of spectacles. & since she was ninety she reads the finest print, & threads the finest needle without their aid. To return: tho' I have but an indistinct recollection of my grandmother at the time of my living in Middletown, yet I well remember my Uncle Micah, & my aunts Phebe & Elizabeth: particularly my aunt Phebe. She was extremely fond of & indulgent to me, bestowed on me many endearing titles, & always took me up stairs with her, when she went to make up the beds; on which occasion I was sure to receive from her several large lumps of sugar, from a barrel that stood behind one of the chamber doors. By this practice I became so attached to sweets, especially to Molasses, that it was necessary to take some measures for the eradication of my appetite. This my uncle nearly effected by setting a large bason of Molasses before me, & allowing me to drink of it till I was satisfied. I made myself sick; & my appetite for sweets was afterwards much diminished.

It is from my residence at my Grandfather Hubbard's that I date my first knowlege of cattle, lambs, & fowls. A heifer calf, the companion of many of my frolics, to which I was particularly attached, was the property of my aunt Phebe. She made me a present of it; & my uncle undertook the care of it, on the usual terms: a care he most faithfully discharged; for from that calf sprung many cattle, with some profit to me. It might have been the foundation of some little fortune, by this time, but for the dishonesty of some poor rogues, & the misfortune of others.

These anecdotes are of themselves of little moment to others; but to me they are interesting. I love to recal their memory, & to picture myself such as I then was, so happy, so healthy, so innocent. Especially since this Grandparent, & this dear Aunt are now no more. My aunt Phebe was my mother's eldest living sister, at the time of my birth. She was a woman of more amiableness than strength of mind; of more good sense, than learning. She married a Mr. Wells of Shelburne, in Massachusetts: then, & still I believe, a rude & newly-settled place. My mother's eldest brother Robert lived there as Clergyman. My aunt's life was solitary. She died in childbed, of her third child, I think, leaving one or two behind her. I have very little recollection of her, after this first acquaintance—till the autumn of 1783—when I made her a visit, at Shelburne, in company with my mother. And singular as it may appear, I can not remember her appearance then, so well as at the early age, when we were so intimate. This is a long digression, but unavoidable from the manner in which I write, where the memory is taxed for every thing; & where, of consequence, it is only by association & comparison that I am able to ascertain the dates & order of events. I conclude, then, that I was under Mr. Swift's instruction either in the autumn of 1774, or spring of 1775; that it was the winter of 1774, when I was three years old, that I spent at Middletown, and that it was the autumn of 1775, in which Mr. Morris commenced his School. Still, I find an uncertainty in respect to the time of my going to Miss Bull's (Mrs. Tracy's) School. She tells me that she first taught me the Alphabet. It must, therefore, have been before Mr. Swift was my Instructor; & this fixes the date in the summer of 1774—the summer before I was three—: & this is probably the true date.[7]

Having settled these points to my satisfaction, I come back to Mr. Morris, for the purpose of relating two facts

---

[6] Proverbs 19:17.

[7] Children who lived at a distance from school were not sent until they were four years of age, but those who lived nearby were sent occasionally at two and often at three. Timothy Dwight, *Travels: in New-England and New-York* (New Haven, 1821) **1**: p. 178.

which made a strong impression on my memory; & one of which had, perhaps, some influence on my character. One day a trifling altercation, the cause of which I forget, arose between my sister Mary & me, which terminated in her striking my head with a pewter pot, & making a considerable cut in the scalp. My head was bound up, & I was sent to school. There, in consideration of my wound, & to protect it from cold, I was allowed to wear my hat. When the School was dismist, at evening, I sought every where for my hat. It was discovered by the master to be on my head, to the great merriment of all the scholars. I say all, for I felt no chagrin at their mirth. The other fact was this. Four of my school-mates, who were displeased with me for noticing their playing, by which I was disturbed, combined to write a note to the Master, informing him that I had been guilty of profanity. This note, at their request, & wholly unsuspicious of its contents, I delivered. They were called upon to maintain their charge; which they all did, with unblushing falsehood. As they were unanimous & all older, it was in vain that I asserted my innocence. I recd. a severe whipping. I can not conceal the indignation which this act of injustice excited in my bosom. If it were pardoned in the master, who sincerely loved me, if the light-heartedness of childhood made soon cease to cherish resentment toward the boys, yet it led me [to] scrutinize charges against others, diminished my confidence in the sincerity of men, & excited my passionate hatred of falsehood. Other events, it is true, have variously modified these sentiments—but so strongly did this event operate on my mind, that I have often, at an age nearly approaching to manhood, recollected it with tears of resentment: not indeed against the instruments, but the injustice. Why, have I asked, is there no certain, no unequivocal language, by which the unsupported voice of truth might speak conviction, & outweigh the united clamours of the legions of Falsehood!

July 4th, 1776, the Congress made the Declaration of Independence. The spirit of opposition was now at its height & military ardor persuaded all ranks, ages, & sexes. This summer I went to School to Miss Hannah Stone—of whom, at this time, I recollect nothing but her severity. Boys & girls, as is the custom in New England, mixed at school, indiscriminately. At this time, there were several misses farther advanced in age & learning than any of the boys. One of these, a young woman of eleven or twelve, took particular care of me. Her name was Olive (if her mother had been a reader of romances, doubtless it would have been Olivia) Marsh. One fine afternoon, the Scholars resolved to erect a Liberty-Pole. A long, dry maple stick of the size of a man's arm was selected for the purpose; & we designed to support [it] by a number of stones at the lower end. They were insufficient. It was agreed, however, that if the end were first sharpened, it might be thrust some way into the earth, & then the stones would answer. The whole school, boys & girls, were assembled. One ran for an axe; & the important business of sharpening the pole was entrusted to my execution. I seized the axe, with equal patriotism & eagerness; placed my left foot on the stick, to keep it from rolling; & began to cut. The wood was hard, & had made but small progress in the business, when the axe glanced, & nearly deprived me of the great toe of my left foot. It was near my father's; & the affectionate Olive & one of her sisters supported me, & bore me in their arms to his house; the whole train following. The cut bled much; but, on examination, the joint proved to be uninjured; my father divided the skin which held the seperated piece; the foot was bound up; & all was right again. The boys proceeded to erect the liberty-pole; and Liberty was triumphant, tho' I, her champion, was wounded. This it was to be a Whig of 1776—: this was, the first wound I recd., the first blood I shed, in the cause of Freedom: & certainly I have as good a right to boast, as many of those doughty champions who chaunt their own praises, & proclaim their patriotism & suffering, in the public News-Papers.

Septr. 1776: Five. About this time, I began to have some relish for reading. My mother pointed out to me the Stories of Joseph, David & Jonathan, David & Goliath, & Elisha & the two She-Bears, in the Old Testament, which I read with great pleasure. But what was more disagreeable than these were pleasing, was the necessity of committing to memory & repeating every Sunday at home, & every Saturday at School, the Catechism of the Assembly of Divines at Westminster; beside the Lord's Prayer, night & morng., & a variety of other pious lullabies in rhyme. These things, of which I comprehended scarce a sentence, often suggested very queer ideas. A favorite dish among the farmers in Connecticut, in the Spring, when Greens abound, is Hung Beef, boiled with Greens. It was often eaten at my father's; & I was fond of it. I mention this to explain my meaning, when I remark that "peace of Conscience," an expression in the Catechism, was supposed by me, at the time, to mean a "piece of Hung Beef boiled." Such is efficacy of fatiguing the recollection & harrassing the mind of infants with Creeds & Catechisms. My chief diet was Milk, with bread & fruits, or apple-pye, for breakfast & supper; boiled indian-pudding, with butter & molasses—of potatoes, butter, bread & cheese, for dinner: my drink, water or small-beer. I scarcely tasted meat; seldom tea; & detested Coffee, & spirituous liquors. A little Metheglin[8] was my occasional cordial. In summer, a linnen shirt, trousers & jacket; in winter laid aside for woolen, with woolen stockings & shoes; formed my apparel.

The winter following—76-77—I think I must have been under the instruction of Mr. Ashbel Baldwin[9]— since an episcopal Clergyman. I recollect little, with certainty, of this winter. I was a second time afflicted with Boils; owing, probably, to my having been repeat-

---

[8] Honey and water.

[9] "The first Episcopal minister ever ordained in the United States—August, 1785," Kilbourne, *Biographical History of the County of Litchfield, Connecticut* (New York, 1851), p. 353.

edly affected with the Itich—from the carelessness of an Apprentice of my father's. From this time, my recollection of several persons, with whom I have since maintained an intimacy, becomes more distinct. Before this time, I remember all the family of Mr. Bradley & Mr. Adams,[10] who were our next neighbors; two boys of the name of Marsh, afterwards my classmates—with their brothers; Mr. Catlin, now of this town, a little older than myself; Mr. Wolcott, Secretary of the Treasure, his brother & sisters; Ruth & Sarah Pierce, & Elizabeth Collins.[11] To these I might add a few others; but I shall not have occasion to mention them hereafter. My rembrance of the three last-mentioned persons, is precise from this winter. The two first of them I had long known. The others not till now. Perhaps it is from the same cause that my memory is so indistinct, in the first of my infancy concerning my parents, that is so of the Miss Pierces: for they were much & often with me: but older. I only recollect them before this winter, on a single occasion; which must have been more than a year before. I had then made myself sick by eating some dried fruits; & I was much indebted to their kind attention during my illness. But this winter much attention was paid to our declamation. We had a quarter-day. I do not remember what I spake, or whether I spake at all—but these three misses (R. & S. Pierce & E. Collins) I think, delivered the dialogue, from Lyttelton's "Dialogues of the Dead,"[12] between *Portia, Arria, & Octavia*, I remember the dress of Sally Pierce. E. Collins, also, delivered a soliloquy from a strange sort of Drama then newly published—wherein the principal characters of the British Cabinet are metaphorically introduced—together with real personages. The Soliloquy, if I do not misremember, is of a woman at Boston, or near by, during the battle of Lexington, or burning of Charlestown.[13] These circumstances served to fix these young ladies in my mind. Miss R. Pierce has since married my friend Dr. Croswell,[14] & Miss E. Collins my friend Danl. W. Lewis.[15] Mr. Baldwin left the School in the Spring.

The military spirit was now fast increasing.[16] In every town the boys formed themselves into companies; were provided with light wooden guns, & all the apparatus of war. I remember our dress, arms, exercises, the officers, the evolutions, & all the parade. We had four companies, which when collected, amounted to more than a hundred. Two drums, five fifes, & four standards, gave life & splendour to our exhibitions. The regular soldiery of the country often took pleasure in instructing us; & we were trained, by frequent mock engagements. These were the schools for the Army; & many of the children then directing these little maneuvers, afterwards engaged "in ruder conflicts & more glorious fields."[17]

The ensuing Summer I returned to Miss Stone's School. It was kept at some distance from my father's; & my sister Mary was my companion. I recollect nothing worth notice, this summer, if I except the malice of three girls older than my sister or myself, which induced them to way-lay us, on our return from school, one evening, & to tie my sister to a tree, when in spite of my resistance they severely beat her: for what reason I am now wholly at loss—but something malicious I remember. Her memory, probably, is more precise.

Septr. 1777—Six. I was now old enough to understand something of the nature of the contest my country was engaged in, & made three attempts to escape from home, & accompany the soldiers to the field. My last was this Autumn, with a party who were marching northward to join Genl. Gates. This party was from Middletown. Fourteen of them stayed at my father's. I recollect the faces, names, & even the arms of several of them: so powerfully was my mind interested by every thing which related to war. When they left Lichfield, I set forward with them, & actually kept pace for near a mile; when I was overtaken, & much against my will, dropped home. Burgoyne surrendered.

The ensuing Winter, Mr. Ashbel Baldwin again was

---

[10] Abraham Bradley was a sea captain, captain in the militia in the Revolution, the holder of numerous town offices, representative to the Connecticut legislature and a judge. Andrew Adams was also a representative, a member of the Constitutional Convention and later Chief Justice of Connecticut. Kilbourne, *Biographical History*, pp. 154-155, 353.

[11] Smith hereafter describes the Marsh brothers, Lynde Catlin and Wolcott. Ruth Pierce and Elizabeth Collins married friends of Smith but have no place in history. Sally Pierce earned an enduring national reputation as mistress of the Litchfield Female Academy.

[12] George, first Baron Lyttelton (1760).

[13] By John Laycock (or Leacock) *The Fall of British Tyranny: or American Liberty Triumphant. The First Campaign. A Tragicomedy of Five Acts, as Lately Planned at the Royal Theatrum Pandemonium at St. James's. The Principal Place of Action in America. Publish'd According to Act of Parliament* (Philadelphia, 1776). A rare pamphlet.

[14] Smith's sketch of Croswell appears hereafter (p. 40).

[15] Daniel Wadsworth Lewis (1766-1837), Yale 1788, studied law in Litchfield, practiced there and became state's attorney. In 1800 he moved to Geneva, New York, then to Buffalo.

[16] Although Smith does not mention it, his father was also much occupied by new demands which there were made on him. In 1774 Reuben Smith was on a committee to collect for the poor of Boston. At about the same time he was chosen at a town meeting to be a member of a "Committee of Inspection" to observe and publish any evidence of unpatriotic conduct. In the fall of 1776 he was appointed with Seth Bird, one of the oldest and best known physicians of the town, to examine all persons in the state who wished to volunteer as surgeons or surgeons' mates for the Continental Army or Navy and to give certificates to those who were found qualified. Shortly thereafter he became selectman for a year and a temporary judge of probate during the absence of Oliver Wolcott at the Continental Congress. He lent his gun to a Captain Bezalial Beebe to carry when he was recruited for a campaign for the defense of New York. Then, near the end of January, 1777, he joined the army under General Wooster. Army life proved too much for him. Suffering from overfatigue and exposure, he was discharged after less than a month of service. In a letter to General Wolcott in Philadelphia, Dr. Smith reported that public spirit was at its lowest ebb in Litchfield. Men preferred to pay the five-pound fine rather than enlist, even for six weeks. As he explained, their reluctance was not a lack of patriotism so much as the fear that their families would starve. Kilbourne, *Sketches and Chronicles*, pp. 90, 91, 96, 107, 108-110, 217.

[17] Not identified.

Master, & I again his Scholar. Was it this winter that I had the Hooping Cough? I am not certain, but am more inclined to refer it to the winter of 1775 or 1776. The event is well enough remembered; but I can not determine the date. This disease almost destroyed me. It held on near five months. I was blind part of the time; my eyes much swelled; & the paroxysms so severe that my life was scarcely expected. Often did a fit of coughing cause the blood to start from my eyes several feet: often did my afflicted parents hang over me in sleepless & anxious expectation, whole nights, fearing each turn of coughing would be the last. I survived: but from this period I date the weakness of my eyes, & a protuberance of them & more than was natural. The winter that this happened, whichever it was, my sister Mary spent at Middletown; where she had the same disease, with scarcely less severity.

Mr. Baldwin quitted the School in the Spring: not much regretted. The first time of his keeping it he was much liked; but on his second attempt he conducted with so little temper & discretion towards the children, & was too prone to neglect & ready to punish, that both the parents & the scholars were rejoiced when his term ended. It was fortunate, indeed, for us—for we made no improvement. All the time was occupied in contriving plans to irritate & disturb him, & in carrying them into effect. I shall mention two. All the boys continued to bore or cut out large holes in the writing tables—perhaps four or five inches deep. These were furnished with wire grates, or glass doors; & were made use of for jails for flies, wasps & humble-bees, which we caught, & confined in them. The number of these insects thus shut up was incredible & the noise they made no less troublesome. It was some time before the cause of it was noticed by the Master; & this happened by his overlooking one of the boys, who was busy with his jail, in which he had five or six large humble-bees. Then, indeed, the Pedagogue was in a rage. The jails were all ordered to be demolished, & himself superintended their destruction. Unluckily for him, he was near the humble-bee jail, when the prisoners were set at liberty—& it was with the utmost & most ludicrous difficulty that he preserved himself from being injured by them. No sooner were the insect Bastiles overthrown than a genius inventive in mischief, conjured up a new machine for vexation to the Master. In the first place, we all cut a hole, about three inches long, & a quarter wide, thro' our tables. Within, on either side, we fixed small pieces of wire. In the middle, a small wheel, which turned on a pivot or axle so as to touch, in turning, the grates on each side. A thin piece of the desk was preserved on the top, which when put in its place completely hid the spot where the machinery was fixed. The wheel was turned by a cord which went over it, & had the ends hang down, under the bench. When the school opened, & the Master was seated; & had put things in train a little; & while all the boys were apparently busy at their books, on a signal given, every one set his wheel agoing, & immediately an indescribable buzzing was heard in every quarter. We enjoyed this trick, undiscovered, for more than a week, to the great annoyance of our Teacher.

There was some difficulty in obtaining a schoolmaster the following summer, and I have some doubt whether we had any school during the whole of it. I have searched in vain among my Journals for a fact which would solve the difficulty. The exact time at which Mr. Tracy[18] commenced his school in Lichfield, would decide the question. Meantime, I will continue my narrative. The facts will remain the same, tho' the dates may be incorrect.

I read well—& had begun to write. While the School Committee were in search of a teacher, I was sent to a Boarding-School, about two miles & a half from my father's. The instructor was an elderly man, near sixty, & the father of Mrs. Tracy. He was a farmer: a man fond of children; dilligent in instructing them; of quick passions, great sensibility, & rigidly religious. The school consisted of about twenty children—boys & girls —who all lodged & ate in his house. I slept alone, below: the others, up stairs. I remained but nine days, at Mr. Bull's, when a master was procured in town; & I returned. But these nine days were full of entertainment, in spite of one or two altercations with my instructor. Mr. Bull was a great admirer of Dr. Watts. Of course, all his poems for children: (& pretty poems they are)—were to be learnt by heart—beside catechisms, & hymns, & creeds, & prayers. Our morning & evening exercise was to repeat over these lessons. And this ceremony was executed in the following manner. We were all placed a-row, and, at a signal given by the master, all started forward at once, with much vociferation & what is called *tone*, repeating together, he beating time with hand & foot, & repeating also. This scene, which usually took us an hour, at each rehearsal, was indescribably ludicrous, from the variety & strangeness of our attitudes, expression, & tones. Many other droll exercises were enjoined, & many droll adventures occured—too tedious to particularize. Here, too, I formed my first attachment; for every boy had his sweet-heart; & mine was a very pretty granddaughter of the Master. After School, we were sometimes employed in making hay: sometimes in bringing home the cows, or driving them to pasture; and sometimes we were allowed to ramble in search of strawberries. In all these affairs, as we were all together, we had many frolics.

When I returned to town, I [was] put under the tuition of Mr. Nathaniel Baldwin, of Waterbury. No

---

[18] Uriah Tracy (1755-1807; Yale 1778) after graduation studied law at the school of Tapping Reeve. Admitted to the bar in 1781, he was from 1794 to 1799 state's attorney for Litchfield. He was a member of the state House of Representatives 1788-1793, U.S. House 1793-1796 when he resigned and was elected to the Senate to fill a vacancy created by the resignation of Jonathan Trumbull; he was re-elected and served until his death. Tracy was a staunch Federalist, recipient of many letters from Smith designed to hold him even more firmly in line.

relation of Mr. Asbel Baldwin. To this gentleman all the children were much attached. At this School I found a new mistress; who tho' less amiable than little Miss Bull, banished her from my mind. My new mistress, who will make somewhat of a figure in the memoirs of the succeeding years, was called Anne Frisbie.

Septr. 1778.—*Seven*. At Mr. N. Baldwin's School I improved rapidly in reading, writing, & speaking. We had a quarter-day, which far exceeded any that had gone before. It may be necessary, for the information of that friend who may chance to peruse these notes, to be informed that the quarter-day was, as the name imports, a day set apart every three months, for the examination of the pupils in presence of their parents & friends, in all their studies, which was terminated by declaiming, & the acting of short dialogues, in which sometimes a few, & sometimes many persons were engaged. On the present occasion, I delivered the Soliloquy of Cato;[19] with a broken sword, mended by splints of pine, secured with pack-thread. In the spring, a party of troops had passed thro' town, to join the Army: for Lichfield was on the great road to Camp, had in it a garrison, a deposit for Military Stores, & was the seat of a Commissariate, for furnishing the soldiers with food, clothing, ammunition &c. The men were always freely recd. into the houses of the inhabitants; & of the party now mentioned several lodged at my father's—& among the rest a Lieutenant—who, having broken his small sword by accident, gave it to me: & with this very sword, mended as I have described, did I *enact* Cato, with much applause.

My sister Mary now declaimed for the first time; & tho' I have never seen the lines since, they are correctly imprest on my memory. They were a Toast, from some News-Paper, on the Capture of Burgoyne, & are as follow.

> Success to the States,
> And the brave General Gates,
>   Who fought with courage so fine,
> In the year seventy seven,
> By the blessing of Heaven,
>   He conquered the haughty Burgoyne.[20]

Mr. N. Baldwin's School, to the regret of all, ended this Autumn. I have known him slightly since, but while I was yet a boy. It is many years that I have neither seen nor heard of him: & I am wholly incapable of forming any correct opinion of his character. As for Mr. Bull, I knew the old gentleman, afterward, well; & like all his acquaintance, respected him highly. He lay near two years with the Palsy, before his death; which was in 1788, or 9. His mind was occupied, for many years, with a plan for simplifying instruction; in particular, by increasing the number of characters in the Alphabet, & employing none but such as were indispensible in spelling. The design was laudable; We had, I have been informed, made great progress in a new Spelling-book, on his plan; but he wanted learning for such an undertaking. The following anecdote, which was related to me by the gentleman who then watched with him, will convey a clear idea of the nature of his Plan. During his whole confinement, so much was he esteemed, he constantly had one or more of the gentlemen of the town & neighborhood, to watch with him at night. One night, when the watcher supposed him asleep, Mr. Bull called out aloud—"Why do C O U G H stand for K O F ?" When my informant advanced to his bed-side, to demand if any thing was wanted—the good old man was fast asleep.

It was probably in the autumn of 1778 that Mr. Tracy opened a school in Lichfield, in which he continued till the ensuing autumn of 1779: i.e. his school, whenever commenced, was kept up a year. I was one of his pupils; & in common with the other children, much attached to him. As I shall have frequent occasions of speaking of this gentleman hereafter, it may not be improper to notice such particulars of his history, as I have learnt, previous to his arrival in Lichfield.

Uriah Tracy is the son of a plain farmer, in what was once a parish of Norwich, but is now, I believe, the town of Franklin, in Connecticut. His father was a poor man, & himself brought up to hard & continual labor on their scanty farm, till he attained the age of twenty or upwards. At this time, from I know not what cause, he devoted himself to study; & after a few months only of application, offered himself, & was admitted into Yale College, in the autumn of the year 1774. At College, his proficiency was no wise remarkable; tho' he stood high as a man of genius. His state of unpreparedness, when he entered; the interruptions occasioned by the war; his love of pleasure; & the ill state of his health, towards the close of his collegiate life; may account for his progress not being such as his talents authorized those who knew him to expect. At the same time, it must be observed that he was far above mediocrity in scholarship, & that his Class were remarkable for able men, who have since distinguished themselves. In proof of this it is only necessary to cite the names of Joel Barlow (author of the Vision of Columbus &c.) Josiah Meigs (now Professor of Natural Philosophy in Y. College—) Zephaniah Swift[21] (author of the Commentaries on the Law of Connecticut—) Noah Webster Jr. (The Philoger & Politician—) & Oliver Wolcott Jr.[22] (the present Secretary of the

---

[19] Joseph Addison, *Cato* (performed and published, London, 1713) V, i.

[20] Not found.

[21] *A System of the Laws of the State of Connecticut*. Printed by John Byrne for the author (Windham, Connecticut, 1795-1796).

[22] When Smith refers in the "Diary" to Wolcott, or Oliver Wolcott it is Junior (1760-1833) whom he usually has in mind. He was the first auditor of the Treasury, succeeded Hamilton as secretary of the treasury, 1795-1800, and was elected governor of Connecticut, 1817-1827. His more famous father is "the general" (1726-1797) who was a member of the Continental Con-

Treasury). The Institution, indeed, was particularly flourishing, at this time, as it respected instructors. For, not to mention other names, greatly respected but less likely to be handed down to posterity, John Trumbull, the Poet, & Timothy Dwight, the present President, were of the number. To return to Mr. Tracy—When he came to Lichfield, he was without friends, money, or health. He had only a common recommendation as a School-master; and his design was, should his health permit, (which was very doubtful,) to pursue the study of the Law, under the direction of Mr. Reeve,[23] (since a celebrated teacher) while the emolument derived from his School should form his support. I remember the first time I saw him. He was much emaciated, which made him appear tall; but his eye gave a spirit & vivacity to his countenance, which the languor of disease, & the anxiety of uncertain support, could not extinguish. This man is now a Senator of the United States; & when he quitted the Bar, to devote himself to public life, stood high in reputation as an advocate, was in ample practice, & in the rapid accumulation of what is thought a fortune in Connecticut.

Under Mr. Tracy I pursued my attention to reading, penmanship, & declamation; but I have little particular recollection of the events of this year, as connected with him & his school.

Septr. 1779.—Eight. It must have been before this time, and I think in the preceeding autumn, that I became so passionately attached to reading. I was familiar with the adventures of "Jack Hick-a-thrift," "Valentine & Orson," renowned heroes! & with all the tales contained in Mr. Newberry's little book intituled "Entertaining Stories"[24] (many of which are truly excellent,) which I had been presented with by my aunt Elizabeth; but they had not triumphed over my love of play. This was an honour reserved for "The Fool of Quality"[25]—a work that, with many exceptions it is true, I still read with pleasure & approbation.

My father was a man of a more cultivated taste, than is generally found, even now, in our little country towns. Nor had he suffered his relish for polite literature to decay. He had a small, & for that time, choice, collection of books. Among these were "Paradise Lost," Tickell's edition of "Addison's Works," Mallet's of "Thompson," the "Essay on Man," the "Night Thoughts" & "Satires" of Young, "Venice Preserved," "Jane Shore," the "Lyrik Poems" of Watts; several of the Periodical works, some books of History, Theology, a number of miscellaneous plays, & a few novels, beside professional authors. Into none of these books had I looked, except Watts's Poems & Mrs. Rowe's, (of which I had learnt several by heart) & some of those which are usually called *Good Books* & almost universally put into the hands of children, among us—such as "The Youth's Instructor," "Dodridge's Dialogues" &c.[26] One day, the Master brought with him, to School, "The Fool of Quality," & instead, as was usual, of directing the First Class to read in the Bible, he bade one of the children read from the Novel. The passage selected—most happily I think—was the Story of the *three little silver trout.* This copy of the work belonged to a neighbour. There was, likewise, a copy in my father's library. But the title had never caught my fancy. Beside, I had often seen some of older members of the family perusing it on the Sabbath: another reason why I felt no inclination to take it up. For as all but books of devotion were strictly prohibited us on that day, I naturally concluded "The Fool of Quality" to be a work of that sort. It is probable, however, that, tho' the religious discussions with which it abounds were the pretext for reading in it on Sunday, yet that its entertaining form was the real, tho' possibly not the acknowledged cause; & that the pious eye often wander from the conversations of the enthusiastic Mr. Meekly & the repentant Earl, to the gayer adventures of Harry & Ned, the loves of Mr. Clinton & the wonderful Louisa, the sorrows of Vindex, & the marvellous tales of the Reprobate. This, if true, shews how easily we deceive ourselves, & is another proof of the extreme folly of impossing certain kinds of

---

gress, a signer of the Declaration of Independence, and Governor of Connecticut, 1796-1797.

[23] Tapping Reeve (1744-1823; College of New Jersey 1763) became a resident of Litchfield in 1772. A year later he married Sally Burr, daughter of President Burr of the College of New Jersey. Her brother Aaron came to live with them for a time and did some reading under Reeve's guidance; he is usually called Reeve's first pupil but this is not proof that he read law under him. Reeve formally opened his law school in 1784, generally described as the first law school in America, although the claim is disputed by the College of William and Mary where a professorship of law was established in 1779. The distinction is a technical one, depending on the question as to whether the establishment of a "Chair" meant that the law school then actually came into being. (See an item in the Hartford *Times* for Aug. 10, 1920, commenting on an earlier article in the New York *Times*.) In any event, Reeve's school became nationally famous as its graduates, mostly sharing his strong Federalist conviction, achieved prominence. Reeve did much to codify developing American law. He became judge of the Superior Court and of the Connecticut Supreme Court of Errors, of which he became chief justice in 1814.

[24] Newbery [*sic*] was a London bookseller, not an author, among the first to sell children's books combining religious instruction with attempted amusement. As a result his books were regarded with suspicion by many from about 1750 to 1800.

[25] A novel by Henry Brooke which went through numerous editions. Probable first publication in five volumes appearing at various times between 1767 and 1777.

[26] Among Reuben Smith's books, those not well known today: *Venice Preserved* (1682), a tragedy by Thomas Otway; *Jane Shore*, probably the tragedy by Nicholas Rowe, produced 1714 (there were two other tragedies about this amazing woman). "Mrs. Rowe's poems": Elizabeth Rowe (1676-1736-1737), *Friendship in Death in Twenty Letters from the Dead to the Living* (London, 1728); another edition to which were added *Letters Moral and Entertaining in Prose and Verse* (London, 1740); *The History of Joseph, a Poem* (London, 1736). D. Stephens, *The Youth's Instructor* (London, 1698). Doddridge [*sic*] was the author of a list of tracts and sermons; his most popular work was *The Family Expositor; or a Paraphrase and Version of the New Testament with Critical Notes and Practical Improvements* (1760-1762).

reading as a duty—which are tiresome to all, who are not wedded to them by principle & habit, & are peculiarly detestable to children. The Story of the Trout was read. I listened with eager & breathless attention.

"I was all ears,
And took in sounds, that might create a soul
Under the ribs of death."[27]

The dismissal of the school, for the day, was the signal for me to quit my companions, & forsake the customary sports, to hurry home to the Book. I yet remember the speed with which I ran. No sooner had I entered my father's, than I asked for, & got the book; perused & re-perused, read & read over again, the fable of the *silver trout,* with a transport not to be described, an interest that thrilled to the remotest fiber in my body, an eagerness that almost devoured the pages. In the evening, all was still. The children were in bed; my father was absent; & my mother, unwell, had lain down. I was permitted to have a candle by myself, & to sit down once more to read the favorite tale. When I had satisfied my curiosity, & imprinted every material circumstance, to the very words, upon my memory, I began to look over the book. I soon found that much was said of a boy called Harry. My attention was vividly excited; & I determined to begin the work, & read it thro' in course. I commenced, instantly; read for several hours, without raising my head; & only quitted my book, to be forced off to bed, & to ponder & dream on what I had read. The next morning I flew to my novel. It may well be supposed that I skipped over the religious dialogues, the impertinent conversations between the Author & his Friend, & the tedious & unintelligible dissertation on the English Constitution. I stuck closely to the narrative. Here was a Revolution of mind! A New World seemed to open upon me. A world ever present to wish. Not to be banished by the most busy scenes around me; & most enjoyed when most alone. A World peopled with all the visionary & fantastic beings that infantile imagination could conjure up & set in action. From this moment my passion for books began: From this moment the waking dreams of a fancy ever native, full of adventures, of plans, & projects,—profuse of flowers—but, alas! penurious of fruits. "The Fool of Quality" was long my favorite work. I wished it to consist of a thousand volumes, & was never tired of the perusal. This vehement love of reading, thus excited, henceforth knew no bounds; I became a very *glutton of books*; & searched every where for new Harries, & other Mr. Fentons.

I have said that my love for little Miss Bull, who I left behind at her Grandfather's, was banished by a passion which sprung up for Miss Frisbie, who I found at Mr. N. Baldwin's School, when I returned to town. I have hinted, too, at the cruelty of this fair tyrant. It is time to bring this most relentless of my infantile mistresses upon the stage.

[27] John Milton, *Comus,* 11, 558-560.

Anne Frisbie had a sister somewhat younger, called Mary, with whom my play-mate Elijah Adams, a little younger than myself, was captivated. Mary was tolerably disposed to return his love, had it not been for the counsel & influence of Anne. This gave an air of capriciousness to her conduct which was the occasion of much anxiety to poor Elijah. As for me, my lot was uniformly severe. Yet it was only from the disdain of my mistress that I suffered; for I had no rival. Elijah & I tried every art, of solicitation, attendance, & gift-offering, to propitiate our little divinities. In vain. It were tedious to enumerate our patience, & their contumelies. We were nearly driven to despair. Of this some conception may be formed, by the following history of one of our many projects. The date must have been, before the period now spoken of—& as early as the spring of this year—1779.

Elijah & I, by the assistance of his brother Andrew, a lad four or five years older than I was, had constructed a little Hut, of poles & covered with Bark, in the center of a piece of wood, scarcely a quarter of a mile from our parent's! This was a favorite place of retreat; where, with these two boys & their two sisters, Eunice & Mary, I was wont to pass many hours, in the sports & occupations suited to our years.

This May the boys of our age had planned a dance, on the evening of the anniversary State Election. Elijah & I were of the number of dancers. Our amours were as untoward as ever, & we regarded this occasion as the crisis of our fate. Anne & Mary Frisbie were allotted to us as partners to be invited—as they were known to be our *Sweet-hearts*: & each boy was to be the gallant of his beloved. To be rejected & refused, at such a time, was thought peculiarly disgraceful. In our situation, both pride & love were interested; & we determined not to survive, in Lichfield, the mortification & affliction of a denial. This, however, was rather to be expected, than the contrary. If it really befel us—what were we to do? After much consultation, we determined to bid a secret & silent farewell to our native town, & trust to fortune for the event. We had fixed on our hut for the place of rendezvous; had determined on our course; the provision of food & cloathing we should take with us; the mode of conveying them, unsuspected, to our Hut; & the time of departure. Every thing was settled. We had even conversed on the probable consequences; the alarm; pursuit; & all that could be likely to happen. Let no one who may read these pages, in the dignity of manhood, smile at our childish passion & ridiculous project! In what respect do they differ from the loves, the fears, the plans of twenty, or of thirty? In the eye of reason & of truth, both are equally absurd: or if there be any disparity, it is favor of the amours of children. But, some unexpected & forgotten event, prevented the dance; our solicitations, refusal, disgrace, & flight. Had the first happened, I have little doubt that the others would have followed. We continued our attachment, which every day gave us cause to lament. So merciless, yet so enchanting, so irrational, yet so omnipotent is Love!

Was it in the Summer of 1779 that Mary Adams died? I suspect so. She was a lovely child. M[ar]y we beloved as a sister. I was a sincere mourner. The school walked in procession to her grave.

How corrupt a child was her eldest brother! And how much did his example serve to debase my mind! It is none of the least of those evils which are inseparable, I fear, from public schools, where children of various ages and habits are brought together, that they corrupt each other. The more daring & dissolute, the timid & unpracticed; the older, the innocent younger. I know the difficulties which beset every plan of general instruction; & I am not ignorant of the delicacy & importance of the controversy concerning the relative excellencies of private & public education. I mean not now to discuss this point. For myself, with my experience, & with my principles, while I had life & health, & intellect, nothing should induce me to trust my children, were I a father, in a public school. But all are not capable of teaching their children: few, who are, are disposed to do it: the example of others might be worse than any their offspring could be exposed to at school: and even of those who are most sensible of the danger, & best able to prevent it by their own labours, there is scarcely one who has the courage to make, (as it is shamefully called) the necessary *sacrifice* of time, & business, & pleasure. I revere my native State, above all things, for its provision for public instruction. It is the best, because the only practicable method, in the present state of things. It is the great national bulwark of liberty, & order, & morality. But, much more might be done, in addition to the legislative provisions, to improve this plan. Much ought to be done. I shudder when I reflect on the physical as well as moral debasement in which children are inevitably exposed, at present, by this indiscriminate & unmodified intercourse. I speak not of the indiscriminate mixture of sexes: for this I consider rather fortunate, than otherwise. But children of all ages, & educated at home in the most different habits, mingle without restraint. This should not be. Some restraint is absolutely necessary: And it yet remains for the real philanthropist to devise some means of engaging the passions of children so entirely in active occupation, however trivial, when out of school, that they shall have no leisure for the low pursuits of vice. I recollect, with shame & sorrow, that, in all the schools which I have known, in all I have been informed of, children, of both sexes, under the age of twelve, have, perhaps without a single exception, been initiated in the nomenclature & imitation of vice, which their immature years incapacitated them from practicing, or even rightly comprehending. What must have been the effect, when a few years had increased their capacities, & enlarged their conceptions! Self-pollution, in all its detestable forms, & with all its miserable consequences. A premature & licentious intercourse of sexes, no less destructive of the final cause for sexual intimacies, than of all just notions of virtue. What horrible perversions of the moral sense, of the infantile understanding, are these! Shall I be believed when I affirm, that the example of one or two youths, like the one just mentioned, were sufficient to propagate practices (doubtless derived originally from boys who had preceeded them in the school, or from low & vicious men) the most detestable, & render them almost universal? We, in our turn, delivered them down to others. From the age of four, to that of fourteen, the vice of man, was general. Nor was it confined, probably, to one sex; if I may judge from this circumstance, that occasions were only wanting to affect between the children of either sex, imitations of riper intercourse. In our towns, girls do not often continue at the common schools after eleven or twelve. Or if they do, they are by that age guarded from such intimacies. But does the remembrance of them cease? Do they never seek a selfish & beastly gratification, when appetites have come with the increase of growth? For my own part, I can testify this of the youth. Few have courage to resist solicitation, example, desire. That shame which should preserve them from pollution, is made the grand instrument of their seduction. I speak not of individuals, whom more fortunate circumstances may have kept from this knowledge, & who may be ready to doubt the facts—but I speak of youth in general—& I have, unhappily, too ample & too certain knowledge, to doubt. I wish to involve no individuals in the censure of having surrendered themselves to such vices; nor do I wish to screen, myself. It may perhaps be necessary to authenticate this statement by an acknowlegement, that, in common with many of my acquaintances, I had not the virtue, so deeply was the habit fixed, of wholly emancipating myself from this pernicious practice, till after I had entered my eighteenth year: till love & science elevated my mind above the low & exclusive gratification of the senses.

But I return to a date which all these relations & discussions should have preceeded. Septr. 1779, when I was eight years old. It was this winter that I recd. some instruction in Psalmody, from Mr. Webster—the classmate of Mr. Tracy—& now Editor of the Minerva &c. Before this some instruction had been afforded me by a Mr. Brunson, or Brownson. My voice was fine, my ear good, & I was very conspicuous on the Counter in our parish meeting-house.

Let me not forget to note that my youngest sister was born on the 3rd. of February 1779.[28] She was named Fanny. I recollect the time of *her* birth, perfectly; & remember that in the morning, when she was shown to me, her little face, & little hands, were so red & black, that I could hardly be persuaded that she was my sister.

The winter of 79-80 was distinguished for its uncommon severity & continuance. The snow was terribly abundant; & food & fuel were procured with the greatest difficulty. This winter proved fatal to the greater

---
[28] Fanny was born in 1780, not 1779. Litchfield Records, I, 36.

number of the oaks in my father's meadow, which formed a grove where my infant feet loved to wander. I doubt whether we had any school this season. If we had, the Teacher was a Dr. Wolcott—a cousin of Mr. Olivr. Wolcott. My mother lay dangerously ill, with I know not what disease, all this winter. Indeed, I was the unintentional cause of a relapse, after she had begun to recover; which nearly cost her her life. One of our neighbours, a man just turned of thirty-six, vigorous & healthy, & with a numerous family of small children, foolishly, in a fit of low spirits, hung himself. This, naturally enough, in our little town, excited great disturbance. I had been to the house, & coming home, incautiously mentioned it in the room where my mother lay ill. The shock was too great; & the long period of Danger which succeeded made a deep impression on my mind.

The ensuing May, (1780.) I began to study the principles of the Latin language, from the "Accidence of the late Mr. Ezekiel Cheever,"[29] under the direction of Dr. Wolcott.

It was this season, also, that, disgusted with the unrelenting & unjust contempt of my mistress, & charmed with the superior beauty & amiableness of another fair-one, with whom I formed an acquaintance at this year's Election Dance, that I forgot my long & unfortunate attachment, in a new & more successful one. Miss Hannah Jones & I were partners &, like David & Jonathan, thenceforth our hearts were *knit together*. With this lovely girl I have since been intimately acquainted. Our amour was interrupted by her removal to another & distant town, & mine to College. Since the completion of my academic studies, the intimacy was renewed, at Lichfield; whither as well as myself, she had returned. I was to her as a brother; & she to me as a sister. She is now a wife, & a mother. At the time of our first acquaintance, our amour was the source of great & uninterrupted pleasure. I do not recollect that any bickering, or any partial alienation of affection, ever took place. I brought Hannah to my father's, & created an intimacy & friendship between her & my sisters, which subsists to this day. As my attachment was fervent, it was sincere, & virtuous. I found companions in others, in her a friend. I forgot every other girl in her presence, sought her only, made her the depositary of all my sentiments, the sharer in all my pleasures. Our confidence was reciprocal. Precious friendship! which harmonized my mind; & repaid me for every anxiety, & every mortification.

Surely there is something highly to be prized in these puerile attachments; much as men of the world & women of fashion, may affect to despise them. They are, perhaps, among the best preservations of early innocence. The intercourse is more refined & delicate than between two of the same sex; & their tender age deprives it of all sensuality. To love, & to be loved, is the mighty charm. To be selected from all her mates, how flattering! to be the beloved, of the loveliest among the female throng, how captivating! There is some vanity in this: but there is much sentiment. Proportioned to ages & conceptions, never were lovers capable of greater disinterestedness than were Hannah & myself. Again I am at a loss whether it was this, or the preceeding Summer, in which I sustained a partial fracture of my left leg. The event, too, is of consequence enough to be remembered distinctly, for it came near to mortification, & confined me almost three months, & I still bear the scar. The fact is sufficiently descriptive of my character at that time, to merit a formal statement. My father was absent, on a journey. As, at this time, he was in none or very little business, he had no apprentice: and he never kept a servant. It was my Duty, while he was away, to drive the cows regularly to pasture in the morning, & bring them back at night: & I had some reason to fear chastisement if any neglect was observable in this respect. I spent the most of the day in the shop, which was left to the occasional visits of a pupil of Dr. Hopkins, now of Hartford. It was Wednesday—there was a frame to be raised in the lower street, where, as usual, there was a great collection of boys, as well as men. I was impatient to be present; but fearing a denial from my mother, I went without demanding leave. The boys united to bear a pretty heavy piece of timber to the place where it was wanted. I was near where we had rested it on a rail; & standing with my left foot in advance, recd. the shock of the rail, when it came down, with the timber on it. It seated me: made a deep hole a little above the ancle, on the skin; & laid it bare up to my knee. A drunken surgeon, who happened there, covered the wound with tow, soaked in rum, sewed my handkerchief over it, & all was covered by my trowsers. If I cried out, like other children, when I first recd. the blow, my lamentations soon ceased, from the necessity of concealing the extent of the injury. I made light of it; & as I contrived to walk off without assistance, & with little limping, the attention of the by-standers was not enough attracted to make the accident a matter of conversation, & of sufficient importance to be reported to my mother. This was what I wished to prevent. For, as I had left home without liberty, I was apprehensive not only that I should meet with no compassion, but should receive some chastisement for my playing truant. Nor had I any idea how much I was hurt. My endeavors to hide what had befallen me, were successful till the friday evening following. Then a limping extorted by the severe pain as I made an effort to do something directed by my mother, discovered that all was not right. I evaded questions; but actual examination discovered the injury: & concealment was no longer necessary, as it could no longer be useful. My father returned the next day; part of the mortified flesh

---

[29] Ezekiel Cheever was a teacher for seventy years, more than half of that time as master of the Boston Latin School. Among his pupils were Cotton Mather and Judge Sewell. His *Accidence: A Short Introduction to the Latin Tongue* (before 1650) is probably the oldest American schoolbook.

sloughed off—& by the autumn I was as well as ever. While I endured this confinement, I made some little progress, under the direction of my father, in the Colloquies of Corderius.[30]

Septr. 1780.—Nine. It was this autumn, I suspect, that I first saw the illustrious Washington. Then too, and then only, I saw La Fayette, who was with him. Of the first, I have a perfect recollection, as he then appeared. I remember the air with which he mounted his horse—a fine bay—the furniture without lace or other ornament; & the saddle covered by a black bearskin. Characteristic simplicity! I did not see the countenance of Fayette, distinctly enough, to call it to mind. But his person, his horse, & the rich trappings with which he was decorated, still possess a place in my memory. The spring following, Washington again passed thro' Lichfield. I remember to have carried him a small basket of excellent apples: a rare present for the season; for it was in May. He lodged at a house opposite my father's. When I went over he had walked up the street; but Genl. Knox, the french Genl. Duportail (I believe,) and three aides de camp were there. They learnt my errand, and endeavoured to prevail on me to distribute my fruit, before the return of the Commander in Chief. I was not to be prevailed upon. While I waited the return of the Genl. & examined some large salmon in a back room, one of Genl. W.'s aides—and, from my recollection of his size & appearance, I suspect Col. Hamilton,—entered. This was fated to be a day of mortification to me, as well as of triumph. I had objected to performing my errand in the clothes I had on; for it was Saturday, & I was dirty. But my parents would not indulge my pride. It was soon to receive a severer shock. The officer who now entered, knew my errand, & began to converse with me. He asked of my studies. I was vain of the smattering I had of *latin*, & my vanity led me to return too indefinite answers to his inquiries: so that he was induced to believe my proficiency greater than it really was. He began to examine me; but, unfortunately, his question respected a part of Corderius which I had not then read. I stammered, blushed, blundered—& finally was enforced to acknowlege my ignorance. He recommended it to me to be more thorough & careful in future. A useful lesson; for which I thank him; and which, from the attendant circumstances, was too profoundly engraven on my memory soon to be forgotten. At length, the Commander in Chief came. I made known my business, & presented my fruit. With what a look did he accept my proffered present! It penetrated to my soul! It was full of kindness, full of complacency. Exalted Man! wast thou not born to sway the minds of men with glowing, yet serene admiration? I was led by the Genl. into the room where his officers were assembled; & the fruit was shared with them. The caresses bestowed on me were too flattering not to be lastingly remembered. I forgot, for a few moments, my shabby appearance & my examination. They were about to depart: their horses ready, & they mounted. There was something characteristic in the manner of their taking leave. Washington smiled upon me: Knox said "farewell my little prince": The French General bowed: two of the aids stroked my head: & my Examiner shook my hand. I remember every circumstance, with luminous exactitude. I went home, with mingled emotions of mortification & transport.[31]

Hitherto all had proceeded tolerably well. My masters were, in general, not distinguished for their genius, or science, or perspicacity. In the daily hurry & fatigue of attending to the wants & progress of forty or fifty children, they had little leisure, less desire, & perhaps least of all the capacity, to select the more promising pupils, urge their career, support their spirit, & direct their eaglet flight. But, if this were true, it was no less true, that the same necessity had not yet occurred for such instructors, as did afterward. More depended on the child, & on his parents. The field in which he moved was common to a greater number of minds. More had preceeded, & might guide him thro' it. My ill-luck was soon to commence; & it may be regarded as a matter of surprise that I am, what I am, when the difficulties opposed to my progress, by my tutor, is well considered.

The June following the affair just related, I began, regularly, the study of the Latin tongue, under the direction of the clergyman of our parish; the Revd. Mr. Champion: one of those men who, with some knowledge, or rather memory of words, have a most starved acquaintance with ideas; who, according to Armstrong,—

"Worm the sense out, but ne'er taste the spirit";[32] and whose total want of any conception of the sublime & beautiful is such that—

"Even Maro's self grows dull while they pore o'er him." When I entered his study, I found there, al-

---

[30] Mathurin Cordier (*ca.* 1480-1564) was a French schoolmaster who wrote books for children, his most famous being *Colloquiorum scholasticorum libri quatuor* which was used in schools for three centuries after his death.

[31] Washington is said to have passed through Litchfield six times in 1780-1781. Once he stayed overnight at Samuel Sheldon's tavern on North (now Town) Street near Dr. Smith's residence. See White, *Brief History of Litchfield*, pp. 9-10. On September 23, 1780, he arrived in Litchfield on his way from Hartford to West Point to meet Benedict Arnold. He spent the night in the village "at the hospitable mansion of General Oliver Wolcott." See Kilbourne, *Sketches and Chronicles*, p. 129; also *Itinerary of General Washington from June 15, 1775, to December 25, 1783*, ed. William S. Baker (Phila., 1892), p. 191. The boy's gift of apples to the great man May 19, 1781: "Breakfasted at Litchfield"; *The Diaries of George Washington, 1748-1799*, ed. John C. Fitzpatrick (Boston, 1925) **2**: p. 217. This was probably the time that Lafayette was the overnight guest of Tapping Reeve. See Kilbourne, *Sketches and Chronicles*, p. 114. Major General Louis Le Bèque Duportail, Chief of Engineers, Continental Army, came to America in 1777. *Diaries of Washington* **2**: n. 220. Alexander Hamilton was commissioned in 1776 and became Washington's aide-de-camp with the rank of lieutenant colonel in 1777.

[32] "Taste, an Epistle to a Young Critic," John Armstrong.

ready, four of my former school-mates: but all older, & three of them more advanced, than my-self. With this one (Lynde Catlin) I commenced the reading of Castalio,[33] without a translation. This did not long continue. We went thro' the Entertaining Dialogues of Erasmus,[34] & a new student (Bird) having joined us, we entered on the Eclogues of Virgil together.

I have given some idea of the genius of our preceptor: I reserve the full length portrait till I have sketched the character of each of my companions.

Andrew Adams—the son of an eminent advocate, then in extensive practice & now Chief Justice of Connecticut, was a youth who, with some original activity of mind, falling under the care, or carelessness of an ignorant, vulgar & drunken mother, was suffered to mix with the lowest company, & to guide himself by their suggestions & his own caprice. He was the vicious boy before mentioned; with no proper notion of the value of letters; with an ungovernable propensity to *low fun*; & ever disposed to neglect his own lessons & interrupt those of others. He enticed us to cards—& many other petty vices, beside that already enlarged upon. He was the eldest of the six.

Abraham Bradley, the eldest son of our nearest neighbour, was a youth of some talents, of the minute kind; but full of a pitiful envy, & a sordid selfishness, the effects of a mean education, & the precepts & example of narrow-minded parents. He was always willing to finish his task; but had no higher ambition.

John Bird, the only son of a celebrated Physician, of the neighboring parish, united to a temper & disposition, so early bad, that it might almost be said to have been so naturally, which were rendered still worse by one of the worst of all possible educations, & the unbounded indulgence of a silly mother—fine genius; rapid, and brilliant. His progress was greater than ours. He already had some knowlege of Greek, & had read all the Eclogues. He learnt with great facility; & having perfected himself in his lesson, devoted his time & efforts, to the disturbance of others. His excessive cowardice was his only restraint. As the others were stronger, his abuse was bounded by their forbearance. I was the weak & unoffending subject of all the malignant & dastardly cruelty of his heart.

Lynde Catlin was the nearest to my age; & the most amiable of the five. But his amiableness was always subordinate to his roguery. His mind was active: his body remarkably so, & he excelled in leaping, swimming, & all the exercises which depend on personal address. His father was a neighbour: a cunning man, and cunning was the distinguishing feature in the character of the son. His sensibility never led him to prefer the welfare of others to his own; & rarely to act without some relation to his own interest. His temper was good: Yet he was delighted to see others teazed—& carried himself with an admirable gravity on such occasions. He seldom failed to promote boxing &c.—in others—tho' he took great care never to suffer himself; & as he did not wish to have quarrels proceed to great lengths, he commonly exerted himself to stop them, when his diversion was complete; & this with such success that not seldom he passed with each party as his friend, tho' perhaps the contention had been originally excited by his means. Notwithstanding, he was of an obliging disposition; & as exertion was pleasure to him, was a useful & valuable acquaintance on many occasions. He was always ready to be kind, where he was secure of losing nothing; & as his sagacity exceeded that of many others, his actions had frequently the appearance of generosity, & not unfrequently all the good effects that the most generous motives could have secured.

Frederic Wolcott, the brother of the Secty. of the Treasy. of the U. S. & youngest child of the present Gov. of Connecticut, was a dull, but industrious boy, with great ambition. His family had produced several distinguished men, in the State, and it was a maternal precept not to disgrace the name. To this his mind was submitted. Frigid & unsusceptible, he was led astray from his object by no generous emotions: Proud & selfish, he had little relish for mingling in the equal & free sports suited to his age: Cowardly, he yielded on the first shew of effectual opposition: & his avarice of praise, or rather of distinction, instead of leading him to more animated & liberal toil, while it stimulated him to plodding perseverance, did not protect him from appropriating to himself the products of the literary industry of more enlarged minds. Since he has attained the age of puberty, circumstances have given the shew, & perhaps the reality of some virtues to his character—without greatly impairing the original traits.

Such were my companions.[35] It is necessary to give a more particular description of our Preceptor.

---

[33] Count Baldessar Castilio, *The Courtyer of Count Baldessar Castilio* (1561), reprinted various times.

[34] Possibly Thomas Heywood, *Pleasant Dialogues and Dramas, Selected out of Lucian, Erasmus, Textor, Ovid*, etc. (London, 1637); or Mad. Fauques de Vaucluse, *Moral and Entertaining Dialogues, in English and French for the Improvement of Youth* (London, 1777).

[35] Later in his "Diary" Smith apologized for the savagery of these portraits. Andrew Adams, Jr., although the son of a distinguished father appears to have done nothing to distinguish himself. He died in Litchfield in 1806. Abraham Bradley became a lawyer, then a judge in Luzerne County, Pennsylvania, thereafter from 1799 to 1829 he was first assistant postmaster general of the United States. Kilbourne, *Sketches and Chronicles*, pp. 145, 190. John Bird, Lynde Catlin, and Frederick Wolcott were in Smith's class at Yale. The first two were elected to Phi Beta Kappa. Catlin was a member of the Brothers in Unity. After his graduation Bird studied and practiced law in Litchfield until 1793. He then moved to Troy, New York. He served in the New York State Assembly 1796-1798; he was elected to the U. S. House in 1799 and served until 1801. He died at the age of thirty-eight. Bird was a Democrat, an adherent of Jefferson, noted for his brilliance as a debator as well as for his eccentricity. As Smith notes in this "Diary," he took a strong, lonesome, and ultimately unsuccessful stand in the New York legislature in an effort to secure the emancipation of slaves in the state. Catlin became the wealthiest of the group. In 1797 he became teller of the Bank of New York and held this position

The Revd. Judah Champion would have made an excellent Monk, when monks were in fashion. He was, at this time, about 45 or 46; short; muscular; active. His belly had a little of the canonical rotundity; his face all the redness & fullness of a true friar. He loved a variety, of high-seasoned meats—& tho' he would not have refused any kind of good liquor, his favorite cordial was flip. In this he did not discover much delicacy of taste; nor was it more apparent in his cookery. Quantity, & *gout,* were two essentials: the nicer served, the better; but this was a subordinate consideration. Great activity & constant exercise preserved him from indigestions & surfeits; a head & a stomach immoveable, from drunkenness. This the good parson, with every true saint, held to be a sin & a shame. But he seemed to have no idea that there was any thing improper in gormandizing an ox, or swilling a hogs-head; if neither sickness nor intoxication succeeded. Intellectually, the parson's taste was scarcely less coarse. Two sermons must be produced every week, beside occasional lectures, at funerals &c. For these, the husks of theology answered as well as the most exquisite morsels of literature, eloquence, & morality. The good man put his things together with sufficient celerity for a man of genius. All were plain. He troubled not himself with nice distinctions & subtle arguments. If others did, he was not obliged either to understand, or to read them: And, if materials were wanting, & time pressed, the rent book, & some old discourse, lent their shreds & patches to complete the sermon. The ordinary schoolbooks & books of theology, Mr. Champion, had read, & often. Employed for many years as a teacher, they were imprinted on his memory. He had abundance of quotations at command, which were often happy—because Horace & Virgil, & Cicero wrote well. He could survey a piece of ground, & measure a steeple. He had done this at College. He had taught others to do it. But he never advanced beyond what he had been taught. All that he had done was not to forget. Such was the fact. If there was a rule in Lily, or a Corollary in Ward,[36] he could repeat it. If you doubted, or if they had not furnished an explanation, you must tax your own ingenuity: or rather, there was nothing further to be done.

Mr. Champion was a social man. He loved greetings in the market-places. He had no disrelish to the chief seat at the Synagogues. This was right. "The meek shall inherit the earth,"[37] & was not he a Christian? He loved, too, to sit & eat, & drink, & smoke, & tell stories, with his brother clergy-men, and groan at the wickedness of this back sliding, adulterous, & degenerate generation. He was a charitable man. He freely recd. the clergy & their families, when journeying, into his house. Lodged & fed them, & their horses. It is true he made journeys himself—& as one good turn deserves another, & as he meant at least to do unto others as they did unto him, he did not often sleep at taverns. He was ready to give to the poor—spiritual advice: and sometimes food & raiment—and work. And as it is enjoined on us not to put our light under a bushel, he was free to speak of the charitable things he performed. If any of the faithful went amiss—to be sure it was to be regretted—but men were but men: all were totally depraved by nature: we must be charitable to others, if we would merit them forbearance: & judge not, that 'ye be not judged.[38] If others went astray—anathema: the anger of God: the indignation of the son; the grief of the Holy Spirit. Were his salary not paid (& in truth it was small, & insufficient) the priest should live by the altar: & men paid willingly for sinful pleasures of the flesh, but slowly & with backwardness for the warnings of religion. Did any one treat him unfairly as he thought: to be sure the pious were the victims of the ingratitude of the wicked; it was not on his own account that he was angry; he was a christian, & humility became him; but he could not forget the wickedness of him by whom he had suffered: God do so unto me, & more also. Did his crude discourses & ridiculous metaphors excite a smile—an involuntary & undesired smile —God was despised, the contemners of his word, & his spirit—woe, woe, woe.

Mr. Champion was not the best economist. He was too punctual to all his parochial duties. He was at every wedding, every funeral, every baptism; & he visited all the sick. There were many agreable circumstances attending all these occupations. If his sermon were faulted as meagre, parochial duty was the cause. He was always before his people in the venerable character of the apostle. He was thought to excel in extemperaneous exercises. There are some to whom increase of study, is increase of obscurity. Beside, at these places he always got something good for himself, & often brought something home to his family. He gratified his love of motion; & he was in the way of learning all the history of the families he visited. This came to be habit. Good Man! he thought he acted from a love of duty: & often exposed, & sometimes injured his health, by exertions of this kind. It may well be supposed that he did not occupy his study many hours. He was in his garden: he butchered his own sheep: he assisted in getting in his own hay. In all these occupations we were called upon to assist; sometimes for a day—once or twice a year, for a week. He was faithful at recitation hours.

---

until 1803 when the Merchants Bank of New York was incorporated with Oliver Wolcott, Jr., as president. Catlin was made treasurer. As a protégé of John Jacob Astor, he became president of the Merchants Bank in 1820 and held the position until his death in 1833. Frederick Wolcott, a younger brother of Oliver Wolcott, Jr., had a long but not particularly distinguished career. He was a representative in the Connecticut General Assembly (1802-1803) and state senator (1810-1823).

[36] Apparently the text was the grammar by William Lily (1468-1522) the friend of Thomas More; it was used for centuries. William Ward (fl. 1765) *Grammar of the English Language* (London, 1765).

[37] Matthew 5:5.
[38] Matthew 5:1; Luke 6:3.

At other times we seldom saw him at the book or the pen. We had a respite every Saturday afternoon; and then he, perforce, completed his sermons. He was indulgent to us. We paid him money. He wore a wig. We venerated him. He was on the best of terms with the principal men in the town. Some of them were knaves. He knew it. But they were, also, members of the Church.

This description has reached far beyond the limits I designed. Some might think it light—& overcharged—& perhaps malicious. None such I trust will see it. They are ignorant of my heart. I have no cause for enmity to Mr. Champion. I feel none. I have often toiled to do him good, when the pleasure of obliging him was the only pleasure the exertion gave me. I would willingly, if need were, repeat my labour. I do not respect him, it is true. I consider myself as unfortunate in having been the pupil of a man so little qualified to call into noble action energies which I know I possess; to guide that insatiable curiosity of learning, which devoured me, when I first entered his house. I have endeavoured to paint him such as he was: to pourtray, not his actions only, but his motives: not, perhaps motives acknowleged by his own heart, but those which actually determined his conduct. Nor have I always omitted his real train of reasoning, & series of expressions.

Mr. Champion's family consisted of his wife—a woman of a high spirit & ready wit—unfortunately debased by habitual intoxication; his eldest daughter, a woman known to be a wanton, liable to intoxication, but pretty-well informed, & of a kind disposition; a second daughter, cunning, dark, intriguing, cruel, plausible, active, well informed, a harlot; a third daughter, reduced, while yet an infant, to a state of idiocy, by the administration of ardent spirits by the mother, to quiet her crying, & cause her to sleep. What a family! and how fortunate for the father that his sensibility was small. It was really small, tho' he was very irascible. If, at times, he were reduced to melancholly, trembled with rage, was suffocated with sighs & drowned with tears, others would have been transported with madness, wasted with despair, or expired in agony. Mr. Champion had his hours of distress: Could they have been many, when the vigours of his constitution resisted them all, unimpaired, for more than thirty years, till he was upwards of sixty?

It will be obvious to every one, that, in such a family, we must have witnessed strange events. But let them sleep. I recollect nothing, relative to the family, as such, that had any considerable influence on my conduct. It is time to return to myself.[39]

Bird lived with Wolcott: the rest of us at home. When we rose in the morning, the first thing was to set down to our Grammars. After breakfast, we repaired to Mr. Champion's & the Grammar lesson was recited. We then were directed to perfect ourselves in a certain number of lines in Virgil, by eleven in the morning. At eleven we recited—construed & parsed. This occupied us till twelve, or dinner time. In the afternoon, we applied ourselves anew to Virgil, or some other author, till five, in the summer, four in winter. We recited; & the recitation again occupied an hour: after which we were dismist, with a new grammar lesson to learn by morning. This was sport; as we were versed in the Accidence, or some other grammar, before our entrance into Mr. C.'s study.

I can not recollect what advances we made this season; further than that we must have read Erasmus, Eutropius, Clarke's Introduction to making Latin, & some part of the Greek Grammar—beside the Eclogues of Virgil, & some few of the select orations of Cicero. These were our mental exercises: but we were still more successful in the Gymnastics. It would have been difficult to select an equal number of boys, of the same ages, who ran, leapt, pitched quoit, cast stones, played ball, & practiced swimming, with equal skill & success. It was our constant practice, when the noon & evening lessons were over, to run to the river, & devote half an hour to swimming.

Much is told us of the happy days of childhood: of "the sunshine of the breast": of "the tear forgot as soon as shed."[40] This pleasure is chiefly in recollection. In a certain degree it is true. There is a sort of exuberant elasticity in childhood, which restores the sufferer to joy & vivacity, with the first removal of pain. I enjoyed much during this season, but I suffered more. It is impossible to describe the contumelies & cruelties to which I was exposed, & which I was necessitated to endure. The activity of my disposition, the healthiness of my body, my sprightly temper, the facility with which I learned, & the retentiveness of my memory, were so many fortunate circumstances. But the malignant persecution of Bird, of the selfish indolence of the others, daily prepared for me a scene of mental & corporeal tortures. Bird had already gone over this summer's studies, he learnt as easily as I did & retained as well. It was a light task to master his lesson. Then, the interval between that & recitation was devoted to the perpetration of every species of hindrance & vexation an inventive genius could suggest. From the others, he often recd. the like return. Nor was it uncommon for them, knowing his irascibility, to form & enact plans for his injury. An attempt to revenge on them, did not fail to double his suffering. I could maintain a short combat with him, but was sure to be subdued in the end. Our companions tho' they detested him, preferred their own diversion, to my happiness. They often excited quarrels between Bird & me, till both were much hurt—& Bird likely to be triumphant—when, not from

---

[39] This picture of Judah Champion and his family is unique. Nowhere else is there an account of the man as other than a minister distinguished for his learning, his piety, and his abilities as a preacher. He was pastor of the Litchfield Congregational Church from 1753 until his death fifty-seven years later.

[40] Thomas Gray, "On a Distant Prospect of Eton College," St. 5.

love to me, but hate of him, they affected to espouse my cause, that they might have a pretext for beating him. This sharpened his resentment against me; & his cowardly soul seldom permitted a private opportunity of revenge on me, alone, to escape unemployed. On these occasions, it was in vain for me to expostulate. If the elder youths were desirous to have us fight—it was impossible to avoid it. My alternative was to be beat without resistance, or to resist, & tho' at last overcome, to inflict some pain, in return, on my persecutor. What trials for a benevolence like mine, which, with unsuspecting ardor, would have embraced the universe of being—what cruel exercises of a temper, quick indeed, but prone to an enthusiastic generosity! Is it surprizing if some acerbity, & some selfishness, be now mingled with it? Do I not right to withhold my assent from the idle praises of the poets, as wantonly prostituted on infancy, as on royalty & wealth?

Thus passed the summer of 1781, & with it the ninth Year of my life.

Septr. 1781. Ten Years. I have said nothing of my sweetheart, Miss Jones, for some time. There was nothing to say. Her father had, before this, removed from town; & love had given way to study. I was mistaken, some pages back, when I said her removal was about the time of my entrance into New Haven College.

This autumn I accompanied my mother, for the second time, I believe, to Middletown, on horse-back. We had a vacation. The visit was not of long continuance. I returned: the class were re-assembled: & we re-commenced our studies.

It was in this season, or the ensuing winter, that [I] entered on the study of the Greek Testament. Connected with this I have a fact to relate which, probably, decided my fate as a scholar. The occurrence was mortifying; the consequences have been pregnant in mortification.

It was my father's intention that I should pursue my studies till I was sixteen, before offering myself as a candidate for admission into Yale College. He was not, therefore, anxious to hurry on my studies. He would have been willing that some part of my time should be given to Arithmetic, Grammar, Penmanship, & the more common attainments. Least of all was he eager to hurry me on to the acquisition of Greek. Against this language he had some prejudice, as not thinking worth my while to devote much time to a tongue, for which he supposed I should have little occasion. Beside, there was ample opportunity, in the five years which were to succeed the departure of my fellow-students, & before I was to follow them. All these objections & backwardnesses had given way before the representations of the Master, & the force of example. I was eager to advance with my companions—& Mr. Champion thought it would be less trouble to hear me recite with the others, than separately. Beside, as the Greek must be attained before entering College, it was of small moment whether the time present, or a future period were assigned for the acquisition. My father yielded: but his objections had prepared me to think less highly of my employment than I ought to have done, since I was to pursue it, & moreover exposed me to be more easily discouraged by any adverse circumstance in the outset than was desirable. My companions, beside that they were disposed to learn, had this further motive before them—They were to enter College, the next Autumn. However, we all proceeded together thro' the Grammar, & began the Gospel of St. John on the same day. We had the first six verses for our lesson; & were to render them into Latin. We were perfect; & the hour of recitation arrived. My heart fluttered. I had commenced the study with melancholy presages: & all my spirits were on the wing. Emulation, the fear of committing a mistake, the desire to surpass, the wish to bear home good tidings to my father, the dread of the malicious & unfeeling sarcasms of some of my companions, all agitated my bosom. The two first verses were recited, by those to whom they fell, without mistake. Mine was the third. *Panta* was the first word: the english suggested itself & I forgot that I ought to have translated it *omnia*. Before I could retrieve my error, I was confounded by the horse-laugh of my fellow-students. The indignity mortified me to the soul, the cruelty cut me to the heart. I burst into tears; & my voice was inarticulate with sobbing. At length my grief subsided; a different spirit gained the accendancy: I had formed my resolution, & my eyes were dry. I construed the verse, correctly: parsed every part of the lesson; & immediately left the school. For some days no sollicitations could prevail on me to enter the school. I remained sorrowful, silent, heart-wounded at home; shunning the society of my unfeeling mates; & indignantly brooding over my recollections. Ah! why was I not fated to find, amid all associates of my early years, one heart susceptible of generosity, capable of friendship? The frigid suggestions of my persecutors, "you had better come to school"—"you had better study Greek"—were not calculated to operate on a spirit like mine. The kind exhortations of my preceptor were little better. He meant well—but could have no conception of the nature of my feelings. Nature had denied him her more delicate discriminations, her nicer sensibilities. It was not till my father united his entreaties, with those of the others, that I relented, & deigned to receive those promises of forbearance from my companions which the instructions of their teacher, rather than their own sense of propriety, induced them to proffer. I returned to the study of the Greek, but neither with hilarity, nor satisfaction. I could not avoid associating with it very painful ideas; & was at all times ready to seize every permitted occasion to neglect it.

The April & May following I had the Small-Pox. A Mr. Asahel Strong, a tan-gather for the town, had taken it naturally. His family, of course, were inoculated. Some few persons were allowed the privilege; & among others my fellow-student Bird & myself.[41] Asahel Strong died, before we were removed to his house—which was very pleasantly situated, at the distance of three quarters of a mile from my father's. The interior management of the House was under the controul of Jedidiah Strong; a man, then, in good repute; since, notorious for many vices. His only child, a daughter, deprived in infancy of an excellent mother, & spoiled thro' the absurd indulgence of her paternal aunts, was with us. Her father had conferred on her the fantastic name of Idea. Her petulance was the source of much uneasiness to us all, both directly, & indirectly thro' the captious restrictions of her father, on her account. I felt emotions toward her, with sort of absolute hate. Since, instructed by misfortune, she merits to be considered as an enlightened young woman; & I have the pleasure to call her by the title of sister.

I had the disease with great severity. I was swelled enormously; blind for several days; & unable to take nourishment but with the extremest difficulty. My life was considered as threatened; but my resolution & patience triumphed. This last quality was so conspicuous, that I was saluted by my fellow-sufferers with the appellation of the "second Job." Five weeks passed from my inoculation, to my return home; somewhat more than three of which I was confined in the Hospital. The Small-Pox left me in a very weak state; covered with boils; & with eyes too weak & inflamed to admit of reading or study. This was my most serious mortification. Bird was but lightly affected; he had quitted the House a week earlier; & was now, with the others, pursuing his studies. I continued at my father's, in the use of Bark[42] & other tonic remedies; & restricted from books. I succeeded, at length, in procuring a novel, part of which I read by snatches: the remainder my indulgent mother read aloud to me, to direct the tedious & irksome uniformity of my seclusion. This was "The Fortunate Country-Maid"—La Paysanne Parvenue—but not to Marivaux.[43] After I had in part recovered my health, I made a journey, on horseback, with my mother, as far as Middletown. It was my mother's practice, to visit my paternal & maternal grandparents twice a year. I generally bore her company; & in these little excursions gradually increased my knowlege of persons & places.

By the jaunt this season, my health was restored, & I returned to Mr. Champion's, & renewed my attention of the Classics. Before this, Bradley had relinquished Greek & Latin; but his place was more than supplied by two other lads, of the name of Marsh, the sons of a neighbour. They had been under the tuition of a Clergyman in the next parish, & were about as far advanced in their learning as we were. Thus our number was augmented to seven. There was nothing in the character of the Marshes worthy of particular notice. A thousand such abortions drop into the world every day. The eldest, Samuel, was flighty, inacurate, & vain: the younger Truman, plodding, dull, & pedantic: Both were mean & selfish. Truman was cold-hearted: Samuel had some sensibility—not often called forth; & rather elicited by images of sense than by moral considerations.[44] There was no change in my situation, for the better, by the departure of Bradley, & their arrival. We pursued our studies with tolerable diligence, during the summer. To give some correct notion of our attainments, I shall mention our industry the week but one previous to that in which my companions were to present themselves for admission into Yale College. In this week, we read thro' and recited the Eclogues, & first six Books of the Æneid, of Virgil; Seven of the Select Orations of Cicero; & the four Evangelists, beside other exercises in Grammar, & making Latin. Let me sum up & see the amount of our studies. During our attention to the Latin & Greek, we had all read, Cheever's, Ross's, or Lily's Grammars; Corderius's Colloquies; the Entertaining Dialogues of Erasmus; (Catlin & I had been over a part of Castalio) Eutropius; Eleven of Cicero's Select Orations; the Eclogues & Seven books of the Æneid; Clark's Introduction to Making Latin; the Greek Grammar; & the Four Evangelists in Greek. All these books—particularly the parts of Cicero & Virgil, & the Evangelists had been read repeatedly. The last six times; twice into Latin. Beside this, Bird & Wolcott, who were before any of the others, had read the whole Æneid, the whole of the Select orations, once; great [sic] of the Testament, once; & the first Book of the Odes of Horace. Such were our attainments as Scholars. Of all the others, Bird alone excepted, I was abundantly the best acquainted with English Books: but I had read without system, & with no particular improvement. We had all some smattering of Arithmetical knowlege: I least of all.

The time at last arrived when my fellow-students were to set forward for New Haven, to become Candidates for admission into College. The original laws of the Institution required a more profound & intimate & extensive acquaintance with ancient authors, than they could boast; but these Laws were so far dispensed with that youth of inferior attainments were often times freely received. From the rigidity of the Examiners, therefore, little was to be feared: and all prepared for the journey in great spirits. As I was to be the companion of the others in this journey, my exultation was no less than theirs. A most exaggerated picture had been re-

---

[41] Five years earlier Reuben Smith had expressed qualified approval of inoculation if it were performed correctly. See his letter to General Wolcott, April 17, 1777, as quoted in Kilbourne, *Sketches and Chronicles*, pp. 108-109.

[42] Quinine, the bark of the cinchona tree. It was ground into a powder and taken in a liquid to reduce fever. Sometimes: "Jesuit bark" or "Peruvian bark."

[43] By Charles de Fieux, Chevalier de Mouhy (1736). Translated and published (London, 1782).

[44] The Marsh brothers were Yale 1786. Samuel became a lawyer and Truman a minister "universally beloved and respected." Dexter, 4: p. 493.

peatedly given us of the joys of a College life, by Mr. Champion; & of the magnificence of the festival to which we were soon to be present. Of the first we could only form a sure judgement from a residence at College, & were not likely to be disappointed by a sight of the place: in respect of the last, considering our previous ignorance, there was quite a little reason to fear disappointment.

The town of New Haven, situated on the head of an extensive bay, is laid out with great regularity; and tho' too small to claim much consideration as a city, with those accustomed to the cities of Europe, & a few of the principal towns in America, is well fitted to impress the mind of a child from the interior of the country with new & unknown ideas of grandeur & magnificence. The regular rows of trees, the spacious square in the middle of the town, the number of public buildings placed near to each other, all conspire to raise lively & pleasurable sensations in an inexperienced bosom. At the conclusion of the American War New Haven was a place of some consequence in a mercantile view; & the number of privateers & trading vessels constantly at their Long Wharf, gave it an appearance of life & activity which has long since nearly vanished. At the Commencement this liveliness is much increased by the presence of several thousand strangers, from various parts of the State, & the adjacent States. The chief officers of the Government, the Clergy, the principal literary & political characters, & the beaux & belles of the country, annually repair to this festival. Tuesday the candidates are privately examined. The same evening the Collegiate Buildings are illuminated, & there is a display of fireworks in the College Yard, with music. The next day, the new Graduates, (Masters, & Bachelors of Arts) the whole body of Collegians, the Teachers & Professors, & Trustees of the Seminary, the Clergy &c. form a Procession, from the College to one of the Churches in Town, where the whole number of gentlemen & ladies is collected, to hear the exercises of the day. The bells, the procession, the booths scattered over the green, the flags flying in the air & the crowds of men & women in their gayest attire, give an interesting animation to the scene. This parade is several times repeated in the course of the day—which concludes with one or more Balls. Various literary Institutions meet at this time in New Haven. The annual Discourse to the Clergy is preached by one appointed the preceeding year: the annual lecture on the Evidences of the Xtian. Religion, is also delivered on one of these days: the Society for the Abolition of Slavery meet & a Discourse is pronounced before them; & an Oration is addrest to a Collegiate literary Society. These, & other things of the like nature, are so many allurements to all who have leisure, or curiosity, or interest, to be present at the Commencement.

There are two descriptions of persons, at least, to whom this minute statement would not be tiresome. To the Youth with whom all is yet novel; & to the Philosopher. I have related them more to display the causes which affected my young mind with so much pleasure. To the Philosopher it will be interesting to contemplate the effect of an annual meeting such as that I have represented, on manners & morals; especially when he is informed, that it rarely happens on these occasions, that a drunkard is seen, or a quarrel heard, in the streets.

For our parts, nothing could exceed the gaiety of heart with which we set out for New Haven. Mr. Champion & his two oldest daughters accompanied us. The distance from Lichfield to New Haven is forty miles. We rode thirty four the first day. Nothing material occurred; the road was bad, but the ride pleasant: I had never ridden an equal distance in a day: we supped together & went tired to bed; & rose early & refreshed in the morning. None of us had ever seen New Haven, nor the Sea. It was a misty morning, but we climbed up the highest hills, & clambered up the steepest rocks, in the hope of descrying the steeples of the town, or the broad expanse of water beyond. This was dimly, but exultingly discovered. After breakfast the Parson, who with his daughters had affectionately sojourned with a brother clergyman, three miles back, came up with us & we proceeded together, in due order. As we advanced, every eye was bent to discover the town; every step occasioned some new remark, or presented some new object for surprize. At length "the many-steepled town arose."[45] I can not express the transport & wonder with which I entered the city. The number, width, extent, & beauty of the streets; the regular & extensive rows of trees; the size of the houses, & their proximity to each other; the public buildings, the distant view of the sea; & throngs of gaily drest people, which seemed to inundate the town; affected my imagination with astonishment & delight. All, I thought, was life: all happiness. Alas! how little did I then know of cities! How little did I suspect the hollowness of all the artificial pleasures they boast of! I was a child, ravisht with the splendid hues of the rainbow, & thought the nurse's tale was true —that it was composed of rubies & of diamonds.

We arrived early in the forenoon of Tuesday, the day preceeding the Commencement, and, by the assistance of our acquaintance from the same town, who now entered into his Seniority, were readily accommodated with lodgings. The remainder of the forenoon was spent in strolling about, visiting public places, & above all the Long Wharf & the Shipping in the Harbour. This was a principal object of our curiosity. But the impressions on our senses were too rapid & tumultuous to admit of distinct recollection. I rather felt, than observed. "I remember a mass of things &c."[46]

Meanwhile our Instructor waited on the Teachers of the College, & learnt that the Examination was fixed for that afternoon. On our return, my companions were apprized of this, & desired to be in readiness. The ques-

---

[45] Not identified.
[46] "The baby figure of the giant mass of things to come." Shakespeare, *Troilus and Cressida*, I, iii.

tion now occurred to me, whether I should not also be examined with the others. I was to be left alone, a child, a stranger, in a wide & thronged town, for several hours: I was curious to observe the mode of proceeding, & to mark the success of my fellow-students: was I not as well prepared, as the greater number of them? It was not material if I failed—since I had five years more in which to prepare myself for the ultimate trial, if I succeeded, how honorable for my youth! Would it not gratify my parents? My instructor had no doubts; he would be proud to have prepared a child so well, at so early an age. I had brought no books; but they were easily obtained. My companions were earnest for my being with them. The subject was discussed at large; & I resolved to venture. The afternoon came. We repaired to the place appointed, not without some anxiety. We found about thirty young men, of various ages, assembled for the same trial; & our examiners came in. In the confusion, we were separated, & seated in different parts of the room. Wolcott was alone: The two Marshes & Catlin sat together: & Adams, the poorest scholar of us all, was placed between Bird & myself. As each side of the room had its separate examiner, we knew little of the manner in which the others acquitted themselves. Our principal attention was directed first, to ourselves; & next to those on either side of us. The examination went on, with various success. Mr. Goodrich[47] of New Haven, was my Examiner. In Greek, our having partly accustomed ourselves to translate into Latin, & partly into English, was the cause of some embarrassment at first. Notwithstanding I mistook but in a single instance: *mesouses*, "in medio"— said I, & before I could pronounce the english, it was supplied to me by the Examiner. In Latin, & in the Grammar of either language, I was perfect. A slight examination was held in Arithmetic. Mine was a single & a simple question, to which I gave a blundering answer. It was unexpected, & I was fluttered. Mr. Goodrich saw it—& turned to the next.

The examination over, the Tutors consulted together, & the result was that all from Lichfield were admitted, freely, & with great approbation. Of the whole number, six only were referred for a second trial. Who now exulted in his success? I might summon to the enquiry all the Heroes of Plutarch, & all the chiefs who have borne the desolating standard of the french Republic, & demand of them whether on the highest day of their fortunes they experienced a more entire, sincerer triumph—with little fear of an affirmative reply.

My youth, & the handsome manner in which I had acquitted myself, excited some curiosity concerning me, in the minds of the Tutors & others. Mr. Meigs,[48] particularly, who was a Tutor at that time, interested himself considerably in my destination. My replies to his many questions were apt & simple. I was flattered by his attention. His recommendations to join the College, at the end of the vacation, weighed upon my mind.

The next day we had business enough to observe the proceedings; & were all highly entertained.

On thursday we had planned to set out on our return; but, when the morning came, my horse had made his escape. Here was a dilemma! My fellow-students & the Miss Champions proceeded; Mr. Champion remained with me. As I had been especially placed under his protection, he could not leave me. He was faithful to his trust, & devoted the whole day, successfully, in search of my horse. Meanwhile, I passed my time pleasantly enough. I was allowed to remain in the College Library, & had free access to all the books. Here, for the first time, I met with Plutarch's Lives; & as it is nothing new for the juvenile readers of this work to peruse it with eagerness, it is not surprizing that I rather devoured than read it. But there were many curiosities to divide my attention. Here were Burning Glasses—which I had never before seen. I was delighted with the Camera Obscura, & the Microscope. I first saw the Air-Pump. Beside, I had a lively & interesting companion, of my own age, the young brother of Mrs. Meigs: De Lucena Benjamin. "*O fallacem hominum spem &c!*"[49] This young man was destroyed by 125 convulsion fits, which succeeded each other, within 24 hours, when he had nearly completed his studies in Medicine, of which he seemed to be destined the ornament & improver.

On Friday, after the most fatiguing day I had ever experienced we arrived in safety at my father's. My fellow-students had all reached home before me; the news of my admission had been reported to my parents; & they felicitated themselves with an honest pride, on an event, in their eyes, so honorable to the talents of their Child. I had entered my twelfth year exactly one week preceeding my Examination & admission. Here, then I terminate the history of the first period of my life.

---

[47] Elizur Goodrich (1761-1849; Yale 1779; tutor 1781-1783) had a long and distinguished career mainly in Connecticut politics and as a Yale professor and officer. He was secretary of the Board, 1818-1846.

[48] Meigs, mentioned earlier, was a tutor during Smith's undergraduate days, later professor.

[49] "O treacherous hope of man. . . ." Not identified.

Reuben Hitchcock

The following abridged account of one of Smith's roommates at Yale was written during the first week in September, 1796, about two years after Hitchcock's death.

"Now the man Moses was very meek, above all the men which were upon the face of the earth."—

Reuben Hitchcock, the subject of this article, was born in the town of Cheshire, in the State of Connecticutt, on the 4th, of January 1764. His father, Valentine Hitchcock, who is still alive, continues, as he has always been, a poor, but industrious Taylor. He commenced life without property, married young, and had a numerous family. Reuben Hitchcock was the eldest child. In his infancy he was dreadfully afflicted with the Rickets, which rendered him quite deformed; subjected him to continual ill-health; and, according to the mistaken practice of Connecticut, condemned him to a sedentary life. Having neither health nor spirits to mingle in the rude exercises of his infantine companions, he naturally sought for pleasures more within his reach & better suited to his condition; and his father being a man of some relish for books, they were placed in the hand of his son, & laid the foundation for his future attachment to letters. The hey-day of youthful blood prompts to employments very different from the patient exertion of intellect. My friend felt nothing of this; on the contrary, he was directed, by the very want of it, to reading, observation, & especially to thoughtfulness. There are few parents who are above feeling some partiality for the first-born. In that pride & tenderness are equally gratified, & the desire of offspring & of novelty alike administered to. Healthy & robust children excite very little of that extreme solicitude which is called forth, in the bosoms, of parents, by the sickness, feebleness, & continued ill-health of their progeny. And who knows not the power of solicitude to multiply the tenderness & strength of love? It is in this, as in all things else, we value the object by the difficulty of obtaining or retaining it. It will be obvious that these remarks are intended as the rationale of that particular care which the parents of my friend always employed for the promotion of his welfare. From his father he was rarely permitted to part, except to visit a neighboring Clergyman, who ministered to his love of study, & seized on the seriousness of his mind to turn it, from earthly & temporal concerns, to the contemplation of eternity & heaven. Thus my friend became a student of theology & an apprentice, at the same time; & literature & morals divided his attention with the needle & the goose.

It was, probably—for I am unable to determine precisely—in the year 1780 that the design of obtaining a Collegiate education was first conceived of by him, & in the autumn of that year that he entered on the practical pursuit of his project. It required a temper & appetites subdued like his, & a sense of duty as constant & as forcible, to persevere in a purpose, the execution of which, if it promised some pleasures, must inevitably be attended with many cruel mortifications. His trade, some trifling occasional assistance from his father, & the transient emoluments arising from exercising the functions of a teacher, himself, in the vacations, was all that he could depend on. Mr. Foot, the Clergyman above mentioned, generously remitted to him the customary fees for his academic instruction; & the then President of Yale College, Dr. Stiles, passing thro' Cheshire, saved him the expence of a journey to New Haven, by admitting him, in Septr. 1782, after a private examination, & kindly permitted him to remain at home the two first terms of his First Collegiate Year. This was indeed a kindness, for, if I am not mistaken, in this period of eight months, he played the Tailor & the Schoolmaster to so much advantage as to make some decent provision for the necessary expences of the third & longest Term.

At the time of my entrance into College, I was a mere child; and, as I had rooms out of the college building, it was thought necessary that one of the most sober & elderly of my Class should be placed with me, to watch over & guide my studies and my conduct. In making a choice, the Authority of the Institution seem to have been influenced by the simple consideration of age; for they pitched upon a person who had no other of the desirable qualities, to temper almost every bad disposition that could possibly be comprized in one heart. Happily, however, my destined companion never joined me, & I was left to run wild by myself. The experience of a few months was sufficient to prove that this would not do; & my own Tutor received me into his room. This was a pleasing change at first, for I was in want of company before, & here, beside a student of some standing in College, & some genius, I found a class-mate of my own age, & who loved play full as well as I did. Our Tutor, however, was one of the most stupid & worst qualified of Tutors. A short time sufficed to inspire me with disgust at his conduct & contempt for his attainments; and this disgust & contempt was heightened into indignation, when, a passion for study having seized me, he discouraged my efforts, & discovered that he sought not to develope the capacity of his pupils, but to hide his own incapacity; not to promote their welfare, but to obtain his salary. I longed for the end of this dismal year; & with so much the more eagerness as I hoped to recover a portion of my liberty, & to be once more delivered up to the guidance of my own discretion. But I could not be entrusted to myself. Some student of superior age, & of patient acquiescence to the order marked out, must be found, who would willingly live with me, & to whom I might be committed. In vain I sought thro' my class. One was cold & suspicious; another ignorant & brutal; one was comfortably settled with companions to his mind; & another felt no inclination to become the Mentor of a rattle-headed boy. I was repulsed on all sides. But the more numerous the obstacles which with stood my purpose, the more obstinately was I bent on it's accomplishment. No dawn of promises had broke upon me, and the twilight of hope yet dimly lingered, when Hitchcock joined the Class, about the middle of the third term of the First Year.

It was a common trick, with those of the Freshman Class who had resided the whole time, from their entrance, at the College, when any novice joined it, to assume the air & character of a Superior, & attempt the exercise of his authority. The two most important privileges of Supremacy were the power of disciplining, & the right of sending on errands, the unfortunate Freshman; and as no Freshman was permitted to wear his hat, either in the College Yard, or in the building itself, to be covered, at once distinguished the Superior from the Inferior. Hitchcock lodged out of College, & alone; he had never met the Class; & was now in one of their rooms, for the first time. A Student who lived in the same room, gave me the information, & incited in me the desire to attempt the ordinary imposition. I have often smiled at the recollection of this first interview between two persons, who were destined to be united in the bonds of the tenderest friendship & the most perfect esteem. It was worthy of the pencil of Hogarth, or of Bunbury;[50] & no doubt, had it been sketched by either of them, would have commanded the eternal admiration of the lovers of the Ludicrous. I rapped, with the violence of authority & with the cane of a sophomore, on the door. It opened. Imagine to yourself a figure four feet high, whose fat limbs & jolly person might become a cloathed Bacchus, & whose round, smooth & ruddy visage was surmounted by a large, three-cornered, cocked-up hat, & terminated by a long, flaxen *queue*. A long, white wand, the emblem of command, was florished with his right hand, & a dutch pipe, whose stem nearly equalled the length of the holder, & which seemed to have been just removed from his lip, struggling to suppress a smile, graced his left. A voice shrill & clear, laboring after the tone of dignity, sharply demanded, if a freshman who had lately come to College was not there. At the entrance of this magisterial figure, half-a-dozen of the Class, who were seated around, rose, with an air of respect; & the object of inquiry turned his face to the inquiring voice. I had received no intimation of the peculiar appearance of my new Class-mate, & still less did he expect to be subjected to the domination of children. Time, acquaintance, and intercourse with the world, mended & improved the countenance & figure of my friend. At this time, he was about four feet, ten inches high (he never exceeded five feet, three inches) & his head, which disease had enlarged so as to give to his whole figure the appearance of a pyramid supported on it's summit, seemed to overshadow his person. A monstrous mass of thick, stiff & ragged brown hair covered his head & shoulders; & his nose, like the gnomon of a dial rose from the plate of his face. His coarse apparel corresponded with his person. Time, acquaintance, & intercourse with the world, as I have already remarked, improved my friend's appearance. In growing four or five inches in height, his head was not enlarged, his skin became softer, his countenance assumed a higher tone of benevolence—& the tonsure of his head, which followed his entrance into the Ministry, assisted greatly in giving a more pleasing air to his figure, & expression to his aspect. But I return to our first interview. Imagine, then, these strange figures contrasted with each other; the duckling majesty of the one, the fearful yet inquisitive submission of the other, & the assumed & impatient gravity of the spectators. Our mutual astonishment held us in ludicrous & breathless suspence—which was at last interrupted by the vociferous & reiterated laughter of our companions, forcible & protracted, from the violence of the effort which had restrained, & the novelty of the grotesque scene which excited it. Here ended the farce—the authority which had been assumed was laid aside—the submissiveness which feared it was forgotten—the new, was introduced to the old, classmate—& we sat down to converse & be merry.

It may seem strange that two persons so different in age, temper, & mental qualities, should grow attached to each other. It is above all unaccountable to me, how the attachment grew, on my part. Not why I should love my friend, when I had really gained a knowlege of his character, but why I was not repulsed by the difficulties in the way of gaining that knowlege, & even by the first interview. I was not, however, but I was assiduous to cultivate his good opinion & to win from him his consent to take a room with me, the ensuing year. He, doubtless, viewed me, at first, with a suspicious eye, if not with positive dislike; he might, perhaps, discover that my errors were rather of circumstances, than of original badness of heart; but my perseverance must have subdued him. Few tempers are proof against persevering testimonials of respect & love. It was, at last, determined that we should inhabit the same room, & share the same bed, for the Second Year of our Collegiate life. Preparations were made accordingly; and when we returned to College, at the conclusion of the Autumnal Vacation, we commenced our plan of joint-tenantry.

Little, worthy of being recorded, passed during this year. I studied with more attention, under his tutelage; & my petulant vivacity sometimes banished his equanimity of temper. For the most part, all moved harmoniously between us. Two circumstances conspired to interrupt our felicity. Disagreable companions were

---

[50] Bunbury (1750-1811), who followed Hogarth by half a century, was also an engraver and social satirist of great skill, but his humor was gentler and kindlier than Hogarth's.

forced upon us, for a time, by the Authority; & we were plagued by the rudeness of our Classmates, during the Winter, who had been permitted to use ours as a Recitation-room—the emolument arising from this use being a desirable acquisition to the scanty revenues of my friend.

I know not by what concurrence of unpleasing circumstances we were separated for the ensuing year. He was absent, I believe, part of the time; & I was condemned once more to co-inhabit with my sorry Tutor.

It is hardly necessary to mention, I believe, that what might be called the superfluities of our establishment, while we lived together, both at first, & when we were afterward reunited, were provided at my expence. Hitchcock did not need them, and his means denied them to him: fashion rendered them necessary, & I was not disposed to hoard.

Those of the collegians who had rooms in College, boarded in what was called The Hall. This was no other than a large dining-room, connected with the necessary Offices for preparing the food, & rooms for the accommodation of the people employed for that purpose. The Students were seated by the side of long tables, arranged agreable to their order in College. It was a privilege allowed to certain of the most respectable members of the Junior & Sophimore Classes, who added poverty to their other recommendations, to act as Servitors—or to wait on the Tables of the other Students—bring on the victuals, carry them off, change the dishes—&c. As a reward for such services they received their board, free of other expence. Mr. Hitchcock was a Servitor, during his Sophimore & Junior Years; & by this means discharged the heaviest part of the expence of education.

Two events, worthy of notice, as far as I now recollect, occurred, in the course of his Junior year. In the Spring of that year, several Students, who were considerably intimate, determined on the exhibition of three Plays, in one of the country towns, during the Vacation. Lichfield was pitched upon, as the place of exhibition; a Presbyterian Meeting-House for the Theatre of action; & "Tamerlane," "Kimena," & "The Busy Body,"[51] were chosen for the purpose. Mr. Hitchcock took the inconsiderable part of the *Dervise*, in "Tamerlane," & enacted *Marplot*, in the "Busy Body." Allowance is to be made, no doubt, for the easily-excited admiration of youth, but I have had opportunity of seeing this character well performed by Mr. Hallam of the Old American Company, without half the effect, either on myself, or on the audience, as the performance of my friend. A thousand, and perhaps fifteen hundred, spectators, obliged the performers to a third representation of one [of] the principal scenes. Who would have believed that the meek & religious, the humble & timid Hitchcock could have assumed, with any tolerable effect, a character so totally the reverse of his own? Yet he often, while at College, personated the Rake, the Villain, &

---

[51] *Tamerlane* (1702) by Nicholas Rowe; *Kimena,* not identified; *The Busy Body* (1709) by Mrs. Centlivre.

the Fop, with universal applause. I am not certain whether it was not on this occasion that he first became domesticated in my father's house. Sure I am, that from his first becoming so, he was loved as a son, more than treated as a guest. It was, indeed, a singular spectacle, to behold him quitting family devotion, to rehearse the speeches of a reprobate; & to see the same house, on Thursday, a Theater, & on Sunday, a Church.

In the Summer of the same year, there happened, at College, what, in the technical dialect of Pietists, is denominated "A great *Stir*." Many students went thro' all the grades, from *security in sin,* to the acquisition of *the New Man—awakening conviction, repentance, conversion, regeneration* &c. &c.—& were received into "full communion." A more than ordinary warmth of devotion was awakened in the bosom of Mr. Hitchcock—who had little of that rampant zeal which distinguished the new converts—& this increased piety terminated in his reception into the pale of mother church. Thus ended the Junior Year; we returned as Seniors, after the Vacation; & once more occupied the same room.

By this time my friend had reached the summit of collegiate reputation. One class-mate, alone, ventured to dispute the prize, without enmity—& the event proved that the modesty of Mr. Hitchcock alone could have left room for doubting so long. Two others, whose attainments were confessedly inferior, were examined with them, for the Berkleian Bounty. Mr. Hitchcock was declared "The Dean's Scholar." To understand this—it is necessary only to observe, that the celebrated Berkley devised the annual income of an estate belonging to him, in Rhode Island, under certain limitations & agreable to certain formalities, to the best classical Scholar in the Senior Class—for three years, if he continued to reside at the College so long, after receiving the Degree of Bachelor of Arts. But Mr. Hitchcock's attainments were not restricted to Languages alone; he stood eminent above others, for his historical knowlege, for his acquaintance with Polite Literature. To a pure, correct & manly prose stile, he added the rare merit of a flowing & chaste versification. His talent for verse-writing was never exercised, at least to my knowlege, after he left College; and, probably, his early compositions have been long since destroyed.

Our Senior Year was spent together in the utmost harmony. The year ensuing was devoted, by Mr. Hitchcock, principally, to Theological Studies—at New Haven, where he continued that he might receive the Dean's Bounty—having now determined to enter into the Ministry. I was at Greenfield, and now commenced that correspondence, which terminated only with his life.

It was, as I suspect, in June 1788, that I received a visit from Mr. Hitchcock, at my father's House; & it must have been about this time that he was invited to take charge of the Academy then newly founded, at Sunbury, in Liberty County, State of Georgia. Whether he was licensed to preach, before he first went to the Southward, I am unable to determine; tho' I believe he was. By the answer to a letter of mine, I find that Mr. Hitchcock was busily engaged at Sunbury in the autumn of 1788. He returned, on a visit to his friends, to Connecticut, the ensuing Autumn (1789)—at which time he again paid me a visit; & I then first heard him preach. This was in October, & he had received full Ordination, at Cheshire, on the 30th. of the preceeding month. He went back to Georgia in November, & resumed his former occupations. In the Autumn of 1792 he revisited Connecticut, & spent some time with me at Wethersfield, & we went to Lichfield together. I saw him several times during his stay in Connecticut—which was protracted by some doubts concerning the duty of returning to Georgia. He, at length, determined to return; & I saw him no more. His health, which had suffered very much in his two first residences in Sunbury, became so bad, as to oblige him to take a final leave of it, in June or July 1793. I heard of his return in August, & prest him to hasten to Lichfield—for I was then preparing to remove to New York, and feared I should not see him, for some time, if he did not accept of my invitation. It was out of his power. We agreed to meet in New Haven, when I went on to New York; but an accident called him away, and we were disappointed. His health continued to grow poorer & poorer, every day, from this time. For tho' slight changes happened for the better, they were only temporary—the last glimmerings of the expiring lamp. This excellent person died on the Third of July 1794—wanting only one day of being 30½ years of age.

[The remainder of this essay, about 1,800 words, is of little interest and has been omitted.]

Thomas O'Hara Croswell

The following biographical sketch of the man whom Smith called "my earliest friend" was finished during the first week in August, 1796. In addition to presenting some evidence of the severity of the struggle of a young professional man without family backing it also furnishes a number of facts about Smith's activities between 1787 and 1790.

"O Cassius, you are yoked with a lamb,
That carries anger as the flint bears fire;
Which, much enforced, shews a hasty spark,
And Strait is cold again."[52]

While I was yet a child, at the English School, in Litchfield, I made some acquaintance with a little boy, a few years older than myself, who came to the same School. His parents were honest people, in low circumstances, living in the parish of West-Division, in Hartford. His father was a man of a shrewd & observing mind, of much mechanical ingenuity, had formerly been a Captain of a Vessell in the West-India trade, was now much reduced, afflicted with the Rheumatism & exercised the trade of a Blacksmith. His sagacity & contrivance in mechanics, were hereditary in his son; who lived, as a sort of half servant, half child, with Mr. Reeve; excelled all the boys in making little guns, carriages, rulers, walking-sticks, &c.—kept the finest pens, the nicest red ink, cut the neatest flourishes, wore a red baize great-coat, was ready to help every one, & because it would pester him, was a hundred times a-day, saluted by the nick-name of "Old-Harry." This was a mischievous corruption of one of his names; but the force of it will be lost on those who are ignorant that "Old Harry" is one of those appellations with which Lucifer, "the bright & morning star," "the old Dragon, & Satan," is oftentimes complimented, by the good yeomen of New England. Little Tommy, indeed, was of a most excellent disposition, with the worst temper imaginable. He would lend you his fine cherry ruler, his new, & shining leaden plummet, & his nice red ink, on the slightest intimation that you stood in need of them; shew you how to use them; & even if [necessary?] use them for you himself. In short, there was no act of kindness which he was ever indisposed to perform, & with the most indefatigable activity. But, beware, of the devil! It was not a dark, malignant, sullen devil, but if you touched him ever so tenderly, he was terrible for a moment, then most submissive. The phrase "Old Harry" was sufficient to burst asunder every long-established bond of amity, and to arm with all the weapons of vengeance which a lightning-like invention could conjure up; but the heart shrunk back from the pain the hand was ready to inflict, & the flames of revenge were quenched in the dews of returning love. A mind like this, so irritable, so tender, so sagacious, & so ingenious, united with an active pliable & vigorous body, was calculated to effect great things, or to sink in melancholly obscurity, according as it received a fortunate, or malignant direction. All the children loved Tommy; & all loved to teaze him.

Soon after this, he returned to Hartford, & I went to a Grammar School. We saw each other very little for near two years; tho' he came back to Lichfield, & lived with a Mr. Seymour.[53]

The October, or November, 1782, after my admission into New Haven College, Thomas came to live, as an apprentice, with my Father. And now commenced our friendship. During my continuance at College, & for a year after, when I resided at Greenfield, we maintained a constant & copious correspondence. Never, I believe, were two hearts more united in each other, more unreserved in their communications, in every respect more *One*. Our mutual good offices were often needed; & in particular, I, who was volatile & prone to go astray— &, as may be seen hereafter, part of the time deeply in love, demanded the exercise of all his ingenuity & affection.

The qualities which distinguished the boy at school, expanded in the apprentice. My Father's own temper was too much of the same sort not to give rise to frequent altercation; but the good-sense of both, the parental attachment & care of my father, & the fidelity, & zeal of Thomas, seldom failed of speedily subduing their mutual resentments.

Thomas devoted himself to Medicine. My Father gave him up a year of his apprenticeship; & employed him, with a small salary, from the age of twenty, to that of twenty-one; at which time he quitted the Shop, & put himself under the direction of Mr. Sheldon, a physician of much reputation, in the neighborhood, to complete, as far as his slender means, would permit, his professional preparatory studies. At this time we had quite a Medical School, for I had now commenced the study of Physic, there being six of us engaged, in the same line of reading, & professedly, under Mr. Sheldon's direction. He, it was true, seemed desirous that we should make progress; yet, either thro' indolence, or inattention, paid but little attention to the manner in which we read; so that each was left to the guidance of his own

---

[52] *Julius Caesar,* IV, iii.

[53] Mr. Seymour cannot be positively identified because there were others of that name in Litchfield. It was probably Major Moses Seymour, town clerk for thirty-seven years, who, during part of the Revolutionary War, had charge of David Matthews, Tory mayor of the city of New York. Kilbourne, *Sketches and Chronicles,* p. 120, notes that Seymour commanded a Litchfield Company of cavalry at the surrender of Burgoyne.

caprice or discretion. This was injurious to all; to Croswell particularly, as he was without instruction in elementary sciences. His knowlege of medicine was, of consequence, more the effect of memory, & of casual observation, than of profound views & careful investigation. He had, however, a talent for observation.

It was in the Autumn of 1788, if I do not mistake, that Mr. Croswell commenced Practitioner of Medicine, in a settlement called Cat'skill, on the river Hudson, in the state of New York. His practice, here, was very confined; & his prospects quite discouraging. The people, too, were vulgar, uninformed, & vicious. The place had not then, as it has since, become a flourishing place of trade. Of his feelings the following Extract of a Letter, which bears date Decr. 21. 1788, will convey an idea, as also the character of the people among whom he resided. "To gain the affections of the Dutch people, and do any kind of business, it is in some measure necessary to enter into all their foibles; drink grog with them, praise their homes; & do ten thousand other disagreable things. A man's sense is, among the most vulgar of them, weighed by the largeness of the oath he takes, & the quantity of grog he drinks.

"You will conclude that, as I live in a Tavern, many of my hours are past with much uneasiness."

The effect of such a situation on a mind like his may easily be conceived. Preyed upon by ten thousand sensibilities of which none of those around him could form a conception, without friends, poor, destitute of resources, even of books—for he was unable to purchase them—every movement of his intellect was retrograde. The letters which he occasionally received from his friends formed his only consolation, & were the slender threads which held him from sinking to the level of the herd he so much despised. Another circumstance, perhaps, operated, at this time, to increase his depression. His heart had been rendered sensible to the charms of a young woman of the place he had so lately quitted. As modest, as he was tender, this passion was concealed in his own bosom, to be cherished, & to torment him, in secret; and this torment was not much lightened by flattering probabilities of success. It requires all the force of experience to convey an adequate idea of a wretchedness so complicate. It is a theme for the most impassioned eloquence; but the most impassioned eloquence, unassisted by experience, could only attain to a faint & inexpressive outline.

Things wearing so dismal an aspect in Catskill, Mr. Croswell was induced to remove to a part of Dutchess County, called Clinton Plains, & since North-East Town; there to exercise the double functions of Physician & School-master. This happened the ensuing year—1789. This situation was not better than the former, either in respect to profit, or society. He sustained himself, which was the most he could do. An offer being made him of returning on more advantageous terms, to Catskill, he made a journey there, continued some months, & was on the point of forming a connection in business, when an event, unexpected to him, recalled him to Lichfield, & protracted his ultimate establishment for a considerable time. This happened in the Autumn of 1790, & he had returned to Catskill in the preceeding spring.

On my return to my father's house, which was in the autumn of 1787, I entered as a sort of Apprentice, into his Shop; where Mr. Croswell then was, as Clerk, & commenced the study of Physic. I quitted this situation, in the Autumn of 1790, to place myself in the Medical School of Phila, for the completing of my professional studies. My removal was likely to be disadvantageous to my father's affairs, unless my place was well supplied by a person more capable than a sorry apprentice which he then had. Domestic concerns, & increasing years, as the first occupied much of his time & the last rendered any irregularity in the distribution of his time extremely painful, led my father to conclude that he was unable himself to go thro' with the discharge of the active part of his concerns. In this dilemma, he thought of Mr. Croswell. He recollected his ingenuity, faithfulness, knowlege, & activity, & he knew that they had been unproductively exerted in his profession. To do good was habitual with my Father; to raise up such a man as Mr. Croswell was highly pleasing, in prospect; & his benevolence was doubly active in finding occasion for a partner, the idea being once suggested. The end of this was, that he made an offer of engaging in a partnership with Mr. Croswell. I had the pleasure of communicating this offer to my friend; who came to Lichfield, before I went to Phila.—& when the terms were speedily arranged. He did not, however, fix in Lichd. till after I had reached Phila.

I was absent eight months. During this period I had several letters from Mr. Croswell. I did not find in them except in a single instance, that full unbosoming of the soul to which I had been accustomed; & was ignorant of many events, which happened in my absence, till after my return.

It appeared that the irregularity of life to which my friend was subjected, during his residence in the State of New York, had formed itself, in some measure, into a habit; & that his principles had not altogether escaped that taint, which, soon after his re-settlement in Lichd. became evident in his manners. In particular, his temper had been injured; he was more impatient of reproof, & correction; this added to his partner's desire to correct; which, again, led to contumacy—& ended in complete inattention to the injunctions of his partner. It had, also, another unpleasant effect—it induced Mr. Croswell to take many measures, without consulting my father—& which, as it happened, for want of the information which he must inevitably have derived from so consulting him, proved unproductive, at least, & sometimes expensive. This led to frequent altercations. But differences of this nature did not appear immediately. One of the principal motives which determined Mr. Croswell to accept of my father's invitation of partnership, was the hope of being placed in a situation to press his suit, with the young lady to whom, as I have before hinted, he was attached. The opportunity, indeed, occurred; it was not suffered to pass neglected; his love was proffered; but unsuccessfully. His suit was rejected with many expressions of sincere, but sisterly, affection. He attempted to renew it; but the object of his passion was no coquet, & he was obliged to desist.

While there remained any hope of success in this affair of the heart, the conduct of Mr. Croswell was wholly irreproachable. It was not till after his rejection that the change in his temper & opinions became evident, & that he ceased to aim at their concealment & control. Alas! what is Man, when delivered up to be the prey of insatiate & furious passion! What is the world to him, it's pleasures, it's wealth, it's honors, & it's opinion, who

> Within, without, obscure & void,
> Feels all is ravag'd, all destroy'd?[54]

Where is the wretch, so lost to every sentiment of humanity & justice, that dares, in a moment like this, to exult in lacerating derision over the sufferings of one so cast down & trampled under foot of sorrow, & hug himself, in detestable self-applause while he indulges in reprehension of the failings & errors of the unfortunate? How rare are they who love without selfishness, & can bear rejection with undiminished virtue!

By degrees the tranquillity of Mr. Croswell returned. He renewed his attentions to business; & tho' every thing did not go on with all it's ancient smoothness, yet harmony seemed in a good degree restored. His heart, ravaged by an unfortunate passion, attempted to find consolation in another which was listened to with greater indulgence; & when I returned from Phila. I was soon informed, by himself, that he was addressing Miss Ruth Pierce—who not long after became his wife. This marriage was solemnized, if I do not misremember, in the Summer or Autumn of 1791; & the Winter following, the new-married couple commenced housekeepers.

Mrs. Croswell was, at the time of their marriage, & has continued till now, a delicate woman, with frequent interruptions to her health, by sickness. She is of a very amiable temper & disposition, united with good sense, which has been cultivated with care. She has both read & thought.

The honey-moon over, matrimony had not restored my friend to his youthful uniformity of conduct. The good qualities of his heart & mind were not extinct; they shone forth, occasionally, with all their luster; but it was only occasionally. His irascibility, impatience, & unsteadiness, manifestly increased. (A letter recd. from him at the time I was in Phila., which I have just read, is wonderfully descriptive of the situation of his mind.) It was necessary to the happiness of both parties, that the partnership should subsist no longer. Croswell was the first to perceive this; & he determined, in secret, on a second removal from Lichd. His measures were all taken before my father recd. an intimation of his design from himself. The terms were soon agreed upon: Croswell was fully sensible of his own faultiness: my father retained a paternal fondness for him: they parted without regret: but without animosity. They are still friends.

In the spring of 1792, Mr. Croswell returned to Catskill to exercise a variety of functions. His brother, a stupid, good-natured, idle, card-playing fellow, who had been bred a printer, engaged with him in a newspaper;[55] which the printer executed, & the Physician edited. To this they joined Book-binding, & some book-printing, in the small way. Beside this, Thomas Croswell opened a Druggist's Shop, & entered, anew into the practice of Physic. Since this time I have seen him but twice, & have recd. but two or three letters from him; & am but, generally & slightly acquainted with his affairs. A summary statement, as far as I am possessed of his situation, shall conclude.

Mr. Thomas O'Hara Croswell, is now about twenty nine years of age. He is somewhat above the ordinary height of men, but slender. The vicious indolence of his brother obliges him to exert a never-ceasing & distressful industry; the effect of which is much diminished by fickleness of temper. His ingenuity is unabated; but exhausted in expedients. His life is too active for study, or for continued reflection; but he observes quick, adapts readily, & remembers lastingly. His disposition has lost none of it's excellence; but his temper has augmented in vivacity, & being constantly subjected to irritation, constantly leads him astray.

He would submit his head to the block for his friend; but if the executioner accosted him roughly he would precipitate him from the scaffold, bid defiance to a host of armed men, &, with the subsidence of passion, weep if a child had been injured by his fury. He is therefore still the same, as when at school. All the events of his life have operated unkindly. He may die in obscurity—but what would not such activity, such sensibility, such generosity, have produced, if it had been steadily & benignly directed! I was struck, when I last saw him, with his thin & pale countenance. It discovered the ravages of incessant inquietudes. It is not probable that we shall, henceforth, preserve much intimacy—but this was my first friend. Circumstances, tho' I do not expect it, may yet bring him forward; our intercourse may be warmly renewed; & he may yet occupy a conspicuous place in my Memoirs.

I reserve some anecdotes, to a future opportunity.

---

[54] Not identified.

[55] The *Catskill Packet* (1792-1799), Clarence S. Brigham, *History and Bibliography of American Newspapers 1690-1890* (Worcester, Massachusetts, 1947) **1**: p. 564.

THE "DIARY"

Notebook No. 1: September–October, 1795

September 1795
Friday, 4th

A new, and third volume of my Journal—and how, & with what intentions, should I begin it? That a plan, like the one I have pursued, might be rendered eminently useful, I doubt not. That, even in the method adhered to, by me, hitherto, it has not been altogether useless, I do not question. That I may enlarge it, & deduce still higher & more valuable consequences, from it; seems equally sure. And it is certain that, with a design so to do, I have commenced this volume. Yes! and I have commenced it, with an assurance, a positive assurance, that all my designs, in respect to it's general copiousness, & importance, shall not prove abortive. I determine, that this tome shall exhibit more of a picture of my mind, than either of the preceeding. That is shall be fraught with richer treasures of reflection, more enlarged narrations of events, & more copious transcripts of scenery & fiction. Let us see how this determination will stand.

It is my purpose to have devoted no small portion of this afternoon to this journal. But various interruptions prevented, & diverted my attention to objects, almost if not, equally agreeable & important. The circumstance of beginning a new volume; the more firm persuasion, I now have, than before, that my labour would not be vain; the more consistent turn my notions have lately taken; considerations on the line of consequent conduct it behoves me to adopt & pursue; the events of the last month, generally; and, in particular the recent occurrences of the last six days; in short, the very day itself, on which I actually write; all invited me to amplify, in an uncommon degree. Opportunity, however, tho' suspended, is not lost; and, doubtless, I shall have both occasion & leisure to reflect & write upon every thing, hereafter, on which I was desirous, this afternoon, to have enlarged.

This day is my Birth-day. I am now twenty-four years of age. Twenty-four years! It is impossible to give language to the variety of ideas which so simple a fact, at once, suggests to my mind: neither will I attempt it. To some this period, on looking back, would appear short: a moment; a span; a dream: Such are the terms in which people are accustomed to speak of time past. Are there any to whom it seems long? Yes, I am one, to whom the years which have passed, appear in all their extent. Indeed, I am, at times, at a loss to conceive how it is that I have lived no longer. Well! How have I lived? This is an inquiry much more important. Not for the purpose of gratifying a mean vanity, or a more shameful pride; not to indulge in vain regrets, & vicious remorse; but to draw instruction, consolation, resolution. My opportunities have been both great, & small; have been both used, & neglected; & all in a manner which admits of explication in no other way than by recurring to the history of my life. My attainments certainly surpass those of most persons of my age; at least, in this Country. It is probable that the same is true of my talents. With no less sincerity it may be affirmed that I might, & ought, to have acquired greater stores of knowlege, than I have acquired; & that my talents, having never been truly & fully called forth, their extent & force is imperfectly known. But, what is of most importance, is, that, at last, I seem to have gained, at least, some glimmering idea of truth; while men, in general appear to be either immerged, or submerged, in error. This conviction once fixed, I think, I shall not be backward in attempting to resolve the question, Whether is it truth, or not. Nay, I think, I shall no longer want a motive for action; shall no longer lament the dissolution of the fairy fabrics of visionary & passionate delusion; but shall keep my eye, & my heart, fixed on the majestic, simple, sublime, & venerable temple of Truth. On this subject, however, it imports me not to presume too much. To be as far from the error of unfounded enthusiasm, on one hand; & as from the misfortune of pusilanimous distrust, on the other. And, in all things, to cultivate that even & patient temper of perseverance & fortitude, which best becomes him who aspires after the illustrious character of *The Wise*.... It is time to quit generals, for particulars.

I arose at 7. The day has been remarkably fine; & the evening, also, truly Autumnal. I had time, in the morning, to arrange my little affairs, & to put an end to the preceeding volume, before the arrival of company. The remainder of the time, till dinner, was occupied in a successive attention to visitants. Mumford, Alsop, Adams, our neighbor Mr. Boyd, & Mr. Gahn, were all here;[56] & Mr. Gahn furnished me with "Equisse d'un Tableau Historique des Progrès de l'esprit humain. *Ouvrage posthume de Condorcet.*"[57] He, (Mr. Gahn,)

---

[56] Mumford and Alsop have been previously cited. Charles Adams was the son of John Adams, then vice president. Boyd was probably William Boyd, Smith's neighbor and occasional companion, treasurer of the Tammany Society, a merchant who was associated with the Suydams, one of the largest dealers in tea, wine and spirits in the city. Mr. Gahn was a young Swede who owned a counting house and lived at least part of the year in Perth Amboy. He was an intellectual who frequently lent Smith papers, pamphlets, and books published in Europe.

[57] Marie Jean Antoine Nicholas Caritat, Marquis de Condorcet (1743-1794) was a kind of moderate revolutionist, philosopher, and mathematician. Smith would find him well suited to his cast of mind in some ways, for his anticlericalism, love of abstract justice, and interest in dynamic perfectibility.

borrowed it, for me, of M. Roulet,[58] a gentleman who has lately settled in N. York, a Swiss, I think, by birth; &, if I remember right, last from Genoa. Adams was married, on the evening of last Saturday. Of Mumford I have much to say; &, therefore, must wait for a future occasion.

In the afternoon, I had several errands to do. When I came home, Mumford & Alsop, came, separately. Our conversation did not take a turn sufficiently consistent, to admit of character, or denomination. They left us, to attend to their business. W. Johnson[59] & I, went to Mr. Lovegrove's.[60] We found Mrs. L. at home, alone, and at tea. We took our seats at the table. I told her of Amboy; & of the place, there, which I had pitched upon for Mr. L. She has finished *Anna St. Ives;* estimates it's literary worth highly; & adopts the doctrines in all their extent. An accident happened, however, which shewed that she was not yet able to practice that severe truth which she so much admired. Thro' some neglect, her boy, her infant son, who was quietly sleeping on the bed, up stairs, rolled off. The blow awakened him, in a fright; & he screamed violently. The mother was frantic. She knew not the extent, or nature, of the supposed injury; & her active & maternal imagination, supplied the defective knowlege, by a hundred horrid fantasies. Wm. supported her. Meantime I ran up stairs, & found what had happened; & that the child had sustained no injury. At length all was quieted, again; & a conversation ensued, which, I doubt not, will not be inefficacious, in preventing equal alarm on a similar occasion. Mr. L. returned. The Amboy project was repeated. Conversation, again, took a general turn. We discoursed on the nature of the First Cause: On freedom of inquiry, & opinion; on Rousseau, & Petrarco; on "Anna St. Ives"; on the means of extinguishing false sensibility; & finally, in an imperfect manner, on my own passion, experience, cure. We separated about ten: & I think this one of the best, most pleasant, & most instructive, evenings, I have ever past. To this house I never go, without deriving some advantage from my visit: from it I never depart, with that entire dissatisfaction which is the inseparable consequence of having visited at many other places, to which a stern necessity has hitherto, sometimes, forced my steps.

It is now near 12, & I must conclude. For I would not defer executing what I have done, till another sun should arise. Mumford is to breakfast with us; & I know not what obstacles might obstruct an attention to my diurnal duty.

Saturday, 5th

Wm. W. Woolsey knocked at our door, just as the clock struck 6, this morning. I awaked, & Wm. Johnson rose. He has accompanied Woolsey to Amboy, & returns on Monday. Sleep thus driven away from me, I got up, & had time to read over the letters recd. day before yesterday, before Mumford came. He breakfasted with me; & stayed till 10; & during his stay, & while he was employed in reading News-Papers, I read twenty pages, in the work of Condorcet, which I obtained yesterday.

Mumford is equally fleshy as before his removal. He is somewhat browner; & more neglectful of his dress, & more attached to tobacco; whether in form of hay, twist, or segar. His gravity is almost unassailable; his words come forth slowly, & lingeringly; he chiefly confines himself to answering questions, without much attempting to keep conversation alive: in short, he seems to have acquired a tenfold share of *vis inertia*. At the same time, the equability & amiableness of his temper & disposition appear to have undergone no change. It is so difficult, owing to this slowness of his, to maintain a connected conversation with him, that, hitherto, my inquiries have only drawn from him, a few, imperfect portions of information. It seems that they, (M. & my sister,) are conveniently situated; that there is a pretty good neighborhood; that the place is healthy, & pleasant; & that his affairs wear an aspect of prosperity.

After M's. departure, I went to the Minerva office; but not finding Webster there, I called on him, at his house. We had considerable talk; both on the subject of the proposed connection, & on other topics. Mr. Morton, his fellow-proprietor in the Daily Advertiser,[61]

---

[58] M. Roulet, the Swiss, played much the same part in Smith's continuing education as did Gahn.

[59] William Johnson (1769-1848; Yale 1788) was a Middletown, Connecticut, man and therefore perhaps known to Smith from childhood or, in any event from their days at Yale where he was a member of the Brothers in Unity. The date of his moving to New York is uncertain but was probably about 1793. A lawyer, he was living at 117 Pearl Street in 1794 (see *New York Directory, 1794*). Shortly after this date he became Smith's roommate or housemate and remained so until Smith's death. As did Smith, he became acquainted with James Kent and rose to prominence with him as a reporter in his courts. Some thirty volumes of case reports are his monument. His relationship with Smith is strange in that, although he is mentioned scores of times in the "Diary," he does not appear to have expressed his opinion on much of anything, at least nothing that Smith felt like recording. He is "W. Johnson," "Wm.," or "William" of the "Diary." There are many other Johnson's in these pages including another William Johnson. Smith's roommate had two brothers Seth and Horace, also frequently mentioned; they were unsuccessful storekeepers in New York.

[60] Mr. and Mrs. Charles Lovegrove were an English couple, the husband a business man of some wealth whom Smith obviously considered a cypher; the wife a lady with pretensions to culture, who claimed acquaintance with a number of minor literary people in England. At first Smith was much impressed with Mrs. Lovegrove who is occasionally referred to as "Mrs. L.," but eventually Smith's disenchantment was sudden and as puzzling as it was complete.

[61] John Morton was a professional newspaper man. See *Memoir of the Life of Eliza S. M. Quincy* (Boston, 1861), p. 56. Eliza Morton, upon whom Smith and Johnson frequently called, was his sister. Her marriage to Josiah Quincy of Boston in 1797 was the social event of the season. The *Minerva*, for which see earlier, became the *Advertiser*.

is absent; & nothing can be ultimately resolved on, till his return. Webster, however, promised me, some account, in writing, of the Expenditures & Receits of the Paper.

From Webster's I went to Kent's. He was at Court. I chatted a short time with Mrs. Kent, & came home.

Mumford was here, again, a few minutes; & after his departure, Alsop.

I sat down to posting; & continued at it, till dinner. After dinner, I returned to my Ledger, & finished posting. Alsop came in, & inticed me to accompany to a French Book Store; where he kept me, tumbling over Books, till 7. I bought Tissot's Works—on Onanism,[62] on the diseases of the Studious, & on the Epilepsy.—We returned together. He went to the Coffee-House; I to Woolsey's. I found G. Muirson Woolsey there, as I expected, & soon after Mumford came in. We chatted; Mumford went away, on business; Woolsey to Mr. Rogers's;[63] I came home; about nine.

As Alsop & I walked along, we had some talk on the project of my engaging in the Bookseller's business. It seems that he has had a conversation, with the Johnsons, on the subject; & that they still think of it, as a plausible & promising plan. Alsop, himself, would be glad to become interested in a scheme of the kind.

Three different projects of life, principally engage my tho'ts, at present. The News-paper, the Book-Store, & the Apothecary in Lichfield. Each has it's allurements; each it's objections. The two first are full of risk. They must, inevitably, confine me to this place; & that almost constantly. An immediate support it is scarcely to be supposed that they would confer. Support would come soon; & in the mean time, I could have credit. Should I be ordinarily fortunate, in six, or eight years, I shall have acquired a sum, the legal interest of which would furnish me with an annuity, adequate to my support, in the country, where I should retire. But, for this period, I must, not only relinquish the hope of leaving town, but must give up study, & composition, mostly. On the last plan, I should secure an immediate & adequate support: & my business would allow me much leisure, every day, for study & composition. But then, as the proceeds would only equal, or but just exceed, my expenditures, I must continue, for an indefinite time, my attention to business. I could scarcely hope ever to attain that independency which would place me above the fear of want, & necessity of labour; & which would allow me to devote all my time to the service of my fellow-men. It is not to be dissembled, that another cogent dissuasive is the unavoidable disclosure of my peculiar sentiments. A disclosure of this sort I do not fear, either because I doubt their truth; or am apprehensive of the censure of men, & punishments of the Law; but that I dread their effects on an excellent, beloved, & pious mother; on a respected, worthy, & religious, father.[64] They must know them, at some time. Yet I would fain put off the time, to "a more convenient season"; to a period, for which they may be, gradually prepared. But this I could not hope for, living with them. In this state of affairs, I am irresolute. I find it difficult to form an opinion as to the duty of the case before me.

Sunday 6th

Last night was the night for the meeting of the Friendly Club, but no meeting took place. Johnson told me that there was none, on the preceeding saturday night. It is necessary to notice the cause of this double failure; especially, as a sufficient number of members was in town, at each time. The Club, originally, consisted of ten Members; Wm. Dunlap, Wm. W. Woolsey, G. M. Woolsey, Prosper Wetmore, H. S. & W. Johnson, T. Mumford, & E. H. Smith. Catlin met with us, but three times, & not in succession. He married; & the "cat-ish fondness" of his wife, & perhaps, his own indifference prevented his ever associating with us, thereafter. Seth Johnson was unwell with a rheumatism; which had confined him several months; & tho' getting better, was unable to go out. Of consequence, he was present at no meetings but those which happened in his own, or the turns of his brothers. As soon as he was able, he journied; & thenceforth he has been uniformaly absent, & no turn has been assigned him: and this has been, I believe, for about a Year. Mumford removed from hence, about a year since; I thus left his place vacant. P. Wetmore has always been distinguished by his want of punctuality in attending; so that we have, several times, been on the point of dropping him. H. Johnson was pretty punctual, till about two months previous to his marriage; from that time, till now, six months, he has altogether, absented himself. Since the secession of Catlin, & the removal of Mumford, James Kent, & Charles Adams, have been admitted. They, & G. M. Woolsey, have been about equally punctual. They are absent about one fourth of the time, W. W. Woolsey, W. Dunlap, W. Johnson, & Smith, have been punctual,

---

[62] Simon Auguste Andre David Tissot, physician, *L'Onanisme* (1760).

[63] This is not Dr. David Rogers of Greenfield Hill. It may be a "Parson Rogers" of New York.

[64] In 1784 Connecticut passed a general toleration act which freed a dissenter from the necessity of paying a Congregational tithe if he deposited with the clerk of the ecclesiastical society in which he lived a certificate declaring himself to be a member of some regular society recognized by law. Richard J. Purcell, *Connecticut in Transition, 1775-1818* (Washington, etc., 1918), p. 12. Smith, however, belonged to no such society. There was still in existence, should the authorities choose to enforce it, a law for the punishment of atheism and deism. Anyone convicted of such beliefs could be deprived of all ecclesiastical, civil, and military offices. For a second offense the culprit might be deprived of all rights in court and the right to be guardian of a child, executor of a will, or administrator of an estate. *Acts and Laws of the State of Connecticut in America* (Hartford, 1796), p. 183. Purcell found no instance in which the law was enforced. It would have been necessary to punish thousands of the sons (and some of the daughters) of the first families of Connecticut.

with scarcely any exception, when in Town. It is evident, therefore, that their absence must, materially, affect the meetings of the Club. On Saturday evening before last, G. M. Woolsey, Dunlap & Smith, were out of town; Adams was married; Kent was sick; P. Wetmore, & H. & S. Johnson, busied; W. W. Woolsey, & W. Johnson, alone remained. There could be no meeting. The absences had now so deranged the order of the meeting, that no one knew it; & it appeared as if nothing but re-commencing, could establish order. In this state, last evening came. W. W. Woolsey, W. Dunlap, W. Johnson, & Adams, out of Town; P. Wetmore, H. & S. Johnson, as before; Kent, G. M. Woolsey, & Smith, might have met, but knew not where.[65] It is now probable that the meetings are broken up, till the end of October. It is possible that they will, then, be resumed with added punctuality & advantage.

I rose late this morning, tho' I went early to bed: unexpectedly over-sleeping myself. Neither Mumford, nor G. M. Woolsey, breakfasted with me; tho' they partly promised it. Mumford was here a few minutes, & Alsop, in the forenoon. G. M. Woolsey past near here two hours here. We conversed much; on varied topics; but chiefly on subjects connected with the doctrines of Godwin: I say of Godwin, tho' I have not read his Book, because my friends, who have read it, pronounce my opinions to resemble, in many respects, those therein contained; & because to say my opinions, would convey no idea, unless I were to state them at large; which can not, now, be done. The remainder of my leisure, till dinner, I employed, in making various estimates &c. of my Expenditures &c. for the year past. The general result of which, is as follows.—

A conjectural estimate of my expences from Septr. 5. 1794 to Septr. 5, 1795, including what I now owe, makes the sum	826. dols.
A Ward-robe so supplied that it is supposed equal, at least, to one half the expence, incurred the present year; & therefore will diminish the next year's expence one half	75.
Articles of furniture, purchased this year, still good, but from the cost of which a deduction is made, as second-hand, estimated at,	50.
Medicine still on hand, & estimated, in proportion to the supposed cost—including furniture attendant	65.
Supposed value of one half of the house furniture, low, as	25.
	215. dols.
Conjectural amount of Business, from Sept: 5. '94, to Sept: 5, '95; including Practice, Editing, Writing, &c.	500.
Estimate of monies actually recd., as the reward of labor, from Sept. '94, to Sept. '95	300.
Estimate of monies due me, as appears on my Book	210.
Probable loss on what is due to me	40.
Estimate of money now due from me to others	262. dols.

It appears, from the above, that, after all the assistance recd. from my father, & if everything was paid, which is due to me, I should fall in debt, notwithstanding. It is, however, equally clear, that the ratio, between my expenditures & receits, has considerable diminished; or rather the difference between my expences, & charges. For, whereas, last year, it did not fall short of one sixth; now, it scarcely exceeds three eights. Another might, probably, furnish me with the means of support, without recurring to any other than my profession for aid; if certain occasional deviations, such as Editing, which do not counteract it all, be excepted.

After dinner, & after writing the preceeding page, I went to Mr. Riley's.[66] It was four o'clock. There, with the family, & Alsop, & a visitor, I tarried more than an hour. From thence I went to H. Johnson's. He was at home, his wife, & brother; & I found there Mr. & Mrs. Lovegrove. We drank tea. Amboy being mentioned, in the course of the conversation, gave occasion to Seth to relate his danger of being wrecked on South Amboy coast; & of the gratitude, or attachment, of a negro slave to his master. The circumstances, briefly, were these. The stage Packet left there, with about 50 passengers, men, women, & children; & attempted to boat to N. York, against a strong tide & a violent wind. After proceeding three or four miles, the fears of the people on board were so excited, & many were so sick, it was tho't most prudent to return. Accordingly, they turned about; & the united violence of wind & tide bore them rapidly along, over a tumultuous & surging sea. They were now within an hundred yards of the wharf; the

---

[65] Dunlap, W. W. Woolsey, Thomas Mumford, Horace, Seth and William Johnson, James Kent, and Charles Adams have been cited earlier. Shortly before his marriage to Smith's sister Mary, Mumford had moved to Aurora, New York. Prosper Wetmore was a black sheep of the Wetmore family, merchants who had Middletown, Connecticut, and New York connections. He was a smuggler, a relative (cousin or second cousin) of William Johnson, and also a friend of Richard Alsop. Catlin was Lynde Catlin, Smith's boyhood friend, a bank clerk in New York.

[66] Isaac Riley, mentioned earlier, was a Middletown, Connecticut, man (Richard Alsop's brother-in-law) who sold books and other merchandise there. After moving to New York in 1795 or earlier he became a publisher as well as bookseller. In Richard Alsop, *A Hartford Wit* (Middletown, Connecticut, Mattabesett Press, 1939) Karl P. Harrington speaks of him as probably a founder of the auction book trade in New York; this is unlikely since Smith, an enthusiastic attender of book auctions, does not mention him in this connection. He was a wild and reckless plunger, often deeply in debt, and an associate and sometime partner of that strange man, Hocquet Caritat, for whom see later.

sails were lower'd; when the unfastened boom, driven by a sudden flaw, struck the master over-board; who was at the helm; & the vessel being, thus, surrendered to the guidance of the sea, those on board were under the cruel necessity of seeing him perish, without the power of attempting assistance. The vessel drove to the wharf. Every one expected she must be dashed to pieces; when some person sprang to the helm; the vessel obeyed; the end was turned from the wharf, & the side violently beat against it. Instantly men, women, children, in mingled agony of terror & exultation, precipitated themselves on shore. The confusion was infinite. The master had sailed, in this business, for near thirty years; & with him his negro man. And now, when the faithful slave learnt the fate of his master, he set up a most piercing cry. He lamented, in fearful & heart-rending ravings, his master, his mistress, himself. No sooner was he landed, than he thrust an old & half-rotten boat from the wharf; & threw himself into it; & rowed towards the place where the body disappeared. The storm grew more tempestuous; the sea raged terribly; & the boat sank under him. He swam to the shore; & was recovered, half-dead, & with the utmost difficulty. He rested a few minutes; & renewed his search, along the beach; with dismal lamentations, & for two hours. This story introduced several others: instances of African attachment, fidelity & gratitude: Most of them too imperfect to admit of narration.

Among others, I related, from an imperfect recollection, some circumstances, which were mentioned to me, by Eli Todd,[67] Physician at Farmington, (Connec.) which happened to him, while in the West Indies. I am not certain, whether the pursuit of health, or gain, induced the voyage; which was made before he commenced physician; &, for ought I know, before he commenced the study of physics. I do not, now, recollect by what means he became acquainted with two Africans; or in what way it was that he rendered them some service. Yet some service he did render them. They were not ordinary Blacks. They seemed to have had a good education, in their own country, & to have been of consequence there. Todd supposed them to have been Priests. They both wrote, & wrote well. And Todd shewed me a specimen of either's writing, which he keeps. The characters are well-formed, & as I then judged, bore some resemblance to the Arabian. He made them repeat what they wrote; & he wrote down after them in our character, agreeable to their pronunciation; & as they said was right, when he read it. The structure of the composition is poetical, as far as I could judge. While Todd was in the West Indies, he fell sick, of the disease of the country. These men were his unceasing & unwearied attendants. He gained so much strength that it was deemed expedient to remove him. When they found he was going, they came to him; they fell on their faces, before him; embraced his feet, his legs, his knees; kissed them, & bathed them, with their tears. They put his feet on their heads, in token of gratitude & attachment; they followed him to the ship; pursued the ship in boats; & the last objects which struck his dejected eyes, were their waving & farewel hands. These narrations excited some remarks on the nature & qualities of the Africans; on the iniquity of the Slave Trade; on the celebrated Book of Camper;[68] on influence of climate, soil, food, & other physical & moral causes; & on the probable effects of education. Mrs. Lovegrove mentioned some facts, related to her by an eye-witness, concerning the condition of the natives of New-Holland;[69] corroborative of the general accounts of their bestiality & doubly-deep ignorance; & others of their capacity for improvement. The most material was, That, when her informant came away, there were two natives, a boy & girl, about ten years of age, who had been instructed, in the european method, in readg., writing, &c. who exhibited all the talents & ingenuity which european children usually do. Soon after this, Mr. & Mrs. L. took their leave. Some company came in. I sat a few minutes; & then went out.

The clock struck eight a short time before; & I called at Mr. Webster's. I found him at home, & his wife returned. I congratulated this amiable, this lovely, woman, on the complete restoration of her health. We had some conversation, on contagion; particularly the Influenza. I know not how we fell upon Physiognomy; but so it was. Camper's Book was again mentioned; & Lavater.[70] No new light was thrown on the subject. I took my leave soon after nine. I sat down to my journal, pretty soon after my return home; & it is now past ten.

Monday, 7th

A thousand ideas, of various kinds, coursed thro' my

---

[67] Eli Todd (1769-1833; Yale 1787). A wealthy New Haven man who set out for a long trip abroad immediately after graduation, caught yellow fever in Trinidad, returned home and shortly thereafter lost his fortune. He studied medicine, practiced chiefly in Farmington, Connecticut, became president of the Connecticut Medical Society in 1813 and was largely responsible for the Retreat for the Insane opened in Hartford in 1824.

[68] Pieter Camper (1722-1789), Dutch physician: *Dissertation physique sur les différences réelles que présentent les traits du visage chez les hommes de différents pays et du différents âges; sur le beau qui caractérise le status antiques et les pieces gravees.* &c., published in French and Dutch (1781).

[69] Dutch name for Australia.

[70] Johann Casper Lavater (1741-1801) minister, poet, writer of mystical works, observer of his fellow men and, in his young manhood, a friend of Goethe who collaborated briefly with him. His work on physiognomy was entitled *Physiognomische Fragmente zur Beförderung der Menschenkenntnis und Menschenliebe, 1775-1778.* It was translated into English by Thomas Holcroft, *Essays on Physiognomy, Designed to Promote the Knowledge and Love of Mankind* (1840). Melville had a copy and read it with some care. These conversations on Camper and Lavater and physiognomy are a tantalizing anticipation in New York in September, 1795, of a series of private lectures that Franz Joseph Gall was to give in Vienna in 1796 when he began to discuss his new "science," phrenology.

mind, last night; so that I did not sleep, till long after the twelfth hour. It rained violently toward morning. I rose in tolerable season; & read, some distance, in Condorcet's book. While reading, something suggested to me the probability, or possibility, of my being prosecuted, on the Statute against Blasphemy, should I once again reside in Connecticut: a subject on which I had several conversations with Dunlap & Brown, while at Amboy. I could not get it out of my head, till I had run over, in imagination, the manner in which such a prosecution would, probably be conducted; the part I should act; the conduct of my friends, & others; & the result of the whole. I think I do not fear it. After laying Condorcet aside, I wrote a letter to Elnathan Smith.[71] I was busied on one to my sister Mary, when a Welch clergyman, of the name of Rhees, bro't me a letter from Joseph Strong.[72] The man's physiognomy pleases me; & his conversation. Strong speaks highly of him; & I shall be glad to do him any service in my power. Mumford was here a few minutes. They went away, nearly together. I finished my letter to Mary, & wrote also to Abby. To Mary, for the first time, I declared sentiments adverse to the common superstition. It was, now, near two; & I amused myself with looking over some of the chapters in Volney's Ruins.[73] As I went to dinner, I met Mumford, who was going to my house. I found him there when I returned. We walked. Our return just, luckily, saved from a severe wetting, by a very copious shower. I took up Condorcet's book; & have read, in it, this day, more than 50 pages. I deliver my opinion of it's merits, when I have read it thro'.

We drank tea at Mrs. Bradley's (a boarding-house,) in company with several others, but particularly, John Mumford, the brother of Thomas; who resides, customarily, in Alexandria, Virginia. From thence, we went to W. W. Woolsey's house. Such has been the weather, that neither he, nor W. Johnson, have returned. We found G. M. Woolsey there. We had a stout argument, on the subject of Medical, & other Collegiate, Degrees; which Thomas defended, & I maintained to be impositions. The question is simple enough; & in my opinion, susceptible of a ready decision. Diplomas are certificates of erudition; are, & ever have been, bestowed, alike, on bad & good, on the learned & the ignorant; they are, therefore, no actual evidence of skill; people, in general, suppose them to be so; they are, of consequence, imposed on. He who, knowing this, consents to receive a diploma, or seeks for one, countenances a fraud; & is chargeable with a violation of the duties injoined by morality. We viewed the matter in various lights; a number of examples were cited; but these are not material. Soon after a visitor came in; & the remainder of the evening was not productive of much improvement. I came away at nine.

I had nearly forgotten to mention, that Dingley[74] called on me this afternoon. He stayed an hour. His discourse was chiefly confined to the prevailing Fever; which he has no doubt is the same with that which desolated Philadelphia; & which has appeared here, in some partial manner, for three years past; & indeed, in various parts of the Country. In short, that it differs more in name, than nature, from the Putrid Fever of Sydenham & Huxham. He augurs a sickly Autumn; & indeed the annual recurrence of a similar complaint, while things continue as they are. He mentioned numerous cases, stories, &c. incapable of abridgement; &, probably, not worth insertion, were they susceptible of it. This man is increasing in business & popularity. He has enterprize; intrigue; a powerful mind; good medical information; no small share of general knowlege; application; a talent for observation; & a strange sort of address, which somehow, *constrains* you to do as he would have you, without, at the same time, your being pleased with him, or satisfied with yourself for doing as he wishes. He will, questionless, become eminent in his profession; & his science & judgement will entitle him to eminence.

Tuesday, 8th

Restlessness, heightened by the buzzings, & bitings, of musquitoes, prevented my readily falling asleep. About 12, I was awakened by a rapping at the door. It was W. Johnson; who had been detained, till then, by contrary winds. I rose. He was well; his journey, on the whole, had been pleasing; he left all well at Amboy; W. W. Woolsey returned with him. I slept badly; & rose late. Alsop came in, soon after breakfast, & passed a short time with us. I wrote to Joseph Bringhurst. Mumford came, & Wm. & I walked with him, on the Battery, till one. Conversation principally concerning our bookselling project. Mumford dined with me. After dinner, I read about 30 pages in Condorcet's Book. I called to see Dr. Rhees,[75] but did not find him. I called on Mr. Roulet; found him at home; & spent a short time with him. Returned by way of W. W. Woolsey's Store. He & Mumford were there. Chatted awhile. I drank tea with Mrs. Kent. Kent is on Long-Island, attending a Court. While there, Miss Susan Rogers, the daughter of the Physician of that name, at whose house I boarded, while I lived at Greenfield, entered. She came from

---

[71] A cousin who lived in Berlin, Connecticut; Yale 1788.

[72] (1770-1812; Yale 1788), a physician who was a pupil of Dr. Rush in 1791-1792, lived briefly in Middletown, Connecticut, and then served four years as an army physician in the Northwest Territory (Ohio). In 1796 he settled in Philadelphia where he died of yellow fever.

[73] Smith may have read C. F. Volney's *Les Ruines etc.* (Paris, 1791) in the original, but it was available in a translation by Joel Barlow—*The Ruins; or Reflections on the Revolutions of Empires* (London, 1792). The book was popular in America for many years. Anti-clerical, rejecting everything concerning revelation or the metaphysical, it was one of a number that Smith read continuing the message of Tom Paine.

[74] Amasa Dingley (Harvard 1785), a New York physician. Dunlap's *Diary* 1: p. 340, carries the information of his death in the entry for September 21, 1798, almost certainly from yellow fever, two days after Smith's demise.

[75] Rhees, also Ries and Rhys, a Welsh minister.

visiting her sister, who is married in Phila. She is much grown, & improved; & appears both pretty & good. I spent the evening at Woolsey's. We conversed somewhat on the Book-selling project; but more on the propriety of seeking to gain favor, & shewing civilities to people, for the sake of inducing them to purchase commodities of us, or otherwise to advance our pecuniary interest: which I determined to be wrong. From this subject, we, insensibly, & undesiredly, by me, got on to perfectibility of man; or his nature; on reason; &c. &c. which we left as we begun.

Wednesday, 9th

The musquitoes were so troublesome, last evening, that it was impossible to write, with any comfort; I therefore quitted the pen, & went to bed. Here I fared little better; tho' my interrupted & imperfect slumbers confined me to it, till eight. Mumford, & after him, Alsop, were here in the forenoon; & between them both, I talked much, to little purpose. I found time to write to John Williams, my quondam host, at Wethersfield. I also read a few pages, in Condorcet. Dr. Rhees called, at two. We dined together. The following information, recd. of him, appears worthy of note. The Welch language is still, vulgarly, & spoken in Wales; & religious service, & court proceedings, carried on therein. The Bards are still numerous in Wales; & there are a number of very eminent & able persons, now, of that profession. Their Songs, are, generally, recited; tho', sometimes, sung. They compose in the modern Welch dialect.

The writings of the Ancient Bards, are illegible by the common people; the dialect having undergone great changes in the last two centuries. The Bards have an annual meeting; in some sort national; where all produce a Poem; & the national prize, as I understand it, is decreed to him who excels. They have, also, a prize, instituted among themselves, for him who produces the best extemporaneous verses. The subject is fixed, both in the one case, & the other. The Dissenters are numerous, & respectable in Wales. Dr. Rhees shewed me a number of letters, from thence, which evince the aversion of the people to the present Administration, & War; & prove that they have high ideas of civil & religious liberty. He tells me, That a young gentleman, John Evans, is, now, penetrating this Western Country, along the Missouri, in search of the Welch Indians—the descendants of Prince Madoc & his fellow-adventurers.[76]

Evans was taken up, & confined, by the Spanish Commandant at Fort Louis. It happened that Judge Turner, of the North-Western Territory of the U. S. was holding a Circuit Court, in the vicinity; & had an interview with the Spanish Officer. The Spaniard stated the case of the Young man, he had confined. Luckily Turner had heard of him, & was able to explain his design to the Commandant; & had influence enough to prevail upon him, to assist Evans in it's accomplishment. In consequence of Judge Turner's interference, solicitation, & recommendation, the Commandant has furnished Evans with a passport, in English, French, & Spanish; has bestowed on him money, & suitable presents, for the Indians; & has put him under the protection of the Missouri Company—an Association of Spanish Traders, who carry on trade 1500 miles up the Missouri—where the farthest white settlement is. From thence Evans is to trace the Missouri to it's head; & to proceed on till he discovers the Welch Indians, or to the Pacific. Dr. Rhys informs me, that there are several printed accounts of Wales; & that, should he be here next Spring, he shall be able to furnish me with the best.

I never knew, till now, that Jos. Strong wrote verses. Dr. Rhys shewed me a copy of Verses, written by him, on the fourth of July; which had many incorrectnesses, & some merit. He says, that Strong has written several Poems, of much value; & which he has seen. He leaves town in the morning; & we bade each other farewell.

I had returned from dinner, about 4, & had just finished writing the above, when Alsop entered; &, not long after, S. Johnson. We chatted awhile, & then walked. Returning from out of town, Wm & myself, went to Mr. Lovegrove's; where we drank tea, & spent the evening. Our conversation was various, animated, & a wholesome exercise of the understanding. The topic was, principally, Education. I can not say, that any of us started any new ideas—i. e. new to me. It is evident that the accident which happened, when we were last at the house, to the child; or, rather, her conduct, dwells on this lady's mind; that she thinks it was wrong; & especially, that she has a diseased sensibility to what she supposes are our impressions to her disadvantage. Some pains were used, by both of us, to set her right, in this respect. A future opportunity may be more favorable. To shew no marks of alarm on an occasion of this nature, to exhibit no signs of grief when our friends suffer, is the part of true wisdom; of that wisdom which feels, without indulging useless regrets, sorrows which impair our powers to perform our duty. But, as things are, with all our previous habits, wisdom so sublime, whatever may be the convictions of our understanding, can scarcely be expected of us. Knowing this, were we to see that a person discovered no tokens of interestedness, in such a situation, the irresistible conclusion

---

[76] Apparently Smith was disposed to believe the story about Mr. Evans despite the fact that in America in the 1780's there were many stories afloat regarding ancient Indian fortifications and relics that were said to be evidences of the existence of an invasion of America by Madoc and his Briton and Welsh followers about 800. Smith must have known well *The Anarchiad* by Barlow, Lemuel Hopkins, Humphreys, and John Trumbull, a fiction in verse and prose purporting to present fragments of an ancient poem in English (accompanied by the authors' comments) found among the Indian ruins. Humphreys is said to have taken the idea from an English work, the *Rolliad*, attributed to Fox, Sheridan and others. For later comments on the Welsh Indians and John Evans see *The Monthly Magazine and British Register*, March and September, 1798. See also Southey's poem *Madoc* (1805).

would be, that he was an idiot, or a brute. But, when we see persons of fine & intelligent minds, endued with this keen sensibility, tho' we might think it a want of the most perfect philosophy, still we must ever behold in it's displays the encouraging promise of future excellence, the unequivocal evidence of an excellent soul. Such a mind as this, when it shall once come to be truly & deeply sensible of the extent & vigour of it's own energies; when it shall have learnt duly to appreciate the severe simplicity, the divine one-ness of truth; when it shall see that, tho' perfection may be, to itself, unattainable, in the present state of things, yet is not to man unattainable, & by itself may be nearly approached; when it shall be brought to love sincerity, even tho' sincerity may wound it's most darling prejudices; when it shall aptly distinguish between abstract excellence, & relative fitness; & when it shall be convinced, that the clearer our views of truth, the more we must see the difficulties in the way of attaining it, & the more indulgent we must be towards the frailties and errors of others; such a mind, when it shall so think, & so it may, by no difficult process of illumination, be bro't to think; such a mind, may be made, all of perfect that the present state of things will admit; while, that dull, that insensible, heart, on whom misfortune inflicts no wound, accident impresses no terror, must ever—"to dumb forgetfullness a prey"[77] slumber with it's kindred brutes. Mrs. L. has a soul.

> That, like the needle true,
>   Turns at the touch of joy or woe,
> But, turning, trembles too.

A juster appreciation of her own powers, would give her more confidence in her own strength; would enable her to see herself with the eyes with which we see her; would teach her, suitably, to estimate her own excellence, & the arrested, but not subdued energies, of her own intellect; & would animate her with "a spirit" which

> Could look superior down
> On Fortune's smile or frown;
> That could, without regret or pain,
> To Virtue's lowest duty, sacrifice
> Or Interest's, or Ambition's, highest prize;
>   nay, which would induce her with—
> A prudence, undeceiving, undeceived,
> That nor too little, nor too much, believed;
> That scorns unjust Suspicion's coward fear,
> And, without weakness, knows to be sincere.[78]

And this I must say to her. A woman like her, ought to be above even self-distrust. Of the purity of her intentions she can have no doubt; & intention, so far as the actor is regarded, sanctifies the act. And, if, owing to human frailty, we are deceived into error, from wrong judgement, the illusions of passion, or a surprized & unguarded sensibility, we ought to confide that a single error, or many such errors, can not shake the durable esteem of those who value us for our good purposes; & we ought to derive the utmost assurance that conviction can afford, from their undiminished esteem, their unwavering respect, & the unabated fervency of their zeal for our welfare.

I can write no longer: the musquitoes have not left me any comfort; & I must shelter my wounded philosophy, under the friendly covering of my bed-cloaths.

Thursday, 10th

In the course of the conversation, last evening, something was said concerning the little boy of those we were visiting; which is really a fine, healthy, child, & has an intelligent countenance. An anecdote was told, relative to him, which is sufficiently characteristic, of the father, in one respect. The child had scarcely been born two hours—the exclamations of joy, on the part of Mr. L. were numerous—& this one—"Dear little fellow! one day he will be able to go a Cock-shooting with me!"

On our return, from our walk, yesterday, speaking of the effect of certain works, on the opinions of mankind, I could not fail making an eulogy on the Press; when my friend Wm. exclaimed—"The press is to the moral world, all that the wished for fulcrum of Archimedes would have been to the physical world."

Yesterday, I read Peter Pindar's new Poem, on the Hair-Powder Tax.[79] It possesses the usual qualities of his Performances; almost all of which evidence uncommon talents, but under the direction of a vicious, an unprincipled, mind.

Among the many plans which have, at different times, engaged my individual attention, & that of the Friendly Club, none seemed, for a while, to be viewed with more pleasure, & with greater assurance of success, than that for establishing & conducting a Periodical Paper; somewhat on the plan of the Spectator. We even went so far as to allot parts to several, to form schemes of composition, & to nearly conclude on a name for our Publication. But this, like many others, "worthy a better fate," fell thro': owing, perhaps, more to indolence, than any conviction of our want of capacity. At this time, I sketched out the order of a series of Essays, on the Principles of Education in the which, after having combatted, & exposed, the mischievous tendency, of those usually employed, I should have proceeded to lay down, & explain those which I tho't the proper ones. No doubt there would have been many errors in my Essays: yet I think there would have been in them a nearer approach to truth, than is observable in most

---

[77] Thomas Gray, "Elegy Written in a Country Churchyard," xxii.

[78] Mrs. Greville, "A Prayer for Indifference" in *Poems selected [from Goldsmith, Gray, Pope, etc.] and Printed by a small Party of English, who made this Amusement a Substitute for Society, which the disturbed Situation of the Country Prevented Their Enjoying* (privately printed, Strasburg, 1792).

[79] Pseudonym of John Wolcott (1738-1819). *Hair Powder; A Plaintive Epistle to Mr. Pitt; to which is added, Frogmore Fete* (London, 1795).

writings on that important subject. Since then, my opinions have taken a more consistent form; but the little which I wrote, at that time, will shew how closely I touched upon the real motives, which ought to be excited into action. The order & titles of the Essays, were to have been nearly as follows:—viz.

Introductory Essay.
On the Evil of Fear, as a motive to the acquisition of knowledge.
On the Evil of Envy, as a motive &c.
On the Evil of Ambition, as &c.
On the Evil of Avarice, as &c.
On the true motive, to &c.

That false motives & false education, will be cause & effect to each other; and that just motives & right education, would, also, be cause & effect to each other. In the execution of this design, I proceeded no farther, than to compose, but not correct, an Introductory Essay; to throw together a few ideas, towards one on the second head; & to, occasionally, commit to paper, a few detached tho'ts. The Introductory essay was written in a style rather unsuitable to the subject; being far too declamatory; but would have been corrected, had it ever been determined to prosecute the undertaking. It is as follows.

INTRODUCTORY

Returning the other day, from an excursion into the country, my attention was suddenly excited, by the loud sobbing of a child. On looking round me, I found that the sounds proceeded from a little Boy, who was seated on the steps of the adjacent village School-house. There is something, in every gentle bosom, which is in unison with the tones of distress; and, most of all, with those of infantine distress. I approached the mourner; and the following dialogue ensued. "My little fellow, what ails you?" In a voice, scarcely articulate, he replied—"Master says he will whip me." "And have you done any thing naughty, that you should be whipt?" "I can't learn my lesson"—answered the child. "Is that all?" "Master says I *won't* learn it." "O, that's quite a different affair! But, come! let me sit down by you! dry up your tears; & let us talk over this matter." He rubbed his eyes with the sleeve, and then with the skirt, of his coat; but his heart had been deeply affected, his sobbing continued, and the tears *would* come. "So, your Master is very cruel?" "Yes Sir"; bursting into tears again. "Well, Well, never mind it! cheer up! Do you love to go to school?" "No Sir." "What, not love to learn?" "No Sir." "Well, do not cry any more; you shall not be forced to learn." The Boy looked into my face, with an air of surprise, & immediately began to be composed. He pointed me the way to his home; I took him by the hand; & we proceeded. The evening was uncommonly serene & beautiful. The birds were saluting the sinking sun, with a lively song; the cattle lowed along their homeward way; the labourers were seen returning from the fields; a small cloud rose in the south, & occasionally sent forth pale flashes of light. Much, indeed, must that spirit be deprest, which would not feel some pleasure at a scene like this. My companion, gradually, recovered his cheerfullness; & began to prattle. "How sweet that bird sings!" said I. "Where is he? I can't see him!" rejoined the little boy. "Should you like to see how he looks?" "O yes! I love birds." "Look yonder! see! the sun is setting." "What makes it look so red?" demanded the Boy. "Should you be glad to know?" I inquired. "O! above all things! But what makes it lighten so, down south?" "Would you know the reason?" "I wish I did"—earnestly. "And is your Master very cruel?" "Yes" with a sigh. "Would he whip you; if you learnt your book?" "No sir! but I can't learn it." "Do you try hard?" "O, very hard!" But would you not try harder, if you could find out how all the birds looked, why the sun was so red, & what made it lighten?" "O Yes! Can I?" "To be sure, you can; & many more fine things; only learn your book." "O, I'll answer for it, I'll learn!" "Well, don't forget your promise." We had reached his home, & now separated. As I walked slowly onward, musing on what had just past, a train of reflections arose in my mind, concerning the injudicious methods, so common among men, of enforcing children to learn. The tyranny of parents & teachers, the wrong principles on which they act, & the unworthy motives which they place before youth, afflicted my heart; the tear rolled down my cheek; & I exclaimed in grief—"Alas! how short is the life of man; how many calamities must he, unavoidably, experience, what disastrous & adverse circumstances has he [to] struggle with! And yet, as if these were insufficient evils, how assiduously do we labor, to render that short duration of no value; & to embitter this little period, with increased misfortunes! By our own follies & excesses, the distresses, of the future man, are commenced before his birth. Scarcely has he tasted the vital air, when new forms & varieties of torment, are provided for him, & inficted on his unresisting & feeble frame. His first ideas are modified by false impressions, & received thro' confused mediums. Hardly can he totter about, when the rod is lifted over his head, & he is scourged to the acquisition of sounds, destitute of meaning; & obliged to fix those eyes on the fantastic characters of books, which anxiously seek to wander over the delightful images which nature, every where around him, profusely offers to his contemplation. A little older, his young bosom is made to receive the poison of envy; & he is taught to regard every companion of his play, as one jealous of his advantages, & eager to wrest them from him. Then, too, fame, power, & wealth, are presented to his imagination; ambition & avarice are leagued together; & the book of science is converted into an exhibition of coaches, palaces, stars, ribbons, & garters; the uniform of the general, the robes of the judge, & the coffers of the miser. Fear, envy, ambition, & avarice, are almost the only incentives to industry, which instructors employ. And thus is knowlege, from which only can virtue & usefulness proceed, tainted, while yet in the bud; & perverted, in it's expansion, to poison & corrupt, rather than to heal & purify, the heart. Unfortunate, truly unfortunate, is the lot of man!"—and my heart was deeply oppressed. This subject has since, considerably, engaged my reflections; and I design to lay the result of my tho'ts before the Public, at convenient intervals, in several Essays. The true principles of government & morals which have been slowly unfolding, for a few centuries past, begin, now, to be understood, and to obtain general attention. But never can their full effect be felt; never can those beautiful Systems, which some truly philosophic minds have conceived, obtain universal operation; till Knowlege is viewed in it's proper light, & valued for it's real use. And, never can this be the case, till the mode of education has undergone great, & essential, alterations; till, fear, envy, ambition, & avarice, have become no longer the chief agents of instruction; & the human mind is lead forward, in the path of knowlege, to the discovery of truth, by gentler methods, & juster motives. Vain, or if trifling advantage, will be the finest moral & political theories, while, "from the cradle to the grave," parents, teachers & societies, & nations, busily plant, and cultivate, and protect, all those violent & selfish passions, which are interested in the concealment & destruction of truth. The evil must be attacked in the root. Then, while it is yet small & feeble, it may be destroyed. But, if it be allowed to send forth it's fibres, on all sides; if it is permitted to give out it's shoots, & increase to a vigorous stock; in vain shall we attempt to prevent it's mischievous effects; it's flowers will float their poisonous exhalations thro' the whole atmostphere; the sun will ripen it's seeds; & the winds scatter the pestilential fruit, to the four quarters of the earth.

In copying the preceeding Paper, I have only made two or three verbal variations. It was composed about 13 mos. ago. The following, is a part of an intended Essay, on the Evil of Fear, &c. It was never finished; not even corrected; as the design was given up. After some introductory remarks, in the fictitious character of the Essayist—I proceed—

[Omitted here, four manuscript pages "On the Evil of Fear, &c."]

I have now completed my copying, on this subject. In this I have occupied myself, the most of the forenoon. Beside this, I have only written a short letter, to my father; & devoted a few moments to reading one recd. from my sister Fanny; & a short time, to Mumford & Alsop, who severally called here. Fanny informs me, that she has begun on her Diary; & that her little friends, Sally Tracy & Charlotte Sheldon, are pleased with the scheme of letter-writing, which I proposed; & on which, therefore, I presume they will begin, when I have furnished them with my promised blank book, for the purpose. This I design to do, when I go to Lichfield.

At dinner, this day, James Morris, a fellow-boarder, informed me, that he asked Wm. Wilcocks,[80] the other day, what he meant, by a publication of his, in the News-Paper; & recd. for answer, That there was an intercepted letter, in Town, written by a man high in office, or who had been high in office, in this Country, to some person, in Europe; which letter contained an account of a Plan, famed [framed?] to overturn the present Constitution of this Country; detailing the Plan; & mentioning the names of the Principals. This letter he, Wilcocks, determined, if possible to persuade the person, in whose hands it was, to publish. Mr. Morris further informed me, that he spoke of this letter, to Mr. Harper, a member of the House of Reps. in Congress, from S. Ca.;[81] that Mr. Harper informed him, that, at the time of the Western Insurrection,[82] he, Mr. H. recd. a letter from a man, high in office, in the U. S. telling him, that the Excise was merely the ostensible object; that the real object was to destroy the present Govt. & re-establish the absolute independency of the State Govts.; that, it was expected of him, & the friends to their plans, to form a sort of military establishment, in the back parts of S. Ca.—independent of the Militia; that a vigorous co-operation might be effected, if necessary, with the Western Insurgents. This letter, Mr. H. says he burnt; but sent an answer to the Writer, at the time, assuring him that he, Mr. H. was attached to the present Constitution; & desiring no further intercommunication, on similar subjects. The name of this person, Mr. H. did not mention. After Mr. Morris had finished speaking, Mr. Adams, Charles, said, That he had good reason to believe that a deep plan was laid; that Genet was one of the principals in it; that funds were furnished them, or had been, by France, & other assistance promised; that Fauchet carried with him, despatches, relative to these affairs;[83] & that, for the purpose of inciting them to throw every possible obstacle in the way of our present Govt., certain Merchants in this City, were furnished with a credit on France, to an unlimited extent. To all this, my inquiry is—What is the object? "To overturn the present Govt. And what

---

[80] Plot not identified. Strange that Smith should feel such obscurity necessary in his private diary. For another view of the French see George Gates Raddin, Jr., *Caritat and the Genêt Episode* (Dover, N.J., 1953).

[81] Robert Goodloe Harper, U.S. House 1795-1801.

[82] The Whiskey Rebellion in Western Pennsylvania in 1794.

[83] Charles Adams obviously knew much more about what was going on in Philadelphia than did the average citizen. Less than a month earlier Washington had put into the hands of Edmund Randolph, the Secretary of State, certain captured French documents directed by the French Minister, Fauchet, to his government. On receiving these papers Randolph resigned. Unquestionably the French were attempting to bribe American officials in high places. Genêt was a likely person to suspect in this instance for he was still very active. A few months later he was part of a plan to send George Rogers Clark with a group of frontiersmen to attack New Orleans. F. J. Turner, *Amer. Hist. Rev.*, 3, 4 (1898): p. 652.

then?" To make their fortune, & secure lucrative & distinguished posts, in the squabble. But, when we are separated, & become independent states again, there can be nothing very great, if ambition is to be gratified, for ambition to feed upon. "They have not got their Constitution settled." Then we shall overturn them. I must own—I do not, yet, despair of the CommonWealth.

The scheme, above referred-to, for my Sister & her little Friends, is this. They have been in the habit of writing letters, to each other, under fictitious characters. One is a lady, travelling in one part of the World; another, in another part; & so on. From their remote places, they write, in their assumed characters; either describing the country, or their adventures there; & either conforming to Historical truth, or indulging in the fictions of the imagination. These letters have been written on detached papers; & are liable to be lost. My proposition was, That they have a Book, in which one shall write, & then the other take it, write, immediately after it, her reply. Thus, the several letters will succeed each other in their proper order; will form a species of novel; & will be preserved. Thus, too, they will be excited to take some pains to write well, correctly, & with more attention to accuracy of tho't & expression. How much pleasure will they receive, some years hence, from looking over, together, these joint efforts of juvenile friendship!

I read the greater part of a late english pamphlet, called a Letter to the Prince of Wales;[84] & some passages in Caleb Williams;[85] & the News Papers. I drank tea, & past part of the evening at Webster's: the remainder, at H. Johnson's. Neither he, nor his wife, were at home; but their sister, & Seth & Wm. were there. Seth shewed me his new purchase, of the French Encyclopedia, in 35 vols. folio. It is a most superb work; & cost him 340 dols. We talked of the Book-selling Plan; but nothing definitively. Wm. & I walked an hour; & endeavoured to get a little pure air: without success.

Friday, 11th

Some part of this morning was consumed, in attention to a professional call, & in making those medical inquiries of books, which the nature of the case demanded. The remainder of the fore part of the day, till dinner, devoted to the perusal of Condorcet's Book; in which I proceeded about 40 pages. I shall take this Book with me, to Lichfield; & read it at my leisure.

Since his resignation, of the office of the Secy. of State, to the U. S., Mr. Randolph has been to Newport, R. I.; &, as it appears, to see Mr. Fauchet; the late French Minister. He sent Fauchet word, That he should call on him, at a set hour, in the evening. When he arrived at Fauchet's lodgings, the servant informed him, that his master had gone to the Theater. He left word, that he would call at ten, in the morning: & recd. for answer, That Mr. Fauchet would not be disengaged till 12. At twelve he waited on him, but Fauchet had gone on board the Medusa; & Mr. Randolph did not see him. After this Mr. R. was at the lodgings of J. B. Provost, (a young lawyer of this Place) & related this conduct, with many execrations against the rascality, as he termed it, of Fauchet. This Provost told J. Morris, who related it to me. It is reported, that Mr. R. was obliged to resign his Office—as, it was alleged, he had maintained too strict an intimacy with this same Fauchet.

All these rumours & movements must mean something. I pretend not to conjecture; but I mean to observe.

The heat of this day is very oppressive; & renders exertion disagreable, & unproductive. It was my intention to have dilated, somewhat, on several plans of composition, which I have conceived; but this weather makes bending down to write very unpleasant; & I fear it must be yet longer delayed. My health does not suffer, yet, tho' that of the City, as appears by the Reports of the Committee of Health, is sensibly & dangerously affected, by the sudden change, from cool to sultry, which we have experienced, within a few days.

One of the first Plans of writing of any extent, which I formed, was a Poem, intituled—"Indian Manners"; & the object of which was, to exhibit, in a connected view, all those circumstances, in the history, character, manners, customs, & opinions, of our aborigines, which distinguish them from other nations. The history of this Plan, & of my progress towards it's execution, would require more time for recollection & writing, than I can now spare, or than is at all material, in this place. My design, now, is, to write no more on it; except what may be necessary towards the preparing of some parts, which are composed, for the Press: for I purpose that they shall form a part of the Second vol. of American Poems. I had always, that is, ever since my dealing much in verses, a strong propensity towards that form of composition denominated the Ode; & long since planned to write Odes enough to form two moderately sized books; to contain about twenty each. I went no further, than to fix on the subjects; & to run over, mentally, the general manner in which they were to be managed. The change in my sentiment, on several of the subjects, will forbid my handling them; &, indeed, I now, much doubt whether I shall ever act on this project. Another scheme was, to compose a set of Hymns, in blank verse; religious hymns. The death of religion, in my soul, long since banished this design. A fourth purpose was, to write a Poem, somewhat on the plan of Hayley's Triumphs of Temper, to be intituled "The Trials of Virtue." These trials were Pleasure, Ambition, Avarice: in each of which there were to have been inferior trials; & the hero was to have surmounted all. A more useful plan, now, occurs to my mind; but the writing of the

---

[84] "Authentic Copies of Mr. Pitt's Letter to the Prince of Wales," by Rt. Hon. William Pitt (1789), in *A Compilation* by W. S. Hathaway (London, 1806).

[85] A novel by William Godwin, *Things As They Are; or The Adventures of Caleb Williams* (1794).

Trials of Virtue, has been given up, near a year. In the dramatic line, three pieces had early engaged my tho'ts: one, to be called "Valvaise & Adelaide"—an Opera, on the Italian model; one "Epaminondas," on the model of the Ancient Greek Tragedy; & the other, "Quatimozin" in which I should give way to the frenzy of imagination. On these plans, I still think, with some resolution to act: particularly, on the first. My last, grand, poetical plan, was, for an Epic Poem; the fable of which was built on an idea of this kind—That the interior of America had once, been inhabited by a polished People; but had been conquered by the progenitors of the present inhabitors. My Poem would have been named, perhaps, "The Conquest of America"—& would have given, an opportunity for an accurate delineation of the present Indians; & for a bold fiction, to account for the remains of fortifications, &c. On this, I suspect I shall never act. These several plans—most occupied my tho'ts; &, at different times, I have resolved to accomplish them. Thousands of others have held temporary possession of my brain; but these most, & longest. My prose plans have been—"A Collection of Medical, Botanical, & Chemical, Essays"; "Travels thro' the U. S."—on the plan of Coxe's thro' Swisserland &c.; & a "History of Medicine": this last, to be my greatest work; & the one on which to rest my claim to reputation. All these, are now relinquished.

My present determination extends only to three things: The Opera of Valvaise & Adelaide—My own History; & a didactic Poem, somewhat on the plan of "The Task"; for the purpose of disseminating & enforcing those principles & doctrines of Morality, which I think true. Concerning these, I have much to say; but not now. The history of my own life has been long in contemplation. I have also, which was forgotten before, had a notion of writing a work on a new mode of spelling, of hand-writing. On this, I shall dilate, considerably, in the course of my journal.[86]

I spent two hours with Woolsey, at his Store. Mumford was there part of the time. Woolsey & I went to Mrs. Rogers's; who is alone. We stayed there till eight. I went home with him. Mumford was there, but went soon to bed. He has been somewhat unwell, for two days; & still complains of head-ache & pain in the bowels. I came home at nine; found that I had a call abroad; attended to it; & returned before 10.

My reflections have been less agreable, this day, than I could have wished. The precariousness of my situation; & a restless uncertainty as to what plan I had best adopt; have perplexed me more than I ought to let them. Thousands are worse situated than I am; enter life with worse prospects; struggle with more opposition; & surmount greater difficulties. Considerations of this kind have made me half ashamed of relinquishing my Profession. What could I not accomplish therein, if I would exert the resolution of a man. After all, if I should not succeed, misfortune could not be imputed to me as crime; &, while health & activity remain to me, I need never despair of the means of prolonging my existence. Were I to renew my application to professional studies, with all the assiduity & perseverance of which I am capable; were I only to cultivate those means of obtaining notoriety[87] in my profession, which I might, without a dereliction of principle, or a mean submission; were I to attend, faithfully, to whatever business fell in my way; cherish a cheerful temper, retrench unnecessary expences, & exert myself to procure that collateral aid, which might, possibly, be obtained, with no great breach made in my arrangements for study; what might not be effected in a few years? Would not another year furnish me with enough to answer all it's demands? And what might I not hope for, when once I should have acquired merited reputation? And could I not deserve it? And, if I did deserve it, could I fail of acquiring it? And, should I not do mankind, in this way, more service, than in any other? Certainly, I will, yet, think further on this question. I ought not, lightly, to discard that aid, which it has been the labor of many years to gain.

Saturday, 12th

I have been twice, this morning, to see Mumford; who still continues unwell; tho' he is not necessarily confined. One professional call, terminated all avocations of that sort. I went to visit Dingley; but did not find him at home. From thence I visited Dr. Mitchill, at the College. I past more than two hours with him: the time chiefly occupied in reading, the memoirs of Dr. Torquid, in the History of Hobart, a noted American Adventurer, who was hanged at Tyburn. Some useful remarks are contained in it. The iniquity of law; & the absurdity & wickedness of superstition, a slightly, but forcibly, pourtrayed. Here, too, for the first time, I saw Burton's Anatomy of Melancholly; & a huge Satire, of Danl. defoe, on Passive Obedience, Non-resistance, &c. Mitchill has put his Memoir on Contagion,[88] to Press.

Soon after my return home, John Wells[89] came in, & chatted near an hour with us. He is a lawyer, a young man, resident in this town; & with whom I first became acquainted thro' his intimacy with Charles Adams. Of his history I know little. I have been told that he was born in this State; somewhere on the Hudson; & I believe he was educated at the College in this City. His appearance is interesting; & his person, tho' moderately-sized, manly; as are his countenance & conversation.

---

[86] His plans for the "History of Medicine" became the *Medical Repository,* and he remained faithful to the "Diary" which was to serve as the basis for his autobiography. In the brief time that remained to him he was able to complete none of the other projects.

[87] Smith uses the word correctly. In 1795 it meant "being publicly known." (*New English Dictionary.*)

[88] The only thing Mitchill is listed as having published at this time is *Remarks on Gaseous Oxide* (New York, 1795).

[89] Wells became a prominent New York lawyer. Oral Sumner Coad, *William Dunlap* (New York, 1917), notes, p. 18.

His mind seems much superior to that of most young; but seems to have been cultivated casually, as fancy & necessity dictated. His sentiments are, therefore, not the result of proper investigation; it may be said, of consequence, that he has much yet to do. To this, he seems but little inclined; having, from habitual aversion to long-continued, & systematic attention to investigation, acquired a disrelish to mental exertion, of the regular kind. This defect does not appear, either constitutional, or irremediable; & he may, yet, possibly, assume that rank, in the republic of intellect, which would belong to industry & talents.

Immediately preceeding, & succeeding, dinner, I found time to read 20 pages, in Condorcet. Two hours were employed in the performance of several errands, & a visit to Mumford. Wm. & I walked out of town; & returned by the way of Mr. Lovegrove's; where we drank tea, & stayed till half after eight; interested as usual. I came away, at that time, that I might see Mumford; Wm., that he might go to his brother's. I found Mumford asleep—& have concluded to return, & sleep in the house with him. He is still considerably unwell. W. W. Woolsey went to Amboy to-day; & G. M. Woolsey, sleeps at his Store. These circumstances, unavoidably, contract the record of this day; for it is, now, after nine; G. M. W. will be impatient; & I must hasten back.

Sunday, 13th

I slept at Woolsey's last night. Mumford was restless, all the fore part, but more quiet the latter part, of the night; his medicine operated kindly, & he is much better this morning.

On our walk, yesterday afternoon, Wm. & I conversed, chiefly on this project of Book-selling; & on the different motives, for me, to continue Physician, or commence book-seller. I tho't, at the time, that I would devote some part of this day, to reflection on the subject; and, if possible, come to a determination, by the exercise of my own mind. This day is wet, & uncomfortable for going abroad; &, therefore, favorable for such a purpose; but I feel that I can not resolve this matter, by myself; & come to a determination so settled, that new circumstances, & the opinions of friends, may not cause me to change it. My conclusion is, therefore, to adopt no ultimate plan, till I have been to Lichfield, & learnt what are my father's schemes. After that, I am fixed on adopting some permanent rule of life, as soon after my return as may be.

I have no expectation that my proposals, to Mr. Webster, will be acceded to, by him & his partner; and I have very little anxiety that they should be. On consideration, I am disposed to believe, that it will be better, either, to sell books, or to practice physic. Should my decision be in favor of the last, my plan will be, nearly, as follows. To do justice to my employers; to act with reputation, & with satisfaction to myself; to gain any new accession of medical knowledge; & to increase the sphere of medical science; all of which ought to be the determinations of the physician; a resolute & undeviating application must be made. No method of accomplishing myself in my profession, must be neglected. It will not be sufficient that a single branch of learning is acquired; the science must be pursued thro' all it's ramifications. For this, a method must be adopted; books must be had; expence incurred; & the event hazarded. Mathematics, Natural Philosophy, Mineralogy, Botany, Zoology, Chemistry, Materia Medica, Pharmacy, Anatomy, Physiology, Surgery, the Theory & Practice of Physic, all these must be mastered: they must all be studied scientifically; & an arrangement of facts, opinions, & reasonings, on each particular subject, which they concern, accurately made. This is not the pastime of an idle hour; the entertainment of a casual & uncertain leisure; the business of [a] single day, or labour of a single year; it must be attended to, dilligently, chiefly, every day, many hours every day, for years; nay, for life. Other plans of study must be relinquished; or pursued occasionally; or collatterally, & as they can be made to harmonize with this general plan. To do this, I must renew, double, & out-do, all my former dilligence; I must sacrifice amusements, company, & journeying; I must become the steady tenant of a fixed place; & every motion therefrom, must be only for the increase of this knowlege, or for the exercise of that skill, which it's attainment is meant to confer; & which, indeed, forms an essential part of this knowlege itself. To do this, what do I need, beside persevering resolution? I need the means of support: & especially Books, which as they are only to be obtained by money, may be placed on the same foundation with food, shelter, & clothing. How am I to procure Money? Here it is necessary to pause. My practice, at present, furnishes me with a scanty sum. If I cease to visit, frequently, those with whom I am acquainted, will not that practice, probably, be diminished? Will they not feel a sort of resentment at my neglect, which will determine them to apply, elsewhere, for medical aid? It is impossible that they should know my true motives. Were I to state them, in all probability, such is the unhappy temper of many, I should not gain belief. They would not be persuaded, but that there was something personal meant, by my absence. They never would suspect, they never would credit, that I avoided them, that I might be the more able to assist them, when they should need assistance. At first, therefore, whatever might be the ultimate effect, I must expect a diminution of that pittance which I now derive from practice. Beside, as I should not extend my acquaintance, I must not look for any new accession of employment. How then should I be able to supply my wants. Have I no useless habits of expence? One I certainly have; & one that I mean to be freed from, at all events. No barber shall, henceforth, receive any portion of my slender income, as a reward for disfiguring me. But, further retrenchments must be made, somewhere; a new source of supply must be found out. Medicine I must have; it is indispensible to my business; but of that my supply is, perhaps, nearly as great as I shall need. Shelter is necessary; & my health, & convenience, will admit of no change, in that respect. Service, also, is unavoidable, situated as I am; & fuel. In diet, I may make some reduction. At any rate, after my return, I drink no wine. Of clothing, no new stock will be necessary, except some provision for the winter; & I design to exercise as much frugality as is compatible with my profession. As for diversions, mine are not very expensive; & those few, in which I have indulged, I can readily relinquish. But, after all, retrenchments will not afford a saving, equal to the supply of my wants. A question then occurs—In what way, other than my business, but compatible with it; compatible with my principles; can I gain any additional aid? My Pen:—what can I do with my pen? At present, I have but a single product of it, which is at all in a state of preparation for the Press: & that is my Opera.[90] This is destined for the Stage. It may be, or may not be, exhibited. If it be, so precarious is every thing of the kind, in America, that I have no right to reckon on deriving any gain therefrom. I may; but it is not probable. At the least, I can publish it, whether it be acted, or not. If I do, shall I derive any pecuniary aid, from this circumstance? Probably, some. I think I shall not do wrong to calculate upon 100 dollars. This, excepting books, may be considered, as one sixth of my expence. Now, can I not derive further assistance from my Pen, in the same way? My pieces may as well be dramatic, as of another kind: they may, in this shape, as much advance the cause of truth, as in any other; I must have some relaxation from severer study; & that may as well take this form, as any other. The stage may furnish me with some help: if it does not, I can print without. Beside, there are other ways in which my pen may be employed; & was it ever the case, that resolute, persevering, industry, failed of it's end?

Monday, 14th, 1795

It was impossible to proceed any further. The little, which was written, was done, by snatches, at different parts of the day. I left Mumford, apparently well, but weak; & designed to have returned to him, after breakfast, & after the short conversation, which I had planned to have with myself; & a part of which really happened —as above. But Alsop & Dingley were here almost the whole forenoon; their conversation was agreable; I could neither go out, nor write. After dinner, I went in search of Mumford, but found him not. I sat down to my journal, & wrote a little while when a *young man* of our acquaintance, came to tell me, that he was at *his* father's, & more unwell. I went to him. He had a return of fever; pretty severe. I stayed till it's violence appeared to have abated; & returned. Wm. & I had engaged to drink tea with Mrs. Lovegrove; we sat off soon, & by the way of Mumford's. His fever had returned. I gave him a potion, designed to promote sweating. He seemed better, & we continued our walk. At Mr. L's, we found that *queer* man, Dr. Williamson of N. Carolina. He possesst himself of the whole conversation; & told us his long stories, with all his fantastic gesticulations, & strange contortions of countenance, till we were heartily tired. He left us; & we past a most agreable evening. I came back to Mumford. The potion had puked him, contrary to my intention; but, I believe, without injury; & he had a brisk diarrhea. I exhibited suitable remedies; & left him, at one, in the morning, in a sleep, refreshing, & which continued, with few interruptions, till morning. I was surprized to see him enter my chamber, while I was yet in bed. He complains of being weak; his diarrhea still hangs upon him, but he is much better. At the house where he was, I picked up "Herman of Unna";[91] & made considerable progress in the first vol.—I have heard much of this Book; the little I have read promises something; & I shall peruse it with some avidity.

This has been a most disagreable day: hot, close, the air scarcely respirable. It must be that the health of the citizens has suffered proportionately. As for my friend & brother, Mumford, his imprudence—who would ever suspect his being liable to that charge?—or perhaps, necessity, has bro't back, with redoubled severity, his fever. After going from hence, he sat down to business. An hour's attention, convinced him of the impracticability of pursuing it—& he betook himself to his bed. Excepting occasional, short, absences, partly on his account, & partly on my own, I have past the day in his sick chamber. My only amusement has been "Herman of Unna"; & I am nearly half thro' the second volume. It is a Dublin Edition. I left Mumford, for the night— about half after eight. His brother John watches by his side.

W. W. Woolsey returned, from Amboy, to-day. Our friends there he left well. Dunlap has not heard from C. B. Brown, since his departure. I have never heard from him. What can be the reason? This question I have repeated, mentally, I know not how often. My ready fears suggest that he is sick. The daily expectation of hearing from him, has, hitherto, prevented my writing. It shall no longer; if circumstances do not forbid, on the morrow. This night, I feel neither spirit, nor capacity, for the purpose.

Tuesday, 15th

It is come, the morrow; it is more than half past; and I have not written. I have been all this long forenoon, with T. Mumford. He is much better; & has been free of fever all day—hitherto—& it is now near two o'clock. I have finished "Herman of Unna"; but have read it in

---

[90] *Edwin and Angelina,* of which more hereafter.

[91] Dublin edition not found. The first London edition (1794) perpetuates a curious bibliographical tangle. The title page reads, "Written in German by Professor Kramer." "Professor Kramer" was Gottlieb Cramer, but the book was written by B. E. Naubert. Translator not given.

too hurried a manner, to judge, accurately, of it's merits. The style is not remarkable for it's excellence; either in point of elegance, or force. On the contrary, many careless expressions, which it is hardly probable would have escaped the author, justify a suspicion that the Translator has not done him justice. The story is interesting; yet, in my opinion, loses much of it's force, from the disjointed manner in which it is related. That address, which contrives to introduce all necessary details, without interrupting the thread of the narration, which displays every character, in it's just relation to every other, & to surrounding circumstances, without circumlocution, & unnecessary & fatiguing deviations from simplicity of story; & which keeps the principal personage of the work constantly in view, without losing sight of those to whose adventures it is equally indispensible that we be not strangers: in short, the address of forming a regular, connected, interesting, tale; no part of which shall be independent of the other; & in which the interest is constantly increasing to the *denoument*; this address appears not to belong to Professor Kramer. At least, we are at liberty to judge so, from reading this work. At the same time, we should do him injustice, were we not to acknowlege, that many parts have great interest; that his characters are, in general, well conceived & ably supported; & that the author calls in the aid of terror, on several occasions, with considerable effect. But to be more minute, would require a new reading; & both more time & more attention, than either my situation, or the subject itself, will justify. Many passages, discover, in the Author, a love of justice & humanity, & a sense of liberty, both civil & moral, which do equal credit to his heart & understanding.

Thomas escaped his fever, till about four; from that time, till seven, it increased in violence, till it was nearly as powerful as yesterday: tho' neither his bones nor bowels were as much affected. From seven, till 10, it decreased; & at 10, very little of it was left. I sat with him, from 3 till half past 6; & then drank tea at H. Johnson's; & went, from thence, with Seth & Wm. to the Bath. I was with Thomas before 8, & staid with him, till 10. During my sitting with him, I diverted the moments, not otherwise employed, by reading the Memoirs of Tate Wilkinson.[92]

The day has past; I have not written to Charles: If he is well, why does he so trifle with our feelings as not to write? It grows late.

Wednesday, 16th

This day has been excessively hot; &, in most parts of the city, equally close. In some high situations, a gentle breeze was sensible. My whole day, with little exception, has been either spent with Mumford, or in running backward & forward for him. I flatter myself that he is better. While sitting by his side, fanning him, & administering to his various necessities. I have diverted myself with Tate Wilkinson's whimsicalities. I wrote a few lines to C. B. Brown. The heat was unusually oppressive at the time; & it required all my resolution to finish even those few lines. I past an hour at Kent's, in the afternoon; & another hour, at Webster's, in the evening. It is now a little after 8. P.M.

This whole City, is in a violent state of alarm, on account of the Fever. It is the subject of every conversation, at every hour, & in every company; & each circumstance of terror acquires redoubled horror, from every new relation. In reality, there is reason to be alarmed. I am told that 24 persons died, yesterday: i.e. in as many hours. It is true, however, that of the number who are sick, & who die, there are few of the natives & long residents of this Place. Far the greater part, are emigrants, poor Irishmen; who, coming from a cooler country, in crowded vessels; changing a vegetable, for an animal, diet, & in the worst season of the year; living in narrow & nasty streets, on the border of our worst slips & docks; in cellars; or half-underground rooms; nasty, ill-provided with food, & the little they have bad, & badly cooked; hard laborers, & hard drinkers; fall the first & most numerous victims to disease. It is very evident, that these circumstances, of themselves, are enow to convert, what would otherwise be only a simple Remittent, to what is now denominated a Malignant Fever. My kinsman Reuben Smith,[93] was engaged in loading & fitting out, the ship Connecticut, which lay at the wharf, or near the wharf, where the fever first appeared. He, & four of the people on board, were taken sick, in the same manner, & at the same time. They were either on board, or in the neighborhood of the ship, & all died. Perhaps their treatment was injudicious: but of this I know nothing certainly. However, they all died of the Fever which then, & now, spreads so much alarm. Mr. Smith lived in an airy part of the City; kept himself very quiet; was scrupulously attentive to cleanliness; I purged him twice or thrice; then gave him the bark &c.; he was unwell about a week; & then was perfectly recovered. I mention this as a proof that the same Cause will produce different effects, on different persons; & that all these disputes about Names for Diseases, is trivial & contemptible; & that the *State* of the Patient is, alone, worthy of attention.

I had resolved to visit Lichfield: & I meant to have gone this week. Mumford's illness prevents that, were I ever so much inclined. Now, I have no business. A single Siphilitic Case, & his, are all in which I have any concern. But the prospect is, that the present Fever will become more general. Should [it] be as much so, or half as much so, as in Phila. in 1793, my presence will be useful; as there will be as much business as all the Physicians can do. Some of my friends may be taken with it. At any rate, it will have a bad appearance, in the eyes of the country people, & will injure the city,

---

[92] Tate Wilkinson, *Memoirs of His Own Life* (London, 1791).

[93] This Reuben Smith was a partner in Gaylor Smith and Company, a shipping concern. Thereafter he and Elihu almost never met.

if any medical man, however unimportant his presence may be, shall be known to have quitted it. His true motives can not be known; & motives injurious to him, & pernicious to others, will be surmised. Thus thinking, I have resolved to continue here, till the Fever disappears, or is confessedly fast decreasing: and so I shall write my father word, on the morrow.

Thursday, 17th

After making the preceeding notice of yesterday, I spent near two hours in reading Rush's account of the Yellow Fever of 1793;[94] & this morning I read another hour in the same excellent work. I was desirous of learning how far things here, corresponded with those, there. Most of this day has, as heretofore, for several days, been spent with Mumford. I have had the pleasure to see him escape his fever for 22 hours; & can not help looking on his speedy recovery as certain, if no new misfortune happens, to dash the cup of promise from my lips. While with him, I have pursued the zig-zag ramblings of Tate Wilkinson still further. I wrote a few lines to my father. Such chronicles has the day produced to the present hour—5. P.M.

Thomas continued without fever till 6; it then came on, but by no means so violently as formerly, & at 10, was not entirely gone; tho' nearly so. I drank tea at Mrs. Miller's; & divided the evening between Thomas & W. W. Woolsey.

Dr. Dwight made me a present of his Sermon, intituled—"The true means of establishing public happiness."[95] The passages in it, which I have cursorily read, are handsome, & have no small portion of truth to recommend them.

The constance of my attendance on Mumford, leaves little time, either for reading or reflection. This is sensibly evident in the narrow traces in my journal; which I do not enlarge, as I have nothing interesting wherewith to fill it. To think, read, or write, to purpose, not only leisure, but repose, is wanting: repose of mind; the serene exercise of all the powers of understanding, & the ready recollection & combination of all the treasures of imagination. This my present situation denies me. In vain do I strive to fix my attention on any object; some petty concern steps in to interrupt those moments which I steal from the sick bed of my brother; & by his side, & watchful of his wants, tho't is put to flight, & study dares not to intrude.

Yesterday I dismist my Barber; & to-day I combed my own, unpowdered locks. This is the commencement of a reform, to the putting in effect of which, neither care, nor industry, shall be spared; when care & industry can effect any thing. What will be my triumph, if I can save enough, by the sacrifice of unnecessary, to provide for real, wants!

Friday, 18th

Mumford past a restless night; owing to the irritation of the place where he had a blister, from whence his tossings had removed the dressing. He had been proportionately feeble & unwell to-day; tho' he had no or very little fever, at three, this afternoon, which is an interval of 17 hours.

A few line from Dunlap, in a letter [from] his Clerk, induced me to write to him, for the first time. My letter was short, & hurried.

Study I seem to have done with. The universal theme is the Fever, the Disorder, the prevailing Epidemic; & these words, so often repeated, buz continually in my ears, & rattle incessantly in my head; so that I can think, consistently, on nothing.

I have spent much time with Mumford, some with W. W. Woolsey; some, in reading Dr. Dwight's Sermon—in which I find many truths, &, as might be expected, many errors. The first are as brilliant, as the last are deformed. Alsop here, a short time, in the morning.

The project of Bookselling, grows dim, to the eyes of my fancy. So many difficulties surround it, so many envellop every scheme, where money is the main-spring of action, & where those, who are called upon to act, are destitute of it. To continue in my profession; to succeed in it, by dint of industry & merit; & to rise over the stupid heads of those who now regard me with contempt, or indifference, worse than contempt; is, I own, of all others, the desire dearest to my pride. But I have learnt to distrust the suggestions of that hateful emotion; even when, apparently, directed to a useful end; & I have not, yet, had leisure to exercise the matter, thoroughly, on the score of utility, & duty. This I design to do—as soon as may be; unless some circumstances, now unknown & unexpected, should occur, to put all uncertainty out of question. My wishes, my views, my plans, do not yet put on a uniform, a consistent, appearance; all my endeavours can not be brought to point to one end. That they should do so, is extremely desirable; but that they can not, is certain, while there is any want of precision in my notions; while I am not averse to the principal deductions flowing from one principle, & while I have any remaining doubt how I ought to act. Were I satisfied that my duty required any sacrifice (as it is called) of the desire of reputation, as connected with any one pursuit, more than another, I am sure that I have courage enough to make it; & sufficient fortitude to endure, without either murmurs or regret, all the sneers, & all the affected pity, of those who might rejoice, or feel any sort of gratification, at what they might consider as my abasement. But, it is not be concealed, no, I can not so far deceive myself, as not to feel, that an almost peculiar sensibility to the burthen of Debt, & an habitual indolence, long fostered, & now, almost,

---

[94] *An Account of the Bilious Remitting Fever* (Philadelphia, 1794).

[95] This sermon was delivered before the Connecticut Society of Cincinnati, July 7, 1795. Now a rare pamphlet. It was the custom of the time for ministers to print their sermons and for doctors to print their own articles.

a part of my existence, are the most deadly foes to my success, in whatever line I may strive to excel, or labor to acquire the means of independence. I flatter myself with the belief that, were I possest of a competency, a mere competency, in the country, & such as would not exact of me, any settled & unavoidable intercourse with the world, or the pursuit of any of the other common means of gaining a living, I should apply to study, with alacrity; & employ my pen with as much assiduity, steadiness, & boldness, as becomes a professed laborer in the vineyard of Truth. Perhaps this is all self-flattery. Yet certain it is, that it can only be, by a most violent struggle, a struggle which may, perhaps, cost me my life, that I can overcome my present evil habits of indolence & gossipping. And, most unfortunately, my profession, not only, countenances, but absolutely, as here exercised, demands, the last; & to me, unmarried, & unencumbered by business, seems to be peculiarly requisite; & of me, especially expected. But all these obstacles must be overcome, all these impediments burst & broken down, & at whatever expence, & hazard of health, fortune, & resentment, if ever I mean to become distinguishedly useful, in my profession; either to myself, by the wealth, credit, knowlege, & opportunity of doing good, I may work out; or to others, by the relief, happiness, & increased information, I may afford them.

I stayed near two hours with Mumford; & I confess that, several times, I felt alarmed, when I considered his extreme weakness, & the uneasy motions which were frequently observable. I began to fear that I had carried the debilitating plan too far. By degrees, I became reassured; & when I reflected on his youth, constitution, his uniform temperance, on one hand; & on the fidelity with which I had adhered to those modes of practice, recommended by the most celebrated physicians, on the other; I felt a conviction that accident alone, could wrest him from me. I had, previously, designed to begin, to-morrow, with the administration of the Bark, & other supporting remedies; & this evening determined me. I allowed him Porter, diluted with Water, & sweetened; for which he seemed inclined; & which, I think evidently, did him good. I past the evening at Mrs. Lovegrove's. I had not been there long, when Seth & Wm. Johnson, came in. The fever, & some domestic arrangements, took the place of better conversation. A visit to Thomas, as I returned, terminated the day.

Saturday, 19th

My time, till dinner, was divided between attention to Mumford, a visit & conversation from W. W. Woolsey, & Alsop, & the translating a part of the Introduction of Condorcet's Book. I dined with H. Johnson, & the day being remarkably clear, cool, & refreshing, ate very heartily. I visited Mumford, & Johnson & myself walked, several miles. I spent the evening with the Johnsons, partly; &, partly, with Wm at Mr. Riley's, with the family & Alsop. I sat up, all night, with Thomas. He past a very restless night; & my anxiety on his account, & on the account of all his friends, especially my sister, is extreme. Poor Girl! she knows nothing of his illness; & did she know it, is too remote to yield him any assistance. What grief, what anxiety, must be hers, should she hear of it! What misery—should he—! But no! it cannot, shall not be! If my cares, if the cares of all his friends, if the art of medicine, can preserve him—& I trust it can—he shall be preserved. Mary now, in pleased imagination, places him at her paternal board; there also she seats her brother; & wishes, vainly, fondly, wishes, to be by their side. Unfortunate girl! thou knowest not, that thy husband is languishing on the bed of sickness; nor that a thousand apprehensions distract thy wretched brother.

But, I know not how I have thus strayed. I, I ought not, I will not be discouraged. Be firm my heart, and all shall go well.

I recd. a letter from Joseph. Charles[1] has returned & is well.

Sunday, 20th

I left Thomas at half past five, this morning; & was in my own bed by six. I arose at half after nine, & found Dingley here. He gave me a melancholly account of the state of things. According to him, the Health Committee are but partially informed, & the disease is spreading rapidly. For five days, past, he thinks not less than 40, a-day, have died. After he went away, Aaron Catlin & G. M. Woolsey came. I breakfasted, & drest, & went to Mumford's. He was easy; & had a little fever. His brother John was there. I returned, & wrote the short memorandum of yesterday, & did some little things, about house. It was twelve when I went back to Mumford; & I stayed with him, till near two. Dingley is to go to see him, with me at three.

My soul is opprest with melancholly. A thousand dreadful apprehensions darken my imagination. The weather too, which is cold, dark, & rainy—for it is about the Equinox, adds to my gloom; & the heaviness, from last night's watching, exhausts my spirits. But I am resolved to be firm, I will not be cast down. No timidity, no ill-timed despair, of mine, shall palsy my powers; & prevent me from doing the little good I am able to do. I grow more composed while I write. Composed! I have constantly been so: I grow more assured. I will rise above fear for others, as far as I am elevated beyond dread for myself.

After dinner, the wind shifted, & it became clear, but still cold. I found my cloak as useful to defend me from cold, as it had been to shelter me from rain. I called on Dingley; we went to see a patient of his; & then to visit Mumford. As we walked along all my depression of spirits, & all my heaviness of body, departed. Exercise & a more salubrious air, dissipated both corporeal & mental inquietude. We found Thomas without fever; better than yesterday; & I again went on with the In-

---

[1] Adams in all likelihood, rather than Charles Brockden Brown.

fusion of the Bark. All the afternoon I was with Dingley, visiting his patients. Only one appeared dangerous, to me; & I saw no great cause for distinction, in their cases, from Mumford's. I again saw him, at 7. A watcher was necessary; & at last I found Wm. Johnson, who agreed to go, with perfect readiness. Wm. & I talked awhile at home; & about nine went to Mumford. Thomas was now restless, & mentally disturbed, as last night; but [not] as much so. I left them a little before ten.

Wherever you go, the Fever is the invariable & unceasing topic of conversation. When two persons meet, the Fever is the subject of the first inquiries. People collect in groups to talk it over, & to frighten each other into fever, or flight. I saw, in Maiden-Lane, this morning, a Carman, at a Cabinet-maker's, taking in a load of Coffins. A number of persons, of various colours, ages, & sexes, were staring, half dismayed, at this unwelcome sight. Here was fresh matter for discourse. In one shape, or other, the fever is constantly brought into view; & the soul sickens with the ghastly & abhorred repetition.

Monday, 21st

I slept late, this morning, & thus made up for my want of sleep, the night preceding. Mumford required my first attention. He was restless in the night, but not as much as the two nights immediately before. This day, & this evening, have been the best he has had, since his illness. I left him at nine this evening, much easier than on any evening, for near a week. This forenoon I devoted, pretty much, to accompanying Dingley, in his professional visits. Most of his patients appear to me to be lightly affected. All bear bleeding, or very strong purges, advantageously; & cool air, as much as in the Small-Pox, or Pleurisy. A man, who was bled, last night, sixteen ounces; & who took three ounces of purging Salts; lost a pound of blood, this morning, with great advantage. A strong cathartic was ordered; & I should conjecture that an equal bleeding will be necessary tomorrow. The blood was of a dark purple colour.

Alsop was at our house this afternoon—two hours; I spent half an hour with G. M. Woolsey; I drank tea, & past an hour at Mrs. Miller's; the remainder of the afternoon & evening with Mumford.

This day has been extremely cold, for the season. I have been cold all day; & found a fire very comfortable. The sick do not find the cold troublesome. This change of weather neither prevents deaths, nor new cases of the Fever. Tho' it is not yet certain whether there have been as many new cases, yesterday, & today, as while the weather was sultry. Should we have a turn of warm weather after this, the effects, most probably, will be terrible.

The number of people who have left this City, can not be less than 12, or 15,000. The markets are thinly attended, & all articles very dear. No wood is bro't; & that which is sold, is at 22/—the load—i.e. 11 dols. the cord. These things are here noted as matter for future reflection. Most of my friends are out of Town; & I have no patient, with the fever, but Mumford.

Tuesday, 22nd

I spent much of the forenoon with Mumford. Both Dingley & Alsop were at our house this morning. I was with Dingley, in the afternoon, about a letter, recd. from Dr. Currie of Phila., & addrest to the "College of Physicians of N. York." The rest of the afternoon, chiefly, with Mumford. In the morning, I read a few pages in Condorcet. W. W. Woolsey came home, from Amboy, this evening. He came, with G. M. W. to Mumford's; & I returned, with them, to their house. We talked of various matters. I recd. letters from C. B. Brown, and W. Dunlap, to-day. I past the rest of the evening at Mumford's; & left him, a little after nine, in a sweet sleep. He has no fever, neither has had any to-day. I think he will be well, if no accident happens. His recovery will be slow.

My mind was somewhat agitated in the morning; since, it has been firm, & full of hope.

Wednesday, 23rd

Thomas did not sleep much, last evening, but lay easy. He has slept this day, somewhat; & is gained exceedingly in strength. I spent part of forenoon, afternoon, & evening, with him. In the forenoon, I wrote letters to Dunlap, Joseph, & Charles. I spent, also, some time with Woolsey, & some at Rivington's Book-Store, with Wm. Johnson, & Alsop, looking at his new Books. The afternoon, beside being with Thomas, I was at Woolsey's, & at H. Johnson's; where I drank tea. Wm. & I walked on the Battery, & then went to Riley's. Woolsey was there; & he, Wm., Alsop, & myself, past a few hours, very pleasantly. The conversation was various, animated, & interesting; so that the Fever—that incessant & inquiet subject of universal talk, was forgotten. Thence Woolsey & I went to Mumford's—where Saml. Jones Jr.[2] & I fell into a discourse, on the probability of a Future State—& on the consequences that would flow from the belief, or disbelief, of such a State. It is needless, perhaps, to remark, that I argued in favor of the non-existence of such a State. We talked much; he in his accustomed rambling manner; & we ended, as pub disputants usually do end, in being as wide from each other as when we began.

The weather still continues very cold & clear; tho' it has moderated somewhat, this evening. As far as I can learn, the fever is decreasing. I hope this may be the case; tho', if it be, the panic does not seem to be much diminished.

---

[2] Samuel Jones, recorder for the City of New York; in the list of charter officers for the city his name appears immediately after that of the mayor. Among his other duties the recorder presided over certain criminal trials. He was a trustee of Columbia and a friend of Kent's. Four other Joneses appear in the "Diary"; Smith usually identified him as "Recorder Jones"; he was, however, shortly to become controller for the State of New York.

At this moment, I feel comfortable, & unclouded; & for the first time, for several days. It is an instant worth pausing upon. Why can not one always feel so? O for that energy of mind, which would enable me ever to lift off depressing ills with an undiminished elasticity of intellect! Such, purely, should the good man, the rationalist, be possest of. But in this period, so solitary, so dismal, "when the countenances of all gather blackness,"[3] & when every melancholy event is swelled into tenfold consequence & poured upon the loathing ear, it requires more than ordinary philosophy to preserve equanimity: especially, when our friends are sick, when we are ourselves disappointed, unwell, & surrounded by adverse or untoward circumstances. I meant to have past this month, pleasantly, at my native place, & in the midst of my natural & early friends. The season, the wishes of those friends, my own business, conspired to favor my inclination & to promise me more than ordinary felicity. At that time, & thus situated, I purposed to have settled on the plan I should thereafter, steadily pursue. Now, I am confined here, & must be, inevitably, till too late; & to no useful purpose, if I except the care of Mumford: which, probably, would have been unnecessary, had we gone in season. But it is too late to be helped. Justice, therefore, demands that I be resigned; &, in my present temper, resignation is no difficult lesson. It is not yet certain that I have stayed to no purpose.

Thursday, 24th

This day, after visiting Mumford, & finding him much better, I went, with Dingley, to see several of the sick. I returned, & wrote to my father. Alsop past a short time with us, & I with Woolsey. Most of the afternoon I was with Mumford. Wm. & I, then, walked, several miles, & returning, spent the evening at Mr. Lovegrove's. It passed off agreably. The conversation was rather loose & general. Wm. read several of the Introductory letters, of Sullivan's View of Nature.[4] I was with Thomas a quarter of an hour, on my way home. He has sitten up considerable part of the day; eaten with a good appetite; & written a letter. He does without a watcher—for the first time.

During the prevalence of this Fever, & the consternation occasioned by it, many affecting events have taken place. As Dingley & I were walking along, together, a negro woman passed us. "What has become of the boy?" he inquired of her. "He is dead." "My God!" exclaimed he. "What boy?" I demanded. "A poor man, in Dover Street" (the Street where the fever first appeared) "died of the Yellow Fever. I had never seen him; but was called afterwards, to visit his widow, who, as well as her mother, a woman of eighty, was sick, with the same disease. For the old lady I could do nothing; the other I prescribed for: but, at the end of three days, they both died, within 15 minutes of each other. They left behind them, unprotected & deserted, a fine child, a boy, of 18 months. I took the child under my protection, & wrote, in it's favor, to the Chairman of the Health Committee. By the Committee, it was sent to the Poor House; & is now dead." As we returned from our Circuit, I mentioned my friend's (C. B. B.) plan, for a Tale—& was surprised to see the tears trickle down Dingley's cheeks; & to find him, for several minutes, unable to make any reply. It impressed me, more than any thing I ever saw in him, in his favor. This man, under other circumstances, might have been as open a combattant for truth, as his talents would, then, have made him a successful one. How much it is to be regretted, that poverty has depressed him to seek for independence, the independence of fortune, by a thousand little contrivances; by the suppression of opinions; & at the price of a thousand generous emotions!

Friday, 25th

My father's letter, which I should have had yesterday, I recd. this morning. I past most of the forenoon with Mumford. In the afternoon I attended the funeral of Col. Wentworth, of New Hampshire,[5] a gentleman of 78 years of age, who died here, this morning. As Wm. & I came home, Alsop overtook us. He, & Dingley, past an hour with us; after which, I went to Mumford, then to Catlin's, where I stayed an hour; & then returned, & spent the remainder of the evening, with Thomas. He is now well, & only wants a little of his usual strength; which, however, he is very rapidly acquiring.

Conversation, &c. had induced a belief that the Fever was on the decrease. I learn, this evening, to the contrary; & that the number deaths, this day, surpasses any previous numbers in the same space of time. This, I am told, has increased, to a greater height than ever, the consternation, which, before, was fast declining. I know not where this matter will stop, nor how the irritable minds of the community, can be quieted. Nothing is more evident than that Fear produces, the worse effects. One would think, from a few facts which are related, that all the horrors of 1793, were renewed: renewed in the apprehensions of many: So terrible is the idea of a Yellow Fever. Yes—there have, already, happened instances, of persons being deserted by all their connections. A man, of the name of Casey, an Irishman, (as I hear) was found dead, on the floor, & alone, this morning. All his connections, beside his wife, deserted him, either before yesterday, or early in the

---

[3] Not identified.

[4] Richard Joseph Sullivan, F.R.S., F.A.S., *A View of Nature; in Letters to a Traveller among the Alps; with Reflections on Aetheistical Philosophy now exemplified in France* (London, 1714).

[5] Colonel Michael Wentworth, closely related to the Marquis of Rockingham and the Earl of Strafford. After long and honorable service in the British army he came to America in 1767 and in 1770 married the widow of the late Governor Benning Wentworth of New Hampshire, a very wealthy woman. John Wentworth, *The Wentworth Genealogy, English and American* (3v., Boston, 1878) **1**: pp. 290-291.

morning thereof: & she left him last evening. There certainly prevails some disposition to Insanity. Persons who exercised even the ordinary share of reason, would never, otherwise, so act. It is time that something was done to relieve the minds of the ignorant from this overwhelming, this destructive Terror: this malady of the mind, a thousand times more dreadful & pernicious than all corporeal evils.

Saturday, 26th

The alarm concerning the fever is greater than ever, since yesterday's Report of the Committee. This morning, I observed houses & stores closed, which, yesterday, were open; & that very near the Coffee House; tho' few instances of fever have been in that quarter. Where it will stop I can not tell. In the mean time, I never was more idle in my life. I have no professional engagements; & the perpetual buzzing in my ears, relative to this disease, keeps me in a state of mind very unfavorable, & indeed absolutely hostile, to study.

Mumford is well. I was with him great part of the forenoon; & finished Mrs. Smith's "Celestina"[6]—which I have been reading, at intervals, during my attendance on him. I was at G. M. Woolsey's Store an hour. I dined at H. Johnson's. Wm. & I walked several miles, & returned to tea at Mr. Lovegrove's. We stayed there till seven o'clock. He went to his brother's; I called on Mumford; from thence, went to Mrs. Miller's—where I tarried till nine; & then came home.

I recd. a letter from Bringhurst, this morning; & wrote him an answer.

An anecdote was related yesterday, which diverted me much. The relation will soften the gloom of these pages. Oliver Phelps, now better known, by the appellation of Col. Phelps, a man very wealthy, & distinguished by his extensive & profitable speculations in Western Lands, was, formerly, a poor boy, in the town of Suffield, in Connecticut. He was, at length, entrusted with the disposal of a Cargo of Wooden-Bowls. The town of Suffield is remarkable for the manufactory of Wooden-Bowls. Men are employed, who put great numbers of these bowls in sacks, which are thrown across horses, & thus transported, & vended, in every part of the country. Young Phelps was returning from his first adventure, without having made sale of any bowls. Others, in the same trade, had been before him, & the market was glutted. Musing melanchollily along, & now at no great distance from home, in the morning he was accosted by a man, who was making Brush-fence, by the road side. "So, my friend"—said the laborer—"you seem to have had bad luck: I do not see that you have got rid of many of your bowls." "Yes"—replied Phelps—"very bad luck.—" "Well"—continued the laborer—"I will buy your bowls." "And I"—rejoined Phelps—"shall be glad to part with them. But what will you give me for them." "Give you for them?" said the doctor of fences—jocularly—"Why I will give you fifteen rods of brush-fence." "It is done"—said Phelps. The joke took; the fence-maker recd. the bowls; & gave Phelps a written obligation for the fence, to be delivered at Suffield, on a set day; & both bade each other farewell, with equal marks of satisfaction. At length the day of payment came. No brush fence made it's appearance. The laborer had taken all in jest, & had forgotten his note, never more expecting to hear of it. That was not the case with Phelps. His memory happened to [be] very good—in this instance, at least. He immediately commenced a suit, on the obligation; for damages & costs; & which he recovered. The profit on his load of bowls amounted to 50 pds. This readiness delighted his employer; he was continued in the business; & in this way laid the foundation for his present ample fortune: a fortune, in all probability, raised upon many tricks, not more to his credit, than the one related.

Sunday, 27th

While at breakfast, I was called to a woman, supposed to be sick with The Fever. I saw her; but she was not very unwell. Thomas complained of some headache, & I administered a cathartic. I was with him good part of the forenoon. A whole hour was occupied in making pills. After dinner, I read the first Book of Alsop's "Charms of Fancy"[7] which has been quietly reposing at Dunlap's house, ever since he left town, & which I took from thence to-day. I called on Thomas. He was asleep, & I did not disturb him. I went to H. Johnson's; & with the most fervent delight, devoted two hours to the contemplation & admiration, of Lacombe's edition of Engravings of the Pictures &c. in the Florentine Gallery.[8] After tea, I called to see my patient; & sat, & chatted, with her, & the family, half an hour. Where people, in their condition of life, are clever, I love to talk with them; & mingle in their society, with the most perfect equality. Their rude honesty, their native sensibility, tranquillizes my soul, after mingling with more refined persons, & after having employed my mind on abstruser topics, & more elevated themes, than their conversation presents.

Leaving them, I went to see Thomas. His medicine had operated; he had slept three hours; he had drunken tea; & was well. I stayed with him, till near nine; the clock now strikes; & I have been home a short time.

---

[6] *Celestina*, a novel in four volumes by Mrs. Benjamin Smith (1791). She was an amazingly prolific woman, twelve children and almost twice that many novels.

[7] Apparently Smith read it in manuscript in Dunlap's possession. Harrington, in *Richard Alsop*, p. 78, notes that Alsop wrote his "Charms of Fancy" before he was twenty-seven, but that it was not published until 1856. Harrington describes it correctly as a "versified tour over a large part of the civilized world," and gently suggests that it was derivative: "Based on a wide reading of English literature."

[8] *Galerie de Florence. Tableaux, statues, bas reliefs, et camées de la galerie de Florence et du palais Pitti, dessines par Wicar et graves sous la direction de Lacombe et Masquelier, avec les explications par Mongez l'aîné, etc.* (Paris, 1789; various other volumes until 1821).

Yesterday, I learn, thirty-one persons died. The morning was fair; the afternoon cloudy, & windy; the air close, all day. It began to rain, about three, this morning; & has rained all day, with little intermission; & part of the time, very fast. We have had high wind, some part of the day; & now, it still drizzles. This rain, I think, must be salutary. Our streets must feel the effect. It will—

"purge the foul body of the infected" *Town*,[9] & reanimate the sinking hopes of our citizens. This is a most desirable effect; for fear, more than contagion, wages war with the physician.

Monday, 28th

It has been a fine day, tho' warm; & a most beautiful evening, tho' moist. I went to see my yesterday's patient; found her much better; & persuaded her that she was well. With Mumford I past two hours. Wm. & I read parts of "The Charms of Fancy," together; Alsop came, & with him we walked; &, after my return, I read an Act in Goethe's "Iphigenia in Tauris."[10] I spent the afternoon, with Mumford; with G. M. Woolsey, at his Store; & at H. Johnson's, with them, & with Alsop, looking over Lacombe's edition of the Gallery of M. d'Egalité,[11] in Engravings. The Engravings are not executed in a style equal to the Florentine Gallery, but, still, are inexpressibly fine.

Wm & I called at Mumford's; &, thence, went to see W. W. Woolsey, who had just returned from Perth-Amboy; & with him & G. M. W. we spent the evening.

I learnt to-day, from Revd. Mr. Bisset, that Dr. Rush is about to publish a second volume on the Yellow Fever; & that he has, already, prepared it for the Press.

The alarm, in this City, still goes on. With what reason for fresh alarm this day has furnished us, I have not, yet learned. The season, is now, so far advanced, that we may promise ourselves to see an end to the ravages of the present Fever, in about a fortnight. In the mean time, the desertions from the city have been so extensive, we need not apprehend the loss of any great number of valuable citizens. In all probability, if the weather does not exhibit a variety of rapid & excessive changes, the deaths will continue to diminish, from henceforth. Perhaps, this is more desirable, than probable. We shall see.

Tuesday, 29th

It rained, most furiously, this morning; & cleared off, into a cool & beautiful day, about twelve. I passed an hour with Mumford; Alsop was with us two hours; Wm. & I walked on the Battery; the remainder of the forenoon, occupied in translating Condorcet. The above interruptions prevented my making much progress. The afternoon till four, with Mumford, who then took leave of us, to go by water, to New London. He has not yet recovered his strength. He designs to return here, next week.

W. W. Woolsey went from hence, this morning, with an intention of remaining at Amboy, till the Fever has departed. The Johnsons, Alsop, G. M. Woolsey, & myself, are all that remain of our circle.

[Omitted here, one manuscript page with the heading "Language I."]

I had just finished the preceeding commencement of my plan for reforming ortho- & chiro-graphy, when Johnson came in, & with him Alsop. We rambled several miles, out & in; & it was sun-down & dusk, when we reached home. We had chatted, merily, on trifles, as is too apt to be our wont, & returned in more than ordinary spirits, for Yellow-fever times.

As Wm. & I went to the battery to-day, we had a glimpse of Miss Morton, at her brother's window, in Broadway. I determined to visit her, this evening. We went there together. She returned from her tour, to New York, Boston, & Connecticut, this morning. She is well; has had a most agreable jaunt; & seems quite in raptures with the places she has been to, especially with her ride thro' Connecticut. We stayed till near nine, our time spent in those mutual inquiries which, tho' they make no figure in narration, are exceedingly necessary & pleasant, after so long a division, & so unexpected a meeting.

Just before going abroad, I recd. a short letter from Mason F. Cogswell. When I came home, I wrote an answer. On the Fever—as most of my letters have been, of late. It was scarcely written & not yet read over, when Dingley came in. Tho' it was late, he was full of something, & I led the conversation, by reading my letter, to the subject on which he wished to speak. His friend, Wm. M. Johnson, the translator of Boulanger's "Christianity Unveiled,"[12] has been, as a Physician, at the Belle-Vue Hospital.[13] There he has been attacked with

---

[9] Not found.

[10] *Iphigenia auf Tauris* (1787). Goethe's third version of this play was probably what he was reading. He could read German, but with great difficulty.

[11] For some reason this particular "gallery" of Lacombe's not listed if, indeed, it was his. "Gallery" at this time was used interchangeably for the display room or building and also for portfolios or groups of engravings.

[12] Doctor William Martin Johnson (*ca.* 1771-1797) was the author of poems which Smith ("Diary," December 11, 1797) praised as poems that "would not disgrace the first poets of our language." The son of a pair of drunken beggars, Johnson was adopted by a hard-drinking, retired sea captain and given a fairly good education. For a time he was a roamer himself, as an itinerant schoolmaster and also probably as a sailor. In 1790 he became a school principal in Bridgehampton, Long Island, and shortly thereafter began studying medicine while working as a teacher and carpenter. He then went to New York to continue his medical training, supporting himself as a newspaper man and occasional teacher. Apparently pressed by poverty he translated this work, an act he is said to have much regretted. *National Cyclopedia* 8: pp. 90-91. He is treated by John Howard Payne in a series of articles, "Our Neglected Poets," in the *Democratic Review* in 1838.

[13] Bellevue Hospital for contagious diseases was founded in 1794 and located up the East River about three miles, a safe distance away from town, so it was thought.

the Fever; & dangerously. Dingley recd. a note from him, to this effect, this afternoon; & requesting his presence. With this note he went to a Mr. Stymets, who is one of the Health Committee, & desired him, to make an order for the Boat to go to Belle-Vue, if it should be necessary, & bring Johnson in. Mr. Stymets signified his willingness—but wished Dy. to accompany him to John Broome's—the Chairman of the Committee.[14] I pass introductory circumstances. "Will you make out an order for the Boat to bring in Mr. J. to-morrow, or this evening, if he should desire it, or it should be tho't essential to his recovery?" said D. to Mr. Broome. No direct answer followed this. Meantime, Cathill, the crazy tailor, came in; & J. Broome, winking to Dingley, entered into a trifling conversation with Cathill. After waiting some minutes, Dy. rose, & took his leave. Stymets appeared uneasy, & asked if he, D. would let him know, this evening how Johnson was. Then the great J. B. said—"I do not think myself at liberty, as one of the Committee, to give leave for Mr. J. to be removed into the City." Dingley left him. Would any other than the Man of Reason, hesitated to have loaded him with curses? Dingley bade me good night. I finished my letter. It is now eleven.

Wednesday, 30th

G. M. Woolsey breakfasted with us. S. Johnson left this place, this morning, for Boston; where, it is probable, he will reside the greater part of the winter. After breakfast I sat down to the translating of Condorcet, for two hours. I then walked an hour, including a call on G. M. W. & read the Papers. From then, till dinner, employed in translating, as before; &, after dinner, till near five P. M. Thus I have advanced near 40 pages, in the whole; & about 20 to-day. We drank tea with Mrs. Lovegrove, who was alone. Mr. L. returned, & we stayed there till near ten. We had a most pleasant evening. Conversation, as too often the case, multiform, tho' interesting, fugitive, yet instructive. A comparison between America & Europe, with many exemplifications, as to facts, customs, descriptions, manners, & individual histories. One fact, related by them, struck me particularly: not as new, in practice; but as a new illustration of a common theme of regret on their part, & triumph on ours: the triumph of humanity, for here, children have little else to do, but to learn, & to play. So that we almost regret their premature subjection to that discipline which is requisite to their instruction; & would rather that the "wee-things" should . . . "pass sweet hours at play";[15] & taste, ere they perish forever, the fleeting bliss of infancy. But there, in their numerous manufactories, children of three years old labor, all day, for a *penny*; labor, from morning till night, for a *penny*; & that at a wheel, where at each revolution, the child, the fondling, *must leap up*, to be tall enough to force it round. The tinsel splendor of the arts of luxury dazzles our eyes, & we are made blind to the wretchedness of which they form the splendid covering; but when I think of these things, & when, O my country, I look upon thy homely & russet simplicity, blest as thou art with morals, knowlege, & liberty, I can not but exclaim, "Perish the fine arts, if they must be purchased at a price so monstrous."

This day has been an autumnal day: clear, cool, airy. This evening, without cloud; illuminated by the pure splendor of a beauteous moon; balmy, & health-giving. It must revive the sick. It is also the last day of the month; a month worthy of remark.

October 1795

Thursday, 1st

I went, this morning, in pursuance of a written request, of Dingley, to consult with him, on the case of his friend, W. M. Johnson; & in this way employed great part of it. When I returned, I found a letter from Dunlap. I went out, again, to purchase, for him, "The Secret Tribunal"; a contemptible play, written by James Boeden,[16] & founded on the story of Herman of Unna. Dunlap, last year, conceived the design of writing, himself, a Tragedy, on that Story; &, I believe, went so far as to form a plot. It was this, & his having, once before, chosen the same subject with this Boeden, which made him desirous of seeing this "Secret Tribunal." I read the Piece. I wrote a few lines to my father. The rest of the forenoon, & some part of the afternoon, busied in replying to Dunlap. Alsop was here, both before & after dinner, with a piece he had been writing, to ridicule the crazy tailor—Cathill. It is humorous. The remainder of the afternoon, spent in attending to a professional call, & in visiting W. M. Johnson. Dingley was not with him. We had some conversation, for he was better—more than I ever had with him, before; & I found him to be a sensible, & well-informed, man.

As I went to H. Johnson's, I met Alsop & Wm., & we proceeded together, to Riley's; where we sat, talked, &, as is usual, when Alsop is one of the company, laughed, for an hour or two. We found G. M. Woolsey there. He returned, to our house, with Wm. & me; & stayed till near ten.

Thus a day has passed, in which I have read nothing, & written nothing: & in which, I have, especially, made no progress in my translation of Condorcet. My attention to that work must be resumed to-morrow.

It was my design to have looked over, & commented upon, the memorials of the past month: but circumstances forbid for the present.

---

[14] Broome was a wealthy merchant who became lieutenant governor of New York.

[15] Not found.

[16] Boaden, not Boeden. The usually charitable Dunlap (*Diary* 1: p. 222) refers to him as "that poverty-stricken animal Boaden." A dramatist. *The Secret Tribunal* (1795).

Friday, 2nd

I went, in season, to see my patient. He appeared somewhat better, tho' he had not recd. any benefit from medicine, as his pills had not operated. His pulse was, now, more low, & less frequent. I directed a brisker cathartic.

The translation was resumed, & I made some progress in it. While employed upon it, Dingley came in; &, in a few minutes, I recd. notice that my patient was worse. I hurried to him; & now found, what I had before suspected, that the feebleness of his pulse had been owing to the violence of his disease: for his physic had operated, & his fever was more severe. I determined to bleed him. He tottered out to a chair in the yard. I took away 18 oz. He rose, & walked, with a steady step, to the end of the yard; & after a discharge, returned; went down stairs, & returned to his room. It being in a lodging house, it was necessary that he should be removed; & he was, accordingly.

In the afternoon, I was, with Dingley, to see W. M. Johnson, who is not better. He bears his sickness like a man. There is the greater probability of his recovery.

Mr. Gahn was at his lodgings. He came into town this day, & leaves it again, in the morning. I drank tea with him; &, afterwards, we went, together, to see Mr. Roulet. I was pleased with him, & with the mother of his wife: a pleasing old lady; but who speaks no english. We were difficulted to converse, as I scarcely understand French, when spoken, & make a still worse figure in attempting to speak it.

I spent the evening at H. Johnson's. Wm. was there. We read poetry; chatted, & laughed. M. de la Garenne came in; & helped our sociability very much. We talked on french verse: does it admit of harmony, without rhyme? What might Racine, Dispreàux, & Voltaire, have done, towards freeing it of that incumbrance?—& of the pauses.

G. M. Woolsey left town to-day. Alsop meant to have gone, but a contrary wind detained him.

We shall soon be deserted, if the Fever continues.

Saturday, 3rd

I made some, tho' but little, progress, in my translation, this forenoon; for I was called off at eleven o'clock, to correct the press, for a piece of Alsop's, in ridicule of the tailor—Cathill. I visited W. M. Johnson; & conversation with Dingley, & one thing & another, occupied the remainder of the time, till dinner. We sat sometime at dinner; it was later than usual. Wm. read to me what he had written in his journal, which he commences the first of this month. We walked out of town; it was very pleasant; & our conversation rambled from one thing to another. It was sundown when we got back.

We drank tea at Mr. Winthrop's.[17] Col. Hamilton came there. Conversation settled on to the Fever, & he detailed the history of his own Case, in Phila. 1793, & of the mode of treatment pursued. He speaks very correctly, & sensibly; but with more hesitation than I expected in a man, so accustomed to public speaking. His conversation would have borne impression; nor could it have disgraced it.

I called in at H. Johnson's, on my return. Wm. went to make a visit; I came home. It was eight. I learnt, at H. J.'s, that Alsop left town, for Connecticut, this evening. Horace, William, & myself, are all who remain, of our particular circle.

The circumstances of the times, engage too much of my tho'ts & attention. I would avoid it, but can not. If I have no patients of my own, others call on me to visit theirs; they have done me like favors; & I can not refuse them. This is a rich season for superstition; a fine opportunity for priests to play upon the terrors of the ignorant: neither do they lose it. If any thing were surprizing, if we could be astonished at any sort of folly in men, surely it would merit wonder, that times of calamity, wherein reasonable beings ought to awaken their intellectual powers into new energy, should palsy & pervert them. How is God dinned with prayers! All the churches, on the Continent, are, I suppose, now opened to besiege the Almighty, as he is called, with petitions. At this moment, a Methodist, who dwells in the house opposite, is beseeching the Deity, with nasal twang; & praying him to remove *his judgements*, from New York. To-morrow floods of intreaty will deluge the earth. It was only last Sunday, that Johnson's barber, whose pliant conscience had ever before allowed him to dress his customers on Sunday, found out that it was damning him; and our Corporation or Magistracy have tho't fit at this time, to renew the laws for the religious observance of Sunday; & for restraining the Goats from going in the Streets. But there is no end to the absurdities on this subject.

Sunday, 4th

It is a very, very long time, since I have recd. a letter from Dr Leib.[18] My late, contained a request, unpleasant, I suppose; &, it is possible, that it offended his pride. He is most violently interested in politics, which occupy much of his time. A coolness, & inattention, to the milder calls of friendship, may be considered as no improbable effect. But, be the cause what it may, he has not written to me since last February. He had no reason to be angry with *me*, on account of my letter: it was with *himself,* if any one, that he should have been angry;

---

[17] Probably Benjamin Winthrop, 27 Pearl Street, or Francis at 29 Wall. See *New York Directory* (1795). The other Winthrops mentioned are definitely of a lower social order. His guest was Alexander Hamilton. Smith's casual treatment of the meeting is characteristic of his usual reaction in meeting individuals now legendary.

[18] Michael Leib, a graduate of the University of Pennsylvania, served as a surgeon in the Revolution, member of various committees, state House of Representatives 1797 and 1798, Democrat in U.S. House 1799-1806; Senate 1809-1814; postmaster of Philadelphia 1814-1815, and other offices. His liberalism annoyed Smith.

for his conduct, in this instance, has been unworthy of him, unworthy of any good man. He subscribed for twelve copies of the American Poems. The volume was published in 1793, & the twelve copies, together with two others, free of cost, agreable to the terms of the subscription, were sent. As many others were subscribed for, in Phila. all were sent to Jos: Bringhurst Jr.; & Dr. Leib was notified of it. More than twelve months elapsed, before he took them away; & he has never sent the twelve dollars subscription money. My last letter contained an extract of a letter from Collier, the publisher of the Volume, in which he desires me to procure, for him, the payment of the monies due to him, on this account in Phila.; & representing himself, as was true, in great want of them. Dr. Leib ought to have paid the small debt, instantly. He has not; he has not written to me. Still, I have tho't it would be wrong to give up a friend, for a single error. Last evening, I wrote to him, on our situation here. To this letter I hope he will reply. As I was finishing it Dingley came in. Cathill still continues to persecute him; by going, whenever he hears D. has a patient, & telling the sick man that he will kill him: thus destroying confidence in him, & injuring his fortune, as well as usefulness. I advised to him to state the circumstances to the Mayor, & request his interference. I was surprized to see G. M. Woolsey enter. He returned, from L. Island, the last evening, & came to tell me that he should breakfast with me this morning, & then go to Amboy. He did breakfast with me; & has since left town.

Alsop came to see us this morning. The wind prevented his leaving town last evening, as he had intended; & he was to have gone at eight this morning. The people sailed at seven; without giving him notice. He is now in search of another conveyance. After his departure, I wrote to Mr. Hodgkinson,[19] on the subject of my Opera; & to communicate some information to him, concerning the state of this City.

[Omitted here, two manuscript pages with the heading "Language II."]

I was employed, on the preceeding notes, till after one P.M. Then I took up "The Curiosities of Literature," & amused myself till dinner. Young Mr. J. Mulligan,[20] my host's son, a very amiable & agreable young gentleman, had returned from the country, & I was induced to sit longer, on his account. When I returned, I resumed the Curiosities of Literature, & read some time. I was hesitating, whether I should proceed, or go to H. Johnson's, when Dingley entered. We chatted a while, & I went with him, to see one of his patients. The man was well; we sat some time; & then came out, & parted. When I came home, I found that Wm. had gone out: it was five; I read a little, & then went to Mr. Lovegrove's whither we, yesternight, agreed to go this evening. I found them alone, & at tea; & so took my seat at the table. Shortly after, Wm. came. We past a most interesting & enchanting evening. Conversation rapid, varied, & unusually entertaining. It is impossible, either of abridgement or detail. She, rather L. read us a part of a most sensible letter, from her friend, of whom she often speaks—Miss Sally Morton. She is the *veritable* representative of the *Ideal* Anna St. Ives.[21] The late John Hudson, Miss Hannah More & her sisters, Mrs. Yearsley, The Maid of the Hay-stack,[22] &c. &c. engaged our attention: concerning all whom, Mrs. L. who was personally acquainted with each, related numerous & new anecdotes. Never did she appear to equal advantage. Her voice, eye, manner, the inflections of her countenance, & her language, was uncommonly eloquent, & irresistibly engaging & commanding. How much it is to be lamented, that the pen is not as rapid, & as vividly descriptive, as the memory!

Monday, 5th

I devoted all this forenoon, indeed till dinner, to translating Condorcet. The day was close, & sultry, more even than yesterday; I did not feel very well; & made no extraordinary progress in my labour. I gave up Alsop's name, (who left town yesterday, I suppose,) to the printer, as the author of the piece ridiculing Cathill, as young Broome, who was touched in it, had called to demand the author.

I recd. a few lines from Mumford; informing me of his safe arrival at New London; his increasing health; & his purpose to return here, the present week. I wrote a few lines in reply.

Our table, at dinner, was unusually full: i. e. unus-

---

[19] John Hodgkinson, an English actor in his late twenties was brought to America by John Henry, owner of the Old American Company, in 1792 to play in New York and Philadelphia. In 1794 an actor named Hallam bought the company and sold half to Hodgkinson who became manager. Hodgkinson thereafter sold a part of the company to Dunlap who was thoroughly unhappy from that day forward. The petty intrigue, conniving, cheating and daily displays of temperament by the leading members of the company are almost unbelievable. Despite his shortcomings as a human being, however, Hodgkinson was an excellent actor and possessed great charm. Smith, although he knew him well, and although he was often a merciless judge of weaknesses, nevertheless liked him. See Dunlap, *Diary*; Dunlap, *A History of the American Theatre* (New York, 1832); *John Hodgkinson, A Narrative of His Connection with the Old American Company, from the Fifth September, 1792, to the Thirty-first of March, 1797* (New York, 1797).

[20] John Mulligan (1774-1862), was a graduate of Columbia College, a lawyer, strong Federalist who knew Jay and Hamilton. Smith ate his meals at the elder Mulligan's table until May 5, 1796, when his need to economize decided him to make his own meals, mostly bread and milk.

[21] Thomas Holcroft, *Anna St. Ives* (1792), similar in spirit to William Godwin's *Caleb Williams,* in defense of revolutionary ideals.

[22] John Hudson, not found. Hanna More was a writer of clever verse, a witty conversationalist, in the Dr. Johnson, Reynolds, Garrick circle; she was also the author of some plays of little importance and a philanthropist of considerable effectiveness. She discovered and promoted Anne Yearsley, the milk-maid poetess, who was known as "Lactilla." Not clear from context whether she was the Maid of the Haystack painted by William Palmer.

ually for the present circumstances. Some of the boarders having returned, for the day. I sat some time after dinner, to read a publication of Dr. Rush's on Bleeding. I called at Jones'. They are so so. I think it probable that Samuel will be sick again, & more so than at first. From thence, I to the vessel, to put in my letter to Mumford. Returning, I called at Genl. Lamb's.[23] Some chat. His son, the physician, is to shew me, to-morrow, a letter he lately recd. from Phila.—from a physician there. I came home. Wm. & I read, alternately several articles in "The Curiosities of Literature." I drank tea at Mrs. Miller's. Mr. Miller, the clergyman, there. The Fever occupied the conversation, principally. I spent the residue of the evening at home: reading D'Israeli.[24]

The deaths increased greatly, yesterday; &, probably, the sickness likewise. This day, which has been of the same sort, must have added much to the sickness. A light rain is now falling. But it will do no good. Nothing but a heavy rain, followed by frost, & durable cold weather, can effect a cure of our "distempered atmosphere."

I have mentioned "The Curiosities of Literature." I have read a number of articles, in this work, but miscellaneously. They are all highly entertaining. The author writes with great spirit & elegance; & with an uncommon exuberance & force of wit & satire. He appears to have read, & reflected well on what he has read. His taste appears equal to his erudition; & hence the latter leads him to apply the former with critical acumen, & learned sensibility. He is evidently the friend of civil & religious liberty; tho', from the little I have read, I should suspect that he would not be for carrying the first to that extent which I deem proper; but would fear too much the ills of anarchy, if a great deviation were attempted from established customs, laws, & institutions. Perhaps I am wrong. Further reading, may refute or corroborate, the idea. Many articles, in this work, might receive useful & entertaining additions, from this quarter of the world. For my part, I have determined to dedicate some future pages of this work, & some future portion of my time, to the recollection, & insertion, of several brilliant follies of wit, beautiful felicities of expression, & curious incidents in life, which have fallen under my own observation, been related to me by creditable persons, or thrown themselves in my way in the course of my reading.

I hardly know whether it is fortunate, or unfortunate, that I have so little to do, in my professional line, during the prevalence of the reigning Epidemic. Instances, wherein the disease appears to have been communicated by Contagion, i. e. where one person had been infected by contact, or near approach, or continuance with another, who was sick—seem to multiply. If it be true that it is thus propagated, I might, were I much employed, thus receive it, & death might put an end to all my hopes of usefulness. Besides many bring on the Fever by over fatigue, which might, also, be my case, even if there were no contagion. On the other hand, money, that first good of the multitude is only to be acquired by extensive practice. Extensive practice, in this period, must throw many into my hands, or under my care, who are unable to pay. Here would be loss, fatigue, anxiety, & risk, without any profit. No! I should thus acquire knowlege of the disease & it's remedies. But, a more interesting inquiry arises. Should not I be likely to do much good, were I employed? Is it a foolish vanity, which deceives me, when I suspect that I am less under the influence of prejudice than many; & that I should venture my reputation freely to do good; & that no bigottry to a peculiar system would prevent my readily yielding any notion, which I had once entertained, if I found it false? I think not. Is it not certain that many, very many die? Is it not equally true that various & opposite modes of practice are in use? All can not be right. Am I not convinced that one is better than another? And have I not courage to make the experiment, fairly? I think I am: I think I have. Do I not see ignorance, pride, stupidity, carelessness, & a superstitious veneration for foreign writers, & a mean jealousy of an illustrious writer of our own country, go hand in hand, & as it were, conspire, against the lives of men? I think I do. I think I have had sufficient opportunity to determine that his principles & practice are equally & certainly sound. I think I should apply them, in nearly all their extent. I feel confident that the effects would be salutary. And, with a mind, armed, as mine is against terror, & the idle fear of death; with a spirit animated by a sacred love of truth, & filled with an ardent humanity & tender zeal for the welfare of my fellow creatures; could there be any danger that I should be sick? or, if sick, that I should die? It is on the best principles that I wish, for greater employment. I could fill whole pages in descanting on the possible [word cut off].

Tuesday, 6th

As I had nothing to call me abroad, I stayed at home, & worked away on my translation. I had time enough just to get thro' my ordinary portion, when Adams

---

[23] General John Lamb a leader of the "Sons of Liberty" in New York and thereafter captain of an artillery company in the attack on Quebec during which he unfortunately met Aaron Burr. He later became collector of the Port of New York. In 1796 he lent Burr the then huge sum of $23,000 to buy land on Lake Ontario. When Lamb's assistant embezzled a large amount of money, Lamb resigned and his property was mortgaged to replace the funds. He asked Burr for his money. Burr, caught in a land-poor position, did everything possible to help him, even selling all of the furniture in his great house. Nevertheless, Lamb lost everything and died about two years later. Herbert S. Parmet and Marie B. Hecht, *Aaron Burr, Portrait of an Ambitious Man* (New York and London, 1967). Lamb had a son, a physician, with whom Smith had a passing acquaintance.

[24] Also J. D. Israeli, J. DeIsraeli, Isaac D'Israeli, *Curiosities of Literature; consisting of Anecdotes, Characters, Sketches, and Observations, Literary, Critical and Historical.* **1** (London, 1791); **2** (1793; revised and expanded edition London 1794; **3** (1817); **4, 5** (1823). Added to all this, it was issued anonymously.

came in, & shortly after Dingley. We had much talk about the Fever; which Dingley considers as worse now than ever. I was surprized to see Alsop enter. A letter from home, informing him that his Wife, Theodore & Abby, who are not at Boston, will not be back till next week, will keep him here some days longer, as disappointments in conveyances have kept him here so long. We walked a short time on the Battery, before dinner. Since dinner, Alsop was here a few moments; Wm. has gone to walk with his sister; & I have amused myself, for near three hours, with "The Curiosities of Literature."

My time passes away, & is employed to little purpose. The circumstances of this city, as well as the state of mind induced by them, alike prevent the adoption & execution of any plan, a part of which consists in a residence here. I know not when I shall be able to arrange my ideas with consistence, to fall on some determinate & settled plan of action, & be endued with sufficient energy of mind to persevere & not be diverted from it. The question which I began to examine, some time ago, still remains unsettled, uncanvassed. I say question—but it was, more properly, an inquiry into the relative, or rather comparative, advantages & disadvantages, of several modes of life; to the end that the one which promised most should be adopted & strictly adhered to. Certain it is, that something must be done. As yet I am a very child; the dandling of parental indulgence. Hitherto, I have not supported myself. But I ought, & will do it. With such a resolution, it becomes me to look about, & see how it is to be effected. Why should I hesitate to earn my bread by those very arts of labor which thousands daily practice? Or, if I can better employ my time, why indulge in the absurd & pernicious gratification of a thousand appetites & vanities, the expence of whose maintenance is all that simple nature, the wants of reason, ask for, or recd.?

Nor grieve that slander, with malicious rage,
Fierce war against thy glory wage:
Beneath a grim, ferocious sway,
Palmyra's ruins gloom'd the desert way;
But wide o'er earth their fame forever flies;
    Amid their vernerable shade,
    Oft hath the musing pilgrim stray'd,
    There, oft, the Genius of the waste,
    Wanders, & thinks upon the past;
Counts o'er the mouldering piles, & sighs.

Nor yet, tho' factions' busy imps defame,
And load with every word of shame,
    Think that the offspring of thy mind,
    Was e'er for mischief's evil aid designed.
    The man may suffer in the rude affray;
    But rancour's deadly rage, nor time, it's blessings e'er can stay.
Beneath a ruder, barbarier power,
    Rome, the high mistress of the world,
It's glories doom'd to rise no more,
    To fierce destruction impiously was hurl'd.

The gloom of twelve long ages past,
Her slumbering genius rears at last;
    O'er Europe first his powerful wand he waved,
    Her sons by superstition long enflamed,
    Rouze from their torpid trance:
    See Science now her standard swift advance;
    Up spring the Arts; her sword see Freedom raise;
    O'er distant lands the light of knowlege blaze;
Now would appear, new nations crowd the files
And Roman poets sing in trans-atlantic wilds.

What is the meaning of all this? It was so dark, when I finished these lines, that I could not see to write an explanation. When I have heard Mr. Jay[25] very much censured, & his Treaty much abused, I have tho't on Aristides, Socrates, & many others, the benefactors of their nation & of mankind, & have resolved to address to him an Ode. The idea occurred to me this afternoon, as I had just finished the preceeding page, & the two principal tho'ts in the above stanzas: the inspiration was not to be resisted, & I wrote.

I was at Riley's, a short time, in the evening. The church bells rang. We could not determine whether for *prayer* or *fire*. When we got into Broadway, we found it was for prayer. Alsop came home with me, & stayed till eight. Then, he went to the Coffee-House, & I to H. Johnson's. Wm. was there; & the time was pleasantly spent, till after ten.

Wednesday, 7th

I was employed, by snatches, on my translation, till dinner. I had gone out, early in the morning, to see a man who was sick; & Adams, Alsop, & Dingley, severally called, & took up, each, some time. I dined with Johnson, at his brother's. After dinner, I was engaged in two consultations, & in visiting several sick, till six. I went to Riley's, & drank tea there. Alsop & I came away together. He went to the Coffee-House; I to see the sick. I did not get home till ten.

There was to have been a meeting of the College of Physicians,[26] but Dingley's & my absence prevented it. We called between nine & ten; but found that those who had met, had returned home. We meet to-morrow evening.

---

[25] Jay entered on negotiations from what most Americans thought was a position of strength. It is now generally conceded that he was badly outmaneuvered by Lord Greville. The main questions to be settled were the continued refusal of the British to abandon the Northwest Ports, money owed by American citizens to British citizens, and claims for reparation for damages inflicted by British warships on American (presumably neutral) shipping. Jay, acting largely on Hamilton's advice and anxious not to provoke hostilities at a time when they would do vast damage to America's financial position, came home with a treaty that all Democratic-Republicans and many Republicans thought thoroughly unsatisfactory. The treaty dealt with reasonable ways of settling problems of trade and the evacuation of the Northwest Ports but did not come to terms with the British attacks on American shipping. Reactions in America were violent and there were calls for Washington's impeachment. The Senate, nevertheless, approved the treaty in 1795.

[26] Smith was corresponding secretary.

G. M. Woolsey returned to-day, from Amboy,[27] where he left all our friends well; & whither he returns, either this evening, or on the morrow. He bro't me no letters, for myself. Dunlap has finished his letters to Godwin, & Holcroft, & has sent them to me to forward. I must attend to this to-morrow.

I have not time to make any remarks on the verses on the preceeding page. I meant to have done it. I shall only say, that they are too diffuse; & do by no means keep pace with the spirit of the tho'ts. They want the hand of culture. This might bestow on the ideas, a versification & flow, neither unworthy of them, or of the fancied object to whom they are addresst.

Thursday, 8th

Immediately after breakfast, I went out, with Dingley, who called for me, to visit some patients of his, to whom he, yesterday, called me to consult for, with him. We found them both, in a situation nearly hopeless. One I considered so, from the first, & I declined calling again. The other's case did not appear equally desperate; tho' there was little ground for hope. I returned, & set down to translate. I made no great progress. The day was far advanced when I began; & recd. a letter, from my father, which required an answer, & some business to be done. I wrote my answer, & did the business, in season for dinner. After dinner, I went instantly to see Mr. Webb, an apothecary, the patient of Dingley, mentioned above. Dingley was with him; & we stayed, from three, till five; & two more melancholly hours I never past. I must spare myself a detail so painful. All hope was now at an end; & nothing which we could devise, seemed to answer any purpose. We were near an hour employed in attempting to stop a bleeding which took place from a vein which had been opened before. The blood was intirely destroyed in it's texture; the man stupidly insane; the house deserted; a negro nurse only remaining; except a drunken relation of the landlord, who with oaths & imprecations, refused to allow our moving the sick man, from an apartment five feet wide by twelve long, into an unoccupied, airy room. We did it however—& exerted every thing in our power to restore sensibility & hope to a man, thus forlorn, & without relation or friend near him, to yield any assistance.

I went from this house of despair, to visit a patient of my own. He is in a good way. When I reached home, I found Alsop here. We talked an hour, & my spirits revived. Wm. & I drank tea, together, at his brother's. We passed a couple of hours very pleasantly. The bells rung for fire. We went out. I was surprized at the number of men collected, & the alacrity displayed. It seemed as if every person tho't the town deserted, & his own efforts necessary on the present occasion. I have met with nothing, for some time which gave me so much pleasure. Still, this satisfaction was impaired by the recollection that such an event happened at Phila. in 1793, & was supposed by Dr. Rush to have induced the fever, in several instances. The fire was soon extinguished.

I went to the College of Physicians. We had a thin meeting: talked a little: but were unable to do much business, from the absence of a Fellow, from whom a report was expected, relative to Dissections, made in the present Disease.

We have had a most copious rain. It began in the night, & cleared off at sun-set. The day has been quite cold. The wind constantly, during the rain, at the time of clearing, & since, North-West. The night is clear, a brisk wind, & cold. I hope we shall have frost.

This event can not fail, I think, of proving very favorable to the health of the city, unless it should be succeeded, which is not probable, by very sultry weather. I am informed that but seven deaths were reported to the Committee this evening. If this be true, the declension of the disease, within a week, & since the change of weather, from hot to cold, has been rapid, beyond all expectation. If prayers were ever of any avail, it would be worth the while to *clap to*, in Yankee dialect, all hands, & pray for cold weather after this rain. Indeed, the prospect is not discouraging; & a gleam of hope burst thro' the thick gloom which surrounds us.

Friday, 9th

When we reached Mr. Webb's, we found him, as I expected, dead. I went with Dingley to make some arrangements about his funeral, but, being disappointed in not finding the Alderman we called on, we parted; he to apply elsewhere. When I came home I found I had a new call. I attended to it.

After getting business out of the way, I sat down to translate. Wm. was reading Quintillian's Institutes;[28] he occasionally fell into discourse; my head became confused, & I threw by my work. I have, to-day & yesterday, done little more than ten pages. We walked an hour on the battery; & when we had returned, I took D'Israeli, till dinner.

John Wells, who has returned to town, dined with us. I sat longer, of course, than usual. When I came home, I had recourse to D'Israeli again; not being in a humor for more serious study. Alsop came in. He sat an hour. All reading was laid aside, while he stayed.

I went to visit my young patient. He is quite sick; & the people where he is, are so negligent, & his mind so totally inelastic, that I fear he will not recover. Nothing on my part shall be wanting; but I have as many apprehensions as hopes.

I put Dunlap's letter to his friend Brewer, which, I suppose, includes copies of his letters to Godwin & Hol-

---

[27] Perth Amboy about twenty miles south of New York was Dunlap's birthplace where he frequently spent his summers. It gradually became the summer resort of his friends. Smith, because of his work and poverty went there only for short visits.

[28] *Institutiones Oratorias*. What Quintilian had to say about the importance of education and training uninterruptedly from infancy would have a great appeal to Smith.

croft, in the letter-bag of the Ship Tigon, bound to Liverpool; there being no vessel now ready to sail for London.

I drank tea, & spent the evening, at Mr. Lovegrove's. Johnson came there after tea. In the former part of the evening, the child was *tewsome,* & we exerted ourselves to divert & pacify it. Afterward conversation began. We rather chatted, than conversed. The difference in manners &c with some particularization—between our country & Britain, was more than any thing, our topic. I did not feel in very good spirits. My mind, involuntarily dwelt upon the situation of my little patient. His condition, & the difficulties in his way, dwelt upon my imagination, & almost made me melancholly. How great a draw-back on the happiness of a physician, is this constant anxiety: & which a man of any sensibility must feel! When shall I be able to satisfy myself, when I have done all in my power, under the circumstances— even tho' the event should prove unfortunate? But the difficulty lies in knowing, when we have done all in our power. Yet will dissatisfaction do any good? Will it not impair our talents for future usefulness?

Saturday, 10th

I found my little patient better, this morning.

I sat down, with more spirit to translating, & did a tolerably good forenoon's work. After this was thro' I walked till dinner, on the Battery.

After dinner, I visited W. M. Johnson. I had not seen him for a week. I found him much better. We fell into conversation, & I stayed with him two hours.

I found my patient in a fair way to recovery. This gave me the more satisfaction, as my anticipations concerning him, had been rather melancholly.

Learning that Alsop had not left town, I went to Riley's, in the hope of seeing him. He was not there. I stayed there two hours, & drank tea. From thence I went to H. Johnson's. They all dined at the Bowery, but had returned. Wm. & I came home at little after nine. We found Dingley here, & he sat, & talked with us, till after ten. He thinks the fever no better, & that those who are now taken sick, are more violently siezed; & have the disease run on more rapidly to indirect debility. He says he inquired of a watchman, from whom he learnt, that only one of their occupation had been affected by the disease; & that one a man, who had been out of the city for some time; returned; entered on his business again; caught the fever, & died. This may be attributed to the effect of habit; which renders the noxious atmosphere of our streets, which is still more deadly in the night, harmless.

"The monster Custom, ...
. . . . . . "is angel yet in this."[29]

---

[29] "That monster, custom, who all sense doth eat, Of habits devil, is angel yet in this. . . ." *Hamlet,* III, iv.

Sunday, 11th

It began to rain in the night, & rained violently, I imagine, during the whole night. It is now ten o'clock, in the morning, & it still rains violently. If rains can do us any good, good will be done to us; for we have many & severe ones, lately. The City will, at least, be washed.

When I visited my patients, this morning, I found them better. Since my return, I have been employed in writing an Official reply, as Corresponding Secretary of the College of Physicians of New York, to a Communication of Dr. Currie of Phila. of the 20th ulto.

PUNS

There is, in the Spectator, if I do not misremember, a long Paper, and I believe several papers—on Punning.[30] It is so long since I read it, that I forget how the subject is handled; & whether the writer decide in favor, or against, Puns. Some persons affect to despise them, altogether; not only as childish, but as destitute of any pretensions to wit. Others, regard the Punster as a sublime genius, & are ever on the hunt for a pun. Both are wrong, in my opinion. Nothing is more easy, &, at the same time, more foolish, than to acquire a habit of punning. It is, beside, a very difficult habit to conquer. Habitual punsters are among the most tiresome of companions. The infinity of execrable puns which they incessantly fatigue you with, is by no means repaid by the few good ones which they occassionally produce. And how irrational, how absurd, is that labor, which is ever on the stretch, for some new ambiguity of expression. But contemptible as this truly is, we, occassionally, meet with, & hear, puns, which have some claim to merit. I will not say they are *witty*; for that would be entering into a new controversy: Wit being a thing as little decided on, as Contagion: but I shall proceed to notice a few, which appear to me worthy of preservation.

My friend Theodore Dwight is distinguished for his love of every thing, which promotes conviviality & merriment. He is noted for puns; &, considering the fertility of his punning faculty, he may be called a good punster, & has produced many celebrated puns. To collect all he has scattered, would be like attempting, at this day, to gather the leaves of the Sybils. Puns, too, owe much of their success to the circumstances in which they arise: so that to make them intelligible to readers, would require a narration so tedious that the force of the pun itself would be destroyed. The following, requires but little previous explanation.

Some company dined at Col. Wadsworth's, in Hartford; it was at the time when it was fashionable to wear the Soals of shoes, extremely narrow—especially, just

---

[30] Addison wrote a series of six papers on "false wit," *Spectator* papers numbers 58 through 63. Number 61 was on puns as was part of the following paper.

by the heel. Dwight was there; dinner was over; & the company had retired into another room. Col. W. is noted for his wealth, in that city. Much merriment was a-foot. Mr. W. the son of Col. W. was standing by a chair, into which he put one knee; thus displaying the soal of his shoes—which was a fashionable one. Something was said of his having, by & by, a large estate. Dwight, who stood behind him, replied, pointing, at the same time, to his shoe—

> He's but a wretch, with all his lands,
> Who wears a narrow *soul* (*soal*)[31]

The quotation is from Watt's Lyric Poems.

Mr. Asa Hopkins, an Apothecary in Hartford, a gentleman distinguished for his humor, was to see Mr. Dwight. The family he lived in, went early to bed; he had stayed late; & the night was escessively dark. He rose to go. Dwight entreated him to sit longer.—"If I stay longer," he replied—"I shall be shut out, into *outer darkness.*"

A Mr. Lord of Lichfield (Connec.) humourously described the return home, of some young men, from a drinking party, where they became nearly intoxicated—by saying, that "they proceeded thro' the Street, with great *circumspection.*"

We were at Mr. Rogers's, one day, & were jocularly talking of Sir Jno. Temple's method of thrusting his nose into the face of the man who is talking with him (Sir Jno. is deaf). Says W. W. Woolsey, "You must, in return, thrust your nose into his ear, if you speak to him." "Dovetail it?" said another. "That," replied Dunlap—"would be *fineering*"—(*fine-ecring*)—(*fine-hearing.*)

Mr. Decius Wadsworth was standing by the side of one of his acquaintance; & taking hold of the hair of his friend—"You have very little hair"—said he—"and how short it is!" His friend replied—

> Man wants but *little* here below,
> Nor wants that *little* long.[32]

A gentleman, of whose name I am ignorant, was sitting by the side of a lady in New-Port, on whose gown he observed a small *spot* of *grease*; which, by some accident, we will suppose, had found it's way there. "Your gown, Madam," said he—"has been a great traveller I see." "How so?" demanded the lady; somewhat alarmed. "Has it not been in *Greece?*" asked the gentleman. "Fye, fye! That was far-fetched." "Nay, not at all," rejoined he—"For I made it on the *spot.*" (This was related to me by Dr. Mitchill.)

But this is trifling; & let us have done with it.

[Omitted here, two manuscript pages with the heading "Puns."]

Dingley came in. I shewed him my letter to Dr. Currie,[33] which with a correction, he approved. I copied it. We walked on the Battery; & then went to see Alsop; with whom we stayed till dinner. After dinner, I read "The Curiosities of Literature," till five. I then visited my patient. Returned by the way of H. Johnson's. They were out. Wm. came home with me; & we spent the evening at our own house. I finished reading the Second Volume of D'Israeli.

The rain went off before ten A. M. It was warm till the middle of the afternoon; then it clouded up; grew cold; & rained a little: then cleared, but remained cold. In a month, all will be as if nothing had happened.

If I spend the winter in New York, which I probably shall do; & spend it studiously, as I design to do; the following are my intended studies.

Medicine:—some portion of this every day: I think about three hours; & in some measure systematically. *The Mathematics*: beginning with arithmetic, & proceeding on to the highest branches, regularly, & scientifically: devoting, perhaps, two hours, every other day. *History*: to be read, regularly, with Wm.; the two last hours, of each day, before going to bed; beginning with Herodotus, & reading all, of character, downward. *French*: to make a part of the business of every day; but, chiefly, as connected with some of my other studies; & not merely as a study of itself. *German*: to be attended to one hour, every other day. *Composition*: to be carried on, in various ways, but on some subject, almost every day. *Morals*: some portion of each week, to be given to this study. *Letters*: the amusement of leisure hours, & interrupted moments. *Copying*: to proceed occasionally, till completed. Here, now, is work enough for one poor mortal. To do any thing, with all this mass, requires exertions which, I fear me, I shall never make. Indolence, thou delightful fiend! let go thy hold.

It is late. I can go no further. Dingley interrupted me; & had just departed, after an hour's dissertation on equalized & unequal, Excitement.

Monday, 12th

Visited my patients, and found them better. The forenoon chiefly devoted to translating. Wm. & I walked, from one, till two. After dinner read the Newspapers. When I came home, found Alsop with Wm. We talked till near five. He went away. I visited my patients, & found them still better. The day has been very clear & fine.

It has been a favorite project of mine, at some future period, to undertake the compilation & publication of a Literary Journal. Not a Review; but something between a Review, a Register, & a magazine; or compounded of all three. I scarcely can tell how, but, in our conversation to-day, the idea was started of our (Wm. &

---

[31] Isaac Watts, *Horae Lyricae*, "False Greatness."
[32] Oliver Goldsmith, "The Hermit."
[33] Smith corresponded with a Dr. Currie in Philadelphia and also with another in Liverpool. A good guess would be that this letter was addressed to Philadelphia and contained a description of some aspect of Smith's studies of yellow fever.

myself) engaging in a publication of the kind, together; & to begin it, this winter. We made calculations on the expence, support, necessary labor, & product. It is well enough to make such plans; but let us look a little into it; & see what we might do; & what would be our materials.

1mo. A series of Papers, selected from the best authors, tending to illustrate & explain the most interesting Phenomena in Meteorology, Hydrology, & Geology; with accounts of the best works, & instruments, therefor; & some biographical memoirs of their authors.

2ndo. New, forgotten, & interesting Memoirs, relative to either of the three remaining divisions of natural History; particularly, on the philosophy thereof; critical account of Books; memoirs & anecdotes of authors.

3tio. Original communications in any of the branches of Medicine & natural Philosophy.

4to. Statistical accounts of every part of the United States, & of America, generally; with historical &c. comparisons with modern Europe, & times ancient & modern.

5to. American Biography; including memoirs of characters distinguished, in any respect, from the first settlement, to the present time; accurate lists of the works of such as have written; anecdotes, &c.

6to. The Literary History of the U. S. in particular, of America generally; including a list of publications of all kinds, critical & historical notes, anecdotes of books & authors.

7mo. A republication, either of the whole, of parts, or an abstract, of all the pamphlets, tending to illustrate the history of this country; especially of the late revolution, & the characters who conducted it.

8vo. Curious, literary, critical, biographical, &c. anecdotes—: & here much use may be made of "The Curiosities of Literature," & similar publications; & to these may be added things of the like kind, which have fallen under our observation, or been related to us.

9no. Occasional insertion of the best moral, political, literary, &c. essays; either from our own, or foreign authors.

10mo. Tales; original, translated from other languages, & selected from the English authors; having reference, as much [as] may be to the circulation of some useful truth.

11mo. Republication of the time-pieces, particularly of a humorous nature, which have appeared in America; with notes, comments, & historical anecdotes.—Lycurgus,[34] the Anarchiad, &c.

12mo. A selection of the best English small poems, from Spenser downwards; with short criticisms; some account of the authors, & of the poems.

13tio. Papers, original & selected, relative to Arts, Commerce, & Agriculture; with comments, anecdotes of authors, &c.

14to. Memoirs, facts, &c. relative to the antiquities of our country; & the present state of the interior.

15mo. Miscellanea: including original communications, of every sort, that do not properly rank under the preceeding heads.

I must defer any continuation of this subject, till to-morrow.

Wm. & I drank tea at his brother's. We were sitting, & talking about visiting at Mr. Lovegrove's, when some-one wrapped at the door, & inquired for me. It was Charles Adams. His Wife was somewhat unwell, & he wished me to see her. I went with him. I was introduced to her, for the first time. I did not find her very unwell. I however prescribed something for her—put it up—& returned to H. Johnson's; from whence Wm. & I went to Lovegrove's. They are weaning their little boy; & we found him in a fine crying humor. Our entrance served to amuse him; & we put him off good-natured. We stayed till ten. The conversation was rambling—but, as usual, entertaining.

I recd. a letter from Thomas Mumford, to-day. He is on the recovery; tho' he gains strength slowly.

The above sketch of a plan for our Paper, was written, partly, before tea, & partly, since my return from Mr. L's. Wm. & I have conversed considerably upon it, to-day; & mentioned it to Alsop, when he was here. He approves of it; &, if we go on, engages to yield us some occasional assistance.

Tuesday, 13th

The necessary professional calls over, I sat down to translate. In this I did more than I expected, having been diverted, for some time, by Alsop's taking us to see about some French books.

After dinner, read in D'Israeli. Made some calls. Saw C. Adams, & found his wife better. Dingley was here a short time. He has heard from London—from Dr. Hawes & Lettsom.[35]

Wm. & I spent the first part of the evening at Riley's; I found a letter from Hodgkinson, when I returned; from which I learn that the music for my Opera, is nearly in readiness;[36] the music for Dunlap's also. This is good, & unexpected, news. It will be so to Dunlap, in a particular manner; for he had given up all expectations of ever bringing an Opera to the stage: judging

---

[34] Apparently a minor political satirist who wrote for newspapers. Only one extant publication in book or pamphlet form carries his name: *War or No War* (New York, 1807).

[35] William Hawes and John Coakley Lettsome. Like so many other doctors in the eighteenth century they did not restrict their studies or interests to medicine but wrote on a variety of subjects.

[36] Smith's opera was *Edwin and Angelina* the music for which was written by a musician playing the "first horn" for the Old American Company in New York. His name is rarely spelled twice the same way: Victor Pelissier, Pellesier, Pelesier. Dunlap's play (or opera) was probably *The Archers*, music by Benjamin Carr, for which see later. However, Pelissier did write the music for Dunlap's *Sterne's Maria*, first played in 1799. Dunlap's *Diary* 1: p. 75. Incidental music, songs, etc. were often introduced into plays at the time so that the normal distinction between play and opera is occasionally blurred.

from the delay, heretofore experienced, in relation to musical pieces.

As for my Opera, I scarcely expect that it will succeed. It is serious. In blank verse. Yet it is impossible to make any calculation on the subject. Should it be well played; the music be good; the scenery pleasing; it may live along, it's three nights. Greater success can not possibly be hoped for it. Caprice may dignify, caprice may destroy, it. The experiment is worth making, after the trouble I have been at. It may be necessary for me to publish it, as a means of making some slight addition to my slender funds. If it is damned, publishment will be my appeal to the judgement of people at large; if well-recd., applause will justify my laying that before the reader which the auditor did not find fault with. Variety of opinions, will excuse my making it public, as the best way of affording to each an opportunity to fortify, or overthrow his opinion, or that of his adversary. At any rate, it must be printed. If it should succeed, it would be a new proof of the crudeness of the public taste, which could relish this piece, in preference to much better ones of my friend Dunlap; if it fail, it will still be an evidence of the miserable injustice of the public, who crown with applause foreign productions, which, to compare with this, *"are, as a Satyr to Hyperion."*[37] After all, I feel no great anxiety; as I have neither much to hope, or much to fear. If I succeed, I shall not be overjoyous; if I fail, I shall not be greatly disappointed.

Wednesday, 14th

After breakfast, I called on Dingley. He shewed me the letters he recd. from Lettsom & Hawes; & the books & apparatus sent by them. Lettsom appears to be a plain, sensible man, from this letter, & other things of his, which I have seen; but no wise distinguished for gifts of genius. Hawes, is a strange, good, methodistic, man, as all his publications, & this letter, bear witness. Dingley being somewhat unwell, I devoted great part of the morning to visiting his patients. I visited also my own.

Mr. Lovegrove called to let me know that he tho't of visiting Amboy, to-morrow, for the purpose of viewing a place there, which I had recommended to him to purchase, & build on. I had promised him a letter to Dunlap. I wrote this forenoon; & also wrote to Hodgkinson.

Alsop called to take leave of us. I have not heard whether he went, or not.

The afternoon pretty much occupied with visiting one or two patients; & attending to a little other business, of no recordative importance.

I drank tea, & spent part of the evening, at Mrs. Miller's. They are all well. Some talk, with the parson, relative to Mr. Randolph[38]—whose letters are now a topic of conversation.

From Mrs. Miller's, I went to Mr. Lovegrove's. I found them at home, & alone; & passed two hours pleasantly. We talked on the perfectibility of man. I mentioned some things of Dunlap's: of his dramatic performances—(introduced by my letter to him); theatrical subjects thence spoken of; & some eulogiums on several celebrated English performers.

Soon after my return, Dingley came in, & stayed till after ten. Various talk. He informed me of a letter of Barlow's, which he had seen, in which Barlow explicitly condemned Christianity, & disavowed it. He also mentioned a new Poem of his; an eulogy on "Hasty-Pudding."[39] Conversation, on Trumbull, Barlow, Dwight, &c. with some anecdotes of each mentioned by me.

Thursday, 15th

I visited my patient, returned, wrote a letter to my parents, & sat down to translate. In this I made a little advance. I called on Adams, at his office, to learn how his wife was, & finding, from him, that she was better, did not visit her. After this I read in "The Curiosities of Literature," till dinner.

It had been rainy all the forenoon; raining very hard, from very early in the morning. It cleared off, & Wm. & I walked to a French bookseller's, in Chambers Street, purchased some books, & returned. The man did not appear to have much knowlege of the character of the authors, whose works he dealt in—& Wm., as we were returning, facetiously remarked, that "he was a *man of Books*, in the same way that Bauman was a *Man of Letters*." Bauman is the Post Master. As we walked along, we took notice of a negro, very flippantly drest, if I may be allowed the expression, with legs like two semi-circles. "He is"—said Wm.—a very great beau (*bow*)—*about the legs*."

After we reached home, we chatted awhile, & then I went to make a professional call. I returned to H. Johnson's, where we spent the evening very agreably.

Dingley made us another unseasonable visit, just after we got home. There is something peculiarly unpleasant in such interruptions, just as one is preparing for bed, & when we want the last hour, before sleep, to commune with ourselves, & to reckon up the busy events of the day. Last evening, Dingley related some anecdotes of a crazy man, of Boston, whose name was Coolidge. This man was covered with vermin. One day, he picked one off from his body, &, as he killed it, observed—"that his *bosom/friends* had become his *back-biters*." At another time, [when] he was walking thro' the streets of Boston, in a soaking rain, & passing the Store of a China & Glass Merchant, his situation excited the Trader's mirth. He addrest Coolidge thus—"Pluit tantum, nescio quantum, scis tu?" Coolidge, irritated by the joke, threw a stick against the bow window, with such force as to break a large number of glasses—retorting

---

[37] "Hyperion to a satyr. . . ." *Hamlet*, I, ii.

[38] The secretary of state whose relations with the French were still a matter of public concern.

[39] Joel Barlow wrote this mock-epic in France, probably in 1793, but it was not published until 1796. Dingley must have seen it in manuscript.

—"Fregi tot, nescio quot, scis tu?" The Trader forgave the injury, for the sake of the repartee.[40]

Friday, 16th

The rain, which returned & was incessant & prodigious all last evening, cleared off, before bed-time, & this morning was one of the most beautiful I have ever seen.

I returned from a professional call, which I made immediately after breakfast, to my translation. At this I continued till near twelve. Wm. did not feel disposed for study, & the day invited us abroad: we accepted the invitation, & walked four or five miles. I read D'Israeli, after my return, till dinner. After dinner, I again sat down to translate, & wrote till five. It was about four that I recd. a few lines from Dunlap &, strange to tell, he promises me a *long letter*!!! But I must write to him first. O the modesty of this friend of mine!

I went out, & did an errand, which Dunlap requested. I made a visit at Catlin's. Catlin the younger is going to Lichfield, tomorrow. I sat down to write to Fanny. C. Adams sent to desire to visit his wife. I did; found her better; stayed there an hour. I found Dingley here when I returned. He stayed till near eleven. We talked on various subjects—chiefly medical. I wrote a short letter to Fanny, after he went away.

Saturday, 17th

I found my young patient, tho' yet weak, at work. This case has done better than I feared. I spent part of the forenoon, in translating; & part of it, & of the afternoon, in posting my books. I dined with Wm., his brother & family having gone to the Bowery, & he left alone, with Richard.

I recd. a short letter from Mumford. He is fast gaining strength.

I can account for my not having heard from C. B. Brown, only by supposing him busily engaged on his Work, of which he spake in his last letter. He has not written to Dunlap; as this last informs me. I feel no small curiosity to see how my friend will manage his plot. But I have no doubt of it's being worthy of it's Author. What different sentiments will it excite! And how much rancour, & misrepresentation must he encounter! And not he alone, but all those who are united to him, by the ties of friendship, & bonds of resembling opinions. Hitherto, in respect to public misfortunes, our lives have glided forward, smoothly enough. A calm like this can not be durable. Storms & tempests hover over our heads, ready to burst, or are gathering in slow & sullen vengeance, to break, & overwhelm us with destruction. But I trust that we shall put forth the conductors of virtue, & turn aside, or disarm the lightnings of superstitious fury.

We drank tea, & spent the evening, at Mr. Lovegrove's. Mrs. L. had taken cold, on friday, which prevented her husband's going to Amboy, & we found her quite dispirited. We succeeded in engaging her in conversation; by degrees her vivacity returned; she forgot her illness; & we left her quite well, to appearance.

This circumstance, of conversation, when interesting, removing, or superseding, the sensation of pain, which is so common as to be known to every one, is no mean argument in their favor, who maintain the superiority of mind over matter—or, to speak more properly, of the intellectual, over the physical, man. If we have power to banish, subdue, or destroy, pain, or disease, in one instance, why not in a second, in a third, & so on forever? Who shall say to the intellectual tide, "thus far shalt thou go, & no farther"? The power & efficacy of volition, in the alleviation & cure of diseases, has never been thoroughly illucidated, explained, understood, or enforced. It would be a labor worthy to occupy the life of a sainted sage. And it must, & will, be accomplished. Hitherto, men seem to have been groping in the dark, in search of they know not what. Avarice & ambition, envy & heedlessness, speculation & ignorance, audacity & cowardice, superstition, & credulity, have leagued together to betray, corrupt, & destroy, mankind. False observations, false relations, false reasoning, false applications, have continued the deception & the distress. A ray of light darted from the school of Leyden, a serene & steady lustre shone from the university of Göttingen, a dazzling glory beamed from the hills of Scotland; the mirror of Brown caught, concentrated, & reflected, but in unequal angles, their combined splendor; & the prism of Darwin illuminated & beautified the dazzling reflection, with the primitive radiance of reason, & the rainbow hues of fancy. But who is he that shall hold up the convex & transparent glass, & cast upon the mental eye the pure, unwavering, lovely, & eternal beam of truth?

So much for rhetoric, into which I know not how I have strayed. This day, has been cool, & windy. It rained, hard, in the morning; but soon cleared off. The night is clear, wholesome, & cold. There must be frost in the country. Fever must fly before this weather.

Sunday, 18th

We had not yet breakfasted, Wm. was not up, when G. M. Woolsey entered. I was surprised & pleased. He has returned to stay with us. All friends are well at Amboy; but do not think of returning immediately. Woolsey stayed with us, till ten. I sat, musing, till eleven—on transforming a pretty, ignorant, vain, young woman, of sixteen or seventeen, into an unaffected, learned, & cheerful, woman, of three or four & twenty. All this was effected, with no great difficulty, by the aid of imagination: I wish it were done as easily, in reality: How many *ladies* would vanish! & how many *women* start up! From eleven, till one, I wrote a letter to Dunlap; excepting occasional turns of chatting with William. Then, we went to Riley's, where stayed till two.

---

[40] The principal interest in this particular anecdote lies in the fact that both of the participants could joke in Latin, weak though the joke is. "It is raining so hard, I don't know how hard, do you?" Answer: "I've broken so many, I don't know how many, do you?"

Since dinner, I have written a letter to C. B. Brown.

This is the most barren Sunday memorandum that I have made, for I know not how long. But I am wearied with writing. Beside, the evening may furnish matter enough to fill out the page: perhaps to fill the remainder of the volume.

I read an hour, in D'Israeli.

I drank tea, & spent the evening, at H. Johnson's. Wm. was there. We talked on various topics, but to no particular edification. Fanny had the head-ache, & W. & H. complained of their eyes. The conversation did not become spirited. It was ten when we returned.

The day has been cold; the wind southerly; & the aspect of the skies variable. A little rain fell. The evening is clear.

The greater part of this day has been occupied in making arrangements for the winter, in visiting booksellers' shops, & in consulting & making inquiries relative to our projected Journal. To this last business the whole evening has been devoted; except a small portion of it, spent at H. Johnson's, where we drank tea. Beside this, I have read, a little, in D'Israeli; & cursorily, perused Dr. Mitchill's treatise on Contagion—or—as he calls it, on "The Gaseous Oxyd of Azote."[41]

We have, as yet, come to no conclusion, on the subject of our Periodical publication. It is probable, however, that the scheem will be laid aside, or determined on, before the end of the present week. I feel some earnestness to proceed; & am eager for a speedy decision, as I mean to visit Connecticut next week, & wish to take some steps, when there, in favor of our Work. If we do not miserably deceive ourselves, it will not materially interfere with our professional engagements & pursuits, & may be made extensively useful to ourselves & others.

Tuesday, 20th

The note which I have to make of this day is singular: I have spent it all at home. For the going to dinner & returning, & the making a medical visit, of a few minutes, in the evening, scarcely deserve notice, as exceptions. If it be expected that some deep matter has engaged my attention, disappointment will be the consequence. The principal part of the time, till dinner, was spent in translating. Some persons were in here, I read a little, & thus went off the remainder. After dinner, young Mulligan came home with me, & stayed a short time. I busied myself in looking over, & arranging some papers, & in reading D'Israeli. In the evening, G. M. Woolsey, & Mr. [word blurred], were here. They stayed till eight. I read D'Israeli, after they went away.

I recd. a letter from Dr. Leib to-day, much to my satisfaction. He writes short—but his letter is a pleasing one. It would seem that the violence of his political feelings has not impaired his friendly ones. I shall write to him soon, again.

[41] *Remarks on Gaseous Oxyde* (New York, 1795).

That knowlege is essential to liberty & virtue, is a truth which few, at the present day, will be bold enough to controvert. Those times exist no longer, when the credulity of men was made the measure of their goodness, when ignorance was preached up as the promotive of order, & deception extolled as the guide to happiness. The wisdom of later ages, has demonstrated how intimately the enjoyment of our rights & the fulfillment of our duties, is connected with our knowlege of their nature & extent; & has established the foundations of the happiness of society on justice, comprehended, & practised by all. To the glory of modern times, these principles have gained the assent of all enlightened men; & to the distinguished glory of our country, their practical application is made the basis of all that is dear to us in government, or precious to us in morals.

I intended the preceeding paragraph as the introduction of our address to the public, on the subject of our proposed Periodical Work; but it appeared to me too formal, labored, & I dropped it. It is a fault easily slidden into, to make a solemn affair of an introduction. Dr. S. Johnson is remarkable for this. His exordium would have been equally solid & sententious, were he writing the preface of a Primmer, or of an Encyclopedia. It is well to discover our faults: it will be better to mend them. Let me take care not to err on the other side. To disgust as much, by improper familiarity, as I should offend by ill-placed reserve & stateliness.

This day, has been April weather. We have had sultry and frosty hours; a clear & a cloudy sky; a warm & joyous sun, & a cold & drizzling rain. The fever has not yet disappeared. Some few new cases, as I am told, occurred yesterday & to-day.

FACTS, RELATIVE TO THE FEVER. I.

I went on to Bunker's-Hill, this morning, that I might survey the town, in all it's parts, advantageously, & at my leisure. Between the street by Col. Rutger's, & the beginning of Cherry Street, north & South & from the Middle Road, & the East River, west & east, is the lowest part of the city. From the beginning of Cherry Street, to where Oliver St. intersects it, there is a rapid descent—& at Oliver St. is the lowest part of the city. Water St. which is nearer the East River, than Cherry St.—is also lower: i. e. there is an easterly slope, from Cherry St. to the river. This is particularly observable, in Dover Street.

Many of the buildings, comprehended in this space, are wooden; newly-erected; slight; & on the ground.

There are several pools of stagnant water, in this space; the largest of which is the Fresh-Water Pond. (A mistake—I believe)

The Streets, in general, are narrow; many of them crooked; most of them flat, so that the water (as rains) does not readily run off; & many of the streets & alleys are not paved.

The inhabitants, except directly in Cherry St., are

mostly poor, laborers or mechanics. Numbers are crowded together in one small building.

This part of the city has much less opportunity for free ventilation, than the other. If the wind come from the East, or N. East, it only blows over a narrow sound—& the force of it is broken, by L. Island, on the East, & Morrisania, on the North-East—both of which are higher. If it come from the North, all the ground, north, is much higher—so that the highest rooms in their houses, are the only ones that can receive the full force—& many can not feel it at all. If it be west, or south, or southwest, the other part of the town takes it—as it does the north-west, also. So that, in it's sunken situation, there is no chance for very free ventilation, in summer, even were it perfectly well laid out. If to this we add the badness of it's disposition, it is still more evident that it must be very deficient, in this respect.

[Omitted here, three manuscript pages with the heading "Introduction to a Proposed Periodical."]

The two foregoing pages were designed to collect, in some measure, my scattered tho'ts to preface our intended publication. The design was not completed, from want of time, & from my having come so near to the conclusion of this volume. It will, however, be continued, in the next; in which, too, I hope to compose a perfect or rather, satisfactory—introduction.

It was, thro' mistake, almost three, when I dined; &, falling into conversation, I sat till four. I found Wm. at home, when I returned, & we read & conversed till near six. We drank tea, & stayed till ten, at Mr. Lovegrove's. Mrs. L. was alone; he being gone to Amboy. We had a story-telling, homespun, pleasing evening; & I came away, more & more charmed with her.

Wednesday, 21st

I have finished a first reading of "The Curiosities of Literature" this morning; &, in general, find no reason for retracting the favorable opinion with which I was early impressed, in regard to it. I recollect but two instances in which I tho't the author, or editor, uncandid: one, in relation to the literary character of the Germans; the other, in respect to the scenic decency of the Holland Stage. The host of elegant writers, which has arisen, in Germany, of late, ought to have obtained a more warm eulogium on their literature; & the well-regulated Theatre of Amsterdam, should have, at least, softened the asperity of the censure on follies, no longer tolerated, or only tolerated at particular times—on festivals, when the lowest of the people are the sole frequenters of the theatre.

The greater part of the fine forenoon was occupied in a long walk, which Wm. & I took—for the first time, in several days. Dingley & Wm. M. Johnson, called here, just as we returned, & stayed till near one.

I have now brought this third volume of my diurnal memoirs, to a conclusion: and did the time permit, I might indulge in recollection, to some advantage. Compared with the two preceeding volumes, it must be acknowledged a great improvement. It far surpasses them, in copiousness & importance, & affords a pleasing presage of my future success, in this species of mental labour. My subsequent tomes must increase in value, if, (what I think is not probable,) I do not decrease in industry. If the ensuing Winter be occupied agreeably to my expectations, my mind must, necessarily, take a wider & more precise range; & the treasures which it will bring back, for reflection & recordation, must be proportionately numerous & important. I hope to be able to devote more time, & different hours, to this employment of diarizing. As I now proceed, what I write is less the result of my reflections thro' the day, (generally speaking) than the ideas which the moment suggests. And these, oftentimes, are slight & trivial—& by no means exhibit a just, & accurate picture of the operations of my mind. The difficulty lies in abridging the multifarious ruminations of the day: & in making such a judicious selection, as shall neither speak too much in one's favor, or detract from one's real merit—& which, at the same time, will be useful to direct, or admonish thereafter. But this difficulty must be gotten over. I think a better method of time will allow me to do this, &, when I return from the country, I think, nay am sure, that I shall make the attempt.

Notebook No. 2: October, 1795–March, 1796

Thursday, 22nd

The commencement of a new volume, like that of a new year, seems to demand a retrospect of the former, & new, good resolutions, in respect to the present. The day, which is gloomy, & unpleasant abroad, naturally invites to reflection, while it confines me at home. Yet, and I scarcely know why it is so, I feel little inclination to retrace the events of the last & the present month; & still less to indulge in fairy dreams of the future, & in the formation of new schemes of conduct, & determinations to adhere to them. This is not because I have more than usual to reproach myself with, in this last period, or that I have less sanguine anticipations, than I was wont to entertain. On the contrary, my journal exhibits evident traces of greater industry; & is equally the evidence of greater perseverance in the resolutions I have made. But my mind seems more disposed, this day, for sober duties, & less prone to busy itself in framing pictures of visionary bliss. To this disposition I shall oppose no struggles; but, on the reverse, allow it to effect all it can. I have before me the necessity of composing an Address to the Public, on the subject of a Periodical Publication, often mentioned, of late, in my last volume. Hitherto, my attempts have neither been fervent, nor effectual. It is for this volume, perhaps, for this day, to accomplish that which the others have been unable to. On this same subject, I am still doubtful: doubtful, as to the real determinations of my friend—to engage in the Work, or not—doubtful, as to our ability to support it reputably, without more labor than we now imagine, doubtful, as to the degree of success which it would meet with. It remains to resolve all these doubts, by experimenting. The executing of a Prospectus, will determine on the first; it's publication, on the last: &, on the other, we can only be satisfied by several weeks trial. Success, in every of these three particulars, would be as advantageous, as it is desirable. In my view, it only requires method, & persevering industry, to make it certain. Perhaps, should Wm. give up all ideas of engaging in it, Dunlap might be induced to write with me, & the project still be carried into effect. But, may this not be necessary; may Wm. become my fellow-laborer; & may we, our friends, our country, the whole world, be benefitted, by our labours!

The favorable reception which Literary Journals have met with, in various parts of Europe, the avidity with which some have been sought after, and the numerous & important advantages which have consequentially resulted to Letters, to Morals, and the Arts, render similar publications, in our own country, exceedingly desirable. Their absence has been, at certain periods, well supplied, by the peculiar excellence of our News-Papers; and did that excellence still exist, any attempt towards an establishment, of the kind referred to, must prove equally injurious & abortive. This truth has been experienced, in all it's severity, by almost all who have endeavored to gain public patronage for Magazines, Pamphlets, Museums, & Repositories. The superior cheapness, & the more frequent impression, of News-Papers, were strong recommendations to the enlightened, inquisitive, & frugal, yeomanry of the United States; while the universality of their circulation, affording a wider field for the operation of all the impressions they wished to make, made them, not only the most convenient, but the most valuable, vehicle for the compositions of our writers. The self-esteem of an author might be wounded, when he reflected on the perishable nature of performances, thus sent abroad; and the man of taste might be disgusted, at times, with the multifarious page; but the benefits which were thus extended to all were so numerous & so great that the regret was temporary, & the defects patiently tolerated. Thus, while tranquillity abroad, & order at home, went hand in hand; while men of letters had leisure to write, & men of business opportunity to read; the weekly, or daily, pages of our Journals, abounded with serious & profound disquisitions, in polity, morals, & letters, & were adorned with the more airy & graceful ornaments of wit & humor. The moralist, the statesman, & the interpreter of nature, the poet, & the novelist, made them the repositories of their various & accumulated treasures.

But this happy state of our Journals, was not of many years continuance. The adoption & operations of a new government, at home, and the interesting scenes, daily exhibited in Europe, as they became more & more the topics of conversation, gradually usurped that place in News-Papers, which, till then, had been carefully reserved for communications of a less immediately interesting, but more permanently useful nature. The novelty & importance of these wants justified a change of this nature, at the time, tho' it was to be wished that it might be temporary. The two last years have shewn us that we have little to hope, in this respect; & that elegant & useful communications have been wholly banished, to make room for details of battles & debates, for the history of public contests & private intrigues. They contain every thing to gratify the eager curiosity of the politician, but nothing to satisfy the more temperate appetite of the scholar, the philosopher, or the man of literary leisure. To that Sex, which has been so rudely & pertinaceously thrust from all share in the great questions of national concern, they present nothing but an eternal dearth.

It is for men, who are accustomed to regard the liberty & virtue, the tranquillity & happiness of a nation, as intimately connected with the knowlege they possess, to calculate the possible effects of this alteration. For the imperfect history of daily transactions is but one species of knowlege; & that which, perhaps, the least of any, enlightens the understanding & improves the heart.

An event of this kind would be less to be regretted, were our countrymen in the habit of seeking, in other periodical publications, for additional amusement & instruction. In Europe, Pamphlets are almost as universally & habitually purchased, as bread; in the United States, the author may think himself more than ordinarily fortunate, if he is not obliged to pay his printer himself. There, every week, at least, presents them with a variety of pleasing & useful matter, in the form of a Magazine; while here, the narrow precincts of a single city, contain all the patrons which such a publication has ever durably obtained.

It would occupy too large a portion of this Address, were we to delineate the progress of these publications, & expose the causes of their failure. This last has been done already, in part, & the remaining causes must be obvious to all, who have considered the subject, with any attention.

The change in the nature of our News-Papers, of which we have been speaking, will deserve to be regarded as fortunate, rather than a subject of regret, if a successful establishment can be effected, of a Journal of an opposite character: if an equal circulation can be given to a Paper wholly devoted to literary & scientific entertainment, as to a Paper entirely occupied in detailing the news of the day. The circumstances of the times, and the state of knowlege in this country, seem peculiarly to demand & encourage such an attempt.

The United States is distinguished, above every other country, for the uniform & universal education & intelligences of it's inhabitants. Men, versed in all the minute & profound erudition, of the Europeans, are, indeed, rare; but, from the poorest laborer, to the chief magistrates, with few exceptions, all are able to read, & all desire to know. Universally devoted to business, & obliged to depend on this own industry for their support, they have no leisure for profound & laborious investigation; but their early habits preserve in them a love of learning, & a relish for works of science & of taste, which to their honour, they fondly cherish & assiduously cultivate. This which is true, in the strongest manner, of men of business, is scarcely less so, of those who engage in, what are called, the learned professions. The duties of the Divine, the Civilian, & the Physician, admit of extensive research, for the most part, only in matters relative to his profession. He may indulge, occasionally, at other streams; but that he must exhaust. To men like these, a publication, like the one hinted at, must be inestimable. For here they might catch, with a single glance of the eye, the laborious results of the scientific investigation of ages, muse on the various fate of nations & of empires, glow at the revived lustre & success of the benefactors of mankind, & sport with the attic pleasantries of ancient & modern ages. Neither is this the only way in which such a publication would be valuable, to men, occasionally indulging in literary exercises, or to the public at large. As literature is not a profession in this country, it is true, that few can devote themselves to the composition of considerable works; yet, among those who have cultivated the sciences, with any success, there are scarcely any, who do not, at times, divert themselves by lighter compositions, or by writing on detached parts of those sciences to the study of which they have especially attended. Performances, of this kind, are by no means infrequent, in America, & doubtless would have been more numerous, had they been provided with a repository, whose respectability would have secured to them that duration, which they merited. Such a repository a literary journal would present them with. To the public, in general, the advantage would be no less. The information would be afforded in as cheap a manner, & in a form much less perishable.

But the benefits of such a periodical publication, would not be confined, to the collection & preservation of the productions of our own country. Whatever the accumulated industry of ages has collected, interesting to man, in Art or Science, in Polity, Morals, or Physics, would equally claim & obtain a place in it's pages. Not in the dry & tedious form of minute & laboured detail, but in the pleasing & instructive dress of Anecdote, & short, judicious Abstract, & useful Remark. Thus, while the most grave & learned reader, should not fail to find something wherewith to gratify his love of profound investigation, the gayest & most volatile should also be attracted by that which would continue their cheerfulness, & while it corrects their vivacity, should administer to their love of amusement.

Great & important discoveries, it is tho't, are often lost, for want of some cheap & convenient vehicle of information: how long, the most interesting truths, on every subject of value, have remained concealed, or partially known, from a similar cause, must be known to every one, who is in the least acquainted with the history of the progress of man. Even at this day, & in our own country, how much has the philanthropist to lament, on this account!

It is impossible for men, even with the best dispositions for mental improvement, to quit their several occupations, & plunge into the mazes of contradictory opinions, & explore after truth; the ponderous & mouldy folios of neglected authors. To them the more convenient octava of modern authors, presents a labor beyond their leisure to accomplish. The weekly & scanty pages of the Journalist, are easily read over. They may be taken up, or laid aside, at pleasure. To these the man of business can recur, while he waits for an expected guest, lingers at an ill-attended appointment, or patiently submits to the operations of his hair-dresser. From these, even the self-complacent beau, & the fashionable fair-one, may catch an unexpected ray of knowlege, while they sip their morning coffee, or their evening tea. To the pages of a literary journal, America may be indebted, for a Petrarch or a Robinson, who else had floated down the tide of frivolity & dissipation, into the oblivious pool of eternity.

It can not be denied, that Essays, Extracts, & Short pieces, of the kind spoken of, if judiciously selected, & neatly arrayed, may be of the highest usefulness. Their brevity & dress, while it allows & invites all to read with little labour, & some pleasure, is more likely to impress the mind favorably & lastingly, than graver & more elaborate disquisitions. They refresh the minds of the learned, the studious, & the reflecting, they awaken curiosity & stimulate inquiry in the young. Active minds want *Hints* only. In them they excite trains of reflection, while they enliven & invigorate thought. The mind is thus gently directed in the road to truth, without being deprived, either of the advantage of exercising itself, or being forestalled in the pleasure of investigation. In short, there is no individual, whatever may be his situation in life, to whom it will not be useful to multiply *hints*. To him, such a Work, as the one referred to must be valuable, whether as the companion of his contemplative, or of his convivial, hours. And thus, while it reaches to every division of literature & while it comprehends, at once, in its ample, but transient, survey, letters & arts, customs & manners, the history of nations & the peculiarities of individuals,—it becomes alike the *Manual* of Science & of Conversation.

A work of this sort, we are desirous of presenting to the Public. Sensible as we are of it's importance, & the rare talents it requires to give it it's highest value, we are far from confidently promising either that Public, or ourselves, that we shall attain to the excellence we aspire after. This, we are well convinced, must depend as much on the benevolent assistance of others, as on our own private resources. We pretend not to offer an Original Work, our devotedness to our professions, & the duties & labours which they demand of us, preclude the possibility of this; but we present the fruits of a leisure employed in literary amusements; the treasures of a youth of study; & the collections of hours of relaxation from the more serious pursuits of professional business. In so doing, we hope to render an agreable, if not a useful, service, to our fellow-citizens of the United States; & to communicate to them by this diffusion of our selections, some portion of that pleasure which we have derived from their formation. Neither will the Articles selected, be found altogether foreign to our particular professions, or unuseful to those who are, like us, engaged in their study & exercise: for, beside from that thing, as Cicero has well observed, "A Common Bond of Union among the Sciences" we hope, to be able, occasionally, to illucidate some of the abstruser, & less cultivated, parts of the Arts we especially delight in; or, at least, to incite the industry of others.

Books always present an innocent & useful resource to those, who are fatigued with the abstruser studies of professional science, & the daily avocations of business.

The principles of Polity & Morals are essential to all; a knowlege of History is indispensible to a good education, for any business; & biography, & elegant literature, delightfully recreate the wearied mind. A change of reading, like a change of air & of scenery, gives a new spring to the intellect, & reanimates the dropping energies of the soul. Were we to pursue the allusion still further, we might regard the more serious inquiries into morality & jurisprudence, as the deep, solemn, & awful grove, where contemplation loves to ruminate & wander; while the lighter paths of literature, the elegancies of criticism, & the charms of poesy, might be compared, to fertile & luxuriant meadows, watered by winding streams, enamelled with flowers, & diversified by sunshine & shadow. It is true, that we are not to linger here, for our whole life; but it is allowable, occasionally, to indulge in their delights; from which we return, with a keener relish, & a more elastic activity, to our proper employments. At least, an indulgence of this kind, is far less censurable, than the too common method, of killing time; & purchasing a short reprieve from mental lassitude, & the pressure of *ennui,* by pleasures, which impair the corporeal powers, while they do not enlighten the understanding.

In the execution of the proposed publication, the Editors hope to present nothing to their subscribers, but what may be considered as valuable. That every portion of their Work should be equally agreable to all, is not to be expected; but, that in the variety of matter, every taste, which is not absolutely vicious, shall find something to gratify it, is, they think, within their power to perform, & certainly is conformable to their expectations. In addition to extracts from authors, they have every reason to expect much original assistance from their friends; & they, thus publicly, solicit the contributions of the men of leisure & information, thro' out the United States. They design to bestow particular attention on whatever relates to the Literary, Civil, & Natural History of their Country; but their success, in this particular, will be much increased by the communications of men, who have a more intimate knowlege of the individual States.

In the arrangement of their materials, some general heads will be observed, to facilitate references to the several numbers; but these will not be particularly insisted on, but will undergo alterations, as convenience, or utility may dictate.

We shall now proceed to lay before the public, the particulars of our Plan, & the Forms on which we purpose carrying it into execution.

CONDITIONS

1. The Title of the Publication, to be "Proteus."
2. To be printed weekly, on fine paper, & a good type; —each number consisting of sixteen close-printed octavo pages.
3. To contain no advertisements, or news of the day; but to be intirely devoted to entertaining & useful performances, relative to the Arts & Sciences.

4. To be afforded to purchasers, at three dollars a year, paid in advance—quarterly, half-yearly, or yearly: delivered, free of expence, to city subscribers—sent into any part of the country, as directed, the subscribers being at the charge.
5. A regular Index, gratis, every six months—with a title-page: the publication making two octavo volumes, of more than 400 pages, annually.

N. B. Papers, with the Conditions are left at &c.—for the annexing of the names of such as encourage the Work. If 500 names appear, by the 1st of Jany. next, the first number will be published, the Wednesday following. Subscription payments recd. only by the Editors—No. 13. Cedar St.—New York.

Such is the first sketch of the Address to the Public; on which I bestowed the most of this day. I wrote it, principally, in the forenoon; but, receiving a letter from my father, was obliged to leave off, & do a little business, & write him an answer. After dinner, till near five, I was busied in doing a number of errands, & with W. W. Woolsey & his family, who have returned to Town.

I read, for an hour, in Mary Wollstonecraft's translation of Salzmann's Elements of Morality,[42] which I purchased, for Mrs. Lovegrove, at her request.

I drank tea at Mrs. Miller's; where I likewise, stayed till seven o'clock. I returned; wrote a letter to Mr. Gahn; & concluded the Address. When I had done this, Wm. came in. We conversed on the subject of "Proteus." My first doubt is resolved: it is only a project: we shall do nothing. I shall, however, insert the list of Titles, which we determined on, a few evenings since: they may, hereafter, be serviceable.

The Arts.	*Fine Arts.*	*Medicine.*	*Natural History.*	*Physics.*	*Antiquities.*
	Painting.	Anatomy.	Meterology.	Mechanics.	American.
	Sculpture.	Physiology.	Hydrology.	Pneumatics.	European.
	Engraving.	Surgery.	Geology.	Harmonics.	Asiatic.
	Architecture.	Physic.	Mineralogy.	Hydraulics.	African.
	Music.	Chemistry.	Botany.	Hydrostatics.	
	Mimics.	Mat. Meda.	Zoology.	Optics.	

Commerce.	*Agriculture.*	*Economics.*	*Morals.*	*Politics.*	*Religion.*	*Laws.*
						Education.

Criticism.
Language.

Polity.	*Statics.*	*Biography.*	*Literature.*	*Anecdote.*	*Poetry.*	*Manners.*	*Miscellany.*
Government.	Domestic.	American.	American.	Historical.	American.		
Jurisprudence.	Foreign.	Foreign.	Foreign.	Philological.	Foreign.		
Political	Parallels.	Ancient.		Critical.	Selected.		
Economy.		Modern.		Literary.	Original.		

Friday, 23rd

The memorials of this day, contrary to my expectation, are very scanty. I designed to have pursued my inquiries, relative to The Fever; & to have recorded the result. From this the dampness of the morning deterred me, till it was too late. Some errands employed me till ten: I read in Saltzman's Elements of Morality till twelve: Wm. & I walked on the Battery, & bathed, till two. After dinner, I went to see Dingley; but, not finding him, returned, & read Salzman, till near six.—We drank tea, & spent the evening at W. W. Woolsey's.

I recd. a letter from C. B. Brown.

Saturday, 24th

This day, like yesterday has been spent to little purpose. I called on Dingley, but he was absent, on business; & I returned, & read in Saltzman, till dinner. After dinner I did the same, till after four: then Wm. & I walked several miles—& returned to Mr. Lovegrove's, to tea—: where we spent the evening, till near nine.

My sensations have been unpleasant, all day; & this evening I did not feel much fitted for conversing. I read two tales, in Saltzman; with which all were pleased. Mr. L. has just returned from Amboy. He seems undetermined what to do; yet talks of buying the land—recommended by us. Dunlap thinks of coming up, on Tuesday.

I recd. a good letter from Mr. Gahn. He can not accompany me; &, indeed, I know not when I can get away. At present there is no vessel here from New Haven.

My faculties seem weighed down, by an universal torpor. How pitiful—thus to be the slave of physical impotence! In the prime of life, how vigorous, active, alert, & elastic, ought I to be—instead of being, as I am, the sport of every change of temperature, & variation of atmospheric gravity. Let parents, friends, teachers, let their first study be, to give health to children, who fall under their care. "*Mens sana, in corpore sano*"[43] is all that men ought to, or need, desire.

How much of my present depression is the consequence of viciously indulging in submission to the

---

[42] (London, 1790 or 1791); date disputed.

[43] Juvenal, *Satire* X, 356.

causes of it? This is an important question. Why should I not rouze myself, & determine to banish uneasiness? I will. It is but a little resolution—& bodily inquietude, & mental impatience, vanish from the view. The bare idea makes me feel better.

Sunday, 25th

It is now near one o'clock, P.M. and I have not been out. Some cold, taken yesterday, or last night, affects my spirits, & feelings: which are, both, better, than they were an hour since. I have written to Dr. Leib, & to C. B. Brown. W. W. Woolsey called here, & sat an hour. Wm., who had been out, returned, & we had a conversation—various, & interesting. They went to walk: I stayed at home to finish my Letters.

It has several times occurred to me, and perhaps I have before noticed it, that it ought to be mentioned. That the thoughts of the day, are, by no means, regularly registered, in these volumes. At evening, when I sit down, to make up the account of the day, it is not always that I can, immediately recollect all that I have done—tho' my life is very simple; far less is it in my power to reassemble all my ideas; or even the most important of those, which, during the day, have coursed thro' my head. And, were it possible, such are the circumstances under which the recollection would be oftentimes made, that it would be so near to impracticable to record them, that they would not be recorded. To effect this, a degree of patience, leisure, & industry, would be essential, which rarely falls to the lot of man. For me, subdued as I am by a thousand bad habits, & the very slave & sport of indolence, & physical ailments —"fiends without a name"[44]—it is vain to think of it, or resolve about it: it can not be done. So far am I, from registering the thoughts of the day, that oftentimes I can think of nothing, worthy of record; & most commonly, the ideas, or the sentences, are such as the moment suggests—The crude offspring of uneasy sensations. There is no other way of making my Journal important, than by making it the table-book of my studies & my compositions. And this I design it shall principally be, hereafter. My plan is, to copy into a regular series of volumes, all of any importance, that I have written:—so as to form materials illustrative of my life. To copy every thing which I have written, will be impossible. Many of my first pieces are completely destroyed; of others I neither have, nor could easily procure, copies; & the greater part of my Prose Scraps, are only worthy of mention, as they serve to fill up the history of my mind. These, I shall content myself with merely reffering to.

After dinner, I amused myself with the Dictionary of Anecdotes,[45] till between four & five, when I went, with Wm., to W. W. Woolsey's. We drank tea there; & I spent the evening. As for Wm. he went to his brother's, at seven.

My cold has made me feel dull, all day; & this evening, in particular: so that I neither walked with my two friends, this morning; nor with Geo. M. Woolsey, this afternoon.

Dingley was here between one & two. We are to go over that part of the town, where the sickness has most prevailed, to-morrow.

Monday, 26th

I walked with Dingley to see several of his patients, & was with him most of the day. In particular I went to see, with him, a woman in labour. It was the first time; & my inexperience did not allow me to profit much by the opportunity: especially, as, after waiting the greater part of the day, the true pains did not come on. I did not feel well enough to return in the evening; but, as our house was in confusion, we having whitewashing &c. going forward, I went to H. Johnson's; where I stayed till near two—then came home & went to bed. A cold, which I first perceived Saturday evening, afflicts me exceedingly.

Mr. Gahn came to Town to-day—& I spent a quarter of an hour, very pleasantly with him. He returns to-morrow, to Amboy.

FACTS RELATIVE TO THE FEVER. II

I walked thro' Dover, Water, Rosevelt, & James, Streets. Dover St is built on a declivity, running from Cherry, to Water St. The sun must rest upon it, in the summer, from it's rising, to three P. M. It is narrow, & has neither gutters, nor side walks. The houses are many of them small, & tippling houses. Since they were built, the street has been raised several feet—so that the surface of the street is up to the middle of the lower windows, many times,—& the cellar is still lower. The yards, remaining as before, are, of course, several feet lower than the street: & they have no vent: so that the water, & all filth, must stagnate there. Add to this, in many of these yards, there are little, miserable huts, where are collected still more wretched & poor people.

Water St. above Dover St. is almost wholly composed of wooden buildings. The same is true here, of the situation of the houses, & yards—for this street also has been raised. This too is exposed to the full influence of the docks—whatever that may be—& is exposed, in summer, to a broiling sun: as it nearly faces the East. Of Rosevelt & James Streets, it may be observed that they are equally affected, with the two, before-mentioned, from having been raised; tho' several new buildings have been since erected. The alleys, leading from them, are unpaved; so that, after a rain, the water stands in puddles.

All these streets abound with tippling-houses. All are inhabited, mostly, by poor people. Most of the houses

---

[44] Not found.

[45] DePrezel Lacombe, *Dictionnaire des portraits historiques anecdotes et traits remarquables des hommes illustres* (1768).

have several families in them: even in the underground apartments.

Tuesday, 27th

I felt so unwell, last evening, that I could not write; & this morning, tho' scarcely any better, I have made the preceeding notes: which had been more ample, had I been less indisposed.

Our neighbor Boyd returned to-day. He looks fat & hearty. Mr. Gahn called to bid us farewell. He has returned to Jersey.

I was busied, till after one, in moving & arranging my things, up stairs: such being our determinations, for the Winter. Johnson removes his bed, below; into the little room where we used to breakfast; I take his, for my sleeping room; & use my former sleeping room, for my study. After this was done, we walked on the Battery, till dinner.

After dinner: I found no vessel for N. Haven, till friday or saturday. I shall therefore take the Stage, on Thursday. I stayed a little while with G. M. Woolsey, & a little while with W. W. Woolsey, at their respective stores; & made Mrs. Woolsey a short visit at the house. I stupefied at home, two hours.

Mr. & Mrs. Webster returned last evening, as I learnt this morning. I drank tea with them, at their house, & spent the evening. Mr. Lagarenne,[46] & Wm. were there part of the evening. Much talk about the Fever.

Mr. W. who has been at Philadelphia, during his absence, gave us a long account of many circumstances, relative to Mr. Randolph's—the late Secy. of State—affairs; now so much talked of. I forbear to detail them; as, probably, they will all be, ultimately, stated before the public, at large. It appears, plain enough, that the Ex-Secretary has been traitorously inclined. His detection is now begun: his infamy must be complete.

Neither T. Mumford, nor Dunlap, as far as I can yet learn, have arrived. This delay, on the part of the former, is almost unaccountable; & must prove distressing to my sister. What I very much fear is, that it will prevent her visiting Lichfield, the ensuing winter. If this should be the case, the misfortune would not end there; for, I suppose, Abby would also remain at Aurora: & her stay, which has, already, been protracted to near twice the original limit of it, would then become very painful & inconvenient for our parents. To herself, & to Fanny it would be scarcely less so, as it would make a still greater & more unfriendly impression on their time for improvement.

Wednesday, 28th

This morning was occupied in various employments, previous to my departure; which is fixed for to-morrow. Mumford returned to day, in perfect health. He proceeds to Lichfield, & thence home, in a few days. I got all my errands over by one, & till three amused myself with The Gallery of Portraits of the National Assembly.[47] H. & W. Johnson, Mr. Sebor,[48] & myself dined at Mr. Lovegrove's; whence we returned at seven. The afternoon was pleasant. When I came home, I found that Dunlap had been here. I found also a letter from El. Smith jr.—by which I learnt that he was well; returned; & to be married, the last Monday. I called on a patient. I then went to W. W. Woolsey's—the family were there, & Mumford, & W. Johnson. From there, I went to Dunlap's. I found his wife & children returned also, (which was more than I expected—) & all very well. I stayed an hour with them; & spent the remainder of the evening at Woolsey's.

I am to inquire, when in the country, for a little girl, for Mrs. Lovegrove: about ten—& to live with her till nineteen.

Thursday, 29th

This morning was divided by numerous little businesses. Dunlap & Mumford were at our house; I called on my patient & on W. W. Woolsey; wrote a few lines to my father; was in the Stage at twelve; & a little after we sat off.

Stage Coaches are generally supposed to be so many regions of ludicrous adventure; but I am disposed to believe that more depend on the peculiar temper of the traveller, than on the strange associations which are formed in these vehicles. For my part, I, who am no humorist, derive but little store for merriment, & humorous description, from these casual adventures.

We were six, beside the driver: an old, greasy, gouty, lecherous Jew; a huge Irish manufacturer of Fleecy Hosiery; a South Carolina Merchant; a middle-aged, decent Frenchman; a young mercantile Hamburger who spoke French & English; & myself. The Israelite was for fun & singing; but no one sung. He & the Irishman discust politics & the Fever. The Frenchman & the German, first fell on the French Emigrants, next on the Fever—& lastly upon this country. All these topics they handled, with prodigious volubility, in French. The Carolina growled a little, & muttered something on merchandise: I was silent. We reached our place of destination, in season; where we supped, & then thought of retiring. A rambling talk, on religion, at Supper, gave opportunity to all the guests to discover their infidelity; & the Hebrew, in particular, disclaimed Moses & the Prophets; & emphatically, pronounced this sentence, that—"from Genesis to Revelations, all is trumpery."

Friday, 30th

We rose about half past three, & in less than an hour were on the road. We arrived at New Haven, at seven. This day offers nothing worthy of remark; except it's unusual pleasantness, for a season so advanced.

---

[46] Mr. Charles Lagarrenne of 112 Liberty St., no profession listed after his name in the *New York Directory* for 1796, probably a "gentleman."

[47] Supposedly the work of the Count de Mirabeau. Only available copy, L. C. (Dublin, 1790).

[48] Jacob Sebor, a New York merchant.

Saturday, 31st

All my inquiries, last evening, after a conveyance for my trunk, were fruitless: my attempts to procure a horse for myself, were no less so. I debated in my own mind, as to further attempts; & a fine morning served to make me more anxious: but it soon clouded over, & the question was determined. After breakfast I set off to see Dr. Dwight. I stopped a few minutes on my way, to talk with Mr. Chauncey. I found Dr. Dwight well: we talked: I delivered him the letters &c. I had for him; accompanied him to Mr. Hillhouse's; thence to the College—& there left him. I spent an hour at Mr. Beers's —partly in his Store & partly with Mrs. Leffingwell; who is here from N. York. After dinner, I past an hour, with Mr. Chauncey, at his house. His representations induce me to believe that the Connecticut Agricultural Society is likely to become something. He read me their Minutes from which it appears that they are disposed to be active. From hence, I went to see Dr. Dwight again & spent the whole afternoon with him & Mr. Ingersoll. The Fever, & Mr. Randolph's affairs, the principal topics of conversation. I drank tea there, & stayed till seven.[49]

I waited on Mr. Meigs, the Professor of Natural Philosophy; & stayed an hour. We talked of the Fever (every one asks me of *the Fever*) of politics—& the state of literature &c in this college. Some improvements have been made, since I was here; many are yet necessary; & there seems to be reason to suppose that they will be effected, after a while.

At Mr. Beers's Store I found Dr. Stiles's singular book on the Judges of Charles I. of England[50]—who fled to this country. Into this I have dipped a little; & promise myself much curious entertainment from it's leisurely perusal.

I have seen H. Johnson's charge—young Mr. Quince —to whom I delivered the articles for him. He is well & well-satisfied.

It has rained some to-day; & this night is excessively windy & dark: a night proper to usher in the melancholly month of November.

On this month, well might I indulge in reflection, & profitably might I speculate, were my situation favorable. But here, in a tavern, & ill-provided with the accustomed accommodations for undisturbed meditation & composition, I must postpone, at least, if not neglect it. At my paternal dwelling, should circumstances so far favor me as to admit of my things, as well as myself, seasonably arriving there, I may freely engage in any occupation of thought to which reason or feeling shall incline. Yet it is possible, that even there, my mind may be so much occupied with what surrounds me, with the passing scenes, as to unfit it for the active duty of transcribing the images which they present.

They are all retiring. This is a dull, dismal place. I also must have recourse to my pillow. Ah! how different from those social hours of converse, by which the conclusion of the day was illumined, when I sat down with Wm., in Cedar Street.

November 1795
Sunday, 1st

The night was windy & cold, the morning clear. I went to Chappel; where Dr. Dwight preached. His discourse was against Indifference in Religion. It was eloquent, in some parts; handsome, in all; &, admitting his principles, just. I conversed with him, a few minutes, after coming out; & spoke with Mr. & Mrs. Meigs. This is the first time that I have attended the Christian Service, on Sunday, for more than a Year. This afternoon I have preferred a seat by the fire, to one in the cold meeting-house. I have amused myself, near an hour, in looking over a volume of the Massachusetts Magazine, for 1792. This is a miserable compilation— in which the contemptibleness of the authors, is exactly proportioned to the Editor's total want of Taste.

This place, (New Haven,) is, to me, by no means agreable. I seldom willingly rest in it; & while I do, find my time drag heavily along. Such, also, are the feelings of Wm. Johnson, as he told me, just before I left home. Yet, in this city were we educated: & here were passed four years, at an age when life is most full of enjoyment. The reason is not obvious—but that which suggests itself to my mind, is satisfactory. When lived here, it was in the company of numerous class-mates— who were, at the same time, the companions of our pleasures & studies. We formed no acquaintance with the inhabitants of the place—at least, no intimacy; for we felt not the want of it. Thus, when we left College, we left New Haven, as much strangers to it's citizens, as when we first went to it. Now, we no longer find those, here, with whom, while here, we used to associate. The contrast diffuses a gloom over the place & we quit it without regret, since nothing remains which used to interest us.

I have thought, for some time, of writing a Poem, somewhat on the plan, or of the kind, of Cowper's Task. On his principles, it could not be, since many of them are hostile to mine; but in that stile of moral precept-giving, for which he is so remarkable, & in which he is oftentimes so happy & so just. To the execution of a plan, such as I have contemplated, much previous study & reflection is necessary; & more of method is indispensable, than Mr. Cowper has adhered to: for my design is no less than, thus, to convey & enforce accu-

---

[49] Dr. Dwight was Timothy Dwight, president of Yale for the preceding seven weeks. Mr. Chauncey was Judge Charles Chauncey, LL.D. James Hillhouse (Yale 1773) was elected to the U.S. House in 1790 and served until December 1796, when he was elected to fill a vacancy in the Senate, thereafter in the Senate until his resignation in 1810. Beers ran a bookstore. Mrs. Leffingwell is Beers's daughter, Sally, married to William Leffingwell (Yale 1786), New York stock broker.

[50] *A History of the Three Judges of King Charles I* (Hartford, 1794).

rate notions & suitable adherence in practice, on & to, all moral questions & requisitions.

The great difficulty in the way of spreading the moral truth, is that of making people think. This is true, in respect to all subjects, but especially in relation to morals. For here, you have to conquer, not indolence alone, but apprehension. The first thing, then, to be done, is to convince mankind, that they have a right to think. And not only that they have a right, but that it is their indispensible duty to exercise it. That they ought to hesitate, to doubt, to inquire, & not to sit down in any belief, which is not founded on rational conviction. It will be easy to shew, that the most devoted adherents to religion, & to Christianity, in particular, do no less; & the necessity of so doing may be forcibly exemplified in various ways. Thus, supposing Christianity true, & Popery a corruption of it—all men must have remained in the belief of this corruption, had not Luther & others, doubted, inquired—substituted their own convictions for the dogmas of the Church of Rome, & ended in openly opposing them. If this be allowable in Luther & in Calvin, in Zwingle & Melancthon,[51] it must also be allowable in every one else: if it was their duty, it is also ours. Having established, by a variety of arguments, the right & the duty—& exemplified, by many illustrious instances the advantages arising from the exercise of that right—the writer should proceed to seek out the true ground of morals, the basis on which all our reasoning must rest. What is man? How is he situated? Hence what are his duties?

I found so much difficulty with poor pens & poor ink, that I threw by my Journal in despair. I went to the Stage house, & secured a passage to Farmington. Thus I shall see some others of my esteemed acquaintance. From this time, till six, I was at Mr. Chauncey's—where I drank tea. We had much talk; about new books, &c. I sat off for Mr. Meigs's—but met him & his wife; & went with them to see Mrs. Stiles. I was much pleased with this short visit. The general conversation was animated & interesting; & Mr. Meigs gave me some account of Dr. Stiles's papers &c. which I must defer inserting, till a future opportunity. I went to Mr. Ingersoll's a little after seven, & stayed till nine. Here also was much conversation: but too various for the small time, I now have, to allow me to abridge.

Monday, 2nd

This morning I left New Haven, in the new Line of Stages, & went by Cheshire &c. to Farmington.

It is surprizing to observe how communication between every part of this country, is expedited & facilitated, by these Stages; & all within a very few years. Ten years ago, there was not a Stage went thro' any part of New-England. Now, there are no less than three, which steadily ply between Hartford & New Haven.

At Cheshire I called on the parents of my late friend Hitchcock; & found them comfortable & well. There I recd. as many of my Letters to him, as could readily be found, on so short a notice; & was offered the perusal of any of his Papers that I pleased. The opportunity did not allow me to avail myself of this liberty; tho' I hope, hereafter, to do it, to the advantage of those who made it. I saw among his papers, some Memoirs of himself. These I feel particularly desirous of looking over. His father shewed me a portrait, which was designed for him; It is a bad picture; & bears but little resemblance to my friend.

As the Stage ran along, I passed within a mile & a half of the dwelling of my paternal aunts. It was with some reluctance that I submitted to the necessity of pursuing my journey, without seeing them.

The valley in which lies the township of Southington, is one of the pleasantest & best cultivated parts of New England. Here, more than any where, that I know of, are discoverable, the traces of those simple & interesting manners, for which this country was once so distinguished, & which now are nearly banished by the gradual progress of more accurate knowlege, & by that barbarism which seems to connect the primitive & the refined stages of society.

I arrived at Farmington, to a late dinner. I went to Mr. Lewis's, the father of my friend Daniel—whose mother & sister—excellent women, I saw. I next made some inquiries relative to my journey to Lichfield—& then visited at my kinsmen's—Saml. Smith's. This is a good family. I drank tea with them. I spent the whole evening at my friend Todd's—the physician—with his sisters & Miss Lewis. He was out on business—& did not return, in season for me to see him. I slept at Mr. Lewis's.

Tuesday, 3rd

This morning I made several visits. At length, I found Todd. We met as friends who had long wished to see each other. We had but a few minutes together—which I had the more regretted, was he not to be in Lichfield the next week.

I left my trunk in Farmington, & sat off on horseback. This town, (Farmington) has improved somewhat in it's appearance, since I was there last—which is now more than two years. It is pleasing to observe the progress of improvement, on this road. In many places, very good houses & cultivated farms, have succeeded to wild woods, & quagmires, & barren rocks.

I reached my father's a little before sun-set. He was at home, & Fanny, & Sally Tracy on a visit. How these girls have grown! All was joy & happiness. My mother was out, on a visit but soon returned. She was no less pleased. Mr. Tracy called in a few minutes. He is in good health. Mumford has not yet arrived. Mr. J. Morris was here, also, a few minutes. Our mutual salutations were hearty & sincere.

The evening was spent in temperate enjoyment.

---

[51] Hildreich or Ulrich Zwingli or Zwinglius (1484-1531) Swiss reformer who collaborated with Calvin. Melancthon, German reformer who collaborated with Luther.

Wednesday, 4th

The notices of the two preceeding days have just been written. It is the first convenient leisure I have had, for the purpose. Dr. Sheldon has been in to see me —& we have talked of—The Fever. This detestable *Fever* will never be at an end. From New York to Lichfield, I have been incessantly wearied with questions concerning the Fever.

I have, also, recd. visits from several of my infantile friends. It is time, now, that I take my turn of visiting.

My first visit, was to Mrs. Tracy. I found her, & her children well. Mr. T. was in Court. Our conversation was general; indeed we could have no other; for Mr. Mitchell of Wethersfield, who has lately been appointed a Judge, came in, & did not go out but a few minutes before I did. From him I learnt that all were well at Wethersfield. I was rejoiced to find Mrs. T. in better health & spirits than I have seen her for several years. This is as it should be. How much of this may attribute to the extraordinary share of business, which she has had on her hands, since her husband's removal to Congress? She recd. me with as much friendship as I could wish.

After dinner, I visited, successively, at Mr. Lord's, Miss Pierce's, Dr. Sheldon's, Danl. Lewis's, Mr. Collier's, & Mr. Buel's:—& found my friends all well, &, apparently, glad to see me. Mrs. Lord's two youngest boys, are fine children:—Sally Pierce looks well, & her school maintains her, comfortably: Danl. Sheldon & his sister Charlotte are much grown—he talks like a man, & tho' only sixteen, was tho't fit to sustain a legal examination, this autumn, which, however, the Court refused him, on account of his Youth. Danl. & Bessey Lewis look better & in better circumstances, than when I was here last; & their little boy seems to me a finer child than the one they lost. Collier has built him, by piecemeals, a snug little house; & enjoys all the comfort of *home*. Miss Buel is still more unwell; than when in New York. The probabilities are not in her favor.

Mrs. Tracy drank tea with us. Dr. Sheldon, D. W. Lewis, & Mr. F. Wolcott, spent the evening here. After the fever was discust, Mr. Randolph's affair became the subject of conversation; from which, by a train of conversation, which I can not, now, recollect, we branched out into considerations & discussion on education, the best government, the original bias of the mind or the cause of the varieties discoverable in children &c. &c. There was nothing remarkable in the argument in either side—except that my friend Lewis seems to me, fast verging towards Christianity.

I was born on Wednesday, the 4th of Septr. 1771—at two o'clock in the morning: so says my mother.

Thursday, 5th

I called on D. W. Lewis, this morning, & went with him into the Court House—where I met with a number of my acquaintance. There was spent most of the forenoon. About twelve I went to see Sally Pierce, & dined there, & stayed till three in the afternoon. Miss Wells, the sister of the two Physicians of that name, of my acquaintance, was there; & a Mr. Asa Bacon—originally of Canterbury in this State—educated at Yale College—& now a student of Law, with Mr. Reeve. We passed several sociable & agreable hours.

After my return home, I went in to see Mrs. Tracy. She was preparing to ride out: I helped her on to her horse, & went back. At home I conversed with my Mother & sister: & the last allowed me to look over the Diary which, at my instigation, she has commenced, it is now two months. She has done pretty well. I shewed her some parts of my own; & gave her some further instructions. Doubtless she will improve.

I wrote a letter to Roger Hitchcock.[52] How could I forget to notice the receit of letters from my sisters, at Aurora, the day of my reaching Lichfield? Mary's was of a good length, & an excellent letter. Abby was of unexampled length, & better composed than her letters usually are. Both gave me great satisfaction.

We had just drank tea, when our cousin E. Hubbard first of Middletown, came in. He is the son of my mother's brother—about 18—just out of College—& has come hither, to study Law under Mr. Reeve. He seems clever; & possest of good sense.

Dr. & Mrs. Catlin also came in. They spent the evening. I left them, for an hour & a half, to spend that time at Mr. Tracy's. He was not at home; but Mrs. T., her neice, & Mr. Lewis, were there; & afterward Judge Mitchell came in. We talked on general topics. Mrs. T. seemed pleased with "Caleb Williams." Lewis admires the style, but does not approve the plan. He says that, were it not the design of the author shewes itself, here & there, it might be supposed written for directly the opposite purpose for which it was. That is—written to make people contented with whatever government they happened to live under. I told him he had *retrograded* in his principles, within a few years: he acknowledged that his sentiments had *changed*, in that time. What the particular changes are, I have not yet learnt.

Mr. Reeve spake to me, when I was in the Court House. He asked me if an uncommonly brilliant Aurora Borealis was observable about the middle of September. I did not see it—& I had heard of no such thing. I have not seen this phenomenon for a great length time; & Mr. Reeve tells me, that none has appeared for more than three years:—except, occasionally, slight flashes. Mr. Reeve's Father, who is an intelligent Clergyman, now upwards of 80, remarks That, from diligent observation, he has learnt, that sickly seasons always succeed the disappearance of the Aurora Borealis. This observation may be of some importance. Mr. Reeve, himself, has made numerous & accurate observations on this phenomenon; the result of which he once mentioned to me. This I must get him to repeat—that I may preserve it. Both himself & his wife are enthusiastic *Observateurs*—& have treasured up much curious in-

---

[52] Brother of Reuben Hitchcock, apparently rather unstable.

formation. They are both in unusual health. Their only child, their son, is now at Nazareth, near Bethlehem, in Pennsylvania.

Friday, 6th

We sat up, my parents & myself, last evening, to converse on various subjects—particularly on plans of life; & I explained to them, in part, my Printing & Bookselling projects. This forenoon was chiefly spent with Mrs. Tracy. We conversed on a great variety of subjects. She accounted to me for her long epistolary silence, & in [a] way which was equally unexpected & astonishing. It is to the unfounded malice of one who is under the greatest obligations to us both, that we owe this suspension. This note is sufficient to preserve the facts in my memory; & I will spare myself the odious task of detailing them. We talked of Miss Wollstonecraft's Works—of Caleb Williams—Political Justice[53] &c. This last is in Town; & Mrs. T. will read it. She gave me, to read, a letter which she wrote to a kinsman of mine, who desired her opinion on Miss W's Rights of Women. It is full of good sense—& much in it's favor. An equal education would have placed Mrs. T. far before Miss Wollstonecraft. The rest of our conversation was on topics of neighborhood concern & not of sufficient importance to be dwelt upon, in this place.

After dinner, Mr. Collier made me a visit. He seems even yet, unsettled—still thinks of going to New Haven, &c. &c. The American Poems will lie untouched, for a time.[54] It is very probable that I shall yet be the Editor, at my own risk.

I went into the Court-House, in hopes of speaking with Allen; but he was earnestly listening to Mr. Reeve —& after waiting near an hour, in vain, I went out. From thence I went to see Lucy (Lewis) Parmele. I found her well; & stayed half an hour.

I drank tea at home—or rather, ate milk: for such is my country diet; & was just about to go to D. W. Lewis's to see him & Allen,[55] when the last came in—& spent the evening. And now was a new discussion of the Fever—the Treaty—& The Randolph. These subjects have become so hackneyed that it is painful to converse upon them. Luckily my circumstantial information is more accurate than that of those with whom I converse, or it would be still more insipid.

The man by whom I expected my trunk, returned from Farmington, without it. My acquaintance there, who were so ready to promise, have been as ready to forget. I should have secured myself from the possibility of this mistake.

Saturday, 7th

While we were yet at breakfast, Mumford, whose coming we had begun to despair of, entered. He brings me word that all friends are well in N. York, & that I shall hear from Wm. by the mail—this day.

With Mumford I went to D. W. Lewis—to Collier's, &c. I spent a little while at the Court House, & a little while at Mr. Brace's.[56]

The whole afternoon was passed at Mr. Tracy's. I went there for the purpose of reading to her some parts of "Political Justice," which I had procured of Mr. Allen; but, owing to frequent interruptions, I was only able to read her a single chapter—that "Of Justice"— which I meant as preparatory to several others. I found there Serina Bull, who is as pretty as ever, except that, now, she did not appear in usual good health. Mr. Holmes, D. W. Lewis, & Judge Mitchell, were there most of the time: Mr. Tracy, but a few minutes; being called away on business.

In the evening I recd. an excellent letter from Wm. Johnson, which also inclosed one from J. Williams.

I spent the evening in reading the New York Papers, & in domestic conversation.

While waiting at the Post Office, for the arrival of the Mail, Mr. Reeve, Mr. Allen, Wolcott & Dr. Sheldon, & others, present, we fell into conversation—in the course of which I first heard mentioned the name of a Mr. Periam—originally of Georgia—educated at Princeton College—& for a long time, Tutor there—& while Mr. Reeve was also tutor, at that place. This Mr. Periam, Mr. Reeve thinks to have been the greatest man—for genius & erudition combined, he ever knew. He was also, a most eloquent & able writer; & distinguished himself by many pieces, written at the commencement of the Revolution. He was at first a Tory; afterwards a Whig, on Tory principles—obeying the precept which directs us to "yield obedience to the powers that be." He studied divinity with Dr. Bellamy —became a Sandiminian—crazy—& is now dead. At the same College, & at the same time, a Mr. Halsey was Tutor, who was a monster of Erudition. He wrote the celebrated Piece—intituled "Join or Die."[57] This Piece Mr. Reeve carried in MS. to the Printer.

Sunday, 8th

The record of this day is simple. Instead of going to Meeting, I stayed at home, both parts of the day, & wrote letters—to Mary, Abby, & to Wm. Johnson.

In the evening we had considerable company here. Sally & Polly Pierce & Idea Strong; Mr. Skinner[58]—

---

[53] William Godwin, *Inquiry Concerning Political Justice* (London, 1793). Of all the books that Smith read this was probably his favorite.

[54] Only suggestion that any copy for Volume II had been given to the printer.

[55] John Allen (1763-1812), was a graduate of Reeve's Law School, admitted to the bar in 1786, member of Connecticut House 1793-1796, U.S. House 1797-1799, Connecticut Supreme Court of Errors 1800-1806. Kilbourne, *Sketches and Chronicles*, p. 185.

[56] Jonathan Brace (1754-1837; Yale 1779) was a successful lawyer who served in the Connecticut House for six sessions between 1788 and 1794, became state's attorney for Hartford County, U.S. House, 1798-1800, mayor of Hartford 1815-1824, other state offices.

[57] No longer so celebrated. Not found.

[58] Richard Skinner (1778-1833), a graduate of Reeve's Law School, was admitted to the bar of Litchfield County in 1800. At twenty-three he was state's attorney for the county of Ben-

Parmele—& Gold. We sat up late, to converse after the company went away. The conversation was too broken to admit of analysis.

Idea Strong is an excellent young woman. She is the daughter of that Strong, who was, ultimately stripped of all his offices, by my exposure of his villainy, or rather, by my exciting others to it's exposure. He is now a poor drunken wretch—& wholly despised & neglected, after having been one of the County Judges, a Senator of this State, & once chosen a delegate to the Old Congress; while his daughter is universally beloved & respected. Public opinion is unusually just in Lichfield.

Monday, 9th

It began to rain last night, & continued thro' the whole of this day, & evening, with very little remission. At first it was accompanied by violent wind, from the south-west. I lay in the southwest corner of the house, & lay awake two hours, this morning, to enjoy it. The sense of our security is rendered doubly sweet, by the tempests which howl around us, & ineffectually beat against our shelter.

As Mumford could not ride, we made several visits together:—thus occupying the forenoon—in which nothing, worthy of notice, occurred.

The afternoon & evening were mostly spent at Mr. Tracy's; & most of the afternoon in conversation with Mrs. T. Numerous little matters, & many of ancient times, were talked over. The only general conversation we had, was on the principles of morals. I am tolerably sure that when she has attended somewhat more to the subject—read Godwin, & other authors, which that will lead her to read, we shall not widely differ. As yet she can not talk on these subjects with sufficient calmness: —so much has she suffered from the calumny of others, that she ventures timidly, at times, & at times, boldly, on inquiries which may subject her to new misrepresentations. I often observed the tears in her eye, as we discoursed yesterday.

In the evening Mr. Tracy & Mr. Mitchell were there all the evening: Mumford in the last; D. W. Lewis in the first of it. We had a very agreable time of various talk.

I recd. a letter from Bissell Hinsdale, clerk of Saml. Richards, trader at Farmington—in which he informs me, that as my trunk had not been sent to the Store, he had bro't thither, & would forward it to me, the first safe conveyance.

This mark of kindness & attention, in a young man to whom I am a stranger, & with whom I never spake but once, gave me much pleasure, & he imprest me very strongly in his favor. I must not forget to acknowledge this to him.

Tuesday, 10th

Mumford left us in good season, this morning. I spent much of this forenoon at home—talking with my mother & sisters; & some of it [with] Collier, & at the Court-House. About eleven, I went to see Sally Pierce—& stayed till twelve. She is to see about getting a little girl for Mrs. Lovegrove—having mentioned one to me. She gave me many particulars, respecting Idea Strong's situation. After her father's public trial, she was taken to live with him; & for several years was his slave—writing, reading, & visiting, almost altogether by stealth. Her reason at length acquired sufficient energy to enable her to throw off his tyranny, which had now become insupportable. This was about a year ago: when she came to an open determination with him—since which she has enjoyed a considerable share of liberty. She now visits who she pleases—but makes choice of those times when he—thro' intoxication—is too insensible to be conscious of her departure & return. Hitherto she has constrained herself not to oppose his positive prohibitions, how capricious soever may be their motive.

Sally Pierce has quarterly exhibitions in her school; the three last of which have gained it much reputation. At the last, her scholars acted a dramatic piece which she copied, or rather drew, from "Cecilia"—& another which Danl. & Charlotte Sheldon, took from "Evelina." These & several smaller ones, manufactured in the same way—were played very well by her scholars, to a crowded auditory.

In the afternoon I called on Almira Catlin & Mrs. Cowles—& drank tea & spent several hours at Sherif Lord's.[59]

I spent the evening at D. W. Lewis's. John Allen was there part of the time: (Todd has not come.) Our conversation was various & interesting. Both of them talk of visiting New York ere long. I gave them some account of our Friendly Club; & to Lewis, in answer to his inquiries, particulars concerning Dunlap.

Wednesday, 11th

I scarcely recollect how this morning flew away. About eleven I went over to Mr. Tracy's, & spent the remainder of the forenoon, till dinner, with Mrs. T. & the children: conversing of various matters. Caroline—the youngest—came to me, for the first time; & we had a fine frolic.

After dinner, Fanny & I walked to South Farms, to James Morris's; five miles. We went by the way of the plain, & had a very pleasant walk. Marks of increased cultivation are evident all along this road. We reached our place of destination, in good season.

James Morris married my mother's youngest, & now, only, sister. He is a man of 43 years of age. His occupation is that of farming, to which he added a school: & he

---

nington, Vermont, a member of the U.S. House at thirty-five (1813-1815), elected governor of Vermont 1820-1823, chief justice of the Supreme Court of Vermont 1823-1828.

[59] Lynde Lord was for twenty-nine years high sheriff of Litchfield County, this despite the fact that at all too frequent intervals prisoners escaped from his jail. His son Lynde Lord, Jr. (Yale 1783) was a deputy sheriff.

is also Justice of the Peace. His school is now beginning to assemble; & he already has nine young women boarding in his house. He was occupied with them, & with some Society business, much of the evening. Amos Chase, too, the parson of the Parish, came in, & held us some time engaged. We talked of various matters, chiefly of moral kind, till late bed-time.

Thursday, 12th

The same conversation was renewed, with still more spirit, this morning; tho' the shortness of the occasion did not allow either of us to be very full. This man is a Calvinist; & believes, of course, in the *total depravity* of the human heart. It need scarcely be remarked that my sentiments were quite the reverse; & never was I more explicit, in the same period, & with the same opportunity. We love each other—& parted in the continuation of it. He is to send me, soon, his history of himself—which is mostly written.

Fanny & I reached home to dinner. We came back, by the way of Pine-Island—as it is called. This is much the pleasantest road—tho' clearing the adjacent grounds, has impaired it's charms. Still we were much pleased—: I, probably, the most—as it is long since I have traced this way.

Both yesterday & today we, Fanny & myself—have conversed with great constancy—: chiefly on plans of study for her. She is a good girl.

I forgot to mention, that my long-wished-for trunk arrived yesterday—after it's many perils & delays.

I spent a couple of hours with Mrs. Tracy & her family. We talked some on the subject of education—in mutual confirmation of our notions—& I read her some passages from my Journal, on that & other topics.

I shall succeed, I believe, in procuring a little girl, for Mrs. Lovegrove; & I hope to her mind. Sally Pierce went with me to the house of the parents of Sophy, the child in question, & they have consented. As for Sophy —she is in fine spirits on the occasion.

I spent the evening at Dr. Sheldon's. We had much conversation—for all were at home. The Theatre at Hartford—at which Danl. had been—& Dr. & Mrs. Sheldon—was suggested by the exhibitions here, in which Danl. bore a principal share both as actor & author—& was the theme of copious disquisition. From that, on to other theatres—the stage—it's effect, &c. &c. —Danl. was reading "Perigrine Pickle"—& lo! a discussion on Novels. Medicine & Law, were also handled; & last of all—speaking of studies for Danl. this winter— Moral Philosophy; to which Politics became attached; & with this the evening ended—for it was now ten.

I have some reason to be satisfied with the fortitude I shewed this day, at Mr. Morris's, in combatting the doctrines of the christian religion. I long to throw off the veil of concealment, altogether—& yet dread to do it. The occasion of so doing has, as yet, been avoided—as far as my parents are concerned. I too much fear the consequences of such a discovery, on them, to hasten it's arrival.

Friday, 13th

This morning I called to determine the matter, about little Sophy: all is settled; she is to go; & her parents are getting her ready. I called to see Polly Buel, & spent an hour with her. She is much altered; tho' she has neither lost her spirits, nor her hopes. Her sister Sally is quite grown. Collier was not in his Office. I went up into the Court room, & conversed an hour, with John C. Smith, of Sharon,[60] & D. W. Lewis.

In the afternoon, soon after dinner, I sat off—& after crossing *Bantam River* struck into the woods. Thro' these I rambled, till I came to the northerly Chesnut-Hill road; & then passed along that, to Phins. Baldwin's —whither I went about some butter, which I am to have, for this winter. The woods are pleasant, even yet, & stripped, as they are, of leaves. What name shall we give to that vivid & soft, & gentle sensation & sentiment, which is inspired by being buried in the embowering shades of thick woods? I never felt it—fully, on York Island. The road to P. Baldwin's is remarkably fine. I was so forgetful of this transcendently excellent prospect, that it struck me like something new. What a picture of majestic & beauteous repose, did the western view present! The town of Lichfield, the West mountain, the Lake, the blue & distant ridges of New Milford —the chasm, by which they are, in part, exposed to the eye—but I will not trust my untutored pen with a description of the scene. Thy pencil Charles, my friend Charles to thine doth it belong. I lost, I know not how, much time, in gazing. My tho'ts next turned to my several friends—& my fancy summoned them all around me.

It was two miles further to Capt. Bull's, & I reached thither, at half past three. He was not at home—but all the rest of the family were, & Julia Tracy. Mrs. B. & Mrs. T. are sisters. They have made quite a convenient —almost an elegant, mansion, of the old farm-house— in which I once recd. some of my infantile lessons. Everything around them wears the best face of thrift and improvement. The scene around is pleasant; & the distant prospect, designed, by nature, for future wondrous beauty. Such vales! such hills! Such woods! Mrs. B. looks ten years younger than before this marriage. We drank tea—it was sun-down—& I walked home, two miles & a half—in half an hour.

I had been seated but a short time, when some [one] rapped—& my friend William Buel, very unexpectedly, entered. I have not seen him, before, for more than two years. We were not sorry to meet. He sat an hour— the time principally consumed in general inquiries—&

---

[60] John C. Smith (1765-1815; Yale 1783), lawyer, member of Connecticut General Assembly 1793, 1796, 1800; U.S. House 1800-1806, lieutenant governor of Connecticut 1810, governor 1813-1818.

then sat off for his father's. He is to be in town to-morrow.

I went to Danl. Lewis's—& there, also, saw Collier. Danl. & I went to Mr. Reeve's & had the good fortune to find him at home, & his Wife in spirits. We spent two hours in very cheerful conversation.

While I was at Mr. Reeve's, Roger Hitchcock came in. He had been to my father's—& learning where I was, followed me. I proposed my plan to him—& he seemed to fall in with it: informing me, however, that it had been thought on before, by himself. He moreover told me that he had tho't of using his brother's sermons, himself: of commencing Preacher. I had not sufficient opportunity of telling him how absurd I tho't it would be. There was a wildness in his manner, which made me fear he was about to revert to his insanity. I found that my mother had observed it, when he was at our house.

I was a few minutes at Lewis's on my return.

Saturday, 14th

It was ten when I went out; & I determined to make a number of little visits. I first called at Dr. Catlin's; where I found Buel, & where, contrary to my first intention I spent the whole morning. Nothing material passed. Buel dined with me. We conversed about the Western Country; whither he has been, with a design of establishing himself; which he has since relinquished. We conversed, also, of the Fever which has prevailed, the last summer, in Sheffield, where he now resides. I hope to receive some account of it, from him.

In the afternoon, we made Sally Pierce a visit—called at Dr. Sheldon's—& spent the rest of the afternoon at Mr. Tracy's.

Buel returned, in the evening, to his father's on Pheasant-Hill. I spent the evening, reading the News-Papers—sadly disappointed that I had not a letter from William.

Sunday, 15th

The solicitations of my parents, much against my inclination, drew me to Church; where reason & religion, & every thing else was wretchedly tortured, by a certain Mr. Tailor. Buel was also there, & came home with me. We spent the afternoon much more profitably, in pleasant conversation with each other—concerning our several situations, prospects, &c. Buel is to be married within six months. He will send me an account of the Fever which has prevailed, in his vicinity, the last summer.

In the evening John Allen, D. W. Lewis & his Betsey &, afterward, Judge Mitchell & Mr. Tracy, were here —& we spent a sociable evening.

My Father & I sat up some time, after the company retired, to converse on our various matters.

I meant to have spent part of this evening, at Dr. Sheldon's, with Buel—but the coming in of this company prevented me.

Monday, 16th

Buel sat off for Sheffield this morning.

I had an hour's agreable rambling conversation, with J. C. Smith, D. W. Lewis, & U. Holmes,[61] in the Court-House; after which I went to Govr. Wolcott's—where I saw him, his son, & their House-keeper—my father's quondam Maid.

Part of the afternoon was devoted to my father—relative to some purchases to be made in New York. I saw Mrs. Tracy a few moments. Sally Pierce, Mrs. Lord, & Miss R. Sheldon, drank tea here. Lively conversation. In the evening I was, with my mother, a short time at Mrs. Talmadge's (the Col. is at Marietta). Sally Pierce was here when I returned—& we went over to Mr. Tracy's. I had a short conversation with Mrs. T. after which I went with Mr. T. into his office. We talked of the Politics of our country—a few words on "Aristocracy."

I am to speak to Mr. Sands, in New York, (the gentleman who hires Cash)—a negro man of this Place —on the subject of sending part of his pay to his wife— who is here, & in great distress.

Since my stay in Lichfield, I have, generally, written the Notes of each day, in the morning of the day after.

I have read a little in the Dictionary of Anecdotes— in Stile's Judges—in Political Justice—which I found here—during my short stay.

I wrote a few lines to Wm.

My Father made me a present of Thirty Dollars—& let me have one hundred; which are charged to my private account. I also recd. Three hundred & forty to expend for him, in N. York.

I shall leave word to have my trunk sent to the Coffee-House, in New Haven—or, if they do keep open house there, to Carrington's, the Stage-House.

Tuesday, 17th

Mr. Allen called here this morning, as I was in the bustle of packing up, to bid me farewell; & to request a renewal of our decayed Correspondence.

I bade adieus to my family, & friends, about ten, & with Sophy, sat off on my return. The morning was unpleasant & cloudy. It cleared away before noon, & the rest of the day, was pleasant, for season. Sophy's horse was very troublesome, & she was somewhat fatigued when we reached Southington; which was a little after sun-down.

This house has undergone a great interior change, since I was here, last year. My two Aunts still remain: but my cousin, Dr. Root has removed to Hampden, a town twelve miles below—& his brother has taken his place. Every thing here looks neat & patriarchal, as usual. My aunts grow old—but they are still affectionate & careful.

I played with my cousin Root's children—chatted

---

[61] Uriel Holmes, a lawyer. He was a justice of the peace in Litchfield in 1808 and an associate judge 1814-1817. Kilbourne, *History of Litchfield,* pp. 208-209, 212.

with him & his wife, read the newspapers—& went early to bed.

Wednesday, 18th

Contrary to my expectations, this morning proved to be very pleasant.

I forgot to note, yesterday, that I have recd of Sally Pierce two dollars, to purchase for her—if it will do it—two copies of the "Triumphs of Temper"—& one of "The Honest Farmer"—a dramatic piece, by M. Berquin.[62]

My grandmother Smith's sister, Mrs. Upson, is yet alive—in her 92nd year.

We sat off a little after nine. The day was unusually pleasant. We reached Hampden at twelve & dined with Dr. Root—whose situation is remarkably pleasant.

We reached New Haven in season. I made all the inquiring I could, relative to getting forward; but all left me uncertain. I went to Dr. Darling's—& after some fresh inquiries—returned there, & spent the evening. This man married a cousin of my mother: a clever couple. I brought a letter for them; & their daughter is to ride back the horse which Sophy rode down.

Nothing material this day worthy of notice—the conversation, in the evening, was equally uninteresting.

Thursday, 19th

Rose late—wrote a few lines to my father—& arranged matters with the Post, about taking back the horses.

The greater part of the day wasted, in fruitless attempts to procure a passage to New York. Drank tea at Mr. Chauncey's. Nothing particular occurred there. Spent the evening at Mr. Meig's. Much conversation. I was made particularly unhappy by the political turn which the conversation took in the beginning of the evening; as Mr. Meigs's is a strenuous democrat & Frenchman in politics—which I am not. A literary conversation relieved me; & the rest of the evening was very agreable.

Friday, 20th

The wind still contrary—we took places in an *extra*-stage. Mrs. Greene, the widow of the late Genl. Greene, her son & daughter—a Mr. Lloyd & Rosevelt of N. York—& two others. We reached Norwalk. A disagreable day, in respect to our getting forward—pleasant weather—excellent company—various & interesting conversation.

I have long wished to see this lady. She is a fine, sensible woman—of a lively & spirited mind: her daughter a pretty woman.

We spent the evening sociably, together.

---

[62] "The Triumph of Temper," a long poem by William Hayley (Newbury-Port, 1781). *The Honest Farmer* (New Haven, 1794); Arnaud Berquin was the translator; author is not named.

Saturday, 21st

We proceeded within seventeen miles of New York. Master Greene left us at Stamford; where he is put to school. We found excellent accomodations.

This morning opened beautifully, & promised a fine day: a promise, however, but scurvily fulfilled—for it soon clouded over; & drizzled thro'out the day. Shut up as we were, in the carriage, we felt it but little, & it made but little impression, either on our spirits or conversation. When we had gotten supper out of the way, we sat down, around a cheerful fire, in a room by ourselves, & the spirit of conversation was again awakened. I designed, at the time, to have recorded the principal parts of this conversation—but it is now too late.

Sunday, 22nd

I reached home, this day, a little before One, in the afternoon. We had, previously, seen the ladies safely at their lodgings. I made all haste to arrange myself a little, & accompanied Sophy to Mrs. Lovegrove's. I found them all well—& dined there. After dinner I came home, & thence to H. Johnson's where I found his family & William. There I past the afternoon. Wm. & I went to Mr. Lovegrove's to tea—& thither came Dunlap & his wife. We spent the evening. Wm. & I called Woolsey's—in our return. They are well—except his youngest child—which is quite unwell.

I found at home—a letter from Wm. Buel—of which he spake to me, when we were together, in Ld.—I delivered several letters.

Monday, 23rd

The preceeding notices have been written, at such hurried & indeterminate intervals of motion, that they are very imperfect: neither can I promise myself leisure to do much better, for a week to come. When I have a little disengaged myself from business, which now pours upon me, I hope to review the transactions of the last three or four weeks, & give some more importance to that part of my life.

The forenoon principally dedicated to business—of my father. I found time to call at Woolsey's, whose youngest child is unwell.

Dined at H. Johnson's—& sat there till after four. Alsop came here—& stayed half an hour. He has been to Middletown since I saw him. All well there.

I was at Woolsey's a little while in the evening. His child seems better. The remainder of the evening at home—looking over the late News Papers.

On Saturday, as we came thro' a place called *The Saw Pits*—Mrs. Greene informed us, that, in that place, a woman, the wife of a respectable man there, had been delivered of two children, within *six weeks* of each other. This happened in the time of the last War—the children are now grown up—& she thinks alive. The father had a formal & authenticated account of this remarkable fact drawn up, & sworn to by all the witnesses.

Tuesday, 24th

The whole of this day devoted to making purchases for my father. I hope to complete this business in two days more, at farthest.

I drank tea at Kent's. They are well.

I spent most of the evening at Webster's. Mrs. W. severely afflicted with a Cold. Mr. W. is collecting materials for an account of the late Fever.

At my host's—Mr. Mulligan's—no other change than what is occasioned by the marriage of Miss Betsey—who eloped, & united herself to a man, disagreeable to the family, during my absence.

The funeral of Lawrence Embree was numerously attended, this day. He was of the Society of Friends—in this City. His loss must be much deplored—as he was a man of distinguished & active benvolence—of good sense, influence, & universally respected.[63]

Wednesday, 25th

This day, like the two preceeding, chiefly devoted to my father's affairs. Still, in this period, I have found time to run over the first vol. of Miss Williams's last letters from France[64]—& Charlotte Smith's Elegiac Sonnets[65]—which fell in my way; & to prepare the notices for a Special meeting of the Manumission Society.

I drank tea at Woolsey's—& spent an hour at Dunlap's. He was not at home. The remainder of the evening at home.

It was with great pleasure that I learnt, from Miss W's letters, that Genl. Miranda was safe. This man travelled thro' part, if not all, of the United States. It was my second year in College that I saw him at New Haven. He was then meditating a revolution in South America. This strongly imprest me in his favor—& his demeanor was calculated to heighten that favorable impression, which a knowlege of his design had made. I recollect with what keen regret I heard a fictitious account of his having fallen into the hands of the Spanish Court—by means of their emisaries.[66] In looking over some letters of mine, to my friend Hitchcock, which I had restored to me, a short time since, I find mention made of this report, in terms of sorrow, which the instant suggested.

Are we not always more interested in the fate of those extraordinary men whom we have seen, than in that of strangers, altho' their superiors?

Thursday, 26th

This day, contrary to my expectation, being universally observed as a day of Thanksgiving, & service performed in all the churches, I was, much against my inclinations, compelled to defer the completion of my father's business, till tomorrow. It was fortunate, perhaps, for the Manumission Society; to whose business I gave up most of the forenoon.

Wm. & I made a short visit to Alsop. I recd. a business letter from Frederic Wolcott & wrote a few words in reply. I also wrote a short letter to my father; & recd. a letter from Wm., which had been sent to me at Lichfield too late, & was now returned. Still it was acceptable.

After dinner, I made a visit, relative to the business of the Manumission Society. Then I spent an hour & a half at Mr. Lovegrove's, very agreably.

Wm. & I drank tea at Dunlap's; & thence we all repaired to the Mann. Socy. where multiplicity of business detained us till late. Wm., Dunlap, & myself, are of the number chosen to represent the Society, in the next Convention.

Friday, 27th

I returned to business, with renewed vigor, this morning; & it is nearly accomplished. I wrote to my father; & a few line to Sally Pierce; whose commission I have, in some sort, fulfilled; expending all her money; tho' not altogether as she wished—that being impossible.

I drank tea, & passed two hours, at Mrs. Morton, with her, & Miss Susan. I have not conversed so long with them, together, for many months. So many, that I can not now recollect when was the last time I saw them together. They are well—& in good spirits.

I never had a convenient opportunity of reading "The Castle of Otranto" before this day. It is among the books I purchased for Sally Pierce. I have nearly finished it; & design to finish it this evening. Certainly, Vicesimus Knox,[67] this is not "a poor production." If not equal to the inspired poesy of Chatterton—still it is far from mean. Nay, it deserves to be ranked high among performances of this kind.

Saturday, 28th

This day, like most of the preceeding, since my return from the country, consumed in various affairs. Thank heaven! I have completed my father's business. I added a few lines to what I wrote yesterday, wrote a short letter of business to Bradley & Huggins, merchants, in New Haven.

---

[63] "The same whose conscience refused one hundred dollars for the poor, because it came from the manager of a playhouse." Dunlap, *History of the American Theatre* (London, 1833) **2**: p. 323 (note that this is the London edition not the '32 Amer. ed.).

[64] Helen Maria Williams, *Letters from France; containing many New Anecdotes relative to the French Revolution, and the present State of French Manners.* Revised edition in four volumes (London, 1792-1796). Smith was reading a six-volume edition, not found.

[65] (1784); a spectacularly successful publication; five editions followed in the next five years.

[66] Miranda died in a dungeon in Cadiz, but not until 1816.

[67] See Knox, *Essays Moral and Literary* (Dublin, 1786). Knox's strong religious leanings, the subject of much of his writing, were not calculated to arouse Smith's admiration. Smith may have been rebutting "On Novel Reading," *Essays Moral and Literary* (Dublin, 1786) **2**: pp. 68 ff.

Aaron Smith[68] of Lichfield came to town this morning, & brought me a letter from Thomas Collier. Collier wishes to reprint the Ghost-Seer;[69] & I made ineffectual efforts to procure the copy for him. I wrote a few lines to him; & also to Frederic Wolcott, on whose business I have, hitherto, been able to effect nothing.

I read some medicine, to inform myself respecting a particular case, on which I was consulted, a few days since.

I spent an hour with Henry Gahn, at his lodgings.

Wm. & I drank tea at Horace's; & from thence, went, together, to Charles Adams's, where the Friendly Club were to meet.

The meetings of the Friendly Club, which so many accidents had concurred to interrupt, were formally renewed on Saturday evening, the seventh inst. while I was in the country. But tho' this is the fourth night, the unusual hurry of business at this time, owing to the long delay, occasioned by the late Fever, prevents their being prosecuted with vigour, & attended to with exactness. Adams, Dunlap, W. Johnson, & myself, were all that attended. Adams read us Hume's introductory essay "On Parties." We conversed, soberly for the most part, on a variety of subjects & separated at ten—considering the evening as having been well spent.

I finished the Castle of Otranto, last evening. This book has great merit—but, I confess, not equal to my expectations. The conclusion falls far short of what the principal part of the work had led me to expect. The author seems to have employed a machinery too vast for his powers to manage. The enormous casque, the gigantic sword, & the giant leg & arm, excited expectations, which were never satisfied. I looked to see something grand & overpowering produced from them; but, like the prophecies of the Harpy Caleno, they all end in nothing. But what is still more reprehensible is, what the author is pleased to call the *Moral* of the Story. The death of Conrad was well enough, perhaps. At least, the insignificance of his character, & the little the reader knows of him, make him no object of regret. But that the amiable Matilda should be killed, to punish the crime of her father, as it appears wholly unnecessary, so also it appears wholly immoral. Her innocence, & her virtues, deserves a better fate, & other ways might have been found of scourging the ambition of Manfred, more consonant [page mutilated]

Sunday, 29th

Most of the day was employed in engrossing the Minutes of the Manumission Society, & in writing connected therewith. About four, in the afternoon, William & I went to Mr. Lovegrove's, where we stayed till nine. The conversation was very rambling, part interesting, & part not. Too much time was wasted in talking about an Englishman of the name of Ray; a detestable wretch, unworthy of existence—and in enumerating instances of his selfishness & depravity. They are full of their plan of building. We had much to say on the scheme of a house. Mrs. L. has read "Iphigenia in Tauris", while I was in the country; &, (as she ought to do) admires it. They have a fine engraving of the Maid of the Haystack—Louisa—from a painting of W. Palmer—a friend of Mrs. L's.—& they say it is a striking likeness. She is beautiful. They have, likewise, a fine engraving, from a painting of Palmer's, also, of John Henderson. Mrs. L. says it has not his healthy countenance. She shewed us a miniature, by Palmer, which is perfectly like: more so than any picture ever taken of him. The head is capacious—the eye mild, penetrating, inquisitive, a little enthusiasm—great delicacy, as well as force, in the nose—which is unusually beautiful—the mouth not handsome, but full of sensibility. It is much to be regretted that a man, so universally spoken of, as of profound erudition & uncommon genius, should never have benefitted the world by presenting it with the fruits of his inquiries, & the offspring of his talents. He died in his thirty-second year.

I had scarcely reached home, when a professional call forced me out again. It rained, & still rains, most violently. I went.

I have read a little in Miss Williams's sixth volume; & purpose to make still further progress in it, tho' the evening be far spent.

Monday, 30th

Helen Maria Williams's letters from France engaged my attention till breakfast. I was employed in adjusting my hair, when Uriah Tracy of Lichfield entered. He brought me a letter from my father. His family, & all my friends, there, are well. Dunlap, & H. Johnson, were here & various talk interested most of the forenoon. I accompanied Tracy to James Watson's—where we spent two hours. He dined with Noah Webster, I at home. After dinner, Letters from France, again, gained my attention, till after four, when Tracy returned. We made many calls. We drank tea at Kent's—& spent the evening at Dunlap's. W. Johnson there—& the Woolsey's. We talked on the politics of the day—& afterward had a lengthy argument on the perfectibility of man—the effect of knowlege—the populousness of the world—&c. &c. in which Tracy & W. W. Woolsey, were opposed to Dunlap, Johnson, & myself. It was near ten when we separated. Tracy took leave of us. He proceeds, early tomorrow to Philadelphia.

This month, which is now at an end, has been a season of hurry, in which I am rather surprised that I have written so much, than that I have done no more. After

---

[68] Aaron Smith (1771-1834; Yale 1790) is no relative, at least no near relative. Born in Waterbury, he studied law in Litchfield and settled there. Representative in the Connecticut House 1808-1814.

[69] Two editions, translations of Schiller's *Der Geisterseher* (1787), appeared in America within a few months after this diary entry, from the presses of T. & J. Swords in New York and W. P. Young in Charleston. It was also serialized in the New York *Weekly Magazine.* Collier changed his mind about printing it.

all, what I have written is, for the most part, very trivial; rather a dry catalogue of occurrences, than an interesting & expanded view of sentiments. Since my return from the country, I have been more engaged than before; & have not settled myself down to quiet study. This I hope to do, before another week. Unhappily, in some respects, in others fortunately, perhaps, in about three weeks more, I must undergo a new change of scene; & must, again, have to acquire, thro' many fluctuations, a fixed state. The visit to Phila. should I make it, will, of necessity, interrupt me for a fortnight. Notwithstanding all these impediments, I feel, untoward destiny excepted, that I shall not, altogether lose this winter.

December 1795
Tuesday, 1st

In commencing the memorials of another month I ought to feel better fitted for composition than I do at present: and that, because no time is so proper for casting the mental eye forward, gaining some conception of what is to come, and arranging as far as may be, the temper of my mind, the nature & order of my exertions. But, this evening, I have a strange, crowding sensation, in my head, which, in great measure, incapacitates me for reflection & enjoyment. I must, therefore, content myself for the present, with merely noting the little business of the day.

The forenoon was mostly employed in settling some little affairs, purchasing some books, & chatting with several acquaintance. I was just going to dinner, when I recd. a message from Dingley, that he had injured his knee, & desiring me to call on him. I did so. He is hurt —but not dangerously. How is it that physicians, in sickness, are so much more wanting in fortitude, & filled with apprehension, than other people?

The remainder of the afternoon devoted to looking over the books I have bought, & reading their Prefaces, Introductions &c.

I drank tea at Abijah Hart's. They have a child— since I saw them. What sight is more interesting to all the best affections of the soul, than a tender & intelligent mother caressing her infant? But a mother who is not intelligent—fye!

I came home at seven; it is now near nine; & in the interval I have been writing letters for the Manumission Society.

Tracy went to-day. I heard from Cogswell.

Miss Wms, whose letters I finished yesterday, writes in a very interesting style. Mde. Roland appears to have been a very uncommon woman. The satire of Camille Desmoulins has great merit.

Wednesday, 2nd

To Charles Brocden Brown.

The earnest desire which I feel to hear from you would have prompted me to give you earlier notice of my return to New York, had not a variety of pressing concerns occupied all my time, till now.

I reached this city, about ten days since, after an absence of a little more than three weeks, & after a journey & visit pleasant beyond my expectations. The lateness of the season made me apprehensive of that disagreable weather, which usually prevails at the close of autumn; but all my anticipations of gratification, from my excursion, were heightened, by the additional charms of an unclouded sky & a mild temperature.

You are not ignorant of the delight which all hearts of sensible mould, are conscious of, when they revisit the scenes—

> Where once their careless childhood stray'd,
> A stranger yet to pain.[70]

even if that visitation is made under circumstances of sorrow & want; you know likewise, how greatly this delight is increased, when all things proceed prosperously, when tranquility & plenty surround the dwellings of our friends, & when they meet us in vigorous health, & augmented felicity. Fortunately, my friend, a happiness so pure had been prepared for me. I will not ask you to forgive me for dwelling on this subject; for I am sure that to you, as well as to me, it can not fail of being grateful. You must be pleased, for I am pleased; you must be rejoiced, for you know the value of these friends; you can not be insensible to it, for they are acquainted with & esteem you. You were, often, the object of their solicitude & inquiries, & the subject [of] our mutual congratulation & discourse.

Shall I tell you, my friend, that I sometimes indulged the hope of hearing from you, while I was at Lichfield? A thousand circumstances, I know, might prevent your writing. I recollected this, & was not disappointed by your silence. But I am now in this city; the communication is so direct; it is long, very long, since you wrote to me; can I doubt of your seizing the first leisure to dilate on all those numerous topics of discussion, which my previous letters must have presented to you?

Farewell,
E. H. Smith.

Wednesday, Dec. 2. 1795.
Cedar St. No. 13, New York.

To Joseph Bringhurst, Junior.

I returned, from Connecticut, about ten days ago. Since that time, I have been perpetually busied, & have only taken up the pen to answer the demands of business. I am, now, just beginning to gain a little tranquillity, & seize on the first moments of it, to inform you, where & how I am, & how much I desire to hear from you.

---

[70] Thomas Gray, "On the Distant Prospect of Eton College," St. 2.

At present, it is incompatible with other engagements, of some importance, to write to you as lengthily as I would be glad to write, & as, you know, I am accustomed to write. Neither do I regard my friend as that punctilious & urgent being, who penuriously hoards up his talents for communicating happiness to others, & who rigidly insists on the "uttermost farthing,"[71] before his debtor is restored to the exercise of a right which ought never to be restrained. But, my friend, am I the debtor? It is a foolish question—& I will not insist on it. I am sure that you will do all that friendship & duty demand of you; & that the impulses of your own heart may be securely trusted to, as unwavering conductors to every act which will diffuse pleasure around you, & to those you love, when some higher duty does not interpose it's sacred obligations.

You will be gratified with knowing that there are strong probabilities of my being in Phila. the last of this month; but, ere that time, I hope to have recd. frequent letters from you; to which let this be considered as an incitement & example.

My love to our common friends.

Farewell.

E. H. Smith.

Wednesday, Dec. 2. 1795.
Cedar St. No. 13, New York.

It is but lately that I conceived the design of preserving copies of all my letters. There can be no doubt of the numerous advantages which would result from making it effectual. I wish there was as little of my perseverance. I find that I am very apt to *begin* well: it will not do, therefore, to augur much from what I have done to-day. Beside both the preceeding letters are very short, & written with little care. How shall I act, when I commence my long-letter-writing? "Aye there's the rub!"[72]

It is not every one whose destiny it is to be constantly in interesting situations: it is not every day, even of a great man's life, that is important: what right then have I, to complain—that all is uniform & dull? And, indeed, how little reason is there, for one, in my situation, to expect to see the days crowded with incident! It is in my own mind that I must look for something to interest. From thence I ought to bring the treasures of memory, the riches of reflection. Of what consequence is it, that this self-moving machine, directed it's advances towards the east or the west, rose at this hour & lay down at that, here added to the mass of it's solids & there of it's fluids? The mind! the mind! "The mind's the standard of the man!"[73] Thank thee, good Isaac Watts. I shall improve on thy hint, by & by, &, no doubt, prove myself to be, mentally, at least six feet high. For the present, however, I must be contented with being just as little, & just as low, as heretofore.

I transacted Frederic Wolcott's business, this morning, as far as circumstances, would permit. I spent some time with Dingley. I wrote the two preceeding letters to my friends.

In the afternoon, I purchased a translation of Schiller's "Cabal & Love";[74] & read part of it; & have finished it this evening. The piece, I should conjecture—bating some faults—must be good, in the original: and some scenes masterly. The translator has murdered it, in a most savage manner. It is neither English nor German, neither prose nor verse, but a strange, anomalous, preposterous, confusion of all.

Dunlap came here, just after sun-set. I went with him to his house. The Woolsey family were there. I came home a little before eight.

Thursday, 3rd

To Wm. Buel.

Your letter, of which you spake to me, when we were together at Lichfield, I found waiting for me, when I returned to New York; & I should have replied to it sooner, had I not been prevented by business of a less pleasing kind.

No, my friend, our mutual attachment shall neither perish, nor be impaired. We have esteemed each other; our esteem, I trust, is not founded on unworthy motives; & we will continue to esteem each other. It must not, however, be denied, that frequency of intercommunication is a great agent in preserving the vividness of attachment; & that almost all the advantages of friendship are lost to persons removed at considerable distance from each other, when they cease to correspond. This consideration ought, at least, to make us attentive to maintain our epistolary intercourse; & I hope that, hereafter, it may assume a more important character than can even be conferred on it by general & loose expressions of affection: and I acknowlege myself obliged to you, for kindly suggesting the idea, & pointing out the way. At present, it will not be convenient for me to attempt any thing: neither is it to be desired—For you have promised me a more full account of the Fever which has prevailed with you; & the little I have to remark on the late Sickness of this city, may be better subjoined to my reply, then, than added to this short letter, now.

In giving me the history of the Fever, which has appeared, for two successive years, in Sheffield, I must desire you to be as minute as circumstances will admit of your being. Would it not be well to take some notice of the situation of the place, generally, as well as particularly; of the Fever, in former years; of the diseases which generally prevail there; of those which preceeded

---

[71] Matthew 5:26.
[72] *Hamlet* III, i.
[73] Isaac Watts; *Horae Lyricae*, Book ii, "False Greatness."
[74] Schiller, *Kabale und Liebe* (1784) published in translation, *Cabal and Love* (Philadelphia, 1795); it appeared in London with the same title the same year.

& succeeded those in question; & to compare the success of the usual treatment, formerly, & now? I expect you to add as complete an account, as you can, of the Fever you saw at the Westward. To this Letter of your's, I design to reply, by giving you as perfect a history of the disease which afflicted this place, the last season, as the opportunities I had for observing it, & the effect of medicines on it, will permit. But this must be very incomplete—& I hope before that time, to be able to supply you, from other sources, with better information.

You will expect me to send you Samuel Latham Mitchill's Pamphlet on contagion: but I shall not send it, at present. He is about to publish a new edition, with additions equal to the present treatise. When this appears, I shall forward it to you, as soon as possible. This, I think, will be better than to pay for it twice. Still, if you are very desirous of the perusal, I will send the first edition, by the first conveyance, after receiving such an intimation.

I am well.

E. H. Smith.

Thursday Decr. 3. 1795.
Cedar St. No. 13. N. York.

The bells sounded the alarm of fire, just as we were sitting down to breakfast. Johnson was drest, & did some good; I did none. The fire was subdued in two hours; but not till it had done much damage. Several people, very unable to bear any loss, have suffered in consequence.

I have done but little, to-day. I have written, on business, to F. Wolcott; beside the foregoing letter, to Buel.

I have read several little matters; & have been twice to see Dingley, who is ill.

Alsop was here towards evening. He had a letter from Theodore. From him I learnt that Chauncey Goodrich[75] & his wife were in town. I waited on them—& also saw several of our national legislators who were with them. Since my return, I have been reading the Catechism of Health.[76]

Why is it that I feel so dull? Heavy, heavy, heavy. My intellect seems ponderous, & my body nerveless. I am unfit for any noble purpose.

Friday, 4th

I have done nothing this day worthy of record; as the memorial of it will shew. The business of dressing &c. is pitifully & shamefully long. It was after ten, this morning, before I was in a condition to go out. I went to see Dingley—he was better—we began to talk, & I stayed there till half past eleven. Yet this conversation left nothing worth remembering. I ought to have been at the Monthly Examination of the African School at eleven. This over-staying made me half an hour too late —there were only three Trustees of us there, & so nothing was done—that ought—or as it ought to have been done. Wm. & I went to a Book-Store. He bought some books—I wasted an hour: & another hour, in groaning about it, till dinner. Gahn & Roulet had been to see me, while I was out. Thus I lost the pleasure of their visit.

In the afternoon I went to see David Hosack—the professor of Botany in Cola. College; with a design to look over his books: but he fatigued me for two hours, with a pedantic display of his medical &c. science—& I came away, with a determination to lose no more time in visits to him.

I drank tea at H. Johnson's—with his wife & sister—& Wm.; & here I spent an hour of repose, at least—& it was very grateful to me.

We past the evening at Charles Lovegrove's: & I think the least interesting evening I ever spent there. There was his architect to pester us awhile; Dunlap came, said a few words, & hurried away; Mrs. L. was unwell, with a Catarrh; the child had a long crying spell; & the coal fire burnt dismally. It was ten when we reached home.

Saturday, 5th

I had a letter to deliver to Mrs. Watson, & I past half an hour at the house. From thence, I went to several Book-Stores, & devoted the greater part of the morning to looking over, & picking out some books.

This morning I finished reading a little treatise, of a young physician of Connecticut, named Thaddeus Clark, on Scarlatina Anginosa.[77] He is not an unpromising man.

I have read, too, Faust's "Catechism of Health." With some exceptions, it is a good book. Much of it is excellent. As far as I can judge, the Germans much excell us, in works of this kind. More of their men of learning & genius have turned their attention to the composition of their initial books—for the aid of children—& the unlearned.

Wm. & I spent much of the afternoon at Kent's—where we drank tea. We went to see on affairs of the Manumission Society—but, after discussing & arranging them, had much general talk. We all went, together, to Dunlap's; where the Friendly Club were to meet. Present, Dunlap, the Johnsons—H. & W.—the Woolseys—Kent, & myself. Dunlap read to us one of the letters in H. M. Wms's Letters from France—3rd vol. (supposed to be written by Christie) wherein the writer gives a very interesting account of his situation, in a tavern, on the frontiers—when he was following the course of the army. This introduced a mention of a story in Smollet's "Count Fathom"—a discussion of

---

[75] Yale 1776, a Hartford lawyer who held many offices including U.S. House, 1797-1801, U.S. Senate 1807-1813, mayor of Hartford 1812, lieutenant governor of Connecticut 1813.

[76] Bernhard C. Faust, *Catechism of Health for Use in Schools* (Philadelphia, 1795).

[77] Thaddeus Clark, *A Treatise on Scarlatine Agninosa* (Norwich, Connecticut, 1795).

Smollet's merit & character of a novel-writer—of Fielding & his novels—Richardson—Charlotte Smith, Holcroft, Godwin, &c. & of novels & novel writing, in general. We past on to dramatic writing—& discussed the subject, in several parts—& with relation to several performances: more particularly "Gustavus Vasa"—on which there appeared to be a variety of sentiment. I forgot what introduced a long discussion on Abbé Spallanzani's Experiments on Generation, & on the subject generally. A recent case, introduced a discussion of some questions on the law of insurance—& on the justice & policy of admitting the decisions of Foreign Admiralty Courts as conclusive evidence. Some other questions of general policy, were partially handled. We met at a little after six, & separated a little before eleven.

This evening has been better spent, than usual.

Sunday, 6th

To Mary S. Mumford.

I have been waiting, for near a week, with great impatience, in expectation of hearing from you. There was every reason why some of you should write, at least to our parents, as soon as Thomas reached home; and the calculations of all of us, brought the letters by the way of New York, & a week earlier than this date. As I have recd. none, I conclude that you have found a direct opportunity: for I can not, for a moment, suppose that you would delay writing, where the feelings of all your friends were so deeply interested. For myself, my anxiety is constantly on the increase. The long & unexpected absence of Thomas, could not fail to be the occasion of great inquietude to you, even if it were of no more dangerous inconvenience. He is with you, unquestionably, before this, & desire, most ardently, to learn that he found you well; &, tho' wishing for his return, yet not suffering from his absence. Your peculiar situation, too, increased my earnestness, & still maintains it; not so much because I was fearful of the issue; as because I was apprehensive least it's novelty might distress you, & the more his being away—with unnecessary anxieties & terrors. I can not but hope that all is well, & as it ought to be; that you have written, & your letters will soon reach me; & that your reply to this will be the occasion of joy, in more ways than one.

By Thomas, you recd. ample evidence of the undiminished attachment & affection of your friends. My poor, imperfect, letter, made but a sorry figure amid the copious epistles of your Lichfield correspondents. Still, I would willingly flatter myself, that it did not entirely fail to give you some satisfaction. It contained the expressions of more than brotherly love; which, alone, ought to make it of some value. It is in the same light that you must regard what I now write. After so serious an agitation as a journey to Connecticut occasions me, it takes a long time for me to get settled. The *lees* continue, for many days, to be intermixed with the *liquor*, & will not allow it to run off clear & sparkling. If it be not absolutely vapid, you must be content—"for the present."

I left Lichfield a week after Thomas—or about three weeks ago and, as it is possible that you may not have heard from thence, since he left there, I will inform you that I have heard repeatedly, & that all are very well. Our parents, (especially our mother) are better in health than I recollect to have seen them, for several years. The same is true of Mrs. Tracy; & most of our friends, in Lichfield. This, you will not doubt, augmented, in no common degree, the pleasure of the visit.

I have not time to write to Thomas & Abigail now. Give my love to them.

Farewell, my dear sister: Be careful of yourself; & write soon, to assure me of your health & happiness.

E. H. Smith.

Sunday, Decr. 6. 1795.
Cedar St. No. 13. New York.

You may have heard that your friend Lucy Parmele has a son. This event happened while I was at Lichfield.

E. H. S.

I had just written the above letter when Dunlap came in, & after some conversation, we, with Wm. walked out of town. Before walking Dunlap shewed me a new dialogue in his "Euphrasia."[78] During our walk, we had much general & agreable conversation. We walked several miles, for the day was remarkably pleasant—& it was dinner-time when we returned. I dined at H. Johnson's. There were there, beside the family, Miss Stuyvesant, & Miss Wirkam. We passed the afternoon together—& had some lively chat. After tea, I came away, with a design to visit at Woolsey's—where—strange to tell! I have not been for near a fortnight: but, when I came home, I found here—Elnathan Smith Jr.—a guest equally unexpected & wellcome. I was overjoyed at seeing him. Shortly after, Henry Gahn entered—they are acquainted—& spent some time; but went away, with a promise to return. Soon after his going out Timy. Pitkin jr.[79] came in—& all three past the evening, very sociably, together. Johnson came home, at the close; & Gahn returned in time to bid us good night.

Smith brought me two letters, from himself: one very long, & giving an account of his Western Tour. Johnson & I have sat, till it is near twelve at night to read it. Need I add that it is interesting?

Monday, 7th

After copying my letter, to Mary, & sending it to the Post Office, I sat down to the study of Anatomy, & read steadily on it, (excepting an interruption, hereafter to be mentioned) till dinner: about three hours.

---

[78] Not mentioned in Dunlap, *Diary* or Coad, *Life of Dunlap*.
[79] Timothy Pitkin (1766-1858; Yale 1785) was admitted to the bar for Hartford County in 1788, a representative in the Connecticut General Assembly for 22 sessions 1790-1805, 1805-1819, again a representative in the General Assembly until 1830. Author of *A Statistical View of the Commerce of the United States* (Hartford, 1816); *A Political and Civil History of the United States . . .* (New Haven, 1828).

I have resolved to review all my studies, & to extend them; & have chosen to begin with Anatomy, as that is most connected with the immediate subject of my practical attention. I have, therefore, added to my small stock of books, & am resolved still to add, as opportunity & fortune will allow. To-day I have only, as it were, begun upon the preface—reading the preliminary remarks & definitions of authors & impressing them on my memory. To-morrow I purpose entering on Osteology. A thousand disadvantages surround & hedge in every attempt of mine, of this kind. Poverty renders it impossible for me to see dissections, obtain preparations, skeletons, & even such plates as are best fitted for the end I have in view. I must depend on my recollection of what I have seen before—& on the assistance of such plates & books as my straitened circumstances will allow me to purchase. Still, I hope to effect something.

The interruption above referred to, was by Gardiner Baker, the keeper of the Museum[80] in the city, who wishes to publish an account of the fever; & has addrest a circular letter to the physicians—desiring their aid. He talked half an hour, or more—till I was heartily sick of him. I told two or three facts: he may use them, if he pleases: I can not write for him.

After dinner, I went to see Dingley, half an hour. He is still confined to his bed. When I returned Elnathan Smith Jr. was here. We conversed till sun-down. Thus I had no time for French, this day. He went out, on business, & I to W. W. Woolsey's. Before going thither, I recd. letters from Aurora, by which I learnt that Mary was safely delivered of a son—& that all were well. This news gave me inexpressible satisfaction. The letters were from Abby & Thomas. I drank tea at Woolsey's —from whence I came about seven. When I came home, I found that Henry Gahn had called for me, & left word for me to call at his lodgings. I did so & found there, beside himself, both Smith & Pitkin. I stayed till nine; & past the two hours very pleasantly.

Johnson & I entered on our course of history, this evening, for the first. Our plan is to read all the ancient Historians; & we commenced with Beloc's Version of Herodotus[81]—in which we read till half after ten—an hour & half—when, he feeling unwell, we dismist the book for this evening; & I only have sitten up to write these notes. No French—no Arithmetic—but letters, Medicine, History—this is something. Courage!

Tuesday, 8th

MEDICINE, I

The bones are said to be composed of the Phosphoric Acid & Calcareous Earth. In the Rickets, to the want of which of these component parts is the diseased flexibility & sponginess of the bones owing? If to the acid—of what is composed, & how may it be administered so as to afford relief? If to the earth, in what manner may it be applied, in it's proper form, so as to combine with the superabundant acid?

This day, which has been rainy & windy, has been spent much as it ought to be, when there is no particular business to call me abroad. I read a little German; employing an hour upon it, & attaining the knowlege of one sentence. From that time, till dinner, I read Anatomy. After dinner, I read French—in Tissot—till sundown. Dunlap past half an hour with me—which brought it to five. I made a visit to Mrs. Miller's— where I stayed till near seven. There I saw two sensible men, from Geneva—who have fled the commotions of that unhappy city, to take up their residence in America. One is a Calvinian clergyman—named Duby: the other, whose name I do not recollect, was Professor of Languages in the University of Geneva. I was pleased with them both. After returning home, I applied myself, till nine, to Arithmetic—which I am undertaking to study scientifically; & so mean to proceed on thro' every branch of the Mathematics.

Johnson not being in, at nine, I took up a new medical author, & read till ten. when he came home—& we pursued Herodotus till half after eleven.

Elnathan has [not] been here, thro' the whole day— what is the reason? I trust I shall not fail to see him, tomorrow.

This sedentary life is fatiguing, from long disuse, it must be owned; & I feel heartily tired. But then, the satisfaction of having done, in some sort, one's duty is so sweet—it more than counterbalances all fatigue. I have applied myself ten hours, to-day. This is more time, than I expect to have, in general—& indeed more than I wish, till I become a little more accustomed to it. Beside, there is danger of setting off too furiously—of soon expending one's forces; & I hope, at length, to proceed, with moderation, but with perseverance. Suppose an application of seven hours. This will amount to something in as many years; And, in as many years, I hope to quit this city—forever—as a place of residence. This Winter will, probably, determine whether I can persevere in any plan of study; this year, may resolve me, whether I shall longer continue a citizen of this city, & a practitioner of the art of Health.

Wednesday, 9th

I wrote a few lines of introduction, for Elnathan Smith Jr., both to Joseph & Charles. After this, I read anatomy, almost without interruption, till dinner-time. After dinner, I read the papers, & also went to a Bookseller's, after Condorcet's Work—having left the copy of Mr. Roulet's, with my trunk, in Connecticut. I came home & read in Condorcet till after sun-set; except that Elnathan past half an hour with me. Then I made a visit, of half an hour, to Dingley; leaving whom, I went to Moses Rogers's; where I drank tea, & stayed till near seven. At M. Rogers's I saw Mrs. Colt of Paterson, who

---

[80] The American Museum, supported by the Tammany Society occupied a room in City Hall provided by the corporation.
[81] William Belloc (1756-1817), *Miscellanies; Consisting of Poems, Classical Abstracts, and Oriental Apologues* (London, 1795).

was well, seemed pleased to see me, & politely re-invited me to their house. I was just seated at my Arithmetic, when Elnathan came in, & Johnson with him; & shortly after H. Gahn; & in a few minutes, Ty. Pitkin jr. They stayed till nine; & the talk was lively, tho' not to much purpose. When they were gone, we sat down to Herodotus, & read till near eleven. Then I took up arithmetic; & looked over some part of what I attended to last evening: so that I have made no advances, in the System.

I am thus minute, in detailing my method of studying, at first—because, for the most part, hereafter, when I pursue my reading regularly, I shall content myself with a bare mention of it. Thus it will be understood, that every other day, I read German for one hour, in the morning & then devote myself, till dinner, to Medicine; that, after dinner, I read French, till sun-set, & then visit till seven; & that, from seven to nine, I apply to Mathematical studies, & from that time, till eleven, to History. These regulations, admit, systematically, of some interruptions: as, for instance, Sunday is occupied in writing, or in Moral reading: & Saturday evening devoted to the Club. Beside, every study gives way to professional calls, & often to those of friendship: & I must lay my account not to escape, without frequent interruptions, from the visits of those I love, & those I am indifferent to. This arrangement secures to me, apparently, the leisure for medical studies; to which it is most important that I should attend; & of which I hope to effect a pretty general & thorough review, as far as the authors I possess, & may possess, will enable me, in the course of the next two ensuing years. In that period, likewise it is possible, if no misfortune happen, nor no new plan of life be determined on, that I may go thro' with the general authors on Mathematics, & acquire such a knowlege of that all-important division of science, as will fit me for pursuing the study of Natural Philosophy, & of other sciences which depend upon it, to profit, & with pleasurable ease. French, German, & History, are almost matters of course.

Thursday, 10th
To Reuben Smith, of Lichfield.

The inclosed letter was recd. on Monday evening last, together with others, directed to me, & which contained the information which is, undoubtedly conveyed in this. I felt my mind relieved of a great burthen of anxiety, at the news of an event, so desirable in itself, & rendered so much more so, by the circumstances of distress & apprehension—(at least to us) which preceeded it. I felicitate you, my mother, sister, & all our friends, on so fortunate a termination of all our fears.

As yet, I have recd. neither my trunk, nor the other articles, which were to accompany it. I trust, however, that they are on their way, & that they will speedily come to hand. I think you must have gotten your medicine &c. home, by this time; & hope that you found them equal to your expectations. I shall inclose Philips & Clark's receit for a second hundred dollars—& also Geo: Bunce & Co's. for another year's Herald.

When I was last at Lichfield, you may remember, I spake to you, on the subject of hiring a small sum of money, for a certain time; & which you supposed might be obtained, on proper security, at the rate of 10 per cent. The more I reflect on my present situation & future prospects, the more I see the absolute necessity of some aid of this sort, & am convinced of my future ability to repay a loan equal to that which I shall solicit. At the lowest estimate, what I am now in possession of, can not be worth less than 500 dols.; & it is a kind of property, the value of which admits of but little fluctuation—being chiefly books & furniture. What I want is, to procure two, three, four, or five hundred dollars, if possible, for three years: i.e. I wish to borrow that sum of money, with a certainty of not being called upon to pay it before that time, but with liberty to pay it, within that time, if I please: and for the use of this sum, I will consent to pay, yearly, & punctually, 10 per cent. interest, or at that rate, till the whole of the principal is paid. I am tolerably sure that I can not only pay the interest, punctually, but also, that, within, or by, the time specified, I shall be able to discharge the loan. At any rate I consider myself as possest of sufficient property, to answer the demand—if it should ever come to be pressing. Now, what I would further request, is, that—(if the money can be had on these terms, at Lichfield, & if the lender is not willing to loan it on my simple note,) you would consent to sign the obligation with me; & I will, if you request it, secure you, as far as my note will render you secure. If the time of payment may be still further protracted than three years, I shall be the more pleased; & I would obtain the highest sum mentioned, if it may be had. I wish you to reply to this part of my letter, by the earliest opportunity. I would not urge a request of this kind, did there not appear to me the most unavoidable necessity for adopting some measure of this nature; & were I not satisfied that, if effected, it would be, not only in my power to answer every obligation which it imposes on me, but, greatly for my advantage. You must decide.

To my mother, sister, & friends, present my most affectionate remembrances.

E. H. Smith.

Thursday, Decr. 10. 1795.
Cedar St. No. 13. New York.

The regular business of this day has been variously broken in upon. In the morning, by the necessity of writing the above letter (which inclosed one, from Aurora, to my mother, conveying the news of the birth of a grandson) by the reception of letters from the President of the N. Jersey Abolition Society, & from Frederic Wolcott; doing some business & writing a short letter, to this last; & by a short visit from El. Smith Jr.—who left town, for Phila.: In the afternoon, by some business of accounts, & a visit from Alsop: & in the evening, by staying from five, till nine, at Mrs. Lovegrove's. Mr. L. is at Amboy—Wm. came there, & I left him there. I read no German—We read no history

—&, except on the *Arithmetic,* my other studies were not attended to their usual length of time—*that* occupied the historic hours—as Wm. was absent.

Mrs. L. seemed somewhat out of spirits. She was deprest by the reading of Miss Williams's Letters—which her accumulated sensibility rendered too afflicting to her. Conversation, with us all, very egotistical; but fruitful in nothing deserving of particular note. It is after 12 at night. Good night, [line missing.]

Friday, 11th

It was in July 1794 that I commenced the history of my own life. I had contemplated such an undertaking for a long time, & when I began, proceeded to sketch out, rapidly, & by the efforts of my own memory, the events of my childhood. In this manner, I had brought down the narrative to the end of the first term of my Collegiate life, when I discontinued the composition. This narrative was merely a thread of facts, which was designed to be interwoven with many others, expected to be derived from the communications of parents & friends; & with a recital of the sentiments connected with them, at the time of their taking place, & the reflections which now occurred to me, on their revision. It would require an effort of memory, to which I am not now equal, to determine what were the particular causes of this interruption in the completion of my Story—which has been extended to the present time. It is most probable that it may be, principally, ascribed to one alone—Indolence. Be that as it may, it is fortunate that I proceeded no further; for the undertaking was commenced under the influence of feelings which ought, surely, never to mark a performance of the kind: under the still vigorous influence of impressions hostile to virtue & destructive of energy. Had they continued, they would have diffused over my narration, as they then already had over my soul, an air of melancholy, & querulous repining, unbecoming a man—& most of all a man whose profession, as well as his duty, requires an undiminished & unwavering fortitude. As the history, if it ever be written, will be continued under very different impressions, I have thought fit to insert, in this place, that I may preserve, the Introduction to what I then wrote: not only, because, it can, hereafter form no part of the work itself, but because it serves to illustrate the history of my mind, & mark it's progress, from error to truth, from despair & inactivity to assurance & energy.

"When, with a retrospective eye, I survey the days which are past; when I arrest the fleeting images of former times, and consider what I have done, and what I have felt; tho' ruddy youth still blooms upon my face, I become astonished at the length of my existence; and can scarcely believe that I am not already in the wane of life, and near the termination of it's strange, eventful period. To me, however they may appear to others, the years, which are gone, seem numerous and long; they exist, to my imagination and memory, in all their extension; nor does the future elongate itself so far in perspective, as the past stretches back towards the commencement of my being. And, if the consciousness of duration depend rather on the succession of ideas in the minds, than on the diurnal & annual revolutions of the earth, an obvious solution of this paradox appears: for my life, tho' outwardly, neither very deeply or curiously variegated, has been marked with many revolutions of opinion & sentiment, of success & delight, of passion and distress. Events, considerable in number, and powerful in effect; events, operating on my mind with uncontroulable & afflictive energy; and dressed by my imagination, and arrayed by my heart, in fearful & ruinous importance; have exercised, over every power of my soul, and every action of my life, a wondrous, tho', mostly, a concealed, influence.

"Sweet were the days of my childhood! embittered only by little anxieties, and trifling disappointments. Hope swiftly succeeded to distrust; and the dimple hollowed itself under the tear which yet stood on my cheek. War, which then ravaged my country, was, to me, rather a pastime, than a terror. Unconscious of it's many & dire calamities, my heart exulted in the sound of the trumpet, the fife, and the drum; the glistering arms pleased my eyes; and tales of victory ravished my fancy. My bosom beat, and my soul panted, to follow the soldier to the field; to mingle in the glorious conflict; to wrest the sword from the destroyer, & turn the thunder of the oppressor upon himself.

"Delightful days! with what fond enthusiasm do I look back, & reflect, upon ye! What joy does it still convey to my bosom, to review & reconsider the innocence which reigned in my heart, the wanton and guiltless frolics of the day; the peace which waited on the hours of serene repose; and the tranquillity which welcomed the departure of refreshing sleep, & the approaches of awakening morn! O days! ye days of bliss! days crowned with delight! few and transient indeed ye were; yet still does your recollection refresh & invigorate my mind. With melancholly pleasure do I love to compare your calm, contented progress, with the stormy & afflicting advances of later years: to trace the origin of error, to view the birth of misfortune, to lift the concealing veil from treasured griefs, and dissolve the mystic charms which bind, in stern enchantment, the melancholly thought, to near & pressing misseries.

"What is of more importance, to man, than the knowlege of man? What so useful, to an individual, as an acquaintance with himself? And how shall this science be obtained? And where are the most certain means of discovering to our own hearts, what they really are; and of bringing our actual character before the penetrating eyes of our own understandings? To have all our secret sentiments & wishes, all our hidden & open actions, exposed to our reflection, and arranged in regular succession & array—what method gives more ample promise of obtaining self-knowlege? Man is so variable a being, susceptible of such infinite changes, and capable of such wonderful diversities, that, in no other way, than by composing an actual history of himself, can he come to a thorough knowlege of his true nature & absolute constitution. How faint & evanescent are our ideas of what we have been, till, by the aid of memory, we have methodically disposed & reviewed our lives!

"To see what I have been, therefore, and to have a connected view of actions, feelings, and opinions, from my earliest years, are, in part, the motives which have influenced me to undertake the composition of the history of myself. But these are not the only motives. No! —I would record what are my present sentiments of those things which have already past; & which are daily passing; I would trace the rise, and delineate the progress, of all those connections with my fellow-beings, which have been to me such fertile sources of delight and grief; I would fix, while yet the recollection lives in my mind, the sentiments, the actions, the characters, of my friends—of their friends—finally, of all those distinguished personages, with whom, accident, or design have made me acquainted.

"Minute circumstances rapidly escape, how lasting soever may be their coincident impressions. But how important are these minutiae! How much does the explication, of every considerable event, depend of these very things, which common minds regard as too trifling to deserve attention!

"With mingled sensations of pleasure and distress, do I commence, & shall I continue, this undertaking. To record every thought, wish, action, and suffering, how arduous, yet how useful, the task! How many pleasing, how many mournful, images, must I recal! What instances of folly and of vice! What moments of wisdom & of virtue! Difficult, truly difficult, is the labour which I have imposed on myself. Yet, what benefit shall I not derive from it! For, tho' I replunge myself into the midst of darkness & despair; tho' anguish & agony, disappointment, and almost death & infamy themselves, surround me; still, will there not be many preceeding scenes of joy, many subsequent pictures of resignation? If the fairest fabric of human happiness be overthrown; if every hope of joy, every expectation of fondly anticipated delight be wrecked; yet, will not some scattered fragment of the edifice, some wandering recollection of the vanished bliss, still remain, to comfort, if not console me?—Yes, assuredly, there will: Patience may unnerve the arm of grief; and Peace may steep her poppies in the cup of woe, and occasionally cheer the dark, dark gloom of melancholly remembrance.

"To thee, my dear, my long-tired, my unshaken, friend, whoever thou art—whether the fertile Connecticut receives thy form; whether thou delightest to brave, with sinewy arm, the lordly Hudson; or to dip thy tender foot in the stream of shady Schuylkill; to thee do I address these accents of my heart. It is thou, and thou alone, who canst fully comprehend, and rightly estimate, what thou seest before thee: for to thee only am I known. O, read not with too severe an eye! Few, few indeed, are they, who have not, sometimes erred; & whose lives exhibit one unvaried spectacle of harmony & beauty. On myself heaviest do my errors fall: Aggravate them not, by thy disdain; increase them not, by thy detestation. Thou canst not hate me more, for the wrong I have committed, than I hate myself. Alas! is not self-condemnation a sufficient curse?"

It is evident, from the preceding paper, that I thought my life had been an almost unexampled series of misfortunes; & it is probable that such an idea would have prevailed thro' the whole History, had it then been written. It is true that I have not been fortunate & happy, beyond example—a sufficient proof of which is that I should ever, seriously, entertain such a belief, as "The Introduction" evinces me to have entertained. But it is not true that I have been so wonderfully, so markedly, unfortunate—neither was I, at that time, so wretched, if I had consulted the voice of reason, as much as I did that of passion. Were there no other argument against the indulgence of passion, than what a consideration of the instance before us would furnish, the conclusion must, inevitably, be against it. Truth can never dwell in the same bosom with Passion. At the very moment, when I was painting myself as the most wretched & miserable of men, as one devoted to despair & hopeless of relief, I was, beyond the lot of mortals, happy in numerous & exalted friends, in competence, in peace, in a reputation beyond my deserts, & in the possession of stores of knowlege—not usual, at least in this country, to persons of my age. Such are the vicious effects of the passions; & of that Passion which has been called the ennobler of hearts, & saviour of mankind.

The regular business of this day, also, has been interrupted: tho' not so much as yesterday's. I have read German, Medicine, French, Arithmetic, & History: tho' neither as much as I wished. In the forenoon much time was occupied, in endeavoring to collect a small sum of money. I met, at the Coffee-House, S. A. Law—who I had not seen, since we were separated in New Haven—where we met & meant to have journeyed hither, together. I learned, to my surprize, that Decius Wadsworth was in town. In the afternoon I was still more surprized at seeing my earliest friend, Thos. O'H. Crosswell, enter. He stayed here two hours—during which time we had a long, domestic, series of conversations. The family were out, at N. Webster's, where I called—& also at Woolsey's. I went to Dunlap's—where I found the last, & also M. Rogers's family. I stayed there till seven &, coming back with Woolsey, stopped, half an hour, at his house. Returned—I applied to arithmetic till nine—& then to writing on the preceeding Paper—which—this day, I have not finished, but hope to, to-morrow. We read history till eleven. Since then, I have written of the Paper, above-referred to—& thus far, on this day. Wadsworth called here, while I was out.

Saturday, 12th

Things went on regularly till dinner. I recd a letter,

from C. B. Brown, accounting for his long & mysterious silence. As I was returning from dinner, a woman, who was sweeping in the street, flirted a broom-full of dust into my right eye. This accident occasioned me some pain, & still does, & effectually prevented me from reading. This deprivation lasted three or four hours; which were enlivened by the society & converse of Wm., Dunlap, Alsop, & Decius Wadsworth;[82] the three last of whom severally called on me. Decius is well, & looks better than I expected, & seems in better spirits. He stayed but a short time, & is to call again. Dunlap read me some passages from his Novel of Charles Tomson[83] in which he has made some little progress. I was pleased with them. In the evening—Friendly Club met here, in Johnson's turn. Present, Dunlap, Kent, the Woolseys, Johnson & myself, & Alsop visitor. We had much, & very interesting, *conversation*; but too variegated for me, now, to methodize—late as it is, & much as my eye complains—of my having written, since my friends went away, the 57th & 58th pages—& these notices of to-day.

Sunday, 13th

To John Allen.[84]

If I have not written to you as early, after my return to this place, as you may have expected, and if I should not, now, write to you with my wonted copiousness, you must attribute it to the pressure of various concerns, coming upon me, immediately after my arrival, & which I have not, even yet, entirely freed myself from. Beside, this reason, which is sufficient for a delay in writing to all my friends, operates with peculiar force, in the present instance. For, where a correspondence has been so long interrupted as to furnish no immediate topic for discussion, it requires more than ordinary mental tranquillity to enable me to re-create it, & to fashion, by the exertion of a single energy of the will, a subject & method, the first of which shall not fail to interest, nor the second to delight. You can not but have observed how various are the powers of men, in this respect; & how contemptibly the minds of some appear to have dwindled, when they come to give a written language to that, which, in ordinary conversation, seemed to possess no little share of brilliancy & truth. There are so many resting places, in common *talkings* (for they scarcely deserve the name of *conversations*,) so many ways of sliding out of difficulties, by means of an apt illusion, a pun, a repartee, or a new subject, that men of superficial minds, & scanty information, oftentimes, obtain

---

[82] 1768-1821; Yale 1785; a lawyer who in 1792 accepted a commission in the army, resigned in 1802 with the rank of major. Rejoined the army, 1812-1821.

[83] Apparently never completed. He was "thinking" about his novel August 2, 1797; August 21, 1798 he wrote a short (new?) first paragraph. Dunlap, *Diary* 1: p. 127; 2: pp. 331-332.

[84] John Allen (1763-1812) moved to Litchfield from Great Barrington, Massachusetts, Litchfield Law School, admitted to Connecticut Bar 1786, member State House 1793-1796, U.S. House 1797-1799, Connecticut Supreme Court of Errors 1800-1806.

great credit, where they deserve none. The touch-stone of these, is the pen. When men venture to assume this instrument, we looking for something more than the *passable*: we expect precision, pertinence, method: and, in no other species of composition do men so miserably fail, in these particulars, as in letter-writing. This is, perhaps, because they mistake the purpose of letters. For "a letter," they say, "is of no consequence." They regard it as a thing of trivial concern, & make it the slovenly vehicle of crude & contemptible opinions. But, surely, you, my dear sir, do not think thus lightly of the importance of these substitutes for conversation. (You will bear in mind that I am not speaking of mere letters of business.) You do not think it sufficient to have scrawled half-a-dozen, almost unintelligible lines, concerning some report of the day, & to have dismist the abortive thing, under the title of a Letter. Much as you may love your friends, and dearly as you prize their welfare, you will not be satisfied with mere testimonials of the continuance of their affection, assurances of their happiness, & wishes for your own. Letters, in your mind, must certainly assume a higher, a more dignified character. What this character is, becomes evident enough, when we have reflected, for a moment, on their design. Had I been absent from my friend, for many months, hearing nothing from him, no communication subsisting between us, and were we, after such an absence to meet, should I content myself with bare inquiries after his health, & his pecuniary prosperity? & would be satisfied with corresponding information respecting myself? Should we both, be likely to suppose that the purpose of our meeting was then effected; & quietly return to the same remote situations, & to the same long-continued silence? Is it not more probable, nay, is it not certain, that we should indulge, ardently, passionately, & reasonably, indulge, in many long, & to us, interesting, conversations? That we should not feel each other's company a burthen, for one, two, three, or even more hours? And, that, tho' our health & prosperity might, reciprocally, claim some part of our attention, we should seize on the occasion, with avidity, to discuss all those questions, which, during our absence, from each other, had greatly affected us? impressed us with strong convictions of their truth or falsity, & influenced our sentiments to become more fixed, or less stable? Should not we seek, in fine, to unfold the treasured volume of our soul, & expose the variegated pages to the inspection of our friend? If this be true, if it be true that "letters are intended as the substitute of discourse," can there, any longer, remain a doubt as to what they should be? Is it not clear, that the more copiously they treat of important, of useful, matters, the more valuable they become, & the more perfectly they answer their true end? It has been remarked, of the celebrated Grotius, & greatly to his praise, that he wrote numerous letters, & that all his letters were complete treatises. Compared with such a standard, what would be the character of the infinitude of puny existences which daily arrogate to themselves the sacred appellation of Letters? Shall I answer you in the spirited & forcible language of my friend Charles B. Brown? Speaking on this subject, in one of his Letters, he says—"Letters, indeed, as they are usually written, are the ghosts, the skeletons, of Conversation—'with bones as marrowless & blood as cold' as any gibbetted representation of "death whatever. Of such mockeries of wit & ease, such shadowy resemblances, of life & nature, it is not easy to speak in any other language than that of anger or ridicule."

With such ideas of what letters ought to be, & of what they too often are, (how much soever allied to their common condition my own may customarily appear,) you will not wonder that I was somewhat slow not rashly to adventure on what I regard in so serious a point of view. A few letters have, a long time ago, passed between us, but I consider this as the commencement of a new correspondence, & would wish to make it a fertile source of entertainment & instruction to each of us. If this idea please you, if you feel disposed & will endeavour to conform to it, nothing shall be wanting, on my part, as far as I am able, to realize so just a notion, & to effect so desirable consequence. To this end it is not necessary that we should write frequently; but it is necessary that, when we do write, we write copiously. When communications are frequent, they are apt to become very brief: & in short letters, all the real use of such an intercourse is lost, by frivolous inquiries, tiresome introductions, & impertinent conclusions. They are like fashionable tea-parties; where all is hurry & confusion while the company are together; where every one is under constraint by the fear of not doing every thing just as it ought to be done, or of injuring her fine cloathes; where the value & merit of fans, ribbons, & muslins, are the topics of discussion; & where, in fine, each guest is glad when the company separate, & the hostess happy to see her visitors depart. But long letters, when not very frequent, are like those visits which our distant friends make, when they come to stay with us, occasionally, several days, in the true family way; where all things take their accustomed course; & where we are more anxious to enjoy their society, than to display the richness of our habiliments & the magnificence of our furniture.

Do you feel this subject, as I do? For it is important, if we mean to maintain an epistolary intercourse, that on this point, at least, our minds should harmonize. If you do, let me hear from you speedily; & in the mean time be assured of my firm & increasing esteem.

Sunday, Decr. 13. 1795.
Cedar St. No. 13. New York.   E. H. Smith.

P. S. When I was in Lichfield, you had some expectation of visiting N. York & Phila. this winter. I would inform you, that Dunlap & myself, & perhaps Alsop & Johnson, shall go to Phila. the last of the present month —so as to be there on the first day of Jany. next—& that we shall return in about a week, from that time. Why can not you accompany us?

My love to Danl. & Betsey.
                    E. H. Smith.

You are, perhaps, not unacquainted with the character of James Kent, the Professor of Law in Columbia College, &, possibly, may have seen an Introductory Lecture, to his Course last year, which was published at the request of the Trustees. He is now printing three additional Lectures—the next, in succession, to that which he has already published. They will be out in a short time; & will, no doubt, do equal credit to his head & heart; & be the cause of as much pleasure to his readers, as of reputation to himself. I have desired him to put into my hands thirty copies; which I design to transmit to you, & hope you will not hesitate to take upon yourself the trouble of disposing of them, on the most advantageous terms. I have not time to express to you the insensibility, which, almost universally, prevails here, in respect to the merit of this man; & I should feel a deep regret, were this effort, which he is making, with the noble design of awakening the sluggish minds of the youth of this city to a just apprehension of the importance of the profession they have chosen, not only to fail of it's effect, but involve it's disinterested author in an expence he is little able to bear. When I send you the Pamphlets alluded to, I may, perhaps, enlarge on a theme, fruitful, & shamefully fruitful, in numerous, important, & interesting topics of discussion & inquiry.

Monday, Decr. 14. 1795.
Cedar St. No. 13. N. York.   E. H. Smith.

After writing the preceeding letter, and adding the first P. S. I went to see Dingley; who, having imprudently gone abroad too soon, was reduced to almost as bad a predicament as at first. From thence, I visited a patient of his, & returned to dinner. After dinner, I visited at A. Hart's, principally with the design of obtaining, of Elias Cowles, some facts, in respect to his case, which had escaped my memory. I did obtain them. Then I visited Dingley again. I went to Woolsey's, to see his child; &, unexpectedly, stayed there to tea, & till after six. There I read Sir John Shore's first discourse to Asiatic Society—on the literary labours of Sir Wm. Jones.[85] From Woolsey's, I went to Mrs. Lovegrove's— (he is still out of town) where I found Johnson & Dunlap—who had, severally, come there. Dunlap stayed but half an hour, after I came in. We talked constantly —on the President's speech—& chiefly on Swedenborg —Air—Animal magnetism—& subjects connected therewith. Some stories were told; but no light gained. After

---

[85] Jones, president of the Asiatic Society of Bengal, died in 1794. His friend John Shore, Lord Teignmouth, succeeded him and delivered an address on the "Literary History" of his predecessor which was first published in 1795 and frequently republished. He also became Jones's literary biographer.

Dunlap went away, I read Mrs. L. my friend El Smith's Letter, on the Falls of Niagara, &c. with which she appeared much pleased. The remainder of the evening was chiefly devoted to conversing on Amboy—& circumstances connected with their removal to that place. Some little incidents had lately turned up, which affected the mind of Mrs. L. very powerfully; & we endeavoured to collect as many topics of consolation & encouragement, as the time & circumstances would suggest: not, altogether, without effect.

The opposite page, & this, so far, has been written, this, Monday, forenoon—it being very late when we returned home, last evening.

Monday, 14th

I had just gone thro' with my German exercise, when Mr. Gahn entered my room, & with him, Nathaniel Terry.[86] I was gratified with this visit, because I always esteemed Terry, notwithstanding those vices which once deformed his character, but which ill-health, & the operations of his own good sense, have jointly contributed, long since, to bannish. They stayed with me an hour, & we all repaired to the lodgings of Decius Wadsworth with whom we were another hour. I then visited a patient; & had just finished the preceeding, & part of this page, when it was dinnertime. After dinner, I copied my letter to John Allen. This held me till near sun-down. Then I sat out to get up, from the landing, my Trunk, & some other things from Lichfield, which a short letter from my father had informed me had arrived. This I effected. I drank tea at Noah Webster's —where were Jedidiah Morse[87]—author of the Geography—a brother of Mrs. W's—& her niece Eliza Elliot; the same agreable young lady who was here last May or June. I stayed till seven—When I returned home—I past an hour in overlooking my newly-arrived trunk, & some of the Papers it contained; & also read Alsop's "Stow Wood"[88]—a poem. It had numerous beauties; but is deficient both in order, & in the want of an object. There are some inelegant expressions in it; & many single words, quite inadmissible. I sat down to Arithmetic for two hours. Thus Medicine & French have been lost this day. Wm. came home at ten. We might have had one historical hour: but he was indisposed for it, & we diverted ourselves with President Stiles's History of the Judges.

I had almost omitted to mention that Dunlap was here in the morning, to inform me that the Commedians were soon to be here, & that I must make the necessary dispositions, in respect to my Opera. From the account he has recd the Company is unprecedently efficient. I am afraid that this business will not a little interfere with the plan of study I have marked out for myself.

On Saturday, for the first time, Dunlap mentioned to me—that Mr. Burns, the Physician of Amboy, is about to leave that place. We talked on the subject to-day— for Dunlap wishes me to fill the vacancy. He thinks it would furnish me with an ample support. I can come to no determination to go there—at present.

Tuesday, 15th

To Mrs. Tracy.

A longer period has elapsed, without my having written to you, than I expected when we last parted. But this has been unavoidable; and, as I know you have confidence in my sincerity, I shall not engross any part of this leisure to detail the reasons why it has been so. It is sufficient, that they have nothing of the unfortunate connected with them, but this interruption to our correspondence, to which I have alluded.

When I look back upon what passed at Lichfield, during the few days which I spent there, I find that, of the many lengthy conversations which I had previously planned, few have taken place; & that more than half the purpose of my visit was completely uneffected. I am now convinced of the folly of expecting any thing better; unless it were possible, (which it is not,) to confine my visits to a single family, & almost to a single individual. Lengthy visits I can not make to Lichfield: both my interest & duty forbid. And, when I am there, the number of those on whom duty & inclination prompt me to call, is so great, that my time is absolutely frittered away, without my being able to satisfy either those I wish to see, or myself. What then remains for me to do? Or is there any other remedy for this evil than the Pen? You know not, you can not know, how much was suspended on a single determination, which you hesitated to make. Had you resolved to cease to write, all power of affording mutual assistance, & deriving mutual aid, must have forever been at an end: for, in the few & hasty conversations, which a few days annually allow us, what could we have known, what could we have done? Perhaps you did not view the subject in this

---

[86] Terry was Smith's classmate at Yale; he wrote him a rather remarkable medical letter six days later in an effort to get him to help make clear the nature of his illness. Terry obviously recovered his health. He practised law in Hartford, represented Hartford in the General Assembly from 1804 to 1815, was chief justice of the County Court in 1807, a member of Congress 1817-1819, a member of the convention for framing a new Connecticut constitution in 1818, president of the Hartford Bank from 1819 to 1828, and mayor of Hartford 1824-1831.

[87] 1761-1826; Yale 1783; D.D. University of Edinburgh, 1794, studied theology under the Rev. Jonathan Edwards (the son, Princeton, 1765) and became a preacher; held the pastorate of the First Congregational Church in Charleston, Massachusetts (1788-1820). He had a great and, for the time, unusual interest in the condition of the Indians, investigated the situation as a government agent for the War Department and published a report at his own expense (1820); he was also interested in plight of the Negroes and was one of the incorporators of the American Board of Commissioners for Foreign Missions. His bibliography contains some thirty-two articles, books, and published sermons; his most important contribution was the first geography in the United States, *Geography Made Easy* (New Haven, 1784) which went into many editions, revisions and enlargements. Father of Samuel F. B. Morse.

[88] Not mentioned in Harrington's biography of Alsop.

light; & I was fearful of pressing any argument, as far as I could have wished, lest I might appear more actuated by the spirit of selfishness than of truth, & lest you might yield that to my importunity which your own better feelings & sounder judgement would have withheld. But now, since it is decided that our correspondence shall not be given up, & since this decision has been the result of your own, unbiased, reflections, I feel myself at liberty to speak freely on the principle which I, while with you, but partially hinted at.

With whatever fooleries of superstition mankind may choose to adorn morality, & whatever they may determine on as it's real & permanent basis, all, who pretend to reason at all, must allow that there is, concerning all questions, but one opinion which is true, and concerning all actions, but one line of conduct which is just. Truth must be one, & Justice must be one. You will forgive the repetition but, of consequence, there can not be two opposite opinions, concerning the same subject, equally true; nor two opposite modes of conduct, with respect to the same thing, equally just. What then is our duty? Is it not, to seek, earnestly, after truth; to embrace it, when found, at every hazard; & to cling to it, as the only *pearl of great price* which the universe contains? Is it not equally our duty to pursue, with a disinterested zeal, the path of justice; to exercise it on every occasion; & to sacrifice, on it's pure & holy altar, & before it's sacred shrine, & according to it's rigid & eternal law, every prejudice, of how many pleasurable emotions soever it may to us have been the source? If this be true—and it can not be denied—we have but one inquiry to make, concerning any action—"Is it just?" This answered in the affirmative, it becomes our duty to perform it; from which to swerve, even in a tittle, is to be criminal. Few persons, fewer than, at the first glance, you would imagine, act from motives of duty. The greater part never make the inquiry, concerning any action proposed to them, (to perform it) whether it is their duty or not; they catch at hazard the little morality they ever possess; & continue, thro' life, the blind & passive machines of imitation or fear. This being the case, it is no more to be expected that they will form proper opinions concerning the actions of others, than that their own will be according to an intelligent perception of right. It follows, of necessity, that, as there are few who are competent to judge, there are few whose judgements ought to influence our conduct. Another necessary consequence is, that the actions of those who are influenced by motives of duty, must, forever, be liable to misconstruction. From a consideration of these things, two important truths result. One, founded on the very nature of duty; the other, the irresistible admonition which is forced upon us by this condition of mankind. If it be clearly right for me to perform any action, it is my duty to perform it, & no consideration ought to have any force with me to prevent it's performance: And, as it is unavoidable that, in the course of the performance of my duty, for any considerable period, I should avoid unjust & ungenerous imputations, from persons not competent to decide, & as the fear of subjecting myself to such imputations, would tend to restrain me from the performance of my duty, were I to indulge it; it becomes, equally, my duty to act without reference to the opinion of the generality of mankind, as much as it was, before, my duty to perform what I thought it right for me to perform. In short, the whole is reducible to this: to *mere opinion* I am to give no heed; I am bound to examine, candidly & attentively, the *arguments,* of all; but I have no right to *substitute the convictions of another, for those of my own mind.* As the consequence of error is unhappiness, so the consequence of my own error, is my own unhappiness, & this, whether I am singly affected, or whether others are involved in the effects of my erroneous conduct. It is, therefore, my peculiar business, property, & duty, to examine & determine for myself; for on me must rest the evil or the good.

You will see, in an instant, whither all this tends, You will perceive, at the same time, that the only real question, in reference to what gave rise to this discussion, is whether it is right for us, situated as we are, to maintain an epistolary intercourse. For myself, I have no secrets—I have nothing of which to be ashamed—I have not compact to make with the compassion of the world: my sentiments, as well as my person, are the property of the species. If I am wrong—why should I hide error? let the world know it, & I shall have a greater chance of being set right. I pretend not to perfection, but I do pretend to integrity. And what is there to be feared? The *malice* of mankind? Ah! are you not, long since, convinced, that the most inflexible adherence to justice can not secure you from *it's* ferocious & empoisoned attacks? When the mists of slander would attempt to dim the meridian lustre of the glory of Washington, what have we, who have neither name, nor fame, nor ought but the conscious glow of honesty to guard us, what have we to screen us from the infectious power? Who are we, that we should expect to escape

The slings & arrows of outrageous fortune,[89]

When their conjoined & unremitting violence does not fear to assail a Man, the invariable terror of whose life, & the unwavering splendor of whose virtue, have realized every fairy model of benevolent & seraphic imagination, & cast a wide & refulgent beam of light over the history of man?

If I am erroneous, in applying arguments of this nature to you, you best know how to pardon my mistake. But I really deem it important that we should clearly understand each other; so that, acting from a thorough conviction of the propriety of our conduct, we may not be, hereafter, subject either to mutual crimination, or the reproaches of our own hearts. And I have been the more ready to notice this matter, as you seemed to lay

---

[89] "The slings and arrows of outrageous fortune . . ." *Hamlet,* III, i.

more stress on the opinion of the world, than I am willing to allow to be your duty. I know that when the misrepresentations & the malignity of mankind have long persecuted any one, the mind of that person becomes exquisitely (will you forgive me, if I say *diseasedly*?) sensible to every new attack: at least, this is too often the case. Instead of this, the mind ought to derive new energy, & new fortitude, from every attempt at injuring it. But, after all, what is the world to us, or we to the world? You will answer—much: this I acknowlege, in certain respects, to be true in the highest degree; & I know the interesting topics which you have to urge, in support of those measures, which your feelings, rather than your reason, would induce you to adopt. To all, I must reply, that these arguments apply not to the particular subject in question: that it is, on affairs of this nature, absolutely impossible to avoid misrepresentations, by paying homage to the opinions of the multitude; & that, if it were, still it would be vicious to do so, if you, thereby, neglected the performance of any thing which deserved the name of duty.

This view of the subject, will, I hope, serve to render you still more satisfied with the determination you have made, relative to it.

What is the object of our correspondence? Is it not to confer mutual pleasure, & derive reciprocal advantage? Nay, to extend that pleasure & that profit, to others? To make us better members of the great society of mankind? Can any situations which we can ever be in, in respect to others, make such an intercommunication criminal? Are there any in which it may not [be] the means of rendering us more serviceable to our fellow-creatures? What, then, have we to fear? Not the malice of others, surely—for an exposure of our letters, (& this may at any time be done,) can only display the purity of our hearts, & the benevolence & uprightness of our intentions. They may contain paragraphs not rounded with the happy elegance of more accomplished writers; they may contain sentiments slight, trivial, & even false; but they contain nothing which ought, or can, ever criminate their authors, in the eyes of mankind. What, then, have we to fear? We may defy the malignity of man or fiend.

  Beat on, proud billows; Boreas blow;
   Swell curled waves, high as Jove's roof;
  Your incivility doth show,
   That innocence is tempest proof:
  Tho' surly Nereus frown, my tho'ts are calm;
  Then strike, Affliction, for thy wounds are balm.[90]

Were I writing to any other than you, it might become me, perhaps, to demand forgiveness, once again, for troubling you so long on this topic: But I left you reading "Political Justice"; & I should pay an ill compliment to the author, & to your own understanding, were I ever after to speak to you in any language save that alone of "truth & soberness." I will, therefore, suppose —that you will receive this long homily with pleasure, read it without yawning, & reply to it without resentment.

Since I have mentioned "Political Justice," you will gratify me, if you make it so far the subject of your next letter, as to deliver me your opinion upon it. If you have not read it thro', I will not ask any thing more than a general sentiment, on such parts as you have read.

  My love to all yours.
            Farewell.
Tuesday, Decr. 15. 1795.
Cedar St. No. 13. N. York.   E. H. Smith.

P. S. It was not till last Sunday that I saw Cash Africa; he having removed from our neighborhood, & we being ignorant with whom he lived. I saw him, then, by accident. I made a proper representation to him, of the condition in which his wife & her children were; & made use of your name, as you desired me. The fellow *promises well*. That, you know, he always does. I have, however, found out with whom he lives; &, if he does not fulfill his engagements, I shall apply to his master. He promised to bring me five or six dollars, before Thursday noon. If he should, I shall take the liberty to inclose them to you; & have no doubts of your applying them, to their best use. He has further engaged to do something more, for his family, at intervals, as he shall be able. I hope to effect something for the poor animals;[91] but fear that it must be, as it now is, uncertain.

            E. H. Smith.

This morning I devoted to the composition of the preceeding letter that part of my time which, yesterday, was employed on German; & wrote the greater part of it. It was finished this evening. In addition to the regular business of study of this day—which has been regularly pursued—I have visited two people, for Dingley, & himself likewise; & I drank tea, & spent an hour, at Lynde Catlin's.

            Wednesday, 16th

Two professional visits, one carrying me a considerable distance, Frederic Wolcott's business, & an unsuccessful call on N. Terry, bro't me to near one o'clock. I then, drew up a Paper, relative to Wolcott's affair—& had just finished it, when Terry came in. He stayed with me till two; &, in part, stated to me the history of this present complaint. He had several recurrences of them, while here, which I forbear to describe because, as he has consulted me as a Physician, I mean to make out a regular History of them. After dinner, I was busied, till

---

[90] Sir Roger L'Estrange, "Loyalty Confined," or "In Prison," or "Liberty and Requiem of an Imprisoned Royalist." All three titles given.

[91] The tone of these lines makes abundantly clear the fact that Smith's interest in the Manumission Society by no means carried with it any fellow feeling for Negroes.

sundown, in copying the preceeding letter, & in attending to getting in Wood. I called at Charles Adams's, but he was out. I drank tea, & spent part of the evening, at Mrs. Morton's. Nothing particular there. Devoted near two hours to Arithmetic—two, with Wm., to History—one to copying. It is after twelve.

Thursday, 17th

Of all my studies French & History only have recd. any attention; & the former very little. Professional business, & that of F. Wolcott & the finishing the copying of the letter to Mrs. Tracy, having occupied the chief of the day till dinner; a part of the afternoon spent with Terry; & the evening, till nine, divided between a visit to Mrs. Lovegrove & Mrs. H. Johnson. I recd. letters from my Father, N. Tracy, & F. Wolcott. Mrs. L. was in very good spirits.

I have at length bro't F. Wolcott's business to a kind of conclusion; & in the following manner, which I am the more particular to insert, lest any misunderstanding should hereafter arise.

Oliver Wolcott of Phila. possesses a tract of land, on the outlet of Lake George, in this State, contiguous to Lands of Alexander Ellin, an English merchant, of commerce, now in this country. F. Wolcott, is agent for his brother & has agreed to sell this land to A. Ellin; & he has commissioned me to carry the bargain into effect. He has agreed to sell it to Mr. Ellin for 6,000 dols which Mr. Ellin has consented to pay. Wolcott wants, but does not press for all the pay down: Ellin is willing to pay half now, & the rest by the first of Feby., but will pay the whole, if urged. He purchases this land, that he may the more readily get rid of his own—the situation & quality of this being much better—& therefore likely to help the sale. As he is soon to return to England, he wishes to conclude the bargain, that he may make his arrangements to dispose of this property. He expects, too, to go to Albany, every day; & it is there that he wishes to make his arrangements. Oliver Wolcott possesses this land, in right of his Wife: It is necessary that the deed be signed by both, & acknowleged before a Judge of the Supreme Court of the U. S. When this is done, the deed is to be sent to me. Now the Deed is not recd.; F. Wolcott does not know that his brother insists on the immediate payment of the whole sum; but considers, as does Mr. Ellin, the bargain as complete, as if the deed were really delivered & the money paid. In this situation—I have ventured to take the Step, which the following writings will explain.

"It is understood by us, Alexander Ellin & E. H. Smith, subscribers to this writing, that Alexander Ellin, the first-named subscriber thereto, has purchased a certain Tract of Land, (the property, heretofore, of Oliver Wolcott & his wife, of Philadelphia) lying on the outlet of Lake George, (being all the land they did own there,) in the State of New York, together with all the improvements on said Tract of Land; for which the said Alexander Ellin is to pay, to the said Oliver & his Wife, the sum of 6,000 dollars, (in manner hereafter mentioned,) & is to receive, from the said Oliver & his Wife, a Warranty Deed thereof. And, whereas, the said Deed is not, now, ready to be delivered, by reason of some necessary delay, it is further understood by us, the subscribers, that the aforesaid Alexander Ellin is to pay, to E. H. Smith, (the second subscriber to this writing, & who is authorized, by Frederic Wolcott, Agent for the said Oliver & his Wife, to receive the money & deliver the Deed,) immediately, on the signing of this writing, the sum of Three Thousand dollars: that E. H. Smith is to place the Warranty Deed, abovementioned, in the hands of Alexander Ellin, or Alexander Pfister, his Agent, as soon as may be after he, E. H. Smith, shall have recd. it; & that the said Alexander Ellin, also at the time of signing this writing, is to put into the hands of the said E. H. Smith, his Note, or Order, on Alexander Pfister, his Agent aforesaid, payable, with interest, after the delivery of the Deed aforesaid, on the first day of Feby. 1796, for the remaining sum of 3,000 dollars. And, furthermore, it is understood by us, the subscribers, that, henceforth, the right & title to the aforementioned Tract of Land, does rest in the said Alexander Ellin, as fully as tho' the formal deliverance & acceptance of the said Warranty deed, were actually performed, & that he, the said Alexander Ellin, is authorized to act, in regard to it, in the same manner as he would be, were he actually in possession of the abovementioned Warranty Deed.

New York. Decr. 17. 1795.   Alexander Ellin.
                            E. H. Smith.

"New York, Decr. 17, 1795. Then recd. for Frederic Wolcott, in behalf of Oliver Wolcott & his Wife, of Philadelphia, of Alexander Ellin, one of the subscribers to the preceeding writing, the sum of 3,000 dollars; being the first payment stipulated in the said preceeding writing. Then, also, recd. for Frederic Wolcott, in behalf of Oliver Wolcott & his Wife, of Phila. a draught on Messrs. Pfister & Macomb, of New York, for the remaining sum of 3,000 dollars.

E. H. Smith."

It may be well to note, that the first 3,000 dols. was not cash, but a draft on Col. Ward of this city—which he, this day, engaged to pay next Saturday. The above writing is to be left with Alexr. Pfister; & I am to take it up, when the Deed is given, & the 3,000 dols recd. which he is to pay me.

Friday, 18th

When next I write to John Allen, W. T. Broome desires me to request him to send back Mr. Burr's Argument in Chancery.[92]

Several professional visits, including a visit to Ding-

---

[92] Not found in usual search of biographies, bibliographies, catalogs of major libraries; possibly a magazine article.

ley; some further trouble on Wolcott's business; & attention to procuring W. Buel's Miniature *set*; (which he requested of me in a letter of a few lines, recd. last evening) took up so much of the forepart of the day, that I had no time for German & only an hour for Medicine. N. Terry dined with me—I spent half an hour with him, at his lodgings; which finished the afternoon. I drank tea at Dunlap's—having first called upon him at his Store. I went from his house to Woolsey's, with Mrs. Wy. senior—where I stayed half an hour: then came home; applied two hours to Arithmetic; then Wm. & [I] read Herodotus, till half after eleven; & thus concluded the day.

Saturday, 19th

German recd. it's stated share of attention; & medicine employed two hours. I then made a visit to Terry, with W. W. Woolsey. We found, at Terry's lodgings, Nathaniel Smith[93]—member of Congress from Connecticut—& conversed an hour. Some business held me till dinner. After dinner, I made some professional calls—& business, generally, held me till evening. Evening, at Club—at Woolsey's—Present, the Woolseys—H. & W. Johnson, Dunlap, myself—Alsop, & Gahn visitors—& much to our regret, Wetmore. Conversation was heavy —& the evening, on the whole, unpleasant. No small part of this may fairly be ascribed to Wetmore's presence. It is a long time since he has met with us; &, in the mean while, he has been discovered to be guilty of some conduct, which made us all wish that he would never frequent our little circle again. Of this, however, no one wished to speak; & this general contest of feelings generated a general embarrassment, & heaviness. The explanation of this is, that Wetmore, & his brothers, with whom he is in partnership, in trade, have been discovered to have been guilty of smuggling, in several instances, & for very paltry savings. The dereliction of principles which conduct of this kind involves, has changed his character, in all our eyes, & makes him no longer an agreable, or fit, associate for us.

Sunday, 20th

To Nathaniel Terry.

To the thorough and satisfactory comprehension of the nature of that Malady, by which you are afflicted, it will be necessary to go far back, into the History of your Health, &, perhaps, to commence our inquiries, with some questions relative to your infantile ailments. A slight sketch of these will, in all probability, be all that is requisite; but, from the age of puberty, the relation must be more in detail; & no small degree of minuteness should mark your account of that period which immediately preceeded your first sufferings from your present calamity. Thenceforward, the History will be that of the Disease itself. I know that this will be an exercise of memory, perhaps, greater than you will be able, perfectly, to affect; but it will not be an useless one: and, tho' you have, already, made me, in part, acquainted with previous circumstances, the advantages, obviously attendant on an entire & connected view of the subject, are too many & too great, to make me fear lest you should decline the task. Nothing is more pernicious to the patient, as well as deceptious to the physician, than that *half-knowlege* which, in chronic complaints, is so generally communicated, & so universally acted upon. Where diseases become part of the constitution, itself, as it were—which they oftentimes seem to do—it is indispensible to understand the constitution, if it is designed to comprehend the disease. In the explication of your constitution, & in the detail of the history of your Malady, I trust that the following Inquiries will be found useful: both as they may suggest topics, to which, otherwise, you would not have attended, & as they may tend to simplify & abridge the labour.

Inquiry 1st. Had you any ailments, in Infancy, except such as are common to Children? & did these, if any, leave any permanent local, or general, consequences?

2nd. Was your diet, in childhood, simple, or the reverse? & were you confined to a sedentary or indulged in an active life?

3rd. Were any particular consequences of your mode of life observable? or, do you, now, recollect any, worthy of notice?

4th. As you grew up, did you perceive any important effect to follow from any of your infantile ailments?

5th. Between infancy—or the first seven years—& puberty, were you subject to any new diseases, with any permanent effects, worthy of remark?

6th. Did there, about the age of puberty, happen any remarkable change in your mode of living—i. e. as to air, diet, &c.

7th. From puberty, till within a year of the time you first perceived any of the symptoms of your present ailments, were you subject to any diseases which seem to have considerably—&, in any degree, permanently— affected your system? If you did, what were they & what their effects? It will be proper, also, to notice the method of cure: not particularly—but generally.

8th. At the time of your being affected, as you now are, or for six months, or a year before—How was your Sleep, Food, Situation as to Air, Exercise, & general Habit of Body—including the Functions of the intestinal canal?

9th. What was the commencement of your present Complaints? How were you first affected? How long did the same symptoms occur simply? When, & under what circumstances, did new symptoms appear?

10th. What is your present, general, condition? What your, present, particular, situation? I mean, in respect to the complaints to which you are subject.

11th. What effect, if any, has a stimulating diet?

---

[93] Nathaniel Smith (1762-1822), member State House 1789-1795, of U.S. House, from Woodbury, Connecticut, 1795-1799, State Senate 1800-1805, judge of Supreme Court of Connecticut 1806-1819. Probably not a relative.

What, Excess? in quality or quantity? Solids, or Fluids? What Company, & Retirement? The converse of friends, or of Strangers? What study, or exercise? What temperance? What Abstinence? What early sleeping & rising? What late hours? in crowded Assemblies, more particularly? What the various, ordinary, combinations of these?

These questions are so much connected with each other, that I have thrown them into one mass.

12th. What is the effect of costiveness, & the reverse? and of a Lax? Have you taken any Medicines? If you have, what have been their effects—as far you can judge, *simply*? And what, as viewed in connection with any of the preceeding circumstances—of Inquiry 11th?

13th. How far, & in what form, do the reflections of your own mind—not immediately influenced by the circumstances abovementioned, effect the *general* condition of your body; & it's *particular* condition, as relative to this Disease?

You will perceive that many of these Inquiries have been put to you, &, in part, replied to, before. My design, in repeating them, is, (in your Answers,) to bring the whole subject, together, in a connected view. Partially acquainted with your Complaint, as I now am, I can only venture on a few general recommendations. To cultivate equanimity of mind, and an equable state of body, by all the means in your power; to avoid all occasion of fatigue, without foregoing the wholesome use of exercise, in the open air; to use a diet neither deficient, nor excessive, in it's stimulating qualities, but moderately incentive; & to maintain regular & seasonable hours for sleeping & waking; appear to me, absolutely essential; & as means which, tho' they may not, of themselves, effect a cure, yet, without which no cure is to be expected. Of this you are already aware; & I should not have repeated it, but that I know, whatever is so indispensable to our welfare can not be enforced too often.

Should you see fit to favor me with Replies to the foregoing Inquiries, it shall be my business, as it will be my pleasure, to investigate the subject, as fully as I am able, & to transmit to you, whatever of promise shall result from my inquiry. In the mean time, as I expect to be in Phila. the last of this month, suffer me to lay your case, as far as I am acquainted with it, before Dr. Rush. His regard for one who was once his Pupil, & the philanthropy for which he is so much & so justly distinguished, will not suffer him to conceal any information concerning it which has been already, & may hereafter be the result of his Studies & Observation.

With the sincerest desires for the restoration of your health & promotion of your happiness, & wishing you a safe & pleasant return home.

I am,

Sunday, Decr. 20. 1795.   Yours affectionately,
Cedar St. No. 13. N. York.   E. H. Smith.

I began the preceeding letter, in the morning; but, on account of various interruptions, did not finish it till after dinner. My longest interruption was from Saml. A. Law, who stayed here two hours. I dined at Woolsey's. After finishing my letter, I visited a patient, came way out of town—notwithstanding the snow, which fell fast—& returned by the way of Mr. Lovegrove's. He is still at Amboy. I found Mrs. L. well & in good spirits. Dunlap was there. We had general & interesting conversation. He went away, about seven; & I, quite inconscious of the lapse of time, remained till near ten. I compared Alsop's Incantatory Song,[94] in his Scandinavia, with the Incantation to Lok, in the last of Dr. Sayers' First Drama.[95] I read, also, several of his pieces, to her, & of others, in the American Poems. She indulged me in some notices of her own life—which were necessarily interesting, & we had much minute talk, chiefly concerning her acquaintance in this Country, & some which she is soon to make.

Monday, 21st

To William Buel.

I have attended to your several requests. As you gave no particular directions, concerning the setting of the Miniature, I have procured it to be done plain. The expence was six dollars: which have been paid. I shall inclose Mitchill's Pamphlet with this hasty note. I have not time to write a letter. You will expect one, in answer to that which you have promised me; and I trust I shall have leisure to compose one, when I have recd. yours. My best regards are for you.

Farewell,

Monday, Decr. 21. 1795.
Cedar St. No. 13. N. York.   E. H. Smith.

It is my misfortune to be necessitated still to lament frequent & trivial interruptions. All my arrangements for study are, constantly, impeded, or set aside, by petty avocations: partly, on my own concerns, but, chiefly, on those of others—& from which I derive neither knowlege nor emolument. Thus has this whole day been wasted; without the happening of a single circumstance worthy of notice.

Johnson & I drank tea with Kent; & stayed two hours. General talk. I have, since, devoted near two hours to Arithmetic—& one to reading Beddoes's preliminary remarks, to his Edition of Brown's Elements;[1] which appear to me to be sensible—& in some degree, novel.

I have been more sensible to chilliness, & experienced greater derangements of head, eyes, & stomach, & thought, this day—than for some weeks, before. Perhaps

---

[94] Alsop, *The Conquest of Scandinavia*, unfinished, published by Smith in *American Poems* (Litchfield, 1793), pp. 271-284.

[95] Frank Sayers, M.D., *Dramatic Sketches of Ancient Northern Mythology* (London, 1790).

[1] Beddoes was an English physician-scientist (1760-1808). John Brown's Work, *Elementa Medicinae* (1780), contains his theory that all diseases result from an excess or deficiency of the "exciting power," with most diseases in the second category.

it is in consequence, that I have reflected on the low & unpromising state of my Finances—& on the little prospect there, also, is, of my acquiring extensive knowlege, & becoming greatly useful.

[Smith's copy of a letter written by Mrs. Tracy to James Morris.]

Lichfield, Jany. 25. 1794.

Dear Sir,

You request me to give you my opinion concerning Miss Wollstonecraft's Plan. I have read her Work,[2] with as much attention as my domestic avocations would admit, & with as much pleasure as any book. Perhaps I have read with some enthusiasm:—But away with this —and let me say—I think it a sound performance, consistent with itself, and consistent with reason.

As to her ideas concerning the present Female Character, I am willing to suppose they apply, with more propriety, in European Countries, than here: still, I think there is much justice, as well as much severity, in her remarks when applied all over the World: I mean with exceptions.

As to her proposed amendments in the Education of Women, I confess I see no objection to the attempt: and, if it do not succeed, lay it aside, after a *fair* trial. To eradicate a single folly,—above all, to expel a single vice, from the character of Woman, is worth the united exertions of Mankind, for, at least, *one* Century. For, after all, Women are of great importance in the world; even with their present, narrow, views of things. Let them, then, possess, *legally*, that Liberty which they now, obtain, by their illicit operations on the minds of their male acquaintances & connections. This will shew whether they will bear a reasonable independence; whether they will bear to be, lawfully, of consequence. The term which was first applied to Woman—"Help-Meet"—carries, to my understanding, an idea of *Equality*.

This plan of Education must be tried on the Infant. You can not, so effectually efface a habit, or a prejudice, as to leave no trace behind. Many of her (Miss W's) small plans, as well as her main object, must come to the test of experiment, before we can decide upon them absolutely. In some cases, she takes things for granted, which, perhaps, may be disputed: And, I believe, if sentiments, of the kind she has exprest, were now generally diffused & adopted, they might make, here & there, a *grown up fool* wise in her own conceits, only to her own destruction—: but you & I might live to see children more naturally educated, & men & women forming more perfect human characters.

The light of science, where it has only beamed on *half* a Nation, (for Women, *nationally*, have never partaken but of the reflected blaze,) has shewn us wonders. Suffer it, then, to have indiscriminate extension, to men & women, and I believe it will have, indiscriminately,

---
[2] *A Vindication of the Rights of Women* (London, 1792).

good effects. As we are the work of the hands of the same God, and, independently of each other, accountable beings, I can not conceive why women ought not to be so educated that they can *think* for themselves. It is allowed, on all hands, that exercise of mind, as well as of body, tends to strengthen it's faculties.

I believe the Deity sees latent talents, in the human mind, which will, in his own time, be drawn into light & into use; and that the means appointed to this sublime end, are to be found in the *mutual* exertions of *Mankind*. I have sometimes indulged the thought—that the whole human character is yet in it's infancy. We daily see men stopping short, when they have but half ascended *the hill*, discouraged with the thought that *they* can never attain the summit of perfection, which has been attained, much less go on to an ideal state. *That* is as dark as midnight. We are all in a habit of viewing things dangerous—nay, impossible—which are only *difficult*. A little more light, which would dawn upon us, if we would shut our eyes to prejudice & open them to reason, might excite astonishment, how we could have been so long in ignorance of simple truths, respecting one half of the human race—who interweave themselves with the *happiness* of the other half.

I much admire Miss W's sketches of a plan of national Education. I hope she may live to fill up her outlines. I am well convinced that the training of useful animals will be more perfectly attended to, than training the young of the human race, to their proper destination, until the subject do become a grand National concern. This can not take place now. Our national heads are too much occupied to admit these domestic concernments.

Universal Love must gain ground, in all hearts, & Science spread, universally, it's pure lights, before women will be completely emancipated from the chains of ignorance, & consequent folly; or men from their passion to tyrannize. I speak collectively, not individually. I do not call all men tyrants; nor all women slaves, or fools, or samples of blind ignorance. No! There is, here and there, a being, among both sexes, so enlightened, & so good, that Nature may hold them forth, &, in the language of Minerva, say—"These are my Children."

I have only perused this Book once thro', and, therefore, can only touch it's prominent features: but you will be able to gather, from what I have written, my general opinions; which was all you asked; Nor have I given them with diffidence: because, *you*, I know, will not deem it an infringement on Modesty, that a *Woman* should venture to speak what she believes; & were I to give my sentiments otherwise, than under the influence of unreserved freedom, depend upon it they would be artful disguises, not genuine principles. But mark! I do not expect to give new ideas, on subjects which Miss W —has handled; or to sketch with her firm hand and "prophetic fire."

I do not wish to be understood to say, no author has written good & just sentiments, on Education, save the lady in question. I hold lord Kames's "Hints on Education"[3] in high estimation, & which, if you have not read, I will send you; But I am not so inconsistent as to approve *all* he has advanced. He has many sentiments in common with all those who have written on that subject.

I need not comment on Mr. Day's "Sandford & Merton."[4] You have read it. I am disposed to give it the highest praise.

A considerable number of years ago, a gentleman, a friend of mine, put into my hands Rousseau's "Emilius";[5] and, after praising it highly, he laid before me this inducement to read it: that if I had ever regretted the situation in which I, or my sex, were placed in the world, I should feel perfectly contented with it, after reading this Work. I told him, I had no reason to regret my particular allotment; & that I had, hitherto, lived among my acquaintances, full as well respected, as I thought I deserved to be. I read the Book; &, whether it deserves praise or blame, I confess I read, by much, the greater part, with secret indignation. I viewed his principles as corrupt, as his mind was enthusiastic. You will easily imagine then, that I have look'd patiently on, while Miss W. (to use a vulgar phrase) has *cuffed his ears*.

Sunday night

You request me to make all the remarks I can think of. Alas! I have so many cares, and so many kinds of employments, that I am hardly left with sufficient leisure to take my rest. If I could rise at midnight, when my mind is calm; when all is stillness round me, & my recollection of every thing, which has previously employed me, is clear; I might give you some thoughts, not altogether unworthy your attention; something more systematic. But, perplexed as I often am, & hurried from one subject to another, I have been tempted to destroy what I have already written—as a thing incompetent to my own wishes, & your expectations. But I will regard my promise as a sacred engagement; and, however, in *substance*, I may fall short of the performance, I will send the *form*.

Miss W's idea, that Women ought to learn certain professional business, I see no objection to. Indeed, I think, with her, they are the natural proprietors. I know that great courage & fortitude are necessary to surgical operations; & I hold that females do possess these qualities, & united with the tenderest humanity. All *Men* are not destined to the same employment, let the bent of their genius be what it may: then, why should *Women*? They, too, differ in genius & capacity. Why not make surgeons & physicians of some? I know many men, whose genius is better fitted to superintend a kitchen, than to practise in any learned profession, who, however, have spent the morning, & the evening, of their life in such ill-directed manner: *pretending* to acquire, & *pretending* to practice, what their wives & sisters *know* more perfectly—without having *devoted* themselves to it, or having been instructed. On which side must this be determined? Equal rights, equal claims, is all I ask for.

I highly approve learning women some mechanic arts, by which they may earn honest, honorable, independent bread. The only resource left to a woman, who is destitute of *natural* support, is, to repair to her needle, or the spinning-wheel. The latter is a healthful employment; but mantua-makers & milliners are, almost without exception, weak in mind & weak in body: for the simple reason that *both* are in want of exercise. And to speak generally, they are, also, more unfit, than *Scholars* are, to manage any thing, in the domestic circle of business, besides the *sewing* of the Family which is so unfortunate as to fall under their direction.

The situation of Woman, in the world, is somewhat like the following example—Two men go into a field to labour together, to obtain a certain object. The one, is possest of a competency to begin those occupations; *he*, of course, assumes the right of *proposing* every scheme, and *ordering* the execution. The effect of this difference in their circumstances is, the one becomes most capable of governing, by having exercised his faculties *independently*; the other, incapable of directing, even himself, & must be lead; because he has been in the habit of being *led*, & *directed*, by another. I will touch the picture once again, now the effect is clear. The former, is a cunning tyrant; the latter, a simpleton, at least.

Women, with a few exceptions, are not allowed to manage *property*, or considered as any body, in Law, where matters of property come in question; (yes,—they are allowed to make a last will & testament!) &, to treat the matter humourously, we are, as a kind of compensation for this exclusion from privileges, exempted, personally, from Taxation. But, seriously—we are sometimes called, late in life, to the management of property, (where we have to look carefully around us, as well for our children as ourselves;) & property, too, under the most difficult & embarrassed circumstances. We can easily discern, here, the want, & the worth of independent sentiments. But, even under the most difficult view of this case, I have seen women display superior capacity in management.

Is there danger in enlightening the understanding of Woman, as it respects practical religion, & the great

---

[3] Henry Home, Lord Kames, *Loose Hints on Education; chiefly concerning the Culture of the Heart* (Edinburgh, 1781).

[4] Thomas Day, a humorless London barrister (1748-1789) whose highly moral works were devoted to social reform. He attempted to amalgamate Rousseau and his own moral code, particularly regarding the education of children (in what now seems a particularly "modern," way) by stimulating their curiosity and enthusiasm. *Sanford and Merton*, a children's tale, was published in three volumes 1783, 1787, 1789.

[5] A "considerable number of years ago" Smith would have known little if any French. The edition he probably read was *Emilius, or an Essay on Education,* translated by Thomas Nugent (London, 1763).

duties we all owe to God's Family on earth? For myself, I think, in proportion to numbers, I have seen, among the enlightened of my own sex, more sacred regard paid to religious duties, than among the ignorant. Why not *better*, if more enlightened? I have, it is true, seen pious, well-meaning, ignorant women; whose intentions charity bids us hope are accepted—(for God looks at the heart) but can they comprehend *why* they *ought* to be virtuous? Is not a woman, who has principles of her own—who acts right, because her reason tells her it is best, a character more desirable to contemplate?—a more desirable friend, wife, or mother, than she who is only a conformist to rules learned by *rote*? Which of these characters would men be most liable, or necessitated, to watch?

Has well-directed, scientific knowlege, made *Men* worse? It makes Women pedantic, they say, to have *read* much. I have but a short answer to this hackneyed speech: I never saw a Man, or a Woman, pedantic, who had *reflected* much. Is it envy which leads Men to dispute, with Women, the claim of almost every talent in common with Men? or is it thus? Women, in the aggregate, are not in the habit of cultivating their talents; & where, here & there, one does gain some knowlege, she is *flattered*; she exalts herself; & loses the merit, by the indulgence of a passion; as common to men, as to women. A learned man, is not infrequently to be met with; if it were so, in regard to women, we should see, the *ugliness*, & the *oddity*, of such a figure, vanishing together.

But I must have done, or my *letter* will take another name; & I shall appear to be attempting what, by Education, I am unfitted to perform.

S. T.

The preceeding letter was written, by Mrs. Tracy, to my kinsman James Morris of Lichfield—in consequence of a conversation, which passed between them, on Miss Wollstonecraft's "Vindication of the Rights of Women"; to which conversation the letter constantly refers, & which was terminated by Mr. Morris's desiring Mrs. T. to send him her opinion on the Work, in writing. The effect of her letter is much lost, by the miscellaneous manner in which her tho'ts are thrown together. This will find some excuse, in the recollection that—she bore constantly in mind the conversation which induced the letter—&, probably, follows very nearly, the order of that conversation.

Tuesday, 22nd

I read some German & some Medicine, this forenoon: but an interruption, in the line of my profession, & an agreable visit from Dunlap, shortened the time for both. At our dining home I found Mr. Randolph's Vindication—in which, after dinner, I read till four. Then I made a call on a patient; &, according to previous appointment waited on Mrs. Lovegrove to Dunlaps. We stayed there till near eight—the conversation rambling —& I returned with her, to her house. There I tarried till after ten. The time occupied in various chat, relative to her previous & present situation, her plans in future —&c. &c.

Wednesday, 23rd

To Oliver Wolcott, of Phila.

I write to you sir, at the request of Mr. Ellin, the gentleman who is about purchasing of you a certain Tract of Land, in this State, to explain to you the situation he is in, respecting it, & to express to you his wishes that such an arrangement may be made as will accomodate him, without disobliging you.

At the request of Mr. Frederic Wolcott, I undertook to transact the business, with Mr. Ellin. Mr. Wolcott desired me to receive the sum of six thousand dollars of Mr. Ellin & deliver him the deed: expecting to send it me, himself, & to have me send him the money. After waiting some weeks, Mr. Ellin informed me that he was about to leave this place for Albany, that he wished to have this business first settled; that his object in purchasing the Land, was to aid the sale of some lands of his own, which lay adjoining it; that he considered the bargain as completed; & that he was willing to pay the one half of the sum, immediately, & would give his Note, payable, for the remainder, on the first of February—on the expectation of having the Deed lodged, by me, with his Agent, soon after my receiving it. His reason for wishing to conclude the bargain, was, that, when at Albany, he might take measures for disposing of the land: & his motive for wishing to postpone the payment of one half the purchase money was, that he had remitted his money, before hearing from your brother, to England, must now draw to disadvantage, & would have the sum required due to him, here on the first of February. I wrote to your brother, & informed him that I should consent to such a disposition of the business, if he did not insist on it's being otherwise. His letter did not decide on it; he considered the bargain as completed; & he appeared uncertain, merely, as he had not heard from you. He moreover, informed me, that you would forward the Deed to me. In this situation, & as the deed did not arrive, I accepted Mr. Ellin's offer i.e. I recd. 3,000 dollars of him, & a draft on a house, in this city, payable the first of Feby.—with interest from the time of their acception of the deed, for the remaining 3,000 dols. This was the state of the business, when Mr. Hamilton recd. your letter, with the Deed. As Mr. Hamilton can do nothing, other than as you have directed, & as it will be most convenient for Mr. Ellin to have the business so ordered as to proceed agreable to our arrangement, he hopes that you will signify your disposition to have it so, to Mr. Hamilton. If, however, it is a matter of necessity, that the whole sum be immediately paid, Mr. Ellin will, how much soever it may be to his disadvantage, complete the payment, by the 1st of January. A speedy reply is requested by him, as he will leave town as soon as his health will permit, & as, at present, nothing can be done with the money which is now in my hands.

Wednesday, Decr. 23. 1795.
Cedar St. No. 13. N. York.   E. H. Smith.

This whole day has been one continued series of uneasiness; &, in it, I have scarcely done any thing as it ought to be done. I recd. a few lines from El. Smith Jr.—; wrote the above letter, to O. Wolcott—; attended to a visitor; looked over the late minutes of the Manumission Society, & made some memorandums; & spent the remainder of the time, till dinner, in drawing off some accounts. In the afternoon, I read a little in several late pamphlets—& visited N. Terry; at his lodgings. I spent the evening, with Wm., at his brother's. After we came home, we read in Herodotus an hour & a half.

Thursday, 24th
To Uriah Tracy.

The only reason why I have not replied to your letter, before now, is, that I have had nothing of sufficient importance to justify communication. It is true, the situation of things has not varied much, in that respect; but I would no longer leave room for a suspicion, of neglect on my part, to creep in, by continuing silent. My letter, if it serve no other purpose, may have a tendency to convince you, that my taciturnity did not originate in forgetfulness.

The House of Representatives continue to *stand still*. But tho' their proceedings do not furnish us with much matter for general conversation, the *ci-devant* Secretary of State has kindly lent his assistance, to help us thro' this dreary interval of repose. On this publication,[6] as I have had time & opportunity only to read a small part, I shall not venture to pronounce an opinion. Neither is it yet time to begin to collect opinions on it. Every body is reading, but few have read it. And I have been, in some sort, out of the sphere of political conversation, for a week past. But, if opinions are not already in circulation, they can not long remain stationary. Public expectation has never been more excited, & was never, I believe, more forcibly drawn towards any pamphlet. Our venders of such commodities vie with each other for the sales; Every place of public resort is filled with hawkers, loaded with baskets-full; every news-paper teems with advertisements; & the corners of all the streets are covered with placards. One sarcasm, extorted, perhaps by the spirit of party, from many virtuous & amiable minds, is general. It is contained in this remark—"Mr. Randolph will make money by his Pamphlet."

On general politics, or rather on those our Country at large, as I have before intimated, I have had opportunity of talking but little, of late; &, consequently, of collecting but few opinions. The little which I have learnt, & which is confirmed, or countenanced, by the Papers, seems to shew us, that the tide of popularity is turning, or has turned; & is setting strongly in favor of the President, & of the Government, generally.[7] One fact, which has lately occurred here, is, perhaps worth noticing; as it may have more effect, than is ordinarily expectable from single changes in the opinions of individuals. Most of the Dissenting Clergy, in this city, have, till within a very short time, been violently democratic: and these are, chiefly, pretty able men. The late violent conduct of their party, has opened the eyes of the priests. They begin to suspect that those, on whom they have so long relied, are not as honest as themselves. The effect of this has been, to render all very temperate; & to produce a total change in the principal persons. On the Thanksgiving, which we had here, some little time ago, for the restored health of the City, two, if not more, of these gentlemen, preached discourses abounding in Federal sentiments, & reprobating the conduct of the Democrats in the strongest terms. In a place like this, where the priest-hood is greatly reverenced, it is easy to conjecture what must be the effect of so open, & so vigorous, a dereliction of long-cherished, & long-enforced, opinions.

In looking over these local changes, & contemplating the picture which the several State Legislatures present to our view, our little band, here, indulge many pleasing anticipations. All are well, & desire remembrances to you.

I design to be in Phila. next week.

Thursday, Decr. 24. 1795.
Cedar St. No. 13. N. York.   E. H. Smith.

The knowlege of a few circumstances, connected with the following little Poem, is necessary to it's being understood. A strict intimacy had subsisted, for some years, between Miss Sally Pierce, & my two eldest sisters. Of these, at the time the "Verses" were written, Mary, the eldest, was supposed, as was actually the case, to be engaged to marry her present husband, Thomas Mumford. Sally Pierce, was, at the time of writing these lines, just beginning to acquire, by her own exertions, some feeble knowlege of Drawing. The three young

---

[6] The reference is to Edmund Randolph, and the pamphlet everyone was reading was his "A Vindication of Mr. Randolph's Resignation" (Philadelphia, 1795). Despite rather convincing evidence of his innocence of the charge of seeking a bribe from France (made in an intercepted letter from the French minister, Fauchet, to his government), many continued to regard him as guilty of stupidity if not treason, this even after Fauchet apologized. The fact that he was deeply in debt to the government may have helped keep suspicion alive. It was Randolph's job as secretary of state to preserve good relations with France while Jay was negotiating the treaty with England.

[7] The unfortunate "Jay treaty" with England (signed November 19, 1794) was the cause of widespread dissatisfaction. Randolph, however, was the only cabinet member who opposed the treaty. See his letter to the President in *Amer. Hist. Rev.* **12**, 3 (1907): pp. 587-599.

women were together; it was evening; Sally had shewn them some of the productions of her pencil; & they were, sportingly, conversing of their different destinations. The conclusion was, that, when Mary left them, the other two should unite, & spend their lives, together, "in single blessedness." This idea once started, it received numerous additions, & the whole economy of a house, & of life, was readily arranged & determined on. Before separating, it was agreed that Sally, should design a house suitable for each, & sketch the surrounding scenery. This, as soon as my sisters were gone, she sat down to do. Her first care was directed towards accomplishing a plan for Mary; whose lot being more certainly decided, demanded the earliest attention. The inexperience of Miss Pierce, in the art of design, made her progress both slow & painful; so that, when she had effected her first picture, by the aid of the pencil, she had recourse to a readier instrument, & relied on the pen for a sketch of the second. And, lo! this is the landscape which she drew.

Verses,

written in the Winter of 1792, & addressed to Abigail Smith Jr.—by Sally Pierce.

On rising ground we'll rear a little dome;
    Plain, neat, and elegant, it shall appear;
No slaves shall there lament their native home,
    Or, silent, drop the unavailing tear.

Content and cheerfulness shall dwell within,
    And each domestic serve thro' love alone;
Coy Happiness we'll strive, for once, to win,
    With meek Religion there to build her throne.

And oft our friends shall bless the lonely vale,
    And, social, pass the wintry eves away;
Or, when soft Summer swells the fragrant gale,
    Delighted mark new beauties as they stray.

Pleased with the scene, by Fancy's pencil drawn,
    The various landscape rushes on my view;
The cultivated farm, the flowery lawn,
    That sucks the fragrance of the honied dew.

The fertile "meadows trim with daisies pied";
    The garden, breathing Flora's best perfumes;
And stored with herbs, whose worth, by Matrons tried,
    Dispels disease, and gives health's roseate blooms.

Here vines, with purple clusters bending low,
    And various fruit-trees loaded branches bear;
There roots of every kind profusely grow,
    Bespeaking plenty thro' the circling year.

See yonder hillock, where our golden corn
    Waves it's bright head to every passing breeze;
Yon fruitful fields our sportive flocks adorn,
    Our cows at rest beneath the neighboring trees.

As misty clouds from silent streams arise,
    Yon distant Town attracts the gazer's view;
Yon mount, whose lofty summit meets the skies,
    Shelters the Village on the plain below.

Behind our lot, a Wood defies the storm,
    Like those where Druids wont, in days of yore,
When Superstition wore Religion's form,
    With mystic rites their unknown Gods adore.

Within this grove we'll oft retire to muse,
    Where Contemplation builds her silent seat;
Her soothing influence she will ne'er refuse
    To those who wander in this blest retreat.

A river solemn murmurs thro' the shades,
    The whispering pines, in echoes soft, reply,
Then, hoarse o'er rocks, it seeks the distant glades,
    Forming a rain-bow in the moistened sky—

Nor leaves us here—but thro' the Village winds,
    Where simple elegance, in neat array,
Might teach even pomp that, not to wealth confined,
    Genius & taste might to a cottage stray.

In front, a level grass-plot smooth & green,
    Where neighboring children, pass sweet hours at play,
And Fairies oft, (if Fairies e'er have been,)
    Will featly foot the moonlight hours away.

Our plenteous store we'll freely give to all;
    Want ne'er shall pass, in sorrow, from our door;
With joy we'll seat the beggar in our hall,
    And learn the tale of woe that sunk his store.

But chiefly those who pine, by sickness prest;
    Whose merit, known to few, unheeded lies;
How sweet, to banish sorrow from the breast,
    And bid fair hope shine sparkling in the eyes.

Thus, humbly blest, when youthful years are flown,
    (Proud to be good, not wishing to be great,)
And swift-wing'd Time proclaimed our moments run,
    Resign'd to heaven, we'll cheerful bow to fate.

Placed in one grave, beneath a plain, smooth, stone,—
    Where oft the tear unfeign'd shall dew the face,
The sick, the poor, shall long our fate bemoan,
    But wealth & grandeur never mark the place.

This simple Epitaph the stone adorns,—
    Which calls, from artless eyes, the frequent tear—
Matrons & maids shall often stoop to learn,
    And all the Village think it passing rare.

The Epitaph.

Beneath this stone two female friends interr'd,
    Who past their lives content, in solitude;
They wish'd no ill, yet oft, thro' ignorance, err'd;
    Reader! depart, reflect, and be as good.

In the way of study I have done nothing, thro' this whole day, but devote a single hour, this evening, to

Arithmetic. I have written the preceeding letter to Mr. Tracy, & copied it; finished the copying of Mrs. Tracy's letter to James Morris of Lichd.; copied the verses of Sally Pierce; made a professional visit; visited Dingley; drank tea at Riley's—& talked two hours; there, with Alsop, & the others; read Citizen Fauchet's Letter; & done several errands. I recd. a short letter from Oliver Wolcott of Phila.—but written before mine; of course, not containing the information I wanted. Dunlap spent an hour with us, in the morning.

Friday, 25th
To C. B. Brown.

You, undoubtedly, expected an answer to your letter, of the 10th, before this time: but I have been constantly & variously engaged; and, as you know how many circumstances must concur to enable me to write, you will not wonder at my silence. Indeed, at the present moment, I either have not, or, which amounts, very nearly, to the same thing, think I have not, leisure sufficient to compose any thing which will deserve the name of letter. Instead, therefore, of replying to the several parts of your letter, which you might, reasonably enough, expect, I shall, in imitation of your illustrious example, talk on almost any thing else. But, not to under-rate the value of your communications, I must acknowlege that they were quite as important, in my eyes, & full as dear to me, as would have been a dissertation on Atheism, or some question of morality; which, in truth, was what I expected. But, I am straying from the purpose of this letter; which is, to inform you that, if "the fates, & destinies, the sisters three, & such odd things"[8]—do not determine otherwise, I shall leave this city of N. York, next Wednesday, & be with you on the evening of the Thursday following. I shall come alone—i.e. unaccompanied by any of our particular friends; &, as you rightly conjecture, on the business of the Manumission Society. Both Johnson & Dunlap are on the Delegation; but neither of them can attend.

My love to Joseph, his, & yours.

Farewell.

Friday, Decr. 25. 1795.
Cedar St. No. 13. N. York.   E. H. Smith.

To John Williams.

You, my dear sir, will be satisfied that no part of the delay, which has arisen, in respect to the answering of your letter, has been occasioned by a loss, or diminution, of my esteem for you, when you are made acquainted with the following circumstances.

I recd. your letter, while I was in Connecticut, sometime in November last, & while busied in paying & receiving visits, in my native place, & after a long absence. Thus situated, I had neither leisure, nor opportunity, for writing. Time flew away too rapidly; & at the end of my stay, I found as much to do, as on the day of my arrival. My return to New York was slow & tedious; & I did not reach home till the last of the month. When I had returned, I found numberless affairs crowding, all at once, upon me; and all my embarrassments heightened & increased, by the business which I brought with me, & the lateness of the season. The mass of occupation was shouldered off, before many weeks; but, even yet, & when I am on the eve of a new journey, I have not completely restored things to their wonted regularity. Of my numerous correspondents, you are one of the first to whom I have written. Even several members of my own family, & who have written to me, remain, hitherto, unnoticed, in the epistolary way. This, with you, will, surely, be enough to plead & obtain my pardon, for all apparent neglect; & I appeal to my former, & to my future, conduct, in evidence of the firmness of my attachment.

To your letter, multifarious, yet unity, as it is, I scarcely know how to reply. I would, willingly, change the subject, & introduce something new—so long have we been confined to the same—but that I am at a loss for a topic which will justify me in being lengthy, by it's interesting nature. Is it imitation or nature which so forcibly & uniformly directs the thoughts & the pens of the unmarried & of bachelors, towards matrimonial discussions? For myself, much as my mind may have, in former times, felt interested in determining whether to marry or remain single, I do not, now, find that I am very constantly contemplating the subject; & I can not but be surprised that, from the commencement of our correspondence, to the present moment, we have never failed to make it the principal theme of our discourse. This is not as it should be. Love is a phantom, too fugitive, & too unsubstantial, to deserve so much of our attention. Let us, then, even let it flit away, & mingle with it's kindred shadows; hover over the midnight couch of youths & maidens, just ripening into maturity; but haunt our sober, waking, & chastised imaginations, no more. Of how much affectation & nonsense, how much real & imaginary distress, of what phrenzy & cruelty, waste of genius, health, & usefulness, hath it been the cause! Let us, then, foster & support it no longer; but, fixing our eyes, steadily, on the simple, sublime, & radiant, reality of Reason, recollect that we are men; & that passion is the play-thing, or tyrant, of the ignorant, & of children.

You complain that I oblige you to make yourself, too much the subject of your letters: yet what is the object of letters? Is it not, at least in part, to acquaint ourselves, mutually, with each other, our situation, health, happiness, sentiments, & discoveries? Can any thing be impertinent, or unworthy of notice, which relates to a friend? And why should he talk to me of ideal existences, of men in the moon, rather than of himself? No! my friend! it is of ourselves that we *should* speak to each other. Have I a fault? does my friend know it? & will he not strive [to] correct it? Have I penetrated,

---

[8] "Fates and Destinies and such odd sayings, the Sisters Three . . ." *Merchant of Venice,* II, ii.

in a new direction, into the region of undiscovered truth? & shall I not impart, of the fruit of my discoveries, to my friend? Will not he, who, perhaps, surveys mankind, & nature in general, with a calmer, & more instructed eye, teach me to temper the ardency of pursuit, to retract hasty conclusions, & soften extravagant descriptions? Shall we not, mutually, by becoming reciprocally admitted into the very inmost soul, each of the other, be better & more enabled, to draw forth the latest qualities which lurk there unimproved & perhaps unknown, & bring them out to day, & cultivate them into useful importance? Can cold, irrelevant, & generalized, communications, do this? Have they the genial warmth necessary to stimulate the slumbering germ of benevolence, foster it's slowly-unfolding bust, support it's feeble stalk; & expand it's fragrant blossoms to bless & beautify the world? No! this is no property of theirs. This only can be hoped from unfolding, as it were, the interior of the heart. And this should letters do. Why then regret that such is their actual effect? It is not to be regretted: we will not regret it: on the contrary, it shall be more & more our practice, shall it not?

Shall you not visit us this winter? I hope you will. I shall go to Phila. next week, & return the week after. From that time, I hope to be, in a manner, disengaged. Beside—Winter is the season for social converse. The long evenings invite to friendly discourse; & the retirement & stillness which the altered temperature forces upon us, seem to remove the world at a distance, & unite the friends who are together, in all the sweet community of silence & solitude. In such situations, my soul often springs forth, to those who are away, embraces them in idea, & seats them by my side. Ah! were the reality equally easy of accomplishment. How often should I surround my little hearth with those whose kindness & hospitality endeared, & does still endear to me, the banks of the Connecticut!

Remember me to all who affectionately ask after me.

Friday, Decr. 25. 1795.
Cedar St. No. 13. N. York.   E. H. Smith.

I wrote the two preceeding letters, this forenoon; copied & dismist the first, & in part, the second. I should have finished it, had I not been agreably interrupted by the entrance of Rufus Stanley[9]—who sat an hour with me, & gave me much pleasure unfolding to me the mildly prosperous state of his affairs.

I dined at Riley's; & spent the afternoon there, with Alsop, only—Mr. & Mrs. Riley having ridden out. Alsop made me a present of a Work of Richard Morton[10]—who, I take to be the rival of Sydenham; but, as it is in Latin, & the title-page gone, & as I have not yet had sufficient time to examine, on this I can not decide.

---

[9] Not known except for the fact that he lived at Fort Montgomery. He may have been the son of Oliver Stanley (Yale 1768) of Wallingford, Connecticut.

[10] Richard Morton, M.D. (? -1698) wrote a number of medical works in Latin. This is the only suggestion of recognition of Christmas in the "Diary."

From Riley's I went to Mrs. Lovegrove's. I found Wm. there—& Mr. & Mrs. Dunlap came there. The two last stayed there till nine; Wm. & I till eleven. Much conversation—which I feel incapable of sketching.

Saturday, 26th
To Abigail Smith, Junr.

Your letter, of the 20th of Novr., my dear sister, gave me more, and more various, pleasure, than I can well express. I recd. it on the evening of the very day in which I had dismist a letter, for Aurora, full of that anxiety, which I could not but strongly feel. How pleasing, how delightful, to learn that all cause for apprehension, on our sister's account, was joyfully removed; and that she had presented us with a new argument for gladness, in a living & healthy child! But, consoling & agreable as this event was, it scarcely gave me more satisfaction than to observe the spirit of improvement, which your letter, every where, manifested. Assure yourself, my dear friend, that thus to feel, is half to accomplish your victory; and that your continued resolution is all that is wanting, to your being both wise & useful, learned, & happy. Never lose this spirit, but mature it into habits; & extend it into every minutest concernment. Correctness & order, industry & perseverance, even in little matters, exert a beneficial influence over the whole conduct, and render their application, to more important affairs, easier, & more satisfactory; while the great principles, which determine our actions, on every momentous occasion, are, thus, assisted, in their endeavours to become incorporated into *every* action; & we become, more readily, the children of reason, in all situations; & more enabled to distinguish & perform our duty towards all mankind. Have I exprest myself too abstractedly? as I fear I have—and will you apprehend the foregoing remark to mean?—that the application, or extension of the spirit of improvement, to the most minute parts of our conduct, is of the utmost importance: not only, as it may rightly direct them, but, also, as it may influence us in respect to things of higher duty. It is unnecessary for me to descend to particularize: a thousand examples will be immediately suggested to your own mind, on the slightest reflection. Yet, that I may be completely intelligible, and as the instance is connected with the subject, & prest upon me, by seeing it before me—I will mention *Your Writing*. Of this I have spoken to you, before; but never in this light. Correctness in this particular, in the formation of your characters, & in the disposition of your lines, would, unquestionably, tend to introduce correctness in your orthography, your punctuation, your stile, & above all, into your thoughts. Correctness in your thoughts, on one subject, would extend it's influence to every other subject; & this precision of thinking, would lead to rectitude of conduct; & rectitude of conduct, to happiness—the crown of all our labours, the bright & inseparable reward of virtue. You will not misunderstand me. I do not intend that all this great good would result from writing correctly, alone, but only that writing correctly would, so far as it has any influence, & some it must have, favor such an effect: and I instanced the direction of the spirit of improvement to this particular, because your letter, which lies before me, proves how much it's direction thereto is needed. But, not to harrass you on this subject, I will say, that, both your stile of writing & of thinking, in this same letter, is more than usually correct; & affords a promising prospect of future & rapid improvement. I will add, that I have but little doubt of you effecting all that ought rationally to be expected of you, if you continue to advance as fast as you have, lately, appeared to advance—Go on, my sister & my friend, & the most happy consequences can not fail to flow from your exertions!

In respect to the books you mention, I shall give you my opinion, freely. I think you have done well, in reading Blair's Lectures;[11] & that you may read them a second, and a third, time, with advantage. Perhaps, you would do well to examine some of your own compositions—(some of your letters, for example, which have been leisurely written) by his rules; and to endeavour to apply them. Were you not too much engaged, I would further recommend it to you, to attempt an arrangement of your notions, on some particular subject, in the form of an Essay; with reference to the rules laid down in the Lectures, & for the purpose of improving your stile of thinking & writing. With regard to the "Philosophical Dictionary"[12]—I think you will act most wisely in laying it aside; &, also, all M. de Voltaire's Works, unless they should be his dramatic works; & of these I recommend to you his Tragedies only; & to which you may add, now I recollect it, his Henriade.[13] I do not give you this direction under the influence of the prejudices so common against this most ingenious Writer, but because I think you may, now, alone as you are, find more intelligible & sound writers on Morals & Philosophy; & because you ought to read his Philosophical Works under the direction of some person both able & willing to point out to you his errors.

Of two subjects: concerning which I am particularly curious, you have not spoken: Arithmetic & Journalizing. I wish to learn that you are still attentive to the one, & that you receive delight & advantage from the other. Can you, sincerely, assure me of the gratification of this my wish? Of the importance of the first, having so often spoken I need say nothing now; of the value of the second, if you have carefully adhered to it, for two months, you must be an adequate judge. May they both prove to you, sources of permanent, as well as present, advantage & pleasure.

You mention your having written to me, immediately on the birth of our little kinsman: but this letter I have never received. Possibly, were you to inform me how it was forwarded, I might be able to obtain it. Your letter, for Lichfield, was sent in season. I have heard from thence, several times since, & all are well.

Farewell.

Saturday, Decr. 26. 1795.
Cedar St. No. 13. N. York.   E. H. Smith.

The necessity of doing some writing, soon, has induced me to lay aside my regular studies, for the present. This morning I have finished my letter to J. Williams—& composed the one to my sister Abigail. I also, made out the general & particular Certificates, for our Delegates to the Abolition Convention. The remainder of the forenoon I spent in reading Mr. Randolph's Pamphlet.

Afternoon: I did some business, & continued to read Mr. R's Pamphlet. Drank tea at Horace Johnson's. Seth returned to-day, but was absent; so that I did not see him. Club met there—Present—Dunlap, Kent, W. W. Woolsey, H. & W. Johnson. Horace read us Dr. Aikin's Letter to his son—*An Improvement*.[14] We then, after a slight discussion of it, proceeded to discuss & determine on the conduct we ought to pursue, in respect to Prosper Wetmore. This *conversation* was interrupted, by the entrance of Wetmore himself, accompanied by Alsop. *It* now took a general turn; the politics of the day were discoursed of very largely. Wetmore felt himself ill at ease—for he could not avoid observing a marked coolness in our conduct towards him. After this, he stayed but a short time; & Alsop & he departed, together. The discussion was, now, renewed; & it was, ultimately, determined—that we should, collectively, address a letter to him—stating the reasons of our estrangement to him—& pointing out the terms on which we must in future, associate with him; & Dunlap & myself were desired to prepare the letter. And thus the evening ended.

Sunday, 27th

I copied the letter to my sister. Dunlap came here, I drew up a letter to Prosper Wetmore, which he made a few alterations in, & agreed to. Wm. did the same. Thus was spent the forenoon. After dinner, I made a professional visit; &, returning, called in on Dingley, & sat some time with him. I drank tea at Woolsey's— whither Dunlap came; we examined, altered, & Woolsey agreed, generally, to the letter. Woolsey & I went to Moses Rogers's:[15] my business being to see him,

---

[11] Hugh Blair, Scottish minister (1718-1800), professor of rhetoric: *Lectures on Rhetoric* (1783).

[12] *The Philosophical Dictionary, or the Opinions of Modern Philosophers on Metaphysical, Moral and Political Subjects* (London, 1786).

[13] A poem in 10 cantos by Voltaire on Henri VI. Voltaire's epic appeared first as *La Ligue ou Henri le Grand* in 1723 and as *[The] Henriade* in 1728.

[14] *Letters From a Father to His Son, on Various Topics, relative to Literature, and the Conduct of Life* (London, 1796). John Aiken (1747-1822) was a tireless writer not only on medicine but on literature, sociology, and geography. He also published some poetry.

[15] Moses Rogers (1750-1825), a wealthy New York merchant, husband of Mrs. William Dunlap's half-sister Sarah (Woolsey) Rogers. He was governor of the New York Hospital 1792-1799.

concerning our going to Phila. He was not at home—& I waited for him, in vain, till after nine. I went to H. Johnson's, I found Wm. there—& Seth, who I had not seen, before, since his return. He is fine health. Both H. & S. read the letter—& agreed to it. And thus has past the after part of the day.

Monday, 28th

I have been on the run all this day; partly on my own business, partly on that [of] others, & partly on that of the Manumission Society. This almost constant motion has only been interrupted by a visit, of an hour, from Mr. Post—surgeon & physician—till, after having spent two hours, at Mr. Websters, where I drank tea, I have sitten down at home; & part of the time reading loud to William, & part of the time silently to myself, I have devoted near four hours to Mde. Roland's "Appeal to Impartial Posterity, Part I."[16]: and this, with inexpressible satisfaction, on most accounts—on all which relate to her—except her sufferings—& yet even in regard to these, in some measure—since they called forth that wonderful, that sublime, display of energy & virtue, which elevate her character, in my eyes, far above that of any woman who I now recollect to have become celebrated in the history of nations: a woman, in whom appear to have been concentrated & consolidated, & warmed into living perfectness, all that dignifies & adorns, that consoles & instructs, humanity.

Tuesday, 29th
To Thomas Mumford.

It was my intention to have written to you, at some length; but a thousand interruptions have prevented me; and, now, I am obliged to set off, on a journey, to-morrow, & can only write you a few lines. I am going to Phila. as one of the Manumission Society's Delegates; & their business has kept me on the run for some days, which would have been better spent in writing to you & Mary. To her I wrote a few lines, the day before receiving your letter. These I hope she has recd. The inclosed letter, to Abby, has been since written; & at a time when I trusted that I should have had leisure to write to you all; otherwise it would have been the bearer of congratulations, which must now be omitted, as I have not time to offer them. But, assure yourself, my dear friend, no person can more rejoice in the welfare of you, & of yours, than I do; no one has your happiness more at heart; no one more sincerely loves your virtues. The additional blessing which is now presented to you, in a son, will be heightened, to the benefit & joy of all, if your attentive zeal should inculcate & nourish in him, those principles which I trust his parents, equally, possess. This, I doubt not, will be the unceasing object of your care; & that it may be rewarded by complete success, fervently prays,

Your brother,

Tuesday, Decr. 29. 1795.
Cedar St. No. 13. N. York.   E. H. Smith.

This day, as yesterday, has been hurriedly devoted to petty businesses. I have, notwithstanding, snatched time to finish Mde. Roland's Book; to make a short visit to Mrs. Lovegrove; to spent two hours at Woolsey's, this evening; and, since my return, to write the preceeding short letter.

The weather threatens to be bad: yet I shall set forward, to-morrow; and, on friday evening, hope to embrace Joseph & Charles.

Wednesday, 30th
To Reuben Smith, of Ld.

I am just on the point of departing for Phila., &, as I expect to [be] absent near a fortnight, I tho't it best to intimate it to you; lest you should be disappointed, were you to send any business for me to transact.

My trunk, with the cheese & butter, arrived safe, & in good condition. I am pleased that the medicines are such as you wished, but disappointed in respect to the Figs: for I had a box opened, which appeared to me, to be pretty good—& I sat them one side, for myself; & this was, I believe, the box sent. It seems as if fortune was determined we shall have nothing, of this kind, as it ought to be.

In respect to the payment due to Philips & Clark—I believe that there will be no difficulty, even should it over-run the time. If they are likely to be much in want of the money, I will give you notice: &, at the worst, I may be able to satisfy them here—for a while. But I do not expect any trouble from them.

We have nothing new here, beside what you will see in the Papers.

My love to my mother, sister, & friends.

Wednesday, Decr. 30. 1795.
Cedar St. No. 13. N. York.   E. H. Smith.

This day was one continuous bustle, while I was in New York; &, at a little after two I sat out, on my journey to Phila. Between the Ferry & Newark, I met El. Smith Jr. who was returning from Baltimore & Phila., & who gave me a letter from C. B. B.—in which, I am kindly solicited to take up my residence with him, while I remain in Phila.

We reached Elizabeth Town, to spend the night, after a very disagreable & fatiguing jaunt of fifteen miles.

Thursday, 31st

We set forward at two in the morning, & reached

Moses and Dr. David Rogers of Greenfield, Connecticut, were sons of half-brothers. In 1792 he took William Woolsey as his partner in Moses Rogers & Co. In 1793 the firm name was changed to Rogers and Woolsey. Barrett, *Old Merchants of New York City,* pp. 317 *passim.* Two other Rogers are cited: Parson Rogers and Dr. John R. B. Rogers.

[16] Madame Marie-Jeanne Roland, a counselor and adviser of the moderate Republican party (Girondists) in the French Revolution, was executed in 1793. Her "Appeal" was published in 1795.

Trenton, fifty miles, at dark. It rained very hard—the roads were almost impassable, & we were constrained to stop. Nothing remarkable happened this day—which concludes the Year. I postpone those remarks, which the season, & other circumstances naturally suggest, till my return to peace & liberty, at New York.

January 1796
Friday, 1st

Contrary to my wishes, I am constrained, by the situation in which I am, to make the record of this, & probably the succeeding days, during my residence in Phila. more than usually short. I must be content with barely noticing transactions & events, without allowing myself to indulge in those remarks & speculations, which they would naturally suggest.

We reached Phila. by three in the afternoon, in a most pleasant day. Immediately after dinner, I sought out Charles. We went together to W. Franklin,[17] the Secretary of the Abolition Society here, to learn where the Convention met. At the hour, I was there; & found several of my acquaintance: particularly Dr. Rush & Griffitts: with the former of whom, before we went to business, I had some conversation. The Convention was organized this evening; & I was placed on the Committee of Arrangements. After the adjournment of the Convention, the Committee devoted an hour to business.

At this house, (the house of the father of C. B. B.) I now first saw James Brown, an older brother of Charles. This evening we had some talk—& I read Charles some parts of my journal.

It was late when we slept.

Saturday, 2nd

All this day, doggedly employed, in the Committee of Arrangements. The Convention met in the evening: so that I have not had a moment's leisure.

After supper, Charles read me a few pages of his Journal, & also of his projected Novel. I recd. letters from Wm. Johnson, & my father.

Dr. Wistar was present at the Convention this evening; & I renewed my acquaintance with him.

Sunday, 3rd

After I had brought up my Journal to this day—(for I had been obliged to neglect it till now, ever since my leaving home,) I visited Mr. Tracy. I found him, & four others of the Connecticut Representation, well. I stayed with him till dinner, having much general conversation, & then returned hither. After dinner Charles & I went to his brother Armit's—where we tarried till near tea-time. From thence we proceeded to Timothy Paxon's.[18]

---

[17] The Abolition Society had two secretaries at the same time, Walter Franklin (1729-1813), attorney and counselor at law, and James Todd. Franklin served at least one term on the Common Council in 1797. See *Stephen's Philadelphia Directory for 1796*, p. 26; *Philadelphia Directory* (1797), p. 26.

[18] Timothy Paxon. The *Philadelphia Directory* for 1796 labels him a "flour factor."

I have long had a curiosity to see this man & his wife. It has now been gratified: but I have not leisure to dwell on this subject now. Beside, I am to see them again. Here I remained till eight in the evening—when I took my leave, & sat off for Mr. Wolcott's. There, with him & his wife, Mr. & Mrs. Goodrich, who live there, I spent the rest of the evening.

Monday, 4th

To William Johnson.

We did not arrive, in this city, till after three o'clock on Friday. The roads were inconceivably bad, & the weather, for the most part, very disagreable. Friday morning proved a cordial to us all; &, ever since, the temperature & sky have been more those of Spring, than of Winter.

The Convention met at five; but was not numerous. Several of the Societies are not, even now, represented.

You know the course of procedure on the first evening. A Committee of Arrangements was appointed, of whom I was one. We sat more than an hour, after the Convention broke up; and, beginning again, at half past nine, the next day, we were busily employed, with the exception of an hour, till six in the evening; when the Convention met, & kept us till ten. I was thoroughly jaded—so that, yesterday, I was glad to be able to snuff a little fresh air, & hunt up some of my friends. Your letter, with the inclosure, was all that I had to make the situation tolerable, till yesterday. Short as it was, it excited pages of ideas, more brilliant, & more soul-satisfying, than the view of all the splendors of Philadelphia.

"Brissot came to see us." You recollect some remarks which fell from me; on the passage, just before I left New York. I have seen Charles, Stella & her husband; &, tho' the visit was short, & embarrassed by many of those circumstances, which often impair the satisfaction which one would, otherwise, receive from a first interview, still it has left pleasing impressions behind. These Friends of Philadelphia, cheerful, intelligent, polished & well-informed, how infinitely are they removed, from the cypress-visaged, & selfish *Quakers* of New York! Covered by those Waist-coats with ponderous flaps, & by those triple-walled stays, bosoms beat, with high, heroic, love of man. Understanding beams from forth those bushy locks; & wit sparkles from underneath that close-eared cap. If the few insuperable awkwardnesses of their language & garb were removed—all might, here, see the reality of those sweet, simple, & intellectual forms, which have so often in vision delighted our imaginations.

We are all well here. Charles remembers you all. Present my affectionate regard to all, with you. To Mrs. Lovegrove, &, if he has returned, to Mr. L. remember me particularly.

Yours.

Monday, Jany. 4. 1796.
Phila. No. 117. So. Second St.   E. H. Smith.

This day I have visited the Halls of the Senate & Representatives of the U. S. & of the Representatives of Pennsylvania. In this last I found my old friend Michael Leib; we had some conversation, & went together, to call on several acquaintances; who, unfortunately, were not at home. I called, ineffectually, at Jno. Fenno's. I have seen Peter Thomson, been at his house—& he accompanied Charles & me, around the city, to observe the late improvements. The evening, at the Convention.

Tuesday, 5th

I called on Mr. Miller, ineffectually—he was not at his lodgings. I attended Dr. Rush's Lecture, &, afterwards, accompanied him to the Hospital. I called, in vain, at Mr. Wolcott's & Dr. Griffitts's. I visited a number of Book stores. Such were the occupations of the morning. I dined at Dr. Wistar's—where were some company, agreable conversation—& where I stayed till after five P. M.—Charles & I went to see his friend Miss Atmore—where also, are found his friend Miss Biddle, & where Peter Thomson came. We spent an hour, very agreably. From seven till ten—at the Convention.

I was greatly, but joyfully, surprized, to learn, at Miss Atmore's, that Joseph Strong was in town—had learnt that I was to be there, this evening—& had called after me. I can not see him till tomorrow.

Wednesday, 6th

Was with Joseph Strong, from ten, till twelve—in company with Charles; Then we spent an hour and a half at Timothy Paxon's. When returned home, Charles read to me, from his Novel, till three. We dined with his brother Armit. I drank tea with parson Rogers—& was at the Convention all the evening. A terrible stormy night.

Thursday, 7th

A fine day. Spent the forenoon with Mr. Tracy. Met Joseph Strong in the street, & had some talk with him. Dined with Michael Leib. When I returned, learnt, of Charles, that Joseph was in town. We went to him; & stayed half an hour with him. Drank tea at Saml. Coates's. His wife a fine woman. At the Convention all the evening. Convention adjourned *sine die*.

Friday, 8th

I divided the forenoon between a visit to Joseph, & one to Mr. Wolcott's family. Charles read to me, another portion of his Novel. I called on Th. P. Cope.[19] Then on Tracy; & together, with several of his Colleagues, spent the evening at the Theater.

Saturday, 9th

I have called on a number of persons, this day; & ineffectually. I waited on M. Wertmüller,[20] & was highly gratified by seeing several of his pictures; of which more hereafter. I saw the celebrated Volney. I spent the whole evening with Joseph.

Sunday, 10th

Charles & I visited at Timothy Paxon's—& saw there, T. C. Cope. I spent an hour with U. Tracy. I dined, & stayed till six P. M. at Oliver Wolcott's—where stay Mr. & Mrs. Goodrich, & where Mr. Ellsworth[21] also dined. We had a long argumentation on, what the three gentlemen, who all opposed me, termed the French Atheistic Philosophy. I called at Dr. Rush's—but he was not at home. Charles, Joseph, & I, spent the evening at Paxon's.

Thursday, 14th

I arrived at New York, yesterday, a little before two P.M. after a fortnight's absence. My journey had nothing in it, worthy of remark. The roads were excessive bad; the weather part of the time very bad, partly very fine. Company tolerable. Samuel M. Hopkins overtook us at Prince Town—on his return from Virginia—& journeyed in our company most of the day. I found that Danl. W. Lewis had been here in my absence. A note from Mumford—& letters from Mrs. Tracy, Sally Pierce, Joseph Strong, & the father of Sophy, were waiting my arrival: & this day I have recd. others, from my Father, sister Abby, Dr. Buel, & Theodore Dwight. I spent the principal part of yesterday evening at Dunlap's & Woolsey's; after having called on Miss Morton —for whom I had letters. This day, also, I have been at Woolsey's—& at M. Rogers's. Mrs. Woolsey has been delivered of two sons, during my absence.

---

[19] Thomas P. Cope (1768-1854). From 1786 to 1790 he was an apprentice to his uncle Thomas Mendenhall and for two years thereafter his partner. Going into business for himself he acquired a line of packet ships sailing between Philadelphia and Liverpool. He became one of the wealthiest men of his day. His fame, however, rests in considerable degree on his refusal to flee the city as did many of the rich during the yellow fever plagues of 1793 and 1797; instead he applied himself vigorously to helping the sick and the poor. He was a founder of the Mercantile Library Company (of which he was president for many years) and he also gave generously to the Institute for Colored Youth to found a Scientific School. His interests and the direction of his charitable activities were much like Smith's, the difference being that he was able also to back his charity with great sums of money.

[20] Adolf Ulric Wertmüller (1751-1811), a Swedish-American painter, trained in Sweden and France. His Danaë is said to have shocked Philadelphia. He did a portrait of Washington (one of several reproductions of which is in the Metropolitan Museum), and a portrait of Marie Antoinette. Smith mentions him later as a friend of Gahn and notes (September 30, 1796) that he is about to sail for France.

[21] Oliver Ellsworth (1745-1807) attended Yale, graduated from Princeton 1766; Connecticut General Assembly, senator from Connecticut 1789-1796, lawyer, Connecticut state's attorney, chief justice of the United States Supreme Court 1796-1799, envoy extraordinary and minister plenipotentiary to France; many other offices.

Friday, 15th

Two professional calls; some calls of business; short visits from Dunlap & Alsop; & attention to posting my books; have occupied my time this day. I spent the evening at Mr. Lovegrove's. I do not, yet, get time to be more copious. It is late at night. A letter from Theodore Dwight.

Sunday, 17th

To Reuben Smith, of Lichfield.

I have recd. two letters from you, my dear father, since I last wrote: one, including an hundred dollars, the other, two hundred. I was in Philadelphia, when I recd. the first; from whence I returned on Wednesday last; but was too much engaged on thursday to write. Since then I have paid over the two hundred dollars to Philips & Clarke, according to your direction; & shall forward, to you, their receit, by the first safe conveyance.

I found Mr. Norton waiting my return. He appears to deserve the good character given of him. I have introduced him to Philips & Clarke, & he is getting his medicines put up at their Store. This will engage him for several days; & when he leaves this, I expect to send my letters by him.

Sophy's parents have, undoubtedly, heard from her before this time—as both she, & the lady with whom she lives have written to them. I shall write, notwithstanding, to Mr. Pierpont—in reply to his letter, & give him every information in my power.

Our winter has, hitherto, been very open & warm—& I fear will continue so, to the prevention of the intended journey of my sisters, to Lichfield. It is possible that you have had snow, when we have only had rain; if so, they may venture to come. I have heard nothing very particularly from them, for some time. While I was at Phila. a few lines were recd. directed to me, from Thomas—informing me of their health, & serving as the cover to a number of letters for Lichd.—which were forwarded by Mr. Lewis. If they come at all, it is now the time for them to set forward. What their intentions are, in this respect, you are probably acquainted with. I hope nothing will prevent their visit.

Nothing could have more opportunely happened than the arrival of the money, which you kindly sent me. We had been long in arrear for Rent: We are now free. Indeed, I can not express my sense of your unremitted exertions in my behalf. All other debts are hateful, burthensome, oppresive: all other debts I hope to be able to discharge: but this which I owe to you, is both grateful & unoppressive—& I have no reluctance to it's perpetuity. To love can not be painful.

Present my best regards to my mother—to my sister. I can not bannish some little wonder, at the long silence of Fanny. I have not heard from her, since I saw her.

Sunday, Jany. 17. 1796.
Cedar St. No. 13. N. York.   E. H. Smith.

To Evelyn Pierpont.

You will not accuse me of any neglect, in not answering your letter before this time, when you learn that I was absent from the city when your letter came; & that I have been at home but a few days. Had I been here, when Mr. Smith came, I would gladly have accompanied him to see your child. Your anxiety, on her account, has been removed, I suppose, for some time; as, no doubt, you must have recd. letters both from her, & from Mrs. Lovegrove. Those letters will best explain to you, the principal subjects of your solicitude & inquiry: I shall, however, answer your questions as fully as I am able.

I saw Sophy night before last: she was well; & has been well, ever since her coming to live here. I suppose you know that she has not had the Small-Pox—& are also acquainted with the reason why she has not had it. There has been no Small Pox in N. York this winter. I have two persons to innoculate, beside Sophy, & I have been on the hunt for *matter* to innoculate with, since I returned from Lichfield,[22] & have not been able to find any. None of the Physicians have been able to find any. Thus, you see, it has been impossible for her to have it. In the meantime she has been in no danger; for, if the City were full of it, in the retired situation in which she lives, she would not be exposed. But she will be inoculated as soon as *matter* can be obtained for the purpose.

I am happy to inform you that Sophy seems well pleased with her situation, & that the people with whom she lives appear to be equally satisfied with her. She has probably informed you that Mrs. Lovegrove pays particular attention to her improvement in reading, writing, & sewing. I am not a judge of the last, & I have never heard her read—but in both she has no fault found with her. As I have, sometimes, set her copies myself, I have had opportunity to notice some improvement in her writing: to which she devotes a part of every day, regularly. On the whole, I do not doubt, but that, both she, & her employers, will have equal reason to be satisfied; & that, if things go on, as they now do, you, & Mrs. Pierpont, will have cause to felicitate yourselves on the proper conduct & success in life of your daughter.

Sunday, Jany. 17. 1796.
Cedar St. No. 13. N. York.   E. H. Smith.

To Sally Pierce.

On the common principle of "Like for like," I should be justified for sending *you* a short letter; but I have disclaimed that principle, I hope, am actuated by a bet-

---

[22] Smith, like his father, believed in inoculation for smallpox. He followed the usual procedure, found someone with the disease, took a small amount of pus from sores on the patient and rubbed it into scratches or small cuts on each of the arms of the recipient. The results were usually violent; the procedure could be fatal. One of the most famous victims of the practice was the great Jonathan Edwards in 1758. See Matthew D. Davis, *Memoirs of Aaron Burr* (New York, 1847) 1: pp. 119-120.

ter motive, at this time, even tho' my letter be short. Indeed, I am too much hurried to make it long: otherwise, I have subject enough for copiousness, furnished me by your letter, brief as it is.

I am pleased to learn that you are satisfied with the use I made of your money. I assure you that, under the circumstances, I tho't it doing the best in my power. I should have been better pleased, could I have followed your directions, literally. But that was not possible.

I concur with you, in part, in part not, in your remarks upon the Castle of Otranto. The machinery of that Piece appears to me equally magnificent & impressive. The feelings which it excites, in my breast, are those of awe & expectation. It is defective, as the Author has managed it—because the scattered parts are never formed into a whole; & the story is concluded without their appearing to influence directly, the conclusion. Here, I confess, I was disappointed. The objection which you make to the morality, is, likewise, in my opinion just. And yet, it is Christian morality—the morality of the Ten Commandments: "for I am a *jealous* God—visiting the iniquities of the fathers, upon the children—to the *third*, & *fourth*, generations." How do you reconcile *jealousy* & *revenge*, to your ideas of *justice*? Yet such is the divine character, as exhibited in the Old Testament, & as adopted & preached by Christians: & I repeat it, the morality of the Castle of Otranto is perfectly conformable to these models—prest upon us, for our acceptance & direction, for ages. How are we to act, in this place? Shall we press boldly on, & strive to form to ourselves some more suitable conceptions of the Source of Animation? Or, must we "put off our sandals —for the ground on which we tread, is holy ground"?[23] I should be highly gratified by your reply to these questions: or by your opinions on this interesting subject.

In answer to your inquiries concerning Sophy—I can only tell you, that, those with whom she lives appear satisfied with her, & she pleased with them. She has her health, perfectly; & is, I think, improving in reading, writing, & sewing—the three things most material, at present. I have heard no complaint from Mrs. L. & Sophy always seems happy.

I thank you, with all my heart, for your congratulations; as I am glad with all my heart, for their cause.

Sunday, Jany. 17. 1796.   Farewell.
Cedar St. No. 13. N. York.   E. H. Smith.

To Theodore Dwight.

It was on my return from Lichfield that I wrote those few lines to you, of which you speak, & in which I thought that I had mentioned from whence I had come to New Haven. But they were written in the greatest hurry imaginable. I saw a little package, lying on the counter, directed to you; & instantly conceived & executed the design of inclosing Mr. Trumbull's Poem, to you. Surely, you are too well acquainted with the character & temper of my heart, to doubt of the steadiness of my attachment to you, of my deriving pleasure from seeing you, & to suspect me of forming any paltry plans for ostentation. No, my friend, I neither pant for wealth, nor expect it—& one only reason, could ever restrain me from visiting you, when so near you as Lichfield; & of that you must have been informed. While I pretend to do business here, & while I look to business here for a support, my presence, for the greater part of the year, is indispensable. If I visit any where, it is obviously my first duty to visit my parents; & if I do visit them, I have no time to extend my visitation beyond their place of residence. A journey to Lichd. & back, unavoidably takes up three weeks. Were I to go to Hartford, I could not be excused should I neglect riding over to Wethersfield. At Wethersfield—it is only eleven miles to Middletown; &, beside my friends in the city, I have near relations & an only grandparent, whom I have not seen for several years, & who is now near ninety years of age. Beside, Berlin & Farmington are on my road back to Lichfield. All this could scarcely occupy less time than three more weeks—& do any justice to my own feelings, & the expectations of my friends: and six weeks, are nearly one eight of the whole year; & when considered in relation to the nature of my profession, & the difficulty of forming an establishment in it, a period of great importance. You will see, in this statement, the true reason why I do not extend my visits to the banks of the Connecticut. As for Wealth—the hope of obtaining it has, long since, fled my bosom; & the expectation of Competency does but hover around it. This will form an answer to the friendly inquiries, by which your letter is concluded; for which I thank you, while, at the same time, I congratulate you, on the brighter promises which the future holds out to you.

The Second Volume of the American Poems—is still in an equivocal situation. There does not appear sufficient encouragement to proceed in it, at present; & Collier seems undetermined what to do. I shall prepare it, for the Press, at all events. If he chooses to go on with it—it is well; if not, I design, at some future period, to publish it, at my own risk. In that case, I shall new arrange the whole affair—& assuming to myself the first volume, shall probably, publish three, or four, handsome volumes. But, if I do this, it will be a work of time. Half of the second volume, on the present plan, is ready for the Press—at a moment's warning; & I could get nearly the remaining half in readiness, in a few weeks. From Alsop, however, I expect nothing. He seems resolved to write no more; & he has nothing, already written, which he will consent to have published.

I hope Mr. Trumbull will prepare his Poem. He can not expect that it should be forgotten: neither, in my opinion, (considering the time at which it was written,

---

[23] "And the captain of the Lord's host said unto Joshua, Loose thy shoe from off thy foot; for the place where thou standest is holy." Josh. 5:15.

& his age,) need he be ashamed of it. If it do not add to his reputation, it will not impair it.

I saw the New Year's Verses while at Philadelphia—& had no difficulty in fixing on their principal author—whose happiest effort I think they are not. Had Babcock any verses this year? I have seen none. I have seen the Middletown Verses: were they written by yourself, or Nathaniel, or both, or neither,—or who were they written by?

As for us, we have all degenerated into plain prose, & downright argument. The Muse has taken her flight; & the Spirit of Satire has all evaporated. Richard left the bung out of the Jug, last summer; & this warm weather has driven it all off.

Wm. hopes to hear from you, speedily. He is well—as are all your friends: some of whom are in a *thriving way*. You doubtless will have heard, before this letter reaches you, that Mrs. Riley has a fine girl, & Mrs. Woolsey two stout boys.

My love to Mrs. Dwight, Mason, Ezekl. &c.

Sunday, Jany. 17. 1796.
Cedar St. No. 13. N. York. E. H. Smith.

The principal part of this day, till dinner, employed in writing the foregoing letters—the first of which I transcribed. I spent the afternoon at Woolsey's; the evening, with him, at Dunlap's—till eight. Since my return home, I have been engaged in reading A Report of the Directors of the Sierra Leone Company, to the Proprietors[24]—an interesting publication which I have nearly half finished. Wm., who came home about ten, spent an hour with me—in conversation.

Monday, 18th
To Mrs. Tracy.

Your last letter, which I found waiting my return from Phila., has given me great pleasure. To a mind eager in the search after truth, & desirous to disseminate it over the whole world; to a mind venturing to adopt opinions, not commonly received, as truths; to one looking for opposition & contumely, rather than support & approbation, & who sincerely believes the doctrines he receives to be essential to human happiness; to such an one, how dear, how invaluable, is every new proof of congeniality of sentiment! Even if it extend no further than a concurrent conviction of the importance of inquiry: For mankind, in general, are more frightened by the necessary labor of investigation, than by any sentiments, how hostile soever to their own. On all moral questions, they are either too timid, or too indolent, to inquire. And, why should they trouble themselves with solicitous & painful examinations, when they pay a man well for devoting his life to such cares; to the business of seeking out what is true, & then pointing it out to them? "We put our property under the safeguard of the lawyer, our health under the guardianship of the physician, our reason under the guidance of the priest; each is learned in his deparment; let him answer for his faithful administration; what is that to us?" That such are the feelings of men, in these respects, the history of all their conduct exhibits melancholly proof. "But this is vile, 'tis infamous!" you say. It is so: & yet, how few adopt an opposite practice! And how strenuously do we hear persons, & of vigorous understanding & cultivated minds, argue in extenuation, in support, of this pernicious system! What! shall I implicitly receive an opinion for truth, & blindly practice what it directs, because you tell me it is truth? Shall I bow my reason to your authority, & tamely yield my faith to whatever you require? By what right do you assume the direction of my conscience? Shew me the patent by which you are commissioned, point me out it's author, and give me proof, unequivocal proof, that he is indeed it's author. You falter! You can not do it? I know it. Your power is usurpation, & you are either deceivers, or deceived—or both. Your system, that monstrous compound of error & of truth—I see that, as a system, it is false. Still, false as it is, it weighs down the better half of men. The ingenuity of ages has been employed in it's behalf. It's legions surround the very temple of Truth; & often, while they seem to invite our approach, are preparing to circumvent, or entangle us in the labyrinths which their unhallowed hands have wrought in the majestic groves which environ it. I see that what mankind have mistaken for the clear sky of truth, is no more than the mist of error; but, tho' I perceive & am convinced of the deception, it forms a cloud too thick for me to penetrate. It is thro' the loopholes only, which the brisk breeze of discussion sometimes forms, that I can discern the celestial azure. What then! is this the less a cloud because it hides the heavens from my eyes? Or am I to believe this mottled intermixture of light & shadow, is all, & one, because I can discover nothing more? Will not the time come, when all these vapours shall be dissipated? And shall I hesitate to call this vapour & that sky, because I am yet unable, with my own breath, to disperse the one, & display the whole extent of the other?

Do not reply to all this, that, "It is talking in the clouds." for, tho' I have been, as it were, seduced into this strain, & had no intention of straying into it, when I began to write, yet I am confident that you can not misapprehend me; & I am tolerably sure that, without further explication, you would feel it to be an answer to one part of your letter. But, I will discuss the question more plainly.

---

[24] Some of the most forward-looking men in England were responsible for the first British effort to establish a workable and humane colony in Sierra Leone. The first effort in 1787 was a failure and the colonists suffered greatly. They were escaped slaves, Negroes discharged from the American army after the Revolution and a handful of not-too-enthusiastic white whores. Everything conspired against them—their inborn shortcomings, disease, the climate and attacks by the natives. In 1791 the Sierra Leone Company was formed and the effort was repeated, against almost hopeless odds. A detailed account of the colony is most readily found in the *Encyclopedia Britannica*, 11th ed.

In all kinds of inquiry, Moral, as well as every other, we must endeavour to come at first principles. When these are obtained, tho' the business of deduction may be occasionally difficult, & the application of principles to many subjects exceedingly delicate, yet the chief labour is accomplished. If I would form a system of morals, I must acquaint myself with the powers, situation, & history of man. When I have accurately obtained this knowlege, my inquiry will be, what follows from this information? If such are the powers of man, such his situation, & such his history, what is he? how ought he to act? & what is to be expected of him? It is obviously my duty, in the pursuit of such an inquiry, to apply myself to it with a mind, as far as may be, unbiased by any particular system: With a pure & earnest desire of knowing what is true; & with a determination to adopt what may appear to me to be so; & to make it the governing rule of my life. Now Truth, in strictness, can be but *one*: and can only exist in the mind of that being to whom all is known. Men can not be expected to attain to the entire knowlege of truth. Should they discover the *principle*, in their present imperfect state, they must, of necessity, err a thousand times in the *application* of that principle, to the affairs of life. All, then, that can be said of any human system, & of any system, or succession of human actions, is, that it, or they, approach or recede more or less, than any other, to or from the truth: And this approach or recession will be more accelerated, or diminished, in proportion as men become more intimately instructed in the relation between the several parts of the moral & material universe. This being true, we have no right to expect perfection, much less to demand it, of any human being, or in any system of morals, or physics. We may demand of all, that they shall strive to learn what is right; & shall never hesitate to sacrifice any error, however dear it may be to them, or how advantageous soever they may deem a continuance in the practice of it to be. Let us apply this to the question immediately before us. Mr. Godwin, we will suppose, becomes convinced that it is the duty of every human being, and therefore his duty, to inquire for himself, & to rest his faith on his own conviction only. In the progress of his inquiries he becomes convinced of the falsity & futility of a number of systems of faith; some of which are no longer supported by partisans, some only by a few, & some by the greater part of the world. The arguments which investigation presents him with, to disprove them, are satisfactory; &, accordingly, he rejects them all. If these arguments are, in his view, conclusive—he is bound to admit their validity, & it is his duty to make that sacrifice which they enjoin. Still, according to the terms of the supposition, he may be far from having discovered what is true. These systems are erroneous—of that I am satisfied—what then is the real system? He proceeds in his inquiry—till, at length, he satisfies himself of the validity of certain principles. From these principles he next goes on to deduce consequences; & these deductions become so many rules, which he lays down for the direction of mankind, in their journey thro' life. Suppose me now, to take up Mr. Godwin's Book & suppose that, after a careful examination, I find his system to be equally false with that of every other man, with every one which preceeded it—does it, therefore, follow—because his is false, that they, or either of them are true? Certainly not! He may have disproved all other systems, tho' he may have failed to discover & unfold the true one. And when we consider the imperfect state of moral science in the world, & how very lately it has become at all a subject of general attention, we should act unreasonably were we to insist on receiving a perfect system from any man; & were we to resolve to hold to the present, of whose falsity we are convinced, till we could find a perfect one, instead of discarding it, as soon as we found it wrong, & applying ourselves to construct a better. This argument is stated, at some length, & with great perspicuity, by Mr. Gisborne, the refuter of Paley; & as his book is now before me, I shall make no apology for transcribing the passage. "I wish stedfastly to fix one consideration upon the mind of the reader; namely, that whatever may be the number or the magnitude of the errors contained in the answer which I shall give," (to the question—What is the basis of morality?) "they can not, in any degree, affect the validity of the foregoing refutation of the rule of general expediency." (Mr. Paley's Rule.) "That rule, I apprehend, has been proved to be inadmissible through it's own radical & incurable defects. It can not, therefore, derive support from the real or supposed mistakes in any other system; for what has thus been demonstrated to be false, can never, by any mode of comparative reasoning, be rendered true. So that is I should unfortunately prove unable to establish, to the satisfaction of my readers, the fundamental principles of morality, which I am about to lay before them, that circumstance will afford them no solid ground for recurring to the standard proposed by Mr. Paley. In that case they will do well to reject both the one & the other, & look elsewhere for a safer guide."[25] Such is the language, which Mr. Godwin might well adopt; & I know not what you can reply to him. "All the systems of Religion"—might he say—"are false. They are founded in ignorance, & imposition; & are destructive of morality. I present you, in my book, with, what I conceive to be, the true system of morals. Examine it attentively: If it be true, adopt

---

[25] Thomas Gisborne (1758-1846) "An Enquiry into the Duties of Men in the Higher and Middle Classes of Society in Great Britain, Resulting from Their Respective Stations, Professions, and Employments." The subject of theological utilitarianism and Paley's place in the development of this line of thinking is both large and complex. Briefly, and therefore of necessity somewhat inaccurately, Paley, a latitudinarian minister, joined with other theologists and philosophers of the time in attempting to refute or rephrase Hobbes by giving virtue and the resultant happiness "to obedience to the will of God." There is little doubt that although Paley looms large in the times and Gisborne is less known that Smith would favor Gisborne.

it: but, if it be not true, do not, therefore, return to those errors, which I have fully unveiled." Is not such language rational? And is it any just cause for retaining particular creed, & for turning a deaf ear to the proof of it's absurdity, that he who opposes it does not present a perfect one?

I did not intend to have gone, so lengthily, into this question; but, since I have done it, I am not sorry. More justice, perhaps, has been done to it, with all my repetitions, than *I* should have done in a shorter manner of discussing it. In respect to Mr. Godwin's Book, as I have never read it, & am only acquainted with parts of it, I ought not, perhaps, to decide on it's merits. I will venture one remark only; that, as far as I am acquainted with it's contents—tho' I would not declare his system to be perfect—I have no hesitation in expressing it as my opinion—that it approaches nearer to truth, than any preceeding system, with which I am acquainted. But this opinion, you will understand to be pronounced on what has been represented to me, as his system: for with his system, as delivered by himself, I am but partially acquainted; having never read so much as the one half of a volume of his Book.[26]

I have now, at some length, endeavoured to remove what seems to be your principal source of opposition to this book: i. e. I have, I trust, established it as just— that Mr. Godwin's Book is not to be condemned, altogether, even tho' it do not present us with a perfect system of morals; & that former systems are not to be adhered to, because his is imperfect. In short, that no man is bound to produce a perfect system because he declares others to be imperfect.

As to what is perfect, what is true, I do not feel myself competent to decide. I am, as yet, but just entering on the great inquiry. I must judge according to the light which is afforded me. I seek with a sincere desire to find the truth with a firm resolution to adopt it, when found; & with a perfect readiness to relinquish any & every opinion, that I do, or may, possess, whenever it's falsity is demonstrated to me. Thus it may happen, that, of all my present opinions, I may retain **no one**, at some future period. And such must be the feelings, & such the situation, of every honest inquirer for the truth. At the same time, we ought not to be too ready to relinquish our opinions; & we should, above all, be on our guard against the suggestions of fear, selfishness, & sensuality; against the imposition of talents, authority, & even virtue—for good men, may act well from wrong motives, & the excellence of their lives is very apt to sanctify their opinions in the eyes of the mass of men.

Do you want a breathing spell? So do I. Let me, then, throw aside the pen, for the present; to be resumed, with fresh spirits, & greater interest.

Monday, Jany. 18. 1796.
Cedar St. No. 13. New York.   E. H. Smith.

---

[26] *Enquiry Concerning Political Justice* (1793).

I was busied for the most part of the time, till dinner, in writing the foregoing letter, & in transcribing those to Mr. Pierpont, & Miss Pierce—& this latter labor occupied some share of the afternoon. Dunlap spent an hour here; & we three, Wm., Dunlap & myself, drank tea at Mr. Lovegrove's; Where we stayed till half past seven. I called at Kent's—they were out. I went to Mr. Webster's—he & his wife were at home, & alone. About nine, Dr. Bollman—he who attempted the rescue of La Fayette,[27] entered; & we had more than an hour of very agreable & interesting conversation—which I design to mention more particularly hereafter.

Tuesday, 19th

Various errands engage me. Spent an hour with Dunlap, at his Store. Adams passes an hour with me, at my room—for the first time in several months. Read the Report of the Directors of the Sierra Leone Compy. &c. Copy my letter to Theodore Dwight. Spend the evening, with Wm., at Kent's. Am very unwell, all day, with a cold.

Wednesday, 20th

To Mrs. Tracy, (in continuation.)

I designed to have written somewhat further, in relation to a very interesting topic, hinted at in your letter: Whether man is to remain in his present condition? but I find myself unable. I have been quite unwell, for several days, with a severe cold, which must excuse some of the inaccuracies in the preceeding part of this letter, & I should not have added any thing to it, but that I might let you know what had been done in favor of the poor woman, for whom you have interested yourself.

When I was at Phila. Mr. Tracy gave me a letter, for Cash, from his wife, which, in the hurry of his passage thro' New York, he forgot. This I delivered, yesterday, to Cash; &, at the same time, informed him that, notwithstanding his promises, his wife had recd. nothing. He assures me, that, on the very day I last spake to him, on this matter, he purchased seven yards of baize, (I think it was,) which he put into the hands of a man, who was going to Lichfield, & who engaged to leave it, at Seymour's Shop in Lichfield. He says that what he sent was sufficient to furnish his Wife & children, with short-gowns, & the children with petticoats. Of this I am no judge. On my representing to him the insuffi-

---

[27] Justus Erich Bollman (1769-1821) was a doctor born in Hoya, Hanover. He studied medicine and practiced briefly in Carlsruhe and Paris. In fear for his life he left Paris in 1792 and went to London and thereafter to Vienna. Learning that Lafayette was imprisoned at Olmütz, he managed to free him with the help of an American named Huger. Lafayette, however, was recaptured and Bollman was imprisoned for a brief time. In 1796 he came to America and was welcomed as a hero. Thereafter, under the patronage of Jefferson, he held a number of political appointments. In 1805 he became an agent for Burr.

ciency of so small a provision, & urging him to do something more for them, immediately, he has promised to bring me something for them, to-morrow—in time to send by the Post: money, or clothing. I fear that this will turn out to be one of his old tricks; & that he neither has sent, nor will send, any thing. It may be well to inquire, whether any thing has been recd. at Seymour's; &, if he does not furnish me with some aid for his family, I shall apply to his master.

Wednesday, Jany. 20. 1796.
Cedar St. No. 13. N. York.   E. H. Smith.

I finished the Sierra Leone Report; transcribed my letter to Mrs. Tracy; partook of a late dinner at H. Johnson's, where I spent the evening; & came home as unwell as I went out. This day has been very snowy.

Thursday, 21st

To Fanny Smith.

Who would have believed that we should have been so long neglectful of each other? That more than two months should have passed, without the interchange of a single line. There is, doubtless, something quite wrong in this; and I can not conjecture why you have been so silent. For my own part, I can more easily account for, than excuse, my taciturnity. But now, since it has happened, & all the talk in the world can not mend the matter, we may as well resolve to do better, & not waste any more time in lamenting our past misconduct.

When I left you, in November last, you had I know not how many plans of study, of your progress in each of which I long to be informed. I had flattered myself with the expectation of being, before this time, made the depositary of your various schemes; & particularly of the result of your consultations with your young friends, how the large blank book should be disposed of. You have, no doubt, filled many of it's pages, by this time, with curious matter; and I anticipate much pleasure from being permitted to look them over, when I shall be next at Lichfield.

Another expectation of mine was, that you would have put me in mind of my engagement to furnish you with blank books, for your Diary. I hope you have not given up your design of continuing it steadily. If you have not, you must either have supplied yourself with books elsewhere, or must have been very scanty in your diurnal notations. Pray, let your answer confirm me in my good opinion of your industry & perseverance. For my part, I mean to leave you without excuse, on one side—for this letter will be accompanied by one or more little volumes, similar to that which you first recd. from me.

And so, you have been advanced to the dignity of an aunt, too, since I saw you! Well, & how does this new honour effect you? Does it make you feel yourself to be much older? And have you gained any accession to your convictions of self-consequence?—Take care! There is something dangerous in this new relationship; & it demands no little share of prudence on your part, to conduct properly. Grandparents, uncles, & aunts, the first & the last, particularly—are always taxed with spoiling children. Recollect this accountability of your's, when your little nephew is with you; & may no part of the errors he may, perhaps, commit, hereafter, be fairly imputable to the misdirection given him by you.

This is a short letter—but I can not write a longer, at present; &, beside, it may be sometime before this is sent. However, it suggests a sufficient number of topics for reply—& if your answer is long, my next letter will, doubtless, be long also.

Thursday, Jany. 21. 1796.
Cedar St. No. 13. New York.   E. H. Smith.

I wrote the preceeding short letter; Dunlap spent an hour with me, in the forenoon—& made me a very pleasing present—The Ghost-Seer. I have read, cursorily, thro' half of Dumourier's Memoirs[28]—my innumerable aches rendering it impossible for me to attend to any thing which required much active attention. Henry Gahn & Alsop past an hour with us, this evening. Wm. & I finished the reading of the first volume of Herodotus. A remarkably fine day—& still finer moonlight evening. How incessantly the sleighs fly past us!

Friday, 22nd

Somewhat better. Finished Dumourier's Memoirs. Made a little progress in Beddoes on Factitious Airs &c.[29]—Alsop here much of both forenoon & afternoon. Evening at H. Johnson's.

Saturday, 23rd

Dunlap was here much of the forenoon; Alsop part of the afternoon. I spent some time in arranging some medical notes I had made of a Case. I read some in Beddoes's Book. Club night: Met at Dunlap's—Present, beside himself—G. M. Woolsey, W. Johnson, E. H. Smith—Alsop, visitor. Here I learnt that Dr. Dwight is in N. York. The evening commenced somewhat dully: the room was cold, & the fire burnt dim. Afterwards we became animated—conversation lively—& at this moment, when I am just returned home, & seated by my own fire, the clock strikes eleven.

I feel better, this evening, than I have felt, since Monday afternoon. I am not without hopes of issuing forth in spirits, to-morrow.

---

[28] *Memoirs of Dumourier, Written by Himself*, Part I, translated from the French by J. P. Beaumont (London, 1794); Part II (London, 1794); Part III, translated by John Fenwick (London, 1794).

[29] Thomas Beddoes (1760-1808) *Considerations on the Medical Use of Factitious Airs and of the Manner of Obtaining Them In Large Quantities*, Part I (London, 1792); Part II (London, 1794).

Sunday, 24th

To John Allen.

The history of the City of New York, is the history of the eager cultivation & rapid increase of the arts of gain, & of the neglect of elegant & useful science, of the arts of genius, taste, & society. Of the numerous attempts which have been made to effect some permanent Institution, friendly to literature & useful knowlege, many have been ill-judged, some happily conceived, a few well-executed; but all have shared the same fate—a speedy dissolution. Curiosity, and a sort of frothy activity, may have, occasionally, given temporary support to such an undertaking; but the curiosity of ignorance is always stupid, barren, & transitory, & that zeal which is founded on any other than just conceptions of the advantages of scientific institutions, if it be not corrected, can never be durable: truths, learnt, with many pangs of mortified hope, & deceived expectation, in this tomb of the elegant, the learned, & the enlightened. My very soul is wounded, and indignation mingles with my grief, when I think of the fate of some recent exertions, in their behalf; exertions which, I fear, must continue to be wholly ineffectual, till some arm is found sufficiently vigorous to arrest the fatal progress of the demon of Speculation.

You must pardon this warmth, my friend! you will pardon it, when you reflect upon the cause. I might, possibly, arouse your indignation, still more deeply, were I to unfold to your view that picture of *humanity*, which our Legislature is not ashamed to exhibit to the world. But I forbear, for the present.

In a postscript to my last letter, I promised to send you a number of Copies, of Mr. Kent's Lectures. I design, to have them accompany this letter. You will readily conjecture that I had their author in my mind, when I began to write; & that the remarks which you have already read, were suggested by what I have before hinted to you to have been the fortune of his Jurisprudential efforts. Some particulars of this fortune, if you are not already acquainted with them, you may not be displeased to learn.

The establishment of a Professorship of Law, in Columbia College, was brought about by I know not what means. One would suppose that some uncommon pains must have been taken to effect it, as the Trustees of that Institution must have viewed the expence as an objection almost insurmountable, when they saw how great a part of the professorships, already created, were no more than Sinecures to men either unqualified, or indisposed, for the discharge of the duties annexed to them. But it having been resolved to erect this new professorship, Mr. Kent recd. the appointment; & the lovers of good sense & sound learning congratulated the College on the acquisition of, at least, one effective Professor. Alas! they did not foresee that the stupidity of his fellow-citizens was about to render his office equally unfruitful with those of his Colleagues. A shew of encouragement was held out, at first; several men, respectable for their years & situation in life, attended the first year; & the Lecturer found at least, thirty nominal, & many real, & constant auditors. The Introductory Lecture was published by order of the Trustees, & received with some applause; & the Course concluded with reputation to the Professor. In the common course of things, the commencement of a new undertaking is attended with difficulty & delay; the progress is expected to be gradual; but the completion splendid & happy. But the City of New York, in respect to every thing literary & refined, seems fated to exhibit the melancholly reverse. That this had, heretofore, been true of other scientific adventures, we knew; but who would have suspected that the malignity of fortune was so persevering as never to relent; & that, in a place like this, where there are near an hundred Lawyers, most of them young men, & almost an equal number of Students of the Law, a Course of Lectures, by a man of acknowledged learning & ability, on that very science which they all profess to cultivate, & on the Constitutions of the Country, should fail of patronage, after an appearance of respectable support in the very outset? Yet this is indeed the fact: & it is a fact destined to fix a stain of indelible infamy on the character of this sordid & purblind city. It will be remembered, when we are not living to be wounded by it, that in the second year of his Professorship, Mr. Kent, the Professor of Law, in Columbia College, publicly delivered a Course of Lectures, on the Laws & Institution of the United States, & the State of New York, in particular, to two Students of those Laws & Institutions. Yes, my friend, it is true, that in a City, where at the Supreme Court now sitting, there are thirty Clerks who offer themselves for admission to the Bar, in that very city, two only are found, who are sensible of the importance of a knowlege of principles: Who have enough of intellect to prefer the study of the science & philosophy of Laws, to the dry detail of shameful & dishonest forms. So deeply has the love of money taken root! so widely has it intrenched upon the empire of science! or so powerfully have *other causes* operated.

In the city of New York there are five or six men of considerable eminence as lawyers, & who derive from the exercise of their profession no little pecuniary emolument. No small part of this emolument results from the premiums they receive for the admission of Clerks into their offices, & from the labors of these Clerks—often employed eight, ten, or even fourteen hours, in a day, as scriveners. Were these young men devoted to their studies, & employed, as they ought to be, in acquiring a knowlege of Law, the principles of Law, how small a part of their time would they be willing to allow for the servile drudgery of an office? A true master lawyer must take care, therefore, how he encourages his Clerk to read; & be very cautious of exalting the science of Law, above the Art: for, otherwise, he might deprive himself of no little share of lucre.

Who will venture to say, that any considerations, like these, affect the present case? A Professorship too—what is a professorship? A matter of 500 dols. pr. ann. —no more. Who, that is in great practice, would accept it? No one, to be sure. And then, as one can not be silent, some persons might chance to be suspected of not knowing more than the rest of the world. It must not be given to a fool, neither; for that would call our own sagacity in question. Well then—we will bestow it on a sensible man; on one qualified to do it justice, perhaps —at least, one supposed capable thereof. The public opinion secures our character for sagacity; &, if he fail, we have put a man, who may chance to be troublesome, out of the way. We must make a show of attending, at first, ourselves; that we may seem to encourage the thing. After all, if it promise to exceed our expectations, & prove dangerous—we know the way—we know the way. The first course of Lectures are at an end. This will not do. It is too well. My Clerks will all be quitting my Office, for the lecturing room. I shall have them asking me questions, instead of receiving my directions. And when I would see them at the Desk, I find them at the Library. Reputation & Profit are both at stake. Young men, Blackstone is a very good book. No man ever equalled him. It is vain to expect it, and we ought to be satisfied. As for principles, you will find them all in him; with a few Reports to refer to. But the practice is the main thing. No one can get along, without this; nobody ever grew rich, in the Law, without a perfect knowlege of the practice. And the practice can only be attained in an Office, by close attention, for a long time. When a person has been writing a long while, exercise, recreation, is necessary. You must take a ride, & go & visit the ladies. If a man understands the practice well, he need have no fears for success. He must gain both advancement & riches.

Now, I will not swear that such means as these have been used, & have influenced the Professorship in question; but, I confess, I can not avoid suspecting it. Of one thing I am certain, that the strenuous recommendations of the principal lawyers, in this city, recommendations which it is infamous in them not to give, to their students, would have crowded the Lecturing Room with Auditors—they could not fail of doing it. At present, the young Clerks pay enormous premiums; drudge on, for several years, as scriveners; devote their leisure hours to every species of dissipation; & die, rich, perhaps, but certainly, ignorant. When you have read this, possibly, you may, cast your eyes a little southward of your Office, & feel an emotion of generous pride, mingled with pity.

Humanity! sacred word, effluence of virtue, daughter of justice, how little understood, how little felt! Good Heaven! Will you believe it? Will it not seem, to you, a burlesque, a satire, on humanity? There is now, before our State Legislature, a Bill for promoting the gradual abolition of Slavery. The parts of the Bill are two—that all children born of mothers who are slaves, after a certain time, (left blank in the bill) shall be free, on arriving at a certain age; &, in the mean time, shall be considered as indentured servants. Of this bill, the only able advocate, the only powerful asserter of the rights of the friendless & oppressed, is John Bird![30] Other advocates there are, indeed, but none, in respect of argument & eloquence worthy to be so, save him alone. The Bill will, probably, be lost.

Farewell.

Sunday, Jany. 24. 1796.
Cedar St. No. 13. New York.   E. H. Smith.

P. S. You will receive thirty Copies of the Lectures. They sell here for 3/8 of a dollar, a Copy. Convert one or more to your own use; & dispose of the others as well as you can. I had almost forgotten to mention, as another mark of the literary character of our City, that not twenty Copies of these Lectures have yet been sold here; tho' they have been printed these three weeks.

E. H. S.

I copied my letter to Fanny, & had made some little progress in the preceeding letter, when Noah Webster jr. entered—& engaged me in conversation, till dinner. After dinner, I had just taken up the pen, when Joseph Strong came in. I was rejoiced to see him—Wm. came home—we talked a while, & then went all together to see Alsop. When we came from seeing him, Strong went to his lodgings, Wm. & I to Mr. Lovegrove's, where we spent the evening. We had much talk. I have finished my letter, since my return. Dunlap was here in the morning, a little while.

Monday, 25th

Recd. letters from Thomas, Mary, & Abby. S. M. Hopkins visited us. Called on Joseph Strong; he out. Visited Dr. Dwight. Strong & I dined at H. Johnson's; where we spent the evening. He came home with us—& sat an hour. Dingley came in, & sat a few minutes.

Tuesday, 26th

To Daniel Wadsworth Lewis.

One would be ready to believe that a malignant destiny over-ruled the actions of men, were it, becoming, or just, to derive a system of faith from the fortune of a single individual or even a single nation. For, surely, there must be something more than usually perverse in my fate, which determines my footsteps to other places, when those of my friends are directed to this; & which contrives so harshly to allay all the satisfaction, I otherwise, should take in the recollection of the pleasures enjoyed in the society of those I visited, by dashing the cup of remembrance with regrets for those I might have tasted in the converse of friends who visited me. So true is it, my dear friend, that we are seldom indulged

---

[30] The supporter of the bill was John Bird, Smith's boyhood friend.

in pure, unmixed happiness. Yet, reflections such as these, often as I force myself to make them, have very little power to temper the vivacity of the regret which I feel for the disappointment I so lately sustained, in being absent while you were here; & I am tempted to demand of those who manage these things above, why it was so? Why you could not have made your journey earlier, or later? Or why, when you were here, you were not persuaded to defer your return, for a single day? I returned from Phila. the very morning you left New York; & within four hours after your departure. How much would the satisfaction, from rejoining my friends here, have been heightened by the light of your friendly countenance, by the warm embrace of one so long, so well-beloved! You found here, it is true, other friends; &, in William Johnson, my second self. In his society, & in that of those to whom he made you known, you recd. much pleasure, I do not question; but all would, I am sure, have been greatly heightened by my presence. The presence of an old friend, warms & vivifies, new attachments; exhibits to either party, & in more captivating lights, the lovely features of each; draws forth, unfolds, & animates, energies else latent & inert; & diffuses over all a tender & attractive grace. Ah! why was I not with you!

This letter is short. You will have the greater courage to answer it. For answer it you certainly must. Some compensation, at least, you ought to make me, for the disappointment inflicted on me, by your unseasonable arriving, & hasty departure.

My love, my best love, to Betsey; & imprint a double kiss, for me, on the lips of little Eli.

           Farewell.
Tuesday, Jany. 26, 1796.   E. H. Smith.

I have neither seen Dr. Dwight, or Strong, to-day. Some errands occupied the morning. About eleven I went to the House of Representatives of this State, to hear an expected debate on the Bill for gradually abolishing Slavery; which being postponed, I came off, & paid a visit to Dr. Rodgers. After that returned home, & wrote the preceeding letter. After dinner, read in Beddoes, till four. Went, with Dunlap, to his house; where I drank tea, & stayed till seven. Went, with him, to Woolsey's; where I stayed, in the vain expectation of seeing Dr. Dwight, till nine. Came home; found Strong had been here; read Beddoes till eleven.

           Wednesday, 27th
Added to my letter to Fanny Smith.

I have said nothing, in what precedes this, on the subject of your visiting this part of the country, in the course of the ensuing season; which, you know, was talked of, when I was last with you. I should like to know what would be your feelings, & the feelings of your parents, in this matter. How would you be pleased with coming here, in May or June, & passing three or four, or, may be, more months, in an agreable family? Perhaps, part of the time, in the adjacent country; where there are many beautiful situations? I do not know that any body will be desirous of receiving you; but, will suppose that such a place is prepared for you: How would you like it? Abby will return in about a fortnight: by the middle of May, you will have seen her three months; & her services will more than compensate, to our parents, for the loss of yours. In the mean time, you may go thro' the Small-Pox, in a kindly season; gain some acquaintance with the world; & be in a situation to receive some aid, in a variety of ways, from your brother. Think on this matter—& let me hear from you, upon it.

The letters which accompany this, (from Aurora) were recd. a few days since. I can not find out from those which I have had, what is the plan of our friends. I wish you, if you know, to inform me, how long Mary expects to stay at Lichfield. If she tarries till May, or June, I shall put off my visit till Spring.

           E. H. Smith.

I finished copying my letter to Lewis, & made & transcribed, the foregoing additions to my letter to Fanny; this forenoon. Strong & I went together to see Dr. Dwight; with whom we spent two hours. Dunlap was there. We called at Dunlap's; where I found Hodgkinson—& thus learn that the Commedians have arrived, & will soon commence playing. In the afternoon Strong was here, & Dunlap, & Dr. Rodgers. The first & the last went away. Dunlap had a new Commedy, of Holcroft's, "The Deserted Daughter."[31] He read part of it. I went home with him—& finished it. It is truly excellent. The three first acts, superior to the two last. From Dunlap's, I called on Strong at the Tontine[32]—& stayed with him, till half past ten. We conversed much on his prospects for the future—among which there is one of removing hither.

           Thursday, 28th

Went to Mr. Lovegrove's this morning, to see his little son—with the Measles. He will do well. Strong called here this morning. The wind has since been fair; & he is gone. Finished Beddoes; & begun his other book, on Calculus, &c.[33] Dunlap called here, this afternoon. Dr. Dwight & Mr. Kent, past some short time here, forenoon. Dunlap, Wm. & I went to Mr. Lovegrove's—where we stayed till eight. We went to Woolsey's—he not at home—Wm. & I stayed till nine. Read near fifty pages in Herodotus. Recd. letters from my father, & J. Wms. of Wethersfield.

---

[31] Thomas Holcroft.

[32] John Hyde kept the Tontine Coffee House at the corner of Wall and Water Streets. Rooms were also available. Opened in 1793, the Tontine became a popular meeting place into which the Stock Exchange which usually met under a tree on Wall Street moved for a time.

[33] *Observations on the Nature and Cure of Calculus, Sea Scurvy, Consumption, Catarrh and Fever, etc.* (London, 1792).

Friday, 29th

Mr. Lovegrove's child better. Stayed there half an hour. Returning, visited Dr. Mitchill. He read me a new Theory of Fevers, &c. on the Pneumatic Plan. Transcribed my letter to John Allen. Dunlap, & Dr. Mitchill both here, in the afternoon. To the latter I read Dr. Buel's account of the Sheffield Fever—the former pointed out some errors, & suggested some slight alterations, in my Opera. Drank tea, & spent part of the evening at Mrs. Morton's. The remainder at home—reading Beddoes.

Saturday, 30th

Finished Beddoes on "Calculus, Scurvy &c."—& made some progress in his Essay on Demonstrative Evidence, &c.[34] Two visits to Mr. Lovegrove's—their child better. Dunlap past part of the afternoon here. Evening, Club night. Met with me, in W. Johnson's turn, as they had with him, in my turn. Present, Dunlap, the Woolseys, W. Johnson, & myself. Grand-Jury, in relation to the case of the Mayor &c., the Distribution of justice, crimes & punishments, education, &c &c. topics of conversation.

Sunday, 31st

To Thomas, Mary, and Abby.

I should not have addrest you, thus conjointly, did there not appear to me some reason for apprehending that what I now write, may not be seasonably recd. Mr. Nicoll's continuance here threatens to be of longer duration than, perhaps, you expected: so that, if you hold to your resolution of leaving Aurora the beginning of next month, there is little probability of his returning, before you set out on your journey. My only hope is, that he may meet you, on your way. But, lest he should not, I have determined to defer, to some future time, any particular reply to your letters; & confine myself, chiefly, to acquainting you with my tho'ts, in respect to seeing you in Connecticut.

From the manner in which you have constantly spoken of your visit to Lichfield, I find myself unable to form any opinion as to what is your plan. The expectation of our friends, there, has been that Thomas would return; that Mary would remain, till May, or June, or till the riding became good; & then, that Thomas would come & carry her home. If this is, indeed, your intention, I shall defer my visit till Spring. It was late in the Fall, when I returned hither, from Connecticut, & the beginning of Jany. I was necessitated to make a journey to Phila. What with these two jaunts, & with several weeks of ill health, in consequence of them, my time has been well nigh wasted—for the whole season. On every account, therefore, I would willingly avoid another winter journey, if possible. If, however, your plan is, to spend a few weeks, together, at Lichfield, & then return home, together, I shall endeavor to meet you there—inconvenient as it will be for me. But I hope that you will fulfill the expectations of our parents; & that a more pleasant season will be chosen for Mary's return; & then, that it may be by the way of New York. Should you receive this letter, before leaving home, or at Albany; I wish you to write to me, by Post, & inform me what are your intentions, in this regard, that I may know how to act.

The letter which you wrote to me, Abby, on the birth of your little kinsman, I have, since writing to you last, recd. by the way of Lichfield. From something in your last letter, I am inclined to believe that you have, still, written one letter, which I have not recd. That is, that you have sent me four letters, since the birth of Mary's child. I have recd. but three.

You, Mary, require of me, what is most difficult for me to perform. Notwithstanding, it is my design, to send you some of my opinions; the result of my own reflections, observations, & reading. If I do, you will excuse me, if I am not very minute; your own understanding will best direct you, in the application of general principles; & we may have more leisure, than we are aware of, to pursue our inquiries, in relation to education.

Farewell, my dear friends; kind fortune, health & happiness, be yours.

Sunday, Jany. 31. 1796.
Cedar St. No. 13. N. York.   E. H. Smith.

To Uriah Tracy.

Since I saw you, I have been quite unwell; and this, in connection with the want of any thing interesting to communicate, has kept me silent, so long. If this do not appear a sufficient excuse for my silence, I must be content to be condemned; for I have no other.

When I saw you last, I informed you that Mr. Kent, our Professor of Law, was about publishing three of his Preliminary Dissertations; & I asked if you tho't that a number of them might be disposed of among the members of your House; & if you would be so kind as to receive them, & direct the manner of their disposal. I think that you replied affirmatively. These Discourses have, since, been published, &, on the strength of what passed between us, I have ventured to send you fifty Copies, which you will receive with this letter, & which I wish you to put off, as much to Mr. Kent's emolument, as may be conveniently done. They sell here for 3/8 of a dollar. You will convert as many Copies as you shall see fit, to your own use; & if you will be so obliging as to forward, to me, for Mr. Kent, that money which you may receive for those Copies which are sold in Phila. you will confer a real favour on one of the worthiest of men, & add to those sentiments of esteem & affection, with which I remain,

Sunday, Jany. 31. 1796   Yours &c.
Cedar St. No. 13. N. York.   E. H. Smith.

---

[34] Probably John Brown's book that Beddoes edited entitled *Elements of Medicine* (1780), cited earlier; *Observations on the Nature of Demonstrative Evidence, etc.* (London, 1792).

Professional visits to Mr. Lovegrove's & W. W. Woolsey's, left me leisure to do little more than write the two preceeding, short letters. I spent the afternoon at Dunlap's—& the evening at Hodgkinson's; much pleased with a new Actress, Mrs. Johnson[35]—a very lady-like woman. Have made some further progress in Beddoes on Demonstrative Evidence, since my return.

February, 1796
Monday, 1st

I stayed at home till dinner, and during a considerable part of the morning, gave myself up to the guidance of Fancy; who assumed the direction of my thoughts last evening, after I had retired to rest, & who renewed her enchantments with my rising; bearing me over almost every empire of Europe, in search of instruction in the Science of Nature, that I might return to dispence my knowlege thro' my own country, to exalt & bless it. From this excursion, so delightful, & so beneficient, I returned, to the contemplation of realities scarcely less pleasing—as exhibited in the little Tract of Dr. Beddoes, aforementioned. To this book my attention was given, with no other interruption than the transitory visit of my friend Dunlap, till near two. Dunlap came to invite me to dine, with Dr. Dwight, at his house. I went; but the Dr. had flown. The temperature of the weather had become milder, & he had set forward on his journey homeward. A violent Catarrh, contracted last evening, harassed me all day, & diminished, in spite of myself, my disposition for sociality. We went to the Friends' Meeting House. Some travellers of the Sect, from Britain were here, & wished for an opportunity of addressing some advice to the *Blacks*; & those of the Sect, who reside here, hoping that it might have a good effect on the conduct of this *People*, had caused their gathering together. We, as Officers of the Manumission Society, were invited to attend. There were, I suppose, about a thousand of the African Race. The Speakers were women; elderly; both still exhibiting evident traces of former beauty: one, of a very interesting countenance, & pleasing voice. Some appropriate advice was delivered, mingled with the ravings of the most absurd mysticism; in terms full of metaphor; & in tones, hardly intelligible. It was sun-down when we came out; & I scarcely know whether pity, contempt, disgust, or laughter, most possest my mind. I went to Mr. Lovegrove's, where Wm. Johnson came; & where, contrary to my first intentions, interested, in despite of my illness, by the conversation, which was varied & pleasing, I past the intire evening. Their little Boy is well.

Tuesday, 2nd

Finished Beddoes on Demonstrative Evidence &c. this morning. Attended the Debate, in the House of Representatives of N. York, on the Bill, for the gradual Abolition of Slavery, in this State. Mr. Alsop, and Mr. Miller, visited me. Drank tea at H. Johnson's, & past part of the evening; remainder at W. W. Woolsey's. Wm. Johnson & Dunlap there. Came home, & did some writing.

Wednesday, 3rd

Several professional visits, & some writing, have occupied most of this day. Dunlap was here, this afternoon. Attended the funeral of Dr. Samuel Nicoll; who died yesterday. Drank tea at H. Johnson's. Was a little while at Woolsey's. Spent most of the evening at Kent's. Came home, & devoted an hour to tumbling over all my books, which say any thing on the Meazles.

Thursday, 4th

This day, well nigh, lost. A little business—the News-Papers—ineffectual attempts to raise the pitiful sum of forty dollars[36]—wasted my time. Dunlap was here, a while, forenoon & afternoon. Dingley was here—two hours. I spent an hour, this evening, with Henry Gahn. Remainder at home, writing.

Friday, 5th

Professional business—a call at Dunlap's—some conversation with him, at my room—the reading of his Opera of "The Archers"[37]—& writings—busied me thro' the day. Drank tea—& spent part of the evening, at Riley's, with Wm.—then we went, together, & past the residue, at James Watson's[38]—chiefly with Saml. M. Hopkins. Since my return, I have transcribed my last two letters.

Saturday, 6th

I began this day with reading a portion of Condorcet's so long-neglected Work. Professional affairs, & copying, occupied the remainder. Dunlap was here, both forenoon & afternoon. He has given out the parts of his Opera.

This night, being Club night—met at W. W. Woolsey's. Present—Dunlap, W. Johnson, Smith, the Woolseys. Several circumstances conspired to render this evening less interesting than usual: a trifling conversation was in part, the cause & consequence. We separated the earlier.

Sunday, 7th

Professional business, the sickness of one of his servants, carried me to H. Johnson's—I stayed there an

---

[35] Mrs. Johnson and her husband joined the Old American Company in 1796; both were excellent actors. According to Dunlap, she played the fine ladies of comedy. Coad, *Dunlap*, p. 48.

[36] "Pitiful" is a strange word for him to employ here. Neither to him nor to others was $40 a "pitiful" sum at the time. It appears to have been approximately a month's wages for a laborer.

[37] Sometimes titled *William Tell;* it opened at the John Street Theater on April 18, 1796.

[38] James Watson (1750-1806; Yale 1776). A lawyer who practiced in Connecticut and moved to New York in 1786. He held numerous state offices; elected to the U.S. Senate to fill a vacancy, he served from 1798-1800. Member of the Board of Governors of New York Hospital.

hour. From eleven, till dinner, I was busied in writing—at Mr. Riley's—thence to Mr. Lovegrove's—where I found Wm. & spent the evening.

Monday, 8th

To Oliver Wolcott, of Phila.

The frequent & pressing solicitations of the gentleman, with whom Mr. Ellin has left the completion of his contract with you, induce me to trouble you, once more, on that subject. That gentleman is now in Albany, but has made provision for the immediate payment of the remaining 3,000 dols. upon the receit of the Deed. The persons, from whom this sum is to be recd., have had the money in readiness, for more than a fortnight; & appear to be extremely desirous to make the payment. Not having heard any thing from you, since I was in Phila. it has been impossible for me to give any satisfactory reply to their inquiries—when the Deed would be transmitted, & when they should be called upon for the money. I can not doubt, for a moment that your delay has arisen from causes altogether unavoidable—& of this they seem equally well satisfied—as they can not conceive that any one would willingly sustain that loss, which has already arisen to you, from not having the use of the money. In the mean time they appear equally eager to dispossess themselves of what they still retain—& it is in compliance with the intreaties of this eagerness that I write. A reply is desirable, on their account; & the more early it is, the more perfectly will it answer their wishes.

With sentiments of respect & affection, I beg to be remembered to Mrs. Wolcott, & Mr. & Mrs. Goodrich, & remain, dear sir,

Yours sincerely,

Monday, Feby. 1796.
Cedar St. No. 13. N. York.   E. H. Smith.

Beside attending the business of my profession, doing some errands, copying great part of the day, writing & transcribing the preceeding letter, &c. &c. I have read fifty, or sixty, pages in Condorcet. Dunlap & Alsop were [here] this afternoon; & Dingley this evening. I was at Woolsey's two hours; & there heard, that Mumford & his family had sat forward, for Lichfield—so that they will probably be there, by this time.

Tuesday, 9th

Medical visits &c. occupied me till near twelve; then I went into the House of Representatives of this State, to hear the Debate on the Slave Bill—where I stayed till dinner. I was witness to a most disgusting spectacle of ignorance, prejudice, corruption, & villainy—feebly illuminated by some transient gleams of good sense, & good intentions. After dinner, Copied. Dunlap was here a short time. I spent a few moments with Mr. Gahn: most of the evening with Dunlap at his house; & call'd at Woolsey's, on my return. Since then, I have applied to the reading of Condorcet—& have, at length finished his book—with great pleasure. Read Mr. Barlow's "Hasty-Pudding," with pleasure.

Wednesday, 10th

At home, all day, copying. Dunlap past a short time here, in the afternoon. I drank tea at W. W. Woolsey's; & spent the evening at the Theatre—with more unalloyed satisfaction than I ever did, before. The Comedy of "The Provok'd Husband"[39]—& the farce of "The Spoiled Child"[40]—were played. Six new performers made their appearance—& all good. We have lost, & gained, ten, performers, since the last season—& the change, is in almost every respect, for the better. It is impossible for me, in justice to my own feelings, to leave unnoticed the excellence of Mrs. Johnson, in Lady Townly—the propriety of Mr. Tyler, in Manly—of Mrs. Tyler—(whose unfortunate figure will ever prevent her receiving her due share of applause—) in Lady Grace—or the Humor of Mrs. Brett, Mr. Johnson, & Mr. Jefferson, in Lady, Sir Francis, & Richd. Wronghead. These are the new performers. The others, of the company as it stood before, did well. Mr. Hallams Ld. Townly was respectable. In the after-piece, Jefferson, as Tag—& Mrs. Brett, as Miss Pickle—were truly excellent. Tho' the day & night have been horribly stormy—the house was full—& all seemed delighted.

Thursday, 11th

Continued to copy: some medical visits: recd. letters from Mrs. Tracy & Thomas Mumford—dated Lichd. & sent a few lines, in reply to the last—& afterward recd. a Script from him, of an earlier date. Dunlap, Kent, & S. M. Hopkins, were here in the P. M. Evening—partly at Noah Webster's—partly at H. Johnson's.

Friday, 12th

The copying, which I have mentioned several times of late, & in which no small part of this day was occupied, has been of my Opera. I have, now, completed the transcription of the several parts; so that they are ready for the Performers. The copy of the Opera, for the prompt book, is to be done for me, by Mr. Dunlap's Clerk. I was at Mr. Lovegrove's, a short time, this afternoon; drank tea at Dunlap's—& went with him to the Theater: after which, as I did not tarry to see the After Piece, I spent an hour at Woolsey's. At the Theater I was much pleased. The Piece was Inkle & Yarico.[41] Miss Broadhurst, who made her first appearance here, in the latter character, exceeded my expectations—which had not been much in her favor. I knew

---

[39] Colley Cibber, *The Provok'd Husband; or A Journey to London* (1728).

[40] Prince Hoare[?], *The Spoiled Child* (1790). Other writers to whom it was attributed at various times: Mrs. Jordan, Sir Richard Ford, Isaac Bickerstaffe, and Mrs. Inchbald. *Cambridge Bibliography of English Literature* 2: p. 460, and other standard references.

[41] A romantic comedy by George Colman, the younger, 1787.

she was esteemed a fine singer—& such she proved to be; but her acting was also pretty good—which I did not expect. Mr. Tyler gave us an opportunity for the first time, to judge of his voice—as a singer. It exceeds all I have ever heard. Little Miss Brett, is a sweet singer—& acquitted herself surprizingly well. She never was on *any* stage before. This Piece is one of Coleman Junr's best. The morality is, thro'out—unexceptionable; & the satire on false education, & fashion, very just & happy.

Saturday, 13th

This day has been filled with nothing of importance. Several calls, visits, &c. filled up the greater part of it. Dunlap & I walked out of Town, in the afternoon. I drank tea at his house—& we went together to the Theater. The Play was Mahomet:[42] we stayed to see the two first acts, only. Mr. Tyler appeared well in Alcanor; Mrs. Cleveland, *so so*, (better than I expected,) in Palmira—Mr. Cleveland—wretchedly in Zaphna.—he has neither voice, action, nor discrimination—in short he has no judgement. It was Club night —we came away. The Club was to have met at H. Johnson's—he was engaged—& so Wm. took his turn. We had a sorrowful meeting. Dunlap, Wm. Johnson, & myself were all; & Alsop, as a visitor.

Dr. Wm. Pitt Smith[43] died yesterday morning at 4 o'clock—& was buried this evening.

Sunday, 14th

I went to Woolsey's, to see his children. When I returned, I found Mr. Gahn here. He sat an hour or two; & we had much pleasant conversation. After he went away—Wm. & I took a walk, out of town—& returned, in season to make a visit at Riley's before dinner. After dinner I did a little writing for the Manumission Society. At five Gahn called for us, & we went to see Mr. Roulet. We stayed at his house till eight; & were agreably entertained; tho' our conversation was a strange motley of languages. Roulet understands English perfectly—but can not speak it. Wm. & I are in the same difficulty, in respect to French. Roulet spake in French—Johnson in English—& I—part of the time in English—part of the time in bad French. But we got along. The other members of Roulet's family—neither speak, nor understand, English; except his brother— (who was there but part of the time—) who speaks it, well. From this house—we called at Woolsey's—& then at H. Johnson's.

Monday, 15th

To Joseph Bringhirst Junr.

There are many reasons which might be assigned, my dear friend, for my long, &, doubtless, unexpected, silence; but I have not the heart, nor the time, necessary for their enumeration. Since I saw thee, I have been much unwell—tho' never very sick; & beside, I have had no convenient & safe opportunity of sending to thee —except by the Mail: which is not, as thou knowest, a proper conveyance, for a package like the present. Thou wilt find, with this letter, which I am not, now able to make longer, the work which thou hast so long wished to see. May it give thee all the pleasure which thy good heart can wish. Our friends are all well: I am well: my love to Charles, his family, thy own, & if they will not deem it presumptuous, to those of thy beloved friends, with whom I had opportunity of forming a slight, but I trust, not perishable, acquaintance.

Farewell.

Monday, Feb: 15. 1796.
Cedar St. No. 13. New York.   E. H. Smith.

I have been running about, great of this day, to find a conveyance to New Haven—for myself & Dunlap: unsuccessfully. We took a walk: I dined at his house. I visited Dingley—wrote, & transcribed, the above lines to Joseph—& talked with Johnson & Dunlap, about translating a publication of Riouffe's. Was at the theater part of the evening; & visited Mr. Miller,[44] the remainder. Seige of Calais[45]—Mrs. Johnson excellent as Julia. The Parson & I, had quite a dish of metaphysics. He deserves to be called a pretty candid man.

Tuesday, 16th

Almost all the former part of this day occupied in endeavours to find a conveyance to New Haven. Wm. W. Woolsey & I, have determined to go in the Thursday's Stage. Translated ten pages of Riouffe, this afternoon. Visited my little patients. Spent the evening at the Manumission Society.

Wednesday, 17th

This day I recd. of James R. Smith,[46] the master of Cash Africa—five dollars—which sum is a part of the wages of Cash—& is, by his consent, advanced to me, for his Wife—who lives in Lichfield. I gave a receit, to this effect, to Mr. Smith.

I was surprized by an intimation from one of the Governors of the Hospital, that, if I would apply for it,

---

[42] James Miller, *Mohamet the Impostor*. This, in fact, is a translation of Voltaire's *Mohamet;* Acts I-IV by Miller, Act V by J. Hoadly (London, 1744).

[43] A prominent New York physician.

[44] Samuel Miller, A.M., a Presbyterian minister, member of the United Presbyterian Churches in the City of New York, also a member of the Manumission Society. Author of *A Brief Retrospect of the Eighteenth Century, Part the First, In Three Volumes; containing A Sketch of the Revolutions and Improvements in Science, Arts, and Literature, During That Period* (New York, 1805). Miller (1: p. xii) claimed that his work was the first handbook of American literature as well as of science and the arts.

[45] Odell (I, 403) gives the bill for this date as *Surrender of Calais* by George Coleman, the younger (1791).

[46] James R. Smith, the master of Cash Africa, was apparently not a relative. He seems to have taken no part in Litchfield official life in a day when practically everybody held one office or another.

I might, probably, receive that appointment therein, (viz. of Physician) which my name-sake, who has lately died—Wm. Pitt Smith—held. Much of my time has been spent in learning what are the duties of the Office —& conversing thereon, with the Governor referred to. I shall make the application. Any thing resembling solicitation & interest-making, is irksome to me: but such is the custom: & he who will not seek opportunities of doing good, when he is capable of doing good—is as much in fault as he who wilfully thrusts himself forward into situations the duties of which he is incapable of performing.

I was at the Theatre, tonight. I went with Dunlap & his Wife—& Mr. & Mrs. Lovegrove were in the same Box. Henry Jones's "Earl of Essex"—& "Rosina"[47]— were the pieces—& they were performed, for the most part, much to our satisfaction.

I sent a letter to Mr. Tracy—which has been long written—with twenty-six copies of Kent's Lectures. Kent had a daughter born last evening. Well done, good Mr. Chronicle!

Monday, 22nd

My friend W. W. Woolsey & I left New York, together, in the Stage, on Thursday noon. In the morning I was variously busied; more especially in relation to the proposed appointment in the Hospital. We reached New Haven, & went to Dr. Dwight's Friday evening. I immediately sat out in search of means for accomplishing my journey to Lichfield—but found none that evening. About eleven next morning I left New Haven in a one-horse sleigh—leaving Woolsey behind me—& having spent a few pleasant hours at Dr. Dwight's. My horse proved to be a sorry jade—tired— & obliged me to spend the night twelve miles distant from Lichfield. I reached my father's, yesterday, just as the people were going to Church. I met my father, & sister Abby—& taking the last into my Pung, drove home. Here I found all the rest of the family. Sally Pierce, Idea Strong, & Abby Lewis (of Farmington) spent the noon-tide here—& Idea the afternoon & evening—& I read to her—& the family—"The Ghost-Seer." At sun-set I slipped off—& went into Mrs. Tracy's, for a half hour. They were all well. My father's house was crowded with visitants all the evening—&, among others, El. Smith Jr. of Berlin was present.

This day, also, has been a day of visiting & being visited. I called at Mr. Pierponts—the father of little Sophy: at the Printing Office, to see my old friend Collier: at D. W. Lewis's: & at Mrs. Tracy's. Idea Strong spent the day here. Mrs. Tracy, Miss Pierce— &c. &c. spent the evening.

Tuesday, 23rd

Mumford, Mary, Fanny, & the little one, are gone:

El. Smith & his companions have left town: we are quite [word blurred] & solitary. Idea spent the day with us. I must send her "The Heiress."[48] In the afternoon I visited at Mr Lord's—the Miss Pierces, Dr. Sheldon's—& Mrs. Tracy's—where I spent most of the evening. Dr. Sheldon past the remainder of it, with us, at my father's.

Saturday, 27th

I left my father's on Wednesday morning last, &, after a very difficult & fatiguing journey, reached Dr. Root's,[49] in Hampden, at nine in the evening—after having passed half an hour with my aunts at Southington. My spirits were unusually deprest during the day —& have scarcely yet regained their wonted elevation. The next morning I went to New Haven. I found that Dr. Dwight had accompanied Woolsey to Hartford— where they both then were. I found Sally Dwight at his house. I dined there—& very soon after dinner got into the Stage—from which I was delivered, after a journey in no wise remarkable—this day—a little before eleven. I find Johnson out of town—where I know not. John Bird came in, almost as soon as I did—& has been gone but a short time—so that, with the little affairs I have found to set to rights within—I have been busied till now—(dinner time—) & have not been out.

Since my return, I have called on Dingley; have visited Woolsey's family; Dunlap—& been with him, to hear Carr play over the music to his Opera;[50] & have spent the evening agreably, at H. Johnson's. I saw there some fine Engravings, from Claude Lorrain & Gaspard Poussin.[51] Alsop came to see me.—W. W. Woolsey & G. M. Woolsey & Wm. Johnson out of Town; no Club.

Once more am I seated by my own fire-side, after an absence of nine days, & a journey of near three hundred miles. This journey was made in an inclement season, a busy period, & when my time had been much broken in upon, & my pecuniary means were low, to visit a beloved sister, from whom I had been absent sixteen months—& who I could not expect to see for a still longer period to come, if I did not see her now—to visit her infant, who I had never seen; to see another sister,

---

[47] Henry Jones's *The Earl of Essex* (1753); Mrs. Frances Brooke, *Rosina* (1782), comic opera. Not to be confused with a novel by the same name, for which see later.

[48] John (Gentleman Johnny) Burgoyne (1786). The play is largely derivative but it is remarkable that he should have written it at all.

[49] Josiah Root was Smith's cousin and gained at least part of his training in medicine as an apprentice of Reuben Smith. He is mentioned in Smith's "Brief Notices Concerning My Paternal Ancestors."

[50] Imminence of production of *The Archers* (April 18, 1796) would make this the vehicle referred to.

[51] Gaspard Poussin and Claude Lorrain. The latter was a pseudonym for Claude Gelée or Gellée, French landscape painter (1600-1682). Poussin was also a French landscape painter (1613-1675), the adopted son of the more famous Nicolas Poussin. Some 200 outline drawings of Claude Lorraine's pictures were engraved between 1635 and 1675. Apparently something of the same was done for Poussin. Smith loved to leaf through portfolios of etchings but obviously never felt that he could afford to buy them.

from whom I had been absent an equal time; & to visit a third sister, from whom I expect a removal of similar duration; such were the principal motives to this journey; in addition to which may be mentioned the delight I always receive from my visits to my parents & friends —& especially the satisfaction I knew it must give the former to see their children once more together. I have accomplished this journey & I am repaid for all my trouble. Mary is very little altered in appearance. She says less than formerly—but looks more. She doubtless converses less—& thinks more. She is an excellent woman: & of this I become more & more convinced every time I see her—read her letters—& contrast her character with that of people in general. The fortitude with which she parted was particularly noble. Her child is a fine child: her husband unchanged. Abby has grown very fat: I saw, & conversed with her too little—for all was hurry: her heart is too sensible: a husband firm, yet tender, is necessary for her. Fanny accompanied Mary. She has grown beyond her sisters: she is an excellent girl. My parents—Mrs. Tracy, Sally Pierce, D. W. Lewis &c. are as they were wont to be. I have seen more of Idea Strong—& we have agreed to correspond. I can not write!

Sunday, 28th

Dunlap entered my room, while I was busily employed in transcribing the Minutes of the last meeting of the Manumission Society. I had before, and while waiting for breakfast, read Dr. Sayers's fine drama intituled "Starno." My friend came by appointment; and went to Mr. Hodgkinson's. We found him without visitors; and, tho' we stayed with him more than two hours, suffered but little interruption from them. It should seem that both Dunlap's Opera & mine will, certainly, be played. The principal delay, apparently, arises from the Music; which is complete for his, &, it is said, nearly so for mine. A Finale, however, (which I designed to omit, & have not written, from having observed that few attend to it, at the representation of a Piece, & from a conviction that mine was as well without one) is said to be necessary.—This, therefore, must be done. Unfortunately—as it will, no doubt, delay the presentation much longer—considering the Composer's wonderful talents for procrastination. I shall set about it directly. Dunlap has made some additions & alterations in his "Fontainville Abbey":[52] judicious—as representation is regarded; in other respects not material. Hodgkinson read us some scenes from the "Wheel of Fortune"[53]— Mr. Cumberland's new Comedy—which are really good. After we came out, we walked on the Battery. I dined with Dunlap; & spent most of the afternoon at his house —While there I read, with him, & for the first time, J. J. Rousseau's "Devin du Village"[54]—which I found to be a pleasing little drama. The music accompanies my friend's copy; & if, on examination, it proves as pleasing to us, as it is said to be in France, we think of translating, & fitting it up for our stage. I read also a M.S. Piece intended to be a Drama of Three Acts, called "Bourville Castle"[55]—which Dunlap had recd. of the Managers; it having been offered to them for acceptance. It is professedly the composition of a young man—and, tho' it is not altogether deficient in marks of talent, is eminently wanting in dramatic propriety.

I drank tea & past the evening, at Mr. Lovegrove's. Variety of conversation, as usual; &, as usual, not susceptible of condensation. H. Johnson there, also, great part of the time: we came away together. Little Sophy seemed glad to hear from her Parents & family.

A letter of Du Paty's—gave rise to conversation on Views &c. &c. & I expatiated on several remarkably grand views of hills, & mountains, & valleys, & clouds, & woods, of whose sublimity I was never before so sensible, & which the road from Plymouth to Bristol, in Connecticut, by way of the Forge & Hitchcock's Mills, presents—over which I passed in my return from Lichfield to New Haven. The whole road is exceedingly abundant in rude & rugged grandeur, & must be powerfully interesting at every season of the year. It was doubly so now, to me—when the hills were covered with snow, & when a tempest seemed to brood over them; descending from the gloomy sky. Several times did the tears start, involuntarily into my eyes; & my bosom seemed too narrow for my laboring heart.

While at Lichfield I paid Cash Africa's Wife the money which I had procured, of his master, for her. She gave me her receit.

John Allen left town monday morning—so that I saw him not. I left my letter to him, behind; but delivered the Pamphlets of my friend Kent, to my kinsman E. Hubbard Junr.[56] to be disposed of. I added a P.S. to my letter, to fullfil W. T. Broome's commission—i. e. to remind Mr. Allen of the Argument of Mr. Burr which Broome wishes him to return.

I carried a copy of "The Ghost-Seer" to Lichfield, for Collier to republish.

Monday, 29th

I finished arranging the minutes of the Manumission Society, & transcribed the Resolutions &c. I composed a Finale for my Opera; parts of which had pestered me for considerable time, after going to bed last evening. I read, before breakfast, several of Sayers' Poems—as also last night, before going to bed. I am greatly charmed with this Poet—who appears to possess uncommon genius, erudition, good-sense, acuteness & taste. Wm. Johnson, unexpectedly, & to my great joy, returned this afternoon—from Albany—where he saw Mumford, &

---

[52] Played at the John Street Theatre, February 17, 1795.
[53] Richard Cumberland (1795).
[54] *Divin due Village; a Musical Entertainment* (1752).
[55] The author was John Blair Linn. The play was presented by Dunlap, January 16, 1797.
[56] There were two Elijah Hubbards, father and son, Smith's uncle and cousin; this is the cousin.

learnt of him, that my sisters & nephew were well. I have been employed, much of the afternoon & evening, in reading Ireland's Hogarth Illustrated.[57] I drank tea at Kent's —&, afterwards, past near two hours at Webster's.

March 1796
Tuesday, 1st

To William Buel.

In compliance with your wishes, and in return for the Communication with which you lately favored me, relative to the Diseases which prevailed in the neighborhood, where you reside, for the three last years, I have put together all the scanty information I possess, respecting the Fever which was the occasion of so much distress to this City, in the last summer and autumn. I regret my inability to communicate any thing more than a few facts which fell under my own observation. Various circumstances conspired to render the sphere thereof very narrow; and this may have led me into erroneous conclusions, which more extensive practice, by furnishing opportunity for longer-continued & wider observation, would have corrected in me, & may have corrected in others. Of the persons who habitually, employ me, few are so situated as to be obliged to remain in Town; & on the occasion of the Fever of which I am speaking, most of them did actually remove into the Country. Those who stayed behind had a sufficiency of the goods of fortune to render themselves comfortable, & had discretion to direct their application. The few who suffered, thus circumstanced, were more lightly affected: for it was on the poor, the intemperate, & the stranger, that this calamity fell most heavily. Among these last, I was often led, by different motives, not necessary to be enumerated here; & it was almost only among them that I saw this Disease in all it's horrors.

To form an accurate idea of the Fever of 1795, it is necessary to consider it in respect to it's *Origin, Nature, & Method of Cure*:—and on each of these heads I shall deliver my own observations & opinions, with such additional information as I can rely on as accurate.[58]

[Omitted here, three manuscript pages with the heading "Origin, season, situation of the Fever of 1795."]

No inconsiderable part of this forenoon was absolutely wasted by the presence of tiresome visitors, whose conversation was scarcely rendered tolerable even by the aid of Alsop & Dunlap, who were here, for a few moments. When left to myself I wrote the preceeding part of a letter to Wm. Buel. Dined, very late in the afternoon, at H. Johnson's, with much company; spent part of the evening there; remainder at Mrs. Morton's: Miss Morton not at home. Since my return have read an hour in Ireland's Hogarth.

Wednesday, 2nd

Very busy, all the forenoon, in doing various errands, & making several calls. Put my "Finale" in the hands of the Manager, in the afternoon. When at Dunlap's Store, found Mr. Hallam there—& Dunlap taking down Notes for his intended history of the American Theatre.[59] Dunlap here, in the afternoon. Drank tea with him—& we went to see the "Deserted Daughter"[60]—performed —expecting much delight. I was deceived—& tho' some of the characters were well played others were so badly, that I resolved never to see it murdered a second time, in this way.

[Omitted here, eleven manuscript pages: continuation of the letter to Wm. Buel.]

I read a few pages in "Bonner on Bees,"[61] before breakfast. After breakfast, I went on with my letter to Buel, till Dingley came in; when I read what I had then written to him, & he refreshed & added some new matter to the stores of my memory. Mr. Gahn called on me, a few minutes. It was eleven o'clock when they went out. I went to the Monthly Examination of the African Free School, & did not come away till one— the Trustees having business. There I saw Thomas Eddy,[62] & from what he said to-day, & Mr. Rogers yesterday, I deem my election as a physician to the Hospital, as probable. When I came home, I made up the minutes of the Trustees, & then wrote on my letter till dinner—& a short time after dinner. I was interrupted by the entrance of Dr. Mitchill—soon after Dunlap—& soon after Johnson. We talked, & laughed, till near sunset. I drank tea at Dunlap's, & we went to the Theater. A new Comedy of Cumberland's—"The Wheel of Fortune"—was played—& very much to my satisfaction. Hodgkinson's—Penruddock; Tyler's—Sydenham; Johnson's Weezle; Jefferson's—Davy Daw; Mrs. Brett's—Old Woman; & above all, Mrs. Johnson's— Emily; were exceedingly well played. The Piece is, with very slight exceptions, moral—the principal moral fine, & impressive—& the whole exhibition, of the best of our Theater.

Since I came home, I have read the first Chapter of Du Marsais' "Essai sur les Préjugés"[63]—& written a few lines on the opposite page.

---

[57] John Ireland (?-1800) a self-taught English etcher and engraver who exhibited at the Royal Academy in 1765. Between 1780 and 1785 he etched many plates of Hogarth's work. His natural son, William Henry Ireland, was the notorious forger of Shakespearean manuscripts.

[58] The letter which Smith copied here continued at length (with interruptions) and then developed into ten letters, copies of which Smith interspersed in the Diary until April 19. All of the letters were published and, therefore, are omitted. For publication see hereafter.

[59] Dunlap eventually published *A History of the American Theatre* thirty-six years later, in 1832.

[60] Thomas Holcroft (1795).

[61] James Bonner, *Plan for Speedily Increasing the Number of Bee Hives in Scotland* (London, 1795).

[62] Thomas Eddy, like William Eddy of Philadelphia, was a wealthy New Yorker. He made a fortune in speculation when the national debt was refunded. Eddy and Smith were associated as officers in the Manumission Society, see Minutes, Manumission Society, VI Jan. 1785-Nov. 1797, New-York Historical Society.

[63] César Chesneau Dumarsais, *Analyse de la Religion chré-*

Saturday, 5th

[Omitted here, six manuscript pages: continuation of letter to Wm. Buel.]

Read a little in Dumarsais—was interrupted by a visitor—Dunlap spent a short time with me—occupied in making a few corrections in the Prologue to his "Archers"—which he is about to print;[64] rest of the forenoon spent in writing on the letter to Buel. After dinner—hunting over News Papers in search of the publications, on the Fever, during it's prevelance in the city. Dunlap brought us Cumberland's "First Love."[65] Alsop came in—& I read it aloud, to them & Wm. It is a charming Piece. Dunlap & I went to the Theater to see "The Inconstant"[66]—reduced by Hodgkinson, to a Piece of three acts. We were pleased. Went to Kent's—Club night—Present—Wm. Johnson, Dunlap, Kent, & myself. Talked—separated at ten.

Sunday, 6th

To Oliver Wolcott Junr.

You will not be surprized at receiving the inclosed pamphlet, when you recollect your having, formerly, requested me to procure for you a copy of An Elegy on the late right honorable William Pitt. This Poem is contained in the number of the New-York Magazine, now sent. On inquiry, I find it to have been republished from the Edition of the Poem printed at Lichfield; & it may, therefore, be supposed to be tolerably correct. Some few verbal, or literal, errors I observed in reading it over; but of a kind to be readily discerned, & obviated. The Editors of our Magazine have no other merit than that of being neat, &, for the most part, correct printers; you will not wonder, therefore, at the alteration which they have made in the title of this Elegy, tho' it may provoke a smile at their stupidity. One would have tho't that the Dedication, which, for fear it would take up too much space, they have seen fit to omit, would have saved them from the commission of this absurdity; but it is too much of a piece with the general state of elegant literature in this place, to excite any profound astonishment.

My best wishes are for your happiness, & the happiness of the several members of your family.

Sunday, March 6. 1796.
Cedar St. No. 13. New York.   E. H. Smith.

P.S. I am still importuned on the subject of my last letter to you; to which suffer me to press for an answer.

E. H. Smith.

To Charles Chauncey, Senr.

Since my return to New York, I have made the usual inquiries, in our Book-Stores, but can not learn that any new Publications, of distinguished merit, have been lately imported. Publications relative to Agriculture, are more infrequently found in them, than on most other subjects which have become objects of so general curiosity & attention, & I know of none, worthy your perusal, except those which I mentioned to you, when I last had the pleasure of being at your house. In particular, there are no Copies of the County Surveys, made by order of the Board of Agriculture, for sale. Sir John Sinclair's Statistical Account of Scotland, & Mr. Arthur Young's Tours, thro' various parts of Britain & France, you are doubtless possest of, or, at least, well acquainted with. Should you, however, not possess them, you will be pleased to learn that they may all be obtained here, if I am not mistaken, & in as reasonable terms as books of that kind are usually sold.

I have taken the liberty to send you Mr. Bonner's treatise on the Management of Bees &c. of which I beg your acceptance. It appears to be a plain, unornamented, practical Work; &, therefore, I think, more likely to inspire general confidence, than a performance marked with more brilliancy of genius:—of which our *practical* men seem, still, to entertain many fears.

My best respects to Mrs. Chauncey, & your family.

Sunday, March 6. 1796.
Cedar St. No. 13. N. York.   E. H. Smith.

Read part of Sayers's "Descent of Frea," & of his "Moina"—before breakfast. Afterward, wrote & transcribed the preceeding letters. Went to Riley's—saw Alsop's prints—dined there: called on John Bird—who was not at home: at Woolsey's—he not returned: drank tea & spent part of the evening at Mr. Lovegrove's—read them Barlow's "Hasty-Pudding": past the remainder of the evening at Hodgkinson's—agreably—Mr. & Mrs. Cleveland there:[67]—agreable young people.

Monday, 7th

[Omitted here, three manuscript pages: continuation of letter to Wm. Buel.]

A number of errands kept me on the trot till dinner. After dinner, as I had called on Dingley in the morning, he returned my visit—& we rubbed up our memories, somewhat, on some parts of last summer's transactions. I wrote what goes before, on the Fever. I was at Dunlap's, in the morning. He is writing a Historical Memoir, relative to his "Archers." Nobody at Woolsey's—when I called there. He returned last night—& I saw him to-day. Went into the Theater, a short time, with Dunlap; who I met in the street. Visited at Catlin's —where I have not been before, for several months. Came home & finished the second Chapter of Dumarsais.

Tuesday, 8th

[Omitted here, six manuscript pages: continuation of letter to Wm. Buell.]

Wrote the foregoing pages, under this date, in the

---

tienne; Essai sur le Préjugés contenant l'apologie de la philosophie (London, Amsterdam, 1770; Paris, 1795).

[64] This was a compressed history of Switzerland.
[65] (1795).
[66] Reduced from *The Inconstant; or the Way to Win Him* by George Farquhar (1703).

[67] Actors in the Old American Company. Most of the Company was composed of married couples.

morning. Various errands &c. employed me till dinner. Saw Col. Tallmadge,[68] now on his way home, from Marietta. Recd. a letter from Roger Hitchcock, inclosing part of his brother's private Journal. Dined unusually late. Alsop here when I came home. Went with him to see some books. Dunlap here when we returned. Both stayed till dark—Alsop till after seven. Wm. & I spent the rest of the evening at Woolsey's. Dunlap & his Wife there.

Wednesday, 9th

[Omitted here, five manuscript pages: continuation of letter to Wm. Buel.]

Spent the morning in writing the above pages—having finished Sayers' "Moina" before breakfast. Dunlap brought the first Proof of his Opera. We looked it over, & corrected it. Many errands, some business, till late dinner. Read Dr. Leib's Speech in the Pennsylvania House of Representatives, on the Virginia Resolutions.[69] A pretty handsome thing. Made some progress in Dumarsais. Alsop came here; bringing some pieces, in various News Papers, relative to the Georgia Land Purchase, with which we had some diversion. Evening, at the Theatre: "Deserted Daughter"—somewhat better played than before; less applauded: "Agreable Surprize"—what miserable trash it is!

Thursday, 10th

[Omitted here, five manuscript pages: continuation of letter to Wm. Buel.]

Wrote the following pages, under this date: Corrected a proof-sheet for Dunlap: several calls: read the newspapers: made some progress in Dumarsais: visited Charles Adams—John Wells there: spent the evening at Woolsey's—partly conversing with Alsop, who I found there, but who soon went away—partly in assisting Dunlap in correcting proofs &c.—but chiefly, on the business of revising the Constitution of the Manumission Society.

Friday, 11th

[Omitted here, five manuscript pages: continuation of letter to Wm. Buel.]

Wrote the above, of this date: assisted Dunlap in correcting his piece: made several professional calls: progressed, considerably, in Dumarsais: spent much of the afternoon, in business of the Manumission Society: drank tea at H. Johnson's: past the evening at Mrs. Morton's—very agreably in Company with Wm.

---

[68] Benjamin Talmadge (Yale 1773) had been an aide to Washington. He first suspected Arnold's treachery in 1780 and almost prevented his escape. He had custody of Major André until his execution. U.S. House 1801-1817. Kilbourne, *Sketches and Chronicles*, pp. 150-156.

[69] One of several sets of such "Resolutions." What are now known as the "Virginia Resolutions" followed passage of the Alien and Sedition laws in 1798.

To Thomas, Mary, & Fanny.

There is no doubt, I believe, but that Mr. Nicoll is, at length, about to depart, for Aurora. His journey happens most opportunely, to convey to you my most ardent wishes for your happiness, my congratulations, as I hope, on your safe return. Wm. Johnson caused me, to experience an unexpected pleasure, by the news he brought me, of your safe arrival, as far as Albany. It would have been greatly heightened could he have had an opportunity of receiving, from the lips of my sisters, a kind message for their brother.

I reached home, in good health, after a fatiguing jaunt; having left Lichfield, the morning after you. Since then, I have been well: but have recd. no intelligence from our family; in which respect, I hope you have been more fortunate.

When I reflect on the distance which separates us; on the many months, perhaps years, which must inevitably pass away, ere we meet again; on the length of time which elapsed, before I saw you, Mary, in particular, at Lichfield; I can not sufficiently regret the fewness of those moments which were allowed us, to see each other; & the numerous interruptions, which robbed me of half the satisfaction those few moments might have bestowed. When, alas! shall we sit down together, as we were wont to do, & give way to all that unreservedness of heart, that embosoming of the soul, which was at once a display of our character, & the delight of our lives? When, again, shall we ramble, together—"hand linked in hand"—over our native fields —deceiving the rugged way fall it's weariness [*sic*], by reciprocal offices of affection, unaffected descants on the various scene before us, & sincere & lively converse on literary & moral topics! Alas! my sister, few have been our social enjoyments. An evil destiny seems to have been ever bent on separating us, from each other, since the germs of reason & taste began to expand in our bosoms. We have never known each other, as we ought: our very hours of confidential intercourse have been but snatches from the rapacity of disuniting occupation: our souls have flowed towards each other, but a cruel intervention has forced them to distant regions, in the moment of their confluence. You were too happy, to conceive of my sorrows, when I was afflicted; & I loved you too sincerely to poison your felicity, by a disclosure of my own misfortunes. Those days are past: I have nothing to complain of: but the opportunities of confidence exist no longer. Our situations in life, now, call us to more important meditations; & we may yet be more than merely useful to each other. Our letters must assume a serious aspect; & be worthy of those duties which demand our performance. Let them be as frequent, & lengthy, as love & mutual benefit, could wish for, or require.

And you, my sister Fanny, you must not suffer your recollections of your brother, to diminish, as you journey from him. Remember, he is your friend, as well as brother; & if his zeal be not according to knowlege, it is true to all the knowlege he possesses. Much leisure will, now, be yours. Use it discretely. Forget not those studies which engaged your attention, while in Lichfield: you will find an able instructor, in the brother with whom you reside. In particular, look to that sister, who now embraces you: Learn, like her, to reflect, & act: &, above all, copy her equanimity of temper, her heroic fortitude.

I would wish to lay some inducement before Thomas, which might cause him to give a freer scope to the friendly effusions of his pen. If I am brief in my letters to him, it is only that his unchanging example of brevity, has fixed in my mind a conviction that a greater copiousness would be unpleasing. If I am mistaken & I hope I am—let him prove it to me, by one act; he shall see what new strides I shall make to regain his former indulgence.

I am pressed for time. All friends are well.

Fare ye well.

Friday, March 11th. 1796.
Cedar St. No. 13. New York.   E. H. Smith.

Saturday, 12th

[Omitted here, four manuscript pages: continuation of letter to Wm. Buel.]

After having written the letter, of yesterday's date, I went to bed; but had not lain long, when I was rouzed by the cry of fire. The appearance of the fire, at first, boded much mischief; Fortunately, however, it did not do very great damage. I worked in the ranks till near two, in the morning: and it was after that hour, when I regained my bed. This morning, I wrote the preceeding pages, of this date—transcribed my letter of this date—& made some professional &c. visits. Progressed in Dumarsais. Dunlap & I, walked out of Town in the afternoon. Returning, met Mr. & Mrs. Lovegrove, & Seth Johnson. Turned back, & walked with them. Drank tea at their house. H. Johnson & his wife there. Club night—with me—Present—Dunlap, W. W. Woolsey, Kent, Wm. Johnson, & myself—Alsop, & J. Mulligan visitors. I read several of Dr. Sayers' smaller Poems. Much desultory, but pleasant conversation. Evening spent very agreably. Recd. a letter from my cousin Samuel Smith.

Sunday, 13th

Rose late—breakfasted late—was dressing when Dunlap entered. Assisted him, for an hour, in correcting his Opera: settling the disputes between *ands* & *ors*; & comas, semi-colons, &c. Made my professional visits—visited Dingley—Dined with Woolsey—After dinner Woolsey, Dunlap, & myself—walked out of town, several miles—returned & drank tea at Dunlap's. Visited, & had an agreable visit, at Mr. Roulet's—who I met in the street. He has two most charming children. Gahn came there. From thence I went to Dunlap's—a few moments: thence to Hodgkinson's—where I past an hour very agreably. Never saw the little woman look more sweetly. Made a short call at H. Johnson's.

Monday, 14th

Till near two o'clock, my time divided between attention to my own business, & that of the Manumission Society. I read an hour, or two, in the first volume of "Memoires secrets & critiques des Cours, des Gouvernmens, et des mœurs, des principaux États de l'Itale.[70] Par Joseph Gorani,"—looked over a miserable Sermon of Dr. Linn's, & finished reading Mr. Harper, of South Carolina's, respectable Address to his Constituents. Adams, Wells, & Mulligan, were here most of the afternoon—& thus my time past away. Drank tea at Kent's—saw Mrs. Kent, for the first time, since the birth of her Child—saw that, too—& spent an hour, or so, very pleasantly: From thence to the Theatre; where I met Dunlap. "School for Scandal"—of which I saw one act—poorly played; & "The Quaker, or &c."[71]—which I saw well played—& was delighted with. It has no powerful recommendations to this piece, but it is all very simple, & sweet—the music is peculiarly so—it is sweetly performed here—& simplicity & purity are so rare in After pieces, that they charm from novelty, at least, if from nothing else.

To William Buel.

Were it necessary, my friend, for me to offer any excuse to you, who are so well-convinced of the sincerity of my attachments, for my long silence, never was I furnished with one better, or more suited to remove any doubt, which my taciturnity might have exerted, to my disadvantage. I sent you a verbal message, from Lichfield; which was all that the time allowed me to do. I would have gladly written, but the circumstances, under which my visit was made, forbade it. Since my return, so far have I been from forgetting you, that every moment which I could spare from the calls of duty to others, has been devoted to you. Yes, it is because I have been busily engaged in writing to you, that I have not written long before this time. And, now, I should not have sent this short letter, were I not apprehensive that your patience might be nearly exhausted; & that you might, incautiously, do me injustice, while ignorant of the cause of my delay. You will, questionless, comprehend my meaning: you will understand the task I hint at, as having occupied my time, to be no other than the arrangement of those facts, concerning the Fever which prevailed here last season, which have been so long promised to you. In truth, my friend, I know not when I shall be able to gratify your curiosity. Your letter gave me much satisfaction; & I feel emulous of acquitting myself as much to your approbation, as you have to mine. When I took up the pen,

---

[70] (Paris, 1793).
[71] *School for Scandal* by Richard B. Sheridan (1777); *The Quaker*, Charles Dibdin (1777). See also as less likely, *The Young Quaker*, John O'Keefe (1781).

I thought to do this, in fewer pages than you had written; but I find my undertaking more arduous than I expected—

"Hills peer o'er hills, & Alps, on Alps, arise."[72] & I have yet, a long way to travel over; & you may think yourself well off, if you escape the reading of five times the number of pages you sent me. In the rambling manner in which I have, hitherto, proceeded, I believe I may have blotted ten or twelve sheets, already—& I can not get thro' with less than three, or four, beside. But, I hope, when all these disjointed members come to be fitly put together, they will occupy less space, & offer a more agreable spectacle, than in their present state, to the eye of the beholder. In the meantime, do not be impatient: & remember, that, if I do delay, it is only that I may give you the greater satisfaction.

Monday, March 14. 1796.
Cedar St. No. 13, New York.   E. H. Smith.

Tuesday, 15th

[Omitted here, two manuscript pages: continuation of letter to Wm. Buel.]

To Reuben Smith—Lichfield.

Mr. Collier arrived in town this morning, & delivered me your letter. His unexpected visit gives me great pleasure; tho' he intends it shall be of short continuance. I shall send by him on his return, the Instruments, for W. Fowler, the Sand—& some Soda. The quantity of this last is small, but being all I have by me, & it not being convenient for me to go out for more, at this time, I thought it as well to wait till I heard from you again before I forwarded any more. From the manner in which you speak of it, I am unable to form any opinion, as to it's having been of use, or otherwise. What it is designed for is, to alleviate, or remove, the painful symptoms, attendant on Calculous Affections. As these are not constantly present, how useful soever the Medicine may be as a preventative, it can not be expected to have any sensible effect, in removing what does [not] exist. But if these symptoms are present, & the medicine has no beneficial effect—after a due trial—I would give it up. Now, perhaps Mr. Lord has not one of his ill turns upon him. If he has Not, how can we tell but that the Soda has prevented one from coming on. If he has, I do not think that a trial of sufficient time has been made. If it continues to purge him, a smaller quantity may be used—at greater intervals—or combined with Opium: tho' I would prefer the trial of it, by itself, as that is the fairest way of determining it's efficacy.

I heard, verbally, from Mumford & my sisters, when they were within fifty miles of home. The sleighing was very poor, & his horses much fatigued; tho' the person who brought the news thought they would be able to get home, without very great difficulty. I mentioned that I had heard from them, at Albany—in a short letter,

---

[72] Pope, *An Essay on Criticism*, Part II, 1. 32.

put in the Book sent by the Post, of which you say nothing. I hope you received it. The book was for Idea Strong.

Col. Tallmadge left New York, this day week; & has doubtless arrived at home before now. He was in good health when he past thro': I saw him but a short time.

Coffee, I have not purchased, & shall not at present. It is 25 Cts. the pound. There is a probability of it's being lower, in the course of 5 or 6 weeks, & none of it's being higher. So that I think it best to wait.

	dols.
The teeth-instruments cost	3..50 cts.
The Swiffle Key	3..75
The Sand	—..19
	7..44

Present my best love &c. to my mother, sister & friends: I hope, soon, to be more at leisure, than at present; & shall then write. In the meantime, they would oblige me, were they a little more loquacious with their pens.

Tuesday, March 15. 1796.
Cedar St. No. 13, New York.   E. H. Smith.

I was writing on my letter concerning the Fever, when Mr. Collier entered. He spent some time here; & we chatted about Lichfield affairs. After he went away, I transcribed the letter, written last evening, to W. Buel; made several visits—did some business—wrote & transcribed the letter to my father. After dinner, read in *Gorani*. Dunlap & Alsop were here. Drank tea at Woolsey's. Spent the evening at the Manumission Society. Nathaniel Lawrence,[73] formerly, Attorney-General of this State, was impeached—before the Society—; but overcome by the eloquence of Mr. Hamilton & by motives of expediency, rather than by the defense of the accused, or just notions of justice, the Society ordered every trace of transaction to be erased from the Minutes.

This is the first opportunity I have had of hearing Mr. Hamilton speak; & I heard him with pleasure, tho' he opposed me. His method is clear, his style precise, his argumentation pointed & forcible, & his manner emphatic. This manner is calculated to have as much effect, as his argument.

Wednesday, 16th

[Omitted here, one manuscript page: continuation of letter to Wm. Buel.]

I have done very little, to purpose, this day. Dingley was here, & Dunlap, in the morning: after them came Collier; & stayed with me till noon. I then went out to pay some money, & get some books. I read an hour in Gorani. Alsop & Dunlap were here, after dinner. Made some professional &c. visits. Drank tea, & spent two hours, at Mrs. Miller's. Went from thence to the room

---

[73] No further information is available. It is not referred to at any time thereafter in the Minutes.

where the Humane Society were to have met: Not enough to make a quorum. A most dreadful snowstorm, doubtless, prevented their attendance. The Theatre I found full, when I went there. I did not see the Play, which was "The Deserted Daughter"—a great favorite here—but I saw some pretty good French dancing—& a most contemptible After-piece, called "Poor Vulcan" —of Dibdin's,[74] I believe. Thank Heaven! our audience was not stupid enough to relish it—stupid as it generally is; for never did I see any piece recd. with less applause, or obtain so much disapprobation.

Thursday, 17th

Th: Collier breakfasted with us—after breakfast, we fell into conversation, which lasted some time; &, while he was here, Dunlap came in—then Alsop—then Mr. Gahn, & so on—till I had only time to run out, & pay a few professional visits: last came Saml. M. Hopkins, who brought me a large packet of letters, from Lichfield, for Aurora—& one letter, from Abby, to me. I recd. also, a letter from John Allen.

Dunlap & I dined at Hodgkinson's—beside his family, there was a large collection—all of the Theatre, beside us & Mr. Cozine.[75] We came away about twelve o'clock at night, after one of the most pleasant afternoons & evenings I ever enjoyed. The company was intirely made up, on the theatre side, of our new performers— Mr. & Mrs. Johnson, Mr. & Mrs. Tyler, Mr. & Mrs. Cleveland, Mrs. & Miss Broadhurst, & Mr. Jefferson: all are well-bred, agreable, & of very good information & good-sense. We had much good conversation—& *a great deal* of very excellent singing.

Friday, 18th

This day, like yesterday, has gone by, with little exertion, and less improvement. I arranged & transcribed the Minutes of the Manumission Society, & did somewhat towards the revision of the Constitution. Dunlap, Alsop, & Collier, were here, some time; & I assisted the first in correcting &c. his Opera. I past part of the afternoon with Dingley—conversing on Medical subjects. Johnson and I drank tea, & spent the evening at Mr. Lovegrove's. Returning, I stept into the Theatre & stayed half an hour. I have read some, in Gorani; & have recd. a short letter from O. Wolcott jr.

To Samuel Smith.

I recd. a letter from you, a few days since, in which you complain of my silence; and express some surprize at my not having applied to your repeated letters. This reply, should it ever reach you, will justify me, I have no doubt, to your satisfaction.

The last letter I recd. from you, (before the one I am now answering—which is dated Feby. 16. 1796) is dated Nov. 23rd 1794—I recd. it the 29th of Decr. 1794—& answered it the 11th of January 1795. These circumstances I can not be mistaken in, as they are all noted in my Journal. Since then, I have never had any direct information of you, till now: so that, if you have written, I have never recd. your letters. I thought it strange that you did not write; & the more especially, as Mr. Aron Catlin[76] had letters from you, once or twice, & I had none: but I supposed that you were engaged by business, or wanted opportunity, & I did not suspect you of wanting friendship for me.

In the letter, which I wrote to you, a year ago last January, I informed you that Mr. Mumford had seasonably attended to your business; and that the Survey had been delivered into the Land Office, according to your wishes. It is so long since—that I have lost all particular recollection of the business; & only know that it was completed.

Mr. Mumford has removed to one of the back Counties in this State—about three hundred miles from hence—& about the same distance from Lichfield. My sister & he have been married about fifteen months; & have a fine, hearty boy, near four months old. I saw them, last month, in Lichfield—where they were, on a visit; & whither I went to meet them. They enjoy fine health. I returned by the way of Southington; but had only time to stop an hour, with our Aunts. They were well; & told me that your father's family were well also. Your brother Calvin has removed, to Norfolk—& is well settled there—on a good farm. Dr. Root has removed to Hampden, & his brother takes his place at Southington. I spent the night with the Dr. & found him happily settled in his new situation.

In addition to all this budget of news, I have to inform you that your sister, Mrs. Jocelin, has made you an Uncle—but whether to a boy or girl, I can not, now, remember; tho' I believe it is to a boy.

I am happy, my dear Cousin, to renew, & shall be pleased to continue, our correspondence. Be assured, however neglectful I may appear, at any time, to be— there is no person who maintains a more steady & warm affection for you.

Friday, March 18. 1796.
Cedar St. No. 13. N. York. E. H. Smith.

Saturday, 19th

To Abigail Smith, junr.

Your letter, my dear sister, found me under so many engagements, of one kind and another, that I had no time to attempt answer till now; and now, I have no opportunity of sending to you—as Mr. Collier has just left us. I shall write, notwithstanding; for, at this time of the year, we can not long remain in want of a conveyance.

You request my opinion & direction, in three concerns—and then inform me that you have decided on

---

[74] *Poor Vulcan* by Charles Dibdin, a burlesque (1778).

[75] An acquaintance of Smith's and Dunlap's who was dead of yellow fever by September 17, 1798. Dunlap, *Diary* 1: p. 339.

[76] Aaron, brother of Lynde Catlin, died of yellow fever in Jamaica before July 31, 1796.

one. This is according to the usual course of advice-taking; where resolutions commonly preceed inquiries. But, pleasantry apart, I will give you my opinion, as well as I am able, considering the little information I possess of particulars.

"What shall *you* read?"—"What have you read? It will be very difficult to give a minute answer to the first, without having had a reply to the last, question. You know that the studies I have constantly pressed upon you, as the most important, in your situation, are Arithmetic, Geography, Chronology, & History. If you are not perfect in these, you stand in no need of further direction, as long as you have authors & instructors in each of them. The first of these, I must again repeat it, is indispensable; & you ought to acquire a perfect command & application of it, at all hazards. Let it, then, be your first care to devote as great a portion of your time to the cultivation of it, as circumstances will permit. For the rest, as you have made a general acquaintance with History, it is not very important, placed as you are, in what point you begin your review of it. Take up any period of History which best pleases you; read all the books which throw any light upon it, that you can procure; & make yourself mistress of so much geography, chronology, & biography, as relate to it. I know the difficulties you will labour under in respect to books; but, by the aid of those which there are in Lichfield, you may obtain more than an ordinary share of historical information. You may take up, for instance, that period of the Roman history, which commences with the death of Julius Cesar, & is terminated by the accession of Tiberius to the purple. This period is extensive, splendid, interesting, & important, beyond any other in the history of the Romans. In studying it, do not confine yourself to the mere detail of military operations, proscriptions, & triumphs, but endeavour to become intimately versed in the literature of the times, the character of the most celebrated personages, & the changes that were wrought in the civil administrations. This period was rendered illustrious by the united labours of Virgil, Horace, whose names are, in some sort familiar to you—& many others, whose works you will obtain with more difficulty; & who are less deserving of your attention. To comprehend the value of these men, & the importance of this period, you should not only collect the opinions of others, but endeavour to form opinions for yourself. Read, therefore, the Works of Virgil, of Horace, & such others as you can find. Virgil has been well translated by Dryden & Pitt—& one, or both, of their translations may be found in Lichfield. Mr. Reeve, formerly, possesst Francis's translation of Horace;[77] it is a poetical translation; & is held to be the best. The famous Orator, Cicero, perished in the early part of this period. You would obtain some notion of his merit, by reading some his Orations—translations of which you will meet with, almost every where; &, from certain of them, would gain additional information respecting the history of the times. But it is needless to enlarge: you will find the several writers mentioned by the historians; & will read such of these works as may fall in your way. On the whole, I think it will be well for you to revise this part of the Roman History, with great care. With respect to other reading, it will be best to direct your principal attention to such writings as will assist you in forming just notions in morality & criticism. In the former, read Stewart's "Philosophy of the Mind,"[78] & Godwin's "Political Justice"—you will get them both of Mr. Allen—as also Smith's "Theory of Moral Sentiments":[79] in the latter, read Kames's "Elements of Criticism"—& Blair's Lectures. I mention these books, because I know that you *can* obtain them; & because they are, perhaps, as good as any you can procure.

Your Diary ought to be a faithful portrait of your mind, each day; & an exact register of your actions. Further than this I need not direct you. If you follow this direction, it will be ample, interesting, instructive. Such it should be; & such I hope to see it.

As the distribution of parts is completed, I know not that I can render you any service, in your theatric course. The part of Miss Hardcastle is an arduous undertaking, for one so much a novice as you are; yet, I see no reason why you may not acquit yourself as well as most of your companions. You should *study* the character. It is not enough to get the speeches by heart; you must endeavor to realize the situations of Miss Hardcastle, figure to yourself what would be her conduct, & strive to lose yourself in her. You have my hearty wishes for your success.

Farewell.

Saturday, March 19. 1796.
Cedar St. No. 13. New York.   E. H. Smith.

This day has been, as it were, a day of scraps: filing letters, receits, looking some books lately bought; doing errands &c.—Collier called to bid me farewell; Hopkins called; Dunlap several times, & I on him: wrote the above letter; corrected one Act of a new Copy of my Opera—made by Dunlap's Clerk; finished the first volume of Gorani. Walked—Johnson, Dunlap, Alsop, & I, in the afternoon. Drank tea with Dunlap—Club night—At his house—Present, Alsop, Dunlap, Kent, W. Johnson, Smith, the Woolseys.

Hodgkinson has made Dunlap a proposition, of becoming Manager of the Theatre—& to own one fourth of the property—&c.

Sunday, 20th

Made a professional visit—at some distance: transcribed my letter to Saml. Smith: walked with Wm.:

---

[77] Philip Francis (?-1773). English clergyman. His translation of Horace was first printed about 1743, the eighth edition or printing in 1778.

[78] Dugald Stewart, *Elements of the Philosophy of the Human Mind* (London, 1792).

[79] Adam Smith, *The Theory of Moral Sentiments*, etc. (London, 1759).

dined, spent most of the afternoon, at H. Johnson's: remainder, & part of the evening, at Woolsey's—from whence Dunlap & I went to Hodgkinson's. Since I came home, I have amused myself for an hour, with the Monthly Review. I find a Mr. Clutterbuck asserts great things of Mercury, as a cure for disease from Saturn.

Monday, 21st

[Omitted here, two manuscript pages: continuation of letter to Wm. Buel.]

A strange sense of weariness, & incapacity for bodily or mental exertion oppresses me—& has opprest me, today, & for several days: and this does not, in the least, serve to put me in better humor with myself. I attempted to write, to-day—but was obliged to throw aside the pen—I have made some attempts at reading, but with scarcely any more success: my conversation was laborious—& even my walk, in the course of my circumscribed practice, a great fatigue. I have finished the correction of my Opera—or rather of the new copy of it: I have looked over three numbers of the Monthly Review—I have dedicated an hour or two to Dunlap, on his proffered opportunity of becoming Manager of our Theatre[80]—I have spent an hour at the Theatre—chatted a while with Alsop—& lost most of the afternoon in assisting a hysterical girl.

Tuesday, 22nd

Visited my patients—assisted Dunlap in correcting his proof-sheets &c.—wrote the Introduction, in my new Journal—made a new professional visit—& the same in the afternoon—Dunlap here again, & we aiding him—drank tea at H. Johnson's, where we spent the evening—Miss S. Morton & Miss Smith there—Wm. & I went home with them—have looked over several numbers of the Monthly Review—read some in Gorani.

My letter to Wm. Buel, on the Fever, seems to be pretty much at a stand; &, indeed, my laziness, and a little business which I now have, make me fear that I shall do no more towards completing it, for some time. Still, I hope, before long, to be at leisure, to sit down to it, & complete it, in a decent sort. When I began to write, I had no idea of any thing more than a mere, private letter, to be dispatched in two or three sheets: since the matter has so much accumulated on my hands, the idea of preparing it for the press has several times occurred to me. On this I have, as yet, made no determination. Should I do it, there will be a necessity of throwing it into a somewhat different form; & there will be a use in a greater number of references to authors. This will require some reading, & writing: & this I think to do, whether I do, or do not, publish. I must think further on this matter.

Wednesday, 23rd

[Omitted here, three manuscript pages: continuation of letter to Wm. Buel.]

I have, at last, brought my letter to Buel to a sort of conclusion—& this the sooner because my attention had become so scattered, that it was impossible for me to proceed, in this loose way, any longer, with advantage. I shall now make it my business to reconsider all these loose notes, with care—to compare them with the best authors—digest them under proper heads—& give to the whole, as far as I am able, a systematic form. On the whole, I am determined to throw what I shall write, into the figure of several letters—& adapt them for publication. They can not be the worse, for my friend, on this account—even should they not be published—& I may be, in this way, led to write more carefully, than if I were scribbling merely for his private perusal. I have thoughts, too, for sometime past, of addressing a letter, to the Poor of the City, on the means of prevention—so far as depends on themselves; & if I should do this, it will form a useful appendix to my Letters to Buel. But all this requires more thought.

Professional business occupied most of the forenoon—concluded, after the above fashion, my letter on the Fever—made considerable progress in Gorani—Dingley & Dunlap here in the afternoon—Evening at the Theatre—"The Clandestine Marriage"[81]—Mr. Hallam's "Lord Ogilby"—Hodgkinson's "Lovewell"—Tyler's "Sir John Melville"—Johnson's "Sterling"—Mrs. Johnson's "Fanny"—& Mrs. Brett's "Mrs. Heidelberg"—all excellent—Mrs. Hallam's "Miss Sterling" pitiful—on the whole much entertained: meant not to have stayed to the "Midnight Hour"[82]—but Miss Morton, persuaded—& I was not sorry: it was well played—& her conversation was an Entertainment still superior.

Thursday, 24th

All the morning doing business, out-doors. Corrected Dunlap's "Historical Memoir." Afternoon, Mr. Laffert, here on a visit from Phila., called on us—spent an hour or more, very much to our satisfaction. We made some calls with him: Dunlap was here, & Mulligan. Drank tea & past the evening, at Mr. Webster's. R. Flint[83] & Kent there. Talked much on politics, education, & perfectability—to no purpose. Came home & read "The Mountaineers" of G. Coleman jr.[84] Pretty good: tho' does not leave much impression, when you have finished it. Read some in Gorani.

---

[80] Dunlap made clear in his *Diary* that he relied heavily on Smith for advice in the appalling series of problems and difficulties that followed his taking up Hodgkinson's offer.

[81] Garrick and Colman, the elder (1766), *The Clandestine Marriage;* Elizabeth Inchbald, *Midnight Hour* (1787).
[82] Elizabeth Inchbald (1787).
[83] Royal Flint was a New York merchant.
[84] Colman, the younger (1793). Odell notes that this play with music by Arnold and accompaniment by Pelissier was first presented in America March 30, 1796.

Friday, 25th

Dunlap spent part of the morning with me. I then went out & attended to my business. Yesterday Hodgkinson applied to me, to write an Ode, something of the kind, to be recited on the public meeting of the Anacreontic Society—which is to be next Thursday evening—& when a considerable number of the ladies of this city are expected to be present. I did not think of doing any thing, in consequence of this application—but, while I was walking, a thought struck me—& when I came home I sat down to write; & finished an Ode—before dinner—notwithstanding several interruptions. Dunlap came in, & agreably surprized me, by shewing me letters, which he had recd. from Holcroft & Godwin—in reply to his. They are both fine letters—especially Godwin's. Johnson came in—& the Woolseys—to see the new Satire, in the Connecticut Courant, on certain members of Congress: they all read the letters, & with pleasure. To accommodate D. & myself—who wish to see "Jane Shore"[85] performed—the performance of which is put off till to-morrow evening—because this is Good Friday—it was agreed, that the Club should meet this evening. As, in consequence of a change, made some time since, we seldom get done with dinner, till 4 P. M. I have very little afternoon. I sat awhile with Kent: returned & copied my Ode: made a professional visit: called at Hodgkinson's: drank tea at Dunlap's with Johnson—& then all came here. Johnson's night—Present—himself—Dunlap, Kent, the Woolseys—myself. Kent read the above-mentioned letters, & those of D. which gave rise to them—with great marks of satisfaction. Johnson read us Gibbon's character of Mahomet. Some talk on both these things. My Ode was called for—& read. Desultory conversation. St. Pierre's Theory of the Tides. Johnson read Sullivan's abstract of it—which gave rise to a lengthy conversation—with which the sitting terminated.

Saturday, 26th

Writing &c. for the Manumission Society—a little

[85] Nicholas Rowe, *The Tragedy of Jane Shore* (1714).

business, &c. occupied all the forenoon. Made still further progress in Gorani. After dinner, Johnson, Dunlap & I, walked out of Town. Went to the Theater—& saw "Jane Shore" well performed.

March 29, 1796

It would have been doing as I ought to have done, to have drawn up whatever remarks, I had to make on the business of this month, so far as detailed in this volume, & on the manner in which this volume has been conducted, immediately on coming to the conclusion of it, & while the facts, opinions &c. connected with it, were, to a certain degree, more fresh in my memory. But I have not done this—& now shall conclude this volume, with a few thoughts which strike me at the moment.

This month is in my favor, on the whole. The beginning promised, more than the end fulfilled. My notes on the Yellow Fever, notwithstanding, & loosely as they are arranged, even should I never do any thing more, in relation to it, will be valuable; & bear a testimony in my favor—as an observer. The records of this month, in other respects, are more than usually scanty. This may be imputed, in part, to the fatigue, & consequent disinclination to writing, occasioned by so steady a use of the pen, as is apparent for a considerable part of the time.

In respect to my studies, this month—my notes on the Fever excepted—& all the rest of the volume, bear lamentable marks of falling off. The testimony of the preceeding volume, on the contrary, is much in my favor. Some part of the cause must rather be considered as my misfortune, than fault—but, after all, it is impossible to excuse my conduct. It is to be hoped that my Memoirs, in future, will be more to my credit.

I have, now, not only brought a fifth volume of my Diary to a close, but have extinguished the thing itself—hoping, with a new title, & somewhat different form, to catch a better spirit. This the event, alone, can determine. The attempt is good; & let the Journal spring up, like the new Phenix, from the ashes of the Diary.

Notebook No. 3: March–July, 1796

Jam nova progenies—[86]
Virgil.

JOURNAL. 1796. MARCH.

With a new title, and a new book, I have commenced a new plan, & with new resolutions. Experience, it is true, does not present me with any flattering prospects, as to the success of the one, or the stability of the other. May it be my fate, notwithstanding, as, if it should be, it will prove my happiness, to give the lie to all melancholly presages, & evince to myself, in one instance at least, the utility of the former, & the unchangeability of the latter.

In the present undertaking, if circumstances should so far favor me, I hope to give still more unity, system, & order, than has, hitherto been uniformly observable in my Diary. Where each day presents nothing remarkable, in itself, or where a week passes away, whose days are of this common cast, it is my design, as far as possible, to melt the whole into one little narrative. Still, I do not intend to omit the notices, or minutes, of any day: but, rather, to make them mere notices, unless, indeed, the spirit, or the interest, of the moment, swell them into importance. To each week, I further hope to prefix some prefatory matter; and, at it's conclusion, not only a review of what has past in it, but of what has not been effected, which I meant to have effected; of what have been my feelings; what ought to have been; & such remarks as the review shall suggest. So much for my particular history of each week. To every month, a more general preface, & a more ample postscript, must be added. It is, however, not improbable that this order will be subjected to many aberrations— from caprice, after-thought, &, perhaps, necessity. So far as it may proceed, aside from these hindrances, I *now* feel resolved to pursue it.

The last Volume of my Diary exhibits an example of a vigorous, but temporary, application to professional study & inquiry. I feel it to be probable that this will not be a solitary example in the course of my private Memoirs. This Volume, I am well assured, will not only perfect what that will leave undone; but will contain the more wide & minute researches of my mind, on various other subjects, connected with Medicine. I do not expect to compose systems, or even systematic Essays, in this book: I shall limit myself, principally, to collecting the materials, & reasonings,—& arrange & polish them, in other forms—if designed for public inspection. To these, as to other collections, relative to different studies, I shall prefix a general Head; the more easily to dispose them, in my future Index. Thus, my Journal, will not only exhibit the tenor of my life, and the temper of my mind, but, also, the history of my various studies. Neither will there be any interruption in the Journal of actions, from these speculations; but the bounds of either will be so marked, that it's course may be separately pursued.

My Letters, too, being composed in this book, & thus preserved in it, will exhibit, at the same time, in some sort, a view of my business, feelings, sentiments, the condition of my friends, &, occasionally, perhaps, the history of former periods. In respect to this last point, I hope to do more than I have ever done. The many schemes with which my head is filled; the increasing aversion I feel for composition, except by starts; the engagements, of various kinds, by which I am surrounded; & the numerous interruptions to thought & action, that I am constantly subjected to; make me more than ever, doubtful of my effecting any thing, to the purpose, for some time to come, on my own History. Thus circumstanced, I have long thought, & have now resolved, to devote a portion of this volume to the character, and, as far as I am able—to the history, of my friends: and this in the order of my *intimate* connection with them. The facts, and opinions, which I shall give, may be more important than any which simply relate to myself: at the same time, they will, in no small degree, explain my own story. To those, into whose hands my Papers may come, when I cease to exist, they will be valuable: for my connections, in many instances, have been with those, who either have been, or promise to be, in some good measure, distinguished actors in the scene around me. Should leisure & inclination conspire to the composition of my intended Memoirs, this previous exercise will have it's use. Should they not, it's place will be nearly supplied thereby. In either case, then, the design is interesting, & deserves accomplishment. If my present resolution hold, this plan will not be limited to those who merit to be called my *friends*; but will be extended to a variety of characters—perhaps, more interesting, on some accounts to the Historian & Philosopher.

Were it possible for me to fill up the Outline which I have just traced, this new Series, would claim some rank among the Records of my knot of brothers. It would deserve a Title no less honorable, than that of "The History of the Feelings, Sentiments, Actions, Studies, of E. H. Smith; with critical & biographical anecdotes & remarks concerning his Friends, & others." But, alas! this sportiveness of imagination, is too unreal: it wants that persevering energy of Volition, which would embody & array it. The history of myself, is that of precipitate resolutions, precipitately abandoned: of transient activity, and long-continued inaction: of unlimited

---

[86] "Jam nova progenies caelo demittitur alto . . ." Vergil, *Eclogue* IV, 7. "Now the new progenitor is sent down from the high sky."

desires, over-powered by a wayward sensibility, or childish timidity, & an eloquent indolence. This portrait of myself, which even these very traits prevent me from making more full, & which every day becomes more strikingly just, & resembling, cautions me against too firm a reliance on that self-confidence with which I am apt to commence every new undertaking. This caution, has been attended to, for once: of which this very Introduction is a proof. There yet remain many unfilled pages, in my Diary; & I do not intend to pursue this Journal, till they are filled. When I procured this Book, & resolved on this new Plan, I resolved, likewise, to write this Introduction some days before the book would be wanted. I knew myself too well, to trust what might be my feelings at the moment when it would be necessary to use it. That heavy sluggishness of my powers—that spiritual inanity, & corporeal inertness, which so often wrest the pen from my hand, or incapacitate me for directing it—might then possess me; & the particulars, even now so imperfectly displayed, would then have limped along as lamely, as the pen which traced the character would have moved indistinctly. This is mortifying; but it is true. May the conclusion of the volume before me, shew it to have become less so. Then, indeed, may I exclaim, in the language of my Motto, & in the joy of my heart, "Jam nova Progenies!"

Tuesday, March 22nd[87]

First Week

Sunday, 27th

PREFACE

The preceeding pages sufficiently explain the intentions which this volume is designed to fulfill, and the resolutions with which it is commenced. It is now my duty, agreable to the plan I am to pursue, to enumerate, in some sort, those things which it is incumbent on me to attend to, in the course of the present week: and, of all these, my Studies claim the first notice.

I began this Winter with strong expectations, & with some endeavor after their accomplishment. 'Till my journey to Phila. some faithfulness, on my part, was observable. Since then, a variety of accidents, new engagements, & above all, a disgraceful indolence, have concurred to dissipate, or interrupt my application. At this time, it may be as well, perhaps, to form no particular determination, concerning certain of these studies, and to confine myself to those which more immediately demand my attention. For some time, Medicine has lain neglected: even the letter to my friend Buel, which I began upon with so much spirit, remains in it's rude condition; & none of that reading has been entered upon, which should preceed the attempt to Methodize the composition. Hither, then, should my first thought be directed; & it shall be understood to be one part of this week's business to accomplish as much of this preparatory reading, as circumstances will admit of. As for all other medical reading, tho' events, not now foreseen, may demand it of me, it does not fall in with my design to cultivate it, till the present business is completed. Of all my studies, that which I have least neglected, perhaps, is French. Few days pass away without some moments given to that; and I am encouraged to believe that my knowlege of it is more accurate than ever. Still, much remains for me to do & learn; & while it is so, this language must not be neglected. Of the German, I know not what to say—but of this, of History, of Mathematics, I must not think, at present. Medicine, French, my own language, must be my first care.

With regard to the exercise of my profession, no new resolutions are necessary. It must be my primary duty to attend to it: and, during this month, I have nothing, on this account, with which to reproach myself. All that I have done has been successfully done.

Much neglect is certainly chargeable to me, both on the score of correspondence, & visiting: and I impose it on this week to make some progress in the removal of this reproach. I can not help lamenting that my profession renders so much of the latter necessary; but since I must lose time, that I may gain it, let me strive to lose it most advantageously. For my correspondence—as my pen must labor on my medical studies, it is probable, that this must not receive the highest notice. A little time will, I hope, put it on it's true establishment.

Much of my time has been occupied, since Dunlap began the printing of his Opera,[88] in assisting him in the correction of his M.S. & of the proof-sheets: a labor the more necessary, as he is unacquainted with the rules of punctuation, & not well versed in those of grammar. But to this business a conclusion is near at hand; as the Piece is almost finished. When it is, one diversion from my proper occupations will be ended.

It is certain that the Theater engages too many of my thoughts, and attendance on it, too many of my hours: and here I am most doubtful of my strength. The merit of the new performers, which have graced the Stage, this season; the excellence of the general run of the Pieces; the novelty of others; the example of some friends; the few diversions I indulge myself in; the inexpensiveness of this; & my love of the drama; all vigorously concur to lead me to be present at theatrical exhibitions. My attention, too, has been drawn this way the more, perhaps, from the expectation of having my own Piece performed; & from the necessity of devoting some cares to this object. But, henceforth, I must not, idly, visit the Theater.

---

[87] Readers may be puzzled by overlapping dates in the last two entries in the preceding volumes and the date of this preface for "New Series, Volume I." What Smith did was to write the introduction on March 22, but he continued to make daily entries in the previous volume through March 26. He then picked up his daily entries in the New Series Preface for March 27. Two days later he went back to write the conclusion to the previous volume.

[88] *The Archers.*

The line traced out, for this week's adherence to, may be varied, & broken, in numerous ways. Against accidents no one can absolutely guard. Neither do I expect to find myself, at the end of it, to have pursued the track, with undeviating steps. This would be to count upon strength which I never yet found myself to possess; & to slight the testimony & admonition of experience. Let me hope, however, that, if I do vary very much, it shall not be from causes, & in a manner, which shall justly excite strong self-disapprobation.

LETTERS

To Charles Brockden Brown.

You will, probably, receive a letter from Dunlap, at the same time with this; which will render it less necessary for me to be minute, on one subject, than I should, otherwise, have thought it. You will learn, from him, that he has recd. answers to his letters to Godwin & Holcroft; and of such a sort as might be expected from the authors of those works which we have read together, with so much delight. Our friend will, no doubt, make you acquainted with their contents; & in the best manner which the distance you are from us will admit. We have all wished you to be present, on this occasion, with an eagerness the less becoming, as it was of necessity unfruitful. Let, however, these communications strengthen your heart, and give new activity to your hands. We must do something to convince these men that we are worthy to receive some moments of their consideration.

The length of time which has elapsed since I have heard any thing, particularly, of you, opens a wide range for the exercise of your epistolary powers. You can not have been idle, all this time; & you know that I have a right to demand of you, how you have been busied, & to receive precise information, in return. You shall have no right to complain of me, in this respect; for I shall be sufficiently minute.

Soon after my return from Phila. I was called to Lichfield. My sisters were there, & Mr. Mumford; & the eldest was immediately to return, & my youngest sister to accompany her, instead of Abby. I went; & had the opportunity of interrupted conversation with them, for two days: spending only three at my father's. The extreme badness of the roads, made my journey long, tho' my visit was short.

These several visitings have very much broken in upon all regular exertion & application: my winter, of consequence, has been productive of very little. Since I came from Connecticut, my attention has been mostly directed to my professional studies; &, in this line, I have composed the rude outline of an account of the Fever which prevailed here in 1795. Should I finish this to my liking, perhaps I may publish it: but this is quite uncertain. Further than this, in the way of composition, I have done little more than make some corrections and additions, to the dramatic piece, which you have seen; & prepare it for a representation, which I begin to fear it will not attain to, this Season. If, however, contrary to my expectations, it should be played, I think, also, to have it printed: and, of this, I shall give you seasonable notice; as I shall, in that case, stand in need of your friendly assistance.

In respect to reading, I have no information to give, that will be particularly pleasing to you; unless it should be, that I have read Condorcet's book, of which we conversed when last together, with great satisfaction; & have made some progress in a Work of Dumarsais, intituled "Essai sur les Prejuges"; which appears to me to be the fount whence the Philosophers of the New School have drawn their delightful, vivifying, & invigorating, waters; the work which most deserves to be the Manual of the *little children of Truth*. Religious persecution confined this inestimable volume to few hands: the late Revolution, while it threatened the destruction of morality, as well as of religion, opened a way for it's introduction to universal notice. A new, and correct, Edition was published; & is now, probably, to be had in almost every French Book-Store. If you can, let me press you to, procure it. The probability that it will soon appear, in an english dress, is all that restrains my hands from attempting to bestow such a garb upon it. Beside this, we have been considerably amused & pleased with a publication of Riouffe's: a young frenchman, the friend of Louvet &c. who was imprisoned, during the tyranny of Robespierre. I am not sure that I have the title right—but I think it is—"Memoires d'un Detenu &c."[89] You will be gratified by the perusal, if it fall in your way: particularly with a New Religion, which he, & his friend, established, while prisoners. We, Johnson, Dunlap, & myself made some progress in a Translation; but other things have obliged us to relinquish it, for the present. As for Dunlap, he has been busy, in his way, reading, writing, & conversing. The correction of his three Tragedies, copies of which he has transmitted to Holcroft, took up some of his time:[90] still more has been devoted to his Opera—on the story of Wm. Tell.—which is soon to be played, & is now in the press. Our friend risks the impression of 750 copies; & depends on your aid, in the disposal of some part of them. It is, indeed, in part, the purpose of this letter, to request of you to let us know how many copies you can circulate among your friends, & obtain immediate payment for; & how many you suppose you could put in a favorable situation for sale, & for the ready collection of the avails, when sold. The play has very considerable merit, in several respects; a succinct account of Swisserland, & the Helvetii Confederacy, is

---

[89] *Memoirs d'un Détenu, etc.*, translated as *Revolutionary Justice Displayed, or an inside View of the various Prisons of Paris under the Government of Robespierre and the Jacobins* (Philadelphia, 1796).

[90] Dunlap sent his letter and tragedies to Holcroft in March, 1796. In December, Holcroft answered and the letter reached Dunlap in April, 1797.

annexed to it; & the pamphlet will be sold at 50 Cts. We desire you to make it one your first concerns to reply to these inquiries.

I have not recd. a line from any of my correspondents, in Phila. since I was there. It is true, that I have written but little to either of them, & not at all to you. Still I think you ought to have, & I hope you really have, some better reason than this, for your silence. I need not assure you that a letter from you would be the occasion of very deep & sincere delight to me, or that I always remember you, your family, & our common friends, with a heart over-flowing with affection.

Wm. Johnson, his brothers, the Woolseys, all, send much love to you & Joseph.

            Farewell.

Sunday, March 27. 1796.
Cedar St. No. 13. N. York.   E. H. Smith.

P.S. The bearer of this letter will, probably, be Mr. Gahn; the young Swede, with whom you made some little acquaintance, while you were here, last Summer. I can not doubt of your receiving great pleasure from a renewal of intercourse; & I beseech you, should he give you the opportunity, to avail yourself of it, as far as circumstances will permit. You know how highly we estimate his worth; & further intimacy will convince you that it is not without reason. He is intimate with Dr. Bollman, who, if you do not know, seek to know, by means of Mr. Gahn. I could give you some interesting information concerning Dr. Bollman, did leisure permit.

              E. H. S.

MEMORANDA, 1

Even the little business which I have, in the way of my profession, consumed much of this day: more indeed, than is always necessary. Webster, Alsop, & Dunlap, were here, a short time: the two first for me, the last to see us. I had no proper conversation with either. I wrote the preface to this week, the letter to Charles, & transcribed one, from my last volume, to my sister Abby. Wm. & I spent the evening at Lovegrove's. She grows more habitually cheerful.

MEMORANDA, 2

Monday, 28th

Transcribed my letter to Charles; made the necessary calls; & devoted the chief part of the day to medical reading. Mr. Gahn called here, in the forenoon; Dunlap, in the afternoon. I was at the Theater, in the evening. The piece was "The Haunted Tower"[91]—a performance altogether contemptible; but the music exquisite. I came away, but little satisfied. John Johnson[92] arrived from England, this day—a few hours after Seth had sailed for Boston. From the play, I went to H. Johnson's, where I found Wm. & John, very well. We supped there.

I finished the second volume of Gorani, last night.

MEMORANDA, 3

Tuesday, 29th

Walked over the greater part of the city, where the Fever prevailed last season; and surveyed it attentively. Read some Medicine. Wrote the following letter. Dr. Hale[93] called, & spent part of the afternoon with me. Alsop called here. Read some in Riouffe's Memoirs, both in the day, & evening. Walked, before tea. Spent the intire evening at Kent's, till near ten. Both he & his wife are charmed with Godwin & Holcroft's Works; and there is some hopes of their conversion.

LETTERS

To Idea Strong.

Since my return to this place, my time and attention have been constantly engaged, by a succession of various affairs; some, indeed, trivial; but, others, important, and necessary to be considered; so that, till now, I have not felt myself at leisure to commence that correspondence, on which we, mutually, resolved, when last together. I could have wished that, without waiting for the formality of an introductory letter from me, you had seen fit to lead the way yourself; and, as it were, provoke me to the field. But, I know that the ordinary course of practice is to the contrary of this; and, tho' you ought to be above such considerations, I shall not venture to find much fault, even if you have been influenced by them. But, how do I know, that your silence has not been the effect of more meritorious causes?

Letters are designed as substitutes for conversation; and that regular succession of them, which obtains the title of a Correspondence, may be considered as analogous to the intercourse of neighbours. Yet, tho' this account of their use be just, it should not be hence inferred, that, like most conversations & neighbourhood visitings, they are to be devoted to prattle & gossiping. Correspondencies, like partnerships & marriages, may produce important consequences, & ought to be engaged in with some caution, & much meditation. Neither caprice, nor vanity, nor ambition, nor any selfish feeling, should have any thing to do in this matter. Little as mankind, in general, reflect on this subject, like every other action, or system, or mode of conduct, it is to be viewed as limited & regulated by the rule of duty; as rigidly subject to the decisions of reason & justice. We

---

[91] James Cobb (1789).

[92] Probably a brother of William and Seth. There was, however, a John Johnson, an actor, mentioned earlier, who was in New York dickering with Hodgkinson for a position in the Old American Company at about this time. Dunlap, *Diary* 1: p. 49.

[93] Dr. Hale, mentioned once and not otherwise identified, may have been a visitor to the city or one of the many who even then tried New York briefly and returned home. Not mentioned in *New York Directories* 1796, 1797, 1798.

are not made for ourselves alone, but for each other; for all. For the benefit of all, therefore, should our lives, our thoughts, our energies, be employed; and each act must be pronounced good or bad; only in proportion as it promotes or impairs the welfare of all. Every action, of consequence, should have a moral end in view; much more every system of conduct. In the proportion of our adherence to this axiom, do we deserve the character, & shall we feel the charms & blessings, of virtue. We may often commit errors; but, acting from a regard to virtue, & thus watchful of consequences, we shall enjoy the approbation of our own hearts, & be most likely to discern our failings, & correct them. It is no sufficient reason, for a continuance in error, that it is pleasant; but it will always be a perfect reason for the relinquishment of any conduct, & any pleasure, that it is error. Of this we must daily become more sensible, as we press truth to our bosoms, seek for it every where, & in all things value that alone. To bring these remarks to the particular subject most immediately before us—Our correspondence must have some good in view: that good must be sufficiently important to justify the devotion of so much time to it, as will be necessary: if this prove not to be the case, it will be our duty to relinquish it. As the whole is composed of individuals, the rendering of essential advantages to one being, may, justly, be considered, as a benefit conferred on all being. This is strictly true, provided the good done to the individual, be not procured for him, at the expence of a greater good to society; & especially, if it be promotive of general happiness. To enlighten one ignorant mind; to confer a superior degree of illumination on one already, considerably enlightened; is to promote the progress of knowlege, the extension of virtue. For knowlege & virtue have an inherent inseparable, & eternal, tendency, like light, to extend in every direction; and every virtuous being, like the planets which diffuse around them a portion of that splendor which they derive from the sun, becomes a new point in the universe of mind, a new & subordinate center of intellectual illumination, from whence originates a new diffusion of that truth & virtue, primarily derived from God, the Source of Animation, the imperishable spring & exhaustless fountain of knowlege, virtue, & happiness. And thus will this wonderful work proceed, till the intermingling rays of moral radiance form a galaxy of virtue; spreading over & comprehending, in it's glorious brightness, all intelligent being; & reflecting back upon the sun of moral excellence, a splendor, dazzling & eternal like his own. The contemplation of a state so sublimely interesting, makes me half regret that I must quit it, for the present, to return to the subject of our Correspondence.

If we can mutually assist each other, in the acquisition of knowlege & virtue; if we can strengthen the dispositions to advance human happiness, which we already possess; if we may be the better enabled to be useful to others; if such will be the consequences of our correspondence, we can not commence it too speedily, continue it too long, or pursue it too earnestly. If the least of these good consequences will flow from it; or if there be a probability of such a result; situated as we are, we need not decline it, we need not fear that we shall violate our duty. And, am I too sanguine, when I think that there is, at least, this probability? Do I deceive myself, when I expect many good effects from it? I believe not. You are not one of those unthinking girls, your mind is not of that trifling cast, to be alive only to the rumors of the day, & the flatteries of fools: and, I—I am not accustomed to flatter; & can, at least, be confident of the goodness of my intentions. To some young women, the seriousness of this letter, & the importance attributed to epistolary communications, would be sufficient to terrify them from attempting to write again—especially to him who could address them such a letter. With you, or I have dreadfully deceived myself —the case will be different. You will be pleased to turn your time to some account; & to derive instruction from a source whence the mass of letter-writers expect only the gratification of vain & foolish imaginations, or a curiosity equally idle, unproductive, & contemptible. You will most be gratified; if, hereby, we can, really, advance each other's true happiness. You will, gladly, enter on the pursuit of those inquiries, which lead to the discovery of the truths most important to be rightly known & comprehended, by rational beings. Of all these proper dispositions in you, I am confident. It remains that they be directed to some particular point. For, to be useful, no correspondence should be suffered to ramble; but should be employed on a clear & certain subject. As this is what equally concerns us both, & as the nature of our first inquiries may be particularly important to you, I leave it with you to select you own subject—either from what has fallen from me in this letter; from our last conversations; or from the choice of your own mind: only, do not let us lose time, in general writing; but, abandoning the formalities of persons less acquainted with each other, cause our communications to assume a determinate form, as soon as may be.

I need only add, that I hope soon to hear from you; & that, in the mean time, I cherish the most earnest & constant wishes for you health & happiness.

Tuesday, March 29. 1796.
Cedar St. No. 13. N. York.   E. H. Smith.

LETTERS

Wednesday, 30th

To John Williams.

By this time, you may, perhaps, begin to think that I partake of that surprize which you express, on account of my writing to you; and have determined to be no longer guilty of such a "mispence of time," as you call it. This is not true, however; and, if I have been silent, it has been with reason. My time has been occupied with many affairs, not necessary to be enumerated; as, I am sure, you will not question my veracity.

Your last letter, my friend, is so intirely devoted to that subject which, henceforth, you have forsworn, that it leaves me almost without whereon to build an answer: & were it not for the occasion you have given me for congratulating you on the increase of your domestic enjoyments, I might be near to despairing of any assistance, from it, in this respect. Accept, then, my warmest congratulations; & may those enjoyments be doubled unto you.

What a sad man you must be, that, with youth, health, solitude, wealth, & leisure, you are unable to pass time agreably; & not only so, but usefully. I could go near to reproving you, now, did I think your philosophy were sturdy enough to bear reproof. But, you would not be patient under the discipline of a young Mentor; & I must forbear. But, have I not, aforetime, ventured to assume the preceptorial style? And, when it has once been tolerated, shall I hesitate to attempt it again when I see occasion? You see whither your submission, in one instance, is likely to place you; & how much I am about to presume on your good nature. Without more preface, then, I was going to remark that much inquietude, much dissatisfaction with your present condition, would be spared to you, would you attach yourself to some systematic, pleasurable, occupation: one which would be likely to engage most of your thoughts; & which, might place you in a situation to be useful to others. If a mere course of study should not suit with your love of action; if you should find it irksome to consult, & possess yourself of, the history of nations, or to investigate the true principles of morality & rational policy; you might fall upon some pursuit, where mental activity & bodily exertion go hand in hand; & where the business of the open field comes in aid of the schemes, principles, & deductions of theory. It gives me great pleasure to observe some steps taking, in our parent State, towards agricultural improvements. Nothing is wanting, but a philosophic spirit, to guide the attempt, to make it more successful in Connecticut than in almost any other part of the country: for no people are better observers, none more communicative. If I do not misremember, you have always had some passion for the business of the Agriculturist. It would be an enterprize worthy of you, of the talents, property, & leisure you possess, to acquaint yourself, intimately, with the principles of the science of Cultivation, & overlook their application to practice, in your own neighborhood. This would be a steady occupation for mind & body, thro' the year; & surely, a delightful one. The winter, you would devote to study; the summer, to the realization of that knowlege the winter had afforded. How, thus busied, could ill-nature, peevishness, or discontent, steal in. No study, morals alone excepted, can be so important; none more engaging than Agriculture. For it is intimately united to every other branch of the History of Nature; & Chemistry & Botany are, as it were, it's twin sisters. And, if the study be so interesting, the practice is no less so. It is, indeed, the most improving method of study; and the unceasing variety to the observation of which it, as unceasingly, solicits our attention, is an unfailing source of entertainment. I repeat it—my friend—It would be an undertaking worthy of you, to attempt the introduction of rational agriculture into your native State. The example, the industry, of a few men like you, would do more, in ten years, than, in the present mode of preceeding, ever has been accomplished, since the settlement, or will be effected in fifty, years to come. I wish I may prevail upon you to think, seriously, of this project.

My best remembrances to your family, & our common friends in Wethersfield.

Wednesday, March 30, 1796.
Cedar St. No. 13. New York.   E. H. Smith.

To John Allen.

Your letter gave me great pleasure; and the more, as I began to fear that I had written in vain, & was not to receive a reply. This apprehension you have kindly banished, and, in a manner highly grateful to my feelings, in every other respect, than, as would seem from some expressions which have fallen from you, that you apply to yourself what were intended merely, as general remarks. If you suppose that I designed a particular application, you mistake; if you have forcibly made the application to yourself, your sensibility is excessive, for it is unjust. Your letters are such as you need not to be ashamed for; & when you compare them with mine, tho' I do not suspect your veracity, I confess I regard your judgement as unduly biassed, by overweening modesty, or an indefensible partiality to your friend.

The copiousness & variety of your letter renders it impossible for me to reply to each part of it, particularly: this would be to compose a treatise on education, morality, & legislation. I shall content myself, & I hope satisfy you, by selecting that part which appears to me, most immediately important; & which by the stress you lay upon it, seems to lie nearest your heart.

According to my System of Politics, the virtue & happiness of every individual member of a Community, or Nation, is important to every other individual; or, in other words, is important to the Nation: and it is not sufficient that the Government of a Nation should not place any obstacles in the way of each citizen to happiness, but it is the duty of every Government to do all in it's power to augment that happiness. For the design of all Political Institution should be to *assist*, as well as *protect*; a design never accomplished where encouragement does not go hand in hand, with restraint. The consequences of a failure in any part of this duty, are no less fatal to the community, than to the individual. And this is one of the strongest arguments in favor of a republican government; where the general will is supposed to direct the application of the common property to the benefit of all; while other governments lose sight of general, in the furtherance of partial interests. But if any government make any other distribution of the public property, than such as is promotive of public prosperity; & if any government fail in directing public property to the promotion of public prosperity—from any private consideration, of wealth, power, pleasure, or any thing else; that government is, to all intents, in this respect, hostile to republicanism. It's members are guided by the ruling principle of all tyrannies—Selfishness—a principle which eternally conducts to self-destruction: and such must be the principle which can blind men so far as to make them believe the offspring of the citizens of a State, private property only; & the protection of that offspring, merely private concern. No opinion can be more false; none more unfortunate for a State, if it's Legislators make it their rule of conduct. The more ignorant the subjects of a Despotism are, the safer for that despotism; but the very essence of Republican Governments rests in Equality: & the more perfect that equality, the more assured is the continuance of the reign of order, freedom, virtue, happiness. Now, the only stable basis of equality is knowlege. Without knowlege, we may vainly look for virtue, or for happiness. The progress of government is towards equality: i. e. towards happiness. None have yet reached it, in any point, intirely; tho' some are verging upon it, in a few particulars. The usurpations of preceeding ages, & the prejudices of the present, are powerful obstacles which must long continue, even in our own country, to withstand the establishment of truth. But if, by these means, inequality has become inseparable, in certain respects, from our forms of government, it is the more necessary to call in the aid of equality in other respects, to the maintenance of those forms. And in nothing is this more important, than as the universal diffusion of knowlege is regarded. The ignorant are ever the slaves of passion; easily swayed by accidents; readily improved upon; & at the command of every intriguer. In them, hatred, envy & resentment, are awaked without difficulty; on them, they operate with uncontroulable fury; & by these may they be led to the destruction, in one hour, of the blessings procured by the labor of many ages. A confident air, an improving tone, a pretended love for their persons & zeal for their interests, makes them blind to every other consideration, deaf to all persuasion, insensible to justice or compassion. What security is that for any government, where this is the character of it's citizens? Even in the State of Connecticut, the recollection of the times of Commutation,[94] to say no more, may read us some wholesome lessons on this subject. Every year, & in every state, & nation, in the world, teems with Lectures, enforcing the necessity of the distribution of knowlege. Men, well-informed, hear, attend, read, reflect, investigate. They trust not to this, or that man;

they suspect all mere assertions; they look for argument, not opinion. On such men, how feeble is the influence of faction. The first, may overturn the very best parts of a government, from an ignorance of their value; or, strong by a cause of the inquiries they find enforced upon them, may rise in dreadful & overwhelming vengeance; bear off friends as well as oppressors; & again become, for a longer period, the patient victims of a new tyranny: the last, knowing, at the same time, both the excellencies & defects of the Institutions they are connected with, submit quietly to the one, to preserve the other; studying, with gentle hand, to remove the bad, as fast as circumstances will permit. Thus, the strict & intimate connection of general knowlege, with general felicity, becomes clear; & not less so it's inestimable importance thereto. How, then, are we to think of that Legislator who strives to confine knowlege to those only who can pay the price of it's acquisition? If he is sincere, he is a fool, & deserves our pity; but if, he makes this sacrifice to avarice, or ambition, he is a *Villain* who all should know; with whose real principles all should be made acquainted.

In my view, the whole property comprehended in a state, is the State's property; & ought to be apportioned to the necessities, & capacities of doing good, of each citizen. But Civil Institutions oppose this, & have usurped the authority of confirming every one in his possessions, in certain ways. What, then, shall they restrain the course of knowlege too? Shall they deprive my children of the benefits of science, shut them out from happiness, because I want that, of which they have unjustly deprived me? Can men be blamed, when they rise up, with all that vengeance which ignorance thus preserved necessarily fosters, against such monstrous impositions? No sir—nothing can be more true, than that it is the business, the duty, of every Government to study the advancement of the well-being of every citizen: that both the existence & happiness of every Government depend on the knowlege & virtue of the citizens: & therefore, that to fail in the extension of knowlege to all, is to violate their duty, prevent individual, & destroy general, felicity.

The State of Connecticut possesses uncommon advantages for the ready distribution of every species of information, by means of it's division into so many regularly organized & small Communities. This, which is perhaps as much the effect of chance, as of knowlege, has been the safeguard & preservative of all it's freedom, all it's order, all it's happiness. And in this respect it is, at least, half a century before New York: and nothing but the most criminal blindness, or indolence, can prevent it's long continuing so. I can not, yet, bring myself to think that the man you mention, or the legislature, generally—will abandon these advantages—as they respect Education, but to introduce something better. A Law, or System better than the one in this State, & much more practicable in Connecticut, might easily be formed; & such a one, I have been informed, has

---

[94] A reference to the difficulties experienced by officers who had served in the Revolution in securing either back pay or pensions.

been contemplated by Mr. Davenport:[95] one, nearly resembling that of Massachusetts. You may, perhaps, be a member of the Legislature, this Spring: if you should, I presume you will not let the subject pass, without exertion of some kind. My attention is too much directed, at present, towards other subjects or I would attempt to lay before you some particular principles, on which I think a Bill might be founded. As it is, perhaps, the few Hints, which follow, may be acceptable.

1. An estimate may be made of the expence necessary, in addition to previous appropriations, to support schools, throughout the State; & a Tax be laid, for this purpose.

2. Each Town be divided into Districts for the formation of Schools. This is done, in part, already & might be accurately accomplished, by means of the County Meetings.

3. A County Commission to oversee the conducting of this business, in each County. This would be better than a Town Commission, as it would be more independent.

4. This County Commission, in connection, with the Civil Authority, or Select-men, perhaps, of each Town, to appoint Committees to each District—determine on building Houses &c.

5. The District Committees to engage Teachers to provide for the schools—repair houses &c. & present their Accounts & vouchers to the County Commission: if passed by them—they to signify the same & draw on the Treasury, for the Amount.

6. An annual Statement to be made to the Legislature, of the condition of Schools—throughout the State—by means of the Co. Commission.

7. If academies could be established, in each Co. Town & under the same guardianship, in connection, perhaps, with the Trustees of Yale-College so much the better.

You must forgive me for offering these imperfect Hints &, also, must overlook such repetitions & errors as you find. Subject as I am to continual interruptions, it is impossible for me to write with that attention to accuracy of method, which is ever desirable.

Wednesday, March 30. 1796.
Cedar St. No. 13. New York.   E. H. Smith.

MEMORANDA, 4

I wrote the preceeding letters, conversed with Dunlap, who came to see me, and spent an hour with Dingley, before dinner. I made a number of calls, afterward, & past the evening at the Theater. "The Mountaineers" was performed for the first time; & pretty well.

Thursday, 31st

[Omitted here, two manuscript pages: Medicine. On the Fever of 1795. Letter First. Introductory.]

MEMORANDA, 5

Wrote the preceeding letter: Dunlap past some time here; and Mr. Miller:[1] was at Lovegrove's, to innoculate Sophy: & spent an hour there: walked over some part of the Yellow Fever region: returned, & read in Riouffe, till dinner. Made some further progress, in his Memoirs, after dinner. Dunlap, Alsop, & Muirson Woolsey,[2] here two hours. Called on John Bird, at his lodgings. Spent most of the evening at James Watson's—himself, Wife, & S. M. Hopkins, present. Afterwards, past an hour at Hodgkinson's. I learn that the Music to my Opera is all composed.

This being the conclusion of the Month, it would be proceeding in consonancy with the design expressed in the Introduction, were I, here, to review the proceedings of this month. This, notwithstanding, I shall not attempt. It would, in a measure, break in upon the unity of my plan; & is, beside, unnecessary—as it has been done, after a sort, at the end of my Diary; & improper, in a degree, as most of the procedures of the month are detailed in that Series of my Memoirs. So far, however, as this Work is concerned with the subject, it may not be improper to remark, that, since I have been engaged in it, it's testimony is not, altogether, unfavorable. Some marks of improvement are observable—how small soever they may be thought. And, perhaps, this may be as much of encouragement, as would be a sudden & violent change: since these changes, in me, are mostly as short of continuance, as considerable while they do last. I have some hopes that I shall, yet, deserve to be esteemed as a man of virtue.

APRIL 1796

GENERAL PREFACE TO THE MONTH

The ideas expressed in the preface to this week, may be applied, generally, to the month now begun. The same faults are to be still further corrected; the same duties remain to be performed. Before the close of this month, it is my purpose to complete the letters to my friend Buel. So much of the reading, as is immediately necessary, has been done already; & the remainder must proceed in connexion with the arrangement of facts & reasonings, in relation to each particular head. In the way of composition, I can hardly expect to effect more

---

[95] James (1758-1797; Yale 1777), brother of John. Among other offices he served in the Connecticut Senate, 1790-1797, was elected to U.S. House to fill the vacancy caused by the resignation of James Hillhouse, December 5, 1796; re-elected and died in office.

[1] Probably Doctor Edward Miller (1760-1812), born in Dover, Delaware. After stints in the army and navy as surgeon's mate and surgeon he attended the University of Pennsylvania Medical School and received his M.D. in 1789. He practiced in Maryland and Delaware and went to New York in 1796. Member of the American Philosophical Society, and later Smith's partner in editing of *The Medical Repository*.

[2] George Muirson Woolsey, who started business in 1797.

than these Letters, this month—aside from my regular correspondence. It is unnecessary, therefore, to anticipate, by hinting at any schemes of composition then to be entered upon. In my correspondence, I have effected something, within the present week: this month will, I trust, enable me to place it on a good footing. My French will, questionless, be well attended to: & as I have now finished certain books of amusement, I shall resume my moral inquiries with my friend Dumarsais. His work, I think, I shall have once read thro', ere the first of May. At least, it is my expectation. Neither do I mean to leave Medical reading wholly neglected, in the meantime, should I finish my Letters on the Fever, in season. Now, let us see how the Postscript, of this month, will compare with it's Preface.

Friday, 1st

[Omitted here, nine manuscript pages with the heading: "Medicine. On the Fever of 1795. Letter Second."]

MEMORANDA, 6

I finished the reading of Riouffe's Memoirs last evening, having perused them with great pleasure, in most respects. I design, either to complete the translation, undertaken, in union with Johnson & Dunlap, or to translate & transcribe some passages into my Journal.

To-day: I wrote on my Journal, letter &c. till eleven: then, went with Dunlap, to the African Free School, it being the Monthly Examination: after that was over, walked with D. & Wm. J. on the battery, till one: returned, & composed on my letter, till dinner. After dinner, wrote a little—made two professional calls—drank tea & spent part of the evening, at Woolsey's—two hours at Mrs. Morton's—& then saw "Florizel & Perdita"[3] at the Theater: came home & finished my letter.

MEMORANDA, 7

Saturday, 2nd

Attended to the calls of my profession. Hopkins spent some time here. Transcribed letters to Idea Strong & J. Wms. & part of that to J. Allen. Read some in Kalm's Travels.[4] Past some hours at Lovegrove's; from whence, Wm. & I went to the Club. Met at Woolsey's. Present—himself, Dunlap, Kent, W. Johnson, E. H. Smith—S. M. Hopkins, visitor. Woolsey read to us the history of Sheik Daher, from Volney's Travels. We conversed on the Eastern Government; on Godwin's "Political Justice," which Kent has just read thro', examining several of the subjects therein treated—particularly, Sincerity & Promises; on the President's of the U. S. reply to the Representatives—which all commended; & on State Politics.

Dunlap had the first Rehearsal of "The Archers," this forenoon.

POSTSCRIPT

The Postscript to this Week need not be long. A slight review of what has been done therein, will show how far I have effected, what, in the Preface to it, I purposed to attempt. And, first, of Medicine. Here, I have been moderately industrious. I have read all that was necessary to be read, before beginning to methodize my Notes on the Fever—and, indeed, more—tho' not all that is necessary to be read, before concluding my letters on this subject; & I have written two letters, one of which is lengthy, & required some preparation & much care.

French. Here I have done enough—in proportion to what has been done in other things.

Correspondence. I can not blame myself, in this respect.

Visiting. I have done pretty well, as to this—tho' not quite as much so as I intended.

Theater. Not altogether right, on Monday evening: so, for the rest.

On the whole, tho' there is no great ground for self applause, from the industry displayed this week, yet it so far surpasses what I have oftentimes done before, that I feel tolerably satisfied with myself. Perhaps I am in the way towards Improvement; &, if I am, tho' my progress may be slow, it would be highly reprehensible either to repine or despair.

SECOND WEEK

Sunday, 3rd

PREFACE

The conclusion of the last week offers some encouragement, for the present. It displays the marks of some dilligence; and, as they were the effects of no uncommon & painful exertion, it may reasonably be expected that an equal industry will be observable hereafter, & be equally productive.

Still, the nature of my duties remains unchanged; & the prospect before me, for this week must nearly resemble that of the last. Yet further attention to medical studies—in relation to the Fever of 1795; & the composition of additional letters, concerning it. French, Correspondence, Visitation, &c. are on the same foundation.

I am sensible to a fault, which I have, in common with several of my friends, & which is mostly obtrusive & busy in their company. The gaiety & frolic which society often inspires, give a looseness to conversation, neither moral, nor becoming. It is my duty to put an end to this, in myself; & to attempt to check it, in others. I will put an end to it. This week will I exert myself, to this end. Now, resolution! fail thou not. *A sin which so*

---

[3] David Garrick (1756).

[4] Peter Kalm (1715-1779), a naturalist and professor of economy at the University of Abo in Swedish Finland. *En resa til Norra America* (Stockholm, 1753-1761). Translated as *Travels in North America, etc.* by John Forster (Warrington, 1770; London, 1771).

easily besets us, which starts up before we are aware, which seduces us so much by example & the desire of pleasing, will be difficult to conquer: so much more glorious, necessary, virtuous, the victory.

MEMORANDA, 8

Transcribed a part of my letter to Allen. Joseph Strong came in, from Connecticut. He is well. Fatigued & sleepy, he left us soon, to refresh himself, for tomorrow. Dunlap, Wm. & I walked till one P. M. Some desultory reading, till dinner. We dine at two, on Sunday. After dinner, went to H. Johnson's: sat awhile: & then, Wm., John, & I, went on board the Henrietta—John's Ship—& afterwards walked some time. Drank tea, & spent part of the evening, at H. Johnson's. The remainder, at Hodgkinson's—where I found Dunlap.

Joseph Strong's presence will, probably, draw off much of my time & attention from my studies, this week. Agreably—perhaps, improvingly—but effectually.

MEMORANDA, 9

Monday, 4th

I was called early, & some distance, to visit a patient. Visited several others, & made some calls. Wrote the following Letter. Wm. & I called on Strong: but he was not at his lodgings. We walked, & met Miss S. Morton & Miss Smith; & continued our walk with them. Afterward met Strong, & walked, conversing, with him. Returned, & read in Kalm's Travels, till dinner. After dinner, took a long walk, with Wm. & Dunlap. Called on a patient & found him better. Visited at Riley's. Came home early, & read an hour in Kalm.

Whether it is my fatigue, from walking, or not, I cannot tell—but I am miserably sleepy; & must retreat to bed—much earlier than usual.

[Omitted here, four manuscript pages with the heading: "Medicine: On the Fever of 1795, Letter Third."]

MEMORANDA, 10

Tuesday, 5th

Rose early, tho' still opprest by a sense of weariness, & walked three miles, or more, with Wm. & Dunlap. After breakfast, visited my patients. Began to write on my Fourth Letter. Strong came in: we talked on his affairs—particularly, as to his coming to reside here: & he stayed till dinner. After dinner, I wrote still further on this Letter—which I had not time to finish. Visited a patient. Read the article New York, in Kalm. Strong came to see me again. Charles Adams called here, a few minutes. Went with Strong to his lodgings. He shewed me two of his short Poems, which I think not good. Recd. a letter from Uriah Tracy.

[Omitted here, fourteen pages with the heading: "Medicine: On the Fever of 1795, Letter Fourth."]

MEMORANDA, 11

Wednesday, 6th

A visit from Strong protracted my delay in visiting my patients. It was late in the morning, when I returned. I began to write on the foregoing letter, which I left half written, yesterday. He came again; we had some conversation, & he took his leave, for Phila. & then for the Western Army. The want of money to render him independent of business, for two or three years, prevents his settling in New York. After he left me, I resumed the pen; dined; returned to my task, & completed it, as above. Walked with Dunlap: drank tea, & spent part of the evening at his house; remainder at home, looking over the Monthly Review for Nov. 1795.

MEMORANDA, 12

Thursday, 7th

Rose early, & walked with Johnson & Dunlap. Made a professional visit. Most of the forenoon, with Dunlap, at the rehearsal of his Opera. Read in Kalm's Travels till dinner, & after dinner. Visited two patients; one of which being at Lovegrove's—spent some time there. Part of the evening, engaged, with the Trustees of the African School, on business of the School: remainder, past at Woolsey's,—where I supped, in company with several others.

I have passed a miserable day—partly from ill-health, & partly, from low spirits. The dangerous condition of a patient, which I have just heard to be still worse, has pressed upon my mind, the whole time; & I have had very little reason, on other accounts, to be satisfied with myself.

MEMORANDA, 13

Friday, 8th

Visited my little patient before, & after breakfast. Made another professional call. Dunlap & Hodgkinson were here, some time. Read in Kalm's Travels till dinner; & after dinner, till near five. Visited my little patient. Drank tea, & spent part of the evening, at H. Johnson's. Went with Wm. to the Meeting of "The Federal Republicans"[5]—as they call themselves; but, not finding any thing interesting there, departed, & went, for the first time, this week to The Theater—

---

[5] "Republicans themselves added interesting touches to campaigns at times. Since Federalist foreign policy was popular in 1798, their opponents practised what has been more recently classified as 'card stacking.' They said very little about international affairs and ran candidates under a 'Constitutional Federalist' or 'Federal Republican' slate, as opposed to the 'Federal Aristocratic Ticket.' Intending to confuse voters by concealing their list under another name, they also avoided distasteful issues." Donald H. Stewart, *The Opposition Press of the Federalist Period* (State Univ. of New York Press, Albany, 1969), p. 509. This "Diary" entry for April 8, 1796, shows that the practice was in vogue somewhat earlier.

where I saw "Bon Ton."⁶ Recd. a short letter from Olivr. Wolcott Jr.

The air, to-day, has been exceedingly disagreable, close, & oppressive: I have been troubled with my wandering, gouty pains: my patient lies, I fear, at the point of death: my spirits, affected by so many unpleasant circumstances, have been proportionately low, & I have been unable to do any thing to my own satisfaction.

MEMORANDA, 14

Saturday, 9th

Rose in pretty good season, & went to visit the child I have been attending, for some days past, & found it dead. It died last evening, within an hour after my leaving it. This is the first patient I ever lost with a pneumonic complaint; & the prospect which I had of the probable termination of the disease, for the two days immediately preceeding it's death, was the cause of great inquietude, & mental oppression, to me. On looking back, I know not how I could have done better, unless I had bled the child, the first day. Two reasons deterred me—the difficulty of so nice an operation, on so very young a child —& a probability, (which the subsequent appearances seemed to confirm, for a time,) of effectual relief, from a blister. Since the event was known to me, my cheerfulness has returned—in despite of the unpleasantness of the weather. After breakfast, visited another patient— & found all things going on well. On my return, visited R. Mitchill.⁷ He shewed me a letter he had recd. from Professor Ebeling of Hamburg. We went, together, to the Hospital. Made several calls. At Fellows' Book-Store,⁸ I picked up the last publication of the Traveller Stewart,⁹ in which I have read some to-day. He came in, & I saw him, for the first time. His countenance is fine—parts of it uncommonly so; & his voice is equally agreable. He spake like a man of sense. I recd., this day, a Commission of Physician to the New York Hospital.¹⁰ The appointment is not lucrative, but honorable; & the more so, on account my youth, confined circle of acquaintance, and the disuse or neglect of the customary arts employed to obtain such places. Drank tea with Dunlap. Club night—met with me—Present, Dunlap, Kent, W. Johnson, the Woolseys, E. H. Smith,—Hopkins, visitor. An agreable evening.

POSTSCRIPT

A review of the transactions & products of this week, will not speak as much in my favor, as might have been expected from the Postscript of the last, & the moderate pretensions of the Preface to the present. The reason of this is obvious, on the face of my Journal; and appears to be, the anxiety of mind, & uneasiness of body, arising from the condition of a patient, & the extraordinary condition of the air. For it is evident that I have devoted less attention to one of the greatest encroaches on my time—the Theater—during the past, than any former, week—since the House opened. Neither did my friend Strong's presence, very materially interrupt my studies. And, so far as composition is concerned, a comparative view will shew my medical application to have exceeded, in this week, that of the last. The summary of the Week, tho' not greatly in my favor, will not be greatly in my condemnation.

Medicine. An industry surpassing that of the last week.

French. Wholly neglected: but the time occupied in reading "Kalm's Travels": perhaps as usefully.

Correspondence. No otherwise forwarded than by the transcription of a letter written last week.

Visitation. Not advanced; but much better in respect to the Theater.

To this may be added, that I have, in some degree as I hope & believe, suppressed my tendency towards the commission of the fault, resolved against, in the Preface to this Week.

THIRD WEEK

Sunday, 10th

PREFACE

The Postscript, to the last week, offers no very flattering presage of the present. It rather leads to temperate expectations, & to a disposition to distrust the tenacity of all my resolutions. Nevertheless, as I can not but intend to do something, I can not avoid a preponderance

---

⁶ *Bon Ton*, or *High Life Above Stairs* (1775).

⁷ R. Mitchill, like Donald G. Mitchill and Captain Mitchell (*e* for *i*?), may have been close relatives of Dr. Samuel Mitchill who visited him in New York at the same time. None of them appears in any *New York Directory* for 1796, 1797, 1798.

⁸ John Fellows (1759-1844; Yale 1783), started as proprietor of a book store and as publisher in New York, 1795. In 1796 he printed one of the political tracts of Joel Barlow. A man of deistic principles, he became an intimate of Tom Paine in 1803. Later in life he was an auctioneer.

⁹ Probably *Travels Over the Most Interesting Parts Of the Globe to Discover the Source of Moral Motion* (London, n.d., but likely before 1794). "Walking Stewart" as he was known, managed in thirty-eight years to walk over most of the civilized and a large part of the uncivilized world. His literary production was as prodigious as his walking. He was an extraordinary man, a complete atheist, fantastically honest, blunt and outspoken almost beyond belief, very humble much of the time and outrageously arrogant and egotistical at other times. De Quincey loved him and did his best to put his shortcomings in the best possible light; he decided that Stewart was half crazy, but in a wonderful way. See "London Reminiscences," *Collected Writings of Thomas De Quincey* (Edinburgh, 1890) **3**: pp. 99, 103, 110.

¹⁰ There were usually four doctors on the staff, but only two served during each quarter of the year. Smith's term began in June and ran for three months. Thereafter, until his death, he served for alternate three-months' periods except for occasional slight variations in the schedule. In 1796 (*New York Directory*) the doctors were Smith, Samuel Bard, John Rodgers, and Samuel Mitchill. In 1797 and 1798 (*Directory*) David Hosack replaced Bard.

of intentions towards me, more than another thing, I shall express what are those objects to which I purpose to direct my thoughts, during the week now commenced.

Medicine will claim my first attention—& here I hope to make still further progress in my Letters on the Fever. French shall receive some share of my studious notice. I will continue my Correspondence; & I mean to make some of my projected visits, to long-neglected acquaintance. The Theater, will, probably, occupy more of my time, this week, than the last, because pieces are to be played which I have never seen—one of them is that of my friend Dunlap. But, if I have good health, my other projects will not be the more neglected. I hope to go on in the correction of the fault, in whose correction I am now most immediately interested. Faultless, I can never expect to be; but less frequent in the commission of acknowleged error, I may, undoubtedly, by a proper & necessary exertion, speedily become.

LETTERS
To Uriah Tracy.

Your short letter of the 4th inst. gave me much pleasure, both in respect to the opinions contained in it, & as it was a renewal of our drowsy correspondence. I do most sincerely hope & believe that the event will justify your prediction; notwithstanding some of our politicians regard the majority on Mr. Blount's Resolutions as threatening evil to the Treaty. To me it appears rather as a gasconading flourish of certain persons, who mean to make a merit of what they will call a republican submission to the will of others, for the sake of preserving the tranquillity of the Union. I can not, yet, be brought to believe that the Opposition will have the courage to assume that high responsibility which would inevitably be attached to them, should they refuse to carry the Treaty into effect. The leaders may vote against the measure, to preserve the appearance of consistency; but not till they are *secure* that a majority will be in it's favor. Am I not right in my opinions?

The present Session of our State Legislature, which is now near to a close, is a remarkable—perhaps I may justly say—an unexampled one. The contentions of party appear to have ceased. If the ensuing Election prove as much in favor of the friends of the Government of the Union, as the last, the tranquillity & federalism of this State will be secured forever. But this is doubtful; & the importance of this Election, as it respects the Federal Government, has given an extraordinary impulse to both parties—especially to the Anti-federal. One circumstance operates greatly in their favor. The Federalists have gained the Elections till all their leading men have become satiated with this kind of Promotion, & averse to a labor which brings so little profit. It is, therefore, difficult to find men of talents, on this side, who are willing to serve as representatives; & nothing but the peculiar consequence of the present Election could have induced several, who are now held up as candidates, to consent to be so. On the other hand, few of the antifederal leaders have enjoyed any considerable share of legislative authority; & to be in possession of it is, with them, as much an object as ever. Of consequence, all their prime men are now brought forward; & some have been so, as in the former case, in consideration of the present occasion. The Antifederal Ticket is, therefore, charged with the names of as many, if not more, able men, than the Federal Ticket; and, when you reflect a moment, you will not be surprized to see Aaron Burr's name, as Senator from this city, in the State Senate.[11] For the next Legislature appoint the Senator who is to succeed him in Congress—&, what is more material, choose the Electors of the Prest. & V. Prest. of the U. S. Mr. Watson is his opponent. So much for Politics.

Our friend Dunlap has written an Opera, on the story of William Tell; which is to be played this week, & is now in the Press. He designs sending some Copies of it to some one of the Booksellers, in Phila. for sale. When he does, I shall advertise you of it; & as the Piece really possesses a considerable portion of merit, I trust your recommendations will promote the sale.

Please to inform me, when you write next, whether you ever recd. a letter from me, with a package of Mr. Kent's Dissertation—forwarded by the Keeper of the Phila. Jail.

Our friends are all well—& return affectionate remembrances to you.

Sunday, April 10. 1796.
Cedar St. No. 13. N. York.   E. H. Smith.

MEMORANDA, 15

Wrote the preceeding pages, & transcribed the letter to Mr. Tracy. Finished the perusal of the Monthly Review for Decr. last, which I began last evening. Read in Kalm's Travels, till dinner. Visited at Mr. Lovegrove's, where I spent most of the afternoon, & whither Wm. came. Passed part of the evening at Hodgkinson's, the remainder at home—when I read still further in Kalm's Travels.

MEMORANDA, 16

Monday, 11th

Rose late. Great part of the morning wasted, as to any valuable purpose, in an attempt to complete a little business for Mr. Wolcott. Attended, equally in vain, a meeting of the Trustees of the African School. Finished looking over Kalm's Travels—a valuable work—but rather to be used as a dictionary to refer to—than as performance to be read. Afternoon nearly wasted—but, at length completed Mr. W's business, & now have much

---

[11] Smith seems to be saying that Burr was running for the New York State Senate but according to the record he was a member from New York in the U.S. House from March, 1791, to March, 1797.

care removed from my mind. Posted my books. Drank tea at Dunlap's, & went with him to the Theater: "The Maid of the Mill"[12] playing. Not liking the music very much, or rather finding it uninteresting, we came off. I went to Mrs. Morton's—where I passed two hours very agreably. I hope to make some medical progress to-morrow.

MEMORANDA, 17

Tuesday, 12th

In the forenoon I wrote the preceeding letter; recd. a visit from Dunlap, & one from Dr. Mitchill; attended the Meeting of the Trustees of the African School. After dinner, I finished a Chapter in Dumarsais' "Essai sur les Prejuges" which I began last evening; & translated the passage concerning Madame Roland. Then Wm. & I took a walk out of Town, & called at Lovegrove's on our return. I spent the evening at Webster's.

[Omitted here, five manuscript pages with the heading "Medicine: On the Fever of 1795, Letter Fifth."]

As there is very little probability that we—Johnson, Dunlap, & myself—shall finish the Translation of Riouffe's Memoirs, which we undertook some weeks ago, I have determined to translate a few passages myself, & transcribe them into my Journal. The following account of Mdme. Roland is from Riouffe—page 66.

[Omitted here, four manuscript pages: "An account of Mdme. Roland, from Riouffe-Madame Roland."]

MEMORANDA, 18

Wednesday, 13th

Both Dunlap & Hopkins were at my room, a little while, this morning. The remainder of the time, till dinner, devoted to the composition of the succeeding letter, which I did not complete till after dinner. As I was finishing it, Dunlap came in, with the Second Part of Paine's Age of Reason. Johnson entered soon after; & we amused ourselves, the rest of the afternoon, with this lively & humorous publication; which caused us many hearty laughing-spells. Dunlap left us, to go to the Theater; & we took a short walk, & returned to H. Johnson's, to tea. I spent an hour there, & then went to Mr. Moses Rogers's—where I made a visit—for the first time in many weeks. I came home in season to have a dish of conversation with Johnson, & to read a chapter in Dumarsais, which concludes the first volume of his "Essai sur les Préjugés." On the whole, this day has been pretty well spent; & if I can give as good an account of every day, I shall not be ashamed of my Journal. Tho' I shall have no occasion for boasting. Resolution! resolution! Courage! courage! Perseverance! perseverance!—with your aid, what shall I not be able to accomplish?

[Omitted here, twelve manuscript pages with the heading: "Medicine: on the Fever of 1795, Letter Sixth."]

[12] Isaac Bickerstaffe (1765).

MEMORANDA, 19

Thursday, 14th

I was employed, very steadily, till dinner, & a little while after dinner, in the composition of the following letter. The notes I had made before, on the questions examined therein, were so loose, that I was obliged, in some sort, to examine the subjects anew. After this I finished reading a chapter in Dumarsais, which I began before breakfast. Dunlap came here, & William & I accompanied him in a long ramble. We returned to his house, where we took tea, & spent part of the evening: much of the time devoted to an attempt to solve one of Stuart—the Traveller's—unintelligibles, in his last publication. Since I came home, I have read another chapter in Dumarsais.

We have had a long turn of dry weather; as I suppose, about a fortnight. People began to be apprehensive of a drought. Last evening it began to rain; & has been showery all this day. It ceased to rain long enough for us to finish our ramble; but commenced again just as we reached Dunlap's. Now, it rains violently; & there is much lightning & thunder; but, neither sharp, nor heavy.

I recd. a letter from Mr. Tracy to-day.

I have suffered more, this Spring, from wandering Gouty pains, than for a long time before. This month they seem to be principally confined to my left great toe; & have, for most of the month rendered walking painful to me.

[Omitted here, ten manuscript pages with the heading: "Medicine: On the Fever of 1795, Letter Seventh," and one manuscript page with the heading: "Bailly. Translated from Riouffe's Memoirs, p. 79."]

MEMORANDA, 20

Friday, 15th

Employed in writing on the succeeding letter till dinner, chiefly. The necessity of vigourous recollection, the irregularity of my notes, & the perusal of Dr. Rush's History of the Phila. Fever, prevented my bringing it to a conclusion. After dinner, finished a Chapter in Dumarsais, which I began in the morning; made several calls; & walked out of town, with Dunlap & Johnson. Spent the intire evening at Kent's, whither Wm. came, afterward, & we returned together.

MEMORANDA, 21

Saturday, 16th

Finished the following letter; read the news-papers; walked with Johnson. We visited Hopkins, & then all walked together; before dinner. After dinner made a short visit; came home, & began to read in Dumarsais, when Dunlap came in, & Lovegrove, & afterward, Mr. Roulet—who stayed here the greater part of the afternoon, much to our satisfaction, &, I may add, instruction.

We drank tea at Woolsey's, where the Club met afterwards; it being G. M. Woolsey's night. Present. Dunlap, W. Johnson, Kent, the Woolseys, & Smith—James Watson & S. M. Hopkins—visitors. Some comparison having accidentally been made, before tea, between the former & present Mr. Pitt—G. M. W. read us two different Characters of the father. He occupied our conversation for a while; but it soon branched out into consideration of the political situation of our Country; & terminated in some abstract discussion of moral & political principles. The sitting was agreable, & unusually long.

[Omitted here, thirteen manuscript pages with the heading: "Letter Eighth, on the Fever of 1795."]

POSTSCRIPT

The week, now concluded, began with no very pleasing prospects. The little that had been effected, compared with what had been resolved upon, in the preceeding week; the vexations, and almost total loss of monday; the expectation of loosing, in some sort, two or three evenings, at the Theater; all contributed to damp the feeble hope with which it was commenced. A review, however, of what has been effected therein, proves that, so far from the events having justified the previous apprehensions, few periods, of equal duration, in the course of my journalizing life, can shew more evidence of dilligence. Others, it is true, have been more distinguished for application; but, then, the consequences thereof have not been so apparent.

In Medicine, I have done more than I expected; in French, as much; in Visiting as much. I have visited the Theater but once & then, but for a short time: two of those Pieces not having been represented, which were designed to be. My Correspondence, alone, has made but little progress. This can hardly be a suitable ground for self-condemnation, considering how steadily my pen has been devoted to a more important purpose. But I have reason for self-congratulation, in that I have passed thro' ano- week, with less impropriety of conduct, in respect to the particular intended to receive correction, than heretofore. On the whole, this week is encouraging.

FOURTH WEEK

Sunday, 17th

PREFACE

Tho' with the great experience I have had of my want of perseverance, & of the little dependence there is to be placed on my dilligence the second day, because I have been dilligent the first, it becomes me to be aware of the delusions of self-flattery; yet, I can not but indulge the pleasing expectation of effecting as much, in the week now entered upon, as in either of the preceeding, whose transactions are recorded in this volume. In Medicine, I design to complete the Letters on the Fever; perhaps, transcribe some of them; & possibly, copy & correct, for the Press, that of my friend Buel which occasioned them to be written.

In French, I mean, if possible, to finish the reading of the "Essai sur les Préjugés"; & translate, from Rioufl'e's Memoirs, those passages which relate to the Religion of Ibrascha.

My Correspondence, has no clamorous demands upon me; I shall, therefore, take no resolution on that point. Neither shall I determine any thing, in respect to visiting.

The Theater will, doubtless, engage that attention, this Week, which unexpected circumstances prevented it's receiving, the last. Still, I hope that it will not, otherwise, derange the economy of my time.

I must continue to guard against my Faults, & to correct my Errors.

MEMORANDA, 22

A day of rest. Wrote the P. S. to last week & pf. to this. Wm., John, & I, visited at Lovegrove's. John left us, & we continued our walk to the Battery. We fell in with Mr. Roulet, on our way; carried him with us; & walked, & talked, till dinner. After dinner, I went to H. Johnson's where I stayed two hours. Wm. & I walked out of town. Returned, & were at Dunlap's an hour—he not at home. We went, thence, to Mrs. Morton's—where we spent the evening—much to our satisfaction.

I have been exceedingly pleased with Mr. Roulet, this day. His conversation proves him to be a man of uncommon reading, reflection, good observation, & good sense.

MEMORANDA, 23

Monday, 18th

In the forenoon wrote the succeeding letter—tho', for great part of the time, I felt so disagreably as to make me fear that I should do nothing. After dinner, read a Chapter in Dumarsais; did some errands; took a walk with Wm.; visited at H. Johnson's; &, at evening, went to the Theater. Dunlap's play—"The Archers"—was performed, for the first time—with "Edgar & Emmeline." The House was very full, & the audience tolerably attentive—tho' a riot in one of the Boxes,[13] injured the effect of the first scene. The sentiments of liberty, with which this Opera abounds, secured considerable applause; & not less was bestowed on the comic parts. The music was rather heavy, on the whole, & there was too much of it. Some of the songs were pleasing; & a March very much so. Several of the per-

---

[13] Riots in the theater were not at all uncommon. Between the date of this entry (April 18, 1796) and March 31, 1797, Smith was present at five. The New York theater often attracted a rough crowd. One of the difficulties arose from the fact that theater-goers brought liquor with them and became progressively drunker as the evening grew late. But, drunk or sober, the audiences were far less inhibited than they are today.

formers, & one in particular, were quite imperfect. For myself, I felt too much interested in the fate of the Play, to be a good judge of it's merits—as a representation.

[Omitted here, ten manuscript pages with the heading: "Medicine: On the Fever of 1795, Letter Ninth."]

MEMORANDA, 24

Tuesday, 19th

Wrote the succeeding letter, & additions to the others. Dunlap spent half an hour. Met Co. Tallmadge of Lichfield, & recd. letters, by him, from my father, from Abby, & from Sally Pierce. In the afternoon, made a professional, & several other visits—particularly a long one, for the first time in near a fortnight, & believe, to Dingley. Spent the evening at Lovegrove's. Mrs. L. was in better spirits than I have seen her for this month, & I past a more agreable evening than I have, there, for twice that time. They are busily preparing for Amboy.

[Omitted here, seven manuscript pages with the heading: "Medicine: On the Fever of 1795, Letter Tenth."]

These Letters, which are now concluded, are addrest to my friend William Buel, Physician, resident at Sheffield in Massachusetts, in reply, or, more properly, in return for his Letter, communicating a History of the Fevers prevalent in Sheffield, in 1793, 1794, & 1795.

[Omitted here, two manuscript pages with the heading: "Additions and Notes to Letters."]

MEMORANDA, 25

Wednesday, 20th

Translated the following articles from Riouffe's Memoirs. Dunlap visited me. Was visited by a black man, who wishes to take charge of the African Free School. He appears capable, & it gave me pleasure to find such a man. Read a chapter in Dumarsais. Company prevented further application. Did a little business. Spent part of the evening at Woolsey's, the remainder at Kent's.

MEMORANDA, 26

Thursday, 21st

Dunlap was here, some time, in the morning. Much of the forenoon busied in marking my linnen &c. Read an excellent Pamphlet intituled "Considerations on Lord Grenville's & Mr. Pitt's Bills &c" supposed to have been written by Wm. Godwin, author of Political Justice.[14] Read also—or rather finished—a chapter in Dumarsais. Much of the afternoon devoted to professional business. Walked with Wm.—spent part of the evening at H. Johnson's—remainder at Lynde Catlin's.

MEMORANDA, 27

Friday, 22nd

Received a letter from my father, this morning, in consequence of which, & of some other little business, much of this day has been occupied in running hither & thither. Finished reading Dumarsais. Took a walk, out of Town, with William. Spent the evening at the Theater. Dunlap's "Archers"—in some respects better than the first night, in others worse. Sheridan's "Critic"[15]—very well played.

[Omitted here, nine manuscript pages with the heading: "Translation of that passage of Riouffe's Memoirs which relates the history of the Religion of Ibrascha. Page 154."]

MEMORANDA, 28

Saturday, 23rd

A strange stupidity, an incapacity, or rather inaptitude, for intellectual exertion, has opprest all this day. I sat down to preparing of a long Report I have to make to the Manumission Society—but could not get on with it, & so laid it aside. In the mean time Dunlap had called, with a letter from C. B. Brown, addrest to us both, & brought by Mr. Gahn, who has returned. I went out to do a few errands for myself, & for my father. I foolishly lingered away sometime in a bookseller's shop. When I returned, I found Dunlap, at my room, with the second Edition of "Political Justice."[16] We compared the Chapter on Promises, with that of the former edition, & found it more perspicuous & precise. We walked out of town. After dinner, Wm. & I compared some other parts of the two editions. I recd. a letter from Bringhurst. Drank tea at Woolsey's. Club night—met at Kent's—Present—Dunlap, W. Johnson, Kent, Smith, the Woolseys—& Hopkins, visitor. Kent read us the article "Robert"—in Mdme. Roland's Appeal to Impartial Posterity—& the characters of Ld. Falkland & Mr. Hambden, from Clarendon's History of the Rebellion. We had much, pleasant, somewhat ingenious, but desultory conversation.

POSTSCRIPT

I have done less, this week, than I promised myself, at it's commencement. I have finished my Letters on the Fever; I have gone thro' with Dumarsais, & have translated those passages of Riouffe which I had resolved to translate; I have done as much visiting as I meant to do, & have devoted no more time to the Theater than I expected; but I have neither transcribed any of my letters to my friend Buel, nor his to me. Instead of doing this, which I ought to have done, & which I must do, I have been lolling in my chair, wrapt in visionary meditation; lounging in the shops of book-

---

[14] *Considerations on Lord Grenville's and Mr. Pitt's bills concerning Treasonable and Seditious Practices and unlawful Assemblies. By a Lover of Order* (London, 1795).

[15] Richard Brinsley Sheridan, *The Critic; or, A Tragedy Rehearsed* (1779).

[16] (London, 1796).

sellers; & strolling thro' streets & fields. The several businesses which I have completed this week, were a great undertaking for me, that called forth all my perseverance; & such is my disposition to idleness that I always sink down in a sluggishness, of greater or less duration, in proportion to the extent or magnitude of the exertion, after every exercise of intellectual & bodily activity. It is to be hoped that I shall not be always thus; but that I may, by & by, contrive a disposition of my time so fortunate, that employment after employment shall succeed, one to the other, in a manner to maintain a steady mental excitement, which shall engender no lassitude, & require no interval of repose.

I grow better, in respect to the error noticed some time since.

FIFTH WEEK

Sunday, 24th

PREFACE

The frequent evidence of departure from good resolutions which the P.S. to my weekly notices afford, warns me not to be over-earnest to mark out the line which is to be pursued in the course of another week. Let me rather summon together the present probabilities of my studies being interrupted during the ensuing period of seven days. In the first place, I have four innoculated patients, all of whom are expected to be sick this week. It is true that children, generally, have not the Small-Pox hard, this spring; but some do; & my patients, or some of them, may be of this number. At the best, as all will require to be visited every day, & as they are distant from each other, they will occupy much of my time. Then, I have, still, some business to do, for my father, which will unavoidably, demand some time, in the beginning of the week; & I must write to him, at least, if to no one else of my Connecticut friends. Beside this, I have a long Report to present to the Trustees of the African School; & there are some letters, from Phila. which require answers. And, if to these be added all the diversions from study which the Theater, visiting, interlopers, pleasing visitors, rambles, & the infinitude of the pleasing illusions which Indolence presents to captivate a feeble mind & win it from it's duty, it is but too evident, that much is not to be hoped from this week. And, if I do busy myself at all, with the occupations which demand my attention—i. e. if I go on to copy my own letters, & that of my friend Buel, the employment is so mechanical, that but little improvement is to be expected therefrom. But, I will neither sink in despondency, nor indulge in promise: let us see what this dimly-opening week will produce!

MEMORANDA, 29

William and I diverted ourselves with "Candide," for an hour after breakfast. I made many & vain efforts to draw up this execrable Report, all the morning; I returned to it after dinner; & I have again hammered away at it, this evening. What ails me? I can write nothing. I can arrange nothing. All the facts are before me: It is only necessary to state them: and yet no enamoured swain ever made so many beginnings, & tore to pieces so many prefaces, as I have done for this same Report, tho' nothing depends on the one, & everything might have rested on the other. I was dull, all day. I stupified an hour or more at Kent's—who was as stupid as I was. I spent part of the evening at H. Johnson's—where I was but little better; & the rest of it as just mentioned. I shall make my last effort, at this detestable thing, to-morrow.

MEMORANDA, 30

Monday, 25th

A number of errands, & the confusion of a house white-washing, prevented my doing any thing, all day—except scratch off a Report to the Manumission Society, & amuse myself with a few pages of Jean Jacques. The evening, at a meeting of the Trustees of the School.—Recd. a letter from Mr. Tracy.—

MEMORANDA, 31

Tuesday, 26th

The whole day occupied in doing a number of errands, partly for my father, & partly for myself, & in making a few professional visits. Wrote a few lines, on business, to my father. Spent the evening at Mr. Lovegrove's.

MEMORANDA, 32

Wednesday, 27th

Made a few professional visits. Transcribed my friend Buel's Letter. Dunlap spent an hour here. Drank tea at Kent's. Past the evening at Mrs. Morton's.

MEMORANDA, 33

Thursday, 28th

Visited my patients—Began the transcription of my letters on the Fever. Dined with John Morton, in company with Wm. Johnson, where we met his brother & wife, &c. &c. passed a very agreable afternoon. Evening, spent at a special meeting of the Manumission Society.

MEMORANDA, 34

Friday, 29th

Visited my patients. Continued the transcription of my letters on the Fever. Wrote a short letter to Mr. Tracy, which I did not compose in my Journal as I think not to do so, in future, unless the letter contain something to be particularly remembered; or be of such a sort as will draw on discussion. Wm., Dunlap, & I walked out of Town. Spent the evening at the Theater, & saw "As You Like It"—for the first time.

MEMORANDA, 35

Saturday, 30th

Visited my patients, as usual. Made several other calls. Continued the transcription of my letters on the Fever. Commenced the reading of Cruikshank on the Absorbent System.[17] Dingley made us a visit. Wm. & I drank tea at Kent's. Club night: met at Dunlap's—Present—Dunlap, W. Johnson, Kent, Smith, the Woolseys. The conversation was pitifully rambling & uninstructive this evening. The late city election, the Treaty, &c. &c. occupied most of the time; during which, one yawned, another stretched himself, a third dozed, & all were stupid. I can not but regret that we do not give a higher & efficient character to this little association, which certainly is not wanting in capacity & information, & ought to be devoted to something better than mere amusements.

POSTSCRIPT

This has been the most unproductive, & worst spent, week of any, since the commencement of my Journal. I am heartily ashamed to acknowlege & to feel it to have been so, but justice demands it of me; &, were I not to do it, the few preceeding pages would furnish sufficient evidence against me. For the most part of the time, I have felt indisposed for business & study; & with me, the indolence whose nature requires constant excitement, & who have only examples of equal indolence in those around me, indisposedness to labour is, alas! a sufficient cause for discontinuing it. How can I answer this to myself? I can not. On every principle, selfish, as well as social, it is highly reprehensible. Let me, then, do better in future! Aye, let me! Feeble exclamation! which neither leads to virtuous activity, nor arouses from vicious sloth. Surely I am an unhappy man, and may be truly called the Self-tormentor, since I so steadily violate my own sober perceptions of propriety; & necessarily entail on myself, thereby, self-crimination, & ceaseless inquietude; & shall I not strive to be happy? I know wherein it consists—this happiness —would that my knowlege were less speculative!

GENERAL POSTSCRIPT TO THE MONTH OF APRIL

Tho' the P. S. to the last week appears so disheartening yet a comparison of the several P. S. of the month of April, & thus of what has been accomplished in it, with the General Preface to the Month, carries with it some consolation, & gives some energy to encouragement. It will appear that, in this time, I have effected every thing that circumstances then led me to hope & resolve to effect. Thus, in Medicine, I have completed my letters to my friend Buel, & have even made some progress in their transcription; and have done a little—very little it is true—in the way of medical reading, as disconnected with those Letters: in French, I have, likewise, somewhat exceeded my expectations, as exprest in this same Preface—having not only finished Dumarsais but Riouffe—translated some from the latter—& read a few hundred pages, here & there, in Voltaire & Rousseau: my Correspondence, indeed has made no distinguished progress; nor has there been occasion for it to do so; but it has done pretty well; and, finally, in Visiting & the Correction of certain Faults, my progress has not been contemptible. On the whole, when I compare what I have done, with what I determined to do, I see very little room for self-condemnation. But these is another light in which this matter is to be viewed: and when I consider how little I have done, with how much it was in my power to have done; when I see so much leisure wasted; so many opportunities neglected; so many faults committed; and so little pains taken to repair my errors, & to augment my vigilance & industry; my heart sickens at the recollection, & is unable to draw satisfaction from the flatteries of the previous statement. Why am I so weak, when the means of becoming strong are within my grasp? Why so foolish, when the treasury of wisdom is opened to my view, & I am invited to partake of it freely? Why so much a slave, when I am called upon to be free, by the accents of persuasive felicity, by the threatenings of deep-wounding remorse, by the animating voice of virtue? Am I then fated—doomed—irrevocably, irresistably, destined—

> to sigh on, from day to day,
> And wish, & wish the soul away;
> Till youth & genial years are flown,
> And all the life of life is gone?—[18]

Surely I ought not to be this child. Having the years, the form, the station, of a man, I should not want his vigour, nor his spirit. To sink in desponding inactivity, at my age, ere time has planted a single wrinkle on my brow; &, while the warm blood dances thro' my veins, to become the unresisting prey of peevish discontent—fye! fye!—it will not, must not, can not, shall not, be! No! never! never!

MAY 1796

GENERAL PREFACE TO THE MONTH

In entering on a new month, my determinations, respecting the business to be perfected in the course of it, should be guided or influenced by two considerations, founded on the preceeding month, in addition to other motives, derived from circumstances extrinsic & intrinsic

---

[17] William Cruikshank, *The Anatomy of the Absorbent Vessels of the Human Body* (London, 1786).

[18] From an untitled poem by James Thomson (for which see Palgrave, *Golden Treasury*) beginning: "For ever, Fortune, wilt thou prove, . . ."

to the month itself. Every succeeding month, should display greater industry & virtue than that which preceeded it; and the outline for the following period should be extensive in proportion as experience has proved that of the foregoing to have been easily filled up. With a conviction of the soundness of these positions, let me proceed to mark out the line which I am to pursue in the present Month of May. Accident, necessity, duty, may all, or either of them, force, or demand, a deviation from it; but, without their interposition, it must be adhered to.

In Medicine: the Letters on the Fever must be transcribed, &, if printed in Webster's Collection, their correction must be attended to. If they are not printed, they must be forwarded—I must read Cruikshank's, Baillie's, Hewson's, Richter's, Fowler's, & Saunders's, Books, before the end of the month. And as I am to commence attendance at the Hospital, the first of June, I must gain all necessary information respecting the Routine, or course of business.

In French: it is my design to take up the reading of "Voyages du Jeune Anacharsis,"[19] where I discontinued it; and, if possible, complete the reading of it, this month.

Correspondence: Here it is my intention to be a little more busy than in the last month. I began, however, to think it best to contract the sphere, or at least diminish the quantity, of my correspondence. It is true, that I have not written either much, or often, to my friends of late: in future, it is my plan to write seldom, & to the purpose; or often, & briefly. But, as business of this sort has somewhat accumulated upon me, latterly, much is to be done the present month. In particular, I must write to my friends Joseph & Charles, in Phila., beside one or two short letters to Mr. Tracy: should Theodore Dwight not visit us, this month, I must write to him, & perhaps to Cogswell: to Williams I shall not write, unless something particular requires it: I must write to Buel; to Sally Pierce, to my sister Abby, perhaps to Allen, Mrs. Tracy, & Idea Strong—in Lichfield: to Elnathan Smith who has been long neglected: to my friends at Aurora: perhaps to Mr. Beers:[20] and, on the whole, if I get thro' the month, with no more than ten letters, I shall do well.

I think I need take no order in respect to other, ordinary, affairs; but, should the effecting of the preceeding plans, leave me any leisure, it shall be devoted to the purpose explained in the Introduction to this Volume—relative to my friends; & this in the chronological order of my intimacy with them.

---

[19] Jean Jacques Barthélemy (1716-1795) *Voyage de Jeune Anarchasis en Grèce dans le milieu de quatriène siecle avant l'ere chrétienne* (1784). An antiquarian's comments on Greek literature, manners, customs, etc. One of the most frequently reprinted books of the time; numerous translations.

[20] William Pitt Beers (1766-1810; Yale 1785), a lawyer who settled in Albany, N.Y., and wrote a number of political essays.

Sixth Week

Sunday, 1st

PREFACE

How much of the business of this month shall be allotted to the present week? In Medicine, I must, at least, finish the transcription of the Fourth, Fifth, Sixth, & Seventh Letters on the Fever, & the reading of Cruikshank's book: in French, the fourth volume of Anacharsis, from where I am to begin: & I must write, at least, three letters.

When I consider my habits, I confess, this appears no slight task. But, perhaps, the execution will prove more easy than I now imagine. At any rate, it shall be attempted. I will call to mind the conclusion of the Postscript to the last month, & will not dare to shrink from any duty which the present imposes on me. How feeble, how contemptible are my exertions compared with those of other men, & often for pernicious purposes. To them, activity is pleasure, & they only complain if their industry be restrained. So should it be with me. Are not my motives as pure, as generous, as exalted, as those of other men? And shall mere sloth palsy my powers, & defeat my projects? Shall I not only yield to indolence, which destroys me? but complain if forced to oppose it? and, instead of striving with my enemy, court, crouch to, & cherish it? It is time to rouze! and I will rouze!

MEMORANDA, 36

Most of forenoon busied in writing the three preceeding leaves; adjusting some accounts; &c. John Johnson visited us. Wm. read me a part of Voltaire's "Micromegas."[21] Visited my patients. Stayed some time at Woolsey's; & at Kent's. Johnson came there. Kent, Johnson, & I, took a long, & very pleasant, walk, into the country. Wm. & I spent the evening at Webster's.

MEMORANDA, 37

Monday, 2nd

A day tolerably well spent. Finished transcribing the Fourth Letter on the Fever. Made some progress in Cruikshank. Read 40 pages in Anacharsis. Visited my patients. Dunlap & Hopkins both visited me; & the former, twice. Spent the evening partly at H. Johnson's, & partly at Dunlap's. Much company at Johnson's—the Woolsey's, & their eldest brother, from New Brundswic, at Dunlap's. Recd. two letters from Mr. Tracy.

MEMORANDA, 38

Tuesday, 3rd

Visited my patients. Several errands took up more of my time than I intended. A meeting of the Trustees,

---

[21] *Micromegas et l'Histoire des Mensonges* (Holland, 1750).

also, hindered me awhile. Dingley called on me, & I on Mr. Gahn. Transcribed the fifth Letter on the Fever. Made considerable progress in Cruikshank—having spent the evening at home: part of which was devoted to the business of the Manumission Society. Recd. a short letter from Mr. Tracy; & wrote the following reply.

LETTERS

To Uriah Tracy.

I have received three letters from you, the last of which was this day, since writing to you; for which uncommon bounty I feel no less thankfulness, than for the interesting events of which they treat. The feelings of our citizens have undergone a rapid & pleasing change, within the few last days; public confidence is restored; & a proportionable variation in the price of our native produce is observable. So many men were deeply interested, in a pecuniary view, that the ultimate decision of the House of Representatives, on the Treaty, should be such as it is, that extravagant demonstrations of joy were to be expected; & as extravagant commendations of those, by whose means it has been effected. For myself, having no interests of wealth, vanity, or ambition, involved in the question, my gladness is far less violent; but, as a sincere friend to my fellow-men, & a fond admirer of order & peace, my satisfaction is certainly as pure, deep, & affecting.

Your account of Mr. Ames's Speech[22] has interested me extremely. Indeed, the highest commendations are lavished upon it, even by his political enemies. The peculiar circumstances in which he stood, could not fail of rendering it impressive. Mr. Wadsworth[23] of Connecticut, who is here now, or has just left us, is no less warm in his eulogium on a late Speech of yours; & has raised my curiosity to an unusual height. The Speech referred to, was a Phillipic against Gallatin.[24] It will, doubtless, be published; & I must beg you to transmit me a Copy. Citizen Bache[25] is engaged, I see, in republishing the Debates on the Treaty, in the Pamphlet form. We shall have his publication: so that, if it will contain, & accurately, the Speech above-mentioned, I will not trouble you for a Copy.

The important question being now decided, Congress will, probably, proceed to business; & we may hope to see you along here, by the first of next month, I suppose. If the Session bid fair to prove much longer, would it not be possible for you to take an airing, of a few days, as far as New York? After so tedious a confinement, it must be doubly pleasant. You can not doubt of our receiving you with suitable tokens of congratulation & wellcome.

Our friend Dunlap's Opera has been twice represented here, with tolerable success. Copies of it were to be sent forward to Phila. yesterday; & to be left, for sale, at Matthew Carey's;[26] where you will probably find them.

All friends are well, & desire particularly to be presented to you.

Tuesday, May 3. 1796.
Cedar St. No. 13. N. York.   E. H. Smith.

MEMORANDA, 39

Wednesday, 4th

Transcribed the Sixth Letter on the Fever. Made considerable progress in Cruikshank. Transcribed my letter to Mr. Tracy, & forwarded it; & recd. a short letter from him. Part of the forenoon & afternoon devoted to business of the Manumission Society. Dunlap visited me. We drank tea, & spent the evening, with considerable company, at Mrs. Morton's. I found there Mrs. Craig Millar, the daughter of the celebrated Cullen[27]—& had the good fortune to be seated near, during great part of the evening. We had much conversation—rambling & interrupted, as usual—but pleasing. She appears to be a woman of good sense & good information.

MEMORANDA, 40

Thursday, 5th

Transcribed the Seventh Letter on the Fever. Made some progress in Cruikshank. Visited my patients. Was visited by John Johnson—by Mr. Mason, a quondam College room-mate of mine,[28] & Class-mate of Wil-

---

[22] Fisher Ames, Harvard, 1744, a lawyer and Federalist. Representative to U.S. House from Massachusetts, 1789-1797. Ames declined to accept the presidency of Harvard because of ill health. His speech mentioned by Smith, sometimes called the greatest speech ever made in Congress, was delivered on April 28, 1796. The House of Representatives, after the Senate's ratification of the Jay Treaty, asked Washington for the papers dealing with the negotiations. Washington refused to release them, claiming that the Treaty was now the law of the land. Ames supported the hotly debated motion: "Resolved, That it is expedient to pass the laws necessary to carry into effect the treaty lately concluded between the United States and the King of Great Britain." The motion carried.

[23] Jeremiah Wadsworth (1743-1804), member of the Continental Congress, Federalist, representative from Connecticut in U.S. House, 1789-1795, also held state offices thereafter.

[24] Albert Gallatin, supporting Madison, was in opposition to Washington in the treaty dispute.

[25] Benjamin Franklin Bache, grandson of Benjamin Franklin, whom Hopkins attacked in the *Echo;* he was a Philadelphia printer and publisher of the *Aurora,* a Republican paper.

[26] Mathew Carey, bookseller and printer, 22 North Front Street, Philadelphia.

[27] Probably the daughter of William Cullen (1710-1790), famous as a lecturer, professor of chemistry, professor of medicine, practicing physician and writer. His last major publication was *Nosologicae Medicae* (1785) in which he classified diseases into four major catgories. This classification was highly regarded by physicians for many years.

[28] Smith's roommate during his junior year at Yale, a New Hampshire lawyer and U.S. Senator, cited in the *Introduction.* There are three other Masons probably not related: Miss Mason of New York; Mr. Mason, a minister; and Mr. Mason (also Masson) an English botanist.

liam's—& by J. O. Moseley[29] of Connecticut, who spent an hour or two with us, much to our satisfaction. Much of the day, & all the evening, devoted to the business of the Manumission Society.

This day I ceased boarding at Mr. Mulligan's—& entered on the execution of my long-projected plan: viz. of dining at home, & relinquishing the use of meat. To-day, I substituted Milk & bread—& have felt well, & in good spirits.

[Omitted here, four manuscript pages with the heading: "Medicine, The Case of Elias Cowles (Singular disease of the eyes.)"]

MEMORANDA, 41

Finished Cruikshank's "Anatomy of the Absorbents." Read thro' the Fourth Volume of Anacharsis. Drew up, from my minutes, the preceeding Case. Posted my books. Visited a Patient. Wrote, & did errands for the Manumission Society. Dunlap called here; I went with him to his Store, & saw a strange sort of a thing, called a Comedy,—in MS.—supposed to be written here. It diverted me; but I have forgotten the title—Evening, at the Theater. Saw Reynolds's new Comedy—"Speculation"—& "The Prisoner."[30] The first has some merit. There is more character in it, than falls to the lot of his Pieces in general. Very little of it, however, among the women of the Comedy; & there want of interest. The after Piece, is a trifle.

This is the second day of my dietetical reform; & I have not felt so much of the *animal* man, these six months.

MEMORANDA, 42

Saturday, 7th

Commenced the reading of Baillie's "Morbid Anatomy."[31] Wrote & transcribed the following Letter. Did some errands. Dunlap & I took a walk out of Town. I drank tea at his house. Club night—Johnson's evening. Present—Dunlap, Kent, W. Johnson, Smith, G. M. Woolsey—Hopkins, visitor. Johnson read us Hume's "Stoic."[32] This, first, excited comments on various modes, & on the best mode, of Reading. Each read, in turn—we criticised—& with some improvement, & much diversion. Conversation followed, on the excellence, evidence, & spirit, of different Religions—& on the proper conclusions to be drawn from a decided preference to either. I read the Religion of Ibrascha.[33]

LETTERS

To Charles B. Brown.

The necessity of attending to concerns, of immediate & considerable importance, has, in part, prevented my replying to your letter, before this time. It is useless to particularize, or apologize: the first would only waste time; & the last, could not repair the mischiefs of the error, if error there has been.

Your letter, my dear Charles, was the occasion of much satisfaction, as well as disappointment & sorrow, to your friends. Sentiments so opposite, yet so intimately combined & interwoven, gave it an interest in our hearts, which sensibility could not but cherish, & which reason hesitated whether she should wellcome or disclaim. Why is it so? Wherefore are you so vigourous, so firm, in thought; & so weak, so vacillating in action? Charles! Charles! if thou hast not strength to contend with the tempter, if thou art not mighty enough to overcome temptation, & trample it under thy foot, doth not wisdom whisper thee to decline the combat, & to fly the field? To encounter danger, to brave death, causelessly, & with the certainty of suffering, the mildest appellation for such conduct is folly; & the person who is guilty of it can only be excused on the plea of disordered intellect. By heaven! my friend! I mourn & am afflicted for you—for myself—(for to my own weakness does this reproof reach) & I "could play the woman with my eyes,"[34] if haply it might warn you to retire, or animate you to conquer.

We must know our errors, or how can we correct them? We must be informed of their whole extent, of their utmost virulence, or how can we apply the remedy? He deserves not the name of Physician, who, thro' fear of giving pain, temporizes with his Patient, when the ulcer threatens his life, & requires instant extirpation. To wound, is to save; to delay, is to destroy. No palliative can reach this case. Nay, tho' it seem to menace but little danger; tho' returning sanity appear to glow around it's edges; trust not! withhold not! the poison sinks inward; a moment, & it preys upon the vitals. You "have been the child of passion, & inconsistency; the slave of desires that can not be honorably gratified; The Slave of hopes no less criminal, than fantastic."[35]

What, my friend, is the meaning of all this? And what am I to learn from it? Or, rather, what are *we* —Dunlap & Smith—to learn from it? If you meant that we should understand you, why were you not explicit? If you had no such intention, where was the necessity of

---

[29] Jonathan Ogden Mosely (1762-1838; Yale 1780). A Connecticut lawyer, representative in the General Assembly 1794-1804, then elected to the U.S. House 1805-1821.

[30] Frederick Reynolds, *Speculation* (1795). *The Prisoner*, an afterpiece probably by Reverend John Rose. *The Prisoner* was probably new when it played at the New Theater, Philadelphia, in the season of December 3, 1794-July 4, 1795. See Thomas C. Polloch, *The Philadelphia Theater in the Eighteenth Century* (Philadelphia, 1933), p. 255.

[31] Matthew Baille, *Morbid Anatomy of some of the most Important Parts of the Human Body* (Albany, 1795).

[32] David Hume (1711-1776). "The Stoic" was a brief essay which Hume wrote when he was thirty in which he rather uncharacteristically concerns himself with the thought of the necessity for cultivating art and industry. *Essays Moral and Political* (ed. 1777), Part I, Essay XVI.

[33] From Riouffe's *Memoirs, etc.* cited earlier, upon a translation of which he was intermittently engaged.

[34] *Macbeth*, IV, iii.

[35] Not identified.

introducing such a passage? Charles! you know we love you. Your heart has told you so, a thousand times; & you *dare not* question it! You know, too, that *real friends*, alone, have the courage to point out the faults of others, boldly to themselves. You know the difficulty, the delicacy, the danger, of the undertaking. You are well aware of the value of sincerity; you see that we stand, as it were, isolated from the rest of mankind; & you must be convinced, that if we are not true to ourselves, & true to each other, we can not hope for aid, correction, & instruction,—candidly & affectionately administered—from any one beside: for the world troubles not itself with these things, or minds them only to the injury of the individual.

This is a solemn strain, you will say; a melancholly & grave preface. It is—& indeed, my Charles, the occasion requires it. Why do you so much delight in Mystery? Is it the disease of Will? or of Habit? Do you, of choice, give to the simplest circumstances the air of fiction? or have you been so long accustomed to deal in visionary scenes, to intertwine the real with the immaginary, & to enwrap yourself in the mantle of ambiguous seeming, that your pen, involuntarily borrows the phraseology of fancy, & by the spell of magic words, still diffuses round you the mist of obscuring uncertainty? The man of Truth, Charles! the pupil of Reason, has no mysteries. He knows that former errors, do not constitute him guilty now—& he has nothing to conceal. He seeks only to know his duty, & perform it, & he has no occasion for disguise. He places, with his own hand, the window in his breast; & he bids the world look in, & comment. Lurks there any deformity within—he blesses the eye that descries it, commends the tongue that proclaims, & kisses the hand that drags it to the light. He acknowleges his error; he owns his weakness; he purifies his heart; & he invigorates his hands.

What do your most intimate friends, my Charles, know of you? What do they wish to know, but that they may be of use to you? Far be from them, that teazing curiosity which seeks only it's own gratification. If there be any thing you think it your duty to withhold from them—withhold it—they will not blame you. If there be any thing you have not the courage to reveal—conceal it still. They will not commend the cowardice, but they will compassionate; will pardon, it. But, when you know that these are their feelings, why will you continue to remind them, that there are secrets? that you have science, which they must not have? Why will you allude to misfortunes of which they are ignorant, & from which, therefore, they can not relieve you? Why will you array each new transaction in the garb of obscurity? Are you, yourself, conscious how much this is a prevailing fault, both in your speech & writing? In this very letter, to which I am replying, in a sort—we only learn, by implication, that Joseph[36] has been imprisoned. The fact is no where plainly noted; & had it not been for his letter, I had still remained somewhat doubtful whether you meant he had been in prison, or not. It would have been much more agreable to us both—D. & S—to have been informed simply of the fact; & the circumstances of it. Again, when you mention the authors you have read—instead of a plain account of them—we behold you, with visionary step printing the sands of Arabia, hovering over the hills of Swisserland on wings of imagination, & exploring the wilds of America with the eye of fiction. I particularize, because you have sometimes complained of our want of precision, when we have attempted to point out your errors. I confess that the style of these remarks of yours is handsome; &, in a Poem, I should have been charmed with it; but in a letter, a mear catalogue, with a slight notice of the character of each book, would have given me much better information. And, in such cases it is information we look for—not amusement—& the more simply & precisely it is conveyed, the better. Beside, we are apt to distrust information so conveyed: & we ought to distrust it; for it often imposes on, & misleads, us. The pen of poesy, Charles, is not often that of Philosophy & Truth. But I will have done with this language—only commending the word *Simplicity*, to be inserted, in Capitals, in your vocabulary.

Joseph, you say, contemns our Philosophy. Ask him if the votaries of Jesus—the sincere votaries—always exhibit in their lives, that virtue they profess? Ask him, if the followers of Paul, the eulogists of Peter, have no moments of weakness? Let him answer you, whether Heaven allures, whether Hell terrifies, whether the Holy-Ghost sanctifies, any human being to unwavering, undismayed, ever-active, & self-approving, virtue? If he can not decide affirmatively; if he find not an unequivocal accordance in favor of some one man, on the part of all the world; where is his mighty boast? Let him hesitate!

There was no mistake in the person, mentioned as having been elected a Physician to the Hospital. I was the person elected. There is no immediate emolument from that place. The appointment is a respectable one & holds up the person, obtaining it, to public consideration, employment, & munificence. Whether this will be the consequence, in respect to your friend, time must determine.

By this time, you have received several Copies of Dunlap's Opera.[37] I wish for your opinion of it's merits; & to know what are the opinions of our friends at Phila. & of others, whose sentiments you can collect.

You will remember me respectfully & affectionately to the several members of your family—to Joseph & his family—to *friend* Paxon's—& all other friends.

Saturday, May 7. 1796.
Cedar St. No. 13. N. York.   E. H. Smith.

---

[36] "Joseph" is Bringhurst. Smith even here misunderstood Brown; Bringhurst was not in prison, for which see later.

[37] *The Archers.*

POSTSCRIPT

This Week somewhat revives my confidence in myself. In looking back on the transactions of these last seven days, I shall be found to have done all, & more than all, I had previously resolved to do, with a single exception. In Medicine, I *have* transcribed those Letters which were mentioned; I *have* read thro' Cruikshank's Book; & I have, further, begun a new one, & arranged my notes on a medical Case. In French, I *have* finished the fourth volume of Anacharsis; & if I have not written three letters, it has only been, because I wanted the necessary information to write to the friend I designed to—& have been obliged to write much for the Manumission Society.

So far, all is triumph: but, then—how little is this all! How much others have done, in the same time! to how much better purpose! how much more might I have done! & how much better! Ought I, then, to repine? Is it not something to have gained even a trifling advantage over my irreconcilable & deadly enemy? Surely, to have maintained my ground, after so many defeats; to have gained some foothold in the adversary's territory, after so many repulses; surely this is matter for some exultation. "Gently, Dapple, gently!"

Seventh Week

Sunday, 8th

PREFACE

In the course of the present Week, it is my design to finish the transcription of my Letters on the Fever; to Copy, for Mr. Post, the Case of Elias Cowles; to finish the reading of Baillie's Book; to read, at least, two hundred pages in Anacharsis; to write letters to Joseph, Theodore, Elnathan, & Wm. Buel. Further than this, I dare not resolve.

I find no inconvenience, as yet, of any kind, from my newly-adopted plan of living. On the contrary, I am sure that I feel better; have purer activity; freer spirits; & unimpaired digestion. While this is the case, I shall continue the disuse of meats—except when at the tables of my friends. My ordinary breakfast consists of three moderate dishes of Coffee, & about six ounces of bread, eaten with butter: my dinner, is a pint of Milk, & about ten ounces of bread: I sometimes drink tea in the afternoon & then take two cups of tea, & a little bread & butter: if I do not drink tea abroad, I eat half a dozen biscuit, & a small piece of cheese, with a glass of water. This is food enough. With this simple fare I am satisfied & well. And, for the year past, except when journeying, I have slept on a Mattrass. There are three advantages in this mode of living—First, it's cheapness: I expect to make a clear saving of 1/16 of my whole expences, in the single article of dinner. Secondly, it's superior healthfulness; and Third, in the saving of time, & the greater aptitude which it allows for study & action.

MEMORANDA, 43

Wrote the P. S. & Pf. which preceed. Visited a new patient, twice, & a former one, once. Then Wm. & I walked out a number of miles, into the country: the pleasantest walk I have had this year. We returned just in time for dinner—which we took at H. Johnson's—where we spent the afternoon. I visited my patient & we past the evening at Kent's.

MEMORANDA, 44

Monday, 9th

Owing to numerous petty interruptions & a little business abroad, I have done no more than transcribe the Eighth Letter on the Fever; with a few lines to the good people at Aurora; & read a few pages in Baillie's "Morbid Anatomy." Wm. & I spent the evening at Riley's.

MEMORANDA, 45

Tuesday, 10th

Transcribed the Case of Elias Cowles, gave it to Mr. Post, & so have done with that. Copied a part of the Ninth Letter on the Fever. Made considerable progress in "Morbid Anatomy." Attended a meeting of the Physicians & Surgeons of the Hospital. Was twice at Mitchill's Room, in the College; & in the afternoon, with Mr. Dunlap & Post,[38] attended there, to a curious inquiry into the Natural History of the Shark. Evening spent, partly at H. Johnson's, partly at Dunlap's.

MEMORANDA, 46

Wednesday, 11th

Transcribed the ninth, & part of the Tenth Letter on the Fever. Made some further progress in "Morbid Anatomy." Did a little business. Visits from Dunlap, Hopkins, & Kent. Wm. & I spent part of the evening at Dunlap's; part of it at Woolsey's—at which last place we met Col. & Mrs. Tallmadge. Recd. a letter from my father. Mr. Gahn called on me.

MEMORANDA, 47

Thursday, 12th

Finished a hurried reading of Baillie's "Morbid Anatomy." Completed the transcription of my letters

---

[38] Dr. Wright Post, surgeon, a professor at Columbia who had an anatomical museum, a friend of Hamilton. He attended him after his duel with Aaron Burr. Mrs. Martha J. Lamb, *History of the City of New York, etc.* (New York and Chicago, 1877) **2**: p. 494. The physician actually at the duel was David Hosack; see Parmet & Hecht, *Aaron Burr*, p. 212.

on the Fever; & wrote a little advertizement, to precede them. Made some little progress in French. Visited my patients. Called on Dunlap. Wm. & I walked out of Town. Spent the evening at Kent's.

LETTERS

Friday, 13th

To Joseph Bringhurst, Junr.

I have been busily employed, & could not reply to your letter earlier: and now, I fear that you will derive but little gratification from what I write, for my mind is far from possessing that luminous perspicacity which is requisite to the perfect comprehension & illucidation of a subject.

Your congratulations on my supposed good fortune are sincere & consolatory; they are not without their effect in stimulating me to become deserving of your commendation; but they are founded on misconceptions of the nature of my appointment, & of the probable consequences. It is necessary that you should be informed that no immediate emolument results from the office of Hospital Physician; & that it's efficacy in promoting, indirectly, the accession of business & fortune is, at least, doubtful. In other respects, I know not whether to rejoice, or be sorry. If there be an opportunity afforded of gaining reputation, so likewise, is there a wider field for disgrace. The mistakes of a private practitioner may pass unheeded or unknown; but he who exercises his profession in a public Charity, is exposed to the observation & comment of other, if not of rival, practitioners; to the sneers & cavils of the malicious; the misrepresentations of the ignorant; the injustice of the base. Superior information, too, is not always accompanied with forbearance, & benevolence. My talents & my knowlege are, perhaps, best fitted for the shade & fortune by contriving to "throw this cruel sun-shine round a fool,"[39] may wreak her vengeance on the physician & the man, at once. But, be this as it may, I shall endeavour to do my duty—the rest remains to be determined.

You do well to indulge the playful sallies of the imagination; they shall divert, but not deter us. If Philosophy can elevate us above apprehension; if she can make us proof against "the stings & arrows of outrageous fortune";[40] if she have power to strengthen us beyond the force of malicious persecution, & unblushing misrepresentation; surely we have little to fear from the sportive raillery of good-humored, but incredulous, rebuke. An awful & sweet serenity reigns in the countenance of Truth, which can impose silence, when she pleases, on the most wanton & loquacious Wit: And Innocence, you know, my friend, hath nothing to fear, not even from Guile; time is, to her, a continued Millenium, in which she may gaze on the serpent without danger, & play with his forked tongue without harm. Wag, then, the head at us, & point the finger—it shall not move our anger, but our compassion.

I rejoice with you, my Joseph, at your prospect of escape from tribulation. You have left us ignorant of the circumstances of your imprisonment: but, no matter: it is at an end; & I hope soon to see you once again established in regular business: Nay, I hope to see you, with competence and content, & Laura. You still adhere to the language of fiction, I see; & really, I think it is, in this instance, somewhat better than the *plain language*. Could I express myself in terms worthy of this better Laura, of a quaker Petrarch, I would say something— some little thing—concerning the pleasure which it gives me, to know that I am remembered of her. Canst thou not divine what I would say? Tell it to her then, for I impose the office on thy lips; on thy eloquent & friendly eyes.

I have made many vain inquiries after the Book you wished for. I shall continue to seek for it; &, if successfully, shall send it, as soon as found.

All friends send love: love to all with you.

Friday, May 13. 1796.
Cedar St. No. 13. New York.   E. H. Smith.

To Theodore Dwight.

I should not have permitted so long a period of silence—at least on my part—to appear in our correspondence, had I not *first* expected to receive a letter, & *then* a visit, from you. It is probable that the same reason, in part, has prevented your writing. You, in all likelihood, thought it unnecessary to write to him, with whom you intended soon to be, with whom you could converse face to face. The time of expectation is now gone by; you have relinquished the design of visiting New York; it is time that you assume the pen; and I write, that I may provoke you to epistolary retaliation.

I know not how it should happen, that we, who were wont to exceed the Post in the quantity & punctuality of our communications, should have fallen into this tardy, interrupted, & starved, kind of intercourse. It is the more surprizing, as I love to write, & you compose with equal facility & pleasure. I hope I have lost no claims upon your friendly bounty; & that you will not cease to do, what you effect with so little labour to yourself, & so much profitable pleasure to others.

Our world affords but little matter, the detail of which will please you; & of all your friends, I am the least capable of administering to your entertainment, by the relation of things connected with myself. Woolsey & Johnson are involved in business: Dunlap, alone, can furnish topics for expatiating upon with interest: and he is so soon to become a temporary resident among you, that I forbear to mention, what you will learn, more amply & advantageously, from himself. Have you seen his Opera? If you have, what think you of it?

My love to yours & to all friends.

---

[39] Not identified.
[40] "The slings and arrows of outrageous fortune..." *Hamlet*, III, i.

Friday, May 13. 1796.
Cedar St. No. 13. N. York.   E. H. Smith.

To Elnathan Smith Junr.

It is a long while since I heard from you, my friend; but you are not faulty, on this account; it is I who am to blame. You were bountiful, indeed, to me; and I have made you no suitable return. It were idle to go into an enumeration of the causes which have chained my tongue, & stopped the course of my epistolary discourses: I please myself with the belief, that were they fairly exposed to you, you would compassionate me, at least as much as you would blame me; & that, tho' you would questionless discover me to have been silent sometimes thro' indolence, you would also see that it was as often thro' necessity. But I can not go into such an exposition; it would take up too much time; & I trust my credit is still so good with you, that my word will be sufficient.

Well then—this preliminary matter being gone thro' with—how are you? how have you been since I saw you? & what have you been doing? Has Health continued to shed her roses upon you? or has Disease, or Sorrow, or the winter of the souls turned them pale? Burns the torch of Hymen as bright as that of Cupid? Or is it true, that enjoyment consists wholly in pursuit & dies with fruition? These are knotty questions, on which it becomes a married man to hesitate & ponder, ere he answer. But, perhaps, coming, as you did, to domestic sway, to domiciliary rule, with regulated wishes, & chastised desires, you have found all that you expected, & enjoy all you asked. Be it so, my friend! From my soul, I wish, & trust it is so.

What man—especially what young man—does not plan out visionary scenes of joy, schemes of future bliss? Who does not flatter himself, that, at some time he will correct such & such deficiencies, accomplish such & such purposes, new arrange the domestic economy of life, educate his family better than others have done before him, & extend his benevolent cares to the society in which he resides? You have, formerly, indulged in such designs, as well as others; the opportunity for execution is now presented; & I hope you will not shrink from the task. Tell me, how stands your resolution in this matter? Nay, tell me of all your concerns. I long to hear that you are happier than you thought to be; that every day adds to your present pleasure, & future expectations; & that, if you find in her to whom you are united, not every possible perfection, you see none necessary to rational enjoyment which either she does not possess, or is not disposed to acquire. May I not venture to assure her, that I am her, as well as your, friend?

Friday, May 13. 1796.
Cedar St. No. 13. N. York.   E. H. Smith.

To William Buel.

You would have received, before this, the information so long promised you, concerning the Fever of 1795, but that I have suffered myself to be persuaded to let the papers which contain it, form a part of Mr. Webster's Collection. I am not altogether displeased with this, as your Communication will be inserted in it, & I shall be gratified in seeing our names united in an undertaking which may, perhaps, prove useful to mankind. I suppose that his people will commence the impression of our papers next week. I shall make it a point to send you the sheets, as they are dismissed from the Press: so that you will have my letters long before the whole compilation is completed; & before any part of it is communicated to the world. I took the liberty, in transcribing your letter for Mr. Webster, to make a few verbal corrections, which were necessary; & with which I presume you will not be displeased. What I have done has been only to avoid the too frequent recurrence of the same words, & to alter some expressions which were not strictly grammatical. The sense is unaffected.[41]

I long much to hear from you; & hope you will not remain silent much longer. Are you not to be married about this time? If the ceremony is past, accept my congratulations.

Friday, May 13. 1796.
Cedar St. No. 13. N. York.   E. H. Smith.

MEMORANDA, 48

Wrote the preceeding letters. Read near an hundred pages in Anacharsis. Visited a sole patient, repeatedly. Did several errands. Past the fore part of the evening at Dunlap's—remainder at Mrs. Morton's. Recd. a long letter from C. B. Brown.

In spite of all my efforts, I find my heart sink within me, for these two days. A little matter discourages me. I have been languid & melancholly this evening. Me thought my company were so likewise—but perhaps it was my disease, that made them appear not well.

MEMORANDA, 49

Saturday, 14th

Visited my patient. Transcribed the letters which I wrote yesterday. Completed the reading of two hundred pages in Anacharsis. Devoted some part of the forenoon to putting together several paragraphs, as articles of a Report to be made to the Physicians & Surgeons of the Hospital—of a Memorial to the Governors. Spent part of the afternoon at Mr. Post's, with him & Dr. Mitchill, on the business of this Report. Drank tea at H. Johnson's. It being Club night, & W. W. Woolsey's turn—we met there. Present—Dunlap, W. Johnson, Kent, Smith, & the Woolseys. Before the others came in—

---

[41] Smith appears to be saying here that he had not yet sent Buel his ten letters but intends to send them in galley proof. See "Ten Letters on the Fever which Prevailed in New York in 1795," in *A Collection of Papers on the Subject of Bilious Fevers Prevalent in the United States for a Few Years Past,* ed. Noah Webster (New York, 1796).

Johnson, Dunlap, Woolsey & Smith, finished their revisal of the Constitution of the Manumission Society. The conversation this evening, has been very desultory; & little calculated to preserve spirits if present, or inspire them when they were not. Both the Woolseys were unwell.

POSTSCRIPT

In the last week, I have done all that my Pf. demanded of me to perform; and beyond my expectation. For several days, I felt considerable depression of spirits, & great inaptitude to exertion. These, & other obstacles to accomplishing what I had previously resolved on, have been surmounted, & the conclusion has been in my favor.

I can not disposses my mind of a constant, and growing, sense of the meanness of my professional skill, & the scantiness of my medical information. It hangs, like a mill-stone, about my neck; and weighs me down. What gives peculiar force to such sensations is, that I am destitute of the means of acquiring extensive information, either from books, or instructors; am called upon to devote much time & attention to extraneous matters; & have demands upon me for the immediate application of the knowlege which I want. To confess my incapacity —when, perhaps, I know as much as others, would not only be a deep wound to my feelings—but deprive me of the little practice I have, prevent the further acquisition of employment—& render useless years of study. Thus I am in a dilemma.

Eighth Week

Sunday, 15th

PREFACE

It is difficult for me to take any precise resolutions as to the business of this week. A single sick person is under my care. He must be attended to. As he seems mending, I hope to be discharged in the course of the week. We are to have a meeting of the Manumission Society; some Committee meetings will preceed it; &, in this way, much time will be occupied. I am on the Committee of the Hospital Physicians & Surgeons, & am to make out a catalogue of Books, to be purchased. This will be the labour of another day. Then it is a plan of Dunlap & myself to go from here on Saturday to Amboy, & return on Monday. Thus two other days are provided for. These are all interruptions; but the application of what time I have will be simple enough. I must continue my medical reading; the perusal of Anacharsis; & write some letters; & the more leisure I gain from the other affairs, the more I must devote to my proper business.

The sentiments contained in the conclusion of the P. S. to the last week, should not be indulged. I am capable of learning; my advantages have been, & still are, greater than those of many others, who have figured in the profession; if they are not as great as some have, I must exert myself the more, that I may remedy such a misfortune; it is no shame not to appear wiser than we really are; & with dilligent & persevering attention, nothing can prevent my gaining knowlege. It is in vain to think of receding from my present ground; I must go forward; & to go forward steadily, tho' it should be slowly, is all that is necessary.

MEMORANDA, 50

Attended to my professional duty. Wrote the immediately preceeding P. S. & P.f. Johnson, Dunlap, & myself, walked out of Town. Wrote a short letter to my father, to send by Col. Tallmadge, who, on inquiry, I found gone & so my letter remains behind. Alsop came in. He returned yesterday. Left all friends well. Is well. Spent the evening, with Wm. at Dunlap's.

MEMORANDA, 51

Monday, 16th

Attended to my little business. Most of the day busied in compiling a Catalogue of Books for the purposed Hospital Library. Spent the evening at Mr. Rogers's.

MEMORANDA, 52

Tuesday, 17th

Business occupied a little time. Read somewhat in Fowler's Reports on Rheumatism. Dined with Mr. Gahn. Dunlap recd. a letter from C. B. Brown directed to us both. Alsop called here. Much of the day, & all the evening, till very late, devoted to the business of the Manumission Society. Recd. a letter from Mr. Tracy.

MEMORANDA, 53

Wednesday, 18th

A heavy day. Most of it spent in writing for the Manumission Society. Read a little in Fowler's Reports. Alsop visited us, forenoon & afternoon. Visited the sick. Visited at Dunlap's. The evening at Dingley's, in the expectation of meeting there the Trustees of the Humane Society. A few came; but not enough to do business.

MEMORANDA, 54

Thursday, 19th

Finished Fowler's Reports. Began Richter's "Medical Observations," which I have dipped into before. Attended to my scanty business. The whole evening, till late, at the Manumission Society.

MEMORANDA, 55

Friday, 20th

The day was the first pleasant day, after many rainy & cold. I walked, & indulged a little in the luxury of fine weather. Visited my patient. Spent two hours with Dunlap—who read me what he has written of a Comedy in Two Acts, which he lately began, imitated—or rather altered & amended from "Jerome Pointu."[42] I was pleased with some passages in Deckar's "Honest Whore." Recd. a short letter from Wm. Buel. Finished Richter's Work.[43] In the evening, at the Theater.

MEMORANDA, 56

Saturday, 21st

A day nearly wasted; of which I can say nothing good. The want of a few dollars gave me a great deal of trouble. Half my time is lost in the gathering together the trifling sums I earn; & in the vexation attendant on delay, uncertainty, importunity, & regret. Thus I loose, in thinking how to live, that time which should be occupied in living that I might think.

Recd. a few lines from El. Smith jr. Wrote a few to Buel. Club night, & my turn—Present—Alsop, Dunlap, Johnson (W.), Smith, & the Woolseys. An ill-spent night. We talked—but foolishly.

POSTSCRIPT

In looking back on the past week, I have, once more, occasion to lament that weakness which, in defiance of numerous & powerful motives to exertion, has enfeebled my hands, opprest my spirits, & subdued me to self-reproachful inactivity. My conduct would almost realize the fable of Araspes,[44] & lead to a conviction of the existence of two opposite & contending souls. For, as if alternately actuated by them, I am now elevated to hope & activity, now dejected in despondency & sloth. My mind, agitated by a sense of duty, a conviction of power, a feeling of error, is subject to perpetual inquietude, & longs for the repose of stable virtue. Why am I not virtuous? Is it that I am deficient in just conceptions of what is to be virtuous? or in inclination to become so? No! not this. It is that I want permanency of conviction—of inclination—a vigorous will. My resolutions are "like the spider's most attenuated web, broken with every breeze."[45] But am I not better than I was? I would fain hope so. Notwithstanding my many misgivings, my numerous relapses, I have then progressed? It should seem so—I will endeavor to draw some encouragement from this.

---

[42] *Jerome Pointu,* by A. B. Robineau, "Beaunoir."

[43] August Gottleib Richter, M.D., *Medical and Surgical Observations,* translated from the German by Thomas Spens (Edinburgh, 1794).

[44] This is a passing reference to a work by Christoph Wieland (1733-1813). Probably the version read by Smith, considering his almost complete ignorance of German, was *Dialogues From the German of M. Wieland: I, Araspes and Panthea; or the Effects of Love. II, Socrates and Timoclea; or, apparent Proud and Real Beauty. To which is prefixed an Essay on Sentiment by the Editor* (London, 1775).

[45] "The spider's most attenuated thread./ Is cord, is cable, to man's tender tie/ On earthly bliss; it breaks at every breeze." Edward Young, *Night Thoughts:* "Night" i, 1. 178.

NINTH WEEK

Sunday, 22nd

PREFACE

Certainly, it is my hope that I shall accomplish more in this, than in the last week. My *hope*: for I hardly dare declare it my intention. I purpose to read the two medical works, which remain to be read, of those mentioned in my general preface to the month. I mean to pursue the perusal of Anacharsis. I design to write several letters. If circumstances permit, I intend to visit Amboy. I have one project further, which is, to make myself acquainted with the routine of business at the Hospital.

The idleness & inaction of former periods, while they should inspire me with diffidence in the tenacity of my will, ought to prove double incitements to future exertion. If I have been weak heretofore, it is high time to become strong: If I have been dilatory, to be now active: If forgetful of my duty, now attentive. In short, watchful that, in all things, I surpass myself; that I may, by some means, retrieve my own good-opinion, & make up, in some sort, for the opportunities I have neglected, & the time I have lost.

MEMORANDA, 57

Dunlap & I walked out of Town. Fell in Mr. & Mrs. Roulet & their children, & sat with them a while. Came back to his house, & dined there. Walked on the Battery. Wrote the two last preceeding pages. Attended to my patient as usual. Made some calls. Drank tea at Mrs. Miller's. Spent the evening partly at Kent's, partly at our neighbor Boyd's.

MEMORANDA, 58

Monday, 23rd

Attended to my business. Commenced & made some progress in Saunders on the Liver. Dined at Kent's. Alsop here. Drank tea at H. Johnson's. Evening wasted, for the last time, I am resolved, at what should have been a meeting of the Humane Society.

MEMORANDA, 59

Tuesday, 24th

Finished Saunders on the Liver, & began Hewson on the Blood. Added a few lines to my letter to El. Smith Jr. & forwarded it. Attended to my professional business. Alsop here. Wm. Johnson left me, to make a visit at Middletown. Called on Dunlap, & spent part of the evening at his house. The remainder at Mr. Hodgkinson's. He was not at home, but I saw Mrs. H. for the first time since her *accouchement*, & had an hour's agreable chat with her.

MEMORANDA, 60

Wednesday, 25th

Attended to my business. Finished Hewson on the Blood, & made some further progress in Anacharsis. Called on Dr. Mitchill. Dunlap spent an hour with me. Past the evening at Woolsey's.

MEMORANDA, 61

Thursday, 26th

Visited the sick. At a meeting of the Physicians & Surgeons of the Hospital. Finished the Fifth Volume of Anacharsis: Spent the evening at Kent's. Dunlap here in the forenoon. Recd. a letter from my father.

LETTERS

Friday, 27th

To C. B. Brown.

My silence & delay in respect to your letter of the 10th inst. my friend, have arisen from necessary & unavoidable avocations; not trifling, but sufficiently important to justify my conduct in this behalf. To that letter I now sit down to frame an answer, but not with those vivid conceptions of the subject before me, which were awakened by the first perusal. The weather, too, which is heavy & stupifying, brings with it a sluggishness of thought, unfriendly to perspicuity & precision. Still, I hope to make myself intelligible to you, & to correct some errors into which you have fallen, respecting my last letter.

You have misapprehended both the purport & the purpose of my letter; the consequence has been that, in your reply, you have wandered wide from the object towards which your attention was meant to be directed; & in so doing, you have perplexed, without satisfying, yourself, & have contraverted, without replying to, the censures of your friends. Let me request you to read over, once again, & with attentiveness, my last communication. Do you find in it a single passage in which your veracity is questioned? I have a copy of that letter before me, & certainly I can not find such a passage. But should you discover a phrase susceptible of such an interpretation, I wish you to be assured that no such questioning was intended. With this explanation, if you do not think it time misused, once more examine my remarks. To what do they tend? They point simply to the correction of a single error; an error, perhaps *once*, of Will—probably *now*, of Habit. By them, you are not charged with intentional misrepresentation of the truth, but with conveying it in such a manner, as to make it difficult of comprehension to your friends, or encumbered with such circumstances, or deficient in such particularities, as to render it unintelligible to them. Here is no charge of falsifying the truth. Here are no doubts expressed of your veracity. Here is no more than a plain intimation of an erroneous manner of communicating information, which those who love you regard as a misfortune,—as an error—persisted in by you, thro' ignorance, & capable of being remedied by you, when fairly exposed to your contemplation.

Among the number of our conversations, at Amboy, some, you will recollect, turned on the subject of your style of composition. It was charged with certain defects, by us, & we endeavoured to make you sensible to them. We were unsuccessful. In the epistolary communications which succeeded, we could not but discern the same faults. The sense was often obscured by imperfect metaphors, tumultuously heaped upon each other; common facts were introduced with a species of poetical periphrasis, which sometimes puzzled us to determine what was & what was not, accurate; & allusions were made to transactions, in relation to which we could neither act, nor speak, neither aid, nor counsel, you—as all, on our part, was conjecture & obscurity. It became necessary for us to renew our remonstrances, on this point; & your letter, in answer to which my last was written, as it offered several examples of the defects we complain of, was made the subject, or basis, of our friendly reprehensions. The manner in which you communicated to us the names of the authors & the titles of their works, which you had been reading, was faulty, as it wanted both perspicuity & precision. The passage in regard to Bringhurst, as I have before remarked, was so obscure as to leave me in doubt. You talked of the terror he had conceived of imprisonment, the value he set upon unimpeached integrity, &c. from whence I concluded that he had been in Jail, & had been declared insolvent &c.—but the plain facts would have been more acceptable: Knowing his character, it would not be difficult to make the proper inferences. Now, in respect to both these instances of a faulty mode of communication, on your part, you will not find that we have charged you with intentional "mystery & delusion." An instance occurs in your letter, before me, of a similar fault—when, speaking of Mr. Laffert, you say—"He resides in the rural neighborhood of this City." I know where he lives—but what information would a stranger derive from that passage? You see, I do not question your veracity: I take it for granted that Mr. Lt. does "reside in the rural neighborhood" of Phila.—but what am I the wiser? Unless it be, that I learn that he does not reside in the City?

But I have dwelt too long, already, on these—which are more trifling circumstances.

What, indeed, is the purpose of our correspondence—if it be not "to disclose our feelings & actions, chiefly with a view to benefit, & be benefitted, in turn, by the communication?" Any disclosure which has not this for it's object, is trivial, impertinent to the design of our intercourse, & undeserving of attention. Any narration or sentiment that is obscure & unintelligible, is defective, since it can neither, as to it's proper contents & intent, be made the subject of comment or controversy, or concurrence. In this situation, what is he to do, to whom it is addrest, but to call for an explanation?—Should such an explanation be demanded, is it fair to infer, that he by whom it was requested, doubted the veracity of the original communicator?

"You have been the slave of passion & inconsistency: & of desires &c." Pardon me, my friend, I do not mean to sport with you—but I did not doubt the truth of the facts, nor mean to question it. But why were they communicated to us? You doubtless had some object in making the communication. Was it not—because you supposed we might "usefully animadvert upon them"? Was it not, that you might, "in turn, be benefitted," by our counsel, or instruction? But how benefitted? On what circumstances are we to animadvert? Here is nothing precise: nothing thoroughly known by us.

How have you been "the Slave of passion & inconsistency?" And what are these "desires which can not be honorably gratified? that are no less criminal, than fantastic?" Do you not see that this partial communication is nugatory? That we can address to you neither counsel, nor instruction—in short, can not be of the least possible service to you, in these respects, without precise information? If you wished our assistance, it was your duty to point out explicitly, wherein we could assist you: to have discovered to us the nature of your danger, & the causes of your weakness. If you either did not need our aid, or was resolved neither to request, nor accept it, why make such a communication? To what purpose could it subserve? Surely none—since we could not "usefully animadvert" upon it; & you were determined not "to be benefitted by the disclosure." Here, then, is the point between us: here is the matter of which I complain—that you will allude to circumstances which you do not choose to explain; & which, therefore, are foreign to the purpose of our correspondence, since, without explanation, we can render you no assistance in regard to them. Not that I question your veracity when you assure me that you have been unfortunate—but that I am pained to be the useless depository of complaints I can not understand, of sorrows that I can not assuage.

I do not mean to call upon you for explanations. I do not want to know to what you allude. I can not find fault with your conduct in concealing the circumstances of your early fortunes—since I neither know what you conceal, nor the motives you have for concealment. I am actuated but by one wish in relation to you—to be of service to you, & to render you useful to mankind. To effect this wish, I am willing to receive what you choose to communicate—if, by my animadversions, or opinions, on such communications, I can advance your wellfare. But I do not love to be needlessly perplexed & grieved: neither should you, needlessly, add to my perplexity & sorrow. In respect to your former communications, relative to the story of yourself, tho' I meant not, in my last letter, to allude to them, I acknowlege, in all sincerity & simplicity of heart, I know not what to believe. You have acknowledged that you *once* thought yourself at liberty to vary circumstances, in the narration—& in those fragments which have been related to me, I find so many & such perfect contradictions, that I am forced to suspend my belief, on all, as I can reconcile but few of them to each other. This has, formerly, been the cause of much pain to me, on your account—it is so no longer. I suppose that, hereafter, should it seem proper in you to disclose the facts, the disclosure will be accurate. In the mean time, I have no curiosity; & my only wish is, that you, by avoiding all allusions to these events of your life, would neither excite doubt, nor alarm sensibility.

This letter is long; & I am weary with writing; you will excuse me, therefore, for passing over, for the present, at least, some parts of your letter. But I can not forbear to add, on the subject which is now before us, that it does appear to me that, at some former periods of your life, you affected to be mysterious—& made ambiguity your delight; That the example of J. J. Rousseau had too many charms in your eyes, not to captivate you, & incite you to imitate him; & that you were pleased to have others believe those misfortunes to be real, which you knew how so eloquently to describe. The transition is natural—& to a mind of sensibility almost unavoidable: you began to fancy that these fictions were real; that you had indeed supposed, enjoyed, known, & seen, all that you had so long pretended to have experienced; every subsequent event became tinctured with this conviction & accompanied with this diseased apprehension; the habit was formed; & you wandered in a world of your own creation. Now & then a ray of truth broke in upon you, but with an influence too feeble to dissipate the phantoms, which error had conjured up around you. *Godwin came, & all was light.* But the Sun himself does not always diffuse around us his benignant beams: clouds & mists sometimes intervene, & shut him from our view. Despair, itself, is dear to the wretch who has drank deep of the delicious poison of Love. Cold, cruel, tho' she be—dead to honour, & "glorying in her shame," the form he loves is dear to him; he fosters, he cherishes her idea in his heart; it is his ruin—but he can not resolve to loose it. With what gradual, what scarce perceptible, advance, is intried to reason, to activity, to virtue! How often does he relapse into his woe, call upon the phantom of his passion, & banquet on the pleasures of despair! Nay, when full of mighty purposes of reformation, how often does his self-love cheat him of his resolution, his actions burst out in all the extravagance, his voice swell with all the emphasis, of passion—while he smiles upon the cheat!

See you any points of resemblance, in this picture, Charles? & a friend of ours that shall be nameless?

Friday, May 27. 1796.
Cedar St. No. 13. New York.   E. H. Smith.

MEMORANDA, 62

Wrote the preceeding letter. Commenced the Sixth volume of Anacharsis. Attended to my business.

Walked, in the afternoon, out of Town, with Dunlap—it having cleared off. Spent the evening at Catlin's.

MEMORANDA, 63

Saturday, 28th

Read a little in Anacharsis. Most of the day devoted to my own, & my father's business. At the Hospital to obtain information of the routine of prescription &c. Wrote a few lines to my father. Called on Dunlap & drank tea at his house. Club night—With G. M. Woolsey—Present—Dunlap, Kent, Smith, & the Woolseys: an agreable evening.

POSTSCRIPT

In the week now terminated, I have done very little, & yet, as much as I expected; & I fear that my greatest exertions will fall far short of what deserves to be called much. In Medicine I have read Saunders on the Liver & Hewson on the Blood—which completes the quantity of Medical reading allotted to this month; & I have, also, read several Papers on the 4th vol. of the Memoirs of the Medical Society of London. I have not made as great progress in Anacharsis, or in the composition of Letters, as I intended—but this has arisen, in part, from the interruptions of business. It is not yet to be despaired of—this Perseverance.

Tenth Week

Sunday, 29th

PREFACE

There is not great probability, I fear, of my accomplishing much, in the way of study, the present week—particularly after the first of June. At that time I commence attendance at the Hospital—& shall have enough to occupy my time & thoughts, till custom has rendered the routine of business familiar to me. It will, doubtless, be a scene of trouble, difficulty, & embarrassment, for some time. Eventually, I hope to discharge the duties of the appointment, with ease to myself, & satisfaction to my employers. What leisure I shall have, this week, will be apportioned, as usual, to my several studies & occupations.

MEMORANDA, 64

Visited my patients. Called, ineffectually, on Alsop. Walked. Dined with H. Johnson. After dinner, H. J. & Mr. Lovegrove—who is here on a visit—& I, took a long walk, out of town. Made a short visit at Woolsey's. Evening spent at Mrs. Morton's: Miss Morton was not at home—so I sat & conversed with her mother.

I am rejoiced to hear that Mrs. Lovegrove is pleased with Amboy.

MEMORANDA, 65

Monday, 30th

My own, & my father's business took up some time. Nearly finished the perusal of the fourth vol. of the Memoirs of the London Medical Society. Walked with Dunlap in the afternoon. Spent the evening at the Theater & saw "Much Ado about Nothing", & "My Grandmother"[46]—both for the first time.

MEMORANDA, 66

Tuesday, 31st

Rose late, having gone late to bed. Dunlap called here before I had finished my breakfast. I went with him to Hodgkinson's. There are great uneasinesses subsisting between the managers, & Dunlap wished me to be present at a conversation he meant to hold with Hodgkinson. I was. Visited my patients. Read two Papers in the Memoirs of the London Medical Society. Lovegrove called here. We dined at Dunlap's. Dunlap & I spent much of the afternoon in walking, in the adjacent fields, for it had now become clear & pleasant. Part of the evening passed at Woolsey's—part at Dunlap's.

Tomorrow, I suppose, tho', as yet, I have had no proper intimation to that effect, I commence my attendance at the Hospital. I can not feel at my ease, in respect to this business. I feel that I am deficient in many qualifications necessary to enable me to go thro' with it, pleasurably, & advantageously. It is, however too late to recede. The trial, however painful, must be made; & custom may render it less irksome.

GENERAL POSTSCRIPT TO THE MONTH OF MAY

Experience, or rather the event, has proved that the outline, traced in the beginning of this Month, was too extensive. Not comprehensive beyond my ability to have perfected, had my endeavors been steadily made; but too comprehensive when viewed in relation to the inconstancy of my resolutions, & the habitual indolence of my mind & body. In Medicine alone do I appear to have effected all that I had allotted to the month of May to accomplish. In French I fall far short: in my Correspondence, I have much wherewith to accuse myself. But, amid all the sensations of self-disapprobation, which so vigorously press upon me on this review, I am somewhat gratified & find some alleviation of my regrets, in observing that the deficiency on my part has fallen on those studies & those exercises, least immediately essential to my situation; & that medicine, imperfectly cultivated as it has been by me, has felt no part of that neglect which has been displayed towards my general determinations. The absolute necessity which I am under, if I continue in my present profession, as well on my own, as on the account of others, of increasing my stock of Medical ideas, & the satisfaction which I have derived from this source, already, & within the

---
[46] Prince Hoare (1793).

present month, encourage a hope that I shall have less to accuse myself of, in future, in this respect, than formerly.

But, on so slight foundations, do all my resolutions rest; so easily are they erected & overthrown; so perpetually do they vary, or contravene each other; that I neither have the satisfaction of discovering what I am able to effect, nor the pleasure of looking back on what I have done & feeling "It is well done." My views of the propriety & impropriety of actions vary exceedingly, at different times; & condemnation & commendation are bestowed now on this & now on that. So, also, as it is with the past, is it with the future: arrayed, at one time, in beauteous colours, at another, wrapped in the melancholly pall of distrust, trepidation, & terror. How immense are my desires! how feeble my powers! how contemptible my attainments! how much more feeble, & much more contemptible my industry! When I look back, all is dissatisfaction & shame; when I look forward, all apprehension & mortification. Such is my present temper of mind—oppressed as I am with a deep sense of my numerous imperfections, & my still more numerous omissions or transgressions. In myself—I am weak; in myself also am I, sometimes strong. It is when I compare myself with others—only—that I find that I have any value; & it is by comparison with others that I discover the extent of my ignorance, defects, & errors. If the Month now past, be better, or worse, than others —it affords, in the first case, no certain ground for encouragement—nor perhaps in the last, for dejection: & on this supposition hangs my feeble hope.

JUNE 1796

GENERAL PREFACE TO THE MONTH

Dejected & disheartened as I feel at this time, it is only in conformity to the plan of this Journal that I affix any prefatory matter to this month. The consciousness of my own ignorance which constantly oppresses me— especially of my professional ignorance, renders the practice of Physic but very rarely a source of any satisfaction to me. This consciousness is now redoubled, by the situation in which I have foolishly placed myself— by the necessity of prescribing in public, at the Hospital in this City. A material deficiency on my part is, my imperfect acquaintance with the Latin language—in which all the prescriptions are dictated. I know not how I shall go thro' this ordeal. I am as yet unresolved— whether to attempt to prescribe in Latin—or disuse it altogether. It is a ridiculous custom; but it is a custom —& to depart from it might be more disadvantageous— than to continue it—even with all my defects. But I must go on—somehow. How that somehow will be— to-morrow must, in part decide.

I have no new plans of study—& therefore, with my present sensations, shall not extend this preface any further.

MEMORANDA, 67

Wednesday, 1st

My professional concerns occupied the morning. From 12 to 2 at the Hospital—to make the necessary arrangements. I prescribed for one of the patients. Wrote a letter to my father, on business. Mr. Lovegrove here—& Dr. Mitchill—most of the afternoon. Made an ineffectual effort to read. The few lines of prefatory matter to the month, sufficiently indicate what have been my mental inquietudes this day. Drank tea at H. Johnson's—in company with Alsop, his sisters, &c.—but spent most of the evening in attempting to relieve a poor sick woman.

MEMORANDA, 68

Thursday, 2nd

From breakfast, till late dinner, pretty steadily employed in my private & Hospital practice. Afternoon— a few errands—& walked out of town with Dunlap. Evening at Kent's.

I have passed a very wretched day. One of my own patients is extremely low—& the cause of much solicitude to me; & my administrations at the Hospital have been truly painful. I prescribed there—for the first time —but with so many embarrassments as nearly to overwhelm me; & I fear very little either to my own credit, or to the advantage of the patients.

MEMORANDA, 69

Friday, 3rd

Engaged almost all day in professional concerns. The evening in company with Mr. Tracy, Mr. Trumbull,[47] Mr. & Mrs. Goodrich &c. who have just arrived, from Phila. A little while at Mrs. Morton's. Somewhat better to-day: my patient beyond expectation better: but my spirits still low.

MEMORANDA, 70

Saturday, 4th

Called on Mr. Tracy &c. this morning. Went with them to see the Elephant.[48] From thence, the gentlemen went to visit Govr. Jay; & I returned with Mrs. Goodrich to her lodgings. Thence I called on Miss Morton & waited on her to see Mrs. Goodrich. The rest of the day, till after three P. M. engaged professionally. I now found the Connecticut friends gone. Dunlap & I

---

[47] Mr. Jonathan Trumbull (1740-1809; Harvard 1759). For some time a representative in the Connecticut General Assembly, representative, U.S. House 1789-1795, Speaker of the House 1791, U.S. Senate 1795, but served only one year before leaving to become Lieutenant Governor of Connecticut and, in 1798, Governor, a position he held until his death.

[48] At fairly regular intervals, traveling animal shows (often with one animal), came to New York. Smith seems never to have missed one. The intense interest and hunger of this man for information of the kind that is often today commonplace for children is sometimes startling.

walked out of town. Drank tea at his house. Evening—Club—at Kent's. Present—Dunlap, Kent, Smith & the Woolseys. Found a letter from Theodore Dwight when I came home.

POSTSCRIPT

The week now closed offers a melancholly spectacle of mental imbecillity to the eye of retrospection. The unhappiness, consequentially impressed on my spirit, is aggravated by a sense of continued weakness; & by the mournful presages respecting the future which are thence derived. Alas! alas!—why am I so weak?

It is certain, however, that I went thro' with my business at the Hospital far more easily, & judiciously, to-day, than on Thursday; & that I felt tolerably well the remainder of the day. Courage! courage! It will, yet, go well.

Eleventh Week

Sunday, 5th

PREFACE

The present week opens gloomily: may it close serenely! The end I have in view is, like all others, happiness: the great object of my labors, knowlege: for we can be happy, only as we know. All my perplexity arises, from the extent of my desires; for I would have all knowlege: from endeavoring to act, with very imperfect information, where no one should act but with much greater: and from a fear that even the little good I am able to do should be abridged, by a discovery, on the part of others, of how little that good really is. Could I trace out a correct & comprehensive method of study; were my situation favorable to the putting of it in operation; could I clearly discern what knowlege was most important to be obtained, at the neglect of others where some science must be neglected; & had I firmness of mind equal to vigorous & unrelenting adherence to this method; doubtless much more information would thus be obtained by me, than I may, now, reasonably hope to acquire; & my happiness would gain a good degree of stability. In this case, the second cause of my perplexity would be nearly destroyed, as well as the first; and could I discover what proportion subsisted between my own attainments & those of others, the third would perish with the others. How much error is perpetuated in the world by these slavish apprehensions: not merely in Medicine, but in all divisions & departments of human science! This is a topic too fruitful in remark to be dwelt upon at this time.

I feel my cares somewhat lighter, and, tho' I make no arrangement for the business of this week, I trust it will furnish more encouragement to perseverance, than the last.

LETTERS

To Theodore Dwight.

I recd. your letter, my dear friend, last evening; & I seize on the first moment of leisure to reply to it. The contents of it, are matter of some surprize to me; but I have no doubts of being able, by the help of a little recollection on your part, to clear up every thing, to your satisfaction, & of preventing all future misapprehensions. The narrative may be a little tedious—because it must be circumstantial—but I can not bear the idea of being suspected deficient in affection for him, towards whom my heart has always gone forth in the full vigor of attachment; & in respect to whom—if it be—

in heaven a crime to love too well—[49]

I am certainly chargeable with guilt.

About two years since, I commenced a diary, or journal, of every day's transactions—studies—& feelings. It was a plan long contemplated by me, but which till then, my habitual indolence prevented me from putting in execution. I have continued this Journal ever since—with more or less exactness, copiousness, & advantage, as I was enabled to bestow attention on it, or prevented therefrom. The inconveniences which I have sometimes sustained from not having preserved copies of letters to my friends; & the history which my letters contain of the state of my mind, & progress of my studies; determined me, near a year ago, to compose, from that time, all my letters—except on mere matters of business—in my Journal. For more convenient reference, I placed the direction, or address, of my letters at the head—instead of the end—which is most common. In copying some of them, afterwards, I followed the same method; which, on reflection, appearing to me the most proper, I have since adhered to. This is the real history of one circumstance which appears to have been the cause of some disquiet to you; & I am convinced that, when you think of it, it will not appear very important whether "Theodore Dwight" be written at the beginning, or end, of a letter. You may, if you please, consider it as whimsical in me, but I like it best, & use it steadily: & surely you can not suspect it as implying any coldness, when you know that in this way I address my parents & sisters.

I do not consider the titles, in use in the United States, as of much consequence—yet I acknowlege that I would rather that they were intirely disused. Titles are nugatory except inasmuch as they are descriptive of the character, or occupation, a man sustains in life. In conformity with this sentiment, I have, very generally, neglected the use of them—except when significant—for sometime past, let me write to who I will. In writing to you—I have generally added "Counsellor at Law"—because, I tho't it respectable, & significant—which the

[49] Pope, "Elegy to the Memory of an Unfortunate Lady," l. 6.

common addition of Esquire is not. When a letter is sent by a common friend, or acquaintance, there is no use in any addition—because no information is contained in it. To a stranger there may be some information—& it may serve as a direction to a Post-Master. Further than this, there is no use in any addition; & where it is not for these purposes, I commonly omit it. This you may think whimsical, also—but it pleases me —& ought not to offend any reasonable being. Many of my correspondents write to me in this manner—& it is now so much a habit with me, that I do it without thought, & as a matter of course.

It is with the ordinary forms of beginning a letter, as with the circumstances which I have just noticed,—they can not very important—different persons act differently, in this respect & after all, the general spirit of the letter, & the general conduct of the writer, are those things on which we ought to decide. It is not from the words "Dear sir," "my dear sir," "my friend," "my dear friend," "my very dear friend"—&c. &c. that we are to judge—for these are inserted, thro' affectation of regard, as often as from a sincere sentiment of their value & import; still less consequential is it, whether they be inserted in the body of a letter, or lead the way to the friendly out-pourings of the heart.

Now let us examine the letters of which you complain.

The circumstances relative to the first are simply these: I returned from Phila. in January, & found my desk covered with letters. It is my practice to reply as speedily as possible to those communications which I receive from my friends; that I may write while my heart is warm with the impressions which what they have written have made. When I feel, & am not hurried, I acquit myself pretty much to my own satisfaction, & sometimes to theirs. But it is the inevitable consequence of writing many letters, at one time, that my mind is jaded, & looses much of it's elasticity. Thus it was when I wrote to you in January: & I find, by recurring to my Journal, that all my letters at that time, were short, & inelegant.

More than this, I see nothing remarkable in the letter I wrote to you—in respect to style or sentiment. The first, is in my ordinary way; the last—does not seem to me so frosty & repulsive as you describe it. But, admitting that it were so—what ought to have been your conduct in respect to me? Had you any uncertainty as to the meaning of what I wrote? did you in the least suspect the sincerity of long-continued friendship for you?—did you do right, to surmise, conjecture, distrust, & still be silent? Was it not the part of a friend to request an immediate explanation—to have all difficulties resolved at once—to have administered correction & reproof, instantly? Ah Theodore! I do assure you—I speak it from my inmost soul—the idea of your brooding over the supposed injustice of your friend, for near five months, without asking of him —whether his heart were true to you or not—is, indeed, the "point-of-the-bayonet" to me. As for my last letter, of a few lines, it was written in a moment of dejection, when my heart was heavy, & my understanding cloudy—in a moment like the present: yet, even then, did I exert myself to write to you—for I shuddered when I reflected on the interval in our correspondence—& thought I could not make too much haste to put an end to it. What, or how, I wrote, I scarcely knew—I tho't not of the tricks & graces of eloquence—my soul knew but one wish, it was possessed but of one idea, to recal to your remembrance one who never had ceased to love you, one, who, for some inexplicable reason, you seemed to have forgotten. I have been solitary, sad, heart-sick, & surrounded by a thousand little embarrassments, for a week past—& my mind sinks under the pressure of so many accumulated uneasinesses. My understanding, sluggish, clouded, & imbecile, struggles in vain to give language to those sentiments of sorrow for your regrets, of love for your love, & of constancy for your constancy, with which it is impressed, with which my bosom swells, & my heart labors.

I will write to you some other time.

Sunday, June 5. 1796.
Cedar St. No. 13. N. York.   E. H. Smith.

MEMORANDA, 71

A single professional visit, of some length—the correction of a proof sheet—& the preceeding writing—took up all my time till dinner; for I rose late, & felt unwell. I was preparing to transcribe my letter, when I was called away to examine whether a person who wanted to be admitted into the Hospital was a proper object of that Charity. Spent the remainder of the P. M. at H. Johnson's. Part of the evening at Mr. Hodgkinson's where Mrs. Brett gave me some account of Mr. Holcroft—the rest at Mr. Woolsey's.

MEMORANDA, 72

Monday, 6th

Made a professional visit. Copied, with several alterations, the letter to Theodore Dwight. Did a number of errands. Corrected a proof sheet. In the afternoon, wrote an additional sheet to Theodore—which I did not copy. I feared that the labor would be too much for me. Dunlap came here. After him Donald G. Mitchell.[50] Woolsey & J. Murray Jr.[51] on Manumission business. Kent & I walked out of town. Saw Decius Wadsworth, for a few minutes on my return. Spent the evening partly at Mrs. Miller's, & partly at Dingley's.

I felt well till a little while after breakfast—from that

---

[50] See previous note #7 for R. Mitchill.
[51] John Murray, Jr., a New York merchant.

time, till near three o'clock, quite unwell—almost distracted—I have been better since—but am not now quite free.

MEMORANDA, 73

Tuesday, 7th

Professional business, at the Hospital & elsewhere, till dinner. Called on Dingley. Made a short visit at Woolsey's. Dunlap & Alsop here. Drank tea, & spent the evening at Dunlap's. [At] Woolsey's—Wm.'s wife & her sister, there—part of the time: Part of it—delighted ourselves with reading portions of "The Fool of Quality."

Rather better than yesterday. Much of the same disagreable sensations—both mental & bodily, as for several days past.

MEMORANDA, 74

Wednesday, 8th

Dunlap here in the morning, & about noon. Attended to my business. Alsop here. Numerous petty interruptions. Began, & made some progress, in, preparing the press certain papers, by the Drs. Monsons[52] of New Haven—relative to the Yellow Fever, as it appeared there in 1794. The papers are exceedingly immethodical. I do very little beside make a few grammatical & verbal alterations. Began Kite's Medical Essays.[53] Called, vainly, on Decius Wadsworth—& at H. Johnson's. S. Johnson & his Wife have arrived—but, to my great disappointment, Wm. has not. Evening at Riley's.

I have felt better to-day, than for a fortnight past. I am not quite well yet; but hope to be in a few days.

MEMORANDA, 75

Thursday, 9th

Read several Papers in Kite's Essays. Attended to my own business, & that of the Hospital. Corrected proof sheets of my letters to Wm. Buel, which have been printing for some time. Finished the transcription & revisal of Dr. Monson Junr.'s papers, on the Yellow Fever in New Haven. Dunlap & I walked out of town. The theatrical troubles seem drawing to a close. We called in at Webster's country residence, on our return. Pleasant place. Kent & his Wife there; Mrs. Cotton, &c. —Drank tea at Dunlap's, with Alsop & sisters—the Woolsey's &c—Evening at H. Johnson's. Saw Mrs. S. Johnson, for the first time. All well.

MEMORANDA, 76

Friday, 10th

Visited my patients. Read papers in Kite's Essays. Made some progress in arranging the papers of Dr. Monson Senr. on the Yellow Fever of New Haven. Dunlap here. Corrected several proof sheets. Drank tea at P. Wetmore's. Evening, partly at Kent's—partly at Boyd's. Had my hair cut behind.

MEMORANDA, 77

Saturday, 11th

Nearly finished Mr. Kite's Essays. Completed the transcription & arrangement of the New Haven Yellow Fever Papers. Corrected several proof-sheets. Attended to my own little, circumscribed business. Prescribed at the Hospital. Dunlap here, in the morning. A call from Capt. Mitchell, & his eldest brother.[54] A visit from Dr. Woodhouse of Phila., accompanied by Dr. Lamb of this place. Woodhouse, who is now Professor of Chemistry in the University of Pennsylvania, was a pupil of Rush; a student at the time I was; left the college at the same time; & entered the Army, in capacity of Surgeon's Mate. His Thesis was on the Persimmon. He has grown fleshy, & handsomer than formerly. We talked of the Yellow Fever—on which subject Dr. Rush is preparing a second volume for the Press—& also an octavo volume in defense of Venesection. Mr. & Mrs. Kent &c. went up the River to Poughkeepsie to-day. Club night. No club. Dunlap at the Theater. Spent the evening at Woolsey's. Recd. a letter from Thomas Mumford. All well.

POSTSCRIPT

I begin to respire. The mist of apprehension, of anxiety, & distrust, which envelopped, confounded, & distressed me, begins to grow more thin, & transparent, before the, as yet, feeble rays of experience, & returning courage. The task is not so immense as I had imagined, the difficulty not so insuperable, my abilities & knowlege not so incompetent. Will not assiduity & study raise me, yet, above all obstacles? Shall I not, at last, be able to deride fortune, smile at calamity, & court difficulty? May I not hope to triumph, where others have failed? to make those bow beneath my yoke, before whom I have crouched in servile despondence? Yes! If I may make new inroads into the empire of death; if I may wrest from him his already predestined victims; & hem him in, within his early bounds; I may indeed exult. And let me not—& I will not—despair of it.

Now would any one say—this is a strange Postscript. But why should we confine ourselves to one dull & beaten track? The week has been passed thro' better than I expected. I have lost many fears; I have gained some hopes. For the first, I rejoice; I exult in the last.

Twelfth Week

Sunday, 12th

PREFACE

I am not without hopes of being able, in this week, to return, in some good measure to my regular studies.

---

[52] Monsons becomes, a few lines later, Monson (also Munson). Aeneas Monson, Jr. was Yale 1780 who, about 1799, left medicine to enter business and became a bank president. No further information about the other Monson.

[53] Charles Kite, *Essays and Observations, Physiological and Medical, etc.* (London, 1795).

[54] See previous note #7 for R. Mitchill.

Medicine, French, & my Correspondence, must be equally attended to. I am now in a situation to find constant exercise for all I know of Medicine, & for much that I have learnt of French—as a language merely; & the calls of my correspondents begin to thicken upon me. Here then is occasion for industry, here it is indispensible. Let me then, with earnest resolution, set to work. The glooms which overshaded my soul, the clouds which darkened my understanding, are passing away; & the physical & moral man are renewing within me. Shall this be, & study not be also renewed? Shall energy be given me, & shall it not be exerted? A ray of comfort & assurance plays around my heart; I feel it's vivifying influence; my bosom is expanded; I breathe with greater freedom; my pulse beat more lively; a mild glow spreads itself over my frame; my limbs are apt for motion; & the voice of hope beckons me away. "Arise! let us be going."[55]

MEMORANDA, 78

Alsop spent much of the morning with me. Visited my patients. Wrote the two preceeding pages. Made several calls. Dunlap here. After dinner went to see him. We read, & walked. Spent the evening at Mrs. Morton's. Miss M. alone—& I had two hours of rational conversation with her.

MEMORANDA, 79

Monday, 13th

Finished Kite's Essays, & the fourth volume of the London Medical Society's Memoirs. Took up Anacharsis anew—& made some progress in the sixth volume. Visited my patients. Dunlap here in the P. M. Met M. M. Rozier[56] & Roulet on the Battery & accompanied the latter home. He presented me with the Three Constitutions of France—the three last parts of Madame Roland's Appeal & Rabaut's Sketch of the Revolution.[57] Evening at H. Johnson's.

MEMORANDA, 80

Tuesday, 14th

I have done very little this day, contrary to intentions: but it has been difficult for me to do much. Company deprived me of nearly all the little time allowed me from the duties of my own, & the Hospital business. In respect to the last, I was unnecessarily detained, by the irregularity of my Colleague—& of a heavy shower, in which, on that account I was caught. I spent the evening, partly at Dunlap's, & partly at Woolsey's.

[55] Matthew 26: 46.
[56] J. A. Bernard Rozier, vice consul for New York and New Jersey for the French Republic.
[57] Probably taken from M. de Saint-Etienne Rabaut, *A History of the Revolution of France*, published in English (London, 1792; New York, 1794).

I have made some progress in the Second part of Mde. Roland's Appeal.

MEMORANDA, 81

Wednesday, 15th

I have read a little medicine, this day—& made some progress in Madame Roland's Appeal. For the rest, a little business—& numerous interruptions, of one sort & another, have allowed me no proper leisure for study.

MEMORANDA, 82

Thursday, 16th

This day, like yesterday, has been nearly lost, as to study. In the morning I attended to my business. Wm. came home—& we had some talking to do. John came with him. I went to the Hospital. Phineas Miller & Dr. Kollock of Georgia came to see me. After them, Alsop & Dunlap. Then Dr. Woodhouse—with whom I conversed much about Medical matters—especially in Phila.—& who spoke with more independence than I expected. I spent the evening at home.

Still reading Madame Roland's Appeal.

MEMORANDA, 83

Friday, 17th

A little business, a visit to Dr. Woodhouse, some pages of Mde. Roland, occupied my time till dinner. Visits from Dr. Kollock, Alsop, Dunlap—some pages of Madame Roland, & a visit to my neighbor Boyd, the afternoon. A walk on the Battery, a visit at Riley's, & a few letters of Mde. Roland, the evening.

My good friends cause me to lose much time.

LETTERS

To Thomas Mumford.

Your letter, my dear friend, of the 25th. ulto. gave me much pleasure. I was on the point of writing to you all, & chiding you, severely, for a neglect equally cruel & unexpected. It was beyond all conception that the wretch to whose care I intrusted letters for you, so many months ago, should not have delivered them to you before. I could not conjecture why you delayed writing so long; I found that others had recd. letters of business from you; I was ready to accuse you very heavily; & at times, was distressed with horrid apprehensions. After all, it appears not a little extraordinary, that I should have recd. not a single line, from either of you, since we were last together, in Lichfield, till this short letter to which I am now replying.

Your letter came to me thro' the Post-Office—& is said to be forwarded by Judge Phelps. You speak to me of letters to be sent by the same person, from my sisters. I have recd. none; & have, vainly, made inquiry, of your brothers, your friend Jones, & every one I thought likely to know any thing about him, or concerning people from your quarter, where this Judge was to be found. I have not been more successful in my attempts to discover by whom the letter really did come. I long, most earnestly, to hear from my sisters. It would seem as tho' they were in concert, to overlook me. Abby has written but once, since we were together; & the rest of my friends in Lichfield, my father alone excepted, are silent & dead to me. I know not what I have done.

I am sure I have left nothing undone to preserve their esteem, that was either incumbent on me to do, or proper, or expectable from me. Pray do not let me be thus passed by, on the part of your family. Can they have ceased to love me?

I heartily thank you for your attention & zeal, in respect to the Circular Letter. I hope some good will result from it. We have great hopes, here, of effecting something erelong; & repose great confidence in the good dispositions, in this respect, of the ensuing Legislature.

Ah! your little son! Would that he could understand the wishes that I have for his happiness & usefulness! That he could feel how many sympathies I have rushing forth towards him, in common with his parents. Shall I bid you kiss him, for me? Or are not the lips of a mother more rich in sensibility—& shall I not request it of Mary?

Mary & Fanny,—you are good girls, for the most part —but you have been sadly neglectful of your brother. Remember him, & do better. I send you here, Mr. John Mulligan; with whom Thos. is somewhat acquainted, I believe; but with whom, if he be not, I am sure he will rejoice to become intimate. He will bring all the news, & more than I, who am less in the way to learn it, could tell you, were you present. Cherish him, for my sake, till you know how much he deserves your love, for his own sake.

Farewell—I shake Thos. by the hand, I kiss little Wm.—& I press you both, my sisters, to my bosom. Our friends all send love.

Friday, June 17. 1796.
Cedar St. No. 13. N. York.   E. H. Smith.

MEMORANDA, 84

Saturday, 18th

Visited my patients. Dunlap here. At the Hospital. Finished Madame Roland's Appeal. Read a small part of Dugald Stewart's Life of Adam Smith.[58] Went into the Bath. Recd. a letter from Mr. Tracy—by which I gain some pleasing intelligence. Idea Strong has fled her father's—where she was cruelly maltreated—& is protected by my father, at whose house she lives, & is supported. This is doing as my father ought to do.

---

[58] *Dr. Adam Smith's Essays on Philosophical Subjects; With an Account of the Life and Writing of the Author* (London, 1795).

POSTSCRIPT

In spite of the rhodomontade with which the Pf. to this week concluded, I have done nothing. Not absolutely nothing, but very little. The Appeal of Madame Roland occupied all those moments which the numerous & long-continued interruptions of visitors left me for reading. Of consequence, all other French, & Medicine have lain quietly on the shelf. In the mean time the pen of Correspondence has nearly slept; & the demands of friendship are as importunate as ever. I begin to doubt of the propriety of the resolution I have taken, to compose my letters in my Journal. It is true that they form, in part, the history of my mind; but, when my aversion to labour is considered, I am not sure that this plan is not, not only the cause of much loss of time, but of my repugnance to writing, & my epistolary delays. It is easy enough to write a letter, when one is in the humor of it; but to sit down doggedly to the transcription, when one might be acquiring real knowlege, is, I know not how great a mispence of usefulness, as well as of time. Are the advantages equal to the disadvantages? I confess I am at a loss. Is it proper to make a change, when unconvinced of the duty of the change? This reason of mine is a snail-paced thing; I must leave it to inclination to decide on these nice points.

THIRTEENTH WEEK

Sunday, 19th

PREFACE

The fresh proof which every succeeding Week continues to bring of the perfect inutility of those resolutions which it's preface contained, towards the effectuating of those scheems of study which they looked forward to, almost deter me from venturing any future determinations, of this sort. Unfortunately I feel stronger, when contemplating what is to be done, than when I attempt the execution; & have clearer views of my duty & of the manner in which it is to be discharged, at those moments when I bring it before my mind in perspective, than when the distance vanishes, I am placed in the midst of realities, & am necessitated to act. Illusion, which exerts but a feeble influence, when remote, too generally bears me away, in triumph, when near at hand. My reason is proof against all her arts; my passions against few. When both are united to oppose her, I am strong indeed; when she binds the latter to her aid, it is seldom that the former gains the victory. A native & almost fastidious sensibility, cultivated by education into a settled habit, a durable & discriminating taste, is my most certain, & nearly solo, preserver in cases of this kind. Where that is fluctuating, uncertain, inactive, & especially friendly to the side of passion—Ah beware the giant Reason! A sad picture! A true one! But it shall not always be true.

To Mr. & Mrs. Lovegrove.

This will be, I am persuaded, an unexpected address, but I hope not an unacceptable one. I designed to [have] spent this day with you in Amboy, in my proper person, but I am prevented from leaving town, by professional calls, & I have recourse to the pen. There is an interest, a life, a spirit, an energy, in conversation, when voice answers to voice, & eye replies to eye, which is vainly sought for in letters: sorry substitutes, indeed—but still substitutes. Their imperfections, however, are scarcely greater, or more numerous than those of modern conversations; for in these, the talking is all on one side; & in those, it is very nearly the same. I will not altogether exculpate myself from the censure herein implied; but, as you have sometimes listened with complacency to my loquacity, when present, I shall venture to expect a similar effort of good-nature from you, now that we are apart. Beside, you will, in your present situation, possess one advantage, at least, which you did not formerly; for you can throw aside the letter, when tired of it, at any time you please; & you could not, always, so easily rid yourselves of the visitant.

The day of your removal was windy, & unpleasant. We scarcely expected that you would venture to set off; &, (as I have already had an opportunity of informing Mr. Lovegrove,) designed to have spent the afternoon at your house. We were, of consequence, not a little surprized & disappointed to find you gone. The disappointment was the more severe, as we had to regret your departure without our having bidden you adieu, & as we had some room to apprehend that you would accuse us of neglect. And certainly, this last is an imputation to which, of all others, we should least desire & deserve to be subjected. Were it necessary, which I trust it is not, to exhibit proof of this, how many hours of sad vacuity might we not bring in attestation of it's truth; hours which the social converse of your house had made to dance lightly away, but which now "lingered like the tale of youthful feats, upon an old man's tongue."[59] Indeed, so circumscribed was our circle of visitation, yet so complete, so pleasantly filled up, that we felt not, nor conjectured, till your removal made a breach in it, how narrow it was, & how much of our happiness reposed on your society. Were I not fearful that the obstinate conviction which you retain of my philosophic insensibility would render you incredulous, I could display before you facts little calculated to strengthen that conviction, & still less to support that character for superiority to gentle affections, which, somehow, against my will, I seem to have acquired. But this is a task the performance of which I must leave to my good friend William: to that friend, who *never having known a scar, still jests at war*;[60] & who, elevating himself above the power of Cupid, is still supposed most open to his seductions. I more than half doubt whether this is intelligible; but if it be not, it is of so little importance, that it were a folly to waste time in attempting to explain it. To return then—You will receive, with a deeper assurance of it's being true, the information which Wm. may chance to give you, of the numerous & pointed regrets which we have felt, shewn, & exprest, for the loss we have sustained in your removal. He best can tell you, how many hours which we were wont to spend in your society, we have past at home in recalling you to mind, & lamenting that it was no longer in our power to be present with you, but in imagination. He can tell you, often we have started forth to visit you, when you were no longer here; & how frequently our steps have turned, involuntarily & thro' habit, towards your late habitation, when we were returning from our rural excursions. He, happy man, has spent three weeks in his native place; whence he has just returned. I have been a forsaken lover, a widowed turtle, for more than three weeks. It was a resolution well taken to raise the cup of solitude to his lips, on the instant of his return; & I had surely made the effort, had not this unfortunate profession of mine, chained my hands.

Seth Johnson & his better half have been here more than a week. She is a charming woman; not handsome, but spirited & engaging, frank & well informed; & they are now comfortably established in their own house. My good friend [William Johnson] is like the Ass between two bundles of hay, in the fable: he runs to this brother & to that; & half the time is on the point of loosing his dinner, thro' indecision with which it is best to take it. For the rest, he has been so surrounded with business, since his return; so envelloped in writs, declarations, pleas, indentures, &c. in newly-written papers, & musty parchments; that I have had but few moments wherein to see him; & still fewer, in which to converse with him. But, I know not how often he has, already, questioned me concerning news from Amboy; how much he was gratified in hearing of your welfare, by the father of your house-maid; & how earnestly he longs to put into practice a scheme which we have formed of seizing on the first leisure to make you a visit together. So much for ourselves.

We are extremely anxious to learn how your new residence agrees with you: Whether it becomes more tolerable, the more you become acquainted with it: How the Cows, & Beans, & peas, & Cucumbers come on: If Mrs. Lovegrove churns the butter, & Mr. Lovegrove weeds the garden. But, above all, we have a thousand inquiries hanging on our lips, & ten thousand affections clustering about our hearts, in relation to the little Charles. He grows finely, no doubt. The country air expands his lungs, & heightens the colour in his cheeks. His little steps already print the soft grass; & his lisping tongue makes some efforts towards language. I must beg of Mrs. Lovegrove to impress on his lips a mother's kiss, on my account. I will hold myself ready to dis-

---

[59] Not found.
[60] "He jests at scars that never felt a wound." *Romeo and Juliet*, II, ii.

charge the obligation, if she require it, when I see you in Amboy.

I dare not hope an answer to this letter; much as so an unexpected a favor would delight me. But if you are not absolutely averse to this chattering, & should it still be impossible for me to visit you, I may again, perhaps, intrude upon your leisure & retirement, in this unceremonious manner.

Sunday, June 19. 1796.
Cedar St. No. 13. N. York.   E. H. Smith.

P. S. Be so kind as to remember me to Sophy. I hope she proves herself a good girl. I feel myself bound to take care that she continue so; & should regret much the necessity of giving a different character of her to her parents. But I am sure that she will always deserve well of all the world; & that Mr. & Mrs. Lovegrove, will speak in her praise to me, when I come to Amboy.

You will understand what use is to be made of this Advice.

E. H. Smith.

MEMORANDA, 85

Copied my letter to Mumford. Visited my patients. Wrote the preceeding letter to Mr. & Mrs. Lovegrove. Dined with Dunlap, at whose house I past part of the P. M. The rest at H. Johnson's. Wm. & I went to Riley's. Thence to Mr. Roulet's—where we spent most of the evening.

MEMORANDA, 86

Monday, 20th

Saw my patients. Dunlap here, forenoon & afternoon. Began, & made considerable regular progress in Bell on Siphilis[61] &c. Saml. Bowne visited us—& pointed out the principal Quaker authors to us. Called to see Boyd. Kent has returned. Drank tea with Mrs. C. Riley. Called at Mrs. Morton's. Miss Morton leaves town to-morrow. Accompanied her to H. & S. Johnson's—with the last of whom spent most of the evening. Made a professional visit. Read Volney's Catechism.[62] The Head has resemblance.

MEMORANDA, 87

Tuesday, 21st

I forgot to notice, yesterday, that I transcribed & forwarded my letter to Mr. & Mrs. Lovegrove. To-day, I have attended to my business, both in private & at the Hospital: Have made progress, equal to yesterday, in Bell's Work. Read fifty pages in Anacharsis. Visits from Dunlap, Dr. Mitchill, & John Johnson. Drank tea at Woolsey's. Spent part of the evening there, & part at Hodgkinson's.

MEMORANDA, 88

Wednesday, 22nd

Visited my patients. Made progress in Bell. Mr. Roulet here two hours. Alsop, Dunlap, & Webster here. The last left me some papers of his to read, & pronounce upon. I mentioned some facts to him—which he wished to have—& I hastily threw together a few remarks. Walked out of town, some distance, to see a patient. Drank tea at Saml. Bowne's. Evening at Woolsey's. Theodore Dwight was there—& I past several hours most pleasantly in his society. Friends in Connecticut well.

MEMORANDA, 89

Thursday, 23rd

Visited patients. Read thro' the first vol. of Bell. Dwight & Alsop here. Called on Kent. Prescribed at the Hospital. Visited a patient out of town. Dined at Woolsey's—in company with Alsop, Dunlap, Dwight &c. Attended a meeting of the Trustees of the African School. Evening at Woolsey's—with Dwight &c.

MEMORANDA, 90

Friday, 24th

Visited patients. Read Bell. Attended an operation at the Hospital. Mr. Roulet brought several pamphlets here. I looked over "Quelques Chapitres" by Riouffe; "L'ancien Comité de Salut Public" &c. a Satire on Jh. Just; & "Les Premiers Jours de Prarial." Dunlap here; & Alsop. Drank tea with the Woolseys, Dwight, &c. at Riley's. All spent the evening at Woolsey's.

MEMORANDA, 91

Saturday, 25th

Attended to my private & Hospital business. Made further progress in Bell. Read the greater part of our Dr. Bailey's Account of the Fever of 1795;[63] of which I have no very exalted opinion—but think it may do some good. Dined at Moses Rogers's—in company with Alsop, Dunlap, Dwight, Johnson, & the Woolseys. Part of the afternoon at Dunlap's. Evening we all went to Kent's.

Dunlap goes to Amboy to-morrow—with his Wife; returns on Tuesday—& proceeds with the Commedians to Hartford some time in the week.

POSTSCRIPT

Considering the many diversions from study, & from my proper business, the week now concluded has been spent to more purpose than I had any reason to expect,

---

[61] Benjamin Bell, *Treatise on the Gonorrhoea Virulenta, and Lues Venerea* (Edinburgh, 1793).

[62] Constantin F. C. Volney, *The Law of Nature: or Catechism of Reason* (Philadelphia, 1796).

[63] Not found.

& than I did expect. In my profession, I have discharged the active duties with more than usual ease & success; & I have pushed my attention to books beyond what my hopes—interrupted as I constantly am, oppressed by indolence, & enjoying the rare society of a long—& well-beloved friend. I have read much French: not much, indeed, in the regular course of my reading of that language—for, inticed by the publications relative to the times, & which a favorable opportunity permitted me to peruse, I have laid the history of former ages aside, & attended to that of the present: full as much to the purpose, I trust. I succeeded better, in my attempts to converse in French, the last Sunday evening, than I have ever done before; & have some hopes of myself in this particular. My correspondence has been too much neglected.

Fourteenth Week

Sunday, 26th

PREFACE

My design & expectation is to pursue this week, my professional & general reading, my private & public business, & my correspondence, with at least an equal degree of vigour, as in the past week. Should circumstances concur to favor my wishes, I intend to make a visit to Amboy, on Saturday, & return the Monday following. An increase of private professional employment will certainly prevent the execution of this project.

This day is very sultry, & heat oppresses me, & makes me incapable of much exertion. My delicate & feeble frame, is thermometrically sensible to every considerable change of temperature; & stands in need of the support of a more elastic & persevering spirit. My mind has much of the pendulum in it—it goes forward—receeds—recurs—vibrates back—forward—is never stationary in ancor, but does not much exceed it's original line of progress—& never holds that firmly which it has once conquered.

MEMORANDA, 92

Visited my patients. Finished Mr. Bailey's publication, relative to the Fever of 1795. Made some progress in a pamphlet published by Meillan—a Member of the French National Convention, & one of the Girondists: a very interesting narrative. Dined with all the Johnsons, now in town, at Seth's; & spent the afternoon there. Evening, partly there, with Theodore—& with him at Riley's—& at Woolsey's. Dwight goes in the morning; so that I have taken my leave of him.

MEMORANDA, 93

Monday, 27th

My business occupied some time. Was at Hodgkinson's. Made some progress in Bell. Finished Meillan's—& several other french pamphlets. Recd. letters from Mary & Fanny. Called on Dingley. Spent the evening at Mr. Roulet's.

MEMORANDA, 94

Tuesday, 28th

Private & Hospital business. Read farther in Bell. Read part of the Travels of Bachaumont,[64] in French; & part of the Report of Camus &c. to the Council of Five Hundred.[65] Dunlap & his family returned. He was here. Left all well at Amboy. Lovegrove came up with him. Wrote the following letter to Mary. Drank tea at Dunlap's. Spent the evening at Jno. Murray Senr.'s[66] at a meeting of the Joint Committee of the Governors, & Physicians & Surgeons of the Hospital.

LETTERS

To Mary S. Mumford.

Your letter, my dear sister, which I recd. yesterday, by I know not whose means, invigorated recollections & sentiments of affection in my bosom; never dormant; now, more than ever, lively & sincere. The proofs which it contains of your love & forbearance are dear to me, tho' it has not been thro' any fault of mine that you had been afforded this new opportunity of disclosing & displaying them. Doubtless, you have, before this time, recd. those letters which were forwarded long since, & which, to my utter astonishment, I recently learnt had been till very lately withheld from you. The few lines which I have had from Mr. Mumford, acquaint me with the fact, & encourage the hope, now exprest.

I hardly know how to assign the causes for so long a delay, in respect to furnishing you with a brief statement of my sentiments, relative to the true principles of Education. I have been busied; sometimes, to good purpose; but particularly distracted with a thousand little affairs, which amount to nothing, & yet require more thought & demand more time, than the most weighty concerns. At present I shall confine myself to reply to the several parts of your letter, merely: after which, if leisure & power concur, I shall enter on the subject which, apparently, most interests you; & which is, certainly, one of the most important of all to which the human mind has ever been directed.

The remarks which you make, relative to the character of "Caleb Williams" & "Herman of Unna," appear to me equally pertinent & judicious. On the merit of the "Mysteries of Udolpho" you seem less decided, & request my opinion. Before I speak further of this Book

---

[64] Claude E. Chapelle, *Voyage de Bachaumont, et la Chapelle* (La Haye, 1749).

[65] Armand Gaston Camus, Director of Archives of the Republic and a member of the Council of the Five Hundred in 1796; such titles of his as have been found seem unlikely for this reference.

[66] Like his son of the same name, Murray was a successful New York merchant, member of the Board of Governors and treasurer of New York Hospital.

it is proper that you should be informed that I have never read it but by snatches, & never intirely. The sentiments which I have formed from this imperfect perusal, & of the general merit of the works of Mrs. Radcliff, therefrom, & from the reading of "The Romance of the Forest,"[67] I shall briefly explain to you. The merit of a Book depends on several circumstances. The highest estimation is certainly due to that work, which has in view the enforcing or displaying, of some truth, or truths, highly interesting to the welfare of mankind, & calculated to promote or secure it, which employs to this end, an exact & luminous method, & enforces every consideration connected with the subject, by force, precision, perspicuity & elegance of style.

Should it chance to be the lot of "The Mysteries of Udolpho" to be judged by this rule, I very much fear of it's bearing away any preeminent marks of approbation. In respect to the principal design of the author, in this work, I am ignorant. The general character of her plan of writing appears to me, simply this: To excite & sustain curiosity, by a succession of contrivances, as long [as] this will answer; & when this is carried as far as it will bear, to clear up all the difficulties, by a disclosure of the insignificant machinery by means of which the illusions have been effected. The great fault of this plan is, that it raises expectations, which it never gratifies. How marvellous the events have been, the causes are trifling; they, therefore, bear no proportionate consequence to them; the mind is fatigued by the former, & disgusted by the latter. It appears the labour of a Mountain, to bring forth a mouse. Neither are these contrivances proofs, as you seem to suppose of a fertile, but, on the contrary, of a sterile, fancy. A rich imagination peculiarly displays itself in the various & well-defined delineation of character, in conjuring up situations calculated to bring the peculiarities of character into complete operation, & in supporting a long narration by the energy of sentiment & character, with but little aid from external & accidental circumstances. In the "*Julie*"[68] of Rousseau, a young man, of a good education, but neither of family nor fortune, becomes the private tutor of a young lady, the only child of a rich & haughty baron. In this situation they become mutually enamoured of each other—a private amour is carried on—is discovered—the lover flies—a friend of the father offers marriage to the daughter—the lover is induced to relinquish his claim—his mistress marries—he leaves the country—returns—is recd. as a friend —& receives her last advice, on her death-bed, where she lies in consequence of an accident. Here are very few circumstances, few events—& yet the spirit is incessantly kept up, by the force of passion & sentiment. This novel is as long as "The Mysteries of Udolpho." In this last, on the other hand, every chapter abounds with tricks, which keep alive your curiosity, on a first reading, but never have that effect a second time. And why? Because, there is very little character, very little sentiment, very little variety; & the style is a constant ringing of bells, & mists, & glens, & port-cullises, & moats, &c. &c. the miserable & tattered coverings of a feeble imagination & a languid & barren understanding. But I have spent too much time already on a book, which you will never read a second time, & which might just as well have been characterized by a single sentence. It would be easy to justify & establish the opinion, which you will gather from what I have written, were I not fatigued, & the weather oppressively sultry. Excuse me, then, for this time: I hope to write more lengthily to you—before this is dismist.

Tuesday, June 28. 1796.
Cedar St. No. 13. New York.   E. H. Smith.

MEMORANDA, 95

Wednesday, 29th

Private business. A consultation at the Hospital. Finished Bell on Siphilis; & the Report of Camus &c. Copied, with many alterations, the preceeding letter. Part of the evening at Kent's—remainder at Mrs. Miller's.

MEMORANDA, 96

Thursday, 30th

Private & Hospital practice attended to. Finished the journey of Chapelle & Bachaumont. A visit from Dunlap, & Charles Adams. Writing for the Manumission Society. Wrote to my sister Mary—but not in my Journal. I have not decided whether to transcribe or destroy it. Read several chapters in the second volume of Hugh Trevor.[69] Called at Boyd's. Spent the evening at Charles Adams's.

GENERAL POSTSCRIPT TO THE MONTH OF JUNE

I know not when I have felt more wretched, or had less confidence in myself, than at the commencement of this month. My heart was oppressed with apprehensions and distracted with doubts, some of which experience has demonstrated to have been visionary, & all of which reason, now that it has room to operate, is convinced were faulty. Still, I can not affirm that I derive that pleasure from my situation which would spring from a conviction of my own ability. I see too clearly the circumscribed limits of my own power, to exult much in it's exercise. I see, too, how impotent it is to save, where, perhaps, others might preserve; & I have none of the trappings of Art to cover the poverty, the tatters, of Science. Were it not that I sometimes think the ornaments, the vain & gaudy decorations of our Profession, all which others possess more than myself, & that in respect of ready apprehension & a facile adaptation of

---

[67] Novels by Mrs. Ann Radcliffe (1794).

[68] *Julie, ou La Nouvelle Héloïse* of Rousseau (Amsterdam, 1760).

[69] Thomas Holcroft (London, 1794-1797, 6 v.).

things to circumstances they might sometimes chance to be my inferiors, I should cease to pretend to medical skill, & surrender up my present foot-hold to those who are more worthy to possess it. But, how is this to be determined? No one has confidence in another. All fear that their ignorance will be detected. Not a soul has courage to acknowlege how little he knows. Physicians, like religionists, are restrained from confession, lest they should appear to be worse than those around them, or from a belief that others are more instructed, they are deterred from acknowleging the inefficacy of their practice, their faith, their art.

In respect to study, this month, tho' better than my fears predicted, offers but little for praise to delight itself in. I have read a few medical, & a few French, Books; but they are few. I fondly hope, notwithstanding, that I have not read them altogether in vain.

In respect of my Correspondence I can not impute much blame, or bestow much commendation.

That is a bad month which allows not of positive self-approbation. Alas! how eagerly does mistaken self-love endeavor to screen it's object from blame! This Month, then, is *bad*.

JULY 1796

GENERAL PREFACE TO THE MONTH

The first pleasant sensation which occurs on the opening of this month is, the recollection that one fourth of my time of imprisonment—for such I feel my term of service at the Hospital—is expired. In three more months I shake my ruffled plumes, clap my pinions, & soar away—the liberated bird. In the meantime, here I must labor; & since it must be so, here I *will* labor, & with dilligence & attention. Haply, my toil may not prove vain: I may restore the unfortunate to health, or comfort: I may gain knowlege, precious, inestimable, knowlege: I may become the means of extending happiness to thousands. That is an idea dear to my heart; & almost the only one that supports it, under it's daily mortifications & sufferings.

Well! shall I not bend the dilligent mind to study? Shall the present month, sultry & oppressive as it must of necessity be, find me not forgetful of my duty? Shall not my arm burst open the portals of science, my feet enter her secret recesses, my eyes devour the mighty & manifold treasures, & my hand bear them captive to my use? Certainly, I must & will strive to know something. "Jove laughs at the perjuries of lovers"[70]—they say—alas! doth he not also, mock at the resolutions of the indolent?

They may say what they will, these talkers, but Industry is assuredly a very rare virtue. I blush when I hear, as I sometimes do, myself praised as industrious. What ideas must those entertain of this virtue, who can ascribe it to me, if they know how little I perform? If they make the ascription thro' ignorance, how severe a reproach! I appear what I am not. I deceive my fellow-beings, & that knowingly. It is in the base & detestable service of Avarice, alone, that men are industrious. Shew me one who is so thro' philanthropy! And can not a noble principle excite to equal activity with an ignoble & destructive principle? It were a libel on the species to say no—& yet—I am on the point of being guilty of the libel. But I will not. The fault is in circumstances, not in man; & I may yet live to see thousands refute it; may, perhaps, live to be a refutation of it myself.

I think that this Volume will terminate with the Month.

MEMORANDA, 97

Friday, 1st

Attended to my business. Wasted much time. Read a hundred pages, or so, in Anacharsis: a little in some other books. Drank tea at Dunlap's. Spent the evening at Woolsey's.

I could not help feeling that Woolsey's manner was less cordial towards me, than it has been wont to be. I fear that his religious opinions will, eventually, estrange his heart intirely from me. These ideas made me somewhat melancholly.

MEMORANDA, 98

Saturday, 2nd

Private & Hospital business. Commenced Adams's Essay on Electricity, & read eighty pages. This book is very deficient in philosophic method; but it is far better, in that respect, than Nicholson's introduction to electricity, in Philosophy.[71] Pursued the reading of Anacharsis. Visited Dingley. From six till nine, occupied professionally.

The Town already begins to be alarmed concerning the Yellow Fever. Two recent cases of Fever, supposed to be the same with that of 1795, have excited much curiosity & apprehension. A Mr. Briggs & his clerk, the first a merchant, his store on Schermerhorn's Wharf—in the neighborhood of the place where the Fevers generally originate—were taken sick last Monday. Briggs died yesterday morning. The young man, his clerk, is now ill.

POSTSCRIPT

My intended journey to Amboy is prevented, by the presence of Mr. Lovegrove; so that it stands postponed

---

[70] John Dryden, "And Jove but laughs at lovers' perjury." *Palamon and Arcite* ii, 758 or 9.

[71] George Adams, *Essay on Electricity, in which the Theory and Practice of that useful Science are illustrated by a variety of Experiments; to which is added, an Essay on Magnetism* (London 1784). See also William Nicholson's Introduction to Electricity in *Experiments and Observations on Electricity* (1789).

to the last of the next week, instead of the present. In other respects, I have done as is my wont. Read a little; & been lazy much.

There has nothing of much importance, in relation to myself, occurred the week now ended. The presence of my friend Theodore Dwight gave me pleasure; & the more, as he seemed to have lost none of his attachment to me. I hope still to deserve & preserve his esteem; tho' I have much reason to fear that his heart is, or will be, estranged from me—in consequence of the difference in our metaphysics. On me, this difference can have no effect of this kind, as I do not love him the less, & compassionate him the more; but he must regard with pain one who he apprehends is doomed to perdition. The same change is to be feared, on the part of several others: but it must be so.

Dunlap sailed for New Haven Saturday—on his way to take charge of the Hartford Theater, this summer.

Fifteenth Week

Sunday, 3rd

PREFACE

As I do not find that my resolutions have any permanent influence on my conduct, I will make none for this week; & as all my plans are so liable to be frustrated, I will, for this week, cease to plan. If my mind pants after exertion, if it is eager to acquire any particular knowlege, it needs no resolution to encourage & strengthen it's endeavours; if it sink in despondency, or be overpowered by lassitude, no previous determinations have efficacy to restore it's elasticity, & animate it to industry. Alas! that it should be so: yet so it is.

It is the curse of Indolence that all it's shameful indulgences leave remorse behind them. The consequence is certain, is clear, & yet the present temptation is always too powerful. The triumph of a single hour, renders that of the succeeding more certain; & perhaps, there never was an instance of the permanent shaking off of the habitually endeared bonds of indulgence. Let me beware!

MEMORANDA, 99

Visited my patients. I never sent the letter which I wrote, on the 27th of May, to Charles B. Brown. To-day I composed a new one—in which part of the former was incorporated. Read a little—miscellaneously. Visited Mr. Kent. Visited at H. Johnson's—where all the Johnson's were collected. Wm. & I walked.

MEMORANDA, 100

Monday, 4th

Made some further progress in Adams's Electricity. Visited my patients. It being the Anniversary of the Declaration of Independence, the day was observed as a festival—& I devoted it to visiting. Called at Kent's—Dunlap's—Woolsey's—Riley's—Boyd's—Dingley's—: Alsop here—He, Wm. & myself drank tea at S. Johnson's. S., Wm. & I went into the Bath—after which we spent the evening at S. Johnson's. Recd. letters from my Father, Abby, & Idea.

MEMORANDA, 101

Tuesday, 5th

A little progress in Adams, & in Anacharsis. Private & Hospital business. At the Monthly Examination of the African School. Walked out of town, to Mr. Webster's. Visited Mr. Boyd.

It is certain that the young man I saw Saturday has the Yellow Fever. I saw him again to-day.

MEMORANDA, 102

Wednesday, 6th

Professional business. Continued the reading of Adams; finished the sixth, & began the seventh, vol. of Anacharsis. Wrote letters to my Father, & Mr. Tracy. The whole evening, till late, consumed in medical affairs.

MEMORANDA, 103

Thursday, 7th

Private & Hospital practice occupied great part of the forenoon. Wrote letters to my sister Fanny & to Sally Pierce. Recd. a letter from C. B. Brown. Made considerable advance in Anacharsis. Read several parts of Rush's Book on the Phila. Fever of 1795, & Thucidydes' account of the Plague of Athens. Visited Boyd. Spent the evening at S. Johnson's. Many visitors in the course of it. Among others, Mr. Laffert, much to my delight. He has made a flying jaunt to the Eastward—is charmed with the country—leaves town to-morrow—& suddenly sets sail for Europe.

MEMORANDA, 104

Friday, 8th

Our servant was taken violently ill last night; I was much disturbed; & slept late this morning. Attended to my business. A violent sultry day—read very little in Adams on Electricity; & a little in Anacharsis. Mr. Laffert made us a short visit in the morning, & Dingley in the afternoon. Dined at S. Johnson's. A small, but salutary shower, with a little thunder. Wind became northerly, & air pleasant. Called at Mr. Kent's. Evening at Mrs. Morton's. We went to the Bath.

MEDICINE

Saturday, 9th

Sketch of the principal Objects of a proposed Periodical Publication—to be called the Medical Repository,—or any thing else.

1. The principal Object, to collect facts, opinions, rea-

sonings, &c. relative to Epidemic & Endemic Diseases of the United States—primarily—or America—generally—& chiefly of the Febrile Diseases—properly so called; with a view to discover their causes, determine their histories, explain their mode of action, ascertain their method of Cure, illucidate their peculiarities, & effectuate their prevention.

2. To record useful Histories of other diseases—whether in America, or elsewhere; & new successful methods of Treatment.

3. Histories of New Medicines.

4. Accounts of general diseases among Domestic Animals—their causes, method cure, prevention, &c.

5. History &c. of Insects injurious to grains, trees, grasses, fruit, &c. Remedies to be used against them—&c.

6. Extracts &c. from authors—in all countries—illustrative of the Nature &c. of our own diseases—& useful to assist in their removal; as also in the treatment of the diseases of domesticated animals—in the destruction &c. of pernicious Insects.

7. American Medical Biography.

8. Some account of former medical publications, in America.

9. Account of New Publications.

10. Medical news.

11. Meterological Observations.

12. Agricultural Information.

13. Observations on the face of the Country, at present, in all the new, or recently settled, parts of U. S. & on the progress of the changes—such as opening roads—draining marshes—cutting down forests—&c.

14. Mineralogical Information.

15. Botanical ———do.

In short, this Plan is capable to any degree of extension, & of embracing the whole concerns of the Universe so far as they involve the physical & moral health of man. The variety of subordinate objects renders it hardly possible that much useful & entertaining matter should not be collected; which will support the value of the Work in it's slow progress towards the accomplishment of it's principal design.

MEMORANDA, 105

Private & Hospital business took much of the forenoon, & some of the afternoon. Visited Dr. Mitchill. He read me two Papers—one a Theory of Hail—connected with theory of Contagion; the other a sort of continuation of the Theory of Fever; both letters. Shopping consumed some time. Alsop here. Wrote a letter to my sister Abby—& sent my letter to Mary & Fanny. Drank tea at S. Johnson's. Wm. & I went to Mr. Roulet's. He was not at home. Thence to Woolsey's. Mrs. Dunlap there. She has heard from her husband; who is at Hartford, & well.

POSTSCRIPT

Had the letters which I have written in the course of this week been composed or transcribed into my Journal, I should have appeared to have done much more than I now appear to have done. I did intend to have copied the letter which I wrote to Mary, as prefatory to some remarks on Education—but it was suddenly & unexpectedly called for, & I had not time. The other letters were not important to be preserved—being merely relative to common occurrences; & the extreme heat of the weather rendered me unfit for exertion. Had I been more capable to business I should have composed them in my Journal, & with more care & copiousness.

So much for my correspondence. My studies have not progressed much. I have been somewhat more busy—than usual—as my business occupied more time; & the heat has made me willing to neglect every thing, so I could only gain coolness. I have not, however, been altogether idle.

I have several times thought of taking up Mr. Webster's Plan, since he has relinquished it, or a larger scale; some persons, with whom I have conversed, encourage the idea; & the notes on the two preceeding pages have been made in consequence. But I have come to no determination.

Sixteenth Week

Sunday, 10th

PREFACE

I design to write a letter to Ch: B. Brown; another to Idea Strong, taking up the subject proposed by her; & another to my sister Mary, on the Physical management of Infants. I further design to put together some sentences towards a view of the plan of such a Work as is hinted at under the date of saturday.

I purpose to complete the reading of Adams on Electricity; to continue the perusal of Anacharsis, & to finish the looking over, which I have already in good part effected, of Mr. Webster's Collection, relative to the Yellow Fever.

Some portion of my time will necessarily be devoted to my own business; as much more, probably, to that of Hospital; & if I have nothing to do on friday, I mean to pay my long-projected visit to Amboy.

Such are my projects for this week; all of which may be frustrated; some of which can hardly be expected to gain intire accomplishment. I shall be too fortunate—to use a common phrase—if I can succeed in executing them all. We shall see.

MEMORANDA, 106

Visited the sick. Called at Mr. Riley's. Made a visit to Dr. Young, who shewed me his Astronomy & Theory of Physic—of which last I read several sheets. Visited at S. Johnson's. Wm. & I called at Mr. Roulet's—they were out. Spent the evening at Kent's. Read most of the remaining Papers in Webster's Collection.

MEMORANDA, 107

Monday, 11th

A number of calls. Wrote a letter to a Dr. Kissam of Long-Island—requesting of him the History or Case which came lately under his care. Finished Webster's Collection. Made some progress in Adams—some in Anacharsis. Visited the afternoon & evening. Walked out, with Wm., to Webster's. Was at Dunlap's.

MEMORANDA, 108

Tuesday, 12th

At the Hospital. Visited patients. Some advance in Adams. Had just taken Anacharsis, when Dingley came in. He sat an hour, or more. We proceeded to visit some patients. It rained; & we were necessitated to make a long stay, on the way. We found both the young man & his mother, with the Yellow Fever, in all appearance, past recovery. The father is affected in a very singular manner—& in all probability will soon be taken down, & die. Our spirits sank much. Yet we have done all in our power, under the circumstances.

Spent the evening at H. Johnson's.

MEMORANDA, 109

Wednesday, 13th

Made progress in Adams & Anacharsis. A fine rain. Visited the sick. Spent an hour or two with Dingley. Several calls. S. M. Hopkins came to see us. Lately returned from Virginia—in good health. Called at Boyd's. Kent here. A visit from Mr. Roulet. Called to Mr. Adams's by him—his wife somewhat unwell—in the evening.

MEMORANDA, 110

Thursday, 14th

Very contrary to my expectations I have been unable to prosecute my studies this day. I recd. a letter from my father, requiring of me to perform certain services. I did them, & wrote him two short notes. I recd. also another, foolish, letter—from Evelyn Pierpont; to which I was obliged to reply with some severity. The fellow's injustice was no longer tolerable. Having sent off my letters more early than I expected, I have not had time to write to Idea, & therefore, probably, shall not do it this week. I found, too, on inquiry, that the man by whom I expected to send to Aurora—has gone, without letting me know of it. So I shall hurry my letter to Mary. I have been at the Hospital—attended to my private business—dined at Woolsey's—& spent the evening at Mrs. Miller's.

(MISNUMBERED—DISCOVERED JULY 24; SHOULD BE 111) MEMORANDA, 115

Friday, 15th

Made progress in Adams & Anacharsis. Visited patients. A call from Capt. Mitchell & Mr. Sandford. Spent the evening at Mr. Kent's. Was at Mr. Dunlap's house. Mrs. D. had heard from him. All well.

LETTERS

Saturday, 16th

To C. B. Brown.

It has not been in my power to reply to your last letter till now, when it is impossible to send to you for two or three days; & when I should not write, would I be certain of having a more convenient moment as much at my command.

I pass over the contents of the greater part of your letter, as it principally relates to matters which have been sufficiently dwelt upon, & come to that paragraph, in which you attribute the gravity of my letter, to a supposed melancholly of my spirits. But you are mistaken. No such melancholly was felt; & my solemnity arose, solely, from the sense I entertained of the importance of our understanding each other, & the earnest desire I felt to render all future explanations unnecessary. I experience, for the most part, a temperate flow of spirits; & tho' I find occasional causes of dejection, in the observation & contemplation of my own ignorance & weakness, I do not often suffer myself to be greatly depressed thereby.

You wish for information concerning your friends, yet can not bring yourself to the communication of particulars relative to your own affairs. My several questions still remain unanswered; tho' my desire to know how you are? what are you doing? what you wish to do? What is proposed for you to do? & What you expect to do?—continues as vivid & anxious as ever. To give you an example of what is becoming in a friend, on occasions such as these, I shall be somewhat minute in recounting my own procedures; not only that I may satisfy your friendly inquiries, but to the inducing of you to return the like to me—tho' there is nothing in my manner of life particularly interesting.

I have long thought that the aid & death of no animal is necessary to man, were his desires & energies limited to their proper objects. His own limbs, the various machines by which he may be enabled to traverse & command the earth, the ocean, & the air, suffice for loco-motion, & for all the purposes of tillage, commerce, & manufactures—even supposing them necessary. Wants he clothing? the Flax & the Cotton, & various other plants, contribute to protect him from the cold of winter, the heat of summer, the chills of spring, & the fogs of autumn. The myrtle, the croton, the olive & various other shrubs & trees, furnish him with a substitute for animal oils, whether for food, or light. The farinaceous & leguminous plants, roots, greens, fruits, &c. are sufficient for his food; their juices, without the pernicious aid of fermentation & distillation, & the limpid stream, form his most salubrious beverage. But, I go farther. Not only are these sufficient for man, but all else is superfluous, is noxious. If this is true, how far can I, depraved by previous habits, bring myself back, uninjured, to the path, the simple path of nature? The example of a few solitary beings, scattered up & down in the history of my species, encouraged me. My first attempt was to incroach upon the territory of cold. (That figure will do for you.) I substituted a hard, for a soft, bed—& I have bidden adieu to the debillitating use of feathers. Distilled spirits I had long relinquished. I have nearly foregone the use of all other liquids than water. Nearly—for it will not do to make too rapid changes. The same is true of animal food—which I rarely taste; & when I do, in small quantities only. I feel better, free from passion, more alert for corporeal & mental exertion; & I think that I shall never return to the habitual use of animal food. So much for my physical conduct.

My time, when not wasted in indolence, (an enemy hitherto insuperable) is principally divided between the active & contemplative duties of my profession. My present situation, in the Hospital, engages some share of my time & attention; my private practice, which, tho' small, is slowly increasing, a further portion. I devote the forenoons to Medical studies; the afternoons to French & various literary pursuits; the evenings, mostly, to my friends. Plans of study, of Composition, & of Life, press upon my mind in turbid & tumultuous assemblages; succeed, & mingle with, each other; & pass away, again, with faint impressions, or none at all. A small part of my leisure has been lately devoted to transcribing for the press some letters, written to my friend Buel, on the Yellow Fever, & overlooking their impression. Public consideration alone induce me to suffer them to be published. They are incorrectly written; & the Printers, as is there [*sic*] usual conduct, have loaded them with some errors which were not their own.

I have no more to add, than love to all friends, & a wish that I may soon hear, particularly, from you.

Saturday, July 16. 1796.
Cedar St. No. 13. N. York.   E. H. Smith.

MEMORANDA, 116(112)

Private & Hospital practice. Finished Adams on Electricity, the Seventh volume of Anacharsis, & read Dr. Caldwell's Thesis. There is much useful matter in Adams' Book, but it is very deficient as it respects method. Wrote the foregoing letter. Spent an hour with Dingley. Was at Mrs. Dunlap's, at S. Johnson's, & in the Bath; with Wm. in the evening.

POSTSCRIPT

I have accomplished all the reading I planned to accomplish, but I have done a small part only of the writing. It is true that circumstances different from my expectation, have rendered the performance of part unnecessary; but it is more than probable that, even if this had not been the case, it would not have been effected. In the mean time, I have done some business; & I am daily picking up crumbs of knowlege, & scraps of confidence in my own judgement. As far as I can judge, my letters on the Fever have gained me more credit than they deserve, & may, perhaps, contribute to my future success. This, if true, can only arise from the astonishing dearth of really scientific men; for no man of profound professional science could be satisfied with what I have written.

SEVENTEENTH WEEK

Sunday, 17th

PREFACE

I have not yet determined what professional work I will next enter upon. In French, Anacharsis must still be attended to. I have made such progress in it now, that I think I shall proceed to the end, without any new wanderings.

If no particular reason operate to forbid, I mean to perform that writing, this week, which was to have been done the last, but which was left uneffected.

In respect to business, company, &c. my resolution is a standing one, & needs no new determination to give it tenacity. To pay all necessary attention to my patients, to discover all suitable attachment to those I esteem, is, with me, as much a matter of feeling, as of duty; what equally engages my reason & my heart.

Amboy—it is vain to resolve.[72]

MEMORANDA, 117(113)

Made two professional visits. Wrote a short letter to Dunlap, & transcribed with some alterations, that of yesterday, to Brown. Dined, & spent the afternoon at S. Johnson's. Called at Riley's—Wm. & I past the evening at Mr. Roulet's.

MEMORANDA, 118(114)

Monday, 18th

Dr. Leib of Phila. left a card on Saturday. I could not discover where he lodged. This day I found the place. He was out; & I have not seen him. Read Jh. John's preface to his translation of the New Nomenclature, & other parts of the book. Began Fourcroy's Chemistry.[73] Commenced the eighth volume of Anacharsis. Read

---

[72] This cryptic sentence may refer either to his rather ambiguous relationship with Mrs. Lovegrove or to some half-formed idea of moving to that town. See the first sentence in the Preface for Sunday, July 24, a week later.

[73] Antoine François, Comte de Fourcroy, French physiologist and chemist, *Leçons d'histoire naturelle et de chimie* (1781). Translations of his *Elements of Natural History and Chemistry* were published in 1782, 1788, 1790.

Thos. Paine on the "English System of Finance."[74] Wrote a Sonnet. Visited Boyd. Made some professional visits in the course of the day & evening. Recd. letters from my sisters Mary & Fanny, with a few lines from Mumford.

MEMORANDA, 119(115)

Tuesday, 19th

Hospital & private practice. Some progress in Fourcroy: some in Anacharsis. Recd. a letter from my kinsman Samuel Smith. A call from Dingley. Drank tea with Mrs. Dunlap. Spent the evening at Mr. Kent's.

MEMORANDA, 120(116)

Wednesday, 20th

It has rained hard & steadily all day. Progress in Fourcroy & Anacharsis. A visit from Dr. Mitchill, in the forenoon; & from Dingley, in the afternoon. Visited at C. Adams's. Spent the evening at H. Johnson's.

MEMORANDA, 121(117)

Thursday, 21st

Progress in Fourcroy & Anacharsis. At the Hospital. Several calls. Drank tea, & spent part of the evening, at Riley's; the rest at Mr. Kent's. Composed a Sonnet. Recd. letters from my Father, C. B. Brown, & Mumford.—Wm. has gone to Albany, this afternoon.

LETTERS

Friday, 22nd

To Idea Strong.

I began to fear that the gravity of my letter had terrified you from the prosecution of a correspondence which promised so little of that liveliness generally expected, in epistolary communications, when your letters came in to dispel my apprehensions. I read them over, with increasing pleasure, several times; because, they were without affectation, without formality, were affectionate—in short, proved you to be such as I expected to find you. It remains to be determined whether our mutual dispositions to pleasure & benefit each other, will be properly & efficaciously exercised.

Your proposal for entering on the consideration of the "Rights of Human Nature," is a noble one, & would lead, if acceded to, to a wide & nearly interminable field of speculation & inquiry. But as this is, of all other subjects, perhaps, the most important, the difficulties, arising from its immensity & partially-explored state, should by no means deter us from proceeding to it's investigation. It should be the object of our particular care, however, to make all necessary, previous preparation. Otherwise, we may find ourselves involved in unexpected intricacies; destitute of a clue to guide us, in this untrodden labyrinth, may discover too late our error; & thus bewildered, be equally unable to proceed on our course, & to retrace our footsteps. In this previous preparation you must take an equal part. As we are to be fellow-travellers, & do not mean to part company, we must be directed by the same motives, guided by the same compass, led by the same genius, & illuminated by the same benevolent planet.

Human Nature! The nature of Man! What is it? Can we reason consistently, without knowing what it is of which we reason? It is hardly necessary to express a negative, it is so self-evident. Our first care, then should be to determine what is the import of the phrase "Human Nature"—What is really meant by the Nature of Man. To gain accurate notions of so complex a being as man, it is necessary to contemplate him simply, without relation to other beings, of his own, or different, species; without regard to any previous, or existing system. What his origin, his structure: what his powers: how do external objects affect him: whence is his determination to motion: &c. &c. Next, he must be considered in connection with his fellow-beings: and here his history, as far as it is known to us, becomes of use. What are the mutual influences of beings on beings: how far is the well-being of each, consistent with that of every other &c. &c. But this is, in a measure, anticipating. To lead you, the more easily, to right & satisfactory determinations, on this head, let us compress the material points of inquiry into the form of a few simple questions—the answers to which will furnish the basis of our future investigations.

I.

Remarks. We observe great varieties in the characters of human beings—as well in their *dispositions*, as in their *powers*—

1. Do these depend on *original* structure or constitution?
2. If so, are they differences in *kind*, or in *degree*?
3. If of *kind*, how are they, certainly, to be known?
4. If of *degree,* only, how far do they depend on original structure?
5. If both of *kind*, & *degree*, how can we, absolutely, distinguish each from the other?

II.

Remarks. Men are exposed to numerous & infinitely varied external impressions—

1. Do these impressions influence human beings?
2. Are these impressions *equal* to the formation of the human character—i. e. of the dispositions & powers of men, *of themselves, solely*?
3. If they are not, how far does their influence extend?

In these questions, my dear sister, are comprized the

---

[74] Thomas Paine, *Decline and Fall of the English System of Finance* (New York, 1796).

several points to which it is necessary that our attention should be directed, previous to any consideration of the subject proposed by you. In your next letter, I shall expect your answers to them. When we have agreed on the proper answers, we shall be in a situation to pursue our inquiry; for the rights of men, are little more than deductions from their nature; & their duties nothing but their rights put in exercise.

Let me hear from you speedily. Assure yourself of my brotherly affection—that I feel the connection, which fortune has so kindly created between us, to be more than nominal.

Farewell.

Friday, July. 22. 1796.
Cedar St. No. 13. N. York.   E. H. Smith.

MEMORANDA, 122(118)

Further progress in Fourcroy & Anacharsis. Dined at S. Johnson's. Attended to some business of my father's, & of my own. Wrote the foregoing letter, & also a few lines to Daniel Sheldon Jr. of Lichd.[75] Dunlap returned. We drank tea & spent the evening, at Woolsey's.

MEMORANDA, 123(119)

Saturday, 23

Some advance in Fourcroy & Anacharsis. Hospital & other business. With Dunlap, & he with me. Busied much of the afternoon, with Dr. Mitchill, relative to the Hospital Library. Evening at Dunlap's.

POSTSCRIPT

The industry of this week is comprized in a small space. In a professional way, I have done as much as common: whether it respects action, or reading: in french, I have accomplished as much as usual: in my correspondence, no great, to the purpose, has been effected. My medical plan has lain by, & I have composed two Sonnets. It is the end of the week, & I am not in Amboy.

It is vain, if it were not also vicious, to waste time in regretting that things should be so. I hope to be able to rise above sorrow, in my attempts to deserve happiness.

EIGHTEENTH WEEK

Sunday, 24th

PREFACE

The path before me is plain; I have only to pursue it steadily, and shall be certain of self-approbation—the

---

[75] Son of Dr. Daniel Sheldon of Litchfield, Smith's one-time teacher. Graduate of Litchfield Law School, 1799, clerk in Treasury Department and then an assistant to Ambassador Gallatin to France to become secretary of the legation. On Gallatin's recall, Sheldon remained as chargé d'affaires. Died in France.

pleasing, the only satisfactory & adequate reward of proper conduct. Doubtless, my progress in Fourcroy will not exceed the usual course: I hope, however, to finish Anacharsis, this week. I must labor a little further, & more dilligently, in my correspondence; & I likewise hope to trace out, at least, the full plan of a Medical Repository. If I do this, if my correspondence be spiritedly pursued, if my Sonnets are inserted in this volume, I may be able to commence a new one, with the succeeding month. This is what I wish.

Charles is to meet Dunlap, at Amboy, this week. They will be there a fortnight. I think it shall go hard with me, if I am not there next week.

[Omitted here, two manuscript pages with the heading: "Fragment." (Copied from loose paper.)]

MEMORANDA, 124(120)

Transcribed my letter to Idea Strong. Copied the preceeding Fragment, from a loose paper, into my Journal. It was written some time since. Spent some time with Decius Wadsworth, at his lodgings—& he shewed me a statement &c. that he is about inserting in the public papers. Dined, & spent all the remainder of the day & evening at Dunlap's. It has rained very hard this afternoon & evening.

MEMORANDA, 121

Monday, 25th

Visits from Decius Wadsworth, S. M. Hopkins, & Dr. Mitchill, & a long ramble thro' booksellers' shops, in search of Medical works for the Hospital Library, prevented me from reading much in Fourcroy. Dined at Dr. Rodgers's—in company with Dr. Leib—went with him to see his sisters—& this, & writing a short & hurried letter to Dr. Rush, prevented me from reading much in Anacharsis. Spent a part of the evening at H. Johnson's. Visited my two patients.

SONNETS

I like the Sonnet. It is, when well managed, an elegant & impressive mode of conveying an important, or tender, sentiment. The cares of Avarice so universally possess men, that they will not read any thing lengthy. A profound & extensive disquisition, a laborious & learned research, an elevated epic or moral poem, is thrown by, unread, or carelessly looked over. Scraps, Anecdotes, Paragraphs, & Stanzas, alone attract curiosity; because on these alone will the mass of readers allow their attention to rest. To this necessity we must submit. Sonnets are short; if well written, & on profitable subjects, they may do good. I have long thought of composing a little book, in this form. Of exhibiting just thoughts, & striking maxims, in this dress. A few evenings since, the plan occurred to my mind, with more than common allurements, as I lay meditating on my bed. I resolved to write a number of Sonnets, & address them to my sister Fanny. They may keep her industry alive; they will form a pleasant mental & poetical exercise; & may, hereafter, undergo such corrections as to fit them for public inspection. Full of this idea, the next morning, the 18th inst. I composed one; & on the 21st a second. They follow.

SONNET FIRST

The Invitation

While blooms the rose of Youth upon thy cheek;
 And health and pleasure sparkle from thy eye,
 Not, with impatient, giddy spirit, fly,
In dissipation's round, delight to seek:
Nor yet, with ductile mind, subdued and meek,
 Conning the school-men's lore forever lie:
 Not with the gay alone doth bliss aby,
Not always truth from learned pages speak.
Up! up! arise! come forth! and cast thy view
 O'er Nature's ample realm that 'round thee spreads!
Nature, the source of pleasures ever new;
 The fruitful source whence every good proceeds;
From the low dust, to man's imperial crew,
 Whose every form some moral lesson reads.

SONNET SECOND

Spring

Light gales of Spring on playful pinions move,
 Sport on the waves, and wanton o'er the land;
 The blade shoots up, the swelling buds expand,
Flowers gem the mead, and foliage crowns the grove.
The torpid tribes a new existence prove,
 Rouzed by the season's life-restoring hand;
 Wings throng the air, fins press upon the strand,
And plains, hoof-beaten, echo sounds of love.
Thus shall the brute & vegetable kind,
 With eager joy improve the vernal hour,
And, idly, Youth, the Spring of Life, resign'd,
 In base inaction wither all thy power?—
Ere habit warp, ere wayward passion blind,
 Each field of science, realm of art, explore!

MEMORANDA, 122

Tuesday, 26th

Hospital & private practice. Called on Dr. Leib, but did not see him. A visit from Dunlap. He goes to Amboy, with his wife & son, to-morrow. C. B. Brown is to meet him there. Some progress in Fourcroy. Finished the eighth volume of Anacharsis to-day. Was at Dunlap's. Spent the evening at Mr. Kent's.

MEMORANDA, 123

Wednesday, 27th

Wrote five pages of the circular letter, commencing on the opposite page; read a chapter in the ninth volume of Anacharsis; made a few professional calls; the remainder of the day occupied in hunting up books, for the Hospital Library, with Dr. Mitchill. Evening—partly at Dunlap's house—partly, with him, walking on the Battery. I wrote a short letter, on business, to my father, yester evening.

MEMORANDA, 124

Thursday, 28th

At the Hospital on the Library business. Read a few pages in Anacharsis. Read the "Memoirs of Planetes"[76] —a work of no eminent merit. A visit from S. M. Hopkins—a visit from John Johnson. Called on J. Mulligan —at Boyd's—on Dr. Mitchill—at Mrs. Miller's—& at Mr. Kent's. Dunlap went to Amboy, to-day. Kent & I were to have followed him. He is restrained on account of business. I have no money.—Recd. letters from Wm. Johnson—& Evelyn Pierpont.—Spent the evening at Seth Johnson's.

SKETCH OF A CIRCULAR LETTER

To the Physicians, &c. in the United States.

Gentlemen,

The importance of an extensive acquaintance, with the facts which relate to every particular division of the general subject of Medicine, can not have escaped your attention. Theorize as he may, no discreet physician will venture far on any other foundation than that of Experience. To bring together & exhibit in one comprehensive view, the mass of facts, connected with any point of medical science or inquiry, has, therefore, always been considered as a useful service rendered to mankind. Systematic arrangements of facts & opinions have, at times, appeared, to attract general curiosity & fix the public opinion; but their influence has never lastingly prevailed, while collected observations, free from the weight of system, have constantly been resorted to, as the surest guides amid the intricacies of practice. Compilations of observations & histories, whether the work of a single hand, or many hands, have, therefore, steadily maintained a high degree of consideration and authority, in the libraries of Physicians; & so universally is their value & importance now recognized, in Europe, that publications of this nature are multiplied in every country, & sought after with peculiar avidity. In America, notwithstanding the numerous advantages, which, from the extent of our country, the variety of climate & disease, & universality of information, & sameness of language, we are possessed of, for giving novelty & importance to Medical Collections, undertakings of this nature have been few, & feebly prosecuted. But the period seems to have arrived, in which they are loudly called for, and may hope for extensive patronage & encouragement. The distressing events which have been so recently witnessed, in various parts of our country, have awaken'd the curiosity of every other class of citi-

---

[76] Not identified.

zens, as well as of physicians; & while they have quickened the zeal & observation of the latter, have excited the eager apprehensions of all. From such a state of the public mind, Science & Humanity have much to hope, if some common point of union can be created, towards which the labors of all careful observers may converge. A late benevolent attempt, of this kind, which has been made by a citizen unconnected with the profession of Physic, tho' it failed of obtaining so large a share of medical encouragement as was to have been desired, affords a reasonable ground for expectation of future success in plans of a similar nature; and it is such an expectation which has given birth to the present address.

The immense advantages which would result to mankind from the possession of an accurate history of Epidemics—or those diseases which, at certain periods, have become general over a considerable territory, or mass of population, have been the theme of medical eloquence for several centuries. Yet so little has been satisfactorily effected in this department of medicine, that a Physician of distinguished reputation has declared his library, of more than 5,000 volumes, totally inadequate to the furnishing even of a simple outline of the History of Epidemics. For the time past it is in vain to attempt to labour; but, surely, it is a matter well worthy the universal attention of the Faculty, to endeavour after the prevention of that reproach which will rest upon them, should the present time afford no better testimony in favour of their industry.

The illustrious Sydenham, more than a century ago, proposed it as problem, "whether a careful examination might *not* shew, that certain tribes of epidemic disorders constantly follow others, in one determined series, or circle, as it were; or, whether they all return indiscriminately, & without any order, according to the secret disposition of the air, & the inexplicable succession of seasons." The problem is recorded; but where shall we find the solution? Has it been that physicians have devoted those hours to the neatly fitting together of ingenious conjectures, which should have been occupied in careful observation & dilligent inquiry, that a question so interesting to humanity has remained hitherto unanswered; or was the resolution of it delayed to form the basis of the durable glory of the physicians of the United States? Was the honor reserved for them, to have turned their attention from conjectures to facts, & to have concurred in the erection of a national edifice sacred to the relief of man? It is fairly presumable that this desirable event may be fully accomplished, if regular information can be obtained, annually, from all parts of the United States, relative to the following particulars.

1. The state of the Atmosphere, in respect to dryness & humidity, heat & cold, serenity & tempestuousness including the direction & face of winds, & the sensible quantity of Electricity.
2. The progress & condition of Vegetation—in respect to growth, vigour, & disease—independent of the ravages of insects, or the particular effects of certain Manures.
3. Accounts of Insects—especially any unusual plenty or dearth of them—whether troublesome to man, or injurious to trees, plants, fruit, grains, grasses, &c. with as accurate notices as may be of the circumstances which preceeded or attended their arrival & disappearance, the remedies effectual against them, &c. &c.
4. Accounts of general diseases among Domestic Animals—their causes—symptoms—method of cure—time of appearing & disappearing,—&c. &c.
5. The habits of the people, among whom a Disease prevails—the local peculiarities of their residence—the time of it's appearing & disappearing—the attendant circumstances—preceeding & subsequent diseases—in sea-ports, the arrival of foreigners, in any considerable number, should be noticed—in the new settlements, the progress of clearings, drainings, opening of roads, & of population: the symptoms, remedies, &c. of the Disease.

To this end it is proposed to institute a publication, to consist of an octavo volume, annually, with the title of "The Medical Repository."[77] The principal design of this periodical work will be, to collect & preserve histories of the Epidemic Diseases, which prevail in all parts of the United States, in every season of the year. Thus, for instance, the same volume will shew what complaints were general in Portsmouth in New Hampshire, in Savannah in Georgia, & in the intermediate settlements, in the same spring, summer, autumn, & winter. And thus, every succeeding volume will form the history of the health of the United States, for the succeeding year; & so on—as long as the Work shall continue.

It is not to be expected that a Plan so extensive, & requiring the aid of so many observers, can be speedily carried into full effect; especially if so many different subjects of attention are taken into view, as are proposed above, & as seem necessary to give the highest value to medical histories. But it is not unreasonable to hope for a complete filling up of this Outline, in the course of a few years, if sufficient encouragment can be obtained for the undertaking during the perilous & uncertain state of it's infancy. In the mean time, that there may be no difficulty in the way of making up a yearly volume, which will be worthy the acceptance of the faculty, & of the public at large, it proposed to extend the Plan of the Work so as to comprehend Communications relative to a great variety of interesting subjects; all of them immediately, or remotely connected with Medicine. These are, in addition to those already suggested—

1. Accurate & succinct accounts of General Diseases

---

[77] Note that *The Medical Repository* at this stage was conceived of as an annual volume rather than the periodical it became.

that have heretofore appeared in any part of the United States, including the method of Cure.
2. Useful histories of particular cases.
3. Accounts of New Methods of Cureing any diseases.
4. Accounts of New Remedies, either for common complaints, or for those hitherto incurable.
5. Interesting Information relative to the Minerals, Plants, & Animals of our Country.
6. American Medical Biography.
7. Accounts of former Medical Publications, in America.
8. Accounts of New Publications (Medical) in America.
9. Medical News.

It is the intention of the Compiler, should his plan meet with encouragement, to publish an Octavo Volume on the first of next May; & to continue the publication annually. Should he not be possesst of sufficient materials by the time proposed, the impression will be delayed till he shall be able to issue such a volume as will do credit to the undertaking. It appears hardly possible that valuable materials should be withheld, so that the design should prove abortive; & the aid & countenance of all dilligent observers & of the learned, throughout the United States, as well physicians as others, is thus publicly & earnestly solicited.

The above is a mishapen mass—heaped together, in haste, & at different times. I must give it some better form; & send it into the world.

MEMORANDA, 125

Friday, 29th

Considerable progress in Fourcroy. Completed the intire reading of the Travels of Anacharsis the Younger. A professional call, or two. A visit from Decius Wadsworth. Walked with him. A call at James Watson's. The evening at Mrs. Woolsey's. Woolsey has gone to Albany.

Advantages of the Medical Repository

1. To discover the Origin, Nature, history, & method of cure, of Fevers, in every part of the U.S.—& thus lead to a knowlege of the means of prevention.
2. Would shew the progress of particular Epidemics, thro' the continent; &, perhaps, afford data for accurate calculation, on this point.
3. Will determine what situations are favorable to particular diseases—& what seasons.
4. May have the way for discovering whether there is, as Sydenham conjectured, a regular succession of general diseases, & return of them, after determinate intervals.

MEMORANDA, 126

Saturday, 30th

At the Hospital. Finished the first volume of Fourcroy's Chemistry. Dined at Seth Johnson's. Made many calls. Spent the evening at Mr. Kent's.

I have been endeavoring for three days to collect, even if it was no more than the pitiful sum of four dollars. Vainly. I now have not a single shilling in the world. Not enough to pay the postage of a single letter. How is it, that men who are able to discharge their debts, will suffer themselves to be requested to pay them; or, being requested, want the spirit, or the justice to satisfy the demand?

I am, at times, nearly disheartened with the little progress I make in the acquisition of knowlege—tho' I read something every day. I am wholly deficient in the article of *attention*. While reading, especially books of science, my thoughts are continually wandering from the subject, on to a thousand matters, wholly disconnected with that before me. Now, I have just read the first vol. of Fourcroy—& I verily doubt whether I am possessed of thirty new ideas—tho' the book contains a fund of information.

POSTSCRIPT

Two causes have very much contributed, during this week, to abridge my opportunities for mental exercises: the expectation of visiting Amboy, with the preparatory arrangements; & the business of selecting books for the Hospital Library. The last is effected—as far as it can be, at present; the first is necessarily put off to another week. Notwithstanding, I have, as I intended, completed the perusal of Anacharsis—& have made some little advance in other studies; little, indeed, & unsatisfactory; as every thing I do, falls far short of my conceptions of what I might, & ought to do.

I have written no letters this week—or at least none worthy of recollection. The same causes which prevented my reading, also prevented my writing. Some doubts, occasionally, arise in my mind, on this matter of letter-writing. Whether it is worth the while to continue so extensive a correspondence; & if it be not more proper to confine the exercise of my pen to some work which may be of general utility. I can not yet decide.

NINETEENTH WEEK

Sunday, 31st

PREFACE

This is the last day of the month of July, and I design to conclude this volume of my Journal, this day. It is of little use, therefore, to trace out any plan for the ensuing week—seeing it must be re-entered in the succeeding volume—or else be disjoined, in great measure, from it's proper connections. Thus, then, let it be dismist.

The notices of this day, the General conclusion to the volume, & the Index, with, perhaps, some other little matters, will fill up the remaining pages, & the new volume will fitly open with a new month. Had I not been the prince of indolence, this would long since have happened; & I should have now commenced a third, instead of a second volume.

LETTERS

To Mary S. Mumford.

A few days since, I received letters from you & Fanny, sent by a Mr. Owens; & a day or two after, a short letter from Thomas, by Mr. Mulligan. You have, probably, by this time, obtained my letters, which were forwarded, half written, by Mr. Phelps. I purposed to have written more lengthily, in pursuance of the subject commenced in my last; but I have had, since that time, very little opportunity to write; & none to send, if I had written. Mr. Isaacs,[78] by whom I expected to convey to you some books, as well as letters, left this place earlier than I expected, & much to my disappointment; & since his departure, I can not learn of any speedy conveyance to you. I shall, therefore, write at my leisure; & be ready to seize the first opportunity.

Your plan of reading is happily chosen, on many accounts; & will be particularly advantageous to Fanny. You will be able to direct her attention to proper objects, & to constrain her, in some sort, to examine sentiments & reasonings, which persons at her age, are extremely apt to hurry over, without reflection. I hope this method of study will be extended to other books, and other subjects, than those immediately before you. United exertions are exceedingly favorable to progress, whether in art or science. The intermingling, combination, &, if I may be allowed the expression, introsusception, of different tempers, understandings, & turns of thinking, serve mutually to support, encourage, & strengthen. Solitude, so favorable to reflection, so necessary a preparatory or aid to great undertakings, would fail of every useful effect if more than occasionally yielded to. Solitary exertion, unless preceeded by combined efforts, rarely produces any thing great. In the repose of retirement, the mind runs over, & contemplates previous conceptions, & carries them, in imagination, into operation; but it is in the lively intercourse of men, that the intellectual faculties are sharpened, that the abstract is made to assume practicability, that the schemes of solitude are brought into complete effect. How useful, too, are the young, to those of riper years, in all great occasions, whether of action, or of thought. Lively, inquisitive, impatient after knowlege, Youth is forever ascending to principles of things. Firm, sober, full of practice, Age, is steadily endeavouring to carry a principle into operation on every subject. Thus Youth, by it's vivacious survey of all things, rouzes & keeps up, & widens the contemplation of Age; & Age, by it's steadiness confines, & brings to use, the volatile spirit of Youth—ever ready to catch at principles, ever indolent in their patient investigation. Something like this mutual aid, this recoprocal re-action, may probably happen between you & Frances. She may force you to inquire, & you her to reflect.

Most parents are guilty of an extravagant estimation of the merits & value of their children; & this on the most selfish principles. A child is no better for being my child; nor any worse for being another's; & I should act very unreasonably to conduct towards a child of the same goodness of disposition, & degree of understanding with my own, in any measure different than towards my own—except in matters immediately dependent on that circumstance. It is the intrinsic worth of the object, not the extrinsic circumstances of the proprietor, by which we ought to be guided in our estimation. Some are so absurd as to carry this ridiculous measure of evaluation to the minutest thing about them. I dare say, you have seen people who never have any thing but what is the *very best*. Their horses, their houses, their lands, their coats, & even garters & sleeve-buttons, are superior, in every respect, to those of all other human beings. We are ready to laugh when this rate of judging is extended so far—tho' in fact, it is not a whit more irrational in this case, than in the former. This ought to make us careful not to over-rate the worth of our possessions. Not that I would insinuate any thing to the demerit of your boy. On the contrary—I really think him a fine, healthy, promising child; deserving of all proper affection; & that you act & think in relation to him, with suitable tenderness & rationality. The true basis of parental love, is the real worth of the child, & the probability that were it neglected by the parents, it would also be neglected by others. Were society properly organized, there would be but little scope for this passion —which, after all, is a great bar to general improvement. For parental love is only amiable from the end it answers—i. e. the preservation & instruction of the child. And were this, as it ought to be, the business of the whole community, there would be no necessity, or excuse, for the indulgence of it. In the mean time, however, that parent will best fulfill the duties resulting from parentage—who strives to render his offspring worthy of the national esteem. So may you do.

From the manner in which you have mentioned Mr. North—I am at a loss to know which of the brothers it is. Dr. North of Goshen, the elder, has three sons, who are practitioners of Medicine. One has been some time in the practice, & is thought to have the brightest parts —his name is Joseph. Another is said, & I believe with truth, to be the best informed & most dilligent—he has been to Phila.—& his name is Elisha. The third, when I knew him, did not promise to be very intelligent—his name, if I do not mistake, is Uzal, or Uzziel. He is the youngest of the three. I do not know whether Joseph or Lisha, is the eldest. If you have got either of the two eldest, you have been as fortunate as you can expect— & quite so, if it is Elisha who has settled with you. I should like to be informed if it is him—as I am somewhat acquainted with him; & should wish to write to him, when he becomes stationary among you.

My own affairs, about which you inquire in so sisterly a manner, have very little interesting in them. I am still groping along, in a blind & unsatisfactory manner. I can not yet be certain that my business is equal to my

---

[78] Probably Benjamin Isaacs (1764-1834; Yale 1781). He was a merchant who lived in Bedford, New York after 1789, member of the New York Assembly from Westchester County at various times from 1807 to 1818.

support; tho' I live very prudently. The last three months, if—(what is quite uncertain—) I receive all that I have earned, will just afford a bare maintenance. But, in the mean time, it is impossible to conjecture, with any assurance of being right, whether this will continue. And if it should, it will not remove the numerous embarrassments with which I am constantly obliged to contend. Courage—is something. Fortitude something more. They sometimes waver—but never long forsake me. So that I preserve pretty good spirits; & tho' my efforts are much restrained, by the narrowness & incompetency of my circumstances, I am not altogether deserving of the appellation "Idle fellow." Will this information suffice, for the present?

Our weather is very warm. It is fatiguing to write. If I have time, before an opportunity occurs of transmitting a letter to you, I shall resume the pen, & pursue the theme of my last letter. If not, let this do, till I have more leisure.

Adieu.

Sunday, July 31st. 1796.
Cedar St. No. 13. N. Y.   E. H. Smith.

To Samuel Smith.

Your letter of the 3rd inst. has been recd. some days. It came very directly. I hope I need not assure you that I read it with pleasure; or that I shall ever continue to communicate with you, with satisfaction.

The late failure in inducing the Indians to make a Treaty is, indeed, as you conceive of it, unfortunate; & no doubt owing to very improper conduct of people claiming the privileges of American citizens. I fear that, owing to the unhappy divisions which have lately become much embittered in your State, we can expect very little permanent tranquillity, in that quarter. The spirit of party seems to have attained to so prodigious a height as to threaten the peace of Georgia for a great number of years, & to introduce disquiet & dissention into every thing, of how little importance soever, in itself. But I hope the friends of good government & of law, will by & by gain the ascendancy; & that your future prosperity will be in proportion to your present calamities.

The settlement of St. Mary's is, as I suppose, the last within the southern boundary of the United States. I am desirous of obtaining some account of it. I wish to be informed how it is situated? What is the face of the country? What proportion of Cold, of Warm, of Dry, & of Wet weather, you have in the year? What are the occupations of the settlers? What [do] they cultivate? What state of improvement the lands are in? How much is cleared up? Whether the waters are swift, or slow, or stagnant? How many inhabitants they are? What sort of accommodations they have? What is their mode of living? What diseases are most common, & at what seasons? What proportion of deaths, & births, to the number? What proportion of Blacks to Whites? & from what quarter the winds generally blow, during the greater part of the year, or at different seasons? Any information which you can give me, concerning any of these particulars, will be exceedingly acceptable; & in return I shall be ready to communicate to you any information in my power. If there is any sensible, well-informed, Physician settled near you, I will thank you to let me know; & also send me his name & address. It will be very agreable to me to open a correspondence with such a man, in your part of the country; & might be advantageous to him, considering my situation.

All our friends were well, the last time I heard from them. You will be grieved to learn, if you have not been informed of it before, that your friend Aaron Catlin is dead. Poor young man! he died of the Yellow Fever, at Kingston, in Jamaica, a few months ago—just as he had formed a very excellent mercantile connection.

Farewell.

July 31. 1796.
Cedar St. No. 13. N. Y.   E. H. Smith.

MEMORANDA, 127

Wrote the two preceeding letters, & transcribed the last. A visit from John Johnson. Read several articles in the New Annual Register. Between three & four, in the afternoon—took a long, devious, & pleasant walk, which terminated at Mr. Webster's. I stayed there two hours. I returned by the way of Mr. Roulet's, where I spent two hours, also, very agreably—& talking horrid French.

CONCLUSION

To a person as ardent in his expectations of being uniformly disposed to carry his resolutions into complete effect, as he was in entering into them, the Conclusion of this First Volume of my Journal would be a source of disappointment & chagrin. For myself, accustomed as I am to observe daily & numerous marks of mental instability & imbecillity in myself, I receive it with all becoming moderation. I may, perhaps, be allowed to say that "It is better than was to be expected."

To comment lengthily on my life, as herein exhibited, I have neither leisure, nor patience. I can only remark that something, not altogether vain has been affected, during the last four months; & that, if all has not been accomplished which ought to have been, but little has been done which deserves severe reprehension, & marked contempt. Sins of Commission do not cluster around my life; it is in Sins of Omission that I am chiefly prodigal & blame-deserving. This serves to display the real state & cause of all my feelings, which are not attributable to any malignity of temper or disposition, to any pertinacious continuance in known & acknowleged vices, but solely, or principally, to the influence of evil habits—early formed, long indulged in, & still powerful. If I know my own heart, it beats with a love as fervent for mankind as that of any man. All it's wishes are for the promotion of knowlege, virtue, & happiness. And this, too, in no narrow, cramped, selfish way; in no one method, more than another, because it is my method, or because I think it right. No person forms more lively, more disinterested, more generous, wishes, or contrives more plans for the propagation & diffusion of human well-being. Thus every thing which depends on principle is not unfavorable to virtue. But, when I come to speak of my actual conduct, of my habits, it is most unfortunately true—that tho' my principles may be gaining some slow & scarce perceptible ascendancy over them—they operate to render of small effect every resolution that I have taken, every design which I have formed. So that I am almost tempted to coincide in the extravagant adage—That a boy had better be busied in mischief, than be idle. For the disposition to mischief may be corrected, but it is next to impossible to restore persevering activity to him who has lost it by long indulgence in sloth, & to communicate industry where early habits of indolence have been allowed to proceed without impediment.

That my convictions of the duty of continued & vigilant endeavors after knowlege, & unremitted exertions for the good of all men, together with the resolutions founded thereon, are not altogether ineffectual, I think, notwithstanding all its defects, this Volume exhibits a proof. An improvement on every preceeding tome it certainly is, as much for the copiousness of it's contents, as for their variety. And tho' it is wanting, in almost every week, in marks of that constant pointing towards general utility which the history of every good man's, of every man's, mind should display; yet, more of the useful, more of consideration, in all things, for actual usefulness, is observable, if I do not deceive myself, than heretofore. How little soever my actions correspond with my resolutions, it will be seen that my thoughts, & correspondent feelings, are more steadily turned towards the subject of doing good, & active in aspirations after the power of so doing, than formerly. To the drowning wretch, a straw appears as an anchor of safety; to the bewildered & nightly pilgrim, the lambent flame that plays over the stagnant pool, seems as the beacon of approaching security; insubstantial & glimmering as is the encouragment which the preceeding observations allow me, still I can not but derive some hope, some momentary vigour, from them. I long for the delights of knowlege, I pant for the repose of virtue, too fervently & too constantly, to be yet willing to relinquish my expectations of either. Dim, doubtful, & disheartening as is the prospect, the term proposed to all my exertions is too radiant in glory, too bountiful in blessings, not to excite resolution after resolution, determination after determination, project after project, for it's attainment. But these, perhaps, are reflections more suited to the commencement than the conclusion of a volume. I will, then, indulge in them, at present, no longer.

Whatever character the future volumes of my Journal may deserve, I shall not be able to look back upon the present one, with emotions of unmingled satisfaction. The imperfect manner in which the purposes exprest in the introduction, have been adhered to, & filled up, can not fail to arrest from me a sigh of regret, how imperfect soever a later period of my life may find me. At the same time, when I compare this volume with those which have gone before it, & especially when I look around & in the (shall I call it becoming, or pardonable?) confidence of my heart, view myself in relation to my fellow-beings, no future period of humiliation & vice will be able altogether to stifle in my bosom a sentiment of partial self-approbation. Feeble as will be my beam of joy, it will nevertheless diffuse some pleasing light over the dungeon of my mind.

> Peace! then thou little, tremulous, anxious, slave!
> That beat'st so lively 'gainst thy prison walls.
> Ten thousand foes combine to work thee woe:
> Dark, sullen Cares; grim Discontents; and Doubts;
> And Fears, and wayward Hopes, and Wishes, fraught
> With self-destroying contrarieties.
> O'er thee Remorse, the child of Youthful Guilt,
> Shakes his vindictive scourge; and Ignorance,
> And Indolence unite, with treacherous guile,
> To blast thy budding joys. Yet, fear thee not!
> False & relentless are thy foes to thee?
> Be true unto thyself! Bear up! be firm!
> May this gentle ray that now, tremblingly,
> Visits, & plays around thy cell, cheer thee;
> Sustain thy purpose, animate thy zeal,
> And make thee bold. Peace, then, thou little Slave!

[Omitted here, seven manuscript pages: "Index."]

Notebook No. 4: August–November, 1796

Ecce iterum Crispinus!

Juvenal.

JOURNAL. 1796. AUGUST.

INTRODUCTION

"Truth must be sought with a simple heart"[79]—saith the tender, the eloquent, the fascinating St. Pierre. It is no less true that all our schemes of life, plans of study, and determinations to action, should be formed, entered upon, & pursued, with simplicity of heart. "A simple heart never pretended to understand what it did not understand, or to believe what it did not believe. It neither helps us to deceive ourselves, nor to deceive others afterwards." Admirable description of that spirit which leads us to the prudent & temperate exercise of hope, to the sincere love & search of truth, to the ready & undaunted acceptation of it, to the free acknowlegement of all former errors, & to the maintaining, cultivation, & diffusion of all we know, & all we enjoy. O sweet Simplicity! eternal Truth! Ye who, "like the dew of heaven," *that ye may be preserved pure,* require to "be received into a pure vessel"[80]—now purify my heart, enlighten my understanding, sustain my courage, & animate & strengthen all my energies!

Were it possible to foresee what be [the] event, much mortification might no doubt, be spared to me, on the score of broken resolutions, and abortive plans. It is my earnest wish not to exceed in projection what I may accomplish in practice. But how can I tell? All my present designs seem to have been well weighed. All of them present so many charms; so many allurements to execution, that I can not convince myself that I shall altogether neglect any of them. And, after all, is it not best to aim high, even if we attain not to the point proposed? Shall we not be the more likely to reach some noble height, than if our humble expectations were bounded by a narrow & low limit? It is, indeed, most probable, that, of all my projects none will be totally overlooked. But such is the instability of my temper, so little is there of perseverance in it, that it was rash, & neglectful of the dictates of Simplicity, to promise myself a wide & active industry. I shall confine myself, at present, to the tracing a simple Outline of those objects towards which I trust this Volume will prove my attention to have been directed.

1. I purpose soon to commence the forming of an Abstract of all the accounts I can procure, relative to those great Epidemics—as they are called—which have been attended with singular mortality: such as the Plague—Yellow Fever—Billious Fever—Putrid Fever —Dysentery—&c. &c. with the view of discovering, if possible whether they are not, as I suspect, & have long suspected, different modifications of one Disease. I shall commence with the Plague of Athens, as described by Thucydides.

2. I design to pursue the composition of the Sonnets, addrest to my sister Fanny.

3. I intend to undertake the composition of an Utopia —for the purpose of shewing what improvements are compatible with the present condition of man, in our country.

4. I mean to write the characters & anecdotes of my Friends &c. as planned in the Introduction to the preceeding volume of my Journal—& hitherto neglected.

Further than these, I have no present plans of composition, other than those already engaged in, in the course of my Correspondence—which will be spiritedly continued.

My Medical Reading will be chiefly confined to the plan marked out above; & I expect to unite the study of French with that of Medicine; by the perusal of several Professional Works in that Language.

Such are the views with which I enter on this the Second volume of my Journal—to which I have none other to add, unless, indeed, I should prosecute the project of a Medical Repository—concerning which I have many doubts.

All these studies, all these closet exertions, must terminate in the extension of physical & moral aid to man, or all are imperfect & abortive.

First Week

Monday, 1st

PREFACE

After what has already been written in this volume, after referring to the date regularly commencing a new week, in the preceeding volume, it will be unnecessary to say more in this place—than—That it is not probable that this week will allow me to effect much. My intention being to visit Amboy on Thursday, I shall rather be busied in feeling, than at leisure to describe. In the mean time, I have many little avocations from thought & composition.

---

[79] Bernadin St. Pierre; this may be a quotation from his *Etudes de la Nature* (Paris, 1784), translated by Henry Hunter as *First Study of Nature* (London, 1796). Something like this quotation can be found in any number of places in the book, but a quick rereading failed to locate the precise language.

[80] Not found.

MEMORANDA, 1

A few medical visits. Commenced, & made considerable progress in the Second Volume of Fourcroy's Chemistry. Walked; made a number of calls; drank tea with Geo. M. Woolsey; & spent an hour at neighbor Boyd's. Recd. a letter from William Buel; & a note from C. B. Brown—by which I learn that he is in Amboy. Mr. Lovegrove is up from there. He is well; & left his family, and all friends, well.

MEMORANDA, 2

Tuesday, 2nd

Cursorily looked over Jackson's account of the Remitting Fever of Jamaica.[81] At the Hospital. Called on Dr. Mitchill. At the Monthly Examination of the Trustees of the African Free School, for the Scholars. The children improve under the care of their new teacher. Wrote the Conclusion to the First Volume of my Journal; and the Introduction to this Volume; & made the Index to the First Volume. Walked; made several calls; drank tea, & walked, with Mrs. Woolsey; & terminated the evening at her house. Received a very flattering & encouraging letter from Dr. Rush.

MEMORANDA, 3

Wednesday, 3rd

No small part of the day spent running round in a fruitless search after money, where I ought to have found it. In the after part of the day, I received enough to answer all my exigencies, whence & where I least expected it.

I have made a reasonable advance in Fourcroy.

Spent the evening at Mr. Kent's, very pleasantly. His brother there. I dined at Boyd's—& had a visit from Mr. Lovegrove.

["Thomas O'Hara Croswell" which followed the above entry now appears early in the text. See pp. 40-42.]

MEMORANDA, 4

Thursday, 4th

I determined to pay my long-projected visit to Amboy, & to set off to-day. I called on Dr. Mitchill, to engage him to prescribe for me, at the Hospital, in my absence. There I prescribed this day. It was twelve before I was ready to depart; it was the hour fixed by the boatmen; Lovegrove called upon me; & we went to the dock. We were detained more than an hour. We then crost the bay, to Staten-Island; &, after some further delay, sat off, in the Stage, for Amboy; whither we arrived between seven & eight, in the evening. Mrs. L. was out, on a visit. L. went after, & conducted her home. She welcomed me, with great cordiality. Some company came in—& among others, Mr. & Mrs. Dunlap, have stayed long. After tea, & a little rest, I went up to Dunlap's—embraced & was embraced by C. B. Brown. I have never seen him look so well—tho' he tells me of his having been unwell this season. I returned to L's, after a short stay with my other friends.

Sophy Pierpont, the little girl that I procured for Mrs. L. & who behaved perfectly to her satisfaction for a considerable time, has lately given them much uneasiness. We sat up late to talk the matter over, & it was decided that during my stay, Sophy should be called in, &, after Mrs. L. had made an ample statement of her several errors, that I should reprove & advise her.

MEMORANDA, 5

Friday, 5th

I rose in tolerable season; breakfasted; & after breakfast, went up to Dunlap's. It was a fine, clear, cool day, & we took a long & pleasant ramble.

Amboy has lost none of it's charms, since last year; & the society of the same friends gave it an interest in my mind, new & considerable. We conversed, as may be supposed, on our wonted themes. Man, Morals, Politics, &c. I opened to Charles some views of, at least, a temporary settlement in New York. He has been idle. A few pages in his Journal, & those, too, written since his arrival at Amboy, are all that he had to shew me.

I dined at Lovegrove's. We had some hours of agreable conversation after dinner. Then, we all went up to Dunlap's. There was company there. We took tea. Mr. & Mrs. L. walked. Charles & I stole upstairs, where we looked over my Journal together. After the company went away, Mr. & Mrs. D. joined us. When I returned to L's, Mrs. L. was a-bed & quite unwell. She is near lying-in, & had exerted herself too much in the course of the day. I relieved her pains, & procured her sleep, in the course of two hours, by means of Opium. I sat up till late to read the seventh vol. of Helen M. Williams's Letters.

MEMORANDA, 6

Saturday, 6th

Mrs. L. was better this morning, & devoted it to repose. I finished the volume of H. M. Williams's Letters, which I began to read last evening. I also looked over some numbers of the Monthly Review, for 1795, which I had not before seen.

After calling at Dunlap's—we—Dunlap, Brown, & myself—took a walk. Conversation various. We seemed agreed, after a long discussion, that but one idea could be received by the mind, at the same instant.

As we were walking along, I began to muse on a tale in Miss Williams's Letters, of an old gentleman, in the neighborhood of Vaucluse, his niece & son—ruined by the horrible blood-hounds of Robespierre. It struck me as affording, in connection with other circumstances, the basis of a good drama—the outline of which my imagination imperfectly sketched, as follows.

---

[81] *A Treatise on the Fevers of Jamaica with some Observations on the Intermittent Fevers of America* (London, 1791).

Suppose a Man, animated by the purest spirit of benevolent Philosophy, to obtain, by some means, the place of Commissary in one of the Departments—i.e. be placed in the situation of Lebon, Carrier, &c. I suppose this to happen after the Department had been subjected to the fury of some minor villain; & before the invention of *Noyades, fusillades,* &c. Our Commissary's plan is to arrest & imprison, that he may save. His prophetic spirit tells him that the Decemvirs must fall, shortly; & that if he can contrive to preserve their victims for a few months, or weeks, the justice of the Nation will then restore them to their homes & fortunes. From the moment of his arrival at the place of his Mission, he new organizes the Tribunals, after the manner of Lebon, with persons who he brings with him, & on whose integrity he can therefore rely. He puts a stop to most single executions. As the denunciations & arrests are very numerous, some instances of persons deserving punishment occur, these are publicly tried & expiate their crimes. But a report is caused to be spread, that numerous victims are recd. into the prisons, & never more heard of. Mean time the inferior blood-hounds are busy. Men, women, & children, are dragged from their homes, on the slightest pretence. The cruelty of these wretches would lead them to put their prisoners to immediate death. Our Commissary derides such feeble vengeance—speaks to them of the Noyades of Carrier, of his treacherous Feasts, &c. &c. To conceal his real designs the more effectually, he causes an immense vessel, on the plan of Carrier, to be constructed. He also causes hideous excavations to be made in the court-yard of the prisoners. His addresses to the people breathe the spirit of patriotism; & the young men of the Requisition are eager to depart. Among these is the Lover of Vaucluse. During all this period his prisoners are always spoken to, by the Commissary, with tenderness; & perfectly well treated. They, however, detest him the more—knowing how such arts have terminated. The Jacobins, too, are deceived, & admire the zeal, & address of their supposed leader.

The Drama may be supposed to open before the arrival of the Commissary in his Department. His first business is to dispatch the young men of the Requisition. Our Lover is torn from the arms of his mistress, & the house of his father—& there is interrupted that picture of felicity with which the piece commences. The lover goes with a conviction of the Commissary's goodness. In the mean time, various incidents occur. The father & Mistress of the young man are denounced, arrested, & placed in prison. Being of Noble extraction, & the character of the Commissary being now supposed, universally, to be like that of his employers, a report easily gains credit that the new prisoners are massacred in private. The exterior conduct of the Commissary countenances this belief, while, in fact, he causes them to be treated with all possible kindness. Their fears, notwithstanding, are boundless. The Lover obtains a furlow. He hastens home, & finds all desolate. He hears of the unprovoked arrestation, & supposed death, of his friends. He determines on revenge. His return from the army affords him a pretext for a private conference with the Commissioner; who suspects his purpose, & is prepared. An interesting scene ensues. The Lover, tho' torn with contending passions, attempts to poinard the Commissary & is seized. He is ordered to be imprisoned; & is told that his punishment shall be inflicted the next day, & in a summary manner. This proves to be, in restoring the delinquent to his friends, & a full exposition of the true character of the Commissioner; who, at this moment receives the news of the Revolution of the Ninth of Thermidor, enlarges his prisoners, arrests the cut-throats, & proclaims the triumph of Humanity.

Such is the imperfect outline which was suggested to me, in the moment, & which I immediately unfolded to my friends, who bestowed on it marks of approbation.

I dined at Lovegrove's. After dinner I read them the passage which I had translated from Riouffe. Mrs. L. asked me if I had not published something on the Fever of 1795; & exprest a curiosity to see what I had written. I read her some passages, from the manuscript in the first volume of my Journal. Her spirits were somewhat heavy; my reading seemed to amuse her; & I continued to gratify her by the communications of several passages from my Journal. The sentiments were not uncongenial; the confidence was consolatory. This alone made the articles of value, & induced the communications. A visitor coming in, I went to Dunlap's. G. M. Woolsey arrived. He went, with Dunlap, to Mr. Parker's. Mrs. D., Charles, & I, went into the next neighbor's—to see Mrs. Turell & Mrs. Brown, with whom I stayed, part of the time, when first at Amboy: i. e. I slept in their house.

We spent the evening pleasantly, at Dunlap's. It seemed more like the Friendly Club, than any Saturday evening in many weeks. Three of the members being to-gether, & a friend, who had been a frequent visitant in 1795.

POSTSCRIPT

Notwithstanding the doubt exprest in the scanty Preface to the week, it is evident, on the face of the volume, that something has been effected. More, indeed, than was expected; but, as will be shewn in a proper place, not so much as appears.

Altho' I am exceedingly weak & irresolute, as every page of my Journal evinces, yet I am ready, at times, to believe that strength is certainly, tho' slowly, acquired. In this opinion my friends, who are present, encourage me. They will not allow that I am quite as idle as I am persuaded is true. They, indeed, judge from these records. Alas! they are ignorant to how little effect are all my studies. They know not that attentiveness is almost wholly wanting to me, when I read; & that many weeks of application lay up for me but a few, solitary, & nearly useless, recollections. While my eyes are fixed on the volume before me, while my tongue articulates the words, my mind traverses distant & disconnected regions of fancy or reality, busies itself with ten thousand trifles, & returns to the subject before it exhausted & unimproved.

Second Week

Sunday, 7th

PREFACE

This week like the last, is destined to be subjected to too many interruptions, for me to indulge a rational hope of much regular progress in study. While at Amboy, in the society of friends so dearly beloved, & with my mind busied in the various investigation & exposition of moral truths, I ought not, & do not, regret it. Their conversation is too valuable, their united aid in this sublime occupation too rare, to make me hesitate for a single moment in prefering my present occupation, to all that a solitary application to professional studies may probably, in a like length of time, produce & realize. From conferences such as these, new intellectual, as well as moral, energy is derived; a fresh spring is given to every noble exertion; & a bolder, firmer point of support is formed for all future benevolent undertakings. "It is good for us to be here."

MEMORANDA, 7

I rose in good season, for I went early to bed. As Mrs. L. was tasting of that repose so necessary for her, & L. busied in domestic matters, I was left to the quiet reading of several articles in the last Appendix of the Monthly Review for 1795. This No. is uncommonly valuable. I was delighted with the Extract from the Conclusion of Wieland's "Agathon." It is very nearly conformable to my philosophy. Girtanner's History of the French Revolution must be valuable, notwithstanding it's many defects. The Reviewers do not exactly agree with me, in respect to certain parts of Mde. Roland's Memoirs. Stolberg's Travels must be worth having. The extracts are all pleasing; & that concerning the effects of the Earthquake, in Sicily, p. 541, contains an interesting physiological fact.

G. M. Woolsey returned to New York. Dunlap, Brown, & I went to walk. Was it this day, or yesterday, that we revisited the three-partile Tree, emblem of our friendship, which we discovered, & made our own, last year? We had some doubt which stock belonged to each. For each of us had fixed upon his own. We readily agreed that the slenderest one, & which grew in the middle, must be Charles's; &, after many examinations, the reason of size determined me that the westermost must be mine.

This proves to be the fact.

We dined together, at Dunlap's. We walked after dinner; & I then, returned to Lovegrove's. Mrs. L. felt in tolerable spirits. We talked, & I read her several articles from the Review. Mrs. Hobson, an English lady, spending the summer in Amboy—Dunlap & his wife, & Charles, agreable to previous engagements, drank tea with us. A young englishman, of the name of Palmer, came in afterwards. They all departed seasonably.

It was agreed that the conversation with Sophy should be held this evening. Lovegrove sent her up, & disappeared for the night. We talked, like friends, to this child, two hours. She appeared much affected; made many promises of amendment; & was dismissed. This was about nine o'clock. Mrs. L. & I conversed till twelve. She read me a most remarkable fine letter, from her friend Mrs. Briggs, formerly Miss Norton. In this letter mention is made of a promising young genius, of Mrs. B's acquaintance, whose name is Coldridge; & who is soon to publish a volume of Poems.

I am more & more imprest with the conviction that Mrs. L. is very unhappy, & destined so to be. Never were minds less allied than hers & Lovegrove's. She took a melancholly satisfaction in dwelling on the scenes she had once enjoyed, in England, & on some slight & transient pleasures of the same nature, in New York. Perhaps she has been disappointed in L's capacity. Certainly, she is now convinced that he is wholly incapable to make her happy. This she did not tell me. But she cannot conceal it. He has a few ordinary good qualities; he is the father of her child; & she is soon to become the mother of a second. These are ties. But he has no taste, education, knowlege, refinement, delicacy, or manners. How every act, every word, every idiot look, of his, wears on her keen, wounded, & diseased sensibility! They can never be happy together; never happy in America. Perhaps, after many years, were he dead, & she united to a man such as she ought to love, & amid her early friends, her agitated spirit might taste the sweets of domestic repose. But will this ever be?

MEMORANDA, 8

Monday, 8th

It was quite late when I retired to bed, & my sleep was interrupted by a sudden & uncomfortable diarrhea. I slept late. Dunlap called on me, a minute, before breakfast; & went away in expectation of seeing me again. Mrs. L. was well this morning. Mr. Palmer breakfasted with us. I left the table hastily, to see when the boat would be ready, for N. Y. I found them going off; & was obliged to jump in, without having a moment to bid adieu to the Lovegrove's, or my friends on the Hill.

The day was pleasant; the tide in our favor, but not a breath of air. We were necessitated to row to Elizabeth-Town Point, fourteen miles. We arrived, without an instant to spare. A light breeze now sprung up; we had the advantage of the other tide; & we sported thro' the Kills—as the strait between Staten-Island & the Northern Jersey shore, is called. In the intervals of labor, I amused myself with Montesquieu's "Grandeur & Decadence &c".[82] When we came into the bay, the

---

[82] Baron de la Brède, *Considérations sur les causes de la grandeur et de la décadence des Romains* (1734).

wind slackened, & the tide opposed us. We landed a little after 5 P.M.—after eight hours sail.

I drank tea at Mrs. Miller's. Mr. Miller & I visited Miss Mason. I have been extremely negligent in this respect; & this is the first visit in more than a year, as I believe. The talk was lively, but trivial. It approached to conversation but once, & only, then, for a few minutes.

Made some calls. Was at H. Johnson's. All well. Has not heard from William in my absence. John gone to Philadelphia.

No professional calls have been made on me, during my absence. Bad, & good.

MEMORANDA, 9

Tuesday, 9th

At the Hospital. A fire broke out, as I was returning. I attempted to make my peaceful way thro' the people, that I might go to the assistance of a widow lady, lately moved into the city, & near the fire. A surly fellow, who pretended to suppose I meant to be idle, but whose real motive appeared to be a desire to disoblige one who was somewhat better drest than himself, without any intimation of his purpose, came behind me, & dashed a bucket of water on me. I lost an hour in drying my clothes. Another hour was spent in fruitless attempts to gain a meeting of the Trustees of the African School.

When I went to Amboy, I had not completed the Article "Thomas O'Hara Croswell." I continued my journal in a little pocket memorandum book. I now finished that article; & transcribed the notes on Thursday & Friday.

In my absence, Mr. Roulet left several french pamphlets. Some I looked over last evening, others to-day. The titles of those which I have read, are—"Quelques Reflexions sur les Fugitives Francais, depuis le 2 Septembre. Par J. *Marchena*"—a light performance; "Rapport &c pour examiner la conduite du representant du peuple Joseph Lebon—par J. B. Quirot"—which fully establishes the villainy of the monster Lebon; "Rapport &c. par Lakanal, sur les livies élémentaires &c" which speaks well of several new performances in this line, which will probably be published; & "Réponse de Guadet, a Robespierre &c" a sensible, and, in some parts, eloquent oration.

Called at Kent's. Spent the evening at S. Johnson's. John returned. He saw Miss S. Morton, & the Miss Smiths, at Princeton, who send compliments, & are well. Recd. a letter from John Williams.

MEMORANDA, 10

Wednesday, 10th

Was unwell in the night; of consequence slept late. I attribute my intestinal disturbances to change of diet, while at Amboy. If so, they will cease in a day or two, now that I have returned to simple fare.

I have devoted all the morning to bringing my Journal, regularly, to this date. It is now effected.

I read the two remaining pamphlets of thise left by Mr. Roulet. One, intituled—"L'Éducation, cause éloignée, et souvent méme, Cause Prochaine destoutes les Maladies"—par F. Lanthenas—an agreable, but superficial, performance; the other, "De la Tragédie Grecque &c." Par A. Auger, a sensible, well-written, & satisfactory Essay.

I called at Mrs. Miller's, & found that Dr. Miller had arrived. Dr. Mitchill was also there. I saw Dr. Rush's 4th vol. Dr. Miller informed me that he was to set off, on a journey to the eastward, to-morrow. He has never been in New England. I promised him some introductory letters. Accordingly, I came home, & wrote letters of introduction for him, to Dr. Kollack, at New Port; Drs. Hopkins & Cogswell, & Theodore Dwight, at Hartford; Dr. Osborn & Mr. Alsop, Middletown; & Revd. Dr. Dwight, New Haven.

I drank tea, & spent the principal part of the evening, at Mrs. Woolsey's.

I have not felt very well any part of this day.

MEMORANDA, 11

Thursday, 11th

At the Hospital. Called on Dr. Mitchill, & sat an hour. Felt unwell, & unable to study. Turned over a volume of the New Annual Register till dinner. Felt better. Made some progress in Fourcroy. Dr. Mitchill here some time. Was at Mr. Watson's. S. M. Hopkins sailed to-day, for Europe. Drank tea at Charles Adams's. They had a daughter born on Sunday evening last. Spent the evening at Kent's.

LETTERS

To William Buel.

I have been out of town, for a few days, to inhale a little fresh air, or your letter of the 18th ulto. would have recd. an earlier answer. I felt the less anxious about the delay, as, the day I went into the country, the Letter of the Health-Officer was published, which contained all the information you could wish respecting the actual condition of this place.

The last two or three weeks of June, & the first week of July, were extremely sultry, with no rains. The consequence was, that we had some cases of Yellow Fever, and a prospect of it's becoming more extensive & virulent than last year. But the rains, & the cool weather, which soon commenced, & have continued, with little interruption, to the present time, have rendered New York as healthy as it is possible for so large a place to be, under like circumstances, & at this season. Indeed, I question whether any of the country towns have fewer cases of dangerous fevers than this.

You speak of the prevalence of Dysentery & Fever among you. In a few cases, in our Hospital, they have evidently been the same disease; the two states alternating with each other. For my part, I have for some years, considered them as the same, or depending on the same cause—only, that, in one case, it is the intestines, or the lymphatic system, perhaps—& in the other, the sanguiferous system, that is effected. I wish you to observe, minutely, with a view to this opinion. The same general remedies, if it is true, must be successful, in both states of the disease. I have another reason for wishing you to observe, & record your observations. I think, as Mr. Webster has relinquished his plan of continuing his Collection, of taking it up myself, on a far more extensive scale, & publishing an annual volume; the principal object of which will be the preserving & collecting of the materials for a History of the Diseases of America, as they appear in the several seasons. If I prosecute this scheme, I shall give you early notice; but, at all events, I wish you to attend to the above request; for our mutual private benefit, if for no other person's.

Dr. Rush has lately published the Fourth Volume of his Inquiries. It contains an account of the Yellow Fever in Phila. in 1794—a dissertation on the Proximate Cause of Fever—& a Defence of Blood-letting. I have had but a few minutes, as yet, to look at it.

I hope to be able to send you the first vol. of Zoonomia,[83] some time next month.

You have, doubtless, recd. a copy of Mr. Webster's Collection, which I forwarded, for you, by the way of Lichfield.

Let me hear from you speedily.

Thursday, August 11. 1796.
Cedar St. No. 13. New York.   E. H. Smith.

MEMORANDA, 12

Friday, 12th

Wrote the preceeding letter last evening. Some time since, Mr. Roulet left with me a Work, in the latin tongue, intituled "Origines Typographicæ. Gerardo Meerman Auctore." Printed at the Hague, in 1765. I have looked over this book this morning. It must be valuable, no doubt. But my ignorance of the latin language is such as to render it next to impossible to derive much benefit from the reading, even if I had, what I have not, leisure for the perusal. The author determines in favor of *Laurentius Joannes filius*—(in plain english, John Lawrence Junr.) as the first typographer; & fixes on 1440 as the era of the discovery. There are several very curious specimens of antient printing annexed to this work.

Wrote the succeeding letters, & transcribed those to Wm. Buel, Evelyn Pierpont, & Fanny Smith—& also the first Sonnet to Fanny Smith, from the first vol. of my Journal.

[83] Erasmus Darwin (1731-1802). He discussed the "laws" governing organic life; his work embodied evolutionary principles in which he anticipated errors of Lamarck. Smith liked to browse in this book and may refer to sections of it without naming the title; for example, "Nutrientia" (entry for October 20, 1796), a section in Vol. II, Part III, under "Materia Medica," Article 1.

Wm. Johnson returned to-day, from Albany, &c. in high health, & good spirits, after a remarkable pleasant voyage, tour, & visit. We dined at Seth's.

I made some further progress in Fourcroy's Chemistry.

Walked with J. Mulligan, in the Triangle; & went home with him, & spent part of the evening. Came home, & looked over some part of the Annual Register.

This day has been quite sultry. Of consequence I have felt incapable of much exertion; & the more so, as, since my return from Amboy, I have not been very well. I think, however, that I am in the mending order.

LETTERS

To Evelyn Pierpont.

I have been doubtful whether to answer your last letter, or not, which is the reason you have not heard from me before. I have at length, determined to write to you; and I hope what I now write will leave no room for any further misunderstanding between us.

You best know with what feelings your letter, of which I complained, was written. I can only declare how it appeared to me; & I freely tell you, that your last letter has not done much to wear off the impression made by the first. But, be that as it may, I have no resentment against you; & shall not be one grain the less disposed to render you, your child, or any of your family, all reasonable service in my power. It is my principle, Mr. Pierpont, to do people all the good I can, whether they do me good in return, or not. If they do me evil, I make it a point to tell them of it; but, whether they amend, or not, I do not think myself at liberty to alter my own rule of conduct. If I do any man evil, whether the act of ignorantly, or intentionally, performed, let it be proved to me that I have done wrong, & I hope I shall never want the justice, & courage, to make him every reparation in my power. If I have wronged you, I certainly am sorry for it, & would request your forgiveness. That I have wronged you I confess I am not convinced; but this is a subject which I am desirous of forgetting.

The design of this letter is, principally, to inform you that I have been to Amboy, & have seen your child. She is well, & has been well—and tells me that she is pleased with her situation. Those with whom she lives, have found some reason to be dissatisfied with Sophy's conduct. This you probably know, before this time—as you have doubtless recd. Mrs. Lovegrove's letter—or rather postscript to Sophy's letter. I had a long conversation with Sophy, & talked to her as if she had been my child. She owned that she had done what was laid to her charge; seemed to be a good deal affected by what I said to her; and promised to amend. I hope that the next account you will have from her, will be much for the better. Mr. & Mrs. L. will not use harsh means; they will use all possible tenderness to reclaim her; and if this is not effectual, I have advised them to send her home.

If at any time you wish to write to Sophy, you will direct to her "At Mr. Lovegrove's, in Perth Amboy"—& if your letter is put in the Post Office, she will be sure to get it.

Friday, August 12. 1796.
Cedar St. No. 13. N. York.   E. H. Smith.

To Fanny Smith.

Want of a proper opportunity of sending to you, has left me silent so long. The hope of some speedy, tho' hitherto, unknown conveyance, determines me now to write.[84] My letter will not be lengthy, for I have little to say. I can do no more than repeat my pressing incitations to continued reading, reflection, observation, & composition. For all these your situation is happily adapted, more so, perhaps, than it will be in future; and you will be inexcusable if you let so good an opportunity pass unemployed.

Your plan of study is well chosen; I have bestowed many commendations upon it, in my letter to Mary; I trust you will pursue it with unabating vigor; & that you will derive distinguished advantages from it. I am desirous, in the mean while, that you should devote some portion of your time to the study of Morals; the most important, but most neglected, of all the Sciences. Your morality is, probably, like that of mankind in general, more a matter of habit, than of reason. It ought to be both. You should be habitually good; but your habits should be founded on a clear conception, & determined conviction, of their propriety & fitness to produce good. To lead you to inquiries of this sort, I send you a question, which I wish you to answer in your next letter. You must not only give me your opinion, but also the reasons on which that opinion is founded. Now, I desire you to think on the question & let me, have the result of your own meditations, without consulting your brother & sister. The question is this—"Will any thing justify a deviation from truth?"—or—"Is it right ever to tell a falsehood?"

I am about to address a series of Sonnets to you, to encourage you in the unremitting pursuit of knowlege & virtue. I inclose the first. May they not fail of their intended effect!

                        My love to you.

August, Friday, 12. 1796
Cedar St. No. 13. N. York.   E. H. Smith.

---

[84] As early as 1789 a post-rider passed through Litchfield on his route between New Haven and Lenox, Massachusetts. In 1790 a post-rider carried letters between Litchfield and New York every two weeks. In 1791 the post went once a week (once a fortnight in the winter) between New York, Litchfield, and Hartford. In 1792 the President approved a Post Office bill establishing a post road between New York and Hartford that included Litchfield. A government post office was then established in Litchfield in that year but it was poorly patronized. Why Smith chose to trust his mail to individual travelers to Litchfield or its environs is not clear. Economy may have been the governing reason. See Kilbourne, *Sketches and Chronicles*, pp. 167-169.

To John Williams.

At length I have recd. a letter from you, and **one** which has given me more pleasure, on several accounts, than any which you have written to me before. We have, now, fairly got out of the old track of love, matrimony, & nonsense, & may lay our account with deriving some benefit from these communications, sparing & interrupted as they may be.

I rejoice to see you engaged in something useful; & hope that your example may have some effect in banishing a detestable spirit, the offspring of prejudice, ignorance, & selfishness, still too prevalent in our native State. You will see to what this points when I remind you how many times we have heard this reply—"I shall never live to enjoy it"—when we have asked people why they did not cultivate fruit trees. Were I the founder of a State, the streets of every town, & the roads in every direction, should blush with fruit, bend down with nuts, & spread forth in shade & timber. A word might effect this—& the health, happiness, & safety of thousands be promoted & established thereby.

I am not certain that I can afford you any immediate information; relative to the business of Engraffing. But it will not be difficult to furnish you with the best authors on the subject—if you will commission me to purchase them for you. I am not sure that I know what you mean by the Plum stock. I have seen the finest peaches raised, in Mr. Reeve's garden, at Lichfield, from Graffs set in the stock of the wild Thorn-Plum. But the difficulty, I take it, is in the operation of Engraffing; which has been represented to me, as somewhat nice, requiring judgement, & in general very badly performed. If you mean to have very fine Cherries, they must be Engraffed on Stocks of our wild Black-Cherry, otherwise, they soon degenerate—& are liable to be killed by the severe cold of our winters.

I can not altogether concur with you in some of your opinions—or rather some of *the* opinions exprest towards the conclusion of your letter. Every reason which can make it worth the care of europeans to bestow much cultivation on their lands, exists for the people in Wethersfield. Land is very dear, & laborers are very few. It is of the utmost importance, therefore, to remedy this mischief by obtaining as much from this small quantity of land, & by means of these few laborers, as, if laborers were plenty, might be gathered from much land. The less shall you have to work in, the more must you force that to produce. And, certainly, it is all the better if you can get as much from one acre, as your neighbor does from twenty. Your acre, in that case, is as good as his twenty acres. You bestow a little more labor upon it, it is true; but he wastes more time in running over his twenty acres, than you expend in this extra work on your one; & without any compensation. No doubt, we can not expect to see the country universally well cultivated, till the increase of population forces men to cultivate it properly, that they may live. But this will be the actual situation of some parts of America, long before it is of others. Indeed, it is the condition of Wethersfield, at this moment. Men can no longer subsist there, by means of that slovenly & wasteful husbandry to which they have been accustomed. They are, therefore, obliged to leave their lands in the possession of a few wealthy people, who are able to let their money lie in an unproductive state, & remove to new lands, where by their accustomed means, they can derive their customary advantages. And so they will go on, till the whole continent is in the same state of tillage. Then they will be obliged to manure their land, & study it's improvement. And there is no need to fear any mischief from this. The growth of population, in an agricultural state, will exactly keep pace with improvements in agriculture. People will not have time to grow luxurious; for the man who has ten sons, must support them. And these ten sons must draw a support for their families, from the same ground from which their father supported his single family. Ingenuity, therefore, & usefulness will go hand in hand—or rather will be the same thing. You have, then, no reason for apprehensions concerning the *morals of Wethersfield*—even were the people to become better farmers. Would they become such, they would be more moral, more happy, & have no occasion for removing to Pittsfield, Genesee, &c.

Love to all friends.

Friday, August, 12. 1796.
Cedar St. No. 13. N. York.   E. H. Smith.

MEMORANDA, 13

Saturday, 13th

At the Hospital. Dunlap unexpectedly entered my room this morning. He came from Amboy yesterday; left all well; & returned this afternoon. He thinks of coming up week after next. Charles will come with him, & will spend the winter here. Read Holcroft's Comedy intituled "The Man of Ten Thousand."[85] This piece has some merit; & a few of the scenes are quite fine. It disappointed me, however; & is much inferior to several of his Plays. I also read Cumberland's "Days of Yore."[86] A very poor piece. The first scene in which Voltimar is introduced is the only one that has any claim to applause—& that has no great claim. Made some progress in Fourcroy. Ezekiel Lewis was to see me this afternoon. He is now a sailor, & seems pleased with his new way of life. I sent letters by him to Lichfield. Wm. & I drank tea with Mrs. Woolsey. Thence we went to S. Johnson's. Thence to the Bath—which was quite refreshing. Thence, home—where we have chatted for more than an hour. After a separation of some weeks, it is like the meeting of husband & wife.

POSTSCRIPT

This hardly deserves to be called an idle week, tho' much has not been effected in it. To have run over, at least, a good number of french pamphlets; to have written several letters; & to have made a progress of more than a hundred & twenty pages in Fourcroy; is doing something. The fruits, however, are small. The pamphlets furnished me with few, if any, new ideas, of value; the letters are trifling; & my attention is too much interrupted & dissipated to derive sound instruction from a scientific author. I have felt unwell, too—which has been another reason for indolence; & the weather has been sultry, for these three last days, which is still another excuse. O for that persevering energy of mind which is impeded in it's course, & impaired of it's vigour, by no oppressiveness of season! which disdains the ardors of summer, & the rigors of winter; & starts forward, with redoubled alacrity, in the beamy hours of spring & twilight soberness of autumn!

THIRD WEEK

Sunday, 14th

PREFACE

I trust that I shall be able to conclude the second volume of Fourcroy, this week; and I hope to make some inroad into the third. For till this work is read, I shall not commence my course of study, on the subject Fever. I design, if resolution & spirit favor me, to compose my Circular Letter—so as to have it ready for the Press. The earlier this is done, the better. But I will not allow a mean thing to issue out with my signature. It would be injurious to the undertaking. I do not want a very elegant Address. This would be mis-placed. But there is a certain neatness & precision desirable in things of this sort; which are very difficult to attain; & which leave favorable impressions on the reader's mind. An idea of the writer's good-sense, steadiness, & information, is afforded—& this is better than the persuasion of his brilliancy; & more likely to gain attention.

Other matters must be, as they come. I have no other resolutions to take.

MEMORANDA, 14

Went to the Hospital. Transcribed the letters to John Williams, & to my sister Mary (from the first volume.) Look over a volume of the New Annual Register. Rode out with Dingley. Drank tea at S. Johnson's. Wm. & I spent the evening at Mr. Roulet's. Visited a patient.

MEMORANDA, 15

Monday, 15th

Visited a patient. At the Hospital, & at Dr. Mitchill's, two hours. Felt dull, but began the Circular Letter on the 49th page. Could not get along. Wrote three pages, & dropt the pen. Read the article "Mercury," in Fourcroy, with very imperfect attention. Wm. & I spent the evening at Kent's. A visit from Donald G. Mitchell.

---

[85] (1796).

[86] Richard Cumberland (1796). This was not played in New York at least until after Smith's death in 1798.

MEMORANDA, 16
Tuesday, 16th

At the Hospital two hours. Visited a patient. Called on Dr. Mitchill. Visited Donald G. Mitchell. Wrote for the Manumission Society. Made some progress in Fourcroy. Wrote, last evening & this afternoon, a little further in the letter following, & commenced yesterday. Spent the evening at the Manumission Society. A thin meeting; many of the most active members out of town; & but little business done.

MEMORANDA, 17
Wednesday, 17th

Made progress in Fourcroy. A visit from D. G. Mitchell. A visit from Mr. Roulet. Recd. letters from my father & from Abby. The evening at H. Johnson's. Visited a patient in the forenoon.

This day I finished the succeeding Letter. I have hardly ever written with more difficulty, or less to my satisfaction. It has seemed, ever since I commenced the composition of this address, as if my mind were totally incapable of exertion. Instead of that simplicity & precision which I wished, I find half the ideas I meant to insert omitted, & the whole spun out so loosely & in so circumlocutory a manner, that I much doubt whether my design can be apprehended from it. I have, therefore, determined that, even if I relinquish the project in consequence, this shall not be it's precursor. I must wait for, or create, a more favorable opportunity for writing.

My father's letter is a little more full & peculiar than usual. It has, accordingly, given me much pleasure.

(Circular)
To the Physicians, of the United States.

Gentlemen,

The importance of an extensive acquaintance with the facts which relate to every particular division of the general subject of Medicine, will, questionless, receive your ready acknowlegement. Theorize as he may, no discreet Physician will venture far on any other foundation than that of Experience. I do not mean by experience the uniform & empirical exhibition of remedies which have somehow obtained a universal reputation in certain cases; but I wish to designate by it that scientific calculation of probabilities, which is the result of united observation, reflection, erudition, & inquiry. To him who is guided by this experience; who incessantly inquires of Nature, & carefully watches her replies; & who is at least as studious to discover the general laws by which the animal machine is governed, in its various operations, as to determine the effects produced thereon by a particular cause; it will be rendering a useful service to bring together & exhibit, in one comprehensive view, the mass of facts connected with any point of the science he cultivates. It is a benefit not conferred on such a man alone but, thro' his hands, on mankind. Such it ever has been, and such it deserves to be considered. It is from collections of this nature that the materials have been drawn with which so many brilliant systems have been constructed, to arrest & fix the public opinion, for a season; and, as their influence has never lastingly prevailed, it is to such collections, freed as they are from the incumbrance of systematized hypothesis, that physicians have steadily resorted, as the surest guide amidst the intricacies of practice. Compilations of Observations & Histories, whether the work of a single hand, or many hands, have, therefore, uniformly maintained a high degree of consideration & authority in the schools of Medicine, as well as in the closets of practitioners; & so universally is their value now recognized, in Europe, that publications of this kind are multiplied in every country, & sought after with peculiar avidity. In the United States, notwithstanding the numerous advantages—arising from the extent of our territory, varieties of climate, descent, manners, & disease, the universality of information, & sameness of language, which we possess, for giving novelty & importance to Medical Collections, undertakings of this description have been few, & feebly prosecuted. But the period seems to have arrived at which they are loudly called for, & may hope for extensive patronage & encouragement. The distressing events which have been so recently witnessed, in various parts of our country, have awakened the curiosity of every other class of citizens, as well as of physicians; & while they have quickened the zeal & observation of the latter, have excited the eager apprehensions of all. From such a state of the public mind Science & Humanity have much to hope, if some common point of union can be fixed, towards which the labors of all dilligent observers may converge. A late benevolent attempt, of the kind above-referred to, which has been made by a citizen unconnected with the practice of Physic, tho' it failed of obtaining so large a share of medical aid as was to have been desired, affords a reasonable ground of expectation for future success in plans of a similar nature; and it is such an expectation which has given birth to the present address.

The countenance which that undertaking received, & the circumstance of it's further prosecution being relinquished by the conductor, induce me to lay before you, for your consideration & furtherance, a design of the same character in every respect, except that of it's embracing a wider range of investigation. It will be obvious that Mr. Webster's Collection, relative to that description of Fevers which ordinarily pass under the name of Billius, is here referred to. Mr. Webster's inquiries were directed to the single purpose of illucidating the nature, operation, cure, &c. of those diseases. No doubt this is a very important subject of examination, &, notwithstanding all that has been done, is still capable of much additional illustration. It will, therefore, continue to be one of the primary objects of the work I have in view, to collect all possible information on this head. But I do not wish to confine inquiry to so limited a topic. A large portion of the United States is never subject to complaints of this kind, in their worst forms; & even those which are most exposed to them, are only so exposed during a small part of the Year. My design is, therefore, to institute a Work, whose main object shall be co-extensive with our country. And this is no other than an endeavor to obtain *an accurate & annual acccunt of those general diseases which reign, in each season, over every part of the United States.* The advantages which must result from such a Plan, if vigorously & judiciously carried into effect, are too numerous & considerable not to be instantly suggested by the slightest reflection. Beside those general benefits which are hinted at, rather than unfolded, in the preceeding observations, the particular good effects to be expected are of the highest consequence. No plan seems more happily adapted for the discovery of the origin, causes, proper situation, season, mode of propagation, progress, cure, & prevention, of febrile diseases; for determining the relative healthiness, & peculiar diseases, of every part of the country; for ascertaining the influence of particular states of society, occupations, temperature, air, institutions, & changes in the face of the earth, on morals, happiness, & health; for resolving the hitherto unexplained & difficult problem, proposed by the illustrious Sydenham—"Whether a careful examination might *not* shew, that certain tribes of disorders constantly follow others, in one determined series, or circle, as it were; or whether they all return, indiscriminately, according to a secret disposition of the air, & the inexplicable succession of seasons"; finally, for the dissemination of professional science, of individual experience, throughout the United States. Some respectable physicians have, I know, exprest an apprehension that a collection so multifarious, & abounding in opinions, reasonings, & plans of cure, so various & opposite, will rather tend to distract, than satisfy the public mind; that the people at large would lose all confidence in those to whom they have hitherto entrusted the care of their health, when they saw how much they were divided in sentiment; & that the profession would be degraded, without benefit to the science. To this objection there are replies of sufficient force, as it appears to me, to justify undertakings of this nature, even were the apprehensions above-mentioned admitted to possess considerable reality. But, it is probable that, a very undue importance has been conceded to them. On all the leading points of dissention, it can hardly happen that men can be more distant in their belief, than they now are. If this difference could ever produce the apprehended effect, it must have already produced it. It is easy to shew, however, that such an effect is nearly impossible; & that men attach themselves to a physician whose opinions resemble their own, with just so much the more vehemence as his opinions are vehemently opposed. Neither is it true that the science will derive no benefit from these inquiries, & that the profession will be degraded. Men who have gained an ascendancy which does not belong to them, may, indeed have some reason to complain that their ignorance is exposed; but men of real talents, learning, industry, & philanthropy, can not fail of assuming a more elevated rank in the eyes of their fellow-citizens, & with their elevation of carrying with them the art they exercise. It should be remembered too, that all opinions will come connected with some facts, with some reasonings, which may be valuable, tho' the opinions themselves are not; & that how ineffectual soever the labours of any individual may be, they will have their weight & value when combined with those of other men. The materials which will be collected may be thrown together without order, without other connection than nearness of position & relation to one design; but here will be the timber, the stone, the marble, the silver, & the gold, the gross & lighter substances with which some master-builder, some future & well-instructed architect, may construct & decorate a noble & national edifice. There is still a further consideration, not destitute of importance. The physicians, as well as every other class of citizens in the United States, are in the constant practice of deriving all their opinions & modes of reasoning & acting, from Europe. The consequence of this implicit confidence in foreign authors, have, no doubt, been fatal in numberless instances to the people of this country. Beside the mischief which a regard to their varying & wild theories has effected, it can scarcely happen that the application of the same practice to diseases passing under similar names, in climates so extremely different, should have been other than destructive. There is no reflecting mind but must be struck instantaneously with this idea. I am persuaded that, to any person who will think candidly on the subject, it will appear scarcely less absurd for us to be governed by the laws of the monarchies of Europe, than overruled & directed by the no less authoritative *dictum* of their Medical Schools.

It should seem, then, that beside the benefit which would accrue to the science of Medicine, generally, from the prosecution of the plan hinted at, it also deserves to be promoted for the particular good it promises to our country. For certainly, if physicians can derive any instruction from accounts of the ordinary appearance of diseases in other climates, they must obtain a more immediate & precise advantage from the knowlege of those symptoms which characterize the diseases of their own.

The considerations now submitted to you, Gentlemen, together with such others as will, no doubt, suggest themselves more persuasively to your own mind, embolden me to request your assistance in the compilation of the Work proposed. I shall content myself with laying before you a simple Outline, by which you will see the whole extent of the undertaking, be apprized of the difficulties attendant on it, of the variety of observations necessary to it's perfection, & the good it may effect, if completely executed. You will observe, further, that it is proposed to include a variety of matter, more nearly or remotely connected with the main design; so that an annual volume, not unworthy of the public's acceptance, may be made up, even if it should require, as it probably will, several years to establish regular communication, with every part of the United States.

The subjects concerning which the most minute & comprehensive information is requested, from all parts of the continent are these—

1. The State of the Atmosphere, in respect to dryness, & humidity, heat & cold, serenity & tempestuousness —including the direction & force of winds, & the sensible quantity of Electricity.
2. The progress & condition of Vegetation, with regard to growth, vigour, & disease—independent of the ravages of insects, & the particular effects of certain manures.
3. Insects, whether an unusual plenty or dearth of them, & whether injurious to men, or to vegetables; with as accurate notices as may be of the circumstances which preceeded, attended, & followed their appearance & disappearance, & the means effectual against them, as well as the mischiefs committed by them.
4. Domestic Animals—if any diseases among them— their causes, symptoms, methods of cure, time of appearing & disappearing—&c. &c.
5. Diseases among men—time of their appearing & disappearing—peculiar manners & customs of the people among whom—local peculiarities of their residence—preceeding, contemporary, & subsequent complaints—symptoms, progress, extent, nature, & cure: in sea-ports, attention to be paid to the arrival of foreigners; in new settlements, to the progress of clearings, drainings, opening of roads, increase of population. &c.

Communications of the following kind, are also requested.

1. Accurate & succinct accounts of general Diseases that have heretofore appeared in any part of the United States.
2. Useful Histories of particular Cases.
3. New Methods of curing Diseases.
4. Accounts of new discovered & applied remedies— either in the cure of common, or of rather & hitherto incurable diseases.
5. Interesting information relative to the Minerals, Plants, & Animals of our Country.
6. American Medical Biography.
7. Accounts of former Medical Publications in America.
8. Accounts of New Medical Publications in America.
9. Medical News.

Such, Gentlemen, are the materials with which I now venture to solicit you to supply me, annually. The subjects noticed, in the first place, appear to me closely connected with the main design of the proposed Work—which is, as before mentioned—"An accurate & annual account of those general diseases which reign in each season, over every part of the United States." The remaining subjects, on which Communications are also requested, are of considerable importance; & the publication I have in view would well merit your patronage, were it confined to such alone. But the plan contemplated, I trust, will be thought of more extensive utility, & be forwarded with proportionate alacrity. Should the necessary supply of materials be obtained by the time, it is intended to issue the first volume of the Collection in the month of May 1797, under the title of "The Medical Repository"; & to continue the publication of an annual volume, as long as professional aid & general patronage shall be afforded. In this event, a few years, it is probable, will give to the undertaking all the stability & perfection to be expected; & the volume of every year, will contain the history of the health of our Country for the year preceeding.

P. S.—It seems hardly possible that valuable materials should be withheld, so that the design should prove abortive: for tho' I address myself more particularly to the professors of the Healing Art, it must be evident, from the outline just drawn, & from the nature of the undertaking, that it will be in the power of my fellow-citizens, generally, greatly to further it; & the aid & countenance of all dilligent observers & of the learned, throughout the United States, is thus publicly & earnestly solicited.

Communications, may be addrest to the subscriber at No. 13, Cedar Street New York.

MEMORANDA, 18

Thursday, 18th

Visited a patient. Two hours & a half at the Hospital. An unusual number of patients recd. within a few days; & many interesting cases. Much time employed in doing a little business for my father; to whom I wrote a letter thereon. Made some trifling progress in Fourcroy. Wm. Johnson, Kent, & I walked out of town. We returned to Kent's to tea; where we spent most of the evening. I waited on Mr. Wertmüller, the Swedish Painter, & friend of Mr. Gahn. Gahn has been to my father's in Lichfield, & is soon to be here.

H. Johnson had a son born to-day.

MEMORANDA, 19

Friday, 19th

Nearly completed my father's business. Recd. a letter from Dr. Kissam, of Huntington, Long-Island, containing a history of a Hectic Fever, occasioned by the accidental presence of a Bean, in the Bronchiæ. A visit from Dr. Mitchill: from Charles Adams. Visited a patient. Several ineffectual calls. Spent the evening at home; and, in consequence made considerable progress in Fourcroy.

MEMORANDA, 20

Saturday, 20th

At the Hospital forenoon & afternoon. The critical condition of some of the patients required it. We have been quite unfortunate there, in respect to the Yellow Fever, this year. All who have come in, have come in, as it has happened, as late as the sixth day of the disease. This has been the case in five instances. Three have died. One is now, as I fear, at the point of death. Another will, I believe, recover. Of these five, two had been very much mistreated; one not assisted at all; one, who died, had good medical attendance, as far as I could learn, but none other; he who is recovering, was pretty well attended before coming into the house.

Finished the second volume of Fourcroy. Finished my father's business. Visited Dr. Mitchill. Spent part of the evening at Mrs. Woolsey's; part of it at home.

POSTSCRIPT

That which I intended to do has been done; but lamely & imperfectly. I have finished Fourcroy—I mean the second volume—but with little benefit. I have composed a Circular Letter, but one unfit for the press. The complaint, which seized me at Amboy, still hanging on me, withers my strength, lowers my spirits, & makes the cold & hot weather equally unsupportable. I feel a remarkable inaptitude to exertion. When I am seated, I wish not to rise; when standing, not to walk; when unoccupied with thought, not to think. It is, indeed, with great difficulty that I force myself to think at all. Mean time my desire for knowlege, my wish to be active, is undiminished; and this opposition between power & inclination produces it's usual effect—self-dissatisfaction & irresoluteness. "O wretched man that I am! who shall deliver me from the body of this death?"[87]

Fourth Week

Sunday, 21st

PREFACE

In my present situation I can take no particular resolution. I shall do all, on my general & customary business which circumstances will permit, & occasion demand; the event must prove whether it be well or ill.

MEMORANDA, 21

Called on Dr. Mitchill, & we went together to the Hospital, where we continued two hours. I spent an hour with him, on my return. Incapable of any regular & efficient application, I amused myself with a volume of the New Annual Register. I dined & spent the afternoon at S. Johnson's. Wm. & I walked on the Battery. We returned at eight—& conversed & read two hours.

---

[87] Romans 7:24.

MEMORANDA, 22

Monday, 22nd

Considerable progress in Fourcroy. Called on Mr. Gahn, who returned last evening. He left all my friends well. A professional visit. Began to trace out the rude & irregular outline of my Utopia. I do not at present design to arrange the articles in any determinate order. On the contrary I shall compose them according to the momentary bias of my mind. Each article must be the subject of particular & successive reflection. A visit. Wm. & I walked on the Battery. Amused myself with a volume of the New Annual Register.

MEMORANDA, 23

Tuesday, 23rd

At the Hospital, forenoon & afternoon. Made tolerable progress in Fourcroy. Visit from Jeremiah Mason—from Jno. Wells. Spent the evening at Mr. Kent's.

MEMORANDA, 24

Wednesday, 24th

Made good progress in Fourcroy. At a meeting of the Physicians & Surgeons of the Hospital. Drank tea with Dr. Richd. S. Kissam. Spent the evening at Woolsey's. He returned on Monday; is well; & left all friends well.

MEMORANDA, 25

Thursday, 25th

At the Hospital. Read a few pages in Fourcroy. At Dingley's, where I saw "Zoonomia P. II" for the first time. Looked over several numbers of the "Analytical Review"—a poor Journal. At Dr. Seaman's,[88] where I drank tea, to frame rules for the Hospital Library. Walked with M. M. Wertmüller & Gahn, most of the evening. Wrote a few lines, on business, to my Father.

MEMORANDA, 26

Friday, 26th

Finished looking over the five first numbers, for 1796, of the Analytical Review. I found many interesting Extracts from books, but the Journalist's part of the publication gave me no pleasure. How different from the Monthly Review—whose judicious & elegant discussions are, oftentimes, so instructive! I went to the Hospital. My poor unfortunate Mad Girl, has in part, recovered her senses. Her feelings are lively; & she shed tears at the interest I could not but discover on her account. I know not that it is to my care that she is indebted for her present degree of restoration; but she is better, & I rejoice at it.

---

[88] Valentine Seaman, New York physician, was the author of the first essay in Noah Webster's *Collection of Papers on the Subject of Bilious Fevers*, etc. (1796), a convinced anti-contagionist.

I made shameful progress in Fourcroy. Of more than eighty pages, do I remember two? Well! well! I have found the Road-Post—I may travel the Road, by & by. I went with Wm. to a Book-Store. He purchased Mary Wollstonecraft's Letters from Sweden &c.[89] & Beddoes's "Essay on the Public Merits of Mr. Pitt."[90] I have read, this evening, sixty pages of the latter, with great pleasure; & a few of the former, with melancholly satisfaction. I am eager to know the private history of the Author. We drank tea at H. Johnson's. His wife and child are charmingly. Jno. Johnson hurt himself. Wm. & I went down to Seth's, where we was. He is better. We spent most of the evening there.

[Omitted here, nineteen manuscript pages with the heading: "Utopia."]

MEMORANDA, 27

Saturday, 27th

At the Hospital longer than usual. Read a few pages, only, in Fourcroy—having spent some time in selecting books for the Hospital Library. Nearly finished Beddoes' Essays &c. but laid it aside to read Mary Wollstonecraft's Tour thro' Scandinavia—which, after having set up till twelve at night I have run thro'. This is more a view of the author, than of the country she travelled thro', there being but little information which is to be treasured up; yet the work is pleasing, & abounds with remarks, not the product of a common mind. At Charles Adams's—at S. Johnson's—at Woolsey's—H. Johnson here—Wm. & I walked on the Battery.

POSTSCRIPT

How stands the account this week? Much after the old sort—but little has been done, & that imperfectly. I am as much fatigued with finding fault with myself—as of making resolutions. I do not find that either has much good effect. My general determinations do not vary, in any considerable degree—it is idle to teaze myself about particular variations.

Fifth Week

Sunday, 28th

PREFACE

This may be dismist in a moment. I design to finish Fourcroy, to write some letters to my friends, & perhaps to begin on some new work, or dash away a little on my Utopia, Sonnets, Characters, or Hints on Education. It is of little importance to which of these subjects my attention is directed.

Dunlap & Brown will I suppose, be here this week.

---

[89] Letters from *Sweden, Norway and Denmark* (1796).
[90] Thomas Beddoes, *An Essay on the Public Merits of Mr. Pitt* (London?, 1796).

They will form a sinking fund for much time, & perhaps redeem some Moral Science.

MEMORANDA, 28

Finished Beddoes' Pamphlet—in which he appears to have perfectly established his point. It is remarkably well written. Visited Woolsey, who is unwell. Finished looking over my late friend Hitchcock's Journal, & read letters written by me to him, & returned since his death. I shall draw up an article relative to him soon. The letters are, many of them, strange things. I shall be more particular when I speak of this correspondence. At Seth Johnson's. Wm. & I called at M. Roulet's. Nobody there. We walked—returned to Woolsey's—where we spent most of the evening. Residue at home.

MEMORANDA, 28 [*bis*].

Monday, 29th

At the Hospital. Visited Patients. Finished Fourcroy. Further professional visitation. Dingley here. Drank tea at Kent's. He, Wm. & I walked on the Battery. Bathed.

MEMORANDA, 30

Tuesday, 30th

Visited a patient. At the Hospital. When I returned, I found Mr. Roulet here. He stayed two hours. His conversation is always elegant & instructive. It was particularly so to-day. I have gained a better idea of the state of Society, in Italy, from him, this day, than from all the published accounts of travellers. They describe only statues, paintings, &c. & the manners of the great: he extends his view to the whole people. Recd. letters from my sisters Mary & Fanny. Wrote the succeeding letter. Drew up some Rules for the Hospital Library. Wm. & I took a long walk. Dunlap & his family, & with them Brown, arrived this afternoon. We spent the evening there.

MEMORANDA, 31

Wednesday, 31st

Wrote the letter to Mrs. Tracy. C. B. Brown & Dunlap came in & stayed till after twelve. Went to the Hospital, to attend an operation & a meeting of the Faculty. After dinner transcribed my letter to Theodore Dwight, & made several professional visits. Spent the evening at Dunlap's.

LETTERS

To Theodore Dwight.

I have entertained a hope of hearing from you, speedily, ever since your return. You have not written, but—do not misapprehend me—I mean not to accuse you, but attribute your silence to the pressing calls of business;

I write you as a lover not a man

for our friend Woolsey gives me the pleasing information that your business accumulates rapidly.

I designed to have written, myself, before this time; but I have been variously engaged, & have not felt myself free. Now, when I have just accomplished the perusal of a lengthy Work, connected with my profession, in the reading of which I have been several weeks employed; I seize the first moment to assume the pen & I sit down with full purpose to enter into a free conversation with you, after the manner of ancient days.

I regretted, at the time, & still regret, the shortness of your visit, which allowed us so little opportunity for conversing together; & the more, as I was exceedingly anxious to remove from your mind every vestige of doubt concerning the state of my feelings towards you —if, indeed, that had not already been effected by my letter, written a short time previous to your coming here. But I had not even the chance of inquiry whether that were, or were not, the case. To have been assured of it, either then, or after your return, would have given me inexpressible satisfaction; to be enabled to prosecute my endeavor, if it is not so, would then & will now, be my next desire. I would fain persuade myself, however, that even were there some suspicions remaining after the reception of my letter, there were none which were not dissipated by my conduct towards you during your visit. I will not conceal it from you, that there was something so new, so abhorrent to all my former conceptions, in my standing, in regard to you, in the light of a suspected person, that my emotions on our meeting were by no means pure & unmingled. A sentiment very different from that transport with which I always embrace you, united itself therewith; & the tears which were on the point of bursting forth would have been half as much those of sorrow as of joy. When a thought glanced towards the subject of our latest communications the querulous expostulation of Helena was rising to my lips—

> Is all the council that we two have shared,
> The *brother* vows, the hours that we have spent,
> When we have chid the hasty-footed time
> For parting us—O! and is all forgot?[91]

and I was ready, in the bitterness of my soul, to exclaim with Hamlet—

> That it should come to this![92]

But I discovered, or thought that I discovered, in your eye, your voice, your manner, that tenderness which I felt in my own bosom, & which once mutually constituted so large a portion of our happiness, & my agitated spirits were calmed. Am I then deceived? Will you, can you, tell me I am not? I do not know whether I ought to estimate your friendship so highly, but whether it be from the sense I entertain of your merits, or from the powerful effect of early associations, there is something in the idea of forfeiting your affection like the pain supposed to accompany the forcible separation of soul & body.

You must not, therefore, be surprized if, in writing on this subject, I use rather the expressions of a lover than a man; for I feel for you all that Jonathan felt for David. The acquaintances which we form when our understanding is tolerably mature, give us pleasure, from the benefit we derive therefrom; they are entered into & prosecuted with a spirit too temperate to have their dissolution inflict any deadly wound; but those which commence in youth, & which grow & become consolidated with the increase of our mental powers & attainments, are, as it were, intertwisted with our very existence: to rend them asunder is to annihilate our greatest joys. It is here, indeed, that a generous & affectionate heart is vulnerable. The envy of rivals, the malignity of enemies, the persecutions of a misguided & false-judging multitude, he can sustain; a just indignancy at their attempts, the conscious purity of his intentions, & above all a persuasion of the good which his exertions will eventually confer on mankind, are able to bear him up above all these common calamities—but to lose the approbation of those on whose approbation he had fondly counted—to find the heart of him he thought his long, tried & inmutable friend, estranged—where is the soul so stern in adamantine virtue as to bear unmoved a shock like this? I know not where—Mine, mine it is not.

> But there, where I have garnered up my heart;
> Where I must either live, or bear no life—
> ———————to be discarded thence—
> ———————Turn thy complexion there,
> Patience, thou rose-lipped cherubim,
> Ay, there look grim as hell.[93]

I fear that I weary you. We will turn our thoughts another way.

You are now laboriously dilligent in your profession, & have nearly thrown aside the pen for other purposes. We have talked so little together of late, that you must bear with me if I am a little troublesome with my inquiries. It will be from no base motive, I assure you.

I want, then, to be informed whether you have, in good sooth, bidden farewel to the Muse; whether you have only ceased from transient & public homage, & woo her more retired & extensive favors. In plain terms —whether you have relinquished your plan of occasional composition, for the pursuit of some connected subject, or have relinquished it altogether, for the present. If the last be true—do you not still intend to bestow some share of your future leisure in the preparation of some poetical, or other, work, for public inspection, delight & improvement? Does your profession, do you intend

---

[91] Helena: "Is all the counsel that we two have shar'd,
   The sisters' vows, the hours that we have spent,
   When we have chid the hasty-footed time
   For parting us. O! is all forgot?"
A Midsummer Night's Dream, III, iii.
[92] *Hamlet,* I, ii.
[93] *Othello,* IV, ii.

that it shall, engross you wholly? Or do you look to political or judicial promotion, & determine to shine as a legislator, or a judge? I wish you would write to me, & explain yourself freely, on these questions.

I could talk to you a long time—for I am now in the humor of talking—but my hand is already weary. If I have time, I shall make additions. Assure yourself of my continued love, & make it acceptable to Mrs. Dwight & the rest of my Hartford friends.

Tuesday, August 30th 1796.
Cedar St. No 13. New York.   E. H. Smith.

To Mrs. Tracy.

What a dreary interval has opened between our once-frequent communications! I am startled when I think of it, and scarce credit that recollection which assures me of it's reality. It is impossible for me to reckon up your losses in consequence, (tho', were I to take for my standard of computation the flattering regard which you have witnessed towards me, I might suppose them something,) but me it has deprived of the charm which chased away melancholly & distrust, me it has deprived of consolation & instruction. For your letters were my great encouragers; not less by those sentiments of virtue & virtuous action, which they contained, than by the ceaseless inquiries after more certain science & more blameless morals to which they incited me. This you can have no difficulty in conceiving. You know yourself too well to doubt it, of yourself; & me too thoroughly to suspect me of not feeling all that I profess to have felt. Will you indulge me in a reply to the inquiry—"Why have you not written?" When I saw you in February you were good enough to assure me that my letter, recd. by you a short time before—should be answered. It was not a trifling one—& I was anxious that you should answer it. The expectation of hearing from you held my pen enchained. I did not wish to divert the current of your reply, by any obstacle which another letter, on a different subject, might cast in it's way. Had you intimated a desire to be acquitted from your voluntary engagement, or had you discovered that it were more agreable not to pursue the theme considered of, I should readily have acquiesced; the disappointment would have been spared me; & we might have renewed our correspondence, on it's ancient basis, & drawn new delight from frequent communications. I will not venture to assign a cause for your silence; I can only lament it. I have the most firm persuasion of the reasonableness & necessity of your taciturnity; & would not dare to hazard a conjecture, which might wound the mimosa-like sensibility of friendship. Alas! how often has it been ravaged by the rude surmises of a temper too ready to suspect. How often have tears of anguish dropped over the impatient sallies of a friend, which ascribed that to loss of affection which proceeded only from a lamentable necessity! I apply not this particularly, but generally: for you can not but have observed how apt we are, when we descend to surmise, to produce that injury to friendship which we supposed already to have happened. How much better is it to repose in the plenitude of confidence on the sincerity of those we love, & to endure every thing rather than to discover a doubt of it's continuance. And when we reflect, free from passion, how little reason do we generally find to conclude against a friend, merely from his silence? Cares, interruptions of business or of pleasure, & that mental imbecillity to which even the best are sometimes liable, occur too often to interrupt the else steady course of correspondence, to allow us any just cause for crimination & complaint. No! you shall never find me so unjust as to complain of *you* for being silent; tho' the sorrow which it occasions me, may often force me to exclaim against that evil destiny which delights to promote it. May it now cease it's persecution—& may this letter provoke a reply.

Our Swedish friend, Mr. Gahn, brought me a most acceptable present, in that, thro' him, you renewed your expressions of friendship. He has had a long, interesting, & pleasant journey; & seems particularly pleased with the Town on the Hill. It is almost superfluous to inquire how [you] like him. No worthy person can dislike him; & the sentiments of regard which he inspires are, I think, not those of an ordinary nature. Few young men write with so pleasing manners, such good sense, study, instruction, reflection, & observation. He seems equally fitted for the closet & the drawing-room. You will say that I am giving you no information. I know it; but I also know that you take a pleasure in discoursing of the acknowleged merits of those who are meritorious; & that it is a still further satisfaction to find others concur with you in the favorable sentiments you have formed. I expected that my friend Woolsey would have shewn himself at Lichfield—which would have been a new gratification to you—but he was too uxorious, & hastened home. His tender & manly spirit would have charmed you, & you would have delighted to contemplate [h]is open & benevolent aspect. I do not speak of it's handsomeness—that is a trivial thing, & my friend's is not handsome—but such faces are sufficiently rare, to deserve study when they are met with. I am sorry that you did not see him.

It is so long since I have heard any thing particularly from you, & your family, that I do not know how to question you about a hundred things, concerning which I am anxious to be informed. I must leave them untouched, therefore, for the present, & intreat you to make yourself & yours the subject of your next letter.

I have lately read a book, intituled "letters written during a journey thro' a part of Norway, Sweden & Denmark, by Mary Wollstonecraft." It has given me some information, some pleasure, but more pain. I could wish you to read it, as it opens a new vista into the soul of this admirable woman, but that I fear it would be the occasion of a melancholly too afflicting, & which you have every reason in the world for wishing to shun. In this work, Miss W. appears wounded, afflicted, desolate.

She is a mother, & is deserted. There is an air of mystery thrown over the whole book, perhaps only so because I am ignorant, of circumstances well known in Europe, but which at this distance I can not penetrate. It has, of consequence, interested me the more, & excited new eagerness to discover what is the cause of her evident unhappiness. At present I will not hazard a conjecture, as, in all probability, I shall soon be able to obtain a true statement of facts. Many ridiculous stories have been propagated; but there are so many fools & so many knaves interested in decrying her, that I choose not hastily to credit what they say. I shall make you a participant in any information I may obtain; meantime, it may be well always to bear it in my mind, That the truth of any sentiment does not depend, in the least, on the character of him who utters it. Farewell, for the present. Mr. Gahn has encouraged me to expect a letter, ere long, from Mr. Tracy; & I wish one from you may be inclosed. Present my affectionate remembrances to him, & to your children.

Wednesday, August 31. 1796.
Cedar St. No. 13. New York.   E. H. Smith.

P. S.

This letter has been written, as you will see, from the date, some time. I have been too busy to transcribe it; & had some hopes of being able to make additions to it's size & interest. As it is uncertain when I shall have an opportunity of sending it, I am resolved to be prepared. What else I would have said may well be reserved to a future occasion. And then I hope your letter, previously recd. will furnish copious subjects for a reply,

                     Adieu.

Sept 11th 1796.   E. H. Smith.

GENERAL POSTSCRIPT TO THE MONTH OF AUGUST

A hundred pages ought, surely, to contain something worthy of preservation; and, yet, how little deserving thereof will be found in those pages which preceed the present. It were an imbecillity of mind worthy of being expatiated upon, that which marks the proceedings of the month now ended, if any practical utility might be thence derived. But, alas! conduct of this kind has become so habitual to me as neither to excite surprize, or determination to amend. Like the feeble Parisians, I see the horrible devastation which surrounds me, contemplate the disgusting spectacle with grief, even with remorse, & yet stupidly remain without power of exertion over with the volcano which grumbles beneath—& threatens to burst forth & overwhelm me. But stop! Since it is idle to regret what is past & inevitable, since not even any future benefit promises to flow from an indulgence in complaints like these, why do I give way to them? What I have not done is evident—let me see what I have done. What have I read?

Fourcroy's Chemistry—second & third volumes;
Miss H. M. Williams's Letters—the seventh vol.—
The man of Ten Thousand—a comedy by Holcroft.
Days of Yore, a drama by Cumberland—
Quelques Reflections fugitives &c.—par J. Marchena—
Rapport &c. sur Joseph Lebon—par J. B. Quinot—
Rapport &c. sur les livres elementaires &c. Lakanal—
Reponse de Guadet a Robespierre—
L'Education cause eloignée &c. des maladies—Lanthenas—
Des la Tragedie Grecque &c. par A. Auger—
Letters from Sweden, Norway, & Denmark—by M. Wollstonecraft—
Essay on the public merits of Mr. Pitt—T. Beddoes—and

beside—several numbers of the Monthly & Analytical Reviews, some detached parts of several Medical & other Publications. This is a pitiful list of reading; & even these few books have not been read improvingly. What have I written? Letters to—Wm. Buel, Evelyn Pierpont, Fanny Smith, John Williams, Theodore Dwight, & Mrs. Tracy—one half of which are of little value—a single Memoir of Friendship, an abortive Circular Letter, & a few scraps on my Utopia. On the Sonnets, & still more on the Medical Abstracts, I have not only not done, but not attempted, any thing. Meantime, if I except my Hospital employment, which, it is true, has been somewhat pressing, my professional business has been a mere cypher. One day would have sufficed for the whole of it. What then have I done with my time? The foregoing pages must declare, for it has been too insignificantly employed to leave recollections sufficiently vivid to enable me to answer the question. Shall I do any better the succeeding month? Aye, shall I? This is an inquiry in regard to which I must leave the preface to that month to speak for itself. The Month may, perhaps, give a still more thorough, if not more satisfactory, answer. Has the month of August been badly spent? There are sins of omission, we are told, as well as sins of commission. I do not know that I have done any thing, in the Month now complete, positively bad—but, then, how many good things have I omitted to do!

SEPTEMBER 1796

GENERAL PREFACE TO THE MONTH

This is the month of my nativity, and to-day the commencement of that season in which, ordinarily, I am most myself. This year it promises to be free from the interruptions of sickness and of journeying. In this month, then, it is incumbent on me to double my dilligence, and turn my time to profit.

The absence of pain, uneasiness, of corporeal inquietude, is necessary, no doubt, to the full & free exercise of the mental powers; but is there not a state of corporeal enjoyment so exquisite & perfect as to render it impossible for the understanding to operate with fixed & persevering energy? When I walk abroad, in the country, the serene heavens, the balmy air, the verdure every where around me, the lofty & thick-growing woods, & the solemn & sweet repose of nature, fill my soul with a sentiment of delight so pure, so glowing, & so entire, that I deliver myself up to it, & am lost to every thing beside. In this state all my heart is satisfied. I do not want to talk; I am still less desirous of study. My bosom seems full; my eyes ready to overflow, but not overflowing; every faculty is absorbed; I stretch out my arms; I feel that I am free. This is enjoyment, but my tone of mind, or tone of body, must be somewhat lower, to render my moral, or scholastic exertions effective. Analagous to these sensations & to this situation are those which I experience in Autumn; and thus it may happen that, tho' I am then most Man, I am also least active in the duties of Man. But I will endeavor to blend both activity & enjoyment; or, rather, will strive to make enjoyment of activity. In regard to the subjects towards which this activity is to be directed, I have no new resolutions to take. Those objects which I proposed to myself, as worthy of pursuit, when this volume was commenced, still hold the same important rank in my estimation. On these, therefore, will my powers be exerted. The circumstance which, at present, appears most likely to impede my progress in my destined course, is the presence of my friend C. B. Brown. His society is too pleasing, his conversation too interesting, & his pursuits too important & connected with my own, not to engage an unusual share of my attention & my time. In his company, in that of my other friends as united with him, & occupied in the discussion of so many high & extensive principles of policy & morals, it is not improbable that I may oftentimes forget to "build the lofty rhyme,"[94] to "exhibit the exact impress & body" of my friends, to trace the mysterious windings of disease, & to lay the aerial foundations of the visionary republic of Utopia. I have good resolutions, notwithstanding; and Time will put them to the proof.

MEMORANDA, 32

Thursday, 1st

At the Hospital. Thence I went to the College. The appearances ex[hi]bited by some blood taken from a sick man, having determined Dr. Mitchill & me to make a chemical examination, we returned to the Hospital, & devoted the remainder of the forenoon to experimenting on it—but without being able to come to any satisfactory conclusions. Dined at S. Johnson's. We all went to see some Optical Tricks, after dinner. My defective eyes prevented my being so completely deceived as my companions. I found C. B. Brown here when we returned. He spent the rest of the afternoon here. I went with him to Woolsey's—where we past the evening. Dunlap, his wife, G. M. Woolsey, &c. were there. I recd. a letter from my father.

---

[94] Milton, "Lycidas," 1.10.

MEMORANDA, 33

Friday, 2nd

I began to read Dr. Rush's Fourth Volume of Inquiries & Observations last evening, & made a little advance in it. This day & evening I have finished it. I have many things to commend, & some to contravert. I shall soon write to him. Mr. Roulet was here, in the forenoon; & Mr. Lovegrove, afterward. Mrs. L. has a daughter—about ten days old. She is quite well; & the child healthy. Sophy behaves better. In the afternoon I went to the Hospital, & busied myself in drawing up, partly from the Prescription Book, partly from my own, & partly from the Apothecary's Memory, the Histories of the unfortunate Cases, which have fallen under my care. Part of the evening at Mr. Boyd's; part at Mr. Kent's: visited a patient.

MEMORANDA, 34

Saturday, 3rd

C. B. Brown breakfasted here. At the Hospital two hours. Visited the sick. Drew up notes on the Case of J. L. jr.—the first, or one of the first of Yellow Fever, which occurred this year. Visited Dingley. At C. Adams's—& with him took a long walk to see a patient. At Dunlap's Store. Wm. & I walked on the Battery, with the Roulets. Spent the evening at Dunlap's. Made a professional visit. Dr. Mitchill here, about one P. M. with Dr. Barton on the Rattel-Snake.[95]

POSTSCRIPT

A week, on the whole, not very badly spent; tho' no part of the composition designed to be performed therein, when the Preface was written, has been accomplished. Yet my correspondence has not been neglected; & I have attended to professional composition, more immediately interesting, & equally connected with my plan of medical Inquiry with the Plague of Athens—or any other plague.

My opinion of myself & my own conduct varies exceedingly, with variation of circumstances. It can not be said that I enjoy any steady self-complacency—yet my chief misfortune lies in not being able to decide on what is best for me to do—what I ought to do.

Sixth Week

Sunday, 4th

PREFACE

What do I mean to do this week? It is a question which I know not how to answer. It is hardly probable,

---

[95] "Memoir Concerning the Fascinating Faculty which has been Ascribed to the Rattle-snake . . ." (Philadelphia, *Trans. Amer. Philos. Soc.*, o.s., **4** (1799): p. 74). This essay by Dr. Benjamin Smith Barton, professor of botany at the University of Pennsylvania, had an almost inordinate interest for Smith.

however, that I shall be idle; tho' it is far from being improbable that I shall do much. I will resolve on nothing. Things must even take their course.

This day I am twenty five years of age. Twenty five! I can scarcely realize it. And, yet, when I look backward on what I have experienced, I am ready to demand "No more than twenty five"? Well! I have enjoyed this day, soberly & sincerely. It has been one of those calm, clear, cool, autumnal days in which I so much delight. It came after two or three days of gloom & rain—sunshiny, & balmy, breathing. The anniversary of my birth, for several years past, has been unpleasant. But this has been of the pleasantest of days. And all my movements have corresponded to it.

MEMORANDA, 35

I rose in moderate season, after a night of perfect repose. As I had nothing to hurry me, I went thro' all my little preparatives with perfect leisure. Afterward I made a professional visit, and found my patient better. When I returned, Dunlap & Brown came in, & we had an hour of pleasing & instructive conversation. I went, then, to the Hospital. D. & B. accompanied me. D. walked on, & B. went in. Everything seemed to be going on pretty well, there. B. was much gratified by his visit. D. now joined us, & we went to his house. Thence I went to Woolsey's. When I came back, Wm. & I walked on the Battery. We dined at S. Johnson's. After dinner, we spent the afternoon in walking. This was the most agreable of many late excursions. We were at H. Johnson's in the evening. Mr. Lovegrove, who was there, came home with us, & sat a while.

PRAYER

I received an early & rigid Calvinistic education. From the time that I could speak, till after my entrance into the University, I was accustomed to repeat to my parents, morning & evening, the Lord's Prayer, with several little Hymns. When I went to College, the continuance of this practice, by myself, was enjoined. I believe that it was not, even at first, very strictly persevered in.

I was not long at College, however, without having all fixed veneration for such practices dissipated. The recollection, it is true, sometimes haunted me; & I did not leave the Institution till after having lost all settled belief in religion. My unbelief, however, was not founded on any proper comprehension of the arguments either for, or against, Christianity. It was rather adopted as a fashion, than arrived at thro' reflection. It is not surprizing, therefore, that the society of Dr. Dwight, & of other sensible & amiable Christians, should restore me to my juvenile orthodoxy. I became, indeed, a sincere & warm religionist. Still *Prayer* had not been habitually adopted. When I left Lichfield, for Phila.—in September 1790, I passed thro' Middletown, where my mother then was, on a visit to my Grandmother—who was thought to be dangerously ill. She gave me, what she deemed, her dying advice. It was, as may be supposed, chiefly concerning Religion—for no person possest more, or more truly amiable, piety. The duty of *Prayer* was especially inculcated. For some time, previous, I had been pondering on the subject, & made it matter of reproach to myself, that I had, therein, been so negligent. The words of my Grandmother had a proportionate effect. They roused up every spark of conscience within me; and I did not give slumber to my eye-lids, till after a fervent offering of prayer & praise, of contrition, repentance, & promise of reformation, in the name of Jesus Christ, to God, the Father, Son, & Holy Ghost. From this time, my morning & evening devotions have been regular; without, as far as I able to determine, the intermission of a single instance. Meantime, they have undergone many alterations. I began to doubt of Christianity. Yet I continued Prayer, as a Christian, because I deemed it improper to discontinue it, as such, till I was convinced of the falsity of Christianity. I became convinced & ceased to employ the name of Christ. It was not long before I questioned the propriety of Prayer. I was satisfied of the impropriety of petitioning the Supreme Being—& since then I have rendered him praise & thanksgiving. My views of things have undergone still a further change, & I have hesitated, for some months, concerning even this exercise of devotion. I have persevered in it, however, because I would be satisfied of the reasonableness of discontinuing it, before I should actually discontinue it. For several days & evenings, lately, I have reflected more on the subject; I have satisfied myself that a formal, periodical exercise of this kind is inconsistent with the notions I entertain of the structure & constitution of the Universe, & henceforth I am resolved to discontinue it. What those notions are, I shall take another, & "more convenient opportunity," to explain.

MEMORANDA, 36

Monday, 5th

Wrote fifteen pages of the article "Reuben Hitchcock." Brown was here two hours. Did some errands; was at Dunlap's Store; commenced the Second Book of Thucydides; drank tea at Dunlap's; & with him & Brown, spent the evening at Mr. Roulet's.

MEMORANDA, 37

Tuesday, 6th

At the Hospital two hours & a half—part of the time employed in compiling Notes of Cases which have been under my care. From eleven, till one, at the Monthly Examination of the African Free School. Found C. B. Brown here, when I came home. Dined & spent the afternoon at Wm. W. Woolsey's—with Brown, Dunlap, & G. M. Woolsey. The two former & myself spent the evening at Kent's. Since my return I have read an account of the "Putrid Billious Fever,"[1] as it appeared at the Havanna, in 1794—by John Holliday—with additional remarks, by Dr. Bullfinch of Boston. No great merit in Mr. Holliday's part—Dr. Bullfinch's contemptible.

MEMORANDA, 38
Wednesday, 7th

Went, in season, to the Hospital, to see two patients admitted yesterday; & stayed there to compile some Cases, till after one o'clock. Part of the afternoon at Dunlap's—Brown & he here. We & Johnson & Lovegrove &c. went to see the Lion—& then walked. Drank tea at Dunlap's—& spent the evening at H. Johnson's. Lovegrove returns to-morrow.

MEMORANDA, 39
Thursday, 8th

Professional visit morning & afternoon. At the Hospital. Tarried to take Notes. Brown here. Finished the article "Reuben Hitchcock." Wrote a few lines to my father. At Dunlap's Store. Brown, Wm. & I drank tea, & spent the evening at Seth's.

MEMORANDA, 40
Friday, 9th

At the Hospital, & prescribed for Dr. Mitchill & myself. When I came home, found Dunlap here. We went to the City Library, to consult all the books we could find, on the article "Lion"; our curiosity having been much excited by his manner of ejecting his urine. We could obtain no satisfactory information. C. B. Brown joined us there. We came here—Wm. came home—& we talked till dinner. Mr. Gahn here in the afternoon. Spent most of the evening at Dunlap's. G. M. Woolsey & Wm. W. Woolsey, Wm. Johnson & Brown there. Wrote the letter to Dr. Rush this afternoon & evening. It is incorrect & hasty; but I have been industrious to do so much. Recd. a letter from Mumford. Fanny has been unwell; but is better.

[For "Reuben Hitchcock" which followed the above entry see pp. 36-39.]

LETTERS
To Benjamin Rush.

The flattering expressions of esteem which were contained in your letter of July 30, and the importance of the subject, would have induced an earlier reply, had I not been anxious to read your 4th Vol. before I wrote, & desirous to communicate to you the result of practice in certain Cases, not then decided. I have just finished the reading of your Work; & desire to communicate to you my thanks for the vast fund of entertainment &, I hope, improvement, which it has afforded me. Some facts which have fallen under my observation, & which have been communicated to me, tend to confirm certain of your doctrines; while others are, in a degree, opposed to them. I presume that you will receive both, with equal pleasure; for it is not your opinion, merely, but Truth, which you wish to prevail. My letter will be multifarious, but I hope neither uninteresting nor insignificant.

The conviction of the Local Origin of the Yellow Fever seems to gain ground rapidly. It was a most fortunate circumstance for this opinion, (as far as New York, & perhaps as the United States is considered,) that the appearance of this Disease in this City, the present year, was early in the season, during very sultry weather, under circumstances sufficient to account for it, & without the least room to impute it to Importation. With the departure of sultry weather, it departed too; or assumed the mild form of ordinary Remittents or Intermittents. Of these, and particularly of the last, we have had an uncommon share, for this place. This I ascribe to the cool & moist season which we have had. For I have not the least doubt of the justice of your doctrine, which considers all Fevers, of this kind, as varying only in *degree*. This is confirmed by the experience of all those Country places, in the neighborhood of Lakes & Marshes, in which a Bilious Fever of uncommon malignity prevailed last year. Dr. Buel writes me, from Sheffield, that the Intermitting Fever was never more common than this Season. For two seasons past they have had Bilious Fevers, in that place, but little short of those of Phila. & N. York. The same is the fact in respect to the Western Counties of New York. In all these places the Dysentery is also prevalent: another proof, if further evidence were wanting, of the unity of the cause of Yellow Fever & Dysentery. Indeed, the Books of Physicians are full of testimonies in favor of that opinion—& abundantly shew that the same situation favors the rise & spread of Dysentery & Fever.

A certain family in Lichfield (Connec.) was afflicted, year after year, with Intermittents. The Physician, Dr. Sheldon, a sensible man, attributed it to a Mill-Pond, which rendered the neighboring ground marshy. The people could not be persuaded that this was the cause. Wearied, at length, with incessant sickness, on every return of every Spring, they turned the course of the Water, the Marsh was removed, & none have since suffered with the Ague. The same intelligent Physician was called to a Man who was then sick, & all whose family had been sick, with Dysentery. A rival practitioner had in vain exerted his skill. Mr. Sheldon sought for the cause. He discovered it in a stagnant pool, directly behind the House. This he had filled up, im-

---
[1] John Holliday (Surgeon of the Royal Navy). *A Short Account of the Origin, Symptoms, and Most approved Methods of Treating the Putrid Bilious Fever, commonly called the Black Vomit which appeared in the City of Havanna, with the utmost violence, in June, July, and August, 1794* (London, 1795).

mediately. The man recovered, by the ordinary means, & no more were seized.

A further proof, is the *alternation* of these complaints —or forms of disease. We have had many Cases, in the New York Hospital, this very season, of alternation of Intermittents & Diarrhea, or Dysentery, in the same persons. In two [or] three instances, this alternation has been several times repeated. The appearance of Dysentery, near a lake or marsh, one year, & of Fever the next, is only a more extended & general alternation. Is it not true that Dysentery most often alternates with Yellow Fever, or highly Bilious Fever, & Diarrhea with Intermittents?

Every fact recorded, when rightly considered, tends to prove, not only that Fevers are of local birth, but that they are rarely exported. The Bulam Fever of Grenada, was of local & not imported origin. The Captain of the vessel supposed to have carried it there, now lives in this State. He is a well-informed man of excellent character. He informed Mr. Webster that the Fever was raging in Grenada when he arrived there. The circumstances have been stated at large in Mr. Webster's Paper.

People make use of this as an argument, That Yellow Fever always first appears or appears only in Sea Ports. The reason is obvious—it is in sea ports, that there is the greatest accumulation of the causes of Fever. In the country, vegetation & ventilation unite to dissipate or neutralize the pestiferous miasma. There is a very interesting Letter, on this subject, in Bailey's Account of the Fever of 1795 of New York—written by Dr. Cogswell of Hartford (Connec.) whose name is suppressed. But, after all, the Fevers among the manufacturing poor of Manchester, as described by Dr. Ferriar, are scarcely less formidable than those of our Cities. The causes are sufficiently clear. It would be, perhaps, impossible to create such diseases, by any importation, in well built, & ventilated towns, the inhabitants of which were temperate & cleanly. The following facts were communicated to me by a Physician who has seen the Yellow Fever in the West Indies, & who recd. his medical education principally in Birmingham. In that populous town, where so many operations in metals (which are commonly supposed to be unhealthy) are carried on, no Fever ever prevails, except in one Street. In this Street the Typhus is found, during the whole year. It consists of two rows of low, damp, & dirty houses, situated on either side of a hill or ridge, higher than their tops, which is only wide enough to separate them, thro' the whole length. A population equal to 80,000 supports only seven practitioners of Physic. Physicians, Surgeons, Midwives & Apothecaries, do not exceed forty; & Fever is rarely found but in this single street—the medical care of which appertains to the Poor-House.

Is it true that the Bile is so peculiarly in fault as to justify the term Bilious Fever? Were this the fact, should we not more generally find the Liver diseased? I do not think that this Viscus suffers, ordinarily, more in Yellow, than in Intermittent Fever. And I suspect that Inflammations & swellings of the Liver will no more happen, in Yellow Fever, where the patient has been properly evacuated, than swellings of the Legs will take place in Intermittents which have been timely cured. Cases of hepatic derangement probably occur more often in hot, than in temperate Climates. In temperate Climates, & perhaps in all, the season may determine the cause of the disease, to act on one viscus, or system, in preference to another; & local circumstances or idiosyncrasy may cause a like preference, (& consequently considerable variations in the seat of the disease) in individuals. This notion, as it respects individuals, appears to me to be confirmed by the circumstances of two cases, referred to by me in a former letter, as instances of the communication & reception of Contagion.

The first persons taken with the Yellow Fever, this year, in New York, were a merchant of the name of Briggs, & his Clerk. I shall have occasion to speak of the former, by & by; the case of the latter, being interesting in more respects than one, you will bear with me if I am somewhat particular in stating it.

J. L. (the Clerk) was a young Englishman of 20. He had been in the United States a year. Had a slight attack of the Fever last year. He was of a full habit, with that universal redness of the face, which is the consequence of free living. His principal food was animal, particularly rare Beef—& his ordinary drink Porter. He had a large quantity of hair, wore a poultice cravat, & a black hat during our hottest weather. The window of the Counting-room in which he wrote opened over one of the most offensive Slips in the City. He boarded at his father's —who lived ¾ of a mile distant, in a street much afflicted by Fever last year, & the whole walk lay thro' the most unhealthy part of the town, now as offensive as ever. So that the young man walked thro' them, in the middle of the day, to eat rare beef & drink porter, & returned to write over this Slip. He ate no acid or acescent fruit—& any thing acid was always offensive to him. A few days before his seizure, which was in excessive hot weather, he was intoxicated, at a party. He was taken on Monday, & violently. The uncertainty of the physician, & the opposition of the friends, prevented his being bled till Thursday. Meantime his bowels were freely opened with Calomel & Jalap. On Thursday, with much difficulty, he was bled; but fainted, & but a small quantity was taken away. A similar attempt was made on Friday, with still less success; & a spontaneous hemorrhage appeared, from the nostrils & gums, particularly the last. I first saw him on Saturday afternoon. Some degree of Coma had now come on. The bleeding from his nose ceased; but from his gums continued. From this time, till his death, which happened on the morning of the 17th day of his sickness, the full effect of Ice, cool drinks, ablution, clysters, & air, was tried—except that the fatigue of the family, (who could gain no assistance, so great was the terror,) occasionally begat some remissness in their application. The bowels were kept constantly open with Calomel &c. & the Cupping-Glasses[2] often applied to the head. The purging & cupping, the last expecially, always afforded temporary relief. We had some hopes till the 15th day. On the 13th day, in getting on to an earthen pot, it broke, & he recd. a wound, in the left buttock, $2\frac{1}{2}$ inches long, & $\frac{1}{4}$ deep. From this wound, his cupping, bleeding, & hemorrhage from the gums & fauces, he lost, according to our estimation, not less than thirteen pounds of blood. Not the least approach to mortification, or gangrene, appeared, either in the wound, or scarifications. On the contrary, most of the last healed by the first intention, before the patient's death. On the 15th day, the right thigh swelled to twice it's natural size, & a similar swelling rose in the groin; both with some slight discoloration. They were not much diminished by the applications made to them. The whole body began to turn yellow on the 7th day, & was excessively so, at death. All the bed & body linnen were tinged, both by the sweat & urine. The eyes were exceedingly pained by light from the first. The most inveterate coma prevailed, from the 7th or 8th day—but the *stomach was not in the least affected*.

The mother of the Young Man, was a woman of near fifty, feeble, & of a sluggish & dispeptic state of stomach & bowels. She was worn out by incessant fatigue, watchfulness & distress; & was taken with the Fever, on the tenth day of her son's disease. A few purges seemed to carry off all her Fever; & she appeared to sink from the want of nourishment alone—which was not regularly administered to her, from want of suitable attendance. She died on the same day with her son. She was yellow —& had a vomiting of Coffee-coloured matter—but her *head was never in the least affected*. Two younger brothers of the young man who died, were also slightly affected with fever. The free & continued use of Cathartics, enabled them to keep about, & restored them.

Two or three days before the death of the two persons above-mentioned, Mr. L. the father, who had most exerted himself, in the care of his family, & was great part of his time bent over his son, assisting him, &c. was suddenly seized with a swelling of his nose; which increased to near thrice it's proper size, became red & painful; & at the same time, a tumor, half the size of a hen's egg, rose over his right eye, & gradually extending, almost closed it. Next both his breasts swelled, as large as those of a woman; & lastly his feet & legs, like those of a person with anasarca. Cathartics, & cold water to the swellings, cured him, in about a week. No others were any way affected, by these persons, or in their neighborhood.

I ascribe the disease of the mother, father, & two brothers, to their attendance on the young man. I attribute it's fixation on his brain to the circumstances noted in the beginning of his Case; & on the stomach of the mother, to her particular debility, in that organ. And here it may be remarked, that when any particular part—whether head, stomach, intestines, breast—or liver—is peculiarly seized upon, the others enjoy, for the most part, an immunity from the disease. If the stomach is affected, the brain is free; if the brain, the stomach is not disordered—& so of the rest. But this is not constantly the case.

The hemorrhagy from the nose & gums, in young L., broke forth on the 5th day of his disease. While we were attending him, Dr. Dingley recd. this information, from an intelligent New England Sea-Captain, of his acquaintance; a man who had been in the West India Trade, for many years. He said—(The Captain) that he had lost many sailors, with the Yellow Fever, & had some recover. He had had it himself. As his vessel & crew were small, they neither had a physician nor a Medicine Chest. All the cases of recovery happened in one way. A hemorrhage broke out, from the nose, gums & fauces, on the 5th day, & continued, till the Fever went off. This was his case; it was the same in five of his hands; & when the bleeding did not appear, the sick always died.

What confirmation is here, (in these facts which seem to prove that there is a determinate period in this Fever) of the propriety of bleeding? How benevolent is Nature, thus to pour forth the offending fluid, herself, when she has not been wisely anticipated! Most persons regard hemorrhagy as an alarming symptom, & hasten to restrain it. It indeed proves that the necessary evacuations have not been made; but I see no reason for attempting to stop it, when it comes in to remedy the effects of our own negligence, or want of skill.

In those Cases of Yellow Fever which have come under my observation this year, whether in Hospital or private practice, there has been no remarkable deviation in the symptoms, from those of the last year. I saw in one patient, the pupil permanently dilated, tho' the eye was excruciatingly sensible to the stimulus of light. This man came late into the Hospital—& at this time had the most obstinate coma. He lay with his eyes closed; & the efforts of his eyelids, to shut, when opened to inspect his eyes, were very violent.

The same treatment, as in 1795, has been successful, & the reverse. Dr. Mitchill, who has been with me in the Hospital this summer, has even gone before me in the application of similar remedies. The harmony with which we have pursued the antiphlogistic plan of cure,[3] has been matter of astonishment & disappointment to the opposers, as well as of gratification to the friends, of Venesection & Cold. These, & their co-assisting remedies, tho' still opposed by prejudice, & partially employed, appear the more efficacious compared with contrary medicaments.

Mr. Briggs, the merchant who was taken on the same day, & at the same place, with the young man, whose

---

[2] Hot horn cup or glass applied rim-down on the head or other parts of the body to draw blood to the surface of the skin. The vacuum caused the capillaries to break; a form of bleeding.

[3] The use of an agent to counteract fever and inflammation.

case I have stated at some length, took an Emetic on the second day of his sickness. He never ceased to vomit till death, (which took place on the 5th day) & for 24 hours vomited blood. Two other persons died, under nearly the same circumstances, & as early in the disease —from the same cause. One of them was brought to the Hospital. He was then vomiting. Cool Water, & Limonade, both rested well on his stomach. He had wine & water with him. He drank of it, & immediately rejected it. Again he took Water. He vomited no more. I saw a man this day, who was seized with vomiting, immediately on taking Bark in Wine, which had continued for several days. A Physician confessed to me that, having given his patient wine, when he was recovering, from a desire to restore his strength the sooner, it was instantly thrown up—& the man told him, he might as well have given him liquid fire. This corresponds with a case noticed in your 4th volume.

In respect to Salivation,[4] we have had but a poor opportunity for trying it. I attempted to produce it in two persons who were brought into the Hospital in a desperate condition. They both died, without it's having taken place. I gave Mercury, as a cathartic, to a woman who had Yellow Fever, in the form of an Intermittent. Her head was exceedingly affected & with a sensation as if the whole Occiput was removed. A few grains salivated her, slightly. She was immediately relieved of all her pains, & was well in a few days. Beside this woman, I salivated a young woman of 17, with mania. She recovered her reason—but under circumstances so complicated as to render it doubtful how far the Salivation was efficient in her restoration.

We can speak of Bleeding with more confidence & precision—for both Dr. Mitchill & myself, have employed it, very extensively, for three months past; & with sufficient success. Indeed, when we have had any thing like a fair opportunity for doing any good, in Fevers, we have always done it by Bleeding. But we have not confined use of it to Fevers, but extended it to Dropsy & Mania. In two cases, Anacarcous legs[5] have been reduced; one Maniac has been completely cured; & a second much relieved, with considerable probability of a cure; by bleeding. In two instances, we have bled *thro' a Fainting Fit,* with great relief to the patients; one of whom is now convalescent & nearly restored. A young man came into the Hospital on the 27th of August, the tenth day of a Bilious Fever. He had been once bled, by a common bleeder, & had received no other medical treatment. He was bled again, copiously, & purged with Calomel; & drank cold water, took wheaten gruel. I had the satisfaction of discharging him well—& he walked away himself, on the morning of the 1st of September. Bleeding & Blistering, cured an Intermittent, of a long standing, & as irregular as those described by Cleghorn,[6] in a youth so emaciated that the Students shuddered with astonishment & horror when the remedies were prescribed. While he was recruiting he was seized with a diarrhea—& when that was removed, his old complaint recurred. Another bleeding & the external use of Volatile Liniment again removed it. He gained health, & had no relapse. But the most remarkable cure remains to be mentioned. This was of a strong Sailor, a patient of Dr. Mitchill's, with the most violent Quotidian[7] I ever saw. He came into the Hospital on the 8th of August, & is now well. Between the time of his admission, & the 22nd of the same month, he lost 176 ounces of blood. Bark did not agree with—even after this. His fits were removed principally by the blood letting; at least they were so moderated, that the common mild bitters succeeded in completing the cure. The man was so sensible of the benefit derived from this evacuation, that he was impatient, when the Fever was on him, till the operation was performed; & always insisted on having a larger quantity taken away, than was at first intended. He has lost a quart of blood, at one time, in several instances.

A Physician, of some respectability in this place, informed me yesterday, that of 60 persons bled by him, with Fever, this season, he had lost but two; one of whom drank himself to death.

After all these testimonies in favor of this Remedy, one would think that the cavillers should be silent. But they, like all others whose prejudices are exposed, become more violent in proportion as their cause is rendered desperate. The last struggles must always be violent. They will soon be over. You will yet live to taste the sweet reward of all your painful sacrifices, in the contemplation of the good you have effected, by leading the way to the free use of this remedy, & will enjoy the deserved consolation for so many calumnies in the general acknowlegements of your countrymen. Old men hate to have the habits & opinions of many years disturbed; young men are inquisitive, forming opinions, & are candid; the age is more turned to philosophical inquiry; the places of the old will soon be supplied by the young; & the triumph of superior reason will be complete & permanent.

We have not found the same difficulty in curing the Intermitting Fever with Bark, this year, when it never was more common, than was found in Phila. in 1794 & 95. I have, in repeated instances cured it, even of long standing, with this remedy, in a week, or ten days. We have also cured it, with Gentian & Orange Peel, with Columbo Root, with Opium, & with Spirits.

In making the following remarks, I have the most perfect reliance on your candor. They contain some objections to a part of your doctrine—or rather to the

---

[4] The production of an excessive secretion of saliva by administering mercury.

[5] Anasarcous: characterized by secretions of fluids: dropsy.

[6] George Cleghorn, M.D. (1716-1789), *Observations on the Epidemical Diseases in Minorca from the Year 1744-1749* (London, 1751).

[7] An intermittent fever which recurs almost every day or every other day.

rationale of it. I trust you will excuse me for making them, even if they shall be thought undeserving of attention.

You seem to suppose Oxygen, in a superabundant state in the System, to be the exciting cause of the Yellow Fever. Some circumstances seem to contradict this sentiment.

1. The odour noticed, p. 54. & supposed by you to proceed from the contagion of the Yellow Fever, is of a kind very distinct from that produced by any known combination with Oxygen.

2. Smoke, which you remark page 59 to be a preventative, is known to be an Acid. It's corrective qualities must depend, then, on it's acidity—which is absurd, if the principle of acidity is the principle of Contagion.

3. The account of Dr. J. Carmichael Smyth,[8] of his treatment of the Spanish Prisoners, with Mr. Veir's explanation subjoined, seems still further to confirm the idea of the anti-pestilential nature of Oxygen.

4. You have noticed here that small Boils prevent Cholera. Lieutaud[9] & others inform us that Consumptive persons & those who have large ulcers, never suffer from the plague. And it is well known that those Rice Swamps, in the Southern States, which most abundantly generate Fevers, always relieve the Phthisical. This seems to prove, contrary, to your supposition, that Yellow Fever & Pneumonia depend on very different states of the system. And so the fact is clearly represented, by Dr. Beddoes, the great apostle of Pneumatic Medicine & by Dr. Ramsay of Charleston—who puts the Consumptions of the Northern in opposition to the Fevers of the Southern States.

This topic might be urged still further, but I will confine myself to one single additional circumstance—& this, principally, because I wish to notice those arguments which are either derived from, or connected with, your own observations.

5. The appearances exhibited by the blood, when drawn in the Yellow Fever, are of a kind extremely different from those which we are taught to expect from hyper-oxygenation. They prove the state of the blood in Fever & in Pneumonia, to be widely different. No person (I speak from observations made by Dr. Mitchill & myself, this year,) who had once compared the blood of a Consumptive & Febrile Patient, could hesitate in pronouncing to which it belonged.

I have seen that appearance of the Serum, which you notice, when it resembles the washing of flesh in water.

I have seen but one instance, in a great number of patients, with various degrees of fever, of that Scarlet sediment which you mention.

The usual appearance of the Serum in Fever has been of a yellowish or brownish green. The upper surface of the Crassamentum always of a faint, purplish red, like that dye which Painters call *Lake*; & the under surface, dark, inclining to green. Blood taken from some maniacal, Rheumatic, & all Pneumonic patients, has had a lively yellow appearance of the Serum; & the Crassamentum, on the top, has resembled the bright Ink made from Brazil wood; & at the bottom, has only differed in being somewhat darker, as if the dye was more concentrated.

In one fever case I have seen greenish black, coagulated Blood. And, on a third bleeding of the same patient, a remarkable appearance, not susceptible of accurate description—but abounding in masses of greenish yellow & darkish green, jelly-like substance.

But I pretend not to decide on this subject. The blood has been very imperfectly examined; it is a most interesting object of curiosity; & much remains to be known. Dr. Mitchill & myself purpose to institute a series of experiments on the Blood, at some future time. Perhaps we may be able to gain some knowlege in this almost unexplored field. It will be my earliest care to communicate to you any thing, worthy of being known, which may result.

Our field of action has been very much narrowed by the timidity of the Governors of the Hospital, which almost excluded all Fever, from the fear of Contagion. It is really astonishing, the terror which is excited by the least rumor of the approach of Yellow Fever. Many other diseases have, at different times, visited various places, with greater mortality. But thousands & tens of thousands may lie with other complaints, & no one dream of danger. A gentleman of my acquaintance was lately at Saratoga—& was informed, by Genl. Gordon (formerly a member of Congress from this State) that in the neighboring Township of Galiway, whose whole population he estimated at 2,000, they had in one week buried 100 persons, who had died of Dysentery. One twentieth of the whole population swept off in one week! Yet, no doubt, these very people would think they could make not too much haste to banish from their town a person who had come from a place where the Yellow Fever prevailed.

Should you receive with indulgence this long, & I fear, tiresome letter, I hope I may be able, at some future time, to offer something more worthy of your acceptation. Mean time, I am desirous of convincing you that, however awkward my attempts to display it may be considered, no person feels for you a more sincere & lively veneration & esteem.[10]

Friday, Septr. 9. 1796.
Cedar St. No. 13. N. York.   E. H. Smith.

---

[8] James Carmichail Smyth, M.D., *A Description of Jail Distemper, as it Appeared among the Spanish Prisoners at Winchester in the Year 1780* . . . (London, 1795).

[9] Joseph Lieutaud, M.D. (1703-1780); probably his *Synopsis universae praxeos medicae* (Amsterdam, 1765).

[10] It is difficult to avoid the impression that the young physician was determined to show his old teacher how much he knew.

MEMORANDA, 41

Saturday, 10th

At the Hospital. At Dunlap's. Made several other calls. Spent an hour with Mr. Miller, in his house. H. & Wm. Johnson, & I went on board "The America," to see John;[11] who is soon to sail. We, afterwards, walked out of Town. In the evening we revived the Friendly Club. We met at Dunlap's—Present, himself, Brown, W. Johnson, Smith, & the Woolsey's.

POSTSCRIPT

The preceeding pages are evidence for me, that I have not neglected the pen, for the week past. They are not very abundant in proofs of industry, in other respects. Still, my time has not, on the whole, been idly thrown away. The article "Hitchcock," is interesting to me, & will, I think, be somewhat so to others. When the several circumstances come to be interwoven, in their proper order, with the history of myself, their importance will be more clearly apprehended. The Letter to Dr. Rush is quite crude. I wish it may deserve to be considered as the bullion, from which some gold may yet be drawn. I must transcribe, retrench, & augment it —before it is dismissed. To do this, to copy my letter to Mrs. Tracy—& a few other little affairs, will render the Notices of the next week, in all probability, sufficiently short. But let the week speak for itself.

Seventh Week

Sunday, 11th

PREFACE

As at the commencement of the last week, I am at a loss to determine what I shall do the present. To copy & correct my letter to Dr. Rush, seems as proper to be done, as any thing. I hope it will be done. I must write to Aurora. One thing further—the third year of my residence in New York is now complete, & has been for some days. I ought to make an Estimate of what have been my Receits & Expenditures during this year; of what I owe, & what is due to me. I have been too busy, hitherto, to effect this. I mean, if possible, to accomplish it, the present week. But, how many things press upon! how little have I done! how little do I perform! how imbecile are my attempts! how irresolute & vacillating all my exertions! Pish! why do I do I repeat this so often? "Sufficient for the day is the evil thereof!"[12] I will endeavor to "do, what my hand findeth to do"[13] & will not be stung with remorse or discontent even if it should not be much. Call again the smile upon thy lip, little Content, & let it sport in the dimple of thy cheek! Look cheerily! Grief was not made for Man.

---

[11] John Johnson, probably brother of Smith's roommate.
[12] Matthew 6: 34.
[13] Smith, according to his usual habit, is quoting "as memory serves" from Ecclesiastes 9: 10.

MEMORANDA, 42

Transcribed, with corrections, my letter to Mrs. Tracy. Dunlap & Brown here, the remainder of the forenoon. Dined, with the Johnsons, at Horace's. Wm. & I walked out of town. Part of the evening at Kent's—part on the Battery.

MEMORANDA, 43

Monday, 12th

Prescribed at the Hospital, for Dr. Mitchill. Dr. Miller passed two hours with me. Devoted the greater part of the day to posting my books, & making certain Estimates of Receits & Expenditures, which I have not yet completed. Visited Dr. Dingley. Wm. & I walked two hours on the Battery; & supped at S. Johnson's. There never was a more beautiful evening. I suppose C. B. Brown left this city, for Phila. to-day.

MEMORANDA, 44

Tuesday, 13th

At the Hospital. Made several calls. Wrote two short & hasty letters to Mumford, & a few lines to my Father. Several calls. Dunlap, Wm. & I walked out of town. Spent the evening, very agreably, with Dr. & Mr. Miller, at their house.

MEMORANDA, 45

Wednesday, 14th

Transcribed, with several corrections, so much as my letter to Dr. Rush as preceeds the remarks on the Blood; reserving them, with several additions, till another opportunity. Dingley here, two hours. Principal part of the evening, with Johnson, Dunlap & family, at Woolsey's. Dr. Mitchill here in the evening, after my return. He shewed us a letter, from Mr. Ebeling of Hamburg, by which I learn that his Pamphlet on Contagion is translating into German, at Göttengen.

MEMORANDA, 46

Thursday, 15th

At the Hospital. The remainder of the forenoon at Dr. Mitchill's Room. Looked over Maxwell's Experiments. Dunlap came there. Mitchill gave us some new anecdotes of Miss E. A. K. Read part of Fourcroy's "Philosophy of Chemistry." Johnson & I walked out to Webster's. We continued our walk—as they were not at home. It was a most delightful afternoon. Yesterday afternoon & last evening, we had a violent thunderstorm. More so than any I ever heard in New York—or, as I am told, any that has been known here in ten years: tho' not more than is common in Lichfield, & other highlands. I spent part of the evening at Mr. Rogers's; part, at Dunlap's.

SUMMARY OF THE STATE OF MY PECUNIARY AFFAIRS

Friday, 16th

I have just finished that inquiry into the state of my affairs, from Septr. 5. 1795. to Septr. 5. 1796—which I had not time to do, on the day last named. The result offers very little of encouragement. Corresponding with that of preceeding years, it leaves me still dependant on a father's bounty, & without any certain promise of future returns, for past & present neglect. There is no advantage in repining, or one might be tempted to inquire, How many more years are necessary to gratify the malignancy of that Destiny, which delights to see me consume my best years in thinking how to live—not living that I may think. Here follows the Result.

Amount of Expenditures, from Septr. 5th 1795; to Septr. 5th 1796—including Rent, Diet, Servant's Wages, Apparel, Books & Stationary, Medicines, Fuel & Lights, Washing, Postage, the expence of three Journeys, Subscriptions, Charities, Amusements, & other incidental expences—most of the several heads enumerated ascertained by bills—the others by estimation—in round numbers—

840 dollars.

Specification of Monies now due, from me, to others.

To M. Robertson—(Tailor's Bill) .... dols.	076..62 cts.
A. Drummond—(bookseller.)	45..62
T. Wood ... (Shoemaker.)	17..—
Philips & Clark ... (Druggists.)	16..66
Bloodgood & Hitchcock ... (Grocers.) .	14..25
Rogers & Woolsey.— (Hardware Merchants.)	7..69
T. Tiffin ... (Hatter.)	2..—
Belles Lettres Club Subscription	5..—
N. Webster ... (on account..about—) .	3..—
Personal Tax	1..50
Petty debts	1..46
Sum.	190..80

Amount of Monies due to me, Septr. 5th 1796, with the state they are in—as to my obtaining them.

	dols. cts.
Debts due—but no probability of payment.	043..12
Debts—the receit of which is doubtful.	046..55
Debts—likely to be paid—or good debts.	258..44
Sum.	348..11

My Charges, from Septr. 5th. 1795, to Septr. 5th. 1796.

	dols. cts.
Bad Charges—or for which nothing is to be expected	074..62
Good Charges—either paid, or likely to be so ..	498..18
Amount of Charges	572..80

My Receits, from Septr. 5th. 1795, to Septr. 5th. 1796.

Money recd. from my Father, in this period, ... Dols.	431..09. cts.
Money recd. on account, ...	340..23
Money recd. for advice & medicine, not regularly entered	20..—
Money recd. as interest on money loaned.	37..50.
Amount of Receits.	828..82.[14]

Of this Sum, as I have only six cents on hand, my actual Expenditure has been, within the period stated—828..76. This has been partly, for the debts of the former, & partly, for those of the present year. So, likewise, the monies now owed by me, are partly for debts contracted previous to the present period—tho' the Amount of such debts is small. Were all that is now due to me recd. it would discharge all demands against me; &, perhaps, somewhat exceed them. Were all that I ever expect to obtain recd., it would go near to make me independent. Apparently, it would do more—from the preceeding statements; but there is not included in them the balance against me on The House account—which, if continued down to the present date, would not fall much short of One Hundred Dollars. So that, after all, I should be somewhat incumbered. Alas! shall I ever feel what it is to be Independent?!

MEMORANDA, 47

I heard, yesterday, that Dr. Leib was in town. I went to see him, this morning, but he was gone. Democracy is of more importance than friendship. Completed, with some trouble, the foregoing Estimates. Most of the afternoon, & part of the evening, professionally engaged. Called on Dunlap, & he on me. Wm. & I took a turn on the Battery, & dropped in, a few minutes, at John Well's. Part of the evening at Mr. Boyd's; part at home. Made some advance in Fourcroy.

MEMORANDA, 48

Saturday, 17th

Three times at the Hospital. Some other professional business. A short walk, with Dunlap, in the forenoon; & with Johnson in the afternoon. Further progress in Fourcroy. Dr. Mitchill called to request me to supply his place, at the Hospital, in his absence; which will exceed the time of our Limited Order. So that, for the ensuing fortnight I shall have the whole care of the Medical Department of the Institution on my hands. Club night—Johnson's turn—Present, Dunlap, Wm. Johnson, Kent, Smith, the Woolseys. A pleasant evening. The successes of the French, Domestic Politics—& the merits of Fielding, Richardson, & Smollet's Novels —(excited by Johnson's reading Count Fathom's Adventure in the Forest) were the principal topics of conversation.

---

[14] The most interesting item in this account is the last one: "Money recd. as interest on money loaned" $37.50. How was it possible for Smith to lend money when he appears to have seldom had more money available than he had when he drew up this account, i.e., six cents? He never explained.

POSTSCRIPT

As much has been done, in this week, as I expected; & no more. So that, if there has been no disappointment, there has been no surprize. There is as little cause for exultation, as for lamenting.

I am far from being satisfied with the manner in which things proceed; but the duty of my profession, in one shape, continually breaks in upon my discharge of it, in another. To each, I have nearly equal bias; except that it is always easier to do things by piece-meal, than by the whole; while there never is the same satisfaction, when we come to reflect.

In one fortnight, I shall be at liberty, from the Hospital. I shall be glad of a breathing-spell. I wish to be better prepared against my next turn of duty. I want, too, to set down, & summon together, at my leisure, the experiences of the last three or four months. I want to apply these to a great work I have in view; & to labour towards the general diffusion of correct ideas, or subjects the most important to the national health.

Eighth Week

Sunday, 18th

PREFACE

For the week now commenced I promise myself but few acquisitions, in the way of study, but few advances in those of composition. As the whole medical charge of the Hospital now falls upon me, and as the business is more than usually pressing & extensive, I expect so large a portion of my time to be there occupied, as will very much break in upon any plan of study I might otherwise be able to pursue. It is in the bits of days, the shreds of leisure, only, that I shall be enabled to devote some flying moments to my more pleasant employments.

I have been promising myself a visit from my friend Wm. Buel, this month; but I hear that Sheffield is very unhealthy, & the people afflicted with pestilence. If so, that pleasure will be denied me. I shall not regret it, if his life & health be spared. He will make a better use of his time, in recording those facts, which this calamity of his town, will present to his observation.

MEMORANDA, 49

At the Hospital. Attended a Medical Consultation. Wm. & I began the reading of "Lavoisier's Elements of Chemistry,"[15] in company. Dined at S. Johnson's. Was at Hodgkinson's. They returned yesterday. Spent the evening at Dunlap's. Wrote a few lines to Dr. Buel.

MEMORANDA, 50

Monday, 19th

At the Hospital. Performed several errands. Wm. & I progressed in Lavoisier. Dunlap here. Finished Fourcroy's "Philosophy of Chemistry." Recd. Home's "Life of John Hunter."[16] C. B. Brown returned from Phila. leaving all well. Wm. & I spent the evening at Dunlap's—where [were] all the Woolsey's & Brown.

MEMORANDA, 51

Tuesday, 20th

At the Hospital. Made some calls. Began to write the following letter. Visits from Dr. Miller, Mr. Gahn, & Dr. Dingley. Several professional calls. Recd. letters from my Father, & sister Abby, by Mr. Catlin—at whose house I spent part of the evening.

MEMORANDA, 52

Wednesday, 21st

At the Hospital. Professional visits. Called at Dunlap's. Late dinner at Dr. & Mrs. Miller's. Professional visit. At Woolsey's. C. B. Brown & I spent the evening at Mr. Roulet's. C. B. B. to commence instruction in English to Mr. R. to-morrow. Returned & supped at Dunlap's. When I came home, found a man waiting for me, to go & see his child, who is sick. Went.

The hurry of this day, has allowed me no time for reading, writing, or reflection. In one fortnight I hope to be able to do better.

LETTERS

To Abigail Smith Junr.

Twenty things, not one of which is worthy of mention, have prevented my writing to you, since the receit of your last letter. The delay has been so long, that I have expectations of receiving another letter from you, before I shall have opportunity to forward what I may now write; & I rather intend this is an introduction to an answer, than as an answer itself.

The account which you gave me of your dramatic exhibitions, was interesting, (tho' you were fearful that it would be the reverse); as much, it is true, from my knowlege of the parties concerned, as from any other cause. It was, however, pleasing from two considerations not necessarily connected with the persons engaged. I am pleased to see the prejudices of people wearing away, in respect to theatrical performances; & still more pleased to observe the spirited share which has been taken in them, by the young women of Lichfield. Every instance of their assertion of their talents & right to use them, in how small a degree soever, is so much gained. It is a good deal to become convinced of their own powers; it is something more to convince others of their capacity.

Your letter encourages me to hope that you persevere in your present plan of study; & that you will turn it to more account than heretofore. I expect to see your atten-

---

[15] Antoine L. Lavoisier, *Traité Elémentaire de Chimie* (1789).

[16] Sir Everard Home, Serjeant Surgeon to the King, *A Treatise on the Blood, etc. by John Hunter; with a short Account of the Author's Life* (London, 1794).

tion more forcibly bent upon Modern History, when you have so far succeeded in your study of Ancient times, as to have acquired an insight into those remote events, which in any considerable degree, influence recent transactions.

I had written so far, & had been interrupted, when your business letter, by Mr. Catlin arrived. I had not time to send you any answer to it, when the Post went out, yesterday; being particularly hurried all day—& with scarce time to send a few lines to our father. At present, I can assure you that I shall do all in my power to execute your commission. *Plumb-colour*—is so vague a description that I am not sure that I shall hit upon what you mean. I suppose it to be a darkish bluish purple. If opportunity offers, I shall send this for further instructions; otherwise you must run your chance.

I have not recd the note you mention, respecting the volumes of Linnaeus. It will be impossible for me to lend them; & if Miss L. knew what they are, she would not request it. She, doubtless, wants books which will give her an insight into the science. Now, she might as well read a Dictionary, as the volumes she wishes for. They can be of no use to her—unless she had some knowlege of plants, & wished to determine to what particular classes, families, &c. they belonged.

Farewell, for the present. I shall not close this letter, till I have a conveyance for it.

Friday, Septr. 23. 1796.
Cedar St. No. 13. New York.   E. H. Smith.

MEMORANDA, 53

Thursday, 22nd

Most of the day & evening, at the Hospital & elsewhere professionally employed. Wrote a few lines to my father. Was at Mr. Kent's an hour, in the evening. Mr. Roulet & C. B. Brown here a few minutes.

MEMORANDA, 54

Friday, 23rd

At the Hospital, & visited patients. Finished the preceeding letter. Dined at Mrs. Miller's—in company with Dr. & Mr. Miller. C. B. Brown, Wm. Johnson, Dunlap & I walked out of town together. Professional visits. Most of the evening at home, reading the "Moniteur" —of Paris, &c. &c. A Mr. Thomas Green Fessenden came, this day, to read in Johnson's office.

MEMORANDA, 55

Saturday, 24th

At the Hospital. Several professional & other calls. Read some numbers of the "Moniteur." Decius Wadsworth came to see me. Read Holcroft's "Road to Ruin."[17] At Hodgkinson's. Corrected some part of the songs of my Opera, as set to Music. Decius Wadsworth

[17] (1792).

here part of the afternoon. Thinks the music good. We walked. Drank tea at Woolsey's. Club there. Present—Brown, Dunlap, Wm. Johnson, Kent, the Woolseys. W. W. W. read us the Conquest of Siberia, from Coxe's "Russian Discoveries."[18] I was called away, to see a sick person. Returned. Some systematic, more desultory conversation.

POSTSCRIPT

As I expected, little, very little has been done this week, except in relation to my immediate business. I ought not to regret, & I do not regret it; because the execution of my particular functions can never be wholly unattended by improvement.

The present moments press too hardly upon me, in my imperfect state of information, to confer that pleasure which I might else derive from them. My consolation is in the prospect of future & better days. I have that within me which will prompt, at least, to the gradual acquisition of knowlege; & the stationary state of most of those who surround me, must by & by suffer me to equal, & perhaps surpass them. In proportion, too, as I know more I shall shake of that constraint which ignorance imposes, & not ashamed to want information of which few are possest, shall thus put myself in the way of gaining all the lights which variety of situation may cast on the darkness which envelopes all medical inquiry.

NINTH WEEK

Sunday, 25th

PREFACE

This week must labour under all the disadvantages for regular improvement with the preceeding. Indeed, under accumulated burthens. Two additional obstacles present themselves—the purchasing Liquors &c. for my father, & the correction & preparation of my Opera for representation. Next week will set me free from the heaviest pressure of business, but will not, in all probability, leave at liberty to sit down to the systematic employment of my time.

It is really laughable to see the mistakes which the composer of the Music for "Edwin & Angelina" has committed, in accent & punctuation, owing to his ignorance of English. Thus in this line—"What bliss the unlook'd for good inspired"—he has made a pause in the music after *unlook'd*—& then continues "for good inspires." Other examples, equally ludicrous occur. Here will be trouble & time, to set these things right.

MEMORANDA, 56

Professional visits. Corrected the songs of "Edwin & Angelina," as copied to the music. A walk on the bat-

[18] *Account of the Russian Discoveries Between Asia and America. To which are added The Conquest of Siberia and the History of the Transactions and Commerce Between Russia and China* (London, 1780).

tery. Read the "Moniteur." A visit to H. Johnson's. Lovegrove there. Left all well at home. At Dunlap's—where I spent most of the evening. At Kent's.

MEMORANDA, 57

Monday, 26th

At the Hospital. A few professional calls. Most of the day consumed in petty affairs. At the Theater in the evening. "The Wonder," with "The Poor Soldier."[19] Both pretty well performed.

MEMORANDA, 58

Tuesday, 27th

At the Hospital. Calls of business & pleasure. Decius Wadsworth & C. B. Brown here. Purchased the four first numbers of a new periodical publication, from London, intituled the "Monthly Magazine." Read some part of each. It promises to be worth possessing. Most of the evening at Woolsey's. Mr. Fessenden, mentioned, on friday last, as having commenced the study of the Law with Wm. Johnson, returned to Vermont, to-day. Poverty is the cause. He seems to be a sensible, observing young man; & is one of a Club who write in "The Farmer's Weekly Museum"—a Weekly News Paper, published in Walpole—in which many popular Essays, in verse & prose, have appeared. The real, tho' not acknowleged conductor of this Paper, is a Mr. Dennie—who has gained much credit, with some reason, for the productions of his pen—of which a Series of Papers, called "The Lay Preacher," & lately collected, are esteemed the best.[20]

MEMORANDA, 59

Wednesday, 28th

At the Hospital. My Father's business. Called on Dingley. At Dunlap's. Read in "The Monthly Magazine." Transcribed my letter to my sister Abby. Wm. & I spent the evening at Seth's—where Wm. read to us the greater part of Bernardin St. Pierre's First Study of Nature.[21]

This is Horace Johnson's Birth-Day. On this day he is Thirty years old. Seth will be twenty nine on the Second of November next.

---

[19] Susanna Centlivre (1714). John O'Keefe (1783).

[20] Joseph Dennie (1768-1812; Harvard 1790). Admitted to the bar, he was nevertheless much more interested in literature. With Royall Tyler (Harvard 1776), lawyer-dramatist-novelist-professor, who was later Chief Justice of the State, Dennie collaborated on a number of literary pieces. The pair became the nucleus of a group of young "wits" something like the Hartford Wits. In 1796 Dennie became editor of *The Farmer's Weekly Museum* of Walpole, New Hampshire. In short order he made it one of the best papers in New England. As part of his vigorous effort to get able young writers he solicited material from Smith.

[21] Either William read very fast or it was a long, long evening. It seems remarkable now that such intelligent individuals could sit quietly listening to this work for hours.

MEMORANDA, 60

Thursday, 29th

At the Hospital. Business. Read Holcroft's comedy intituled "Seduction,"[22] with much pleasure. The forepart, not equal, in point of style, to his later comedies; the denouement & indeed whole fable, masterly. Wm., Brown, Dunlap & I walked out of town. Spent the former part of the evening at Woolsey's—the latter part at Kent's.

MEMORANDA, 61

Friday, 30th

At the Hospital. Business—chiefly of my father. Alsop & Mrs. Riley & Fanny Johnson returned to-day. Dunlap called here. Part of the afternoon at Dr. & Mr. Miller's. At Horace Johnson's. Remainder of the evening with Mr. Gahn, & Mr. Wertmüller—who sails on Monday for France. Found Alsop here when I returned.

Recd. a very affectionate & complimentary letter from Dr. Rush.

GENERAL POSTSCRIPT TO THE MONTH OF SEPTEMBER

The conclusion of the present, like that of most of the preceeding months, offers very little to be satisfactorily dwelt upon. Constant experience of my own extreme weakness ought, perhaps, to guard me from any expectations whose delusive emptiness might seduce me to certain disappointment. Their vanity has, indeed, become sufficiently apparent, but I do not find myself less inclined to indulge in their creation. In respect to the month of September, tempered & restrained as were the propositions & resolutions with which it was commenced, the event has demonstrated that even these were too extravagant. But let me see what has really been accomplished. In this month I have read—

Dr. Rush's 4th vol. of Inquiries & Observations, 1 vol. 8vo.
The 2nd book of the History of Thucydides.
Holliday's account of the Fever at Havanna—pamphlet.
Fourcroy's Philosophy of Chemistry—1 vol. 8vo. small.
Holcroft's "Road to Ruin"—a Comedy.
Monthly Magazine—4 numbers.
Holcroft's "Seduction"—a Comedy—& besides many *here & there*

parts of different books, in the seconds of leisure which I have had. All this is, however, very little, & not equal to one week's attentive reading. Now let me enumerate my feats as a composuist—These will appear equally diminutive.

Imprimis—The article "Reuben Hitchcock."
Item—Letter to Dr. Rush.
Item—Article Prayer.

---

[22] (1787).

Item—Letter to Abigail Smith—with several other petty efforts in the epistolary way.

This enumeration, both of reading and writing, would be too ridiculous were it not possible that it may have some slight influence, at least, on the ensuing month—especially as that will not have the same claims to indulgence—as far as can now be determined—with it's predecessor. With this month my turn of duty at the Hospital expires. This duty has been a topic much insisted on by Mr. Indolence, an intimate acquaintance & pretended friend, in excuse for every indulgence or regard to his solicitations might induce me to allow myself. It were curious to see in how many shapes this terrifying nothing has been presented to my too easy & careless observation. And now that it is gone—absolutely vanished—no doubt something equally useful, ready, & to all cases applicable, will be soon conjured up by his artifices. Even at this very moment he seizes my arm, stupifies my mind, & insists upon it that my present catarrhal indisposition, ought at least to purchase me a reprieve from present intellectual exertion.

OCTOBER, 1796

GENERAL PREFACE TO THE MONTH

The plans of study & composition, with which I commenced this volume of my Journal, have, hitherto, received but a sparing & superficial attention; and there is every reason to believe that, unless the industry of this month greatly exceed that of those now past, the whole structure which I designed to rear will consist of a few scattered & useless fragments. To remedy the consequences of past neglect, present exertion is doubly necessary. I bring to the task ardent desires, but, I fear, feeble resolutions. I am too well acquainted with the tenuity of those which appear most solid, to suspend any weighty portion of faith thereon. It is in the issue only that I may venture to confide.

These ideas repeated, re-repeated, reiterated, & so often re-reiterated, are tiresome, dispiriting. Yet they press upon me in every preface, & with every postscript; & I can not shake them off, for they are always pertinent. They cluster around the Memoranda of each day; & tho' chased away for the moment, return with redoubled numbers & activity to hang on the conclusion of every week.

In this month, no more than in those which have gone before, can I hope to be exempted from interruptions. These, therefore, are always to be left out of the account in meditating on any plan of conduct. That they will more than usually abridge my opportunities for the contemplative cultivation of knowlege, is hardly probable. Overlooking them, then, for the present—It behooves me to apply, with increased carefullness, asiduity & zeal, to the execution of those schemes which are laid down, & partially traced out, in the Introduction of the present volume. I must soon commence the Essay on the Plague of Athens. When that is complete, I must again devote some hours, or days, to Utopia—some spare hours to my Sonnets, some leisure moments to my Biographical Sketches.[23] At the same time, my studies of every kind, & my various Correspondence, are to be pushed, with a spirit the more concentrated, in the increasing uninvitingness of the season to rural excursions, & diminution of external allurements to the senses, dispose to a more retired; sedentary, & contemplative life.

> Here let me pause—and may the blest event,
> Beyond my hope, crown every honest wish
> And every honest act, with full success![24]

MEMORANDA, 62

Saturday, 1st

Completed, or nearly completed, some little business of my father, which had been several days in hand. Corrected "The Score of Music" for my Opera. At the Hospital—where I resigned over my patients to Dr. Rodgers. Some professional calls. Drank tea, & spent the evening at Dunlap's. Club night—G. M. Woolsey's evening—Present, Brown, Dunlap, Johnson, Smith, the Woolseys.

POSTSCRIPT

There is nothing, in particular, to be remarked here —except that the week has passed away much as I expected. In one respect I am better off than I looked to be—I am completely exonerated from the burthen of the Hospital. The ensuing week, therefore, will be pretty much at my own command. Some interruptions, on account of the Music to "Edwin & Angelina," I can not avoid. I hope they will be trifling—as I shall certainly endeavor to render them.

Now that I am my own man, once more I must begin to discharge a load of visits, which have been some time accumulating. Well! well! All in good time.

Tenth Week

Sunday, 2nd

PREFACE

After the prefatory remarks which usher in the month, it remains for me to observe only that the line of action there determined upon, must be pursued in this first week, with as much constancy as circumstances will permit.

MEMORANDA, 63

Having been previously occupied in other matters, it was not till to-day that I had time to make up the slen-

---

[23] Some doubt about what these sketches were. Almost certainly they were not the biographical sketches of the Connecticut Wits which he wrote for the London *Monthly Magazine* and which were published posthumously, for which see later.
[24] Not found.

der account of the last month, sketch out the imperfect outline of the one now opened, & to compose the subsequent notices. This, troubled as I have been with a catarrh, occupied some time. Beside, I have read John Horne Tooke's account of the Action of Debt brought against him by Charles J. Fox—Dr. Mitchill's Preface to the American Edition of Zoonomia[25]—& some detached parts of the work itself. Dr. Miller spent two hours with me, in the forenoon; & I have made some professional visits—& drank tea—& spent the greater part of the evening at Mr. Kent's.

LETTERS
To Fanny Smith.

Your letter, of the second of August, has lain by me, unanswered, a long time. This had been occasioned by a variety of circumstances not necessary to be enumerated. In the mean time you have, probably, received a letter from me, previously written, & in the cover of which the receit of yours, to which I am now to reply, is acknowleged. That letter was accompanied, if I do not misremember, by another for my sister Mary, & inclosed in it the first of a Series of Sonnets intended to be addrest to you. In the *envelope*, were some hints towards the treatment of the disease you were then afflicted with, & from which I hope you are now perfectly exempt. Similar instructions were contained in a hasty letter, addrest to Mr. Mumford, & sent by Post; which you can not fail to have received. The first letters, I hope, gave you some pleasure; & the last some relief. I expected to have heard from you, before this time, & have been exceedingly anxious on your account. If you have none of you written, before the reception of this, let your first business be to give me information concerning your situation. The expence of sending by the mail is a consideration not to be put in competition with a single instant of uneasiness. But I can not think that you have delayed to write till this late hour.

In respect of your studies, much as I wish you to possess an accurate & extensive knowlege of History, I shall not regret your not being able to pursue the study of it, at this time, if you are thereby induced to perfect yourself in the important sciences of Arithmetic & Geography. Without these neither historical, nor any other reading, can be of much value; if indeed that of Morals only be excepted. For Geography is essential to the right comprehension of History, without which not even Criticism can be well understood. Apply yourself, therefore, my dear sister, as soon as your health will permit, with redoubled dilligence to these studies. Do not be damped by slight difficulties, nor deterred from want of the instruction of others. A difficulty vanquished by your own efforts, is a victory doubly useful. It awakens new powers, infuses new spirits, & makes a more lasting impression.

I shall inclose my second Sonnet.

---
[25] (New York, 1796).

Farewell, be careful of yourself; & remember how much & how steadily I love you.

Monday, Oct. 3. 1796.
Cedar St. No. 13. N. York.   E. H. Smith.

THE PLAGUE OF ATHENS. I.

1. What Year?—2. The season.—3. The latitude of Athens.—4. Its climate.—5. The manner of building the city.—6. The part of the city in which it broke out.—7. The diet of the inhabitants.—8. Their dress.—9. Was there any variation from former years?—10. The state of mind of the people.—11. How it spread.—12. Consequences as to conduct.—13. As to moral conduct.—14. Situation of the sick.—15. Symptoms.—16. Favorable or unfavorable termination.—17. Duration.—18. How affected by change of weather.—19. Mortality.—20. Who most subject to it.

1. The Plague of Athens broke out in the Year 430 before the christian era.
2. It first appeared in the beginning of the summer.—
3. The latitude of Athens is about 38.5° or nearly that of Norfolk in Virginia.
6. It broke out in that part of the city called the Piraeus.

MEMORANDA, 64
Monday, 3rd

A professional visit. Wrote a letter to my father, one to Dr. Rush, & the preceeding to my sister Fanny. Read some part of Thucydides, & determined on reading it in course. A visit of farewell, from Mr. Wertmüller—he sails for France to-morrow. A professional visit.

My mind much oppressed by the dangerous situation [of] a patient, the whole day. I have done all in my power—but that all appeared so little that I could not be at ease. In the evening went to the Theater. "Road to Ruin" & "Spoil'd Child." Saw Decius Wadsworth there—& Dunlap, & Brown, &c.—a visit.

LETTERS
Mary S. Mumford.

Tho' your letter, by Mr. Isaacs, has lain so long unanswered, yet, I trust, you have before this time, recd. a reply to a former communication, & an acknowlegement of the receit of the last. I have been otherwise too much engaged to write till now; & now I design, if circumstances favor my resolution, to expiate for my delay.

The letter by Mr. Mulligan, as far as I can recollect, was no otherwise of consequence than as it might serve to introduce him to you—a service which it seems you did not think him in need of. As he has made his visit, & every thing went on as well as if he had delivered the letter, it is of little moment whether you recover it or not.

Indeed, my dear sister, you have entered into a most elaborate vindication of Mrs. Radcliffe, to which I do not feel myself able to reply. My opinion of the character & value of her work was simply founded on the perusal of, perhaps, a hundred pages, & on the reading of her novel intituled "The Romance of the Forest." I can not contradict what you say—tho' I can hardly conceive that "The Mysteries of Udolpho" can contain a profound display of "Italian policy," together with an accurate account of "the situation of the several States, their great towns, and the manners of their inhabitants." Sufficiently profound, and sufficiently accurate, it may be for the purpose of a romance—but surely not so for the historian, moralist, legislator, or even the critic. Beware of false impressions! I read the "Travels of Cyrus"[26] when a child; & it has cost me infinite pains to banish from my memory the anachronisms & fictitious events with which it was stored by that romance. Historical characters & events, policy, morals, manners, arts, &c. &c. stand no chance when once the disfiguring hand of Fiction seizes upon them; they are despoiled of their proper ornaments, or receive new ones; & are moulded into any shape, & applied to any use, which may best suit the purpose of that fantastic architect.

I fully intended, before now, to have continued my remarks on the subject of Education, agreable to your wishes; but, I know not how it is, one thing after another has come in to interrupt & prevent me. Still I design to send you something further; but whether at this time, or not, I can not now determine. But before I go any further, let me clear up a little mistake—nay, an error of some consequence, into which you seem to have fallen.

In reality I do deny the existence of *Innate Ideas*; & so also does Mr. Locke. He was the first, as far as I am informed, who entered into a labored & effected a thorough refutation of that ridiculous & pernicious doctrine. Did you then mistake me? or have you misconceived the nature of Mr. Locke's Work? Or have you erred in the construction of a sentence? "You seem still to adhere to that doctrine, which Locke endeavored to explode, that innate ideas do not exist." These are your words. Perhaps you meant that I still persisted in opposing that doctrine, which Locke had previously attempted to disprove—viz. that *innate ideas* do exist. Was not this your meaning? But be your meaning what it may, the fact is that Mr. Locke & I his humble follower, (in this respect, at least) do maintain that the *senses* are the only means by which the mind can attain any notion or idea of any kind whatever. Now this is a most important truth; & one therefore which should be most distinctly & vividly impressed on the mind of every one. If, then, you have not satisfied yourself of it's reality, do not remain any longer without examining the subject thoroughly. As it must be the basis of all our reasoning, in regard to man, & indeed the very foundation of all true morality & all right education, it may be regarded as of primary & indispensible obligation to fix it firmly & luminously in the understanding, previous to the exercise of maternal duties. Hasten, then, my dear sister, to form your conclusions on this most interesting point. You have a sufficient motive for it in this alone—that whatever I may transmit to you, on the subject of Education, will be wholly grounded on a conviction of its undeniable truth.

I am interrupted. Adieu, for the present.

Tuesday, Octr. 4. 1796.
Cedar St. No. 13. N. York.   E. H. Smith.

MEMORANDA, 65

Tuesday, 4th

Professional visit. Wrote the preceeding letter. Much time spent in the monthly examination of the African School. Continued to read Thucydides. Went with Dingley to see a patient of his—& he with me, to see one of mine. Drank tea at Riley's. Miss Stillman of Wethersfield has returned with Mrs. Riley. While there Elnathan Smith Jr. came in. He stays with me this night —& being unwell went early to bed. I was, afterwards, at Dunlap's. Recd. a letter from Wm. Buel.

MEMORANDA, 66

Wednesday, 5th

Went to bed late. Woke early. Conversation with Elnathan Smith. Brown breakfasted with us. Professional visit—forenoon & afternoon. Wrote the five following pages. Elnathan here. Dined at S. Johnson's. C. B. Brown here, again. Part of the evening at Dr. & Mr. Miller's. Much company there. Gentlemen & ladies. I had called to see Miss Mason, & found her here. Escorted the Misses Linn's home. Was surprized at an intimation from them, with whom I am not at all acquainted, that it has been reported I am attentive in the way of courtship to Miss ———. Found Alsop here, when I returned.

LETTERS

To M. S. Mumford—in Continuation.

In the remarks, preliminary to some hints on the subject of Education, which were included, in one of my last letters, I divided my theme into such observations as had relation to Physical & such as were connected with the Moral Management of Children. I purpose, at this time, to communicate to you some leading principles & explanations on the first point.

You may remember that, in the advice I gave you, as to your conduct at the birth of your first child, that I laid particular stress on the circumstance of allowing a free circulation of cool air thro' your room: contrary to the common counsel of matrons; who stifle & melt

---

[26] The original work was by Andrew M. Ramsay (Chevalier de Ramsay), *Voyages de Cyrus* (1727); translation, *Travels of Cyrus,* by Nathaniel Hook (1739).

their patients, from an apprehension of their taking cold. We will suppose the child born, & healthy. It is first to be remarked that, from two causes, the sensations of new-born infants are vastly less acute than those [of] adults, of children. Their superficial nerves—or the extremities of their nerves & moving fibres, are less organic, & habit has not produced in them that aptitude of discrimination which is the result of long & frequent exercise. Thus the hearing of an infant is scarcely affected even by loud noises; strong lights, thrown directly on the eye, make but a feeble impression; & a coldness from which grown persons would shrink, is scarce perceived. The truth of these remarks will be justified by the most careless observation. And they are equally applicable to the young of all other animals as well as of human beings. You know that several days pass before kittens & puppies *open* their eyes. And tho' the sun, the fire, or the candle, are the first visible objects which attract the curiosity of children, yet it is not excited even by these objects till after a number of days. This seems an exceeding wise provision of nature. For were infants as sensible to external impressions as adults, their sudden exposure to them, at the time of their birth, must subject their feeble bodies to numberless & horrid maladies. The most important use to which a knowlege of this fact seems applicable, is that of the regulation of the temperature of the rooms where the birth takes place. It is a common error of mankind, the opinion that such tender beings must suffer much more from cold than grown persons; & therefore they are always in haste to pile on garment upon garment, & flannels upon flannels, upon the poor thing—thereby frequently exciting fever, & other complaints, & occasioning fits—& premature death. Now a treatment directly the reverse ought to be pursued. The need of clothing is, probably, altogether artificial; & I doubt very much whether an hour's exposure of a new-born & naked infant in a Lapland winter, would be of any material injury to it. Nay, we know, that it is the constant practice of many barbarous nations, as they are called, to plunge the stranger into the running stream: a practice far more rational than that of nations who arrogate the title of civilized. Did our notions of delicacy & propriety admit it, there would numerous advantages result from the total disuse of clothing for children, (except perhaps to protect their feet from the snow in winter,) till they were six or seven years of age—as is the custom in Turkey, & in the Grecian Islands. The rule to be deduced from all this is, that a child is always to be kept cool—that the clothing of an infant should be merely sufficient to cover it's nakedness—& that we need fear nothing from this—because infants do not suffer like adults from cold.

Another injurious practice is founded on the same mistaken ideas of the dangerous effects of cold on infants—i. e. washing them with warm water, or spirits—the last of which is far the worst. Children ought, on every account, to be kept scrupulously clean—but not with spirits. Noah, as we are told, was the inventor of intoxicating liquors; of course none of his predecessors could have made use of them, in any way; & yet the antedeluvians were proverbially long-lived. The eastern nations, all the people called savages, & some nations of Europe, not only abstain from this practice, but actually employ what I recommend. The comparative effects are exceeding important & interesting; & a volume would be insufficient to display all the advantages of washing with cold water. Instead, therefore, of using warm water, vinegar, & spirits, the infant should be washed at least once a day, with cool water.

Another practice founded on guile, or mistaken notions of beauty, & partly on the same apprehension of the bad effects of cold, is nearly universal—I mean that of covering the heads of children with Caps. The head ought never to be covered; & this is especially important as it respects infants, whose heads are much fuller of blood, & much hotter in proportion, than those of adults. Beside the mischief occasioned by caps, as it respects the unhealthy accumulation of heat, many diseases are occasioned or promoted by it. Inflammations of the ears, eyes, & brain—sore ears—colds—scald-head—eruptions of various kinds—& fits. In the coldest nights the head of an infant will feel warmer than any part of a healthy adult's body. And instead of keeping it hot, & washing it with spirits, it should be uncovered, & often in the day bathed with cold water. Thus all the diseases above-enumerated, will be avoided—& the matter of looks—is to be disregarded. That mother must be a wretch & destitute of all just claim to so sacred an appellation, who can prefer a silly ornament to the health & happiness, & perhaps life, of her child.

False ideas of the effect of cold, generate still another custom fatal to thousands—in various ways. I mean that of causing infants to sleep in the same bed with the mother, or with both parents. It is the pernicious practice of the people of this country to bury themselves in feather-beds, & under loads of bed-clothes. So far is this from being natural, that nothing but habit renders it tolerable. To infants it is the cause of inconceivable suffering. But, as if this were not enough, the child is opprest with the additional heat of both its parents. Instead of this the child should always sleep by itself—on a hard bed—& with slight covering. Not only is it more healthy—but it is more safe. No instance of an infant's being overlaid, or smothered, will ever happen, where they sleep alone. Beside—children sleep better, & longer. They will be less restless—less disposed to cry & wake up in the night—& will never, or rarely want food. They will not acquire that ruinous & troublesome habit of wanting suck in the night. But why do [I] heap instance upon instance—when the whole management of Infants is tinctured with false opinion—& when it is sufficient to excite your reflection by a single example? Let the doctrine I have now delivered, be applied thro' out the whole of the Physical education of Children. It's benefits are innumerable.

MEMORANDA, 67

Thursday, 6th

Smith breakfasted with us again this morning. He left town about ten o'clock. Professional visit. Continued Thucydides. Letters recd. from Abby, Idea, & Sally Pierce. Abby's contains the unexpected intelligence of a marriage soon to be concluded between herself & a Mr. Bacon—a native of Stockbridge—just admitted to the bar—& about to settle in the Province of Maine. He is well spoken of, in every respect; but the distance is a painful subject of contemplation. Charles B. Brown, Dunlap &c. here in the afternoon. Found my patient better, this time. On my return, met Miss E. A. K. whose story fills so large a part of the Second tome of my Diary. She is now married, & carries the evidence with her. Drank tea at Dunlap's. At a book auction. Visited at Mrs. Morton's. Read English papers.

MEMORANDA, 68

Friday, 7th

Looked over the "English Review," for June 1796. Judging from this number, I do not think highly of the execution of this publication. A Professional visit—& another, which being two miles out of town, occupied much time—tho' the walk was pleasant. Recd. a letter from my father. Employed on his business. Some errands of my own. Visited at Charles Adams's. Mr. A. only at home. A visit to Miss Mason—at her brother's—who came in, after I had been there a short time. Much, diversified, &, on the whole, agreable, conversation. Her taste is not correct, or her judgement not sound, she could not, else, prefer "The Victim of Magical Delusion,"[27] to "The Ghost Seer."

[Omitted here, three manuscript pages with the heading: "Thucydides."]

MEMORANDA, 69

Saturday, 8th

Wm. Johnson & Dunlap went to Amboy this morning. A professional visit. Brown spent all the forenoon with me. We conversed & read together. Alsop came in afterward. In the afternoon, did some business, for my father & for myself. Transcribed my letter to Fanny, with the second Sonnet. A professional visit. Drank tea at Mr. Kent's. Club night—& my turn—Present—Kent, Smith, the Woolseys. A very sociable & agreable evening. I read two ballads of Bürger, with some account of him, from the "Monthly Magazine." They were considerably pleased with the poems, & bestowed on them their due share of praise.

---

[27] Cajetan Tschink, *Geschichte eines Geistersehers* (1790-1793). Translated by P. Will (London, 1795). Harry Warfel (*Charles Brockden Brown*, p. 110) mentions *The Victim of Magical Delusion* as having been serialized in the New York *Weekly Magazine* and hazarded that "possibly the initial creative impulse and rationalistic theme of *Wieland* came from [it]."

POSTSCRIPT

One fourth of this month has already elapsed & I have effected but a trifling part of what ought therein to be accomplished. Yet I have done more than for some weeks before, & feel as tho' I should, by & by, do much more. I have not yet become habituated to steady application, & have out-door engagements enough to hinder my acquiring the sobriety of autumnal or hyemial attention to study.

Of all the subjects which the past week has presented to my mind, that of my sister Abby's expected connection seems least realizable. I can not but think that her representation of circumstances is as near just as a lover's can ever be, since the consent of my parents can hardly be supposed to follow any except a cautious & sufficient inquiry & examination; but I wish to have personal satisfaction on all those points which are most interestingly & intimately connected with her future happiness. I must contrive to bring this intended brother-in-law upon paper; & try him over the ground of morals.

Eleventh Week

Sunday, 9th

PREFACE

The season is remarkably fine, business is by no means urgent, my health is good, what should prevent a respectable application to study the ensuing week? A thousand things may; & there are ten chances to one that some of these do not operate with sufficient strength. Indeed, all these external causes, favorable to inquiry & reflection, may concur, & yet the cause internal, the impulse which must be obeyed, refuse to unite with them. Let the choicest collection of viands, the rarest assemblage of fruits, the most delicious abundance of wines, solicit the taste, there are to whom all these invite in vain, till after the stimulating liquerer has performed it's office. I am, therefore, by no means sanguine as to what this week may produce. I hate to labour. Labour is, of itself, an evil. It is only by comparison with the consequences, that is can be called good. The persuasion that the effect will be beneficial must, therefore, be clear & forcible to induce me to employ the means. And, unhappily, it is only be starts that I have this distinct, luminous, & irresistible perception of the numerous benefits thence to be derived!

MEMORANDA, 70

Dingley visited & breakfasted with me. We went to see our patient. I transcribed much of what I had written to Mary—with several alterations. C. B. Brown spent most of the forenoon, & part of the afternoon with me. I dined at Catlin's, with Mr. Deming of Lichfield.[28] A professional visit toward evening. Part of the evening at Hodgkinson's—part at S. Johnson's.

---

[28] Connecticut House 1790, 1791, 1798. He belonged to the Temperance Society with most of the other prominent male citizens of Litchfield. Kilbourne, *History of Litchfield*, p. 252.

MEMORANDA, 71

Monday, 10th

Professional visit, morning & evening. Business for my father. Writing for the Manumission Society. Brown here; & Mr. Miller, in the afternoon. Transcribed, with copious corrections & additions, my letter to Mary. Drank tea at Dr. Miller's, with several ladies and gentlemen, & spent the evening there. Recd. a few lines from Mumford—incolsing letters from Lichd. All well at Aurora. Dingley entered, after ten at night, & kept me up till twelve.

MEMORANDA, 72

Tuesday, 11th

My own business as usual. Most of the day, busily employed in that of my father. Looked over the "Monthly Review" for January 1796—& some articles in the late numbers—in company with Brown. Wm. Johnson returned, to-day, from Amboy. Left all well. Read some in Thucydides, some in Zoonomia, second volume. All the evening at a special meeting of the Manumission Society.

MEMORANDA, 73

Wednesday, 12th

Professional business, as for some time past. My little patient seems now beyond all hope, recovering. Blessings on Medicine, if she be! My father's business is now accomplished—at least it is over, for the present. I wrote a letter to him, concerning it, of some length. C. B. Brown here in the forenoon. Looked over some articles in the late numbers of the "Monthly Review." At H. Johnson's, to tea. The evening at the Theater. "Deserted Daughter," & "The Adopted Child."[29] Martin's *Cheviel* very bad. Jefferson's *Michael* very good.

The specimens of Coleridge's poetry, in the Review, are of the best quality. He who could write so well, must have presented a volume to the world worth possessing.

MEMORANDA, 74

Thursday, 13th

Business. A visit from Mr. Roulet—from C. B. Brown in the forenoon, & from Brown & Dunlap—who returned to-day from Amboy, in the afternoon. Spent most of the day in reading the Monthly Review. This work, in several departments, deserves to be read, as a model of fine writing & fine criticism. The whole evening at Dunlap's. W. W. Woolsey & his wife there.

The introduction to the article on Wieland, in the Appendix to the 19th vol. is masterly, & the extract judicious. This, with the passages inserted in the former appendix, excite in me an eager desire to read the works of that illustrious author. Indeed the whole of this Appendix is extremely interesting; & I should [require] some hours to record all the emotions of delight, & express all the interesting trains of reflection, to which the several articles have given birth.

MEMORANDA, 75

Friday, 14th

Business consumed a little more time than usual. Continued the reading of the numbers of the Monthly Review—which I have now nearly concluded. Visit from Alsop, & from Brown. The evening at the Theater. "Yarico & Inkle," & "The Old Maid"[30]—which last I did not stay to see. The first piece is full of that sort of wit which every body can feel, & with which, therefore, every body is diverted. It has the higher & rarer merit of being nearly un[ex]ceptionable & even excellent in it's sentiments & plot, & was very well played. Mrs. Seymour, a new performer, from England, played Marisser—it being her first appearance on our stage. She is a pleasing little, delicate woman—with a small but agreable voice—& a limited, but sweet execution in music. She was well received.

MEMORANDA, 76

Saturday, 15th

Business as yesterday. Finished the Monthly Review. Several errands & calls. At Kent's. C. B. Brown here. Wm. Johnson & I walked out of town. Club night—at Kent's—Present—Dunlap, Brown, Johnson, Alsop, Kent, the Woolseys, Smith, Mr. Gahn, & a Dr. Wheaton (who has lately removed to N. York, from Hudson,) visitors. Mr. Kent read us Brian Edwards on the Climate &c. of the West Indies.[31] The conversation, this evening, has been chiefly on particular politics, desultory, & animated.

POSTSCRIPT

I have been far from idle the past week; yet I have been busy to very little purpose. Every one of my numerous projects has remained stationary, while I have devoted that attention to extraneous matters, which ought, perhaps, to have been solely directed [to] them. If Buffon's definition of Genius be admitted—"That it is nothing more than a greater aptitude to patience"—surely of all men I have the least claim to that faculty, for no person has less perseverance in the execution of any once favorite design. It is, perhaps, true that great energy of intellect will be connected with a zeal proportionately active, & equal to it's complete, or effectual display: or, at least, it may be affirmed—that persevering patience, in a devotedness to one, or a few, considerable objects, is necessary to the development of genius,

---

[29] Samuel Birch, author of *The Adopted Child* (1795), was a dramatist, a pastry cook, and Lord Mayor of London.
[30] *The Old Maid*, Arthur Murphy (1761).
[31] Bryan Edwards, *The History, Civil and Ecclesiastical of the British Colonies in the West Indies* (London, 1793).

& to the building up of our glory in the estimation of men. But it does not, by any means, seem clear, that the exertion of a power is necessary to that power; that all who have genius, should exercise it. Some possess talents, probably, without knowing it; & many who are too proud, or too indolent to exert them. And of all, it may be said, that circumstances must strongly concur to beget a vigorous display.

Twelfth Week

Sunday, 16th

PREFACE

When I wrote the introductory remarks of this month, I was full of the expectation that I should conclude this volume with the termination of the month. The little advancement which the preceeding fortnight has witnessed, is sufficient to dissipate every expectation of the kind; & I must now lay my account with another month of scrap-like progress. This week, like the two before it, in all probability, move on in the same snail-track.

How infinitely superior are the opportunities of acquiring extensive information in most parts of Europe, to those with which we are provided in America! I sicken at the thought of it. To gain a smattering of learning, such as will answer for the ordinary purposes of life, is easy—& easier here, perhaps, than there; but for all beyond, there is no provision. No Museums, Libraries, Collections—not even learned men. In the State of Connecticut, where the Faculty of Physic are, generally, pretty well-informed, there is not one Naturalist, not a single Botanist, not even one tolerable Chemist.

The following lines were composed shortly before the date of their delivery, at the request of the President of the Anacreontic Society. A circumstance which marks his degree of intellectual perspicacity is worthy of mention—The Seventh & Eighth Stanzas were omitted by him, in rehearsal. These lines were hastily written; but I think it well to preserve them, as they may be corrected, hereafter, with some advantage, perhaps.

Ode,
for Music.
Rehearsed, with musical accompaniments, at
the Anniversary public meeting of the
Anacreontic Society;
on Tuesday the 29th of March, 1796, in the presence
of the Ladies of New York.

Hail Harmony! celestial Harmony!
    Be present now!
Let thy full spirit swell this closing strain!
    Before thee, lo! we bow.
Let not thy votaries plead in vain!
So shall they woo thee here again.
    Accept the vow!
    Deign! deign! O deign!
Breathe thy full spirit on this closing strain,
O Harmony, celestial Harmony!

Sweet Power! without thy vital aid,
    The stable earth, the changeful sea,
The arched sky, in vain were made:
    Their various charms they owe to thee;
And all the tribes that o'er and thro' them rove;
And worlds that 'round in glorious order move.

In man how bright thy bounty shines!
    From race, to race, extends;
In each successive age refines;
    To each new luster lends.

The infant's smile, the mother's gaze,
The sympathetic joy that strays
    Thro' sweet-consenting, youthful hearts;
The husband's ardor, patriot's fire,
Thou canst, blest Power, alone inspire;
    Thy touch divine alone imparts.

Each charm of Music comes from thee:
The Song, the Catch, the merry Glee,
    From thee their power receive:
Thou giv'st the answering chords
    New, lofty words;
Bid'st lively joy, and soft desire,
Tremble and languish on each wire;
And call'st, from every speaking string,
    Such sweet, such soul-dissolving sounds,
That, while the merry echoes ring,
    Or while the full-toned strain resounds,
    Or while the mellow notes decay,
Pleasure and Glory fill our breasts, by turns,
    Or die away,
While Love, or gentle Pity, silent mourns.

But ah! how high the rapture glows,
    When mingling Energies combine,
    The joy to swell!
    When, on the strains of Poesy divine,
    Music, a sister Power,
    Bids all her Melodies intensely dwell;
    And lo! in happy hour,
Beauty her pleased, approving smile bestows.

But see this presence heavenly Beauty grace!
    Ah! would she, now,
    Her pleased, approving smile bestow,
Then would these simple lays,
    This simple strain,
    Not flow in vain;
    For Harmony, celestial Harmony,
Sure must have heard, have answer'd to our vow.

And lo! to bless these simple lays,
    This simple strain,
    Beauty, who doth this presence grace,
Her pleased, approving smile bestows;
    Nor yet, to Harmony, in vain,
Have we preferr'd our vows.

Hail Harmony! celestial Harmony!
    Thou'rt present now.
Now thy full spirit swells this closing strain.
    Before thee, lo! we bow.
Ne'er shall thy votaries plead in vain;
Here shall they woo thee oft again.
    Crown thou the vow!
    Deign! deign! O deign!

Breathe thy full spirit on this closing strain,
O Harmony! celestial Harmony!

LETTERS

To Sally Pierce.

Your letter, my dear friend, short & hurried as it was, gave me no little satisfaction. I admire the caution with which you speak of Mr. Bacon; & could not help smiling, when I compared the manner of Abby & Idea with yours. With the first, he is perfection; with the second, not far removed from it; you admit his obvious good qualities, without venturing to decide on his real character. I was glad, however, since this thing, I suppose, must be, that the young gentleman united so many suffrages in his favor; & that your apprehension rose from what you *did not* know; instead of from what you *did* know. These sisters of mine have not had occasion to lament the fate of an early & beloved friend. The chill of suspicion has not tempered their ardor. We have seen reason not to form opinions too suddenly. The figure of Nancy Collins is as lively in my eye, as it was in yours, when you penned the sentence which has given occasion to these remarks.

Whatever good qualities, & whatever great talents & attainments, Mr. Bacon may possess, it is a serious deduction from the pleasure of having my sister form such a connection, that she must be so remotely separated from us. A thousand anxieties, beside those which arise from mere separation, can not fail of affecting us. Experience alone can (& ought) to satisfy us that this man is really what he appears to be. But to gain experience of his goodness, requires time; & in that time there are a hundred ways in which a man may contrive to break the heart of a wife, with such a heart as Abby's, & without giving the world an opportunity of inquiry, or room for suspecting. Then, who knows what may be the unavoidable calamities from a residence so distant? To how many ills, then divided from all the friends of her youth, may she be the feeble prey: ills which had else never befallen her; or which the hand of parental & brotherly, & sisterly affection might have warded off, or removed, or mitigated! So busy, with painful apprehensions, must the minds of her friends necessarily be, till some years have elapsed. And should the one tenth, the hundredth, or the thousandth part of these fears prove well founded, of how little satisfaction would it be to us that her husband was possessed of shining talents & an illustrious name?

My desire to see my sisters connected with men of distinguished abilities, has very much abated. Let their husbands be *good*, & I shall not much inquire whether they are what the world calls *great*. Men of brilliant qualities are apt to be too solicitous to sparkle in the eyes of men, to bestow much pains to preserve a serene luster in the domestic circle. It happens, not infrequently, that they are at least as much dazzled by their own splendor, as are the multitude; and that they are unable to taste any gratification which is not accompanied with the purblind submission & astonishment of others. Yet, when illusions of this nature are not connected with talents & great acquirements, no doubt there is a proportional pleasure from a near alliance with their possessor. They may call forth & support exertions in those who surround them, which else had never been. They may agitate the serenity of connubial life with a lively breeze of joy; & may dignify & adorn, as well as bless.

But, what deserve the name of great abilities? Surely, not those which sustain the petty triumphs of a school, or a College; not the knack of tacking rimes prettily together—which has become so common an accomplishment as almost to cease to be desirable—but I am wrong to enlarge so much on this theme, to you, who doubtless expected from me something more appropriate to our particular correspondence. Forgive me this once—& I promise to acquit myself with more propriety in future. Accept my affectionate remembrances, & make them acceptable to your sisters.

Sunday, Oct. 16. 1796.
Cedar St. No. 13. N. York. E. H. Smith.

MEMORANDA, 77

Business as yesterday. Wrote the preceeding pages under this date; made some addition to a letter to my sister Mary; wrote a few lines to Mumford; & transcribed the letter to Sally Pierce, with some corrections. Geo: M. Woolsey here, in the morning. I at Dingley's in the afternoon. Spent the evening at H. Johnson's.

MEMORANDA, 78

Monday, 17th

Business more than usual—so that much of the morning was occupied in writing a professional letter. Ch. B. Brown was here, & read me part of a new political romance, in which he is now engaged. I was at a meeting of the Trustees of the African School. In the afternoon, beside the interruptions of business, I wrote the following pages, under this date. I am by no means satisfied with the letter to Idea, as it now stands; but what will satisfy me? I hope it will set her on reflecting—which is as much as I can expect to do. As for sentiments got by rote, they are scarcely worth having—& if we would possess others, we must acquire them by reflection, & be able to shew a reason for them.

In the evening I was, to my regret, at the Theater. The play was "The Mountaineers," which I do not much admire—with "Rosina," which I am never tired of seeing. But the house was over-flowing, & I was obliged to stand up, during great part of the representation. Had it not been that the after-piece was well performed, I should have returned sick. As it is, I am dissatisfied with having thus spent the whole evening, when I had effected so little during the day.

LETTERS

To Idea Strong.

Your letter, my sister, contains many correct sentiments, and exprest with tolerable precision. At least, I have not found great difficulty in discovering the import of the greater part of it. But, as we are now placing, as it were, the corner-stone of our intended edifice, it becomes us to use all due caution that it be fixed, in every respect, as it ought to be. You will not deem it impertinent, therefore, in me, to attempt a brief & compact statement of what I conceive to be your opinions, & what are certainly my own, at the same time.

As Man is the subject of our inquiries, we do not trouble ourselves with searching after his origin. It is sufficient for our purposes that we find him here. If there are original differences in individuals, we shall not hunt after the cause, but satisfy ourselves with discovering what they are. At least, this will answer for all present intentions.

It appears to me, then, that Men have a common nature, as contradistinguished from other races of animals—such as beasts, birds, fishes, &c.—but that, with reference to each other, their nature is the same—since their organs of sense, or the inlets of all their ideas, are, in every general respect, intirely alike; their use & distribution the same. Particular causes, after which it is not our business, now, to inquire—whether they are found in diversity of climate, soil, or nourishment, in the qualities of the air, the distribution of the waters, or the elevation or depression of the surface of the earth, have effected numerous diversities in appearances & conduct, or have given a certain modification of this common nature, among different tribes of men, a still more particular modification among lesser divisions, & so on to the formation of peculiar, or individual diversities. Thus, while each individual has something by which he is distinguished from every other individual, he has also something by which he resembles every other, of this province, state, region, hemisphere, & so on. And these resemblances & varieties are not limited to external appearance, but extend to internal organization, or to the whole structure & constitution of each human being. The deduction from this is, that tho' all men are the same *in kind*, yet they differ in *degree*; & that in their original structure & without any reference to their subsequent character. This you have well conceived. Individuals differ in the perfection of their organs. Some are easily impressed by any object, others with difficulty. Of the first, some retain firmly, others feebly; & so of the last: with all the varieties depending thereon. But these diversities in the constitution of individuals are altogether differences of *capacity*. A being without ideas can not possess *power*. For power is the exercise of the capacities, excited into action by external objects or impressions, or by the associations consequent upon such impressions; & is more or less perfect according to the importance of the aim of this exercise or exertion, & the aptitude of the exertion to effect that aim. Capacity, therefore, is a mere nothing, if the surrounding world were removed. Without that man could neither think, nor act, nor exist. On the surrounding world, therefore, or on external impression he is dependent for all ideas, & consequently for all power. But as there is always some peculiarity of capacity in each individual, so the impression of every external object must be modified thereby, & produce a different effect on one, from what it does on another. It is, perhaps, true that no two persons are ever affected, exactly alike, by the same object. This, of itself is enough to display a variety of character, while it goes some way in proof of an original difference of structure —in opposition to those who suppose all to depend on education.

I do not like this. I have rambled a thousand degrees from my intended point. So I shall quit this letter, & begin a new one. I meant to have said all I had to say in less space, than I have already run over. How is it that I incessantly wander off into desultory remarks, when I most intend to be methodical?

To Idea Strong.

Your letter, my sister, abounds with correct opinions; and it is only because our present subject of inquiry is of the utmost importance to our future discussions, that I occupy any more time with it. But I wish that no step may be taken by us, without a clear view of it's nature, & of the necessary consequences. It is therefore, that I shall now attempt a concise statement of what I suppose are your sentiments; which are, at the same time, my own. If there exist any diversity of opinion, or any error of apprehension, it were best that they be removed or corrected in the outset.

Men, as distinguished from quadrupeds, birds, & fish, have a common nature. Different assemblages of men, according to the extent & character of those assemblages, are distinguished still further into various races, nations, cantons, &c—and each individual, while he has something wherein he resembles every other individual, or is allied to a number of beings, has also something by which he is distinguished from this or that mass, from this, that, & every other being. On what does this depend? On original construction, or constitution—and on education. By the first, man is rendered susceptible of an amazing number & variety of impressions; the last is only a name for a succession of these impressions. This liability to be influenced by external objects which we derive from nature, is termed capacity. This capacity is greater or less, perfect or imperfect, in the first place, according to the perfection or imperfection of our organs of sense; & in the next place, according to their simple, or associated, exercise: it being a law of our nature, that the frequent exercise of any organ (provided that exercise be proportioned to it's strength) increases the capacity of the organ. But as the number, general structure, distribution, & purpose of these organs are the same, in all men, it follows that there is no distinction of *kind*, between man & man. Yet, as there are numerous varieties in the structure of these organs, it is equally certain that men are originally constituted with different *degrees* of capacity. And this is all the primary dissimilitude between one individual & another.

From this acknowleged diversity of original constitution, it necessarily follows that, unless it were in our power to regulate the action of external objects with exact relation thereto, it is impossible that there should not arise great variety in the characters of men, even were all original impressions on the organs of sense made in the same manner. But, as it inevitably happens that as great a variety obtains in this respect, as in that of capacity, & that it is wholly out of our power, at present, to measure either one or the other, so it must unavoidably be that still stronger individual peculiarities exist. Numbers of beings are, probably, born with extensive capacity, who never being submitted to a due succession of impressions, or, in other words, wanting a suitable education, perish without ever having distinguished themselves by the display of uncommon powers. Others, there are, who, being fortunately educated, obtain considerable distinction, without any uncommon happiness of primary construction. Hence it follows, that the character of man, principally depends on Education—not in the limited sense of that term, but as used to signify the sum of successive impressions.

We distinguish between that character which depends on happiness or imperfection of original structure; & that which is founded on education simply. We say, this man has great talents, or mean abilities; & that, is a good man. That is, we distinguish between the power, & the use of it; between the intellectual & moral qualities of men. In a certain view of things, this is accurate, & the reverse.

The greater the capacity of an individual, or the more perfect his original structure, the more vigorous may his intellect & the more pure his morality, be rendered. But education may render the exertions of one of mean capacity moral, of great capacity immoral. In no other respect, than as they differ in capacity, can men be considered as originally depraved, or pure. In no other respect than as their intellectual powers are properly or improperly applied, can they be called virtuous or vicious.

Character, then, in the proper sense of that word, no human being has, at the time of it's birth. It has no more than the basis of character. It is wholly, therefore, in the power of education to determine what that character shall be. Not as to *degree*—(if we speak of all human beings,) but clearly as to *kind*. Thus education may render all bad or good; but can not make one of mean capacity as good, or as bad, as one of great capacity: tho' it *may* cause a feebler, to excell in knowlege & in virtue, a stronger.

Thus, we are agreed on the fundamental points, relative to the nature of man. But, let me press it upon you, to think this matter thoroughly over, & ponder it deeply. Be completely satisfied that we are right, before advancing a step further. For most important consequences depend thereon. They are consequences which I hope will not startle you—for if you love truth sincerely, you must be ready to sacrifice every prejudice, when she requires it of you. Write to me, if you are confirmed in the rectitude of these sentiments.

Monday, Oct. 17. 1796.
Cedar St. No. 13. N. York.   E. H. Smith.

MEMORANDA, 79

Tuesday, 18th

A little business. A visit from C. B. Brown, from Dunlap, from Dr. Miller. Dunlap had with him "The Iron Chest"—a drama of Geo. Coleman Jr.[32] He read some part of it, which I thought good. Brown finished the reading of what he had written on his new Romance. I wrote the following letter to my sister Abby. The style is less simple than I wished. But, somehow or other, I slide into a more elaborate style, of late, than I was wont to use. In respect of this letter, it is of no great importance. The sentiments are, I believe, correct. Alsop visited me. I wrote a professional letter. Drank tea—& spent an hour & a half at Seth Johnson's. The remainder of the evening, very agreably & instructingly, at Mr. Roulet's.

MEMORANDA, 80

Wednesday, 19th

Business. A visit from C. B. Brown; From Dingley; from Decius Wadsworth, who stayed here most of the forenoon; from Mr. Gahn. Wrote & transcribed the letter to Wm. Buel. Brown here much of the afternoon. At Dingley's. A Physician, whose name I do not now recollect, gave us an interesting account of a disease, popularly called The Canker, which proved very fatal in The Province of Maine, where he lives. I hope to obtain some further account of it, from him. At Dunlap's, & at Woolsey's, in the evening. Recd. a letter from Dr. Kollock.

LETTERS

To Abigail Smith Jr.

When I wrote to you, my sister, by Mr. Smith of Berlin, I had not received your letter of the 23rd of September. That came, with others from my Lichfield friends, soon after, and excited in me all that surprize, all that tumult of emotion, which you seem to have expected. You wished me to write speedily; to counsel, to instruct you. It has not been possible for me to write earlier; & even now, I scarcely know how to speak to

---

[32] *The Iron Chest* (1796) was a dramatization of *Caleb Williams*. There is general agreement that the adaptation was poor.

you. It is not because I am wanting in affection for you, that I find this difficulty, or that I fear that you suspect my love, or question my disinterestedness; but the information you have given me is so sudden, so unlooked for; the object of your choice, & the circumstances which led to it, so totally unknown to me; that I am at a loss how I ought to address you, or whether it is proper for me to address you at all. For I can have no certainty that any remarks I might make, in relation to the person you prefer would be pertinent, as I am ignorant of his peculiarities, & of the precise nature of that change which a union with him will effect in your situation. The little that I have to say must, therefore, be solely directed to you.

You dwell, with an emphasis natural to one circumstanced like you, on the talents of your friend. But superior endowments are, at least equivocal, & should not, of themselves, form the basis of preference. It is the use which is made of power, not power itself, which should determine our judgement. It were, indeed desirable that all should possess ability, could we be certain that none would abuse it. But how little satisfaction should we derive from a connection with genius misapplied, injurious to itself, & pernicious to others.

Would not the edge of disappointment be rendered more keen, the arrow of affliction sink deeper into the bosom? A just sense of her own intrinsic worth may animate a woman & sustain her above the uncouth & absurd tyranny of a common man; but to see those powers of pleasing which might enchant & bless her, turned from her, turned towards others—those talents which might have rendered earth a paradise, & her little home a heaven, wasted in excess or cabal, or directed to her tormenting—where is she whose spirit is virtue-proof against such woundings?

Trust me, my sister, I do not wish to terrify you with imaginary dangers; I would only put you on your guard against the excesses of your own admiration, & induce you to temper the ardor of your present expectations. Great talents may be greatly abused; the vanity which is gratified by a union with them, should, therefore, give way to discreter motives. Good-sense, a benevolent disposition, an even temper, & virtuous habits, these are all necessary in a husband. If to these talents are added, so much the better; but without these they are of little value; & where these are, talents may be dispensed with. Ask yourself, then, whether the man of your choice be so qualified. For you must recollect that, tho' youth be the season of love, a less social passion claims a higher interest in manhood; & he who has the power to sparkle in the eyes of a nation, will seldom confine his modest beam to cheer the secluded residence of wedlock. And what is the light to you, if it never irradiate your dwelling? You might well dispense with those splendors which are wasted on the dazzled multitude, for the gentle ray which would steadily illuminate your solitude. It is the fate of virtue & talents united to bless each individual, in blessing all.

Have you good reason to believe, that your intended husband will not forget to labour to please you, when he has once discovered that he can captivate the world? Will he not, like other conquerors, fly from conquest to conquest; & be more solicitous to acquire new possessions than retain those which he has already gained? You are, now, ready to answer all these inquiries in his favor; & your fears seem to be less on his account, than on your own. You dread lest you should afford him just cause to be dissatisfied with you; & are apprehensive of a change in his affections, rather from your incapacity to communicate rational support to them, than from any capriciousness in the affections themselves. With such conceptions of the nature of that danger which may possible exist of a want of future harmony between you & Mr. Bacon, you apply to me for instruction how to avoid so great an evil; for counsel which shall enable you to act as to secure all the blessings, without incurring the hazards, of wedlock.

Indeed, my sister, it is a difficult & delicate task which you impose upon me. And yet I ought to be able to administer useful advice; for I have known you long, & intimately. Bear with me then, in what I shall now say, even if it do not perfectly accord with your own inclinations & opinions. I have no other object, I can have no other, than your good. If there be any possible relationship which should preclude suspicion of interestedness, it is that of brother & sister.

It appears to me, then, that the greatest danger that threatens the continuance of your wedded happiness, arises from your own strong & artless love. You, my sister, have not the enviable power of concealing your sentiments, of clothing your face with smiles while your heart is preyed on by sorrow, of veiling contempt under the mantle of civility, & assuming an air of mild indifference when inquisitive anxiety rages in your bosom. Your love & your aversion are prodigally lavished upon their several subjects.

There are two ways in which women of your character are apt to weaken the love of sensible husbands. In the first place, by a profusion of endearing acts & expressions, not always well adapted to time & place. The operation of conduct like this, which in men is called uxoriousness, is to diminish, by cloying or overstraining affection. Testimonials of tenderness are called for, in a swifter succession than men of reflection are accustomed to bestow; & proffered more rapidly than they are ready to receive them. The sweet confection palls their appetite, & the stimulating *liquerer* exhausts their spirits. In the second place, a temper of this sort, is liable to lead to undue familiarity; & to induce a belief that as there is nothing which a wife wishes to conceal from her husband, there is nothing which she ought to conceal. Thus the delicacy of the connubial intercourse being worn off, the husband ceases to respect his wife, & when respect is lost, love does not long remain. If the vessel excite disgust, the sickly imagination soon extends it to the viands it contains.

It is a difficult matter, without descending to particulars, which would be improper, to convey a precise idea of what I mean. But, if you have not already conceived what is my aim, I hope the following general directions how to avoid the evil I have pointed out, will more perfectly apprize you of it's nature.

There is a very important distinction between mental, and personal reserve. I pretend not to novelty of remark, on this subject; my sole design is to communicate useful truths. To your sentiments concerning every subject connected with the duties & cares of wedded life & with the principles on which they are founded & to be conducted, a husband has an unquestionable right. The right is reciprocal. It extends likewise to the history of your sentiments, & that of the general tenor of your life. Further than this, a discreet man will be careful how he inquires, & a prudent wife what she imparts. For we are not always masters of ourselves, & uncomfortable emotions may be excited & recur when we are conscious of the impropriety of indulging in them. But tho' it be true that the most perfect unreservedness should subsist, on all these subjects, between those who are thus united, yet there are others which are & must be wholly personal, & which never can be made otherwise without the hazard of defacing the unsullied fabric of domestic tranquility. Whatever is, strictly speaking, personal, before marriage, should continue to be so afterward; & it should be the study of both parties to fix the attention of either, as much as may be solely on what is intellectual in the connection. At least, all which particularly relates to the person should be cautiously concealed; & nothing should be risked which may lead the imagination to investigate the various offices by which it is prepared to inspire & preserve the pure flame of attachment. At the same time, while real delicacy is so steadily pursued, great care must be taken not to mistake that which is false, for that which is true; a mistake which, by the numerous affectations into which it betrays the unhappy wife, more certainly disgusts a discerning mind, than a hundred of those negligences in respect to decorum, which a lover naturally attributes to the unsuspecting & unguarded temper of his mistress.

It may, perhaps, deserve to be considered as a good direction, in regard to endearments, rather to expect than solicit, rather to repress, than to indulge in them. This is especially to be observed in public; & in private, the more carefully the attention of the husband is directed to nobler objects, the more likely will he be to respect the wife, the more highly will he prize the tokens of reciprocal affection which are rendered to his re-iterated endeavours to obtain them.

But it will not be sufficient for you to avoid the causes of giving offence & disgust, you must seek after the means of affording delight; & the more ready your husband appears to be satisfied with your present powers of pleasing, the more eager must you be to enlarge & variegate them. If he surpass you in genius, you must strive to exceed him in dilligence; & the greater his attainments, the more unremitting must be your industry. It is not enough that your society be tolerable to him, you must labour to induce him to seek it, in preference to all others; or if this be not possible, at least, to make it pleasant to him, when society of a more illustrious character can not be obtained. Let him not only be impressed with a deep conviction of your domestic prudence, & ready to consult you on every subject of household economy, but be earnest to render yourself worthy to be consulted, by him, on the education of your children, on the part he ought to take in life, on the character of ancient & modern sages, statesmen, & heroes; on the writings of others, & if he continues to devote himself to composition, on his own. Nor be deterred by the profound sense you now have of the superiority of his attainments. Much of the life of a professional man, must be devoted to the labours & study of his profession. If the affairs of your family demand as much time as those of his business, still the hours which he must spend in the acquisition of technical science may be applied by you to the cultivation of general literature. With what pleasure will he throw aside, at proper seasons, the ponderous volumes of the Law, to discuss, with you, if you are qualified to take a part in the discussion, the more interesting themes which morals, policy, history, poesy & criticism, unceasingly offer to the consideration of youthful, virtuous, & glowing minds! How delighted will he be to see the image of his own, reflected from your mind; to find your conceptions inflamed by the gentle touches of his suggestions; to behold his nascent & imperfect hints returned to him with ample illustration; & to feel, in the durable felicity of wedlock, the realized & substantial form of all the poetic visions of his early love! When a happiness so great, so intire, as this, is within your reach, can you neglect to secure it? Then indeed, if you do, may you fairly charge the wandering of a husband's love, the failure of a husband's respect, to your own indiscretion. But, no! You will never remit your exertions. A due respect to your own character will preserve you from indiscreet familiarities, from childish fondling, the neglect of person, the neglect of household, & the still more fatal neglect of intellectual improvement. Thus shall you obtain the veneration, while you preserve the love & confidence of your husband; thus shall you find a firm support against all the troubles which must necessarily press upon you in your way thro' life; thus shall you reach the summit of connubial prosperity, & be enabled to look round with satisfied contemplation, on a family, on relations & friends, of which you will form, at once, the guide, the ornament, & the delight.

Farewell, my dear sister! and may this feeble, but well-meant, effort, if it do not minister to your instruction, at least, approve itself to your heart as a new evidence of my tender & unfailing love. Farewell!

Oct. 18. 1796.
Cedar St. No. 13. New York.　　　　　　　E. H. Smith.

MEMORANDA, 81

Thursday, 20th

Made my morning visit. Returned; did some little errands at home, & went abroad to do some others. Met my cousin Elijah Hubbard Jr. He spent most of the forenoon with me. Mr. Lovegrove came in. Mrs. Lovegrove came up with him. I called on her, & went with her to purchase a variety of matters for him, on his voyage to England. He sails Sunday. Thus passed the remainder of the day till two o'clock. After dinner I sat down to copy my letter to Abby; & finished half of it. Went abroad to do some errands, & to make my evening visit to my little patient. Drank tea at Mr. Kent's. Spent the evening at H. Johnson's—with Mr. & Mrs. Lovegrove. Read, in the morning, Dr. Darwin's Article "Nutrientia"—with much pleasure.

To William Buel.

I have delayed answering your letter of the 27th ulto. because, as I had no communication to make to you which would be of any particular & immediate use, I hoped to be able, after some time, to write you something more interesting than my hurry would have permitted, had I replied to you immediately. But I have gained little by the delay; & you, perhaps, will acquire still less. The vast operations in politics, which at present agitate the world, seem to occupy every mind; while literature, & science, and happiness are forgotten. Wealth alone, in this revolutionary hurly-burly, retains all it's importance.

Your situation has been distressing, I have no doubt; but I trust the consequences will not prove so; and if you do not meet with a pecuniary recompense equal to your sacrifices, you will derive an abundant reward in increased knowlege & skill. Enough wherewith to satisfy the demands of nature we can not but desire; but more than this, if we except some little embellishments & casual gratifications, we need not look for from an art which brings with it's exercise, in spite of calumny, so many heart-consoling returns.

By this time, you have achieved some good degree of leisure. When you have refreshed yourself, after the fatigues of this campaign, I want to have you take up the pen & oblige me with it's history. In making this request, I have in view as much your improvement, as my own. There are numerous advantages resulting from tracing the progress & nature of a disease, & the power & impotence of medicine, while all the circumstances are yet fresh in the memory. Beside, we ought to accustom ourselves to review our own practice; to inquire into the reason of it; to compare the subject, with the thing applied; & to search after new & more satisfactory explanations & methods.

Had I thought of it seasonably, I might have sent you Zimmerman on the Dysentery: a book of much merit, but not without defects. It is, however, as far as I know, the best single & extensive treatise extant, on this disease. It is quite probable, that, notwithstanding the propriety of his general plan of cure, there may arise particular indications, originating in the local condition of the place where the Dysentery rages, which will demand particular applications. There is some reason, likewise, to believe, that a mode of treatment, not essentially different from that which is successful in Bilious Fevers, would also prove advantageous in Dysenteries. Bleeding, in small quantities, & repeated perhaps; free purging, certainly; & possibly the use of mercury, with the design of changing, materially, the action of the Absorbent System. But I reserve particular remarks, till I learn your method, and it's success. I presume that you attended to my suggestion, in a former letter, respecting the connection between Fever & Dysentery.

You have never informed me whether you recd. the Collection of Mr. Webster; still less, how far you were satisfied with my share of the work; & with the little alterations I hazarded in the style of your letter. It would gratify me to receive your sentiments on my account of the Fever of 1795. If you should not visit New York, (as I hope & trust you will) I shall endeavor to furnish you with some new facts & practice, in the same disease. I can communicate them to you, face to face, much more satisfactorily, & with larger comment & explanation, than in any other way; but if this may not be, I shall call in the aid of the pen.

I anticipate uncommon pleasure from your visit; & hope you will not be straitened for time. I have a thousand things to shew you, a thousand things to tell you, & a thousand plans to unfold. Here are some people, too, in our way, & some of a different cast, who are worth being known. Suit the period of your journey to your own convenience. I shall be at home, steadily, till next June; if no accident disturb my designs.

Should this letter, as I expect, be forwarded by one of your traders, I shall send with it the First Volume of Darwin's Zoonomia, for which I subscribed for you, agreable to your request. The Second Volume will be put to press ere long. It is already published in England, & a few copies have reached America; one of which is now on my table. As far as I am now able to judge, it is the most masterly performance ever given to the world on the subject of Medicine. I suppose you will desire to have your name continued for the Second Volume; & also for "The Botanic Garden,"[33] by the same author; if, as is probable, it should be re-printed by the persons who are concerned in the re-impression of Zoonomia. Let me know your determination on this matter, by letter, if you do not come here, this Autumn.

Dr. Rush, you probably know, has published a 4th vol. of his Medical Works. You ought to be in possession of all his publications. As he leads the way in professional science, in America, & has obtained no mean

---

[33] Erasmus Darwin's work, *The Botanic Garden,* has a curious publishing history. Part II, *The Loves of the Plants,* appeared in 1789, published anonymously in Lichfield, England. Parts I and II, two volumes, appeared in London, 1791.

reputation in Europe, we, at least, who are his fellow-citizens, should be acquainted with the nature of his improvements & the foundation of his fame.

If you do not let me see you, at least let me hear from you, speedily.

Farewell.

Wednesday, Oct. 19. 1796.
Cedar St. No. 13. N. York.　　　　E. H. Smith.

MEMORANDA, 82

Friday, 21st

Transcribed the remainder of my letter to Abby, & the letter to Idea. A visit from Elijah Hubbard Jr. A professional visit. Read Geo: Coleman, the Younger's, Play, intituled "The Iron Chest." A performance very inferior to "Caleb Williams," but equal to several pieces by the same author which have had greater success. A visit from Dunlap. Drank tea at Woolsey's—with Mr. & Mrs. Kent, Mr. & Mrs. Dunlap, & others. Made a visit to Mrs. Miller. Read the Articles Incitantia & Secernentia" in Darwin's Zoonomia P. III. Wrote a Sonnet.

MEMORANDA, 83

Saturday, 22nd

Business as usual. Visited & spent two hours with Dr. Mitchill, who has just returned from the country—whither he has been on his Agricultural, Geological, & Medical Tour. Much & interesting conversation. He shewed me letters from Gahn, the Swedish Chemist, from Dr. Beddoes, Professor Hope, &c. Writing for the Manumission Society. Read the article "Sorbentia"— in Darwin's Zoonomia. Visit from Drs. Mitchill & Miller. Rambling conversation. Put up medicine & wrote directions for Mr. Lovegrove. Club night—Dunlap's night—Present, Brown, Dunlap, Johnson, the Woolseys —Smith. Interrupted by the cry of fire. Returned—I read aloud the Monthly Review—an excellently well written character of Gibbon's Memoirs; & their witty exposure of Townshend's Defence of Burke. Synonimy —"Mutual & Reciprocal," "Secure & Safe," "Veracity & Sincerity" &c. discussed—the two last settled.

SONNET THIRD
Summer

Fiercely the proud sun darts his sultry rays:
　　The salt wave sparkles to the rising gale:
　　So, there, it bellies out the flapping sail!
There, mid the topmost foliage, lightly plays.

How deep the verdure of the grove! a blaze
　　Pours from yon sunny slope of wheat so pale:
　　The orchard reddens; and the clover'd vale,
With fragrance sweet, the frolic breeze o'erpays.

And, hark! the insect hum, the rustling wing,
　　Thick-nibbling flocks, and grazing herds, I hear:
And hark, a-field, the merry laborers sing!
　　Sure, is not this the manhood of the year?

Farewell, ye pastimes of the idle spring!
　　Wellcome grave thought, and toil of eye severe!

POSTSCRIPT

This has been a week of interruptions, notwithstanding all of which I have done more, were my industry to be judged of by the face of my Journal, than for some time before. Indeed, I am not altogether dissatisfied with what I have done; tho' I have done very little of what I intended to do. But this was not my fault. At least, it was not altogether my fault. Could I thrust out such visitants as waited on me? Could I foresee that so many would crowd upon me, as it were, all at once? And, have I not derived both pleasure & instruction from their society? I might have some right to complain, if my previous conduct displayed any evidence in favor of a belief that I should have employed my time better, had I been left to myself; or should my future exertion, prove that I have endeavoured to redeem, for my studies, the time thus lost to them.

Thirteenth Week

Sunday, 23rd

PREFACE

What fine weather! A new spring seems, suddenly, to unfold itself. How mild the air! how serene the sky! What a gentle breeze sports upon the waters! Hey-day! Here's a pretty opening of a week! Here's a fine specimen of what my industry is to be for the next seven days, if this weather continue!

Well! I will not deny it—there is something in this atmosphere, in this temperature, which lays too powerful a charm on the physical man, to allow the intellectual man much room for the exercise of his talents. There is something in these last smiles of the departing year, that is unexpressibly delightful & enchanting; & if I were to busy myself in finding them, no doubt, a thousand arguments would present themselves to prove that it is very proper for me to indulge in idleness, & that the mind would be greatly benefitted thereby.

MEMORANDA, 84

Business. A call from Mr. Gahn. From C. B. Brown. Wm. & I walked on the Battery. Went to H. Johnson's —& then with Mrs. Lovegrove, on board the Factor, to see Mr. Lovegrove depart for England. Returned, all of us, to S. Johnson's to dinner—& spent the afternoon & evening there. Wm. had Mrs. Inchbald's new novel— "Nature & Art"[34]—: he read about half of it to us; & we were exceedingly delighted with it. If the remainder be equal—this book is a Chapter in the Volume of Truth.

---
[34] (1796).

MEMORANDA, 85
Monday, 24th

Business. Recd. a letter from my Father, which busied me some part of the forenoon. Called on Mrs. Lovegrove. Finished the Third Part of Zoonomia. Read some pages, at different parts of the day, in Gibbon's Memoirs & Miscellaneous Works. The character of this man, & of his Memoirs, is traced by a masterly hand, in the Monthly Review, for August 1796.

Wm. & I walked out of town. We spent the evening at H. Johnson's—& Wm. read to us the remainder of Mrs. Inchbald's Novel—"Nature & Art"—a book, with some exceptions, of considerable merit. Three faults dwell most, as to sentiment, upon my memory, at this moment. The first misconduct of Hannah is held up as a crime too atrocious. That Hannah should deem it so, is not unnatural; that the Author should speak of it as such, does not accord with other sentiments in her work.

The situation in which the two Henrys & Rebecca are left is not *poverty*. In making the comparison, between the condition of the poor & the rich, it is but too evident that Henry takes his situation for the point of comparison.

The concluding sentiments, on the subject of Reform, will justify any enormity whatever. Their absurdity is too palpable to dilate upon; & I hope they are too clearly opposed to the general spirit of this little book to have any undue effect.

MEMORANDA, 86
Tuesday, 25th

Business & errands, as usual.

How many pages I ought already to have written; but yesterday & to-day have been uncommonly warm, & my head has been full—pressed out—& unmanageable. I determined to let the pen rest. To study was little better than to compose. I resolved therefore to read. And I have really buried Mr. Gibbon—i. e. I have advanced to the Appendix in the first of the three volumes. I reserve my remarks till the conclusion of this work; if indeed, I have activity enough to write any.

I spent a short time at H. Johnson's, with Mrs. Lovegrove &c.

I drank tea at Kent's, who read me his Discourse to be pronounced before the Agricultural Society. "It is so so—yet 'tis well."

Dunlap sat an hour with me A. M.—Brown & Alsop here a few minutes.

MEMORANDA, 87
Wednesday, 26th

Business as usual.
Wrote a hurried letter to my father, on business. A visit from C. B. Brown. Some further advances in Gibbon's Posthumous Works.[35] Wrote the four next succeeding pages. They are scanty, contain few ideas, & perhaps many errors—yet they are the fruit of the toil of most of this day. The forepart of the evening at Mr. Boyd's—the remainder at H. Johnson's—with Mrs. Lovegrove &c. She leaves us in the morning, for Amboy.

MEMORANDA, 88
Thursday, 27th

Business the same. Dunlap & Brown here, an hour, before dinner. The former's "Mysterious Monk" to be played next Monday. Brown here again about 4 P. M. He read me some notes towards his *great plan*, drawn from reading Coxe's "Russian Discoveries." Johnson came up. Estimation of Gibbon's merit—of Sir Wm. Jones's—&c. Alsop entered, with J. Ogden Moseley.[36] Agreable conversation. The evening at Riley's—The Woolseys, Alsop, Mr. Moseley, & Mr. E. Williams[37] of Hartford, with whom I talked much of various matters, relative to Hartford & Wethersfield. I came home, & read the Newspapers, according to custom by the map. This always takes up much time—but then every thing is clear. I began this lately—i.e. within two months. In that time I have acquired better notions of German & Italian Geography than I ever had before.

Most of this day devoted to the Plague of Athens. Reading & Comparing DePauw, Potter, & Barthelemy.[38] I have advanced four pages—& with some improvement. Hints are multiplied. I am deceived, if this exercise do not prove of some use to me.

Mrs. Lovegrove left us, early this morng. Read a little in Gibbon.

[Omitted here, eleven manuscript pages with the heading: "The Plague of Athens. II."]

MEMORANDA, 89
Friday, 28th

Pursued the reading of Gibbon till breakfast. Medical visit to the child in Chambers St., my constant walk for some weeks past. De Pauw, Potter, Barthelemy, & Thucydides, the forenoon, & part of the afternoon. Dunlap, Brown, & Alsop here, an hour in the forenoon.

---

[35] Edward Gibbons, *Miscellaneous Works; with Memoirs of his Life and Writings, Composed by himself. Illustrated from his Letters; with Occasional Notes and Narrative* (London, 1796). Gibbons died in 1794.

[36] Jonathan Ogden Moseley (1762-1838; Yale 1780). He was a lawyer who practiced in East Haddam, Connecticut, member of Connecticut General Assembly, 1794-1804, and held various other state offices. He was a member of the U.S. House from Connecticut from 1805 to 1821.

[37] Ezekiel Williams (b. 1765, Wethersfield), apparently a brother of Smith's friend, John Williams of Wethersfield. He prospered in the marine insurance business in Connecticut.

[38] DePauw, not found. Potter was John Potter successively Bishop of Oxford and Archbishop of Canterbury; probably *Archaeologiae Graecae: or the Antiquities of Greece* (Oxford 1697-1699). Nine editions up to 1775 and still being reprinted in 1837. Barthelemy cited earlier.

Dr. Mitchill an hour in the afternoon. He read me his new letter, to Dr. Muhlenberg, on Septon &c. as a manure. Second walk to Chambers St. Called at Mr. Rogers's, with design of making a visit. All out; & such has been the case every time I have called of late. Went to Woolseys. Dunlap came in. Cheerful talk, news-papers, & politics &c. till eight. Two hours, thence, in my study. Have read 84 pages 8vo in Gibbon. Not badly done. These 2nd vol. letters are entertaining.

Recd. a short letter from Wm. Buel to-day.

MEMORANDA, 90

Saturday, 29th

Pursued the reading of Gibbon, till breakfast. Brown breakfasted with us. Then my medical morning visit. A letter of business. A line from Dr. Kollock, introducing a Dr. Farrington, who wants letters up the Hudson &c. being in search of a place. Called on Dingley. Some errands. Sat down, pen in hand, to Thucydides, till four in the afternoon, bating ten minutes for dinner. My afternoon medical walk. Returning, went into Dr. & Mr. Miller's. Stayed there to tea. Club night—at our house—Johnson's night—Present, Alsop, Brown, Dunlap, Johnson, Kent, Smith, W. W. Woolsey. Johnson read us the History of the interior state of France, during the latter part of the reign of Robespierre, & for several months after his fall, written more than two thousand years ago, by Thucydides, but then predicated of Corcyra. Much conversation & lively. Fell, at last, on to the old subject of Truth. Many difficulties. Woolsey, Johnson, & I, maintain that *on all occasions* truth is to be spoken: i.e. that nothing will justify a falsehood; or that utility can never be promoted thereby. Brown & Dunlap pretend that tho', our position is, *generally*, true, yet there [are] occasions when it will be our duty to speak falsely, since by so doing we shall promote the general good. Long discussion—grounds of argument gone over several times—no conclusion.

POSTSCRIPT

So! so! pretty well! better than I expected! Here has been some dilligence, in the last half of this week. Not much to boast of, but nothing of which to be ashamed. No great advances in my journal; but then, notes, hints, facts, out of which something may, by & by, be made.

I begin to be a little reconciled to my chair; & can sit still & pore over a book, with less reluctance & fatigue. I have, in truth, some hopes of myself. Who knows what this winter may bring forth?

Ha, ha, ha!—it is truly laughable, ridiculously laughable, that I, who have so often, so constantly, seen, I mean *found*, the fallacy of all these predictive self-congratulations, should again indulge in them. And what if they are ridiculous? What then? "What fellows?"—as Dr. Edwards[39] would say—Are they not, also, comfortable?

O Hope, O Fancy, ye sister, ye twin-born deities, still deck the future out in smiles! still lead me on to believe I may yet catch the bright reality of Truth, the resplendent substance of Virtue! Ah! without your aid, ye benevolent goddesses, should not I become the helpless, hopeless thrall of Indolence & Shame?

FOURTEENTH WEEK

Sunday, 30th

PREFACE

Speaking without reference to the possible events of the ensuing week, which may disconcert every project, how well-founded soever, it is my design to prosecute, and, if possible, complete my inquiry, into the History of the Plague of Athens. I hope to make a rude draft of an Essay, on this subject, in my Journal, and to perfect it in the first volumes of my Memoirs. Till this purpose is accomplished—still speaking without relation to possible causes of deviating from my present plan—every thing else will be but an object of secondary attention. It will time enough to decide on what shall next be done, when what is now in hand is completed. But I can not avoid looking forward with some intentions of devoting the next cares, at least for a few days, or perhaps a week, to my Utopia. I have many hopes founded on that performance, if it shall ever deserve the name, and am eager to explain, at some length, or rather to embody & substantialize my numerous speculations. Other projects, too, crowd thick upon my mind.

> But who can tell the dew-drops of the moon?
> Or count the rays that in the diamond burn?[40]

MEMORANDA, 91

Rose in usual season, & read Gibbon's Posthumous Works Vol. 2nd till breakfast. Brown had called on Johnson, & they walked. The former breakfasted with us. My morning medical walk. Busied, great part of the morning, in writing nine introductory letters, to gentlemen in different parts of the State, for Doctor Farrington. Then wrote a hasty reply to Doctor Buel's hasty letter, recd. last week; & went out & delivered it. Read four Papers in the second vol. of Asiatic Researches.[41]

---

[39] There are either five or six (one reference is uncertain) Edwards mentioned in the "Diary." Three of them are Jonathan Edwards: the great Jonathan (Yale 1720), his son the Rev. Dr. Jonathan (Princeton 1765), and his son (Yale 1789). This appears to be clearly Jonathan I because his step-by-step method of arguing in his writing is indicated; nevertheless, Smith customarily referred to Jonathan I as "President Edwards," and he almost certainly knew Jonathan II in New Haven.

[40] Not found.

[41] In 1783 Jones, by now a famous master of Oriental languages, was knighted and made judge of the Supreme Court of Judicature at Calcutta. In 1784 he founded the Bengal Asiatic Society and was its only president until his death. *Asiatic Re-*

One on the Literature of the Hindoos—a strange mass of matter, from which I derived very little satisfaction. Two, relative to the Teshoo Lama—interesting, & have excited in me considerable curiosity to become acquainted with this superstition. Who is the Delai Lama? Is he the political sovereign of Thibet? The fourth paper was on the College of the Leeks. Short, sensible, curious. A sort of Quakers. Johnson & I walked out of town. I drank tea at H. Johnson's, with all the Johnsons, except H. who is now in Phila. Visit to Miss Susan Morton, who returned on Friday. Chat. She is as agreable as ever; but, contrary to what Wm. told me, who saw her in the morning, I did not think she looked as well as usual. Came home, & read Gibbon. I have finished his letters. Spirited & light. Such as one would be well pleased to receive from a friend, & much better calculated to give you an intimate idea of his character than his Memoirs. They leave behind them feeble impressions; & contain very little to be remembered to advantage: no useful sentiments, discussions, & truths. He was a miserable political, not to say moral, philosopher. His Journal displays great industry, applied to no illustrious purpose: if the good of man, alone deserve that character.

MEMORANDA, 92

Monday, 31st

Read, cursorily, the Extracts from Gibbon's Journal, till breakfast. His plan of reconciling different ancient testimonies, relative to the time at which an author &c. lived, is ingenious & satisfactory; & his illucidation, by reference to Fontenelle, happy. My customary professional walk. Sat down to Thucydides, & in the course of the day, finished the remainder of the First Volume. This day's reading has added next to nothing to my stock of materials for an Essay on the Plague. Since I have proceeded so far, I think to finish this History. C. B. Brown was here much of the forenoon. We talked —principally in reference to political morality & happiness of man. Drank tea at Dunlap's; & went with himself, Brown, & Johnson to the Theater. Dunlap's Tragedy, intituled "The Mysterious Monk," was played, for the first time, & "The Midnight Hour." I stayed only to see the first. The House was full. The whole of this piece rests on four characters; & the plot is one. The dialogue is, chiefly, between two persons. As to stile, the chief beauty is simplicity & force—too often subsiding to prose, & weakened by faulty inversion for the sake of a verse. The characters are well drawn; the delineation of passion natural & interesting; the situations fine; & the *denouement* or catastrophe, complete, satisfactory, & unexpected. My friend has made a very bold experiment, with a New York audience, & a New York band of Performers. The event is not as well as I could wish, but as favorable as might be expected. The very excellencies of this Play, are so many obstructions to it's popularity. Our people will not bear a simple, unbroken, & artfully natural display of passion; & our Performers are unequal to the task, totally incapable of forcing them to relish it. *Tyler* played the most satisfactorily to me; yet he injured, from total ignorance of recitation, the finest passage in his part. *Martin* exhausted his scanty voice by unnatural violence in the first Act; & was totally deficient in tenderness. *Hodgkinson* was shamefully boisterous, never touching, but sometimes impressive. *Mrs. Melmoth* did not conceive her part; all was affectation; & had no effect on me. Her long soliloquy is too long; & in her hands, was heavy. *Martin* was execrable with the *Letter*. Dunlap committed an oversight in changing the name of his Play—which was, at first, "Ribbemont, or the Feudal Baron." By indicating a Mystery connected with the Monk, every one was watching that personage; & conjecture thus sharpened, foresaw the catastrophe which else would never have been expected. When I heard the Piece first read, the discovery of Nabonne, in Manuel, was a real surprize; tho' there are several hints, scattered along, which lead naturally to the disclosure, & suspicion, when once awakened. But this is not the worst effect—The curiosity of the audience is too steadily fixed on the Monk, to admit of that high interest which would otherwise be excited by the different scenes. The Music to the Ode, is good, & was well performed & received. The auditory bestowed silent attention, during the whole representation; but there was not that glow of approbation which the play merited; but which we should have done wrong to expect. For myself, I was too much disgusted with the conduct of some of the spectators, too little satisfied with the exertions of the players, & too much interested in the fate of the play, to be interested greatly in the play itself. Continued Gibbon. Finished the Second, & commenced the third volume.

[Omitted here, one manuscript page with the heading: "III. The Plague of Athens—contd."]

GENERAL POSTSCRIPT TO THE MONTH OF OCTOBER 1796

Some industry this month, compared with others of it's predecessors; very little, viewed in reference to that which ought to distinguish him who pretends to any accurate notions & perfect glimpses of true morality. But it will be more useful to enumerate my labours this month, than to expatiate on their number or insignificance. From such a prospect of them a more ready estimate of their value may be formed; & a motive to equal, if the exertions have been honorable, to superior, if they have been few & feeble, may, perhaps, be thence derived.

I have read in October 1796.

---

searches was the name given to the published and bound papers of the society, many of them his, correct title: *Dissertations and Miscellaneous Pieces, relating to the History and Antiquities, the Arts, Sciences, and Literature of Asia* (London, 1793).

The History of Thucydides—Vol. I.—the whole; many parts repeatedly; some, with strict attention.

De Pauw's Researches concerning the Greeks—chief of the First Volume.

Potter's Grecian Antiquities—several lengthy Articles in both vols.

Voyage du Jeune Anacharse—several chapters—perhaps—equal to one vol.

Proceedings in an Action of Debt—Ch: J. Fox—& Jno. Horne Tooke.

Zoonomia—P. III intire—Diseases of Volition in P. II. the whole. Miscellaneous passages, beside.

Dr. Mitchill's Preface to the American Edition of Zoonomia—Vol. I.

Gibbon's Miscellaneous Works—Vols. I, II, & part of the III.

Monthly Review, for Jany., Feby., March, April, May, June, July, & Appendix, 1796.

English Review, for June 1796.

Nature & Art—Novel. 2 vols. 12 mo. Mrs. Inchbald.

The Iron Chest—a play, by Geo. Coleman Jr.

Six Papers in the Asiatic Researches.

In the foregoing list are not included the numerous scraps which are unavoidably read, both relative to one's profession, & to other things—& a dozen NewsPapers a week—studied out by the Maps, &c.

I have written in October 1796—

Letters—to my sister Mary—a very long one, an imperfect part of which is contained in this Journal.
    to my sister Abby—contained in the Journal.
    to —————Fanny—also here.
    to ————Idea Strong—the same.
    to ————Sally Pierce.—do.
    to Wm. Buel.————————do.—beside letters to most of these, and to others, no part of which is preserved.

A Sonnet.—

Abstract of Thucydides, B. I.—miserable scanty & imperfect.

On the Plague of Athens, several pages of notes, the result of careful inquiry.

Such is the faithful representation of my mental industry, during the month now complete. And if I have not employed my time to purposes so noble, & with a perseverance so unremitting, as I ought to have done, at least I may spare myself useless reproaches, & indulge some consoling hopes of the future. And where is he who, duly sensible of the value of time, & duty of virtuous toil, finds every little portion of it suitably devoted to the best of objects? Where is he who does not often look back, with condemnation & regret, on the hours irrevocably gone; forever lost in wasteful neglect or frivolous occupation? Next to the madness of an improper use or neglect of opportunities, is the folly of fruitless self-reproach when those opportunities exist no longer.

NOVEMBER 1796

GENERAL PREFACE TO THE MONTH

I am fatigued with this part of the plan of my Journal, and shall certainly relinquish it, with the present volume. My general determinations are very steadily the same, & therefore not allowing of variety, they produce a tiresome repetition at the commencement of every month. The case were far different did I proceed in my several studies which such rapidity or execution, as to have the accomplishment of a design be almost consentaneous with it's conception. Were I endowed with any tolerable degree of industry, this might, in fact, be my conduct. But days are consumed in intending, & resolving, & dreaming, when hours properly employed are all that are needed. This Journal, when it was began (pf. vol. I.) was to contain wonderful things. I know not how many new vistas were to have been opened into medical science. What is the result? The pitiful business of collecting the facts illustrative of so simple an event as The Plague of Athens, has slept in lifeless contemplation for I know not how many months. How many Sonnets was I not to have written? One a day, I thought, was easy. In three months, only one is produced. Memoirs, too—they flow so readily from my pen, it was but to move it over the page, & all was done. Utopia—here, again, I was on my own ground, & the labour of a few days was all that was necessary to expand on paper, a subject, so long & so maturely weighed. But I am sick of renewing complaints, of dwelling on broken resolutions, deserted projects, imperfect executions—"With endless variety of folly." Yet to such an irksome employment, according to my present arrangement, do the beginning & end of every week, much more of every month, reluctantly compel me. Henceforth, therefore, I have done with it. This, or my mind must sadly slumber, this is the last occasion, of the like kind, which the present volume will present me; & with this volume, I change my plan. In my new Memoirs, I will laugh at this petty order, & shake my free plumes in the bounteous space. There is something too cramped, too chalk-line, in these openings & shuttings of every seven days; & I have no notion of being confined to a Dutch Garden, when the Garden of Nature is before me, & invites my steps. But—what shall I do, what *will* I do, the present month. I can not tell; & why should I resolve? If I ask myself what I expect to do, why truly, I see no reason to deviate from my late designs, unless it be in activity & attention. I think a propensity to study is gaining ground within me; but the approaches are so slow as to leave room for many intervening doubts. I think, too, that I can bear to sit still longer, than I could six weeks since; & that my mind is not so easily & completely jaded by a few hours of application. Still, I have a most mortal aversion, a deadly hate, of motion: I mean intellectual motion: motion with the marking, the careful, the scrutinizing, methodizing, Pen. Shall I ever do better? Poh! What a question is that to one who holds to the Perfectibility of Man! True, man may have a wonderful deal of perfectibility—nobody disputes his capacity—it was not that after which I inquired. There is such a thing as Volition, you know. Yes, & I know how feebly it is exerted, where it ought to be rapid & penetrating as the lightnings.

MEMORANDA, 93

Tuesday, 1st

Read Gibbon till breakfast. Visited my patient. Some errands. Ch. B. Brown came in, just after I had taken up my pen to trace out the concluding notices of the last month. Dunlap came in shortly after; & Mr. Roulet, while they were here. It was near two when I was alone. After dinner, I made the necessary additions & prefixes to the past & present months; & read thirty pages in Thucydides Vol. II.

The picture which Mr. Roulet draws, and he never exaggerates, of the municipal regulations of the *Pays de Vaud*, and indeed of all Swisserland, is little calculated to foster our admiration for their liberty & happiness, or to create a disrespect for our own civil & political institutions. Every town, every village, has it's distinct government, & sometimes (as in Lausanne) there are two governments in a single city, independent of, & variant from each other. Every mile, every half mile, you change the territory, & with it the regulations, of this complicated Confederacy. Born a citizen of Zurich, or of Basil, you can not claim a like privilege in removing to Solcure, or to Bern; & tho' you may have exercised, with conformity to Law, a profession at Vevai, you are no longer at liberty to prosecute it when you remove to Lausanne. It is only by submitting to new trials, and at the expence of new impositions, that you are qualified to act in the new, as in the ancient residence. Nay, it is not enough that you are willing to pay the price of the house you would purchase, you must purchase the permission to purchase. And then, the right of property, and not of citizenship, is all that you acquire. Meantime, in the Canton of Bern, the aristocracy assess the tax, & levy it upon you, without a reason assigned, or an account rendered. They send their Bailiff; a petty tyrant whom their favour enables to set at defiance even their Laws in favor of the people, who retain the fruitless right of exposing themselves to new indignities by deputations & petitions.

Visited my patient. A short visit at Mr. Catlin's. Visited, at Mr. Hodgkinson's. Came home & read Gibbon.

MEMORANDA, 94

Wednesday, 2nd

Read Gibbon till breakfast. Made my medical visit. Some errands. Pursued the reading of Thucydides.

Dunlap & Brown here, in the afternoon. Repeated my medical visit. Drank tea at Kent's. Was at the Theater. "Which is the Man?" & "No Song no Supper.[42] Saw the first. A great rout by some foolish & intemperate people. The house rose upon them, & very properly turned them out; but not without some difficulty, & several persons being hurt—themselves the most. Came home, & read the two Prefaces in Godwin's Political Justice—part of his essay & Appendix on Sincerity, & those parts of the 8th & 9th Chapters of the 8th Book which treat of Marriage & Longevity. I can not help thinking, that both Condorcet & Godwin have treated this last subject superficially.

MEMORANDA, 95

Thursday, 3rd

C. B. Brown breakfasted with us. He brought me two french pamphlets—one of which I looked over. Dunlap came in, & we talked over the *fracas* of the preceeding evening. Made two medical visits. Came home, & was sometime employed with pestle & mortar. Read Thucydides. Visit from Jeremiah Mason: From Alsop, Brown, & Dunlap. The last had Morton's play of "The Way to get Married."[43] We read the first act—which has the merit of uncommon stupidity.

Visited at Ch. Adams's. From thence I went to Moses Rogers's. Mr. Rogers just returned from N. England. Came home & read Gibbon. I can not help smiling at his minute research. Were it conjectured that Julius Cesar wore ruffles, & had certain learned fools written folios of controversy on this *important* point, Gibbon would have read them with avidity, & perhaps added some new solution of the difficulty. The refutation of Warburton, which I have read this evening, is complete & elegant.

MEMORANDA, 96

Friday, 4th

I looked into the romantic pages of Gibbon, intituled "Antiquities of the House of Brunswic," but concluded that I could better use my time, at present, than to read them, & having little curiosity to peruse his Essay on the Study of Literature, & still less to examine a Vindication of a History I have never read, I bade adieu to this author, for some time, at least. Made my, now, daily visit to my little patient. Finished Thucydides. I have read the Second Volume of this Work too hastily

---

[42] The play by Mrs. Hannah Cowley (1782); the afterpiece, a light opera, by Prince Hoare (1790). One would scarcely realize from this account that Smith had seen the beginning of one of the worst theater riots of the time. It began during the overture when two drunken sea captains in a box interrupted with a demand for "Yankee Doodle." The audience, as Smith noted, ejected the captains with considerable difficulty and several people were injured. The captains went down to the waterfront, rallied their crews, and returned for further violence which resulted in numerous arrests. Smith subsequently appeared as a witness for the state at a court of the Quarter Sessions, for which see later.

[43] *The Way to Get Married*, Morton (1796).

to derive much instruction from it; but not, as I hope, without some benefit. The first I read with more care. The translation is executed in a very affected & inelegant manner; but sufficiently well to convince me of the excellence of the original, which relates to one of the most important periods of ancient history, & has every appearance of meriting the praises which modern writers have so abundantly heaped upon it. Read in one of the french pamphlets sent me by Mr. Roulet—intituled—"De la force du Gouvernment actual de la France & de la nécessité de s'y rallier. Par Benjamin Constant. 1796."[44] Executed several errands. Visited Dr. Mitchill. He read me a portion of the Geological part of his intended Report to the Agricultural Society; by whose appointment he has been exploring the condition of a part of this State. Visited Dunlap. Dunlap & Brown here, in the afternoon. Former part of the evening at H. Johnson's—remainder at Seth Johnson's. I have looked into Plutarch's life of Pericles—which I mean to read to-morrow: at least so much of it as has any connection with the Athenian Pestilence. As yet I can find no satisfactory account of the time when that disease ceased, ultimately, it's ravages.

MEMORANDA, 97

Saturday, 5th

Read till breakfast in the french pamphlet of Benjn. Constant—"De la force &c." After breakfast read the life of Pericles, in Plutarch, & noted down three particulars relative to the Plague of Athens. Visited my patient. Called, a few minutes, on business, on Dr. Mitchill. Attended the first reading rehearsal of my Opera. I foresee that—or rather I aftersee that, it must undergo several alterations to adapt [it] to the taste, in any degree, of our audience. No matter how often a half-fool, who pretends to be a man of spirit or a fine gentleman, exclaims "God damn it"—no matter how often a pert little miss, cries out "My God"—in a dramatic performance—so tender are the consciences of our people, so careful are they of the name of God, how much soever the character & passion of the fictitious being may require it, this venerable monosyllable is not to be made free with: I must exclude God from my Play. Recd. a letter from Mrs. Lovegrove, to which I returned an answer. Johnson has picked up a new Novel—by the author of "Man as he is"—intituled "Hemsprong, or Man as he is not."[45] He began to read it to Dunlap, who was here, & I threw aside more serious employments, to become one of his hearers. Brown came in. We were pleased; & I purpose to read this new book—whose author seems to be treading in the *profane* steps of "Caleb Williams." Club night—W. W. Woolsey's turn—Present—Brown, Dunlap, Kent, Johnson, Smith, the Woolseys—An agreable, & very sociable evening;

---

[44] Benjamin Constant de Rebecque (1796).
[45] Robert Bage, *Hermsprong, or Man as He Is* (1792); *Man as He Is Not* (1796). *Hermsprong* fascinated Smith and he wrote at least one act of the play which he had decided to draw from it.

tho' nothing of importance beyond the news, politics, & chit-chat of the day, occupied our consideration.

POSTSCRIPT

This week has not been idly spent, tho' but little has been effected. I gain some encouragement, & hope for better things. When I look back on life & consider how feeble have been my exertions, when I attentively view the present time & observe how trifling are my acquisitions & how many years have been expended in their pursuit, & when I look forward & see how short is the probable duration of my existence & how much of that short period is likely to be mispent, I am necessitated, for comfort & support, to call to mind what it is possible to accomplish therein, & that the welfare of man rests but lightly on what I am, & what I do. Of what silly vanity are we constantly the slaves! And how inconsiderable is our real weight in the liberal scale of nature! For tho', in respect to exertion, each should act as if all depended on him, yet no one should indulge the false conceit that all, or even much, does on him depend. Let us exert, but not too highly estimate the extent of our powers!

FIFTEENTH WEEK

Sunday, 6th

PREFACE

I bring with me, to the encounter, the entering week, all the good resolutions with which I commenced the last. May they prove still more efficacious and productive! The succeeding pages, if I mistake not, will bear witness to a further investigation of the subject which has, in part, occupied the preceeding: The Plague of Athens. In these, I design to prosecute my inquiry, in a more systematic manner; or rather, to arrange, in some sort, the materials which have been already collected. Is this for my own conviction, simply? No! But having taken up an opinion, I wish to be satisfied that it is defensible—& not this merely, but also that it is founded in truth. I would, likewise, be able to defend that opinion, should any one choose to call it's validity in question. Beside, if I do not err, it will cast a strong & distinguishing light, on the generally [mooted] subject of what are called Epidemics. I may be induced to communicate the result of my inquiries, & the arguments on which my opinion is founded, to the public; & I certainly shall do it, if I am convinced that any good will thereby be produced.

MEMORANDA, 98

I finished the first volume of "Hermsprong," this morning. I then made my daily visit to my patient. Returning, I called in & paid my respects, to Dr. & Mr. Miller—the last of whom was confined to his chamber by indisposition. I found Mr. Gahn here when I came home. He had with him the first number of a Swedish

Literary Journal—several passages of which he obligingly explained to me. He speaks of it as a work of merit—& it is executed by his friend Mr. (if I spell the name aright) Silverstorpe. I wrote the two preceeding pages; & a letter to Mrs. Lovegrove, to go by Post to-morrow, lest the one of yesterday should not be seasonably recd. Her child's wet nurse has deserted her—& she asks my advice. After a solitary dinner, I took up the second volume of "Hermsprong"; & had proceeded about thirty pages—when, as Johnson was not here to enjoy it with me, & indeed had read it—it occurred to me that Dunlap & Brown would not be displeased in hearing more of what seemed yesterday to give them pleasure. To them, therefore, I hastened. I sat down, with Mrs. Dunlap, & the others, began the volume anew, & did not quit it, till it was finished. The reading has given us uncommon pleasure; we pronounce the book an excellent one; & I have half resolved to undertake the mechanical task of compiling, out of it, a Comedy. This resolution, as it is but half formed, perhaps, is as little likely to be executed, as many which have heretofore obtained still greater maturity.

MEMORANDA, 99

Monday, 7th

Read a few pages in Benjamin Constant. C. B. Brown breakfasted with us. He had gone, & breakfast pretty well out of the way, when Mr. Allen of Lichfield came in. He sat with me, we talked; & thus, & in walking about, but together, we spent the morning. I visited my patient, a new one, & Mr. Miller. In the afternoon, I began my arrangement of the symptoms of the Plague, from Thucydides. I had not proceeded far, when Mr. Allen returned, & I dropt the pen. We conversed, till tea-time—which we spent at Dunlap's, & thence went to the Theater. "The Mysterious Monk"—& "Catherine & Petruchio."[46] A thin house, for the second night of a new piece. My friend has made some judicious curtailments in his piece since the first night, & it was now better performed—but, still, indifferently: indifferently, as it respects just performance, but better than usual for our performers, & therefore very well for our audience. How much of the applause which British Plays obtain, among us, arises from our knowing that they have been well received at home? And, beside the prejudice so universal against pieces of our own manufacture, is there not an intellectual cowardice, a fear lest others should despise his judgement, which restrains the spectator from applauding a cis-atlantic drama?

MEMORANDA, 100

Tuesday, 8th

I finished Benjamin Constant's essay "De la force du Gouvernment &c." It is a sensible performance; calculated, as I should think, to do good in France—if indeed any thing can do good there. I was called to a new patient. "Woes cluster—rare are solitary woes."[47] I meant to have done much, ere this, on my Essay on the Plague; yesterday I was interrupted; & I knew I should be part of this day: but I calculated on having a few hours to myself. I was summoned to the Court of Quarter Sessions, as a witness, on the part of the State, concerning the Riot at the Theater, noticed in the Memoranda of last Wednesday. I was detained, & so the morning was lost. I found Jeremiah Mason here when I returned. After dinner, I had time to read over, hastily, but with great pleasure, the description of the Plague of Athens, by Titus Lucretius Carey, at the end of his 6th book—in the Paris edition *apud Barbon*.[48] Notwithstanding one interruption, I also added near a page to the following remarks. Mr. Allen came—we walked out to Mr. Webster's—where we spent the afternoon. I made a second professional visit. I found C. B. Brown here, when I came home. Mr. Allen came, & we went to the Anniversary meeting of The Agricultural Society; where we heard Mr. Kent deliver a discourse. He has corrected it, & made some additions, since he shewed it me. It is honorable to him, & I think more deserving of preservation than either of those which have been previously delivered. We spent the evening at W. W. Woolsey's. Dunlap & his wife were there. Recd. letters from my father & Mr. Tracy.

[Omitted here, six manuscript pages with the heading: "The Plague of Athens IV."]

MEMORANDA, 101

Wednesday, 9th

The visiting of four patients, in very opposite quarters of the city, occupied no inconsiderable portion of the forenoon; and, in connection with the reading of the Newspapers, the writing of a paragraph for the Minerva, and several other interruptions, left me little leisure for study. Mr. Roulet visited us; & brought with him, for our examination, the first part of the First Volume of "Origin de tous les Cultes. Par Dupris"[49]— I believe I have the title right. I have read a paper, or two, in the Journal of the Paris Lyceum of Arts, which have not imprest me with very high ideas of it's general merit. I found a few moments to pursue my arrangement of the symptoms of the Plague. Notwithstanding that there is much more ground to travel over than I expected, I had long since completed this business, were it not for these incessant interruptions. Mr. Allen & I dined at James Watson's, and spent the afternoon. Mr. Webster, Mr. Spencer of the Senate, and Dr. Brown of

---

[46] David Garrick (1756); made out of fragments of *The Taming of the Shrew*.

[47] Edward Young, *Night Thoughts*, "Night" iii, 1.63.

[48] Probably a reference to some work of Nicholas Barbon, M.D. Possibly in *A Discourse of Trade* (London, 1690); text not available; no Paris edition found.

[49] Charles François Dupuis, *Origine de tous les Cultes, ou la Religion Universelle* (1794).

the House,[50] were of the company. With the last I was pleased. He lives at White's-Town, or near there; & will be able to furnish useful information, respecting the diseases which prevail in the Western County. Contrary to my design, I accompanied Mr. Allen to the Theater: "Such Things Are," and "The Waterman."[51] I recd. a lengthy letter from Theodore Dwight; a letter more flattering to my heart than almost any I ever have recd. from him. He would not, he could not, have written thus, did he not love me. I shall write to him soon; and my letter will explain, what I have not time now to enlarge upon.

MEMORANDA, 102

Thursday, 10th

Mr. Allen breakfasted with us, of consequence, we sat longer than usual. I then made two professional visits—one of them being to Mr. Miller, who has been some time unwell. When I came home, I found C. B. Brown here. It was after eleven o'clock when I sat down by myself. Then I finished the preceeding enumeration &c. of symptoms, from Thucydides. Next I read over those line of Lucretius which relate to this subject—beginning at "Principia caput incensum &c."[52] Drs. Mitchill and Miller came in. They stayed an hour; & we agreed to unite in the prosecution of the plan for a Medical Repository, as projected by me last Summer. I determined to make myself master of the lines of Lucretius, beginning as above—to the end of Book VI. I began to translate literally. Johnson entering, we went over them together; & I made a close verbal translation of forty one lines. This is no bad effort: I do not mean the translating; but the having carefully enabled myself to translate the whole passage of 144 lines; and this, too, in an author I never before perused; who is commonly esteemed difficult; & when I have not read as much Latin for many years. Mr. Gold of the Senate,[53] formerly my class-mate, now resident at White'sburgh, came to see me. He speaks well of Doctor Brown's professional talents; well of a Dr. Kirkpatrick of Whitesburgh; and of Dr. Hopkins of Paris. These, then, are persons to be written to, on the business of the Medical Repository. I wrote short letters to my father, & to Mr. Tracy, to send by Allen, who goes in the morning. He came here. We went together, to Mr. Catlin's. I bade him adieu, & went to Seth Johnson's—where I spent the remainder of the evening.

MEMORANDA, 103

Friday, 11th

Ch. B. Brown breakfasted with us. After breakfast, I finished translating the lines of Lucretius which I read yesterday, & wrote No. 5, on the Plague of Athens, being the result of what I found in the Roman Poet. I sketched an outline of an address to the Physicians &c. of the United States, on the subject of the Medical Repository. Visited my two patients; having, in the course of my walk, met & conversed with several acquaintance—which much retarded me. Visited at Mrs. Riley's—where I saw Mr. Bird, & Mr. Griswold, of the House[54]—who lodge there. Our legislature is now adjourned, to meet at Albany in January. I went to Mr. Mason's, where I spent an hour. Miss Mason was not at home. From there, I went to Mrs. Morton's. I found them all at home, & well. Wm. Johnson joined me there; & the evening passed off pretty well. I came home, & have read several articles in Darwin's Zoonomia, P. II.

MEMORANDA, 105

Saturday, 12th

I began & nearly finished the Prospectus of "The Medical Repository"; & I had completed it, were it not that my attention was diverted, & my time occupied, by several visitors. Ch. B. Brown called on me, in the morning; after him, Dr. Brown of Fort Stanwix, visited me. He stayed here two hours, or more, & we talked over the business of "The Repository." He gave me an account of what they call, in his part of the country, the Lake Fever, & also of the Dysentery as it has appeared there. He has taken notes of the cases which have fallen under his care; & has engaged to transmit to me a minute account of those diseases, with the method of cure he has found most successful, in the course of the coming year. I may count upon him, as a steady Correspondent, in our new undertaking. He intimated a possibility, however, of his quitting the Practice of Physic. He recommends Dr. Hopkins & Kirkpatrick, & a Dr. Moore of German Flatts. They must be written to. Dunlap came to see me. Alsop made me a visit, for the first time, in many days. He was diverted with "Serenus Samonicus,"[55] (Dr. Hopkins of Hartford's satire on Perkins the Vender of Metallic Points) as he is with all odd things. It was Club Night. G. M. Woolsey's turn. Present—Alsop, Brown, Dunlap, Johnson, Kent, Smith, the Woolseys. G. M. Woolsey was hoarse, with a ca-

---

[50] Ambrose Spencer (1765-1848). Three years at Yale but graduated from Harvard, 1783. He was a lawyer, state senator 1795-1798, and held numerous offices. In 1810 Chief Justice of New York Supreme Court, U.S. House 1829-1831, and Mayor of Albany for one term. "Dr. Brown of the House" was apparently a member of the New York legislature.

[51] *Such Thing Are*, Mrs. Elizabeth Inchbald (1787); *The Water Man*, or *The First of August* (1774), Charles Dibdin.

[52] "Principio [sic] caput incensum fervore gerebant..." "First they felt the head burning with heat." Trans. W. H. D. Rouse, Lucretius, *De Rerum Natura*, VI, 1145. The quotation is from the writer's poetic account of a plague at Athens, 431-430 B.C.

[53] Thomas Ruggles Gold (1764-1827; Yale 1786); lawyer, state Senate 1796-1802; from 1797 to 1801 he was also assistant attorney general of New York, later a congressman.

[54] Roger Griswold (1762-1812; Yale 1780), representative from Connecticut in U.S. House, 1795-1805; judge of Supreme Court in Connecticut, 1807; Lieutenant Governor, 1809-1811; Governor of Connecticut, 1811 to 1812.

[55] For Smith's acquaintance with Perkins, a strange, dedicated eccentric, see later.

tarrh. Dunlap read to us his Comedy of two acts, intituled "Tell truth & shame the Devil."[56] He means to bring it on to the Stage, this winter. I fear that it is too moral to succeed. Our audiences must have a plentiful dose of fun, to make even a drop of morality palatable. Came home, & read part of a little Opera, in French, called "Paul & Virginie"; founded on Bernardin St. Pierre's Novel of the same name; but was called away to visit a sick child; & it was too late to finish it, when I returned.

[Omitted here, three manuscript pages with the heading: "The Plague of Athens. V."]

POSTSCRIPT

Tho' I have not yet been able, owing to many interruptions, to complete what I fully intended, at the opening of the week, yet I, when these interruptions are duly estimated, I am not ashamed of the industry, little as it may be deemed, which is therein apparent. Certainly, with a firmer mind, a resolution less wavering, less apt to [be] diverted from it's purpose by the solicitations [of] others, more might have been effected. But I must speak of my own conduct, with relation to my own character; & tho' I hope it will become more virtuous, & even fancy that it daily verges towards propriety, yet till it is virtuous, till there is no longer room to doubt of it's deserving that epithet, every exertion I may make must be measured by the effort which it costs to make it, as well as by the abstract rule of moral excellence. By this last, how unfit am I to be judged; by the former, I will venture to bestow some little commendaion on myself.

SIXTEENTH WEEK

Sunday, 13th

PREFACE

With this week if I mistake not, my Journal will be closed. The various concerns of the week will demand much of time, and perhaps, prevent me from pursuing my lingeringly-executed Essay on the Athenian Pestilence. Indeed, should I have time, I shall pursue my design in my Memoirs; since I have not room sufficient in this Journal. But it is quite probable that what with the avocations of business, professional & of other kinds; what with the project of a "Medical Repository," which must be speedily set on foot; & what with the writing of a lengthy letter which friend Dwight's demands, in answer; I shall find my whole time occupied, & more than occupied. The event will determine. But, beside, have I not corrections to make in my Opera? & perhaps a rehearsal to attend? Ah! how ingenious is Indolence in the construction & array of excuses!

---
[56] Dunlap's comedy, produced January 9, 1797, was an alteration, as he admitted, from a French one-act piece called *Jerome Pointu* (New York, 1797).

MEMORANDA, 106

Finished "Paul & Virginie," an Opera. Read the Preface to "Origine des tous les Cultes." A visit from Ezekiel Lewis, who sails, next week, for the Falkland Islands & for Canton. Ch. B. Brown here. A medical visit. Dined & spent the afternoon, at S. Johnson's; part of the evening at Mr. Roulet's; the remainder at Mr. Riley's.

MEMORANDA, 107

Monday, 14th

Ch. B. Brown breakfasted with us. After breakfast a professional visit. Then called on Dr. Brown, & we went to see Dr. Mitchill at the College. Conversation: & Dr. Brown renewed his engagements to furnish us with all the information in his power. Mr. Kent came in. Several of the Professors commenced their Lectures. Their auditory, & still more their regular pupils, very few. Dr. Brown & I came away. I took leave of him. Finished my Prospectus of a Medical Repository. Several errands took up much time after dinner. Called on Dr. Mitchill. We went to Dr. Miller's. Read, & agreed on the Prospectus; & to have 300 copies printed to distribute privately; & then to have the Address published in all the News Papers. Went to T. & J. Swords—& bargained for the impression. Called on my patient. Called on Dingley—he was out. Read several articles in Zoonomia P. II. A long visit from my neighbor Boyd. Recd. a letter from Mrs. Lovegrove. Our plan of a periodical work is good: if it do not succeed, it will be shameful to the Faculty.

MEMORANDA, 108

Tuesday, 15th

Two professional visits. A visit to Dingley. A visit from C. B. Brown. Wrote eight pages & a half on the letter to Theodore Dwight. Read a number of Articles in Darwin's Zoonomia, P. II. Drank tea at Mr. Boyd's. Spent the entire evening at the Manumission Society.

MEMORANDA, 109

Wednesday, 16th

Ch. B. Brown breakfasted with us. Wrote the Introduction &c. to the first volume of my Memoirs. Made some corrections in my Opera. Visited a patient. Drank tea at H. Johnson's, & spent part of the evening. Remainder, with Wm., at Mr. Kent's.

MEMORANDA, 110

Thursday, 17th

Read several articles in Zoonomia, last night. Wrote nine pages of the following letter, this forenoon. Ch. B. Brown here. And Dr. Mitchill—Johnson & I dined & spent the afternoon at Kent's. Evening called, in vain, at Gahn's—was at Woolsey's—at a fire, which has destroyed, as I am told, most of Mr. Catlin's property—at Dunlap's, who has returned—& at Woolsey's again. Read several additional articles in Zoonomia P. II.

MEMORANDA, 111

Friday, 18th

Some progress in Zoonomia, P. II. Several errands occupied some time. Visit from Ch. B. Brown—from Dr. Hosack—from Dr. Miller—much time thus spent. Dined—spent the afternoon—& part of the evening—at S. Johnson's.

Began to transcribe & correct—in the first vol. of my Memoirs, the letter to Theodore Dwight, which follows. I take all this pains—that I may avoid giving him any cause of offence—& that I may correctly reply to all his remarks. Beside, from the possible use to which this letter may be put, when it has gone from my hands, it is an important paper.

MEMORANDA, 112

Saturday, 19th

Ch. B. Brown breakfasted with us. Visited a patient. Read the news-papers. Visits from Dunlap—& Ch. Adams. Continued my letter to Theodore Dwight—Professional visit. Visited Dr. Miller—& his brother. Sat some time with the former. Medical visit. Drank tea at Dunlap's. Club night—& my night. Present, Brown, Dunlap, Johnson, Smith, the Woolseys. I read Marat's character, by Brissot, from H. M. Williams's letters—vol. 7. Appendix; & a scene from "The Negro Slaves"—translated from a German Play—inserted in the Oracle, a London Paper, of Oct. 10. 1796.

POSTSCRIPT

All my preconceptions & forebodings have been realized, and more than realized. I have not only not done any thing on my Medical Essay, but have not even finished either of those matters, which I did not think, when I wrote the preface to this week, would have consumed half my time. But the week has been wonderfully interrupted—partly by business—partly by pleasure—& in part by company. Yet I have not been idle: and, if I have devoted some hours to the pleasures of the table & of society, I have curtailed as many from those of the Theater, & from evening company. But I hope to effect much more the ensuing week; & to have removed the load which at present weighs me down. A little patience—& I think my patience is on the increase; a little perseverance—& this also I hope I shall not want; will do much. A few days, by their aid, will dispatch a world of writing—& leave [me] somewhat more at liberty.

LETTERS

To Theodore Dwight.

Your last letter, my dear friend, which I recd. a few days since, gave me a pleasure superior to any which you have ever written me. Not on account of the sentiments it contains, tho' they are characteristic of an excellent heart, but for the motives by which you were governed in it's composition. How much soever we may vary in opinion, I can never be insensible to the proofs of uncommon friendship which this letter contains.

The sincerity & freedom which you have exercised, in this last letter, have augmented the delight it has given me. In replying it to it, I shall endeavour to be equally sincere & free. You will at least be convinced that I am honest, that I mean to think & act right, whatever you may believe concerning the real nature of my sentiments & conduct.

On the subject of Titles I shall make but few remarks, in addition to what I have already written. I still consider them as childish, as best; &, on the whole, pernicious; but I would consent to their being retained, & would myself willingly use them, rather than to lose any superior good which might be obtained by employing them. Children are pleased with toys; but when they have attained the age of manhood, they ought to have sufficient good sense, to substitute objects of real utility for those of diversion. But some people continue children all their lives; tho' they live ever so long, they must still have toys. From such persons I would not withhold them. They should be permitted to retain their playthings. Some individuals, likewise, tho' they think & act correctly, in general, have, in relation to some particulars, a perversity of taste or judgment; & if it was necessary, in an affair of any importance, I should no more think of addressing certain men, without adding their titles, than of attempting to administer a drug which was nauseous to a patient & on which his life depended, without sugar, when I knew that he would immediately reject it, unless sugar were added. I might [think] the habit a bad one, but it would be too late, then, to contend with it. But, suppose that, instead of weaning children from toys, as their reason matured, I should strive to fix in their minds a belief that they were important; suppose I should teach them that it was necessary that their clothes should be laced; that persons with laced coats were to be treated with more respect than those whose coats were plain; or that it was essential to tell every man who had lace on his coat, that his coat was laced; I ask whether this would not be perverting the understanding, & busying it about straws, rather than pearls? Every thing must be, in a degree pernicious, which induces the understanding to ascribe a value to any man, or any thing, which does not really belong to it.

In respect to mankind at large, it is precisely as with individuals. Society has it's infancy, & I hope will have it's manhood, like the beings of which it consists. In proportion as the reason of mankind is informed, in that proportion the littleness of titles, & other distinctions than those which are founded on pre-eminent virtue, becomes evident; & in the same proportion should those members of society who discover their nothingness, disuse them, & endeavour to persuade others to lay them aside. For while men continue to attach ideas of excellence to what has no claim to that character, so long are they straying from the right road, so long are they paying that homage elsewhere, which is only due to Worth.

In the allusion to the "seam of the stocking &c." I discover the humour of my friend. Yet, surely, he will agree with me, that if there were any real advantage in the change, it would be proper to make it; & that a man of sense would little merit the appellation, should he be deterred by the ridicule of those who could not, or would not, comprehend the reason of his conduct. But, then, I will allow to you, & more than this I am sure you will not wish me to concede, that, tho' there would be a benefit from such an alteration, no person ought to sacrifice to such a consideration a more material benefit.

As to the probable consequences of the use of titles which now exist—in the view you call upon me to consider them—I have no apprehensions. I have no fear for our civil or political liberties, from any thing which I now observe. Temporary inconveniences we may suffer, (tho' not from these, particularly) but permanent national misfortunes I do not, at present, greatly apprehend.

But why should you discredit my assertions concerning the manner in which I first began to use what you pleasantly denominate "the bald-face style"? What *temptation* do you suppose I could have to misrepresent the truth? Or do you estimate my veracity so lightly as to suppose that any common, or even any, temptation, could have made me *lie*? It is very true that the address I now use, was at first a matter of chance, or imitation, & not of reflection; & even that it had even become habitual in regard to Brown & Bringhurst—& I believe some others—before I tho't of there being more propriety in one mode than in the other. It is also true that, by the same process I first came to direct my letters at the top, instead of the bottom. This was so much the case, that when I sent the unfortunate letter to you, which has caused this discussion, it never occurred to my mind, for an instant, that I had never written to you so before. If it had, I believe I should have made the usual additions: or at least told you why I did not. The reasons on which I ground my practice, or for which I continue it, are mostly subsequent to the commencement of the practice. Nor do they govern my conduct in all cases—because I know there are some people so attached to their adjuncts to their names, that it might wholly counteract the purpose of a letter, were they to be omitted. And if it will give you the least pleasure to have them retained, when I address you, I assure you I am not so obstinate a *Lewellan*[57] as to refuse to gratify you.

I come now to what may be considered as the body of your letter. And here I know not how I can do better than to give you a brief history of my mind, in respect to moral & religious sentiments, and then to add a few remarks on particular passages of your letter. I foresee all the sorrow which this explanation will give you; but it is incumbent on me to be explicit. My duty, both to you & to myself, demands it of me.

It was my happiness to be born the son of parents whose belief in Christianity made them distinguished for the morality of their lives, among christians. They educated me in a belief of the precepts of their religion; & what was more important, in virtuous habits: but they taught me to believe that the religion of Christ was the only foundation of morals.

I shall interrupt my narrative to make some observations, not hostile to your opinions, as I trust; & for which you will give credit to my sincerity.

I have but little doubt that I am indebted to the circumstance of my parents being christians for my virtuous education; because, I know few who disbelieve Christianity, who are as moral as some Christians. It has been to gain freedom from the restraints of morality, that they have generally discarded religion. It is with reason, then, that I regard it as fortunate that my parents were more than professing christians; as, had I been born the son of unbelievers, the chance is that I should have recd. an immoral education. But, I regard it as a real misfortune that I was ever taught to believe morality absolutely dependent on religion. For, when I went to Yale College, I formed acquaintance with several youths, who banished from my mind my conviction of the divinity of the christian doctrine; & with it, in a good degree, my sense of moral obligation. But, you must recollect that, at this time, I was a mere child. The operations of understanding must, of consequence, have been very limited; & my conduct & sentiments deserve to be regarded rather as the result of example, imitation, & false notions of what was spirited & becoming, than of a mind or imbued with just conceptions, of the force of arguments on either side. Meantime, my early habits prest much upon my mind; & tho' I might ridicule belief, it still held a firm footing, in the depth of my heart, which I did not venture to examine. I contracted, however, many foolish habits; some [of] which were quite immoral; & was preserved from others, probably, by my immature age, alone. Such was my situation when I went to Greenfield; & of this I have reason to think Dr. Dwight was already apprized, when [I] arrived. Still he must have seen, (at least so I flatter myself—) that these blemishes, were superficial; that by a proper management they might be removed; & that there was something beside which was worthy of the attempt, even should it prove more laborious than he deemed it. For myself, I came to your brother, with a mind deeply impressed in his favor. I was only fifteen; of an affectionate & pliable disposition: of a temper warm, enthusiastic, but easily manageable. All around me were christians; my early education had been such as he could wish.

---

[57] Possibly, from the context, Fluellen (Llewellyn); Smith could easily have heard the name in conversation with his friends, but there is no evidence that he ever read *Henry V*.

Was it strange, then, that the eloquence, the judgement, the understanding, the uncommon virtue, of Dr. Dwight —the address which he peculiarly possesses of attaching youth to him, the more than paternal kindness which he shewed me—& a thousand other things, beside, which you can imagine, & which I need not enumerate, should gain an easy conquest over opinions, hastily taken up, without reflection; & habits, of slight duration, & in opposition to those of many years?

The cares of Dr. Dwight were rewarded. He restored me to christianity, to morality; he confirmed me in them; because my restoration was now, in a degree, founded on reason, as well as on habit. For this, I thank him. It is to him, more perhaps than to any other man, that I owe that love of virtue, which I now feel, & which is, I trust, daily ripening into more extensive habits of benevolence. Whatever change of fortune, or opinion, he or I may yet undergo—however it may appear to become his or my duty to act—while I retain any sense of the excellence of virtue, I shall not, I can not, cease to love & admire that man; & to ascribe to him a large share of all the little virtue I may possess.

I left Greenfield, then, a Christian. As I reflected on the precepts & doctrines of christian teachers, I grew convinced, more & more, of their truth. Still, some particular tenets shocked me. I could not find it just that those who lived before Christ, & who, therefore, could never have recd. his instructions, should be forever lost. (I purposely avoid minute discussion). When I considered how strict an adherence to the practice of religious duties was enjoined, & how few of all I knew behaved conformably to the injunction—I was startled at the immense disproportion between those who were lost, & those who were to be saved. A doubt once roused, I consulted authors. The argument from scripture was clearly against the Universalists; but my sense of Justice was still unsatisfied. Meantime, the train of thought, which another doctrine led me into, brought me to doubt, on another ground. I believed that there would be a Millenium. When I considered the improvement in the condition of the human species, within the three or four last centuries, I was led to believe that this great event would be brought about by natural means; & in my enthusiasm for the reality of this doctrine, I overlooked the slow progress of knowlege, & boldly affirmed that, the Millennium must be expected, from natural causes, to take place in the year 2000. By natural causes? How was this reconcileable with Christianity? You will see that I had overrun belief, in striving to support it. If natural causes were sufficient—if man could improve his condition, by his own efforts, so as to live free from moral & physical suffering—where was the necessity for superhuman assistance? See here—the origin of my belief in the *perfectibility of man*—a doctrine which you misunderstand—but which I shall by & by explain to you. The progress of an idea is gradual; & I had revolved this over in my mind, in a thousand ways, before it was settled there. It then became a point with which to compare all other opinions. You will see that this tree had a wide-spreading root; & if my former doubts, warred against the morality of christianity (as taught in our churches) the present opinion was no less hostile to the dogmas. The Atonement, Regeneration, Election, the Fall, Original Sin, &c. &c. all fell before it, in orderly succession. I run over, in these few lines, the mental progress of seven or eight years. These doubts & difficulties were fast growing, even long before I left Connecticut. You will be my witness that no evil change was wrought by them in my conduct. No. My disbelief originated in the supposed immorality of the christian doctrines; not, as before, in a wish to excuse vices I chose to be guilty of. In proportion, therefore, as the true ground of moral obligation became apparent, my actions must become more virtuous. But, there was another motive which had great influence. I did not deem myself at liberty to change my mode of acting, & speaking, till I was convinced it was wrong. A doubt whether it was right, did not appear to me, to justify a change. Then I continued exemplary in many of the external duties [of] christianity, while I secretly was half-persuaded that they were not consistent with truth. And my morning & evening devotions, were steadily offered in the name of Christ, till I was intirely satisfied that this name had no superior efficacy to any other. Nor was this alteration rashly made. More than two years passed, while I debated the matter with myself, & before I determined on it. The same is, generally, true of all my opinions. Few have been adopted without thought. None, but from a conviction of their truth; & if of their truth, of their morality, of necessity. In all this lengthy process I have had, I can not have had, any sinister motive. For almost every temporal advantage is on the side of Christianity; & my morality is more strict in it's injunctions, as I conceive, than that of any religion.

From what I have now stated, you will see that my deviation from Christianity, has been very little influenced by any other than the single operations of my own mind. With the writings of those who have opposed Christianity, I am much less acquainted than with those of it's friends; & very little with either. I never read Bolingbroke, or Shaftesbury, or Voltaire, or any but the literary essays of Hume. Of Godwin I have read but a few chapters (tho' I am pretty well acquainted with his principles) & my disbelief was fixed before I heard his name; & my conviction of the truth of several doctrines whose advocate he is. I owe him so much, however, as to acknowlege that what I do know of his writings have confirmed my previous opinions, & given me clearer views of the arguments which recommend them, while they have, at the same time, strengthened by love virtue & desire to practice it, in a tenfold proportion. For no author, as far as I know, has more accurately pointed out what are our duties, more satisfactorily explained the reasons why they are so, or more persuasively exhorted those who love virtue to practice it unceasingly. Benevolence, Justice, Truth, are no where more ably vindicated & inforced. You will allow me to pass this eulogium on a Writer, whose virtuous dispositions you can not but admire, how false soever you may esteem his sentiments. But, to return—Such has been the progress of my mind: not broken, & retrograde, as you have supposed, but uniform & steady.

First, good habits were given me, grounded on false principles. A glimmering light shewed me the falsity of the last, before I had strength of mind sufficient to perceive that the first was not necessarily connected with it. I swerved from the path of right. A friend re-conducted me into it; & urged me to pursue it, for the reasons that he did. My understanding was less convinced, than my heart was affected; & was more convinced of the duty of moral conduct, than of the falsity of religious notions. These last were sustained by the first. But endeavoring to support christianity by morality, I discovered that they were hostile. I adhered to that which made me happy.

It will be evident, from what has gone before, that my dereliction of christianity is not ascribable to the influence of Mr. Godwin's writings; & that the most they can have done is to confirm me in my present sentiments. But you seem to have mistaken the character of this author's writings, as well as the manner of my change. I shall succin[c]tly explain to you certain circumstances which will place the subject in a different point of view.

You exclaim with too much vehemence against theories. What is theory, but the philosophy or explanation of fact? If the explanation is correct, the theory is good, & we are really the wiser by knowing it. If the explanation be false, it is by no means certain that it will be injurious—at least, that it will long be so. For theories which have any ingenuity to recommend them, generally incite men to new observations & more careful collection of facts, that they may disprove or establish them. And, tho' in the course of these inquiries, the theory be overthrown, yet the new spring which it has given to the minds of men is often more salutary than the theory itself was pernicious. But how does the reproach of theorizing—in your sense of the word—that is of framing conjectures or hypotheses, not at all countenanced by fact, apply to Mr. Godwin? I might say very little. No person can say very much. His principal work, to which I suppose you refer, is a system of morals, metaphysics, & politics. It has been said that his morality is drawn from the New Testament. I should call it more pure. But in either case, you can hardly find fault with it. His metaphysics are those of Mr. Locke & President Edwards. If they are visionary, Godwin must be confest to be so. In his politics he lies more open to such a charge—because people who read with preconceived notions of forms of government, are very apt to confound what is said of a certain abstract form of government, with something now existant under the same name, without regarding the modifications proposed by the writer. Thus, if I were to praise Democracy, (attaching to that word a peculiar idea) one would have the idea of what is called democracy in America, excited, & immediately exclaim against all I might say in praise of my democracy, as absurd—whereas all the absurdity would lie with him, who did not know, or would not know what I meant by the term. This is the same conduct which has been observed with regard to Mr. Adams —when he has been vilified for calling England a Republic: His dishonest revilers not having the candour or the understanding, to notice or comprehend his definition of a Republic. There are few of Mr. Godwin's political doctrines which appear absurd or visionary to a reflecting & ingenuous mind, which compares them with the principles on which they are founded. Ridiculous they would indeed appear, if compared with different principles. Beside these, there are several speculations, which are thrown out merely as such; & which are no wise material to the main design of his work. These may be rejected or adopted, as each one pleases. Most persons will stigmatise them as mere fancy pieces; tho' the support of Ld. Bacon & others be given to the opinions.

Various writers have written, at different times, on most of those subjects which employ the attention of Mr. Godwin. He is the first, I believe, who has collected all these detached pieces, & arranged them, after a peculiar method, in one consistent system, rejecting what was foreign, & adding many new illustrations & arguments. Thus you see that he does not pretend to extensive originality. Much less does he deserve the imputation, which is implied in your mention of him, of arrogance.

"The progress of knowlege is gradual; & will forever be gradual." I fully believe it; & this is sufficient to account for discoveries, in the present century, which are very important, & are made by man in no wise equal for talents to many who lived some centuries ago, & yet were ignorant of them. Nor are these discoveries, nor this progress, limited to mechanics. Every branch of physics, & every department of morals, have been illustrated by new facts & reasonings. Undoubtedly there were no more innate ideas ten centuries ago, than now —yet as all moral reasonings were founded on the supposition of their existence, it was, as to all practical purposes, a real discovery on the part of Mr. Locke, that they did not exist; & he has recd. the meed of transcendent glory for the discovery. You will not venture to declare that it was known before, or that no benefit has accrued from the establishment of the doctrine. And yet this great truth—this truth for the explication of which Mr. Locke is ranked among first of men, was hidden from mankind, till the 18th century. Nay, and it is probable that many thousand truths, equally important remain yet to be discovered. For tho' the progress of knowlege is gradual—yet knowlege does progress. There is nothing, then, so very wonderful that we should hesitate to give credit to it, in another important truth, being discovered by another great man. It is what we should rationally expect. President Edwards, who lived after Mr. Locke—has been called "a moral Newton"—& with reason, I believe—for if he did not invent, yet he explained the theory of the mind in a more masterly manner than it was ever done before—so that little can be added & little taken away. He, therefore, is to be ranked among the great moral philosophers, as one who as eminently contributed to ascertain the true basis of moral reasonings. The same argument which you apply to Godwin—would strip Mr. Locke, & President Edwards, of all their well-acquired fame, if it were admitted. But it is apparent, I trust, that no such argument ought to be admitted. I come, then, to the discovery objected to.

The doctrine of "the perfectibility of man," is not a discovery of Mr. Godwin's—at least he was not the first who published it to the world; nor can I certainly tell you who was. So much I may tell you—that Mr. Turgot, in France, Dr. Price, in England, & Mr. Barlow, in America, all had published this as their opinion, (& many others beside) before Mr. Godwin wrote. Indeed, the doctrine had become current long before; & was familiar to my mind as early as 1789—(tho' not in it's full extent) which was four years before "Political Justice" appeared. To originality, therefore, on this subject, Godwin has no pretensions—nor does he make any.

But what is this obnoxious doctrine? I shall tell you. Man is an animal formed with certain capacities. These are not unlimited—for he would then cease to be Man. But they are improvable; & that in two ways—first, by culture or exercise; & secondly, by an hereditary propagation, to a certain degree, of that culture: there can be no doubt that the child of a native of Connecticut is born with a greater aptitude to receive minute impressions, than a child of one of the stupid inhabitants of Labrador. When we read the history of man, we must be sensible that he has undergone a gradual refinement of manners, & acquired, gradually an amazing fund of ideas & consequent powers, which he had not at first. We have every reason, therefore, which our knowlege of his capacities, & of his history, can offer, for believing that he will continue to improve: or, in other words, that he is likely to approach still more towards perfection. This capacity for progressive advancement towards excellence, is denominated *perfectibility*—which, you will observe neither implies that man will ever become *perfect*, nor that he is not vicious & weak, & imperfect, *now*.

But what do we mean by perfection? When we speak of God, we speak of him as a perfect being: i.e. with the perfection of his nature. But there is also a propriety in calling a man perfect—when he is possest of all that excellence which his native capacity admits of. He is then perfect as a man—but not as a god.

Those who admit that man is a perfectible animal, mean that he is an animal susceptible of all the improvement consistent with human nature. They do not know in what consists this perfection of humanity, & as they see that man has constantly been improving, they conclude he will continue to improve; & as they do not venture to set bounds to his improvement, (since hitherto we have attained but a very imperfect acquaintance with the powers of men) they regard his perfectibility, or improveability, as unlimited. Not that they suppose man, can ever be any thing but man—but that they are ignorant of what man may become. "Dr. Dwight says that man may as easily become an angel, as continue a brute"—There is no difference between him & Godwin, but that one calls in the aid of religion, & the other rests on morality. In every other point of view, they agree. Both admit that man *may* become perfect as man—they only differ as to the means. With the general doctrine, therefore, you can not find fault.

I have already admitted that Mr. Godwin does not lay claim to intire originality. He modestly supposes that he has added something to the stock of materials, out of which he has formed his book: And he certainly has added something. But morality is not the less valuable—truth not the less important—because it is old. Nor should I hesitate to receive a moral axiom from any book, how little credit soever I gave to the pretensions of it's author, were I satisfied that it was well-founded. The merit of a new-system of morals, or of one different from the Christian system—must consist of it's being more perspicuous, practical, & just. Morality is a science, as much as Medicine, & susceptible of constant improvement. In forming a new system of Moral Philosophy, it is not only the right, but the duty of every author to engraft into it, all the excellencies of every previous system. This Godwin has attempted to do; & I do not hesitate to declare my belief that it [is] superior to every other system. It is not here that we want originality—we want only truth; & if the whole truth had been published two thousand years since, it would be idle to look for anything further. But I do not suppose that it was—or that it now is; for while I believe that "Political Justice" contains a purer system of morals than the Bible, I am far from believing that no corrections may be made in it. For tho' I might not discover it's errors, morality is an improveable science, man is an improving animal, & no doubt will make improvements in all that we now know. As to truth, that is alone important—that alone ought to be the constant object of our inquiries—& if it be presented by the greatest villain, it should as readily be accepted as from the greatest saint.

When you find fault with me for "speaking lightly" of christianity, do you not view the subject on one side only? Is ridicule ever the test of truth? I suspect not. Can it ever be applied to any subject consistently with justice? I doubt it. For what is ridicule, but a distortion of the thing ridiculed? If a thing be represented just as it is, surely he who so represents it, can not be charged with ridiculing it. Unless he himself doubt whether his representation be true, & design to ridicule it. You see I do not attempt to defend such conduct. I acknowlege that I am often faulty, in this respect, on more subjects than one; but I hope I am mending. But, let us view this matter in a different light. How many thousands of men sincerely believe in all the idle stories of Mahomet. Yet you, who do not believe them, will not hesitate to express your contempt for his pretended conferences with Gabriel, his pictures of a letcher's paradise, & his degrading doctrine respecting the souls of women. Thousands, millions of people, fall down before a stock, a stone, a leek, an onion; place the most implicit confidence in the wondrous transmigrations of Vishnou, the rainbows that surrounded the infant nose of Tohi, and the earthly immortality of Teshor Lama; & thousands, & millions of men, perhaps, repose all their hopes of happiness, present & to come, on these incredible fictions, & would consent to martyrdom in their support. Yet you do not hesitate to load these tales with every epithet of scorn, & to regard the wretches who believe them, with compassion, or horror, or disgust. Do not misapprehend me—I do not mean to compare Christianity to any these religions—but why do you so think & speak of them? Evidently because their falsity & absurdity is apparent to you. Does it spring from any opposition which you have to truth? Are you the less disposed to seek truth & receive it? I hope not. But where is the difference between my conduct & yours? We both refuse to assent to what appears absurd in our eyes; tho' millions receive it as sacred & divine. The only difference is that I extend my dissent to one more subject than you; because I have not faith, & you have. But, one step farther. As you believe christianity —you must, of consequence consider all who disbelieve it, as erring—& their conduct, on so disbelieving, must also appear absurd in your eyes. Let me ask you, then, if you have never made Deism the subject of your ridicule? If you have never "spoken lightly" of the arguments on which their faith was founded? Yet *some believe* them just. In good truth, my friend, it is impossible for us to consider & speak of those arguments as feeble, which so appear to us; & to assert the superiority of that doctrine which we believe the most excellent. It is not, however, proper to do this with scorn, with ridicule—perhaps, in any case—& when a native of Egypt should be with us, I do not think we should act either justly or politely, to speak contemptuously of his humble adoration of the *leek*.

But what argument can be drawn from my having once admitted the truth of Christianity? Many philosophers supposed the earth flat. There is little doubt but some such were alive when the contrary was demonstrated. If they were convinced that the earth was in fact spherical, they must have seen the absurdity of their first belief. Was it, therefore, incumbent on them to treat the doctrine of it's flatness, with any more respect than any other falsehood? Certainly not. It is our duty to acknowledge that to be false, & to declare it to be false, when we are satisfied that it is so.

Your remarks on the manner in which we should conduct towards our fellow-men, are beautiful & true. All men are our brethren. We should love them as such, treat them as such, & as such labour for their good. In this labour persuasion is the grand instrument; & it must be used with sincerity, with benevolence, with reason, & with discretion. All other means are to be abjured. Not merely because of the effects of a contrary procedure on ourselves; but because no other means can promote the end in view. I readily acknowlege my faultiness, in this respect (which is more, you know, than I would do formerly). I see the evil of my rude, peremptory, & dogmatic manner, & labor to conquer it. I can not flatter myself that I have accomplished much, in this way, but I shall not cease to use my endeavours to produce it wholly. Yet I can not agree with you that it is vain to labour for the benefit of others; or that there would be no consolation in having labored, altho' it had been in vain. It is our duty to [do] all the good we can. We can not foresee what will be the consequence— & ought not, therefore, to presuppose that our efforts will be ineffectual. Admit they are so—will it be no consolation, at the close of life, that we have done our duty? And, that, tho' others have been vicious, we have lived virtuously? I never will believe it. You do not, yourself, think so. To leave men free to repair from the execution of their duty, would be to inculcate vice, & to cut up all virtue by the roots. No, my friend—let us do what we feel to be our duty—we may not exactly perform it—but we shall, at least preserve ourselves from remorse.

I have anticipated much of what might be said in reply to your questions concerning the object of unbelievers. I have denied that there was to be found in belief all that was excellent. What is, or ought to be, the object of all moral inquiries? or is it not Truth? If I am convinced that religion is false—I reject it, because it can not confer that happiness, which truth only can confer. Not from any pitiful desire of independence, or superiority over others. If I discover what is Truth—is it not a rational act of mine, which has for it's object the illumination of mankind? Nay, is it not incumbent on me to remove, as far as in me lies, every obstacle in the way of men towards happiness? And if Religion be an obstacle—to remove religion? If I believe it false, I must believe it noxious—for nothing but truth can be salutary. And, as it is my duty to promote the well-being of all, it must be my duty, if I am convinced of the falsity of religion, to endeavour to expose it. In doing this, I ought to proceed with all due care —& proportion the application of the remedy, to the nature of the disease, & the strength of the patient.

CONCLUSION

It is now some time since this volume, &, with it, my Journal, have been brought to a termination. At that time, my mind was deeply employed on other & interesting themes, & I had not leisure to put the finishing hand to it. At present, I find but little inclination to dilate this summary into any very extensive review of my life & studies, during the three months of which it forms the history. In that period, my application has neither been severe, not unusually remiss. If I have done less than I intended, I have effected all that I expected. Tho' no great is done, on any of the several plans which I had sketched out; yet none has been altogether neglected. It is with consolations such as these, I fear, that I must continue to comfort myself, at the end of every volume of my Memoirs. What then? Are they not suitable consolations? Or should I do well to sit down in idleness, or pine with remorse, because every thing went not according to my impatient spirit's desires? I can not regret than I think more justly—how much soever the acknowlegement might, in the eyes of some, derogate from my sensibility.

But why view the matter in this light only? If to have composed this volume in less time than the preceeding, be a mark of increased industry, that mark is evident. And, if circumstances were not as favorable to a certain sort of medical composition, may I not affirm that my professional speculations, in this volume, are no less important—as far as they extend—than those in the first; & that the other materials are much more so? The conclusion, then, is clearly in favour of my conduct; & it will appear that I have improved some, if not as much as I ought. In future, may the evidence of progressive knowlege, industry, & virtue, be less & less equivocal!

Notebook No. 5: November, 1796–September, 1797

Memoirs or Notices concerning the Life, Studies, Opinions, and Friends, of E. H. Smith

NOVEMBER 1796.

PROEM

The plan pursued by me in my Journal, tho' apparently well suited for my purposes, was attended by several inconveniences, in practice. For one regular in conduct and steady in resolution, it was well-adapted; and I vainly hoped that a rigid adherence to the forms I had prescribed for myself, would gradually have wrought in me an adherence to the spirit of those forms. But, alas! so fickle am I still of mind, so impatient of restraint, that the very means which I had fixed on as best calculated to subdue my irregular volitions, administered assistance to them. The necessity of sitting down, weekly, to comment on what I had done during the seven preceding days, and, weekly, to mark out the line by which my course was to be directed for the seven days which were to follow, gave me a disgust for an exercise, which, otherwise, I might, perhaps, have relished; and if not steadily executed by me, when it had been, it would have been with spirit; whereas, for the most part, it has been performed with languid resolution & all the dispatch of impatient distaste. Hereafter, then, I renounce all forms. I shall, indeed, preserve dates; but farewell to periodic prefaces and postscripts, introductions & conclusions, weeks & memoranda. I will write much, or little; content myself with a bare note, or expatiate freely on the transactions of the day; according as the incitement of the moment shall direct me. Why should I force my tardy and reluctant pen to record what is of no value, and to consign to paper the crude speculations which the tiresome hours of melancholly engender? No! I will have every thing, as far as may be, spontaneous. I would write, because the impulse was irresistible, not from painful ideas of duty, ill-considered and little promoted when not assisted by those of delight.

When I first attempted to Journalize there was nothing but the novelty of the undertaking which made it pleasant. This soon wore off. In prospect the daily recording of minute occurrences appeared tiresome & useless; and the reality was speedily no less so. For once I was blest with perseverance; tho' the notices of my original Diary will shew how impatient I was under the restraint; for they often consist of only two or three, & sometimes of a single line. But, habit has worn off the sense of weariness; and reason has made the task delightful. Were it not for the tediousness of the mechanical part of this labour, I know not how many hours I should willingly spend, in every day, busied with my Journal. Here would I trace the past scenes of my life, & here sketch out the prospects of the future. Here, too, would I investigate all the many questions in morals, literature, and physics, which so tumultuously throng my mind. For, it is only but with the pen in our hand, that we correctly discover our own opinions, and the reasons on which they are founded. The pen is, indeed, the touchstone of all our sentiments, of all our systems, of all our actions. Those fits of desultory reflection in which we so often indulge, however they may, occasionally, present to us new & important ideas, seldom terminate in any comprehensive & profound views of the subject on which we meditate. There, an idea has opportunity to present itself in a thousand various dresses, & thus to impose itself upon us for so many distinct perceptions. But when reduced to writing, when once the fleeting thought is fixed, we have leisure to contemplate it in all it's attitudes; & often find, to our great disappointment, that where we thought we had reflected most, we have, in truth, penetrated least. Till then, we had appeared learned, to ourselves, a hundred times, tho' now, we discover, that it was, like the venerable Mr. Jenkinson of The Vicar of Wakefield, with a single sentence: the different lights in which we had viewed this one idea, & the different times at which it had presented itself to our minds, operating exactly like the several distinct companies of men, into whose astonished ears that profound personage, above-mentioned, had poured the scanty rivulet of his biblical learning. But am I not straying from that which ought to be the purpose of this Introduction? A reflection well slipped in to fill up the pause occasioned by the mending of my pen. What, then, is, or ought to be, my purpose? Is it well to presume on the future, & expose the treasure of anticipations, none of which, perhaps, may be realized? It is, in very deed, a miserable reflection, and the oftener I make it the more afflicting it appears to me, That I can, rationally, confide so little in my resolutions; that there is so little certainty that I shall execute, what I am so ready to project, and so sanguine that I shall accomplish.

With the ghosts of murdered resolutions staring me in the face, I tremblingly venture to proceed, and mark out the line which I am to follow, or rather to enumerate the subjects towards which my thoughts must be directed, during that period of which this volume of my Memoirs is expected to form the History.

1. Under the general head of Medicine may be comprized the regular prosecution of professional studies; the necessary attention to private practice; the performance of Hospital duties; particular researches, con-

nected with such subjects as I select for composition (and here is to be mentioned the completion of my Essay on the Plague of Athens); the formation of a private Dispensatory or Pharmacopoiea; medical correspondence; and such engagements as my share in "The Medical Repository" will render unavoidable & necessary.

This title is of extensive concern and importance; and must daily become more so. Should it gradually withdraw my attention from those which follow, it may, perhaps, for a time at least, be more fortunate than blame-worthy.

2. My projects literary & moral are closely connected: I may, therefore, speak of them under a single title. Of these my "Utopia" deservedly holds the first place in my esteem. On this, I purpose to bestow some thought, ere long; & to fill many pages of this volume with the result of my reflections. Next to this, I now most favourably regard the composition of the "Sonnets." I expect several advantages from them, over any other form of composition to which I have time to attend. Lastly, I may yet indulge in dramatic labour, should there, perchance, open to my hope or prospect of benefiting others & myself, thereby, at the same time.

3. Tho' I have so long neglected to record the slender Memoirs, which I possess, of my several friends, yet I do not mean to relinquish the design. I even intend to do somewhat on the Outline of my own History, before this volume is laid aside. Thus, I shall have some portion of myself displayed, even if I should not, thereafter, be able to complete the portrait.

4. My correspondence forms a very important part of my occupations. With my sister Mary, I discuss Education; with Abby, I purpose, by & by, to explain Economics; with Idea, I have entered into the world of Metaphysic. These are, or will be, laborious correspondencies. When I am separated from Charles, how widely may we not expatiate on Morals! And who can foresee whither my present letter to Theodore may lead us? Without noticing others, with whom I communicate, & not professionally, what a fund of industry must be expended, to maintain these several relations in due vigour! Shall I be equal to the task? Hitherto, of all my concerns, my Correspondence has been least neglected. Whatever may be the merit of my letters, they have been frequent, copious, & extensively diffused. With more than twenty correspondents, there is not one whose regularity & abundance exceeds my own. But many have now acquired a degree of solidity which did not formerly belong to them. More reflection, & therefore more labour, must now be applied to their due prosecution.

I shall hardly open another title for avocations & diversions: these will come but too often. As I belong to several associations, many interruptions must necessarily arise from their agency; as I am one of the general society of mankind, the duties incumbent on me as such, & the accidents to which I am thereby exposed, will still further derange the order, & impede the progress of my studies; and as I am prone to indolence and prone to change, a more serious succession of obstacles is thence to be apprehended. With all proper & becoming reverence for the influence these may exercise over my conduct, I yet am presumptuous enough to believe that I shall effect somewhat on each of the topics enumerated in the preceding titles. May my presumption be punished by unexpected industry and success!

My pen is now well a-going, and why should I throw it aside? I hate to repeat old exclamations, anticipations, doubts, discouragements, hopes, & encouragements, over and over again. Why should I? Will the event be in any wise modified by it? I have a general idea of how much I shall accomplish, of what motives will now inspirit & now dishearten me, of the joys & reproaches I shall successively experience; I have dwelt on them until I have worn out many a goose-quill—and why should I perplex myself with them more? I will not! Hence, ye wayward offspring of a sickly & peevish mother! Hence, I say, and make room for better company!

There was once, in those golden days, when the world was young, when an eternal spring, linked, hand in hand, with an eternal autumn, displayed, at once a profusion of flowers & fruit, of fragrance & of food, when the fish frolicked in the gentle, winding, & translucent waters, when the beasts gambolled on the grassy plains & gentle slopes of the new earth, when every grove & every thicket resounded with the melody of the feathered songsters, & when men were equal, free, and happy, a celebrated Prince—Nonsense! a prince, when men were equal, free, and happy! "Mind your own business. Daniel! and do not meddle with the business of other people Daniel"—Yes, sir, there was a prince, a celebrated prince. A Prince, and men equal! "Well, sir, do you tell the story." "Pardon me, I never tell stories I do not believe." "Then, sir, you—you—are no—story-teller." Very true—but what of this Prince? Since he lived in those times as you say, he must have been a very extraordinary character. What was he like? Like Gallio—"He cared for none of these things."[58] And since you have interrupted my tale, which was purposely contrived to shew the vanity of fretting, & plotting, & doubting, & hoping, about what we neither could, nor ought, to know, I shall bid you farewell, with declaring with Gallio—"That I care for none of these things."

Sunday, Novr. 20. I made two professional visits. Obtained the "Monthly Review" for August, and September, with a second Appendix. Read several articles. Mr. Roulet came to see me; and spent two hours. Wm. and I dined at S. Johnson's. I wrote short letters to Doctor Rush and Mrs. Lovegrove. Drank tea at Dunlap's. Spent the evening at H. Johnson's. Read several articles in the Appendix to the "Monthly Review," Vol. XX. There are some sensible remarks in Emmanuel Kant's "Project to Perpetual Peace"; but the conclud-

---

[58] Acts of the Apostles 18:17.

ing remarks of the Reviewers are more excellent, and breathe a spirit of Godwin. The mention of Salstonstall's "Dissertation on Septon," will be very flattering to Doctor Mitchill. Seaman's Pamphlet on our Fever of 1795 is quite as well spoken of as it deserves to be. How has it happened that neither Mr. Bailey's Account nor Mr. Webster's Collection, have not reached them? I have some curiosity to see how they would treat a certain E. H. Smith, who has said something on this same Fever. The facts concerning the absorbing power of frogs, from Townson's "Physiological Observations," are curious. Much interesting matter in de L'Isle's "Political Testament &c." The review of Herder's "Scattered Leaves" is full of entertainment. A translation, executed by a hand as able as this reviewer's, is exceedingly desirable. There is great felicity of expression, & precision of thought, in the concluding observations. Art. vii—Vaillant's "Second Journey"—is extremely interesting. The effect of Fascination, as it is called, seems simply the operation of Fear. There is no difficult[y] to explain the fact on that principle. All the extracts are judicious. I have been most interested in that relative to the "Houzuana." In this race of man are found the very qualities—I mean physical qualities—which are most desirable: Activity, force, insensibility to changes of temperature, agility, temperance, acute vision. Here is a nation for the purposes of Ch. B. Brown.

Monday, 21.—Visited one, two, three, patients. Ch. B. Brown here, and Dingley. It was after twelve when I took up the pen. Continued my letter to Theodore. A visit from the benevolent John Murray, Jr. Drank tea at Dunlap's. Spent part of the evening at the Theater—much pleased with "The Wheel of Fortune." Visited Kent's child, who was a little unwell. He was prodigiously alarmed; & told me he thought she was dying, & that he could not survive her loss. "Yet you have survived the loss of a child." "It almost killed me—& I am now less able to bear such a stroke." "There is no danger, I believe." Read several articles in the Appendix to the "Monthly Review" Vol. XX.—The extract from "Report made to Louis 18th"—impressive. What a list of abuses! I should be pleased with an opportunity of reading "Historie de la Conjuration &c." of Louis Ph. W. Orleans—fictitious as some of it must be. The remarks of the Reviewers are judicious & well-written.

Tuesday, Nov. 22.—Made four professional visits; and all satisfactory. Returned to the composition of my letter to Theodore; which, in the course of the day, I completed. Dunlap was here, in the forenoon; & again in the afternoon; as was Ch. B. Brown. Wm and I spent the evening, till nine, at Mrs. Morton's. The family were alone & disposed for sociability; and I know not when I have spent a more rationally pleasant evening. Since, I have finished the Appendix to vol. XX, of the Monthly Review; and have read several articles in the Review for August 1796. *Art. xv*: The Extract from Kotzebue's "Negro Slaves," which I had seen before, in a London Paper, is excellent and affecting. The leading thought, & even the turn of expression, seems to me to have been borrowed from the story & speech of an Amazonian woman, to a Jesuit—in the Abbé Raynal's History of European Settlements in the E. & W. Indies. *Art. xx: Durand's* "Elementary Statistics of Switzerland," must be a useful work. The enumeration of the inhabitants of the Canton of Zuric offers two important observations: "the one, unusual in most countries, that the number of men surpasses that of women; the other, almost universal, that more women attain old age than men." The rustic institutions of the village Ormont, are excellent; & present us, probably, with a view of monarchy such as it was in all the early ages of nations; under Cecross & Dejoces. Those of Vevai are of a different kind. Concerning these I must inquire of Mr. Roulet. If I do not mistake, I have been informed that one of his brothers was the Bacchus at one of these strange festivals. *Art. xxi*: The two principles extracts from "Le Spectateur Francais" of *de la Croin*—one full of good sense; as the lesser one is of humor. *Art. xxxii*: Professor *Tiedmann's* "Spirit of Speculative Philosophy," from the exhibition here given of it appears to be an excellent work, a translation of which is very desirable. The unfinished Analysis here given of it, is highly instructive; & the specimens sustain the general character of the author. *No. for August, Art. ii*: the review of Dr. Burney's "Life of Metastasio," is executed with great felicity of expression, and, as far as I can judge, correctness of sentiment. The Sonnet to Farinelli is charming. The letter to Belloy, the tragic muse of Calais, is sensible. *Art. iii: Archeologia*—What contemptible waste of time! *Art. iv: Zoonomia*, Vol. II.—The critics have dismist this great work in a way, at once, both safe & honourable to themselves. *Art. vii*: "A Treatise on the Police of the Metropolis," a most invaluable work: but what an unanswerable argument against cities; & indeed the whole scheme of society, as it is at present! Art. viii: "Memoirs of the Manchester Society &c." Do not Mr. Gough's Experiments & Observations somewhat militate against Dr. Mitchill's Speculations, concerning the use of Azote as a manure? I must ask the Doctor. But I am impatient to possess & read the whole Dr. Beardsley's masterly Paper on Hydrophobia &c. Great God! What a picture of misery! how deep, how ineraseable a stain, is this on the character of that government, in which such an event took place! The descriptive eloquence of the second extract is almost without a parallel.

But the night wears apace, and I must drop the pen.

To Theodore Dwight

Your last letter, my dear friend, gave me uncommon pleasure. Not merely by those sentiments with which it abounds, so characteristic of an excellent and virtuous mind, but by the motives which influenced you in its composition. However we may differ in opinion, I can never be insensible to such proofs of your friendship. The sincerity and freedom with which you have written demand my warmest acknowlegements. Nor shall your example be lost upon me. This letter shall, at least, convince you that I am honest! that I mean to think and act rightly—whatever you may believe concerning the real nature and tendency of my sentiments and conduct.

As it is necessary for me to be explicit, you will pardon me for neglecting that brevity which is inconsistent with a faithful explanation of my sentiments. I shall study to repress all useless digressions. Have the goodness, likewise, to believe that no offence is intended, even should anything offensive remain, after all my care to avoid it. I assure you that I have twice transcribed this letter, with the most solicitous attention to efface every the minutest expression which might be construed into a design to wound. I know that great part of what I must now write will give a certain kind of pain to your friendly heart; that pain which every friend must feel in seeing the conduct of another friend governed by what he supposes to be false & pernicious principles. But I hope not to give you uneasiness in any other way. In this, since we do differ, I cannot avoid it. My own regret, on your account, I venture to believe, is no less than yours on mine; this you will bear in mind; and it will, I hope, mitigate any motion towards indignation which, with all my pains-taking, may be excited.

On the subject of Titles my opinions have undergone no change. In answer to your remarks, I shall briefly assign a few reasons for my sentiments & conduct, which, possibly, may justify, or at least, extenuate them, in your eyes.

Without remounting to the origin of Titles, which would shew them to be usurpations over the rights and consciences of men, obtained by force, by artifice, and by terror, from the weak, the poor, and the ignorant, it is sufficient to observe that in no comprehensive view of polity or morals can they be considered in any better light than as childish. And even this is, perhaps, an indulgence which, abstractedly regarded, they would not receive. For every practice must be, in a degree, pernicious, which induces the understanding to ascribe a value to any man, or any thing, which does not really belong to it. It is true that we are not permitted to estimate things, in every case, according to their intrinsic value. We enter into a world whose habits are already fixed; & are called upon to act with relation to them. If we are convinced that evil results from a compliance with them, it is our duty to effect a change. But in our attempts to produce this change, we must look to the immediate, as well as to the ultimate consequences. The last must be supposed good; the first may be bad. This will be a sufficient reason for patience, gentleness, & forbearance; especially if the final benefit be not great, & immediately important: And our efforts must, in such cases, be rather indirect, than pointed. The whole amounts to this—We are not to sacrifice a superior, for an inferior good.

Toys are deemed suitable for children; but it is expected that, after a certain age, they will substitute something more useful in their stead; & relinquish diversion, for study. But some persons continue children all their lives. Tho' they live never so long, they must still have toys. From such unhappy beings it would be in vain to withhold them. They, therefore, should be permitted to retain their play-things.

Like these children, are certain individuals, who, tho' they think & act correctly in respect to most subjects, have in relation to others a pitiful perversity of taste or judgement. This is to be lamented; but it must be kept in view, in all our connection & correspondence with them. If they set a great value on the titles which custom had annexed to their names, and I were to write to them, on matters of importance, & where their agency was necessary, or might be useful, I should no more think of omitting their favorite titles, in my address to them, than of forcing a patient, whose sickly taste rejected every thing which was not combined with sugar, to swallow a medicine on which his life depended, without having previously seen that it was dully sweetened. I might regret that he was the slave of so idle a habit, but it would be then too late to contend with it.

Where it is in our power to form habits, we must be worse than foolish if we direct them wrong. And this we always shall do, when we lead the infant mind, intentionally, to place an extravagant value on things, at best, insignificant. Were I, as the reason of my child matured, instead of weaning him from toys, to fix in his mind a conviction that they were inestimable, & the proper subjects of desire & preservation; were I to teach him that it was necessary that his clothes should be laced; that persons with lace coats were more deserving of respect than those with plain; or that it was becoming to tell every person who had lace on his coat, that his coat *was* laced; I ask whether this would not be perverting the understanding, and busying it with straws, rather than with pearls? Yet scarcely more rational is it, to inforce so scrupulously the importance of the unmeaning titles so much in use.

Mankind may be considered as an individual of a larger growth; for society has it's infancy, and will I trust have it's manhood, like the individuals of which it is composed. In proportion as the reason of mankind is informed, in that proportion will the meanness and folly of titles, and other distinctions than those which are founded on pre-eminent virtue, become apparent; and in the same proportion should those members of society who make the discovery, disuse them; and endeavor to persuade others to lay them aside. For while men continue to attach ideas of excellence to what has no claim to that character, so long do they wander from the direct path of justice, so long are they paying that homage elsewhere, which is the rightful property of worth alone.

In the allusion to the "seam of the stocking &c." I discover the humor of my friend. Yet, surely, he will agree with me, that were there any real benefit from the alteration he mentions, it would be well to make it; and that a man of sense would little merit the appellation, were he to be deterred by the ridicule of those who could not, or would not, comprehend the reason of his conduct. At the same time, I will allow, (and more than this I am sure you will not require me to concede,) that tho' some benefit might accrue from such a change, no person ought to sacrifice to such a consideration any thing of more importance.

As to the probable consequences of the use of those titles which now exist, in the view you call upon me to consider them—I have no apprehensions. And yet, in all simplicity, I do think them less proper, and less useful, in America, than in Europe. Our government rests on a foundation very different from that which supports most, if not all, of the governments of Europe. Ours is maintained by equality; theirs, by inequality. We, have regard to rights; they, to privileges. Of inequality, & privileges, rank & title form a distinguished part; to them, they contribute a firm support. Nor can a government like those of Europe, subsist without such distinctions; which must, therefore, continue to be useful so long as the government exists. But the reverse of this is our condition: & if we admit titles at all, they should be only such as are descriptive of the office, or profession, of the man. In the last instance, they would confer no privilege, no authority; in the first, they would only confer that which appertains to a public functionary, and would cease when the man returns to the situation of a private citizen. Thus, it would be the distinction of the law, & not of the person. The individual might afterwards be respected; but it would be for those talents, and that virtue, which had elevated him to so dignified a trust.

But I have dwelt too long on this subject, unless I designed, which I do not, to devote the whole of my letter to it. I return with pleasure to more personal & interesting topics.

Why should you dis-credit my assertions concerning the manner in which I was led to adopt, what you pleasantly denominate "the bald-face stile"? What temptation do you suppose I would have to misrepresent, or conceal, the truth? You can not suppose that I estimate my own reputation as a man of veracity so low, however I may regard veracity itself, as to prevaricate about so simple a matter! I do not believe that you meant to offend me, by such an intimation, and therefore shall not be offended—tho' I intended to make a faithful representation of the fact. It is indeed true, as I have already declared, that this simple stile of address was adopted more from chance, or imitation, than from reflection or design; and that it had become habitual for me, in respect to Brown, Bringhurst, and Wilkins (who were educated in Quaker habits) and I believe some others—before I thought of it's being more proper than any other. It is also true, what I told you respecting my custom of addressing my letters at the top, instead of the bottom. And so natural had this become, in a few months, that when I wrote the unfortunate letter which has occasioned all this discussion, it never occurred, for an instant, to my mind, that I had not written to you so before. Nor should I ever, in all probability, have thought on the subject, had not your letter brought it, affectingly, to my memory. Had it been thought of, at the time of writing, I should doubtless have made the usual additions; or, at least, have assigned my reasons for not doing it. These reasons have rather been the fruit of the practice, than the practice of them. Nor do they govern my conduct in all cases. I know too well how much some persons are attached to certain adjuncts to their names, to hazard the consequences of neglecting to affix them. And I generally add their titles when I write to strangers, with whose characters I am unacquainted. But in either case it is no mark of my respect for their good sense. This is a very honest statement; after which you must be content, I believe, to let me act according to my whim, if so you choose to consider it; or agreable to my principles, if you will permit me to speak of my conduct, from my own opinion of it.

I have now replied to all the prefatory part of your letter, & shall next attempt an answer to the most material division of it. And here, I know not how I can do better than to lay before you a brief history of the progress of my mind, from before our first acquaintance, in respect to religion and morality. For tho', when I wrote, I had not, as you suppose, any particular reference to religion, more than to other subjects concerning which variety of opinion occurs, yet, since you have chosen to point your observations principally to that, I were wanting in sincerity should I decline the task you have assigned me. I have but one remark to make, and I shall then proceed.

In this following hasty sketch of my mental history, (which, at some future period, I mean to finish, with ample details,) I purposely avoid all reasoning; & content myself with simple narration. I shall not even go so far as to notice the arguments which influenced me to adopt opinion, after opinion, except where it is indispensable to a ready conception of the connection between one change of sentiment and another: even, here, confining myself to the leading revolutions of sentiment.

Few men, whether they profess to believe in the Christian doctrines, or deny their divinity, are distinguished for the stedfast purity of their conduct. But among those who are called Infidels there are fewer persons of strict morality—so far as my observation has extended—than among Christians. Tho', probably, not in proportion to numbers. In America, it has generally been to gain freedom from the restraints of morality, that men have abjured religion. It is with reason, therefore, that I account it a happiness to have been born of parents, whose belief in Christianity so operated on their lives, as to render them exemplary for the excellence of their morals, among Christians. What they practiced themselves, they endeavoured to persuade me to imitate. They educated me in the precepts of their religion, & in habits conformable to those precepts. And this, which was far the most important, created in me a moral sensibility, which has been my greatest safeguard, amid the numerous temptations to which youth is hourly exposed. But, beside the faulty conceptions which could not fail to be excited & fostered in me, by an obedience to some of their injunctions, they taught me to regard christianity as the only basis of morality: an error the more dangerous as it naturally led to a conclusion, that if religion were unfounded, morality was nugatory.

After such an education, & with a scrupulousness which might have been stigmatized as superstition, even by a religionist, I was sent to College. It has been said that Young Men, with a certain degree of knowlege & reflection, are prone to infidelity. I found many of this character at New Haven. Their sarcasms at first shocked my piety; and their arguments, drawn from the common sources, perplexed me. Custom, familiarized me to the former; & frequent repetition established to my mind, the latter. The young men I speak of, were gay, witty, dissipated. The scene was new to me; and had all the charms of novelty. I was seduced by their example; & then resorted to their arguments in defence of my conduct. Having laughed religion out of countenance, it was not difficult, on occasions which demanded it, to dispense with morality—whose foundation I had supposed religion to be. The vices of a College are not very enormous, in general; and I was preserved from some of the worst, by immaturity alone.

You must recollect that, at this time, I was a mere child; that I could not possibly comprehend the just force of an argument, either for or against religion; that example, to one in my unprotected situation, outweighs a thousand reasons; & that an appeal to the pride or courage of a lively & warm-spirited youth—"You dare not say so"—"You dare not do so"—has an almost irresistible effect. What could be expected from a boy of twelve or thirteen, surrounded by wild companions, all older, more instructed, and more daring than himself; & who had neither parent, nor friend, to counsel or controul him?

Whatever may now be the state of Yale College, when I was there, it wanted only a little address, & almost anything might be effected, that the wantonness of youth panted to perform. Few of my companions had been as strictly educated as myself. Few, probably, had much reason to love & respect their parents. I had; & my regard for them often restrained me, when no moral principle would have done. But, amid this career of folly, I had many misgivings. With my fellows, supported by their merriment & incited by their example, I discarded all my former faith; but, alone, it still operated in my bosom, the interior of which I did not dare to scrutinize. It is not easy to emancipate ourselves from long-established habits—even when we are satisfied of their impropriety; much less when we are not satisfied; and beside my internal monitor, in the last year of my College residence, I was repeatedly checked by my ever-to-be-lamented friend, Reuben Hitchcock.

In the state of mind, just described, debased by vicious habits; denying the truth of a religion which I did not understand, & employing against it trite arguments, rather committed to memory than comprehended, & which I was unable to support by others, when denied or obviated; moreover, with a secret doubt of the propriety of my conduct, & soundness of my objections; I sat off for Greenfield.

I have reasons for believing that Doctor Dwight was apprized of these particulars, before my arrival. But, if he were not, they could not long escape his almost intuitive sagacity. His distinguishing mind must have discerned the real character of my thoughts; must have seen how superficially they lay; must have duly appreciated the influence of early education; and been satisfied that, to effect my cure, it was only necessary to apply the proper motives to the same principles on which those which were improper had been made to act.

For myself, I came under the care Dr. Dwight with an impression in his favour, next to adoration. I was only fifteen; of an affectionate & pliable disposition; of a warm, enthusiastic, but manageable, temper. All around me were Christians; & all whose character was in the least calculated to impress me with respect, were exemplary Christians. Was it strange, then, that the eloquence, the understanding, the judgement, the commanding manner, of Dr. Dwight—his illustrious virtue, his winning address so peculiarly calculated to gain the affections of youth, his paternal kindness, & the marked attention with which I thought he devoted himself to me, that these, and a thousand things beside, which you can imagine, and I need not enumerate, should obtain an easy conquest over opinions, hastily assumed; over habits, of slight duration, & counteracted by those of many years?

At this time, likewise, my reason began to expand. Your brother watched it's progress; and, by arguments he well knew how to select, fixed deeply in my mind a full belief of Christianity. This operation, was attended with a return to a virtuous life. Having experienced the bad effects of vice, which had been connected with a dereliction of religious faith, I was the more prepared to believe that virtue could only flow from christian piety. This revolution of sentiment and conduct, was followed by another circumstance, not less important. In reasoning with me, Dr. Dwight taught me, also, to reason; & while he inspired virtuous resolutions & religious faith, he excited a spirit of inquiry, & a disposition to examine the foundations of that faith & the reasonableness of those resolutions. He was, indeed, a second intellectual father to me. To him, more, perhaps, than to any other being do I owe that love of virtue, and fervent aspiration after truth, which animate me now, & are, I hope, daily ripening into more extensive habits of benevolence. Whatever change of fortune or opinion, he or I may yet sustain; however it may appear his or my duty to act; while I retain any sense of the excellence of virtue; I shall not cease to love & venerate him; nor hesitate to ascribe to his care & instruction the most important share of all the merit I possess, of all the good I may effect.

I returned, a second time, to the embraces of my parents; and I returned a Christian. As I meditated on the doctrines of Christian teachers, & compared them with the Bible, I felt my confidence in the latter heightened, but diminished in the former. There was a wide difference between the senseless jargon of the Revd. Mr. Champion, & the over-bearing, & lucid eloquence of Dr. Dwight. The absurd arguments of our Lichfield Boanerges,[59] made me revolt against the doctrines he delivered. Dissatisfied with his reasonings, I invented others of my own; and all the leading principles of the Calvinistic theologians were reviewed in my mind. The severity of some of their dogmas shocked me. Yet I could not deny their validity, if I admitted their first principles. This led me, naturally, to examine the arguments in their favour. The event was, that I admitted most of the chief doctrines; but modified according to my peculiar notions. The medical doctrine of hereditary diseases, presented me with a new theory of the theological doctrine of Original Sin; and I contrived, what I then thought, a rational explanation of that of the Trinity. Such were the efforts of my mind, to reconcile the character & conduct of Jehovah, with my sense of Justice. But, these did not long satisfy me; & the more I struggled to render the tenets I had embraced conformable to my reason, the less I succeeded: and still my chief difficulties arose from the impossibility of regarding the acts predicated of the Deity, as consistent with my ideas of a supremely moral being. Christ came to save all: But millions of human beings had lived before his appearance, who never heard his name; millions still existed who would never hear it. Were they all to perish?—inevitably?—doomed to eternal, unmittigated punishment, for a crime they knew not of? pursued by inexorable & almighty vengeance? I shuddered —I still shudder, at the thought. When I regarded those around me; when I saw how few there were who were visible members of the church, and how few of these "lived worthy of their vocation"; when I recollected the comparative wickedness of every other Christian country; and reflected how large a part of the world either knew not of, or rejected, Christ; I was filled with horror at the numbers devoted to perdition. The scripture argument was clearly, as I thought, hostile to the preachers of Universal Salvation. "Strait is the way, and narrow is the road, which leadeth unto life eternal—and *few* there be that find it."[60] *Few* there be, who find it! What must I think of a being who having infinite fore-knowledge, must have foreseen the fate of man; who had infinite power to prevent it, if he would—and yet would not? My mind was troubled; but I was yet a Christian. I looked to have all these difficulties removed in due time. Thus did my own sense of morality first lead me to a rational distrust of Christianity.

It would be wearying your patience, and in truth it is impossible for me, at this time, to expatiate on the numerous points which engaged my attention; and, gently & gradually, brought me to the same conclusion. I shall mention but one other.

Among other Christian doctrines, that of the millennium had always captivated my fancy. I gave it the most entire credence; was impatient of every objection; & dwelled, with all the fervent joy of an innocent & benevolent heart, on the blissful scenes which were then to be displayed—when the lion shall lie down with the lamb, &c. &c. You may, perhaps, be informed that very serious objections to this doctrine are made by some denominations of christians, and that the scripture arguments in it's favor are by no means as explicit & unequivocal as it's friends might wish. The want of such, induced me to look abroad, & endeavour to call in the aid of others, to those which I found in the Bible. When I considered the improvement which had taken place, in the condition of man, for the two or three last centuries; when I reflected on the influence which a discovery in any one science has on every other science; and when I observed the impulse which the transactions of our own times have given to the human mind; I became persuaded that natural causes existed, sufficient, of themselves, to bring about this great event—The Millennium. In my enthusiasm for the reality of this expected state, I overlooked the slow progress of human knowlege, & grounding my belief on a popular calculation, boldly affirmed that it might be expected by natural means in the year 2,000. By natural means! How was this reconcileable with Christianity? You will observe that I over-ran belief, in striving to support it: for I had, at that time, satisfied myself that, taking the improvements of the 18th century, or rather the progress of improvement during that period, for the basis of the calculation, the event might be demonstrated with mathematical precision. I sometimes smile, when I recollect the earnestness with which I maintained this position, against the scoffs & sarcasms of older & more incredulous men. But, if natural causes were sufficient; if man, by his own efforts, could so improve his condition as to gain an immunity from physical & moral sufferings; where was the necessity of divine assistance? The maxim of Horace was then familiar to my mind—

Nec Deus intersit, nisi dignus vindice nodus Inciderit:[61]

---

[59] Names given by Christ to James and John, the "sons of thunder," Mark 3:17; Luke 9:54.

[60] "For narrow is the gate, and straitened the way, that leadeth unto life eternal, and few are they that find it." Matthew 6:14.

[61] "And let no God intervene unless the complication (or

I remembered it, and doubted. I stopped to remark, that this was the origin of my belief in the doctrine of *"the Perfectibility of Man"*: a doctrine misunderstood by you; but which I shall subsequently explain.

The progress of belief is gradual; and I had viewed this doctrine, turned it in my mind, and examined it, a thousand ways, before I was satisfied of it's truth. It, then, became a point of comparison; a something that was fixed, & by which everything else might be estimated. You will see that this tree had a wide-spreading root: for, if my former doubts warred against the morality of the Scriptures, the present opinion was no less hostile to their dogmas. Original Sin, the Atonement, Election, Regeneration, &c. &c. all fell before it, in orderly succession.

I run over, in these few lines, the intellectual history of several years.

These doubts & difficulties were fast-growing sometime before I left Connecticut. You will be my witness that they wrought no immoral change in my conduct. No: my disbelief originated in the supposed immorality of some of the Christian doctrines; not, as before, in a wish to excuse those vices which religion & morality equally condemned. In proportion, therefore, as the true ground of moral obligation became apparent, my actions must become virtuous. Two motives concurred to keep me silent concerning these internal movements of my understanding. The first was that mental imbecillity, which is so common, & which renders us too cowardly to incur the hazard of that odium which generally pursues him who departs from received notions in religion: the second, which was more worthy of me, was, that I did not feel myself at liberty to adopt different sentiments from those which I had avowed, and a different line of conduct, till I was fully satisfied that I had hitherto been wrong. A mere inconviction of the truth of the one, & the propriety of the other, did not seem to justify a change. Thus, I continued to admit the justness of each, & was constant in the performance of the external duties of religion; while I was, secretly, half-persuaded of their unsoundness & inconsistency with truth. My morning & evening devotions were steadily offered in the name of Christ, till I was completely assured it had no peculiar efficacy. Nor did I rashly discontinue to invoke his mediation. More than two years passed, while I debated the subject with myself, & was determined in the duty of the omission. Like scrupulous regard to their justness, have I admitted, most of those opinions which I now entertain. None have been received without reflection. None, but from a conviction of their truth; & if of their truth, necessarily, of their morality. In all this lengthy process, I have not had, I can not have had, any sinister motive. Almost every advantage, merely external, is with Christianity. You are conscious how deep is the reproach of Infidelity, in most parts of the United States; & what difficulties he has to encounter, in the road to riches & preferment, who openly acknowleges his unbelief. As I have been led astray by no considerations of interest, so I have not been influenced by a weak wish to gratify any favorite passion, much less to indulge in the gross pleasures of sensuality. On all these points, as my morality is no less strict than that of the gospel, I could gain nothing by the rejection of Christianity.

From what has now been stated to you, you will perceive that my dereliction of Christianity has been little owing to the writings of it's adversaries, and much to the solitary operations of my own understanding. At College, I recd. arguments at second hand; for my repugnance to metaphysical works never allowed me to consult them. After I left Greenfield, I read a few of the most popular writers, in favour of religion; but I studiously avoided those on the other side; and soon, tired of the continual turmoil of argumentation, quitted the perusal even of these. So that in reality, I am less acquainted with the celebrated authors who have unfurled & fought under the banners of unbelief, than with those who have been covered with "the shield of faith," while they wielded "the sword of the spirit." I never read Shaftesbury, nor Bolingbroke, nor any but the literary & historical writings of Hume; I am wholly unversed in the deistical works of Voltaire & Rousseau, of Boulanger & Helvetius. Of Godwin's celebrated work I have read only a few chapters; and these, long since my disbelief was fixed, & my conviction clear of the truth of certain opinions, whose advocate he is. I am bound, in justice to Mr. Godwin, to declare—That what I have examined of his book, has obtained my entire approbation; that by him my previous opinions have been confirmed; that I have gained from his writings more distinct notions of the moral arguments which support those opinions; while my love of virtue, & desire to practise it, have been strengthened in a tenfold proportion. No author, as far as I know, has so well enumerated & displayed our various duties; no one so accurately determined the principles on which they rest; none so persuasively invited men to the unwavering exercise of those virtues which they profess & ought to revere. In no book are Benevolence, Truth, and Justice, so ably vindicated, so zealously inforced; and this, with a spirit so noble, a sincerity so pure, that you, my friend, tho' you might deny the justness of his doctrines, must unite with me in this eulogium on his character. But, tho' I think thus highly of the "Political Justice" of this writer, it is very evident that my change of sentiments is not ascribable to it's influence. In supposing this to be the fact, you are not more misled, than in the notion you seem to have acquired of the nature of the work just-mentioned. You will excuse me, therefore, for offering a succinct account of it; prefacing it with some remarks, in reply to those connected with your mention of Mr. Godwin.

You exclaim, with a vehemence too undistinguishing, against theory. What is theory, but the rational explana-

---

problem) turns out to be worthy of an intervention." Horace, *Ars Poetica* 191.

tion of fact? If the explanation be just, the theory is true, & we are really made wiser by it. To deny this, would be to disclaim the use of the understanding. We should want little beside memory; & even this would be nearly, if not quite, useless to us. We know that part of the 24 hours, which we call a day, is dark, & part light. Is there no benefit from knowing, also, the cause; & the mode of it's operation? And how can we know this, but by the aid of theory? Suppose a theory to be false, unfounded, & insufficient: it is by no means certain that the injury it will occasion will exceed the good it will confer on mankind. Theories, which have ingenuity to recommend them, excite new attention to the subjects of Theories; observations are multiplied—no matter whether with the design of supporting or of overthrowing them—new discussions take place; & tho' the theories be rejected, men are wiser by all the additional facts & reasonings which they have occasioned. How many false explanations of astronomical phenomena preceeded those of Newton: yet he, perhaps, had never written had he not been guided in his observations by the errors of others; or had he written, might have committed the same. It is the destiny of men to come at truth, only by penetrating thro' the mist of error; and we ought to be thankful to those who have excited themselves in this honorable attempt, even tho' they have lost their way in the obscurity by which they were surrounded.

But how does the reproach of theorizing, in your sense of the word—i.e. of framing conjectures or hypotheses not countenanced by fact—apply to Mr. Godwin? "Political Justice," his principal work, to which I suppose you refer, is a system of Morals, Metaphysics, and Politics. It has been said of his Morality that it is drawn from the New Testament. I deem it still more pure. In either case, you will hardly venture to find fault with it. And I had given you both my own, & the opinion of William W. Woolsey, concerning it. The Metaphysics of "Political Justice," are those of Mr. Locke & President Edwards. If they merit to be classed visionaries, I must be content that Godwin be called so likewise. It is in the Political part of his work, that this writer is most exposed to the charge of facifullness: not because there is any *necessary* portion of his theory of government which deserves to be so characterized, but because men who read, without attending to the peculiar & fundamental doctrines of an author, & with preconceived notions of the import of certain phrases, are constantly prone to disregard the definitions of the writer, & the modifications he proposes. Were I to attach a peculiar meaning to the word Democracy, & write a work in praise of a democratical government—half who read it would be stupid or uncandid enough to mistake my meaning, & affixing the common idea of democracy which prevails in the United States (i.e. anarchy) might condemn as absurd, all that I should say in praise: whereas the real absurdity would be on their part, who decided without comprehending or admitting my definition. Examples of like ignorance or baseness occur every day. It is thus that Mr. Adams has been vilified for denominating a Republic; his revilers wanting the sense, or the honesty, to understand or notice his explanation of that term. To an ingenuous & reflecting mind, who attends to the principles on which they are founded, & the limitations with which they are proposed, I am persuaded, there are few of Mr. Godwin's political doctrines that will appear visionary or absurd. But he who reads, must have a head purified from the jargon of authority, & a heart uncontaminated by the mildews of party.

In addition to what may be called the systematic political discussions of "Political Justice," the author has inserted several ingenious & interesting speculations. But he has inserted them merely as speculations, & whether they be true or false, his general doctrines will not be at all affected. They may be adopted or rejected, at the pleasure of the reader.

Numerous authors have, at different periods, & in different countries, written on most of the subjects treated of by Mr. Godwin; & with more or less resemblance to his views. He is the first, I believe, who has collected these detached pieces, and arranged them, after a peculiar method, in one consistent system; neglecting what was foreign or improper & adding many new arguments & illustrations. Nor does he pretend to extensive originality; much less does he deserve the imputation (which is implied in your mention of him,) of arrogance.

"The progress of knowlege is gradual; and will forever be gradual." I fully believe it; and this is sufficient to account for the very important discoveries which are made, in the present century, by men of far inferior talents to those who were ignorant of them in every preceding century. Not mechanics only, but every branch of physics,[62] & every department of morals, have been illustrated by new facts & more correct reasonings. Undoubtedly, there were no more *innate ideas* ten centuries ago, than there are now; yet as all moral & all metaphysical inquiries proceeded on the belief of their reality, it was, to all practical purposes, a real discovery, on the part of Mr. Locke, that they were suppositions; and theologians & philosophers have, with one accord, bestowed on him the meed of transcendent renown. You will not venture dissent from their decree; and yet, if you do not, you must confess that this great truth; this truth, the discovery of which has established Mr. Locke in the rank of the first of men, was reserved in secret & hidden from mankind, till the 18th century. President Edwards, who lived after Mr. Locke, has been called a "moral Newton"—intimating, & with reason, that he was as distinguished for his discoveries in Morals, as other was for those made by him in Physics: For, if he did not absolutely invent, yet he explained the Theory of the Mind in a more masterly manner than had ever

---

[62] Physics, i.e. natural philosophy, treating of the material world.

been used before; so that little can be added & little taken away. He, therefore, is ranked among those who have contributed by their labours to render intelligible the most difficult & most important of all sciences, the science of morals. And what is there so extraordinary in all this? Tho' "the progress of knowlege is gradual," yet knowlege does progress. Why then should we hesitate to believe that, as some great men have found out important truths, concealed till the present century, other great men may not effect similar discoveries in after times? Is it not what we should rationally expect?

"The Perfectibility of Man," is not a discovery of Mr. Godwin's. Traces of this doctrine may be found in the writings of numerous authors, who wrote long before our time, but who have but a glimpse of its nature & importance. Mr. Turgot & Mr. Dumarsais in France; Dr. Price, in England; Mr. Barlow, in America; & many others, had published, on this subject, or casually treated of it, in their several works, before Mr. Godwin wrote. Indeed, the doctrine had been current, many years; & was familiar to my mind as early as 1789—(tho' not in it's full extent—) which was four years previous to the publication of "Political Justice." To originality, therefore, on this subject, Mr. Godwin has no pretensions; nor does he make any.

But what is this obnoxious doctrine? A few words will suffice to explain it.

Man is an animal created with certain capacities. These are not unlimited; for then, he would cease to be man; but they are improveable; & this in two ways: First, culture or exercise—which we call Education; secondly, by an hereditary propagation of that culture —to a certain degree. The child of an instructed citizen of Connecticut being, doubtless, born with a superior aptitude for lively, distinct, & minute impressions, than the imperfect offspring of the stupid natives of Labrador. When we read the history of man, we must be sensible that he has undergone a gradual refinement of manners, & gradually acquired an amazing fund of ideas, and consequent powers with which he was not originally endowed. We have every reason, therefore, which the experience of ages can afford, for believing that he will continue to improve: or, in other words, that he likely to approach still nearer to perfection. This capacity for progressive advancement towards excellence, is denominated *perfectibility*; which, you will observe, neither implies that man will ever become perfect—(as God is perfect—) or that he is not vicious, & weak, & imperfect, *now*. It is, in short, no more than to say that man is an improveable animal; & as the word *improveability* is less liable to be misunderstood, Mr. Godwin has judiciously substituted it, in the greater number of instances, in the new edition of his work.

What do we mean by *perfection*? When we use the term, in relation to the Deity, we undoubtedly mean absolute perfection. We suppose God possesst of certain attributes, in all their excellence. But Man, also, has attributes; & if they existed in any individual, in their greatest possible degree of excellence, he would deserve to be called *perfect*; not as a God, but as a Man. Some of those who maintain the "perfectibility of man," suppose that he is susceptible of perfection, & will actually attain it: i.e. human perfection. Others, with more reason, regard the human improveability as unlimited. For as we yet know but little of what man is capable; & as from what we do know, we have reason to expect he will proceed, as he has hitherto proceeded; it is presumptuous & absurd for us to pretend to set any other bounds, than those essential to humanity, to human improvement.

"Man may as easily be a Saint, as a Savage; and nations as easily enlightened with millenial glory as overcast with the midnight of Gothicism. All that is necessary, on the part of man, is to bring the subject home to his heart, to feel it's inestimable importance, to realize it's practicability, and to make it the chief aim of his fixed endeavours." Such are the words of Dr. Dwight, in a Sermon, abounding, beyond example, with interesting truths in legislation & morals. Mr. Godwin himself could not have been more explicit, or wish for other terms of expression. The general doctrine of these two excellent and virtuous men is the same: They differ only as to the means: for one expects to accomplish that by a simple machine, for which the other would employ one more complicate. With the general doctrine, therefore, you can not be displeased.

The merit of a system of Morality must depend wholly upon it's truth. That any particular system coincides with any other, is no valid objection against it. Not is it at all important from what sources an author has derived his sentiments, provided they are just. It is not here originality that we want—but truth. Mr. Godwin, as I have observed, claims no extensive originality. He modestly supposes that he has added something to the stock of moral knowlege, and he certainly *has* added something. Inasmuch as this is true, his work is better than any which preceeded it: his system superior to every other. But I am far from believing it perfect. For, tho' I may not be able to perceive it's errors; morality is an improveable science, man is an improving animal, and no doubt will, hereafter, correct numberless errors which now exist without our being sensible to them. Meantime, it is sufficient to determine my preference, that this system is better than any with which I am conversant. Truth is the great object of human inquiry, & whether it have existed one, or one thousand years, whether it be presented to me by a villain or a saint, it is to be accepted with equal readiness & delight.

When you insinuate that I am blame-worthy, in "speaking slightly" of Christianity, do you not view the subject on one side, only? Is ridicule ever the test of truth? I suspect not. Can it be applied to any subject, consistently with justice? I doubt it. For what is ridicule, but a distortion of the thing ridiculed? And is it just to misrepresent? But if I represent a fact in it's true light, however insignificant, or base, or foolish, I can not be said to ridicule it: unless, indeed, I were unconscious of the correctness of the exhibition I made, & designed to ridicule the subject of it; which, as I have before said, were reprehensible.

You see I do not attempt to defend such conduct. I acknowlege myself to have been often guilty of it, on more subjects & occasions than one; but I have abjured the satiric pen forever & I shall strive to correct my wayward tongue. But let us view this matter in a different light.

How many thousands of the human race sincerely credit all the idle tales of Mahomet. Yet you, who disbelieve them, will not hesitate to express your contempt for his pretended conferences with Gabriel, his pictures of a letcher's paradise, and his degrading doctrine respecting the souls of women. Hundreds, thousands, millions of people fall down before a stock, a stone, a leek, an onion; place the most implicit confidence in the wondrous transformations of Vishnou, the rainbows that surrounded the infant nose of Tohi, and the earthly immortality of Teshor Lama;[63] hundreds, thousands, millions of men, perhaps, repose all their hopes of happiness, present and to come, on these incredible fictions, would massacre nations in their defence, & consent to suffer martyrdom for their support. Yet you do not forbear to load these tales with every epithet of scorn, to expose them with all the keeness of triumphant ridicule, while you regard the wretches who believe them with compassion, or horror, or disgust. Do not misapprehend me: I design no comparison of Christianity with these religions: but why do you so think & speak of them? Is it not because their falseness & absurdity are apparent to you? It does not spring from any opposition you have to truth, but rather from the love you bear it. At least, you are not, on this account, the less disposed to seek for & embrace it. Where is the difference between my supposed conduct, and yours? We both refuse our assent to what appears to us unworthy of it; tho' millions accept what we reject, as sacred and divine. The only difference is, that I extend my dissent to one more Religion than you; because you have faith, and I have not. But, one step further. As you believe in the divinity of the Christian religion, & receive it as the anchor of your soul & guide of your actions, you must, consequently, regard all who disbelieve & reject it, as fatally erroneous. Their conduct, in so doing, must necessarily, seem absurd in your eyes. Let me ask you, then, if you have never made unbelief the subject of your ridicule? If you have never "spoken slightly" of those arguments which unbelievers have employed against Christianity? of those doctrines which they adhere to, in preference to those of Christ? Let *some believe* them just; & believing them just, make them the regulating principles of their lives. But have you stopped even here? The doctrines of Christians are no less various, than of other religionists, or than of those who cast off all religion: And has no papist, no methodist, no universalist, ever felt the force of your sarcastic sallies? And whither, you will say, does all this lead? In simple seriousness, my friend, the very act of election is an implied assumption that our particular opinions are right, and those which differ wrong; & when we speak of them, if we believe our real sentiments, we cannot choose but assert the superiority of our doctrines, over those of other men. This is always to be done with mildness, except when the situation we are in demands the use of energy. But scorn, satire, ridicule, are, perhaps, never suited to such occasions; & were a worshipper of the onion in our presence, we should behave unseemly, & perhaps unjustly, were we to speak contemptuously of the humble adoration which he paid it.

Can any valid argument be drawn from the circumstance of my having once admitted the truth of Christianity? Because I have once erred, is it a sufficient reason for my continuing to err? Many philosophers, at one period, supposed the earth to be flat. Of these, some were doubtless alive, when the contrary was demonstrated. If they were convinced that the earth was, in fact, spherical, they must have seen the absurdity of their first opinion. But, was it, therefore, incumbent on them to treat the doctrine of it's flatness with more respect than any other falsehood, because it had been formerly recd. by them as true? Certainly not. That which is false, is to be pronounced so; it is the intrinsic character of the doctrine, not the casuality of it's adherent or opposer, which should govern our decisions.

Your remarks on the manner of regulating our conduct towards our fellow-men, are beautiful and just. Here I recognise the warm spirit of the benevolence which so eminently distinguishes my friend. These are the sentiments which should ever distill from his lips & his pen. All men are, indeed, our bretheren. We should love them as such, treat them as such, & as such labour for their welfare. In this labour, persuasion is the grand instrument; & it should be used with sincerity, with benevolence, with reason, with zeal, and with discretion. All other means are to be abjured. Not merely for their injurious consequences to ourselves, but because they are inadequate to the end proposed, or would counteract our designs. For myself, I regard with disapprobation & regret my own misconduct. I see the evil of my rude, peremptory, & sarcastic manner, and strive to subdue it. I cannot flatter myself that I have accomplished much in this difficult enterprize; but I shall not fail in perseverance. "The frequent drops shall wear the rugged rock."

I can not agree with you that it is vain to labour for the benefit of others; or that no consolation would follow our labours, should they prove unsuccessful. It is our duty to do all the good we can. We can not foresee the consequences; and ought not, therefore, to presuppose

---

[63] Vishnu, a Hindu diety; Tohi, fire god of Mayan tribe; Teshu Lama regent of Tibet in the late eighteenth century; i.e. strange gods of other lands.

that our efforts will be ineffectual. Admit they are so: Will it be no consolation, at the close of life, that we have done our duty? That if others have done wrong, we have struggled to prevent it? If some have lived viciously, we have set them a virtuous example? I never will believe it! You, yourself, can not think so! To allow men the liberty of refraining from the performance of their duty is to inculcate vice, and to put the knife to the root of virtue, even before the tender blade appears. No, my friend! let us do, with all earnestness, what we feel to be right. We may not exactly perform our duty; but we shall, at least, preserve ourselves from remorse.

I have anticipated much of what might be said in reply to your inquiries concerning the object men could have in view, when they cast off Religion. Let me ask you what is the object of believers? Is it not Happiness? And Truth, as the only road to Happiness? If Religion be false, it can not confer on me the happiness I seek; & I must look elsewhere. I searched for it in truth alone, not from any pitiful desire of independence, or superiority over others, but because in truth only can it be found. And if I discover what Truth is, is not that a rational act of mine, which has for it's end the illumination of Mankind? If I can point out the road to Happiness to my fellow-men, is it not my duty to disclose it? Nay, is it not incumbent on me, by every honest means, to remove the obstacles, which may impede the progress of the traveller? And, if Religion be an obstacle, to remove religion? If I am convinced that religion is false, I must believe it noxious: for nothing but truth can be salutary: and as it is my duty to promote the well-being of all, it must, in such a case, be my duty expose the nakedness & insufficiency of Religion, to strip her of all her delusive ornaments, point out her hitherto concealed deformities, compare her with the lovely & unsophisticated form of Truth, & hold her up to the temperate regard, & for the rational dereliction; of undeceived & reforming man. In this arduous undertaking, what difficulties have I not to encounter! The more discreetly must I act. The disease is obvious; the remedy certain; but what variety in the character of the patients, in the extent & force of the malady! Here is room for the exercise of judgement; lest in the application of the means of cure, the cordial be disproportioned, and inflict on the sufferer that death, from which it was designed to rescue him.

I touch upon the boundary of this long, and, I fear, tedious epistle. But one more explanation, and I have done.

You will recollect the remarks I made, in a former part of this letter, on applying our own definitions to the terms of others. Had you studied the works of those philosophers you condemn, you would not so have mistaken the import of the moral maxim which you reprobate. "Knowlege" is a word of extensive significance. It's sense is by no means restrained to such narrow bounds as you suppose. It includes not merely Learning or Erudition, but physical & moral Science: especially the two last. For if they were rightly understood, I know not that Learning would be of any use. Virtue may be considered as morality in action; & vice as active immorality. We distinguish between the Act, and the Agent. He only is virtuous, strictly speaking, who acts agreably to Justice; but he, relatively, is virtuous, who performs what he thinks is duty. But how can any one fullfill his duty, who is ignorant what it is? The more clearly he perceives it's nature & extent, the better able is he [to] conform to it; and as no one can be happy who is not virtuous, or happy but in proportion as he is virtuous, the more accurate is his knowlege of the connection between virtue & happiness, & of the consequences which flow from a conformity or opposition to the precepts of morality, the more virtuous will be his conduct. It is to the illusions of the passions, to the want of a clear & steady knowlege or conviction of the importance & nature of virtue, that men are vicious. Had they, in the moment of action, that distinct perception of the unhappiness entailed by vice on all her adherents, which they sometimes have in the hours of peaceful meditation, never would they listen to the deceiver, for whether the mind be obscured by passion or stupidity, knowlege is equally wanting. And thus knowlege, if it be not virtue, is essential to it; and Ignorance, if it be not vice, is it's origin & preserver.

With regard to Physical Science, it is evident, that the more perfectly we comprehend the intimate nature of all the objects which surround, which act, & are acted upon by, us; the more thoroughly we understand their exact relations to each other; the better prepared shall we be for the exercise of justice: so that, in a moral view, none of the offspring of nature are insignificant, or unworthy of our study. In any other than a moral view, they are indeed utterly contemptible: For all learning, all science, all study, all action, except inasmuch as they are designed & able to promote the good of man, are "as a sounding brass, and tinkling cymbal."[64] But if vice be ignorance, or if it depend on ignorance for it's support, what shall we say of the wretches who wander, without a clue to guide, without a glimmering light to direct, them, in the labyrinth of error? Vice is hateful, detestable; the object of the fixed opposition & abhorrence of all virtuous minds: shall we not then compassionate those who are it's unhappy votaries? Shall not our pity be the more abundant, as their darkness is the more profound? and shall not the energy of our benevolence be coextensive, forceful, and persevering, with the measure, strength, and duration, of their errors? Where, then, is there reason to apprehend, that the cultivation of a pure morality should weaken our love for our fellow-men? If the wretch who sells his voice, who sells himself, for pay; if he who prowls on feeble & defenceless chastity, and steeps his hand in murder; if he excite compassion; and lost & loathly

---

[64] "I am become sounding brass, or a clanging cymbal." I Corinthians 13:1.

as he is, it be still our duty to love, & labour for him; how shall we not esteem him, who sincerely searches after truth, & steadily aims to practise justice? To you, my friend, I am bound by a thousand ties: your very errors strengthen my attachment. I might adopt the language which Brutus held to Cassius—

I do not love your faults;[65]

but I love in you an eager admiration of virtue, a fervid zeal in the cause of truth, a heart warm with benevolence, and a hand ready to second it's suggestions. I can not but lament that you have not attained to clearer views of the foundation of morality, & to a more consistent notion of it's injunctions. Were you more perfect, I should have a different interest in you, not a greater. It is this mixture of truth and error which fosters the sensibility of friendship. It is this sense of the want we mutually feel of counsel & support, which binds us to each other. The steady votaries of virtue, find their reward, in their adherence to her maxims. They gain our approbation; but not our sympathy. We commend these; we feel for others. But he, alone, can fix our love and admiration, whose knowlege, equally minute & just, ample & vast, as the infinitely-varied forms & mighty whole, of what relates to man, flows forth in one abundant, distinguishing diffusive, & interminable stream of benevolence to all.

If I have spoken with too much enthusiasm, I must borrow my apology from you, and plead in my excuse the interest excited by the subject.

I have now, my dear friend, with the utmost sincerity, & to the best of my knowlege, replied to your affectionate letter. After this, you will probably, think with me, that every thing particularly connected with religion, in the form of argument, should be omitted, in the further prosecution of our correspondence. There is, I fear, little promise of a change of opinion to be wrought by this means; & we have not opportunity for an ampler discussion of the grounds of faith. As nothing which has fallen from you has, in any degree, affected the unalterable regard I bear you; so I hope that any unintentional cause of offence I may have now, or ever, given you, will be overlooked & forgiven. I need not repeat how sincere an interest I take in all your concerns, & how much your increasing prosperity augments my happiness; but, after this long letter, you will pardon me for not enlarging further on these topics.

With affectionate regards for Mrs. Dwight, I am, as ever,

Your friend

Tuesday, Nov. 22, 1796.
Cedar St. No. 13. N. York. E. H. Smith.

Wednesday, Novr. 23.—A professional visit. Called on Dr. Mitchill, with whom I found Dr. Miller, & we conversed on our medical project. Two calls. Ch. B. Brown, who breakfasted with us, was here again, & Dunlap; to whom, at his request, I read my letter to Theodore. Just as I finished it, Dr. Miller came in, and sat till dinner-time: so that my ordinary concerns were neglected this forenoon. Johnson, Brown, & I, dined, by invitation, at Mr. Boyd's; where we met Mr. Kent, Mr. Radcliff, his friend, of Poughkeepsie, & Mr. Wortman —& where we spent the afternoon. A medical visit. At the Theater—with Johnson & Brown. The play was "Othello"; which I saw for the first time. Othello, by Hodgkinson, bad. A few good touches—but boisterous & senseless, in general. Tyler's Cassio, respectable: Hallam's Iago, excellent; judicious: Mrs. Melmoth's Emilia, good: Mrs. Johnson's Desdemona, graceful, correct, tender, affecting. The short part of Brabantio, by Crosby, well. Martin made me laugh in Roderigo. I am uncertain whether his conception of the character is just. On the whole, this representation is of the best of our Theater. It struck me, while in the house, that one cause of the pleasure which our people takes in the plays of Shakespere, more than in those of most dramatic writers, is, that they are familiar with all the principal dialogues & characters, from their boyish days. Who has not bore a part in the quarrel of Brutus & Cassius, pronounced the soliloquy of Hamlet, & played the orator over the corpse of Caesar?

I came home, and have finished the Monthly Review for August 1796. *Art. xi*: "The life of Lorenzo de Medici &c." by Roscoe, must be full of variety of interest. How flattering are the prefatory remarks of the Journalists! *Art. xii*: The character of Gibbon & of his memoirs is executed with wonderful felicity & truth. The two last volumes are not yet reviewed: I have some desire to know how far the opinions of these critics coincides with my own, respecting the importance of Mr. Gibbon's studies. *Art. xiii*: Spencer's translation of Bürger's "Leonora." There are four versions of this little poem, of which this is the least meritorious. That in the "Monthly Magazine" of March 1796—is by far the happiest. Mr. Florian's plan of Study or Education, (*Art. 19.*) is pretty good: but how much "dancing, drawing, music," & how little *morality*! It is curious that Dr. Hunter, in his "Outlines of Agriculture," speaks so strongly on the use of nitrous acid gas as manure. (*Art. 18.*) I shewed this to Mitchill; who, by the way, was here two hours, almost, this noontide.

There is nothing else worthy of notice in this number.

Thursday, Novr. 24.—Much of the forenoon writing for the Manumission Society. Ch. B. Brown here. He read me some extracts from his Journal. Two medical visits. Recd. last evening, a letter from my father, which ought to have been delivered a month ago. Wrote short letters, on the business of "The Medical Repository," to Dr. Buel of Sheffield, & Dr. Bird and Sheldon of Lichfield. Called on Dr. Mitchill, & we went to the Hospital, on business, relative to the Library. Found Ch. B. Brown here, when I returned. Was at W. W. Woolsey's an hour. Accompanied Mrs. Riley & Miss

---

[65] "I do not like your faults," *Julius Caesar* IV, iii.

Stillman, who were visiting there, home. Came home—wrote letters on "The Medical Repository," to Drs. Hopkins, Fisk, & Cogswell of Hartford, Dr. Orton of Woodbury, Dr. Rockwell of Sharon, & Dr. Carrington of Goshen. Took up the "Monthly Review" for September 1796. *Art. i*:—Mr. Owen is an agreable writer; & the Extracts are lively, & apparently well selected, from his "Travels in different parts of Europe &c." *Art. ii*: the account of Joseph Fawcett's "Sermons," has excited in me a desire to read them: & I will, at least, read some part of them. They are in Mr. Miller's possession. A Priest, delivering the doctrines of Godwin, must be a curiosity. The fault of the Extracts is, too great labour to dazzle. *Art. iv*: The two little Poems of Norgate, are happy. *Art. v*: The criticism on "Hermsprong" is liberal; & the spirit of a Godwinite breaks forth in the selection of extracts.

Friday, 25.—The Anniversary of the evacuation of this city by the British Forces. It has been *martially* observed. I wrote letters to Drs. Osborn & Hall of Middletown,[66] relative to the "Medical Repository." Ch. B. Brown breakfasted here. Finished the "Monthly Review" for September 1796. *Art. xvi*: "Travels thro' &c. Naples. By Charles Ulysses &c." The extracts very pleasing & instructive. The Duke of Martina is, surely, one of the best of nobles, & I admire the economy of his sheep-fold. The Lynx of Abruzzo is well-described. *Art. xvii*: "Letters to William Paley, &c." This criticism is excellent—& the subject of it more than usually meritorious. To be more particular would be to dwell on each idea: which, indeed, merits it; but not now. *Art. xviii*: I know of no work I more desire to be possesst of than the "Essays, Political, Economical, & Philosophical": by Benjamin Count of Rumford &c.[67]—whether from the character of the author, or of the work; which is on subjects of the utmost importance. This man, as far as I can judge, greatly surpasses Franklin—with whom he has sometimes been compared. *Art. 28.* I notice the "Twenty-four Lectures on the Italian Language," by Mr. Galignani—that I may know how to inquire for an ingenious assistant, should I ever wish to learn that tongue. There is taste, as well as ingenuity, in his manner exemplifying a verb. *Art. 29*: "The Parent's Assistant." This, also, is a book to be looked out for; but for a better purpose. *Art. 34*: "Observations, Anatomical, Physiological, & Pathological, on the Pulmonary System" by William Davidson. This is a book I want to read. The plan of author, as far as I can collect it, from the indirect mention of the Journalists, is to prevent any commotion in the system; give mild & gently-nourishing, & but not liquid food; & leave the cure to nature: & this seems to have been, in a degree, successful. *Art. 42*: "Thoughts on the cause of the High Price of Provisions &c." contains some curious statements, tending to confirm my ideas of the unprofitableness of Horses—& to shew how many more men, than horses, may be supported on a given territory. *Art. 62*: "The History of the Isle of Wight." See here a good account of a curious insect, called the *mole-cricket—(gryllus talpa.)* *Art. 69*: "Travels before the Flood." I barely notice this as it gives me an opportunity of remarking how much I have been surprized to see the rapid growth of the "New Philosophy"; & the precautions which writings, more or less, tinctured with it's doctrines, bear to other works, mentioned in the late numbers of this Review. In *Art. 38*: there is an admirable exposition of the principles of votaries of the "New Philosophy," by a man, certainly, nearly, if not quite, ready to admit their truth. I made a medical visit. Wrote a few words, by way of Conclusion to the second volume of my Journal; & finished an Index to it. Ch. B. Brown & Dunlap here. I spent part of the evening at the Theater. Dunlap's "Archers" was the piece. Very badly played. Not a single scene as it should be. But the house was full: chiefly of the middling sort of folk—men—warm with the rejoicings of the anniversary; the play was full of liberty; & every joke *told*. More applause, than ever, was bestowed on the Piece. Alsop here, a few moments. Read a paper in Gooch's Works, Vol. III.[68]

Saturday, Nov. 26.—Employed good part of this cold morning, in executing some little, necessary, out-door business. Found Ch. B. Brown here, when I returned. I read the news-papers; we conversed; & read, together, several articles, & parts of articles, in The Monthly Review. Errands, and a professional visit, in the afternoon. Read a considerable part of the Vol. III, of Gooch's Works, which I procured for the purpose of shewing Brown the History of the Sleepless Man of Madrid; a history which is connected with many important speculations. Dunlap & Brown both here in the afternoon. I shewed the former, a few slight alterations, made in my Opera; which he approved. Club night—at Kent's —Present, Alsop, Brown, Dunlap, Johnson, Kent, Smith, the Woolseys.

Sunday, 27.—Wrote letters, on "The Medical Repository," to Dr. Todd, of Farmington; Dr. Field, of Somers; & Dr. Sylvester & James Wells, of Berlin. Dunlap here a short time. Donald G. Mitchill came in, & sat here till dinner time. Wm. & I dined, & spent most of the afternoon, at S. Johnson's. We found Ch. B. Brown here when we returned. I visited Dingley. Johnson & I spent the evening at H. Johnson's. I came home; & have, since, transcribed the corrections, in my opera,

---

[66] Here and in the following pages Smith will list the names of a large number of doctors to whom he is writing to promote subscriptions for *The Medical Repository*. Since these names comprise no more than a mailing list and (unless noted) he had little other connection with them, they will usually not be glossed. One of the best known was William B. Hall, Yale, 1786, who practiced medicine in Middletown, Connecticut, 1790-1809, credited with being one of the earliest to vaccinate for smallpox.

[67] An eighteenth-century military man, spy, scientist, and adventurer.

[68] Benjamin Gooch, surgeon, *A Practical Treatise on Wounds and Other Chirurgical Subjects,* etc. (Norwich, 1767-1773).

into the Prompt-Book. None but he who has gone thro' the labour of bringing a Play, & particularly an Opera, on the stage, can have any adequate idea of the vexation & fatigue, inseparable from such an undertaking.

Monday, 28.—Ch. B. Brown breakfasted with us. A medical visit, & several errands. Wrote letters concerning the "Medical Repository," to Dr. Sage, of Chatham; Drs. Barker, and Eneas & Elijah Munson, of New Haven; Dr. Root, of Hambden; Dr. Beach, of Cheshire; Dr. Hull, of Fairfield; & Drs. Hulbert & Rogers, of Greenfield, Connecticut. A visit from Mr. Jereh. Mason. Alsop called here, and left "The Monthly Magazine" for September 1796—which I read—but cannot, now, dwell on it's contents. Ch. B. Brown here, in the afternoon. Looked over my notes on The Plague of Athens; & arranged the subject, in my mind, & made a feeble outline on paper. Spent the evening at Wm. W. Woolsey's. Dunlap & wife, Ch. B. Brown, Dr. Mitchill, Geo. M. Woolsey, and others, there. A sociable evening. Kent has got the "New Annual Register" for 1795, at length. He came here to let us know it.

Tuesday, 29.—I had just finished all the ordinary operations of breakfasting, shaving, &c. &c. and was just congratulating myself on having, at last, found a day of leisure, to sit down seriously to my "Essay on the Plague of Athens," when, in comes Dunlap, to tell me he had ordered the rehearsal of my Opera, for this morning. I went—and, what with corrections, new people, music, &c. it was one o'clock when I got home. The music, however, is pretty good; &, if the piece should be tolerably played, may render it tolerable. After dinner, new corrections to make in the parts of some of the performers. Wrote letters, on the "Medical Repository," to Drs. Norton, of Canadaquai; Hopkins, of Paris; Kirkpatrick, of Whitesburgh; Brown, of Fort Stanwix; Moore, of German Flatts; and Croswell, of Catskill. Read some pages in the New Annual Register —which Johnson purchased to-day. Ch. B. Brown here. Most of the evening wasted at Hodgkinson's—whither I went on business which might have been executed in five minutes—had it not been for the interrupting presence of others. Read further in "The New Annual Register."

Wednesday, 30.—Ch. B. Brown breakfasted here, & we attended to the very interesting anecdote of Mr. Howard, written by Pratt, & inserted in the New Annual Register for 1795. Read the newspaper. Wrote the first four & half pages of The History of Epidemics. Visited a patient. Called at Ch. Adams's, to see his child; that I innoculated Monday, & found there his father, the Vice President of the United States. This, tho' not the first time of my seeing him, was the first time of my being in his company; & till now I had a very imperfect idea of his countenance. The opportunity was good, & I spent near two hours with him. Some interruptions broke the chain of a conversation concerning the origin of the American Revolution, which promised to be very interesting. Mr. Adams considers James Otis as "the father of the Revolution." Mr. Otis's publications have never been collected. Mr. Adams exprest a fear lest there should never be any good history of the Revolution written. The ground of this apprehension was, that the material facts have never been published; that they were in the memories of individuals, who were dying, one after another; & that no person qualified for the purpose, was employed in collecting the anecdotes which these individuals might afford. He remarked that, could their papers be published, the most authentic history, or the best materials for such a history, would be found in those of the Tories. He particularized Hutchinson, Oliver, & Sewall, who died a short time since, in Nova Scotia. These men, he knew, preserved notes of all the events, & had the originals of the principal papers; but, events having happened so contrary to their wishes, expectations, & endeavour, it was to be feared that their executors & heirs would suppress or destroy them, from a regard to the honor, or reputation, of their authors & possessors. In the course of some remarks on Pennsylvania, Mr. Adams said—that "William Penn was the greatest land-jobber, that ever existed; & that his successors in the administration of that government, had continued the same policy." The remainder of the conversation was on the topics of the day; & the state of parties in this State. Mr. Adams's manners are more agreable than I supposed them to be. There is no affectation, or pride observable in him; yet he can hardly be called a sociable man. It is not proper to judge from one interview only—but such is the impression left by having been once in his company; &, for at least an hour, alone in his company.

I found Ch. B. Brown here, when I returned. I called at Mr. Rogers's: they had company, & I came away without seeing the family. I called, next, to see Mr. Beers of Albany, but he was not at his lodgings: next, on Mr. Gahn, who was also out. I spent most of the evening at Dr. & Mr. Miller's. The former read me a singular Letter from Dr. Rush—in which he says that he has thrown away his scabbard, & now openly brandishes the disorganizing sword.[69] Came home, & read the articles "Domestic Literature" & "Foreign Literature," in The New Annual Register.

In the month of November now ended, I have read—
Miscellaneous Works of Edward Gibbon—Vol. III— the greater part. 8vo.
Political Justice—three chapters.
History of Thucydides—Vol. II. 8vo.
De la Force du Gouvernement actuel de la France &c. par Benjn. Constant. pamphlet 8vo.
Plutarch—Life of Pericles.
Hermsprong: or Man as he is not. 2 vols. 12mo.
Lucretius—B. VI—lines 144.

---

[69] Dr. Rush had so many running fights going on at once that it is not possible to determine the nature of this one. The most probable subject was the question of whether patients with yellow fever should be bled.

Lycée de Arts—No. II.
Paul & Virginie—french Opera—
Zoonomia, P. II—near one half—
Monthly Review—for August, Septr.—& Appendix to Vol. XX. 1796.
Gooch's Works—Vol. III—half—8vo.
Monthly Magazine—for Septr. 1796.

In this same month of November, I have written—
A letter to Theodore Dwight—equal to 40 common 8vo. pages—
An address to Physicians &c. concerning a "Med: Repos:" equal to 16 common 8vo. pages.
On the Plague of Athens—notes &c.—equal to 20 common 8vo. pages—
Concerning the "Med: Repos:"—thirty letters, from one, to three, pages—
A few letters of friendship & business—short.

DECEMBER 1796

Thursday, 1.—Read several agricultural papers, in the New Annual Register for 1795, before & immediately after breakfast. A professional visit. Wrote two pages on my History of Epidemics. Went to Hospital Consultation, which detained me two hours. A visit from Dr. Mitchill. A visit from Mr. Alsop. A medical visit. Called at Hodgkinson's, to leave the copy of my play—& sat for a few minutes, with Mrs. H. Went to Kent's. Mr. Recorder Jones came there, & smoked me away. Came home; & have read near one half of "Man as He is"—a novel—by the author of "Man as he is not."

Friday, 2.—Ch. B. Brown, & Henry Johnson[70] (Wm.'s youngest brother—who came to town last evening, to spend the winter here—a fine youth—) breakfasted with us. Two medical visits. Dunlap came here; & soon after, Mr. Tracy, Mr. Goodrich, & Mr. Smith,[71] on their way to Congress. Mr. Tracy brought me letters from my Father, Abby, Idea, & Sally Pierce; Mr. Goodrich, from Mason F. Cogswell. All friends well. C. B. Brown here, again. Went with Mr. Tracy to his lodgings—& saw there, besides the gentlemen just mentioned, Mrs. Goodrich, Mr. Davenport, Mr. Hillhouse. An hour spent agreably. They continued their journey to Phila. Congress meeting next Monday. A visit from Mr. Beers of Albany—from Mr. Jere: Mason—&c.—Called on Dingley. Two other medical visits. Spent the evening at the Theater; where I saw "She Stoops to Conquer" and "The Prize."[72] Finished the first volume of "Man as he is."

Saturday, 3.—Two medical visits. A number of errands. Wrote four pages & a half on my History of Epidemics. Read the news-paper. Read some passages in Fawcett's Sermons.[73] A visit from Ch. B. Brown, in the forenoon & in the afternoon with Dunlap. Made considerable progress in "Man as he is." Club night—Dunlap's evening: Present, Brown, Dunlap, Johnson, Kent, Smith, the Woolseys. Dunlap read us the history of Wilkes's famous prosecution, from no. 45 of the North Briton—from Belsham's Memoirs of the House of Hanover; & afterward the account of the retreat of the British Forces, from Holland, into Germany, from the New Annual Register. Some politics of the day, & much trivial talk, not worthy the name of conversation, occupied the meeting. I wish we could devote our evenings to more respectable & useful purposes; but I fear they must be allowed to proceed without restraint.

Sunday, Decr. 4.—A medical visit. Wrote a letter to my father. Ch. B. Brown here. We read & compared a New Year & Birth-day Ode of Pye's with those Warton & Whitehead: Pye's, for 1795; Warton's, for 1786; Whitehead's, for 1784—was it? or 1783?[74] I read the account of the Religion &c. of the Dahomans, in The New Annual Register—extracted from Dalzell's History of Dahomey. Good & bad. Dined at James Watson's. Wm. Pitt Beers there—& other company. The commonplace & incessant rattle of Amasa Learned, & the maukish affectation of Miss Ledyard[75] suffered me to take but little pleasure, from this afternoon. Drank tea & spent two hours at Ch. Adams's. He shewed me two very sensible & well-written letters, from his brothers John & Thomas, to his father. The writers were at The Hague. These young negociators are neither Frenchmen, nor Britons: they are Americans & do honor to their country. I past the evening at Mrs. Morton's. Miss Susan was agreable, interesting, & sensible, as usual. I saw there a Mr. Sullivan of Boston—a young man—handsome, & of pleasing manners. I had not much vivacity in conversation. Circumstances led me to speak of my sisters; & I could not but think how widely we are to be separated, & how seldom we are destined to see each other, more. I finished "Man as he is," last night: a work estimable, on many accounts—less connected & on the whole unequal to Hermsprong; on others, superior. I give the preference to "Man as he is not."

Monday, 5.—I read, last night, a sermon of Joseph Fawcett's, "On the propriety of the Scripture term to express the virtuous character." The text is "The spirits of *Just* men made perfect." In this discourse, he lays down, in many places, the precise doctrine of Godwin. I was pleased. Ch. B. Brown breakfasted with us. Visited a patient. Wrote five & a half pages, on the

---

[70] William's younger brother who became an unsuccessful storekeeper.

[71] Of many possible Smiths, probably Nathaniel Smith (1762-1822) a man of little formal education but considerable ability, for many years in the Connecticut legislature (in which he served in both houses), Connecticut representative in U.S. House, 1795-1799, judge of Supreme Court of Connecticut, 1806-1819.

[72] Prince Hoare (1793).

[73] Joseph Fawcett, a Dissenting Minister, *Sermons Delivered at the Old Jewry Meeting* (London, 1795).

[74] All three are Laureates: Whitehead, who succeeded Cibber, from 1757; Thomas Warton, who followed Whitehead, from 1785; and Pye, who succeeded him, from 1790.

[75] Learned (1750-1825; Yale 1772), preacher then a lawyer and member of Connecticut General Assembly, 1785-1791, representative in U.S. House, 1791-1795. Miss Ledyard, probably a member of the Ledyard family of Hartford, Conn.

following essay: but very little to my satisfaction. Nor have I, since the first day's writing on it, pleased myself. I have had so many interruptions of one sort & another—especially to-day—that my ideas became confused, & my mind unhinged. Drs. Mitchill & Miller, & Mr. Roulet here, in the afternoon. I received a letter from Mrs. Lovegrove, which contained another for Miss S. Morton. I delivered it. Called at Mr. Kent's: At Hodgkinson's—whence I brought the prompt-book of my Opera; & corrected the part of Ethelbert. Called at S. Johnson's. They were out. Went to Riley's—& spent the evening with Alsop, & Mrs. Riley & Miss Stillman.

Tuesday, 6.—Dunlap came to call me to a rehearsal of my Opera. When we reached the Theater, we found a principal performer unwell; & delayed the rehearsal. A medical visit, & errands. Went to the monthly Examination of the African School. Thence, to a consultation, at the Hospital. Came home, & wrote short letters to Mr. Tracy & Mrs. Lovegrove—the first, introductory of Mr. L. to Mr. T. Dined at Dr. & Mrs. Miller's. It was four when we sat down. No advantage from the conversation worth mentioning. Found Ch. B. Brown here, when I returned. He spent the evening—which is very rainy; as the night promises to be. This is our first rain for a long time: several weeks. Recd. a letter from Wm. Buel.

[Omitted here, two manuscript pages: "Sketches of the History of Epidemics—Essay First" and twenty-six manuscript pages: "The Plague of Athens."]

Wednesday, Decr. 7.—I finished, this day, the preceding article, of which I composed nine pages. This task has been executed in a manner very little to my satisfaction; and, I fear, would not much increase my reputation, were it to be published. Should I determine on it's insertion in our "Medical Repository," it must be transcribed, new-modelled, & corrected. I shall let it rest a while. By & by, I may take it up, again, & coming to the subject with a mind refreshed by repose, may bestow on it a decent dress. Mr. Beers was here, a short time. He was in excellent spirits. I made two professional calls. Spent the evening at H. Johnson's.

Thursday, 8.—Errands. Wrote letters to Nathaniel Dwight, and Lemuel Kollock, principally relative to the "Medical Repository." Brown and Dunlap here. Transcribed two pages & a half of my letter to Theodore Dwight. Mr. Beers visited us. Made two professional visits. Drank tea, & spent part of the evening, at Dunlap's. Saw there, Pélisier, the composer of the music to my Opera. Remainder of the evening at a special meeting of the Trustees of the African School.

Friday, 9.—"A fire broke out last night"—but not in the Vatican, Mr. Dupaty. No—It was on Murray's Wharf; And a dreadful conflagration it was; and with an immense destruction of property. I have heard no estimate of the amount.[76] Ch. B. Brown breakfasted with us. I transcribed three pages of my letter to Theodore Dwight. Made two professional visits. Reconnoitered ruins, made by the fire last night. What confusion! I met Sylvester and James Wells,[77] in the Street. They came to town last evening. The former is going to Philadelphia. I wrote letters to Dr. Rush, Griffiths, Leib, Strong, & Woodhouse—partly on the business of the "Medical Repository"; partly introductory of Dr. Wells. I was surprized to find the name of the "Vicompte de Cornillon"[78] on my table; & to learn that he had called in my absence, this morning. I waited on him, & we met with much & mutual satisfaction. He looks in good health; but thinner, and older. He has been several times sick, during his absence; & has been, part of the time, in military service. He is now married; & is going on, with his lady, to Connecticut; of which he designs to become a citizen, for the remainder of his life. We made a call, together, on Woolsey. Made some progress in a lengthy paper, concerning the Tartars, in the New Annual Register. Mr. Beers came in. He spent most of the evening here. Mr. Mason was here, in the forepart of the evening; & Alsop in the morning. I spent the latter part of the evening, with the Wells's, at their lodgings. Too many interruptions, to allow me to effect much.

INNOCULATION

It has lately become a question, in Great Britain, whether the degree of Fever, and quantity of Eruption, in the Innoculated Small Pox, are not modified by the quantity of matter, introduced into the system, by Innoculation. It is the opinion of Dr. George Fordyce, that the number of pustules will be greater, & the fever more severe, when much matter is inserted, than when but little is inserted; and this opinion is countenanced by two Communications, made to Dr. Beddoes, and lately published, by that gentleman, at the end of his translation of *Gimbernat's* "New Method of Operating for the Femoral Hernia."

I wish to call the attention of Practitioners of Medicine to this point. No country is under better circumstances to determine the question than the United States; in which Innoculation is almost universally practiced, & where some physicians have opportunity of making several hundred observations every year.

I have always been of the practice of inserting a very small quantity of matter, by a small incision; tho' not from any expectation of mitigating the disease by this means. When an incision is large, the blood is apt to wash away the matter; or the local inflammation throw it off. Both these inconveniences are prevented by a small puncture. But if a milder disease is communicated

---

[76] Mr. Dupaty not identified. This was the fire which destroyed forty buildings on Wall Street and the east side of Front Street. See Stokes, *Iconography of New York* **5**: p. 1336.

[77] Sylvester Wells (1762-1837; Yale 1781), a physician who practiced in Berlin, Connecticut, until 1805, when he moved to Hartford. He was a member of the convention which framed the State Constitution of 1818, and state senator, 1818-1822. James Wells was probably his older brother.

[78] Not identified or traced.

by it, also, this is a more important reason for observing the practice.

In all the cases which have fallen under my care, I do not remember but a single instance where the patient has had so many as thirty pustules; and this depended on circumstances no wise connected with the manner of performing the operation, & arose from causes sufficiently obvious. My patients have been of varied ages; from two months to thirty years.

On the other hand, I have had occasion to observe, in numerous instances, where the incision was large, the quantity of matter inserted considerable—especially, when the *thread*[79] was used—that the patients either had very sore arms, or great numbers of pustules; and, oftentimes, with several days of severe pain & fever. I do not pretend that this uniformly happens. Constitution, treatment, & accident, may, & must, produce variety. But it seems to be a question worthy of attention & solution, "Whether any, & what, influence is to be attributed to the greater or lesser quantity of variolous matter, introduced into the system, by innoculation?"

Communications are requested, from all parts of the United States, or elsewhere, on this subject.

Saturday, Decr. 10.—Ch. B. Brown breakfasted here. We generally spend an hour in conversation, when this happens. Transcribed near five pages of my letter to Theodore Dwight. Ch. B. Brown read & wrote here, most of the forenoon. I read twenty-three pages in Zoonomia P. II. Made two medical visits. Visited Dingley. Drank tea at Kent's. Club night—Met with Johnson—Present, Alsop, Brown, Dunlap, Johnson, Kent, Smith, the Woolseys, & Mr. Mason, visitor. Johnson read us Pratt's account of Mr. Howard's singularities, from The New Annual Register. A spirited discussion succeeded, on the subject of simplicity of diet, dress, &c. &c. The President's (of U. S.) Address, next talked over.[80] Lively conversation: some investigative talents displayed. A very general disapprobation of the project of a Navy, a Military Academy, &c. Difference of sentiment, relative to a National University; which I defended, on definite principles—not on the apparent foundation of the President. A very agreable meeting. I recd. yesterday, a few lines from Mr. Tracy.

Sunday, 11.—Ch. B. Brown reading & writing here, most of the forenoon. Visited M. de Cornillon. Two professional visits. Finished Chapternu's account of the Tartars, and read considerable part of Thunberg's account of Japan in the New Annual Register for 1795. Dined, and spent the afternoon, at S. Johnson's. Evening at Woolsey's. A medical visit.

There dined at Johnson's, Mr. Henry Remsen, now Teller to the Branch Bank, in this city, formerly chief clerk in the office of Secretary of State, when Mr. Jefferson was Secretary, & before that a clerk in the same office, when Mr. Jay was Secretary. He confirmed, from his own personal knowlege, the accounts which I had before heard, of the licentious & indiscriminate indulgence of Mr. Hamilton (late Secretary of the Treasury—) in the use of women: even those of the most common kind, & in the most common houses. He, also, related an anecdote of this same celebrated man, much less to his credit. When Mr. H. was Secretary, his office was opposite to the Bank of North America. On the day when the subscription was opened for the National Bank, people crowded to subscribe, in the morning. As they were rushing thither, Mr. H. came to the door of his office; &, pleased with the success of his project, which had been violently opposed, by his political antagonists, he stood there, *clapping his hands*, & shewing other marks of exultation for near fifteen minutes. This Mr. Remsen told me, expressly, that he himself saw.

In respect to Mr. H's amours, it does not appear that they influence, in the least, his political conduct.[81] He gratifies his appetite, rather than his passions. He repairs to a brothel; but he has no mistresses on whom he lavishes his fortune, & to whom he surrenders his independence. It is well to know these people, whose names are much bandied about in history; & I would, for facts like these, have more precise records than those of my memory; accurate as it generally is, in matters of biography & anecdote.

Monday, 12.—The neglect of our milk-man, lost us an hour this morning. Ch. B. Brown breakfasted with us. Two professional visits. Transcribed near eight pages of my letter to Theodore Dwight. A visit from Dr. James Wells. A professional visit. At the Theater; where I saw "Romeo and Juliet." I read twenty pages in Zoonomia P. II, last night; and an equal number to-night.

Tuesday, 13.—Two medical, several friendly, visits; and some errands. Transcribed somewhat more than three pages of my letter to Theodore Dwight. Wrote a letter, moderately long, to Mr. Tracy. A professional visit. Spent the evening at Mr. Boyd's. Read forty-five pages in Zoonomia P. II.

Wednesday, 14.—Finished the transcription of my letter to Theodore Dwight, and a few words, by way of Postscript. The composition of this letter is pretty good, on the whole; but I have aimed at perspicuity, more than elegance. A fear of exciting unpleasant feelings, in the bosom of my friend, has prevented me from pushing an argument, in several instances. I have, also, failed in philosophical precision, some times, from an apprehension of being unintelligible to him, unless I

---

[79] A string was drawn through a pustule on the arm of a person suffering from the disease and then drawn through the cuts, sufficiently deep to break the skin, on the arms of the person to be inoculated—normally on both arms.

[80] Washington's eighth and final annual message to Congress, Dec. 7, 1796.

[81] In 1797 a political attack on Hamilton, Secretary of the Treasury, developed into an attack on him for womanizing. Hamilton confessed to having had an affair with a Mrs. Reynolds.

went into details, too extensive for the time & subject. I hope he will be so far satisfied, as to put an end to theological discussion. Alsop here. Voted for Representative in Congress. An hour at Fellows's Book-Store. Dr. Miller called on me. Dined at Mr. Boyd's, in company with a young gentleman, of the name of Higginson, a native of Boston, & lately from Paris—from whom I gained no information worthy of notice. An errand. A visit from Ch. B. Brown—who read me several passages from his Journal. I wish he would turn his Aloas & Astoias, his Buttiscoes and Carlovingas, to some account. He starts an idea; pursues it a little way; new ones spring up; he runs a short distance after each; meantime the original one is likely to escape intirely. Visited, & spent the evening, most sociably, with Mr. & Mde. Roulet. I have read, this day, the remainder of Thunberg's account of Japan; the article concerning the Republic of St. Marino; the Extract from Murphy's Travels in Portugal; in the New Annual Register for 1795. The article St. Marino gave me much pleasure.

Thursday, Decr. 15.—Executed some small part of the labor of forming a pocket Pharmacopoiea. Several errands, after money &c. A call from Dr. Miller. Wrote a hasty letter to Mrs. Lovegrove. Dunlap here; & we marked my Opera, for the Prompter. A medical visit. Spent the evening at our neighbour's—Mr. Riggs's. I have read several papers in The New Annual Register—and, in the Asiatic Researches—"On the ruins at Mavalisuram," "On the Indian Trial by Ordeal," "On the descent of the Afghans from the Jews," & "On extracting the Essential Oil of Roses." Ch. B. Brown was here, from five to six.

Friday, 16.—Read the paper, in the Asiatic Researches, intituled "A description of Assam." Ch. B. Brown breakfasted here; was writing here much of the forenoon; and spent from 5 to 6 here, in the evening: when he read us his "Reply which might have been made, by the Senate of the U. S. to the President." Alsop here, in the forenoon, & in the afternoon. Dr. Miller called in the morning. Dr. Wells returned from Philadelphia. He spent near two hours here, in the forenoon; & Dr. Mitchill about the same time, in the afternoon. With so many avocations, I could not do much. Most of the day devoted to the Pharmacopoiea. Wrote letters, concerning the "Medical Repository" to Dr. Potter, of Wallingford (Connec.)—Dr. Eustis, of Boston; & Dr. Coffin, of NewBuryPort. Read forty pages in Zoonomia P. II. Recd. letters from Dr. Strong, of Phila. & from Mr. Tracy, who is now in that city.

Saturday, 17.—Read three papers in the Asiatic Researches—"On the manners &c. of the Mountaineers of Tipra," "On the Baya, or Indian Gross-Beak," & "An account of the kingdom of Népál." The two last somewhat interesting. The whole forenoon at the rehearsal of my Opera, which is to be played on Monday night—tho' of all the performers, Mrs. Hodgkinson alone is perfect. Some are unacquainted with the music; & one of the principal performers could not read his part. Dunlap thinks it will be ready; & his inclination appeared too fixed for me to contend with. Made two ineffectual calls on Dr. Wells, who, I suppose, left town, this afternoon. Was a short time, at Dunlap's. We called at Hodgkinson's, relative to the Opera; & then took a short walk out of town. Alsop & Brown were both here, today. Drank tea at W. W. Woolsey's—& spent the evening. Club night—& his turn—Present, Brown, Dunlap, Johnson, Smith, the Woolseys. The conversation not remarkably interesting.

A great, & to my apprehension, unnecessary alarm, prevails in respect to the danger the City is in from incendiaries. The citizens, in the several wards, are enrolled, to serve as patroles. Near two hundred are to be on duty, each night.

Sunday, 18.—It has been exceeding rainy, all day, & so continuous; wherefore I have kept house. Ch. B. Brown spent most of the forenoon here; which passed off briskly enough, in varied conversation. The arrangement of my drawers, &c. occupied some time; & some hours were busied in posting my Books, from Septr. to the present day. The remainder of the day has been employed in reading the Asiatic Researches, the Second Volume of which Collection I have now finished. The real title of the book is—"Dissertations, and Miscellaneous Pieces, relating to the History & Antiquities, of Asia." I slightly notice those Papers which appear most to merit attention. "A short description of Carnicobar," is interesting. The equality, veracity, & unceremoniousness of the people are worthy of the Golden Age. "On the cure of Elephantiasis"—this paper is valuable. I had, before, resolved to try the effects of Arsenic, in some shape; I think, now, of experimenting with it in Lues—& in Hapatic complaints. In the season of Intermittent Fevers, I shall attempt to discover it's curative effects, in such disorders. The next paper, "On the cure of persons bitten by snakes," is so unequivocal that I should be desirous of trying the effects of the Volatile Alkali, not only in the cases in the Bite of Rattlesnake, but in Hydrophobia & Tetanus. The method used by this writer was, to put a ligature between the part bitten & the Heart; to give from 20 to 60 drops of Spt. Volat. Caustic. in water, by the mouth; & to wash the part with the same. His reason for applying the Ligature is insufficient, tho' the practise may, perhaps, be salutary. The veins do not absorb, but the lymphatics. The ligature, possibly, may compress them, & thus prevent the circulation of the poison. This, however, does not appear very probable, when we observe that tho', in almost every case, the ligature was applied, yet the effects of the bite were not prevented. The poison of the *"Cobra de Capello"* seems surprizingly to affect the nervous system; & the muscles of the Fauces & Throat. This suggested to me the idea of the possible efficacy of the same remedy, which cures this poison, in Hydrophobia. "Of the Method of Distilling &c." This badly-written paper contains some suggestions worthy of notice. "On the Pangolin of Bahar"—This is a curious & valuable addition to Natural History. There is *some* foundation, probably, for Mr. Burt's conjectures; but it is impossible that they can be true, to the extent he supposes. No analysis of Calcareous justifies us in supposing that it can furnish, even with the aid of water, the constituent elements of animal substances. "Description of the Lácsha, or Lac Insect," is new (at least to me) & worthy of preservation. The two Poems of Sir William Jones are pleasing, fanciful, & happily-illustrative of the Doctrines of the Hindus. What an amazing & disgustful collection of absurdity is the religion of Hindustan—& indeed, are all religions! As a means of elucidating the history of the country, the theology of the Indians is deserving of study; but these men seem actually to acquire a passion for the study of these fables, on their own account, & to attach to them romantic ideas of I know not what beauty, sublimity—& other nonsense. Fye!

Monday, Decr. 19th.—Read on Zooncmia, P. II, till ten o'clock. Then, I went to the last rehearsal of my Opera;[82] which kept me the remainder of the morning: most unpleasantly. For it went on but poorly. Mrs. Hodgkinson, alone, of the principal performers, was perfect; & Mr. Martin, in Ethelbert, was quite imperfect. I found Ch. B. Brown here, when I returned. A long & disputatious argument, "On the difference between poetry & prose"—or rather on "the wherein are poetry & prose distinct"; which ended, as such discussions usually do, without the conviction of either party; & with no clearer ideas on the subject, than before. Spent the short afternoon in reading Darwin's Zoonomia, P. II.—partly; & partly in making several calls. Drank tea at Kent's. Went to the Theater. A thin house. Boxes, better than I expected; Pitt, worse. On the whole, & under all the circumstances, as many auditors as were to be looked for. The performers were more perfect that I had any hopes; still they were quite imperfect. This, which, perhaps, was not observed by the audience, was evident in the heaviness & feebleness which are inseparably connected with it. The music is very sweet & pleasing; & the people seemed pleased with it. They heard the Piece with as much attention as could be desired; with more than I expected; & tho' they bestowed but little applause, bestowed as much of that as I expected. It went off, on the whole, tolerably well; & I believe my friends were, in this, somewhat disappointed. After the representation was over, I went into the Green-room, a while. The performers had been full of anxiety & trepidation; and were as much gratified, as I was, at coming off so well. In the principal Scene between Edwin and Angelina, a fellow in the Gallery, was comfortably asleep; while Mrs. Brett shed tears—the only ones, I suspect, which fell from any eyes, during that Scene—as I told her. I have felt some little anxiety, myself, in the course of the day; & some, tho' not so much, during the representation: less, I believe, than is usually experienced in such a situation, but more than I ought to have felt. As the players were better than I feared, my tranquility was perfectly restored, before the end of the Piece; & I came home, without waiting to see "Florizel and Perdita," & sat down quietly to Zoonomia—in which, I have this day read fifty pages: read—not studied.

I ought to have noted, on the 17th inst. that it was Wm Johnson's Birth-day; who was then 27 years of age.

Tuesday, 20.—Ch. B. Brown breakfasted here. Conversation till ten o'clock. Called at Dingley's, & at Wortman's. A professional call. At a book-store; where I picked up the translation of Baron Haller's "Usong."[83] Found Brown here, when I returned. Mr. Jereh. Mason came in; & sat till near two. He left with me, two works, which he had taken a few days since, from a Circulating Library. The first, is the Chaste Loves of Peter the Long &c.[84]—to which my attention was attracted by the circumstance of it's being a work of Thomas Holcroft's. The work may be regarded in two points of view. As an exact picture of love, in the times, & with such characters, it is admirable; and it is no less so, considered as a burlesque on that passion. I am not perfectly sure in

---

[82] *Edwin and Angelina* was a complete failure. Even Dunlap's great affection for Smith could not override his judgment as a producer. It was played only once. Dunlap in his kindly way described it as being like Smith, "pure and energetic." He added, "But it was not sufficiently dramatic, and the characters of Edwin and Angelina were too familiar to all readers." See *History of the American Theatre*, p. 156. In Dunlap, *Diary* (February 7, 1798) **1**: p. 219, he wrote that the opera was noticed in the *Monthly Review* for October, 1797, "not so favorably as it deserves, tho' they allow it interest." From first to last it was bad theater. The blank verse has a kind of wooden craftsmanship but no art. The plot is involved, disjointed, deficient in structure. Emma, a key figure in the play, never appears at all. Angelina appears for the first time in Act II but Edwin is not seen until Act III. The dramatist scarcely succeeds in getting all of his characters on stage before the final curtain. As Smith stated in his preface, all but one of the songs in the third act were taken from Goldsmith's poem, "Edwin and Angelina." In the scenes between these two characters he made use of Goldsmith's sentiments and, wherever possible, of his phrases. See *Edwin and Angelina; or the Banditti, An Opera in three Acts* (New York, 1797), p. 6. The theme, as Miss Bailey pointed out in her biography of Smith, p. 104, leans heavily on Schiller's *Dee Räuber* in its concern with injustice leading to banditry and a reform finale. Despite all of its faults, however, the responsibilty for the failure of the piece should probably rest on Pelissier, the composer. However poor the book, an opera can survive if the music is good. But Pelissier was no Mozart. In addition, his lack of familiarity with English led him, as Smith pointed out, into frequent small disasters when he tried to fit his notes to Smith's words. Finally, the native origin of the work militated to some extent against its favorable reception. It should be noted that as early as 1786 Smith's friend Cogswell frequently referred to himself in his letters as "Edwin" and to his correspondent as "Angelina." See also a letter from Theodore Dwight to "Edwin," signed "Orlando." Cogswell Papers.

[83] *Usong, an eastern Narrative* (London, 1772), trans. anonymously.

[84] Thomas Holcroft, *An Amorous Tale of the Chaste Loves of Peter the Long,* imitated from the original French of L. E. Billardon de Sauvigny (London, 1786).

which view the author meant to have it taken; tho' I suspect, in the latter. I have also read one volume & a half of the other work—"Travels before the Flood"[85]—of which I now say nothing. I spent most of the evening at H. Johnson's; but found an hour to wait on my kinswoman, Lucy Bull, of Hartford: an hour very agreably employed. Alsop made us a visit this afternoon.

Wednesday, 21.—Ch. B. Brown breakfasted here. I finished "Travels before the Flood." I am pleased with this work, but I have read it too hastily to be able to speak of it judiciously. It certainly contains many wise remarks, & proves the author to be of no ordinary stamp. I do not know that it is worth my while to study out his meaning. At least, I do not, now, feel disposed to attempt it. Made some progress in my Pharmacopoiea. Began, & read the first Book of Baron Haller's "Usong." Made several calls. Drank tea at Mrs. Miller's. Spent the evening at Mrs. Morton's. S. Johnson & his wife, Wm & Fanny Johnson, Lucy Bull, &c. &c. were there.

Thursday, 22.—Turned over the leaves of a "Tour thro' North Wales";[86] I suppose by Thomas Pennant. Johnson read me some passages from Nugent's translation of Benvenuto Cellini's Life,[87] written by himself—indicat[iv]e of uncommon understanding & spirit. Made some little progress in my Pharmacopoiea. Attended an operation, at the Hospital: the usual effect; I felt sick, & found it prudent to quit the Theater. Returned with Dr. Mitchill, to his room—where I saw, for the first time, Count Rumford's Essays Vol. I. the reading of which is promised me. A visit from Mr. Roulet. Ch. B. Brown here. Continued the reading of "Usong." Drank tea at Dunlap's. We went to W. W. Woolsey's, where Mrs. Dunlap was, & where Ch. B. Brown & Geo. M. Woolsey, came. Nuts & apples—of which there was immense destruction. I recd. a short letter from my father. All well. I have obtained Mr. Voght's publication, relative to the establishments for the Poor, at Hamburg; & a pamphlet, in part on similar subjects, from Manchester.

Friday, Decr. 23.—Finished "Usong." This book has great & various merit; which shines thro' the obscurity of a poor translation. To judge properly of it, we must recollect the time when it was written; the plan of the writer; and the political & religious errors which misled his judgement. Not withstanding, I have recd. much pleasure; tho' the information obtained from it has been more concerning the author, than the subject of his work. The most commendable ideas & reasonings have been long familiar to my mind; with ampler illustrations than are here displayed. I read a pamphlet (27 pages 8vo.) intituled "Thoughts upon the Means of preserving the Health of the Poor, by prevention & suppression of Epidemic Fevers. Addressed to the inhabitants of the town of Manchester (Eng.) &c. By the Revd. Sir Wm Clarke"—Not much new information, but a very useful publication. I read "Account of the Management of the Poor in Hamburg, since the year 1788"—printed in 1795 by a Mr. Voight or Voght—of Hamburg—62 pages 8vo. This pamphlet deserves to be studied. I have read it hastily, with unspeakable pleasure; & propose to give it a second reading—perhaps to-morrow. It has renewed, with great liveliness, in mind, the several plans, in relation to this City, which have so long floated there & so often shared a considerable part of my reflections. This pamphlet was bound up with several others, belonging to Dr. Mitchill. Among them was one—"Letters on Emigration"—to America—(76 pages 8vo.)[88] which, attracted by the title, I also read. Superficial—with some sensible remarks. If the people of Great Britain must have incorrect notions of this Country, I wish that they may believe this writer. We should not, then, have so many & such emigrants. It is much to be desired, not for America only, but for the prosperity of the general cause of Liberty & Humanity, that we be left to the natural means of increase. Wrote letters to my Father & Mr. Tracy—I recd. a letter from Mrs. Lovegrove—now in Phila. Part of the morning wasted in futile errands. Drank tea & spent the evening at S. Johnson's. Lucy Bull there, & Jno. Morton. Ch. B. Brown & Alsop here, in the forenoon.

To Fanny Smith

It is so long since I received your letter, of the 17th of October, that I am at a loss for the reason which prevented me from replying to it immediately. I have some faint notion that I had written to you, but a short time before it's receit; and that this circumstance, in connection with some hurry at the time, occasioned the delay. Since then, I have been steadily busied with something; and this is the first moment when I have felt myself at leisure, to write to you. At present, my letter must be short; & I shall send it, to meet you at Lichfield.

Your answer to my question is very judicious; and, I hope, was founded on a more profound consideration of the subject than you were disposed to enter into, in a letter. If you still pursue the plan, formerly recommended to you, of Journalizing, I wish you to examine the question, above-referred to, at your leisure, & in all it's views. This is the more necessary, as we seldom obtain correct notions on any subject, till after much reflection, & having often endeavored to arrange our ideas on paper. In the desultory reflections of successive days, a few arguments & principles present themselves, repeatedly, to our minds; &, thus, as they assume dif-

---

[85] *Travels Before the Flood. An Interesting, Original Record of Men and Manners in the Antediluvian World, Interpreted in Fourteen Evening Conversations Between the Caliph of Bagdad and his Court,* trans. from the Arabic (London, 1797).
[86] Thomas Pennant, *A Tour in Wales* (1778-1781).
[87] Thomas Nugent (London, 1771).

[88] *Letters on Emigration by a Gentleman lately returned from America* (London, 1795).

ferent aspects, are mistaken for different & distinct conceptions. Hence we deceive ourselves; supposing we know much more, & have thought more deeply, than we have in reality. The true method of detecting the imposture, is to recur to the pen, & then, when we attempt to methodize, shall we discover what indeed we do know. We shall often be mortified & disappointed, to find how little it is, when we thought it considerable; but the discipline will be salutary. Have the courage, then, my dear sister, to submit to it.

When you wrote the letter to which I am replying, you had received only my First Sonnet. I am pretty sure that I have, since, forwarded the Second; &, in this belief, I now send the Third. If it should so happen that you have not had the Second, let me know it, & it shall be transmitted immediately. I now send them to you, in the order of their composition; but I design, when I have filled up the outline which exists in my mind, to arrange them after a peculiar method. Meantime, they may give you some pleasure, disconnected as they are.

You are in the wrong to indulge so many misgivings & irresolutions. You can improve, if you will; and you do improve. What is a decisive evidence of your advancement is, the sense you have of the feebleness of your exertions. Cherish the small sensibility, my sister, but only that it may operate as an incentive, not a repressive, of industry. Your own sense of propriety is active enough to convince you of the futility of regret; may it be sufficiently discerning to teach you that the only cure for such regrets is in virtuous exertion!

I shall bid you farewell, by proposing a Second Question, to you, for solution. "Is he a vicious man, who does wrong, thinking it to be right?"

Receive my unaltered love.

Saturday, Decr. 24. 1796.
Cedar St. No. 13. N. York.   E. H. Smith.

Saturday, 24.—Read "Observations on the Small Pox, & on Inoculation &c. by Alexandar Aberdom (93 pages 8vo.)—it being bound up with certain pamphlets read yesterday—a performance of no supereminent merit, and much inferior to that of Walker, whose book he attempts to criticize. Still it has some good practical remarks, not undeserving of attention. Dunlap & Alsop spent some time here, in the forenoon; & also Ch. B. Brown. I wrote letters to Mary & Fanny. Brown was here all the afternoon. He read me part of his Journal; & I him, part of mine—for a fortnight past. We read Moore's[89]—or Brook's—Fables—"Love & Vanity" & the "Sparrow & the Dove." I drank tea at Kent's, who objected, on account of the coldness of the weather, to going out. I left him, & repaired to Dunlap's—where the Club met, in Geo. M. Woolsey's turn. Present, Alsop, Brown, Dunlap, Johnson, Smith, and the Woolseys. Much talk; very little conversation. Recd. a short letter from Mr. Tracy.

[89] Edward Moore, *Fables for the Female Sex* (1744).

The weather is now excessively cold. Night before last, yesterday, last night, & this day, exceed in severity all we have known for several winters past. This morning, at 7½ the mercury was at the zero of Fahrenheit's Thermometer. This cold is not unpleasant to me; tho' I have kept house most of this day. I have, hitherto, had no need of a Great Coat; & my feelings had been remarkably agreable. This weather resembles that of my native hill; & were it to continue, one week would make it quite comfortable. These sudden changes are the greatest trials to the constitution.

To Mary S. Mumford

Your letter, of Octr. 16. has lain by me, unanswered, a long time; but, meanwhile, you have probably recd. one from me, written previous to the receit of yours. I have been busied; and have had nothing to write about, sufficiently important to divert my attention from my proper occupations.

By a letter, from my father, recd. by the last Post, I learn, that your visit to Connecticut will be divided between several places; & that, in all probability, you will not be long at Lichfield. This renders it quite uncertain whether I can meet you there. It will be impossible for me to leave N. York, after the first of February. You will not be in Lichfield till the first, or second week in January; &, as you make your visit to New London immediately, it will not be till the third or fourth week of that month, that you return. This will be too late for me; as I must be here on the first of February. Such is the dilemma in which I am placed, at all events; & beside, it is quite uncertain whether I shall be able to leave this place at all. I regret this the more, as I fear, if we do not meet now, we shall never *all* meet again at the same time. If Abby flies to the eastern extremity of our world, it must be some extraordinary turn of fortune that shall unite us, afterward, in Lichfield. Were it not for this, I should far prefer the summer, for my visit. It is more pleasant, & less busy, than the winter; and this winter threatens to be unusually severe. But this I should not mind—other circumstances favoring. For I despair of seeing Aurora—& can not think of letting two, & perhaps three, years pass, without meeting you somewhere. Yet, if this meeting may not be, as we can not controul, we must submit to our destiny; & with the more readiness as, probably, that which will prevent our meeting, will be the occasion of more good, on the whole, than the meeting itself.

The difficulties which you meet with, in the management of your boy, are common, & were to have been expected. Education is a matter of infinite difficulty & delicacy. Complete success is not to be hoped for, with that degree of knowledge which, ordinarily, falls to the lot of mankind. Our study must be to avoid evil; & where, from our ignorance, we have erred, to retrieve our error, in the simplest & readiest way. In situations like those of which you speak, my observation has led me to place most reliance on persuasion, mildness, & firmness. Does a child act improperly? The parent, in requesting it to desist, should endeavor to make the child perceive the reasonableness of what is required from him. But if he will not listen, or if the *real* reason can not be made apparent to his understanding, the injunction should always rest on it's being more agreable to the parent; & this should be made mildly, but firmly. Where this is not effectual, no punishment answers better than solitary confinement; which should be immediately, silently, & perseveringly, executed. No promise should, in such a case, be listened to. The remission of punishment, or it's abidement, should never rest on any other foundation than the conduct of the child. I would never permit him to make a promise. Above all, in censoring the conduct of children, avoid the trite exclamation—"It is wicked."—which conveys no idea; & rather incites to mischief, than restrains from it. Two other, common faults must be guarded against: making many prohibitions, & many threats. It is much better, on every account, to tell a child, when doing wrong, to be still—& if he persist, to punish him without passion, & without speaking—than to threaten & remonstrate. The ideas of improper conduct & immediate suffering should be steadily associated in his mind. Where prohibitions precede the commission of vice, they stimulate ingenuity & excite a disposition to the perpetration; & where the parent condescends to remonstrate, the child always indulges the expectation of avoiding the penalty.

I have attended to your commission, respecting the Cloak; & hope to conclude it agreable to your wishes, tho' not exactly conformable to your expectations. You will understand this better, when you have been at Lichfield; where, I mean, you shall find this letter. I shall, doubtless, write to you again, while you are there; if I do not find opportunity to join you.

Farewell.

Saturday, Decr. 24. 1796.
Cedar St. No. 13. N. York.   E. H. Smith.

To Abigail Smith, Jr.

The sentiments which are exprest in your last letter, my dear sister, are just and natural; and equally bespeak reflection & sensibility. I rejoice to observe in you such accurate conceptions of the nature of that change which is likely to take place in your situation, and of the consequences which may flow from it. Continue so to examine & so to weigh the importance of actions, & I shall have little doubts of your felicity, and less of your virtue. One of the most indispensable injunctions of Morality is, to scrutinize, compare, estimate, the nature, relations, & tendency of every act. It is not enough to have good intentions, we must labour, unremittingly, to discover what is good. Otherwise, our very exertions may counteract our purposes; and in striving to establish, we may shake the throne of virtue; and employ those arms in the cause of vice, which we had taken up against her.

If there be any thing, previous to the completion of which comprehensive, accurate, and profound reflection is requisite, it is marriage: if there be any contract of extensive import which is entered into without thought or preparation, it is marriage. Is it strange, then, that we hear it, so often, compared to a Lottery? that the groans of connubial anguish, & din of domestic discord, so often resound in our ears? Vanity dazzles, ambition cheats, & avarice goads, the wretch; or Force compels, or Appetite stimulates, or Gratitude constrains him; or Love, the most generous, but least clear-sighted, of them all, places the bandage over his eyes; & only removes it, when it is wanted to form the uniting & indissoluble band of wedlock. I might pursue the metaphor much farther, were it necessary, for how seldom do we see Reason mingling in the councils! Instant gratification is all that parties pant after; and their own future happiness, much less that of their offspring, seldom engages their attention. Provisions are sometimes made for Pin-money; but none for Household Economy, for the Education of Children, for mutual improvement. Personal, not mental, endowments are considered. The temporary dictates of caprice, not the settled directions of opinion, are consulted. The effects of uncertain passion are observed, the influence of permanent habit is disregarded. How are beings, brought together under such circumstances, likely to agree, when every day calls upon them to determine on subjects of immediate, of mighty, & of infinite concern? on subjects, respecting which so great diversity of sentiment prevails, where years of previous reflection are necessary to a right comprehension, where the sages of the earth doubt, hesitate, & despond?—on subjects, concerning which they have never conversed; concerning which they know not each other's sentiments?

Every topic which is likely to interest persons *after* marriage, ought to be fully & freely discussed *before*. In a matter of so great moment childish timidity, & girlish shamefacedness, ought to be banished. Mutual confidence, mutual sincerity & mutual dilligence, should supply their place. No event, which arises in the ordinary process of life, should find you unprepared, & undecided. Every physical, as well as every moral, question should be widely examined. Then, if you want knowlege, have you time to obtain it: if doubts occur, have you leisure to resolve them; if diversity of sentiment prevails, have you opportunity to examine, canvass, argue, & convince. Once settled, all is clear. When the occasion presents itself, you are ready to act: there is no room for delay, no danger of dissention. How few of the miseries of wedded life are unavoidable! How few but what depend on mutual ignorance, & on a false notion, that love alone, & not reason, is to be consulted in forming a correction! Let not an error so pernicious poison the future tranquillity of my sister! May she reflect & act in season! May he who shall be her husband, not then first begin to study & learn her character & sentiments, when he is united to her; but may he enter on the enjoyment of that happiness, which a previous acquaintance with them, has prepared him to expect, value, & improve!

\+ + + + + + + + + +

It is quite uncertain whether I shall be able to visit Lichfield, this winter. I dread a winter's journey. The experience of last year remains with me; & nothing but the strong desire of being once more all together, will overcome my aversion. But I know not that I shall be at liberty to choose. If I do not come next month, I shall lay out to be with you in June. That is the pleasantest season; &, ordinarily, the healthiest. Then, I may venture to spend a fortnight, perhaps, in Connecticut. And possibly, your good friend, whom I am very anxious to know, may, in that event, meet me there.

In reply to my Mother's inquiry, I should be well pleased to have the stockings; & could two or more pairs of fine, white worsted be added or substituted, I should be still more gratified. I am glad you like the Cloak.

My best love to my mother: I propose to write to Idea.

Farewell

Sunday, Decr. 25. 1796.
Cedar Street. No. 13. N. York.   E. H. Smith.

To Sally Pierce

The portrait, my dear friend, which you have drawn, of Mr. Bacon, is pleasing, and, I hope, just. Little, occasional asperities of temper, are to be expected in men whose sensibilities are acute, & whose intellectual energies are rapid & forceful. These may be corrected by a good understanding, if the disposition be good, & the man a lover of sincerity and virtue. That these faults, of which Mr. B. is accused, should be most evident in political debate is not unnatural, when we recollect how little reason is listened to in such controversies, & how hostile the opinions of those who surround him are to his own. There exists, in Lichfield, as well as in most parts of Connecticut, a degree of political intolerance repugnant to every just sentiment of liberty of opinion. These village giants, like some of the tyrants of old, are for a forcible equalization of principles & creeds. The rack must be employed to stretch faith [when] it is too short; & the axe to shorten it, when it is too long. That a man of spirit should assert his own independence, in opposition to the levellers, is all in his favor. To constrain men to be free, is a solecism; yet it is daily attempted.

I hope no friend of mine will become the tool, or the leader, of a party. Should I ever know Mr. B. I shall not be wanting in my endeavours to check any tendency he may have to engage, with such feelings, in political life: and this I should as strenuously aim to accomplish, were it directly opposite to what it is represented. A Federalist, & a Democrat, in the party-acceptation of those terms, are equally detestable. But, from what I can learn, Mr. B's opinions are founded on more comprehensive views of the nature & end of Government, than those of his adversaries. His error lies in notions too enthusiastic of the ease with which just principles may be carried into effect. He draws his inferences, too much, from the character of *Man*; &, too little, from the principles of *Men*. If my ideas concerning him are just, it is only necessary for him to reflect & observe, at a distance from public life, a few years longer, & he will relinquish his errors, while his principles will be confirmed: he will advocate *federalism* on the foundation of *democracy*. I may be mistaken; and, should he prematurely engage in politics, probably shall be. I now speak without knowlege; & by conjecture only. The acquaintance of a day, will determine me on this subject. Till then, let us quit it. You may be sure, the regard I bear my sister, will not blind my eyes.

Your conjecture was just, in respect to Abby's letter; and your domestic intelligence was very acceptable. I have many filial feelings for Lichfield, tho' it has sent me forth "into the wide world, to seek my fortune." On one subject, in which I feel some interest, you are all silent. You are at liberty to continue so, if you deem it most proper—but I shall ask you the questions—What is true concerning Sally Tracy's forming a connection with James Gould? And what part has Mrs. T. taken in this affair? I was surprized, and grieved, when I heard of it; & I have not, (to my utter astonishment,) recd. a line from Mrs. T.[90] since I was in Lichfield.

I am glad that you find reason to be pleased with the wives of Todd & Smith;[91] as I presume I shall, likewise. With Dr. Wells I am well acquainted, and esteem him highly: with Mrs. Wells I hope to be on the same terms, erelong. At present, I am uncertain whether I ever saw her.

Present my affectionate remembrances to your sisters & to Miss Rhoda.

Farewell.

Sunday, Decr. 25, 1796.
Cedar St. No. 13. N. York.   E. H. Smith.

Sunday, 25.—Wrote the letters to Abby, Sally Pierce, and Idea. We dined at S. Johnson's—in company with Mr. Atkinson and his family; spent the afternoon there & part of the evening. Thence we (Wm. & I) went to Mr. Denning's—to see Miss Bull, I—Wm to see the family, as well as her. We found some company; but stayed after they went away. Time past off agreably enough. We called in at H. Johnson's on our return. When we came home, Wm finished reading aloud,

---

[90] The wife of Senator Uriah Tracy.

[91] William B. Todd was a merchant whose address was 36 William St., *New York Directory*, 1797. Todd and Seymour are listed as merchants in 1796, but Todd and Smith does not appear as a firm name.

Thomas Paine's Letter to George Washington,[92] which was commenced in the forenoon. Concerning this we have but one opinion, that it is full of impudence, egotism, misrepresentation, & falsehood: especially as relating to Mr. Washington, & several other distinguished characters in the United States. The publication of it, at this time, by Benjn. Franklin Bache; & the numerous similarities of sentiment & expression between this & the letter of Mr. Adet; leave room to suspect both to be a part of a concerted plan, the final cause & issue of which are yet secret & uncertain. Conjecture may be busy; but not profitably. Whatever the design may be, the effect of this publication will be more injurious to Thomas Paine, than to George Washington.

To Idea Strong

The present leisure will not permit me to write lengthily. My sister will not, therefore, impute to me any design to neglect her. She must be sensible that just conclusions, on all moral subjects, must be the result of her own reflection & investigation; that no friend can, here, supply her place; & that she rather needs hints, & directions how to proceed, than ample illustrations of every principle proposed for her adoption. The truth of a proposition may be evident, the instant it is placed before the mind; but it is doubly satisfactory when the same conviction has been attained, by a chain of thought, & by our own efforts. All it's relations & supports are then seen; & beside, the mind is invigorated by the exercise.

The conclusions to which we arrived, in our last letters, made deep & wide inroad into many of the present received opinions of men. It was an undertaking worthy of your mind to examine the principal doctrines of moralists, in relation to them. This might well be accomplished, in the Journal form; where you can break off, & resume, your inquiries, at your leisure; & are not bound down to any formal line, but may divide your subject into as many heads as you find convenient. I shall be ready to give you every assistance in my power, whenever called upon; & wish you to propose difficulties, when they occur, with all sincerity.

If man be born with capacities only, if he depend entirely, on external impressions for character, in what sense can he be considered as a Free-Agent? If his actions are the result of necessity, where is the criterion of virtue & vice? What propriety is there in the idea annexed to Crime? What is the object & nature of Punishment?

These are, all, important topics; & require much thought, & separate, yet connected inquiry. No moral being can be excused from the labor of attempting their elucidation. On that hang the essential principles of social & political welfare. You will not shrink from the task: a soul like yours, will court difficulties, and invite occasions for exertion. Assure yourself of my ready co-operation, and stedfast regard.

Sunday, Decr. 25. 1796.
Cedar St. No. 13. N. York.   E. H. Smith.

Monday, Decr. 26.—Ch. B. Brown breakfasted here. I had been writing a short time, when Jereh. Mason came in. He sat a little while, when Mr. Dana,[93] of Middletown, (Connec.) on his way to Congress, entered—having, unfortunately, fallen on the ice, near our house, & dislocated his wrist. The rectifying of this mishap, & his visit occupied us till two. After dinner I resumed the pen. But, before sun-down, went to see Mr. Dana at his lodgings. Found Alsop & Brown here when I returned. The latter stayed till 7. I then went to Moses Rogers's, where I remained till 9, & then came home. I have transcribed my letters to Abby, Fanny, Idea, & Sally Pierce. I have recd. letters from Drs. Cogswell & N. Dwight. I have read 27 pages in Zoonomia, P. II.

Tuesday, 27.—Our milk-man played us a trick, a second time; & we lost an hour in moment expectation of his coming. I was not ready to go out when Dr. Kissam called to go to visit Mr. Dana. We found him comfortable. I transcribed my letter to Mary; & wrote one to Mrs. Lovegrove. Then I called on Lucy Bull, & went with her, to see Mrs. Johnson, the actress. We spent an hour with her, & her husband, agreably; & are to dine with them on Tuesday of next week. I have read somewhat more than seventy pages in Zoonomia, P. II—this day, & evening. Alsop & Brown here. A medical visit. Spent the evening at Dunlap's.

Wednesday, 28.—Ch. B. Brown breakfasted here. Read a few pages in Zoonomia. A visit from Lynde Catlin, & his father—Mr. Catlin, of Lichfield. Went with Dr. Kissam to see Mr. Dana. Called at Fellows's Book-Store—where I saw an engraved portrait of General Buonaparte. He looks very much like one of our Indians. Visited Mr. Webster, at his office. Went to see Dr. Mitchill—who read me a Mss. account of his Experiments &c.—on the Tartar of the Teeth. While there, Mr. Robertson—formerly, Dr. Stark, of Bath (Engd.)[94] came in. He seems a sensible man. I brought away with me Count of Rumford's Essays—and I have read, with peculiar pleasure, on many & every accounts, the first & part of the second, Essay. Wrote a letter, last evening, & another to-day, (the first to Dr. Elisha North of Goshen, the other to Dr. Joshua Porter of Salisbury—Connec—) relative to "The Medical Re-

---

[92] One of the most detailed discussions of the numerous attacks on Washington by Paine and others is to be found in Stewart, *The Opposition Press of the Federalist Period*. Specific ref.: "Letter to George Washington," Dec. 25, 1796. Published by Bache.

[93] Samuel Whittlesey Dana (1760-1830; Yale, 1775) from Wallingford, Connecticut, Lawyer who practised in Middletown. Connecticut General Assembly 1789-1796; Federalist who filled vacancy left by Tracy in U.S. House, 1797-1810; U.S. Senator, 1810-1821; Mayor, Middletown, Connecticut, 1810-1830.

[94] Smith never sees fit to enlighten us as to why Dr. Stark became Mr. Robertson although he is occasionally mentioned hereafter.

pository." A professional visit. Spent the evening, chiefly, at Mr. Catlin's.

Thursday, 29.—Visited Mr. Dana, in company with Dr. Kissam. An errand carried me to Dunlap's; & to Woolsey's Store. Here I saw M. B. Whittlesey, of Danbury. Came home, and finished my letter to my father. Dunlap came here; read, & was extremely pleased with, one or two chapters, in Count Rumford's Essays. Dined at Woolsey's—in company with Mr. Timothy Edwards,[95] of Stockbridge (Mass.) A long walk, to see the Lichfield Post. Recd. a letter from Mumford, who is at Lichd. with his family. Went to Mr. Catlin's—to leave letters for Ld.—& executed two other errands. Ch. B. Brown here—& read much in Rumford's Essays—& much to his gratification. Drank tea at Dunlap's. Kent & his wife, & Mrs. Woolsey there. Called at Riley's—but they were not at home. Spent two hours at Boyd's. Came home, & read in Rumford's Essays—till after eleven. I have now finished the Second & Third Essays—& my veneration & love of the man increase with every page.

Friday, 30.—Ch. B. Brown breakfasted here. Medical visit, as usual. Errands. Finished the First Volume of Count Rumford's Essays. I have read this book with great pleasure, but with great haste. This last was a matter of necessity; as my time is limited. It has (I mean the book) given me some new ideas; revived, strengthened, & extended previous conceptions; led to interesting trains of thought; & will, hereafter, be one of my School Books. I long to see the additional volume, or volumes. Began President Edwards's essay, "on the nature of True Virtue."[1] Alsop here in the afternoon. He went with Kissam & me to see Dana. We spent an hour or two, very agreably there. At the Theatre. "Siege of Belgrade," first played here—"Modern Antiques"[2]—I saw for the first time. The last, nonsense; the first, a showy piece, of harmless nothingness, with the exquisite music of the late Stephen Storace.

Saturday, 31.—We made our last professional visit, to Mr. Dana, this morning. An errand. Jh. Mason, Alsop, & Brown here, in the forenoon. Read the newspapers. A visit from Dr. Mitchill. Finished Edwards's Essay, intituled, "The Nature of True Virtue." Alsop here, in the afternoon. A visit from Decius Wadsworth—who comes from Phila. & is going to Georgia to spend the winter. Club night—& my turn—late in collecting—Present—Alsop, Brown, Dunlap, Johnson, Smith, the Woolseys: Kent goes to Albany tomorrow. I read the Introduction, & first & seventh chapters of Count Rumford's First Essay—with which all seemed pleased. The meeting was not productive of much entertainment. W. W. Woolsey had been on the Patrole, last night; Geo. M. Woolsey, had ridden twenty three miles in the wind; Dunlap was here but a few minutes—there being a Play acted to-night; & no one seemed to feel any generous elevation of spirits, or ideas.

Here endeth the week; and with it, this month of December; and, therewith, the good Year 1796.

Industry of December 1796

Have read in this Month—

"Essays, Political, Economical, and Philosophical." by Benjamin Count of Rumford. Vol. I. pages, 464—8vo. common print.

"The Nature of True Virtue." an Essay by Jonathan Edwards Senr.—83 pages—12mo. closed-printed.

"Account of the Management of the Poor in Hamburgh, since the Year 1788." by Mr. Voight. p. 63—8vo. common print.

"Letters on Emigration, by a gentleman lately returned from America."—p. 76.—8vo. loose print.

"Observations on the Small Pox, & Inoculation," &c. by Alex. Aberdom. p. 98—8vo. common.

"Zoonomia," P. II.—4th. p. 336—large; & common print.

"Man as he is." Novel. Vols. 2.—12mo. Thick, close-printed—p.—

"Usong." An Oriental Tale, by Baron Haller. Large 12mo. Close print—p—300—about.

"Travels before the Flood." 2 vols.—small 12mo.—large print—p. perhaps—400.

"The chaste loves of Peter the Long &c." by Thos. Holcroft.—18°.

"Asiatic Researches"—Vol. IInd.—(except six papers —) 8vo.—common print—p. 300.

"Thoughts on the means of preserving the health of the Poor &c." 8vo. p. 27.

"Thomas Paine to Geo. Washington." 8vo p—

Miscellaneous Papers in the New Annual Register, for 1795—large 8vo & very close print—p.—300—and upwards.

"On the propriety of the term, usually employed in Scripture, to express the virtuous character."—a Sermon, by Josh. Fawcett. large-printed 8vo.—p. 27.

Have written in this Month—

On the Plague of Athens—equal to 40 common 8vo. pages.

Letters—copies of which are here preserved—equal to 12—pages.

A short scrap on Inoculation.

Ten or twelve Letters, on the Medical Repository.

Several others of friendship, of various length.

---

[95] Mr. Timothy Edwards of Stockbridge, Massachusetts (1738-1813; College of New Jersey Princeton 1757). He was the sixth child and oldest son of Jonathan Edwards; member of the Continental Congress; one of the commissioners to settle the boundary between New York and Massachusetts in 1784; judge of probate for Berkshire County, Massachusetts, 1778-1787. William H. Edwards, *Timothy and Rhoda Ogden Edwards of Stockbridge, Massachusetts, and their Descendants* (privately printed, Cincinnati, 1903), p. 20.

[1] Jonathan Edwards (1703-1758). *An Essay on the Nature of True Virtue*. Published, apparently for the first time (New London, 1785).

[2] James Cobb, *The Siege of Belgrade* (1791). John O'Keefe, *Modern Antiques, or the Merry Mourners* (1791).

Labored, somewhat, on my intended Pharmacopoiea. To this may be added the mechanical industry of transcribing my long letter to Theodore Dwight.

MEMOIRS. 1797. JANUARY.

Sunday, 1st.—Read the three first of Dr. Van Troil's "Letters on Iceland."[3] Wm. and I made several visits: to Mr. Dana, H. Johnson, S. Johnson, S. Riley's—& he to others, & I at Hodgkinson's. We dined late, at Mr. Atkinson's, & spent the afternoon. Called on Miss Bull, in the evening—who was not at home. Visited Dana. Were on the Patrole all night.[4] In the intervals of duty, were at home—reading Count Rumford's Essays.

Monday, 2.—It was late when we rose. Ch. B. Brown came in while we were at breakfast. Called upon Mr. Dana; who, as I suppose, left town to-day. Johnson & I visited Miss Bull & Miss Denning. Thence, we went to Mrs. Morton's. We dined at H. Johnson's. Found Brown here when we came home. Alsop called here; & Dunlap. At the house of the last, I drank tea & went to the Theater with Miss Parker, Mrs. Dunlap, & her children John & Margaret—who went for the first time. "Much ado about Nothing"—& "The Sultan"[5]—both well played. Mr. Hodgkinson's *Benedick*, & Mrs. Johnson's *Beatrice*; & Hallam's *Dogberry*, & Jefferson's *Verges*, were excellent. Recd. a short letter from my father.

Tuesday, 3.—Most of the forenoon employed in making out a catalogue of books sent to me, by Mrs. Lovegrove, to be sold at auction. A medical visit. An errand. A call from Mr. Miller. Waited on Miss Bull, & went with her to Mrs. Johnson's. Came home, & looked over Lempriere's Travels,[6] till dinner time. I dined with Mr. & Mrs. Johnson; of our Theater, in company with Miss Bull; & past the afternoon pleasantly. Mr. Jefferson, his wife, & her sister, drank tea there. Accompanied Miss Bull to Mr. Denning's—where I heard her play on the harp—(the first time of my hearing that instrument,) & Miss Denning on the Piano Forte. A medical visit. Amused myself—not being in a humor for study, with Thicknesse's Memoirs[7]—which Alsop left here yesterday—in which I read 100 pages, after 10 o'clock.

Wednesday, Jany. 4.—Made some further progress in compiling my Pharmacopoeia. Alsop & Ch. B. Brown here. A medical visit. Errands. Read the Newspapers; & some pages in Thicknesse's Memoirs. Much of the afternoon at Dingley's. The evening, partly at a special meeting of the Trustees of the African School; partly at W. W. Woolsey's. I have not felt equal to much exertion this day; & have given way too much, to my feelings.

Thursday, 5.—Some writing for the Manumission Society &c. and some errands, occupied most of the forenoon. Called on Miss Bull—who goes to Hartford, tomorrow. Finished "Memoirs & Anecdotes of Philip Thicknesse &c." 8vo.—common print—Dublin edition—pages 421—a book which I have read, for the same reason that some people get drunk, to drown care & banish unpleasing reflections. Wrote a few lines to my father. A medical visit. Spent the evening at Dunlap's. The circular address, concerning "The Medical Repository," was published in this evening's Minerva.

Friday, 6.—Ch. B. Brown breakfasted here. A medical visit, & another. Agreed with a printer for 50 subscription papers for my Opera. Alsop twice here. Read in Zoonomia, P. II, from p. 336, to p. 442. Drank tea at Dunlap's. At the Theater, in the evening—where I saw "The Man of Ten Thousand"—it being the first presentation. Thin house; players, mostly imperfect; pretty well played, notwithstanding; piece went off pretty well.

Saturday, 7.—Medical visit. Alsop here, several times; and Brown; and Dingley. Executed some errands. Recd. a letter from Wm Buel. Read, in Zoonomia, P. II—from p. 442, to 504, inclusive. The evening, being Club night—& Dunlap's turn—at his house—a thin meeting. Present—Brown, Dunlap, Smith, & the Woolseys. Two alarms of fire—which proved to be only from chimneys—did not contribute to our amusement. Trifling conversation, for the most part. Dunlap is printing his comedy of two acts, intituled "Tell Truth and shame the Devil."[8] The piece is to be played on Monday evening; & advertised for sale, on Tuesday morning. I fear with no great success, in either respect. Show & bustle, for interest & character & plot; & eating a pudding, for wit & humour; pass off better, with an audience, than Othello & Iago, Benedick & Beatrice. It is the infirmity of the times, & must be endured, for wisely saith the proverb—"What can't be cured, *must* be endured."[9]

Sunday, 8.—Drew off several accounts, from my Ledger, for collection. Wrote a letter to Mr. Tracy. Read, before breakfast, several articles in Mrs. Piozzi's Italy.[10] Called at H. Johnson's. Dined, and spent much of the afternoon at S. Johnson's. Wm & I drank tea at Riley's. Saw there, for the first time, a Miss Howland,

---

[3] Uno von Troil, M.D., *Letters on Iceland; containing Observations on the Civil, Literary, Ecclesiastical and Natural History etc.* (London, 1780).

[4] The Patrole comprised a volunteer group of about 200 citizens who took turns patrolling the streets to guard against fires.

[5] Isaac Bickerstaffe, *The Sultan: or, A Peep into the Seraglio* (1775).

[6] William Lempriere, *A Tour from Gibraltar to Tangiers, Sallee, Mogadore, Santa Cruz, etc., and Thence over Mount Atlas to Morocco; including a particular Account of the Royal Harem, etc.* (London, 1791).

[7] Philip Thicknesse, *Memoirs and Anecdotes of Philip Thicknesse, late Lieutenant-Governor of Languard Fort, and unfortunately father to George Touchet, Baron Audley* (1788-1791).

[8] This was an unusual procedure, printing a play before it was performed. See later.

[9] Burton, *Anatomy of Melancholy*, Part ii, Sec. 21, Mem. 3.

[10] Mrs. Hester Lynch Piozzi, *Observations and Reflections made in the course of a Journey through France, Italy, and Germany* (London, 1789).

of Norwich; a pleasing young lady. Spent part of the evening at Mrs. Morton's. We came home; & I have, since, read from the 504th p. of Zoonomia, to The Theory of Fever; & also the additions, which follow it. I must defer the reading of this Theory, for the present: especially if I determine on visiting Connecticut.

Monday, 9.—Ch. B. Brown breakfasted here. Wrote several snip-snap letters, to inclose subscription-papers for my Opera. Alsop here. Visited Dr. Mitchill & Mr. Miller. Read the three last lectures, of the third volume of David Williams's lectures,[11] &, in the evening, the five first, of the first volume—in all, 136—very loose-printed 8vo. pages. I am much pleased with what I have read. Dr. Mitchill, Mr. Miller, Brown, & Alsop, all here, in the afternoon. Drank tea at Boyd's. Went to the Theater in season to see "Tell truth, & shame the Devil"—for the first time. The night was extremely cold—the audience thin—the piece moral—is it wonderful that it did not produce bursts of applause? Yet there was some, in several parts. But not enough to satisfy the wishes of one, who longs to see a deserving piece well received.

Tuesday, 10.—I have finished this day, forenoon, afternoon, & morning—reading it by snatches, the first volume of Williams's Lectures; a work of uncommon merit. Various errands, which occupied much of the morning. Dunlap, Alsop, & Brown here. In the afternoon, walked out to Mr. Webster's, where I stayed till six. Was at Dunlap's—& at Mrs. Kent's, till nine. Have read since, in the work of above-mentioned; & hurriedly, but sufficiently, turned over the leaves of Don Silvio de Rosalva[12]—of Wieland—a book which lies among other rubbish, on my floor—which several of us have thrown together, to be sent to the auctioneer.

Wednesday, 11.—This day has been most unprofitably spent. Ch. B. Brown breakfasted here. Most of the forenoon occupied in making out a Catalogue of old books, for auction: for the last time, as I trust. Alsop went to Connecticut to-day. Several errands. Felt very stupid after dinner. Mr. Roulet visited us. Looked over Blacklock's Poems,[13] for amusement—but found none. It rained this evening—Ch. B. Brown spent it with us. Discourse on the idea of a God: Theism & atheism. Since he went away, have yawned over the Jockey Club[14]—second part. Better have been in bed. But I am unfit for serious employment, in my irresolution concerning a visit to Ld.

Thursday, Jany. 12.—I fully intended to have begun my journey to Lichfield tomorrow; but I found, on inquiry at the Stage office, that it was impossible; and, if no accident present, I shall proceed, on Monday next. Several errands, &c. occupied most of the morning. Ch. B. Brown here. Dunlap came in; &, with him, James Brown—Charles's brother, from Phila. He sat here an hour. Jerh. Mason spent another hour here. I gave him copies of the Medical Address, to send to New Hampshire & Vermont. Recd. letters from Mr. Tracy & my Father. Wrote to the latter. A long walk. Dingley here, much of the afternoon. Before he went away, Ch. & Jas. Brown came in. The last stayed till seven, in the evening; the former, till nine. Since then, I have written a letter to Wm. Buel.

Friday, 13.—Ch. B. Brown and James Brown breakfasted here. Dunlap came in, after breakfast. It was eleven when I sat down to labour on my Dispensatory. After dinner, I read the first lecture, of the second volume of David Williams's. I went to Dunlap's. He, Charles, & I walked out of town, and it was after four when we returned. Dunlap came home with me. James Brown came in; & sate till six, when he & Johnson went to the Theater. I spent the chief part of the evening at H. Johnson's. Since my return, I have read in David Williams's Lectures—& have made progress, this day —175 pages.

Saturday, 14.—Read the News-Paper, which was uncommonly interesting. One column of the Herald is equal to three octavo pages. Fifteen columns, therefore, form a busy hour's work. I have laboured, much of the day on my Dispensatory. Dr. Miller has returned; & made me a visit. Ch. B. & James Brown were, also, here. The former, in the afternoon. Continued the reading of David Williams's Lectures—and have attained to the 252 page, of the second volume. This being Club night, & Johnson's turn, the members were to meet here. It has been rainy, all day; & rained hard, in the beginning of the evening. Present, Brown, Dunlap, Johnson, & Smith. Johnson read the three first lectures, from the second volume of David Williams—much to our pleasure. Dunlap read us some passages from his play, on which he has been employed, at intervals, so long—and which, I believe, he designs to call "The Fall of Robespierre."[15] What he read was pleasing.

Sunday, 15.—Most of the morning busied in making preparation for my journey. Ch. B. & James Brown here. Wm. & I called at H. Johnson's; & dined, & spent the afternoon, with James Brown, at S. Johnson's.

---

[11] Rev. David Williams, *Lectures on Education; read to a Capital Society for promoting reasonable and humane Improvements in the Capital discipline and Instruction of Youth* (London, 1789).

[12] *Don Silvio de Rosalva,* trans. from the German (London, 1773).

[13] Thomas Blacklock (1721-1791), a blind English poet. He published at various times, 1754 ff. The volume Smith had was probably *Poems, together with an Article on Education of the Blind* (Edinburgh, 1793).

[14] Anonymous publication of Charles Pigott (d. 1794). *A History of the Jockey Club* was a gossipy and abusive attack on London society as seen from the inside (London, 1792). It was followed in 1794 by *A History of the Female Jockey Club.* The first mentioned book went into at least twelve editions in the first year and was reprinted in America.

[15] Coad, *Dunlap,* pp. 179-180: "For two titles in Dunlap's bibliography I have no data. *Forty and Twenty* and *Robespierre* were apparently neither acted nor printed and I am unable to say whether they were written, or whether they were originals or translations." It is obvious from the "Diary" entry that at least part of the second play was written and, by implication, was original. See also entry for January 30, 1796.

There I saw General Lincoln, if not for the first time, yet for the first time to any purpose. I shall now remember him. Wm & I walked on the Battery; & then drank tea at Riley's. Geo: M. Woolsey was there, & informed me that Dr. Dwight was in town. I went to William W. Woolsey's. I found Ch. B. Brown there. Soon after Dr. Dwight came in. We had—all of us—a long, various, & interesting conversation; & parted at ten.

Monday, 16.—Finished the second volume of David Williams's Lectures, & wrote a letter to Mr. Tracy, last evening. Ch. B. Brown breakfasted with us. Made several calls. James Brown came to see us. He goes to Phila. to-day. Left New York, in the Mail Stage, at a little past eleven A. M. No company worthy of particular notice. Reached Rye.

Tuesday, 17.—Came to New Haven this evening—safely: 57 miles. Waited on Mrs. Dwight, this evening. Found all well. Genl. Lincoln[16] overtook us, in his extra carriage, this evening; & I relinquished my seat in the Stage to him. Have a prospect of a direct conveyance to Lichfield, in the morning.

Wednesday, 18.—Saw Mr. Todd & Mr. Burt, from Lichfield. Fine sleighing. Left N. Haven, in a one-horse sleigh, with a man of the name of Pope, about one P.M. We reached Lichfield at ten in the evening. I found Mumford, Mary, & their little son, still here; & with all the family quite well. This has been a safe & pleasant journey. Expences on the road:

Stage, from N. York to New Haven	6..10
Food &c. from N. York to Lichfield	3..34
Sleigh, from N. Haven to Lichfield	3..00
	12..44
Expences on my return	9..31
	21..75

Thursday, 19.—Spent the chief part of the day at home. Drank tea, with most of the family, & spent the evening, at Mrs. Tracy's. All well. The children have grown exceedingly; except Sally; with the propriety of whose manners I was much pleased.

Friday, 20.—Danl. W. Lewis called here, to-day; as did Mr. Lord, yesterday. I went to Lewis's, called on Mr. Allen, & Mr. Collier. Drank tea & spent the evening, at Dr. Catlin's—with my sisters, & Mr. Mumford.

In a settlement of my private acct. with my father, this day, I gave him my Note of hand for £413..4..5½ Connecticut Currency—being, if I mistake not, equal to £552..5..11—money of New York; or 1380 dols. .. 74 cts.—Thomas Mumford & Daniel Huntington[17] witnesses.—1380..74

Saturday, 21.—Spent the forenoon at home. I looked over one tome of Abby's Journal. It is more ample & valuable than I expected. More so as a picture of her affections & sentiments, than as an exhibition of intellectual operations, as distinguished therefrom. After dinner, visited at Miss Pierce's & Mr. Lord's. When I came home I found Mr. Morris here, with his wife & daughter. All well. In the evening, recd. a short letter from Ch. B. Brown; read the News-Papers, conversed —&c.

Sunday, 22.—Spent the forenoon at home. I have read, since I have been here, by snatches, more than two hundred pages in the London edition of Dr. Aikin's Letters to his son.[18] Mr. Ezekiel Bacon appears, from his letters to my sister Abby, which I have this day read, a sensible & worthy man. The solicitations of my parents, contrary to my inclinations, prevailed on me to accompany them to Church. The preacher, a Mr. Huntington, a young man, now a tutor in Yale College, gave us a handsome & moral discourse; with which I was more pleased than I expected. I was at Mrs. Tracy's a short time, in the evening. She gave me a letter—lest we should not have opportunity for a conversation. I have read it with mingled emotions of pity, pleasure, & indignation. It increases my respect for her; & is a new, & interesting mark of her confidence. I was recalled to receive company at home. Mr. Wolcott, Allen, Holmes, Skinner, Todd, Burt, Sheldon, &c. were here. Dr. Buel arrived about nine o'clock. We lay together [not clear]; & have indulged in medical & friendly conversation.

Monday, 23.—Buel & I called at several places—Collier's & Allen's, in particular. He went over to Chestnut-Hill. Mary & I called at Mr. Lord's & Miss Pierce's. In the afternoon, Mumford & I visited Govr. Wolcott & Mr. Reeve. We drank tea, & spent the evening at Danl. W. Lewis's. His wife seems more amiable than ever, & he has a fine child. A long & animated conversation, on Education & several collateral subjects, which occupied us the whole evening, was occasioned by the boy's suddenly throwing his shoe into the fire, & being whipt by his father. As usual, no conviction followed our debate.

Memoranda

Subscription Papers—for Edwin & Angelina—

No. 28, 29—left with	Dr. Buel.
30.	Mr. Hubbard.
31.	Mr. Allen.
32.	Mr. Collier.
27.	R. Smith.

— — — — — —

Just before I left New York—I had paid for Mr. Mumford, for the materials for a cloak, for

his wife, ...	21..25
I had recd. from him	12..50
	8..75

---

[16] Major General Benjamin Lincoln (1733-1810). In the Revolution he succeeded Howe and attempted to drive the British out of Georgia. In 1787, commanding federal troops, he broke up Shay's Rebellion in Massachusetts.

[17] Daniel Huntington (1774-1864; Yale, 1794). Licensed to preach as a Congregational minister, 1796; tutor at Williams College, 1794-1796, and at Yale, 1796-1798. He became an assistant to Smith's old teacher, the Rev. Judah Champion, in 1798.

[18] John Aikin, M.D., *Letters from a Father to his Son, on*

My father sent me 20 dols. out of which I was to pay three for his Herald a year.

The sum above, subtracted from the 20— is— . . . . 11..25
Deducting the three . . . . 3.
                                                 8..25

Which should be the charge to Cash, on my book, instead of—5..25—as it now stands. & Mr. Mumford still owes me for two years' Herald.

The three dollars, for my jaunt from New Haven, were paid by my father.

Tuesday, 24.—I was disappointed when I learnt, this morning, that Mrs. Tracy was to spend the day at the South Farms. I meant to have devoted the forenoon, at least, to conversation with her. Dr. Buel went to Chestnut-hill. Read my sister Fanny's Journal. It contains marks of industry—equal, not to my wishes, but to my expectations. Most of the day conversing [with] my parents & sisters. At Lewis's a little while, in the afternoon. Our family drank tea at Mr. Lord's. I came away about six, & went to Mrs. Tracy's; where I spent the evening. We talked on various topics.[1] Her children, & niece, were all present. I found that when Theodore was at Lichfield, my conduct & sentiments were a subject of conversation between him & Mrs. Tracy; & that he had, then, mentioned his desire of writing such a letter, as he has since sent me. I thought it proper to acquaint Mrs. T. that the letter had been recd. & replied to. As Theodore had discoursed with sufficient freedom, not to be misunderstood, of the nature of our difference in opinion; there appeared to be no impropriety in shewing her his letter. I carried this with me, suspecting (from something said by Mr. Allen, when last here,) that Theodore had spoken to several of my friends, on the subject; & determining to be explicit with all—even my parents—if need were. In this case, I meant to have laid his letter, & my reply, before them—as being, perhaps, the best method of explaining myself. But for this, so far as related to my parents, there was no occasion. When I had read Theodore's letter, I proceeded to read my answer. For this I had several reasons. In the first place, there was nothing in it which I wished hid from any body: I was especially desirous of acquainting Mrs. T. with my sentiments, in a more methodic manner than I could well do, in conversation; because they were my sentiments—because the opinions were likely to have some effect on her mind—because, I thought them just, & important to be recd.—& because some better sources of information, on points therein treated of, were interdicted her. Further than this, it appeared to me probable that my letter would be shewn, by Theodore, to many of our common friends; and I did not wish any to suppose I was driven by such a circumstance, to shew, what I would otherwise have concealed; but, on the contrary, that I had a willingness & even a desire, to acquaint them with its contents. Nor who I influenced (as I believe,) any farther, by this motive, than as I regarded the consequences which might be drawn, from a contrary step, to the prejudice of what I believe to be the truth. In addition to these reasons, I thought it not improbable that a knowlege of the opinions contained in my letter, might, gradually, extend to many of my acquaintance; & that some of them might come to converse with Mrs. Tracy on the subject, as tho' she were also acquainted with them. In this case, were she ignorant how far how I had been explicit, she might be awkwardly situated; &, knowing the effects of the cry of infidelity against any one, might feel obligated to preserve silence, or equivocate, or explain away my meaning. From this dilemma I wished to preserve her, from an ample disclosure of all that any body could know. Thus she might not be obliged to conceal any thing; & could, with the more effect, contradict misrepresentations, if any should, by any means, appear. I proceeded, therefore, to read my reply. All her children were present. But, what I had to read, was true—was important: if she saw no objection, I could have none. They continued in the room during the whole reading—which lasted more than an hour. One was of an age, & of a mind, to comprehend the whole; & two others could well perceive that the big book, called the Bible, was spoken of, as of no import & value, in a religious view. Mr. Gould, a gentleman who boards there; has lately been admitted to the Bar; & was formerly a Tutor in Yale College; came in, while I had five or six pages to read. I did not stop. Mr. Allen was to visit me, at my father's. I left word, when I went out, where I was going; & requested him to follow me. He entered Mrs. Tracy's, when I had a page or two to read. I finished my letter. Some little talk ensued, when I had gone thro'; but it was late; & I took my leave. I wished for further opportunity of conversation with Mrs. T.—but have not time. I shall write to her soon; & mean to lead her to a more precise delivery of her own notions, on questions of the nature above-referred to, than she has yet indulged in. If I am not greatly deceived, her opinions have been gradually changing, for some years past. She gave a moral impulse to my mind; my sentiments must have influenced hers.

Wednesday, 25.—I did not see Idea, to take leave of her this morning. She went to spend a day or two with an Aunt—before her journey with Mary, to Cayuga. This young woman has a remarkably vigorous understanding; with some obstinacy & asperity of temper, but an excellent disposition. Persecuted as she was by that wretch, her father; deprived, in great measure of the means & opportunities for instruction; it is wonderful that she is so amiable, as she appears, & that her mind has made such bold advances. I presented her with Condorcet's Posthumous Work. I left Fawcett's Sermons with my parents—& recommended their perusal, on explicit grounds, to Mrs. Tracy. Mary carries with her, my copy of Aikin's Letters. This excellent sister appears rather to have improved, than otherwise. Her child is a fine boy; & rather handsome; of an

---

[1] *various Topics, relative to Literature, and the Conduct of Life* (London, 1796).

active, lively, affectionate, & tractable disposition: as such, a proper object of love to all—especially to parents. I have rarely seen as much good sense discovered by parents, as by Thomas & Mary.

Mr. Allen, & Mr. T. Pierce, were at our house this morning, to inquire concerning the latter's coming to New York, to complete his medical education.

Dr. Buel & I sat off, in an open sleigh, for Sheffield. The day was severely cold; we rode north; & the wind was in our faces. We stopt in Goshen—where I called at Mr. Kettle's, Dr. Jill's, & Mr. Hooker's. All well. We reached Sheffield (30 miles) in good season. I was introduced to Mrs. Buel. She appears mild, modest, sensible, & amiable. Her figure is delicate & interesting —& rendered still more so, by a first pregnancy. Her face pleasing, rather than handsome; & her mouth peculiarly sweet. It is a match of affection, more than passion; & seems likely to continue. We were hardly yet warm, when the father of Mrs. Buel came in. He was Captain, in the late Continental Army: a man of observation & sound sense. Buel tells me that he never saw him out of humour in a family of five daughters—tho' he is of a warm & glowing temper: for it is tempered with a philosophy of better ages. He sat half an hour. We conversed. There was a little too much of the soldier in what he said: But a man can not always be known in half an hour. Supper over, we learnt that there was to be a Dance near by. I perceived that my friend would be glad to join the company, for a short time; & to have me go with him. I thought of it with some reluctance, at first; but the novelty of such an act gave it some recommendation. But we had a medical consultation to go thro' with, first. To ride thirty miles directly north of Lichfield, that I might reach New York, which is more than a hundred to the south west; to accomplish this journey in one of the severest days, of a severe winter; to consult, gravely, on the health of a sick man; & then fly to a dance; were circumstances & performances too charmingly incongruous not to come with many recommendations to a mind in the frame mine then happened to be. So we drest for the Ball; went to see our patient; & then repaired to the Assembly-room. The valetudinarian was Mr. Lee; a man of some learning & ability; & of considerable eminence as a lawyer in his county. His case was complicate; & we devoted an hour to examination, & history, & interrogatories. We found at the Ballroom, near forty pairs. I danced twice, (for the first time, I believe, in more than three years—) & both times with Miss Polly Bacon, a fine looking young lady & the sister of Mrs. Buel. Not more than ten of the young ladies collected here, would have been called ordinary, in New York— & as many as ten, were quite handsome. We came off, in season. We had, then, to discuss Mr. Lee's case. We did so; & I proposed a method of cure—for the present; & a plan for a permanent restoration; for the mind of our patient seemed as much distempered as his body. During our ride, we had talked much on professional topics: they engaged our attention afresh; & we made some verbal arrangements relative to a part of our concerns. The conversation, now, took on a more general turn; Mrs. Buel bore a part in it; & it was near twelve, when we separated to repose—after the various labours of the day.

Thursday, 26.—I took leave of my Sheffield friends, & got into the Vermont & New York Stage, at 10 this morning. We were six passengers in all: A Young man, who had been up to the ball, the preceding evening, & who left us, after riding four miles; a rum-drinking, tobacco-chewing, germano-gallic barber, baker, balloonist & wit, with his humble satellite, an english beard-clipper & politician; the fiddler, who had so musically invited us to the exercise of our toes, the last night; a pretty young miss, who was going from Sheffield, where she had been at School, on a visit to her parents; and myself. As I was a passenger for the whole distance, I was complimented with a back seat; & that being a matter of politeness, also, the young lady was placed by my side. The sleighing was remarkably fine; seven miles & less than an hour, brought us to the house of my fair companion. The School at Sheffield is of the higher kind; & under the sole management of my friend Dr. Buel; who procures teachers, &c. &c. There are more than thirty young men & women there —chiefly from neighboring towns—who are instructed in Arithmetic, Penmanship, Geography, Grammar, Elocution, & the Greek & Latin Languages. They are now preparing for a Quarter-day; when they are to exhibit several dramatic & other pieces. My companion gave me the cast of "The Heiress," which was one of the pieces; & in which she had a part of some consequence. After leaving her, we proceeded, right dully, to Salisbury, where we dined; & I left all my company, save the sawer on the fiddle. He, indeed, had much entertained us all, on the former part of the road; torturing his instrument in unusual combinations of sound; to the great delight of the driver—who shuffled his feet, whipt his leaders, & urged his wheel-horses in symphonious unison. After dinner, we proceeded together in an open sleigh. The weather was mild, the sky clear, and a gentle breeze played from the south. The scraper of cat-gut began now to exhibit himself in a new light; & of a sudden broke forth upon me as a moralist & philosopher. He descanted, very feelingly, on the advantages, for business, which arose from the long period of fine going we had experienced this season, "but," said he, affectingly—"there is never a convenience, without an inconvenience, as the old saying is—never was such a scant time known for water. Difficult to get grinding; wells dried up; brooks' most dry; people have to go some miles to water cattle; some melt snow for 'em. But we must take it as't comes—the lean with the fat. Have you ever heard"—said he, abruptly changing the subject—"have you heard any *account* for the cold weather, after so much warm?" "Now"—continued he —"we have had scarcely any sleighing at all, for six or seven winters back. No business done. A little snow—then rain—all mud & *splash*. Some people think that our globe has been out of it's way; several degrees to the south; where it's warmer. What do you think?" "Why," replied I—"if it has been to the south, for some years past, it must have come back now—for we have as cold weather this winter, as we used to have." "So I tell 'em"—says he—"& for my part, I can't see any *propriety* in talking about the globe's going out of it's way. They might every bit as well talk of God's going out of his way. I believe all goes on fair & square." Here an unlucky breeze bore away the hat of my philosopher. It took some minutes to recover it. He then resumed his topic—but with an apparent forgetfulness of the opinion just delivered by him. "There's room enough"—continued the philosopher fiddler—"for the world to go every way." "To be sure"—rejoined I. "It's much warmer to the southward"—said he. "You think so?"—replied I, questioningly. "It's warmer," he answered—"a plaguy deal—& I believe that our globe has got out of it's way, some winters back, two or three degrees to the south." Just at this moment a sleigh passed, which contained one of his acquaintances, who was going to his home. He broke off his physical lecture & left me to proceed alone. The town of Sharon is a very pretty little settlement; neat, & well-built. This day's ride was remarkably pleasant; the country was new to me, & it's novelty, & romantic intermixture of mountain & valley, wood & water, rendered it peculiarly delightful. We reached a sorry inn, at Dover.

Friday, Jany. 27.—The moment of quitting New England & entering the State of New York, you find yourself in another world. The traces of cultivation, & population, except here & there, visibly, & strikingly decline. A house, here, is almost as rare as a village there. The country, notwithstanding, is healthy, well situated in every respect, & the soil good. What causes are assignable for this difference? Before the late revolutionary War almost all this region, for perhaps sixty miles, belonged to a few large proprietors, or manor-holders; & this is the present situation of many parts of it now. Confiscations took place of parts, in the meantime; troops were stationed here; & some people were scattered. Nevertheless, at the end of the war, the population was near ten to one, what it is now. This my informant assured me he knew, from the militia muster-rolls. After the war, peace was made with the Indians on the frontiers—the New England people began to settle the north-western parts of New York; there were no patents of the manorial kind, there; & the people of this territory followed their example. The country is now almost desolate. This is particularly true, when you come upon the Manors. The upper part of this country was, originally settled by Connecticut people; & was a part of that State; but was afterwards exchanged for Greenwich &c. on the Sea-coast. The people of this part—i.e. of Dover, Nine-Partners &c.—tho' not so industrious & wealthy as those of Sharon & the neighboring parts of Connecticut, are much superior to those who reside on the manors. The reason may be that they are proprietors of the soil. The differences of this in their looks—dress, & the improvements about their houses. On the manors, no repairs seem ever to have taken place. Large tracts of natural meadow are totally useless, for want of draining, which might be done at a small expence, & with great profit; & the wood is almost all cut down, near the houses, before it is half grown. I was surprized & pleased, however, during all this jaunt, at the singular beauty, or comeliness, of the people. Our landlord at Dover was a plain man—but comely; his wife fleshy, but still comely; seven or eight children, all handsome; & one little girl, beautiful. We left Dover—which consists of a few stragling houses, scattering along for some miles a little before sunrise, in an open sleigh. I had now, a companion—a good-natured, carrotty-pated son of Crispin. This day's ride was also pleasant; & the distant view of the Catskill Mountains romantically magnificent. I pass over the horrors of our breakfast, the comforts of our dinner, & come to Bedford—where we arrived in season, & put up, for the night, after a ride, on runners, of 45 miles. At Bedford, 46 miles from New York, we found a clean & comfortable house. An obliging landlord & landlady, with two sweet girls—that would be admired in the Houses of our Gov. Chancellor, or wealthy merchants—a good fire, good supper, wholesome bed, & the Herald for the week past. All these were so many conveniences which were to be shared with a Stage-full of people from New York, & two who had now joined our Carriage. We past the evening merrily. They were a "motley mixture" who came from the city. Two were Drovers—one of 45, & one of 23. The elder, & one of the others, thought the other a fine singer, & prest him to sing: he was good-natured & complied. He entertained us with three most delectable ditties—one teemed with the philosophy of Epicurus, & had for its further independence & content: one was a famous Masonic song—about King David, who told King Solomon "how far to build" the temple; how King Solomon sent unto King Hiram of Tyre; how King Hiram sent unto King Solomon, the widow's son Hiram, of the tribe of Dan; how all the materials were got together—the stones squared & fitted, & brought on wheels—

> So that no hammer might be heard,
> On that fine building for to sound.

The third song was a word of advice to all young men, against committing the grievous sin of Matrimony. This was thought so good, that it was repeated, for the benefit of the young ladies, who sat down to supper, after the guests had finished theirs. The song begins with a caution *not* to "trust to any of women-kind," who "are more changing than the *winds*"; & the concluding verse of each stanza is "A single life's the rarest." The melodious Mentor commemorates the fate of Samson—who was a very brave man; killed a vast number of

Philistines—& was not afraid of thunder, or a cannon-ball—

> He feared no cannon ball
> Nor roaring claps of thunder—

yet was ruined by a woman, who—"proved to him false-hearted." In the course of the song, three descriptions of women are particularly excepted against—the young, the tall, & the proud—

> Wed not with one that's proud, she'll never seem to love you.
> Nor marry one that's young, for she will play the fool.
> Nor yet with one that's tall, she'll always *feel above* you.

After assigning so excellent reasons, the bard comes to sum up all by shewing the consequences of marrying contrary to his injunctions—

> For some the seas have crost;
> And some their lives have lost;
> If young, they'll breed or brawl;
> They'll scorn you, if they're tall;
> And pride must have a fall:
> So the best is none at all:
> A single life's the rarest.

We slept soundly; rose early; proceeded on our way without any accident of importance (—except breaking down the carriage, five miles from Kingsbridge, & loosing off a wheel, in the streets of New York—) & I arrived early in the evening of

Saturday, Jany. 28.—At home. after a journey of near 300 miles. The riding, this last day, was bad—for the road is bad—yet better than usual: ice & snow filling up the ruts, & suffering the wheels to proceed with a more than usual facility. We had eight passengers, from the White plain's—among whom were a buxom damsel, & goodly to behold—under the protection of a middle-aged sea-captain, who might be her husband, or suitor. He was not without a spice of jealousy; & I suspect she was of a disposition to afford some cause for it. It was not altogether an unpleasant employment to watch & mark the secret workings of this lively & circumspect passion, in a man of some understanding, towards a woman who "had a roguish twinkle in her eye." They quitted us before we reached the Stage-house; & before the wheel ran off.

I found a letter, at home, from Saml. M. Hopkins, now in London: an excellent letter. William came in, soon after, & we spent the evening together, in mutual inquiry & recapitulation, till the hour of reasonable slumbers.

Sunday, 29.—Ch. B. Brown breakfasted with us. Put things in order. Attended a consultation at the Hospital. Wm. W. Woolsey called here. Made a call, myself. Dined, with Wm. at Seth's—& spent the afternoon. Spent the evening at Mr. Dunlap's—with Wm.—Came home, & wrote pages 92, 93, 94, & 95—in my Memoirs.

Monday, 30.—Wrote five pages immediately preceeding. Ch. B. Brown here, & Dunlap twice. The former read me some pages in his Journal; the latter, read me some passages, lately written, from his "Fall of Robespierre"; & left with me his little Opera of "Sterne's Maria"[19]—which I went over with great pleasure. These friends were here in the afternoon—& Wm. W. Woolsey. Recd. a letter from Mrs. Lovegrove. Made a short visit at Mr. Woolsey's. Drank tea at Dunlap's—& went with Mrs. D. & Miss Parker, to the Theater. "The Mountaineers" & "The Romp"[20]—played. Mr. Collins made his first appearance, on our stage, in the part of Kilmallock—which he played indifferently well.

Tuesday, 31.—Called at Swords's—respecting the printing of my opera. Visited Mrs. C. Riley. Called at Rutgers's, concerning the Books left with him, to sell at auction. Called on Woolsey; on Catlin, at the Bank, at Fellows's; at the Minerva Office; to see Mrs. Kent; & on Dingley, who was out. Repeated my call on him, after dinner; & finding him to be absent, went in, & sate a short time with Wortman &c. Ch. B. Brown here, in the afternoon, & Dunlap. In the evening, called at Riley's—all out; at Dr. Miller's—all out; at Prosper Wetmore's. Sate two hours, with Mrs. W. Came home, & have been reading such part of Mr. Pickering's letter to Mr. Pinckney, as is already published in the Minerva. So far as I have proceeded, the letter appears to be well written; and the arrangement, & arguments, happy & forcible.

The Month now terminated, has been too busy, & too much divided by petty cares, & little labours, to have effected much. The difference is apparent on my Memoirs. But the causes are also apparent; & will extenuate, if not justify, the narrow remains, & scanty testimonials, which these pages afford of industry & improvement. I shall be too happy, if future efforts place the succeeding months on a footing more respectable, in regard to it's predecessors.

Industry of January 1797

I have read, in the course of this month—

"Zoonomia"—large 4to. common print—from p. 336, to the Theory of Fever—and also the Additions. Lond. Edit.

Lectures on Education &c. by David Williams—the two first volumes. these are 8vo.—loose print—& may contain 500 pages. Lond. Edit.

"Memoirs & anecdotes of Philip Thicknesse &c."—8vo. —common print—pages 421—Dublin Edit.

Aikin's Letters to his son—large 12mo. common print— more than p. 200—Lond. Edit.

"Letters on Iceland &c." by Uno von Troil—8vo. loose print—near p. 60. Lond. Edit.

"Don Silvio de Rosalva"—translated from Wieland— 3 vols. 12mo. loose print—the greater part.

---

[19] *Sterne's Maria; or, The Vintage.* For some reason Dunlap did not present this opera until January 14, 1799, some months after Smith's death.

[20] Isaac Bickerstaffe (1792/3).

"The Jockey Club"—P.II.—8vo. Common print—greater part—Lond. Edit.
Piozzi's Travels—several articles—perhaps p. 50.
Lempriere's Travels—perhaps, p. 50.

I have written, in the course of this month—
On my Dispensatory, no great in effect,—tho' with labour & care equal to the composition of 20 pages 8vo.—close.
Letters, to various correspondents, of various length—nine or ten—equal, perhaps, to 20, or 30—pages—

The above is but a beggarly account of a Month's work; but I have been, much of the time, in a journeying state; & have been, otherwise, more diverted, than usual, from my proper employments.

MEMOIRS. 1797. FEBRUARY.

Wednesday, 1.—Read, in the "Letters on Iceland," from p. 58 to p. 220. Went, according to notification, to the Hospital. Dr. Mitchill & I were to have commenced our Tour of duty to-day; but, by an arrangement, for the accommodation of the Clinical Lecturer, Dr. Rodgers—we shall not enter thereon till the first of March. I accompanied Mitchill to his apartment. After dinner, read the Herald; & a pamphlet, published in 1771, by Dr. Samuel Bard, of this City, intituled—"An Inquiry into the Nature, Cause & Cure, of the Angina Suffocation, or Sore Throat Distemper &c.—which is remarkable from the writer's constantly confounding Cynanche Trachealis, & Scarlatina or Angina Maligna—& treating them as one disease. It is a pamphlet in small 8vo. of p. 33. Ch. B. Brown here, most of the day; and quite sick, in the evening, from indigestion, & consequent cholera—induced by Clams for dinner. At the Theater, in the evening. "The Comet"—a new musical comedy, in V acts, by Mr. William Milns—a Teacher of some eminence, in this city, and an Englishman, was played, for the first time. It excites much laughter, & was much applauded, by a pretty full house. The day has been rainy, with some hail; & the rain still continues. The night is dark; & the walking excessively bad & dangerous. I was therefore the more surprized to find so full a house. I came home, without staying to see the farce of "The Spoil'd Child"—and have amused myself with looking over the second volume of Camilla, Mde. D'Arblay's new novel—now republishing, here, by subscription.[21]

Thursday, Feby. 2.—The chief part of the forenoon was consumed in errands of business. I visited Dingley. Ch. B. Brown was much better to-day. A visit from Dunlap. Continued the reading of the "Letters on Iceland"—& progressed from p. 220, to p. 319. Read, also, a pamphlet—"Observations on Accidental Fires; with an account of those that have lately happened within the United States"—8vo.—p. 40—close print—Ch. B.

[21] Printed by John Bull for Samuel Campbell (New York, 1797).

Brown, as usual, spent most of the day here. We conversed, two hours, in the evening. The remainder, passed by me, at Moses Rogers's.

Friday, 3.—Before breakfast, read 64 p. in Camilla. Errands. Put the MS. of the First Act of my Opera, into the hands of the printers. Finished. "Letters on Iceland: &c. by Uno von Troil—&c." Edit. Dublin—8vo.—p. 400—Loose print, Dunlap here. We walked. Drank tea at his house. Read Dr. Mitchill's Letter to Sir Jno. Sinclair—in the New York Magazine for January. Mrs. Dunlap, the mother, informs me—That Sir Jno. Sinclair is a native of the U.S.—born at Trenton—where his father, Sir Jno. Sinclair lived; & after whose death, the present Sir Jno.—went to Gt. Britain, at the age of 10 or 12. Spent the evening at Mr. Roulet's. Mde. R.—who I saw, for the first time, since her *accouchement*, looked remarkably well. Came home—& finished the first vol. of Camilla—N. Y. edit.—p. 232—12mo. & fine print.

Saturday, 4.—Read "A Memoir, concerning the Fascinating Faculty, which has been ascribed to The Rattle-snake &c." by Dr. Barton of Philadelphia. 8vo. p. 70—common print. Wrote the head of an analysis of the Memoir—with some remarks—designed to be corrected, & enlarged—for The Medical Repository. Wrote the following letter, to Mrs. Lovegrove. Wrote, also, a hasty letter to Mr. Tracy. Read the Newspapers. After dinner, walked out to Mr. Webster's. Spent an hour there. Found Ch. B. Brown here, when I returned. Conversation. Spent the evening at Mr. Riley's: Beside the family, Mrs. H. Pollock, & Miss A. Rowland—& others of less note. The latter a very amiable, fine-tempered, well-disposed young lady. Found Charles here, reading "Camilla"—when I came home.

Yesterday, was my sister Fanny's birth-day. She is now 17 years of age. She seems very much like *the girl*; which is what I wish. It gives time for the improvement of the mind; & she will be more of the woman, in consequence.

To Mrs. Lovegrove

You have, probably, been informed, by Mr. Howlet, that your letter, from Amboy, informing me of your return from Phila., was recd. I hope you experienced no chagrin from a mere verbal message. I was busy, and my mind pre-occupied, when Mr. H. called to receive my commands; & I could not write satisfactorily to myself; & therefore, not to you.

I have been a long journey, of near 300 miles in all, to meet my sisters, from the western wildernesses. It will give you pleasure, I am sure, to learn, that they, & all my friends, were well. This visit has taken me away from my affairs; & the situation in which I found them, at my return, necessarily occupied my attention, till now. You will, hence, perceive why I did not reply to your letter, in better season.

I supposed that you had returned, by a letter I recd.

from Mr. Tracy, just before my journey to Connecticut; & my friend William confirmed my conjecture, by informing me that Miss Morton—whom I have not seen these five weeks—had heard from you, in my absense. The contents of the letter to her agreeing with mine, leave me no room to doubt of the satisfaction you derived from your journey; & enable me to receive, with self-congratulation, the testimonies of friendship with which you have honoured me, on this occasion. But I were a miserable wretch, indeed, were I incapable of a joy, more deep & more sincere, on your account, than on my own; & all I have to regret is, that the circumstances under which your journey was made, the shortness of your stay, & the situation of some of my Phila. friends, rendered it impossible for me to afford you all the aid, & communicate to your visit all the pleasure, that I was anxious you should receive. On the account of one friend, I have some explanations to offer; which, I doubt not, will prove satisfactory. Mr. Tracy was to have called upon you, the morning succeeding the last evening you were together, at Mr. Wolcott's. You might, possibly, observe that Mr. T. was affected by a Catarrh, on that evening. It grew worse, in the night; & confined him to the house, for a week or ten days. He requests me, to express his regret to you, for this prevention; & presumes that the cause will exculpate him, in your mind, from any imputation of neglect.

Your remarks on the character of this gentleman are just. He has risen, in the world, by incessant struggles with adverse fortune, & powerful antagonists; & in the early part of his career, thought himself justified to employ the same weapons against others, which they exercised against him. His passions, likewise, which were lively & violent, often & long, led him astray. If success, maturer years, & more enlightened contemplation, have rendered the use of such means less necessary, have tempered his ardor, & brought him to juster conclusions, in some respects; still, it can not be expected that they should have wrought miracles, & overturned, in two years, the habitual bias of five & thirty. To commence life, with the strongest & most irresistible incentives to obtain power & property; to have engaged in the active scenes of business, with no fixed principles, or at least no sound principles, of morality; to have been extensively employed, in the tricking profession of the Law, among a subtle people; & to have entered, early, into the career of politics; are circumstances very unfavorable, if not absolutely abhorrent, to the attainment of just, pure, & comprehensive notions, concerning the nature & distinction of man. Mr. Tracy has been more fortunate than some others. Events, calculated to impress a mind like his, in a manner terrible & profound, have operated such a change in his character, as renders him deserving of high estimation; tho' they were of a nature little adapted to strengthen any opinion in favour of the virtue of mankind. Of this, it is hardly possible that he should not doubt; but the mind which could rise superior to doubt, in such circumstances, might claim affinity to all we imagine of divine.

In answer to the remark you make concerning the expression of Mr. Washington's countenance, I may observe—That you, probably, saw him in unfavourable circumstances, to judge accurately. The habitual character of his *sober* face, is solicitude, or rather thoughtfulness. This was true of his youthful face; it must be still more so, of his face when old. When animated, in conversation, or with his family, his aspect clears up, his eye lightens; & a smile of placid enjoyment plays upon his features. You would scarcely reconize him. Such is the representation what has been made to me, by those who have known him intimately. The parade of a levee, & a drawing-room has very little in it, to call forth emotions of pleasure, from a man like him.

But I shall weary you, with my prating pen.

I have disposed of the principal part of the books; & hope to be able to collect, & transmit the money to you, soon. I am afraid the sales will fall short of your expectations. Those that were privately disposed of, were sold advantageously: But, at the Auction, Religious Books found no eager purchasers.

How does the little boy? & how, the young lady? They must prove better amusements to you, than any letters. I hope Sophy gives you no further cause of uneasiness—& that she improves in her reading, writing, &c., as much as while here.

Our friends, in New York, are all well, as I believe, & are those who have been sometime otherwise. My good friend is entrenched, up to the very ears, in parchments &c.—but he finds a port-hole thro' which to transmit his best respects.

Saturday, Feby. 4. 1797.
Cedar St. No. 13, N. York.   E. H. Smith.

Sunday, 5.—Transcribed my letter to Mrs. Lovegrove. Read p. 60, or thereabouts, in Camilla. Ch. B. Brown here. Wm. & I dined at Seth's. We walked after dinner. Came home. Read to about the 120th page in the 2nd vol. of Camilla. Wm. and I left Charles here, reading Camilla; & drank tea, & spent the evening till eight, at Mrs. Kent's. I came home the more willingly, as I meant to continue Camilla; & was somewhat disappointed when I found H. Johnson had sent, & taken it away, in our absence. Mrs. Inchbald's "Simple Story"[22] lay on the table. I had never read, but a part of the second volume, and that, some time ago: all speak well of it; and I admire her "Nature & Art." Wm., too, was intent on "Camilla"; & Charles had departed. I do not know what other circumstances would have induced me to read "A Simple Story." In my present frame of mind, a more serious employment would have been irksome. I have read the first volume

---

[22] Published, London, 1791; reprinted Philadelphia, 1793, two volumes in one. Smith says "two vols." Possibly a different edition or a different binding.

of "A Simple Story"—with great interest. It is now after twelve; and bed-time.

Monday, 6.—It rained hard, till near sun-down. Dr. Dingley was here great part of the forenoon; Ch. B. Brown, much of the day. I finished "A Simple Story," and this with the greater haste, as I must hurry thro' "Camilla"; which is in urgent demand. Of this, also, I finished the second volume. The rapid manner in which these books are run over, allows me little opportunity of reflecting on them, themselves; less of drawing useful influences from them; and least of all, of entering into an examination, moral or critical. Still, they will not have been read wholly without profit. They remain to be reconsidered, in after meditations. The facts are tolerably well imprest on my memory; & may serve for [so??] to many musings on life & the purposes to which it should be put. Were this hurried reading confined to these books, only, it were less a matter of moment & regret; but I have so much of every thing to read, so much of every thing to reflect upon & examine, that nothing is properly read, reflected upon, or examined. I spent the evening at Mrs. Morton's. Miss Susan was unwell. I did not see her. We talked some. Mrs. M. read the Magazine; John, the London papers; & I looked over the English Review, for Octr. 1796. A superficial & unsatisfactory publication.

Tuesday, 7.—Various trivial concerns occupied the morning. Dr. Mitchill came in. We went, together, to look at some books; & thence to the monthly Examination of the African School. This held on till dinner. I have said that the morning was occupied with trivial concerns. I forgot, at the moment, that John Fellows was here; & made me a proposal of being his partner in the Pocket Magazine, which he intends reviving. This I declined; but exprest a willingness to be the Editor; provided I should receive a certain sum, wholly independent of the success or failure of his undertaking. This seemed to hit his fancy. But we parted without coming to any positive conclusions. In the afternoon, corrected the first (proof) half sheet of my Opera; & went to the printers', to give some directions. Returning, stopt in at Horace Johnson's, & got the 3rd vol. of "Camilla." Spent the remainder of the afternoon, and the whole evening, at home. Ch. B. Brown here, and Dingley; and I corrected the second proof, of the first half sheet of my Opera. The rest of the time devoted to "Camilla"—& I finished the volume before twelve.

Wednesday, 8.—Ch. B. Brown breakfasted with us. Made some progress in my Dispensatory, to which part of the forenoon, and of the afternoon, was devoted. At a consultation & operation, at the Hospital. Charles here in the afternoon. Read the Herald. At my printer's. He sends me a request, this evening, which is quite inconvenient, as well as unexpected. He wants me to advance 55 dols. for the purchase of paper, when I have not five dollars in the world, of my own. I must cast about, tomorrow. Called at Mr. Woolsey's. Company there I did not know: would not stay. Drank tea at Mrs. Miller's. Spent part of the evening at Mr. Catlins. The remainder at the Theater. I went to see Johnson's exquisite face, in the part of *Simon*, in "All the World's a Stage."[23] The play was "The Comet"—the third night. I saw part of the IVth and the Vth Act. The House was full; and there was great applause. This piece has met with great success; chiefly, from its power of exciting a laughter, and from the contagious influence of laughter: For, when we inquire for nature, character, & sentiment, we must look elsewhere. I heard a merchant, who was delighted with "The Comet," dissuading his friend from coming to see *that stupid thing*—"The Man of Ten Thousand."

Thursday, Feb: 9.—Errands &c. occupied much of the morning. A visit from Mr. Johnson—the Player. Read Hoole's translation of the "Hipsipile," of Metastasia;[24] with new & augmented delight and admiration. Nearly completed my Dispensatory. Ch. B. Brown here. A visit from T. Wortman. Visited Dr. and Mr. Miller. Drank tea at Mr. Hodgkinson's. Spent the evening, very agreably, till nine, with Mr. and Mrs. Johnson—comedians—at their apartments. Have since read the eleven first letters of Sullivan's "View of Nature."

Friday, 10.—It has rained, excessively hard, all day; & so continues; with high wind. Continued, this day & evening, the reading of "A View of Nature &c."; and have gone thro' with the 12th, 13th, 14th, 15th, 16th, & 17th Letters. Some hours engaged, unpleasurably, with a sick man. Dunlap here in the afternoon. Ch. B. Brown, in the afternoon, & evening, till near ten. He read us, from his Journal, of Carlovinga &c.[25]

Saturday, 11.—Two tedious visits to my patients, occupied too much of the day. Some time at Fellows's —conversation on the "Pocket Magazine." Brown here, forenoon & afternoon. We read, together, with new admiration & delight, Milton's Hymn on the Nativity, and his two best Sonnets: "The great Emathian conqueror," & "I waked, she fled, &c." Dunlap was here, in the afternoon. He had been writing a Song; in his new piece, intituled "Sterne's Maria." He shewed it to me. The first stanza was pretty; but I disliked the second. I wrote one. He was pleased with it: but wished to preserve two lines in his own. I altered the other two, & he was tolerably satisfied with the stanza. The song is in the character of Nannette—& commences thus—

---

[23] *All the World's a Stage*, an afterpiece by Isaac Jackman. Played in Philadelphia in 1790 (Pollock) and possibly written as early as 1777.

[24] John Hoole (1727-1803), a minor English poet known now chiefly for his translations from the Italian. Metastio, whose real name was Pietro Antonio Domenico Bonaventura Trapassi (1698-1782) was, in his day, a well-known writer of lyric dramas for which others wrote the music. One of his lesser works was *Hipsipile* or (L.C.) "Hypsipyle" or (Metastio's biography) "Issipile" first produced in 1732; n.d. for first performance after translation.

[25] These names were perhaps sarcastic inventions of Smith but more probably were names of characters in some abortive fragment of fiction that Brown had read to him.

I laugh, I sing, &c.

The stanza I composed is as follows:

> Let Time my cheek with furrows plow,
> And o'er my tresses sift his snow;
> Let Death his fatal shaft prepare;
> My solace in my breast I bear:
> 'Tis Innocence, sweet Innocence.
> Youth must be gone; and all must die;
> One charm can every loss supply:
> 'Tis Innocence, sweet Innocence.

I labored on my Dispensatory; and have, at length, completed it—at least, for the present. Wm. & I spent the evening at Wm. W. Woolsey's. Dunlap was there, & G. M. Woolsey. We have had no regular Club, for some weeks; owing to various circumstances; but are to meet, in due form, at our house, next Saturday evening.

Sunday, 12.—Visited my patient. Read the 18th and 19th Letters, of "A View of Nature." This work, hitherto, does, by no means, equal my expectations. The author has availed himself, very sparingly, of the late discoveries in Chemistry; & his arrangement is obscure & unsatisfactory. Water, Air, Earth &c. are all *elements*, with him. Notwithstanding, some of the Letters are valuable; & almost all contain something to the purpose. Ch. B. Brown here. We walked on the Battery. The day was unusually fine. We, then, called at Mr. Riley's. Johnson met us there. We all dined at S. Johnson's. After dinner we walked out of Town. I called at G. Mumford's—All were out. A professional visit. Spent the remainder of the evening at Mrs. Morton's.

Monday, 13.—Ch. Brown breakfasted with us; and has been here most of the day. He began to dramatise "Hermsprong":[26] a task which I had allotted for myself; but which, since he has undertaken it, I shall be spared the execution of. So much the better: I shall have the more time for other purposes. Most of the forenoon busied with my printers, proof-sheets, &c. Read the 20th, 21st, 22nd, 23rd, and 24th Letters from Sullivan's "View of Nature"; & like him somewhat better. In the evening, at the Theater: "Man of Ten Thousand" & "The Critic." I saw there, among others, Nancy Mumford—the sister of Thomas. She spends the winter in town. I was near forgetting that I wrote letters, to Dr. Dwight & Isaac Beers, in N. Haven, to inclose Subscription papers for my Opera: they were short: to Dr. Cogswell, in reply to his concerning the "Medical Repository"; & recd. a short letter from Dr. Kollock, from Savannah. He appears to have written in haste; and mentions nothing of his own affairs—so that I am ignorant whether he suffered by the fires, or escaped their repeated ravages.

Charles has, also, recommended his Phila. novel; so fiercely undertaken in the Autumn of 1795.[27]

Tuesday, Feby. 14.—Read Letters XXV and XXVI in Sullivan, with some satisfaction. A visit from Dunlap. New commotions in the theatrical world. Mr. & Mrs. Hallam are determined to try the philosophy of my friend.[28] Wrote a short preface for my Opera. Ch. B. Brown here most of the day, and all the evening. Wrote the following letter to Joseph Strong. Arranged, in new order, my letters from my friends. We drank tea, for the fifth time, I believe, since we have kept house. Charles has been all day, writing verses. He read them to us—after a sad manner, this evening. He also read what he has composed of his novel. William read what he has written in his Journal; & I, the contents of mine, from the time of my setting off for Lichfield. We conversed. I corrected the first half sheet, of the second act of my Opera.

Wednesday, 15.—Wrote the following letter to S. M. Hopkins. Transcribed the letter to Strong. Corrected, to correctness, the first half sheet of the second act of my Opera. Ch. B. Brown here, all day, writing. Dunlap here, in the afternoon. Drank tea at his house, & stayed till seven o'clock: then went to a special meeting of the Board of Trustees of the African School. Came away at nine. Have finished, this afternoon, & this evening, the first volume of Sullivan's "View of Nature"—in all 502 pages. The last part of this volume is improved. The author is not master of every division of his subject; nor does he seem possest of all the discoveries which have been made: but this is a deficiency unavoidable in books which are written while a science is in the course of advancement.

Thursday, 16.—Wrote the subsequent letter to Mrs. Tracy. Dr. Mitchill, and, afterwards, Dr. Miller, came in to see me; and it was two o'clock when they went away. Called at my printer's. Corrected the proof of the fourth half sheet of my Opera. Commenced the second volume of Sullivan's "View of Nature," & have read the 32nd, 33rd, and 34th letters, this afternoon & evening. Ch. B. Brown has been here most of the day—writing. Called to see Miss Mumford, but she was from home. Drank tea, and spent part of the evening, at Mrs. Kent's. Mr. K. is to return next week. Passed the principal part of the remainder of the evening at Mr. Dunlap's—who goes to Connecticut, tomorrow.

To Joseph Strong

The long interval, between the receit of your last letter, and the present moment, has been so steadily, and so variously occupied, that I have not, till now, felt real leisure to write to you. For, of what value are

---

[26] David Lee Clark, in *Charles Brockden Brown* (Durham, North Carolina, 1952) p. 192, speaks of Brown as being a novelist of purpose, that purpose being the dissemination of radicalism, rather than a Gothic novelist. He traces the influences on him to revolutionists Thomas Holcroft, Godwin and Robert Bage. Bage's *Hermsprong*, a thoroughly revolutionary work naturally attracted him. Quite as naturally, perhaps, it did not hold him long.

[27] Harry R. Warfel, *Charles Brockden Brown* (Gainesville, Florida, 1949) p. 54 believes that the "Philadelphia novel" was *Arthur Mervyn*.

[28] Smith uses the word "try" in the accepted sense of "test." The Hallams almost drove Dunlap mad as Mrs. Hallam continued to drink and Mr. Hallam continued to be devious. See Dunlap, *Diary*, variously.

hasty, or even lengthy letters, when the mind is distracted by other cares; and can not devote itself exclusively to the object which demands its more particular attention? And, how much do those communications delight us, how short & transient soever, in which the soul seems to concenter itself—whether of friendship, or of science!

You have loved; you have wooed; you are wedded. What a series of new & interesting events; which have all come into existence, since I saw you; and rendered life precious to you, by fresh ties, & more endearing sentiments. Are any changes of opinion, any revolutions of ideas, any variation of character, consequences? Do you view things, with different eyes; and tho' you love your friends as much as ever, love them from different principles? How are pleasures and how science, affected by this change? The flame of Love often outblazes the rays of Ambition; Connubial Joy saddens the once-pleasant calls of Friendship; & paternal care extinguishes the lamp of benevolent Investigation. Do none of all these miserable deviations haunt your recollection? I trust not. If you were actuated by ambition—I look to see it revive, with added lustre; if by Friendship, to behold it expanded & ennobled by the new exercise of social affections, to which you have been called; if you have aspired to the possession of knowlege, from an ardent zeal for the interest of mankind, to view this zeal increased by all the additional & more precise motives which the participation of your offspring in the common fate of men, may present to your contemplation. Shall I be disappointed? Ay—*shall* I?

When we were last together, you spoke to me of certain papers, which you had committed to the flames, on your quitting the Western Territory. The contents of them related to Medicine, & were valuable. They have taken such possession of your memory, that you supposed yourself able to reproduce them at pleasure. You acknowlege the importance of the Plan presented to you, in the Address I sent you; you expressed a readiness to further it, by all the means in your power; can you do it more conveniently than by furnishing us with the papers I referred to? If you can, or if you can not, will you withhold your assistance?

You must not mistake the nature of the earnestness which I manifest, on this subject. Reputation, & riches, fame & money, are wholly out of the question. In respect to the first, it is obvious that the writer of each paper will appropriate to himself the merit, or demerit, of his communication; & with regard to the last, we have but an uncertain prospect of defraying, immediately, the expences of publication. But, much good may be accomplished, eventually, if, by any means the undertaking can be so supported, at first, as to gain consistency. To practitioners in the country, it will be more immediately, advantageous, than to those who reside in town—but what incalculable benefits would result from converting the great mass of physicians, thro' out the Union, into rational, observing, reflecting, prac[ti]-tioners? This consideration, I doubt not, will have due weight with you; & urge you to send us some of *your* "treasured sentiments" with convenient speed.

Our friend Alsop has been unsuccessful, here, in his business; and has bidden us farewell, to reside in Connecticut. He is now at Middletown. Johnson is here, in usual health, & more than usual business. I saw Danl. Lewis a fortnight since, at Lichd. He is well, & begins to prosper. Salstonstall[29] is verging towards success at Canandaigua, in this State; & Elnathan Smith has become a father. Here is intelligence!

Tuesday, Feb: 14. 1797.   Farewell.
Cedar St. No. 13, N. York.   E. H. Smith.

To Samuel Miles Hopkins[30]

Your letter, my dear sir, of the 28th of Octr. had a tedious passage; and was not recd. till the last of January. Leisure and opportunity, for reply, have been wanting, till this moment; when, a little disengaged from the pressure of other concerns, I feel myself at liberty to devote an hour or two to conversation with you.

You write with the same spirit with which you converse; and I am delighted to see that the old world has not been able to damp that keen, investigative temper, which led you on, so successfully, to the detection of error, in the new. Undoubtedly, we are made the slaves, here, of ten thousand impositions. The vanity & ignorance of our own people, and of the emigrants, conspire to misrepresent, and distort into hideous magnitude, the picture of the countries of Europe. The contradictory accounts which are published of our country, ought to inspire us with a salutary doubt of the accuracy of those which are given of every other. The sources of these multiform absurdities & falsehoods, are too well-known to you, to render it necessary, or useful, for me to descant upon them now. You are equally well apprized, with me, how seldom the footsteps of the traveller have been guided by the torch of inquisitive, sagacious, & philosophical sincerity. But have not you, yourself, in some measure, fallen into the very snare, the meshes of which you have, in part, discovered? Should Bacon[31] survive the present Mr. Pitt;

---

[29] Dudley Saltonstall (1770-1824; Yale, 1791) studied law with Reeve, moved to Canandaigua, county surrogate there 1798-1809, but ultimately an unsuccessful lawyer.

[30] Samuel Miles Hopkins (1772-1837) Yale, 1791, half-brother of Dr. Lemuel Hopkins of Hartford. He attended Reeve's Law School and was admitted to the bar 1793; went to New York in 1794, became a business associate of James Watson (cited earlier) and for a time he sold Virginia land in Europe. Thereafter, until 1810, he practiced law in New York before trying farming. In 1800 he married Sarah, daughter of Moses and Sarah (Woolsey) Rogers. U.S. House 1813-1815; State Assembly 1820 and 1821; State Senate 1822. He also held other offices including membership on a committee to superintend the construction of Sing Sing Prison.

[31] John Bacon (1740-1799) was a British sculptor of the neoclassical school who specialized in commemorative busts and monuments. His best known work is the bust of Warren Hastings in Westminster Abbey.

or should a statuary like to Bacon, or his superior, arise, in future times; and be called upon to perform that office for the son, which has already been executed for the father; might not his warm, pictorial imagination bestow equal, or transcendent, excellences, on another block of marble? And how would the observer be misled—(if indeed Lord Chatham were the orator we have been told—) when he should behold the energies of the elder, dwindling into insignificance, before the superior genius of the younger? The chissel of some new Leusippus[32] may clothe the "sculptured form" of William Pitt with a dignity & force, an impassioned fire, or a seductive tenderness, compared with which the noblest staue of Bacon, celebrated as he is, shall stand abashed in stupid tameness. "Ne crede colori"—put not confidence in sculptors, and painters, & poets. If we would have truth, we must seek for other sources of information. I do not make these remarks from any doubt of the superiority of Lt. Chatham to his son; for the living witnesses of the powers of each have testified, & must be believed; but I confess I *do* doubt whether the former was so very wonderful as we have been informed. On all these subjects, I am well persuaded, we foolishly suffer ourselves to be deceived. How much has been said of the ancient orators! Of Themistocles & Pericles—Yet neither of these celebrated men used any gesticulations; & the orations of the latter, as preserved by Thucydides, do not impress us with the idea of any divine gift of argument or persuasion: Of Eschines[33] & Demosthenes—of the first I say nothing—& of the last, I must doubt whether, with all his vaunted energy, he pronounced any thing equal to Ames's speech on the British Treaty. When we consider facts coolly—& throw aside the prejudices of the College, we shall see nothing so unaccountable in all this. In ancient ages, few had the benefits of instruction: those who had, like the priests of the dark ages, were regarded as surpassing the perfections of mortals, arrogated to themselves a sort of divinity, & were confirmed in the usurpation by the exaggerations of succeeding poets added to the gaping praise of contemporary ignorance. Now, men are generally educated: the means of instruction are accesible to all: some, use them more dilligently than others, & excell: they are praised accordingly: but they are seldom regarded as prodigies, except when their talents have been trumpeted across many leagues of ocean, to countries, where the mass of men have not opportunity to correct the information of others, by personal observation.

What a dissertation I have, insensibly, strayed into! Pardon me! I will endeavor after something better; tho' I know not what I can write, that will be particularly acceptable to you. Had you pointed out any one subject, concerning which you wished information, I would have devoted myself to it, with pleasure. But I am so little in habits of intimacy of some of your correspondents, that I am fearful that I may, tediously, repeat intelligence, which they have communicated in more acceptable forms. For Politics, I must refer you to the Papers. They will give them to you, with plenteous intermixture of speculation & abuse. Indeed, I know not which party is least decent. The Journals on either side, are full of disgustful falsehoods. In Congress, notwithstanding, a more than usual moderation has prevailed; & the turn which the election (for Prest. & V. Pt.) has taken, will, I hope, assure our tranquillity. Violent partisans, on both sides, have been disappointed; but the people, at large, grow every day, more & more satisfied. The conduct of the French, is near having completed the painful cure, undertaken a few years since, by the British; and a total aversion to all foreign connections seems fast gaining ground. Even the leaders of the Democratic party acknowlege the conclusiveness of Mr. Pickering's reasoning; & unite, with their adversaries, in condemning the ridiculous aspersions of Mr. Adet. In our own State, an increasing spirit of unanimity, promises to render Mr. Jay's administration fortunate for himself, & beneficial for the people.[34] The removal of the Seat of Government & the Public Offices, to Albany—which is now provided for, will, probably, preserve the union of the different parts of the State, some years longer, than it might, otherwise, have continued; & allow time for the preponderating policy of the New England Settlers to infuse the ferment of improvement, into the else torpid pool of the primitive Batavian intellect.[35] The only danger arises from the ardent temper of the many young men who represent the western & northern Counties. They feel their power; and are almost too fond of exercising it; they perceive their own superiority & are too prodigal of contempt for the imbecillity of others. Mr. Kent,[36] who is a member, from the City, this year, forms the simple, firm, & judicial column, round which, for the most part, they consent to rally.

Having dwelt longer on the condition of the political world than I intended, I must be proportionably brief in my notices of literary transactions. The few months

---

[32] Leucippus, in Greek mythology, lover of the nymph Daphne. Disguised as a woman he went hunting with her. Apollo, also in love with her, suggested to her that the girls go swimming naked. Leucippus, "unveiled," was torn to death by Daphne and her maids.

[33] Aeschines, an Athenian orator, member of a committee of ten selected to make peace with Philip of Macedon. He opposed Demosthenes, another committee member who refused to accept the peace terms.

[34] Jay, now Governor of New York, was said to have once slighted Adets, the French minister. See Stewart, *The Opposition Press of the Federalist Period,* pp. 286-287.

[35] Smith seems to equate "Batavian" with "stupid." The Batavian Club was a group in Holland in sympathy with revolutionary ideas. They managed to organize a government in 1795 that made peace with France and thereafter they secured a French-style constitution. Crane Brinton, *A Decade of Revolution, 1789-1799* (New York, 1934), pp. 232-34.

[36] Governor Jay, who had made Kent master of Chancery, was also responsible for his being made recorder for the city of New York about two weeks after Smith's "Diary" entry.

you have been absent, have not been wonderfully productive of morsels worthy of the palate of taste or science. Our friend Dr. Mitchill continues to instruct the public with his monthly lucubrations on Contagion, its influence on Animals, plants, &c. These speculations do credit to his industry in research & ingenuity in application; and will confer on him considerable celebrity. You will see, by a paper, which I propose to inclose to you, that we have undertaken, in conjunction with Dr. Miller, a work which may be, eventually, of great importance. You will be pleased to learn, that we have a prospect of some success; & are making preparations for the publication of the first *Fasciculus*. which will be a pamphlet of 100 p. 8vo.—& will, probably, appear in May next. Mr. Gallatin's ingenious book "On the Finances of the U.S."[37]; Mr. Wolcott's "Report on Direct Taxation"; & Mr. Pickering's "Letter to Mr. Pinckney"; have, all, too strict & important a connection with the state of our public affairs, not to be sent to you, by your friend Mr. Watson—who is more conversant with politics than I am. I should only remark, that their authors have, severally, derived some credit from their performances. In respect to publications, or performances, which appertain to what is called *polite literature*, I do not recollect any thing, but dramatic works; & these are all confined, hitherto, to New York. Early in the season, Mr. Dunlap brought out his tragedy —"The Mysterious Monk"—which was repeated with some applause. He does not print it. Since then, he has given out another piece—a Comedy in two acts; which has merit; & being printed, I mean to send it to you. You, probably, know Dr. Linn—one of the Dutch Clergy—or rather Dutch Church Clergy. His son[38]— a young man who has formerly published two volumes of miscellanies—has also presented us with a Serio-comico-musico-Drama, in three acts. It was played three times; but with no great success or applause, except by his friends, who exerted themselves in his favour. It is a juvenile performance; & is not published. Mr. Milns, a teacher of some character in the city, & an Englishman, has reproduced, this winter, with considerable additions, a piece, intituled "The Comet," which was performed, for some player's benefit, in England, in 1789. It is now in five acts, & interspersed with songs; & has been very successful; being to be played, the fourth time, this evening. You may have seen a serious opera, written by me, several years since, when at Phila. This has been represented, also, this winter. But, tho' as favorably recd. as I had any reason to expect, it had not sufficient attractions for our laughter-loving citizens; & is laid aside for the present. It is now in the press; & you shall receive a copy, in due season. So much for the Theater; which, you will observe, has been unusually prolific. Nor must I forget to mention, that we have the promise of several new Pieces, still; & that one or two, are advertised as ready for presentation, at the rival theaters in Boston. Boston, indeed, is stage-mad, now; as, formerly, it was church-mad. Thirty years ago, a congregation divided, & created a church, which they called "The Revenge": now, the patrons of the Theater quarrel; & two larges houses are built, in a town which has not more than 20,000 inhabitants; & where, five years since, a player was in prison for exhibiting dramas, without a legal sanction. What would the burners of heretics, & drowners of witches, say, could they rise up, and observe this "wicked & perverse generation"?

I laid your letter before the Club; to all of whom it gave great pleasure. They are all well; & send many remembrances. Johnson will, I believe, write to you. Dunlap will forward the introductory letters you request: probably, by the same conveyance with this.

I have been to Connecticut, where I found all our friends in health. My sister &c. were down from the Western World. They are happy; & have a fine boy. I heard of your family; who were also well.

Write to *me* often & long. You can write nothing which will not interest me: nothing, which will not furnish matter of useful meditation & inquiry. Have I not proved to you, that I prize your favors?

Yours sincerely,

Wednesday, Feb: 15. 1797.
Cedar St. No. 13. N. York.   E. H. Smith.

Friday, 17th—February—Transcribed, & arranged six pages & a half, from my medical notes. Several errands, & calls. At my printer's. Corrected a proof morning & evening. A Professional visit. Ch. B. Brown here, all day, writing. Read letters 35, 36, 37, 38, 39, 40, 41 in Sullivan.

Saturday, 18.—A professional visit. One, two, three, four, calls. Read the Herald—wrote a short letter to Mr. Tracy. Visited Dr. Dingley. Recd. a letter from

---

[37] Smith in his suggestions for his friend's reading covered wide ground. Albert Gallatin published his book *A Sketch of the Finances of the United States* (New York, 1796).

Oliver Wolcott's [Junior] Report on Direct Taxation. The letter from Secretary of State Pickering to Thomas Pinckney, minister plenipotentiary from the United States to the Republic of France, was dated January 21, 1797. It is said that Pickering, a notably hot-tempered man with no love for France, wrote some original drafts which were revised by Washington himself. The final letter dealt coolly and precisely with the confused and dangerous charges and counter-charges between Adet, the representative of France, and various members of the government of the United States and newspaper editors. See Gerard H. Clarfield, *Timothy Pickering and American Diplomacy, 1795-1800* (Columbia, Missouri, 1969).

[38] The literary illusion is notably vague. Dr. Linn's son was John Blair Lynn. The comic musical, in three acts, was *Bournville Castle, or the Gallic Orphan*. The music was by Carr, harmonized by Pelissier. The two volumes of miscellanies are, *Miscellaneous Works, Prose and Poetical* (New York, 1795). Milns (or Miln, or Milne) for whom no first name is available wrote a piece called *The Comet* which, as Smith says, was considerably revised after its English production in 1789 and played in New York in 1797. Milns was a school teacher who seems to have been theater-mad and who occasionally wrote little introductions or did other work for the producer. Odell calls him "useful."

Elnathan Smith. Read Letters 42, 43, in Sullivan. Visited Mr. Mulligan Jr. called on Dr. Mitchill, who was out. Visited Dr. Miller. Drank tea, & spent the evening, at Mr. Woolsey's. Mr. Dunlap out of Town; no club—Corrected proof sheets as usual. Ch. B. Brown, here. most of the day, writing.

Sunday, 19th.—Transcribed Bürger's ballad of "The Lass of Fair Wone,"[39] for Alsop: also, a part of my letter to Mrs. Tracy. Brown here, and Boyd, & Dr. Mitchill. Charles & I walked. Wm. & I dined at Seth's. After dinner, we called on Dr. Mitchill & went, with him, to Mr. Webster's. I spent the evening at G. Mumford's—but came home so as to read p. 76 of "Hai Ebn Yohdhan."[40]

Monday, 20.—After correcting a proof-sheet of my Opera, I went with it to the printer's. There I found the October & Novr. numbers of the "Monthly Review," & of the "Monthly Magazine"—I devoted most of the morning to a hasty & superficial examination of their contents; of which I say nothing, now, as I hope to peruse them, more at leisure, hereafter. Professional visit. Read thro' the fourth volume of "Camilla." Ch. B. Brown writing here, most of the day. At the Theatre, in the evening. Saw "The School for Arrogance"[41]— played here, for the first time. An excellent play; well performed; & well received: promises to be popular. Was at Wm. W. Woolsey's, after the play, a short time.

Tuesday, 21.—Finished the transcription of my letter to Mrs. Tracy. Two professional visits. Mr. Johnson, the Comedian, called upon me. Corrected proofs, & at the printer's as usual. Finished the reading of Simon Ockley's translation of "Hai Ebn Yohdhan," with his "appendix"—12mo. close print, p. 195. This is a curious performance, & not without great ingenuity; yet totally false. All we know of savage nations, who, of necessity, have much traditional information, is proof that the progress of the human mind, when wholly unassisted, could, in no degree, resemble the picture exhibited in this book. It was written at the close of XIIth century; & is evidence of the universality of religious enthusiasm, among men enlightened to particular point. The writer seems to have been a Mahommedan Quaker. Spent the evening at J. Riley's. Read thro' "Rosina"[42]—vol. 1st: which I procured at Fellows's, this afternoon.

To Mrs. Tracy

You have given me another, and pleasingly-painful proof of your confidence, in the paper which lies before me. I have read it over & over, and considered it with great attention; yet, scarcely know how to reply to it. I can not but compassionate your situation; but, in sincerity I must regard that of another, as still more pitiable. He must, indeed, be wretched who fears inquiry; who so doubts the soundness of his faith, as to tremble at every opposition. I could have wished that you had read the Book; but it is not so absolutely, so indispensably, necessary. Important truths are, therein, directly unfolded; but the same doctrines may be attained by a more circuitous, yet, perhaps, not less pleasing, course. At all events, no censor can restrain the operations of intellect. He who possesses the undisturbed faculty of thought, may well deride the pigmy violence of a thousand Omars. Yet, I say not this from any indignation I bear against Mr. T. on this occasion. My only emotion is regret: and more on his account, than on yours. He knows, you know, and the whole tenor of my conduct is evidence, that I value him highly; & have no feeling in relation to him, which I either fear or would hesitate, to display. But, at the same time that I do justice to his virtues, I am not obliged to forget his errors; nor do I feel more anxious to spare my own, than those of others. You will understand the force of this declaration, & will see the propriety of making it. You will see that I act from no vain motives of ostentation, but from a simple & fixed regard to justice. I earnestly desire that, in all our correspondence the motives which influence us may be evident & unequivocal; and I have, no longer, any *personal* reason for concealing any letter which I have ever written you. You once requested my leave to impart the contents of certain of my communications to Mr. T.: I was foolish enough, at that time, to have objections. They have, long since vanished. Hereafter, I would willingly have the world my confidant. I do not know that this tardy consent will be of any value to you; but should you ever find occasion to avail yourself of it, you will, doubtless, recollect what respect may be due to the prejudices & feelings of a lovely woman; and the disclosure will be made with proper restrictions.

I have been, insensibly led into conversation on this subject; but, since it is mentioned, I will add, that, should any future conversation point that way, there may be an advantage in laying all my letters, freely, before Mr. T. Not because he has any *right* or any other person to require it, for every individual is, in every thing of this sort, independent, & self-sufficient; but I would not, needlessly, excite a momentary sensation of pain, in the mind of any one; much less in his. And, perhaps, there is no readier way of removing any unpleasant doubt that may sometimes overcast his mind. I know those letters contain many foolish, and many false, opinions; that they exhibit a picture of miserable imbecillity, which, but for you, might have terminated in self-destruction; but there are no erroneous positions which I shall not be as ready to condemn, as any other person; there are no follies exposed, which I shall hesitate to disclaim. In respect to our future correspon-

---

[39] Gottfried August Bürger. See Collected Works, *Sammtliche Schriften*. (Gottingen, 1796-1798).

[40] Simon Ockley, *The Improvement of Human Reason, exhibited in the Life of Hai Ebn Yokdan, written about 500 Years ago by Abu Jaafar Ebn Tophail*, translated from the Arabic and illustrated with figures (London, 1708).

[41] Thomas Holcroft (1791).

[42] This *Rosina* is a novel, not the play, by Miss Pikington (London, 1793).

dence there will be, there can be, no possible reason for withholding any part of it, from every person whose situation admits of the colour of a pretence for a right to see it. I say this for myself. With regard to what you may write, you need not fear either my delicacy or discretion. You will not fear it. There is a wide difference between carefully secreting all our thoughts & actions from human eyes & pertinaciously foisting them upon the world. We may not wish to be the subjects of general discourse, tho' we have no reason for apprehending any thing from such an event.

In the foregoing pages, I have explained myself, fully, on the most tender point of our intercourse. Hereafter, I shall observe a continued silence, on this subject, unless you make a particular call upon me. You will understand me as leaving every thing I send you wholly in your power. You will exercise your own discretion concerning it. You will decide, whether anything, and what, shall be withheld, or exposed; when, & to whom.

I have been weak enough to regret, exceedingly, that I had so little opportunity of conversing with you, when I was last at Lichfield. I say weak—since regrets avail nothing. But I had a thousand things to say, and as many to hear. At least, I wanted to have heard your opinions, and remarks, on many subjects, there was neither time, nor opportunity, so much as to mention.

Your mind must have undergone several revolutions, in the course of your life; and these probably, have been multiplied, within the last six years. Or, more probably, this period has been marked by a steady progress of your intellect, towards an entire change of sentiment, on some of the most important subjects which can engage the attention of mankind. As we had not a moment for explanation, after a lecture that occupied so much of the last evening I spent in Connecticut, I came away with an eager, and unsatisfied desire, to be made acquainted with your opinion. I can not prevail on myself to think otherwise than that it preponderates on my side of the question. Convinced as I myself am, of the truth & soundness of my reasonings, it is painful to admit a doubt of their failing to carry conviction to your mind. Why will you not so far imitate my example, in that letter to which I refer, as to make me the depositary of your sentiments? You can not doubt the purity of my motives in wishing this disclosure; and we may never have an opportunity for personal, unrestricted conversation, on such topics. Beside, if any incertitude yet remain with you, if any particular questions are still obscured by doubt, what service may I not be able to render you, by pointing out to you the best, or the only, sources of information? Indeed, have I not a right to claim this act of confidence from you? Can you have any reason for hesitation? I can conceive of none. Yet it is possible you may have: or may think you have: and, in such a case, I refer all to your own discretion. There ought to be no reason; yet there may be; and I am not a stranger to the apprehensions which disturb the recent rationalist. I have seen children attempt to walk.

There is another subject, on which I wish information from you. Not, indeed, from any foolish, girlish, impertinent curiosity, but from the sincere and deep interest I take in every thing which may, in any way, affect your happiness. Some months before I left New York, at New Haven, and at Lichfield, I understood that it was generally credited that a union was, hereafter, to take place, between the gentleman that I saw at your house, and your eldest daughter. You will naturally suppose I did not hear this, as I should a similar piece of information concerning a stranger. It occurred to me, instantly, how much your future tranquillity must be involved in the fate of this child; & I was not insensible to the merits of the young lady. This interest was increased when I had opportunity to observe her improvements, in my late visit; & compare them, at her tender age, with the inferior attainments of others of her sex, whose years considerably exceeded hers. Of the facts, connected with this topic, I know nothing, certainly; of the character of the gentleman, very little. You are not apprized of the celebrity which attended a late secession, on his part, from an engagement he is said to have formed. How far justice is done him, I know not. But, if his conduct be fairly represented, the inferences drawn from the supposed countenance he receives from you, at this time, are unfavorable to the future peace of your child. For my own part, as I *know* nothing, I *judge* nothing. But incalculable advantages will arise from a decided conduct on your part. If such a connection is to happen, I do not doubt but you are satisfied of it's propriety; & with the conduct of the man you have selected. If the whole is surmise, a free avowal of it, (which may easily be managed, without any expence of delicacy,) would operate most powerfully in Miss Sally's favor. But, why do I trouble you on this topic? Do you know what is said? If you do not, who but a friend, a disinterested friend, will venture to tell it you? May I not appropriate that character to myself? Can I, in any more unequivocal manner, prove to you the sincerity of my friendship? You will pardon me—I am sure you will.

To obviate any unpleasant suspicion, concerning the source of my information, it is proper that I assure you that it was recd. previous to my visiting Lichd.; that, there, the subject was spoken of, to me, with a delicacy unusual, in matters of this nature; and that Fanny told me that her friend had disclaimed any such connection, in the most unequivocal terms. The sincerity of lovers we are accustomed to doubt. They think, & general practice countenances their belief, that they have a right to dispense with the obligations to speak truth, on such occasions. I hope the morality of the rising generation will receive, at least, *partial* improvement, in this particular. To sum up all—Have you any objection to imparting to me the real state of this affair? (If you have, I do not wish you to say more than that "you have.") I am anxious to be able to justify you from even the slightest imputation. Do not misapprehend me: I do not mean that your conduct is condemned: all that any pretend to say is—to express their surprize that you admit any connection—and they account for it, by presuming you to be ignorant, either of the thing itself, or, if not, of the character of the man.

This is a delicate subject, and I hope what I have written will not affect you unpleasantly; but I felt it my duty to speak to you, of what I supposed few others would venture to do. The important connection it has with your welfare, will excuse my zeal; even should you deem it misplaced.

I purpose, by the first conveyance that offers, to send my sister Abby, Mr. Godwin's Novel of "Caleb Williams." You have hastily perused it already. Permit me to recommend it to you, to be read & meditated; and be kind enough, at some future leisure, to communicate to me the result of this new examination.

When you will receive this letter is uncertain. Whenever you do, it will witness for me, how much I prize your friendship; and how eager I am to merit the continuance of your epistolary favours. Be not niggardly of them; but write often: I will not say long; tho' I wish it were in your power to make your letters so. On no account, however, let such an interval again, elapse, without writing. I would rather receive a line, once a month, than a sheet at the end of the year. In such a tedious period there is too much room for painful fears. My best love to you & yours. I send the Poem.

Thursday, Feb: 16. 1797.
Cedar St. No. 13. N. York. E. H. Smith.

Wednesday, Feb: 22.—Two professional visits. Proofs &c. as usual. Ch. B. Brown here, writing. Read the IInd, 3rd, and 4th vols. of "Rosina," & made some inroad into the Vth. Drank tea at Dunlap's, with his mother, & Geo. M. Woolsey—who accompanied me home, & spent most of the evening here—principally employed in reading the last letters which past between Theodore & me. This is the Birth-day of Washington; & has been observed with a festivity & magnificence which has gone near to make me sad. A sum has been wasted, in this ridiculous apery of monarchical formalities, which might have relieved our Finances from their present embarrassments, or bestowed permanent felicity on a thousand wretches.

Thursday, 23.—Finished "Rosina." Read the 44th & 45th Letters of Sullivan. Proofs &c. as usual. Recd. a short letter from Mr. Tracy. He has been sick—& I have, thereby, been somewhat disappointed in my expectations of subscribers for my Opera, thro' his means. It remains to be determined how the Other Paper will succeed. Visited Dr. Mitchill. A professional visit. Brown here, as usual. Drank tea at Boyd's. Went to the Theater: not because I wished to see either of the Pieces to be exhibited; but from an apprehension of some disturbance there; & with the intent of discovering the leaders, should such a thing happen, in the absence of Dunlap. Wearied, & disgusted, I continued till the last; but all went on quietly.

Friday, 24.—I was surprized, this morning, when Johnson informed me that he had spent the preceeding evening with Mrs. Lovegrove; I was still more surprized when I saw my friend Danl. W. Lewis, enter, who breakfasted with us; & most of all surprized, when I learnt, by a note, that he left town at noon—when he had two hours before assured us, that he should stay, with us till Monday. He was well; left all well in Lichfield; & brought me a short letter from my sister Abby. Proofs &c. as usual. The last half-sheet printed off, today. Professional visit. Brown here, writing. Read the 46th, 47th, & 48th Letters in Sullivan. Several interruptions & errands. Drank tea, & spent part of the evening, with Mrs. Lovegrove—who is remarkably well, & in fine spirits: the remainder of the evening at H. Johnson's. Mrs. J. nearly well. Read several articles in "The Monthly Magazine" for October 1796. The Letter on "The Use of Lime, as a Manure," probably right: that on "The Agriculture of Asia," valuable; & the facts respecting "Cochineal" very curious. The "Life of Dr. Arne" induced me to read the Nos 155 & 160 of the Tatler; which I perused with great pleasure. I like Mr. Nitsch's Letter; & hope he will give us better information concerning *Kant*.

[Omitted here, three manuscript pages with the heading: "Intermittent Fever (a series of cases treated in hospital)," and eight manuscript pages with the heading: "Fevers (a series of cases treated in the hospital)."]

Saturday, 25.—Four professional visits, in the course of the day, and a number of errands, engaged much time. Finished the second volume of Sullivan's View of Nature—in all—460 pages; & read the 41st letter, in the third volume. Finished looking over "The Monthly Magazine" for Octr. 1796. The acct of the "Lyceum of Arts" & "The Republican Lyceum" valuable; Particularly that part which gives a sketch of 1st & 2nd Sittings of the former. Several articles are here noticed, concerning which minute information is very desirable. The article "New Patents," is an improvement on former publications, of this sort; that of this month quite interesting. The article "Anecdotes" seems well conducted. Dr. Beddoe's Verses are good; & those of Mr. Coleridge particularly so. This Magazine deserves to [be] ranked among those periodical works which are most worthy to be received. Looked over, attentively, "The Monthly Review" for November 1796. Art. 1. "Studies of Nature." This work has been in America several months; & appears to merit the eulogies of the Critics. The extracts are pleasing. *Art. VI.* Miss Lee's tragedy—"Almeyda, Queen of Granada." The extracts are calculated to impress the reader favorably. Mr. Dunlap thinks well of it; & we shall, probably, have it brought upon our stage. *Art. IX.* "General View of the Agriculture of the County of Lancaster." I was disappointed in this article: neither the work, nor the criticism please me. The extract concerning "raising early potatoes"—& that which relates to the "Gooseberry," seem alone to deserve notice. Some curious calculations might, probably, be deduced from what is said of the productiveness of this berry. *Art. XIII.* Dr. Wells' Observations, Relative to Metallic &c. influence, appear to merit attention. *Art. XVII.* Mr. Burke on a Regicide Peace. This article is a masterly piece of writing—both for the extracts & the comments. The sentiments of the Critics appear to me, to be just, for the most part. I can not altogether subscribe to their eulogium on William III—nor do I think that they perfectly comprehend the character & merit of Washington. The extracts deserve all that is said in their praise, & the second extract contains many just sentiments. *Art. 67.* "Original Letters &c. of Sir John Falstaff &c." The letters inserted in the Review are exquisite, characteristical imitations. They have given me uncommon pleasure, in the perusal.

Our Club, seems nearly annihilated. Yet, I still encourage a belief, that when Kent & Dunlap return, we shall, once more assemble; & proceed with, at least, our usual spirit.

I forgot to notice, yesterday, that I paid a short visit to Mr. Gahn.

Sunday, 26.—Two medical visits. A visit from Dr. Miller. Wm., Charles & I, called on Mrs. Lovegrove. She accompanied us to S. Johnson's; where we dined together; & whence we did not separate, till after eleven at night. Brown slept with me. We had multifarious & interesting conversation.

Monday, 27.—Professional visit. one, two, three, four, errands, which required some time. In the afternoon, a visit to Dingley. Called at Mrs. Kent's—she was out: at Woolsey's, a short time; spent the evening, agreably, at Mr. Roulet's. Ch. B. Brown here most of the day, writing. Looked over the "Monthly Magazine" for July 1796. "Dr. Beddoes on Etymology" curious & valuable: "Songs of the Negroes of Madagascar," poetical & interesting—especially if dependence may justly [be] placed upon them: "Imitation of Wieland's Dialogues" —as far as I can judge—happy; & with no mean portion of good sense: the remainder of the articles are usual. Looked over "The Monthly Review" for October 1796. *Art. 1.* "Principles of Legislation. By Charles Michell &c." The criticism & the subject respectable. Both the French philosophers & Mr. Michell seem, to me, to have diverged, somewhat, from the truth; & chiefly from inattention to the fundamental principles of Society. If we mean to declare the fact, it is absurd to say that all men are born with equal rights. On the other hand, *right* & *duty* are reciprocal. They cannot be separated. It is my *duty* to exert all my powers to promote the welfare of mankind; I have a *right* to enjoy, in proportion to my virtue: i.e. in proportion as I advance the general weal. Nay, I must enjoy in this proportion. *Art. II.* "Inez. a Tragedy." The sentiments of Pedro— (in the Extract) are excellent, & well-exprest. *Art. V.* "Stemmata Latinitatis &c." Salmon's New Latin Dictionary appears, from the account here given of it, a very important acquisition to the library of the student. *Art. VI.* "The History of the Poor." by Thos. Ruggles. The imperfect acct. given of this work is just sufficient to re-excite & re-invigorate a curiosity concerning it, long since awakened, by various commendations bestowed on it by divers authors. *Art. VII.* "The Pains of Memory." Mr. Merry really seems to have improved. *Art. IX.* This critique on Mrs. D'Arblay's "Camilla" perfectly corresponds with my sentiments, & those of friends, Johnson & Brown, except that I can not speak so favorably of the Revd. Mr. Tyrold's Sermon. I have not, yet, read the 14th vol. *Art. X.* I am desirous to obtain Hunter's translation of "Letters of Euler to a German Princess." *Art. XI.* "Letters to Mr. Archdeacon Travis"—by Mr. Marsh. Apparently, a learned work, & which completely overthrows the foundation pillar of the Xtian. doctrine of the Trinity: the Algebraic argument diverted me, not a little. *Art. XV.* Roscoe's "Lorenzo de' Medici"—the review continued. This criticism is written with great spirit & elegance, & must be extremely flattering to Mr. Roscoe—the Extracts from whose work raise in me an eager desire to peruse it. I can not but hope that he will engage in the work here recommended to his attention. *Art. XXIV.* "A Dissertation on Respiration" by Dr. Menzies—valuable; & to be sought after.

Tuesday, Feb. 28.—Transcribed, with some corrections, part of my letter to S. M. Hopkins: also pages 133, 4, 5, 6, 7, from my loose notes of Cases. Mr. Roulet called here, & we went to the Auction of paintings & engravings. Was at Woolsey's. Errands. Brown here. Spent the evening at S. Johnson's. Mrs. Lovegrove, Mrs. & Miss Wilkinson, Miss S. Morton, Miss Sedgwick, Stillman, Howland, &c. Mr. Gahn, Morton, W. Johnson, &c. there. We accompanied some of the ladies home; & sat half an hour at Mrs. Morton's.

Industry of February 1797

I have read this Month—

"A View of Nature &c." by Richard Joseph Sullivan: Edit. Lond. 8vo. common print—vols. I & II, & part of the III—in all p. 999.

"Letters on Iceland &c." by Uno von Troil &c. Edit. Dubl. 8vo. p. 400—loose print.

"An Inquiry into the nature, cause, and cure of the Angina Suffocation, or Sore Throat Distemper &c." by Samuel Bard—Small 8vo. p. 33. close print.

"A Memoir concerning the Fascinating Faculty which has been ascribed to the Rattle-Snake &c. by Dr. Barton of Phila.—8vo. p. 70—common print.

"Observations on Accidental Fires, with an Acct. of those which have lately happened in the United States —8vo. p. 40—close print.

Simon Ackley's translation of "Hai Ebn Yohdhan"— 12mo. p. 195. close print.

"Rosina"—a novel—Edit. Lond.—5 vols.—loose print—perhaps p. 250 each vol.

"Camilla"—a novel—by Mrs. D'Arblay—4 first vols. Edit. N. York—12mo. close print—perhaps 250 pages, each vol.

"A Simple Story"—novel—by Mrs. Inchbald—Edit. Phila.—2 vols. 12mo.

"Hipsipile"—Opera of Metastasio—translated by Hoole.

English Review, for Octr. 1796.

The Monthly Review, for Octr. & Nov. 1796.

The Monthly Magazine, for July & Octr. 1796.

MEMOIRS. 1797 MARCH.

Wednesday, 1.—This day has been, mostly, consumed in unproductive runnings to and fro. I visited Dr. Mitchill, and Dr. Miller—and, with the latter, called, ineffectually, on Mrs. Lovegrove. I dined, with them, & Mr. Miller, at Mrs. Miller's—where we past much of the afternoon. I spent the evening, at Mr. G. Mumford's. Ch. B. Brown here. I looked over the "Monthly Magazine" for June 1796.

Thursday, 2.—Finished with some further alterations, the transcription of my letter to S. M. Hopkins. Read the 52, 53, 54, 55, 56, & 57th Letters of Sullivan. Ch. B. Brown here, as usual. Dunlap returned to-day: was here in the afternoon: not very well: brings me no letters: all friends, in Connecticut well: Alsop finished his translation of "Julius of Tarentum";[43] Theodore has shown my letter, to several friends: some condemn, some defend: asked about my Opera, but not about me. Wm. & I spent the evening at Mrs. Morton's, Mr. & Mrs. S. Johnson, Mrs. Lovegrove, Dr. Miller, & Mr. Gahn, there.

Friday, 3.—Called on Dunlap, in the morning, who is still somewhat unwell. Errands. Visited Mrs. Lovegrove—& afterwards, at Mrs. Riley's. Errands. Read the 58, & part of the 59th Letter, in Sullivan. Wrote a short letter to Evelyn Pierpont. Drank tea at Dunlap's. The evening, at the Theater: "Chapter of Accidents" & "Double Disguise."[44] All our N. England belles there; & much pleased.

Saturday, 4.—Numerous errands—principally relative to the Opera. Very unexpectedly summoned to commence my tour of Duty, at the Hospital. Went thither —& received the patients from Dr. Rodgers. Dr. Mitchill went out of town (to Albany) yesterday—so that I am alone at the Hospital. A visit from Dr. Miller. Read the Newspaper, & the remainder of Sulivan's 59th & his 60th Letter. Recd. a letter from Joseph Dennie Jr. Editor of the "Farmer's Weekly Museum"—a paper printed at Walpole (N.H.)—This comes by means of Jerh. Mason. Dennie writes me that he will insert the Address, relative to "The Medical Repository," & can procure some subscribers for "Edwin & Angelina." I drank tea at Woolsey's—where I spent most of the evening. Dunlap, & Geo: M. Woolsey were there.

Sunday, 5.—Wrote the succeeding letter. A medical visit. Called at Wortman's—on Dr. Miller—& visited Mrs. Lovegrove. Waited on her to H. Johnson's. Called at Mr. Kent's. He returned yesterday—& is very well. Dined, and spent the afternoon, & part of the evening, at H. Johnson's. Mrs. L. S. & W. & F. Johnson there, & Jno. Morton, beside the family. The remainder of the evening, at Hodgkinson's. Mr. & Mrs. Johnson—Comedians—there.

Monday, 6.—Ch. B. Brown breakfasted here. A reverie after breakfast, which idly occupied my mind till I was called out. Errands, & two professional visits. Went early & staid late, at the Hospital. After dinner went to visit a poor woman, the object & subject of the benevolence of Mary Stansbury & Mrs. Miller. Called at Mrs. Kent's—all out. Spent the evening at Mrs. Riley's— Miss Stillman & Miss Howland there part of the time. Finished the Third volume of Sullivan's "View of Nature."

Tuesday, 7.—Recd. a letter from Rhoda Pierpont, the wife of Evelyn Pierpont, and answered it. Drew up proposals for the "Medical Repository." Looked over the three last volumes of Sullivan's "View of Nature" —but thought my time might be better employed than in reading them. Was a little while at the Monthly Examination of the African School. One, two, three, professional calls. Went to see Dr. Miller. Visited Dingley—& borrowed of him Jno. Hunter "On the Blood &c."[45] in which I have read his life, by Mr. Home. Drank tea at Mr. Kent's—& spent the evening at Mr. Rogers's.

Wednesday, 8.—I have read, this day, p. 65 in Hunter on the Blood. Prescribed at the Hospital. A medical visit. Met Mrs. Lovegrove, on my return from the Hospital, & went with her to S. Johnson's. At Fellows's—at Dunlap's a few minutes: drank tea, & spent part of the evening, at W. W. Woolsey's—the remainder at the Theater—where I saw the two last acts of "The Wheel of Fortune"—& "Lock & Key,"[46] for the first time.

Thursday, 9.—Corrected my proposals for "The Medical Repository," & with Dr. Miller's approbation, gave them to our printer. Spent near two hours at Dr. Miller's—and, while there, read several Articles in the Medical Commentaries of Edin: of some importance.

---

[43] Alsop was working from a German play by Johann A. Leisewitz (1752-1806) *ca.* 1776. It was also translated into English by Peter Will before 1800. Alsop's translation has apparently been lost; it is not mentioned by Harrington in his biography (1939) nor by Alexander Cowie who wrote an introduction to a photographic reproduction of the volume for the Wesleyan University Press (Middletown, 1969). In addition to Greek, Latin, Italian, French, and Spanish, Alsop obviously knew some German.

[44] *Chapter of Accidents*, Sophia Lee (1780); *Double Disguise,* John O'Keefe (1784). The afterpiece is a comic opera in two acts with music by Hooke.

[45] John Hunter, *On the Blood* (Philadelphia, 1796).

[46] *Lock and Key* by Prince Hoare (1796).

Called, with Dr. M. on Mrs. Lovegrove—ineffectually. Was at Mr. Adams's. A professional visit. Dunlap here, in the afternoon. He goes to Stamford, tomorrow, after his wife. Drank tea, & spent part of the evening, at Mr. Boyd's. The remainder with Mr. & Mrs. Johnson —Commedians. Progressed thro' the first Chapter, in Hunter's work.

Ch. B. Brown spends great part of every day here— writing, reading, &c.

A Letter from Wm. Buel—

To Joseph Dennie Jr.

I feel myself still more indebted to Mr. Mason for the intercourse which he has kindly facilitated between us, than for his friendly attention to those concerns which are the immediate subject of your letter; much as I am bound to him on that account. I thank you for the interest you take in them, & hope that the Medical Project, with your assistance, will, eventually at least, derive both countenance & aid in your quarter. The Opera is now published, here, & whatever number of Copies may be subscribed for, in your neighborhood, shall be forwarded by the first conveyance you shall point out to me. I am fearful that the friendship which has long subsisted between Mr. Mason & myself, may have led him to speak of this performance in terms more favorable than it deserves. You must not be disappointed should it bear the characteristics of juvenility: it was truly a juvenile production.

The Paper which you conduct has long attracted my attention; nor was I a stranger to the peculiar talents of it's Editor, when his Essays formed the principal recommendations of the Eagle. The Weekly Museum,[47] thro' the agency of Mr. Fessenden Jr. has formed a part of our weekly entertainment, for some time: My friend Mr. Johnson, who resides in the same house, receiving it regularly. But, it will please me to possess a separate copy of the Paper; & I beg you to add my name to the List of your subscribers.

You caution me against expecting much from the Country; I must repeat the caution to you, with relation to the city. Commerce, News, & pleasure, are the giddy vortices which absorb the whole attention of our people; & a literary undertaking would meet with far less encouragement here, than in many parts of the country. The mass of inhabitants, are too, ignorant; & all, are too busy. I shall shew your Proposal's & Address to such persons as may be likely to subscribe; & may, perhaps, obtain a few names for you. This, I presume, is all that you expected. You must be too well acquainted with the state of society here, to have any expectations of obtaining literary aid.

On this subject permit me to recommend a few things to your consideration. Perhaps they may lead to some improvement in your plan. Near one half of your Paper is, now, devoted to literary matter. Mere literature, you must be sensible, forms but one, & that an inconsiderable, means of human improvement. Natural & Moral Science, are the great agents in this important process. For the last, (tho' considerably tinctured with the unintelligibleness of puritannic times,) a portion of the Museum is reserved. Of the former, I do not, at present, recollect to have seen any succession of original or selected, essays. You must be best acquainted with the temper of the people with whom you have to deal—but would it not comport with your Design, & further the success of your Paper, to spare a weekly column to Economics, & that division of Natural Science which immediately relates to Domestic improvements? In this way, the minds of the people might be gradually seasoned with useful knowlege, & the love [of] science, & passion for it's application to rural & civil purposes, might displace & succeed that ardor for party contention & debate which now continually poisons our national tranquility. There are many foreign periodical publications which would be of great service to you, whether you extend your plan, as I have suggested, or confine it to it's present purposes. With the character of most of them you are, probably, acquainted. I shall mention but four: The Monthly Review, The Monthly Magazine, & The Morning Chronicle—published in London; & the Moniteur, or Gazette Nationale, printed in Paris. The Monthly Review has an established reputation; & is, no doubt, more valuable than all the other publications of the kind. The Monthly Magazine is an entire original Miscellany, lately undertaken, & which promises to increase in value. It has been published about a year. The others, as you know, are daily Papers. Our city printers receive them merely as Newspapers; & when the news is extracted, throw them aside. But they exhibit a concise, well-written, & pretty accurate view, of Literature, in the two capitals; & would be useful to you, in that respect. The Chronicle is conducted by Woodfall, so celebrated for his surprizing memory.

You appear to have a number of writers at your service; but I must take the liberty to caution you against placing entire dependence on the writer of the Article which relates to Criticism. I was both surprized & displeased with the manner in which one of the most important publications in the language was treated, in a late paper; & certainly by a person who could never have read the work he condemned. I allude to Godwin's "Political Justice." The source of this writer's information must have been from some misrepresentations of a New York Editor. Nothing, however, advanced by him, is so wide from the truth, as the remarks which were made by your Critic. The manner of "Political Justice" is truly philosophical, & as little popular as that of Hume, & Adam Smith; & so far from abounding with "The cant of patriotism," the philosophy of Mr. Godwin, goes to the utter extirpation of that selfish & exclusive principle. It will not, perhaps, be worth the

---

[47] Probably *The Eagle: or Dartmouth Sentinel*, Hanover, New Hampshire; owned at this time by John Dunham and Benjamin True. The *Weekly Museum* glossed earlier.

while to bring up the subject anew in your paper, but this injustice done to one of the most enlightened, humane, & benevolent of philosophers, ought to operate as a restraint on a disposition to criticize which overleaps the bounds of knowlege.

I have written, Sir, with freedom, on these points, because I feel a sincere zeal for the promotion of your design. I wish to see your paper long & widely successful; & consider such publications as possessing the moral power, if rightly conducted, of regenerating mankind. Every deviation, of consequence, impresses me with a deep & lively mortification; nor am I willing to spare any effort for its prevention. If you possess that real desire for human improvement, & that rare good sense, which I have heard attributed to you, you will consider the frankness which I have used—not as the impertinence of a stranger, but—as the affectionate interference of a friend.

Sunday, March 5, 1797.
Cedar St. No. 13—New York.   E. H. Smith.

Friday, March 10.—Went, with Dr. Miller, to see Mrs. Lovegrove. He accompanied me to the Hospital; and, afterwards, to see a patient. Called at Mrs. Miller's, on my return. Errands. Called on G. M. Woolsey, & at W. W. Woolsey's. Wm. & I drank tea, & spent part of the evening, at Kent's: the remainder at H. Johnson's—where were Mrs. Lovegrove, Miss Morton, &c. I accompanied Mrs. L. & Miss Johnson, to S. Johnson's—& Mrs. L. thence, home. She leaves town tomorrow. I have read near 50 pages in Hunter, to-day.

Saturday, 11.—Snowed almost all day. Transcribed, with some slight additions, my letter to Jos: Dennie Jr. The remainder of the day, chiefly, employed in arranging my House Acct. & a few others. Went out to do a few errands. Mr. Goodrich, of Hartford, called upon me. Mrs. G. is in town, with him. They are returning, from Phila. to Connect. Charles tells me he is going to Phila. this next week. This resolution is sudden—but fortunate. The Club was revived this evening—& convened at our house. Present, Brown, Johnson, Kent, Smith, & the Woolseys.

Sunday, 12.—Wrote a few lines to Cogswell, Theo: Dwight, Jno. Williams, & Dr. Buel. Visited Mr. & Mrs. Goodrich. A professional visit. Dined at S. Johnson's, & spent part of the afternoon there. Called again on Mr. & Mrs. Goodrich. Went with him to Woolsey's—where we drank tea, & stayed most of the evening: remainder at home: Conversation, on domestic topics, with Johnson.

Monday, 13.—Ch. B. Brown breakfasted with us. Our plan of domestic happiness is threatened with a dissolution. A very unexpected, unpleasant, & unkind notice from our landlord, claims the house, for his own purposes, the ensuing year—at this late period. It is uncertain whether we can accommodate ourselves, or must part. My spirits have not been altogether unaffected by this circumstance. Prescribed at the Hospital. The afternoon much broken up, by several errands; principally for the Manumission Society. Set out to visit Catlin. Met him, near his house, going out, after his wife. Called at Riley's. The ladies out, did not stay. Spent two hours at Mr. Kent's. Some part of the forenoon, afternoon, & evening, devoted to Jno. Hunter's book—on the Blood &c. in which I have read near p. 70—to-day. This writer is not always perspicuous; he is frequently fanciful; but he is an original writer; & many valuable hints are scattered, up & down, this work.

Tuesday, 14.—Read about thirty pages in Hunter on the Blood &c. A professional visit, & some errands. Mr. Roulet here. Dr. Miller here, most of the afternoon. Various errands. Drank tea at Boyd's. Spent the evening partly there—partly at Dunlap's, who returned this day—& in part at W. W. Woolsey's. Obtained Mr. Burke's Pamphlet on Regicide Peace &c.[48] & read about 70 p. in it.

Wednesday, 15th.—Finished Mr. Burke's pamphlet—"Two Letters &c. on a Peace with the Regicide Directory &c." Lond. Edit. Rivingtons—p. 188—8vo. Finished the first vol. of Hunter on The Blood &c. Wrote a short letter to Mr. Tracy. A visit from Mr. Roulet. Rufus Stanley called, to let me know that Lucretia Collins was unwell, in town. I went to see her. Her complaint weakness & inflammation of the eyes. Prescribed at the Hospital. Dunlap here. Errands. Boyd here. Wm. & I drank tea at Woolsey's—went to a meeting of a special committee of the Manumission Society—& returned to finish the evening at Woolsey's—where were Dunlap & wife, & G. M. Woolsey.

Thursday, 16th.—Anxiety on account of one of the patients carried me to the Hospital soon after breakfast. I looked over part of Mr. Ford's Treatise on the Disease of the Hip Joint. A case is now under my care, in the Hospital, & I was pleased to see that my practice accorded pretty nearly with that recommended by this writer. Charles determined to set off for Phila. to-day. I called, ineffectually, on Miss Collins, & then went to Dunlap's & assisted Brown in his preparations. While there, I read Mrs. Fangeres' little drama—"The Fortunate Prisoners."[49] I wrote a few lines to Joseph Bringhurst. Charles took his leave. He went away, apparently, not with the best spirits. I fear he will effect but little, in Phila. I wrote the following letter to Dr. Kollock. I read a few pages in the second volume of Hunter on the Blood &c. This dismal weather still continues—it unfits me for study & activity. I visited Dr. Miller. Politics, literature, medicine: our invariable topics. I drank tea, & spent part of the evening at Gordon Mumford's. Miss M. was absent. I passed the most of the remaining part, at Mr. Riley's. Miss Stillman at the Assembly. I came home, and read some pages in Volney's travels. Wm. was finishing Mr. Burke's Letters. He read the last pages aloud—this brought on a

---

[48] Edmund Burke, *Thoughts on the Proposal of a Peace with the Regicide Directory of France, in two letters* (1796). *A third Letter on the Same* (1797).

[49] Apparently Smith read this play in manuscript. No evidence has been found that the play was either performed or published.

conversation, on various matters connected therewith, which carried us well into the evening.

Friday, March 17.—All the morning busied in writing a letter of medical directions for Miss Collins, who (I forgot to mention,) I visited yesterday afternoon. Was at the Hospital, two hours. Dunlap here in the afternoon. Read about 30 p. in Hunter, with great difficulty. This hateful atmosphere still oppresses us. Began "Hermsprong"—& have read near half the first vol. this evening, with a view to dramatising it: for I do not expect Brown will do it. Wm. & I drank tea, & spent all the fore part of the evening, at Mrs. Morton's.

Saturday, 18.—It cleared off about 10. The pleasantness of the sky, & some matters of business &c. called me abroad. About one, we had a thunder storm. All was clear before three. It had been sultry—it was now pleasant. Dunlap called—& we walked. When we returned Woolsey came in, & Boyd. Much talk. Woolsey went home. Johnson, Boyd, Dunlap & I walked again. I came home, & read news-papers. Drank tea at Dunlap's. Club night: W. W. Woolsey's evening: present—Dunlap, Johnson, Kent, Smith, the Woolseys. W. W. W. read us Savary's account of Egyptian marriages; Johnson the same writer's description of the Baths of Egypt. Literature, Morals, general & particular, foreign, national, & state politics. An agreable evening. I have finished Hermsprong—I recd. a letter from Dr. Buel.

Sunday, 19.—I felt something like industry, & activity of mind, inspired by this change of weather: so I kept my room. The first part of the day was employed in sketching out—imperfectly enough, the outline of a play from "Hermsprong." When this was done, I sat down to transcribe, & unite, retrench, & add. This occupied the remainder of the day—save ten minutes for dinner—solitary dinner—till after five. I then drest—called on Mr. Stanley & Miss Collins, who were out—& then at S. Johnson's. Wm. & Jno. Morton were there. We teaed. Morton took leave. Wm. & I went down street. He to Coit's[50]—I, to Riley's. Found there, Miss Howland, & Miss Mumford. They went away. Johnson came, & Morton. Came home before ten; & have finished the first act of my new Play.

To Lemuel Kollock

Your letter, my dear Sir, of Jany. 30. came to me, I scarcely know how, and has lain by me, unanswered, I hardly know wherefore. One little concern, after another, comes to prevent the accomplishment of my designs, and to interrupt that continued intercourse which I am anxious to preserve with distant correspondents. Like every one else, when I have the means of conveyance, I have not always time to write; & when leisure occurs for this employment, the uncertainty of what I might then say will not be antiquated when there is opportunity to send, restrains me from profiting by it. We are too apt to flatter ourselves with future fortunate conjunctions of circumstances. At this moment, it is but an unexpected instant of repose that I am possest of; & I am ignorant whether I shall have a chance to forward, what I scarcely have a chance to write; but I can not content myself with suffering more time to elapse, without an effort to testify to you the pleasure which the receit of your letter gave me—more especially on account of the kind interest it proves you to have taken in a project I have much at heart, foreseeing, as I do, that it's success can not be unimportant to the welfare of mankind. I shall inclose to you three subscription papers for "The Medical Repository," which I do not doubt you will make use of to the best advantage. It will be unnecessary for you to return them to me. Should there be any subscribers, I will only trouble you to transmit me their names, address, & directions how, & to whom, the Numbers of the work, should it go on, may be sent. Is there any bookseller in your place, who will receive & distribute such copies as may be required?

I do not much expect that the first number of the work can be got out, as early as May; tho' I hope there will be such a subscription as shall not oblige us to delay the impression, much beyond that time. We feel ourselves greatly indebted to you, for your promise of assistance; & hope you will not be disappointed in your expectations of sending us something. We constantly & eagerly look for Communications.

You are silent respecting your particular condition. In the distressing scenes which your city has witnessed, it is scarce possible that you should have wholly escaped the misfortunes which have fallen "so thick & plenteously" on your townsmen; but I augur favorably from your silence; & trust that your fortune has not thereby been materially impaired.

When you see Mr. Miller, remember me affecy. to him.

Thursday, March 16, 1797
New York, Cedar St. No. 13.   E. H. Smith.

Monday, 20.—Read p. 23 in Hunter on the Blood &c. vol. II. Rufus Stanley called on me, morning & afternoon. Errands. Recd. a letter from Thomas Crosswell, of Catskill. Went to the Hospital. Two consultations. Dr. Mitchill came, having returned from Albany. I prescribed for the patients; & we made a division. He came here after dinner—& Thos. Eddy & Val. Seaman were here also. Mitchill left me a long letter from a Mr. Owen, in Campo Bello—near Passamaquady, which I read. I read "Cadmus: or a Treatise on the Elements of written language. By Wm. Thornton—M.D.&c."—8vo. p. 110—loose.[51] Went to Kent's. Thence to Roulet's—who was absent. Spent the evening at Catlin's.

Dr. Thornton's "Cadmus," in great measure, supersedes the necessity for such an Essay as I once designed to have written, on this very subject of Orthography. It

---

[50] Joshua Coit (1758-1798; Harvard 1766), Connecticut General Assembly off and on 1784 to 1793, Connecticut representative in U.S. House 1793-1798.

[51] William Thornton, "Cadmus; or a Treatise on the Elements of Written Language, Illustrating by a Philosophical Division of Speech, the Power of each Character, thereby mutually fixing the Orthography and Orthoepy; with an Essay on the Mode of

nearly corresponds with my ideas. In some respects it is better than I should have written, with that knowlege which my previous reflections had produced; in others, I deem it as presumption to say inferior. There are, certainly, more than thirty letters in the English Language, in constant use. Those wanting should be supplied, to render the plan perfect. An additional defect is, that Dr. T's new characters can not, well, be written so as to unite with the established ones.

Tuesday, 21.—I have read, in the course of this day, p. 139 in "Observations on the disease of the Hip Joint &c." by Edward Ford. Recd. a visit from Jno. Fellows. Was two hours at Dr. Mitchill's room. Saw there Mr. Stuart—Atty. Genl. Asst. [always hereafter "Stewart"] —for the western Counties. At the Hospital—A lengthy visit from Dr. Miller, in the afternoon. Drank tea at Dunlap's, with the Woolsey's—& Johnson. Dunlap, just returned from Amboy, left Mrs. Lovegrove well. All the evening, till late, at the stated meeting of the Manumission Society.

Wednesday, 22.—I wrote short letters, on the business of the Medical Repository, to Dr. Osborn, Newbern, North Carolina—Dr. Hull, Fairfield—Dwight, Hartford—Sheldon, Lichfield—Munson, New Haven— and Field, Somers—Connecticut. A visit from Mr. Roulet. At the Hospital. Much writing for the Manumission Society. Dined, with company, at Dr. & Mrs. Miller's. Evening at Kent's.

Thursday, 23.—Most of the day writing for the Manumission Society. Further progress in Ford's "Observations &c." Read some part of Chardin's Travels.[52] Johnson recd. a note from Ch. B. Brown; & I, a few lines from Theodore Dwight. A visit to Dingley. Johnson & I walked out of town. We overtook M. Rossier & the Roulets, & walked back with them. I drank tea, & spent part of the evening, at Woolsey's. The rest, at Hodgkinson's—who read me his drama "The Man of Fortitude, or The Knight's Adventure."[53] It appears well calculated for stage-effect; & the language is more correct than I expected. He who has read "The Mysterious Monk," "The Knight's Adventure," & "Edwin & Angelina," will be able to detect numerous resemblances, in character, situation, sentiment, & even expression. I think, in all, except, perhaps, the second—not mended. I read "Volney's Answer to Dr. Priestley"[54]—a pamphlet of, perhaps, a dozen pages.

Friday, 24.—Finished "Ford on the Disease of the Hip Joint—" 8vo. loose print—p. 258. At the Hospital from 10, to 1; where I prescribed; & took down, minutely, the History of a Case of Diseased Hip Joint. Read, in the course of the afternoon, & the latter part of the evening, the Fifth volume of Camilla—12mo.— close print—p. 295. Wm. & I drank tea at Woolsey's. We went, thence, with him, to attend a Committee of the Manumission Society, for preparing the Annual Report to the Convention. Dunlap was one. We accompanied him home, after the Committee broke up; & stayed till after ten. Since I came home, it is, that I have finished Camilla.

Saturday, March 25.—Wrote a letter to Thomas O'H. Croswell. Read the paper—this day equal to p. 30 8vo. Ld. Malmesbury an able negotiation. Manifest from his letter to Ld. Grenville. Barras' reply to Mr. Munro, stupid, perverse, & impudent, in the highest degree. Mr. Dana came to see us. Mr. Dunlap here. We walked. Errands. At the Hospital. Teaed at Dunlap's. Club night—his night—Present, Dunlap, Johnson, Smith, W. W. Woolsey. Recd. letters from Mr. Tracy (who is better) & from Jno. Williams. Have p. 26 in Chardin's Travels.

Sunday, 26.—Read several passages in Chardin's Travels. Wm. & I visited Kent—at Riley's—at Mr. Dana's—H. Johnson's. We dined, & spent the afternoon, at S. Johnson's: the evening, at Riley's. Much company—Miss Howland, Mumford, Sedgwick, Smith, &c. and several gentlemen.

Monday, 27.—Wrote short letters to Dr. Osborn of Middletown, & to Theodore Dwight. A visit from Mr. Miller. Read considerable in Chardin's Travels—& composed the following pages, "Concerning Colchis." I prescribed at the Hospital. A long visit from Dr. Mitchill —who read me his Remarks on the Law which removes Tallow Chandlers &c.[55] He is about publishing them. Dunlap was here. He is about to relinquish his concern in the Theater. Called at Moses Rogers's—but found nobody at home. Spent the evening at James Watson's. I have read in Chardin about p. 300.

Tuesday, 28.—M. Roulet called to inform me that a french physician, of his acquaintance, was returning to France, & would dispose of his library. We went, together to examine it. I found there many valuable works. I read more than pp. 60 in Hunter on the Blood &c. Visits, & errands took up some part of forenoon & afternoon. I was at Mr. Gahn's—at Dunlap's—& Dunlap was here. I drank tea at Mrs. Miller's—whither I went to see Mrs. Coe. I was at Seth Johnson's, in the evening —the chief of which Wm. & I spent at Roulet's. Mr. Gahn saw Ch. B. Brown in Phila.—& Mr. Laffert. Both were well. Mr. Tracy is on the recovery. The Prest. U.S. has called the Congress together, the 15 of May. I hope their session may be distinguished by an honorable & spirited unanimity.

Wednesday, March 29.—Further progress in Hunter on the Blood &c. At the Hospital—whither I went at an early hour, & took down a lengthy case, as well as went thro' with the ordinary business. Called, ineffec-

---

Teaching the Deaf or Surd, and Consequently Dumb, to speak" (Philadelphia, *Trans. Amer. Philos. Soc.*, o.s., 3 (1793): p. 262).

[52] *The Travels of Sir John Chardin, into Persia and the East Indies, through the Black Sea, and the Country of Colchis, etc.* (London, 1686).

[53] Hodgkinson's extraordinary effrontery is never so clearly demonstrated as in this incident. He not only read Smith his play which was an outrageous plagiarism of Dunlap and to a lesser extent of Smith, he also produced it with Dunlap's aid. Hodgkinson admitted that there were "some similarities."

[54] *Volney's Answer to Dr. Priestley* (Philadelphia, 1797).

[55] The beginning of the anti-pollution movement.

tually, at Mitchill's Apartments. A visit from Mr. Gahn. Errands. Teaed at Dunlap's. The evening at the Theater: "The Fashionable Lover," and "The Quaker."[56] A riot there. Hodgkinson was hist—& a call made for Mrs. Hallam—who was brought out by her husband. This done by a concert—& by a party of young men. The respectable & greater part of the audience favorable to him, & not to her. He was so interrupted as not to be able to proceed. At last the play went on. From this time our Company is ruined, for I know not how many years.[57]

Thursday, 30.—I read, yesterday, Porcupine's Political Censor for Jany. 1797.[58] To-day, I have finished Hunter on the Blood &c., have read Mr. Morris's account of David Williams, with the Letter to Garrick—& also p. 140 in Williams's Lectures on Education vol. III. Wrote a short letter to my Father. Two professional visits. Errands. Dunlap here, repeatedly. Mitchill here much of the afternoon. Read the long account of the destruction of the fifth Austrian Army in Italy. Spent the evening at Mr. Kent's.

Friday, 31.—Finished the 3rd vol. of Williams's Lectures on Education. Read newspapers. Two medical visits. Prescribed at the hospital. Went, with Mitchill & Johnson to see Dr. Gaubert's books—those to which I had been conducted by Mr. Roulet. We could not see them till tomorrow. Wm & I stopped in at a print-shop, & looked over the Shakespere Gallery.[59] A visit from Dunlap. & from Mr. Beers, bookseller, of New Haven. Teaed at W. W. Woolsey's.

Went to the Theater. Disturbance there, which ended in the interruption of the performance, & in Hodgkinson's departure from the Stage. He has been ill-used. Returned to Woolsey's. Thence Dunlap & I went to Hodgkinson's. Talked the matter over. Arrangements made for the Benefits.[60]

Wrote the following letter.

---

[56] *The Fashionable Lover* by Richard Cumberland (1772); *The Quaker* by Charles Dibdin (1777).

[57] Hodgkinson had been feuding as usual with the Hallams. On the evening of March 29, 1797, as he entered the stage from the right in a performance of *The Fashionable Lover*, Mrs. Hallam, who had no part, appeared from the left and began to read a statement of her woes. A claque applauded her and silenced Hodgkinson. Hallam appeared beside his wife and asked that she be heard. A messenger was sent for the magistrates. An argument ensued between Hodgkinson and members of the claque, a number of whom were armed with clubs. Several gentlemen of substance in the audience rose and endeavoured to make peace. At length Hodgkinson, with superb presence, obtained the permission of the audience to continue and the Hallams left the stage. Dunlap, *History of the American Theatre*, pp. 165 ff.

[58] "Peter Porcupine" was the pseudonym of the eccentric William Cobbett, a Federalist pamphleteer. *Porcupine's Political Censor, or a Review of Political Occurrences Relative to the United States* appeared between March, 1796, and March, 1797.

[59] An art gallery in which D. Longworth, editor of the *New York Directory*, exhibited his collection of prints, most of which were illustrations for Shakespeare's plays. S. Mitchell, *Picture of New York* (New York, 1807), p. 153.

[60] Apparently a continuation of efforts of Mrs. Hallam's friends to promote discord, an effort which amounted to little. Dunlap does not mention it.

To Uriah Tracy

Since the receit of your letter, my dear sir, events have crowded upon us, in interesting succession. In many views of the state of our political affairs, I am disposed to allow that they seem melancholy, and to join with you in lamenting that they should be so. On other accounts, I rejoice at the extremity to which things appear to be brought; & hope that salutary, tho' unpalatable, wisdom will be the result. We suffer, we have suffered, from the want of a common, national sentiment; & we have had to deal with the two nations of Europe who possess it—especially the French—in it's highest degree. We feel the effects of their exclusive selfishness; may it teach us self-respect! It is time for us to call to mind that we pretend to be a people—a free people, an independent people. It is for the interest of all the world that we should be so. But the real interests of nations have never been generally understood; they have never been calculated on any other principle than that of monopoly. We have given France credit for more enlightened notions, till she has nearly reduced us to bankruptcy. It is now plain that her whole policy towards us has been a refined system of swindling. The people are almost ripe for entire conviction; & the moment must be seized to press it upon them. We have been wanting in self-respect. We have been too supine. We have talked to France too much in the style of submission, & petition, & remonstrance. We have played the political hypocrite; & echoed back their unmeaning talk of magnanimity, & virtue, & generosity, when they were plundering us, when we knew it, & when they were convinced that we knew it. The Government have been deficient in Justice to themselves, & in sincerity to the public. They have failed of the effect which a dignified tone has, at the same time, upon a foreign people, & upon their own.

Moderation does not consist alone in supplication, or expostulation, or even remonstrance. Firmness, courage, fortitude, should at least be seen, if they are not active. We are injured; we know it; the French know it; and yet they have the insolence to speak in the language of an offended, & justly irritated people & we reply only with exculpations. We say we have not committed injustice; but we have not said that France is the aggressor. Are we afraid to say this? I hope not. If we are, we are fit to be slaves; & shame should seal our lips, if apprehension did not. But what have we to fear? Offensive war we can not dream of undertaking. We must defend ourselves, even in our present hermaphrodite situation. We suffer more than all the external inconveniences which could result from a state of war, with almost all the internal. We have some of those wretched advantages, as they are called, which sometimes attend on war; &, thank heaven, can not have, in a contest with France. She has no commerce, to invite privateering, & ruin the little morality that speculation has left us. But do I wish to provoke the french to a declaration of hostility? No. But I deem the declaration unimportant, if the fact exist. What are we then to do. I am venturing, perhaps, on forbidden ground—since I am no legislator, & not more than half a free man; but I have a love for my country, from the best wishes to mankind, & I can not repress my opinion at this time, & when writing to you. The measures which ought to be taken seem to me sufficiently simple; but it must constantly be borne in mind, that we have higher calculations to make than of mere mercantile profit & loss. No mere merchant can possibly feel the propriety of right principles; yet they are, after all, the only ones which can permanently operate to his advantage. Our commerce is destroyed. It is not, therefore, to be thought upon, in the case before us. If the adventurer, alone, could suffer, he should be permitted to incur any hazard he pleased, & have liberty to defend his rights; But thousands suffer thro' his means. The possible success of an individual, therefore, must not be put in competition, for a moment, with the probable loss of numbers; &, thro' them, of the community. *Let there be an indefinite Embargo.* The pillagers of our vessels, thus disappointed, may be authorized to destroy our towns. *Fortify our Harbours.* It must be done, at some time: when will there be a better opportunity, a fitter occasion? If the means are demanded: *Apply the credit of the States to their own defence.* Connecticut & N.Jersey, at least, are equally concerned with New York, that it's harbour be impregnable. They may be convinced of it. One thing further: *Withdraw all American Agents from french dominions*: let the french remain here, if they please: *assume the tone of an injured people*: let our memorial declare how we are wronged; let it note our forebearance, patient almost to pusillanimity; let it manifest our determination to resist, but not to inflict, injury; & let it declare that, when France shall return to sentiments & acts of moderation & justice, we shall be glad to renew & strengthen our bonds of amity: till then, (& we will judge of this,) all intercourse is suspended. Such is the language we ought to hold; & France would turn pale amid all her victories. "Thus conscience doth make cowards of us all."[61]

Need I assure you of the pleasure it gives me to hear that you are recovering? I intend to have satisfaction of presenting my personal assurances, in the course of the next month. I suppose you will, *now,* remain in Phila. All friends well—& send remembrances.

Friday, March 31. '97.
Cedar St. No. 13. New York.   E. H. Smith

Industry of March 1797
Reading

"A Treatise on the Blood, Inflammation, & Gun-Shot Wounds, by the late John Hunter. To which is prefixed a Short account of the author's life, by his brother-in-law, Edward Home." Edit. Phila. 2 vols. 8vo. close print pp. 625.

Ford on the Disease of the Hip-Joint: Large 8vo. loose print. Edit. Lond. pp. 258.
"A View of Nature &c." by Revd. Josh. Sullivan—the third volume.
Chardin's Travels—(see p. 157)—about 300 pages.
"Hermsprong: or Man as he is not": 12mo. close print—two vols.
"Two Letters &c. on a Peace with the Regicide Directory &c." Edit. Lond. Rivingtons. pp. 188. 8vo.
"Cadmus"—edit. N. York. 12mo. close print—the Vth vol.—pp. 295.
"Lectures on Education &c." by the Revd. David Williams—edit. Lond. vol. 3rd—8vo. common print—pp. 346.
Thos. Morris's account of David Williams, with the Letter to Garrick—edit. Lond: 8vo common print—pp. 68.
"Volney's answer to Dr. Priestley"—a small pamphlet.
Monthly Magazine, for June 1796.
Several Articles in the Med:Comment: Edinb: for 1796.
"Porcupine's Political Censor" for Jany. 1797.
"The Man of Fortitude or The Knight's Adventure"—Ms. play by Jno: Hodgkinson.
"The Fortunate Prisoner"—Ms Drama by Mrs. Faugeres.

Writing

Hermsprong, a Comedy—compiled—Act First.—equal to 15 pages—common 8vo.
Medical Cases, at the Hospital—equal to—p. 10—8vo.
Letters to friends & for business—p. 20—8vo.
Notes on Colchis—&c. . . . . p. 10—. . . . . 55—at least.

MEMOIRS. 1797. APRIL.

Saturday, 1.—A medical visit. Errands & calls—Dunlap & I walked. Called at Riley's. Went, with Miss Stillman & Miss Howland, to see Miss Mumford. Heard, indirectly, from my sister Mary &c. that they were well. Professional visit. Went, with Dr. Mitchill & Wm. Johnson, to see Dr. Gaubert's books. I stayed behind some time, & selected a number of volumes for the N. Y. Hospital Library. Drank tea at Dunlap's. Geo. M. Woolsey returned from Phila. left all well. Club night; & Johnson's—Present—Dunlap, Johnson, Smith—Mr. Davenport of Connec. & Mr. Gahn, visitors.

Sunday, 2.—Two professional visits. Went to see Dr. Mitchill. Saw, at his apartment, Le Brun's picture of the Battles &c. of Alexander. A visit from Dr. Miller. Transcribed my letter to Mr. Tracy. Sent it, by S. Johnson—at whose house I spent the afternoon. Wm. & I passed the evening at Mrs. Morton's.

Monday, 3.—Wrote three letters, to E Smith, Mary, and Idea. Dunlap came here, bringing Hodgkinson's Appeal,[62] to look over with me. We went partly thro'

---

[61] *Hamlet* III, i.

[62] *A Narrative of His Connection with the Old American Company, from the Fifth September, 1792, to the Thirty-first of March, 1797,* by John Hodgkinson (New York, 1797). This

hours of silent handholding

it. A visit from Boyd. Another from Charles Adams. A professional visit. Prescribed at the Hospital. Wrote a few lines to Wm. Buel. Calls & errands. Professional visit. Drank tea at Mrs. Miller's. At the theater, a short time. All went on smoothly. Wm. & I spent most of the evening at Riley's. Godwin has published a new work—intituled "The Enquirer."[63]

Tuesday, 4.—Wrote the succeeding letters to T. Mumford, A. Smith Jr., F. Smith, & A. Smith. Dunlap here. Dr. Miller here. We went to the Monthly Examination of the African School. Errands. Dunlap & I looked thro' Hodgkinson's Appeal. I wrote him a letter, containing my opinion on the subject, & offering him a plan for his narrative. Dunlap & I went to see him. We conversed upon the matter; & H. is to re-write his Appeal. Two professional visits. Drank tea at Dunlap's. Woolsey & I went to see Mr. Elsworth. We did not find him at his lodgings. We spent the evening at Mr. Watson's. I have, since my return, transcribed the letters to Mary & Idea. I copied that to Elnathan, last evening.

Wednesday, 5.—Wrote the Criticism on Dr. Barton's Memoir—as far as to the quotation from Vaillant. Two medical visits. Prescribed at the Hospital—whither I went in season to take down a Case, at some length. Errands. Read the Papers. Drank tea at Kent's. Spent part of the evening at Gordon Mumford's; part at H. Johnson's. Transcribed the letters to Mumford & Abby.

Thursday, 6.—Finish the review of Dr. Barton's Memoirs. Wrote the letter to Sally Pierce. Dr. Mitchill out of town. Prescribed for him at the Hospital. Looked over Mead & Russell on the Plague.[64] A professional visit. Errands. Dunlap here. We looked over, & made some corrections in Hodgkinson's Narrative—which he is recomposing. At the Library—turning over several books. Dunlap & I walked out of town. I read, again, the letters which he recd. a day or two ago, from Thos. Holcroft, & his friend Brewer. I drank tea at his house; where I read Dr. Priestley's Letters to Mr. Volney. Called at Dr. Miller's: all out. Spent the evening at S. Johnson's. He is in Phila.

Friday, 7.—Tumbled over the Athenian Letters, Watkins's Travels, & a Life of Homer, in search of information respecting Attica & Athens. The little which I found, is noted p. 172. Mr. Miller called in the morning. Mr. Roulet spent an hour & an half with me. A professional visit. Prescribed at the Hospital. Mr. Gahn here, two hours. Medical visit. Samuel Bowne

here. The evening at the theater. Saw "The Way to get Married"[65]—which was played here, for the first time. We miss Hodgkinson very much.

The numerous & long interruptions of this day, have prevented me from devoting much time profitably.

To Elnathan Smith Jr.

Ever since the receit of your Last Letter, my dear friend, I have been seeking a conveyance to Berlin: hitherto, without success. I should have written by post, to the care of some friend in Middletown or Hartford, but that I wished to send on, at the same time, "Edwin & Angelina"; which has been published about a month. I shall forward the number of copies you require, by the first conveyance that offers. Perhaps I may send a few more. In either case, I shall expect to receive pay for those, *only*, which you dispose of. I shall not permit the generosity of your temper to lead you to purchase things which you do not want, from an idea of benefitting your friend. I can not *so* be benefitted.

The translation of Madame Roland's works has never reached New York. If I am not mistaken, I either saw it advertised in the Boston papers, or was told that it was for sale in Boston. If you do not get it elsewhere, and it ever comes here, I will send it to you, on the instant.

Expressions of sympathy, and condolements with friends, are matters too common-place to admit of variety, and among those who are really attached to each other, can answer no other purpose than to fill up the paper. We must suppose sympathy where there is friendship; & my friend will not doubt my affection, even tho' no profession should ever escape my lips. Have we not often held each other's hand, & looked one at the other, hours, in silence? And, how expressive is such silence! How much more consolatory to the heart, than all the clamorous compassion of fools! But your health is restored, your family are well, and were we not to meet, it would be, not with a melancholly squeeze, but, with a hearty shake of the hand. I am interested in the tale of your old Cambrian. Let me have some particulars, when you are able.

Monday, April 3. 1797.
Cedar St. No. 13. New York.   E. H. Smith.

To Mary S. Mumford

What can be the reason that I have not recd. a line from either, of you, since we separated? Or, have you written letters which I have not received? Or, have you found no conveyance hither? I am extremely desirous of hearing from you, and should have written, long since, had any opportunity presented itself, for sending what I might write. I am now in daily expectation of being able not only to transmit this letter, but some of the books which I promised you. How many, will depend on circumstances. If the person who goes can,

---

work is a fairly concise statement of Hodgkinson's case against Hallam, Mrs. Hallam and Dunlap. Considering its content it is remarkable that it was written with the advice and assistance of Dunlap. Smith is not mentioned except obliquely as a "gentleman witness."

[63] A series of essays (London, 1797).

[64] Richard Mead, M.D., F.R.S., a physician of great distinction: *A Short Dissertation concerning Pestilential Contagion, and the Method Used to Prevent it* (London, 1720), many editions thereafter in English, Latin, French and German; Patrick Russell, M.D., F.R.S., *A Treatise on the Plague*, etc. (London, 1791).

[65] Thomas Morton (1796?).

conveniently, take a number, I shall send them. Otherwise, you will receive but a few, or a single one. I feel most desirous to have you read Downman's "Infancy," and Dr. Faust's "Catechism of Health"; a work designed for children, but more proper for parents, & those who have the immediate charge of children. These relate, immediately, to a subject we have long been engaged upon, and, as they very much coincide with me in sentiment, your perusal of them will save me the labour of continuing the series of remarks which I undertook.

In addition to these little books I shall send you Mrs. Inchbald's "Nature & Art"; & perhaps "Man as he is" & "Man as he is not"—two novels by the same author,[66] but who is yet unknown. Indeed, were a convenient chance to offer, I might make you up a clever little parcel of books, enough to employ your thoughts pleasantly for several months, in the interval of more indispensible engagements.

I hope soon to hear from you, particularly. Write to me, as you have been accustomed, freely & fully.

Accept my fraternal love.

Monday, April 3. 1797.
Cedar St. No. 13. N. York.   E. H. Smith.

To Idea Strong

You should not oblige me, with every interruption of our correspondence, to renew it myself. I wrote last. The letter, then written, as it forms part of our chain of intercommunication, demands an answer. I write now, principally, to remind you of this, and to prevent the introductory steps we have taken from being in vain. We have proceeded thro' the vestibule of definition & arrangement, and may fairly expect to be led into the interior of the temple of knowlege, if we persevere. The clue is in your hand. Let no childish terror seize you. Proceed. I am at hand. If your heart fail, I will resume the guidance.

I purpose to send, with this letter, and for your perusal, "Godwin's Political Justice." Thomas does not like the book; in part, I believe, from never having read it. With the principal part of it, no moral man can be dissatisfied. Perhaps, from Mumford's aversion to it, he will not be inclined to peruse it: perhaps, he will wish Mary not to read it. They must arrange this among themselves. In either case, it need not influence your conduct. It is the second edition which I shall send you—in which many things are altered which Thomas, & some other friends, thought most objectionable. For my own part, I know of no work more truly valuable; nor can I conceive of happier beings than men might be, were they guided by its precepts: unless, indeed, they were to be endowed with new capacities.

The books which I send Mary, you will, of consequence, have the reading of. I presume that you have, already, examined Condorcet; & I expect your opinion with some impatience.

Monday, April 3. 1797.
Cedar St. No. 13. New York.   E. H. Smith.

To Thomas Mumford

The long and, even for you, unusual silence which has prevailed since we were together, makes me hope that there are letters on the way, for me, from Aurora. The solicitude which this interval has occasioned me has been quieted a little by the letter which your brother received the last week. This sufficed to inform me that you were & had been well.

I left Lichfield in a fortunate moment; my journey was safe & pleasant; & I had snow till the last day. Had I tarried one day longer, I should have been obliged to pound over the stones, and flounce thro' the mud, for more than a hundred miles. Since my return I have been well; as have also all our friends.

Your sister Nancy is still here. It has been quite a winter for New-england belles. We have had near a dozen fair damsels here, from that part of the country; some of whom have been quite admired. Several have done every thing but commit matrimony; and your cousin Ben Mumford seems to be laboring dilligently to prevail upon one of them to be guilty of that extravagance: nay—it is rumored he will not meet with any long-protracted opposition.

I shall send you some copies of my Opera—at least; and, probably, several other books will accompany this letter. Saml. Jones Jr. tells me that he expects to meet you, in Albany, this month. If no conveyance offers, earlier, I shall give him charge of whatever I may forward. How is the boy?

Tuesday, April 4. 1797.
Cedar St. No. 13. New York.   E. H. Smith.

To Abigail Smith Jr.

I should have replied to your letter, by D. W. Lewis, on his return, had he remained in town as long as he gave us reason to suppose, when he first came in. His sudden flight, I might almost say disappearance, left me wholly without conveyance; and a letter which was then lying here for Mrs. Tracy, has kept it's place ever since. But if I have had no conveyance, has this misfortune equally extended to you? If it have, I trust your pen has not been wholly idle, and that when opportunity does favor you, I shall be repaid, by a lengthy letter, for this long period of deprivation.

During my short visit, our opportunities for conversation were few and short. In the progress of things, we must expect them to become more & more infrequent, less & less protracted. We parted, now, with a thousand things unsaid, that we wished to say; we shall part, hereafter, with accumulated sentiments which our brief interviews will forbid us to communicate. Shall we ever

---

[66] Smith is confusing here. Mrs. Inchbald wrote *Nature and Art*, but the "two novels by the same author," *Hermsprong, or Man as He Is* and *Man as He Is Not,* are by Robert Bage, cited earlier.

love each other less? I am sure neither wishes or believes it possible. What remedy for these barbarous, these unavoidable, separations? Is it not the pen? Apply yourself to this faithful assistant, my sweet friend & sister; tell me of all your interests; & I will make them my own. In two years, we have spent eight days together. In two years your heart has admitted the validity of a claim which may soon separate you, for many tedious years, from all your friends—especially from your brother. In two years how many things must have occurred of which I have yet to learn. I am fixed to listen. I am anxious to be made acquainted with all that relates to my sister. I would sustain her by my principles, & protect her by my counsels. Write to me soon.

I send you "Caleb Williams," & "Edwin & Angelina"; you will read them both; you will study the first; you will accept the last.

Farewell.

Tuesday, April 4. 1797.
Cedar St. No. 13. New York.   E. H. Smith.

To Fanny Smith

Have you forgotten, my dear sister, that you have, yet, an answer to give to the question which terminated my last letter? I assure you, I have waited for it, with some impatience; & I hope it will be a little more at length than your reply to my past inquiry. You have had plenty of time to study it; and will, no doubt, have viewed the subject in all its various lights. The more correct, therefore, will be your solution.

On what other matters, or how else, have you busied yourself, for these two long months? I must have an account. I like to see how young women employ the best years of their lives. One may, thereby, judge how they are likely to conduct themselves, when every day, & every hour, calls upon them to act, as well as think. You know, I have always labored to protract your moments, your period, of reflection. I would not have you plunge into active life, wholly unprepared for action. I wish you to possess, within yourself, the means of happiness, independent of circumstances: At least, independent of circumstances which often destroy common women; of circumstances to which, you, as well as they, are exposed. A moral being, I wish to see you possessing the attributes of a moral being, of which to think yourself is one of the first. And, as you ought to form sentiments for yourself, my earnest desire is to see you qualified for that distinguished exercise of intellect. Women, I have told you, are formed for something nobler than merely to be wives & mothers. Can you wonder if I would learn how far you have proceeded in such an employment of your capacities as may render you worthy the character of a rational being? Write me of your studies.

Receive my love.

Tuesday, April 4. 1797.
Cedar St. No. 13. N. York.   E. H. Smith.

To Abigail Smith

With this letter, my dear mother, you will receive a dramatic poem, the first attempt of the kind which your son has made, and, being his first publication, which he has dedicated to you, jointly with his father. This little drama, so far enjoys the good opinion of those who have read it, as to be called moral & decent; so that it need not give you any pain, or put you to any shame, if it should not flatter your parental love, or interest your own self-regard. I should have consulted both you & my father on the inscription, had I not feared such objections from your modesty as would have made obedience painful. I was bent upon the address; and thought it would be less difficult to reconcile you to what had happened, than to obtain your consent for it to be done. Have I offended past all forgiveness? I hope not. I hope you will find such pleasure in this testimony of my love, as shall repay you for any transitory sentiment of dissatisfaction at its publicity. It would grieve me to have it otherwise; for I would make any reasonable sacrifice to accommodate the feelings of others; & I believe I may say, there are few sons who more sincerely & warmly esteem their parents. In proportion as my knowlege of mankind increases, I feel this love of those to whom I owe my being augmented. I will not pretend to say that I am less sensible to what may be called their errors ("for all have errors") but, I am more possest of the extreme difficulties which surround the business of education; & deem more highly of a faithful performance of what are thought to be the injunctions of duty. Will not my mother address a line, at the close of one of my sister's letters, to assure her son of the continuance of her maternal tenderness?

Tuesday, April 4. 1797.
Cedar St. No. 13. N. Y.   E. H. Smith.

[Omitted here, one manuscript page with the heading: "Notes on Attica. From 'Travels through Switzerland, Italy &c. part of Greece &c.' by Thomas Watkins. Outline of book."]

Saturday, 8.—Read the newspapers. Dunlap here; & we looked over the remainder of Hodgkinson's Narrative. I learnt from Dunlap, that Theodore Dwight & his wife arrived in town yesterday afternoon. Jno. Murray Jr., Thos. Eddy, & Saml. Borne here. He brought some papers, relative to Africans; & detained me near an hour. A professional visit. Went to Woolsey's. Theodore not there; nor his wife. Hence to the Hospital. Found Mrs. Dwight at Riley's—whither Theodore came. We dined there, together; & spent most of the afternoon. He returned with me; & sat awhile. Recd. letters from Jno. Williams, Cogswell, & N. Dwight. Teaed at Dunlap's. Club night—G. M. Woolsey's evg. Present—Dunlap, Johnson, Smith, G. M. Woolsey—& Mr. Gahn visitor. Dunlap shewed us the new tragedy of "Bunker Hill"[67] (played in Boston, with such success

---

[67] John Burk, *Bunker Hill, or the Death of General Warren.* Not to be confused with *The Battle of Bunker Hill . . . by a*

this winter); & the impudent letter of the author. Disgustful.

[Omitted here, fourteen manuscript pages with the heading: "A Memoir concerning the Fascinating Faculty which has been ascribed to the Rattle-Snake, and other American Serpents. By Benjamin Smith Barton, M.D."]

Sunday, April 9th.—Last evening & this morning, looked over a file of London Papers. Executed some part of the Outline of the Annual Report of the Manumission Society, to the Convention; on which I labored somewhat longer this evening. This business is rather troublesome than pleasing, & calculated to be sufficiently puzzling, without admitting any opportunity for the display of talents, or the impressing of more extensive sentiments of humanity. In all these things, the old, beaten track must be pursued. If you deviate into new regions, or attempt to spring forward to future & more comprehensive designs, the herd are startled, & shrink back from an undertaking too mighty for their powers, or too vast for their conception. A medical visit. Wm. & I walked. Called at Riley's. Dined at S. Johnson's—who has returned. Spent most of the afternoon there. Walked out of town. Drank tea & spent the evening at Woolsey's. Theodore & wife, Dunlap, & wife, Mrs. Riley, G. M. Woolsey &c. &c. there. Theodore read some part of St. John Wyllys's Romance—intituled "The Fugitive Prince"—which is an extraordinary production for a youth of 18—whose character is such a mixture of idiotism, lunacy, & wickedness, as his is said to be—Wm. Buel is in town, & has been here, in my office.

To Sally Pierce

You have been accustomed to confide in my sincerity, I hope you will not withhold your confidence, when I assure you I was both mortified & grieved that we were so totally deprived of opportunities for conversing together, when I was last in Lichfield. I can hardly tell how it happened, but I seem to have come away without having visited any body. And yet, I thought I did a great deal, while I was there. I almost despair of ever, again, spending any convenient time in my native place. Difficulties & obstacles seem constantly to multiply; and, if they do not shut out hope, they exclude expectation. I shall sustain this deprivation with very little of the spirit of a philosopher, I fear, if my friends, there, desert me; if they do not cheer my absent hours with frequent letters. You have not, yet, relinquished all connection with me; tho' your communications are short & uncertain. Still, as I have but little claim even for this indulgence, & as you are mostly occupied with much more important concerns; I pretend not to complain. I would rather make my acknowlegements, & supplicate for a continuance of your favors. It is to do this, more than to communicate any particular good tidings, or weighty matters, that I write at present. I am so little independent, my happiness reposes so entirely on the persevering affection of those I love, that I am uneasy at any symptom; how slight soever, of a diminution in their esteem for me. I do not expect to raise my character in your opinion, by this confession; but it is proper that you should know my weakness, that you may aid in supporting me under it.

Thursday, April 6. 1797.   E. H. Smith.

Monday, April 10.—Wm. Buel breakfasted & spent most of the day with me. A professional visit. At the Hospital, as usual; whither Buel accompanied me. A visit from Dr. Miller. Executed a draft of the intended report from the Manumission Society, to the Convention. Buel & I made some calls. We separated at evening. I went to Moses Rogers's—where were Dwight, Dunlap, & Woolsey, with their wives, Mrs. Riley, & Miss Dwight. Theodore & I accompanied some of the ladies to Jno. Broome's to see Miss Whittlesey of Middletown—who was not at home. I went with Mrs. Riley to her house—& thence, with her, to Mr. Coit's—with Johnson, also, who had now joined us. There we found a large collection—among others—Mrs. Seba & Mrs. Polloch, Miss Morton & Miss Stillman, G. M. Woolsey &c. We spent the remainder of the evening there. Johnson began to remove his goods to Pine Street.[68] I recd. a letter from Mrs. Lovegrove.

Tuesday, 11.—Wm. Buel here, part of the forenoon. We went to the Apothecaries together, where I left him, & called at Woolsey's, to see Theodore. He was not there. A Professional visit. Commenced the removal of my furniture &c. In the intervals of attention to that, read in Davidson on the Pulmonary System. Prescribed at the Hospital. Dined at Dunlap's. Mr. & Mrs. Dwight, Mrs. Woolsey Senr., W. W. Woolsey there, beside the family. Theodore left us, to go to New Haven, by water. Dunlap & I walked. Drank tea at Dunlap's. Beside the dinner party—were there—Mrs. & Miss Rogers, Mrs. Woolsey & Miss Dwight, Mrs. Riley & Miss Stillman & Miss Mumford—Dr. Buel & Wm. Johnson. I left them, awhile & went to Mrs. Morton's to meet Miss Rush, the daughter of Dr. Rush, & Miss Stockton, the sister of Mrs. Rush. Returned to Dunlap's. Dr. Buel went to the Circus—the rest of the men to the Manumission Society. It was nine when we broke up. I was in at Woolsey's near an hour, on my return home.

Wednesday, 12.—Buel called at our breakfasting hour. We were both invited to breakfast with Dr. Miller. We partook of our own; and completed the meal with the Millers. I went early to the Hospital—as I was moving, & of course much engaged. Another reason was, the common hour of prescribing was that at which the Annual oration before the Manumission Society was

---

Gentleman of Maryland (Philadelphia, 1776), by Hugh Montgomery Brackenridge, later Hugh Henry.

[68] The new quarters of Smith and Johnson at 45 Pine Street were in the residence of Alderman Waddell who lived on the second floor. Dunlap, *History of the American Theatre* 1: p. 277.

to be delivered. Samuel Miller was the Orator. His Discourse was handsome, but the auditory was small. I dined at Woolsey's—late. Mr. Mrs. Miss & Mr. Rogers, were there—Mr. & Mrs. Dunlap—Mrs. Johnson—of Stratford, Connec. & G. M. Woolsey. Spent the evening at S. Johnson's. Much company. Half-a-dozen Broomes—two Brushes &c. & Miss H. Whittlesey. Recd. a letter from Mr. Tracy. Slept in Pine Street—No. 45. for the first time.

Thursday, 13.—We breakfasted here, for the first time. I completely moved my furniture, & am now nearly settled. Buel called. We went to see Mitchill, at the College. Buel went with him to the Hospital. I came home to arrange my things. A most violent north-east storm, of wind & rain soon commenced; which lasted till night. A professional visit—& another. —Wm. Stockwell of Lichfield called. He brought news that all my father's family are well; & a Cheese—an acknowlegement from Mrs. Lord, for my medical aid, rendered when I was last in Connecticut. Buel returned here—& partook of my simple dinner. He spent the afternoon here. Mitchill came. I read them my Review of Barton's Memoir. I have read, to-day, a number of Papers, (Reports, Letters, &c.) relative to the Manchester (Engd.) "House of Recovery." A visit from Mr. Roulet. Medical visit. Spent the evening at Riley's.

Friday, 14.—Dr. Buel breakfasted with us. After breakfast, I went with him to several book-stores, &c. We parted about eleven—& he is gone. one, two, three, four, professional visits. At the Hospital, as usual. Called at Boyd's. Dunlap here. Wm. & I walked out of town. Two medical visits. We drank tea at H. Johnson's —where I spent the evening. S. & his wife were there, to tea; Fanny, to supper. Wm. went to Mrs. Riley's. I wrote a short letter to Mrs. Lovegrove.

Saturday, April 15.—Two professional visits. Read further in Davidson on the Pulmonary System. Transcribed letters to Fanny, my mother, Sally Pierce—& wrote & transcribed the letter to John Williams. Dunlap here. Calls & errands. Club night—my evening—Present—Dunlap, Johnson, Kent, Smith, G. M. Woolsey; Gahn visitor. I read David Williams's Lecture on "Mental Reformation."

Sunday, 16.—Wrote & transcribed the letter to Mr. Tracy. Two calls. Read a few pages in Davidson. Wm. & I dined, & spent part of the afternoon, at S. Johnson's; & part of the afternoon & evening, at Riley's: the remainder of the evening was spent with Mr. & Mrs. Johnson—Comedians. I read Mr. Merry's "Pains of Memory"[69]—& wrote forty verses, after my return.

---

[69] *The Pains of Memory. A Poem. by Robert Merry, A.M., member of the Academy Della Crusca, at Florence, Author of the Della Crusca Poems, Laurel of Liberty, Paulina, or the Russian Daughter, Lorenzo—A Tragedy, etc.*, A New Edition (Philadelphia, 1796). Merry, a Londoner, who lived for many years in Florence was a member of the Academy Della Crusca and contributed to the *Florence Miscellany*. He is credited with founding the Della Crusca School of Poetry, an affected (sometimes characterized as "silly and pretentious") form of verse

Monday, 17.—Wrote and transcribed the letter to Ch. B. Brown. A long visit from Mr. Day of Onondaga. Called on Dr. Miller. At the Hospital, as usual. Finished Davidson on the Pulmonary System. Read some pages in the Botanic Garden, & in Van Swisten. Most of the afternoon writing &c. for the Manumission Society. Two professional visits. Drank tea & spent part of the evening, at Dunlap's—the remainder at Wm. W. Woolsey's.

Tuesday, 18.—A professional visit. Wrote a few lines to Aurora. Visited Dr. Dingley. Read some in the Botanic Garden & part of Haygarth on Innoculation &c. Two professional visits—the last of which being at Riley's, I spent the evening there. Mrs. Dwight is still there. Came home & read Mr. Alsop's translation of Julius of Tarentum. Continued my Elegy.

Wednesday, 19.—Two professional visits. A call from Dunlap; & from Mr. Tod, now a student of Law at Lichfield. He brought me letters from my Father, & from Abby & Fanny. I recd. also a short letter from Dr. Elijah Munson of New Haven. At the Hospital—as usual. Visited Dr. Mitchill, on my return. He shewed me his review of Onvieres' pamphlet, &c. Read the News-papers. Drank tea at Dunlap's. Most of the evening at a meeting of a Committee of the Manumission Society. Finished "A Sketch of a Plan to exterminate the Casual Small-Pox &c." by John Haygarth. London. Johnson. 1793. 8vo. pp—570—2 vols. common print.

To John Williams

About ten days since, my dear sir, I recd. a few lines from you, dated March 22d and a few days after, your letter of Feby. 27th inclosing the subscription for my Opera. This letter is valuable to me, (tho' not without many misapprehensions of my principles & conduct,) as it is evidential of your interest in my temporal & eternal welfare. I receive it, therefore, with much sensibility, & many acknowlegements for your kindness & friendship.

I desire, with equal earnestness, to avoid those discussions which you deprecate so much; & I shall, certainly, do nothing to induce them, at this time. It may, however, afford you some satisfaction to know that I have never read but a small passage of Mr. Paine's Book; & that then, disgusted with the temper in which it was written, I threw it aside, & have never opened it since. So far as I have been informed what his principles are, they do not appear to have much resemblance to mine. Boulanger I have never read; & know nothing of. It will be early enough to speak of Godwin, when you have carefully & candidly perused his works.

In answer to your question, relative to Paley's Evidences—I may inform you that I took up the Book, with a design to read it; but the author sets out, with assuming as proved, the very things which, in my opinion, require to be demonstrated. Can you wonder, then, if I deemed it an unnecessary waste of time to attend to the details of a superstructure erected upon such a foundation?

I respect the sincerity of your faith; but you must not expect me to admit this as evidence of its soundness. Should future reflection induce you to relinquish your present opinions, I should not, like you, regard such a change as necessarily implying any caprice in you. To have given up convictions, founded on patient inquiry, is rather a proof of having dilligently investigated their foundation & evidence, than of having acted lightly & precipitately. Your induction, therefore, is not sound.

In regard to Engrafting—have you seen the "New Annual Register" for 1795? You will find in it, Two Papers, on this subject, from the Philosophical Transactions. They appear to me to be ingenious. You will probably find the Register at Hudson & Goodwin's.

I can not avail myself of your permission for purchasing books, unless you designate the kind of books—or, at least, the extent of expence to which I may subject you. I am afraid of having this matter left to my discretion.

I return you the Subscription Paper. I shall send twenty Copies. The one in blue you will please to accept, as a mark of friendship. There are seventeen subscribers. The remaining copies, if you can not dispose of them, present them to any of my Wethersfield friends.

Present my respects to your family, & remember me affectionately, to all friends.

Yours

Saturday, April 15. 1797.
Pine Street, No. 45. N.Y.   E. H. Smith.

To Uriah Tracy

I recd. your last letter amid the confusion attendant on a removal to this house. A few days have so reduced things to order that I have leisure to take up the pen.

The sentiments & feelings of our citizens, as may naturally be supposed, vary considerably in respect of our national concerns. There are, notwithstanding, few who venture, openly, to defend the conduct of the French: few, who do not freely censure them. I see very little party violence here; indeed, it seems a season for breaking up parties. Our Representative may preserve his zeal, from notions of consistency; but it is, at least, as probable, that, with the knowlege he must unavoidably possess of the temper of the people here, he will endeavor to regain the old Livingston ground of "devotedness to country." Most men, in a commercial country, measure their politics according as their interest is affected. It is not wonderful, therfore, that some of our most violent democrats have been brought nearer to reason, by the losses they have sustained from french piracies. I was agreably surprised, a few days ago, to hear a man, who was formerly a warm partizan of the French, & whom I have often seen with their cockade in his hat, honestly acknowleging his errors, & avowing an entire change of sentiments. This, too, unprovoked by me; & accompanied by information of similar revolutions in the opinions of many others.

Mr. Woolsey, who has lately been thro' part of the country, gives a like favorable idea of the alterations which have taken place in the feelings of the people, & all our accounts from the Northern parts of the State, from New England, are as favorable as could be wished. The obvious differences of opinion, whatever the secret varieties may be, are more on the conduct we ought to pursue, than how that of France is to be regarded. The great object & wish of our democrats, both open & concealed, is to have an Envoy Extraordinary sent to the Directory. I am not certain that I fully comprehend what you mean by a prostration of our country to France, but to me, it appears as if no measure could well be more humiliating & useless, than this. There is no analogy between our situation as to the French, & our relation to the British when Mr. Jay was made Envoy. And who should we send? It must be Burr, or Maddison, or Gallatin, or neither the French, nor their American adherents would be satisfied. But we can not put any confidence in these people. If Ellsworth, or Hamilton, or any other distinguished federalist were sent, he would not be recd. & the French would pretend to consider the mission as an insult. No man in the United States could, reasonably, be more unexceptionable than Mr. Pinckney—the man they have refused. The very idea of an Envoy, to the present people in power, in France, is absurd, delusive, & intended to deceive.

I am not certain that your reasoning is not just, concerning an Embargo; tho' it varies from that which I have been accustomed to use on this point. But, you consider the subject under a different light from that in which it was viewed by me. It was not because I expected an Embargo would be injurious to the French that I advocated it, but because it might be useful to ourselves. If, as you suppose, it could not be preserved for a long time, it would, indeed, be nugatory, or worse. If, on the other hand, it could be continued, till business should find out new channels, & the restless enterprise of our country gain a new direction, I am persuaded no measure could be more salutary. I am not willing to believe that so much stress ought to be laid on the revenue side of the argument, as the federal members of Congress seem to suppose. It is Commerce, principally, which creates this demand for revenue; & the consequence would fall with the cause. Had we maintained no commercial intercourse with Europe, during the present War, our prices would have been unaffected by it, & the same nominal, would have been the same real,

---

writing. Griswold (*Poets and Poetry of America*, p. 81 n). Merry exercised during twenty years a greater influence than any other individual had ever had upon American taste in poetry and other kinds of writing. He married a famous actress and accompanied her to America in 1796 where he died shortly thereafter. Mrs. Merry was for a long time the star of the Philadelphia Theater group.

value. A country which possesses such amazing internal resources as this, has no need of external commerce, & can never, in the end, derive any advantage from it. It needs only a necessity strong enough to oblige the people to turn their industry another way, & seek their prosperity from other sources, & they will never return to the vexatious pursuit of gain, on seas, & in distant regions. Do you want examples of a policy such as I point at? You will object to China, perhaps—well then,—what think you of Swisserland? The Swiss have no foreign commerce, not even a single ship; yet they continue to enjoy considerable prosperity, & derive a revenue sufficient for the ordinary exigencies of their government, in time of Peace. In War, they are under disadvantages, because they want money. They are in debt, too, on account of former wars. But, our situation is far more fortunate. Peace is our policy; peace is the universal desire of the people; & nothing but a folly, too prodigious ever to possess our national rulers, can ever plunge us into an offensive war; if the spirit of commerce, & the naval force it must bring with it, be restrained. When, therefore, we have fortified our frontier, we may sit down in tranquillity; & yielding up our pretensions to rival all the earth in traffic on the ocean, & devoting ourselves to internal improvements, we shall find, them produce a revenue equal to all our wants. I do not say that it is practicable, at present, & at one blow, to bring our country into the situation, but I would be willing to incur any moderate hazard & expence to effect an object, in my opinion, so desirable. At present, so far as regards an Embargo, the question is, will not our interest be promoted by it? If it will, we do not want seamen: if it will not, our merchants must be allowed to defend themselves; tho', I think, no consideration short of the absolute consequent loss of all, should engage us to depart so far from republican principles as to authorize reprisals. The morality of the nation is sacrificed, by the first public permission of privateering.

The remaining measures, proposed by you, seem to me alike just & necessary; unless, perhaps, that of keeping an Agent in Europe, authorized to treat with the French. After what has passed, it becomes them to seek; & we should act, (circumstanced as the world is,) unworthily of the dignity of outraged virtue, were we to return to the language of supplication or proposal. This, however, will depend, in a good degree, on issue of the late Election in France.

Our friend Theodore Dwight has been here, lately. He thinks there is very little doubt of Mr. Allen's being elected; if he will consent to be. Mr. Daggett has declined, you know.

Mr. Reeve is very much affected by the loss of his wife; shuts himself up; & has dismist his students. People, in general, at Lichfield, as I have learnt within a few days, are well.

Sunday, April 16. 1797.
Pine Street, No. 45. N.Y.   E. H. Smith.

P.S. On looking over my letter, I observe an inaccuracy which may mislead you as to my real meaning. By External Commerce, is intended, particularly, that which is pursued abroad, by our own citizens; or, more properly, the Carrying Trade. I have no objection to furnishing other nations with our commodities, provided they will take them away.

To Charles B. Brown

Did you think a mere note of business, more worthy of the clerk of a counting-house than a benevolent friend, sufficient for those you left behind, that you have neither solicited the continuance of the correspondence of either, nor, replied to him who snatched a few minutes from the pressure of accumulating occupations to write to you? I say nothing of myself, because, ignorant as you are of the causes of my silence, you may think me equally reprehensible—but what will you answer respecting the Dunlaps, & Roulet? He, the last, has called here, repeatedly, in the vain expectation of hearing from you, of receiving the promised, but neglected, letter. He even forgets the philosophy of his character: & the gestures of his surprize proclaim him, not a Swiss, but a Frenchman. If you have any good reason for this delay, let us have it. I long to be able to justify you to myself, & to our friends. If you have employed your time better than in writing to us, I shall rejoice. But, pardon the sincerity of my friendship. I fear it.

Now for information which may be more pleasant to you than this reproof. Dunlap & I shall be with you in about a fortnight: i.e. we shall be in Philadelphia. We expect to spend a week or ten days there. I wish you may impart this intelligence, seasonably, to Joseph; so that, if possible, he may contrive to meet us. To see him, will greatly enhance the pleasure of our stay.

You may have heard of the revolutions in our Theater. I fear they are likely to affect our friend's welfare. At present, all is confusion & uncertainty. He has lately received a letter from Holcroft;[70] and such a letter—

---

[70] Thomas Holcroft (1745-1809) was one of the eccentric geniuses of his day. Son of an itinerant shoemaker, a stableboy at thirteen, he was almost entirely self-educated and, in addition to his excellent knowledge of English, was skilled in French, German, and Italian, so much so that when he was in France in 1783 and wanted to steal the *Marriage de Figaro* of Beaumarchais and was unable to find a copy, he attended performances of the piece until he had memorized it in French. He then translated it under the title *The Follies of the Day,* and presented it in Covent Garden in 1784. No one knows precisely how much Holcroft wrote. His bibliography so far as it is known extends to three columns of fine print in a quarto volume. Much of it was written anonymously. His stay in France made him enthusiastic about the French Revolution, although he was not at all in sympathy with the slaughter that followed. In November of 1792 he became a member of the Society for Constitutional Information. As a result of this he was imprisoned and charged with high treason although he was released after a few months without ever being tried. Nevertheless, he was a man who thoroughly frightened most of the worthy people of England, with the notable exception of Lamb and Godwin. He was a man of extraordinary energy, impatient with those less able or dedicated than himself and so quick in apprehension that he

but you will see it, when we meet. There are pretensions in it, which make me tremble. I see nothing like it; & I dread lest he impose upon himself & us.

Remembrances to all friends. How are they? I purpose to send this by the Revd. Mr. Miller.

Monday, April 17. 1797.
Pine Street, No. 45. N.Y.   E. H. Smith.

Elegy

Farewell ye passtimes of my boyish days!
  No more ye charm my renovated soul;
Your colours fade in manhood's brighter blaze;
  Your tiny spells no more my sense controul.

What? when the lively blood of gay seventeen
  Dances, in frolic maze, my veins along;
When the young spirits, sensitive and keen,
  Dart thro' the brain and to the bosom throng?

What? when the voice with bolder accents swells;
  The eyes with fiercer, softer radiance glow;
When on the cheeks a deeper crimson dwells;
  And tingling sympathies the nerves o'erflow?

When first I feel and know myself for man,
  And see how empty & how vain ye are,
As when in hot pursuit I eager ran,
  Still shall I court, and still account ye fair?

No: to each season it's peculiar rites
  Be paid, as it's peculiar joys are felt:
I welcome now youth's yet untried delights;
  Freeze with it's terrors, with it's raptures melt.

Tranquil and uniform my days have flown,
  In sweet seclusion, 'mid these village hinds;
Nor other passions has my bosom known,
  Than such as use to sway o'er infant minds.

Ere yet the tongue forgot it's baby phrase,
  With mates of either sex, the school I sought,
Shrunk from reproof, grew emulous of praise,
  And all the ardour of ambition caught.

The peering morn surprized me at my book;
  In vain the clock proclaim'd the noon-tide hour;
Intent to read, the day the page forsook;
  The dim moon lent her insufficient power:

Sleep fled the eye-lids, while the taper's light
  Dispers'd a sickly, solitary day;
Slumbering, wild dreams possess the tossing night,
  And forms fantastic o'er the fancy stray;

Nor yet, to sports, and pranks, less fierce I flew:
  The top, the cot, the race, the rapid ball,
From the grey dawn-break, to the fall of dew,
  Saw me, insatiate, answer to their call.

To Mason F. Cogswell

I recd. yours by Theodore, inclosing the Subscriptions. We have been on the move, since then, and I have not been able to reply. By the first conveyance, and I hope by the same which takes this to you, I shall send the copies of the Opera. Thirteen are on your list: the one in blue you will accept: the remaining seven place at Hudson & Goodwin's—who will sell them at the usual allowance.

With respect to "The Medical Repository"—send us as many Cases, which are interesting, as you can, but do not forget that what we think most important, is, a regular Report of the State of Health, in your quarter—with all attendant circumstances. This Spring, for instance, you have, I am told, a peculiar sort of Pleurisy—something like that which prevailed in Phila. in 1794, the winter after the Yellow Fever, & which Dr. Rush supposes, in part, owing to the same cause. Is this account of your Hartford disease accurate? If there has been any thing peculiar in it, let us know; & in what it consisted; the mode of treatment; cause; mortality; &c. &c. It is a proper subject for our work.

Do not fear being too late for our first number. Your communication will do for the second, if not for the first. And we can not tell when we shall begin to publish. We have materials enough of our own—if obliged to have recourse to them; but we had rather receive papers from others. We wait only for subscribers, to begin. I have not time to write to Nathaniel—but as soon as any number are subscribed for, worth mentioning, we shall be glad to know. Did you ever hear Hopkins or Fish say any thing, on the subject? Accept my love, & present it to all friends.

Tuesday, April 18. 1797.
Pine St. No. 45. N. Y.   E. H. Smith.

What hand more daring seiz'd the topmost bough,
  And bade the rattling nuts amain descend?
While, with spread 'kerchiefs, meetly rang'd below,
  Stood the gay sweet-heart and the timid friend.

Ere the red dog-star scorch'd the summer air,
  Who, more triumphant, sported on the wave?
When reign'd the Fiend of Frost, more free of care,
  To the glib ice the rapid iron gave?

Anon, in all thy wondrous charms array'd,
  Thou, Nature, burst upon my ravisht sense!
Each mountain, hillock, sea, stream, pathway, glade,
  Correcter beauty, wild magnificence—

---

found the intellectual reaction of others maddening. It is evident from Dunlap's comments that Holcroft was somewhat impatient with the things that Dunlap had sent him to read. In July, 1797, Dunlap wrote him, "In April last I received your letter of December. Placed in a country where men, although devoted to literature are so rare, that, I yet, have never known one, the idea of a man whose time is so unremittingly employ'd in literary pursuits as that the reading of a Tragedy, or attending to a request for a pamphlet, should be serious interruptions was never forcibly impressed on my mind; I must therefore hope to be excused for the intrusions I have been guilty of. My expectations in regard to my Manuscripts, were, that you would look them over, and inform me in a few words whether you thought them worthy of the stage or publication . . . Your reasons for not attending to them are satisfactory, especially after having read the Drama you call Wm Tell: Your opinion in respect to that publication I think just & the knowledge of that opinion is, to me, salutary." Dunlap, *Diary* 1: p. 118.

The rock, whose viewless summit touch'd the heaven;
  The plain, sky-bounded, the sky-mingling sea;
The thunderous tempest, black thro' ether driven;
  Forests of endless pine that break it's way;

Green meadows, where the fickle Zephyr plays,
  And wantons with the lily-of-the-vale;
Light-scattering copses, whom the streamlet strays
  Beside, & listens to the whistling quail—

(Who basks him in the sunny spot, & waits,
  From ploughed fields, on whirring wings upborne,
His swiftly-wheeling, dusky colour'd mates;
  Couch'd ere the eve, and harbingers of morn:—)

The corn-fields waving, and the maize-crown'd steep,
  Those golden-glowing, *this* in tassell'd pride;
At night, the moon-beam flickering on the deep;
  By day, the sun upon the mountain' side:

Such and so various, Nature, to my views,
  Sublime & beauteous, bountiful & just,
Dazzling, yet winning, did thy graces shew;
  Inspiring wonder, more inspiring trust.

Hence, in my mind; a gradual change began;
  A change of manners and of life succeeds;
Each day the child retires, each day the man,
  With step more sure, his novel progress speeds.

Untaught, or misdirected, from his birth,
  What wonder that the youngling's active mind,
Scarce looks to heaven, scarce meditates the earth,
  To idle sports, or tyrant schools, confin'd!

But, rouz'd and nature-struck, his rapid glance
  Snatches, on every side, a swift survey;
Wonders new-born, with sudden joy entrance;
  Thrill to his soul, and on his fancy prey.

[Omitted here, one manuscript page: "Remarks on Haygarth Continued."]

To William Pitt Beers

The postscript of your letter, relative to my Opera, was communicated to me, by Mr. Johnson, soon after its reception; but, in truth, other matters have so entirely engrossed my attention, that I had entirely forgotten it, till this evening, when it has been suggested by I know not what circumstances.

I am sorry to have given you so much, & such fruitless, trouble. I knew the low state of public curiosity, concerning all that pretends to literature; I knew that local politics & the calls of avarice, divided & occupied the minds of men; and I expected little. The possibility of the objection you mention, did not occur to me, or it might have been easily obviated. The omission of my name, in the Proposals, was as much a matter of accident, as any thing else. No secret was ever made about the author. The Piece was known to be mine, for months before its representation; & my name is inserted in it. However, the event has proved it of little consequence. I send you fifteen copies. Be kind enough to place twelve of them in Webster's Book-Store—(he to sell them, if he can, on the usual terms—) or otherwise dispose of them, as you may think best. One copy I take the liberty of requesting you to cause to be sent to Cornelius Roosx, of Albany—who subscribed on a paper which Mr. Kent had—&, if you please, receive the pay. One copy will be for yourself; & allow me to beg the favor of Mrs. Beers to receive the other, as a mark of my respect & esteem.

I wish, exceedingly, to renew our former correspondence; from which I derived great pleasure; and I would enlarge, at present, would the late hour permit. I shall resume the pen, on the first intimation that it will be agreable to you.

April 20. 1797.   E. H. Smith.

Thursday, April 20.—Great part of the day writing for the Manumission Society. A visit from Mr. Lee of Sheffield; who has nearly recovered his health. Calls; & two professional visits—the last of which being at Riley's, spent an hour with the ladies. Called at Kent's—all out: at G. Mumford's—all out: drank tea with Mrs. Morton—& stayed till eight. Miss Susan absent. Remainder of the evening at home. Continued the reading of Darwin's Botanic Garden. Wrote & transcribed the letter to Mr. Beers. Recd. a letter from Mr. Tracy.

Friday, Ap. 21.—Writing for the Manumission Society. Calls of business, which took up much time at the Hospital. Continued the Botanic Garden. Called at Riley's, to see my patient. Found Theodore there, who had returned from New Haven. Spent part of the afternoon there, with him. He accompanied me home. Hence we went to Woolsey's—where we spent the evening. Mr. & Mrs. Dunlap there. Mrs. Dwight & Mrs. Riley came there. I went home with them. Since my return have made some slight additions to my letters to Abby & Fanny.

Saturday, 22.—Still more writing for the Manumission Society. Wrote a short letter to my father; & added a few lines to one to Mrs. Tracy. Numerous errands, which consumed much time. Medical visit. Spent two hours with Theodore. A visit from Dunlap, & from Dr. Miller. Recd. a letter from Joseph Dennie. Club night—at Kent's—Present, Dunlap, Gahn, Johnson, Kent, & Smith. Saml. Jones senr. there. We were entertained by his obstinate good-sense & perverse absurdity, & smoked into a head-ache by his eternal pipe. After our return, Wm. & I compared all the transcribed copies of the Laws, concerng. slaves.

Sunday, 23.—It rained all day. I was employed the greater part of it in writing for the Manumission Society. A visit from Saml. Boyd. Continued the Botanic Garden. Added a Postscript to my letter to Dr. Cogswell. Wm. & I spent the evening at Riley's. Theodore & his wife, & Miss Stillman there.

Monday, 24.—Rainy weather continues. Theodore here, in the morning. Read further in the Botanic Garden. At the Hospital—where I began an arrangement of the Cases under my care; & wrote an hour. Dr.

Miller there. Met Dr. Mitchill, on my return, & he came home with me. A visit from Mr. Roulet. At the Theater in the evening. Mrs. Johnson's Benefit: "Cymbeline." Mrs. J's *Imogen* pretty good; & so of Tyler's *Iachimo*.

Tuesday, 25.—Completed the preparation of the Report of the Manumission Society, with the documents accompanying it. Continued the perusal of The Botanic Garden. Visit from Dunlap. Errands. Various petty interruptions. Cleared off, about one P. M. Dined, drest, went out, walked. Called at Riley's: all out. Met Miss Howland, Miss Stillman, & Mrs. Coit, on the Battery. Accompanied Mrs. C. to Mrs. P's. Rejoined the young ladies, & went with them to various places—last to Mr. Woolsey's—where we drank tea, with many friends. Returned with them. Went with Miss Stillman to S. Johnson's—& again home to Mrs. Pollack's—where I sate some time. Rest of the evening at Riley's.

Wednesday, 26.—Finished the First volume of the Botanic Garden. Four hours at the Hospital, writing & prescribing. Read the News. A letter from Mumford, Mary & Idea: one poor, half-made thing, patched up among them all. They are well. Called to see Mr. Tod, who was out. Went with Theodore & his wife—the Woolseys & Dunlap's &c. to see The Elephant. He has grown a third since he was here. Teaed at Dunlap's. Spent part of the evening at Mrs. Morton's—part at Woolsey's—part at Riley's.

A very fine day. Another such, & I shall have a pleasant ride to Phila.

Thursday, 27.—Almost all day upon the run; preparing to set off for Phila.—with friends—doing business &c. Theodore, his wife, & Miss Stillman, left town. Dined at Dunlap's. Teaed at Woolsey's. Recd. letters from my Father, Mr. Tracy, & C. B. Brown. Wrote a short letter to my father. The evening, at Dunlap's—& here & there.

Friday, 28.—Dunlap & I left New York, together, this morning—& proceeded as far as Woodbridge, in the Stage; where he left me; & went to Amboy, & I went on to Princeton. We had people enough with us, but none worthy of mention. I spent the evening, agreably enough, at Dr. Smith's[71]—the President of Nassau Hall. The young ladies recd. me politely, & even affectionately. I was more pleased with Fanny, than when I saw her last; & always more so, than with her sister. Their brother seems a sensible young man; or, at least, means to pass for such. The father was rather distant; the mother, but so so.

Saturday, 29.—We arrived in Phila. about two. The weather has been fine; the roads very bad, in part, & partly, tolerable. The season is at least ten days in advance, here, of what it is around New York. After dinner, I found Mr. Tracy; & am, for the present, lodged with him: i.e. in the same house. In the afternoon, we went to Dr. Jackson's,[72] where I saw Miss Morton; & where we drank tea. After this, we called on C. B. Brown. He spent the evening with us—till 10. We sat up late—conversing.

Sunday, 30.—Brown called in the morning. Afterward I was at his father's. The chief of the forenoon with Mr. Tracy. Called at Mrs: McLane's. In the afternoon, went with Mr. Tracy to Mr. Wolcott's—where we stayed till evening. In the evening, called on C. B. Brown, Mr. Cope, Dr. Rush, & Dr. Griffiths—ineffectually—none of them being at home. Wrote a few lines to Bringhurst—& read part of the Strictures &c. on Mr. Burke's Two Letters—ascribed to Roscoe—the Medicean Historiam.[73]

Industry of April 1797
Reading

My reading, in the course of this month, has been more miscellaneous, or rather more confined to particular points, which required the partial examination of several works, than usual. Some of it, also, has been unprofitably wasted on matters of little moment. Still I see no sufficient reason for deviating from my customary conduct, & omitting the usual summary of my studies, with which the Notices of the month have been concluded, hitherto, in the present volume.

"A Sketch of a Plan to exterminate the Casual Smallpox &c." by John Haygarth. London. Johnson. 1793. 8vo. pp. 570—2 vols.

"The Botanic Garden; a Poem, in two parts." Vol. 1. Edit. Dublin. Moore. 1793. 8vo. pp. 315—including Notes—very fine print.

"Observations &c. on the Pulmonary System &c." by Wm. Davidson. London, S.Lon. 1795. 8vo. pp. 226.

Merry's "Pains of Memory"—a Poem. Edit. Phila.

Alsop's "Julius of Tarentum"—a Tragedy. (M.S.) from the German.

Priestley's Letters to Volney.

Papers, Reports, &c. relative to the Manchester (Engd.) House of Recovery.

Athenian Letters, Life of Homer, Watkins's Travels, Van Swiston, Mead's Works, Russel on the Plague, &c. &c. & turned over—in relation to my Essay on the Plague of Athens—but with very little benefit.

Strictures on Burke's Letters—attributed to Roscoe—part.

London, Paris, U.S. Newspapers.

---

[71] The Rev. Samuel Stanhope Smith (1750-1819; College of New Jersey 1769), born in Pequea, Lancaster County, Pennsylvania. Smith taught at Princeton, became a missionary, then the founder of Hampden-Sidney Academy and president of that institution (later, college). In 1779 he returned to Princeton, first as a professor and, after 1795, as president of the college. How Smith became acquainted with him is not known. He does not appear to have been a relative.

[72] Dr. David Jackson (1747?-1801), for many years a trustee of the University of Pennsylvania; 1792 elected member of the American Philosophical Society.

[73] [William Roscoe] (1753-1831?), *Strictures on Mr. Burke's Two Letters* (Philadelphia, 1797).

Writing

Composition.

Letters to various friends, preserved, equal to pp. 17. Many, not preserved.

Review of Dr. Barton's Memoir on Fascination—pp. 13.

Verses, Notes on Haygarth &c. pp. 7.

Report, for the Manumission Society, to the Convention—XV pp—4to.

Medical Cases, at the Hospital—equal to pp. 30.

Transcription.

All those letters which have been preserved.

The Report to the Convention.

Extract from Mr. Kent's Lecture on Slavery, as an Appendix to the Report; & various other articles, for the same purpose.

MEMOIRS. 1797. MAY.

Monday, 1.—Called on Ch. B. Brown. We went to Cope's; to see Mrs. Robinson—formerly, Miss Atmore; & Mr. & Mrs. Paxon. He was not at home. I called on Dr. Wistar; & saw him. Ineffectually on Drs. Rush & Griffiths.[74] Strong, who came to see me, yesterday—has not called to-day—as he promised. Dined with Charles—& read Joseph's letter. Went, with Dr. Wistar & Judge Turner, to the Bettering-House[75] & Hospital. The latter has a vegetable powder, which he proposes as a certain cure for Cancer. The principal object of our search was a suitable case in which to try it. One was found. In the evening, at the Theater. I saw Mrs. Merry, Mr. Cooper, Mrs. Oldmixon, & others whom I have before seen. I defer remarks at present. The Play—"All for Love"—the Farce "Dead & Alive."[76]

Tuesday, 2.—Went with Mr. Tracy to see Mr. Adams, the President. He invited us to a family dinner.[77] Next called at Dr. Jackson's. Stept in at Fenno's. Dr. Strong here. Met Dr. Leib in the street. Called at John Riley's—my quondam host's. At Charles's. Went with him to James Bringhurst's, & Armit Brown's.[78] Went, with Mr. Tracy, to Levee; where I saw the Secretaries; the Atty. Genl.; the British Minister & Consul Genl.—& other gentlemen. We stayed till the whole was over, & then went in to dine. Nobody—except the Prest., his Secy. & us. We sat till near seven. Dunlap arrived; & I—with him & Ch. B. Brown, went to Lailson's Amphitheater.[79]

Wednesday, 3rd.—Dunlap & I called on Brown. Bringhurst arrived yesterday. Not to be found. Called, together, at the Theater. Could not find Wignell. Called at Jno. Leib's.[80] Then we went to see Laffert. He recd. us affectionately, but was just ready to mount his horse to leave town. Mr. Volney absent from Phila.—so we had no opportunity of seeing him. Went to several book-stores & purchased some pamphlets. Among the rest, we were at Cobbet's—(Peter Porcupine—)—He is a stout, plain-looking man, with a countenance neither indicative of much ability or amiableness, but not destitute of marks of good-sense. We returned to Brown's—& found Bringhurst. Met Dr. Rush in the street. Brown & Bringhurst with us, in the afternoon. I visited Dr. Leib's parents & family—he not at home. Convention commenced it's Session at 6 this evening & held us till nine & after. Time occupied in receiving Communications from the Societies.

Thursday, 4.—We went to see Federal Frigate, now building here, with Mr. Tracy & Brown. Then to the Convention. After going thro' the Communications, they were referred to a Committee of which I was made Chairman. We immediately fell to work, & labored till near two. Then I went & dined at Brown's, with Dunlap & Bringhurst. After dinner, again at the Committee, till after seven. Came home—found Tracy & Dunlap in, & Mr. Wolcott here, & Mr. Lee, the U. S. Atty. Genl.[81] We engaged to dine at Mr. Wolcott's on Saturday. Brown here. I went to Dr. Jackson's—Where I spent an hour & half very agreably. Miss Morton was not there. I wrote, this day, a short letter to Wm. Johnson.

Friday, 5th.—Dr. Mitchill arrived last night. I found him this morning, & sent him to our lodgings. On the Committee again, from nine till two. Dined at Dr. Wistar's, with Genl. Bloomfield[82] & Mrs. Coxe, of

---

[74] Dr. Griffiths, cited earlier, was on the Committee of Correspondence of the Manumission Society.

[75] Bettering House (the Philadelphia Almshouse) was a hospital for the poor and also an employment agency for them. In all likelihood Dr. Wistar was there in a professional capacity, Smith to observe; Judge George Turner (1750-1843) probably went along for the ride. Turner was judge of the Northwest Territory and something of an authority on Indians.

[76] *All for Love*, John Dryden (1678); *Dead Alive, or the Double Funeral*, John O'Keefe (1781). Mr. Cooper was Thomas A. Cooper, adopted son of William Godwin and protégé of Thomas Holcroft. At this time he was in his early twenties and although a fine actor had not yet become the great tragedian he was destined to be. See Pollock, *The Philadelphia Theatre*, p. 60.

[77] It is difficult to believe that Smith could have spent several hours in conversation with the President of the United States without thereafter making even one comment on what was said. It is all the more strange since Smith was aware, as he wrote elsewhere, that his "Diary" might some day have historical importance.

[78] Armit Brown was a clerk in the Bank of Pennsylvania.

[79] The "Circus" was a huge building (considerably larger than the "New Theatre" which held 2,000 people) with a dome about ninety feet high. Laitson, a Frenchman, built it for both theater performances and circuses (which usually consisted of a caged animal or two and an equestrian troupe). Plays were presented there between April 11 and July 27, 1797. The next spring Laitson opened on March 8 and lasted until April 7 when he sold out and returned to France leaving his company to find work where they could. On Sunday morning, July 8, 1798, the dome collapsed and destroyed the building.

[80] John Leib, an attorney at law, who resided at 445 North Front Street, Philadelphia.

[81] Charles Lee (1758-1815) appointed by Washington, 1795-1801.

[82] Joseph Bloomfield (1753-1823), lawyer, officer in the

Burlington, (N. J.) members of Convention, & Blair McClenechan.[83] Miss Wistar & Miss Eddy are sensible & agreable women. Went to the Convention at three P. M. sat till seven. Then to the Theater. Prigmore's Benefit, very thin house. Execrable play. After Piece "No Song no Supper."[84] Not well played. Came home at eleven.

Saturday, 6.—Mitchill & I called to see Dr. Strong: he was out. We called on Dr. Rush—& found him absent. Went to some bookstores, & purchased a few pamphlets. Met Dr. Barton in the street, & went home with him. We spent two hours at his house. He shewed us a memoir of his, now in print, for the 4th volume of the Philosophical Society's Transactions[85]—also some proof-sheets of an Essay of his, now in the press —in which he supposes that he has proven the asiatic origin of all the american Tribes. He shewed us a part of the jaw-bone of the Mammoth—comprehending all that part, on either side, which forms the chin. This is probably, the only thing of the kind now known. We called on Dr. Woodhouse; he was from home. Went to Moreau St. Mery's. Mitchill was acquainted with him, & I wished to purchase a pamphlet. Mr. Tracy, Dunlap, Mitchill & myself dined at Mr. Wolcott's—& spent the afternoon very agreably. Dr. Strong joined us, & we went to the Theater. "The Way to get Married" & "Lock & Key." The Comedy, on the whole, better played than with us. I did not see the after piece; but stayed only to see the finest dancing I ever did see, by Mr. & Mrs. Byrne—in the *"Pas Ruse."* Dr. Leib here in the morng.

Sunday, May 7.—Mitchill, Dunlap & myself breakfasted with Dr. Barton, with whom we remained till near twelve o'clock, much to our satisfaction. His conversation was entertaining & instructive. He shewed us, among other things, many elegant drawings, some coloured & some plain, executed by himself, of various animals & plants. He also related several curious facts, which I only neglect to notice here—as they are to form part of the Transactions of the Philosophical Society—vol 4th now publishing. Dunlap & I went to see Ch. B. Brown—where we fell into an animated discussion on "Courage, Fortitude, Intrepidity &c." Tracy, Dunlap, & I dined at Dr. Jackson's—& spent much of the afternoon. Dunlap went to our lodgings—Tracy & I went to see Josh. Strong. He was not at home. We came back to Mr. Wolcott's—where we spent two hours very agreably, & saw, a little before coming away, Mr. Harrison, the Auditor of the U. S. & his wife. Mr. T. went home, & I to Dr. Jackson's. I found Dunlap there —& a room full of company—among others—Miss Durham, of Brunswick (N. J.) & Mrs. Levy—who, with Miss Morton, are to be our companions to N. York. Mrs. Levy is a beautiful woman—& I engaged with her in a spirited & varied conversation for more than hour. When we came home, we found Mitchill here, & Dr. Wistar—who stayed but a short time. Mr. Allen Miller of Connecticut came here to-day.

Monday, 8.—Mitchill, Dunlap, Brown, myself, &c. &c. went to see the Jail—& spent two hours, with great satisfaction. I had been reading Turnbull's account of it,[86] in the morning—which is called the best—but it is very imperfect. Information, to be useful, to aid other States in forming similar institutions, should be much more minute. Brown & I visited Strong. Dunlap & a number of the Delegates, dined at James Todd's—one of the Pennsylvania representation. Convention met at three, & sat till near eight. I then called at Ch. B. Brown's—Mr. McLane's (the brother in law of Dr. Miller)—& at the Paxon's. The last were not at home—I followed them to a Mr. Thompson's—where were Josh. Bringhurst & Mrs. Robinson. Stayed till near ten. Josh. came home with me. Bedded at twelve.

Tuesday, 9.—Mitchill & I sat out to see Dr. Leib, but met him—& we all went together to Mr. Beckley's[87]— to see Miss Mason of N. York—she was out. Went to Convention. We adjourned, *sine die*, about two P. M. Mitchill, Dunlap & I dined with Dr. Rush—& spent most of the afternoon with him. After that Dunlap & I visited the Library—Ch. B. Brown & Mr. Cope were there. I saw Poulson—who shewed me Spencer's Translation of Büerger's Lenora—with it's fine engravings. Hence we went to Dr. Jackson's—& thence, with Mrs. J. to Mrs. Levy's. There was much company. We saw little Miss Butler, & her younger sister Penelope: both remarkably beautiful. We were pleased with Mrs. Levy's execution on the Pianoforte—more with her singing: but we were enchanted with Miss Butler's execution. From this we visited Mr. Cope. Charles was there. We came home about ten.

Wednesday, 10.—We took leave of our friends—& about eight, Mrs. Levy, Miss Morton, & Miss Durham, Dunlap & myself—with three other passengers, entered the Stage: the day pleasant. At Trenton, we saw Miss Smith of Princeton; at Princeton, Miss Frances Smith. We reached Brunswic—where Miss Durham was at home.

Thursday, 11.—A beautiful morning. We were on our road, by four in the A. M. Reached N. York, with-

---

Revolution, Attorney-General of New Jersey, 1783-1792; Governor 1801-1812 during which he promoted legislation which with amendment almost eliminated slavery in New Jersey; trustee of Princeton; U.S. House, 1817-1821.

[83] Blair McClenechan and P. Moore, merchants, 33 Front Street, Philadelphia.

[84] Prigmore's benefit: the play was titled *The School for Citizens*, not found; there was also a third offering called *The Sailor's Landlady* probably by O'Keefe; *No Song, No Supper* has been previously glossed. Thomas C. Pollock, *The Philadelphia Theatre in the Eighteenth Century. Together with the Day Book of the Same Period* (Philadelphia, London, 1833), p. 339.

[85] *Trans. Amer. Philos. Soc.*, o.s., 4, 11 (1799): pp. 74-113. His work on the Indians was entitled *New Views of the Origin of the Tribes and Nations of America* (Philadelphia, 1797).

[86] Robert James Turnbull, *A Visit to the Philadelphia Prison* (Philadelphia, 1796).

[87] Mr. John Beckley, clerk of the House of Representatives.

out accident, about 12. After cleaning, & dressing, went to Dunlap's. Called to see Mrs. Lovegrove—twice—she was out, both times. Drank tea at Dunlap's—& we went to see our ladies—they were out. He went home. I to Mrs. Morton's, where I found them. All pretty well there. Saw Mr. Quincy,[88] the gentleman said to be the lover of Miss Susan Morton. Went home with Mrs. Levy & Miss Morton, to Mr. Morton's. Went to Woolsey's. Was at Mr. Kent's, in the P. M. Johnson & all friends well. Recd. a letter from my father.

Friday, 12th May.—Read the various magazines, recd. during my absence. Visited Mrs. Lovegrove, & Miss Morton & Mrs. Levy. Three hours at the Hospital. Met Dr. Miller in the street. Called on him, in vain. A call from Mr. Dana, & from Mr. Webster, & from Dr. Seaman. Went to Riley's Miss Alsop is there. Saw Mr. Hosmer there. He has grown quite fleshy. Called at H. Johnson's—drank tea at Seth's. Principal part of the evening at home. Read M. de Liancourt's pamphlet "On the Prisons of Philadelphia."[89]

Saturday, 13.—Visited the Hospital. Great part of the day consumed in petty calls &c. Wrote a few lines to El. Smith Jr. & to my sister Abby. Dined with Dr. & Mrs. Miller. Dunlap here. We walked. Medical visit. Drank tea at Riley's; & spent part of the eveng. there. Mr. & Mrs. Coit & Miss Howland, Mr. & Mrs. Seba & Mrs. Yates, Mr. & Mrs. Woolsey & Miss Dwight, & Mr. & Mrs. Dunlap &c. there. Part of the evening at Mr. Kent's. Read the newspapers. Read Dr. Logan's little pamphlet of Experiments on Gypsum &c.—& Mr. Peters's Publication, on the same subject.

Sunday, 14.—Some progress in Mr. Bordley's pamphlet on "Rotation of Crops." Medical visit. At the Hospital. Wm. & I went to Riley's. Thence, on the Battery. Separated. I called on Mrs. Lovegrove. Next, ineffectually, at Mr. Morton's—to Mrs. Levy &c. At Mrs. Morton's. At Mr. Catlin's. Dined at H. Johnson's with the whole of them, & Mr. Cragie of Cambridge (Mass.)[90] & spent the afternoon. Medical visit. Evening at Mr. Morton's—with Miss Morton, & Mrs. Levy.

Monday, 15.—Finished Bordley's pamphlet "On Rotation of Crops" & Dr. Priestley's "Considerations on Phlogiston &c."[91] & made some progress in St. George Tucker's "Dissertation on Slavery."[92] Dunlap here—& Gahn. Much of the forenoon posting books. Attended the Introductory Lecture to the Botanical Course, by Dr. Hosack. At the Hospital. A visit from Mr. Roulet. A visit from Mr. Chauncey Jr. of New Haven.[93] Teaed at Dunlap's. Mr. Miller here. Eveng. at a meeting of the Trustees of the African School.

Tuesday, 16.—Finished Tucker's Dissertation on Slavery—& looked thro' the Monthly Review for Jany. & Feby. 1797, which Mr. Roulet left with me. At the Hospital. Looked over some articles in Zoonomia. Drank tea at Kent's. Evening, at the stated meeting of the Manumission Society. I have felt remarkably languid, sleepy, & incapable of mental & corporeal exertion, all this day—which has been spent to little purpose, & been quite unhappy. I must exert myself to throw off this oppression. Since my return from the Society, I have read about 30 pages in the Phila. edition of Godwin's Political Justice.

Wednesday, 17.—Continued Godwin, about 20 pages. Some progress in Mr. Adet's reply to Priestley. Much of the forenoon at the City Library, turning over books, in hopes of finding something further, relative to Athens. At the Hospital. I have been opprest with a remarkable disposition to stupor, ever since my return from Phila. If I sit down to read, especially in the afternoon or evening, it is almost irresistable. Dunlap is affected in the same way. I was obliged to have recourse to exercise to avoid it. I called at Dunlap's—he was not at home. I found him at Hodgkinson's & we went out to Webster's—whose infant I inoculated. We extended our walk a little, & returned. I drank tea at Mr. Coit's—Mrs. Riley, Miss Alsop, &c. were there. Rest of the evening at Mrs. Lovegrove's lodgings. Recd. letters from Mr. Tracy, & my kinsman Saml. Smith of Georgia.

Thursday, 18.—Rain all day. Call from Dunlap; visit from Mr. Roulet. Writing for the Manumission Society. Finished Adet's reply to Priestley—in french. Read Mitchill's Letter to Dr. Percival, in the New York Magazine for April—& several other articles in that publication. Looked over the NewsPapers—read the President's Speech (which is as it ought to be—)—& continued Godwin. At Gurdon Mumford's part of the evening—the remainder at Mr. Morton's—to see Miss Morton & Mrs. Levy. Wrote a short letter to my father.

Friday, 19th May.—Dunlap here—informed me of Mitchill's return. Went to see him. Conversation &c. We went to the Hospital together; prescribed; & made some new arrangements. Read the "Case of the Soapboilers & Tallow Chandlers"[94] & a Dissertation on Oxy-

---

[88] Josiah Quincy (1772-1864), Harvard, 1790, member of an old, distinguished and wealthy Massachusetts family. He married Miss Morton (glossed earlier), a famous beauty. Quincy, who appears a number of times hereafter in these pages, was in his long life a member of the Massachusetts Senate 1804, 1805, 1813-1820; U.S. Senate (as a Federalist) 1805-1813; Massachusetts House 1821, 1822; municipal judge 1822; mayor of Boston 1823-1829; president of Harvard 1829-1845.

[89] [François Alexandre duc de la Liancourt], *Des Prisons de Philadelphie* (Philadelphia, 1796).

[90] Probably Andrew Craigie (note difference in spelling) (1743-1819), Revolutionary surgeon at Bunker Hill and siege of Boston; first to fill office of Continental Apothecary created in July, 1775; during connection with the army he acquired large fortune by buying government certificates and other speculations; one of directors of first U.S. bank; in 1791 bought large house in Cambridge which had been Washington's headquarters: later known as "Craigie House" and "Craigie-Longfellow House."

[91] *The Doctrine of Phlogiston Established*, obviously published by May, 1797; only located copy. (Northumberland [Pennsylvania], 1800) L.C.P.

[92] Philadelphia, 1796.

[93] Mr. Chauncey, Jr. of New Haven was born in 1777 (Yale 1792), studied law but was too young to practice before 1798.

[94] *The Case of the Manufacturers of Soap and Candles* (New York, 1797).

gene. Afternoon Mitchill & I went, by appointment, at Miller's—& we settled some matters, in relation to the "Medical Repository." We called to see Miss Eddy, of Phila., now in town. Teaed & spent part of the evening at Woolsey's—remainder at Moses Rogers's—Miss Whittelsey, there.

Saturday, 20.—Read Alexander Hosack's Dissertation on the Yellow Fever of 1795—distinguished only for some misrepresentations of fact—in respect to transactions in the New York Hospital—last evening. Made some progress, this day, in Professor McLean, of Princeton's—answer to Dr. Priestley—in which I was engaged, when I recd. a note from my father—who arrived in town last evening. I hastened to seek him. On my way, met Dr. Pleasants of Phila. with whom I had a few minutes conversation. With my father, I found Mr. Allen, of Lichfield, who is now on his way to Congress—having been lately elected. Mr. Woolsey came in—& we went to his house. Thence my father came with me, here. We returned to Woolsey's to dinner. Allen there. After dinner, we went to the Apothecary's. There I left him—& came home. Thence, a few minutes, to Mr. Kent's. We drank tea, & spent the evening at Woolsey's—where my father stays. Allen was there, & Dunlap & Johnson. Recd. letters from Abby, Fanny, & Danl. Lewis.

Sunday, 21.—Wrote a letter to Mr. Tracy. Wrote also a Note, transmissive of Edwin & Angelina, to the Secretary of State.[95] A professional visit. Wm. & I sat off, to seek Dr. Osborn of North Carolina, who is now in town. We met him in the street, walked round the Battery; & dropt into Riley's—where I left them & went to Woolsey's, to see my father. Dined at S. Johnson's. About 4 P. M. Wm. & I went to Woolsey's. My father had been to Church all day. He came home—& went with us out to Webster's—where we drank tea. Came back to Woolsey's. Mr. Allen joined us. We spent part of the evening. Allen & I the remainder at Dunlap's.

Monday, 22.—Mr. Allen went to Phila. this morning. Most of the day with my father—piloting him about town, & assisting him in the purchase of his goods. Dr. Osborn accompanied me to the Hospital—where, one of the patients dying, we tarried some time to examine the body. Dined, with my father, at Dunlap's—& drank tea there. We called to see Miss Mumford—& Mrs. P. Riley; & spent part of the evening at Mr. Catlin's—& the rest at Woolsey's.

Tuesday, 23.—Finished Professor McLean's answer to Priestley, last evening; & to-day, have read Bay's Inaugural Dissertation on Dysentery.[1] Most of the day occupied with my father—assisting him in his business. Professional visits. Dined at Woolsey's—with my father. Drank tea at Riley's—with Miss Alsop &c. Called on Miss Morton & Mrs. Levy, ineffectually. Spent part of the evening with Mrs. Lovegrove—the rest at home. Recd. letters from Dr. Griffiths of Phila. & from Mary & Idea of Aurora.

Wednesday, 24.—Breakfasted with my father, at Moses Rogers's. We did some business—& made several calls on some of his old acquaintance. At the Hospital as usual. We dined with Mr. Kent. After dinner, went to Mr. Watson's. I left my father there, & went to Mr. Webster's, to see his child. Returned to Woolsey's to tea. Thence my father & I went to H. Johnson's—where we spent most of the evening. He went home—& I spent the rest at Dunlap's. Recd. letters from Mr. Tracy, & Mr. Pickering.

Thursday, 25.—Accompanied my father, on his business &c. We visited Dr. & Mrs. Miller. I called to see Mrs. Lovegrove. Professional visit. Called to see Mrs. Levy & Miss Morton. Saw the last. Dined at Woolsey's. My father & I went out to see the new Jail, the Hospital &c. A call from Dr. Osborn. We drank tea at Mrs. Lovegrove's. I went to see Miss S. Morton—saw also, there, Mrs. Levy, Miss Howland, Mr. Quincy &c. Part of the eveng. at Woolsey's. Mr. Gahn there. Part at Dunlap's. Recd. letters from Abby, & from Sally Pierce. Wrote to Dr. Griffiths—concerning the business with the Chancellor of the French Consulate[2]—on whom I called.

Friday, 26.—My father breakfasted here. Wrote short letters to Abby & Fanny. Went with, my father, to various places—among others to the African School. Called on Mr. Miller. Dr. Miller sat off for Phila. to-day. At the Hospital from 11 till 2—on business of the library &c. My father & I dined at John Broome's. I called, in the morng. on Mrs. Levy & with Dunlap in the afternoon. She was unwell, & we did not see her. At Gahn's in the afternoon. Drank tea, with my father & Mr. Roulet, at Dunlap's. After tea, Dunlap & wife, R. S. & E. H. S. went to The Theater. "Chapter of Accidents" & "Tom Thumb."[3] both well played. Master Stockwell's *Tom Thumb*, admirable. My father much pleased. I called at Mr. Kent's, on my return, to see the child. Found it better. Mrs. Levy well enough to be at the Theater where I saw her & Miss Morton. Miss Eddy was there also—I conversed with her a few minutes.

Saturday, 27.—My father came here. A call to see a patient in a new family, Mr. Radcliff's—lately moved into town. Visits, or business, &c. with & without my father. Dr. Osborn here: & Dr. S. Osborn. Called on Mrs. Lovegrove. Found there Mrs. Levy & Miss Morton. Accompanied them to Mrs. Morton's. Dined, with my father, Dunlap, & G. M. Woolsey, at Woolsey's. Went with R. S., Miss P. Dwight &c. on board the

---

[95] Transmission of *Edwin and Angelina* to the Secretary of State within six months of application for copyright was in accordance with prescribed procedure as detailed in the *Copyright Law of 1790*.

[1] One of the requirements for a medical degree was that the candidate write a dissertation. Smith appears to have been given copies of these by his medical co-workers in Philadelphia and New York. They will not usually be glossed.

[2] Information not found. Possibly the affair had something to do with the problem of the manumission of slaves.

[3] *Tom Thumb* by Henry Fielding (1730).

vessel. They sat sail for New-Haven. Dunlap & I drank tea, & spent the evening, at Mr. Morton's—with the family, including Miss M. & Mrs. Levy—& with Miss S. Morton & Mr. Quincy. The night is stormy—rain & thunder—I hope no inconvenience will arise to my father & his companions.

Sunday, 28.—A visit from Dr. Mitchill. Called at Kent's—repeatedly—his little girl unwell. Johnson & I walked out of town. Called at Roulet's. He was absent. Visited Mr. Lagarenne, at his new house. Called at Riley's. Dined at H. Johnson's—with S. J. & his wife, Mrs. Lovegrove, Miss Stuyvesant, & Miss Johnson. H. J. is in Phila. Mr. Kent & I went out to Webster's. We drank tea there. A remarkable fine day. Went to Mr. Morton's. Saw Mrs. Levy & Miss Morton. Went with them to Mrs. Morton's. Returning, called in with them, to see Miss Denning. Mrs. Levy goes to-morrow. I took leave of her. Dropt in at Mr. Kent's, on my way home. Little girl better. Mr. Silas Wood of L.Id. there.

Monday, 29.—Commenced the transcription of my review of Dr. Barton's Memoir, with corrections. Made some calls & settled some accounts. Professional calls. Prescribed at the Hospital. After dinner called on Dr. Mitchill—concerning business referred to us & others, of the Hospital. We went to see R. J. Kissam about it —but he was absent. As part of it had relation to a design, I called on Dunlap—but, after more than an hour's labor, we could not hit on any thing satisfactory. I drank tea, & spent most of the evening, at Riley's. After my return a professional visit. The morning was pleasant, & the afternoon & evening cloudy, chilly, windy. I have felt unfit for mental exercise all the afternoon; much as I did on my return from Phila. The sudden change of weather now, as then, may be, in part, the cause. Two others occur to me. At Phila. my mind was constantly in lively employ. It has been so here, during the stay of my father. At Phila. I returned to the constant use of animal food, once, & sometimes twice a day. On coming home, I reverted to my simple fare. While my father was here, I dined abroad every day, & ate of meat &c. This day I returned to my usual food. A change so sudden & entire, in diet, may be the cause of my sleepiness & imbecillity. I shall attend to this—& exclude meat altogether from my food. The habit of doing without it will soon be again confirmed, & I shall feel my wonted alertness. I am much better this evening. In the course of this day, I have looked over a Natural History of Birds for Children, which I purchased this day; & several medical articles, in Cullen & Darwin. I have read in the First & Third volumes of the Asiatic Researches—the articles—"On the Second Classical Book of the Chinese," "On the Plants of India," "On the inhabitants of the Yarrow Hills," "On the Nicoba Isles & the fruit of the Mellon." "On the mystical poetry of the Persians & Hindus," & the two short articles concerning Indigo.

Tuesday, 30.—Two medical visits. While at Mr. Kent's, saw W. P. Beers of Albany. Wrote a little on my essay on the plague of Athens. Wrote a short letter to Mr. Tracy. My sleepiness came on this day before dinner. It was not worse after than before; but it oppresses me exceedingly. Read several papers in the 1st and 3rd vols. of the Asiatic Researches—in all perhaps, 200 pages—with very little improvement. A visit from Mr. Roulet. Two medical visits. Drank tea, & spent part of the evening, at Mr. Boyd's; part, with Mr. & Mrs. Johnson, Comedians; part at home. Visit to Dingley in the morning.

Wednesday, 31.—This day, like yesterday, a fire has been comfortable. It began to clear off about ten in the morning. Continued the reading of Asiatic Researches. Three professional calls, in the course of the day—& various others, on business &c. Read the Papers. Mr. Beers here, when I was out. He out, when I called on him. At the Hospital, as usual. Less sleepy to-day, than yesterday—but still opprest with lethargy—after my spare & simple dinner. Perhaps avoided before dinner, by my walk to & from the Hospital—& my mental employment there. Drank tea, & spent the evening, at Woolsey's. Johnson & Gahn there. Mr. Roulet here, in the afternoon. After our return from Woolsey's, Johnson & I sat down to the comparison of Morse's Geography, & Winterbotham's View of the U.S.[4]—till eleven.

This month, which is now come to an end, is distinguished by less of application than any preceeding month, for some time. Still, it has not been wholly without improvement. My visit to Phila. & the time devoted

---

[4] William Winterbotham published *An Historical, Geographical, Commercial, and Philosophical View of the American United States and the European Settlements in America and in the West Indies* (London, 1795). John Reid, a New York bookseller, reprinted it (New York, 1796). Jedidiah Morse promptly sued Reid in the Federal courts in New York claiming that Winterbotham's book was virtually a copy of his *American Geography, or a View of the Present Situation of the United States* (Boston, etc., 1789). Smith is surprisingly reticent about the matter but what happened was this: in the spring of 1797 Smith and Johnson received a commission from the United States Circuit Court to compare the two works. On April 17, 1797, Judge Kent wrote to Morse to tell him that counsel on both sides had agreed to having Johnson and Smith act as referees to decide two points: (1) whether or not Morse's book was an original work (about which, said Kent, there was no doubt); (2) whether Winterbotham's book plagiarized it and violated Morse's copyright. Morse had been a tutor at Yale during Smith's senior year; they had also met at least once at Webster's, but it would seem that Kent was unaware of it. In his letter he thought it necessary to describe Johnson and Smith to Morse as "very upright, ingenious & literary men. The one is a lawyer & the other a physician." It is hard to see how Morse as a good Yale man could have been anything but delighted to have two other good Yale men as referees. On July 26 Kent again wrote to Morse to tell him that he had seen one of the referees that day and had been informed that the comparison was finished. Kent did not ask what their decision was and the referee did not say; nevertheless, said Kent, he believed that the judgment would be in Morse's favor. Kent was correct in his surmise. The referees declared that Morse's work was original and that Winterbotham's was almost a complete copy. The court, acting on their decision, found for the plaintiff. For Kent's letters and a copy of the Smith-Johnson report see manuscripts in the Morse Family Collection, Yale University Library.

to my father while he was here, have occupied me too much to allow of regular medical study; but, if the last have been marked by pleasure, the first was not destitute of gratification—not merely to curiosity & the craving desire of fraternizing with old friends, but to the eager love of information, which in some measure found itself satisfied.

In this period I have not found, till within a few days, much professional employment. But, within a few days, I have obtained some & from new quarters, in part; so that my prospect seems a little to brighten. I may now consider myself as physician to eight or nine families. A small number it is true, but with twice that number I should be secure of a support; & now I almost dare to promise it to myself.

Industry of May 1797

Reading

Asiatic Researches—papers in the 1st & 3rd vols. equal to 450 pages.
Sketches on Rotations of Crops &c. Phila. Cist. '96—8vo. pp. 76.
Agricult: Experimen: on Gypsum &c. by Geo: Logan. Phila. 1797. 8vo. pp. 18.
Agricult Enquiries on Plaister of Paris &c. by [?] Phila. 1797. 8vo. pp. 118.
A Chemo.: Medl. Ess. on Oxygene—Benj. De Witt—Phila. 1797. 8vo. pp. 35.
Inaugl. Dissertn. &c. on Dysentery. Wm. Bay.—N. York—'97. 8vo. pp. 62.
Considns: on Phlogiston &c. Dr. Priestley—Phila. 1796. 8vo. pp. 39.
Experiences & Obs. par. Dr. Priestley—translated into french by Adet, with Mr. Adet's reply—in all—pp. 70 —Phila. '97. 8vo. fine print.
Professor McLean's, of Princeton, reply to Priestley— about pp. 100—8vo.—Phila. '97.
Turnbull & Liancourt's pamphlets on the Phila. Jail— about pp. 150 8vo.
Professor St. George Tucker's "Dissertation on Slavery"—printed in Phila.—of about pp. 130 8vo. close print.
Hosack's Query: Dissert. on Yellow Fever of 1795—N. York—about pp. 40. 8vo.
Spencer's translation of Büerger's Leonora—equal perhaps to pp. 6. 8vo.
Mitchill's Letter to Percival—equal to pp. 10—8vo.— common size.
Godwin's Political Justice—perhaps pp. 70—8vo.
Monthly Review Enlarged, for Jany. & Febry. 1797.

Writing

Report of the Committee of Arrangements of Convention of Delegates—from the Abolition Societies— equal to pp. 14—8vo. close print.
Letters to friends—equal to pp. 10—8vo.
Transcribed, in part, with corrections, Review of B's Memoir. This, beside News-Papers, occasional medical reading—&c.

MEMOIRS. 1797. JUNE.

Thursday, 1.—Read the annotations annexed to Creech's translation of Lucretius, so far as related to those lines wherein the Plague of Athens is described. A professional visit. Met Dr. Mitchill in the street. Walked & talked with him: Met, also, Mr. Beers— who came home with me—& sat a while. A call from Mr. Miller. Called upon Mrs. Lovegrove. Wrote over a small part of my first medical essay. A call from Dr. R. S. Kissam, on Hospital business. At the time when my stupor usually occurs, worked on my essay. I felt it slightly. The day very fine. I am in great hopes of wearing it out. At three called on Mr. & Mrs. Beers; & stayed till four. Then on Mrs. Lovegrove—& we walked into the country—& returned a little after seven. I drank tea with her. A medical visit. The remainder of the evening at Kent's. Mr. & Mrs. Beers there. Recd. letters from Jno. Allen & Nathl. Dwight.

I am astonished when I seriously consider how little I perform. My time seems to vanish away, while I have just sense enough to see that I do wrong, to condemn my own folly, & to resolve on the cure. Alas! when shall I apply the only remedy!—industry?

Friday, June 2nd.—Medical visit. Writing on the Medical Essay No. 1. At the Hospital. Medical visit. Drank tea with Miss Howland. Company there. Spent the evening at Riley's, with Mrs. R. & Miss Alsop. Have altogether escaped my sleepiness to-day.

Saturday, 3.—A medical visit, which, obliging me to go to the cutler's, the hospital &c. and to make preparations for a small operation, which, after all, was not performed, occupied two hours. Read the Papers, containing long Speeches in Congress &c. An hour or more at the Library—looking over the Reviews, in the vain hope of finding some extracts which might assist me, in my Essay. Made some progress in this essay. At Mitchill's. Read there, letters of Dr. Barker, of Portland, Maine, on Alkaline practice in Fevers; & since, an abstract of his Theory of Consumption. Three hours, with R. S. Kissam, Post, & Mitchill, on a Committee on Hospital business. Medical visit. Gahn & I went out to Roulet's—where we spent the evening. Looked over Beddoes on Scurvy, after my return. Recd. letters from Mr. Tracy, Dr. Griffiths, & Dr. Buel. Wrote to Mr. Allen.

Sunday, 4.—Medical visit. Dunlap called upon me, to accompany him to a meeting which was to take place, between himself, Hallam & Hodgkinson, concerning their affairs. I went with him to Hodgkinson's—& thence we three went to the Theater at 10 A.M., where we met Hallam & a Mr. Basier. They conversed till eleven—& nearly came to terms. I went to Gahn's Counting-house—according to appointment, where I met him & Roulet—& we called on Miss Eddy—who leaves town on Tuesday. I returned home. Wm. & I called on Mrs. Lovegrove. Thence we went to S. Johnson's. Mrs. J. unwell. I dined with Gahn—& spent most of the afternoon. Medical visit. Visit to H. Johnson's, who has lately returned from Phila. Wm. came in—& we went to Dunlap's—where we spent the remainder of the evening. Came home, & wrote letters to Nathl. Dwight, & Wm. Buel.

Monday, 5.—A little progress in Essay First. Medical visit. Calls. Went to see Mr. Miller. Recd. Dr. Smith of Princeton there. At the Hospital. Looked over parts of Hippocrates. Called to see Mrs. Riley & Miss Alsop. Saw the first. At Mr. Kent's. Read there a number of Pages, in Howard on Prisons,[5] relative to the Plague & the Jail-Fever. Called at Mr. Leffingwell's. They out. Visited at Charles Adams's. Was at Woolsey's. Miss Alsop came there, as I came out. Went to Mrs. Morton's. Saw none but Jno. Morton. So I shall not see Miss S. Morton again. I met Miss Morton, in the street. She is well. Have read about 80 pages in Garat's "Account of my Conduct"[6] &c. Recd. letters from Mr. Tracy & Mr. Morris. The letter from the last containing an interesting sketch of his life.

Tuesday, 6.—A medical visit, which occupied some time. Read thro' the book commenced yesterday—"Memoirs of the Revolution; or, an Apology for my conduct &c." By D. J. Garat—translated by R. Heron—Edinb: 1797—8vo. pp. 281. A long visit to Dr. Mitchill. Wrote the following letter to Dr. Barton. Called on Mrs. Lovegrove, & we took a long walk out of town—in the course of which we called at Mr. Webster's. I drank tea with Mrs. L. We spent the evening at S. Johnson's. Since my return, I have transcribed my letter to Dr. Barton, & written a short one to Dr. Wilkins of Baltimore.

Wednesday, June 7.—Most of the morning looking over various medical articles in several volumes of the Monthly Review Enlarged. Wrote letters to Mr. Morris, Danl. W. Lewis, & Mr. Tracy. At the Hospital, as usual. Read the news-papers. Read several chapters in "Political Justice." Drank tea at Dunlap's. We went to the Theater; Johnson's Benefit: Hodgkinson's play, intituled "The Man of Fortitude, or the Knight's Adventure"—first performed: with much effect & applause. Read the Preface, & some part of the work of Le Clerc—called "Historie de la Medicine."[7] Dunlap & I walked on the Battery. A very fine day, & evening. Left off my Flannel vest, next my skin. Recd. a short letter from Ch. B. Brown.

Thursday, 8.—Recd. letters from my Father & from Mr. Tracy; & replied to both. A medical visit. Errands. Reading in Hippocrates Sect. VII—in Le Clerc's Historie de la Medicine, in Thucydides, in the Annotations on Creech's version of Lucretius—& in Political Justice & Shakespere. Wrote, also, a few pages on my Medical Essay No. I. Errands, in the afternoon, & news-papers. Called at Kent's. Johnson & I took a very pleasant walk out of town—& returning paid a visit to Roulet & his family. We came away in sufficient season for the Warm Bath. A remarkably pleasant day.

I have, now, collected all convenient materials, within my reach, for the completion of my Essay, & wait only for the answer to my letter to Dr. Barton. This paper is not well written. The first Section is in too oratorical a style—but in some sort purposely so: I hope to attract common, as well as medical, readers—& they must be amused. The taste of our professional men is not yet sufficiently correct to relish the beauties of a simple style.

To Benjamin Smith Barton

I regret that, after a delay which to you may have been unexpected, it is not in my power to transmit to you the information which you desire, & which I promised to use my endeavours to obtain for you. Immediately on my return, I wrote to friends, in various parts of the country; but, hitherto, have recd. no satisfactory replies to either of my letters. As soon as I receive any information, I shall hasten to forward it to you. In the meantime, it is possible that the following facts may not be impertinent to the subject.

We left Phila. May 10th. That day we saw two *male* Bob-lincolns, in a field near Bristol. The next day, we saw about 15 or 20 *males,* near Woodbridge. On the 17th, in a walk which I took out of town, I passed thro' a public garden, two miles out. I observed the Strawberry in full blow. It appeared to have been in that condition some days; & the *garden* Strawberry does not blow so early as the *field,* or *wild,* plant. It is probable that it was in blossom, in N. Jersey—when we passed thro'.

My Father, who has lately been here, tells me that the Bob-lincoln had not made its appearance in his fields, when he left home—May 16th. He lives in the northwestern part of Connecticut. He also tells me that he never heard any other name for the bird, than the Strawberry-bird, till after leaving Hartford County (Connec.) in which he was born.

I have a letter, dated May 21st.—from the western part of Connecticut, in which I am informed that the bird is there called *The Meadow-bird*; that it usually appears about the beginning of May; that the female is of a dirty brown; & that the writer had then observed no Strawberries in blow. The wet season keeps them back; & we have not *yet* had any on our tables.

We are now engaged in preparing the materials of our First No. of the Medical Repository for the press; & I think we shall put it into the printer's hands by the first of July. Meanwhile, we shall thank you to send us

---

[5] John Howard (1726-1790), *The State of Prisons in England and Wales: with Preliminary Observations, and an Account of some Foreign Prisons* (Warrington [England], 1777), other similar studies in 1780, 1789.

[6] D. J. Garat, *Memoirs of the Revolution; or, an Apology for my Conduct etc.*, translated by R. Heron (Edinburgh, 1797).

[7] Daniel Le Clerc, *Histoire de la Médecine* (1696), other later editions.

those Papers which you kindly promised. Our friend Dr. Miller will be in Phila. on his return from Delaware, this week or next. We hope he may see you, & be the bearer of such communications as you shall make. I am not without fears lest our publication appear less interesting than some expect. Many who have given us promise of assistance, seem to wait to see what we shall do. But, as our Work is calculated for a long period, & to contain much miscellaneous matter, we hope for the patience & candor of the public.

When I was at your house, if I do not misremember, you informed me that you owned the Biblioth: Med: Prac: of Haller. In a work which lies before me, I find reference to an opinion of Haller's, said to be contained in this Bibliotheca—that is interesting to me. Will you be so kind, if the passage is short, as to transmit me those words of Haller, (with reference to the page—or sect. & edition—) which contain his opinion on the Cause of the Plague of Athens—described by Thucydides? Or, if the opinion be lengthily exprest, a mere intimation of what it is—& a referrence to that part of his work, where it may be found? I would not request of you, what may put you to some trouble, but that no copy of this work of Haller's is to be found in New York; & the passage may be of some importance to me, in the composition of an Essay, designed for our Repository.

My friend Mr. Dunlap desires me to present you with his respects; & to request of you the List of American Plants of which good Drawings are wanted, & which you were obliging enough to offer to make out for him. He is soon to move, for the summer, into a part of the country, rich in vegetable productions; & under circumstances very favorable for attention to them.

Tuesday, June 6. 1797.
Pine Street No. 45, N. Y.   E. H. Smith.

Friday, 9.—Reading in the Monthly Review—Fawkes translation of Moschus—Political Justice—Cleghorn—Sydenham—Le Clerc—Morton. A visit from Dingley: and from Mitchill. At the Hospital, as usual. Wrote the three following letters. Copied the two first. Johnson & I walked on the Battery, with Kent. We called at Riley's. Spent most of the eveng. at S. Johnson's; remainder at home.

Saturday, 10.—Wrote & transcribed the letters to Mumford & Brown. That to Mumford is a piece of pleasantry. He has never written me a letter of any length or importance since his residence in the County of Onondaga; & for several months I have not recd. a line from him. I anticipate some diversion from this indirect appeal to his friendship; & think it not improbable that he will suppose the letter misdirected, & designed for some other person. At any rate, I hope it may induce him to write. I have tried direct solicitations in vain. Recd. a letter from Mr. Tracy, of a few lines. Errands. Read two Elegies of Tibullus, in Grainger's Translation. Read Mr. Miller's Discourse before the Manumission Society; & Mr. Burke's Letter to the Duke of Portland.

Made further progress in Godwin's Political Justice. Johnson and I drank tea at Kent's, after which we three walked out of town. We were joined, in the fields, by M. M. Rossier—& Roulet; with whom we had some conversation. When we returned to town, I separated to make a second visit to my only patient. Then I called at Dunlap's; He & his family gone to Amboy. Went to Mr. Rogers's—where I spent the evening. Then took a walk on the Battery, by myself. A fine moon, amid a cloudy sky. How beautiful!

How will the Peace between the Emperor[8] & France, of which we have news to-day, be likely to affect us. Suppose the war to continue between England & France. Britain had just voted large sums to Austria. These she may retain for her own use. Her navy is triumphant. It is more than equal to defend her coasts from invasion. In the West & East Indies she is equally well-situated. The war appears as likely to be in her favor, as in favor of France. In this situation, will they not make Peace. If they do—the French can not expect to wound the British Commerce thro' us. Will they relinquish the dispute? Or will they seize the occasions thus delivered from every other dispute, to oppress us? What can they get by a quarrel? Nothing, but the gratification of their thirst for domination? They may have an interest in cultivating our friendship in time of peace, for the reestablishment of their Colonies. We have done much in sending Commissioners. If the new Third are Moderates, we may confidently look for accommodation. Still, we ought to lose no time in putting the country in a state of defence. The occasion now lost, may not soon recur; & still worse consequences may arise, than have arisen, from our unpreparedness.

To Mary S. Mumford

Congratulate me, my dear sister, I have had a visit from our father. He was here nearly eight days. I have heard from him since his return (yesterday) and he was well. The whole family were in health. As good luck would have it, or providentially, as the parsons say, my father was here when your letters came; & was himself the bearer of them to Lichfield. He had not been here in more than thirteen years; and but five days in about twenty-seven years. Of consequence he found a new city; and, for the most part, a new people. He visited, with me, repeatedly, all our friends, & examined most of the public Institutions. Nor did he neglect what are commonly called the Curiosities & Entertainments of the place. I was with him, at the Theater, the evening before he left town; and was at least as much entertained by observing the satisfaction he recd. from the Representation, as by the Exhibitions themselves. On the whole, this visit has been very gratifying to me; and, I make no doubt, extremely serviceable to him. The journey, change of air & diet, the new face & rapid suc-

---

[8] Francis II (who became Francis I after the Restoration settlement of 1815) the Emperor of Austria or of the Holy Roman Empire. Peace came with the Treaty of Campo Formio, October 17, 1797.

cession of objects, will improve his health; while the daily occurrences of the voyage, & particularly of his residence here, will furnish a fund, not soon exhausted, of reflection, narration, & remark. I have no doubt but that I shall be reminded of many circumstances which glided by me, some ten years hence; should not a future visit efface the impressions made by the present.

It gives me pleasure to hear that my Opera has been the cause of pleasure to you. Yet I can not allow that it merits great praise. More, in the closet, I am well aware, is due to it, as a drama, than on the stage. And more will appear, to you, to belong to it, than to persons accustomed to dramatic representations, & who have duly considered what ought to be the object of dramatic compositions. I shall be satisfied if it do no harm, & communicate some delight. Applause I do not expect it to confer. I hope to merit that by more useful, & more able, productions.

You have, in all probability, recd. my letter by Mr. Day, before this. You will see how he disappointed me. I wish, very much, to send you some books; which are lying here unused; but I know of no opportunity. I hope, however, that the little work I sent you, by Mr. Day, will supply the place of many others—at least, for the present.

Hitherto, your conduct towards your child has been very proper & successful. Your great object must be to excite an active & persevering curiosity, & to turn it towards natural objects. Books, as auxiliaries, must be called in, by & by; but never suffer them to become substitutes. According to the ordinary process of education, we learn much of books, & little or nothing of nature. Birds, insects, reptiles, domestic animals, trees, plants, flowers, &c. are all so many objects, towards which the attention of a child may be attracted by no great effort. If no immediate & apparent advantage be hence derived, it is not fair to infer that none ever will be. Much depends on our being able to impress the infant mind with an habitual bias to observation & examination. Time will ripen the fruit, which these seeds will produce. In short, almost any determination of the mind, if not to purposes absolutely bad, is better than none. All the energies are dissipated, & the faculties rendered sluggish, by that variable, inactive, or superficial care which children so often receive; & which terminates in something, or in indolence which is worse than nothing. This infects others, while it destroys him or whom it preys. It is here that all your maternal caution must be employed. The father is not altogether exempt, the mother not more so—& what shall I say for uncles & aunts?

Your town, you say, is increasing: does your society increase proportionably? I wish you could gain a few intelligent & well-informed neighbors. As for Mr. & Mrs. Kent, we are too much attached to them ourselves, to lament much, very much, on your account.

        Farewell.

Friday, June 9. 1797.
Pine St. No. 45. N. Y.   E. H. Smith.

To Idea Strong

Our correspondence has so little of method in it, or rather so long intervals divide letters and replies, that it requires some effort of memory, and more than I always possess to apprehend the connection between what I receive & what I transmit. This is a perpetual embarrassment, which I know not very well how to avoid, & must therefore submit to. It will oblige me, however, to a more irregular course of inquiry & suggestion than was originally designed, or is altogether pleasing to me.

Your replies are brief, but comprehensive. Still, I wish to see them more expanded. I would learn by what process you came to the conclusion that all wrong conduct originates in & depends upon false judgement. An axiom so extensive in its application, & which topples down, if once established, almost all the present systems of faith, created by so great labor, embraced by such numbers, & defended by so much zeal, learning, & genius, ought to be well considered, before it be admitted for truth. I pretend not to contravene its authenticity; but I desire to know by what arguments you would inforce it. Thousands deny its justice; with what language would you address them, to convince them of their error?

If man be not a free agent, & you declare that he is not, on what basis do you place Morality? If man have no selection of motives, with what propriety can you expect him to form good resolutions? to seek the means of improvement? to embrace this, and reject that? But is not man a free agent? Different motives, it is true, present themselves to his mind, in respect to every action where it is questionable how he ought to act; but has he not the power to say "I prefer this motive to the other"—even tho' he knows it to be a motive improper to influence his decision? Do you suppose there was ever a Murderer who, either before or after the commission of the act of murder, seriously supposed the act a virtuous one? if we except certain enthusiasts in religion & politics. How came he, then, to perpetrate the murder?

I must request you to reconsider each of the great questions, here noticed, with reference to all the subordinate ones; & to explain yourself to me, more copiously. Take your own time; but do it.

There was such a report in circulation, respecting Mrs. Woolstonecraft, as you mention; & I believe it was I who spoke of it at Lichfield; but subsequent inquiry has proved it to be false. At least, I have seen no mention of it, or allusion to it, in any english paper or publication; nor have I heard any thing of it, from english people, who have come to America since the time when the fact is said to have happened: I, therefore, disbelieve it.

        Yours, affectionately,

Friday, 9th. 1797.
Pine St. 45. N. Y.   E. H. Smith.

To Sally Pierce

Your letter, my dear friend, gave me uncommon pleasure; & I would add unmixed, did it wear an air less melancholly. Time was that I should have wooed this same melancholly, & perhaps replied to you in strains pathetic & disheartening. But, tho' habit & other odd causes sometimes bring me to this temper—the inquiry "what good did melancholly ever do"? has recurred too often, to make me anxious to indulge in it myself, or willing to see those I love a prey to its demon influence. Your case, my friend, is not singular; you have come to one point in the progress of affection; it depends on yourself whether the next step shall be fortunate, or the reverse. In early youth, we naturally form friendships among our mates, where amiableness & vivacity allure & attract. But, as we grow up, there is as much difference in destiny of minds, as in that of persons & employments. In the first state, our cares are few, directed to simple objects, & we have much leisure for indulgence of our affections. Afterwards, we are called more to the exercise of our intellect; & those who have employed it least before, have less time for friendship then. Thus it mostly happens, except in the case of those who live near each other & in a simple state of society, that marriage & the care of providing for their own & the subsistence of their family, extinguish the flame of ancient love, or damp its ardor. Common minds, & minds that have recd. but small improvement, have no room for more objects of affection than their own families present. They may be neighborly, but they cease to love. It sometimes happens that an old friend is also a neighbor. In this case the attachment may subsist unimpaired. There is, beside this, another source of interruption to friendships formed in early life. Young people live together. They do not, therefore, write to each other. When separated, they have no means of regular communication. If occasional separations preceeded the final one, then letters turned on common topics. Marriage, a family &c. almost wholly change the course of ideas, in those who have reflected little. They find all their former fluency at the pen annihilated by the variation in their condition & by the uncomprehended weight of notions now pressing upon them. In addition to all these causes, you must add indolence. In a single state, it is sometimes a relief to write. In different circumstances, relief is more readily, & according to the rhetoric of indolence itself, more duteously, obtained. You have, no doubt, been a witness, in more instances than one, of the pleasure with which old friends, who have not written to each other for years, or perhaps never, enter into long conversations, when they meet; & how, for some days, all their ancient amity seems to revive. This, at least, shews that absence & silence have not wholly extinguished it. It is impaired, no doubt. This new state soon becomes irksome; & the friend is forsaken to attend to the ordinary course of domestic affairs.

So far you have read, with some impatience to discover what is to be inferred from all this. It is, that we are not to expect a great deal from early-formed friendships, as such; & that, therefore, we ought not, greatly, to regret them: That, of those by whom we are deserted, the greater part are ordinary minds—Latter to be esteemed as amiable, than valued as intelligent: That we must seek, everywhere, for superior minds, & where we find them, endeavor to attach them to us: That the nature of the acquaintance, more than its duration, is to be considered: & That, in all these things, we should strive to connect ourselves with the intellect rather than the persons, of others. But I should tire you, were I to enlarge on this topic. Your own reflections will direct the application. We have, hitherto, tho' separated & variously busied, maintained our alliance unbroken, & I hope unimpaired: thanks to the pen, & some community of sentiment. By these instruments be it still preserved; & may it thrive abundantly, & grow both luxuriant & fruitful, under their more frequent & vigorous operations.

Friday, June 9th 1797.
Pine Street, No. 45. N.Y.   E. H. Smith.

To Thomas Mumford

I can not, my dear friend, sufficiently thank you for your copious and excellent letter. The picturesque views which it exhibits of your particular situation, of the country in which you reside, & of the state of improvements & manners; the ingenious & profound remarks on politics & morals, with which it abounds, and the interesting sentiments it discloses concerning subjects of more intimate concern, of life & letters; render it, at once, instructive & inestimable. Amid the continual bustle with which I am surrounded & harrassed, how often am I tempted to look with envy on your happy retirement, which, while it includes enough of business to provide for your support & to press you gently into the current of the world, heightens your intellectual pleasures by contrast, and allows you ample leisure for every elegant pursuit of literature & every recondite investigation of science! Thus employed, at the same time laying up store for physical & moral wants, improving your own mind & preparing to enlighten the understandings of your species, how kind it is in you to cast some thoughts upon those you have left behind, in the busy world, & to other less prosperous & more plodding hours, with the beams of fancy & of reason! But, my friend, what can I say to you, in reply? I know not. Cares, little, pitiful, & hourly cares, surround me; and if the dews of Lethe do not actually oppress every flower of taste & science which I once delighted to cultivate; the thorns & briars of a busy life choak or envelope them. In return for your engaging pictures of the scenery which encircles, of the intelligent minds which commune with, and of the simple manners which enchant you, I can only hold forth to view the sickening prospect of multitudes crowded together, hurried on by the demons of ambition & cupidity, & with here & there a solitary exception, lost to the endearments & delights of social & refined intercourse. For morals, the horizon is no less dreary. While you are animated by the contemplation of a continued progress in virtue, and are ready to exclaim that Astrea has returned & the reign of truth & justice has recommenced on earth; every step presents us with cause to doubt the future melioration of mankind: in every street the father of some rising Flaccus might exclaim "this let my son avoid." In Politics—it is only by limiting your view to your own country that you find so much cause of joy. Here there is little for congratulation to feed upon; & if we look to the General Government, the melancholly spectacle of a divided people is poorly compensated by the compact & irrational union of a superior & more enlightened party. In regard to Literature & Science—but I spare your sensible & affectionate heart the discouraging detail. Farewell! Remember me, again & again to each dear member of your family; & let me often have occasion to thank you, for your generous & instructive communications.

Saturday, June 10, 1797.   E. H. Smith.

To Charles B. Brown

I should have written to you before, and without waiting for a letter from you, had I possesst any information worthy to be communicated. Beside the want of such information, I have been occupied with my father, who has lately made me a visit; have had many letters to write to others; & have been much engaged in various little matters connected with my profession, & with the Hospital. Hence you will perceive that, how methodical soever my pursuits may be, they can afford but little whereon usefully to comment. I have made no new discoveries; have lighted on no new works, have composed nothing new myself.

Neither of the Novels you mention are to be found in New York; nor, were they to be found, have I leisure for their perusal. Dr. Moore's "Edward," which I might have read, is yet unexamined. Instead of works of fancy, I am laboriously decyphering Hippocrates & his commentators, & tracing the history of medicine under the auspices of Le Clerc. Have you read "Edward"? &, if you have, what is it?

Mr. Roulet has long designed answering your letter. Indeed, he has already commenced his reply; but he composes slowly in english, & has not much leisure to devote to it. I do not recollect Dunlap's No. nor is it of the least consequence. A letter directed to him, can not fail of being received.

June 10.   E. H. Smith.

Sunday, June 11.—Three medical visits. Visits, with Wm. Johnson, to Mrs. Lovegrove & Riley's: alone, to Miss Morton. Part of the afternoon, tea, & part of the evening at H. Johnson's. S. & his wife went up the river, yesterday, for White's-Town. Wm. & I walked out of town. Part of the evening at Mr. Leffingwell's. Further progress in Godwin's Political Justice. Read Matthew Green's "Spleen."[9] Read, also, several letters in Anna St. Ives.

Monday, 12.—Four medical visits—in the course of the day. A call from Mr. Miller, by whom I sent a few lines to Alsop. Called at Kent's. Mrs. K. has returned, & the child, well. At the Hospital, as usual. At Mr. Gahn's, a short time. At Wm. Woolsey's: all out. Went to Riley's. Mrs. Woolsey there. Spent most of the evening. Went home with Mrs. W. Remainder of the evening there. Read the remains of Bion, & the rest of Moschus; Fawkes' translation. Finished the first, & made some progress in the second, volume of Godwin. Recd. a few lines from El. Smith Jr.

Tuesday, 13.—Medical visits as yesterday. Read Fawkes's Musaeus, last night, & his Anacreon to-day—with the Notes. Made very considerable progress in Political Justice. Gahn here. Drank tea, & spent part of the evening, at Kent's. Remainder, at Mr. Catlin's.

Wednesday, 14.—A number of medical visits—& a mistake of my servant in carrying some medicine to a wrong place, prevented a patient from having it in season—so that much time has been thereby lost. A visit from Dr. Mitchill in the morning. At the Hospital, as usual. Johnson & I went on with our examination of Morse & Winterbotham—in the afternoon—after which we walked out of town. In at Mr. Kent's, a few minutes, in the evening—& we & Boyd, who was there, walked on the Battery. Before going out in the morng. read the Prolegomena & First Book of Cooke's Hesiod. Read the News-Papers.

Thursday, 15.—Finished Cooke's version of Hesiod's "Works & Days," with the Notes &c. Further progress in Godwin's Political Justice. Read several numbers of "Moniteur, ou Gazette Nationale." Medical visits. A visit from Mr. Roulet forenoon & afternoon: & from Dunlap, in the forenoon. Dined at Dunlap's—where I spent two hours. Spent two hours with Dingley, at his room. Johnson & I walked on the Battery; & drank tea, & spent the evening, at Riley's. Dunlap & wife there.

Friday, 16.—Medical visits. Some progress in the Theogony of Hesiod; and in Godwin. Looked over part of a vol. of the Analytical Review for 1791; various news-papers, particular the "Moniteur, ou Gazette Nationale," & Lyson's Medical Essays. Visit from Dunlap. Called at Mitchill's—he out. In the afternoon he called here. At the Hospital, as usual. In the P. M. Wm. & I proceeded with our comparison of Morse & Winterbotham. Evening at home. Recd. a letter from Jno. Allen. Thunder-storm of short continuance, yester-eve—with the sharpest lightning & most powerful thunder I ever heard in N. York. It struck in two places in Broad-Way. Two thunder-storms this day. Rainy all the evening.

Saturday, 17.—Medical visits, in various parts of

---

[9] "The Spleen," a good poem, now almost forgotten, suggesting a retreat to nature and to simplicity as a relief from the boredom consequent on sophistication.

the day. A call from Mr. Roulet. Called on Dr. Mitchill. &c. Drank tea at Moses Rogers's. Spent part of the evening at Mrs. Morton's. Finished looking over, hastily, the Analytical Review vol. IX. This is certainly a superficial performance. Finished, also, the perusal of the file of french Papers—the "Moniteur"—lent me by Mr. Roulet. Completed the perusal of Cooke's Hesiod, with all the Notes &c.—and read all the prefatory matter to Fawkes's translation of Theocritus. Continued the reading of Godwin's "Political Justice"—in which I have made considerable progress to-day, & shall soon conclude. Read the News-Papers.

Sunday, 18th June.—A medical visit. Wrote and transcribed the following letter to Joseph Dennie Jr.—medical visit. Visit to Mrs. Lovegrove. Wm. came there. We went to H. Johnson's—where we dined and spent the afternoon. Medical visit. Called at Kent's. Returned to H. Johnson's—where I tarried till nine. Came home. Read the first Idyll of Theocritus, with the notes, by Fawkes. Read, also, various scraps of my own to Osborn.

Monday, 19.—Early visit from Dunlap. His purpose to invite me to dine, at his house, with two gentlemen from Boston. Some progress in Theocritus. Medical visit. Met Mr. Roulet & conversed with him. Went into the Minerva Office & read many News-Papers. Visit from Mitchill & Miller—who has just returned. Long conversation. Medical, chemical & agricultural; & on our Repository. At the Hospital as usual. Dined at Dunlap's. The Bostonians unexpectedly flown off to Phila. Went to Sword's & bargained about the printing of our Medical Repository. Medical visit. Dunlap & I walked out, three miles, to Mr. Sharples's[10]—a painter, & whose wife is also a painter; whither Mr. & Mrs. & Miss Rogers & Mrs. Dunlap had preceeded us in a carriage. They are agreable people, & have a pleasant house. They chiefly take likenesses, small, & in crayons. Their profiles accurate—full faces, generally, bad. They have a collection of most of the principal characters in the U. S. The husband also paints in oil, & I saw several pretty things done by him thus. The wife is exquisite with the needle. Some of her pieces bear the most exact resemblance to etchings, & at a short distance, can not be distinguished from them. One, cost her a year's labour. Time ill-bestowed. A fine afternoon. Spent the evening at Hodgkinson's. Mr. & Mrs. Johnson—Comedians—there. Came home, & made further progress in Theocritus. Composed, also, the outline of two Sonnets.

To Joseph Dennie Junr.

Your short letter of April 15th led me to expect a more ample communication from you before this time. In this expectation I have continued silent. I waited principally from a desire to be informed how I might convey to you several papers, without subjecting you to the expence of Postage—an expence they would but ill repay. Since you have devoted a corner of the "Museum" to the subjects pointed out by me, I have laid aside several european papers which may not improperly come under the head of Economics. This practice, should it prove agreable to you, I shall continue, as occasion may offer. As for doing any thing myself, in matters of this kind, you must not expect it. It is not personal reputation which I so much desire; above all I have no relish for that fame which is disproportioned to the art supposed to merit it. The great object of all our labors must be to enlighten our fellow-men & render them more happy. The more complete is the information conveyed to them, the better. Nor can I conceive it of any importance whether they receive it from you, me, or another. I should, therefore, be exceedingly backward to dabble in matters, so much better understood, & discoursed upon by others. All that I can do, & all that I ought to do, is to send you, from time to time, with the least mutual expence, such essays as appear to be worthy of notice from their rational sentiments, & the reputation for veracity, learning, & experience of their authors. These communications will be scanty no doubt—but I trust not altogether undeserving a place in your paper. Various lighter productions have fallen into my hand, & been laid aside by me, when looking over files of european & american papers. Of these I purpose to transmit some to you. They shall be forwarded, by the first inexpensive & safe conveyance.

You deal much in selected, as well as original, verse; & I am pleased to see the lives of the Poets occupy a portion of your Journal. I have a suggestion to make, on this head, which may, perhaps, deserve consideration. It is probable that many of your subscribers preserve the "Museum." Any thing which would considerably enhance its value would be likely not only to increase their care, but to augment your subscriptions. There is

---

[10] James Sharples (or Sharpless) b. *ca.* 1751 in England, emigrated to America with his wife Ellen in 1793. For a time after coming to America the pair wandered about the country in a specially constructed carriage drawn by a big white horse. Both man and wife were artists. Sharples himself invariably used crayon for his portraits and had a strong partiality for profiles which he was particularly successful in rendering in a true-to-life fashion. For many of the Sharples portraits it is not clear whether he or she or both did the drawing. Sharples rather carefully cultivated Smith and some three months later (September 26, 1797) Smith sat for his portrait. According to Dunlap: *A History of the Rise and Progress of Arts and Design in the United States* (New York, 1834) **2**: pp. 70, 71, Sharples charged fifteen dollars for a profile, twenty dollars for full face. Smith's portrait was profile but he did not buy it; he remarks that the portrait was for Sharples's collection. As will be seen later he had Sharples do a copy for him (not entirely satisfactory) which he gave to his family. Sharples did a number of people in Smith's circle including Johnson, Alsop, Brown, Catlin, Hillhouse, Hosack, and Kent as well as the famous, including Hamilton, Washington, and Lafayette. See Katherine McCook Knox, *The Sharples, their Portraits of George Washington and his Contemporaries, a Diary and an Account of the Life and works of James Sharples and his Family in England and America* (New Haven, Yale University Press & London, Oxford University Press, 1930), pp. 8 *passim*.

no where a complete collection of all the best smaller poems in our language. What think you of devoting a column, or more, as it may be, to the republication, in an order as nearly chronological as is convenient, of these Poems? I do not mean that you should go back to the days of Chaucer & Gower, but should begin as early as when the verse of our poets becomes intelligible to common readers of some education. Nor do I mean to exact a precise attention to chronology. It will be sufficient to take up a poet, say the eldest in point of time, & publish all his best small pieces together; & then pass on to the next. Suppose the poet to be Milton—you would insert his Allegro, Penseroso, Lycidas, Ode on the Nativity, & some of his Sonnets &c. indeed all which might be comprehended in a News-Paper. To make a design of this sort valuable, it is essentially necessary that you give copies which may be referred to with confidence. It will, therefore, be indispensible that you take them from the most correct editions of each author's works, & that the utmost accuracy be observed in reprinting them. Nor will this be difficult in a weekly paper. Their beauties would be more relished if an explanation were inserted of unusual words which occur; & if the shorter comments of some editors were annexed to each poem. For instance those Thos. Warton to Milton, & of Gilbert Wakefield to Pope. But this is not so material as to be insisted on; & Johnson's, Bell's or Anderson's editions of the Poets may be safely copied, without recourse to the separate publications of more minute editors. You will readily comprehend the additional value which an adherence to this plan would confer on your Paper, in the course of a few years. It would supersede the necessity of a large library of poetry; it would induce many to read what otherwise they might never think of; & could not fail of making some favorable impression on the minds & manners of the people at large. But, this is merely a project—which I submit to your judgement. One word more on the subject of Poetry—are you not almost too unmerciful to Mr. Merry? I see you bestow great praise on Philenia, who is a servile imitator of Della Crusca, with all his faults, & half his genius. Have you seen his last Poem—"The Pains of Memory"? You will be pleased with it, I think; & will discover that he has corrected most of the affectations of which you complain; with so much reason.

Now for a little business. I have been so fortunate as to receive all your Papers, since I became a subscriber. Mr. Johnson has not been equally so. In particular, the Numbers for Jany. 24th, Feby. 7th, March 7th, April 25th, & May 2nd, 9th, 16th, & 23rd—have never reached him. As he wishes regularly to preserve the Museum, it will oblige him if you can supply his loss. Since his paper & mine have been inclosed in a common wrapper, they have come without difficulty. We therefore wish this practice continued.

I send you the names of three subscribers—

John Sigismund Roulet—Greenwich Street.
Tunis Wortman—No. 3. Cedar St.
Wm. W. Woolsey—332 Pearl Street.

In respect to payment, we shall accede to any scheme you may propose. Perhaps the subscriptions for the Opera, may be turned this way.

Sunday, June 18. 1797.
Pine St. No. 45. N. Y.   E. H. Smith.

P. S.—The materials for the First No. of The Medical Repository are nearly ready for the Press. We expect to put them into the printer's hands the first of July. I believe I sent you our Proposals. If I did not, I will just inform you that each No. will contain about 100 8vo. pages—& will be sold for 50 cents. If you can procure subscribers, with you, the Nos. shall be regularly forwarded. May I ask how you came to prefix to our Circular Address the whimsical title of "A Dissertation on the Yellow Fever"?

E. H. Smith.

Tuesday, 20.—Progress in Theocritus. Medical visit. Visit from Dunlap; & from Kent. Medical visits. Finished the transcription of the review of Barton's Memoir, with some corrections. Finished "Political Justice." I have read this excellent work too hastily & with too many interruptions to pronounce decisively upon it. Certain parts, particularly in the 5th & 6th Books failed to carry conviction of their soundness to my mind, as I read them over. It may be that this was only from want of attention to the author. I must read it again, by & by. Medical visit. Johnson & I went on with our comparison of Morse & Winterbotham. We spent the evening at Riley's. Further progress in Theocritus.

Wednesday, 21.—Finished Theocritus, & the Combat between Pollux & Amycus. Medical visit. Visit from Dunlap. At the Hospital as usual. Resumed the transcription of my Essay on the Plague of Athens, of which I copied & corrected several pages. Wrote a few lines to Dr. Barton. Read the News-Papers. Dunlap & I drank tea with Miss Morton. We spent the evening at Woolsey's. Returning, I spent an hour at Dunlap's. Came home & read "The Rape of Helen &c." translated by Mr. C——[11] from Coluthus Lycopolites, a Theban poet, who lived in the reign of the emperor Anathasius—500 years after Christ.

Thursday, 22.—Finished the transcription of my Essay on the Plague of Athens—with various corrections & additions. Called at Kent's. Medical visit. Errands. Went to the Hospital to see a particular patient. Visited Mitchill. We spent some time in purchasing a few books for the Hospital &c. We then went to Miller's—where

---

[11] "The Rape of Helen, translated from the Greek by Mr. C————." See Robert Anderson, M.D., *A Complete Edition of the Poets of Great Britain* (London and Edinburgh, 1792-1795) **13**, p. 323.

we spent the remainder of the afternoon in business relating to our Medical Repository.[12] Two calls. Went to see Mrs. Lovegrove—& waiting for her, took tea. She did not come home. Visited at Mr. Watson's. Saw only Mrs. W. Called at Mr. Coit's—all out. Went to Mr. Leffingwell's—where I saw Isaac Beers of New Haven, & settled with him about a few books for the Hospital. Came home, & finished the first book of Fawkes's Apollonius Rhodius' Argonautica, commenced in the morning. Recd. a letter from my father to-day.

Friday, June 23.—Medical visit. Mitchill & Miller here, near three hours—busied, with me, on the materials of the Repository. We agreed to commence the printing; & I put my Essay into the printer's hands this afternoon. At the Hospital. Medical visit. Various calls & errands. Drank tea, & spent the chief part of the evening, at Kent's: remainder at home. Finished Fawkes's Apollonius Rhodius. The two last books much superior to the two first—really merit to be considered as poetical & interesting.

Saturday, 24.—Medical visit. A number of calls. At the Hospital, to see two particular patients—where I was detained near two hours. Medical visit. Read the Papers. Translated the speech of Fourcroy, in the Council of Ancients, on the formation of Artificial Nitre-Beds—which is lengthy—& in some parts difficult. This is but a rough & imperfect translation, as yet. Medical visit. Johnson & I walked out to Webster's. He gone to Boston. We drank tea with Mrs. Webster. I scarce ever knew a more pleasant evening. We called at Woolsey's. They out. I went to Mr. Coit's. They out. To Riley's. Found Mr. & Mrs. Woolsey there. Spent the evening. Miss Howland &c came in. Some progress in Grainger's Tibullus. Recd. a letter from Mr. Tracy.

To John Allen

I am convinced that you will believe me, when I assure you that indispensable business alone could have prevented my replying to your letter of the 15th—till this time. The preparation of materials for a medical publication in which I am engaged, & which is now in the press, has engrossed all the leisure which might otherwise have been devoted to Correspondence.

My last letter was written more with a design of stimulating you to exertion, than of augmenting your apprehensions by the display of my own. I know the opposition that you meet with, of the Right Side, but as you are strongest, & as no argument will do good with your adversaries, I wish you to put forth your strength, & rely more upon it than upon your reason. As for the rest, I confess your fears exceed mine. I do not imagine our situation so dangerous, as you seem to do; but I wish to see the country prepared to meet every possible calamity, & able to repel it successfully.

Are your Speeches misrepresented in the Papers? or are you, indeed, so warm for War? As I can not concieve how we are to effect any thing, with any european nation, by means of war, it is impossible for me to conceive myself that any of my friends can propose it, even in idea, except as strictly limited to self-defence. I wish, therefore, to be able to justify you more safely than from my opinions of what your sentiments would be, judging from what I know of your character & information.

June 25. 1797.   E. H. Smith.

Sunday, June 25.—Mr. Gahn called to have me walk with him, while I was yet in bed. I was sleepy, having been up till one last evening, & did not rise. Medical visit. Progress in Tibullus. Wrote the letter to Allen. Wm. & I went round the Battery. Called at Mr. Coit's, & at Riley's. Dined, & spent most of the afternoon, at H. Johnson's. Remainder at Dunlap's. Evening, with Mrs. Lovegrove. Came home—& wrote the letter to Tracy—& letters to Drs. Holyoke of Salem, Eustis of Boston, Coffin of Newbury Port, & Senter of Newport; on business of the Medical Repository.

Monday, 26.—Transcribed the two letters to Tracy & Allen. Mitchill called here, & we went to Miller's—where we were much of the forenoon—on business of the Medical Repository. Medical visit. At the Hospital. Progress in Tibullus. Errands. Wrote a few lines to Theodore Dwight & to Mason F. Cogswell. Mr. & Mrs. Kent, Johnson & I teaed at Woolsey's. Went home with Kent. Thence with him & Mrs. K[ent] to Mr. Radcliffe's. Returned—progress in Tibullus.

Tuesday, 27.—Finished Tibullus & Sulpicia, with the notes. Three medical visits, in succession—one of which occupied some time. Dr. Jno. Osborn Jr. of N. Carolina, returned here to-day, from Connec. & made us a visit. Read a number of Articles in Valmont de Bomare's Dict: d'hist. nat.—Read Mitchill's original publication on Contagion.[13] Medical visit. Errands. Read several articles in The Monthly Review Enlarged Vol. XXI. A walk with Johnson. We drank tea, & spent most of the evening at Jacob Morton's. Medical visit. Came home & corrected the first proof of the Medical Repository.

This day has been quite like summer; & tho' the heat is considerable, yet, after so much cold weather as we have had, I find it not unpleasant.

To Uriah Tracy

If I have delayed writing a longer time than you expected, it has only been from the urgency of other concerns, & the insignificance of any thing I might have to communicate. Your letter was the more acceptable,

---

[12] Through the "Diary" we get scarcely a hint of the kind or amount of work done on the *Repository* by Smith's associate editors; however, from what is known of their natures and capacities, particularly so for the dynamic and talented Mitchill, it is clear that they also were very much engaged in the details of publication. The decades of successful publication after Smith's death also give evidence of their abilities.

[13] A work, probably a pamphlet, which Smith referred to several times, apparently by subject rather than title. Tentatively identified elsewhere.

therefore, as it proved you needed not the monitor of a complimentary phrase or two to remind you of your friend.

You, certainly, have cause for condemning the dilatory & imperfect proceedings of the House of Representatives. But is not much of this owing to the federalist's themselves? Are they still to be taught the inefficacy of argument where it is opposed by determined prejudices? In times past, when they were fewer in number than their opponents, they did well to argue & dispute; because the public mind became enlightened, & forced their reluctant antagonists to adopt right measures. But, now, when they have a decided majority, & when the general sentiment out of doors is more with them than usual, they do wrong to waste time in speeches which will produce no effect within & are unnecessary without. Why occupy time with declamations on the danger of our country, & the intrigues of foreigners, which are well enough understood, when it might be so much better employed in preparing the outlines of every measure proper to be proposed & adopted? Let the others speechify, if you can not prevent them, but these should be brief in reply, persevering in action. I see no imminent cause for melancholly apprehensions; but there is cause enough for vigorous preparations. Danger may not come; & we should not be terrified, if it should it come; but we ought to be prepared to meet it. It is this preparedness which is the surest guarantee of our tranquillity. What is most provoking is that, they who complain most of the address & management & success of the opposers of administration, are least attentive to the only true means of vanquishing them. They meet together & rail, & they declaim in the House, when they should be busy out, & watchful within. With superior abilities, & more general knowlege, they crouch beneath those, for whose utter overthrow they want nothing but industry. They are unsuccessful because they are lazy; & curse their rivals, when they ought to condemn themselves; and they execrate a virtue in a cause which they deem bad, while a just cause can not inspire them with a similar energy. If what ought to be done, is not done—it will be more from the indecision of the federalists, than from the superior talents of the democrats.

Have you heard from your family lately? How were they? I had a letter from my father, on Thursday. He does not mention any thing of their health. But he wrote only a few words; being yet very feeble, from a late severe illness—an inflammation in the head, as he tells me.

Our friends here, are all well. Those with you are also in health, as I hope. My remembrance to them.

Sunday, June 25, 1797.
Pine St. N. 45. N. Y. E. H. Smith.

Wednesday, 28.—Three medical visits in the forenoon. Much of it occupied on business of the Medical Repository. Read the News-Papers. At the Hospital as usual. Read several articles in the Monthly Review Vol. XXI. Johnson & I made some little progress in comparing Winterbotham & Morse. Visit from Dunlap. Visit from Drs. Mitchill & Wheaton. Medical visit. Dunlap, Johnson & I walked out of town. Saw the *Magnolia Glauca* in blossom for the first time. Returning, I spent the evening at Mr. Roulet's. A fire broke out, as I came home. The uncommon grandeur of the scene stayed my steps more than [an] hour, in the most favorable of all situations for seeing it. The building being such as not to endanger lives, I was less affected by melancholly considerations than usual. Stopped at the Hospital. Mr. Gahn there. We came home together. Corrected the second proof of the first half sheet of the Med: Reposy.

Thursday, 29.—Medical visit. Transcribed & corrected my translation of Fourcroy's Speech. Mitchill called & I accompanied him to a Bookseller's to procure a few books for the Hospital. Errands. Two medical visits. Dunlap here. Dr. Osborn here, a short time. He sailed for North Carolina, this afternoon. Recd. a letter from Saml. Coates of Phila. with the decree of the French Convention, emancipating the Negroes, & the minutes &c. of the late Convention of Delegates &c. which I looked over. Went to H. Johnson's. Fanny sailed to-day, for Connecticut. Wm. & I accompanied her to Mrs. Lovegrove's, & thence to the vessel, where we were long detained. Went to Riley's. Miss Alsop & I walked on the Battery. Returned—& had a long, interesting, & by-ourselves, conversation—for two hours. Read a number of articles in the Monthly Review, morning & evening.

Friday, June 30.—Read several articles in the Monthly Review. Corrected a proof sheet of the Repository. Medical visit. Recd. a short letter from Elnathan Smith Jr. Visit from Dunlap. Read part of the article Arraigné—in Valmont de Bomare's Dict. de' Hist: Nat:—Visit from Dr. Miller. At the Hospital as usual. My term of service expired this day. This duty, which was originally quite burthensome, has become quite pleasant. Before, I quitted its exercise with joy; now, with some regret. The attendance is a school of perpetually increasing improvement. Wrote, very hastily, the following pages, on the Grasshopper—of the Ancients, which are, doubtless sufficiently incorrect. Dr. Mitchill here. Medical visit. Gahn shewed me the beautiful medal struck in honor of the Swedish Poet Kellgren,[14] & the fine head of him, in his works. At Swords's on business of the Repository. Corrected a second proof sheet. Drank tea at Kent's. There got some butter on my new silk coat—which employed Mrs. K[ent] & me all the evening, in attempts (I fear insuc-

---

[14] Johan Henrik Kellgren (1751-1795), a minor poet and dramatist, editor of the journal *Stockholmsposten*, librarian and private secretary to Gustavus III, member of Swedish Academy from its foundation in 1786. He collaborated on dramas with the king, Gustavus furnishing the plots and Kellgren the versification. Among the plays, *Gustaf Vasa*.

cessful) to get it out, & deprived me of the pleasure of walking. Came home at nine, & was occupied near an hour in the correction of another proof, which was unusually incorrect. Afterwards read a number of very interesting articles, in the Monthly Review. I meant to have gone into the Hudson this evening, but the correction of this last proof occupied me an unexpected length of time—till it was too late—& much to my regret, I was necessitated to postpone my swimming sport.

Thus ends another month—employed to somewhat better purpose than the two preceeding.

[Omitted here, five manuscript pages: "On the Grasshopper of the Ancients."]

Industry of June 1797
Reading

A complete edition of the Poets of Gt. Britain—by Anderson—very large 8vo. double volumes—& on a very small type—Lond. Vol. 13.—so much of this volume as contains Cooke's Hesiod; Fawkes's Theocritus, Anacreon, Sappho, Bion, Maschus, & Appollonius Rhodius; Mr. C's Rape of Helen from Coluthus Pycopolites; Grainger's Tibullus & Sulpicia; & so much of the notes to Creech's Lucretius as relates to the Plague of Athens—in all—pp. 470.

The remainder of "An Inquiry concerning Political Justice Wm. Godwin. Second Edit. Lond—equal to pp. 900—8vo. loose print.

"Memoirs of the (french) Revolution &c." by D. I. Garat, &c. translated by R. Henon—Edib. 1797. 8vo. pp. 281.

Letter from R. Hole. Ed: Burke to Duke of Portland &c. Edi. Phila. 8vo. pp. 56.

Discourse &c. before N. Yk. Manumission Socy. by Sl. Miller—8vo. pp. 36.

Documents accompg. the President's Speech—8vo.—pp. 63.

Minutes of Convention of Abolition Societies—8vo. pp. 59.

Howard on Poisons &c. 4to. pp. 30.

Historie de la Medicini &c. Le Clerc—4to about pp. 40.

Hippocrates—Edit. Foesic—folio—about 20 pp.

"The Spleen" poem by Mat: Green; a file of the Moniteur; part of Thucydides; part of Shakespere; letters in Anna St. Ives; various articles in Valmont de Bonare's Dict: d'Historie Nat:—; Mitchill on Contagion; part of Lyon's Medical Express; various articles in other Medical Authors; one vol. of the Analytical Review; & several numbers of the Monthy. Rev. Enld.

Writing

Letters, copies of which are retained—equal to 20 pages —these transcribed, with others of which I have no copies, equal to—pp. 24.

Transcribed & corrected my Essay on the Plague of Athens—& most of Review of Barton's Memoir.

Translated, & retranscribed part, & corrected Fourcroy's Speech—equal to p. 12.

On the Grasshopper of the Ancients—pp. 5. Two Sonnets.

Compared Morse & Winterbotham; corrected Proofs, &c. &c.

MEMOIRS. 1797. JULY.

Saturday, 1.—Medical visit. Business of the Repository. Errands & calls. Dunlap here. Made out the table of Industry for May—which I had neglected till this time; & also the table of Industry for June. Some articles read in the Monthly Review. Two medical visits. Johnson & I drank tea at Dunlap's—after which we, according to a previous plan, went over to Hoboken. We found the place pleasant beyond all expectation;[15] & after a very agreable walk, came home, supped; & got into comfortable beds.

Sunday, 2.—We rose at four. Dunlap & I walked to Mr. Stevens's place, examined his grounds; & had a long conversation concerning them, with his gardener. Met Johnson on our return. Breakfasted. The morning had been cloudy. It has cleared away; & the sun came out warm, with a fine southerly breeze. Again we went over Mr. Stevens's place—which, for magnificence & beauty of prospect, surpasses any place I have ever seen. Thence we strolled on, thro' wood, marsh, & road—visited several hills—whence we had delightful views—& reposed under shady trees, on the sweet grass. Called at a Cottage—& ate bread, & drank excellent milk. Returned to Hoboken. Dined. Imbibed the delicious breezes on the grass before the door, till six in the evening. Came home. Dressed. Two medical visits. Wm. & I at H. Johnson's. Thence at Riley's. I returned & corrected a proof of the Repository.

I scarcely remember to have enjoyed an excursion so much as this. The variety of singing-birds added much to our pleasure.

Monday, July 3.—Looked over the NewsPapers & the Magazine. Visit from Dunlap; & from Roulet. Two medical visits. Corrected a proof sheet of the Repository. Called on Mitchill—he was out. On Dr. Miller; he was in. Recd. a letter from Mr. Tracy. Read from dissertations of Sir Wm. Jones—On the Literature of Asia, on the Hindus, the Arabs, & the Tartars. Called at Dunlap's—at Mrs. Woolsey's, who was out. Teaed at Moses Rogers's. Called at Mr. Boyd's—all out. At Dr. Miller's, with the design of asking him to accompany me to see Miss Mason. He was out. Called to see Mrs. Lovegrove. She was from home. Visited Miss Morton. Thence went to Riley's. They were out. Went on to the Battery. Met, coming off—Miss Mason, Miss

---

[15] This comment is important as being, perhaps, the last kind thing ever written about Hoboken; even so, the compliment has a slight element of ambiguity.

Nicholson, Mr. Miller, & Dr. Mitchill. Some talk. Walked. Returned to Riley's. They had been on the Battery; but Miss Alsop concluded to return. We went round twice. Returned to Riley's, & had an hour of pleasant conversation.

Tuesday, 4.—The anniversary of American Independence—celebrated with increasing parade & noise. Read two Dissertations of Sir Wm. Jones, on the Persians, & on the Chinese. The last, & part of the first, this evening. Mitchill called—we went to Miller's—where we were two hours busied on the Repository. Johnson & I compared Morse & Winterbotham two or three hours. Dined at Mrs. Miller's. Mitchill recd. a package from Edinburgh—& I looked over two numbers of the Monthly Magazine that formed a part, & some News-Papers. The remainder of the evening, at H. Johnson's —where were Mrs. Lovegrove, Miss Alsop, & Wm. Waited on Miss Alsop home, & returned to read Sir Wm. Jones. The day has been pleasant for the season —but I do not feel remarkably well this evening. Recd. a letter from Mr. Tracy.

Wednesday, 5.—Read a dissertation of Sir Wm. Jones "On the island of Hinzuán or Johanna"; another, "On the borderers, mountaineers & islanders of Asia"; & another "On the origin & families of nations", making, in all, with those before read, in this month, in the 1st & 3rd vols. of the Asiatic Researches, pp. 236. Visit to Dr. Miller. Visit from Dunlap. Recd. a letter from Joseph Dennie Jr. Visit to Dr. Hicks. Read a number of articles in "The Annals of Medicine Vol. I." Writing & errands on acct. of the Medl. Repository. Medical visit. Johnson & I teaed at Dunlap's—who goes to Amboy tomorrow, for the summer. We spent the evening, with them, at Mrs. Woolsey's. Medical visit. Fine evening. Called on Miss Alsop, & we walked on the Battery. Returning, saw Miss Morton standing on the steps of her house—conversed with her some time. She had heard from her sister & from Mrs. Levy. Both well. Came home, & read the News Papers.

Thursday, 6.—Two medical visits. Called on Miller —& we went to Mitchill's; where we were two hours on business of the Med: Repository. Afterwards some time at our printer's. Two medical visits. Considerable progress in the Annals of Medicine Vol. I. Errands. Two medical visits. Johnson & I walked on the Battery. We spent the evening, principally, with Miss Alsop. A medical visit. Called at H. Johnson's. Wm. came to me there—& we went into the Cold Bath.

Friday, 7.—Finished Duncan's Annals of Medicine Vol. 1. Read also several papers in the XXth vol. of his medical Commentaries. Four medical visits, in the course of the day. Many errands & calls, on account of the Repository, & private business: particularly, at the Hospital, where I conversed with Dr. Hosack; at Dr. Miller's; & at Dr. R. S. Kissam's. Read Dr. Warren's Acct. of the Boston fever last year. Drank tea at Kent's. Called at Adams's—they out. Evening at Boyd's—Rest at home, reading. Wrote to my father, a hasty letter.

Saturday, July 8.—Some progress in the XXth vol. of the Med: Comment. Edinb. Writing for the Med: Repository. Dr. Miller here. Two medical visits. At Swords's. Gahn here. Wrote a few lines, for him, to Dr. Dwight & Mr. Alsop. Read the News-Papers, & the Prests. Message &c. respecting Blount & the Spaniard.[16] Further progress in Med: Comment. Edinb. Mr. Gahn & I drank tea with Mrs. Woolsey. Medical visit. Continued the Med: Comment. for 1795. Have last read the Case of *Rabies Canina*—by Alexr. Johnston. It has excited some reflections; which I have not time to detail, or pursue. I hastily mark a few.

1. Ague, like that which precedes fever; thirst; anxiety; oppression; nausea; yellow vomit, of a bitter & sour taste; faintness; costiveness; hard & quick pulse; offensive & bilious stools; were symptoms—& in the opinion of the physician constituted a Yellow Fever.

2. Towards the close of the disease Salivation occurred.

3. Salivation sometimes occurs in the Yellow Fever.

4. The bite of the *Cobra de Capello* produces similar symptoms with those of the Mad-Dog. They are removed, as well as those occasioned by the bite of the Viper, by Alkalies.

5. The Nitrous Acid, according to Dr. Scott, salivates.

6. Dr. Barker cures the Yellow Fever by means of Alkalies.

Sunday, 9.—Three medical visits. Visit from Jeremiah Mason. Wm. & I dined & spent the afternoon at H. Johnson's. It was extreme hot, & we stupified. Recovered a little, I read a few letters in Anna St. Ives. Two medical visits. Wm. & I walked out to Roulet's— where we spent the evening—which has been very pleasant. We met there, again, Mr. Duchesne—who has just returned from Connecticut—having resided there two months, & visited most parts of it—among others Lichfield. He seems much pleased with the country & people. We returned, & bathed in the Hudson.

Monday, 10.—Read a Paper or two in the Med: Comment: Edinb. 1795. Three medical visits. At Swords's. Corrected proof sheets. Calls on me, an errand. Wrote a Sonnet, to be intituled Autumn. Medical visit. Recd. a line from Isaac Beers, with Moseley on Tropical Diseases, & Beddoes' Considerations on Factitious Airs, complete. I read several hours in this last, with indescribable eagerness & satisfaction. Medical visit. Visit from Mr. Roulet: From Dr. Miller. Medical visit. Visited Miss Morton—& Miss Alsop.

Tuesday, 11.—Pursued the reading of Beddoes Considerations &c. thro' the day—when not engaged as to be mentioned. Eight medical visits in the course of the day & evening. At Swords's—& corrected a proof sheet.

---

[16] Senator William Blount, former governor of the Southwest Territory, was like many other prominent men of the day, deeply involved in land speculation. For his letter (characterized as *"High Treason!"*) see Stewart, *The Opposition Press*, pp. 264 ff.

Visited Dr. Seaman. A long vist from Jereh. Mason. Called, ineffectually, at Dr. Rodgers's. Visited Dr. & Mr. Miller. Wrote the two succeeding letters, of this date. Visited & drank tea with Dr. Wheaton. Visited & spent some part of the evening with Miss Alsop. She has heard from her brother. All well. Walked on the Battery—by the fine moon. Encountered there, John B. Mulligan—& we took a turn together.

We gave Cammel notice, this day, to look out for another place. He has become too lazy, proud, & selfish; & this step is equally necessary for him & for us.

Wednesday, July 12.—Read a little in Beddoes P. III —before breakfast. Immediately after, drest & went out. Medical visit. Do. to a patient, very weak, Double Tertian,[17] who had taken Arsenic this morning, for the first time, by my direction; & now first used by me. She took 5 drops only, at 5 A. M. of a Saturated Solution, made according to Darwin. Read the Newspapers, with the Official Documents, Blount &c in it. Medical visit. Called on Dr. Miller—(corrected proof sheet while there) we waited on Kissam, & all three on Hicks[18]—I having an appointment with him to go to the Poor House, to look out some Bad Cases of Syphilis, on which to try the effect of the Nitric Acid.[19] We went. Read over Scott's & Baynton's Accounts. Hicks agreed with the physician of the Poor House, to look out some Cases, & let us know to-morrow. Just got home, & summoned to my Tertian patient. She took four drops more at nine A. M. Ague came on at 11 A. M. Now violent pain & spasms of the stomach—no doubt chiefly owing to the Arsenic. The paroxysm, notwithstanding quite short—3 hours—when the Sweat came on. Was there near two hours. Home; found a note from Mr. Tracy & Allen. Swallowed my dinner, & went to them. Saw also Dana, Hofner, Griswold, Coit, &c. Stayed with them till they went off—to N. Haven —near 6 P. M. Three medical visits. At Swords's— where corrected proof sheet. Read a few pages of Beddoes at home. Ineffectual calls Dr. Rodgers & Miller. Saw my Tertiana. Easier. A drop of the Solution did pretty well. At Dr. Rodgers's. At home. Miller came there. An agreable hours. Came home. Corrected proof sheet. Wrote "Medical Hints, Facts & Inquiries"— Chiefly. Busy day, near one A. M.

To Charles B. Brown

I have expected to hear from you, till I have become sick of expectation. Were I of a careless or revengeful temper, I might let you go on in silence, & with like indifference on my part cease all communication. But I have something to propose, which may be worthy your attention, & I can not *find in my heart* to hold my tongue.

You saw, while here, several numbers of a paper, published by a Mr. Dennie, in New Hampshire. He has some pretensions, you know, to literature; & these are communicated to his Journal. By the kind offices of a common acquaintance, a correspondence has been generated between us. You saw my first letter; & may well suppose that a stranger who could take it kindly, could not be an altogether ordinary man. Well—This same Mr. Dennie—(heaven help him!) has conceived a prodigious notion of my learning, & taste, & judgement—and all that; which is well enough, you know, to begin with; & is continually pressing me to commence dribbler & scribbler in his paper; as likely to be much for the improvement of the people of his State &c Now this Paper has acquired much reputation; & there are about 3,000 copies circulated every week; & it gains subscribers constantly. Here is an opportunity for an adroit disperser of *the truth*; if he be careful to make his approaches with gentleness, & to intermix the lighter pictures of fancy, & the delicate effusions of literature. What think you of contributing a weekly essay to this miscellany? It is impossible for me to do any thing; but I have a project, which I hasten to explain. I think it very probable that Dennie would willingly make pecuniary remuneration for assistance of this kind, regularly afforded: especially if the compensation were moderate, & within his means. I think to propose the matter to him, as in behalf of a friend, concerning whom such aid is probable, with mental reference to you. Would it comport with your plans to engage in such a design, on any terms? I consulted Dunlap about it—& he has engaged to give me several Scraps, to be sent to Dennie, gratis—as specimens of that sort of Moral Philosophy, which he may expect from this quarter, if he receive any. If you like the scheme, & would be willing to further it, will you not send some little Fragment also? Beside, give me some intimation on what terms you will write—if you write at all. Think on this subject—it may be important to the success of virtuous principles in others as well as yourself—& let me soon hear from you, in reply.

Love &c. to all friends.

Tuesday, July 11. 1797.
Pine St. No. 45. N. Y.   E. H. Smith.

To Henry Wilkins

I received your letter, by Dr. Bay, & feel myself exceedingly obliged by the frank & kind interest you take in the success of our Repository. Be assured, my dear sir, any communications which you may favor us with, will receive an early attention; and we shall be too happy if a like spirit shall be found to pervade our medical brethren, in the different parts of the United States.

Since writing to you, we have commenced the print-

---

[17] Malaria. The "double" in the term probably meant two infections so that instead of fever days interspersed by days of normal temperature the fever continued without remission.

[18] Dr. Hicks apparently was either John Hicks, physician, of 1 Magazine Street or John B. Hicks, physician and surgeon, of 69 Bleeker Street. *New York Directory*, 1796.

[19] Nitric acid for syphilis, used externally to destroy the chancre is mentioned as a medical practice as late as 1910. *Encyclopedia Britannica* (11th. ed., 1910-1911).

ing of our first number; of which 72 pages are now worked off. We shall certainly get it out by the first of August; perhaps, a short time before. I venture to insert your information concerning the Seneka, among other articles of medical intelligence.

I thank you, particularly, & my colleagues are no less obliged, for your mention of a bookseller. As soon as our pamphlet is ready for sale, some copies shall be forwarded to Mr. Rice. Will you, if it be not too troublesome, just write me a line—& inform me what probable number of subscribers may be immediately expected? & how many copies of the first Number we had best send?

I do not know that I informed you that, in addition to the 100 pages mentioned in our proposals, we shall have an Appendix of from 10 to 20 pages. This will consist of the best British Essays; & such as have appeared in our own Papers & Magazines. Our type too being small & our page full, one of our *numbers* will contain nearly as much as a *volume* of the Medical Commentaries. I mention this to shew that we labour to diffuse as much, in a small compass, as possible; & that our Appendix alone may be expected to comprize as much matter, in the course of a year, as a volume of any of the publications of the foreign Societies; & being selected from all, probably a more valuable mass of information.

In the course of our Work, We hope to give the most authentic account of the State of Medicine & medical literature, in the United States. We shall be much beholden to you for any communications, on these points, relative to Maryland: Such as Legislative Acts, respecting the Practice of Physic—Constitutions & Officers of Medical Societies, if any; Schools for Medicine; & Medical Publications.

When I write next, I hope to be able to transmit the first prints of our Plan.

Hastily, but sincerely yours,
Tuesday, July 11. '97.
Pine St. 45. N. Y. E. H. Smith.

Thursday, 13.—Finished Beddoes' Third Part, the additions in his third Edition of the 1st & 2nd Parts; & read some Papers in the Fourth Part, of his Considerations &c. Seven medical visits, in the course of the day. Corrected proof sheets—was at the printer's—at the College, & at the Hospital—on business of the Repository. Visited Mr. Dana. Dined at Kent's, & sat two hours. It was too warm to do any thing. Visit from Dr. S. Osborn. Johnson & I walked on the Battery; & spent part of the evening at Riley's. Mr. Hosmer there. Various calls & errands. Finished the Medical Facts, Hints & Inquiries. Recd. the Circular Letter & of the late Convention, from Phila.

Friday, 14.—Continued the reading of Beddoes. Three medical visits. Called on Dr. Miller. At the printer's, & corrected proof sheet. Many errands, for myself & others. Three medical visits. Visit from Mr. Aron Smith of Lichd. who brought me letters from my father & sister Abby. Errands. Visit to Dr. R. S. Kissam & to Dingley. The last came here with me, where he stayed an hour. Johnson & I drank tea at Kent's. All three walked on the Battery &c.—Medical visit. Came home. Transcribed the letters to Dr. Wilkins, & C. B. Brown; & wrote a letter to Samuel Coates of Phila., who sent me the late Convention Papers &c. & a letter to Wm. Pitt Beers, in reply to one recd. from him, day before yesterday.

Saturday, 15.—Finished Beddoes, except those parts which relate to the use of the Apparatus for the production of Airs. Six medical visits, in the course of the day. Twice at the Printer's. Several calls—among others at Dr. Miller's. Jereh. Mason breakfasted with us & left town soon after. Wm. & I spent the evening with Mrs. Lovegrove.

Sunday, July 16.—Five medical visits, in the forenoon. Two in the evening. Wrote letters to my Father, & sister Abby. Visited Mrs. Woolsey—& Wm. & I, called at Mr. Coit's & Mr. Riley's. Dined & spent the afternoon, at H. Johnson's. Mrs. Lovegrove there. After tea we walked out of town. It was eight o'clock when we returned—& it was after that, that my professional visits, was made. One was at Mr. Kent's. Dr. Hitchcock, of Washington County, is there.

Monday, 17.—Our new servant, Nathan Johnson, a black man, came this morning. Three medical visits. At the Printer's. Calls & errands. Two medical visits. Commenced Moseley on Tropical Diseases, & read upwards of 60 pages. He writes in a rambling manner, & affected style. Met Mr. & Mrs. Wolcott of Phila. in the street. Went with them to Mrs. Morton's, where I spent an hour. Dined at Kent's—Teaed at Mr. Radcliffe's. Medical visits. Part of the evening at Mr. Watson's. Mrs. Wolcott there. Called at Mr. Stansbury's[20] & at Mr. Adams's. Visit to H. Johnson's. Mrs. J. goes to Middleton (Connec.) tomorrow.

Tuesday, 18.—Read in the Pindariana.[21] Three medical visits. Errands. At the printer's. Writing for the Repository. Two medical visits. Progress in Moseley on Tropical Diseases.[22] Medical visits. Wm. & I called at Woolsey's. He has not returned. Mr. Gahn has. He went only to New Haven. Wm. & I went to the Manumission Society School-House. There was to have been a meeting; but there were not enough members to do business. I visited Miss Alsop. Called in at Kent's, on my return. Recd. a letter from C. B. Brown.

Wednesday, 19.—Medical visits & calls. Learnt that Mitchill was in town. Went to Mrs. Miller's, to the College, & to Mrs. M's again, in vain search after him. Visited Dr. Miller, who is unwell. A long visit from Dr. Wheaton. Pursued the reading of Moseley' book.

---

[20] Not enough information to identify this Stansbury among the many mentioned in the *New York Directory*, 1796.

[21] "Peter Pindar" was John Wolcott, *Pindariana; or Peter's Portfolio* (London, 1795).

[22] Benjamin Moseley, M.D., *Treatise on Tropical Diseases and on the Climate of the West Indies*, etc. (London, 1788).

Went to the Printer's, & busy there, some time, in correcting the press &c. Found Mitchill here, when I returned. Dr. Seaman also visited me. Got Dr. Barton's "New Views of the origin &c. of the Indians," of which I read the dedication & preface. Got also the Monthly Magazine for March 1797. Read some part of it. Dr. Mitchill & I went in search of an Austrian Professor who is now here. We did not find him. We drank tea at Mrs. Miller's. Parson Miller was there. Conversation of morals, &c. Mr. Miller & I walked on the Battery. Conversation continued. System of Godwin, of the french philosophers &c. Medical visit. Went into the Hudson. Read in the Monthly Magazine—some in Pindariana, in the course of the day.

Thursday, 20.—Four medical visits; one of which, being at some distance, occupied more than an hour. Visited Dr. Miller. He is better. Corrected proof sheets. At the printer's. Visited Mrs. Lovegrove. Medical visit. Finished the Monthly Magazine for March. Read the "Preliminary Discourse" in Dr. Barton's "New Views &c."—& examined some of his comparative Tables of American & Asiatic languages. Two medical visits. Visited Miss Alsop. Walked on the Battery. Recd. letters from Mr. Tracy & Wm. Buel.

Friday, 21.—Continued the Pindariana &c. Four medical visits. A visit from Mr. Roulet. Visited Mitchill & Miller. Corrected proof-sheets. Continued the reading of Moseley's work. A visit from Mitchill, who introduced to me the Swiss Calvinist (french) clergyman, Mr. Albert, (the successor of Mr. Duby,) who has come here to reside. A sensible man. At the printer's. Three medical visits. Johnson & I walked on the Battery. Spent the evening at Catlin's—chiefly in hearing Mrs. Catlin & Miss Taylor on the Piano Forte. Came home, found a message, & paid a professional visit.

Saturday, 22.—Six medical visits. Twice at the printer's. Corrected proof-sheets. Looked thro' the Monthly Review for March 1797. Continued Moseley. Three medical visits. Drank tea at Kent's. Evening at Woolsey's, who returned yesterday. His brother Benjn. here, on a visit. Finished Peter Pindar, Vol. IV.—Edit. Lond. pp. 500.

Sunday, July 23.—Wrote the succeeding Preface &c & the letter to Joseph Strong; which last I transcribed. Medical visit. Wm. & I dined at H. Johnson's. At four we three got into a coach, took up Mr. Kent about two miles out, & made Lake's tour. Wm. & I quitted the carriage two miles from town; walked to Woolsey's, where we sat awhile; & thence I came home. Read a few pages in the 2nd vol. of De Pauw—on the Spartans.

Monday, 24.—A visit from Mitchill. Wrote the letters, of this date, to Buel, Dennie, Brown, & Tracy, & transcribed the letter to Buel. Finished the reading of Moseley on Tropical Diseases. He is sufficiently dogmatic—but the remainder of his book, after he has done with dysentery, is more sensible & better written than the rest. Calls & errands. At the printer's. Corrected two proofs. At Mitchill's. He out. He recd. to-day, communications from Dr. Hedges, of this State; two from Dr. Mease, of Phila.; some, thro' Dr. M. from Dr. Davidson, of Martinique. I read the last, while at the College; & brought all of them off with me. Visited Dr. Miller. Drank tea at Kent's. When I came home, found that Dr. Barton had been here to see me. Called at the Tontine Coffee-House, where he lodges, but did not find him. Visit to Miss Morton—to Riley's. Came home, & read the other three Communications, to Mitchill, for the Repository. I do not think *very* highly of either of the four.

Tuesday, 25.—Tho' I went to bed late, I rose early, & read several papers in the Med: Comment: Edinb. 1795, before Dr. Barton came—who breakfasted with me by invitation. After breakfast, we went to Miller's & Mitchill's—& these visits filled up the forenoon. A little business separated us a short time. I corrected a proof-sheet. We dined at Miller's. Mitchill there. Returned to Miller's. Took Coffee. Miller, Barton & I walked on Battery. Barton & I went up to Mitchill's, where we spent the evening. I left B. there. A fire afterwards.

[Omitted here, four manuscript pages: "Preface, (intended) to the First Number of the Medical Repository."]

Wednesday, 26.—Tho' it was late when I went to bed, & still later ere I fell asleep, I rose very early, after about five hours repose. Walked. Miller & I breakfasted with Barton & Mitchill, at Mitchill's apartment in the College; after which B. took leave of us, & has sailed up the Hudson. The others came to my room; & agreed to the Preface above—with some slight variations made by me in the transcription. At the printer's. Errands &c. Transcribed the letters to Dennie, Brown & Tracy—the last with some additions—& forwarded them. Visited Woolsey. G. M. Woolsey has returned—I saw him. All friends well in Connecticut &c. Wm. & I walked out to Roulet's, where we spent the evening. Roulet shewed me a letter from Dr. Maret—a Swiss physician—a friend of his, to whom he had sent Webster's Collection on the Fever of 1795. This man reads english, & expresses himself favorably of the work. I purpose to write to him and transmit our Repository &c. Read some Articles in the Monthly Review; & finished Med: Comment: Edinb. for 1795—Edit. Phila. pp. 214—close.

To Joseph Strong

I do not know that I have any reason to complain of your silence, as I have not written to you myself, since I was in Phila.; but this I know, your silence has been an unpleasing thing to me. I want to hear from you often; & tho' the pressure of an extensive correspondence, may prevent me from provoking all my friends to write, by being first to write to them, yet they may be sure that I shall never leave any of their letters unanswered. I wish this information may have due weight with you, & determine you to communicate freely & frequently.

Our Medical Repository No. 1. is in the press, & will be out, in less than a fortnight. I must trouble you to call at Dobson's, & on Dr. Barton—both of whom, as well as yourself, have subscription-papers, & let me know how many copies are subscribed for in Phila. Will you be so kind as to undertake this unwelcome drudgery for your friend? I do not know who else to write to, for this purpose. I do not expect much encouragement from your proud City; in part, because I do not suppose much pains will be taken to seek encouragement for us. But time may do something; & should our publication once gain credit, I do not doubt of its receiving, at least, pecuniary aid from your quarter.

This letter is, necessarily, but short. I am hurried with other things. Mr. Woolsey has just returned from Connecticut—where he found & left all friends well.

Sunday, July 23. 1797.
Pine St. No. 45. N. Y.   E. H. Smith.

To William Buel

I recd. yours of the 11th inst. only four days ago, and I have been otherwise engaged, till now, or I should have replied immediately.

I hope your health is perfectly reestablished, by this time; tho' I rather wonder that you apply so tedious & unpalatable a remedy as Bark, when others as sure, & less nauseous are at hand. We have had an unusual quantity of Intermittents this year: the favorableness of the season, & the greater cleanliness of the streets, preventing them from becoming Remittents or Continued Fevers, as in other years. Our Intermittents are uncommonly disposed to recur, in seven or fourteen days—or thereabouts; & I have found it difficult to make my patients retain the Bark. It makes them sick, is rejected by vomit, & sometimes excites fever, like that from indigestion. I wish you to try my method of cure. It has never failed me. If the paroxysms come on at a certain hour, four hours before the recess, give a grain of Opium; in one hour, another; the next, another; the next, another. Four or five, will seldom fail to suspend the most violent intermittent. On the next day of the fever, you may begin an hour later, & give one pill less; & so diminish gradually. On the intermediate days, & in the absence of the fever, give good food, & any bitters you please, to restore the tone of the stomach, & increase the appetite. A small blister, or large Anodyne plaster,[23] on the back, will very much assist the cure. I want you, likewise to try Arsenic; & if I can find an opportunity, I will send you some prepared as I have given it, successfully, this season. It is a saturated Solution, of which from three to ten drops (from a two ounce Phial) may be given in any convenient vehicle, every three or four hours. Ten drops, three times a day, is a sufficient dose for the strongest man. If any disagreable sensations of the stomach occur, they are easily obviated by opium. The great excellences of this remedy are, that it has no disagreable taste, excites no nausea, & may be given without any reference to the presence or absence of the paroxysm.

There is still another remedy I wish you to try. That is Compression. By applying a tourniquet, or any thing which will effect the same, so as to stop the circulation in an arm & leg at the same time, just as the Cold Fit is expected, it will certainly be prevented, & the remainder of the fit be light; & by persevering in this method for a few days, the disease will be vanquished. My trials convince me that Angostura Bark is about four times as efficacious as, Peruvian, in the cure of Agues. It may be given in the same way. Dr. Osborn, of N. Carlina, confirms the truth of my opinion, by the result of his own extensive experience.

I very much thank you for your attention to our subscription; & will send you a Paper. Our first Number will be out in a week. Send me word how many I shall send you, & how. I suppose by the Stage. In that case, you must make each pay you his part of the postage; & you must let no person take a copy, without at first paying the subscription money—one dollar; which I will thank you to forward as soon as recd.

I rejoice that your fears for your child are at an end. My best remembrance to Mrs. Buel.

Monday July 24. 1797.
Pine St. 45. N. York.   E. H. Smith.

To Joseph Dennie Jr.

For near a month I have been so much engaged in superintending the printing of the first No. of the Medical Repository, that, with other ordinary business, it has left me no leisure for writing to you. And at present, I fear I shall meet with too many interruptions to be as copious as I wish.

I sent Mr. Carlisle, a short time since, a few extracts from Papers, as a sample of the communications of that kind, which you might expect from me. I shall transmit others, now, or shortly. As for books, I know of none that will be worth the trouble of transporting back & forth, that are not worthy to be purchased; & none that will particularly aid your design, that you should long continue without. The Monthly Magazine may be procured here, for 1796, bound in two volumes; for two dolls. a volume. If you wish them, I can procure them for you, & the remaining Nos. may be sent, as they arrive. Several persons here receive subscriptions.

There is one other periodical work that I forgot to mention. It is now discontinued. The Literary Magazine—in 12 vols. It is almost wholly a compilation; but the best, I think, that I have ever seen; & will furnish you with abundant, & rare, & valuable materials for

---

[23] Any plaster designed to assuage pain; a mixture of tar and beeswax was, for example, recommended for this purpose in mid-eighteenth century.

every part of your paper, except News. The value of the New Annual Register you must be acquainted with.

I am not much in the habit of consulting the Critical Review; tho' it is a respectable Journal. It is, I believe, still bound to Church & State; but with some moderation. The British Critic is the *violent* supporter of the *good old cause*. The Monthly Review is, I suppose, carried on by men of various professions, & principles: tho' with some *general* resemblance in theological & political principles. A very able clergyman of the established Church was a long time a writer in it. He is now dead. Some one or more of the writers are not christians. At least I judge so from internal evidence. One, at least, is a Republican. Others are monarchy men. I think the steady perusal of this Journal will lead you to adopt the same opinions.

The Gentleman's Magazine is still directed by Nichols —tho' surely not deserving the approbrious title you give him. It was formerly devoted chiefly to literature; now to antiquities. These are the passion of the Editor —who is one of the most industrious men living; concerned in numerous extensive, laborious & useful works; & remarkable for giving a great plenty of matter, at a reasonable price. See the acct. of his last publication, in the Monthly Review. I do not think, however, that his Magazine would be useful to you. Antiquities are not much relished in America.

I have seen the "Monk";[24] but the representation I recd. of it, did not induce me to read it. The "Castle of Otranto" of Horace Walpole, & the "Ghost-Seer" of Schiller, have caused an inundation of imitations; some of which have a little merit; but none are worthy to be compared with the originals. Schiller's performance, particularly, is inestimable for the excellence of its morality. If you have not read it, you can not make too great haste to enjoy the delight of perusal.

I regret that you do not read French. I would send you some valuable originals; but I have no time for translations.

So much in reply to the inquiries of your letter. In regard to original communications, I must again assure you, that it will be wholly out of my power to do you any personal service. Most of my composition must be professional, & directed to the maintenance of a very extensive & increasing correspondence. The leisure for composition which these leave me, must be employed on Plans, which will take much time to accomplish, if ever accomplished; & which are of more importance, in my view at least, than any thing I could perform by a different application of my time. I have, however, one thing to propose to you, which may merit your consideration. I have a friend, not in New York at present, but with whom I could readily communicate, who is very capable of enriching your paper by original composition. He has both taste & learning, & is accustomed to compose. But he is poor: absolutely destitute. His pen is his only support; & he chiefly employs it mechanically. I am certain that if you could afford him a very moderate compensation for his labours, you might so far command his assistance as to be certain of one or two weekly essays, critical, literary, or moral; either in a continued series, or under different titles & signatures, as you should deem best. To this proposition I wish a speedy answer, if you accede to it: as it will take several weeks to establish the intercourse with you & him regularly.

I sent the 20 copies of Ed: & Argus. by Mr. Mason. He will deliver them to you. The Medical Repository No. 1. will be published next week. Any number of copies that may be demanded in your quarter, shall be sent, by such conveyance as you point out.

Monday, July 24. '97.
Pine St. 45—N. York.   E. H. Smith.

Thursday, 27.—Looked over one volume, & part of another, of the Monthly Review. At the printer's, & bookbinder's some time. Corrected several proofs. Visited Dr. Miller. Concluded the Annals of medicine, Vol. 1. pp. 262—edit. Edinb. 8vo. Close print. Johnson & I walked. Called on Mrs. L. She out. Drank tea at H. Johnson's. All three walked on the Battery. I went to Dr. Miller's—& we visited Miss Mason. Miss Nicholson was there. Lively conversation. I spent two interesting hours of conversation & reading with Miss Alsop, this forenoon. I have not felt fit for study, all this day.

To Charles B. Brown

I am tired of assigning want of leisure as a reason for not writing sooner, tho' it is really the true cause of my delay. The superintendance of the press, which is now in travail with the first No. of the Medical Repository, has held my pen silent.

I rejoice at the readiness with which you adopt the suggestion of my last letter; & only wish your perseverance may be as great. I have just written to Dennie, & shall probably be able to send you his terms in the course of a month or three weeks.

In respect of my letter to which you refer, you do me wrong. It was short; but the causes of that brevity were obvious. Nor was it more brief than yours frequently are. In general I am much the most copious. It was only by comparison that this was short; not by comparison with yours, but with my own. I was busily employed, in a professional way, at that time. In any reasonable return of a letter, you would have found me differently engaged: for I shortly after took up, & have read thro', the second edition of Political Justice. Do not be so hasty, therefore, in future, to draw inferences favorable to your aversion to epistolary composition. If my views had been different, they could scarcely be so important. At least, it would be well to intermix moral ones. Whose duty was it, then, to insinuate these sublime & inestimable considerations? You know too well how easily I forego professional enquiry, to listen to other

---
[24] *Ambrosio, or the Monk,* by Matthew W. Gregory ("Monk") Lewis (1795).

topics. Nor can you be ignorant how great & how seducing the influence of friendship over my bosom. These might be reasons for some delay in writing to me, but they do not appear to have been your reasons. You were out of humor with the brevity of my letter; & the causes of it. One would suppose, from your reply, that superstition, & not medicine, were the subject of my studies at that time. Your impatience, then, would be intelligible. You speak of my being "absorbed" in tracing the pedigree of *Hypocrites*"—I do not wonder that you thought the philosophy of Godwin would ill agree with an employment so "sublime." Did you mean a pun. If so, it was not quite so apt as his who called the *tower of Babel*, the tower of *Babble*.

Seriously, & in earnest, I both doubt the sincerity of Mr. Dennie's praise; & was more mortified than pleased with it. He is in the careless habit of extravagant commendation & blame—with no bad intentions, I believe, but certainly without himself believing all he says to be justly merited. Where there is so little judgment, or so little discrimination, it is possible only for the most gluttonous desire of praise to find delight. Still, it is very true, & I lament it, that "Praise finds in me a faulty degree of sensibility to her charms." We think *somewhat* differently on this subject, I know. You have too low a sense of the value of reputation. You do not seem to regard how great may be its instrumentality in promoting the cause of truth. You are therefore faultily negligent to obtain praise; & your powers slumber unemployed. There is errror on either hand. But mine is, perhaps, the more dangerous. I can not therefore but regret that you have so long delayed an attempt to correct this vicious propensity in me. And I still hope that you will collect sufficient perspicuity to state it fairly. I am the more earnest, because I shall have your own view of the subject, which will be always important to me—whether it be the just view, or not. Nor can any remarks, on this topic, be altogether without their use. Sensibility to praise implies an equal sensibility to blame; & here are principles to operate upon, so as to generate right conduct, even on erroneous motives. If I know my own heart, how apt soever it may be to be captivated & led astray by praise, how much soever it may pant to obtain commendation, the motive is really benevolent. I may deceive myself, even here; but I hope not: & this hope, induces me to believe your counsels will not be wasted on me.

Love to all friends. Dunlap &c. are at Amboy.

Monday, July 24. 1797.
Pine St. No. 45. N. York.   E. H. Smith.

To Uriah Tracy

I wish it were in my power to make you an answer that would give you equal pleasure to that which I recd. from your letter; tho' it is not without matters sad & doleful; but our town, & my head, afford little of moment. A healthy season, a clean city, & friends in good condition, are all agreable things, but they do not furnish much theme for discourse. Battles, tornadoes, mobs, & plots, are the fertile topics of conversation, from which, thank heaven, we are as yet tolerably free. This calm may portend a storm, but, notwithstanding the low grumbling in the South-West, things in France seem to look more like accommodation. I hope your sad presentiments may all be converted into cheerful expectations. It were very easy to speculate on these points, if the disposition to do so were prevalent. When we know so little, there is a wide field of conjecture. But as I am determined that every thing is yet to go right, I am also willing to leave the course of events to proceed undisturbed. Hopeful of good, but not unprepared to meet the worst, I will not suffer the cup of present joy to be dashed with any melancholly anticipations of future distress. Nor will you, I presume, at this moment, be inclined to waste many hours in hunting after causes of apprehension, in the flying rumors of the day. Once more in the midst of your family, you look back on the weary days, that have now expired, like the sailor who enters the peaceful haven, after a perilous tempest; & are ready to exclaim, with Othello,

> O my soul's joy!
> If after every tempest comes such calms,
> May the winds blow, till they have weakened death:
> And let the laboring bark climb hills of seas
> Olympus high; and duck again as low
> As hell's from heaven. If I was now to die;
> 'Twere now to be most happy; for I fear
> My soul hath her content so absolute,
> That not another comfort like to this
> Succeeds in unknown fate.[25]

I see a drop glisten in Mrs. Tracy's eye, as she reads this, over your shoulder. When these lines produce so fond an effect, it were ridiculous pedantry to apologize for the quotation. I wish they may also remind her of me, sufficiently to induce her to bestow on me a long-neglected mark of her remembrance: a Letter.

I delivered Mr. Miller his letter; & should occasion present will look at yours to Webster, & give you my free opinion. But he is in trouble; & you must forgive a little pettishness. He will be sorry for it himself, when he reflects.

All friends are well; & send remembrances. Mine, again & again, with unimpaired sincerity & warmth, to you & yours.

Monday, July 24. 1797.
Pine St. No. 45. N. York.   E. H. Smith.

To William Dunlap

Johnson shewed me a short letter from you, a few days since. It is very uncertain whether I visit you this summer. Still I hope to do so, before long.

---

[25] *Othello* II, i. Unlike many of Smith's quotations from memory, this passage is almost correct. Line 6 in the best texts usually reads: "If it were" for "If I was."

Mitchill thinks the *Rice Bunting* & the Boblincon are the same. I know nothing of the Rice Bunting, by that name, but what I find in Galston's History of Birds. If his account is just, they are not the same. He says they did not appear in Carolina, till the Rice was introduced; & that they only dwell where there is rice. Now, I have been familiar with the Boblincon from my infancy; & no Rice grows in New-England. Beside, neither the definition nor the figure of Galston are those of the Boblincon.

Since you have been absent, this very week indeed, we have had a visit from Dr. Barton of Phila. He stayed with us one day, & part of another; & we— Mitchill, Miller, & myself, were constantly with him.

His apology for not sending the promised catalogue is the occupation of business & of printing his new work—which is now published. He is going to Niagara; & possibly may return this way, in about seven weeks. While here, he made out the inclosed Catalogue of Trees & Plants, natives of America, of which there are no correct drawings or plates. It is not as ample as one he had formed; but which, being packed away among his things, he could not readily get at; yet I think there is work enough for you in it.

You doubtless know that Hodgkinson has left Hartford—much to the dissatisfaction of the people; who are incensed against him; & he has opened in Boston, with The Grecian Daughter & The Romp. But perhaps you do not know that Wignell is to play in Rickets's Circus, from the first of next month, I know not how long; & that he is in town, with part of his company, already. If you come up, you may now, probably have an opportunity of seeing Mrs. Merry & Mr. Cooper in their best parts.[26]

I had a short letter from Charles, some days ago. As usual, it is difficult to learn from it what he is about. He, however, relishes the proposal of writing for the New Hampshire paper. I have written to Dennie on the subject.

Munson has returned, fat, ruddy, & in spirits. Your brother Benjn. Woolsey is here. All friends well.

The first No. of the Medical Repository will be published next week. Shall it be sent you? Respects to your mother: Love &c. to Mrs. Dunlap & the children.

Thursday, July 27. 1797.
Pine St. No. 45. N. Y.   E. H. Smith.

---

[26] The theatrical scene was, as usual, chaotic. Dunlap had retreated to his summer home in Perth Amboy to watch birds and be with his children. Following his unfortunate experience with Mr. and Mrs. Hallam and the close of the New York season in June, Hodgkinson took the company to Hartford, Connecticut, where, for some reason, it was badly received. In desperation, he moved most of his regular players to Boston, leaving another group under Mr. Solee in Hartford. The Boston run was also a disaster. Apparently *The Grecian Daughter* by Arthur Murphy (London, 1772) was a poor choice for the opening. Meanwhile, the Philadelphia Company under Wignell and Reinagle endeavored to break the Old American Company's monopoly in New York by opening at Rickert's Circus, a building normally used for equestrian exhibits.

SONNET IV

Early Rising

Shrill crows the cock, the matin peals proclaim
    The near approach of morning's beauteous Queen:
    And now the grey manes of her steeds are seen,
Like waving mists from dewy meads that steam:

And now their white necks in the orient beam;
    Rapid they dart along, the clouds between;
    The ruddy chariot, rich in dazzling sheen,
Bursts on the view; the golden axles gleam:

And lo! the Form divine, with graceful bend.
    Waves the light lash and shakes the lucent reins,
The Hours, the Loves, her purple course attend:
    Her floating hair the glittering band disdains,
And Zephyrs lift her rosy veil in air:
Spring from thy couch, and hail the heavenly Fair.

(Composed Monday June 29. 1797.)

SONNET V

Cold Bathing

See how the dew on yonder lily strews
    A thousand pearls, that twinkle to the morn!
    Each opening flower what glittering gems adorn!
The snow-drop crystals, rubies deck the rose.

What rain-bow hues the morning meads disclose!
    How hang the drops upon the scented thorn!
    And there, from winding streams, in wreaths upborne,
The mist, slow-waving, o'er the forest flows.

Bath'd and renew'd, the vegetable race
    Shed sweeter odours, cast a wider shade,
And livelier hues and fresher green efface
    Marks of decay that yester sun had made.
Health, youth, and beauty court the dashing wave,
And in the gelid stream delight to lave.

(Composed Monday June 29. 1797.)

SONNET VI

Autumn

Mute are the fields that late so tuneful were,
    And all the meadow's gaudy hues are fled:
    Yon grove that lifts its venerable head,
In gayer foliage glistens from afar.

There, as you walk, low murmurs fill the air,
    The deep leaves rustle to your sweeping tread,
    And, from on high, in yellow, pied, and red,
Flow [Slow?] circling down, the present Fall declare.

How sweetly pensive now is every thought!
    How much this holy calm Reflection suits!
Invite her then, and, by her lessons taught,
    When comes thy Fall, like bountiful in fruits,
Ripe & full fraught, as hang these nuts, thy mind,
As yon fair apples, lovely and refin'd.

(Composed Monday July 10. 1797.)

SONNET VII

Cleanliness

1

Perfumes more sweet from many a flower exhale,
    And gaudier colours many a blossom bears,
Than hover round the lily of the vale,
    Than the pale violet of the meadow wears.

Yet, cull'd from all the daughters of the field,
    With *this* thy chestnut locks thou love'st to deck;
Preferr'd o'er all the lavish gardens yield,
    That rests upon the ivory of thy neck.

These simple flowers what secret charm endears?
    Ah if it be so pure, so neat, they seem,
Bath'd in the dew of morning's costliest tears,
    Or tinged with evening's last declining beam,
So may'st thou emulate their virgin art,
Please every eye, and live in every heart.

(July 28. 1797.)

SONNET VIII

Cleanliness

2

Hark to the quaker Wren, whose chattering note
    Proclaims the rapture of his little heart!
Hark how the Robin swells his mellow throat!
    How the brown Thrush essays his rival art!

The twittering swallow skims along the ground,
    Or, beating, mounts upon the buoyant gales;
Now darts, in rapid whirl, the pool around;
    Now, on the breeze, with silent pinions, sails.

List to the Lark, that on the topmost bough,
    Of yon high oak, his waving balance keeps;
Sweet is the Oriole's voice, loud caws the Crow,
    And chirps the Sparrow, and the Grass-bird peeps:
Their plumes composed, they hail the genial Spring,
Joy tunes the song, and health unfurls the wing.

(July 28. 1797.)

SONNET IX

Cleanliness

3

Health, beauty, joy, their tiptoe steps attend,
    O white-stoled Goddess! who fulfill thy law:
O, in my sister, may they find a friend
    Whom want and sickness from thy temple draw.

But, be the wretch who, careless of thy rites,
    Basks him in vain in fortune's sunny ray,
By all rejected; from the dear delights,
    Of social life excluded, thrust away.

Why should he poison, with infectious taint,
    The wholesome purity thou breath'st around?
Virtue disclaims him, prophet call'd or saint;
    They, they alone, by Virtue shall be crown'd,
Lov'd and acknowledg'd by the heav'nly Fair,
    Who, thro' thy temple, to her fane repair.

(July 28. 1797.)

SONNET X

Dress. 1

O sweet Simplicity! thy maiden veil
    Unclose, and yield thee to my wishful eyes.
The glittering swarms that every sense assail,
    The fools of Fashion, prompt my secret sighs.

O sweet Simplicity, arise! arise!
    In all thy nameless charms thy form reveal.
O teach the fair, thy precepts who despise,
    That dress was meant to cover, not conceal:

From the keen air the tender limbs to guard,
    From scorching suns with cob-web folds to hide,
From chilly damps of early spring to ward,
    And foggy autumn's ague-bearing tide:
Not to enshroud in gorgeous piles abhorr'd:
    Grace laughs to scorn the cumbrous pomp of Pride.

(July 28. 1797.)

SONNET XI

Exercise

1

Up, up! arise! haste, haste! the vernal morn
    Purples the orient sky; and see the rays
    Of the young sun the east hill's groves emblaze:
Ten thousand pearls their sparkling boughs adorn.

Quick, quick, the simple robe, the hat of chip,—
    Let thy loose ringlets flutter in the breeze:
    Soft, soft glide down the stairs; thy hand I seize;
Mount we our coursers, and the gale outstrip.

How fresh the air! how mild the early sun!
    How ring the wild notes thro' the neighboring wood!
Dustless the moist earth as we gallop on;
Rattle the pebbles of this shallow run;
    Thunders the bridge:—Ha, ha! in drowsy mood,
Toss on the uneasy down who will—we, we are flown.

(July 28. 1797.)

SONNET XII

Exercise

2

Come, the meridian sun forsakes his height,
    And downward now he seeks the western wave;
Eastward the trees extend their mimic night;
    O be not thou of indolence the slave!

Repose is sweet to Exercise alone;
    The sons of Sloth on softest down in vain
Invite her presence; for, to them unknown,
    She flies to bless the tiller of the plain.

Nor only woo the meditative Power:
    Fruitless her bounty if seclusion dim,
Or selfish silence, hide it from mankind.
Yes—give thy murmurs to the idle wind:
    Cherish full vigour in each active limb:
And live for *all* till age's wintery hour.[27]

(July 28. 1797.)

Friday, July 28.—Composed six of the foregoing sonnets, & transcribed them all. They are part of my long projected series; and are inserted here, without any corrections. Being written at different times, tautologies, or repetitions, occur; which must be weeded out, & the whole revised, at some future time. Corrected the last proof of the 1st No. of the Medical Repository, the printing of which is now completed.[28] Was at the printer's this afternoon. Posted my books—but have not yet done. Evening at Woolsey's. Gahn, who returned yesterday from Phila. was there. Read a number of articles in the Monthly Review.

Saturday, 29.—Transcribed the letter to Dunlap. Read several articles in the Monthly Review. Medical visit. A visit from Mitchell & Miller. At the Hospital on business, & then at Mr. Eddy's. Errands. Drew up the succeeding case of Mania from my notes, made at the time. Read the papers. Wm. & I walked on the Battery. We spent the evening at Riley's. Recd. a letter from Thomas Mumford.

Sunday, 30.—Read several articles in the Monthly Review. Wrote the subsequent pages—ending p. 319.—concerning my paternal ancestors; taking them chiefly from notes originally put together in August 1794. My present intention is merely to collect the materials for my long-projected History of my own Life. What is more immediately important is, to fix dates of early transactions, before those are removed whose memory may be able to supply any deficiencies & correct any errors of my own. A visit from Dingley. Wm. & I dined at H. Johnson's. In the afternoon, we walked out to Mr. Stuyvesant's, at the Bowery—where we drank tea. It was eight when we returned. Spent the evening with Mrs. Lovegrove. Read in the Monthly Review.

[Omitted here, seven manuscript pages: "Case of Mania, successfully treated by Salivation."]

SONNET XIII

Dress. 2

Nature, chaste goddess, erst by all ador'd,
    Enrob'd the sex in modesty alone;
The waist comprest not, ear nor nostril bor'd,
    Constraint and cruelty to her unknown.

No formal folds, no studied pleats, disgrac'd,
    No dangling ornaments deform'd, the fair:
The pliant fabric every limb embrac'd,
    Or the loose robe fell floating on the air.

In *this,* reclining 'mid some favorite bower,
    Minerva and the Muses blest the Maid;
In that, invigor'd by their bounteous power,
    She flew, unmanacled, to misery's aid.
Break, break the spells of Fashion! generous Fair!
Health, grace, and liberty, reward your care.

(July 31. 1797.)

["Brief Notices Concerning My Paternal Ancestors" which followed the above entry is now *Appendix 1*]

Monday, July 31.—In the course of the day read a number of articles in the Monthly Review. I am dissatisfied with myself for this desultory reading; yet I am obliged to run out & in so often in the day, that indolence very readily finds an excuse for it. Read the Newspapers. Medical visits to & from patients. Errands. Transcribed the preceeding pages, relative to my parents,

---

[27] Although these sonnets are no enduring monuments to the muse they are, nevertheless, highly respectable examples of the sonnet in late eighteenth-century America—which is to say that most sonnets published about that time are appallingly bad. In verse forms these are somewhat more orthodox than his earlier efforts when he was a medical student in Philadelphia. Several are fairly regular Petrarchan sonnets except for the closing couplet which is, of course, unusual but less so than once supposed. Four are attempts at the Shakespearean form. The diction repels us but it remains that as exercises (and that is more or less the way Smith thought of them) they are passable.

[28] The first issue contained the "Circular Address" which Smith had written in November; a section entitled "Medical Facts, Hints, and Inquiries," principally composed of notes on hospital cases which are to be found scattered throughout the "Diary"; an introduction, in which he explained that lack of material would prevent his completing what he had hoped might be a full set of essays on the plagues of ancient times; "The Plague of Athens," first of the proposed series; and a review entitled "A Memoir concerning the Fascinating Faculty which has been ascribed to the Rattle-snake . . . etc." It is possible that some of the other unsigned reviews may be Smith's work.

In subsequent issues of the quarterly he was a frequent contributor. The second number carried his article, "A Case of Mania Successfully Treated by Mercury." A poem, "The Doctrine of Septon" (Septon was Mitchill's term for a quality of the air which he believed responsible for disease) appeared in the second number under Mitchill's signature. About fifty of the one hundred forty verses are Smith's. Certain stylistic peculiarities suggest that he was also the reviewer of Joseph Priestley's pamphlet, "Considerations on the Doctrine of Philogiston and the Decomposition of Water." For the fourth number of volume one he wrote an essay entitled "On the Origins of the Pestilential Fever which prevailed in the Island of Grenada, in the Years 1793 and 1794." The same number also contained his remarks on the diseases of infants, which he entitled rather ambiguously: "A Case Similar to Those which Form the Subject of the Preceding Article." Two of his essays appeared posthumously in the *Repository* in 1799, "On the Pestilential Diseases which, at different Times, appeared in the Athenian, Cartheginian, and Roman Armies, in the Neighborhood of Syracuse," and "Concerning the Elk." All of these essays, as well as the column or section which he edited, are well-written but of little interest now except to a student of medical history.

with additions, from notes made August 1794. Composed & transcribed the XIIIth Sonnet, with which I am not much pleased. Spent the evening at Wm Woolseys—chiefly. Mrs. Woolsey returned saturday. Sat half an hour with Geo: M. Woolsey. The rest of the evening at home.

Another month completed—not altogether idly; but not industriously. I have done more professional business in this, than in any preceeding month.

Industry of July 1797
Reading

Annals of Medicine Vol.I. Edit. Edinb. 8vo. pp.462.—loose.
Med: Comment. Edinb. 1795. edit. Phila. 8vo. pp.214.—close.
Mosely on Tropical Diseases. edi. Lond. 1795 8vo. pp. 551.
Beddoes on Fact: Airs—P.3.4.&5. addenda to the 1st.
Asiatic Researches—part of Vol. 1 & 3—equal to pp. 236—8vo.
Peter Pindar's Works. Vol. IV—edit. Lond. 8vo. pp. 500—loose.
Barton's "New Views &c."—edit. Phila. 8vo.
Monthly Review, Monthly Magazine, many numbers; News-papers,&c.

Writing

Composition.

Letters, preserved in the Journal, equal to pp.16—thereof.
Do.—not preserved—equal— —to pp.12.
Eight Sonnets.
Medl:Facts, Hints &c. (in the Med. Reposy:)—to pp. 4.
Medl:News. (do.—)—pp.4.
Preface to Med:Repository 3½
Case of Mania &c. ....pp.7.

Transcription. All the above Letters.
  "   "   "   Sonnets.
Med:Facts, News &c. Preface &c.—equal—8.
Brief Notices transcribed & composed—12½
Posted Books.
Compared Morse & Winterbotham.
  &c.   &c.   &c.

MEMOIRS. 1797. AUGUST.

Tuesday, 1st.—Much of this day devoted to errands & calls. Read a number of articles in the Monthly Review, & the Newspapers. Miller & I at Mitchill's, in the forenoon. He was absent; but we met there a Mr. Goetz; formerly a professor of Moral Philosophy in Vienna. He wants a place, of some kind, in one of our Colleges. I wrote a letter, in his behalf, to Dr. Dwight. Mitchill & Miller here, in the afternoon, on business of the Repository. Mitchill & I went to Swords's on the same. Evening, partly at Kent's; partly, at home.

Wednesday, 2nd.—Read Hosack's Essay on the Fever of 1795,[29] made an outline of a Review of it, & proceeded thereon, thro' the five first pages. Read several articles in the Monthly Review. Also the News-papers, & in the evening Mr. Fox's celebrated Speech on Mr. Grey's motion for a Parliamentary Reform. A visit from Mr. Sharples the Painter. At the printer's. Gahn called here. We drank tea at Dr. & Mr. Miller's—& spent the evening, till nine, at Roulet's. After at home, readg. Mr. Fox. Conversation, an hour, with Osborn.

Thursday, 3.—Read a few articles in the Monthly Review, in the morning. Took up Darwin's "Theory of Fever"—on which I read till dinner; carefully; & marking with my pen a brief analysis. I continued it a little time after dinner. But Roulet came in & brought me the Monthly Review for April 1797. I read almost all, & looked it thro'. There are several interesting articles, tho' this number is not remarkably valuable. The most interesting article is Miss Hays's "Emma Courtney"—& the letter is really fine. Wm. & I spent the former part of the evening with Mrs. Lovegrove. I came home, & resumed Darwin. The day has been rainy.

Friday, August 4.—From a little before nine, till after five, with the interruptions hereafter noticed, employed in reading Darwin's Theory of Fever; continuing my Analysis. The interruptions consisted of Dinner, as usual—which occupied, perhaps, ten minutes: I had recd. letters from my Father, & from Abby—these were read: there accompanied them, letters from my sisters &c. to Aurora—very long—these were read. After five, I went out, to do several errands: at the printer's for one. Returning, I called on Mrs. Lovegrove, to inquire how her little girl was; without any intention of continuing there longer than to have the inquiry satisfied. However, some questions were asked &c & tea came in. To that I must stay. In laying aside my cloak, Mrs. L. discovered that I had pamphlets in my pockets. They were two copies of the Medl. Repository. She had seen the advertisement, & so looked at the pamphlet. The article concerning the Fascinating Faculty &c. caught her eye. She wished me to read it. After that, she would hear so much of the Essay on the Plague of Athens, as did not immediately relate to the symptoms &c. This carried out the eveng. to nine. Since my return I have read various articles in the Monthly Review. I suspect that I have discovered the author of the "Elegy on the late Rt. Honle. Wm. Pitt," in Mr. Day, the author of "Sandford & Merton." The stanzas quoted in the review of the acct. of this excellent man, much resemble that Elegy.

A subject has suggested itself for my Manumission Oration—viz. on the best means of civilizing, or making good citizens of, the Negroes. I wish also to write an essay on the best means of civilizing the Indian—& on the true obstacles to their civilization.

---
[29] *A History of Yellow Fever* (Philadelphia, 1797).

Saturday, 5.—Read various articles in the Monthly Review. Visit from Dr. Mitchill. Visit to Mr. Gahn. Continued the reading & brief analysis of Darwin's Theory of Fever; & have now reached to the Recapitulation. Johnson & I went to Watson's to see Mr. Hosmer of Hudson, who stays there, & has just returned from a visit [to] Connecticut. We stayed there some time; then walked on the Battery; & with Hosmer went to Riley's—where we spent the evening.

Some days since I wrote to Dr. Dwight in behalf of a German Professor, who wishes a regular establishment in some College. I found a short answer, when I came home, giving no encouragement.

Sunday, 6.—Read a number of articles in the Monthly Review. Johnson & I visited Mitchill, at the College. There we saw several publications, among others some by Dr. Dickson, Professor of the Practice of Medicine in the University of Dublin, who is now in New York; having come to America to reside. We dined & spent the afternoon at H. Johnson's. A Mr. Stewart was there & Mr. Hosmer. The Johnson's, Hosmer, & I walked all the evening. A very social day. I forgot—Wm. & I visited, also, Mrs. Lovegrove, in the forenoon.

Monday, 7.—Finished Darwin's Theory of Fever. I have read it with some attention; but not sufficient. I must repeat, & repeat the reading—indeed, of the whole work. I can only denominate it, at present, admirable. Read an Oration, by Dr. Wheaton of this city, before the Friary. Read the News Papers, which are uncommonly full & interesting. Recd. a letter from C. B. Brown—containing "Alcuin; a Dialogue"[30]—which I have twice read, with much pleasure, & some approbation. Mr. Hosmer was here an hour, or two, in the morning. I went with him to a Bookseller's. In the afternoon various errands. Learnt that Dunlap had returned. Two ineffectual calls to see him. Drank tea & spent the evening, chiefly, at W. W. Woolsey's. Miss Alsop, Hosmer, Johnson, & Dunlap there. Went home with Miss A. & spent an hour there. I first heard, this evening, that the *Cats* are sickening, in New York. I must not forget to pursue the inquiry.

Tuesday, 8.—It rained all day. It ceased at 6 P. M. I was at home, during the rain. Dr. Miller was here, in the forenoon. Dunlap spent most of it with me. I read him C. B. Brown's "Alcuin," some articles in the My. Review for April; my Sonnets &c. He read me a long letter he has been writing to Holcroft. He was here, also, much of the afternoon. Mitchill, likewise, was here. The rest of the time I read The Monthly Review. Dunlap & I drank tea at Riley's. Johnson was there a few minutes. He departed. Dunlap followed, not long after. I spent the evening. I read several articles in the N. Y. Review to Miss Alsop; & finished the reading to her, of "Alcuin"—which I commenced last night—I have

---

[30] Smith's decision to edit and publish this work became firm by December 18, 1797, when he expressed his intention to Alsop. For his difficulties in dealing with the unpredictable Brown, see later.

heard more of the *Cat*-distemper to-day; & must make some inquiries tomorrow.

Wednesday, 9.—Read several articles in the Monthly Review. Business for my father & errands called me abroad. Called at Miller's, at the Hospital, & at Mitchill's. There I read two Papers in the Trans: of the R. Irish Acady.—being an account of the Fish Mummies, & of the Preservative Power of Alkalies over meat. I brought away the 2nd & 3rd vols. of the Medical Extracts—which I have nearly looked thro'. Returning, met Dr. Moore, & went into his house a short time. Dunlap went to Amboy to-day. Errands. Drank tea with Geo: M. Woolsey. Visited the Miller's. Spent most of the evening at Mr. Morton's. Rest at Kent's. I hear more of the disease among the Cats—but can not, yet, get an opportunity for making any observations.

Thursday, 10.—Wrote the next succeeding letters to Reuben Smith, Thomas Mumford, Abigail Smith Jr. & Joseph Bringhurst. Read a number of articles in the Monthly Review—finished the 3rd vol. of the Medical Extracts—& read Inaugural dissertations, published at Phila.—by Fisher, Jones, & McKenzie—of each of which I wrote some account, as may be seen in the following pages. Read also Mr. Cooper's Essay on the Datura Strammonium. At our printer's. Visited Mrs. Lovegrove. Called on Mr. Gahn. Walked out of town. Went to Mr. Webster's. Returned in the evening—& called at W. W. Woolsey's, on my way. Nobody at home. Came home & read. Mr. Wr. told me that several Cats had lately taken refuge at his house, from the pestilence in the city.

Friday, 11.—Read several articles in the Monthly Review. Read the Inaugural Dissertations of Messrs. North, on Rheumatism; Allston, on Dropsy; and Black, on Fractures: on the two first of which I wrote a short criticism. Visit at Dr. & Mr. Miller's. Dr. Mitchill returned. He has recd. a letter from Dr. Beddoes, informing that Hepatized Ammonia—& even Ammonia alone—has been discovered to be a complete remedy for Diabetes. Errands. Dined, & spent the afternoon, with Geo: M. Woolsey &c. Nothing passed worthy of note. Wm. & I walked on the Battery. The evening at Mr. Kent's. Mrs. K. has returned—well—& the child.

Saturday, 12.—Read a number of articles in the Monthly Review. Completed my review of Hosack's Essay on the Yellow Fever, as it now stands. This critique is much more incorrect that I intend it shall be, if it be thought best to bestow so much attention, on so slight a performance, which I use rather as a text to comment on, than as anything else. Read Huger's Inaugural Dissertation on Gangrene & Mortification, & the chief part of Church's on Camphor. Wm. & I walked out of town—having first called a few minutes at Dr. & Mr. Miller's. Returning, we were caught in a shower, & were obliged to stop at S. Johnson's House—who is still out of town. Here we spent the evening, by ourselves, in free & friendly discourse; & I seldom have spent three hours so intirely to my satisfaction. I stopped at Miller's, on my way home, & got the Analytical Review from December to April, inclusive—& have read the account of Godwin's "Enquirer" with great pleasure; have run over the whole number for April, & some articles in some of the other numbers. I find many works noticed here, & many unnoticed, which are reviewed, & neglected by the Monthly Reviewers.

Sunday, 13, August.—Read several articles in the Analytical Review. Transcribed the letters to Reuben Smith, Thomas Mumford, Abigail Smith Jr. & Joseph Bringhurst. Wrote also a few lines to Fanny, inclosing a copy (now made) of the fourth & fifth Sonnets. Wm. & I dined with H. Johnson. about four we three walked out of town & returned a little after seven. Wm. & I spent the evening with Mrs. Lovegrove. Miss Morton & her youngest brother were there part of the time.

Monday, 14.—Finished looking over the Analytical Review for Decr., Jany., Feby., Mar: & April last. A visit from Dr. Mitchill: from Wm. W. Woolsey: from Mr. Shethar [?] of Lichfield. All well there. Called on Mitchill, & together with him, Miller, &c. went to see four Elks: two males of two years old, a female of three, & a fawn. Medical visit at Woolsey's. Calls & errands. Spent part of the evening at Riley's—with Miss Alsop. Johnson there some of the time. Remainder at home. Finished Church's Essay on Camphor, & read part of Johnson's on Carbonic Acid Gas.

Tuesday, 15.—Was surprized by a visit from my cousin Josiah Root. He is well, & left all friends so. He spent an hour or two with me. I visited Mitchill at the College. He shewed me the Proceedings, Lectures &c. which he had just recd. from Dr. Valentin—& Valentin's Letter. He also gave a paper of Valentin's on the Actual Cautery to read, which have since perused. We looked over Pennant's very incorrect Article, in which described the Moose & Elk as the same. His figure of the moose, is not like the Elk's now here. Read thro' Johnson's Essay on Carbonic Acid.[31] It merits to be called ingenious. Read several articles in the Monthly Review & various NewsPapers. Wrote & transcribed the letter to Dr. Buel, of this date. Calls & errands. Drank tea at Dunlap's, who arrived this eveng. We went to Woolsey's. They out. To Mr. Rogers's—Saw Miss Rogers. To Kent's—where we spent the eveng. W. W. Woolsey was there, & Mr. Boyd.

To Reuben Smith

The letters and money came safely, by Mr. Clark. I inclose Philips & Clark's receit, in full; together with the receited Bill of the Wine. The cask was put on board of Capt. Bradley's[32] vessel, last evening. I shall keep his receit will you give me notice of its being safe at New Haven.

The letters for Aurora are still here. I know of no opportunity to send them; but shall avail myself of the first that offers. I had a letter from Mr. Mumford, a few days ago; but it is not dated. I suppose it must have been written about the middle of July. All were, then, well.

The first Number of the Medical Repository is now published. I am somewhat disappointed in finding so few subscribers in Lichfield County. Professional curiosity seems to be at a low ebb, there. I hope, however, that it will increase. The first suitable conveyance, I shall forward a dozen copies, as you suggest. If either of the gentlemen, who have subscribed, wish it, their copies can be sent on immediately, by Post. You will please to recollect, when they do come to hand, that no Copy is to be delivered, without the subcriber's paying a dollar at the time. To non-subscriber's, a single number is three quarters of a dollar.

I am sorry to hear that Gov. Wolcott is so unwell, & low-spirited. The sudden and unfortunate death of Mr. Davenport, will be very apt to sink him still lower. The State of Connecticut, & the Union, have sustained a loss in Mr. D. which will not be soon repaired.

When you were here, you mentioned to me a curious fact, relative to the Robin which generally builds on the Pine-tree, before the house. I do not recollect all the circumstances so minutely as I wish; & will, therefore, thank you to relate them to me, in your next letter.

I did not know that my Aunt had been sick. I hope that your next news from her will be that she is in her usual health. Abby writes me that my mother has been lame. This she recovered from; which I am happy to hear.

The Woolsey's &c. are well; & return your comps.

Love &c to my mother.

Thursday, Aug: 10. 1797.
Pine St. No. 45. N. Y.   E. H. Smith.

Wednesday, 16.—Medical visit. Dunlap called on me. We were together for some time. Posted my books. I am surprized to find, that, by my Cash Acct. I have accounted for near an hundred dollars more than I appear to have had. I can not discover how this inaccuracy has happened but by a minute examination, which I am not disposed to make, & which after all might be useless. But I am resolved to be more careful in future. Calls & Errands. Wrote & copied the letter to Alsop. Read several articles in the Monthly Review. Visit to Dr. Root, on board of the Packet. Two medical visits. Drank tea with Dunlap. We walked. Afterwards I walked on the Battery with Miss Mason, Miss Nicholson, Dr. & Mr. Miller.

[Omitted here, fourteen manuscript pages: "An Inaugural Essay on the Yellow Fever, as it appeared in this city (N. York) in 1795."]

August, 17th.—*Thursday.*—Dr. Root breakfasted with me. Two medical visits. I expected Dr. R. to return. He did not. I read several papers in the Monthly; but I was unable to give them much attention, & felt myself wholly indisposed to mental exertion. This sense

---

[31] Apparently never published separately.
[32] Captain Bradley: Abraham Bradley of Litchfield, father of one of Smith's boyhood associates.

of inability has been heightened not a little by a pain in my left hip, which has been nearly continual, for near a week—perhaps more. I find it difficult to obtain entire ease in any position. At length, determining to do something, I took up my notes, made in August 1794—concerning my own life—& transcribed, with various corrections & additions, somewhat more than six pages. Afterwards read a few other articles in the Review. Wm. & I went to see Dunlap, & found him gone to Amboy. I visited Mr. Post, the Surgeon. After this, Wm. & I went to Riley's—where we drank tea with Miss Alsop, & spent the eveng. Since my return, I have read a few more articles in the Review.

Friday, 18.—Medical visit. A long visit from Dr. Root—who took leave of me for home. Read various articles in the Monthly Review. Pursued the further arrangements of my Notes of the first years of my life—making additions, or rather enlargements on particular points—so that I have written to-day nearly eleven pages in my fine hand. Various calls. Drank tea with Mr. Boyd. After tea we went together to the old Theater.[33] This is at present occupied by a company, under the care of Mr. Sollee, who is the Charleston (S. C.) manager. He has taken the Federal Street Theater in Boston, for a Winter Theater; & Hodgkinson the Hay-Market for a Summer Theater. The two Boston Companies are broken up. Out of them, with some additions, Sollee has formed two companies—one for Boston, in the winter, the other for Charleston in the winter. The Boston company to play in Hartford in the Summer, & the Charleston one in Phila. It is this which is now here. They played "The Wonder"—& "The Spoilt Child": I did not stay to see the afterpiece, as Mrs. Williamson, who was to have played *Little Pickle* was ill, & could not play. Opinions to-morrow.

To Thomas Mumford

I recd. a letter from you, my dear friend, a short time since, by I know not who; and, as it is without dates I can not tell how long it had been in performing the journey. It is but of little consequence what my last was meant for, since it has procured me the long-wished for favour of a letter from you. I rejoice to find, that, as there must be some cause for your silence, it is one which will every day diminish the necessity for its own continuance. For I trust, if you have much business, you have also some lucre. But I submit it, as a question to your prudence, whether it be not best to snatch, even if it be only a few hours & occasionally, some little portion from mechanical employments, to be devoted to friendship & science. You do not always mean to drive the quill, day after day, "from morn to noon, from noon to dewy eve";[34] you will give some future hours, you will allot some coming years, to more improving occupations. But you know the tendency of an undivided attention to any one employment, to incapacitate us for the right & pleasurable exercise of every other, even tho' that one employment be irksome. It is no more that wise, therefore, to preserve the connection between our love of, & pursuit of science. How slightly soever, amidst all the jargon of technical labours, till we are completely at liberty to review it more intimately, & establish it more permanently.

I recd. the inclosed Bill. The advertisement is charged at nine dollars. The Herald another year, at three & a half. I have directed Mr. Webster to carry them to my acct. so that you will now owe me, eight dollars & a half.

I do not know of any opportunity of sending to you, at present. When I do, I shall forward with this, a large packet of letters from Lichfield; &, if possible, some additional books.

Thursday, Aug: 10; 1797.
Pine Street, No. 45. New York.   E. H. Smith.

To Abigail Smith Jr.

It is so uncertain that I shall have leisure to write, when I have opportunity to send, that I avail myself of my present leisure, tho' I am ignorant of present opportunity. It will be, however, to write only a short letter, for I have nothing to say of sufficient importance to be lengthy about.

Your remarks concerning Mr. Bacon are evidential of a proper degree of consideration; and I can not but hope that every thing will turn out to be such as you wish it, & better than your timid friends fear, & your political acquaintance predict. I should be well pleased to see & know him; but there is no probability of my being in Connecticut this year. If he is desirous of being acquainted with me, there is a ready way of affecting such a circumstance.

Your opinions concerning "Camilla" coincide with my own, in many particulars: not in all. If Edgar & Camilla were to blame for that want of confidence in each other, what do you think of the father & guardian, who first inspired doubts, suggested artifices, & tempered with suspicion every generous emotion? They are the source of all this mischief. Even the sermon of Mr. Tyrold, excellent as it is, in many respects, is not without several inculcations of partial insincerity. Eugenia is, indeed, an interesting character; but not to be imitated. There are many similarities between her & Susan Tracy; who, sweet girl, I hear must exert her fortitude to bear up under one of Eugenia's misfortunes. But she is superior to Eugenia in knowledge of mankind. In respect to Lionel, I see nothing but what happens every day. Always from home, young, associating with profligate youth, beyond the inspection of his parents, he could not profit by their example; & had he been the child of a saint, the result would have been the same.

I shall send your bundles of letters, to Aurora, by the

---

[33] The "Old Theatre" was the John Street Theatre. A new theater on Park Row was being built by a group of businessmen who had agreed to lease it to Dunlap and Hodgkinson. It was not yet ready.

[34] Milton, *Paradise Lost,* Bk. I, 742.

first conveyance. I fear you write too much, to write carefully; & that your sisters will be as much fatigued, as gratified, by so immeasurable a mass.

In answer to your question, I have no linnen to make up.

Remembrance to friends.

Thursday, Aug: 10. '97
Pine St. 45. N. Y.   E. H. Smith.

To Joseph Bringhurst Jr.

I was thinking, the other day, on our past friendship, and on the frequent testimonies of it that we were wont to interchange. The silence which has so long separated us had something in it so cold and sad that it chilled & opprest my heart. It was not becoming to weep; but I resolved to write. Behold me, then, at the pen; may its accents revive in you the dormant spirit of correspondence, that it may once more speak to me, & cheer me!

I have nothing to reproach you with: this long & wide blank in our intercourse is as much my fault as yours, if not more: but I wish to see it vanish—banished by renewed & lively, & lengthy communications. I wish to see the times arrive again, when every week promised a letter, & fulfilled its promise. When the expectation of hearing from each other was one of the charms of life, as the disappointment was one of its most vivid sorrows. Can friendship subsist, in all its energy, on uncertain recollections? Does it not, like every thing else, obey the laws of habit? And what are those laws which are fulfilled by their own violation? It is in vain to attempt to conceal it, we do not think of each other as often, we do not love each other as well, as we once did. How can it be otherwise, when almost all the usual means, when almost all of every means, are neglected, whose office & end it is to foster & augment the sensibilities of friendship? We even meet with less ardor, associate with less interest, & part with less regret. Are you conscious of this? If you doubt the truth of it; recollect yourself. Remember our conduct, & dare to scrutinize your own sensations. We love each other still, warmly, disinterestedly: we deserve each other's love: we ought to love each other. I am persuaded that the idea of becoming indifferent to each other, or of each other, would shock us both. But this is the inevitable tendency of an absence habitually silent. Need we then, such a stimulus to invite us to renewed intercommunication? Ah! that the habit of correspondence may once again revive! that it may become as necessary & as dear to us as the daily sun, the air, food, & re-creating sleep!

How do you devote your days? What of business? of studies? of composition? of pleasures? I would know them all.

> To sport with Amaryllis in the shade,
> or with the tangles of Neæra's hair[35]

surely does not wholly occupy you. Well—remember me to this Amaryllis, who is too grave to sport; this Neæra, whose quaker hair is never entangled. I commend thy judgement, as I value thy friendship. She, too, perhaps, will deign to recollect to me; & will not think me less deserving, for loving thee.

Our friends are all well. Adieu, adieu, a thousand kind wishes. Write to me soon. Again farewell.

Yours as ever,

Thursday, Aug: 10. '97
Pine St. 45, N. Y.   E. H. Smith.

Saturday, August 19th.—Read a number of articles in the Monthly Review. Continued the arrangement, transcription, and enlargement of my notes on my own History—& have progressed thirteen pages. A visit from Roulet. From Gahn at breakfast time. At a book-store. Wm. & I were at Woolsey's. We saw only Mrs. W. We walked. Drank tea—& spent part of the evening at H. Johnson's. Wm. went away. H. & I walked on the Battery. I came home, & read the first Six Essays in Godwin's "Enquirer" with great pleasure, & much approbation. I defer particular remarks till I finish the work.

The Theater last evening.[36] Mr. Barret, the principal male performer, is a man upwards of fifty—but remarkably handsome for his years: tall, plump, & well made. He has rather too much belly—& his countenance indicates nothing noble. He is evidently a coxcomb—& ignorant. He has spirit, but little judgement. His defects, are those of ignorance & vanity—his merits those quick parts & imitation. He played *Felix*. Mrs. Barret, his wife, played *Violante*. She is tall, well made, & still handsome: but too corpulent; not graceful in her movements, nor tasty in her dress. She possesses power; is mostly formed by imitation; has too much tragedy rant in her seriousness, too much of farce flippancy in her vivacity. Notwithstanding, in several scenes she hit near to nature & truth, & was pleasing. She is second to no actress, that I have seen, in genteel comedy, except Mrs. Johnson. To her she is every way inferior, except in voice. In this she resembles Mrs. Melmoth. Mr. Williamson, the *Col. Briton,* is a fat, broad figure, which seems to exclude the idea of gallantry & spirit. Nor has he any great natural vivacity. He seems, however, to possess more judgement than either Mr. or Mrs. Barret. Mr. Jones, the *Lissardo,* is a man of some parts—but an ignorant buffoon, spoiled by over-rated applause, & continually prone to address the audience, instead of his companions on the stage. Mrs. Jones, *Flora,* has more equal merit, in her line, than either of the others; & supported the character with considerable propriety. Downie, *Frederic,* performed the part much better than I have ever before seen it; & very well. He discovered judgment & genius. His behaviour is pleasing. Mrs. Graupner, *Isabella,* tolerable.

Sunday, August 20.—Read from the sixth to the

---

[35] Milton, *Lycidas,* 11. 68-69.

[36] The play was *The Wonder, or A Woman Keeps a Secret* by Mrs. Centlivre, cited earlier.

fifteenth Essay in the Enquirer. Wrote & transcribed the letter to Mr. Allen, of this date. Wm. & I dined at H. Johnson's—with a Mr. Allen, an Englishman—polite, & agreable. We spent the afternoon there. Evening—walked. I called at Dr. Miller's. Mr. Josh. Miller, a brother of the Dr's—there. Visited Mrs. Lovegrove. Her little girl is unwell. Her boy not very well. Returning, went into Kent's. Wm. there. Thence home: where I have read the Saturday's News-paper—& part of the Enquirer—the other part having been read in the morning.

To William Buel

As you say nothing in respect to the conveyance of the copies of the Repository, I conclude that you expect me to send them by the Stage. They will, accordingly, be forwarded. I still wish you to let no copies go out of your hands, (except for the Ontario subscribers) without the pay: one dollar from subscribers, & three quarters of a dollar, for a single No. from non-subscribers. It is as easy to pay so small a sum first, as last; & we had rather keep our books, than circulate them on any other terms. As our impression is small, we have no fear of wanting subscribers enough, & of getting rid of all we have printed, by the end of a year. In regard to the Ontario subscribers, I wish you to propose it to them to procure their copies here, in future; which will save both you & them trouble; & moreover will render their pay to us more speedy & certain. Be kind enough, also, to remind them of the dollar in advance. Indeed our pamphlet, as books sell, is well worth a dollar; & if printed as is usual in Gt. Britain, would fetch two, or two & a half. I send you a little pamphlet published by the College in this place. If you have not had Dr. Bay's Essay on Dysentery I will send it likewise: therefore, let me know. I can inform you that a very bad Dysentery has been cured by the exhibition of Soda, or Carbonate of Soda, given by mouth & glyster.

I inclose proposals for the Botanic Garden. Perhaps some body may subscribe & *pay*. Do you wish the remainder of Zoonomia? Swords has given up the idea of printing the Second & Third Parts; because Dobson of Phila. had printed them before him. They have, therefore, made an exchange, & if you wish it Swords will send you Dobson's two vols. They will come to two dollars a vol., I believe; & certainly contain the best system of practice ever published. I shall send the Solution of Arsenic, as you desire. So much for business.

You will see under the title of Medical News, in the Foreign Department, notice of a work by Mr. Kellie, preparing for the Press, on the subject of Compression, in Intermittents. If his book does not come out too soon, we shall insert his original Paper in our Repository. The theory of this cure is not difficult to conceive, on the Pneumatic Plan; & I find that Dr. Beddoes explains it just as we did, here, before his book reached us. The Lungs take in a certain quantity of Oxygen, for the whole system, at each respiration. If you diminish the extent to which it was to be applied, without diminishing the frequency & perfectness of respiration, it is evident that the remaining parts receive a larger portion of oxygen, than in common. This increase of stimulus, may be supposed to prevent that torpor into which the system, or certain parts of it were disposed to fall; & thus obviate the fit. This being repeated several times, the tendency to torpor is destroyed; & the patient cured: and thus you may explain the efficacy of Bark, or any other stimulant, perhaps. I should suppose that the practice of Compression might be advantageously employed in all Low Fevers, to obviate the exacerbation; & should hope great benefit from it. I wish you may make the trial.

With regard to opium, many writers have mentioned it as a remedy for Intermittents—but for the particular mode in which I prescribe it, I am indebted to [a] Dr. of Phila. Ample experience on his part, & some on mine, concur in evincing its intire success, in all cases where there is any thing like regularity in the return of the fit—whether of quarter, tertian, quotidian, or any other type. Angustura Bark has been introduced into the Materia Medica, about five years, I believe. There have been accounts of it published, but I have seen none; nor indeed any thing concerning it, except a paper of Dr. Lettsom's in the London Medical Memoirs, which is little better than nothing. I found our people, here, using it; but I could learn but little from them. I therefore made my own trials; & now think my experience as much to be trusted as any body's. I believe I told you that Dr. Osborn's (of N. Ca.) trials, & mine agreed. We think it near four times as powerful as common Bark. It is less nauseous to patients in general. To one, I have found it more so.

I wish much to try Camphor in Intermittents. I am persuaded that three grains, given every hour, for four hours, & on the hour of the fit, i.e. 15 grs. in five hours, would prevent the Cold Fit—& so the disease; & I recommend you to try it. I do not expect to have another opportunity this year.

One piece of news, & I have done. Dr. Beddoes has just sent us word that Volatile Alkali is discovered to be a cure for Diabetes. The substance of his letter will form an article in the News of our next No.

We want to begin to print the 2nd No. by the middle of Septr. May we depend on the Communication you have promised us, by the first of Octr.?

Comps. &c. to Mrs. B.
Yours &c.

Aug: 15. 97.
Pine St. 45. E. H. Smith.

To Richard Alsop

This is a fine cool day, & well adapted for journeying; I am resolved, therefore, since circumstances will not permit me to travel on horse-back, or in a carriage, to pay you a visit in imagination. There is, you know, a wonderful facility in this matter, in some sort appropriate to us poor rogues who have all the wishes in the world with scarce any of the means to gratify them. Well then my ride is soon over, & behold me at your door. The first question, on dismounting & taking you by the hand, would naturally be after your health & that of your family. Suppose it asked then, & recollect that you are to give me an answer. For the present I will suppose it replied to as favorably as heart could wish. We walk in, & after wiping off the dust & perspiration, the customary inquiries after news, & usual offices of hospitality, I begin to respire a little, & conversation commences its according to ancient laws. It is a long time since you have been in Middletown. Yes, a melancholly period; & I delight to see it at an end. I find it as beautiful as ever; the air as pure, the prospect as picturesque, the inhabitants as kind. Time, which has augmented the size, developed the features, & added new charms to these children, seems neither to have impaired the spirit & amiableness of one parent, the passion for letters of the other, nor the benevolence of either. Once more, I find myself where I have so often enjoyed life, where I have so often vainly panted to enjoy it. By this time, I know not how many questions interrupt my rhapsody. I shall answer them as briefly as I may. All friends are well. Mrs. Riley has a fine fat girl—who is to be called Ethelinde, or Celestina, or Matilda, or Patience, or some other soft romantic name. Miss Alsop is the same wild thing as ever; & Isaac as sluggish & immoveable as he used to be: The Justice grows in dignity every day; Woolsey has stopped payment; Dunlap's plays are idolized as much as O'Keefe's; Duer is Govr.; & New York has become the central point of taste, science, & disinterestedness. Having satisfied your curiosity on all these points, allow me to take my turn of inquiry, & ask you what you read? what write? what do? what purpose?

You have lately had a long & pleasant visit from Hosmer. Did not his presence, as it must have renewed many youthful associations, renew your ardor for composition? We lamented, together, that you did not either apply yourself to the finishing your poem so near complete, or to the completing that but just begun. But all the common topics of persuasion have already been exhausted, & we have ceased to hope, tho' not to wish. Why not devote the present uncertain & uninvited leisure, which from the dearth of society must hang heavy on your hands, to a purpose of all others, one would think, the most interesting & delightful?

What could give me more pleasure than to spend some days with you? Yes, Mrs. Alsop, for all you look somewhat doubtingly upon me, I want to sit down by your side & convince you that, if I have not visited you these four long years, I deserve none of your resentment, but four years of your compassion. I am sure that we should part better friends than ever. But—hark!

> The blasts athwarte the hawthorn hiss,
> I may not harbour here;
> My spurre is sharpe, my courser pawes,
> My hour of flight is nere.[37]

Adieu—

Aug: 16. 1797.
Pine St. 45.

E. H. Smith.

To John Allen

When I was in Lichfield last winter, you spoke to me concerning Mr. T. Pierce's coming here to spend a few months for medical improvement. As some variation of circumstances has arisen, since last winter, it may be proper for you to receive some further information on the subject, if the design is not relinquished. This is the occasion of my writing to you at present.

To derive any considerable benefit from residing here, Mr. Pierce should attend the Anatomical, Chemical, Obstetrical, & Clinical Lectures. The two first are indispensable; the last scarcely less so. The expense of these courses may be estimated at forty or fifty dollars. The Chemical Lectures, this year, begin about the end of September: The three other courses early in November; & all are terminated by the first of March, or before. The Anatomical Lectures likewise include a short course of Surgery. In respect of practical improvement, or instruction in the practice of Physic, by attendance at the Hospital, Mr. Pierce, by appearing as my Pupil will be admitted to the House, & to the use of the a valuable Library, without expence. Dr. Mitchill & I commence attendance there the first of October: a few days after the Dr's course of Chemistry begins. We shall continue in the Hospital that month & the next. Then Dr. Rodgers, the Clinical Professor, will attend for four months. During his attendance, he will deliver the Clinical Lectures; & no student can attend the practice of the House, while this course proceeds, without paying the fee for the Course. If Mr. P. intends coming here, he should be here by the 20th of Septr.; & if possible, should not leave us before the 1st of March. At all events, he should come at the time mentioned, whether he do, or do not stay so long. He had better loose some part of the other Courses, than of the Chemistry. By coming early, he will have that entire; & will also, have the most essential part of the other Courses.

The expence for Instruction, I think I have rated full as high as it will be, by placing it at fifty Dollars. Other expences will depend very much on his own prudence & independence. The dress of a student is of no consequence, provided it be clean, whole, & decent: nor has he any occasion for seeing fashionable company. The same dress which is proper at Lichfield, will, with very little variation, do perfectly well here. Board is another *item* of some importance: & this, too, may be reduced to a small expence, comparatively, if a young man is temperate. I have good dinners every day—& they do

---

[37] This is translated (possibly by William Taylor) from Stanza 16 of *Leonore* by Gottfried August Bürger: "Lass sausen durch den Hagedorn etc."

not cost me fifty dollars a year. I have paid fifty pounds for those which were no better. One source of expence may be wholly cut off, if Mr. P. relishes the proposal I made last winter. He is wellcome to read in my room from sunrise, till nine in the evening. This, it is true, will not entirely exclude the necessity for a bed-room somewhere else, where he may, occasionally, be alone, see company, & have a fire: but it will greatly diminish expence—of fuel, candles, & rent: for he will not, then, want any thing more than a sleeping room; & the other accommodations, will be only now & then wanted. In fine, with prudence, the whole expence of his five months residence here, will not exceed two hundred dollars. Perhaps it will fall short of that sum. At any rate, the advantages & cost, bear no proportion.

I have stated these things to you—because you have only a month to consult upon them, & determine.

I have expected to hear from you—for some weeks. I need not assure you that it will give me much pleasure, at all times.

Aug: 20 '97
Pine St. 45.   E. H. Smith.

Monday, August 21.—Two medical visits—distant. A visit from Dr. Miller, with his brother Mr. Joseph Miller. Continued the notes of my life, & wrote thirteen pages. Visit to Mrs. Lovegrove, with whom I drank tea. A visit from Mr. Boyd—in the forenoon. Called & saw Mrs. Morton. Spent the evening with Miss Morton, chiefly, at Jacob Morton's.[38] Finished the first part of the "Enquirer"—& read the four first Essays, in the second part.

Tuesday, 22.—Read the 5th, 6th & 7th Essays of the "Enquirer" P. II. Mr. Kent here. Two medical visits. Visited the Millers—where I spent an hour or two. Found there, & brought thence, Miss Hays's "Emma Courtney"[39]—which I have since read thro'. It contains a fine moral lesson, on the subject of love; & the more valuable as the remedy is constantly pointed out—or rather the preventative. It is very well written. Errands. Wrote a few lines to Jereh. Mason. Two medical visits. Part of the evening at Roulet's—remainder at Riley's.

Wednesday, 23.—Continued Godwin's "Enquirer"— & have nearly half read the last Essay. A number of medical visits. Mr. Kent & Boyd, & their wives set off for New England to-day. A long visit to Dingley, this forenoon—Continued my "notes &c." three pages further. Dunlap returned & was here. We & G. M. Woolsey went to the Circus, which Wignell[40] has converted into a Theater for his company, & saw "Venice Preserved" &c. This Tragedy was better performed, on the whole, than I ever saw any piece: particularly any tragedy. Mrs. Merry's "*Belvidera,*" Cooper's "*Pierre,*" & Moreton's "*Jaffier,*" were excellent. Mrs. Merry was uniformly excellent.

Thursday, 24.—Five medical visits in the course of the day, beside calls & errands. Read a little in the "Enquirer." Dunlap here several hours, at different times in the day. In the afternoon here also, with Mitchill, & we went together to see the Elks. Dunlap made a sketch of one—& I took some notes. Thereby we shall be able to correct the mistakes of Mr. Pennant & other european naturalists, concerning the unity of the Elk & Moose. Concluded my Notes on the first eleven years of my life —on which I wrote six pages to-day. Drank tea with Dunlap, & we went to the Theater, to see the Boston Company. "The Gamester"[41] & "The Romp." Both badly played. I went out & paid a visit to S. Johnson who with Mrs. J. returned yesterday. I met Daniel Wadsworth of Hartford in the street & afterward in the Theatre.

["Notes from Recollection of My Life, from My Birth to the Age of Eleven" which followed the above entry now constitute the opening pages of the text.]

To Joseph Strong

I have waited for your reply to my last letter, with some anxiety. This has increased with the alarming accounts we have from your city, of the progress of the Yellow Fever: & the more, as, from what I can learn, your house must be situated in the immediate neighborhood of the present sickness. I cease, therefore, to urge an answer, in relation to the business I wrote to you upon last month, but I am extremely desirous of hearing from you, what is your own health, & what is true respecting the condition of Phila. If you have leisure do not fail to write. If hurried, at least forward a line that I may be assured of your personal safety & welfare. The old dispute is, I see, revived concerning importation & non-importation. What is the fact? or, if some cases have certainly arisen from imported contagion, have any, as has been pretended, originated from local causes? How do you treat the disease, yourself, & with what success? I ask these questions for my private satisfaction; & you need not fear in me the indelicacy of publishing any letter you may write, without your direct assent. Communicate, therefore, freely.

I fear my last letter did not reach you. I was ignorant of your number & directed to Pine Street only. Send me your address. I shall direct this to your former lodgings —where, I suppose, Mr. Jones continues.

All friends here are well. Our city never was so

---

[38] Probably a businessman and related to the numerous other Mortons whom Smith knew. The only specific information on him makes him a lieutenant, company commander, Third Regiment, Brigade of Militia, New York. *New York Directory.*

[39] Miss Mary Hays, *Emma Courtney* (1796), a disciple of William Godwin.

[40] Rickett's New Ampitheatre, 82-84 Greenwich Street, opened 1797; run later as Wignell and Reinagle's Greenwich Street Summer Theatre. Also known as Rickett's Circus—see earlier.

[41] *The Gamester* by Edward Moore with the help of David Garrick (1753). Smith had seen it once before, at Wethersfield, on November 3, 1791, when it was performed by his friends.

healthy. Uncommon, but not sufficient, pains have been taken to keep it so.

Aug: 25. '97.
Pine St. 45.   E. H. Smith.

To Charles B. Brown

My letter must be a thing of shreds & patches. I have no leisure to make it otherwise. I wish to reply more at large to your letter, which is full of topics for discussion. But on what topic might not one usefully enlarge?

The reason why I have not written before is, I have been waiting an answer from Dennie. He is in Boston, I suppose, & I was desirous of communicating something certain to you, when I did write. I hope to hear from him next week.

"Alcuin" is still with us. I have read it repeatedly, with pleasure. Dunlap & Johnson have also read it. And I have permitted two ladies to peruse it, whose minds I thought equal to the subject. It is now in the hands of Roulet; & as Mrs. S. Johnson returned two days since, she will have an opportunity of seeing it. I can not go into particulars at present—&, perhaps, may never be able to—but I may remark, in general, & in this all who have read concur with me, that the Dialogue is well written, (those who know your style, say more correctly than anything of yours they have seen—) & the sentiments interesting. Some difference of opinion exists, as to the merit of the respective arguments; some doubt of the soundness of your conclusion.

The following note from my Journal is all I have time to say to you concerning "Political Justice." "June 20. Finished Political Justice. I have read this excellent work too hastily & with too many interruptions to pronounce decisively upon it. Certain parts, particularly in the 5th & 6th Books, failed to carry conviction of their soundness to my mind, as I read them over. It may be that this was only from want of attention to the Author. I must read it again."

I have this day completed the perusal, the hasty perusal of the "Enquirer." It deserves what you say of it; but there are sentiments contained in it which should be well considered before they are acted upon. His remarks (Godwin's) are too general to be altogether satisfactory. A very unpleasant circumstance is, that, while he batters down every thing before him, he erects nothing on the ruins. He is aware of this objection; but he evades instead of obviating it.

I must repeat it—we have not the novels you recommend. They are not to be found in the city. Have you seen a late novel, in two small volumes, by Mary Hays, intituled "Emma Courtney"? If not—find & read it. If so—your sentiments.

Dunlap is now here, & sends love to you. You do wrong not to write to him. Summon your courage to the attempt. The longer delayed, the more difficult. Is this tardiness becoming a disciple of truth? Think of it!

Johnson is still busy. He remembers you. He leaves us on Monday for Connecticut, where he will stay a fortnight. All well. Write me of the health of your city: immediately: what true: what false. Remembrances as usual.

Aug: 25. '97.
Pine St. 45.   E. H. Smith.

Friday, 25th.—Finished the "Enquirer." the preceeding letter contains all that is necessary to be noted at present. Four medical visits in the course of the day. Most of the forenoon at Mitchill's room. He read to me his review of Priestley's & Adet's pamphlets. Brought home the two first numbers of Nicholson's Journal; in which I have read several articles. Wrote & transcribed the two preceeding letters. Dunlap here an hour. Drank tea with him. We went to the Greenwich Street Theater together; but were immediately parted, & saw him no more. He is to return to Amboy early in the morning. "The Road to Ruin" & "The Prize"—beside Dancing as usual. They were badly prepared in the Play. Warner's *Dornton* bad; Francis's *Sulky* execrable; Cooper imperfect in *Milford*; Molton not equal to Hodgkinson, in *Harry*; Harwood's *Silky* well; Mrs. Oldmixon's *Mrs. Warren* well; Mrs. Merry's *Sophia* pleasing. Harwood's *Lenitrice* much inferior to Hodgkinson's—& all the rest inferior to our Company. Recd. a letter from John Williams.

To Theodore Dwight

I sat down to write and took up the pen with a determination to say nothing of the long interval in our correspondence. Having resolved to write to you by Johnson, I intended that this topic, at least, should occupy no share of my letter. But I find no other subject so pressingly present to my mind; and I can not avoid some expressions of regret for a circumstance so unpleasant for reflection. I can not forget that there was a time when so tedious an intermission of letters on either side would have been viewed with surprise & anxiety on the other, and have been the theme of many successive inquiries. I can not forget our former eagerness to write, equaled only by our desire to receive communications. I can not forget the unreserved intercourse which subsisted between us, extending to the minutest plans, of life & study. But I remember them only to lament that they exist no longer, and to contrast them with the increasing distance & reserve that threaten to separate us. One would incline to believe, that having, in some sort, taken our leave of the Muses, we had bidden adieu to each other. That, relinquishing the bond of union which was created by the combined & consentaneous cultivation of one department of literature, there is left between us no common center of attraction, no medium of connection. Can this be true? I hope, & trust it is not. I wish to persuade myself that the causes lie not so deeply; that they may be discovered; that they may be obviated. Much I know may be attributed to change of situation, to the cares of the world, to the graver turn which the mind assumes in passing from youth to manhood, to professional correspondencies, & to a more diffused interest in new acquaintances. But are these the sole causes of our diminished intercourse? I fear not. I fear that some real change has taken place in our affections. Certainly not from any good motives: probably from motives little considered & partially understood even by ourselves. Do not misapprehend me! I accuse neither you nor myself. The immediate, the original cause may have been slight & unsuspected. It may be doubtful where it was conceived. Yet I dare not absolutely doubt the fact. Still less am I hardy enough to believe it not to have originated in the difference of sentiment, on certain subjects, now, I fear, confirmed between us. This difference ought not to affect our friendship, while we are mutually satisfied of each other's purity of intention. It is my desire to destroy this affect, by exposing the cause.

We have loved each other, Theodore, long & tenderly. Let not our friendship be lost or impaired! Why should it be? I know that where we love sincerely, & where we have fixed on principles as essential to our moral well-being, it must be painful to see those who possess our affections, disdain our principles. This painful feeling, operating one way, may increase our interest in them, or may diminish it, by a contrary tendency. So, with the objects themselves, an apprehension that this change will affect the esteem which others bear them, may induce a variation of conduct such as would follow it if had actually happened. And such I suspect to have been the latent occasions of our retrocession from the intimate union in which we once delighted. I have been restrained by the fear of offending; you alienated by your love of principles no longer the guide of my life. I do not vindicate myself. I have been too apprehensive. Better fill every letter with discussion, better arouse every power, every energy to this contest of reason & of passion, than sink into a tranquillity, a lethargy rather, so frigid & annihilating. But why forsake me? If erring, expostulate, reason with, at least engage me. Let not your aversion for erroneous principles deprive you of compassion for your friend. At least preserve your hold on his affections; & guide him by the reins of love, if you can not by those of reason. Much as you may disapprove my notions, you can not but applaud my sincerity. You can not but acknowlege the purity of those motives which have enabled me to hazard to much by so free a disclosure. This conduct, surely, should elevate me in your eyes, & endear me to your heart. Superior in years, if you saw me hesitating to write, & sinking into silence, you should have exerted the influence so long possessed over me, to have drawn me back to the duties of friendship; should have forgiven me, & taught me to forgive myself. You know my heart, you know my habits. too well to doubt of my readiness to accept every offer of benevolence, to double every dilligence of zeal, to prosecute every toil of affection. To have written to me, would have secured a reply. Rising superior to my prejudices, an act of confidence on your part, when I seemed best inclined to frankness, must have triumphed over all my apprehensions, & bound me captive to your love in bonds more firm than ere. I feel my heart too much affected by this subject, & must dismiss it. But do not cease to love me—(I call not for protestations—) do not cease to write to me. A few letters, & our correspondence will drop the appearance of effort, & take a regular form. We shall again expatiate on literary topics; again mingle recollections of past social pleasures; again exult in the hope of future meetings & enjoyments. Do not forget me.

I have just recd. the Monthly Review for May, which I presume you have not seen. It contains a few extracts from the 5th or 6th translation of Bürger's "Leonora," together with some stanzas from a new ballad, by the same author, intituled "The Chase." I transcribe a specimen of each for your amusement.

Have you written any thing, since I saw you, beside declarations & pleas? I sometimes amuse myself in tacking a few rhimes together, in the sonnet form, for the encouragement of my sister Fanny in active & virtuous habits. As a specimen I send you one in favor of Early Rising, a virtue of whose value I am the more sensible by wretched experience of a contrary practice. Shew these verses to our common friends, but do not suffer any copy to be made of them. I shall thank you for your opinion.

I have recd. a few lines from Mason, & mean to write to him, by Johnson. If I have not time, now, I shall soon write. My love to Mrs. Dwight, Cogswell, Nathl & all friends.

Aug: 26. '97.
Pine St. 45.   E. H. Smith.

Saturday, 26.—Medical visits. Read several papers in Nicholson's Journal. Composed & transcribed the preceeding letter, with the verses referred to in it. Read the newspapers. A visit from Mr. Roulet, who brought me the Monthly Review for May last, the greater part of which I have read. Wm. Johnson & I called at Mrs. Lovegrove's. She accompanied us in a walk out of town. We returned—Wm. went with Mrs. L. to make some calls. I went to S. Johnson's. All out. Next to Horace Johnson's—where I spent the remainder of the evening. Wm. & I went into the Cold Bath.

I suppose Dunlap returned to Amboy this morning, as I have seen nothing of him.

To Mason F. Cogswell

I received your letter, my dear friend, with the money, in good season; I return you my thanks for the cares you have bestowed on this concern. But it seems always to happen when you write to me that the women are, or have been, holding you in durance. Sometimes, you are busy in assisting to obviate the bad consequences of cohabitation; and sometimes, in preparing them to enjoy the good consequences: at one time, you are helping people out of the world; & the next, bringing them in to it: maid, widow, & matron, conspire against your friend, by subjecting you to a continued round of prescription & exhibition. What am I to do? I can not consent to be turned off with these dribblets from a half empty cask; these half-made & sleep-engendered "how-d'yes" & "farewells." "In short Lappet"—to employ the words of Lovegold, in the Miser—"I must touch, touch, touch, something real."[42] I must receive from you one [of] those letters, which, in the spring time of life & imagination, when every fair-one was a divinity & every friend a hero, you delighted to compose. Then your heart swelled with love faster than your head could conceive how to express it, & language came to your mind more rapidly than your busy hand could trace it on the paper: Poetry & wit mingled their fascinating accents with the eloquent voice of friendship; & an orange, a cake, a feather, or a journey, became interesting in their combined song.

> Hark! Friendship calls! his salient spear, fierce-driven,
> Pierces the spongy armour of the Fiend,
> Indolence. His trenchant blade descending,
> Cleaves the Demon's head, hews his hideous trunk,
> And scatters o'er the earth his recreant limbs.
> Hark, Friendship calls! & waves his mystic wand.
> And lo, dissolving in the potent charm, swift fleet
> The loathsome landscapes of the expiring Fiend,
> Like the light chaff before the mountain-storm.
> The massy pillars of his prison-house crumble to earth;
> The ponderous roof falls shattering
> And the deep base, upheaving, rolls apart,
> In melancholy fragments o'er the plain.
> And, now, nor landscape, castle, ruin, rest,
> Nor trace remains of all that erst was here;
> But, to soft notes and liquid airs divine,
> That permeate & thrill the etherial vault,
> A Glory in the nether sky appears,
> Soft-moving on, by cherub-wing upborne,
> And angel-form attended. Hark! the clarion
> Sounds; the splendor opens; & the fairy
> Dome, on graceful column resting, light, free,
> Of heavenly architecture, firm the base,
> Of spacious entrance, & of ample concave,
> Charms the sight. Without, around, enchantment,
> Or Nature's lavish & diffusive hand,
> Spreads each variety of hill & dale,
> Of copse & wood, of torrent, stream & lake,
> Rude, or fair-cultur'd. Within, the Genius,
> With selection rare, beyond the boasted
> And rapacious choice of Gaul's proud chieftain,
> Each master-piece of art, curious, had placed.
> Nor needed there ought that the mind informs,
> Delights, enlarges, or that moulds the frame,
> By happiest care, to execute her will.
> Waked with the earliest dawn, by song of birds,
> The grey light, or the purpose bold, divine,
> Restless within the soul, & spurring it
> To the high labour of benevolence,
> Thither an active, meditative throng
> Repair. With them no day sleeps unimprov'd.
> They hail the great constructor of the place;
> They feel his influence & record his power.
> Friendship, by some, with selfish zeal, confined
> To one poor mortal, tho' in them it glows
> Intensest ever towards the virtuous mind,
> In its wide scope includes the mighty whole.
> Ah! Vision of blessedness! that form! that form!
> Say, is it not my friend? The fond, the fair,
> Welcome ideas of our former joys,
> Are busy in his brain; his hazle eye
> Beams with delight; and lo! his fingers hold
> The playful, tender, recompensing pen.

You may laugh as freely as you will at these verses, which have rushed, uninvited & unexpected, into my quill. I had not the least idea of stringing lines together, in this manner, when I began to write. "All's one for that."[43] If they bring me a letter from you, I shall not complain, even if it consist of abuse on my rhimes.

You know, I presume, that the first No. of the Repository is published. As soon as you send us directions respecting subscribers & the mode of forwarding to them, the copies you may require shall be transmitted.

Aug: 27. 1797.
Pine St. 45.   E. H. Smith.

Sunday, Aug: 27.—Composed & transcribed the letter to Cogswell. A visit, with Wm. Johnson, at Woolsey's; another at Mrs. Lovegrove's. We dined at H. Johnson's; J. & Mrs. S. Johnson there. Remained till near five. Wm. & I went to Roulet's. He was absent. Some company were there; Mr. & Mrs. Rossier, &c. We stayed till after sun-set. Drank tea with Mrs. Lovegrove. Visit to Riley's. I left Johnson there, & went to Dr. & Mr. Miller's—where I spent the rest of the evening. Finished the May No. of the Monthly Review.

Monday, 28.—H. & Wm. Johnson left us to-day, for Middletown. Wrote a few lines to Mr. Kent. Professional visits, & errands. Composed & transcribed the letter to Mrs. Tracy. A visit from Mitchill. Read several articles in the Monthly Review. A visit from Professor Gözi. At the Greenwich Street Theater: "The Fair Penitent."[44] I stayed only to see the Play. Mrs. Merry, Moreton & Cooper played well; but I do not greatly admire this tragedy. The fifth Act is altogether outré, disconnected, unaffecting, & ridiculous. Read part of a Paper in Nicholson's Journal.

Tuesday, 29.—Finished a paper, on three kinds of Carbonated Hydrogen Gas, in Nicholson's Journal, of which I read a small part yesterday. Medical visit. Errands. Visit from Dingley. Composed the two succeedings letters to Dr. Thornton of London & Dr. Muret of Vevai (Canton Berne)—the first of which I transcribed. Visit from Woolsey. Being dull after dinner, owing probably to the sudden change of the weather to cold, I banished my stupidity by reading several let-

---

[42] Henry Fielding, *The Miser* (1733), I, i.

[43] Robert Burns, "Is There for Honest Poverty," from memory. Smith never mentioned Burns in this "Diary" but he could easily have read his poetry in a volume of Burns's work, *Poems, Chiefly in the Scottish Dialect* printed in New York (1788).

[44] Nicholas Rowe (1703).

ters in "Anna St. Ives." A call at Dr. & Mr. Miller's. Spent the evening, very agreably, at S. Johnson's. Returned & read Mr. Beaume's paper, or rather the Editor's abridgement of it, in Nicholson's Journal. Recd. a letter from C. B. Brown. The accounts of the state of the sickness in Phila. appear to be very contradictory. Dr. Rush writes to his son that the disease is on the decline.

To Mrs. Tracy

How capricious and unfortunate is my lot, in respect to you! We are destined to distant & long-continued seperation I can write to you but seldom; and when I do write, my letters must inevitably contain some portion of remonstrance & complaint. When I had the pleasure of conversing with you last, we regretted the circumstances that had interrupted our correspondence: circumstances doubly painful to me, as the interruption they occasioned necessarily afflicted my mind with many doubts of the continuance of your friendship. You knew & acknowleged the unpleasantness of my situation, & kindly banished every suspicion of its recurrence. I left Lichfield with a firm & sweet persuasion, that every difficulty was happily removed; & that no future delays would protract the interval between our reciprocal communications. Affected by the term, as I thought it, of a recent & melancholly breach in our epistolary intercourse, I applied myself to the pen, on my return, & wrote to you with a freedom & sincerity calculated to display, at once, the depth & disinterestedness of my friendship. The subject was important. It had relation to our common interest; it was intimately connected with your particular happiness. At the conclusion of that letter I besought you to write to me, even tho' it were a line. I protested against the renewal of that afflicting silence, so destructive of all the advantages of friendship, so threatening to its very existence. As the theme was difficult & delicate, as my remarks were dictated by a fervent & unaffected regard for you & yours, I could not but be deeply interested in the event of what I wrote, of being greatly concerned to know that you approved my zeal, tho' you might reject my counsels. I intimated this to you. I intimated how much anxiety your silence would occasion me. Six months, & more, have passed, & neither letter, nor line, nor message has been received. Alas! how am I to interpret this? What am I to think?

I have reflected on this mysterious lethargy of your pen, but am wholly unable to satisfy myself of its cause. Conjecture succeeds to conjecture, only to be considered & dismist.

Am I to suppose you offended by my interference in what may be regarded as your family concerns? I dare not do you the injustice to admit the supposition. Were my interference improper, & from improper motives, one error could not merit so severe a punishment. Much as you might have blamed me, you must have recollected my long & faithful friendship, & the general character of my sentiments & motives. But, were not my intentions good? did they not flow from a heart over flowing with zeal for your welfare? If the act were ill-timed & injudicious, should not such motives sanctify it in your eyes? Should they not rather raise his character, in your opinion, who hazarded even your displeasure, when he thought it necessary to serve you?

Is it possible that your conduct has been governed by the fear of improper inferences; inferences unjust to me & cruel to you; to be drawn from the continuance of our correspondence? It is with an unwillingness not to be exprest that I allow such a suggestion a moment's consideration, after the repeated & satisfactory explanations, we have already entered into on this head; after the unlimited permission I have granted for the exposure of our whole correspondence to those who alone are interested in it. It is vain to hope for escape from the malice of those who dare every thing. It is probably vain to expect the approbation of all whose esteem is desirable. Instances not seldom occur of long-continued prejudice against the best & most virtuous of human beings. I grant that we should do nothing inconsiderately; nor procure ourselves on trivial gratification with the loss of that respect which might greatly advance our usefulness, tho' the loss ought not to follow the gratification. But let us not be too sensitive on this point. That malignity which persecutes all our actions must defeat itself. No one can be so absurd, except in the heat & hurry of indignant passion, as to believe even a murderer absolutely incapable of every virtue. Distinguished excellence ever has been, & must long remain, the object, the selected mark, for fools to point at. It will, probably, on every just & comprehensive view of the subject, be found to be our duty to select such a line of conduct as shall most conduce to good, & to pursue it, without suffering ourselves to be dismayed, or too much alive, to the misrepresentations of the ignorant & the vicious. It is in this light that we have hitherto placed the question. Has any thing happened to vary the aspect it has so uniformly assumed? I tremble when I make the inquiry; tho' I doubt the possibility of an affirmative reply.

It has sometimes occurred to me, as within the verge of possibility, that you have been induced to change your opinion of my character & principles. It is only as *possible*, that I have admitted such a suspicion. That such a change has been wrought in you I have believed improbable from the years of minute observation you must have made on my conduct & sentiments; from your often repeated approbation of them; from the many proofs I have exhibited of unbounded confidence in your friendship & virtue; & from your very silence. Yes, paradoxical as it may appear, that very silence which engendered the apprehension, produced a suggestion to combat & defeat it. To believe you to be suspicious of my friendship, without affording me a chance of vindication, is to suppose you destitute of justice, destitute of common humanity, of that cold consideration which our very laws intend to the basest reputed villain. The idea, therefore, like every other, has only presented itself to be instantly rejected. Each, in its turn, has been discarded; but the melancholly impression of the fact it would explain, is left, to wear the spirits & perplex the understanding.

I cease to detail other hypotheses. After reading what I have written, you may ask why I have repeated any, since all are so little satisfactory. Is it possible, then, that you can not conceive my purpose? to display the pernicicus consequences of your silence: consequences fatal to that happiness which your friendship ought to confer; fatal to the tranquillity of every hour that may admit a thought to glance that way; fatal to every liberal & benevolent purpose that might be executed by our correspondence. Indeed, whither & to what will not these evils extend? what friendship will not be tinctured with suspicion, when that supposed most durable, & most prized, is shaken? By what effort of fortitude are such repeated & extensive shocks to be sustained? The armour of that philosophy I cherish is not such "thick-ribbed steel" as to repel the attacks of a fortune so malignant. I have not yet attained to a firmness so adamantine that I can behold all the tender & long-cherished sympathies of life perish around me unmoved, or undismayed. My ear is still open to the accents, my eye still languishes for the sight, my heart still pants, for the confidence of friendship. How worthless soever I may be deemed by others, I can neither deprive myself of consciousness nor sensibility; I can not anihilate the distinction between pleasure & pain; I must seek the one, & avoid the other. The meanest worm writhes under the foot that tramples on it.

When I commenced this letter I meant to avoid all querulousness. I intended to state my regret for your silence simply & sincerely; to ask for an explanation; & to request that your letters might no longer be withheld. It was far from my desire to display how much I am affected by your taciturnity; & least of all to attempt to derive that from your compassion which was denied me by your justice & your friendship. I have deviated from my original purpose. I have discovered both my weakness & my esteem. What the effect will be I dare not conjecture. I feel assured of the honesty of the motive. If this letter fail of procuring me a reply, I shall deem it sufficient evidence of a disposition in you to put an end to our correspondence; &, whatever my own feelings may be, I shall have too great a respect for yours to persecute you with letters no longer acceptable. I still cherish brighter hopes.

Remembrances to Mr. T. & the family.
Aug: 28. 1797.
Pine S. 45   E. H. Smith.

To R. J. Thornton

The interest that you appear to take in the advancement of medical & natural science and their application to promote the welfare of mankind, encourages me to believe that you will receive favorably an address from a person in some measure engaged in the same pursuits, tho' personally, & perhaps wholly, unknown to you. For the same reason, I venture to hope that the distance from which this address proceeds, will be a further argument with you for admitting it to some share of your attention.

The pamphlets which accompany this letter, more particularly that intituled "The Medical Repository," will afford you some notion of the immediate design in solliciting your correspondence. With the name of Dr. Mitchill you are doubtless familiar. His Essay on the Gaseous Oxyd of Azote must have given you some idea of his abilities & information as a chemist & medical philosopher. The plan of the publication of which we, with our friend & associate Dr. Miller, are editors, you will observe to be very extensive. So extensive, indeed, that this first No. can hardly be considered as the preface to its execution. Still, such as it is, we have no immediate prospect of making the succeeding numbers much more respectable. You will determine from this to what degree of credit & esteem the publication is entitled.—Men qualified & willing to observe are not numerous in our country, tho' the number is increasing. Of those who have observed, few are in habits of committing their remarks to paper. And a more serious difficulty arises from the narrow fortunes of men of information, generally, & their scattered situations, which deny them the means of procuring the implements of science, & the benefits of frequent communication. We must look to Europe, for a long time, for a large portion of our scientific improvement.

In the prosecution of our work, we feel it of great importance to form correspondencies with gentlemen who have something more than a cold & selfish regard for the progress of medical knowlege. Without intending to subject any person to particular inconvenience, we are desirous of maintaining an intercourse with one who would take an interest in pointing out & assuring to us, the best & most speedy means of obtaining the discoveries in England, relative to the objects of our publication, as they may arise; & who would be willing to think himself in some degree repaid by such similar returns as the differences in our circumstances, (arising from the different state of science in the two countries,) will permit. The animated part you have acted in promoting the success of the Pneumatic Practice led us to regard you as likely to receive an application of this kind favorably; & it has fallen to my lot to manage the correspondence should you accept our invitation.

We wish to procure from London all periodical works, connected with our purpose, as fast as they are published. With respect to subscriptions, we shall make immediate provision for their payment, as soon as the method of accomplishing it is pointed out. What we most desire is that pains may be taken to convey to us, as soon as possible, these several publications. In an undertaking like ours, the more we can anticipate others in the diffusion of information & improvements, tho greater curiosity & improvement shall we be likely to excite & promote. This is a task that we do not presume to request of you; but we presume there are booksellers in London who would readily accept such a commission, & we trust the importance of it's execution to the progress of the art we cultivate will induce you to take the trouble of selection, both in respect to the works, & the agent. Beside periodical publications, all single pamphlets & small works, of peculiar merit, will come within our plan of purchase.

On our part, beside making provision for the remuneration of the agent you may designate, & the reimbursement of such sums as may be expanded by him for us, we shall cheerfully transmit to you, from time to time, whatever shall appear worthy your notice, on this side of the water. The pamphlets now sent you will please to consider as a sample. In addition to the original Essay of Dr. Mitchill, Saltonstall's Dissertation on Septon—which I presume you have seen, the Essay on the Dysentery & that relative to the manufacturing of Soap & Candles—now sent, the Dr. has published, at different times, various smaller Essays, all tending to the establishments of his peculiar doctrines. Without pretending to support his Theory, we believe them of sufficient importance to deserve a more extensive circulation. Accordingly, they will be collected, & in the course of our publication, laid before the world in a more formal & direct manner.

The collections & essays relative to the Fever which prevailed here in 1795, we suppose you to have seen. If we are mistaken, they shall be forwarded on the first intimation, with such others as you may be desirous of examining.

Should you be willing to accept our offer of correspondence, I shall hope to receive a reply to this letter, as soon as may suit with your convenience, after its receipt. Meantime, I take a pleasure in assuring you of the esteem of my associates as well as my own; & am respectfully yours.

Aug: 29. 1797.   E. H. Smith.

To Dr. Muret

Our common friend, Mr. J. S. Roulet, lately imported to me a paragraph of a letter he has received from you, by which it appears that you have read with some approbation the publication on our Fever of 1795, which he had transmitted to you. The favourable reception that you have given the Book referred to, induces me to address you at this time, in the hope of being honoured with your correspondence, and that the pamphlets accompanying this letter will prove acceptable to you. Should you authorize this hope, I shall take great pleasure in communicating to you such printed & private information, respecting the state of medicine & science in general, in our country, as you may desire to receive & I capable to afford. In return, I need not assure you how much satisfaction it will give me, and how agreable it will prove to my associates in the periodical work now forwarded, to be made acquainted with the progress of medical & natural knowlege in Swisserland, & of such new discoveries in their practical application to the cure & relief of human maladies, as chance & experiment have suggested.

The aspect of Febrile diseases has, of late, become so interesting a spectacle in the United States, that you will not wonder at its engaging a very large share of our attention. The resemblance between the state of society & the diseases of our two countries, will serve, in all probability, to illustrate each other; & the remedies which prove most successful here, promise to apply with considerable advantage with you. At the same time, the number & reputation of the enlightened medical observers & philosophers of Swisserland, & the long course of experience which must have enriched the minds of practitioners there, allow us to presume that the most successful practice of your country might be transferred, with singular benefit to our own. The merit & writings of some of the most illustrious of the Swiss have been long known to us, by aid of the French & English; but, hitherto, little direct communication has existed between the United States & the Helvetic Cantons. Do I wrong in expressing my desire that the effectuating an intercourse so beneficial may commence with us? Will you flatter the presumption of a young man so much as to accept of his invitation to an epistolary interchange of professional & friendly letters? I dare believe that your consent will be not altogether productive of chagrin & disappointment; that my country will occasionally furnish me with materials deserving of your curiosity & consideration; & that the industry of my associates will console you for any imperfections in one who subscribes himself, with great respect.

                                         Yours &c.

Aug: 29. '97.
Pine St. 45.   E. H. Smith.

Wednesday, 30.—Found a man here from Lichfield, by whom I sent the Med: Reposy, &c. Medical visits, errands &c. occupied the forenoon. Gahn & I rode out to Mr. Sharples's (the Painter) to dinner, by invitation. Sir Jno. Temple[45] & family there—Dr. Morse the Geographer—& Mr. Guillemard, the friend of Beddoes. We spent the afternoon. Returned; drank tea with Mrs. Lovegrove, & went with her to the John Street Theater. "Isabella"[46]—Mrs. Whitlock—a respectable actress, but inferior to my expectations, inferior to Mrs. Merry. The rest of the performers execrable.

To John Williams

I received your letter, with the inclosed bill, a few days ago, with a mixture of pleasure & regret: Pleasure

---

[45] Sir John Temple was the English consul general.
[46] *Isabella, or the Fatal Marriage* by David Garrick (1757).

for the proofs it contained of your friendship; regret, for the trouble & expence to which I fear you have unfortunately subjected yourself. I have too much respect for your peculiar feelings, or I should not consent to retain the sum sent, under the circumstances. I am sorry that you did not demand the subscription at the delivery of the pamphlet, a measure which would, probably, have spared some mortification on all sides. The copy which Mr. Dwight had was a present from me, & does by no means, (nor will he so consider it) exempt him from the subscription. He could not doubt my sending him a copy at the time of subscribing; & probably meant to have a second for his disposal elsewhere. With respect to the remaining copies, do with them as you please. I do not know who has, & who has not copies in Wethersfield; but if you are at a loss, present one to each of your sisters—& the other to Mr. Marsh, if neither have a copy.

You have had so much trouble with one subscription paper, that I shall not send you another; but, as you are turned Farmer, & have some interest in your friend, I shall recommend to you, as likely to deserve your patronage, a publication in which he is engaged; & which will contain many things interesting to men in your situation: I mean "The Medical Repository." The title may, perhaps, repulse you, but the plan of the Collection is by no means confined to mere Medicine, & we shall take great pains, in the course of the work, to collect the best Agricultural Essays. In addition, to this, another recommendation will be, that it will contain the most authentic account of the state & progress of natural knowlege, in our country, that can be obtained. You are to consider the Editors as the mere conduit-pipes, in conveying this information to the public, & encourage the publication less on their account, than on that of the country at large. We shall hope for some communications from you, should your agricultural experiments furnish you with any thing new & curious.

Remembrances as usual.

Aug: 31. '97.   E. H. Smith.

Thursday, 31.—Transcribed the letter to Dr. Muret. Wrote & copied that to John Williams. Wrote the subsequent pages on the Elk; which are merely notes of what I have collected from seeing the animal, their keeper, & the persons accidentally there. I must make more inquiries—& look into Buffon &c. Called on Mrs. Lovegrove. Dined at Woolsey's with Revd. Dr. Morse, Gahn, Mr. Gracie,[47] the three Miller's, G. M. Woolsey, & Mr. Campbell of Virginia. He tells me he has seen the head of the Elk (cranium) & that the cavity from beneath the eye into the nostril is large enough to admit the thumb. He says the moose & Elk are distinct in

---
[47] Archibald Gracie emigrated from Scotland to Petersburg, Virginia where he prospered exceedingly in trade and moved to New York. Here, as a prominent and wealthy merchant and banker, he interested himself in public affairs, especially in free education for children.

Sir Ashton Lever's Museum.[48] Pennant's mistake is the more strange. Dr. Morse very obligingly offers to assist us in the Med: Repository, to Obituary & Meteorological notes & to Subscribers.

In the eveng. to see Miss Morton, at Mr. Morton's. I met there Mr. & Mrs. Merry. She an unaffected, sociable, & well-bred woman; he a gentlemanly, sensible, & agreable man. I was pleased with both.

Took a walk on the Battery. This month has been tolerably well spent.

Industry of August 1797

Reading

"The Enquirer" &c. by Wm. Godwin—Edit. Lond. 8vo. pp.
Zoonomia—P. 11. "Theory of Fever"—4th. pp.
Inaugural Dissertations—all in 8vo.—by Alex Hosack Jr. "On the Yellow-Fever in N. York 1795"; by Saml. Cooper, on the "Stramonium"; by Josh. Johnson, on "Carbonic Acid Gas"; by Colin McKenzie, on "Dysentery"; by James Fisher, on "Dysentery"; by Edward North, on "Rheumatic State of Fever"; by Wm. Allston, on "Dropsy"; by John Church, on "Camphor"; by Robert Black, "on Fractures"; & Francis K. Auger, on "Gangrene & Mortification".—equal to pp. 480—common print.
"Emma Courtney"—by Mary Hays—edit. Lond. 2 vols. 12mo. pp. 350 (perhaps)—
Nicholson's Journal—Nos I, II.—about half—4th.
"Medical Extracts"—most of the II & III vols.—8vo. loose print.
Several Papers in Vol. V of Transact. of R. Irish Acady.
"Oration &c". by Leir Wheaton—8vo. pp. 22.
Several Articles in Vol. I. Arctic Zoology—by Thos. Pennant.
"Alcuin"—MS. Dialogue, by C. B. B. equal to pp. 20 8vo.—Essay on the Actual Cantery, by Dr. Valentin.—equal to pp. 10.
Analytical Review—& Nos.
Monthly &c.—two or three volumes.

Writing.

Composition.

Notes &c. of the first Eleven Years of my Life	pp. 52
Letters—preserved in this volume	pp. 34
Do. not preserved	pp. 08
Medical Reviews	pp. 17
On the Elk	04
Analysis of Darwin's "Theory of Fever", equal to	pp. 10

Transcription.

Of the Notes on my Life .. about	pp. 20
All the Letters preserved	34
Various other matters	26

---
[48] Lever, an English naturalist, died in 1788 and his famous museum, a "must" for sightseers in London, was dispersed.

MEMOIRS. 1797. SEPTEMBER

Friday, 1st.—One of the warmest, most muggy, & disagreable days we have had this year. I have felt quite unwell all day, & was obliged to lie down almost all the afternoon. Recd. a letter from Dr. Strong. Visited Mrs. Lovegrove. Her children mending. Went to Mitchill's room. Found there Dr. Robert & Mr. Owen.[49] The last politely invited me to visit his collection of plants & minerals. Mitchill shewed me some verses, in which he has attempted to display his doctrine of Septon, after the manner of Darwin—with more success than I should have expected, but not without many prosaic lines & low expressions. We went together & called on Professor Gözt: we found him at home. Next we called at the lodgings of Mr. Guillemard; he was absent. Next, on Mr. de Liancourt;[50] he was absent. Next on Mr. Schaubert, a Silesian, & Mr. Stewart of the Western Counties, who lodged in the same house. They were at home. Last at Millers. They out. I adjusted my Cash accounts &c. for the month past; & drew out the preceeding table of industry. Read several articles in the Monthly Review. G. M. Woolsey here. Called at Woolsey's—all out. Met, in going thither, Saml. A. Law, who is returning to Connecticut from Phila. He saw Dr. Rush the morning he left Phila.—who told him the fever was decreasing. Drank tea at Riley's. Miss Alsop & I walked on the Battery. A beautiful evening.

My memoirs have grown rapidly during the last month. It is not to be expected that they will increase as fast during the present. I hope, however, at least to terminate this first volume; which, tho' not every thing I intended, equals my expectations.

Saturday, 2.—Medical visits & errands occupied the whole forenoon. Finished looking over the two first Nos. of Nicholson's Journal, in which I read all that I could understand. Read a number of articles in the Monthly Review. Visited the Miller's. Called, ineffectually, at Hosack's. Walked on the Battery. Spent the evening at Catlin's. Looked over several late London papers. I see that Holcroft has published the remaining volumes of "Hugh Trevor"; & the account of Godwin's marriage is confirmed, as I think, by a copy of pitiful satirical verses on the occasion.

Sunday, 3.—Overslept myself. Two medical visits. Finished looking over the file of Papers, began last evening. Read a number of articles in the Monthly Review. Visit at S. Johnson's. Drank tea with Miss Rogers—at Mr. Kent's House; Called at Riley's. Miss Alsop & I went to Woolsey's—where we spent the evening.

Monday, 4.—Rose in good season. Read several articles in the Monthly Review. Went, with Mr. Tinsdale, the Designer & Engraver, to see the Elks, of which he made a drawing, to be engraved for some future No. of our Repository. This occupied much time. A medical visit & several calls. Looked over considerable part of a file of the "Moniteur"—left here by M. Roulet, in my absence. Wrote a number of introductory letters for Mrs. Lovegrove, who is going to New England. Calls. Spent the evening at Mr. Roulet's. The day has been remarkably pleasant, & the evening is no less so.

This day is my birth-day. I am now twenty-six years of age. I find no disposition to moralize, to lament past evils, or anticipate future joys. This day is no more to me than any other. Why should it be? Of what consequence is it on what day, or in what country, I was born? The whole world should be the theater for my benevolence to display itself in; & every hour should renew & vary the scene & the motives to my virtuous exertions.

Tuesday, Septr. 5.—Medical visit. Visit of a patient, for advice. Visit from Dr. Wheaton. He came to consult me on the case of a patient. We agreed on a consultation. Composed the following diagrams, & wrote the first page on the Districts, of Utopia—my desire of writing something on this subject being renewed. These few pages appear very little—yet they cost me some labour & more time. It is somewhat necessary to carry along a regard to every part of my plan—so that each line is the result of many thoughts, & of some comprehensiveness of views. Was a little while at the African School House—being summoned, by mistake, to a meeting of the trustees, to which body I no longer belong. Went to Dr. Wheaton's. We visited our patient—returned to his house, determined on some measures—& after tea, I went to S. Johnson's—where I spent part of the evening; the remainder at Woolsey's. Read over several Paris papers. I have now been four years in New York—having come here on the afternoon of the 5th of Septr. 1793—& in neither of these years have I been able to derive a support from my own exertions.

Wednesday, 6.—Wrote eight pages on my Utopia. Read a file of London Papers; & nearly finished those from Paris—*Moniteur.* Made some calls before dinner. Read the News-Papers. Medical visit with Dr. Wheaton, at whose house I spent some time, & again drank tea. Called at Dr. Hosack's. He was from home. Spent the evening with Miss Alsop. a small fire: soon extinguished. A remarkably clear, cool & pleasant day.

Thursday, 7.—Composed the short title "Of the County," & the subsequent letter—which I also transcribed. Wrote a few lines to me father. A visit from Dr. Miller. Three medical &c. visits. A consulting visit, which, as it carried me some distance, occupied much time. Finished the file of the "Moniteur." Read all the articles in Pennant's Arctic Zoology under the title "Deer"—except what he says on the "moose": that I had previously perused, as likewise some part of what

---

[49] Dr. Robert, not in *New York Directory* for 1796 or 1797. Mr. Owen, probably Luke Owens, merchant at 37 Broad St., *Directory,* 1797, 1798.

[50] Possibly the Duke de la Rochefoucauld Liancourt, famous traveler and writer glossed earlier; Mr. Schaubert has not been identified; "Mr. Stewart of the Western Counties" was Assistant Attorney General for Onandaga, New York.

I now perused. Read a number of Articles in the Monthly Review. Commenced the Introduction to the Second Volume of these Memoirs. Drank tea with Mrs. Miller. Spent the evening at Mr. Moses Rogers's.

To Joseph Dennie Jr.

I have waited, with some impatience, a reply to the latter part of my last letter, written in July. In answer to your solicitations for original communications I informed you that, tho' my own time was so much employed in other concerns as not [to] allow me the pleasure of contributing to your miscellany, yet that I had a friend whose talents were of a kind to confer value on any scheme of a literary nature in which he should engage, & that I was confident a very moderate compensation might induce him to yield you such stated or occasional assistance as you would require. I hoped that you would have given me a definitive answer on this proposition because other plans sufficiently advantageous for the gentleman I speak of suggest themselves to me, & I only wait to put them in execution on his behalf, till I can hear from you. I may inform you, that he is not ignorant of the proposal, nor averse to it. He leaves the terms wholly to us: & has sent me a manuscript as a specimen of what he may do, provided you think proper to engage his pen. I request your speedy answer.

I believe an acknowlegement of a mistake is due from me to you, on account of what I observed in my first letter, concerning "The Foresters." Perhaps Mr. Belknap is the author. I am doubtful. This tale appeared, continuatedly, in a Magasine published at Phila. of which Mr. Hopkinson was the Editor, about the time of my residence in that city. It was uniformly attributed to him, & by his friends: nor did he contradict the report, to my knowlege. It was on this ground that I ventured to doubt the correctness of your Critic. I supposed, at the time, that the Tale was included in Mr. H's works, which have been published since his death. But not finding it there, I conclude that he is not the author. I see advertised in your paper "The Algerine Captive &c." This I am informed is a novel, & written by Mr. Tyler, the gentleman mentioned in one of your letters. I presume from the manner in which it is spoken of, that it is a publication of merit, & request the favor of you to transmit to me, by the first safe & private conveyance.

Mr. Swords I believe sends you his Magasine. If so you will find some good articles for the Economical department in his last number.

Yours &c.

Septr. 7. 1797.
Pine St. 45. N. Y.   E. H. Smith.

Friday, 8.—Two medical visits in the morning, one of which occupied some time. Two in the afternoon. A visit from the Revd. Dr. Morse. Wrote three pages of the "Proem" to the next volume of these memoirs. Collected the materials for an Index to this volume. Drank tea at Charles Adams's. At the Greenwich Street Theater in the evening. Mr. Fennel made his first appearance here. The play "The Revenge"[51]—Moreton *Alonzo*, Cooper *Carlos*, Mrs. Merry *Leonora*, Fennel *Zanga*. This tragedy wholly fails of affecting the softer passions. Here are none of the tender touches of Shakespere, Otway, Southern, or even Rowe. It is interesting notwithstanding. The character *Zanga* has much force in it, in spite of the inflated style & too frequent apostrophes which characterize the whole piece. I know not if I ever saw a play so completely executed. Fennel is certainly an Actor of considerable merit. I say considerable, for as our taste becomes refined in dramatic representations we are less apt than before to be prodigal of commendatory epithets. His person & face are admirable; & he were a fit model for some Statuary who would represent a Theseus or an Agamemnon. He is certainly superior to any tragic actor I have yet seen. *Leonora* is too trifling a part for Mrs. Merry. The after-piece was "The Adopted Child." Cooper's *Michael*, contrary to my expectation, was very well. Mrs. Oldmixon's *Nelly* excellent.

Saturday, 9.—Wrote the article Medical Institutions under the title Utopia, in the second volume. Wm. Johnson returned just as I finished it. Immediately I had several matters to attend to, that occupied me till dinner. I had made a medical visit in the morning. In the afternoon I made three or four & several other calls. I found that Dunlap returned last night, with his family. I drank tea there. Miss Alsop, Riley, B. Pomeroy & I went to see the *Learned Pig*. It is difficult to conceive by what means this animal has been instructed to perform his several exercises. Undoubtedly, I think, he has not committed to memory all the letters, figures, multiplication tables &c. The number of signs by which he is directed must be much fewer & simpler. Still he discovers a tractability & memory very uncommon & surprizing. The patience & ingenuity of his instructor are no less extraordinary. I went to Dunlap's. We visited the John Street Theater. I did not enter in season to see any part of the contemptible piece called "Bunker Hill." I was there merely to see Mrs. Williamson's *"Little Pickle."*[52] She plays this character very well. Every one else was contemptible. I recd. a letter from Nathl. Dwight. Dr. Miller was here a short time in the afternoon: Dr. Wheaton in the forenoon.

Sunday, 10.—A visit from Dunlap. Some time after called upon him & went to Woolsey's—to see his second daughter. They were out, riding with her. We walked. I made a medical visit out of town. Returned to Woolsey's. Dined there. After dinner came home. Mr. Trott the painter here. Conversation on Theaters & performers. Mention of Mrs. Merry led to speak of Mr. M.[53]—of his poetry—application for the Laureatship—com-

---

[51] Edward Young (1721).
[52] *Little Pickle* by Mrs. Williamson ([1792?]).
[53] Mr. Merry is the Della Cruscan poet mentioned earlier.

parison of Pye, Warton, & Whitehead. Read three of the latter's Odes & one of Warton's. Drank tea with the Miller's. Mr. Josh. Miller goes to Delaware in the morning. We went to Baker's Observatory in the Exchange to see the Comet of which so much is said. We found the Planet Venus to have been mistaken for the Comet, by our sagacious observers. Went to Riley's. Thence to S. Johnson's—where I spent the remainder of the evening.

Monday, Septr. 11.—The forenoon employed in the examination from which the following "Summary &c." is deduced. One additional remark is necessary. The sum expressed as my Expenditure the last year is to be considered merely as the money actually paid out by me. Much of it for debts incurred the year preceeding. Now, in former years, the sum charged to Expenditure is meant to express the expences of the current year. What the expences of the year now ended have been I can not rightly imagine. Perhaps a careful inquiry might shew. I am persuaded, however, that, notwithstanding the increase of some articles, part of the time, as Rent, Service &c. they are less than for the year '95-'96.

After finishing this Summary, I was some time in doubt what to do; & in this doubt I was likely to do nothing. My Muse was contumacious & refractory—but I resolved to force her into service. With some exertion I wrought out a Sonnet—to be transcribed into the next volume—not, indeed, with that felicity of expression which flows from the irresistible impulses of an awkward & vehement imagination, but with some sober decency:—at least I hope so.

Two medical visits: one out of Town. Returning stopped in at G. M. Woolsey's Store. Read there a file of London Papers. Drank tea at Dunlap's. We went to the Greenwich Street Theater. "Romeo & Juliet." Mrs. Merry's *Juliet* above all praise; Mr. Morton's *Romeo* very well, but not equal to my expectations; Mr. Bernard's *Mercutio* so so—the last scene *well*. Mrs. Oldmixon sang with great sweetness in the chorus—her solo exquisite.

Mr. Garrick studied stage-effect; & it must be acknowleged that the idea of Juliet's awaking while Romeo is yet alive is fine, & the situation interesting; but he has spoiled it. The composition is contemptible, & suffocates the emotions of tenderness that were rising to suffuse the eyes.

Recd. a letter from Wm. Buel.

Summary &c

I have been looking over my Accounts for the year commencing Sept. 6. 1796, ending Septr. 5. 1797. They are not in a situation to furnish me with precise results. The following can not be materially incorrect.

My *Charges* from *Septr.* 5. '96. to Sept. 6. 97.
Good—or such as have been or are expected to
be paid . . . . 475.
Doubtful—or such as are uncertain . . . . 103.
Bad—such as I have little or no hope of receiving . . . . 52.
                                                    630.

On a fair calculation I think one half of the Doubtful may be added to the Bad . . . 76.—

Excess of Charges over the last year . . . . 57.—

My *Receits* from *Septr.* 5. '96, to Septr. 6. '97.
From my Father . . . . 254.
On Account . . . . 377.
For Material Advice & Medicine not formally charged . . . . 65.
For Edwin & Angelina, Books Sold, & repayments of small sums expended on the joint dinner acct. of J.[54] [?] & myself . . 100.
                                                    796.

Excess of Receits over charges . . . . . 166.

My *Expenditures* from *Septr.* 5. '96, to Septr. 6. 1797.
As near as I can conveniently ascertain . . . 857.—

Excess of Receits . . . . 61.

Excess of Charges . . . . 227.

Extent my Debts as the present time . . . . 310.—
N. B. this does not include what I owe my Father . . . .
Monies due to me at this period.
Good Debts—such as are likely to be paid . . 244.—
Doubtful Debts . . . . 117.
Bad—such as are not likely to be paid . . . 100.
Due to me for Edwin & Angelina . . . . . 53.
                                                    514.

Remarks.—Perhaps there is owing to me a **larger** sum than fifty three dollars for Ed: & Angel. This, however, is more than [I] expect to receive. In this sum is not included what may eventually be due to me from Booksellers, who have some copies still on hand.

It is probable that, were all paid to me that I shall ever receive on acct. my debts might be discharged without difficulty. In the above statement are not included about thirty dollars due from the Hospital & Manumission Society to me.

My Business appears nearly stationary. Yet it has certainly increased in the last year; & I can not but suspect more than is evident from this Statement. Yet I know not how any mistake of consequence can have insinuated itself.

The difference between Receits & Expenditures would probably vanish had I leisure to compare the sides of the

---

[54] Manuscript is not clear. It seems to read "for J[ohnson?], [?] and myself."

Cash Acct. carefully. It arises from having credited Cash for money paid out for others, & afterwards recd. again. The Article Expenditures in this Statement is taken from the Credit Side of the Cash Acct.; the article Receits is made up by a strict collection of every sum recd. as noticed in the Statement, & is not many Cents different from the absolute Receits.

This Statement offers very little encouragement. I do not mean that it shall cause any despair.

Conclusion

I have allowed but a single page for the concluding remarks to the present volume. And, indeed, there is little or nothing to say. It were useless to repeat the tales of mortification which occur so often in all my journals, at the inferiority of the execution compared with the design. Much as such sentiments press on my mind, they have [been] dwelt upon till even my mind is sick of considering them. & it is more encouraging to regard this volume in the pleasing light of an improvement on its predecessors; as comprizing within its pages many papers of some importance in the rational view of any man, of considerable as I myself am the subject of inquiry. It is probable that the materials that compose this volume are more valuable than all which are included in my former volumes of diurnal memoranda. I do not doubt of their indicating considerable improvement in the arts of thinking & expressing my thoughts. I seem to be sensible of this improvement in myself: & tho' it is far beneath my ambition, far short of my desires, it affords me some gratification. Considering the embarrassments in my way to Science, both early & now, I do not absolutely despair, from what I have experienced in myself, of attaining some respectability in a series of years. I am far from flattering myself with the expectation of fame as a great discoverer or great scholar, but I hope to stimulate abler men to investigation, & do some good by increasing a spirit of attention to other objects than the mere pursuit of wealth.

Notebook No. 6: September, 1797–September, 1798

Memoirs: or Notices concerning the Life, Studies, Opinions, and Friends, of E. H. Smith

1797. SEPTEMBER

PROEM

The First Volume of these Memoirs draws near a close. In a few days I shall deposit it with the preceeding notices of every day's concerns and occurrences. The spirit of procrastination while I have time, the temper of hurry when leisure remains no longer and every moment presses for execution, for action, these and the extensive empire of unforeseen circumstances, all warn me not to delay whatever words of Introduction I may design for this Volume till its immediate use is demanded. I obey the suggestion, while I acknowledge once more my weakness that inspires it. I have a few remarks to make, and I hasten to commit them to these yet unsullied pages.

The experience, ample I may call it, of near ten months has demonstrated the superiority of the plan of these Memoirs to that of the Journal, & to that of the Diary. During a part of the time employed in the composition of the First Volume, my industry, compared with former periods, has been respectable. The traces of my pen bear testimony to some portion of improvement as well as toil. Much, very much remains to be done; and I acknowlege that I am very little satisfied with my own and still less, if possible, with my attainments.

This is a topic on which I have already sufficiently enlarged; and I well know all the extenuations that may be pleaded by an eloquent indolence. I am also aware of the futility of resolutions entered into at times when we feel capable of every thing arduous and commendable but which are to be accomplished amid the occupations, impediments, & misgivings of every day. One of the greatest obstacles to distinguished improvement in science is the want of companions in our researches & labours. Solitary exertion is pleasant to few minds, and least of all to those whose temper and habits lead them to cultivate experimental inquiries in those kinds of knowlege that have a direct relation to human happiness. The metaphysician, the mathematician, the mechanist, may delight to pursue their trains of thought, & their various operations, in silence & seclusion. But, even they must sometimes languish for society, & feel the necessity of intercourse with others whose conversation may direct their reflections to new views of their favorite studies, & whose observation may call upon them for additional ingenuity in the construction & practical application of their designs. With the chemist, the physiologist, & the physician, congenial minds & fellow-labourers are still more desirable. There is so much nicety in all their observations, so much delicacy in all their reasonings, so much at hazard in every experiment, that few dare or ought to venture to decide singly & unadvised. To this may be added the embarrassments from the very nature of these pursuits, inseparable from unsocial & unaided investigations. But these difficulties equally beset the american & the european. They may be triumphed over by minds of uncommon energy, on whom fortune has bestowed her favours, & to whom science has presented her manifold & costly implements. To those in America who are disposed to seek for information, both fortune and science seem to have played the niggard. Judging from my own observation, these are few. I do not know a single man of that ardent enthusiasm which laughs at obstacles, & regards every new difficulty but as a signal for fresh exertions. Some would inquire, experiment, labor, if they had all the conveniences of art about them, & a leader to direct their labours & inspirit their endeavours. Some would be indefatigable were speedy wealth the sure result, till that wealth were obtained. A few will condescend to occasional industry to preserve their reputation, humble a rival, or gratify their vanity. Who is there that labours to know, that he may know? Who toils to understand that he may instruct others in the way to health, & competence, & peace?

I believe that I comprehend the character of my own mind. I know both its defects & its powers. Some exertion I must make. Such is the force of habit that some intellectual novelty is essential to my existence. Unaided by some example, unexcited by pressing & powerful motives, I should never effect, except by accident, any thing illustrious & praise-worthy. Animated by the example, assistance, & social exertion of others, there are no heights of science too arduous for me to attempt to surmount. It is the want of such friends that sickens me to the soul. I look round & survey this busy multitude all eager for wealth & little thoughtful of knowlege & reputation but as instruments to acquire it; I detach the foremost individuals from the throng which follow tumultuous at their heels—I analyse their motives as I observe their conduct; I see one too dull & one too proud to learn, this too lazy to inquire & that satisfied with former investigations, these busy in oppressing others, from whose humiliation alone they expect distinction, & those fertile in expedients to magnify their own attainments, & incessant in petty artifices to spread their own fame; I see the most virtuous & powerful minds rather satisfied to receive than to acquire knowlege, rather employed in collecting the scattered relics of their predecessors than in constructing some beauteous & durable monument of their own, rather wasting their lives in empirical trials of means suggested by others than indefatigable in researches after new implements to combat disease & death; I look round, I analize, & I see all this—& my sad thoughts turn in upon my own heart: Hope & expectation are converted into disappointment & chagrin; and the enthusiasm which promised to support me in the most perilous & protracted enterprizes dissipates in fruitless speculations & idle dreams, & is succeeded by vapidity & self-condemnation. The deeper & more extensive folly of others is a poor, but it is the only consolation. How much soever my vanity may be tickled for a time by the applause occasionally bestowed on me, in the sober moments of self-examination I derive little satisfaction from the praise of those who are too ignorant to discern with accuracy, and too indolent to estimate the scanty sum of my industry. Thus situated & thus feeling & thinking, I am oftentimes half-determined to break thro' every obstacle, to burst every band which impedes & withholds me, to encounter every hazard & sustain every suffering, that, leaving my native country, I may mingle in the scenes of experiment & industry, of learning, & of science, that grace & enlighten the foremost empires in Europe. These resolutions are made but to expire. They are conceived; but perish in the womb, & fall dead-born on the lap that receives them. I seem doomed, by a thousand causes, to remain where I am, with all my ignorance, all my poverty, all my desires, & all my indolence. The hope that sometimes flutters in my bosom barely soothes, the energy which should permanently reside there, has been hitherto a capricious & infrequent visitant. It depends, in some measure, on this volume to determine whether I may steadily hail it as my inmate.

Tuesday, Septr. 12.—I was called out of bed last night to visit Mrs. Lovegrove, who was ill with Odontalgia.[55] I have visited her three times this day—morning, noon, and evening—and she is essentially better. Indeed, my time has been chiefly occupied in calls & errands, so that I have not had leisure to conclude the preceeding volume, & arrange the Index, as I intended. I wrote a short letter to Dr. Barton of Phila. & another to Mr. Kent, to meet him at Hartford. I called on Mr. Stewart, the Assistant Attorney General for Onondaga, & entrusted to him letters for Mr. Mumford. Called at Riley's, & had an hour's conversation with Miss Alsop. In the afternoon, a medical visit out of town. Called at Swords's, & agreed to commence the printing of the Second No. of the Medical Repository next week. When I returned this forenoon from my visits, I found here the Monthly Review for June, & the Appendix to the XXII vol. I have hastily run over the greater part of the No. for June. *Art. 1. Moleville's* "Private Memoirs of Louis XVI" are interesting & well-written: The introductory remarks of the Reviewer are correct: the author's character of Neckar coincides with my own long-entertained opinion. *Art. III. Lyson's* "Environs of London &c." the extract valuable—containing the history of the Greenwich Observatory. *Art. IV. Whitehead's* "Life of John Wesley"—well written, & apparently worth reading. *Art. VI. Daulby's* "Catalogue of Rembrant's Works." I could not read these pleasing quotations without emotions of disgust at my own crude & artificial style, & a renewed longing for powerful, copious, & correct simplicity. *Art. VIII.* "The Henriade"—introductory remarks apparently just; & the extracts authorize the commendations of the critic. *Art. XI. Edward's* "Historical Survey of St. Domingo." Tho' I far from coinciding with the author in *all* his sentiments, yet I am too well acquainted with his merit as a writer not to wish for the possession of all his works. The present, both from its subject & its manner, is particularly deserving of attention. *Art. XVI. Onseley's* "Oriental Collections"—a work to be sought after. *Art. 28.* "Prison Amusements"—the verses to the Redbreast have the rare merit of simplicity. *Art. 30.* "Epitre a mon Pere"—the quotation tender & *naive. Art. 31.* I am much pleased with the citation from Dr. Aikin's Essay prefixed to his new edition of Pope's Essay on Man. *Art. 34.* There are some affecting anecdotes of the French Revolution.

Wm. and I walked on the Battery. On our way thither we stopped, & spent a half hour with Miss Morton. I had seen Mr. Götz in the forenoon. He informed me that he had discovered the Comet, & should observe it, from the Battery, this evening. We could not find him there. We called at Riley's—Miss Alsop was absent. We went to S. Johnson's, where we spent the remainder of the evening.

Wednesday, Sept. 13.—Mr. Stewart, the District Attorney, breakfasted with us. He leaves town for the Western Country this day. A medical visit. Visit to Dr. Miller on business of the Medical Repository. Read the News-Papers. Concluded the preceeding volume, & completed the Index—a tedious piece of business. A visit from Dr. Mitchill. Another from Mr. Sharples the painter. Two medical visits, one out of town. Drank tea at the Miller's. Dr. M. & I went to see Miss Mason. She was not at home. We spent the evening at Dr. Hosack's. He talks very much with the air of a man who thought his opinions of great importance. He was civil. His sister seems a well-bred young lady. Miller & I walked on the Battery. Since I have come home, I have read the Minerva of this evening, which is crowded with interesting european intelligence. There seems little hope of repose in Europe, for many years. I have finished the Monthly Review for June 1797. *Art. VII. Adam Smith's* "Philosophical Essays"—concluded. This analytical account of the work is well executed, & has given me much pleasure. The extracts are all pleasing. Extraordinary as it may appear, & high as is the reputation of Dr. Smith as a writer, I have never read any

---
[55] Mrs. Lovegrove has a toothache.

of his works; nor do I know when I shall have time to examine them as they deserve.

To Nathaniel Dwight

I recd. and thank you for your letter of the 5th inst. Capt. Chatwell of Hartd. sails tomorrow, or next day. As his prospect is pretty certain of arriving in season, I purpose to forward the copies of the Repository by him: For I have no correspondent in New Haven that I can venture to request to take the trouble of sending them from that place. I shall deliver to Capt. C. three bundles, each containing one dozen copies. One bundle is directed for Dr. Field, to your care; the others to you. I would willingly believe that there will be no difficulty in procuring subscribers in your County, for the two dozen—especially as the work is not confined to medical subjects, but is likely to interest all persons who take any interest in the progress of science. In this city, we have as many subscribers who are not, as who are physicians. I believe more.

Our subscription is small: not half adequate to the expence. It is, however, on the increase. When all our papers are returned, we hope it will prove not far short of the unavoidable expence. I must request you to allow no copy to go out of your hands, but in conformity to the Conditions of Publication. If we fail here, we fail altogether. I will thank you, likewise, to transmit to me the names of subscribers. We design to insert a list of their names, in our last number of the present volume.

We shall commence the printing of the second No. tomorrow. I think we shall not want for materials. We have had several interesting communications.

How is health in Hartford, this season? Have you seen or heard any thing of the Cat-distemper among you this summer? If you have made any observations, we shall thank you for them, how brief or slight soever they may be. It is difficult to ascertain the truth, but the general opinion here is, that not less than 4 or 5,000 have died in New York.

I am called out. Excuse this brevity. I shall write & inclose a few lines to Dr. Field.

Sept. 14.   E. H. Smith.

Thursday, 14.—Called on Miller, & we went to Mitchill's, to converse on the business of our Repository. Post was there a short time: And Mr. Owens. We agreed to visit his collection of Fossils &c. tomorrow. Mr. O. is a gentleman of Belfast, who comes to reside in our country. He has studied Chemistry in France, probably elsewhere—& seems well versed in all branches of Natural History. I have met him several times at Mitchill's. We also agreed to visit Kosciusko[56] tomor-row. Called on Mrs. Lovegrove. Medical visit. Call on Mr. Gahn. Errands. Wrote a few lines to Dr. Field of Somers, Connec. & wrote and transcribed the preceeding letter. Transcribed likewise the XIVth Sonnet. Mitchill & I walked out of town (3½ miles) to Mr. Sharples's, the Painter's—where we drank tea. We returned in the evening; called at the Hospital: went thence to Dunlap's, where we spent the remainder of it. I forgot to notice that I spent a short time in the forenoon with Mr. Götz, & that Mr. Webster was here fifteen minutes this afternoon.

In the course of the day & evening, I have nearly finished the perusal of the Appendix to the XXII vol. of the Monthly Review. *Art. I.* Griesbach's "Novum Testamentum Græce." I have been entertained by the history of editions of the New Testament. It is a new proof of the fallacy of religious pretensions. *Art. II.* Pappelbaum's "Codicis Ravani Examen." This article is less interesting, but is no less important as a particular exemplification of the remark. *Art. III.* Heeron's "Ideas relative to the nations of antiquity." The observations on polygamy deserve to be reflected on. The author's opinion—& I may add the critic's—of Herodotus, correspond with my own. *Art. IV.* "Sesostris &c." the elegy of pleasing. *Art. V.* Wieland's Works. The elegant hand of the reviewer of the preceeding volumes of this collection is still evident. The account of Wieland's Works is remarkable for the peculiar talents of the writer for discrimination. His style, with great excellencies, is certainly faulty in being constructed with too much appearance of art. *Art. VII.* This less interesting than the former articles relative to Herder. From the specimen here given, I am inclined to doubt the soundness of his critical code. *Art. VIII.* Tissot's "Life of Zimmerman." This article is valuable. The late publications of Z. had prepared me for a lower estimate of him, than I formed from reading his medical works. His character has many defects: but certainly some excellencies. Tissot is since dead. *Art. XII.* De Saussaune's "Travels in the Alps"—an inestimable work, which I must contrive to cause Mr. Roulet to import. *Art. XIV.* "Historical Essay &c." This performance seems eminently calculated to amuse. Much solid instruction seems scarcely derivable from it. The extract p. 546 of Review is sufficiently curious. *Art. XV.* Hottinger's Life of Gesner—is analysed in a pleasing manner; the remarks of the Reviewer are correct; & the extract from the biographer full of good sense & founded on observation. *Art. XIX.* Rulpiere's History of the Revolution in Russia in 1762—very valuable. I shall seize the first opportunity on reading a work that promises so much.

SONNET XIV

Truth 1

If the clear sun on yonder dial shine,
   The faithful gnomon indicates the hour;

---

[56] Tadeusz Kosciusco, or Kosciuszko (1740-1817), Polish gentleman and soldier of fortune who was of great service to the cause of the colonies in the Revolution. Subsequently he took an active part in the defense of Poland against Austria, Prussia, and Russia. Eventually, Kosciusco was severely wounded, taken prisoner and sent to Russia where he was held until 1796. Late in that year he was released and returned to America. He located in Philadelphia until 1798 and then returned to Paris.

But passing clouds, that drink the light divine,
    Impair or waste its salutary power:
And when the heavens a deeper gloom conceals,
    And casts o'er earth an universal shade,
No more the hour the darken'd plate reveals,
    Its purpose frustrate and its virtue dead.

So the lost mind, in falsehood's moral night
    Deep plung'd, in vain for happiness inquires;
So *truth's* half-hidden, half-discover'd light,
    Leads to false views and kindles base desires:
Reveal'd, full-seen, *its* bright, unerring ray
Points to the object and illumes the way.

(Composed Septr. 11th 1797.)

Friday, Septr. 15.—Finished, this morning, the valuable Appendix to the XXIInd vol. of the Monthly Review. *Art. XXII.* Klaproth on Minerals &c. Tho' I know very little of Mineralogy, yet I have an earnest desire to obtain a correct knowlege of it, & have so much acquaintance with it as to perceive the importance of this work—the analysis of which, here presented, is not uninstructive. Soon after breakfast Timothy Pierce of Lichfield arrived here. He is to pursue his medical studies, under my direction, the ensuing winter. He brought me letters from my Father, & sisters Abby & Fanny. The principal news is from Aurora. Mary has a daughter, & is very well. I went out to procure Mr. Pierce lodgings. Called on Dr. Miller. We determined, notwithstanding it was a drizzly day, to put our design of visiting Kosciusko in execution. At twelve Dr. & Mr. Miller, Dr. Mitchill, Mr. Baldwin,[57] & myself, got into a carriage, & went to Genl. Gates's.[58] We saw the Washington of Poland—(had the event crowned our wishes) —& one of his companions. I am not certain which. The other was absent. Kosciusko came in, leaning on a crutch, & with one assistant. He is tall, muscular, & his face somewhat thinner than would be expected from his limbs. His complexion is light & delicate, with a slight intermixture of red; his eye blue; his hair short, dark, & unpowdered. The countenance is more indicative of reflection than of fancy, of fortitude than of force. He appears to have been laden with care, & anxiety. The ready flexions of his brow bespeak him to have suffered great & long-continued pain. He recd. numerous wounds, & was confined in a solitary dungeon many months before they were any way cured. Nothing but a most vigorous constitution could have supported him. He has nearly lost the use of one thigh; & a sabre-wound on his head is not yet healed. He speaks english, but not correctly, & with a foreign accent & pronunciation. His demeanor is interesting & proper. We talked of the Comet; & he appeared well versed in Astronomy. A reply made by him to a remark addrest to him by me, marks the simplicity & sincerity of his character. Speaking of his residing again in the United States I said to him—"You will find a great many old friends, & a great many new friends." He returned "that he had made some new friends, whose acquaintance gave him pleasure, but that his principal delight was in the society of his former friends." His companion, who is a young man, & has very much the air of an American, speaks english correctly.

Mr. Webster came to consult me concerning one of his children. I made a medical visit out of town. Went with Mitchill & the Millers, to Mr. Owen's. We were much pleased with his collection of Fossils & of Plants, & spent two hours in looking them over. Mitchill has recd. a very flattering letter from a German Professor of Medicine at Erlangen, by which it appears that his doctrines concerning Septon &c. have attracted some attention & gained him some credit in Germany. The professor appears to have adopted them himself. Miller & I went to Swords's, & gave him materials for commencing the IInd No. of the Med: Reposy.

Drank tea at Mrs. Miller's—where Mr. Pierce is to board. Spent the evening at Riley's; chiefly with Miss Alsop.

To Joseph Strong

Your letter has lain by me, unanswered, several days —not from want of inclination to reply to it, but in the expectation of hearing from you again, as your epidemic varied its appearance & situation. I am sorry to learn that it is fast extending, on all hands; & that the mortality equals that in 1793, if the present emptiness of the city be regarded. This being the case, and you likely to continue where you are, my interest in your welfare & desire of being made acquainted with the progress of the Fever, induces me to request of you not only a reply to this letter, but occasional communications, however short. I shall be glad to hear from you once a week, while the Disease prevails; & I will make you the best returns in my power for your bounty in this respect.

I have no more doubt of the possibility of importation, than you have of the local generation of pestilential diseases. But I suspect the instances of importation are very few; & where the diseases are evidently propagated from the crews of vessels, it appears more probable, to me, that they were generated in the vessels themselves, than that, (according to the vulgar metaphor) the *seeds* of the disorder were taken on board in some tropical sea-port. But *is* it satisfactorily proven that your present Fever, or its Contagion, was imported? Some deny it altogether. Those who believe it are divided as to the vessel, or the means, by which it was introduced. There is, therefore, some uncertainty at the very threshhold of investigation. There always has been. Should not this uncertainty inspire doubt as to the reality of importation? The mere exemption of any place from disagreable smells is not a sufficient proof of its healthfulness. The

---

[57] Probably a resident of Litchfield where he could have been one of several: Ashbel, the Episcopal minister glossed earlier; Eli, who became an Ohio politician; Jehiel, known chiefly for having lived to 102. See Kilbourne, *Litchfield Biography*, pp. 353-354.

[58] In 1790 General Gates freed his slaves and moved from Virginia to Rose Hill Farm about ten blocks south of the present Grand Central Station area.

most offensive odours are not always, perhaps not often, noxious. You will find some curious facts on this point in the Preface to Mr. Jh. John's translation of the New Chemical Nomenclature.

Your treatment is unobjectionable, when called in the commencement of the Fever. It is simple, & well-established. Should you see much of this disease, you will probably be required to prescribe for many other symptoms. You will come to your patient when he has been many days sick, when his head is much affected with coma, or delirium; when hemorrhages burst forth from various parts of the body; when the extremities are cold; & when he has black-vomit. These are all very difficult symptoms to manage. Much debate still exists concerning their proper management. You will observe carefully, I make no doubt, & practice judiciously. Should experience teach you any thing successful, or prove the unsuccessfulness of any proposed remedy, I must beg you to communicate the result to me—for my private information, if you please.

Our friends here are all well; nor have our citizens ever experienced a more healthy summer.

Sept. 16. 1797.
Pine St. 45.   E. H. Smith.

To Ch. B. Brown

Your engagement to write to me soon, again, has restrained my pen for some days. As the Fever appears to be on the increase, I feared that you might have left town, and that my letter, should I write, would remain in the Post Office, instead of reaching the place of your retreat. But my anxiety to learn how you are, & where you are, overcame other consideration. "It is but writing a second letter, when his retirement is discovered"—said I—& I took up the pen.

In the first place, then, where are you? & how do you do? If still in Phila.—whither I now direct—what is the condition of that unfortunate city? To this question, indeed, you may be able to make a sufficient answer, even tho' you may have gone into the country; for you will probably remain in the neighborhood.

The account you have given me of your labours has raised in me a very lively curiosity to see their fruits. Is there no way of gratifying my desire? Can you not safely transmit the copy of this precious Romance? Send it—& make your own stipulations. It shall be returned when you please. It shall be shewn to as many & as few as you shall direct. It shall receive general, or particular criticism, or none at all, as is most agreable. But you do not so much as inform me of the nature of this performance: whether it be something altogether new, or the continuation of some one of those plans which occasionally occupied your mind while here. Be more communicative.

I have a similar desire to see your continuation of "Alcuin." In this, at least, I am not singular. Mrs. S. Johnson has read the 1st & IInd parts, & is anxious to know how all this is to end. She commends the performance, on the whole—particularly the style; thinks there is much truth delivered on either side of the debate: but is at a loss to know what is the writer's ultimate design. From what she has seen, she infers his object to be to render women satisfied with their present civil condition. I can not pretend to enlighten her.

I do not hear any thing from Dennie. I do not know that my first letter ever reached him. I have written again; & shall communicate the result, as soon as known. Meantime, "Alcuin" rests with me.

You speak of other works by the Author of "Emma Courtney." Did you misapprehend me, or do you know of others by the same hand? If you do—what are they? I presume you have seen this Novel, or the Review of it, before now. I shall omit, of consequence, any further account of it, than that it is written by a woman who appears to have studied Godwin, Holcroft, &c. with assiduity; & who has produced a fine exhibition of the miseries of an improper indulgence of love in a mind not otherwise far remote from what it ought to be. To say more, if you have read a criticism on it, is useless; & if you have not, may weaken the effect of the Novel upon your mind. Enquire after & read it.

Your love-project cost us some tears—from laughter. It will perish where it was engendered.

I do not think indolence a sufficient justification of your silence towards Dunlap. The longer its duration, the more difficult the remedy.

My sister Mary has a daughter. She was in fine health, with her new relation, & all her family, a month since. The same is true of all friends at Lichfield, Hartford, Middletown, & here.

Love & Respect to those with you. Adieu.

Sept. 16. 1797.
Pine St. 45.   E. H. Smith.

Saturday, 16.—Read the Herald. Dunlap came here, & we went to see the progress of the New Theater, from the north side of which, on the roof, we were presented with an unexpected & pleasing prospect. Descending, we walked a few miles out of town, & collected some flowers. On my return I made vain attempts to discover the names of three of them. I could not even satisfy myself as to their Classes. After dinner I wrote the preceeding letters to Brown & Strong. Mr. Boyd came in. He has just returned—& Mr. Kent of course. They are & have been well. Recd. a letter from Charles Chauncey Jr. of New Haven—& went to my printer's to make some inquiries in consequence. Johnson & I drank tea at Mr. Morton's—by invitation. We expected to have met Mr. & Mrs. Merry there, but were disappointed. Mrs. Merry plays tonight—contrary to custom: saturday evening not generally play-night. Johnson went to the Theater. I made a medical visit & then went to see Mr. & Mrs. Kent. They seem pleased with their journey. Mr. Kent gave me a rapid account of it, according to his usual method. They are very well.

In the course of the day I have read several articles in

the XXIIIth vol. of the Monthly Review Enlarged. *Art. I.* Beddoes on Demonstrative Evidence. I have read the work, which merits all the praise here bestowed on it. The plan of teaching by the senses is both ingenious & just—& in this method I have little doubt of the practicability of imprinting, in an intelligible manner, the minds of children with mathematical principles. *Art. XIV.* Murphy's Tacitus—concluded. I read, sometime ago, the preceeding part of this criticism—which should be read with the work itself. I am very desirous of perusing Mr. M's translation—but, with many other valuable performances, it must remain untouched by me, for a long time yet to come.

Sunday, 17.—Transcribed the preceeding letters. Gahn called & desired me to accompany him to see Kosciusko. I went. The day was remarkably pleasant. The same Pole was with him to-day. His name is Nemochivitch—or so pronounced. I was equally interested in them this visit as the first. I left Gahn there, & returned. Visited at Riley's. I found her mother, Mrs. Alsop & brother, Josh. Alsop[59] there. Dined, & spent the afternoon at Seth Johnson's. Medical visit. Drank tea at Woolsey's. Spent the evening at Dunlap's. W. Johnson was there also. Webster was here in the morning, & I was at Catlin's a few minutes.

Monday, Septr. 18.—Wrote a few lines to Ch. Chauncey Jr. of N. Haven. Dunlap here, twice; a few minutes each time. A medical visit. Another. A third, to Mr. Webster's at Corlaer's Hook. A fourth, at Mr. Woolsey's, on my way home. A fifth, at the last house in Broad Way. All this occupied my time till late dinner. After dinner, I read several articles in the Monthly Review Enld. vol. XIII. *Art. XVI.* Foot on Lues Venerea. I have been in the habit (perhaps unjust) of thinking lightly of this winter. The criticism now read will induce me to look over this work when time & an opportunity favor the design. *Art. XVII.* West's Discourse to the Students of R. A. This article is pleasing, & the principal extract full of good sense. *Art. XVIII.* Pennant's life. It was a singular whim that produced this publication, which, as well as all other of this author's works, I desire to read. *Art. XXI.* Memoirs of the Manchester Society—Vol. IV. P. I. This appears to be a very respectable collection of papers, & to support the character acquired by preceeding volumes. Hitherto I have not had it in my power to do more than look at the outside of them. I hope before the end of the year ensuing, to be able to consult them at pleasure.

The City Library was now open. I repaired thither, & looked over the account of Syracuse, in the Ancient Universal History. What is said on the Plague which destroyed the armies, especially the Carthinian, at the time of the seige of that city by Marcellus, is very short, & as I think closely copied from Livy. I hastily turned over the histories of several other Sicilian Cities. I suspect that it was customary with the ancients to denominate all epidemic fevers, Plagues. This Syracusan pestilence, by the concurring testimony of several writers, was altogether of local origin.

Medical visit—& drank tea at Ch: Adams's. Medical visit, & spent part of the evening at Riley's. The remainder at Kent's. Boyd & Johnson were there. Came home, & read in Swinburne's Travels in the two Sicilies,[60] from Sect. 41, to Sect. 50—being 50 pages of the Dublin edition. These pages include his account of the journey from Ginginti to Syracuse, & of Syracuse. Tho' the ancient city is destroyed, & very remarkable alterations have taken place in the course of ages, yet the marshes have neither disappeared, nor lost their unwholesome qualities.

Tuesday, 19.—Read Mr. Hamilton's Confessions,[61] or his pamphlet of 105 pages, exculpating himself from any political crime in his connection with Reynolds &c.—a pamphlet which, tho' it fully answers his intention, he had better never have written. Medical visit. Various calls & errands which wasted much time. Visit to Dr. Miller. Saw Mr. Goetze, & expect to commence the study of German tomorrow. A medical visit, & a call at our printer's, in the afternoon. We have already printed off the first half sheet of the No. 2. of vol. 1. of the Med: Reposy: Wm. & I drank tea at Mr. Morton's. Mr. & Mrs. S. Johnson were there, & Mrs. Merry. We spent the evening. Mrs. Merry was very sociable, & it was passed agreably. Mr. Owens—the gentleman who has the Collection of Natural History was here in the morning. I have read a number of articles in the same Review as yesterday. *Art XXIII.* Dyer's Complaints of the Poor &c.—a well-intended publication by a worthy man. We have poor-rates in America—perhaps they are collected & applied in a better manner: But the abuses in this City, in this respect, are abominable: Not by expressing the poor, but the citizens; not by feasting the overseers, but from want of capacity or information on their part, & negligence on the part of the Corporation, to do better. *Art. 34.* "A Guide for Self-preservation &c." by Dr. Beddoes—a pamphlet I must send for. *Art. 35.* Pole's Acct. of Fever in Somersetshire 1792—worth considering. February 1794—*Art. I.* Thunberg's Travels—the introductory remarks just: the extracts interesting. As I know little of Japan from any other writer than Thunberg, every extract from his Travels has arrested my attention & gratified. The Salivation from White-lead is an important fact, & adds some weight to Mr. Scott's conjectures concerning the operation of the Nitrous Acid & of Mercurial Salts.

Wednesday, 20.—A visit from Mr. Roulet. Three medical visits in the course of the day. A call from Dr. Wheaton—from Dunlap. I was at Miller's, Mitchill's, &

---

[59] The second son of Richard Alsop and Hannah (Wright) Alsop; younger brother of Richard Alsop the poet.

[60] Henry Swinburn, *Travels in the Two Sicilies in the Years 1777-8-9 and 1780* (London, 1783-1785).

[61] *Observations on certain Documents contained in no.* [sic] *V & VI of "The History of the United States for the Year 1796," in which the Charge of Speculation against Alexander Hamilton, late Secretary of the Treasury is fully refuted.* Written by himself (Philadelphia, 1797).

at Swords's. Visited Mr. Trott,[62] & saw his fine copy of Stewart's "Washington," & some other pictures. Dined at Gahn's—with Mr. Neimschivitz, Mitchill &c.—We sat some time, & afterwards walked on the Battery. Drank tea at Woolsey's. Mr. & Mrs. Dunlap were there. Called on Miller, & we went to Mr. Goetze'—where we found Mitchill, & all proceeded towards the Battery to see the Comet. On the way Mr. Goetze pointed out to us the Star which he supposes to be the Comet. This was considered as Jupiter. To ascertain the matter more satisfactorily, we went to the Museum, to observe the Star thro' Baker's fine telescope. The result was that Mr. Goetze retained his opinion, & Mitchill &c were convinced that it was the planet Jupiter, & that they saw both its belts & satellites. For my part, I am too ignorant to have any opinion.[63]

In the course of the day, I have read a few articles in the Review vol. XIII. Many of them are well, but relate to publications well known, & have no peculiar recommendation to notice here. *Art. XV.* p. 192—"The Minstrel." The story is interesting, & the novel seems worthy of perusal. This note is made chiefly to mark how far I have progressed.

I am dissatisfied with the manner in which my time is spent. Yet the weather is too cool for sitting still, & is fine for exercise; & my mind is busied by numerous petty cares. I hope to be able, ere long, to do something to more purpose.—*Nous verrons.*

Thursday, Sept. 21.—Medical visit. At the City Library, looking over various publications, with a view to the History of the Plague of Syracuse. Read the Article "Marcellus" in Langhorne's Plutarch, with disappointment in not finding any thing on the Plague. Read the original passage in Livy—& looked over Thucydides on the Syracusan War of the Athenians. Two medical visits: one out of town. Call from Webster—& from Mr. Sharples. Read Dr. Priestley's "Considerations on Phlogiston—P. II— pp. 38. Johnson & I walked on the Battery. Spent part of the evening at Riley's: remainder at Kent's. Read several articles in the Review vol. XIII. I have now finished for Feby. 1794—but I see nothing worthy of remark in this place.

---

[62] Mr. Benjamin Trott, a painter of miniatures. See George Gates Raddin, Jr., *The New York of Hocquet Caritat and His Associates, 1797-1817* (The Dover Advance Press, 1953), pp. 7-8. For "Stewart" read "Stuart."

[63] Comment by Arthur R. Upgren, acting director, Van Vleck Observatory, Wesleyan University: "I have been fortunate in finding information about the sky on Sept. 20, 1797. Jupiter was indeed very favorably placed, rising about sunset and dominating the sky all night long. It was by far the brightest object up and the only planet visible until Saturn rose about midnight. There was only one comet visible in 1797. It was discovered on August 14. In mid-August, it was about third magnitude, nicely visible but not conspicuous or eye-catching. By the end of August it had faded below naked-eye visibility. I suspect that it was visible but very unspectacular in even a large telescope of that period. From your description, I'd side unequivocally with Mr. Mitchill for Jupiter because the comet was then invisible from the Battery, and also because belts and satellites are Jupiter's indisputable trademark—easily visible in very small telescopes."

Yesterday Woolsey shewed me a letter he had received from Michael Cunningham. It seems that he has recd. one from me, written in 1795—but none from any other friend. It is a strange performance (this letter) but I must write to him again, & more at large.

Friday, 22.—While shaving, the plot of a Comedy suggested itself to my mind. I traced it on paper. This took up some time; for my hand is slow, & one does not mark out the particulars of a plot in a minute. Some of it has refference to Deckar's (is it not?) two old comedies intituled "The Honest Whore," some scenes of which I read with singular pleasure, two or three years ago, & which have at intervals pressed on my mind & called for a rescue from their oblivion. This is the more desirable as I have conceived a few interesting—to me most interesting—scenes which may readily be grafted on to those I should derive from this venerable poet. I am not satisfied with my plan as it stands. There is no hurry about the matter, & when the whim seizes me I shall attempt to make it more like what I wish.

A medical visit: succeeded by other visits & errands. Dr. Mitchill came to see me. He brought with him his verses on Septon, which he has incorporated into a Letter to Dr. Beddoes. He left both with me: all to read, & the verses to correct. I have read—& must at least suggest corrections—for some of the verses are bad.

Most of the day busied in reading Livy's account, in the original, of the Syracusan War, carried on by Marcellus on the part of the Romans; & Thucydides's history (Smith's translation) of the Syracusan War, sustained principally by Nicias, on the part of the Athenians. My collection of facts, tho' scanty, will be to the point.

Visit from Dunlap. Medical visit. Drank tea at Dunlap's. Evening at the Greenwich Street Theater. "The Country Girl"—& "Rosina."[64] Mrs. Marshall; whom I had never before seen, made her first appearance, in this town, in the characters of *Peggy* & *Rosina.* She is small & delicately formed. Her stage face would be pretty, were it not for a very large mouth, disfigured by teeth ill-cleaned. Her action is pretty good—but every thing is *pettite.* She wants comic force, pathetic simplicity, & musical power & expression. She fell short of my expectations; & tho' she will not prevent me from seeing, she will not attract me to see, plays hereafter. I saw her husband, some winters ago, in Phila. He played *Harcourt* & *Young Belville*—both miserably. He has no qualifications for the Stage. Bernard's *Sparleigh* & Moreton's *Belville* were very well—& Mrs. Oldmixon's *Phœbe,* in the afterpiece. Nothing could well be more wretched than Warren's *Moody.*

Saturday, 23.—Read Mr. Pickering's letter to Chevr: de Grugo—(printed but not yet published—) of pp. 37—8vo. Ably & severly written. Read the news-papers. This is no mean task, & is equal to another such

---

[64] Mrs. Brooke, *Rosina, or The Reapers* (1787).

pamphlet. Medical visit. Visit to Mitchill. Visit from Mr. Owen. Dunlap called, & we went to see Trott; but he was absent. Read part of the article "Nicias" in Plutarch's Lives. Read the History of the seige of Syracuse, by Marcellus, in Rollin's Roman History.[65] & various passages in Cicero's Orations against Vares—relative to Syracuse—& the conduct of that officer there: (in the original). Medical visit. Wm. & I walked out of town: returning, we drank tea at S. Johnson's. H. Johnson & his wife were there. (They returned yesterday from Connecticut)—& Mrs. & Miss Alsop. Medical visit. The evening at Dunlap's. We resumed the Friendly Club. Present—Dunlap, Johnson, Kent, Smith, W. W. Woolsey. G. M. Woolsey has this day gone to Norwich, to marry Miss Howland. We were interrupted, by an alarm of fire, about nine; & tho' it was soon extinguished, none but Johnson & I returned. We finished the evening & came home.

I recd. a letter from Richard Alsop to-day. I learn from a letter to Wm. from his sister, that my mother is at Middletown. Col. Tallmadge brings me word that all are well in Lichfield.

This day the sixth person (that I have heard of) died of Yellow Fever. Some others are dangerously ill. As yet I have heard no pretence of importation. I design to inquire into the facts while yet recent, that no misrepresentation may be practiced hereafter with success.

Two or three days since died at (Long Island) Jamaica—William Martin Johnson, Physician, a young man of promising talents & respectable acquirements: best known, in the literary world, by his translation of Boulanger's "Christianity Unveiled."[66] He is supposed to have been a native of Massachusetts—being rescued by an inhabitant of Wrentham, while quite young, from some Gypsies—& educated by him till the age of 12 or 13. He then passed into a Counting House—where he remained some time (in Boston). He was afterwards a School master on Long-Island—where he studied Physic with Dr. Ebenezer Sage (now of Chatham Connec.); afterwards the Editor of a paper in New York—where he pursued his medical studies. He was one of the Belle Vue physicians in 1795; & had the Yellow Fever. Afterwards he went into the practice at George town, South Carolina. There falling sick, after a lingering illness of many months, he arrived here to die.

Sunday, 24.—Two medical visits. Wm. & I walked on the Battery—visited at Riley's, where we saw John Morton, who has just returned from the country, & then went to H. Johnson's, where I dined. At S. Johnson's in the afternoon: Next at Dunlap's, where I drank tea. Part of the evening at Woolsey's—Medical visit—remainder at home. "The Merchant of Venice" is to be played tomorrow evening. I purpose to see it. I therefore, commenced the attentive reading of this play this morning, & have now just finished, with all the annotations, as it is in Bell's Edition[67]—of XX or XXI volumes.

Monday, 25.—Medical visit. Walked out to Webster's to see his daughter Julia, who is unwell. Returned by the middle road, & visited another patient. Went to the Hospital, to attend a Consultation; but the intended subject of it had run away—so it was not held. While there, I looked over several papers in the Transactions of the American Acad: of A. & S. at Boston. Mitchill & I called at Miller's, to converse on the business of the Repository. It was now dinner time. Transcribed my paper on Mania cured by Mercury; & went with it to our printer's. Looked over several works, in expectation of some facts to my purpose, in my essay on the Syracusan Plague—but found nothing. Medical visit. Drank tea at Kent's. Evening at the Greenwich Street Theater: play "The Merchant of Venice." I was less pleased with it, in the acting, than I expected. I never saw Mrs. Merry play so badly. She was not perfect in her part, (by which the trial scene suffered greatly) & even her voice was not pleasant. In some parts only was she like herself. Cooper's *Shylock* was very well, thro' out: in some parts admirable. Moreton in *Bassanio*, Bernard in *Gratiano*, & Harwood in *Launcelot*, were well: the others, as usual, nothing. The trial scene alone seemed to interest the audience very much: & with that they were interested.

I met at the Theater, Wm. Pitt Beers of Albany. He is here with his wife. They leave us to-morrow or next day.

I read the Reviews (for the Reposy) of Masdeval's, Priestley's, & Adet's pamphlets.[68]

Tuesday, Sept. 26.—Medical visit. Called on Mr. & Mrs. Beers. He was absent. Called on Mr. Owens: he was absent. Dingley came to see me. I went with him to look at a patient—an unfortunate young man—who, having applied to a quack for the cure of a Simple Gonnorrhea, had the running supprest by an improper medicine, which brought on inflammation & swelling of the Penis—to which the quack applied the fresh leaves of Stramonium. This application occasioned the most intense pain for two days—which ended in a mortification of half the Penis. Since then he has bled from the part, & is now in the utmost hazard of loosing his life. Dingley was called to him, in this condition. The Carrot & Yeast poultice seems to have arrested the

---

[65] *Histoire Romaine* (Paris, 1738) (Trans. 10 v., London, 1739-1768).

[66] This was probably the New York edition published in 1795 which, however, does not mention Johnson.

[67] John Bell was a printer, publisher and journalist; he was the owner of *Bell's Weekly Messenger* and one of the founders of the *Morning Post*.

[68] Jose Masdevall (*sic*), *Medicamens et Précis* (New Orleans, 1796); of a multitude of publications, Joseph Priestley's pamphlet with a publication date nearest to the date of the "Diary" entry, *Considerations on the Doctrine of Phlogiston* (Philadelphia, 1796) or, possibly, *Letters to Mr. Volney* (Philadelphia, 1797); Pierre Adet, *Authentic Translation of a Note from the Minister of the French Republic to the Secretary of State of the United States* (New York, 1796). This pamphlet appeared in French in Philadelphia with the same date.

progress of the sphacelus, but there is reason fear that the man will bleed to death when the sound parts separate from the diseased.

When I came home, I found Mr. Beers here. He stayed an hour. I then walked out to Mr. Sharples's, the Painter's—according to appointment; & sat for my picture—which is to be added to his collection. He drew me in profile—& tho' the piece is unfinished, it is said to be like me. To my eyes the resemblance is not as great as in Dunlap's picture. Perhaps it will be better, when finished, than it is now. Mitchill arrived about half after two. He sat half an hour, for the finishing of his portrait—begun some days since. The likeness is not very perfect.

Mr. Robertson (formerly Dr. Stark of Bath, Engl.) & his lady arrived, & with us, constituted the dinner party. She appears a very amiable agreable woman. He is a man of good understanding, spirit & taste: rather too much of a frenchman in politics, & man of the world in morality. We stayed till sunset—& all rode in together. I went to Mr. Kent's—where I spent most of the evening. I found Mr. Beers there—& Mr. Boyd came there.

On my return, read several articles in the Monthly Review Enl. vol. XIII—March. *Art. 1.* Malone's Shakespere—concluded. This is a very ingenious article & I admire the correct decisions of the critics. In one instance, where they differ from Malone, I think a slight alteration in the punctuation of the text as he gives it, would at least remove all obscurity, & allow the words to remain unaltered. This is in "Measure for Measure," Act 1. Sc. 5.

Isab. Sir, *mock* me not: your story.
Lucio. Tis true. I would not, (tho tis my familiar sin &c)
. . . . play with all virgins so.

The reviewers would substitute *make* for *mock*, & remove the colon. This may be right: but as I punctuate it, the sense is clear. "Tis true—you are right—I ought not to mock you, I ought to relate my story—nor, tho' it is my practice to jest &c. yet I would not do as with all maidens; & in regard to you, I hold you as a person so pure & excellent, that I ought to converse with you, as with a saint." *Art. III.* D'Israeli on Anecdotes: a wholesome lesson to our ingenious writer. *Art. IX.* Fowler on Animal Electricity. A fair representation of a valuable essay, which I read some time ago, with great pleasure. *Art. X.* Letters from Drs. Withering &c. to Dr. Beddoes. A pamphlet out of print, which I am desirous to possess.

I read, this morning, the MS. Review of Dr. McLean's Reply to Priestley. It will answer.

Some noise has been made, within these few days, on the subject of Yellow Fever in this city. It is certain that several persons have died with it—after suffering by it, in an extraordinary degree. These persons appear to have had no connection with each other, or with any common source of contagion. The disease seems wholly sporadic. As no pretence is yet made, as far as I have heard, of importation, it is the more important to note the facts, as they occur, that no misrepresentation may be palmed on the public, hereafter. I shall note, as I am correctly informed of each case.

Yellow Fever—New York—1797.—1—

Mr. Havens, lieutenant or mate of a vessel from St. Ubes, laden with salt, arrived here about the end of August. All the people on board had been healthy. They continued so. He took lodgings in Oliver St.—attended to unlading & fitting out the vessel again. The vessel lay between the Fly-market & Coffee House Wharves. He felt unwell on Thursday, Sept. 14—more unwell friday, still more Saturday. Sunday confined. He sent for Dr. Zeiss, who administered an emetic—which operated violently. He also gave him Oil of Cinnamon & Tincture of Fetida. He saw him no more. Dr. Dingley saw him Monday night. He was yellow—& had the Black-vomit, with few intermissions. The matter vomited up was very black—mixed with coagulated blood, which sunk to the bottom of the vessel into which he puked. He threw up a great quantity. He discharged by stool like colored matter. He died Tuesday night—the 19th. Those facts I recd. from Dr. Dingley. Oliver St. is a bad street—but not peculiarly so. Nothing in particular has been discovered as the cause of this man's disease: unless his general situation. He was a hearty & full-feeding man.

Wednesday, Sept. 27.—Attended Mitchill's Introductory Lecture; & went with Miller to his chamber afterwards. Visit from W. P. Beers. Medical visit. At our Printer's. The morning & afternoon chiefly employed in making corrections in Mitchill's Verses—for which perhaps he will not thank me. Wm. & I drank tea at Woolsey's. I spent the rest of the evening at Riley's. Read in the Monthly Review Enld. vol. XIIIth —March. *Art. XIV.* Preston's Democratic Rage &c. The extract contains many spirited lines & correct thoughts—better fitted to a didactic or moral poem, than to a tragedy. The two publications concerning Dr. Franklin make me wish to see the more complete collection, so long promised.

Josh. Osborn commenced the study of Chemistry & Medicine.

To Fanny Smith

The length of your letter, & the more than common correctness with which it is written, would have given me greater pleasure had they not been connected with sentiments that I can not approve. Nothing can shew, in a more convincing manner, how unfounded are your complaints than this very letter which contains them. The sole difficulty is evidently in your aversion to mental exercise in composition. Yet, without this, you will probably always remain behind others in improvement, whose faculties are no better, opportunities no greater, & who only excel you in resolution & dilligence. I need not expatiate on this subject. I leave it to you to consider of the frivolousness & unworthiness of the plea you offer.

That you should not reply to the questions proposed to you, some time ago, on moral topics, is not surprising: that indolence which has held you silent on matters which require no previous reflection, may well explain your taciturnity in regard to them. But, I acknowledge, that I observe, with astonishment, that your letter contains no mention of the Sonnets I lately sent you: especially as they had direct relation to the subject of your letter, & were purposely composed for your sake.

You love me! In how strange a manner do you choose to discover it! I write—but receive no answers: I address to you verses after verses—you make no acknowlegement: I do not press you to labour for mine, but for your own advantage—and you deem it sufficient to confess that you are indolent and proud. You can not bring yourself to make such exertions as shall insure success; & you are too sensible of the real cause of your want of success to be willing to shew the imperfect fruits of your partial & capricious attention. Can that love be very strong which produces no effect on the conduct? Or is it a satisfactory evidence of attachment, do you think, for one to exclaim—"I love you, but I am too lazy to give any proof of it"? If that affection you profess for me were really as fervent as you suppose, could it fail of influencing you to the attempt, at least, of conformity to my wishes? You acknowledge their reasonableness; why are they not the guides of your life?

I know not what effect this reproof may have on your mind. Certain I am, that it is from my regard for you alone that it proceeds. It is much easier for me to be silent, than to condemn & censure those I love. Were you really incapable of exertion I should say nothing. But even you do not believe that you are so. It is indolence only that dictates such a confession. Your heart revolts at it, before your pen has consigned it to paper. Act, then, no longer so unworthily of yourself. Apply to some good purpose the talents you certainly possess. Prove by your dilligence that your love is real—that you value my counsels. I wish, no less than you, that you were near me, & could spend the winter in New York. But this may not be; & if it could, it would avail little without a spirit of activity, which of itself, a little more slowly perhaps, will effect every thing.

I shall send you two or three more Sonnets. When you write next, inform me if you have recd. them & those which have already been forwarded.

Thursday, Sept. 28. '97.
Pine St. No. 45.   E. H. Smith.

Thursday, 28.—Visit to Dr. Miller: afterwards to Mitchill, who was out. An hour & a half at the City Library, turning over all the ancient works I could find, in search of information respecting Syracuse; unsatisfactorily. Some time at a Book Store, inspecting Polybius, with like design & like success. Met W. P. Beers in the street, & bade him farewell. He has gone to Albany. In the afternoon, in the City Library again. Read some passages in De Non's Travels in Sicily & Malta,[69] & brought it home with me. Mitchill here—I shewed him my alterations in his verses—which he approved. Dr. Wheaton was here in the forenoon. He is going to Providence—& consigns his patients to me in his absence. We had much conversation on the Yellow Fever, & I read him various manuscript notes relative to the subject. In the afternoon, wrote the preceeding letter to Fanny. Corrected a proof sheet—& went to the printers', to give some directions. Evening, walked out to Mr. Roulet's, where I spent three hours. Returned & transcribed the chief of the verses on Septon &c.—for the Press.[70] There are 140 lines, of which about 50 are mine.

In the course of the day, I have read various articles in the Review—in addition to several read last night, after the notices for the day were written. My. Rev: Enld. vol. XIIIth April. *Art. II.* Cartwright's Journal. I have been much interested in the simple relation of daily occurrences & observations, & desire to examine the work at large. Probably, it will furnish many curious facts relative to the subject of my Medical Essays. *Art. IV.* Trans. R. I. Academy—vol. IV. A respectable publication. *Art. V.* Wood on Stimuli &c. Does not amount to much: *Art. VII.* May on Consumption—the same may be said of this. *Art. IX.* Williams's Poems. In the dearth of good Poetry these Poems may deserve the credit here allowed them. It would be difficult, however, to remember them when read, or to read them twice. How easy it is to imitate! how difficult to invent! how easy to frame verses! how difficult "to build the lofty rhyme"—to

  Scatter, from the pictur'd urn.
  "Tho'ts that breathe, & words that burn!"[71]

To Richard Alsop

Your letter, as is very common for letters, excited mingled emotions: of pleasure, to hear from you at all, so soon, that you & yours were well, & that you had passed a pleasant summer; of regret, that you were still unsettled, resolute to quit your delightful situation, & lost to the Muses & negligent of fame. The copy of verses which you sent me presented me with some hope —short indeed, & perhaps fallacious. They gave me pleasure. Not from novelty of the ideas, but from the happiness with which they are arranged. I do not think that you have preserved all the simplicity of the original; but I know not whether you have not substituted something better. In particular, the Sixth Stanza rather

---

[69] Vivant Denon, *Voyage en Sicile* (Paris, 1788). Published in English under the title, *Travels in Sicily and Malta* (London, 1789).

[70] The poem appears in the second number of *The Medical Repository*, November 1, 1797. Mitchill's verses were based on his belief that there was such a thing as Septon which carried diseases.

[71] Not found.

claims the character of sublimity than of Simplicity. I observe in it, however, an incorrectness which should not pass. "And *endless* Horror &c." How does this epithet accord with the image of being either seated on a throne, or busied in it's erection? For the rest, I pronounce my approbation, & applaud your design of sending them to the editor of the Museum. Why is it not possible to prevail on you to employ your leisure in something still better? in preparing what you have written for the press, or in filling up the grand Scandinavian outline so happily traced.

Who has told you stories concerning my business? I assure you that it is more in promise than in enjoyment; & little every way. Yet I have been here four years. I admire the spirit which dictated the reply of the present Judge Paterson to Mr. Reeve, when the latter visited him, several years ago. In answer to inquiries concerning his success—"I have been in this place," said he—"twelve years, & have not obtained employment equal to my necessary expences; but it is too early to be discouraged." I fear I may find his fortune, but want his magnanimity. If my final success be equal to his, I will not complain.

In respect to the Medical Repository, it is too soon to form any opinion. At present our subscription is small, & not half equal to the expences. It is true we do not yet know the number of subscribers, & it may be greater than we expect; but then we derive no immediate benefit from them, how numerous soever. We never expected to derive gain from this publciation—nor, indeed, desired it. What was most important was to generate a habit of observation & communication among our countrymen, in relation to natural & medical subjects; & if any other persons had undertaken such a work, we had never engaged in it, but would have laboured equally for its success in their hands, as in our own. We intend, should it become a source of any gain, to devote the emolument, whatever it may be, to the distribution of proper instruments in different parts of the country, to aid persons qualified to observe, but unable to purchase the necessary implements. Our first object is to support the work itself. We have very little doubt of gaining a good subscription in the course of one or two years. At any rate, we shall keep up the publication as long as that. Our Second Number is already in the press, & will be ready by the 1st of Nov. as proposed. And, what will surprize & perhaps please you, it will contain a display of Dr. Mitchill's Theory, written by himself, in verse, after the manner of Darwin, & not altogether destitute of merit. If possible, I will send you this part of the No. with this letter: but I rely on your candour.

I have a favour to ask of you, which if it be too inconvenient to grant, you will of course consider as not demanded. I want you to procure for me several *large* specimens—(of from ½ to 3 or 4 pounds) of the Ore from the Cobalt Mine in Chatham, & the Lead Mine in Middletown, together with a few neat pieces of your common free-stone. You can pack them in a Box, & send them round by Water. Whatever expence you may be at I will cheerfully repay. You will further oblige me, if you add a few words of description, concerning the places whence the several specimens are taken: the extent of beds, & quarries, the quantities removed already, the nearness to water-carriage, & the productiveness of the Ores in metal, of the Quarries in money from Sales. At least, send me some specimens, however trifling.

I shall attend to your several requests. A tragedy [of] Schiller's, called "The Minister", I saw by the London Papers, has been lately translated by Lewis, author of "The Monk";[72] I suspect pretty well.

Your friends here all admire your gallantry to Mrs. Kent & Mrs. Boyd. The ladies & gentlemen seem much pleased with their visit to New England.

We are all well, & the town remarkably healthy.

A thousand kind respects to Mrs. Alsop—& remembrances to all friends.

Friday. Sept. 29. 1797.
Pine St. No. 45. N. Y.   E. H. Smith.

To William Buel

I have been expecting to hear from you for some days past, which has prevented me from writing earlier. As I had informed you that your Paper on the Sheffield Epidemic would be wanted by the first of October, I concluded that, if you sent it, it would come about this time. If it be in your power, we should be glad to have you transmit it now; if you have not been able to finish it, we shall expect it for the Third Number. The Second is already in the press; & we are printing of the second sheet to-day. It will be ready by the time; & will contain a greater variety of matter than the First.

When you write next, please to send me the names of such subscribers as have made payment; & hereafter the names, as they pay. We design to give a list of subscribers, with the Fourth Number. In respect to the Ontario subscribers, I hope that you did not neglect to make the proposition to them, which I made to you. I think it will take some unnecessary burthen off from your hands, & diminish trouble on all sides.

I shall send you copy of Bay's Dissertation by the first private conveyance; & if you have not recd. a copy of Mitchill's publication on Soap & Candle Manufactories, will forward one of them also. If you can contrive to sell the volume of Zoonomia which you have, I think you will do well to purchase a set uniformly bound. If the subscriptions for the Botanic Garden are returned within two months, it will be sufficiently early.

How stand opinions in Sheffield, this year, respecting the *origin* of their Fevers? I wish you may not neglect to note the circumstances of the ponds & marshes, in your neighborhood; the state of vegetation; health of animals; & the symptoms &c. of your present fever. Comps. to Mrs. B—

Sept. 29. 1797
Pine St. 45.   E. H. Smith.

---

[72] Matthew Gregory Lewis, usually called "Monk" after his play of that name.

Friday, Sept. 29.—Read the article Syracuse, in De Non's Travels—pp. 60—A visit from Dunlap. The success of Hodgkinson's Farce, in Boston, has raised the spirits, as it has mended the affairs, of both. At the printer's. Corrected a proof-sheet. Visited Mr. Owens. Called on Col. Tallmadge, who was out. Wrote the letters to Alsop, & Buel. Transcribed the two last, & Sonnets VI, XI, & XII—to be inclosed in my letter to Fanny. Continued the reading of the Mony. Rev. Enld. vol. XIIIth—April—*Art. XII.* Sinclair's Statistical Account of Scotland. The extracts, which form the principal part of this article, are very interesting, & well drawn up. *Art. XIV.* Epigrams of Martial—very well. *Art. XV.* Love's Frailties: the criticism well—the extract admirable. I never saw more exquisite playing than Mrs. Pownal's *Nannette*.[73] Drank tea at Dunlap's. We went to the Greenwich Street Theater. "Othello." I was disappointed, in the first place, by not seeing Cooper in *Iago*: part, by finding Fennell not equal to my expectations in *Othello*. Still he was generally better than Hodgkinson. His voice appeared much more defective now, than in *Zanga*;[74] his gesture too uniform & huge (if I may so express myself) particularly in the first Act. He was not always correct in the words—sometimes, most inharmoniously inserting a syllable too many; & he did not always appear rightly to apprehend the meaning of his author. *Iago* & *Emilia*, were played too badly to speak of. Bernard's *Roderigo* was very well. Moreton's *Cassio*, except in the drunken scene (where he was excellent), not equal to Tyler's: neither of them very good. Mrs. Merry was all that could be wished in *Desdemona*; & she convinced me that Mrs. Johnson played it very well, last winter. I did not stay to see the "Romp": Mrs. Marshall must be very unequal to it—nor is the Piece any where in America, so well played as by our own company.

I met Dr. Hicks at the Theater. From him I recd. the following facts respecting a Case of Yellow Fever, in which he has been lately concerned, with Dr. Tredwell;[75] who was first employed.

Yellow Fever—New York—1797—No. II

A man of the name of Wiggins, died about ten or eleven, night before last, with this disease. He was seized with it on the 20th or 21st. He lived & kept a grocery Store, at the last building, at the right hand, Fly-market—over one of the most offensive Slips in town. He was exceedingly Yellow—bled from the nose & gums—& vomited for some days, matter as black as ink. His stomach was so irritable that, at best, he puked only from taking a teaspoonful of barley-water. He was bled only once, a small quantity, on the 2nd or 3rd day of his attack. A blister over the stomach seemed to increase its irritability (in common language) or sensibility—Darwin. The physicians tried to excite gentle sweats, & kept the bowels open. The reason assigned for not repeating the bleeding was, that his pulse seemed to fail, during the flowing of the blood.

[Omitted here, three manuscript pages: "Notes concerning Syracuse. No. 1."]

Saturday, Sept. 30.—Transcribed the letter to Fanny Smith. Composed the preceeding pages of "Notes concerning Syracuse." Recd. a letter from Mason F. Cogswell; which gave me considerable pleasure. A visit from Dunlap. Some part of every day is spent in conversation with Mr. Pierce, on medical subjects. Visited Dr. Miller, where I met Mitchill by appointment, to converse respecting the affairs of the Repository. A medical visit, out of town. At our printer's. A call on our printers. Another one on Mr. Kent. Club night—Johnson's evening—Present Dunlap, Johnson, Kent, & Smith. Conversation on various topics—Theater—Othello— the delicacy of modern taste, in comparison with the times of Shakespere, of Addison—Of the taste of the Ancients—On the Yellow Fever—Health of the City—Topography of it, formerly—City election of to-day. Johnson read Godwin's Essay, in the Enquirer, on Learning. This gave a new turn to discourse. The utility of various kinds & modes of reading were talked about—Kent recounted his late reading—criticism on the political works of Harrington, Al: Sydney, Sir T. Moore, Hobbes, Locke, Hume, Adam Smith, Sir James Stuart, Arthur Young, the Economists, Godwin—on the metaphysics of Locke, Reid, Beattie, D. Stuart, A. Smith, Hume, Godwin, Berkley, Priestley, Jonn. Edwards, R. J. Sulivan—on the improvements made in Historical Writing, not as to Style, but Manner—Historical may comprehend almost all other knowlege—Machiavel & John Adams—value of the latter's Work as a compend of political History—of the ancient writings in our City library—of Gibbon's Geographical Collections—necessity of a perfect idea of the topography of the scene of historical relations. Kent tumbled over the Enquirer—& was much pleased with it—Dunlap read the character of the Priest, in the Essay on Trades & Professions—Johnson those of the trade & Law[y]er: Hence new discussions—altogether confirmatory of the doctrines, as applied to in[di]viduals generally—Kent & Johnson exceptions to the principal censure of lawyers. Mrs. Kent gone to Poughkeepsie—K. goes after her next Saturday, comes back seven or eight days after, so that we shall not have his company for the next two nights.

To Reuben Smith

As you mention having recd. pamphlets, at the same time with the Wine, I conclude that you must refer to the Medical Repository, which, if I recollect, I sent by Moses Seymour Jr.[76]—& suppose your things went up, with his, from New Haven.

---

[73] A character in *Love's Frailties* by Thomas Holcroft (1795).

[74] Zanga is a character in Edward Young's tragedy, *The Revenge* (1721).

[75] Hicks, one of four doctors of that name in New York in 1797-1798. Dr. Tredwell, either William or his son John, both physicians living at 130 Fly-market St.

[76] Moses Seymour, Jr. (1774-1824) was postmaster in Litchfield and, for a time, high sheriff, son of Major Moses Seymour, one of the most prominent men in the town.

From what I can learn, the first number of the Repository has been as well recd. as we had any reason to expect; & tho' we acquire subscribers slowly, we are tolerably secure of eventual success. We are now printing the Second Number, & it will be out by the exact time. I wish to have this information conveyed to subscribers with you, that they may know that the Work is likely to proceed. I will thank you to send me the names of future subscribers, as they occur. We mean to print a list of subscribers at the end of the volume.

I am much gratified that Mr. Reeve is willing to communicate the facts respecting the Robin—which are more curious than those to which I particularly referred to—for I think I did not misapprehend you. Did you not inform me that a number of birds built on the pine tree, before your house, & drove a Robin that used to build there away? & that after they were chased from the tree, she came back & constructed her nest as usual? It was a correct & circumstantial statement of these facts that I requested. The communication from Mr. Reeve will be additionally desirable & pleasing.

I have heard nothing from Aurora, but in your last letter, for a very long time. I think some of them must have written, & more than once, & their letters miscarried. I hope soon to hear from them.

We continue healthy. All our friends remember you. My best love to my mother.

Sept. 30. '97.
Pine St. 45.   E. H. Smith.

Industry of September 1797

Reading

Pennants "Arctic Zoology"—4to.—edit. Lond. pp. 15.
Mr. Hamilton's Vindication &c.—8vo. close print—pp. 105.
Monthly Review—equal to two vols.
Nicholson's Journal—No. 1 & II—a few papers.
Priestley's Reflection's on Phlogiston—P.II. 8vo. pp. 38.
Mr. Pickering's Letter to Chev. Yurjo—8vo. close print—pp. 37.
The Merchant of Venice—with Annotations—Bell's Edit.
Trans. of Amer. Acad, of Arts & Sciences—several papers.
Files of the Moniteur & of several London papers.
Ancient Universal History—relative to the seige of Syracuse by Marcellus.
Swinburne's Travels—the journey to, & account of Syracuse—8vo. pp. 50—Edit. Dub.
Langhorne's Plutarch—article Marcellus.
Dryden's—Do.—art. Nicias.
Smith's Thucydides—all that relates to Syracuse particularly—
Livy—(original) the War of Syracuse, Marcellus general of the Romans.
Cicero (original) concerning the conduct of Verses in Syracuse.
Rollin's Roman History—War between Roman & Syracusans &. under Marcellus.
De Non's Travels—(translation)—account of Syracuse—pp—60—8vo.

Writing

Composition

Letters, copies herein preserved .... pp.	13.
Concerning Utopia	22.
On the Elk, Yellow Fever, & Syracuse	5.
Summary, Conclusion vol. 1, Proem Vol. II	7.
Sonnet	1.
Plan of a Play & Verses, not here preserved	5.

Transcription

Letters, Sonnets, & Verses .... equal to ...	20.
Case of Mania	7.
Index making &c.	13.

My Memoirs for the Month September are comprized in 71 pages.

MEMOIRS. 1797. OCTOBER.

Sunday, 1.—Last evening I wrote the letter to my father. This morning made out the table of Industry for the last month. In the course of the day, read 188 pages in the second edition of Caleb Williams—a work I never open but with increased admiration. At two Wm. & I went to S. Johnson's, where we remained till near nine. The time was chiefly spent in conversation, only interrupted by the reading of "Alcuin—a Dialogue"—but the conversation was too desultory to admit of abridgement.

Monday, 2.—Read pp. 42 in De Non's Travels—from Syracuse to the end of the volume. I found a few remarks to my purpose. Finished the Mony. Rev: Enld. vol. XIII for April. *Art. 37.* "Letters & Essays, moral & miscellaneous." By Mary Hays. From what I see here, the author afforded some foretaste of the spirit with which she has since executed the novel of Emma Courteney. Visit to Dr. Miller. Read the Phila. & New York papers, for some days. Consulted at my own room. Medical visit. Called on Mitchill. We went together to the Hospital, where our term of service this day commenced, & inspected the condition of House, & made a division of the patients. Mitchill introduced me to Professor McLean of Princeton[77]—a younger man than I

---

[77] John McLean was born in Glasgow in 1771 and entered the University there before he was thirteen. In 1791 he earned a diploma to practice surgery and pharmacy. He left for the United States in 1795 and soon became an acquaintance of Benjamin Rush. Rush advised him to settle in Princeton which he did. Shortly thereafter he was chosen professor of chemistry and natural history at the College of New Jersey. In 1797 he was made professor of mathematics and natural philosophy. He was said to have been for some time the only professor in the college except for the president. Smith was particularly interested in him because while in Paris McLean had been indoc-

expected. A medical visit. When I came home, I found here Mr. Sharples (the Painter). Mrs. S. is unwell, & he wished advice &c. I gave him some medicine. Dunlap came in. I left him here, & went to Miller's, to meet him & Mitchill on business of the Repository. Miller read us his Paper on Abstinence &c.[78] At 4 P. M. Dunlap & I walked out to Mr. Sharples's. Mrs. S. we found much better. Dunlap thinks my picture *like*. Returned to D's to tea. Mitchill there. Came home. Medical visit. Remainder of the evening at H. Johnson's.

[Omitted here, four manuscript pages: "Notes concerning Syracuse, No. II."]

Tuesday, Oct. 3.—The day warm, pleasant, & adapted for sedentary application, was principally devoted to study. I compiled the preceeding pages of Notes concerning Syracuse—in doing which I was necessitated to read not only all parts of the books quoted to this end, but much more in each, to arrive at the exact materials here introduced. A visit in the forenoon, from Saml. Osborn, the Physician at Governor's & Bedlow's Islands: & other interruptions.

In the afternoon, at my printer's—call on Mr. Goetze & on Professor McLean—neither at home. Met Miss Morton in the Street. She accompanies S. Johnson & wife to Boston—day after to-morrow. Drank tea at Charles Adams's. Visited at Mr. Riley's. Miss Alsop & I walked on the Battery—by a very pleasant moon. Called at Mr. L. Coit's—& saw Miss Howland—Miss Susan Howland—Miss Abby Howland, who was here last winter, was married to Geo: M. Woolsey on Tuesday Sept. 20th ulto. Miss S. Howland is pleasing in her appearance: this was all that I had opportunity to discover.

Came home: looked over several passages in Swinburne's & De Non's Travels—particularly the description & history of the Papyrus & the Manna-bearing Ash, in the latter.

Medical visit in the afternoon.

Wednesday, Oct. 4.—Wrote a few lines to Mr. Quincy of Boston.[79] Transcribed the letter to my father. Read various NewsPapers. A call from Dunlap. At the City Library near two hours—in search of additional Notes concerning Syracuse; but was able to find very few to my purpose. Prescribed at the Hospital. A medical visit. A very cold & every way uncomfortable afternoon. I felt unable to pursue any regular occupation. Read various articles & indeed finished the Monthly Rev. Enld. Vol. XIII. Appendix— *Art. VII.* Voyage dans les departments de la France &c. This is an account of the continuation of a very pleasing work—which no doubt contains as much to amuse as to instruct. *Art. X.* Physico-Chemical Inquiries—Mem. III. A very valuable article—I am very desirous to obtain all the Memoirs of these Chemists. *Art. XVII.* Trav: among Kalmuchs &c. an useful & entertaining abridgement, worth possessing, of the large works of [Gmelin?], Pallas, &c. *Art. XVIII.* Scherer on the breathing of vital air. This excellent publication has been superseded by the later & more extensive publications of Dr. Beddoes. The Asiatic Researches I have already read; & I have not noticed the Transactions of the St. Petersburgh & Göttingen Societies, as part of the papers seem of little value —& most of the remainder are unintelligible to me. Drank tea & spent the evening at Dunlap's. Geo: M. Woolsey there at tea: arrived with his wife, about noon: she at her sister's in Greenwich St. Night stormy. Very high wind.

Thursday, 5.—Commenced Darwin's Zoonomia, & read to the 30th p. vol. I. I design to form a regular & careful analysis of this work as I proceed; but this morning was so extreme cold that I shall defer this part of my plan, till I get my winter's wood home, & can have a fire. Made various calls—particular to see the new-made Mrs. Woolsey. Dunlap here. We agreed to go out to Mr. Sharples's in the afternoon. Mr. Goetze called to see me. He is quite melancholly. Saw Mr. Deming in Lichfield. Dunlap & [I] walked out to Sharples's. He & his wife were just going out to dine. We continued our walk, which was remarkably pleasant. Returned & drank tea at Dunlap's & spent part of the evening with Mr. Deming at his lodgings, part of it at Kent's, & part at home. Began the Monthly Review Enl. vol. XIV. May 1794—*Art. 1.* Aikin's Letters to his Son —the remarks of the critics are few & liberal; the numerous extracts judiciously selected. Some exceptions, or rather limitations, occurred to me, on the subject of *strength of character.* They must be reserved to a future opportunity. Art. II. Cogan's Journey down the Rhine. The specimens very lively & entertaining; & the commendations apparently merited.

[Omitted here: "Notes concerning Syracuse III."]

Friday, 6.—Continued the reading of Zoonomia, & have advanced to p. 62. Called on Dr. Mitchill. Prescribed at the Hospital. Medical visit. Recd. a letter from Josh. Strong. He has had the Yellow Fever severely—but is now convalescent. Finished the Mon: Rev: Enld. for May '94. *Art. IV.* Med: Facts & Obs: appears to be a useful publication. Dr. Boag's testimony in favor of Calomel is most immediately pertinent to us. *Art. VII.*—Mrs. Robinson's Widow—a Novel. The reviewers have uniformly discovered an unmerited partiality for the writings of this fair but frail author. *Art. VIII.* Valli on Anm: Elecy. I comprehend too little of the subject, notwithstanding all I have read upon it, to derive much benefit from this author's experiments— the remark, however, concerning the corpses of those who died with the Plague of Smyrna, I think important.

---

trinated in the antiphlogistic theory, Lavoisier's new theory of chemistry. Dr. Samuel Mitchell was also persuaded that the new theory was correct and Smith came to believe in it as opposed to the theories of Dr. Priestley.

[78] If Miller is the Reverend Samuel Miller, the paper could well be one of his many published untitled sermons.

[79] Josiah Quincy, cited earlier, a man who in breadth of interest was very like Smith.

Art. IX. Cartwright's Journal—I resumed with pleasure the continuation of this interesting article, & much desire to possess the entire work. *Art. XI.* Trans: of the Socy. of Arts &c.—the extracts useful. *Art. XII.* Russell's treatise on the Plague—a work which undoubtedly contains much good information, but less than any late medical publication I have ever seen, of the same size. There are wonderful omissions in it—for instance, the local peculiarities of Smyrna, diet of the people & a thousand such physicians might exist & perish without rendering mankind any essential services. It is astonishing that a man in his situation & with the opportunities presented to Dr. Russell, should make no attempts towards the discovery of an efficacious treatment of so formidable & frequent a disease. *Art. XIII.* Philos. Transact. R. S. Lond. I see nothing here but Mr. Young's paper on the Eye, & the acct. is too brief.

Wm. & I walked on the Battery. We drank tea & spent part of the evening as H. Johnson's—the remainder at home. S. Johnson & his wife & Miss Morton sat off yesterday for Boston.

Saturday, Oct. 7. Read to 77th p. of Zoonomia. A visit from Dr. J. R. B. Rodgers. A visit from Dr. Miller. Greater part of the day occupied in moving into this southerly room, from the northerly one in which I have hitherto been. This is pleasantest for the winter—that for summer. Met several of the Faculty of the Hospital at Dr. Rodgers's, concerning some business of that Institution. Club evening—W. W. Woolsey's night—Johnson & I repaired to his house. Kent out of town—G. M. Woolsey "had a wife & could not come"[80]—Dunlap had not arrived, after waiting an hour. We adjourned. I called at Dunlap's. He had been detained by company. I spent the evening with him.

Monthly Rev. Enld. vol. XIV—June 1794. *Art. I.* Sulivan's View of Nature &c. I have read three volumes of this work. The review of it here given was perhaps merited. It, however, deceived me into an expectation of something much more valuable than I found. *Art. II.* Moore on the Mat: Meda.: a sensible Essay. *Art. III.* Lettice's Tour in Scotland—the extracts very pleasing—apparently but little valuable information in the work.

The week now concluded has been spent very little to my satisfaction. Much time has been wasted in trifling employments, or idleness, which is worse. I hope to keep off the numbing attacks of morning & evening cold a little better, in my new apartment, than in my old.

Sunday, 8.—Completed the removal of my books &c. into this room. Visit to Mr. Post (Surgeon & Physician) who has been sick with fever. Called at Dingley's—he absent. Found Dunlap here when I came home. Wm. & I walked on the Battery. We dined & spent part of the afternoon at H. Johnson's. Afterward we, with Dunlap, walked several miles out of town, & being caught by a thunder-storm at his house, on our return, spent the evening there. In the morning & evening continued Mon. Rev: Enld. vol. XIV—June 1794—*Art. V.* Mease on Hydrophobia—I remember to have thought pretty favorably of this Essay when I read it—but I am now less disposed to believe in the soundness of its doctrines. I should be well pleased to see the effect of Mercury fully tried in it, & of Bleeding & other antiphlogistic remedies. *Art. VIII.* Sir H. Englefield on Comets. I read this article with pleasure, tho' I know nothing of the subject. *Art. IX.* Edward's Hist. of Brit. W. Indies—The commendations conferred on this work, in a very elegant & animated style, are justified by the analysis of its contents, & the uncommon beauty of the Extracts. *Art. X.* Biographia Brita. by Kippis &c.—a valuable work: inestimable to every man of Letters. *Art. XI.* Doig on the Savage State—a bad cause ably & virtuously supported. *Art. XIII.* Pettier's Picture of Paris—a publication rather to be read than believed. *Art. XV.* Carey's Acct. of Phila. Fever 1793. a successful catchpenny—with little other merit than what was conferred on it by its first reaching the trans-atlantic nations.

Monday, 9.—Continued Darwin, to the 100th page. Visit from Dunlap. Calls. Medical visit. At the Hospital. Called on Dr. Miller, as I returned. Had fire in my room, for the first time this season. Medical visit. Transcribed the Reviews of Phila. Medical Inaugural Dissertations, in the 1st Vol. of these Memoirs. Drank tea & spent the evening, & supped at Dunlap's—where were Mr. & Mrs. Coit—Mr. & Mrs. G. M. Woolsey, Mr. & Miss Rogers, Miss Howland, Mr. Aspinwall,[81] & Mr. Dwight—& a stupid evening we had of it. Read several articles in the Review, in continuation. *Art. XVII.* Robertson's Tour thro' the Isle of Man—worth possessing—the tale of Ivar & Matilda romantic & well-told. *Art. XVIII.* Mayo's Chronological History of the European States—a very useful dictionary—& for the most part (if we may believe the reviewer) well executed.

The weather cool, but seasonable. Town healthy.

[Omitted here, six manuscript pages: "Zoonomia."]

Tuesday, Oct. 10.—Began Zoonomia anew, & in the course of the day have proceeded with the reading of the notes as above appears. I hope by this exercise to familiarize myself with the author, & with this work, so that I shall be able to form a correct & perspicuous analysis of his doctrines in a moderate compass. The event will determine. Medical visit. Visit from Dunlap—At an auction of French Books one & a half hour. Saw Mr. Roulet there. Visit from W. W. Woolsey. Visit to Mrs. Gurdon Mumford—part of the evening at Riley's—remainder at home. Finished Mon. Rev. Enld. vol. XIV—number for June 1794. I see nothing to be particularly noticed here, concerning the remaining articles.

This day has been quite cold; nor is the evening less

---

[80] "I have married a wife, and therefore I cannot come." Luke 14:20.

[81] Gilbert Aspinwall was a merchant, 207 Pearl St., *New York Directory*, (1796).

severe. I hope it may operate some healthful change in Phila.

[Omitted here, three manuscript pages: "Zoonomia, contd. II."]

To Mason Fitch Cogswell

The reception & perusal of your last letter gave me uncommon satisfaction. I feel a glow of pleasure pervade my whole frame on reading it over, & reflecting upon it. I gain some sweet assurance from it that my friend will cease, has ceased to be unjust towards me; that he will patiently receive from me this imputation of past injustice—certain as I trust he now is, or soon will be, that as I have never experienced any diminution of the fervor of my love for him, so I did not merit any declension of his friendship for me.

It must, most certainly, have arisen entirely from an expectation that I would be cold towards you, that you have ever thought me actually so. Feeling for you an unabated esteem, my subject only could have caused any difference in the style of my late addresses to you, from those of former days. With me, as no change was felt, none, in appearance, was suspected. And now, when I look over such copies of letters to you as I have chanced to preserve, I am at a loss to discover how I could have expressed myself more your friend, without mingling formal, & as I hope unnecessary protestations of affection with scientific or every day concerns.

In the infancy of friendship, while we are but imperfectly known to each other, it is natural for us to enter into lively & minute discussions of the grounds of rational esteem, & to give language to those emotions which are associated with the sentiments we entertain & promulge. But, in proportion as each becomes satisfied of the rectitude of the others opinion & the cordiality of his professions, such discussions & such declarations are deemed unnecessary, & accordingly give way to more general conversation, or more minute information. Satisfied that as we love we are beloved, that him we suppose our friend is such in reality, we proceed from the considerations which have fixed him such, to those acts of confidence which spring out of our relative situations; which form the bands, & constitute the delights of this endearing & consoling union. Thenceforward renewed expressions of love become the accidental growth of the occasional theme of our letters, & cease to be looked for as essential parts of every communication. A better evidence of its sincerity & continuance is generally supposed to be afforded in the unrestrained intercourse which ensues, & in the readiness with which we impose & undertake the various commissions of each other. I appeal to your own experience whether this is not the common progress of friendly correspondence—I appeal to your own good-sense if it ought not so to be.

Make this then, the rule by which my letters are to be examined. Ask yourself how it was possible to write to any one with more freedom; & with what grace paragraphs of business & of science would have mingled with glowing protestations of unchangeable regard.

Our first letters were almost exclusively devoted to friendship. I do not recollect the expressions they contain; but I venture to assert that they were faithful pictures of my mind, & that they leave nothing to be desired in respect to fervancy of affection—From this subject, engaged as we then were in the tastes of the Muses, we proceeded to poetical & literary topics. Our own verses occupied our thoughts, & many pages of our letters were filled with minute statements relative to various plans & matters of business which were occasioned by them. An interval followed, which was filled up with personal communications, amid which our attachment continually fostered, continually increased. We were again separated. The sallies of imagination had now principally ceased, & were well supplied by the graver & more important toils of science. Plans, as before, flowed out of these new employments. As before, they constituted much of the business of our letters: improvingly so, as I thought: nor did I suspect you of thinking otherwise. Enough had been given to profession, enough consecrated to the causation & confirmation of that friendship by which we were united—it was time to reap the benefits it was fitted to bestow. Look at our literary, & look at our scientific correspondence —compare the letters of 1790, & 91—with those of '95 & 96—if you retain them, & point out their differences. I have no copies of those of the former period, few of those of the latter. Yet I am bold to assert that, if any differences are apparent in respect to expressions of friendship, they can only have arisen from this circumstance, that protestation of love became every day less & less necessary, as time added strength to our mutual esteem, & discovered the solid foundations on which it rested.

It were easy to trifle on this subject, & to expose by ludicrous example the strange combinations which inquiries concerning diseases, & remarks on medical publications & subscriptions for medical works, would have formed with rapturous expressions of passionate attachment & glowing descriptions of the pleasures of friendship as for instance—"Be assured, dearest of friends, that while a dreadful epidemic hurries thousands of Cats to untimely death, my friendship for you suffers no abatement. The mortality which surrounds me, operates but as a caution not to forego present opportunities, but to taste with eagerness the joys of amity ere I fall the victim to some similar disease. I trust, most beloved of men, that your attention to the progress of this extensive epidemic will be surpassed only by your zeal for the interests of our love, & that the accuracy of your description of the one will be equalled only by the sentimental evidences of the other. You are a subscriber for Zoonomia—O! my friend, when you read that immortal work, may it remind you that we also are physicians, that we also have sought to gain the favours of the Nine, & may we strive to conciliate the regards of

Phebus in his twofold capacity. My best of friends—I hope the subscription for the Medical Repository is successful. How I shall rejoice to see our names united in it—fit emblem of the sacred passion which more strongly unites our souls." But enough of this nonsense. Seriously then—you must have imagined formality in my letters, because you conceived it impossible for me to pressure my friendly feelings amid changes in metaphysical opinions, or you must have been inattentive to the progress of all correspondencies among friends.

In the last case, I have only to appeal to your own reason. In the former, to fact. Imagining that formality & coldness would happen, it was not difficult to find them. You referred only to the first expression of a new-formed alliance, & forgot all the subsequent course of correspondence. I wish not to obtrude upon you those opinions which may be different from yours. Yet I can not but remark that had you been acquainted with the actual state of my mind, you would have seen that those changes of sentiment of which you speak could no other way affect any interest in you, than by increasing it. Augmenting my love of mankind in general, & of each individual in the proportion of his virtues, I could not fail of appreciating still higher the value of those friends whom I may aspire to equal, but dare scarcely hope to surpass. Seeing in them bright & glowing examples of excellence difficultly acquired & rarely attained, I felt my bosom warmed with a deep admiration & my heart yearning towards them with a profounder passion. Virtuous & amiable in this degree by the effect of early habit & indistinct conceptions of the extensive science of morality, what would they not have been—I have exclaimed to myself—animated by a surer code & more comprehensive views! Ah my friend! you know little after all our intimacy, of my heart, little of the principles which actuate it with feeble sway perhaps, but whose truth it fully recognizes, if you could fear an estrangement from you—if you, could apprehend that ever you should become other than you have been —dear to me, & beloved as a brother. Let me throw my arms around your neck & press you to my bosom, in token of my unabated love. Be this letter, & those which have lately passed between us, the second birth of our friendship. Henceforth it is more firmly established than ever. We can not doubt it. Professions shall be deemed unnecessary & our correspondence shall resume it's calm & regular character & march. Farewell.

Oct. 11. '97.
Pine St. 45.   E. H. Smith.

Wednesday, Oct. 11.—Continued the reading of Zoonomia, & made such progress as in indicated by the preceeding Notes (II.) Two medical visits. Prescribed at the Hospital. Visit from Dr. Miller. Called at Mitchill's —he out. An hour or more at the Book auction. Read the Newspapers. Dined & spent the afternoon & part of the evening at Woolsey's.—where were Mr., Mrs. Mr. Jr, & Miss Rogers, Mr. & Mrs. Dunlap, Mr. & Mrs. G. M. Woolsey. Mr. & Mrs. Coit, Miss Howland & Mr. Aspinwall. Remainder of the evening at home. Most of what I executed (of study) done this evening. Wrote the letter to Cogswell.

[Omitted here, four manuscript pages: "Zoonomia, cont'd. III."]

Thursday, Oct. 12.—Three medical visits—one to considerable distance, in the forenoon, one this afternoon. Called on Miller—& on Mitchill at whose room I translated a part of a paper of Fourcroy's, which M. was preparing for the Repository. At our printer's. Forepart of the evening at Dunlap's, where was one of my patients—remainder at home. Continued Zoonomia —& made such progress as appears. Read several articles in Month. Rev: Enl. vol. XIV—July 1794—this & last evening. *Art. 1*. J. E. Smith's Sketch of a tour on the Continent. The extracts are unusually elegant & instructive—little as I know of Botany, they gave me uncommon delight—which was heightened by the biographical information by which the scientific remarks are accompanied. *Art. II*. Taylor's translation of Plato's Cratylus &c. The extract relative to the death of Socrates interested me; the other is curious. The critics lose no reputation by the short introduction. *Art. VII.* A Looking-Glass for a Rt. Honle. Mendicant—contains numerous incongruities, but many spirited & many just sentiments in regard to Xtianity.

Friday, 13.—Medical visit. Called at our printer's, on business of the Repository. Found Dr. Miller here when I returned. We went to the College. Medical visit. Came back to the College. Heard part of Mitchill's Lecture— on Menstrua—first principles &c. Went, with Miller, to his room, on business of the Repository. We visited the monster calf, whose *Heart* is in her *neck*; & were satisfied of the fact. Medical visit. At the Hospital as usual. Medical visit. Another, in consultation with Dr. Seaman. Dined with Dr. Hosack. Dr. Parke of Phila. there. Much medical controversial conversation. Hosack & Parke are Importation folks—Parke & I are bleeders— in Yellow Fever. I have not time, nor is it important, to record the many curiosities of opinion this dinner presented me with. Medical visit. Took tea at Dunlap's. Spent the evening, till nine, at Dr. Wheaton's. He returned, yesterday, from Providence. He gave me much & very interesting communication concerning the Yellow Fever of Providence, Bristol, & Warren. I have little doubt of the local origin, & am satisfied that it is impossible for Hosack, (as he expects) to prove it to have been imported. Wheaton thinks of removing to Providence. We are to converse on this subject—soon. I am flattered with a hope that, in this case, I may receive some increase of business. Medical visit. A busy day— which has not admitted of study. It is now late.

Saturday, 14.—Called up early to see a patient. Most of the day has been spent with him, in conjunction with Dr. Seaman. I have just left him, with very faint hopes of his recovery. Yet this is only the fifth day of his fever,

& he has none of those symptoms which seem to characterize Yellow Fever—in its worst State. The difficulty of bleeding him in the beginning was insurmountable, to any useful degree: and from the want of this necessary evacuation, he appears to be perishing. Was an hour at Dr. Miller's, in the forenoon; & about as long, at Riley's, this evening. He has removed to John Street. This has been a melancholly day to me. Another patient, I recd. word in the morning, was much better, & likely to get immediately well. This evening, I am informed, that she exerted herself too much—being up an hour, for the first time in several days—& is now lower than before. I have prescribed for, but not seen, her.

Abel Beers had complained of a head-ache, (which he was altogether unaccustomed to) for several days. He was a fair-complexioned lad, lively, good-tempered, & active—about 14 years of age. On Tuesday, the 10th inst.—about noon, he was taken with a chill, succeeded by fever, which continued thro' the night. I saw him the next morning, about nine o'clock. He complained of some head-ache—his pulse was a little quick, frequent, & full—his tongue shewed that he had been feverish the preceeding night. He had no sickness at stomach, but he had no desire to eat—he had been costive two days. It may be proper to remark that the weather had been cool, quite cool, for several days, & that he had gone thinly clad, & in a large open store. I attributed his head-ache & slight feverishness to cold & costiveness—& directed a suitable purge of Calomel & Jalap—expecting to hear no more of his illness. The next morning, I learnt that he had had a return of fever in the afternoon, which had continued thro' the night in spite of the operation of the cathartic—which had been sufficiently considerable. I saw him—his head-ache was trifling—his fever more than the preceeding day—but not great. He had eaten nothing of any consequence.— I proposed bleeding. He objected—grew faint—& I was obliged to lay him on the floor, to prevent syncope. His arm was tied up, but no vein swelled. In the mean time both the frequency & strength of his pulse & the heat of his skin were much diminished. I advised to have him put to bed, & postponed the operation for that time. At one P. M. I saw him. His fever was considerable: His skin dry. I had previously sent him a mixture of Tartar Emetic 4 grs. Tincture of Opium X drops—& beat [?] ʒviii—of which he was to take a table-spoon—or ʒss—every hour. This was to be accompanied by warm drinks, if any moisture appeared—& I supposed if it nauseated him, would not injure & might relieve him. When I found it had done nothing—I no longer ventured to defer Bleeding. He objected, & was faint as before; but I opened a vein. With extreme difficulty we supported him till perhaps ʒvii's were very slowly taken away—when no blood would flow—& the arm was tied up. The above mixture was continued. I saw him in the evening. It had puked him, very gently, once. He had taken it, without that effect, twice since: fever higher—no discharge from the bowels—heat of the skin greater. I attempted to bleed him—as he lay, in the other arm. The faintness was almost to complete syncope—& I could only get about four ounces—*guttatim* as it were. I continued the mixture—& ordered another powder of Calomel & Jalap, to be given at bed-time. *Friday morning*. His fever had continued high all night—his skin dry—he restless. His mixture had gently puked him twice—but no irritation of stomach remained. He appeared to have been *flighty* or delirious, in the night. His uncle, who takes care of him, had omitted the purge. It was immediately given—by my direction before I saw him. When I arrived his cathartic had operated freely once; & brought away something like lumped feces. His fever, as on the former days, had remitted at sun-rise. I wished to renew the bleeding, but it could not be done. Water was allowed for drink—milk & apple for food—& he used oranges. At twelve—his purge had operated twice again—but his fever & heat & restlessness had increased; his tongue, which had been white-furred, now had a dry tip, & a dark stripe in the middle—the edges were clean & moist. There appeared in him some disposition to coma. It was agreed to call in Dr. Seaman to consultation. We met at two. The fever & heat increased—the stripe on the tongue larger—disposition to coma greater. His eyes were clear, lively & natural. He had had no more stools.

We agreed to give him alternately—each hour—a grain of Calomel, combined with one eighth of a grain of Opium, & a tea-spoonful of Mindererus' spirit in some water: so that he should take of each once in two hours. We continue his vegetable food—& the washings of the face, hands, breast &c. with tepid water or vinegar & water—occasionally. We met in the evening. Fever & heat rather increased—no moisture—no discharge by his bowels—tongue as before. We omitted the spirit of Mindererus—ordered him to take a pill every hour, & a drachm of Cream of Tartar every hour—& placed a large blister between his shoulders. We had endeavoured to prevail on him to be bled—but he objected to it—& was made sick immediately at the mention; his pulse sunk, his skin grew cool—& he had a desire to puke. When we relinquished the design—all his sickness &c went off—& his disease resumed its course.

Saturday morning. His physic operated freely about IX A. M.—but his blister had been partly slipped off, & had not drawn completely. It was renewed. There was a remission of his fever, but less than heretofore. He was more comatose—& more disposed to incoherent discourse. We resolved to Salivate if possible. In the course of the day more than three ounces of the strongest mercurial ointment were rubbed upon various parts of his body: some of which was, no doubt, absorbed. His Cream of Tartar, being imperfectly dissolved in water, had nauseated him & made him puke. It was discontinued, & the pills of Calomel given every [hour(?)]. He took milk, or some food frequently. He had three or four stools. In the evening we applied a blister to each arm—we rubbed in & laid on his legs, feet & arms, three ounces more of strong mercurial ointment. As he was quite low, Seaman was desirous of giving the Bark, in the afternoon. I objected. He proposed powders of Camomile flowers[82] 15 grs. each every three hours. Unwillingly, I consented. In the afternoon *Abel* had wished for cyder; & small quantities had been given him, mixed with water. He had a very copious stool—but puked while on the chair. What he puked was darkish. His stool was of the consistence & colour of Chocolate with milk in it. He took the powder of Chamomile flowers without difficulty—& we gave 15 drops of Tinct. of Opium, to prevent more discharges. But in the evening the second powder made him puke again—this also was discontinued—but the pills were to be given one every hour. His coma & delirium were increased: His fever & heat greater his eyes & skin slightly tinged with yellow—his pulse variable, but frequent—his tongue dry at the tip—not quite so dark in the middle; He breathed very quickly but at considerable intervals. Seaman was called up at 5 this morning. *Abel* had puked several (four or five) times—in the night—whenever his pills were given him. A little wine quieted his puking. He had a stool early in the morning, which almost caused him to faint—& this was the occasion of Seaman's being called, his uncle thinking the youth to be dying. Indeed, all his symptoms had been worse during the night. We saw him together, at 8 A. M. There was, again, a remission of the fever—& tho' still comatose & incoherent —the youth was more rational & composed than he had been for many hours. We washed all his skin, with tepid soap & water; & renewed three ounces more of mercurial ointment to his legs & arms. He had clean linnen & a clean bed. There seemed to be some disposition to hiccup. We ordered a spoonful or two of milk to be given every five minutes—allowed a piece of orange now & then—& reposed our hopes on the Mercury. In the forenoon his fever seemed less—he was more rational— his stomach did well—& the scurf on his tongue nearly peeled off. In the evening he was more stupid, & more delirious, than ever—we could only get him to take milk by alowing him a little cyder in water—his tongue is red & dry & shining on the end, for an inch or more— the yellowness tho' not great, has increased—heat of the skin rather less—pulse weak & frequent—breathing as before—has had no stool. We continued the Milk, as before: We covered his bowels with Mercurial ointment (two ounces or more) which was kept on—We directed an injection—½c grain of Opium to be given after, lest he should have too many Stools—& we directed a blister to be applied to the pit of the stomach, in case of hiccup or vomiting. The other three blisters have had no decisively beneficial effect.

Abel Beers's Case contd.—After we left him, last evening, he was very restless & wild an hour or two, & refused his milk, & every thing. About nine he had an involuntary stool. Soon after he sunk into a tranquil sleep. About three quarters after eleven, he hiccuped. The Nurse gave him a spoonful of milk, & he was quiet. In about fifteen minutes, he was seized with a vomiting of blood, not only thro' his mouth, but his nostrils, & died about twelve, in a very few minutes after. The corpse, this morning, was yellowish: inclining to purple on the breast, & lower extremities—but perfectly destitute of smell, & all appearances of putrefaction. It is remarkable that he did not complain even of the slightest head-ache on friday, nor ever after; nor of pain any where. When questioned, his reply was that he was better. On the contrary, before he took to his bed, the first or second day of this illness, after eating, after his first cathartic had operated, & indeed constantly, his uniform reply was, that he felt no better. He sat still, & was sober & silent. In short, nothing seems to have affected in any considerable degree, the condition of his disease—which went on uninterruptedly & rapidly to its fatal termination.

Sunday, Oct. 15.—One, two, three medical visits in succession—these, as one of them was at a mile's distance, & the other took up much time, occupied all the day, till dinner—which I took at Dunlap's. Another medical visit. Read several articles in Mon. Rev. Enld. vol. XIV. July 1794—*Art. XI.* Heron's Journey to the Westn. Counties of Scotland—the remarks of the Critics seem candid, & most of the extracts, tho' as proper in almost any other book, as one of Travels, are interesting & valuable. In general, I find the remarks of the writer very consonant to my own opinions. Called at Mr. Kent's. He & his wife &c. have not returned. Visit at H. Johnson's. Medical visit. Remainder of the evening at home. Read, with much pleasure, a number of articles in Selden's "Table-Talk,"[83] which I now saw for the first time. Wrote the preceeding & hurried journal of a patient's case—in which I trust I am sure, there is no material omission—as far as circumstances, (into which I carefully inquired) have come to my knowlege.

Monday, 16.—Medical visit. Made some notes for the title Medical News, in the Repository. Visit from Dr. Miller. At our printer's. Errands. Recd. a letter from Dr. Buel. Medical visit. Had some conversation with Dr. Wheaton in the Street. At the Hospital as usual. Medical visit. Went to Mitchill's & Miller's, on business —both absent. Called at Mr. Kent's—who returned with his family last evening. Medical visit. Visit from Dr. S. Osborn. Wm. & I spent the evening at Mr. Kent's. Miss Bailey came down with her sister. In the course of the

---

[82] Calomel (a purgative), jalap (also a purgative), ipecac (an emetic), and bark (quinine) for the fever were standard remedies for most of the ills of man in the late eighteenth century. If the patient could not recover with the help of these or after bleeding, he was generally out of luck. For those with incurable diseases laudanum sometimes made or helped to make life bearable. Mindererus, a water solution of ammonium acetate, was used to make a patient sweat. Cream of tartar was employed sometimes as a cathartic but it was also used as a refrigerant. Camomile in one form or another was used to make a person sweat or as an antispasmodic.

[83] John Seldon, *Table Talk* (1689).

day have read several articles, & finished the No. for July 1794 of Mon. Rev. Enld. vol. XIV. *Art. XII.* Maurice's Indian Antiquities—The extracts eloquently written—the last two judicious. *Art. XIII.* Weldon on puncturing the Bladder—apparently a correct performance. *Art. XV.* Whitehouse's Odes.[84] The opinions of the critics just. The extracts factitiously excellent. They do not communicate a pure pleasure. The style in general is both redundant and inflated. Notwithstanding, many passages are fine. *Art. 21. 22.* Stewart's Tocsin of Britannia. This man is known to me—& his miserable qualities as an author as here well & wittily exposed. He is no doubt partially insane. *Art. 33.* Balfour on Fevers &c. The whimsical theory of this writer is properly objected to. His practice appears to have nothing new in it. *Art. 46.* Mrs. Robinson's Poems. Again I remark, how tastelessly partial to this lady are the reviewers! Under what a cloud of incongruous metaphors has she obscured a few common & simple sentiments! These Stanzas are despicable. There is much good sense & humour in the manner in which the rest of the rhymers of this month are exposed & ridiculed. —My patient died this morning—& I have not yet recovered the shock. I expected his death—but my anxiety on his account has been very great. The tumult of mind must gradually subside.

Tuesday, Oct. 17.—I designed to devote this day to tranquil study, but have been variously prevented. I have only transcribed a part of my review of Hosack on Yellow Fever, & read a few articles in the Monthly Review. A visit from Mr. M. B. Whittelsey of Danbury, Connecticut. He gave me the most correct & probable account of the cause of the Fever, which has for three years past (or rather summers & autumns) afflicted New Milford, (an adjoining town) that I had before recd. Visit from Dunlap. Another, & a long one, from Dr. Dewees of Phila. He maintains that the Yellow Fever is never Contagious—& of course that it is impossible to import it. Much time occupied in some preparations against cold weather. Visit to Dr. Miller —to Mitchill, who was out—Medical visit. Was at our printer's. Drank tea at Mrs. Miller's—part of the evening at Mr. Radclift's, remainder at Dr. Wheaton's.

Mon. Rev. Enld. August 1794—*Art. 1.* Andrew's History of Great Britain. The extracts are spirited & remarkably entertaining, & the whole work appears to deserve its eulogium. The compliment of Giraldus Cambrensis to Richard Coeur de Lion, who succeeded Henry II. is truly "ingenius." *Mira cano, sol occubuit, nox nulla secuta. Art. III.* Earle on the Stone &c. A very respectable performance of an author now, probably, the first operation in Gt. Britain. *Art. VI.* Memoirs of Dunrourier: entertaining & full of information. The sketch of Roland I have long admired as masterly &, if what is said of his wanting strength of mind, as just. Roland seems to have been almost the only man of his party who had strength of mind. Recd. letter from J. Wms.[85]

Wednesday, 18.—Called on Dr. Dewees, & we attended Mitchill's Lecture—the subject "Light"—after which we spent an hour at his room—& then went to the Hospital—where I prescribed, as usual. We came home by the way of Sword's. After dinner three medical visits, two of which were at considerable distance. A visit from Dr. Wheaton. Made some little progress in transcribing my review of Hosack's Essay—begun yesterday. Drank tea at Dunlap's, where I spent part of the evening—the remainder at Riley's—having previously called at Woolsey's, & found nobody at home. Read the greater part of five Numbers of "Bulletin de la Société Philomatique"—in which I found several interesting things. Read several articles in the M. Rev: Enld. for August 1794. *Art. VII.* Baillie's Morbid Anatomy—a work deserving the character given of it, & that I have read with much satisfaction, & I hope some improvement. *Art. IX.* Bell of the Venerial disease. An accurate & sensible account of a respectable publications, rather distinguished for the excellency of its practical precepts than the perspicacity of its speculations. Recd. letters from Mary & Idea—now at Aurora. The last progresses rapidly in metaphysical correctness. I wish she might as rapidly improve her style of writing.

Thursday, Oct. 19.—Two medical visits—one of them at some distance. A visit from Mitchill. We went to see Dr. Dewees—we saw only his wife. We next called to see Dr. Parke—but found him gone to Philadelphia. Errands for my father & myself. When I returned home, Dr. Dewees came in. He stayed some time. Medical visit. Finished the transcription & correction of my review of Hosack's Essay. Visited Miller. He tells me that Dr. Rush has some thoughts of removing here, if he can be provided with a professorship. His presence would be the making of the medical school here. It would do much towards the complete establishment of the Repository; & greatly benefit the science, in every respect. Called at our printer's. Medical visit. Spent part of the evening at Geo M. Woolsey's—who moved into his house this day—remainder at Dunlap's—where one [of] my patients is. Recd. letter from my father. Read several papers in the Monthly Rev. Enld. August 1794 —*Art. XVIII.* St. Croin's Life &c. of Alexander the Great—a valuable work, & important to a correct notion of the history of this period. *Note.* (Thursday, Oct. 19) —Sailors often come in well from sea: frequent bawdyhouses, on docks, & dirty parts of cities—are intemperate—& are taken sick: they are then supposed to have brought contagion with them,—& an epidemic is charged to their account; when probably, they have been infected on shore, in consequence of change to bad air, & an irregular life.

---

[84] The Reverend J. Whitehouse, Rector of Orlingbury, Northamptonshire, "An Elegiac Ode to the Memory of Sir Joshua Reynolds, late President of the Royal Academy" (London, 1792). Apparently there was a fugitive publication of other odes by the same author.

[85] John Williams, Smith's friend in Wethersfield, cited earlier.

Friday, 20.—Two medical visits. Transcribed, with some omissions & corrections, my letter to Cogswell. Prescribed at the Hospital as usual. Three medical visits. Called on Dr. Miller. Wrote the two succeeding letters to Strong & Buel. Medical visit. Drank tea & spent the evening at Dunlap's: W. W. Woolsey & Wm. Johnson were there. Finished the Monthly Rev. Enld. for August 1794—Appendix. *Art. 1.* Some account of the Aust. Pruss. & Sicilian Monarchies vols. III. & IV—is full of very interesting matter, which bespeaks a valuable work. The following extract is important to my purpose.

Saturday, 21.—Read the papers. Medical visit. Wrote the letters to Idea & Mary of this date. Medical visit. Called on Dr. Mitchill at Mrs. Miller's & brought him home with me, on business of the Repository. Visit from Dr. Wheaton. Errands. Called at our printer's. Read Mr. Palmer's last 4th of July Oration—a superficial & incorrectly-written performance. Medical visit. Evening at home—Club night—& my turn: Present, Dunlap, W. Johnson, Smith, G. M. Woolsey—Dr. Miller & Dr. Mitchill, visitors. I read Ch. B. Brown's "Alcuin." Conversation various, but interesting & instructive. Read several articles in Appendix Month. Rev. Enld. vol. XIV—*Art. VI.* The Literary Journal of Berlin—the Extract remarkably curious & interesting. *Art. VII.* Crell's Chemical Annals—the account deserving of attention.

Sunday, Oct. 22.—Medical visit. Collected various Notes for the Title Medical News, in the Repository. Transcribed my letters to Josh. Strong & Wm. Buel. Dined at H. Johnson's, where I spent most of the afternoon. Medical visit. Drank tea & part of the evening at Riley's—remainder at Mr. Boyd's. Read in M. Rev. Enld. vol. XIV, Appendix—*Art. VIII.* Mirabeau's Friendly letters—the extracts spirited: The last comes near to some important truths. The author, perhaps, was not aware that, with some modifications, what he proposes relative to Germany is calculated to advance the happiness of all mankind. *Art. X.* Gren's Journal of Nat. Philos. This is a valuable article. The experiments on Nitre correspond with others, made by different persons, & are very complete, as far as they go. They deserve to be repeated, varied, & extended. Other papers are curious, but not necessary to be here particularized. *Art. XII.* Akin's Mysterious Exper: on extingg. Fires. Important. I will endeavor to recollect & have this article reprinted in Webster's paper, when cold weather, & fire alarms commence. *Art. XII.* Kastelein's Chem: & Phys: Magazine. This article also is full of interesting matter. The facts relative to the nitrate of silver seem to contravene Dr. Mitchill's Theory. *Art. XV.* Ewald on the Kantian Philosophy. I have seen nothing yet to give me very high ideas of Kant's System. Some of it appears affected, a part unintelligible, some absolutely false: on the whole, there is more of new words than of new ideas: but I pretend not to decide. *Art. XVII.* Life of Muley Seizit Emp. of Morocco: a monster! *Art. XVIII.* This article has repeatedly afforded me information & pleasure; & a complete translation of the work "Portraits of the German Literati"—is, to me, extremely desirable —as it appears well-executed & authentic. *Art. XIX.* Engravings from Sir Wm. Hamilton's Vases. The principal fact derived from this review is, that Vases called Etrurian, are really Grecian. *Art. XX.* Acct. of the Campn. of 1792—under D. of Brunswic. A horrible statement of enormities—& probably authentic. The author seems candid & pretty well informed.

To Joseph Strong

The pains & pleasures of sympathy, my dear Strong, were powerfully excited by your letter. I need not tell you which predominated. I began anxiously to fear that you were sick. Your letter, which brought me the first intelligence of your illness, conveys to me also the news of your recovery. By this time, you are dandling your new-born blessing, in the fullness of health & joy. I congratulate you, & partake of your pleasures.

I see, by the papers, that the number of deaths is not so much diminished, as might be expected. From this I infer either that new cases of fever still occur, or that great numbers have been sick, or that the Hospital practice is inefficient & unsuccessful. What is the truth?

We have had about twenty bad cases of fever, in New York, this season. Nearly all have died who have been sick. This has arisen, in the greater number of cases from the real disease being unsuspected, or from obstacles to right practice which were insurmountable. I have, myself, lost one patient, on the sixth day of the disease. From having been called to him only on the second day, & then during the remission of the fever, I was not apprized of his danger; & when I discovered it, on the third day, I was unable to bleed him. I made four trials; twice opened the vein; but he fainted in every instance; & I could not procure a free bleeding. I am persuaded that a fifth attempt would have destroyed the patient—so great was the effect of the mere proposal of this operation. I then attempted Salivation; & he took large quantities of Calomel, & was covered, as it were, with mercurial ointment, for two days, without effect. Other means were not omitted; but nothing seemed to make any effectual resistance to the progress of the disease. I have another patient, who is now convalescent.

What is the reason that, under some circumstances, you can not salivate? And are there any means of discovering & obviating the impediments? Have you made many observations on this point? If you have, what have been the situations of those patients, in whom you attempted to raise salivation, without success? These appear to me to be very interesting queries, whose solution would go far toward empowering me to subdue the formidable disease in question. I beg your attention to them.

I concur with you in respect to the general treatment of Yellow Fever. The depleting plan, as far as I am able to judge—(or rather the antiphlogistic plan)[86] is the only rational mode of cure. Still, I believe with you, that it may be, often has been, carried too far. There are some of the younger physicians of your city who talk of Bleeding in a style of wantonness that shocks me. Twelve or sixteen ounces, with them are nothing. They laugh at bowls & basons, & call for buckets & tubs. Let us not be afraid to bleed freely, when it is necessary; but let us not needlessly waste blood; nor boast of the enormous quantities we have drawn. Much of the obloquy which is now so villianously cast upon this remedy, would have been spared it, had its friends been prudent. I lament this the more, on account of Dr. Rush. No man has been so infamously calumniated. When you see him, be pleased to make him by best respects, & assure of him of my warm & continued esteem.

The next time that you write, I hope to hear something from you, respecting the Medical Repository—the second Number of which will soon be published.

Oct. 20. 1797.
Pine St. 45.   E. H. Smith.

To William Buel

Your letter of the 12th inst. with the inclosed money has been received, & our printers do not seem displeased with your punctuality. All our receits, as yet, go to them—& more will be necessary, if subscriptions do not go on to increase—which I believe they will.

The pamphlets shall be ready for the first person you shall direct to take them; & I shall add to them, hereafter, such as from time to time appear, that may merit your attention.

In respect to your paper, as we have made up the present number without it, I am glad that it lies over the next. It will be the more seasonable; & probably the better written. If you think of any information that you have not, & that may be advantageous to you in completing it, let me know, & if possible I will transmit it to you. I think we shall not have any difficulty, hereafter, in obtaining materials, & good ones. Practitioners seem disposed to be communicative—but we can not rely on their readiness as to any particular time. This makes us the more pressing with the few friends on whom we may safely depend for assistance. With your paper, even if we receive no other, we can make up the next No. We therefore think ourselves secure. As soon as that, now in the press, comes out, we shall seize the first chance of conveying it to you, & as many additional copies of both numbers as you may require. Those for the Ontario subscribers shall be sent to you, till you or they direct otherwise.

We have had a few, perhaps twenty, cases of Yellow Fever, or of a bad fever, this season. Most of them have terminated fatally. I can not yet learn that there is any pretence of importation; tho' we have those among us who would gladly seize upon & proclaim it, if there were. I have carefully attended to the circumstances of each patient, as far as I can learn them. Most of the cases are to be traced to obvious sources of disease. They may all be considered as sporadic. No instance of contagion has occurred.

With respect to Dr. Rush's doctrines—that of local origin stands exactly where it did, as regards the medical men of Phila. There have been no converts, I believe, to either side of the question—the discussion of which has only been renewed by the sickness of the present season. As to treatment, even Dr. Stevens himself bleeds on the first day of the disease; & all who bled in 1793, still bleed. The principal source of opposition, which is also the principal source of calumny, is in a few NewsPapers; & these have had great effect on the public mind. Dr. Rush has been most outrageously abused—& I must suspect that it will end in his leaving Phila. entirely, & perhaps the profession. Of this suspicion, however, I wish you to say nothing at present. I have not time to explain the grounds I have for it. His Defence of Blood-letting is not printed separately.

Have you made any trial of the Arsenic? I have lately used it, with success, to prevent the Chill of Hectic Fever, in a single case of Consumption.

Yours &c.

Oct. 20. 1797.
Pine St. 45.   E. H. Smith.

To Idea Strong

Your letter, my dear sister, exhibits many evidences of improvement. The style of thinking is generally correct; & your expressions better suited to your opinions than formerly. It is here, however, that you principally fail: in the nice selection & accurate use of language. To this your future efforts must be powerfully directed. And, as it is by means of words that we mostly think, you will gain precision of ideas, with precision of style.

Next to style, punctuation, which, in some sort, may be considered as a part of style, demands your care. One of the greatest embarrassments in reading, intelligently, your several communications, arises from your careless arrangement of points. You even neglect to mark the commencement of a sentence, by a capital letter. This, frequently, obliges me to read over one of your paragraphs several times, before I can be satisfied that I apprehend it rightly. This circumstance claims your immediate attention; & one step towards true punctuation will be to discard dashes — — — — altogether. Nor must you regard this faults as trivial. Nothing is trivial which materially affects the purposes we have in view. Our thoughts must be exprest clearly, forcibly, & even elegantly, or they will fail of attracting the notice

---

[86] The "depleting plan" or the "antiphlogistic plan": the word "antiphlogistic" used in connection with medicine rather than chemistry had to do with the reduction of heat from inflammation. Doctors of this dispensation were bleeders. Well into the twentieth century a black sticky substance called antiphlogistine was prescribed by doctors for the reduction of swollen glands in the neck.

of many minds, if they are addrest to the public; or of enlightening & delighting our friends, if silently conveyed to them.

Hitherto, I have been most solicitous concerning your opinions. You may consider it as proof how well I am content with them, when I descend to the lesser points of style & punctuation. Still, I would not have you suppose that I deem your moral inquiries to have proceeded to their utmost extent. You have only entered upon them. But you have entered as the proper avenue, & with a spirit which, I think, will conduct you rapidly to truth, certainty, & happiness: with a spirit which I hope, and believe, will not suffer you to stay your course, or loiter on the way. I have, therefore, a proposal to make you, which I hope will not startle you. If I have so much confidence in your capacity, surely you need not be dubious of it; & I can not conceive of any more promising conductor to improvement of every kind. The difficulty should only inspirit you the more. Resolutely to encounter & struggle with impediments, is half to overcome them. If the first exertions do not quite remove them, they must fall before repeated attempts. Nothing, of this kind, can long maintain itself against the persevering assault of intellectual energy.

I wish you to select or contrive some fable or story, calculated to admit of the easy & natural display of your sentiments concerning morality, instruction, personal conduct, literature &c. &c.—& to have you frame out of all a connected, & as far as may be, an interesting tale: i.e. I wish you to undertake the composition of a Novel: not for publication, not even for circulation among your acquaintance, if you do not please, but for the consistent embodying of your opinions, for their development, correction, & extension. The task can only appear formidable at first sight. The difficulty will vanish before a well-considered exertion. I would advise you, if you do make the attempt, to prefer a regular & rapid narration. Endeavour to convey all essential information, both as to incident & sentiment, as little didactically as possible. It may be best to make your hero or heroine the narrator. This will, necessarily, keep the author out of view, & will prevent your entering into irrelevant discussions. Much useful instruction may be comprized in a work of half the size of "Nature & Art"; & something in that way might, possibly, be best suited to your powers. I have not proposed this thing lightly; and I beg of you not rashly to decide against it. Let me, when next I hear from you, be told that you have already made a beginning.

I am much gratified to see that you are so engaged in the reading of "Political Justice." I think that you will derive conviction from most parts of the work. The Vth and VIth Books, appear to me the most exceptionable. In these, I have no doubt, the author will hereafter, see cause to make corrections—at least as regards the present condition & welfare of mankind. We are not yet, even in America, sufficiently instructed to bear a purely democratic government. That which now exists is, undoubtedly, with a few exceptions, quite as good as we may be trusted with. The reasoning concerning the President, is particularly faulty.

I have now an article of intelligence to communicate, which, I think, will afford you a lively gratification. Miss Wollstonecraft is now the wife of Mr. Godwin. Her former husband, who was an American, basely repudiated her, in France; & she has lately married the author of "Political Justice." Her situation is probably rendered as eligible, by this match, as she can desire; & as he is a man independent in his circumstances, we may expect that she will have ample leisure for the cultivation of those sciences in which she so much delights, & for gratifying her friends by successive & interesting publications.

Accept my fraternal love.

Oct. 21. '97.
Pine St. 45.
E. H. Smith.

To Mary Sheldon Mumford

Need I tell you, my dear sister, that your letter gave me pleasure? It would be difficult for me to express how much. You had been silent so long, that my desire of hearing from you would have risen to anxiety, had not some information by the way of Lichfield relieved long incipient apprehensions. It was in this circuitous way that I heard of the birth of your daughter, on which event I congratulate you with the sincere satisfaction, as it has taken place with no expence of health to you, nor of accident to the child. You must indeed, be quite a matron, with your two babes. But, let me caution you against too long a continuance of one part of your maternal cares. Tho' your health is good, your constitution may be considered as delicate; & it would be criminal in you to expose it to any shock so early in life which promises to be filled with claims upon your parental exertions. Accustom your children, by little & little, to feed—the best food will be milk—so that you may gradually excuse yourself from the necessity of suckling them, as their size & demands for nourishment increase. It will be dangerous for you to trifle in this matter; nor must you, if you value your own welfare & the future happiness of your family, continue to nurse them, when this office is attended by fatigue & debilitating exhaustion. I know your goodness, & that you will be in danger of hazarding too much, in obedience to its suggestions, if you are not early attentive to the effect which this extraordinary effort may have upon you.

In respect to names—I am not much of a hand for inventing them. Those which you have chosen are pretty; but I should think either sufficient. I would not have you prodigal of them, in the beginning, as you seem likely to have large demands upon the manufacturers of appellatives. What think you of Caroline, Emily, & Harriet? They seem to me about equally removed from the extremes of puritanism & romance.

If a suitable opportunity offers, I will send you a little

package of medicine, for Worms, with directions. In the meantime, take the following. In the first place, you may make a decoction (in the same way that you prepare tea) of Carolina Pink-root: a quart of boiling water to an ounce of the Root. With this you may feed your child, as with any other tea—with milk & sugar; & he may (at Woolsey's age) take half, or the whole quantity, in a day. This should be followed by a brisk cathartic—of any kind. The symptoms will generally yield to this treatment. If the attack is severe, & the child seems sleepy, very feverish, with his bowels swelled, it will be most prudent to administer from 10 to 20 or 30 grains of Calomel, at one, two, three, or more doses, according to the urgency of the symptoms. Very great nicety in determining the dose, is not important. You may give as much as will cleverly lie on the end of a pen-knife, at a time. After either of these medicines have removed the worms, or obviated the symptoms—(and if they do not do it at once, they must be repeated—& if the Calomel causes puking it is no matter) you must allow the child a more nourishing diet than ordinary—for a few days; & great advantage will be found from giving him a few grains of Steel filings,[87] alone or with some spice or bitters, morning, noon & evening, for several days—especially if he be much weakened by his complaint. If the Steel causes a Lax, you may add a few (3 or 5) drops of Laudanum, or a little Elixr. Paregoric, to each dose. Indeed, Steel filings—one or two tea-spoonfuls, at a time, are, of themselves, an excellent remedy—& I have heard that a decoction of the Tulip or white-wood tree, bark, answered very well as a vermifuge. So Common Salt, in small repeated doses will sometimes succeed; & sometimes any purgative medicine. In Woolsey's case, if you feel that he has worms still, I would recommend the Iron filings—as they are easily procured. You may make them into pills, with the soft part of bread—putting in as much Steel as the Bread will take up—& give three or four pills, three times a day—for a fortnight. They will do him no hurt; & he will take them, in this way, without difficulty.

I do not learn from your, nor from Idea's letter, whether you have read all the books that I sent. I wish you to be more particular when you write again; & let me have a few opinions, as well as the titles. Lay one of your nurslings on the bed, & give the other to Idea, while you write.

Some weeks since, I sent letters to you, from Lichfield, by Mr. Stewart, the Assistant Atty. Genl. for your District. I suppose, as you do not mention, that you have not recd. them. Perhaps you may get them the sooner for this information: tho' I do not yet know of a conveyance to you for what I now write.

Last summer, Dr. Barton of Phila. went from here to Niagara. As he mights perhaps pass by Aurora, I gave him an introductory letter to Mr. Mumford. I have never learnt whether, or not, you saw him. Please to inform me.

If a proper conveyance offer, I still design to furnish you with some additional books. But this, you know, is uncertain. When you have opportunity, you may return such as you have sufficiently perused.

Do you visit Connecticut this Winter? If you will delay till May or June, & come by New York, I will accompany you, & make a long visit among our friends.

Oct. 21. 1797.
Pine St. 45. E. H. Smith.

Monday, 23.—Medical vist. A call on Dr. Miller on business. Dr. Dewees overtook me in the street & accompanied me thither. Business for my father occupied some time, forenoon & afternoon. Medical visit. At the Hospital, as usual. Met Mitchill at Miller's on business of the Repository. At our printer's. Medical visit, & drank tea at Dunlap's. Met Danl. & Decius Wadsworth in the street to-day. The former is at James Watson's, with his wife & sister. I spent part of the evening with der of the evening at Kent's. Medical visit to Ch. Mr. & Mrs. Watson—their guests were absent. Remain-Adams's—where I saw his mother & his sister Mrs. Smith. Recd. a letter from Saml. M. Hopkins—London July 26. 1797. Read *Art. XXII.* Append. M. Rev. Enld. vol. XIV. Rev. Age of Louis XIV—very long & entertaining: a history formed out of Epigrams, with occasional notes & illustrations.

Tuesday, 24.—Medical visit. Rainy day & evening. Visit from Dr. Miller, & from Dr. J. B. Jones. Read the whole of the Monthly Review Enlarged, for July 1797—on the particular articles of which I forbear to make any comments at this time, as I design to look over the greater part of them again. I shall only observe that this No. contains an unusual share of interesting matter. Visit to Dr. Wheaton: to Dr. Seaman—with whom I drank tea, & spent part of the evening. He read me what he has written of a letter to Dr. Hosack, on the local generation of Yellow Fever—in which he supports that doctrine, & by an appeal to facts not easily contraverted. We conversed much on the subject. I had some conversation on it with Dr. Bailey, this morning, in Webster's Office. Visit to Dunlap. Remainder of the evening at home—employed in correcting a proof-sheet, & in reading over the greatest part of what we have got printed off of the second Number of the Repository—for the purpose of forming a list of errors: they will not be numerous.

Wednesday, Oct. 25.—Visit from Dr. Mitchill. Occupied in composing, arranging, & transcribing, Medical News, for the Repository—both forenoon & afternoon. A visit from Mr. Webster. He shewed me his first letter to Dr. Currie of Phila.[88] The argument is correct—

---

[87] Iron or steel filings were also used as an ingredient in prescriptions for at least one other ill, epilepsy. See Gurdon W. Russell, *Early Medicine and Early Medical Men in Connecticut* (Hartford, 1892), p. 110.

[88] During the autumn of 1797 Webster, who valued Smith's opinions highly, often asked him to read letters which were part of his correspondence with Dr. William Currie on the subject

but not pushed to the extent it might have been. Called at Dr. Mitchill's, on business of the Reposy—& saw Dr. Dewees there. At the Hospital as usual. Dr. Rodgers there—& he is to come into attendance the first of Nov. —Medical visit. At our printer's. Corrected proofsheets. Called on Dr. Dewees, who was out: at Woolsey's—all out: at Mr. Rogers's—where I drank tea; & where was much dull company. Called at Mr. Stansbury's—all out: at Mrs. Morton's—she out: spent part of the evening at Mr. Leffingwell's: remainder at home, reading Chisholm on the Boullam Fever,[89] as he calls it. I have hastily run over 104 pages. I do this that I may be the better prepared to question Mr. Paiba, with whom I am to dine to-morrow, at Mr. Webster's. I am told that Chisholm has kept back many interesting facts, with which Mr. Paiba can furnish me. Have read our own & the Phila. papers to-day—& a number from London.

Thursday, 26.—Continued the reading of Chisholm. Transcribed the letters to Mary & Idea. Made some additions to the "Medical News." A visit from Dr. Miller—& from Dr. Dewees, to take leave. Met Dr. Tillary in the street, & had a long conversation with him respecting Dr. Rush's removal here &c. All that I have seen of this man is in his favor—& evidences candor & good sense. Walked out to Mr. Webster's, where I dined & spent the afternoon—with Mr. Paiba & his wife. They were of the settlers at Būlam, & he one of the Council. From him Dr. Chisholm derived his mistated information respecting the Bulam Fever, which he pretends was introduced into Grenada by the Hankey. He is a sensible man. I took notes of his information. His wife a pleasing woman. Spent part of the evening at Mr. Woolsey's—remainder at home. Corrected a proof. Read in Wadstrom on Colonization.[90] Read Webster's IInd & IIIrd letters to Dr. Currie. Prepared the Hospital Return, for the last three months, of the Repository.

Friday, 27.—Continued the reading of Chisholm— which I nearly finished. An early visit from Dr. Mitchill. Another visit from Dr. Miller. Another from Dr. Dingley. Another from Mr. Webster. Recd. two letters from my father. Some time occupied in business for him. At the Hospital as usual. A medical visit. A call at Mr. Kent's. Drank tea at H. Johnson's. The Evening at the Greenwich St. Theater. "The Jealous Wife," & "The Irish Widow":[91] both by a Mrs. Harding, who made her first appearance in America. Her person is good— & she went thro' with *Mrs. Oakly* creditably. She is deficient in voice; & her face shews that she is past her prime. In *Mrs. Brady* she wanted spirit till the *breeches* scene—in which she acquitted herself best. Her *breeches* figure is showy. Its principal fault is the broadness of her pelvis, which makes her appear more knock-kneed than she would otherwise: & her knee is not perfectly well made. Her husband, who played *O'Cutter* in the Play & *O'Neale* in the Farce, is a well-looking man, with a remarkably fine voice, & was correct in both, & excellent in the Farce. Bernard's *Lord Trinket* was excellent, Harwood's *Sir Harry* very well. Blisset was perfectly well in *Thomas,* in the Farce.

Saturday, 28.—Finished Chisholm. Read in Wadstrom on Colonization all that relates to Buluma—comprized in 66 pages 4to. Numerous errands for my father & myself. Medical visit with Dr. Wheaton—who sails to-morrow, if the wind be fair. Visit to Dr. Mitchill, on business of the Repository. Drank tea at Kent's—Club night—his evening—Present, Johnson, Kent, Smith, & W. W. Woolsey. Dunlap out of town. Conversation desultory, & leading to no useful remarks. Many interruptions. Woolsey did not come till it was late. The Monthly Rev. Enld. for July 1797. *Art. 1.* Wilberforce on Xtianity.—a methodistic work—the remarks of the Reviewers sensible & pertinent. *Art. II.* The Mysterious Mother.[92] I have read this tragedy twice, some time since, with inexpressible satisfaction. It is, perhaps, superior to any other tragedy—in the language, considered as a whole. The extracts here made are very fine —but not superior to others which might have been made from either act. The opinions of the critics coincide with my own; & were I the manager of a theater, I should not hesitate to bring it before an audience. What a part is the *Countess* for the powers of a Siddons? *Art. III.* Sir F. M. Eden on the State of the Poor. I have read few articles with more interest, whether on account of the extracts from the work itself, of for the remarks of the reviewer, than those which relate to this of Sir F. Eden; of which this is not the least pleasing. *Art. IV.* Melmoth's Memoirs of an Advocate. Very handsome—& very handsome compliments to the author. *Art. VI.* English Lyrics. These are sweet things, which I suspect to have dropped from the pen of Mr. Roscoe. *Art. VII.* The last 3 vols. of Hugh Trevor. If the statement here made is accurate, the sentiments of the reviewers are just. I must see the book before I conclude. The extracts are admirable. The concluding remarks of the critic are not destitute of foundation. Were all men such as they ought to be, there would be no occasion for Law, nor would any law exist. But, while we are as we are, to reason from what is abstractedly right, against what is relatively so, is to oppose—were we to act upon this reasoning—one of the

---

of yellow fever. Webster's twenty-five letters were the continuation of a pamphlet war between Currie and Rush in which many doctors participated. Webster defended Rush. For the letters see *Minerva* (October 26-December 23, 1797); Noah Webster, *A Brief History of Epidemic and Pestilential Diseases* (Hartford, 1799).

[89] Colin Chisholm, M.D., F.R.S., *An Essay on the Malignant Pestilential Fever, introduced into the West India Isles from Boulam, on the Coast of Guinea, as it appeared in 1793 and 1794* (London, 1795).

[90] C. B. Wadstrom, *An Essay on Colonization* (London, 1794).

[91] George Colman, the elder, *The Jealous Wife* (1761). David Garrick, *The Irish Widow* (1772).

[92] Horace Walpole (1768). Theater managers apparently did not agree with Smith. It is improbable that the play was performed in New York in the eighteenth century.

most insurmountable obstacles in the way to virtue & happiness. To abolish all systems of legal restraint, would be to throw us back beyond the 14th century. Mr. Holcroft is certainly wrong, if he would destroy laws before men are generally prepared to conduct conformably to justice.

Sunday, Oct. 29.—Three medical visits—in the course of the day. Two to [a] man, to whom I was called just at the close of his life, from a Fever of 5 days—which has carried him off—aided by the most absurd treatment, on the part of his physician. Visit to Geo. M. Woolsey. Dined & spent part of the afternoon at H. Johnson's. Drank tea with Mrs. Dunlap. Spent part of the evening at Riley's: remainder at home. Looked over several numbers of the Monthly Magazine in the morning—& read thro', principally, the No. for April 1797.

Dr. Wheaton sailed to-day. The man who died was the head of a family which he had usually attended, tho' he did not see this man but just in time to advise their sending for me. This gentleman Dr. W.—has treated with unexpected friendliness; & I have some reason to believe has spoken of me in such terms, to some of his friends, as will be the occasion of their employing me.

Monday, 30.—Completed the article "Medical News" —in the No. II. of the Repository. Finished looking over the Monthly Magazine for May, & the principal of that for June 1797. Read pp. 48 of "Reports on the effects of the Nitrous Acid in the Venerial Disease"— being part of a publication so intituled, recd. from Dr. Beddoes this day. Visit to Mitchill. Prescribed at the Hospital. Medical visit. Visit from Mr. Webster; & read his 4th & 5th letters to Dr. Currie. Visit from Mr. Roulet. At my printer's. Drank tea at W. W. Woolsey's. Called, vainly, at Dr. Miller's, Post, & Hosack's. Spent part of the evening at Gurdon Mumford's—remainder at home. Recd. a letter from Dr. Buel, of a few lines.

Tuesday, 31.—Finished the Monthly Magazine for June. Visit from Miller—and from Mitchill. At the Hospital. At our printer's. Commenced the composition of my Examination of the evidence that the Grenada Fever of 1793, was introduced there by the Hankey, from Bulama. Medical visit. Drank tea at Woolsey's. Was a short time at Moses Rogers's. Came home & wrote a letter on business to my father, to be sent off before sunrise. Just as I had finished it was called to a lady of my acquaintance, who had just, most unluckily, fallen from a door, by mistepping, into the street; cut her face, & bruised her; & worse than all, as she is in the sixth month of her pregnancy, hazarded a miscarriage. Should this follow, as she is a very delicate woman, & of a feeble habit, I very much suspect that it will prove fatal to her. This accident disturbs me very much. Indeed, the whole day I have felt unusually alive to discomposing impressions. I hoped that a quiet sleep would restore my equanimity, & that I should awake refreshed, mentally as well as corporeally. But I am now in dread of a summons to the lady; & scarcely dare to enter my bed, lest I be called upon to leave it, to witness more distressful scenes.

Industry of October 1797
Reading

An Essay on the Malignant, pestt. Fever, introduced &c. as it appeared in 1793 & 1794. By C. Chisholm.— 8vo. pp. 279—edit. Lond. 1795.

An Essay on Colonization &c. by C. B. Wadstrom.— 4to. edit. Lond. 1794—of this pp. 66.

Zoonomia P. 1.—4to. edit. Lond. pp. 85—twice—& 15 pp. additional—once.

The Monthly Rev. Enld.—part of the XIIIth & XIVth vol. & the No. for July 1797—equal to one entire volume.

The Monthly Magazine—the greater part of Three Numbers.

De Non's, Swinburnes's Travels &c. relative to Syracuse—almost all that was read the last month.

Caleb Williams Edit. IInd.—pp. 188.

Selden's Table Talk—about one half the volume.

Bulletin de la Societé Philomatique—five No.

Reports on the effects of the Nitrous Acid in the Venl: Diss: pp. 48—8vo.

Writing
Composition

Notes Concerning Syracuse . . . . . pp.	4.
Analysis of Zoonomia	12.
Abel Beers's Case	4½.
Medical News (not here preserved) . .	4.
On the 1793, 94, Grenada Fever (do.) .	7½.
Letters-here preserved	14.
Do. not presd.	6

Transcription

Of Medical News.
Of Letters
Of Reviews &c. for the Repository.

47.

MEMOIRS. 1797. NOVEMBER.

Wednesday, 1.—Read some part of the Monthly Magazine for July last. Medical visit. Some time occupied in preparing medicines &c. for another patient. Medical visit. At the Hospital, where I delivered over my patients to Dr. Rodgers. Corrected two proofs. Recd. a letter from Dr. Barton. Read the Papers. Visit to Miller—& to Mitchill. The last shewed me a paper from Dr. Ricketson on the Ricinus—trite & improper for publication in its present form. Medical visit. Drank tea & spent part of the evening at Dunlap's—who returned from Amboy to-day. We called at Mr. Watson's, expecting to find Mr. & Mrs. Wolcott of Phila. there— who were gone to Phila. Called vainly at G. M. Woolsey's. I spent the evening at Mr. Catlin's—where I met

Mrs. Holson. The conversation was various, interesting & animated. She is a sensible woman. I saw at Mr. Trott's Room, where I stopped a few minutes to-day, a beautiful drawing of Cosway's;[93] & numerous elegant french engravings.

Thursday, 2.—Almost all the forenoon occupied in numerous errands for my father, to whom I wrote a short letter. In the afternoon finished the Monthly Magazine for July. A visit from Dr. Mitchill, who continued here some time. Corrected proof-sheets. Medical visit. Visit to Mrs. Lovegrove, who returned yesterday, with whom I drank tea, & spent a part of the evening. She shewed me Book I. of Mrs. Morton's (of Boston) "Beacon Hill &c"[94]—I read several passages; which, tho' by no means faultless, are superior in correctness &c. to any thing of hers I have seen before. Part of the evening at Mr. Green's—a gentleman who was one of the employers of Dr. Wheaton—& who, indirectly, by inviting me to his house, has selected me for his physician. Came home & made considerable progress in the Supplement to the Monthly Magazine. Vol. III.

Friday, Nov. 3.—Finished the above-mentioned Supplement. Most of the day engaged in arranging, posting, & settling my various accounts, up to this time. Made out the Table of Industry for last month. A visit from Mr. Webster. At our printer's. Visited Miller; & we went together to Mitchill's. Medical visit. Walked out to Roulet's—where I spent the evening. Corrected a proof-sheet.

Saturday, 4.—Read a file of London papers & the newspapers of the day. Visit from Dr. Miller, Mr. Webster, & Mr. Dunlap. Read Mr. Webster's 8th, 9th, 10th, & 11th Letters to Dr. Currie. Continued my Examination of Dr. Chisholm's Acct. of the Grenada fever of 1793-4. Medical visit. Drank tea at Dr. Miller's —after which we went to G. M. Woolsey's—Club night —& his evening: Present, Dunlap, Smith, the Woolseys, & Miller visitor. A very lively & interesting conversation, on various topics.

Sunday, 5.—Wrote & transcribed the following letter. Wm. & I dined, as usual, at H. Johnson's, where we spent the afternoon. We drank tea & past part of the evening with Mrs. Lovegrove. The remainder I spent at Dr. Miller's.

At dinner &c. we read the "Morning Chronicle" of Sept. 12th which is filled with the account of the revolution at Paris on the 4th[95]—an event altogether prodigious, gigantic, & overwhelming. If it be possible, which I much doubt, that the treachery alleged against Pichegrue be true, it is incredible that the most distinguished men in France, for talents, public & private virtues, could be concerned in any such plot as is pretended. And who are their accusers? Men infamous for every crime.

The intelligence which concludes the paper, of the death [of] Mrs. Godwin (Wollstonecroft)[1] is another deep wound to my hopes. The loss of 50,000 french & as many Austrians, on the Rhine or in Italy, would have affected me less.

To Benjamin Rush

The hurry & pressure of various occupations, at one time; and the hope of being able to address you, personally, in this place, at another; have prevented me from expressing to you, till now, the lively interest which I have taken in all your recent, as in your former fortunes. The shameful & malignant persecutions you have suffered—more disgraceful, if possible, to the city which permits, than to the persons who inflict, them— have awakened; not in my bosom only, but in those of a large & respectable portion of our citizens, astonishment, sympathy, & abhorrence of their authors. In this state of mind, nothing could be more flattering to us, & more triumphant & as we hoped consoling for you, than to quit a situation & a society which can no longer be worthy of you, & to take refuge among those who entertain an opportunity to manifest it. The conduct of the Faculty of Physic in our College has been particularly gratifying to me on this occasion. Could their freely-expressed wishes determine the question, there is no doubt but that every thing would be accommodated to your desires. But, you probably are informed, that other, meaner obstacles are in the way, some of which perhaps it is in your power to remove. As I do not suppose any of your friends here, who are in a situation to interest themselves effectually in your behalf, will have the courage to explain the circumstances fully to you, I have ventured to take this liberty—which, considering my motives, I hope you will not deem impertinent.

Among the Trustees, who have to decide on the proposed measure, are some who will oppose it from motives of personal dislike, some from diversity of political opinion, & some perhaps from the more sordid apprehension of loosing professional consequence & emolument. Among them all, however, it is not probable that the real ground of opposition will be at all disclosed. They will rather seek to defeat the intention of the

---

[93] Richard Cosway (1742-1821), a portrait draftsman who usually worked with charcoal or pen and ink; he was also, however, a famous painter of miniatures.

[94] Mrs. Sarah Wentworth Morton, *Beacon Hill. A Local Poem* (Boston, 1797).

[95] In the spring of 1797, when internal peace was a hope for France, the elections brought into office some conservatives who were influential in repealing a few of the more savage laws. The three radical members of the Directory, claiming that the country was in danger of a Royalist takeover, asked for help from the generals. General Hoche and Bonaparte answered, Hoche sending troops and Bonaparte sending General Augereau. The conservatives were ousted, arrested, or put to flight. Augereau was specifically responsible for the September 4 *coup d'etat*, the "Revolution of the 18th. Fructidor."

[1] Mrs. Godwin, née Mary Wollstonecraft. She died on September 10, 1797, giving birth to a daughter, Mary, who became Mrs. Shelley.

friends to the appointment by indirect means or plausible delays. The most formidable of these objections arises from the uncertainty of the time when you will remove hither & effectively unite yourself to this Institution. And they argue in this manner. "Dr. Rush is now unpleasantly situated in Phila. He feels wounded by the conduct which has been observed towards him & no doubt feels, at this time, a desire to remove. But it is not difficult to foresee that these feelings will soften down, & that his long residence there, the friendships he has formed, & various other considerations, will every day diminish his eagerness for a change of place. Beside, if we appoint him, he has no design to quit Phila. this autumn; & if he do not, half of the advantage the friends of this plan expect from it, will be lost. The students of medicine at Phila. will have gained new motives for remaining there; new arrangements may be made for their benefit; & a thousand means employed to fix them there—for which a whole winter will allow the other professors & persons interested in the success of that School, ample opportunity. In addition to this, we may ask—will not Dr. Rush, if he continues in Phila. this winter, retain his professorship in the University & deliver his lectures as usual? He has not resigned his appointment there, nor given us any reason to believe that he will do it, immediately on our appointing him. And how incongruous will this appear, that he is exercising the functions of a professor in another Institution, while he holds an office in this! Nor must we forget that there is great reason to doubt, whether, if he should remain at Phila.—if his celebrity & success as a teacher should be unimpaired, & if the present animosities should subside, he will be willing to quit Phila. in the Spring. While, therefore, so much uncertainty rests on this business, ought we to be in a hurry to make appointments which, as we have seen in a former instance, only tend to lessen our own dignity, without advancing the interests of our Institution."

You will acknowlege, sir, that there is a plausibility in these suggestions which it is difficult for men who, tho' they feel friendly towards you, are unacquainted with you, to reply to. Nor should it be concealed from you that these fears are not wholly strangers to their bosoms. They naturally wish, therefore, for the means of not merely calming them in themselves, but of shewing them to be utterly groundless. And they reason in this manner: "It is indeed true that it is essential to the full success of this scheme, that Dr. Rush come here this season. If he will leave Phila. about the first of Dec. or about the time when the lectures are to commence in Phila. we have no doubt but that a large number of the students will follow him, immediately—as they will then have formed no engagements with the other professors. It will be only necessary for Dr. Rush to spend a part of the winter here; for which purpose he may shorten his course—which after all will be satisfactory, as it will be much superior to any thing we have yet had here. The remainder of the Course may be filled up by Dr. Hammersley,[2] with whom such an arrangement can easily be made, as will allow of Dr. Rush's visiting his family, once or twice during the winter. And his stay here will enable him to make leisurely preparations for a final removal to this city. Add to this, the éclat of the transition, & the effect it would be likely to have both at home & abroad, in this movement, when the feelings of all are alive on the subject. In short, he must be ready to come immediately: it is impossible to act with spirit, while we entertain a doubt that we are laboring to no purpose."

Such, my dear sir, is the faithful epitome of the feelings & discourse of both parties. I need not tell you how important it is that no doubt shall remain. All your friends have but one sentiment, that the success, the distinguished success of the measure, depends considerably on this point—whether you come immediately or wait till another year. I may add, that there is now a disposition in the Practitioners of Medicine in this City, generally, to receive you with something like enthusiasm; & to make your entrance into New York, a triumphal entry: alike honourable to you & to them. This spirit, however, can not last six months. It must perish amid the frost and snows of winter. Meantime, every narrow principle of selfishness & vanity, which has been overthrown or blasted, by the novelty & greatness of the design, will have time to revive, and to flourish perhaps with obstinate vigour. In fine, this is a moment to constitute an era in the medical history of the United States. Notwithstanding all the exertions which may be made, the contemptible prejudices & disgraceful bigotry of some men, may defeat the measure; but nothing will so much tend to invigorate every effort in its behalf, & to favorably determine it, as the certainty that in this respect, you will be ready to gratify the wishes of your friends. The final vote is deferred till a week from to-morrow: when I hope every thing will turn as it ought to do.

I take my leave, with again requesting your indulgence if my zeal & friendship, have betrayed me into any improper interference in your concerns.

With augmented respect & affection

Yours,

Sunday, Nov. 5. 1797.
Pine St. 45. N. York.   E. H. Smith.

Monday, 6.—Finished the rough draft or sketch of my Examination of Dr. Chisholm's acct. of the Grenada Fever of 1793. Corrected a proof sheet. At our printer's. Errands. Read the papers. Visit to Dr. Miller. We went to Mitchill's. He was absent. Medical visit. Another medical visit. Drank tea at Kent's. Called at Dr. Post's. He out. Spent part of the evening at Riley's—remainder at home. Mitchill came here. I read him my Examina-

---

[2] Dr. William Hammersley, M.D., 109 Pearl St. and 32 Broadway; member of the Medical Society, Professor of the Practice and Institutes of Medicine, Faculty of Arts, Columbia College.

tion of Dr. Chisholm. He communicated some new facts to me—illustrative of my design. He has been composing a new defence of his Theory of Contagion, consisting principally of an inquiry into the composition of the Nitrous Acid of the Shops.

[Omitted here, two manuscript pages: "Preface to the Med: Repos: No. II. Vol. I."]

Tuesday, 7.—Wrote the preceeding Preface to No. II. last evening. A long visit from Mr. Webster. Another from Dr. Miller, to whom I read my Examination of Chisholm. He, in return, read me Mitchill's Inquiry into the nature & composition of the Nitric & Nitrous Acids of the Shops; & we agreed to persuade Mitchill not to publish it—at least at present.[3] Read Mr. Wynkoop's long reply to Dr. Currie. Read also Dr. Gillespy's interesting letter to Commodore Barry: & the newspapers. After dinner, at Miller's—we completed the list of Errors for our No. II. I copied the Preface—corrected two proofs &c. Mitchill came, & we succeeded in preventing the publication of his piece. Some calls. At our printer's. Wm. & I drank tea, & spent part of the evening at G. M. Woolsey's—the remainder at home; when I finished my letter to S. M. Hopkins, which I had commenced in the morning.

Wednesday, Nov. 8.—Read the papers. At the printers. Corrected a proof. Visit to Mr. Paiba's. Saw Mrs. P. Left my MS. concerning the Grenada Fever there. Medical visit. Returning, called at the Hospital; & concluded, with Dr. Rodgers, to make some trials with the Sulphuric & Muriatic Acids in Syphilis. Visit to Mitchill. Read a letter to him, from Mr. Parsons of E. Haddam, relative the disease among Cattle. Read also his own paper on the health of several parts of England &c. Visit to Dingley. Read an Inaugural Essay he sent, by a Mr. Brown, on the Fever at Boston, of 1796. Read also Chs. Chauncey Jr's. oration—in defence of the doctrine of progressive improvement of mankind. It is handsome. I must write to him on this subject. Met, in the street, my old-classmate, at New Haven, Saml. Carrington,[4] who is Druggist & Physician at Old Fort Schuyler. Wm. & I drank tea & spent part of the evening, at Dunlap's: the remainder at home. Read in Hodgson's translation of "The System of Nature."[5] This translation is wretchedly executed.

Thursday, 9.—Transcribed my letter to S. M. Hopkins. A visit from Dr. Perkins, the inventor of the Metallic Points.[6] Visit from Dunlap—we called at Trott's, & Tisdale's—they were both out. Various errands. Our Med: Repos: No. II. is this day published. Medical visit. Another, to Mr. Minturn's[7]—where I drank tea. Called at Woolsey's—all absent. Visit at Catlin's. Returned home. Read several articles in Darwin's Zoonomia, relative to Consumption &c. & read also the chapter on this subject in Cullen's First Lines. I found that the Circulating Library's Proprietor had sent me "Barham Downs"[8]—one of the novels recommended by Ch. B. Brown. I have read about 80 pages in it—(Edit. Dublin) with considerable pleasure. Let who will write a speech, the author is still apparent. I forgot that Dr. Miller was here a few minutes—Mitchill an hour or two—& that I have read the seven last letters of Webster to Dr. Currie.

To Samuel Miles Hopkins

I recd. your letter, (dated London July 26. '97.) the 23rd ultimo; and should have replied immediately, but for the pressure of other concerns. I will say nothing of the pleasure I derived from your communication; but leave it to my answer to disclose my real feelings.

That I may, as far as possible, meet your wishes, I shall send, in the first place, such private & personal information to you, as may be likely to interest you; this will be followed by such literary news as the time affords; a few remarks on public affairs will succeed; & I shall close my letter with some inquiries which

---

[3] It would appear that Miller and Smith were successful in persuading Mitchell not to publish this article. It was one of several theories to come from Mitchell's active and brilliant mind which proved to be inaccurate.

[4] Samuel Carrington (1767-?; Yale 1786). He studied medicine under his father in the town of Woodbridge, Connecticut, and was later an army surgeon at Stockbridge, Massachusetts. He married and for reasons unknown immediately left the country. Except for a letter from Nova Scotia nothing was ever heard from him again.

[5] William Hodgson, M.D., trans. of *The System of Nature. From the French of Mirabaud* (London, 1795).

[6] Dr. Elisha Perkins was born in Norwich, Connecticut (1740 or 1741). He was one of forty-six original members of the Connecticut State Medical Society. In 1795 he invented his metalic points and actively promulgated them in the following year and until his death. The points were tapered pieces of metal about 3 inches long, one brass, one iron. They sold for five guineas a pair. Perkins is known to have been living in Philadelphia in 1797-1798. In May, 1797, the Connecticut State Medical Society disowned him and expelled him. Shortly after 1797 he developed a "cure" for yellow fever. In 1799 he went to New York to stop the epidemic and died of it there. He did not use his points as is sometimes thought in this attempt to cure yellow fever; instead, he used a concoction, "a powerful antiseptic remedy." Smith does not appear to have used the points which Perkins gave him (for which see later), but many other reputable physicians did. The points were drawn slowly over the affected parts in a downward direction for about twenty minutes each time. Thatcher described them as being "used for local inflammations in general, pains in the head, face, teeth, breast, side, stomach, back, rheumatism, etc." The points attracted great attention among doctors in Copenhagen and in England. In a pamphlet published in London (1804), professors from four different universities, twenty-one regular physicians, nineteen surgeons, and thirty clergymen gave testimony to the value of these points. Opponents pointed out that cures were the result of the patients imagination but this was answered by many doctors who used them with the statement that cures had been performed on both infants and even on horses. Thatcher, *Medical Biography* 1: pp. 423-[425]. See also Howard W. Haggard, "The First Published Attack on Perkinsism: An Anonymous Eighteenth Century Poetical Satire," *Yale Jour. Biology and Medicine* 9, 2 (1936): pp. 137-153.

[7] William Minturn, a gentleman, probably wealthy, member of the Board of Governors of New York Hospital.

[8] Robert Bage (1728-1801), *Barham Downs* (1784).

you may answer at your leisure. I have marked out my course, you see, with parsonic method; & the variety of matter will give my letter a motley appearance; but I trust it will not be wholly displeasing to you.

And first for personal annecdote.

News concerning your own family, I presume you will receive from them. I have the satisfaction to assure you that mine are all well. My sister Mary has a second child—a daughter—& the settlement at Aurora goes on rapidly. They have *now* about thirty decent houses, where six years ago there was only the ruin of a wigwam. Eleven have been erected the last season.

Mr. Tracy, I suppose you know, is in the Senate of the United States; but you probably did not know that Allen is one of the Representatives. The premature death of James Davenport, places Mr. Edmonds in the same situation.

Mr. Reeve has lost his wife. This event, which some expected he would scarcely survive, is likely to render him much more useful, as a public man, than before. He bore it with becoming fortitude. It is probable that you will find both him & Ingersoll on the Connecticut Bench, when you return.[9] Gov. Wolcott & Judge Adams are near to death. I recollect nothing further relative to Lichfield, or even Connecticut, that is likely to engage your notice. In this city, your friends remain *in statu quo* pretty much. None have effected any thing very illustrious. I communicated your article concerning the Irish Professor—(whose name you neglected to mention) to Mr. Kent; & I expect to be able to send you his pamphlets, with this letter. Wm. & I still cohabit; & I believe with none of the bad effects apprehended from so doing, by Mr. Godwin. When I mention his name, I can not express to you the pain which the recent news of the death of his wife occasioned me—& I may say most of our circle. Had the Attila of modern Italy & half his legions, & their sturdy & automatic opposers, fallen in battle, it would not have given me half so severe a pang. What an incalculable loss for intellect & truth!

When I speak to you of literary undertakings, it will be natural enough for you to expect, & for me [to] speak, something of myself. We will not sin against Nature.

When I wrote before, I inclosed our Circular Address. I have it in my power now to inform you, that our plan is likely to succeed. Not altogether in the exact shape originally proposed; but with such deviations as you will see. It is perhaps impossible to create a faithful set of observers to a certain point, over so large a territory as the United States, under many years. This will be ultimately effected; & I think our plan will have the merit of having done it. I shall send you the two first Numbers of the Work. From them you will gain some idea of the progress which is making here in medical & natural science. Hitherto we have reviewed not more than half the publications of this kind, which have been made within the last & present years. I do not suppose that you will take the trouble of reading these two pamphlets; but you may be gratified by a careless examination of their contents; & may, perhaps, dispose of them on such hands as shall advance the interests of our undertaking.

The articles "Medical News" will save me the trouble of communicating any further information on the subject of works in this line. In other branches of literature I may inform you that—Mr. Belknap is about to publish a second volume of his "American Biography";[10] that Mr. Holmes is preparing for the press a "Life of President Stiles";[11] that Mr. Morse has given us a very excellent & accurate "American Gazeteer"—a large octavo volume; that a Mr. Stearns, a Massachusetts Clergyman, is soon to publish a Poem, which is well spoken of; that Mrs. Morton has already sent out the 1st Book of her poem intituled "Beacon Hill"—which is much better than her preceding publications; & in some parts quite handsome; that Mr. Paine of Boston has lately printed a new Poem, & is preparing a volume for the press;[12] & that Mr. Royal Tyler has not only put forth one novel, which is said to be popular, but which I have not seen, but has brought out a new play,[13] & is reported to have several other novels & plays ready for impression. So much for Boston. In Connecticut, Mr. Trumbull[14] of North-Haven, has just published his History of that State, as low as 1712: I have not seen it: He is getting in readiness, also, it is said, an Ecclesiastical History of it: Mr. Z. Swift is employed, also, in collecting materials for a History of Connecticut;[15] & Judge Root has issued proposals for his long-talked of Reports.[16] Mr. Strong of Hartford, too, has been guilty of a bulky 8vo. to prove that God means to damn eternally a large portion of mankind, & that it is very just & kind-hearted of him to do so. In New-York all is still at present. Commerce languishes, but literature does not flourish. Our work, some medi-

---

[9] Smith's forecast was correct. Jonathan Ingersoll and Tapping Reeve are listed as assistant judges under Chief Judge Jesse Root, at the Superior Court held in Litchfield on the third Tuesday of August, 1798. Dwight C. Kilbourn, *The Bench and Bar of Litchfield, Connecticut 1709-1909* (privately printed, Litchfield, Connecticut, 1909), p. 122.

[10] Jeremy Belknap (1744-1798) XX, **2** (Boston, 1798). *American Biography* . . . **1** (Boston, 1794).

[11] Abiel Holmes, *The Life of Ezra Stiles, D.D., LL.D.* (Boston, 1798). *The Life* is based on manuscript material which Stiles himself gave to Holmes.

[12] Robert Treat Paine (1773-1811). The volume he was preparing for the press was probably *The Ruling Passion* (Boston, 1797).

[13] Royal Tyler's play was *The Georgia Spec* (Boston, 1797); the novel, *The Algerine Captive* **1-2** (Walpole, New Hampshire, 1797).

[14] Benjamin Trumbull, *A Complete History of Connecticut* **1** (Hartford, 1797). Note that he is the third of that surname in these pages.

[15] Zephaniah Swift's *A System of Laws of Connecticut* **1** (Windham, Conn., 1795); **2** (Windham, Conn., 1796).

[16] Jesse Root, *Reports of Cases Adjudged* . . . **1** (Hartford, Conn., 1798).

cal pamphlets, & some re-publications are all. The Swords's are now busied in reprinting "The Botanic Garden"[17] on their own account; & "Telemachus"[18] for another person; & this last work will equal, for elegance of printing, almost any european Work. And now, when I have told you that the disgraceful persecution which Dr. Rush has met with in Phila. gives us some reason to expect that he will remove hither, I have nothing to add to this part of my letter. We hear nothing from the South in the way of litterature. The Muses are silent, notwithstanding the favorableness of the Clime.

In respect to the political affairs of this State, I have the grief & mortification to tell you that there will be spirited exertions, at the ensuing election, to exclude Mr. Jay, & replace him by Chancellor Livingston;[19] & the party seem full of hope. You may wonder that there should be any danger of this; but the unpardonable remissness of the friends of liberty—I do not mean anarchy—at our city election lost them all their candidates. Among those who are returned for the Assembly, is Aaron Burr—& his activity & capacity you are not ignorant of. Beside, Mr. Jay has disappointed many of his *ci-devant* warmest partizans. The State had been so long managed by favoritism, that these wretches thought they had only to shew great zeal in behalf of the new Governor, & they should secure appointments for themselves, whether qualified or not. In this they have been disappointed. Mr. Jay has acted justly; & justice has no friends. Still, I rely very much on the steadiness of the western people. In other respects, all matters pass on very quietly with us; & if party have not disappeared, it has lost much of that rancour which poisoned all social intercourse a few years ago. The eastern States are as they always have been: Pennsylvania still divided; & the Southern people slowly verging towards a right understanding of our true interests. But much misrepresentation still prevails there; & it has lost no strength by the election of Mr. Jefferson, who is jacobinical almost to lunacy. You have seen the disgraceful imbecillity of our Congress. There are men there who think well enough, but have no courage; & what is worse, the Friends of our National Character & Interests are deficient in industry. There are so many of them so nearly of equal talents, that they can not agree who shall lead, or each feels diffident of assuming the direction. In this situation they suffer an Exotic, more distinguished for application than original genius, to thwart half their measures, & propose his own.

---

[17] *The Botanical Garden, a Poem* [Erasmus Darwin] (New York, 1798).

[18] Telemachus (a pseudonym), *A Wonderful Narrative of Two Families, in Five Letters to a Friend in Great Britain, by an American* (n.p., n.d.). A note in the Library of Congress Catalog describes it as "an argument for peace in the form of a parable."

[19] Partners in a law firm as young men, Livingstone and Jay became political rivals. Livingstone ran for governor of New York in 1795 but was defeated by Jay, abroad when nominated and, indeed, until after the election. Jay was elected for a second term in 1798.

Our disputes with the Spanish are as little likely to be settled now, to all appearance, as six years ago. Our Government, however, has conducted with great prudence, & appears very respectable in every stage of the business. Mr. Pickering rises in the public esteem; Mr. Adams is as popular as we can ever expect any President, after Washington, to be; & the Cabinet is perfectly united, which it never was till the last of Mr. Washington's administration. Notwithstanding, we have many difficulties to struggle with, which I have not time to detail. We have just recd. the *damnable* news from France of their 4th of September Revolution. It is impossible to say what effect this will have on our affairs, tho' you may perhaps know by this time—but we have no reason to expect that it will be fortunate for us, as all the men from whose virtue & justice we had most to hope are included in this savage & unparalleled proscription. But there is an astonishing apathy in our people to such considerations, which are wholly sunk in speculations on the events themselves, & (on the part of some) in seeking justifications for the Jacobins; for you know that our french partizans have always ranged themselves under the banners of terror, as our english partizans under those of despotism; in short, that they only differ in the sides they take, not in the principles by which they are actuated. But it is time for me to stop these political ramblings, & prepare to put an end to this long letter.

The inquiries which I have to propose are chiefly limited to men & manners: & I wish, as much as possible, for the results of your own observation & experience.

1. How far does the state of the people at large, in Gret. Britain & Ireland, compare with ours in America as to general information, morality, & personal independence?

2. What differences do you observe in domestic life, in the two countries? In particular, how far do they resemble us in that equality which subsists between the sexes in wedlock?

3. What seem to be the feelings of the people at large, particularly in the country, towards their government, & their ecclesiastical establishments?

4. How does the face of the country, at large, compare with the best cultivated parts of America—for instance the environs of Boston, Philadelphia, & the banks of the Connecticut River?

5. What are the relative advantages & disadvantages of the two countries for social enjoyment & improvement?

To these questions I have only to add that it will give me great pleasure to receive from you such anecdotes or opinions relative to distinguished men, as may be derived from your personal observation of, & intercourse with them; or from authentic sources of information: in particular, relative to those philosophers & poets whose writings & sentiments you know most engage our affections & command our homage.

How is your health? & when may we expect your return?

Yours &c.

Tuesday, Nov. 7. 1797.
Pine Street, No. 45. N.Y.
E. H. Smith.

Friday, 10.—Too much of the morning busied in putting up some medicines for a patient; in *conserving* powders into electuaries, & *soaping* them into pills. Hereafter I shall say to the Apothecary "Do this, & he doth it."[20] Continued "Barham Downs." An unexpected visit from Mr. Tracy—who brought me letters from my father & from Abby. All friends well. He (Mr. T.) left town in three hours. Our conversation, as we had so little time together, did not dwell long on any thing; & but glanced on his family. Never have I heard a syllable, directly or indirectly, from Mrs. Tracy, since my last letter. My correspondence there is, I fear, at an end. Our friendship, too, I fear. My perplexity on this subject is painful, whenever it occurs to my mind. If this winter pass without a line from her—difficult as the exertion must be—I must relinquish my hopes of a renewal of our correspondence—& strive to forget our friendship. Two medical visits. At the place of the last, met Dr. Hedges—the author of the "Strictures on Brown &c."[21] Returning, stopt at Dr. Miller's—drank tea there—& we went together to see Miss Mason; found her surrounded with a world of company; waited till they withdrew; & then had an hour of social conversation. Came home—& finished "Barham Downs"—Edit. Dubl. 12mo. fine print—pp. 450—or thereabouts. This work often reminds me of "Man as he is"—& "Hermsprong."

Saturday, Nov. 11.—A rainy day. I did not go out till after sunset. Made such progress in Darwin as is indicated by the two next succeeding pages—i.e. finished the XIIth Section. Variously but agreably, interrupted. A visit from Mr. Webster—who shewed me a letter from Mr. Pike, the Mathematician, to him decisive as to the *local origin* of the NewBuryPort Fever of last year. Visit from Dr. Miller. He brought me a letter from Dr. Rush—& he had recd. one himself: both are conclusive that he can not come here this Autumn. The thing, I fear, has fallen through. What a set of drivelers are our Trustees! How infamously have they sacrificed the interests of this Institution. A visit from Mr. Allen, on his way to Congress. He was here but a very short time; & went directly on. Mr. Dana was here also, a still shorter time. Recd. a short letter from my uncle Morris. Called at Riley's. Club night & Dunlap's [turn]. I went round by Dr. Miller's, & carried him with me. There were present, Dunlap, Johnson, Smith, the Woolseys, & Miller visitant. A sociable evening.

Sunday, 12.—Prepared some directions &c. for a patient. Read several articles in the Monthly Review for July 1797—a second time. *Art. VIII.* Count Rumford's Essays, No. 6. The extract remarkably interesting & ingenious. *Art. IX.* Godwin's Enquirer. The criticism well-written, & the sentiments generally correct. On the *end* of Education—it appears to me not impossible to conduct it in such a manner that all that curiosity & intellectual activity, which Mr. G. desires, should be attained, but that it should be in part gratified, at the age of 25. Concerning modes of education, I have seen nothing (in print) equal to some sketches in David Williams's Lectures; but I think a child may be induced to read what he ought to read, & still appear to direct his own reading—& that the remark of the Reviewers on the character of books is just. The observations relative to servants are very little, & in many cases not at all, exaggerated. The Critic scarcely comprehends what is said of professions. Mr. G. speaks of their *tendency*, & not of their *absolute effect* in all cases. The Critic's observations on Style, & on Mr. G's style, are correct. *Art. X.* Southey's Letters from Spain &c. The translation from George Montemayor is exquisite; the original verses pleasing.

Wm. & I dined at H. Johnson's—where we spent the afternoon. I drank tea at J. P. Mumford's, where I was called to a patient. This is one of the families consigned to me by Dr. Wheaton. Spent the evening with Mrs. Lovegrove.

[Omitted here, two manuscript pages: "Zoonomia, Cont'd. IV."]

Monday, 13. Nov.—Visit from Dr. Miller, & from Mr. Dunlap. Medical visit. Errands. Attended Mr. Post's "Introductory Lecture to his Anatomical Course —which is the same he delivers every year & nearly verbatim to the Introduction of the article "Anatomy," in the Encyclopedia.[22] At Mitchill's. Saw Dr. Hedges there. Two medical visits. Read Dr. Coxe's Defence of Dr. Rush, as far as has yet been recd.—published in the Gazette of the United States. Read also Caldwell's Case of Yellow Fever, in opposition to Wistar. Also a letter, with a mass of matter, sent Mitchill by a physician of the name of Ayers, in Morristown, New Jersey. At our printer's. Medical visit. Called on Dr. Perkins—the Metallic Points-Man—who made me a present of a set of his Instruments. Wrote a few lines to Mr. James Morris of Lichfield. Called to see Mr. George Todd—who is now in town, with his lately-married wife. He has fixed on Hartford as his residence. Spent part of the evening at Mr. Kent's; part of it at Mrs. Morton's —& the remainder at home. Finished the reading of Mrs. Morton's (of Boston) "Beacon Hill." Book I.—which I commenced this morning. I find my opinion, in the letter to Mr. Hopkins, quite as high as the poem will bear. It is desultory, incorrect in sentiment & style, & abundant in imperfect & misapplied metaphors,

---

[20] Luke 7:8, from memory. Also Matthew 8:9.
[21] Phineas Hedges, *Strictures on the Elementa Medicinae of Brown* (Goshen, 1795).

[22] The "Encyclopedia" from which Dr. Pike took his lecture (as have many men since) was almost certainly the *Encyclopedia Britannica* for which see hereafter.

& various affectations—of which perpetual alliteration is not the least disgusting. Finished a second reading of the Monthly Review for July 1797. *Art. XI.* History of the Rivers &c. of Gt. Britain: an entertaining article. *Art. XII.* Zimmerman on National Pride: the same opinion may be exprest of this also. *Art. XV.* Trotter's Medicina Nautica. This appears to be a performance much inferior to what I expected from the author's reputation. *Art. 45.* The Nun; by Diderot. The extract has excited my curiosity towards both this novel, & James the Fatalist, of the same author.

Tuesday, 14.—Read Buffon's introduction to his account of "Les Animaux Sauvages," in the original. Medical visit. Errands, which took up much time. At our printer's. Medical visit. Called on Mrs. Lovegrove. Wrote a few lines to Dr. Buel, & a few to Dr. Wheaton. Looked over Francis Hopkinson's Works, in the course of the day & evening—reading here & there an essay. Visited Dr. Elnathan Beach, formerly of Cheshire, Connec. now of this State—who I supposed dead, but is recovering his health. He left town to-day. Met Dr. Hedges in the street, & had some conversation. At Dunlap's. Visit from Dr. Seaman, who read me part of his paper on Yellow Fever—which he was prevented from finishing by the entrance of other company. Visit from Dr. Mitchill—Mr. Beers (bookseller) of New Haven—& Mr. Moss Kent of Otsego. Drank tea at Geo: M. Woolsey's—& spent part of the evening there: remainder at home. Looked over the articles *Cervus & Capra* in the Encyclopedia—made some comparisons with Pennant; & read part of the article "L'Elan & le Renne," in Buffon: also made some additional Notes for my account of the Elk—of which I am more & more convinced no good acct. has been given.

Wednesday, Nov. 15.—Yesterday recd. a few lines from Joseph Bringhurst; to-day from Mr. Tracy. Wrote a few lines to Dr. N. Dwight of Hartford & Dr. Simeon Field of Somers on business of the Repository—to send by Dunlap, who is going to Connecticut & Boston. Wrote also letters of introduction, for George Tod, to Dr. Cogswell & Theodore Dwight. Read the newspapers. Visit from Dr. Seaman—who finished the reading of his Paper on Yellow Fever. Called on business, at the printer's. Medical visit. Medical visit. Visit to Mrs. Lovegrove. Visit to Dr. Miller, on business. At Dunlap's. Errands. Visit from Mr. Tod. Drank tea & spent the principal part of the evening, at Dr. Miller's—where were present, beside himself & his brother—Mrs. Benjn. Kissam & her two sisters, Miss Mason, Bayard (of N. Jersey) Nicholson & Templeton—Mr. Kissam & Roe, Dr. Mitchill & myself: & Mr. Bisset a short time. Dr. Miller & I accompanied Miss Bayard & Miss Templeton to the house of the latter, where we entered, & had half an hour's agreable conversation. Came home, & finished the reading of Buffon's article on "L'Elan & le Renne."

Thursday, 16.—Medical visit. A visit from Mr. Paiba. At the City Library for some time, whence I brought off the vols. of Buffon (translation) Goldsmith, & the Philos. Transact. Abrid:[23] which contain accounts of the Elk—having previously looked them over sufficiently to satisfy myself concerning the general tenor of the information they contained. Two medical visits. Called on Mrs. Lovegrove—but the severity of the cold prevented her going out as proposed. Errands. Visit of business to Isaac Beers, at Mr. Leffingwell's. Two medical visits. Drank tea & spent part of the evening at Mr. Paiba's—where we looked over my Examination of Dr. Chisholm's acct. of the Grenada Fever, & conversed on the circumstances of the unfortunate expedition to Bulama. Remainder of the evening at home. In the course of it, & of the afternoon, read Goldsmith's account of the Elk & of the Rein-Deer,[24] The article, with all the supplementary matter, concerning them, in Smellie's Translation of Buffon;[25] not only Mr. Dubly's short account—but looked over cursorily the principal part of the VIIth vol. of the Philos: Transact. Abridged. Recd. a few lines from Mr. Tracy.

Friday, 17.—A very cold night. Shut my windows for the first time this autumn. Found it snowing when I rose—& it has continued to snow all day, & all the evening. Breakfasted late. Two medical visits, at distant (from each other) parts of the town. Visited Mitchill at the College. He shewed me the commencement of a new paper, in which he attempts to reconcile the Phlogistians & their adversaries, & to prove that the presence of *flame* always indicates the presence of *Hydrogen*.[26] A Consultation at the Hospital. Afterwards a medical visit, beyond the Hospital. All this occupied the time till late dinner. After dinner, commenced the arrangement of my Notes respecting the Elk; but it soon grew so dark that I could not see to write. Pierce came in, & I communicated some instruction to him. Soon after Dr. Seaman came to see me. Drank tea at home. Some lessons, after tea, to Osborn. Sat down to look over & correct Seaman's Essay on the origin, or cause, of Yellow Fever: & completed it. Corrected a proof-sheet of Swords's edition of the "Botanic Garden." Resumed the arrangement of my Notes on the Elk, & have executed, probably, one third, perhaps one half, of the task.

Saturday, 18.—Read the papers. Two medical visits. Called on Dingley—he out. At our printer's—where I wrote a few lines to the Revd. Dr. Morse, on business of the Repository. Errands. Called on Mrs. Lovegrove. Visit to Miller—where Mitchill came. A visit from

---

[23] *Memoirs of the Royal Society; being a new Abridgment of the Philosophical Transactions* (London, 1740) 7: pp. 96-98.

[24] *History of the Earth and Animated Nature* (London, 1744). Goldsmith speaks of the elk in America as being the "moose deer," still a reasonably correct classification. See edition (London, 1857) 1: p. 333. Clarification of this matter is little better than it was in Smith's day.

[25] *Natural History, General and Particular;* From the French of Count de Buffon (Edinburgh, 1780) nine volumes; apparently also printed in London the following year in eight volumes.

[26] Mitchell failed again. Hydrogen is not necessary for a flame.

Mitchill, after dinner—& from Seaman—who stayed till sun-set. Drank tea at Mr. Kent's. Two medical visits. Club night—Wm. Johnson's turn—We sat alone till after eight o'clock—meantime I read several things from the Monthly Magazine, which I bought to-day. At length Kent came in—& we were sociable. Dunlap is out of town.

In the morning, I brought away with me, from one of my patient's, "Scotland's Skaith &c"[27]—which I have read thro' & thro', (8vo. pp. 50.) with great pleasure. The tale is exquisite—& the Ballad no less so. There is much humour in the "Long Apology"—tho' of that kind which the author justly condemns in Burns, in the Tale. A new example of inconsistency!

Sunday, Nov. 19.—Looked over the volumes of the Monthly Magazine, which I purchased yesterday. Three medical visits. Visit to Mr. Catlin. Wm. & I dined & spent part of the afternoon, as usual, at H. Johnson's. Visit from Dingley. Drank tea at Woolsey's, & spent the greater part of the evening there. Remainder at home. Dingley here part of the time—rest, read in Monthly Magazine.

Monday, 20.—Four medical visits. Saw a number of very handsome paintings at the auction-room, Wm. Street. Drank tea at Dunlap's, with his mother. Spent the evening principally at G. M. Woolsey's—where I saw, for the first time, Miss Miller of New Haven. Wm. Johnson was there also. A visit to Hodgkinson, in the forenoon. Continued to look over the Monthly Magazine. Finished my paper on the Elk.

Tuesday, 21.—Commenced the transcription & correction of my Examination of Chisholm, & made some progress in it. Four medical visits. Errands. Recd. a letter from Nathaniel Dwight. Continued the reading of the Monthly Magazine. Visit from Revd. Mr. Miller. Drank tea at home. Evening at the meeting of the Manumission Society.

I find, by our printer's account, that we are very much indebted to them for the Repository: not less than 300 dollars; & my news from Connecticut is less favorable to the sale than I expected.

Wednesday, 22.—Two medical visits—and a visit to Dr. Miller. A very disagreable rain all day & night—which made the walking very slippery & bad—& prevented me from doing several errands, matters of business &c. Read the news-papers. Continued the reading of the Monthly Magazine—with much pleasure & some profit. Recd. letters from Dr. Buel & Mr. Tracy. Wrote a few lines to the last. Wrote letters, also, on business of the Repository, to Dobson, & Rice—booksellers in Phila. & Baltimore. Continued the transcription & correction of my Examination of Chisholm—in which I have made some progress. Medical conversation with Pierce. The principal part of the day, & on all the evening, spent at home. Put on flannel next my skin, on my body, this day: cotton socks to my feet over silk stockings.

Thursday, 23.—Three medical visits, one at some distance. Returning, stopt in at Mitchill's, where I looked over the Analytical Review for August last, saw an original copy of Mayo's Works,[28] & slightly examined the III, IV, & Vth Nos. of Nicholson's Journal. I brought away the first of these. When I came home, I found that Mr. Roulet had been here, & left me the August No. of the Monthly Review. I spent much of the afternoon & evening in looking it over, & have read it thro'. Dr. Seaman made me a long visit. Two medical visits. Drank tea, & spent an hour or two, at Woolsey's: Remainder of the evening at home. Month Rev. Enld.— Aug: 1797. *Art. I.* Warton's Edition of Pope—I see no reason to dissent from the decisions of the critics. The extract concerning the character of Pope is handsome, & near the truth. *Art. II.* Stolberg's Travels. Apparently, a work equally valuable & entertaining—& well translated. The extract relative to "the gladiatorial exhibitions," is descriptive of such horrible depravity of manners as one can hardly credit in the reading, notwithstanding the concurring testimony of all the ancient writers, & the examples scarcely less horrible displayed in modern France. *Art. III.* Hist. of the Campaign of 1796. I am disposed to place some confidence in many of this writer's statement's; but his evident hostility to the French renders it proper to admit many of his opinions with caution. *Art. IV.* Aikin's Journal of a Tour: a walk concerning which I only wish it was in my power to read it understandingly. *Art. VII.* Medical Facts & Obs: vols. V, VI, & VII. These volumes deserve perusal—but what is most immediately interesting to me is, Beddoes "Facts relative to the origin of Intermittent's"—of which I can not but wish that the reviewers had added a few words of further explanation. *Art. IX.* Sir F. Eden on the Poor: the conclusion of an excellent view of an important work. How easy would it be, in a well-constituted republic, to obtain much more complete information, annually or oftener, concerning every parish in its bounds. I hope to develope the plan, in my Utopia. *Art. XI.* Bertrand de Moleville's private memoirs &c. This is a most entertaining article. Could Louis XVI impose on the credulity of his ministers? or did he hope & expect that the Constitution would destroy itself? or did he accept it in the persuasion that it would increase his power? or from a regard to the happiness of his people? The more there is published relative to this wonderful revolution, the more are all the parts of it involved in mystery. One thing, at least, seems clear—that, whatever may have been the views of the original leaders of it, & of the principal men at many subsequent stages, the present rulers are

---

[27] Hector Macneill, Esq. Scottish poet and writer of miscellaneous pieces, *Scotland's Skaith or the History of Will and Jean; owre true a Tale. Together with some additional Poems. Embellished with elegant engravings.* No copy in Library of Congress; British Museum copy is second edition (Edinburgh, 1795); second edition date in bibliographies; no publication date of first edition found.

[28] Charles Mayo, *Chronological History of the European States, etc. 1678-1792* (Bath, 1793).

men lost equally to public & private virtue & regardful only of their personal & selfish interests. *Art. XII.* The Philanthrope—the praises bestowed on this publication are supported by the extracts made from it: the translation from Horace is neat & correct: but I think rather too highly spoken of by the reviewer. *Art. 26.* Elegy on Mr. Mason. These verses are worth something *as verses*; & the compliment to Cowper is equal happy & merited: but the sentiments are stale & puerile. How many thousand elegies have introduced the persons they commemorated & bewailed, among the fantastic corps of angels & saints! *Art. 35.* Lyric Poems—in elegiac measure! Here, too, are some pleasing verses. *Art. 42. & 43.* Clark & Pryce on the Yellow Fever. I very much desire to read both, & soon shall read one, of these performances. The criticisms on Dr. Clark's philosophy seem to be well-founded: nevertheless, the facts he mentions concerning the impurity of the air are striking, & go some way towards the demolition of Dr. Davidson's opinions & statements.

Read, but with little profit, "a letter from M. de Humboldt to Mr. Putet, on the magnetic polarity of a mountain of Serpentine," in Nicholson's Journal No. 3.

To Robert J. Thornton, London

I have the pleasure to inclose to you the second No. of the Medical Repository. Since my first letter no new publications, relative to Medical & Philosophical subjects, have appeared here, except the IInd part of Dr. Priestley's Considerations on Phlogiston, which I do not send as I presume that the pamphlet has been republished, before this time, in London. Should the contrary be true, or should you be desirous of possessing any other publication from this quarter, an intimation will be sufficient.

In respect to the Repository, we have great hopes of its success; for the determining of which a very fair & spirited trial will be made. The third No., which is now in the press, will contain part, if not all, of a paper on the Mineralogy of this state, by Dr. Mitchill, which I have good reason to believe accurate; & which is the more valuable as hitherto nothing of the kind has been published. The same gentleman has transmitted a paper to Mr. Nicholson, (being the copy of a letter to Dr. Priestley,) which contains, as far as I can judge from a hasty perusal, some plausible grounds for a reconciliation of the remaining differences between the Phlogistians & their Antagonists. It will probably appear about as early in Europe, as among us.

I observe, by the London Journals, with pleasure, that you have published a 4th vol. of the Medical Extracts; but with regret, that a work calculated for such extensive utility, is no longer to be continued. In the notice you have taken of the Phila. Fever of 1793—I perceive that you incline to the opinion that the contagion was introduced from abroad. The repeated pestilences which have visited the United States, within a few years, have given importance to every question which relates to them: & to this among others. It is incredible what numbers of appeals to the public, (chiefly in our News Papers) have already been made on this topic, & on the best mode of treatment. The consequence is, I may venture to assert, that the mass of medical men, even of those most distinguished, favors the idea of local origin. The opposers of this doctrine are most numerous, & find the most popular support, in Phila. Here, three fourths even of the people, are convinced of the contrary. I believe our health this year, & the sickness at Phila. are very much to be ascribed to the difference of the general persuasion in this respect.

Before closing this letter, which is unexpectedly long, I may add that Mr. Bay's *alkaline* treatment in Dysentery has been found very successful in repeated trials.

With respect & esteem—

Yours &c.

Nov. 24. 1797.
Pine St. 45. E. H. Smith.

Friday, 24.—Three medical visits. Errands & purchases for my father. Visit to Mrs. Lovegrove. Visit to Dr. Miller. Drank tea at Mr. Kent's. Called on Miss Mason—she was out: at Hodgkinson's—they were out: on Mrs. Dunlap—she was out: at Mr. Rogers's—where I found her, & a houseful of company & spent a part of the evening: the rest at home. In the course of the day—finished looking over the IIIrd No. of Nicholson's Journal—wrote & transcribed with some corrections, the preceeding letter—& performed the laborious task of making up the Minutes of the Manumission Society—& performing a little other writing for them.

Saturday, 25.—Two medical visits. The day being fine Wm. & I walked out to Mr. Sharples's— seven miles out & in. He was not at home; but Mrs. S. came home, while we were there; & shewed us some drawings, in crayons, of american birds, & in water-colours, of english plants: beside, Wm. looked over the collection of portraits. A visit from Mitchill—& from Miller—who were here great part of the afternoon. Visit to Gahn. Drank tea at Woolsey's—Club night—his turn—Present, Johnson, Smith, W. W. Woolsey—E. Miller, visitor. Read the papers. Recd. a few lines from Mr. Tracy.

Sunday, 26.—Medical visit. Called on Catlin. He has been assisting me in making a collection of Coins, current here, for Mrs. Lovegrove. I recd. the last of him to-day. Came home, & made out a minute list of them, with remarks &c. Wm. & I dined at H. Johnson's. Medical visit. Returned to H. Johnson's. Wm. & I drank tea & spent a part of the evening, with Mrs. Lovegrove. Medical visit. Came home & read in the Monthly Magazine.

Monday, 27.—Five medical visits, in the course of the day—one out of town. A number of errands—chiefly for other people. A visit from T. Wortman, on business of the Manumission Society. Visit from Mr. Sharples—he went, with Wm. & I, to see Calvin Philips, the wonderful Dwarf. Thence we went to visit Dr. Haworth, one of Radclift's Travelling Pupils—from England;[29] a handsome man, of moderate understanding. Called at Hodgkinson's. Drank tea with Mrs. Dunlap. Evening principally at home. Read the Monthly Magazine. Recd. a letter from Wm. Buel.

Tuesday, Nov. 28.—Rose early. Wm. & I went down to the river to see Mrs. Lovegrove go off, & take leave. She was not on board the vessel. After breakfast, we returned, saw her, bade adieu, & the "Cheasapeak" left the wharf with a fine wind—which has continued thro' this clear, cold day—& must have blown them beyond the Hook. Two medical visits. A visit from Mr. Sharples. Errands. Consultation at the Hospital. Visit to Mr. Tisdale the Engraver: to Dr. Miller. At our printer's. Drank tea at Mrs. Miller's. Wm. & I spent the evening at Mr. Kent's. Continued the Monthly Magazine.

Wednesday, Nov. 29.—Wrote the four next succeeding letters. Recd. a letter from Thos. O'H. Croswell—to which I replied by a few lines, for the present. Read the papers. A visit from Mr. Roe—an acquaintance of Dr. & Mr. Miller's—who I have frequently met at their house. He called to invite me to dine with him to-morrow. Made a few words of addition to my letter to Hopkins—which I sealed ready for sending. Visit from Mr. Sharples. He finished my picture—which is, I believe, a pretty good likeness. On business, at our Printer's. Wm. & I drank tea at Riley's—& went thence to Signor Falconi's Exhibition,[30] where we spent the evening—somewhat entertained. Continued the reading of the Monthly Magazine.

Thursday, Nov. 30.—Transcribed, last night, the letter to my father—this morning the one to Mr. Tracy. Wrote a single line—"Charles! are you dead?" to C. B. Brown. Two medical visits. Called on Dr. Miller. Errands. Wrote the letters to Abby, Dr. Barton, & El. Smith. Mitchill, Miller, & I dined with Mr. Roe, in company with some others. This important business occupied all the afternoon. Spent a considerable part of the evening with Miss Mason. Mitchill & Miller &c. were there a short time. Remainder of the evening at home. Finished the regular survey of the Monthly Magazine Vol. II. Recd. a letter from my father.

To Uriah Tracy

At length I have found leisure to reply to your several & friendly letters. Till this moment the demands of friends abroad, & business of various kinds at home, have held me silent.

Inclosed I send you the Bill & receit for the Flour; which I have good reason to believe is such as you desired. It was bought at the current price. The receit for the freight, which is on the bill of lading, I shall send to my father, that he may know how to send an order for its delivery to the team he shall send for it. The freight amounted to three dollars, fifty three cents —inclusive of a small box sent my father—which difference he will settle with you. I have, therefore, a dollar remaining in my hands—to be disposed of as you shall order. The vessel sailed with the Flour, for New Haven, yesterday—& is probably safe there by this time.

The Senate, I see, have made a quorum, & will probably report a suitable answer to the President's Address very shortly. I presume that the debates on the answers will not be long. The Address is composed with temperance, & is of such a nature as probably not to awaken all the angry passions which flocked to the standard of debate on the last similar occasion. It has, I believe, given general satisfaction.

The new members of the Senate, from Tennessee, are said to be federal.[31] If this prove true, you have a decided & powerful majority. I hope it will be so.

The House of Representatives seem to be in a halt—not betwixt two—but a great many. I can not yet see who are to be the decided leaders the present Session. Mr. Harper[32] seems very willing to go forward on all occasions, but it requires stronger hands to guide, & a more penetrating & commanding mind to compel, the discordant or heterogeneous atoms of that Assembly into order.

In our own State, the political campaign is soon to open. Lately, we have recovered more courage, & think that there is less to fear from the change in the Representation—from this city in particular, than was originally apprehended. A very stren[u]ous effort, however, will certainly be made, at the ensuing election, to substitute Chancellor Livingston for Mr. Jay: perhaps with effect. The adherents of the first are confident of success—but nothing certain can be augured from their expectations.

All our friends are well; & send Comps. &c. Mine to the gentlemen with you.

Affecty. Yours—

Wednesday, Nov. 29. 1797.
Pine St. 45. N. York.   E. H. Smith.

---

[29] In his will John Radcliffe (or Ratcliffe, but not Radclift) (1452?-1496) one of England's most important physicians, left most of his large estate to Oxford. This included property left to University College in trust for the foundation of two medical traveling fellowships.

[30] Joseph Falconi was a conjurer whose name appears frequently in Dunlap's *Diary*. Earlier in the year Falconi went to Perth Amboy to see Dunlap about renting his theater after his application for Rickett's Circus had been turned down because Wignell had offered a larger rent. On August 16, 1797, Dunlap wrote to Hodgkinson that he had at last rented the John Street Theater to Falconi. See Dunlap, *Diary* 1: pp. 104, 111, 135, 137. See also G. C. Odell, *Annals of the New York Stage* 1: pp. 261, 398, 474.

[31] Joseph Anderson was elected to fill the vacancy left when William Blount was expelled. For one reason or another three other men served as senators from Tennessee in the Fifth Congress: William Cocke, Andrew Jackson and Daniel Smith; the last two were "Democrats."

[32] Robert Goodloe Harper (1765-1825; Princeton, 1785). Federalist from South Carolina to U.S. House, 1795-1801; later a senator from Maryland.

To Reuben Smith

I have omitted writing till now, that I might send you an account of the completion of the business I have been commissioned to execute.

Yesterday, I sent off ten barrels of Flour to New Haven, for you: which is all that Mr. Tracy directed me to buy. He sent me the money. The flour was 7½ dols. pr. bbl. & is such, I believe, as you ordered. The bill & receit I shall send to him. I send you the bill of lading & receit for the freight. You will observe a small Box with the flour. The freightage of this Box was also paid out of Mr. Tracy's money—& was—⅓ Lawful money. The Box contains 12 copies of the No. II. of the Medical Repository; three shirts, which want new wrist-bands &c. & a parcel of Clothes either too much worn, or out-grown, or out of fashion—so as to be of no use to me, tho' they may to somebody else. They are at my mother's disposal. I directed to have the Box sent directly to Lichfield—by the first team, or by the Stage. You will recollect that the subscribers for the Repository are to pay half a dollar on the receit of the present No. I have inserted an advertisement in it, which I expect will remove all difficulties respecting the Condition of Publication which has been misapprehended.

The Butter & Cheese have been recd. The butter is good; & not more than we shall want, as we have one more in our family than last year. The Cheese I have not cut: but Mrs. Woolsey has her's—& it proves to be good.

You have probably learnt, before this, that Platt has paid me the 200 dollars. I send you Philips & Clark's receit for it. They have given you credit for the Essence of Peppermint; & the Acct. is in your name, as you desired.

I also send you a receit of Abraham Bradley for some Wine—which, if you have got the wine, may be sent to New Haven, when you send for the Flour.

I thank my mother for her several presents. The stockings will not be lost. I hope she enjoys her health as well as usual.

I wish that some pains may be taken to procure additional subscribers to the Medical Repository. If Dr. Sheldon & those gentlemen who are subscribers think the publication deserves encouragement, they may render it essential service by promoting its circulation. At present, we have not subscribers enough to pay half the cost of printing. In the hope of increasing encouragement, we shall continue the work, till it makes two volumes—but farther than that we must not proceed, if our funds do not increase. I think, with a little pains, thirty subscribers, at least, might be obtained in Lichfield County. We only want money; materials accumulate in our hands.

Love to my mother & friends.

Nov. 29. 1797.   E. H. Smith.

To William Buel

You must excuse me if my answer to your several letters be short: it is all that present engagements permit.

I inclose Philips & Clarke's receit for the thirty dollars; & Webster's for a half year's Spectator. Our money acct. is very short. You owe me, on Acct. of the Medical Reposy. seven dols. for the 14 copies of No. II. —& 4 (I believe that is the price) for the two vols. of Zoonomia: one dollar & a half I have taken to balance the Opera Acct.—& I have now 1..75 of your money in my hands.

In respect to Philips & Clarke, I believe you make yourself easy. The sooner you can pay them, the better, on every account—but they will not press you.

I shall endeavour to find this Mr. Whiting, & send to you by him. If not, by some other hand.

Do not hurry your Paper. If you can get it ready in season we shall be glad. But let it rather be *well* done, than *soon* done. Tho' I have no doubt but that it will be both soon & well. The reason why we hurry is, that the original papers come first—& must all be printed off, before the other matter is begun upon. I believe we shall do well enough as to Communication—but we are in want of subscribers. At present we have not enough to defray half the expence of the publication.

With regard to Arsenic—it is not only safe to give it to stop the paroxysms, but, afterwards, to prevent their recurrence. You may continue it, as you would Bark, or any other stimulus, till the habit of falling into Ague-fits is intirely destroyed. I do not think that I should ever use Bark in these complaints, but out of complaisance to the prejudices of my patients—it is so bungling & nauseous a remedy. It is well, however, to have a number of instruments.

If opportunities should occur, I wish you to try the Nitrous Acid in Chlorosis, & in Scrofula—in both of which there is great reason to believe it will prove successful. The way to prepare it for use, will be to expose the double Aqua Fortis of the Shops to the air, by leaving the stopper out of the vial, till it becomes pale & colourless; & then to prescribe it in this manner.

Nitric Acid ʒ iss or ʒ ii

Simple Syrup—(or any other) ʒ vi or viii

Water ℥ ii—

Half or the whole of this quantity, or more or less to be taken every day, till the cure is made. If it purges, or gripes, or salivates—the usual means may be used to restrain such effects. The salivation I can assure you, from personal observation, is by no means painful or troublesome.

I have this moment heard from Croswell. He is well.

The article concerning Dr. Rush is premature. He is not coming here: At least, not this winter, if at all.

This town is perfectly healthy.

Comps. to Mrs. Buel.

Nov. 29. 1797.
Pine St. 45.   E. H. Smith.

To Nathaniel Dwight

You have, doubtless, before this time, recd. my letter by Mr. Dunlap, with the Medical Repository No. II. & those for Dr. Field. My letter was sent off, with the books, before the receit of yours of 11th inst. Again I must repeat my regret that we are obliged to occasion you so much trouble. Had I foreseen that there would have been so much indifference to the publication, in your County, I should not have sent so many copies: for, to own the truth, I expected more encouragement from Hartford County, than from any other in the State. After all, I can not but hope that your advertisement will have some effect; & whatever expence you may be at, on this account, we will cheerfully repay. It seems to me impossible that physicians who have any regard for their profession, or who have any desire for improvement in it, can long be insensible to the benefits which must result from a publication like this, if conducted with spirit. As to that I can safely assure you that we are rather encumbered with materials—I mean especially foreign materials, than in want of them; & our correspondence is every day extending: But, then our subscription is not half adequate to our expences: so that the work must be dropt if our funds do not increase. We are determined, however, to persevere till we have completed two volumes, whether we have more subscribers or not. I mention these circumstances, between ourselves, that you may know the true ground on which we stand, & be the more ready to excuse the importunities you receive from us, on acct. of the Repository. By the way, do you hear any thing from Dr. Field? He has not written me a line these some years.

One question further, relative to the Cat-Distemper: when did it reach Hartford? I mean about what time? You see we have given some slight account of it in the Repository. One obstacle to obtaining intelligence on such subjects is the disposition people have to view it in a ludicrous light; tho' in reality few inquiries are more important than the connection between the health of men, other animals, & particular seasons & local situations.

This letter has been unavoidably, like most of my letters, filled with what relates to my particular business. In future, I hope to have less occasion for so much talk concerning it.

Remembrances to friends.
Yours &c.
Nov. 29. 1797. E. H. Smith.

To Abigail Smith Jr.

Yes, my dear sister, you shall have an answer; but it must be, like most of my letters of late, short, & less comprehensive than I could wish. As the number of my correspondents increases, I must contract the size of my letters. At least, I must give more to improvement, & less to mere friendship. This, indeed, becomes a duty; for the weight & number of other duties is continually augmenting, to which it must bear some proportion. Considerations like these will sufficiently account for my silence towards you, when I wrote last to your sister. The few lines I had lately recd. from you, required no reply. They only promised that you would soon write more lengthily. Till you should do so, I thought it proper to reserve myself. But the case was different with Fanny. She had just written to me, & her letter demanded an answer. It was full of sentiments that needed correction. Her whole mind was infected with a poison, for which an immediate antidote was necessary. I attempted the application; & I hope the last remnant of the venom has been discharged thro' her *sore fingers*.

Your journal of the Stockbridge visit interested me. You acted perfectly right in visiting at Mr. Bacon's. There would have been a manifest impropriety in your non-acceptance of the invitation—particularly in the situation you were. Nor can I see the least reason why you should have conducted any other than an indifferent person, whether they knew of your connection, or not: unless, indeed, you should have taken greater pains to recommend yourself to their good opinion than another. In my view of the subject, there is something pleasant & fortunate in this casual introduction. It may spare you no little confusion, on a future occasion; & if, as I have no doubt, you behave with an ordinary degree [of] discretion, this circumstance will be favorable to you, in the eyes of Mr. & Mrs. Bacon, when they come to the knowlege of the relation in which you stand to their son.

As winter is now fast approaching, or actually commenced, I suppose Mr. Bacon Jr. may soon be expected in Connecticut. I regret that it will not be in my power to meet him there. My desire to see & know him, you may well suppose, is not small. While my own feelings are so deeply interested in the fate of my sister, it could not well be otherwise. Perhaps Mr. B may be able to extend his journey to New York. If not, there is an obvious means of introducing himself to me, should he feel any interest in its employment.

Farewell! This letter has already stole upon the limits I originally allotted it.

Nov. 30. '97.
Pine St. 45. E. H. Smith.

To Benjamin Smith Barton

I owe you an apology for my long neglect of answering your letter of the 27th ulto.; but I hope you will not suspect me of equal negligence in respect to the request it contained. The truth is, I have been so overwhelmed with the printing of the 2nd No. of the Repository, some composition for this, & for future Nos. which demanded immediate attention, with my professional & private concerns, & with the commissions of friends & visits of interesting strangers, that I have been obliged to sink the lesser in the greater duty, & neglect my correspondence. But my arrangements for the winter are now mostly completed, & I begin to be at liberty to converse with, as well as think of, my friends; & gladly seize the first moments of this leisure to reply to your letter.

Immediately on hearing from you, I wrote to the Post Master at Albany—desiring him to forward the letter either to you in Phila. or to me here. As I have never heard from him, I concluded that he must have directed it to you; & that it is long since recd. If this is the case, it precludes the necessity of an answer to a certain part of yours: as what I wrote was merely an explanation of the reason for what I had done. The letter never subjected me to any expence.

I see by the papers, that you have commenced your Lectures on the Materia Medica; & of consequence, I suppose, are not inattentive to your intended publication. The knowlege of your design gave us all no little pleasure. Works of this kind, more than any other, are wanting in our country; & relative to our country. European visitants have merely skimmed over the surface; & from their ignorance of our institutions & character have committed a thousand blunders. Whereas, had they been capacitated to observe the country itself, & directed their attention to it, they might have rendered essential service to science, without such unavoidable exposedness to perpetual errors.

We have taken the liberty to announce your intended work, in our second No. which I suppose you have not seen. We are endeavoring to interest some bookseller in Phila. in the sale of the publication—in which case, subscribers & purchasers will be readily & regularly supplied. In the mean time, we shall forward to such subscribers as you may send us, the requisite copies, by any conveyance or to any direction, which they may indicate. We are now employed in printing the IIIrd No. which will contain a large part of Mitchill's Mineralogical Sketch of this State; & thus present a preface, or supplement to one division of your Publication.

As Phila. is, in great measure, the emporium of American science, I must request from you some account of whatever shall appear there this winter, worthy of notice. From this quarter you can expect very little; but should any thing occur, I shall take care to give you seasonable information of it.

With congratulations on the event which your letter announces, & best wishes that it may prove as fortunate as I have no doubt it is agreable, I am yours, very sincerely & respectfully—

Nov. 30. 1797. E. H. Smith.

To Elnathan Smith Jr.

So long & unexpected an interval in our correspondence has happened that I really feel some degree of awkwardness in attempting its renewal. Still I hope my efforts will not prove ineffectual; & that a speedy reply from you will restore to us our ancient habits of frequent epistolary conversation.

Your health, I have casually heard, has suffered much, the last season; & is, or has been, considerably impaired. How is it now? Your silence excites & has for sometime excited many apprehensions in my mind, on your account. May they prove unfounded. A letter from you will dissipate, or modify, or confirm them. In either case, since the fact will not be varied, it is most desirable. If well, I shall rejoice; if a valetudinarian, I may entertain hopes & perhaps contribute to your recovery; if sick, is it not possible that I may suggest something to your advantage? At least, I shall strive to do so. On every account, therefore, I am impatient to hear from you.

If your health is tolerable, how have you employed your time? "The cares paternal & the spousal cares" can not wholly occupy your mind. It must have been much & variously employed; & some of its exertions & excursions must have furnished it with food & matter for communication. Without pretending to very precise recollection concerning our last letters, I believe I was to have recd. from you some account of the poisonous effects of the Sumach, for insertion in our Medical Repository. I still venture to request & continue to expect it. Concerning this same Repository, have you seen it? We have already published two Nos. which are for sale & delivery to subscribers, at Nathl. Dwight's, in Hartford. To you, who have more liberal curiosity than all physicians, & who are equally liberal in gratifying it, I dare to recommend this publication; & I assure you that, tho' it may contain many mere medical papers, which may not be particularly or at all interesting to you, it will also comprize, in the course of time, the greatest body of correct scientific information, respecting our own Country more especially, that has been hitherto communicated to the public. I even venture to believe that you will not be wholly dissatisfied by the paper your friend has inserted in the 1st No. Now I am on this subject, I will ask you whether the Wells's & Todd know any thing of the Repository? I have long expected to hear from them, in relation to it. Dr. S. Wells even promised me one or two papers on interesting subjects. I shall write to them if I can find time—but otherwise I must request you to jog their memories on this point.

I necessarily write in haste. Forgive & answer me. Comps. &c. to Mrs. Smith.

Yours as ever

Nov. 30. 1797.
Pine St. 45. N. Y. E. H. Smith.

Industry of November 1797

Reading

Monthly Magazine—vol.II. looked over—No. for July '97. & Suppl. vol. III. read.
Monthly Review Enl. for August & July 1797—read.
Analytical Review—August 1797. read.
Nicholson's Journal—No. III.—great part read.
Barham Downs—a Novel—12mo-2 vol. edit. Dubl. pp. 450 small print.

Brown's (Boston) Inaugural Dissertation, on Bilious Fevers—8vo pp.
Chauncey's Phi Beta Kappa Oration—8vo pp.
Beacon Hill—Poem—P.I. ... 4to. pp.
Scotland's Skaith & other poems—8vo. pp. 50.—loose.
Hopkinson's Works—equal to p. 300—8vo.
Buffon (in the original)—Pennant—
  Goldsmith—
Scotch Encyclopedia[33]—& Philos. } pp. 70 8vo.
  Trans. equal to—
Darwin—Zoonomia—P. I. Sect. 12. 4to. pp.
Webster's, Currie's, Wynkoop's, Sayeres, Caldwell's, Stuart's, Coxe's, Gillespy's, &c. Letters, in the Papers—on Fever—equal to pp. 30.—at least—

Writing

Composition

Letters here preserved.... equal to....... pp.	24.
Do. not preserved	18.
Examination of Chisholm	40.
On the Elk..........................	8.
Analysis of Zoonomia..................	2.
Preface to Med: Repos: No. II	2.

Transcription

Of Letters	24.
Exam: to Chish.......................	20.
Preface to Med. Rep. No. 2.	2.
Minutes of Manumis: Socy.	6.
&c- §c. §c.	

MEMOIRS. 1797. DECEMBER.

Friday, 1.—Read some part of the Monthly Magazine. A visit from Mr. Owens. Medical visit. Wrote the letter to Dr. Rush. Consultation &c. at the Hospital. Looked over the first & about of the second, volumes of Lavater's "Journal of a Self-Observer."[34] Visit from Dr. Miller. Medical visit. Drank tea at home. Spent part of the evening at Geo: M. Woolsey's. Remainder at home. Hastily ran over about half of the first volume of De Pauw on the Egyptians & Chinese.

Saturday, 2.—Made some further progress in De Pauw. Four medical visits in the course of the day—one out of town. Read the news-papers. Called on Dr. Miller. Read some medical communications for the Repository. Errands. Transcribed the letters to Wm. Buel, E. Smith Jr., Dr. Barton, & N. Dwight. Drank tea at Mrs. Dunlap's. Club night—my turn—Present—Johnson, Smith, W. W. Woolsey—Miller, visitor. I read Gilbert Wakefield's criticism on the Style of Hume—from the Monthly Magazine. Conversation on the style of Hume, Robertson, Gibbon, Gillies, &c.—on the historical fidelity of Hume—Mrs. McCauley & Mr. Whitaker—Dr. Henry's History, & Andrew's continuation—character & conduct of Charles 1st of England—of the Stuart's—Whitaker's defence of Mary of Scotland—his theory of Government—the present David Hume & others—doctrine of the necessity of liberty to profession of science—France—Russia—effects of Peter 1st, of Catherine II.—particular estimation of what she has done—comparative view of other countries—effect of climate—China—its improvements, morality & population—De Pauw read on this last point—Anderson,[35] & Sir Geo: Stanton—Royal Society—compared with other Societies—state of Spanish literature—state of Spain—probability of a revolution—effects—on Italy—France—agriculture of those countries—of America—comparisons—commerce—President's speech—opinions concerning it—comparative literary merit of Adams & Washington—information of American Merchants—physicians—lawyers—bar of Connecticut—Phila., N. York—Georgia claims—memorial to Congress—state of society there—&c. &c. A very well-spent evening.[36]

Sunday, Decr. 3.—Finished looking over the 1st vol. of De Pauw's dissertations on the Egyptians & Chinese—a very considerable part of which I have carefully read—& with pleasure & instruction. Three medical visits. A visit from Mr. Roulet. Wm. & I dined & spent the afternoon at H. Johnson's: the evening partly at Riley's—& in part at home. Transcribed the letter to A. Smith Jr.

Monday, 4.—Four medical visits. Call at the printer's &c. Transcribed the letter to Dr. Rush, and wrote & transcribed that to Dr. Kollock. Visit from Mr. Roe: from Dr. Seaman: to Mr. Owens—ineffectual call on Dr. Bayley.[37] A call on Mr. & Mrs. Johnson, Comedians, in the evening—she unwell. Remainder of the evening at home. Both in the day & evening, superintending the arrangement of the Accounts of the Medical Repository. Continued the looking over of the Monthly Magazine.

Tuesday, 5.—Some further progress in the Monthly Magazine. Considerable advance in my Examination of Dr. Chisholm. A visit from Mitchill, & from Miller. A medical visit. Drank tea, & spent part of the evening, at Mr. Stansbury's; part of it at Dunlap's, who has not yet

---

[33] The "Scotch Encyclopedia" is the *Encyclopedia Britannica*, the result of the work of "a society of gentlemen in Scotland, printed in Edinburgh for A. Bell and C. Macfarquhar, and sold by Colin Macfarquhar at his printing office in Nicholson Street." The first edition was completed in 1771 in three volumes, published in numbers, the two first issued in December, 1768, and was completed in one hundred numbers. The second edition, also published in numbers, in ten volumes, was dated 1778 to 1783. The third edition in three hundred weekly numbers was completed in eighteen volumes in 1797. See the *Encyclopedia Britannica* (11th ed., 1910), "Encyclopedia."

[34] *The Secret Journal of a Self Observer.* Translated from the German original by the Rev. Peter Will (London, 1795). Original by Johann Casper Lavater, the celebrated physiognomist.

[35] George Anderson, *A Traveller in the East through Arabia, Persia, India, China, and Japan, etc. An account of these taken down by Adam Olearius* (Sleswick, 1669).

[36] An unusually detailed and revealing account of what meetings of the Friendly Club were really like.

[37] Richard Bayley was a health officer for the city of New York.

returned; & the remainder at home. Read Darwin's XIIIth Section of Zoonomia, & the notes connected therewith in the Botanic Garden. Sketched out the plan of my Prologue for opening the New Theater; & composed a number of verses—the commencement with uncommon difficulty.

Wednesday, 6.—Read the papers. Two medical visits —one out of town. Visit to Mitchill. At our printer's. Continued my Examination of Chisholm. Read in the Journal of Nicholson Nos. IV & V, equal to pp. 49. Called at Kent's—all out: at Gurdon Mumford's—all out: drank tea & spent considerable part of the evening, at Charles Adams's: the remainder at home.

These Nos. of Nicholson's Journal contain many important papers; & the information concerning the cure of the Rickets will be of almost immediate use to me.

To Benjamin Rush

The pressure of various & urgent business has alone prevented me from answering your letter till this time. And I am sure that when you learn how some portion of my hours has been employed, you will not be displeased with me. I think that I have it in my power to satisfy any dispassionate inquirer that Dr. Chisholm's history of the origin of the Grenada Fever of 1793, 94, is altogether incorrect; & not only that it did not arise from african contagion, but that it did originate in local causes & was destroyed by them. A general account of one part of the evidence has already been published by Mr. Webster; but he has, by no means, exhausted the subject, even as to fact; still less in respect to argument. His letters to Dr. Currie you have doubtless seen; & probably concur with me in the opinion of their utility in promoting the cause of truth. My paper will be published in a future No. of the Medical Repository; & I can not but think it a material triumph over the favorers of importation. I shall only add, relative to this question, that I expect, from Dr. Wheaton, a very ingenious physician lately removed to Providence from this city, a complete collection of facts concerning the Fever of the last summer, in that town; which, he assures me, will incontestibly demonstrate its local origin there.

It is unnecessary for me to express my indignation & regret at the late conduct of certain men in this city. I have the pleasure to assure you, however, that the great body of physicians & worthy citizens, view the matter in the same light: nor are their wishes for your removal hither at all diminished. But one sentiment prevails on this point. The faculty of physic maintain their original determinations so far that, I have authority to assure you they would not hesitate, could you be prevailed on to concur in the measure & remove hither, next Spring or Autumn, to establish a Medical School independent of the College: & this, tho' two of them derive a salary of 500 dollars each, from the institution. I mention this, to shew their sincerity. With such feelings in respect to this matter, we can not but hope that, should you persevere in your resolution of leaving Phila., you will not hesitate in fixing on this city for your permanent residence. But, whatever may be your ultimate decision on this point, it deserves to be highly gratifying & consolatory to you, that, amid all their own dissentions, so large a part of the most respectable physicians in this city, appplaud your conduct & take a deep interest in your welfare. What consistence & fixity would your removal here have given to some of the most important of medical principles! How would it have overborne & overwhelmed that opposition which even now lifts but a feeble head!

With regard to the Medical Repository, in the success of which I make no doubt of your feeling some interest, we only need that sort of patronage which is essential to all undertakings—a large subscription—to establish it completely. Could we prevail on Mr. Dobson, or any respectable Bookseller in Phila. to take any pains in its behalf, the support of Phila. alone would determine its success. May we not hope that it will deserve your recommendation?

With increasing respect & esteem, I remain affecty. yours,

Dec. 1. 1797.
Pine St. 45.   E. H. Smith.

To Lemuel Kollock

It is near nine months since I wrote to you, and near a year that I have heard nothing from you. Tho' I should regret the loss of any letters you might write to me, yet I can not but hope that some have miscarried; for I would willingly persuade myself that accident alone could so long have prevented my receiving some communication from you. But, if in reality you have not written, I hope this letter may be more fortunate than its predecessor.

Since I wrote, the plan referred to in my last has been carried into effect. From the manner in which you spoke of the design I venture to believe that you will be willing to promote it. I have, accordingly, sent you a copy of each No. for yourself; & have taken the additional liberty of transmitting with them, two other copies of each No., should any person in your vicinity be disposed to become subscribers. If these pamphlets arrive safe, I must press you to acknowlege the receit; & it will be a further gratification to me to receive any communications from you & your quarter for the Work, if the sample now sent shall encourage you to venture your name among those which you see there. I need not add that an extensive subscription & demand for the Repository would be a further & very satisfactory evidence of the approbation of your fellow-citizens.

Yours &c.
Dec. 4. '97.   E. H. Smith.

Thursday, Decr. 7.—I neglected to add to yesterday's notices that I wrote a short letter to Dr. Muret of Vevai, Swisserland. This morning, made a medical visit. Finished my examination of Chisholm. Recd. a line from the Department of State, acknowlegeing the receit of the Med. Repos: Nos. 1 & 2. & a letter from Mr. Rice, bookseller, Baltimore—on business of the Reposy. Visit of Mr. Deming of Lichfield, who brought me letters from my Father & from Fanny. Visit from Dr. Seaman. Recd. a letter from Dr. Eustis of Boston. Johnson & I drank tea & spent considerable part of the evening, at Kent's: Remainder at home. Finished looking over Nos. 4 & 5. of Nicholson's Journal—in which I have read all that I understand, & more. Almost every page mortifies & depresses me by the proofs it affords me of my own ignorance in every thing that deserves the name of science.

Friday, 8.—Two medical visits—one out of town. A great part of the morning occupied in business of the Repository: of the afternoon in various errands &c. Visit from Mr. Sharples: to Dr. Miller. Drank tea with Mrs. Dunlap. Called on Mr. Deming of Litchfield.[38] Was at Miln's book-auction a short time. Remainder of the evening at home—labouring away at my intended Prologue for opening the New Theater—of which I "strain'd from hard-bound brains"—a few lines very little to my satisfaction. I begin to fear that I have been so sparingly in the habit of coupling verses of late, that I shall lose my facility of doing it, without some occasional practice. The great difficulty, in the present instance is, to say much in a small space. Multum in parvo should be my motto; but I fear that parvum in multo will be more descriptive of my performance. Recd. a letter from Richard Alsop.

Saturday, 9th.—Recd. a letter from Dr. Rush. Visit from Dr. Osborn & Mr. Webster. Read five of Mr. Webster's Letters to Dr. Currie; the News-papers; a long communication for the Repository; & the Report of the Baltimore Board of Health. Visit to Dr. Miller —he being out, at first, set some time with his brother. Call on Mr. Owens. Dined & spent the afternoon at Mr. Sharples's—where were only a Mr. Dunn—an irish advocate & member of their parliament; a Capt. of the Frigate & his lieutenant—& myself. The Capt. (Tucker) informed me of a Yellow Fever that had proved very mortal in Bermuda, the last summer, chiefly to young persons—& which probably originated there—as the people & physicians could not tell where it came from. Mr. Dunn is the gentleman Mrs. Lovegrove met with, on her eastern tour, at a lodging-house in Boston, of whom she spake in very high terms. Nothing fell from him to-day that indicated any extraordinary powers. His face bespeaks intelligence, & would be handsome were it not that he never looks a person in the face. He seems, at times, buried in a reverie—but which never prevents his hearing & replying to a question, without any change of countenance or attitude. I am ready to suspect that his plan is to penetrate into the character of others, while he conceals his own. In such cases, it generally happens that there is something which requires concealment.

Club night—G. M. Woolsey's turn—present—Johnson, Smith, & G. M. Woolsey—Dr. Miller visitor.

I opened my subscription for "Alcuin" to-day.

Sunday, 10.—Mr. Deming of Lichfield breakfasted & spent all the morning with me. He related me some facts respecting the *Reason* of birds, which I noted, & shall publish. A visit from Dr. Miller. He will go on to Phila. on the business of the Repository. Wrote & transcribed the two succeeding letters. Wrote letters also to Drs. Leib, Dewees, Strong & Woodhouse, Phila., to send by Dr. Miller—& to Mr. James Rice, booksellers, Baltimore, concerning the Repository. Attended the funeral of my out-town patient, who died of pulmonary consumption on friday last. Spent part of the evening at Riley's: The remainder till nine, at Hodgkinson's. He lent me "The Italian Monk"—a play by James Boaden, founded on Mrs. Radcliff's "Italian."[39] This play is poor enough, but is very likely to please on the stage.

Monday, Decr. 11.—Wrote & transcribed the two succeeding letters, having recd. a letter from Dr. Barton this morning. A visit from Mr. Webster, who left me his 24th letter to read. I read it. Two visits for medical advice. Visit from Mr. Stanley of Fort Montgomery. He is to collect me some choice specimens of Iron ores, in his neighborhood. Read a number of poems & letters &c. written by the late Dr. Wm. M. Johnson. All are elegant; & some of the poems deserve immortality, & would not disgrace the first poets in our language. Visit from Mitchill & Miller. Evening at the Theater—which opened in John St. with our own Company—"The Young Quaker" & "The Purse"[40]—a full house, & the players cordially welcomed. Read T. B. Bayley's little pamphlet on *Manures*[41]—which I recd. this day, with a business letter from Mr. Beers of N. Haven.

Tuesday, 12.—Wrote short letters to Mr. Tracy, Dr. Griffitts, & Mr. Poulson of Phila.[42] Errands &c. which occupied some time. Visit from Mr. Webster. Visit to Dr. Miller: to Dr. Mitchill. Called on Mr. Deming. Dr. Miller & I went to see the Dwarf—for the purpose of gaining some account of him. The crowd of company was so great that we could do nothing. Recd. a letter from Dr. Wheaton. Visit from Mr. Roulet. Prepared some copy for our Printers. Began Yates & McLean's (of Calcutta) Book on Fevers &c.[43] Drank tea with Miller, & we went again to see the Dwarf. We saw him, but could not affect our purpose, for the present. Spent part of the evening at Kent's—remainder at home. Some

---

[38] For once Smith spells the name of his home town correctly: Litchfield.

[39] *The Italian Monk* (Haymarket, 1797).
[40] John C. Cross, *The Purse, or the Benevolent Tar* (1794).
[41] Not found.
[42] Zachariah Poulson, Jr., printer and librarian.
[43] Only one title is usually given for these doctors collaborating as authors: William Yates and Charles MacLean, *A View of the Science of Life, etc.* [a thirteen line title which may be their "Book on the Fevers"] ... *and a Dissertation on the Sources of Epidemic and Pestilential Diseases* ... by Charles MacLean (Calcutta and Philadelphia, 1797).

further progress in the composition of the Prologue. I never wrote any thing with more difficulty.

Wednesday, 13.—Read the newspapers. Some little advance in Yates & McLean. Visit from Mr. Sharples: from Mr. Owens—& accompanied to the Bookseller's. At our printers'. Medical visit. Read Webster's 25th & last letter in ms. Added some few lines to what was before written of my prologue. Made some corrections in a piece for the Repository. Visit from Mitchill—who read me his review of Brown's Inaug: Dissert. Dined & spent the afternoon at Mr. Boyd's. At the Theater. Mr. Simpson made his first appearance, here, in *Mr. Hardy,* Belles Stratagem:[44] *so so.* An hour at Riley's. Remainder of the evening at Professor Post's.

To Fanny Smith

Your letter, my dear sister, for which I thank you very sincerely, is a new proof that it is not incapacity, but want of perseverance, which is the only obstacle to your improvement. Observe now, the real difficulty; the real state of your case. On subjects with which you are familiar, & have been accustomed to think, you express yourself clearly, & with sufficient elegance. It is not to be supposed that you should find the same facility in apprehending a new topic & discoursing upon it. No one ever did. But you must not believe from this that it is any proof of want of understanding in you; it is only proof of the real profundity of the subject of investigation. To render it familiar to your mind, you must think, & speak, & *write* upon it. Your ideas may be confused at first, but they will gradually gain precision & propriety. What ought to encourage you is, that men of distinguished talents have applied themselves for centuries, to these inquiries; & after all, there is considerable diversity of opinion. On all leading points, however, so much is learnt that with your advantages, a person of much more moderate capacity, with some dilligence, may conquer every material difficulty. I have effected this, in some degree, unaided. You may do the same. But you are also certain of all my assistance. Apply yourself, therefore! Do not suffer indolence, our common enemy, under the plea, or in the shape, of modest self-distrust, to subdue your spirit. Depend upon it, there is nothing here but what thousands have found as formidable, & thousands have afterwards overcome. There is not the least reason for doubt. All that is necessary is dilligence. Return, then, to the attack; be bold; & be triumphant.

I am still uncertain what Sonnets I have sent you. In your next letter furnish me with the first line of each now in your possession.

My best love to my mother.

Dec. 10. 1797.
Pine St. 45. E. H. Smith.

---

[44] Hannah Cowley (1780). This was one of the plays that Smith and his friends produced while he was living in Wethersfield.

To Reuben Smith

I have recd. your letter, by Mr. Deming, with the money; & shall send you inclosed Philips & Clark's receit for one hundred dollars.

In respect to the Medical Repository, we had no expectations, nor scarcely any wish, to make money by it. All we want is to save ourselves & promote medical & scientific improvement. This I hope will be accomplished, in the end. For subscribers, we have, in New York, more men, not physicians, than who are: more than two to one, I believe. I wish that the example of these gentlemen may be followed. For our work is not meant to be confined to mere medicine, but to include natural history & agriculture, chemistry & the arts.

You mention that you have added your own name to the list of subscribers, & that Dr. Rockwell has subscribed. You sent me but five names at first; & paid me afterwards six dollars. Are there seven subscribers, or only six, beside yourself? If seven, who is the sixth?

We have nothing new.

My best love to my mother & friends.

Dec. 10. '97. E. H. Smith.

To Benjamin Rush

The sudden departure of our friend Dr. Miller, for Phila., allows me little further opportunity of replying to your last very friendly letter than to express my great satisfaction at the event which has contributed to your decided independency & elevation over all the petty struggles & hostilities of short-sighted malignity & blindfold ignorance. Painful as the scenes must have been, thro' which you have passed in the course of some few years, there is one point of View in which they can not fail of affording abundant gratification to a mind like yours. They have been the fruitful occasion of awakening a spirit of research & observation, of discussion & industry, far beyond every thing before known in the United States & which promises to conduct us rapidly to the goal of truth, & summit of medical improvement. Henceforth it must every day become more difficult for men to build reputations on taciturnity, & the mere non-performance of palpable injury to their employers. Some evident & undeniable proof of ability & skill, & science will be required in future; & even the indolent will be driven to study.

I rejoice to hear that your Medical Society are likely to prosecute such inquiries, & to statedly favour the world with the result of their investigation. Every new undertaking of this kind will increase the value of every other, by exciting greater public curiosity as well as competition & science. I hope it may shame the College into silence, or startle it into action. For I think it fortunate, in some respects, that opposition is still made to the doctrine of local origin; since it obliges us to inquire deep & widely, & will be the cause of such investigations as shall elucidate every minute part of the subject, & remove the lightest shadow of uncertainty.

Were this not, now, to be the case, the discussion might be renewed half a century hence; & the whole ground again have to be travelled over.

It gives me pleasure to learn that there is some prospect of the republication of Mr. Webster's letters in Phila. There, where the medical school is so large, it may answer; here, he would be certain to lose by it. The belief of the local origin of Yellow Fever is so general here, that the citizens almost deem further argument superfluous; & are, therefore, little likely to purchase what they may think works of supererogation.

In respect to the distinction between the fevers you refer to, do you suppose it *generic*? I confess that I have been inclined to think with Mr. Webster. The present time does not permit me to labour any argument on this point; but I will submit a few reasons, on this side of the question, to your better judgement.

1. The analysis of vegetable & animal matter shews that a great part of the vegetable race contain the same elements as the animals, only in various proportions—in particular, that they contain that peculiar element without which putrefaction, properly so called, can not or does not take place.

2. Marshes, in whose neighborhood intermittent fevers, & remitting fevers, dysenteries so generally arise, must contain infinite multitudes of little animals, who perish on steady exposure to sun & air, as well as vegetables, & combine their exhalations, with those of vegetables.

3. In cities, especially in cities on low grounds, near marshes, or on made ground, a larger proportion of animal putrefactive matter is united to the ordinary causes of fever; beside those disadvantages in respect to ventilation &c. which are always, in some degree, consequent on such collections of buildings.

4. In some cities the mass of animal putrefaction may be peculiarly increased, by suffering dead bodies to accumulate, unburied.

From these sources it would seem reasonable to expect different degrees of fever, rather than different fevers; as it would appear that all arose from the same cause—putrefaction—but variously concentrated.

1. Thus, in the country, near marshes, in ordinary years, we might look for intermittents, & diarrheas perhaps. In uncommon seasons, for remittants of various degrees of violence, & dysenteries. All these will be modified by the extent of the commixture of animal & vegetable matters. Thus, in Sheffield, one year, when the Bilious Fever was worst, it has since been discovered, that great numbers of little fish were left out of water, & putrefied.

2. In towns, the greater accumulation of causes will, in common years, produce intermittents early & diarrheas—a little later remittants & choleras. In extraordinary seasons, with uncommon negligence, yellow fever, or violent dysentery. And all will be increased by peculiarities of person, place & food.

3. In the rest where local causes may be still more active & prevalent; where, from their cities having been settled for ages & of course animal recrements & excrements accumulated for ages; the mass of animal putrefaction is much greater than in our recent establishments; where their towns are very badly built; & where much less attention is often paid to speedy burial, than among us; the contagion is multiplied a thousand fold, & produces more terrible effects, tho' not more mortal.

This is but a feeble & hasty outline of conjecture, which I have not time to support by evidence; & I must request your forgiveness for the presumption I have used in stating them at this time. But I dare to expect your pardon; & that you will, in proper time, enlighten my mind, if your own ampler researches do not incline you to believe my opinions conformable to fact.

With great respect & esteem, Yours &c.
Dec. 11. 1797.
Pine St. 45.   E. H. Smith.

[*To*] *Benjamin Smith Barton*

Our friend Dr. Miller's approaching visit to Phila. permits me to return a speedy answer to your letter of the 5th inst. which I this moment recd.

The Nos. of the Repository have only been delayed, from want of such an opportunity as you refer to. They will now be transmitted to you by Dr. Miller; together with so much of Mitchill's Mineralogical Papers as is printed in the 3rd. No. The next head, under the first general division, is "The Alluvial Tracts." This will appear in the 4th No. The 5th will probably contain the Islands—& conclude the Account.

I am collecting some curious specimens of Ores &c. from Connect. particularly of Cobalt, & what is supposed to be Arsenic. I hope it will be in my power to forward some of the same to you, if you are not already provided with them, when I have recd. them. As the Connect. River is frozen, this may possibly not be till Spring.

I have obtained a few striking facts relative to the *Reason* of Birds; which I shall publish in the simple form of facts, in the No. of the Repository now printing. They will form an interesting appendix to your collection on this subject. Indeed, we are not in the way of receiving a great variety of communications; & nothing is wanting to the complete & permanent establishment of the Repository but a large subscription. In this respect we venture to repose some confidence in your friendly offices.

I am particularly curious to learn what may be the result of your inquiries concerning the *impression* you speak of. The discoveries respecting the Mammoth, & the Animal whose bones have lately been found in Virginia—(which I presume, from the acct. given me by Mr. Hopkins, who discovered a part of them—to resemble those found near the River La Plata) authorize us to believe that many animals, now perhaps extinct, formerly existed in this country, which were peculiar to it; & lead to a hope that future inquiries may bring forth to public view a great variety of these singular remains. In this case, how many of our remaining difficulties, in all departments of Natural Science, may be elucidated or removed.

I rejoice to find that the spirit for medical pursuits is on the increase, & that your Classes are full: I think the number of students increases here: Tho' it bears no proportion to yours. Dr. Kuhn's resignation is sooner than I expected. Dr. Rush, I suppose, supplies his place for the present—or have you made new arrangements?

Yours sincerely,

Dec. 11. 1797.
Pine St. 45. E. H. Smith.

Thursday, 14.—Some further progress in Yates & Maclean. Completed the rough mass of my Prologue. This occupied me till some time in the afternoon. I wrote more, more easily, & better to-day, than in all before. Still, my piece is two thirds too long, & must be hewn & paired. Visit from Dr. Mitchill—with his Review of Peters. At our printer's. Called at Miller's, and found him gone to Staten-Island. Called at Mrs. Miller's: & afterwards at G. M. Woolsey's Store, & after that at Gahn's —he not at home. Drank tea (& Wm.) at H. Johnson's. We spent the evening, *en famille*, with Mr. & Mrs. Sharples—at their new house, in Greenwich St.

Friday, Decr. 15.—This day has been rainy; &, having nothing, in particular, to call me abroad, I have not thrown aside my morning gown. Completed Yates & McLean's joint publication. They have made some judicious corrections of Brown's doctrine; but, notwithstanding the gross undervaluation of Zoonomia, this doctrine, with all their improvements, is wonderfully inferior to that of Darwin. Some difference probably, perhaps very considerable, is demanded in the treatment of temperate & tropical diseases; but, beside the absurdities & contradictions of which they are guilty, it may fairly be questioned whether their cures were as pleasantly & quickly performed, as might have been effected by other means. The salivating powers of Opium, if the whole be not a mistake, are matter of very curious inquiry. Is it not possible that the systems of the subjects of this event may have been, in every case, pervaded with Mercury, & only determined to this state by the additional stimulus of Opium? Some objections occur to the sentiments, in the "treatise on Mercury" which I have not time to state. The "essay on pestilential diseases &c." contains much valuable & correct, mingled with some absurd & contradictory, reasoning. It is complete as to specific contagion or the communication of the disease by contact—with but few exceptions. The principal fault is that the author overlooks the putrid exhalations of animals, vegetables, marshes &c. Dr. Saml. Osborn drank tea, & spent part of the evening here. Afterwards, I read Mr. Mason's Sermon, intituled "Hope for the Heathen"—an indifferent performance; continued the "Monthly Magazine"; & corrected a proof sheet of the "Botanic Garden"; which Swords is reprinting.

Saturday, 16.—Read the news-papers. Continued the Monthly Magazine. At our printer's. Medical visit. At Dr. Miller's. At a Book-auction. Visit, with Miller, to the Dwarf. Visit from Mr. Sharples. Drank tea at Miller's, after which, we went to see the Dwarf again— of whose history we took notes, for the purpose of giving an account of him in the Repository. Called in at the Theater a few minutes. "Suspicious Husband"[45] the play. A Mrs. Simpson was in *Clarinda*, owing to Mrs. Johnson's illness. I stayed but a few minutes, & saw little of her. Club night—W. W. Woolsey's turn— Present—Johnson, Kent, Smith, & W. W. Woolsey. Came home & corrected a proof of the Repository.

Sunday, 17.—Read & compared with the original & with the translator's of Goethe's "Iphigenia in Tauris," Mr. Stanley's translation of Bürger's "Leonora"—IInd edition. It is much inferior to the other. Continued the Monthly Magazine. Visit to Dr. Miller; to Riley's; to Mrs. Dunlap—(Dunlap had not returned); to G. M. Woolsey's. Wm. & I dined & spent the afternoon at H. Johnson's—where I read "Wives as they were &c."[46] The plot unnatural; but the piece contains some finely-contrived scenes. Visit to Mr. & Mrs. Johnson—Commedians. Called at Riley's. Remainder of the evening at home. Corrected proofs of the Med. Reposy. & of the Botanic Garden.

Monday, 18.—Wrote & transcribed the succeeding letters to Dr. Eustis & Mr. Alsop—& "The Zephyrs,"[47] the translation referred to in the letter to Alsop. A visit from Mr. Tisdale the Engraver &c. who shewed me, in M.S. his well-executed satire on Dr. Buxton. A visit from Mr. or Dr. Morgan J. Rhees, the friend of Josh. Strong, from whom he brought me a lengthy letter. A visit from Dr. Mitchill. Drank tea with Dr. Seaman. Called at Mr. Minturn's, at W. W. Woolsey's, & at Moses Rogers's—& all were absent from home. Called at Mrs. Dunlap's: & at Mrs. Morton's. Remainder of the evening at home. Continued the Monthly Magazine. The Philadelphians do not seem disposed to countenance our Med. Reposy.

Tuesday, Decr. 19.—Continued the Monthly Magazine. Attended Mitchill's Lecture—afterwards at his room, on business of the Repository—then we called at Mr. Garnett's, who was not at home—then at Swords's —then at Berry & Rogers's auction, where I was introduced to Mr. Garnett, & where I met Dr. Kingsley.

---

[45] Dr. Benjamin Hoadley, (1747).

[46] Mrs. Elizabeth Inchbald, *Wives as they Were and Maids as they Are* (1797).

[47] *The Zephyrs* is not mentioned as such in Smith's letter to Alsop (the second letter following the "Diary" entry for December 20). He, however, does say that it was a translation from the German done some time earlier. His most recent reading in German was in Goethe; he also read some of Stanley's translation of Bürger's "Leonora." If it was from Bürger, one possibility might be the rather juvenile poem, "The Breezes of May."

Thence I went to Charles Adams's. He proposed to me to undertake the Editorship of "The Diary," a Daily Paper in this town. The matter was talked of, but nothing concluded. I dined & spent a part of the afternoon, with Kingsley, at his lodgings. He is full of machines &c. as ever; & leaves town tomorrow. At Tisdale's, on business. At G. M. Woolsey's Store. Drank tea, & spent most of the evening, at W. W. Woolsey's. Read Mrs. Woolsey "Alcuin." Rest of the evening at home. Looked over two volumes of "The Poetry of the World"—trash for the most part—& part of a late selection from the Somers Papers.

Wednesday, 20.—Read the newspapers. Wrote the letter to Dr. Wheaton. A visit from Mr. Dunn, the Irish Counsellor & M. P. He left a small package for Mrs. Lovegrove. A visit from Dr. Seaman. A visit from Mr. Stark Robertson. He invited me to dine with him. A visit from Dr. or Mr. Rees or Rhys—the Welch Clergyman. Recd. a letter from Dr. Buel, inclosing a part of his Paper on the Fever & Dysentery, Sheffield, of 1796—which I read—& find well drawn up. Recd. by Dunlap, who returned this day, a letter from Mr. Quincy of Boston—encouraging, as to the Repository. Recd. also a letter from Dobson of Phila. in which he agrees to take XX copies on our terms. Dr. Miller will settle this with him. Visited Dunlap. He is & has been well. Prospects in Boston, for Theatricals, as connected with our Company better. Called at Mitchill's. He absent. While I waited for him, read H. M. Williams's Sonnets in her translation of Paul & Virginie—& great part of the Hermit of Warkworth.[48] Dined, & spent the evening at Mr. Robertson's. Genl. Gates & Lady, Mr. & Mrs. Garnet, Mr. Rutherford, & a Mr. Jones (from Ireland) at dinner. Mr. & Mrs. Sharples spent the evening. An agreable time. Came home, & corrected a proof of the Repository & of the Botanic Garden.

To William Eustis

Lest you should attribute my apparent neglect to a disposition to be guilty of that which is real, it is proper that I inform you that your letter, tho' dated early in Nov. has not reached me till very lately. I should have replied immediately; but the want of a private conveyance (particularly for the copies of the Repository), & the hope of previously hearing from Dr. Morse, held me silent. But, tho' neither this want nor this hope, have been gratified, I am unwilling by any longer delay, to raise a doubt in your mind concerning the temper with which your letter was recd.

I thank you sir, & may express to you the thanks of my associates, for the interest you take in our enterprize, & your favorable opinion of its character. It is our most earnest wish that the publication may increase in merit, & attain to that method which we rather hope for, than speedily expect. But of this we should have no doubt, in due time, could the *essential* encouragement of a sufficient subscription be extended & secured to us. In this, we are considerably deficient, tho' the number of subscribers weekly increases, & is perhaps as great as we ought to expect, in this commencement of a new undertaking. I must acknowlege, however, that I did expect more from the medical curiosity of Boston; nor am I willing to believe that it will remain so limited, should the Repository at all deserve the good opinion of sensible & scientific men. Some Communications from your quarter would, no doubt, have a powerful tendency to excite the attention of gentlemen residing there. On every other acct. as well as this, we shall receive, with pleasure, what ever you may favor us with; on this acct. an early communication will particularly befriend us, & we shall lay aside other materials, which accumulate on our hands, to make room for it.

When Dr. Morse was here, he kindly undertook to make some interest for our Work. For this purpose he carried with him a dozen copies of No. 1. He was to fix on some bookseller, as a suitable person to transact the business, & to send us notice. We have heard of his friendly exertions, but have not been so fortunate as to receive any letter from him. But we have since forwarded an equal number of No. II. & hope soon to obtain some information from him. Till this reaches us, we can not, in delicacy, attempt any arrangement in Boston. We are, however, obliged by your friendly suggestion, & do not mean that any improper delay shall take place in the delivery of the work to such subscribers as are known to us.

I do not perfectly comprehend that part of your letter, which relates to something published in Mr. Webster's Papers. He has nearly concluded a long series of letters to Dr. Currie of Phila. on the origin of the Yellow Fever &c. which are generally esteemed; & he has, before they were commenced, published some paragraphs on the same subject—of which I have no particular recollection. But, (as your remark glances that way) it may be proper to assure you that neither Dr. Miller nor myself, have written any thing for any paper, & Dr. Mitchill only such things as you see his name to.

In respect of manner, as well as matter, I may speak for us all, that corrections will be cheerfully received & attended to. But, you will readily perceive that, to make them useful, they must be particular. It is because you have not been particular, that it is impossible for me to derive advantage from a caution contained in your letter; tho' I admire, & am obliged by, the frankness which dictated it. Should no other conveyance soon occur, the Nos. for yourself & for the gentlemen whose names you sent me, shall be forwarded by Water—& in respect to subscriptions, if it will be more convenient, they may be advanced for a longer period, & sent at your leisure. One third No. is now in the press.

Yours &c.

Dec. 18. 1797.
Pine St. 45.

E. H. Smith.

---

[48] Thomas Percy, *Hermit of Warkworth* (London, 1771).

To Richard Alsop

Your last letter, my dear friend, leaves little opportunity for any other reply than of thanks for your attention to my requests. I hope that they will not prove unreasonably troublesome to you. There must be *some* labour, or you would have no room for the display of your friendship.

I have been hitherto unable to fulfill your wishes, in respect to "Earl Walter's Chace," & "Fiesco." Neither of them have reached us. But, in further return for your Translation from the Italian, I shall send you one of mine from the German—which perhaps you may have seen, as it has not been lately done. It will be new, however, to Mrs. Alsop; & possibly to some others of our friends.

I am satisfied with your opinion of Dr. Mitchill's Imitation; but you say nothing of the Extract from the *Columbiad*—a thing so precious that I expected a volume of comment on it, in your letter. Do you wish the author's tragedy? He has published it here—& dedicated it to Colonel Burr! See what it is to patronise the Muses.

Now for a more serious piece of literary intelligence. I am about publishing, by subscription, a performance of our friend Charles B. Brown. Do you wish to subscribe? It is a dialogue, in the manner of the Ancients, on questions relative to the intellectual equality of the sexes. It is eloquently, & I believe inoffensively, written. When I say inoffensively, you will understand me as referring to religious prejudices. The price of each copy is 50 cents.

Do you hear any thing of our Repository, in your County? We have, in it, only three subscribers; & one of them is Mr. Dana. Is there no way of exciting some more liberal curiosity among the practitioners, & gentlemen there? For you know that we are by no means confined to Medical subjects. Our third No., for instance, will contain a very respectable letter, from the Revd Mr. Parsons of E. Haddam, giving an account of a disease among cattle, in that part of the country.

My letter is a thing of "shreds & patches"—but you must accept it, for the present.

   Remembrances to Mrs. Alsop & friends.
Decr. 18. 1797.
Pine St. 45.   E. H. Smith.

P. S.—When you write next, be so kind as to inform me what you gave for a copy of Strutt's Dictionary of Engravers, which you bought, when you lived here, at an Auction, for Mr. Riley. I have purchased it of him, & am to have it at the exact price you gave. You will recollect the work—it is two vols. 4to—& from the fine Engraving of Adam & Eve, by Strutt from a picture of Rafaelle d'Urbino.

              Yours
Dec. 18. [1797]   E. H. S.

To Levi Wheaton

I have deferred answering your letter of the 21st ulto., which I recd. only about ten days since, in the hope of obtaining for you a copy of the Medical Annals. On inquiry, I can not find it in Town. But, before this letter is sent off, I expect to procure for you the new work from the East Indies—of which you may have seen some mention in our papers. No opinion on it is necessary, as you will judge for yourself; & as some account of it may possibly appear in the Repository.

Mr. J. Minturn has returned from his journey &, from the little I have seen of him, well. I meant to have been more certain of this, but when I have called, the family have been absent from home. In "The Monthly account of Diseases," inserted in the Monthly Magazine for May 1796—I find a note of this kind, on the title *Hectica Adolescentium*—a disorder very frequent in young persons, "during the period of their growth, after the age of puberty. It is characterised by hectical paroxyms occuring every day, pain in the limbs, painful swelling in the joints, loss of sleep & appetite, with great emaciation. If a cough does not supervene, the patients recover in ten or twelve weeks." Now, tho' Mr. Minturn's case is considerably different, in some respects, yet in others there is so much resemblance, that I am not absolutely without hopes that the disease may be obviated. His cough is gone; & his appetite, strength, & colour, have all returned. But I esteem his situation somewhat uncertain, for the two next ensuing years; or, untill his growth becomes more consolidated.

Speaking of the Monthly Magazine—which you know is edited by Dr. Aikin of London—it is a work every way deserving of your reading & possession: especially in your present situation.

From your manner of speaking of Dr. Bowen's letter, I suppose you are desirous of knowing what are its contents, by my means. Hosack has been some time at Phila. where he is marrying. When he returns, there will be feasting &c. so that no temperate opportunity can soon be expected for a conversation which would lead, naturally, to a request such as you hint at: and I am not sufficiently intimate with him to make a direct request. But, probably, this is a matter of little moment; as there is great reason to believe that Dr. Bowen's Letter will never see the light. It is currently reported, among the Students, that Gillespie has given up the matter entirely; & is even offended with Hosack's publication in which his name was mentioned. If this is true, & I suspect it is, nothing will come of it; for Hosack himself will not venture to publish any thing, after what has been done by Webster & others. Beside, the review of his brother's *practical* Essay, leaves him very little reason to expect more favor for a *theoretical* dissertation from the same quarter. I am persuaded, that your Essay will be better, if written without any reference to what Bowen may have advanced; for, then, you will proceed methodically, & as if nothing had been before written. But I will take some pains to ascertain what his letter contains: tho' I think you will do well not to delay your inquiries for the receit of such uncertain information.

Comps. to Mrs. W.

Dec. 20. [1797]. Yours sincerely— E. H. Smith.

To Tho: O'H. Croswell

When I sent you the pamphlets I was too much hurried to make a suitable reply to your friendly & interesting letter. My present leisure will only allow me to send a shorter answer than I originally designed, & one very inadequate to my wishes. For I am exceedingly desirous of renewing, with more regularity, our former correspondence; & if Mrs. Croswell will hold the pen, when your fingers are out of order, I think something might be done both for friendship & improvement. To this, I hope, she will have no objection; since marriage, tho' it has been the murderer of our epistolary intercourse, has been generally considered as allowing greater freedom to the ladies than celibacy.

I thank you, very sincerely, for the pains you have taken in behalf of the Repository. I assure you that many who have *promised* much more, have *done* much less. I suppose that the names you sent me are entirely of physicians? I ask this, as we shall publish, with our 4th No. the names of subscribers, & wish to know their professions & titles. From so promising a beginning, in your quarter, I indulge very flattering expectations of the future. It will be doing a great thing for Medicine, in the United States, if the body of practitioners can be induced to read, if it be only the Repository. It will do more, in 30 years, than all that has been effected since the settlement of the country. For those who read this publication—or a great part of them—will not be satisfied without reading something else. Who is Elijah Adams of N. E. Town?

When I sent you the *Operas* were there only *six*? or did I send *seven*? There ought to have been *seven*. I desire Mrs. Croswell's opinion on this Poem; & hope she will give it freely. Tell her that, tho' poets are called an *irritable race*, she need not be apprehensive of exciting my resentment by any condemnations. I dare not say that her praise will not augment my vanity.

I suspected that your patient's case was irremediable. It presents us with one fact, however, which is very important, & which I may possibly take the liberty of making public, on your authority. I have, now, no doubt that her disease was pulmonary consumption. The fact I refer to is, that an Intermittent should come on, at all, while she laboured under this disease—but especially, that it should not entirely *suspend* the disease. One of two inferences must [be] inevitable & flow from this—either that the human system, (contrary to the doctrine of the celebrated Mr. Hunter & others) will admit of more morbid actions than one, at the same time; or, that the morbid cause of Consumption & Fever is the same. A curious fact, connected with this question, you will find, in the Med: Repos: No. 1. under "Hints, Facts, & Inquiries"—& the subject deserves the most thorough investigation.

Your information, relative to the course of diseases, in Catskill, is very interesting; but you might make it still more so, & such as to render it a public benefit, with very little additional trouble. Allow me to suggest a method. Make a list of all your patients, each month—setting opposite to the name, the disease, & the person's age & sex: Continue this thro' the year. At the end of each month, notice the event of each case; & add any remarks that occur to you, respecting the disease, the treatment, the individual, the weather &c. All this would not require an hour's time in a month to perform; & the information would be invaluable. I wish you would do this—& communicate regularly to me—as often as once a month, or once a quarter. Half a sheet of paper, will contain all that, except in extraordinary cases, will be necessary.

I should like to have some topographical account of Catskill. Have you any Marshes near the Landing, or near the old town? & what distance is there between them? & what number of inhabitants in each? & what their occupations? A brief answer, at least, to these inquiries will gratify me much.

I believe, with you, that nothing can be done, in your vicinity, for Manumission. It must work its way slowly; but it will eventually triumph. Perhaps the condition of the Negroes is as tolerable among the Dutch farmers, as any where. They live, I suppose, pretty much like their masters; & not infrequently enjoy more real authority over the farm &c. than their owners.

I heard from Dr. Buel a few days since. He is well. Our Lichfield friends were also well, ten days ago. Timothy[49] is *well to study* as the N. York phrase is.

My best love to Mrs. Croswell—to yourself the friendship of former times.

Dec. 20. 1797. E. H. Smith.

To Josiah Quincy

I feel much obliged by your friendly letter, by Mr. Dunlap; & am induced to believe that you will receive the following detail, relative to the Repository, without disgust.

When the Original Circular Address was printed, the earliest private opportunity was taken to transmitting a number of Copies to Dr. Eustis, presuming on his politeness & love of science—with a request, as none of the physicians of Boston were known to me, that he would give them a circulation among his medical bretheren. The engagements of Dr. E. prevented his replying till after the subscription-papers were issued. A number of these were also forwarded to him, in season, with a similar request. These, the Dr. informs me in a letter lately recd. from him, were distributed among the Physi-

---

[49] Timothy [Pierce] of Litchfield.

cians of Boston—with what effect is only to be inferred from this circumstance, that, excepting that retained by Dr. E. none has been returned to us, & that with but two names upon it, beside his own.

While I was taking these steps, Dr. Mitchill, who had long corresponded with Dr. Waterhouse, & Dr. Miller, who was personally acquainted with Dr. Spooner, performed the same offices in respect to them. I am sorry to add, that they have recd. no replies from either of these gentlemen, after an interval of some months of expectation.

In this situation of things, you will not wonder that we were doubtful of the success of our publication in Boston. If professional men were destitute of curiosity, or wanted confidence in our exertions, we had little right to look to others who might be supposed less engaged in subjects of Chemical, Medical & Natural knowlege. At the same time, when we recollected how much the country was overrun with subscriptions, & how many scientific projects, had died in the conception, we were less surprized at the inattention of literary & scientific men to our particular enterprize; but not the more encouraged to renew our application to them. While we were uncertain what further to do, in respect to Boston, Dr. Morse of Charles-town, who was here, very unexpectedly & kindly, undertook to carry on with him a dozen copies of our 1st No. which was then just published, & to make some interest for it. He was to take the additional trouble of making some arrangement for us, with a Bookseller in Boston. This we hope has been effected, thro' his agency; & we only wait to hear from him, to adopt a line of proceeding, which shall remove every obstacle in the way to supplying our subscribers with certainty, regularity, & celerity. In the mean time, all possible care will be taken not to disappoint the wishes of such gentlemen as may favor the Repository with their patronage. I shall seize the first opportunity of transmitting the copies for Mr. Davis & Dr. Bartlett—to your care, if you please, at this time, in connection with this letter.

I trust that you have long since recd. the IInd No. of the Repository; & am, with respectful & affectionate compliments for Mrs. Quincy, & with a proper sense of your friendly offices.

Dec. 20. 1797.

Yours &c.
E. H. Smith

To Joseph Strong

I wrote to you, a few days since, by my friend Dr. Miller, with whom, I trust, you are, by this time, well acquainted. Your long & interesting letter, by Mr. Rhees, has since been received, & perused, & reperused, with much pleasure & some improvement. I regret that it is not in my power to make a reply worthy of it. I regret, too, that my numerous occupations & single state do not allow of my witnessing, in the common way, that respect which I really entertain for your friend Mr. Rhees. Should it be necessary, you will be able to explain to him, the nature of my situation, with more propriety than I can myself.

In respect to salivation, I perceive that the determining why Mercury salivates, would go far to explain why it will not salivate. But this action is not peculiar, you know, to Mercury; & late experiments seem to lead us to more consistent notions concerning this singular tendency of this mineral. I have made a few, imperfect trials with the Nitrous Acid; I have salivated one man with it. What was remarkable in this case, was—that the salivation was not painful, the gums neither swelled nor sore, & the breath perfectly sweet. You have doubtless read McLean & Yates' (E. India) publication.

We find, there, some instances of Salivation by Opium; & it is mentioned as a fact of no infrequent occurrence. I confess that I have some suspicion that there was Mercury in the system, before the Opium was administered. But this is mere suspicion. What shall we make of the remarkable abundance of Saliva in habitual drunkards? Has it any relation to this subject? If the principle, concerning Salivation, laid down by Yates & McLean, were true—which I do not believe— some confirmation might be derived from this fact of the drunkards: for their great flow of saliva is generally in the morning, when there has been a subduction of stimulus for several hours—during sleep; & it is generally arrested by the morning dram.

I will not pretend to comment on the Case you have sent me. To do this to any advantage, as you intimate, would be to write a volume, not a letter. It has suggested some topics of inquiry & reflection. I have no doubt that the Sulphuric Acid was very injurious to her. Without it, she might, perhaps, have recovered after a very slight illness. But do you believe the Bile in fault? & that it is any cause of this disease—the Yellow Fever? My sentiments take an opposite course, & incline me to the belief that, as far as it operates at all, it is in counteraction of the Contagion of Fever. This last material may deprave it; but in just that degree, I suspect, is the morbid miasm deprived of its power to injure.

Your opinions, concerning the *modus operandi* of Contagions, coincide with mine. Like you, I should have free recourse to stimuli, of every kind, in the asthenic state of this Fever. Then, I have found not only spirituous fermentations &c. very beneficial, but mercurial frictions peculiarly so; & I have seen the constitution acquire such an appetite for mercury as to languish immediately on its discontinuance: and this was observable, in one patient, for more than a fortnight.

Suppression of urine, & relaxation of the sphincter ani with inaction of the rectum, I believe to be generally, fatal symptoms. But they are not always so; & I will mention to you a medicine from which much may be hoped in cases of this kind. Clysters of tobacco-smoke, or of Decoctions of the plant, most certainly relieve suppression of urine, & remove obstinate costiveness, in others cases[50]—& why not in Yellow Fever? The decoction is the most powerful & certain, in constipation. I have never heard of an instance of the failure of the Smoke in Strangury. I wish you to make trials, when occasion offers, & impart the result. I am indebted to Dr. Hopkins of Hartford for the first suggestion of this remedy in Strangury. I have since tried it, in a case of suppression of urine & of obstinate costiveness, after all the common means had failed, by Dr. Seaman, at my request, & with complete success.

If I have more leisure, before Mr. Rhees goes, I shall add to this letter—otherwise, I am your friend as ever—

Dec. 20. 1797.   E. H. Smith.

Thursday, 21.—A visit from Dunlap. Wrote the letters to Croswell, Quincy, & Strong—all dated, by mistake, yesterday. A visit from Dr. Mitchill. Drank tea at home. Called at Kent's: all out. Spent part of the evening at Gurdon Mumford's—the remainder at home. Some progress in the Monthly Magazine. Corrected a proof of the Repository. Read the printed papers, with the Report of the Committee, on Gov. Blount's affair[51] —in all about 170 pages. Very little satisfactory is deducible from them.

This is the coldest day, of this season.

Friday, Decr. 22.—Looked over the prefaces &c. to Nicholson's "Kirwan on Acids."[52] Put in order & transcribed my notes for the article "Facts, Hints & Inquiries," in the Repository; & transcribed my letter to Mr. Quincy. Recd. a letter from Nathl. Dwight of Hartford. A number of errands. Drank tea & spent the evening at Dunlap's, with Wm. Johnson, Dr. Mitchill &c. While there, read several humorous chapters in R. Tyler's[53] Novel intituled "The Algerine Captive." Corrected a proof-sheet of the Botanic Garden; & read Mr. Strong's (of Hartford) sermon at the late Thanksgiving.

Saturday, 23.—Some further progress in Kirwan &c. Wrote the succeeding letter, & transcribed that to Dr. Wheaton. A visit from Mr. Owens. Visit to Mr. Gahn. At our printer's. Visit to Dr. Borrows—to Dr. Seaman —to Mr. Tisdale—to Mr. Miller. Call at Dr. Rodgers's —at Mr. Kent's. Club night—Johnson's night—present —Dunlap, Johnson, Kent, Smith, the Woolseys—& Dr. Mitchill & Mr. Gahn visitors. We mustered strong, & had a remarkable sociable & excellent meeting: the conversation principally on important topics—well sustained—& to mutual improvement.

Sunday, 24.—Visions of future times accompanied & protracted my hours of cleaning & dressing. I wrote a few lines to my sister Mary—to be sent to Albany by Dr. Mitchill. Wm. & I called at Riley's—walked, met Mr. Gahn—turned back to town—strolled on the Battery—& went to G. M. Woolsey's—where I dined, & spent part of the afternoon. Wm. & I walked out to Roulet's—returned & drank tea at Mr. Sharples's. I spent most of the evening at Professor Post's. There we looked over a Phila. Dissertation on Fractures. He has written the principal part of a Review of it—for the Repository. I came home—read over the Essay again —& have since made some additions to what he wrote.

This day has been pleasant. A change of wind at eveng. portends a change of weather.

To William Buel

I have recd. your letter, inclosing the first part of your paper on the Sheffield Fever & Dysentery of 1796. I read it with great pleasure, as it contains a number of very important facts. Such I deem the circumstance of the joint prevalence of the two diseases, as they have been thought—proving them to be the same, only in different forms; such, the circumscribed appearance of the epidemic—evidencing its dependence on local causes; & such, the remarkable mortality among children & women, evincing the relation between a soft & sensible fibre, & the superior activity of the disease. Do you any where ascertain the proportion of adults & children who were sick? of Male & female adults; of male & female children? of male & female children who died? If these points can be determined, it may be of some importance.

With respect to *Fogg*—tho' it is not probable that *fog*, as fog—i.e. as the mere condensed vapour of water, was any way pestilential, yet it may have aided the pestilence, in another way than you suppose. As it rose off from these marshes &c. it would naturally (from the strong attraction between gaseous fluids & water), combine with the pestilential miasmata, & thus apply them more extensively, that it is probable they could be applied to the human body in their simple, uncombined state.

I am anxious to see the remainder of your paper. As it has not arrived in season for our third No. I shall read it over leisurely; & if any thing in it appears erroneous, shall exercise the privilege of a friend in mentioning it to you.

Your money acct. is right. I had forgot the dollar on the 15 doll. Bill—as I never made any memorandum of the business.

Comps &c. to Mrs. Buel.

Dec. 23. 1797.   E. H. Smith.

---

[50] Tobacco smoke inserted in the rectum, presumably with a straw or tube, or tobacco in a solution or plain tobacco as a suppository. Tobacco smoke was also sometimes blown into the ear to cure an earache.

[51] William Blount (1749-1800). Appointed by Washington to be governor of the territory south of the River Ohio, 1790-1796; superintendant of Indian Affairs from 1790 to 1796, was first U.S. senator from Tennessee elected to serve from 1796. He was found guilty of conduct unbecoming a senator and expelled in July, 1797. An impeachment procedure was started but was dismissed. Harper (glossed earlier) was one of the managers appointed by the U.S. House to conduct impeachment proceedings.

[52] William Nicholson, *The Controversy between Kirwan and the French Academicians on Phlogiston* (London, 1787).

[53] An author mentioned earlier, Harvard, 1776, lawyer. A friend of Dennie, he became Chief Justice of the Vermont Supreme Court and a professor at the University of Vermont.

Monday, Decr. 25.—Christmas. The forenoon occupied in completing & transcribing the review of Black's Essay on Fractures.[54] Dined at H. Johnson's; where I spent most of the afternoon. Came home & corrected a proof sheet of the Repository. Drank tea & spent part of the evening at Dunlap's—W. W. Woolsey & wife, W. Johnson &c. there. Came home, & made up my bundle for Aurora. Dr. Mitchill & Mr. Miller came in. The first had a letter from Dr. Miller, from Phila. It results from this, that there is good reason to believe Dr. Rush cool, at least, if not hostile to the Repository —& the rest not over disposed in its favor. There does not seem much to apprehend from the publication to be set on foot there. I am even fearful that it will come to nothing. For certainly I wish it success. Something, however, may be effected by means of the booksellers. If twenty copies of the Repository are sold by them, the demand will soon increase. After M. & M. went away—I visited Mr. Kent. Returning from there, I corrected a proof-sheet of the Botanic Garden, & read the remainder of Dr. Buel's essay, which he sent me this day, in a letter of a few lines. When I say remainder—I mean of what he has sent—for there is more yet behind. This Paper will do my friend some credit.

Tuesday, 26.—A considerable portion of this day occupied in several petty errands &c. for the Repository. Recd. a letter from Dr. Miller—quite encouraging. Took leave of Mitchill, who has gone to Albany on his legislative duty. Thrice at Mr. Post's. At Riley's. At Dr. Rodgers's. Corrected a proof of the Repository. At Mr. Miller's. At our printer's. Read Mitchill's letters to Priestley & Haworth, in M.S. Wrote the letter, which follows, to Nathaniel Dwight. Drank tea at home. Evening at the Theater. The play "Hamlet"—which I never saw played before. Mr. Chalmers made his first appearance on our Stage, in *Hamlet*, & performed with tolerable propriety throughout, & in some parts with spirit & even excellence. Mrs. Hodgkinson's *Ophelia* is "neat & sweet." Did stay to see "The Agreable Surprize."[55] Continued The Monthly Magazine.

To Nathaniel Dwight

Your several letters, dated Nov. 20, & Dec. 10 & 13th which all arrived in company, are before me, & I shall endeavour now to make some reply to each. And first, with respect to your kindly-promised Dissertation. We shall be glad to receive it. At the same time, it is proper for me to give you some information which may, perhaps, in some degree influence you on this occasion. The original matter for our IIIrd No. is already printed. For our 4th we have on hand a very lengthy communication of Dr. Buel's, which is intended for publication, & was originally designed for the 3rd. No. We have also, a Memoir of Dr. Mitchill's, which it is important to publish early, for two reasons—1st, because it relates to some new doctrines of Chemistry, which, otherwise, may be broached from some other quarter; & 2nd, because it has been sent to Europe, & we wish to have it first appear in America. In addition to these, I have a long Essay, which it is thought of consequence to print now, as it relates to a question of fact, as well as theory, on which we are likely to be called upon to decide, in quality of critics. These three pieces, therefore, we feel as tho' we were obliged to publish. Beside these, we have several others on hand, if they should be necessary. What part of the 4th No. these papers will occupy, can not yet be known. It may be that there will be no room for additional matter. But, for Vth No. no positive arrangements are made. If, then, you will be so kind as to transmit your Paper, without a certainty of its appearing before next August, we shall be glad to receive it as soon as you please. It may happen that there will be room in the 4th No., but this, as I have said before is uncertain. But, if you prefer it, we will give you timely notice, should we want it for the 4th No. & you may, in the meantime, make some valuable additions. Do not misunderstand our intentions. It is only from their temporarily being of more importance, not from their intrinsic superiority, that we are in haste to publish these essays of our own. We agree to lay aside many other papers, probably of quite as much permanent value, from a regard to the use these may be of at the present moment. After this, it is not probable that we shall at all put back, for a moment, the communications of others; & had yours been sent three weeks ago, it would certainly have been inserted in our present No.

I thank you for your exertions in our behalf, & am much encouraged by your sanguine anticipations of future success for the Repository, in Hartford County. With respect to the suggestion of a Review, I suppose that what has already been done by Mr. Webster in the Herald or Spectator, I forget which, may be something like what you propose. I have only one objection to the republication of his remarks; & that is, that in his acct. of our first No. he has bestowed a disproportionate share of attention on my contribution. On looking over the papers, I find that these articles are included in the Spectator for Octr. 4 & 7th & for Decr. 6th. The last-named paper contains the acct. of the 2nd No.—which is short, & sufficient. In the two former papers there are long remarks by Mr. Webster, & some acct. of two pamphlets, by Dr. Mitchill & Mr. Bay. It will be sufficient, I think, to insert an article of about the same length, & a pretty much the same plan, as Mr. W's notice of the Second No. But I leave all to your discretion. The original Address unfolds our design, the 1st & 2nd Nos. shew how far we have hitherto, been able to accomplish it. Our resources are slightly enumerated in the advertisement to the 2nd No. From all this, the materials may be deduced for all the mention that it is proper to make, or becoming for us to suggest.

I am obliged by your communications relative to the diseases among Cats & Dogs. With regard to this last,

---

[54] Robert Black, *An Inaugural Dissertation on Fractures* (Philadelphia, 1797).

[55] John O'Keefe, *The Agreable Surprize* (Dublin, 1784).

we have similar intelligence from our correspondents in New Jersey. Much mischief has been done in East Jersey, by mad dogs; but, hitherto, I believe it has been confined to brute animals. In consequence of some intimations, to that point, in the Review of Dr. Barton on the Rattlesnake, in our first No.—Dr. Ross of Elizabeth-Town, has tried Alkalies for the cure of Hydrophobia in his own dog—& if I recollect—(for I have not his letter before me) with great alleviation of the symptoms. I wish, very much, if an opportunity occurs, & you will hazard the experiment, that you would try them, in the case of the first animal you know to have been bitten by a mad-dog—or in the first mad dog you meet. Could you not contrive to have a Dog, or some small animal, bitten by one that it is mad; & make the necessary internal & external administrations & applications immediately? I hope we shall have no chance for such experiments among us; but if we do, I shall endeavor to execute them. With so wide an opportunity as you are likely to have, it would be almost criminal to neglect any thing which may lead to successful practice in this very terrible disease.

Decr. 26. 797.   E. H. Smith.

Wednesday, Decr. 27.—Transcribed the letters to Croswell & Strong. Recd. the last of Buel's Essay to-day. I had copied the letter to him last evening, & made some additions to it; I now made some further additions, & sent it off. A medical visit. Visit from a patient. Dunlap here. He looked over my Prologue; & objected to some part of it. In the afternoon, I commenced & made some progress in the corrected transcription. I shall throw away about half the lines, & one quarter of the sentiments: the thing will be much less like what it ought be—a whole—but it will answer the purpose better, & be more thought of. People in general think that a string of verses constitutes a poem. They have no conception that a correct method is as essential in a Song or an Epitaph, as in an Epic Poem or a Tragedy. Went to the Theater to see the after piece—"The Waterman." *Tom* by Williamson, his first appearance. He sings well. A medical visit. Corrected a proof sheet of the Botanic Garden. Read the Newspapers, & the rest of Buel's Essay.

Thursday, 28.—Medical visit. Transcribed, with considerable variations, my letter to Nathl. Dwight. A long visit from J. Graham, the Proprietor of the Diary;[56] but we came to no conclusion. Some further progress in Kirwan & his Answerers. Called at Miller's. Found that he had returned this day. Sat a few minutes with him. He brought me a letter from Dewees of Phila. Dined at Mr. Sharples's: company—Genl. & Mrs. Gates, Mr. & Mrs. Robertson, Mr. & Mrs. Garnet, & Dr. Haworth. An agreable afternoon, & part of the evening. Spent the remainder of the evening with the Millers. The intelligence from Phila. is favorable to our wishes. I think that our publication is now fairly set agoing there; & that we may expect the demand for it to be steadily on the increase.

Friday, 29.—Medical visit. Recd. a letter from Mr. Tracy. Corrected a proof sheet of the Repository & of the Botanic Garden. At our printer's. Visit from Dunlap. Drank tea at Riley's. Part of the evening at the Theater. Saw "A Cure for the Heart-Ach."[57] A miserable play—well performed. Remainder of the evening at home. Corrected a proof. Wrote a letter (to Mr. Tracy), equal to two of these closest pages—which I did not feel willing to transcribe. The rest of the day & evening, except as above, devoted to the reading of Kirwan & his answerers.

Saturday, 30.—Read the newspapers. A visit from Mr. Tisdale, who read me his intended New Year's verses. At Swords's. Met Mr. Garnett, & had some talk with him. Visit from Dr. Miller—from Mr. Roulet. Visit to Dr. Miller. At the Hospital—a consultation, operations &c. Mr. Sharples drank tea with us. We spent the evening at Kent's—whose turn, being Club night, it was. Beside ourselves, only Dunlap was there. The greater part of the rest of the day & evening devoted to the perusal of the Monthly Magazine for August & September 1797. A medical visit.

Sunday, 31.—Continued, & nearly finished the September No. of the Monthly Magazine. Called at the house where Dr. Kingsley lies sick, & found that he had been delirious three days, & that there is great danger of his death. Called to see Mrs. Duryee—late Nancy Mumford. Wm. & I went to Mrs. Morton's. Afterwards we walked on the Battery. We dined at H. Johnson's—where we spent most of the afternoon. We walked again on the Battery—made a visit at G. M. Woolsey's—& returned to H. Johnson's, where we drank tea. Spent the evening at W. W. Woolsey's. When I came home, I found here, from Messr. Swords, the Monthly Review for September with the Supplement—I have looked over several articles, but must reserve more minute notice to a future opportunity.

Industry of December 1797

Reading

Zoonomia P. I. Sect. XIII.
View of the Science of Life, by Yates & McLean. 8vo. pp. 232—close print—Edit—Edit. Phila.
Kirwan & his Answerers—on Phlogiston &c. (a part) 8vo. pp. 165. edit. Lond.
Nicholson's Journal—Nos. IV & V.

---

[56] The *Diary*, at first subtitled *Loudon's Register* had a variety of subtitles between the years of its existence by that title, 1792-1798. The Samuel Loudons, father and son, apparently had no control after the son's death in 1795 after which John Johnson, John Crookes, Robert Saunders, and Cornelius Van Alen owned or ran it. Graham's name (he may have been a silent partner) does not appear in the account of the paper given by Charles S. Brigham, *History and Bibliography of American Newspapers 1690-1820* (American Antiq. Soc. Worcester, Massachusetts, 1947), **1**: pp. 626-628.

[57] Thomas Morton, *A Cure for the Heart Ach* (1797).

Buel on the Sheffield Fever & Dysentery of 1796—MS. equal to pp. 30. 8vo. fine print.
Black's (Phila.) Inaug: Dissert. on Fractures.—8vo. pp.
Mitchill's Letters to Drs. Priestley & Haworth—M S. equal to pp. 12. 8vo.
T. B Bayley on Manures—small pamphlet.
De Pauw on the Chinese & Egyptians—equal to pp. 300. 8vo.
Lavater's Journal of a Self-Observer—12mo. vol. 1. & ½ vol. 2.—about pp. 250.
Papers relative to Blount's Conspiracy—8vo. pp. 170.
Italian Monk—a play.
Wives as they Were &c. a Comedy.
Hope for the Heathen—a Sermon—by Mr. Mason of N. York.
Mr. Strong's (Hartford, Connec.) Thanksgiving Sermon.
Somers Papers—perhaps—pp. XXX. 4to.
Wm. M. Johnson's Remains—M S.—equal to pp. XL. 8vo.
Stanley's "Leonora"[58]..the original—& that of the Trans. of Ipha in Tauris.
Poetry of the World—2 vols. 12mo. looked over.
Monthly Magazine Vol. I. & half of Vol. III. & the Nos. for Aug: & Septr. 1797.
Monthly Rev. Enld. Suppl, to Vol. XXIII. & for Sept. '97.

Writing

Composition

Letters here preserved . . equal to . . . pp.	27.
Do. not Do.	20.
Sketch of a Prologue	8.
Facts, Hints, & Inquiries.	7.
Part of a Med: Review	3.

Transcription

Of this & last month's Letters	34.
Examin: of Chisholm.	20.
Varia for Med: Reposy.	10.

MEMOIRS. 1798. JANUARY.

Monday, 1.—The morning principally at home. At our printer's. Medical visit. Two visits from patients. Visit from Dr. Miller. Wm. & I dined, & spent most of the afternoon, at H. Johnson's: the remainder of the afternoon, & part of the evening, at Mr. Dunlap's. The rest of the evening I was at home; &, in the course of this day, have finished the perusal of the Monthly Review for Septr. & of the Supplement to vol. XXIII—but it is now too late in the night to note any remarks which have been suggested by the reading. Last evening, at Woolsey's, the idea was first suggested, by Johnson & myself, of instituting an American Review. We conversed somewhat on the subject, on our way home; & thought of annexing it to Swords's Magazine. This evening the project was again called up, at Dunlap's.

Appendix to the Monthly Review Enlarged vol. XXIII. *Art. I.* Eichhorn's Introduction to the Old Testament. This is a most interesting article; & the view here exhibited of the Bible is, for any thing that I see, such as might be freely admitted by the most antichristian philosophers. The track now pursued in Europe, particularly in Germany, must, I think lead to the ultimate establishment of truth, & complete overthrow of religion, even in the minds of the clergy themselves. And, after all, this may be the best way; since it will, probably, be the most radical, of exterminating error. The pernicious haste which has been made, in France, by men who had as little morality as religion, & as little discretion as sincerity, will expose that nation to long vacillations—as destructive of temperate conclusions, as of mental repose. *Art. VI.* Saussure's Travels in the Alps. This is a very important & instructive article; & as the complete work is not likely soon to reach America, will be to be often referred to—especially for what relates to the ascent of Mont Blanc. *Art. VII.* Matchisson's Letters. The anecdotes of Gibbon, & of the herbalist Thomas, curious: the whole pleasing. *Art. VIII.* This contains very singular assertions, of which it is difficult to determine how much ought to be received as truth. The same objection lies against a part of "Barruel's Memoirs of Jacobinism"—as against the Conspiracy of Orleans by Mountjoyed. i.e. How could the Abbé Barruel know what he asserts concerning the highest order of Freemasons, without being himself one? If one, which the whole tenor of his book denies, he could not have exposed their secrets. It is desirable to discover whence has arisen this strange belief respecting the agency of Freemasonry in the overthrow of Kings & priests. It is certainly very singular—especially as the general conviction is to the contrary; as the Free Masons are supposed, as far as they profess any sentiment, to be friendly to Xtianity, as the Illuminated, are deemed the most superstitious of men; & as many of the Philosophers here charged with favoring & directing the movements of these sects & societies, have been most active in writing, & otherwise influencing the public mind against them. *Art. X.* Lamarck's Memoirs of Nat. Hist. & Nat. Philos: a farrago which totally destroys all hope of finding any thing worth reading in his pretended Refutation of the Antiphlogistic Theory. *Art. XI.* Delametheries' Theory of the Earth. Not what it should be; but no doubt a book very well worth consulting. *Art. XII.* Bay on Dysentery. The reviewers urge some of the objections that have already appeared in the Repository. They are quite sceptical relative to the Septic Theory. *Art. XVIII.* D'Ussieres—Cyrus & Milto. The younger Cyrus: a philosophical romance: the extract very well. *Art. XIX.* Barère's Montesquieu painted from his works. This whole article—I mean the reviewer's part of it—excellent. The character of the Spirit of Laws

---

[58] Sir John Thomas Stanley, Bart., *Leonora; a Tale;* trans. and altered from G. A. Bürger, new edition 1796.

just, & masterly. *Art. XX.* Wieland's Works. The name of this writer is a security for pleasure. Few articles are more elegant than those which relate to Wieland's works. I read both the critic & the author with delight—nor I do know the name of any poet, whose writings I equally desire to read in the original tongue.

The Month. Rev: Enl. September 1797. *Art. 1.* Townson's Travels in Hungary. This appears to be a valuable work. The extracts are pleasing. The second part promises more instruction. *Art. III.* Darwin's Plan for Boarding Schools. The extract on "Fortitude" is sensible; that on the "Care of the Shapes" appears to be nearly verbatim as inserted in Zoonomia. The purpose of this publication seems to be to recommend a particular school. It is not calculated to increase the author's distinguished reputation. *Art. V.* Townsend's Guide to Health. This is probably a good publication for common purposes; & as such I desire to see it. The Extracts are good. *Art. VIII.* Principles of the Wealth of Nations, illustrated &c. This sensible performance should be read at the same time Adam Smith's Work. *Art. IX.* Vaurien: or Sketches of the times. I should be well pleased to read this work, tho' the philosophy of it is so hostile to that which I profess & believe. The extract is spirited & even elegant; &, in its principal features, probably, is no inapt resemblance of Thomas Taylor. *Art. X.* Maurice's Indian Antiquities vol. VI. When leisure is allowed me for such inquiries, I shall read this curious work. The present volume treats of an important subject, & apparently in an able manner. The extract relative to Tin might be introduced, not improperly, into a course of Mineralogical lectures. *Art. XII.* Abernethy's Surgical & Physiological Essays—vol. III. A valuable publication, & like the two preceeding vols. deserving to be well read. *Art. XIII.* Skene's Donald Bane: a Poem. Here are marks of genius. This extract will not be read a single time, by the lover of poetry. *Art. XV.* The voyage of Harno. Worthy to be read.—*Art. XVI.*—Memoirs of the life of Lord Lovat. Interesting to the historical antiquary. The principal extract, no less so to the moralist. *Art. XVIII.* Sir G. Staunton's Account of the Chinese Embassy. This is, probably, but the beginning of a review, every part of which will be curious & valuable. The work promises to be of great credit & curiosity. *Art. 66.* The Quiz—&c. Here is a curiosity—a french poem, which Goldsmith is charged with having translated & amplified into his celebrated Ballad of Edwin & Angelina: more probably a translation from his poem. It is very literal, in many places—& is beautiful, as that is beautiful.

Tuesday, Jany. 2.—At home all day—till sunset. Dr. Miller here all the forenoon. Mr. Webster a part of it. A call from G. M. Woolsey. Dr. Miller & I were occupied in composing the article "Medical News" for No. 3. of the Repository. The afternoon was devoted to the same business, by me. Drank tea, & passed part of the evening, at Mr. Kent's: the remainder at home. A little more writing for the Repository. Settled my Accounts, for the last month. Finished the Septr. No. of the Monthly Magazine. Wrote the preceding notices of the several articles in the Monthly Review. Recd. a letter from C. B. Brown.

Wednesday, 3.—A day of errands. At Gahn's—at the Dispensary—at the booksellers'—seeking for a vessel to Providence—& to Bristol Engd.—at our printer's—at Dr. Hicks's—at Dr. Miller's—& all, or most, on business of the Repository. A call from Mr. Webster. Met Mr. Dunlap in the street, with Mr. Cooper, Comedian, whom he introduced to me. Two medical visits. A long visit from Dr. Seaman. Drank tea at Dunlap's. He has recd. a letter from C. B. Brown, which I read. Part of the evening at Mr. Moses Rogers's. At the Theater. Saw "The Quaker"—a piece I always see with pleasure. Corrected proof-sheets of the Repository, & of the Botanic Garden. The Johnsons hear that their brother, John Johnson, has died, at Madrass, with Dysentery. He was a fine & promising young man.

Thursday, 4.—Medical visit. Visits from Dunlap, Mr. Webster, Dr. Miller, & a patient. Mr. Webster brought me Dr. Rush &c's answer to Gov. Mifflin, respecting the Fever (Phila.) of 1797. I read it. Finished & transcribed, my Prologue: transcribed it into this book, & wrote the subsequent pages—relative thereto. Drank tea & spent part of the evening, at Dunlap's. Called at Hodgkinson's—all out: at Johnson's—Comedians—he out, she sick—did not see them. Remainder of the evening at home. Read Mr. Fauchet's pamphlet, relative to the Dispute between France & the United States—8vo.—pp. 31[59]—which seems to amount to very little—& contains some ridiculous falsehoods. Recd. a letter from my father. The Repository is doing well in his vicinity. Made up the monthly Table of Industry for November & December 1797. I find, by running over these Tables for the last year, that I must have composed a quantity, of all sorts, not far short of a thousand octavo pages; that I have transcribed a quantity not much less than a thousand; & that I can not have read less than twenty thousand octavo pages. I wish I could add that, from all this, which only appears great in the aggregate, I had obtained any considerable real science.

Friday, Jany. 5.—Three medical visits. A visit from Dr. Proudfit. From Dr. Miller. Continued the reading of Kirwan and his answerers. Drank tea at Dr. Hosack's, where I met the Millers, to visit the new Bride. Called & spent part of the evening, at H. Johnson's—where were Seth, his wife, & Fanny—who all arrived this day—to hear the melancholly news of the death of their brother. Seth brought me a letter from Dr. Morse—the geographer—full of encouragement on account of the Repository, which Johnson tells me is universally well spoken of in Boston. He also informs me that I have been elected a member of the Historical Society, & that I may soon expect a diploma, in due form.[60] This

---

[59] Joseph, baron, Fauchet, *A Sketch of the Present State* (Philadelphia, 1797).

[60] Jedediah Morse appears to have felt that one good turn

an unexpected & I fear undeserved honour. I went to the Theater, to see part of the two last Acts of "Venice Preserved." Cooper's *Pierre* was, as usual, excellent—but did not appear so great by the side of Hodgkinson, as formerly by Moreton. Hodgkinson excelled himself—Mrs. Melmoth was respectable—even after the wonderful exhibition of Mrs. Merry—& all the lesser parts were perfectly filled. In this respect the piece is seldom so well done even in London. Came home—read pp. 70 in Rousseau's Confessions[61] P. 2.—some things in the N. York Magazine for this month—& corrected a proof-sheet of the Botanic Garden.

Saturday, 6.—Five medical visits, which consumed much time. In the intervals continued Rousseau, & read the Papers. Recd. a few lines from Dr. Woodhouse, with his Young Chemist's Pocket Companion.[62] Drank tea at Dunlap's. At the Theater a short time, where I saw a part of Cooper's *"Penruddock"*[63]—which was very well, but did not surpass Hodgkinson's. Returned to Dunlap's—where the Club met—Present—Dunlap, Kent, Smith, W. W. Woolsey—& Moses Rogers, Mr. Davenport (of Connec.), Mr. Sharples, Dr. Miller, & Mr. Gahn, visitors. Came home a few minutes after eleven. Wm. & I have been, since, in constant conversation—a most pleasing *tete a tete*—& it is now near two in the morning.

Prologue,[64]

intended to be spoken at the opening of the New Theater, in New York.

When the first prows attain'd the atlantic shore
One rude, uncultur'd face the region wore;
Nor useful art, nor genial science, smil'd,
Nor social order charm'd the mighty wilds
But, mid his woods, the native savage ran,
And beast, but scarce distinguish'd from the man.
From like beginnings, our adventurous race
The recent history of their fortunes trace.
Like your bold sires, the fathers of the Stage,
Of fate uncertain, brav'd the ocean's rage;
Of future eras caught prophetic views,
And sought a land scarce conscious of the Muse.
Long years of labour mark'd their dubious way,
And fickle Favour oft withheld her ray;
But, as the shades of prejudice withdrew,

Fair, and more fair, the cheering prospect grew;
Till light and life the bright'ning scene endear'd,
And the gay bow of promis'd peace appear'd.
O! if, in future, as in former days,
Their true descendants meet your generous praise,
Propp'd by your smiles, this Stage, a stately tower,
Lifts its proud front, and scorns misfortune's power.

Great is the task, and nice the art requir'd,
To raise such scenes as Dryden erst desir'd;
But greater still, & far more nice, the art
To fix the impressive moral in the heart;
To voice, form, feature, motion, accent, give
Appropriate force, and bid the picture live.
This asks the poet's fire, the player's skill,
Minds that discern, and souls that know to feel;
Applause that cherishes, as well as cheers;
And time, that mends, and softens, and endears.

When first the spell of gothic art was broke,
And, from its tedious trance, the Drama woke,
Mysteries and Masks the new-born Stage disgrac'd,
The monkish structures of perverted taste,
And many a year, and many a lustrum, fled,
Ere giant Shakespere rais'd his hallow'd head;
Ere Britain's earlier Roscius grac'd the scene,
And the first Barry mov'd and look'd a queen.
With patient ear our wise forefathers heard;
With kind applause the actor, poet, cheer'd;
Till, by successive trials, well sustain'd,
Nature and skill the improving pair attain'd;
From infant weakness rose the scenic art,
And truth and genius charm'd the hearer's heart.

Let not your fiercer, more impatient doom,
Blast our young flowrets in their timid bloom;
But shield them from the inclement skies, and hope,
In future years, a rich and various crop.
If noble toils, if triumphs more sublime,
Your boast and glory to remotest time,
To different scenes the glowing mind impell'd,
The watchful senate and the embattled field,
And chiefs and sages, theme of every tongue,
Awak'd, alone, the consecrating song,
While the neglected Stage from foreign shores,
A motley mass! deriv'd her various stores,
Yet, now, by you encourag'd and allow'd,
Dramatic bands your native scenes shall crowd;
And native bards awake the slumbering lyre,
While gain & glory goad them & inspire;
Proud competition struggle for the bays,
And find a new existence in your praise.

So shall new Bettertons and Booths arise;
New Quins and Garricks ravish and surprise;
Another Pritchard charm with varied powers;
And Woffington & Clive again be ours.

So shall come modest Congreve's juster wit,
With keener sallies, more your taste delight;
Some happier Jonson's classic humor charm;
Some gayer Cibber spread no chaste alarm;
Some livelier Farquhar virtuous wishes move;
Some Steel inflame with pure and lawful love;
A graceful Cowley elegantly sway;
Another Inchbald point her sex the way;
Another Sheridan, with nobler zeal,
Convulse with mirth, or teach the heart to feel;

---

deserved another. Morse was a member of the society, and though he did not nominate Smith, he very probably had something to do with bringing the nomination about. So also, no doubt, did Smith's part in the publication of *The Medical Repository*. See *Proc. Mass. Hist. Soc.* (Boston, 1879) 1: p. 108.

[61] Available in French from 1782.

[62] James Woodhouse, M.D., *The Young Chemist's Pocket Companion* (Philadelphia, 1797).

[63] Penruddock is a character in Cumberland's *Wheel of Fortune*.

[64] This prologue is worth at least as much attention as all of the rest of Smith's verse combined. It is no rhetorical collection of neoclassical clichés but an intense, passionate statement of Smith's thoughts about the American theater and his hopes for its future. Certainly Dunlap's timid reservations did nothing to improve it.

A native Holcroft, sovereign of the Stage,
To perfect morals form a future age.
 So shall a loftier Dryden rouse your fears;
A tenderer Rowe beguile you of your tears;
With wondrous verse, a virtuous Otway scourge
Unheard of crimes, and half to madness urge;
With thrilling horror shake the secret soul,
And give the tears of agony to roll;
A perfect Shakespere, nurst by every Muse,
Shake from his manly locks the pearly dews,
Which the fond Graces, all-delighted, shed,
When their fair fingers, round his infant head,
Twin'd flowers & laurels from Parnassus' height,
And rule the scene with uncontested right;
Grief, rage, despair, & joy, and hope, & love,
Destin'd, by turns, their monarch's art to prove,
Vanish, appear, or perish, or revive,
As the soul's master bids them die or live.
 Then shall this Stage, of fame, of praise, secure,
Like this fair Empire, flourish and endure;
Alike in ample strength and beauty rise,
Joy of the earth and wonder of the skies.

Such is the Prologue, very inadequate indeed to my wishes, that I have composed for the approaching opening of the New Theater. I know that it is disproportioned; & that there is a miserable poverty of ideas in it. The reason is, in part, this. The original sketch which I made contained many ideas not altogether conformable to the opinions of Mr. Dunlap. They were however so interwoven with the rest, that the Poem might be considered as a whole; & tho' too long, might have been comprest, by repeated revision, into 100 lines. As he did not seem willing to have this done, I have been obliged to cast away the exceptionable parts; &, by adding a few connecting lines, to endeavor to form a whole, out of what was intended but as a part. This is the outline of the original Essay.

"The first settlers of America found it savage. From this rude begining, they have attained to their present improved state; & our future improvement is secured by our civil & political institutions."

Wide where Virginia spreads her golden plains
Debark successive the adventurous trains;
With different zeal, mid bleaker skies, a band
Of pious exiles seize the desert land;
With patience the doubtful gloom they dare,
And brave the rage of inexperienc'd war:
Destin'd thro' scenes of fearful strife to pass,
And bid, sublime, on virtue's solid base,
In ample strength, thy tower O'Freedom! rise,
Joy of the earth & wonder of the skies.

Next followed the lines relative to the establishment of the Stage in America, & forming a counterpart to those which preceded.

I came, then, to the consideration of what was necessary to such an establishment; & having noticed the difficulty of erecting an unimpeachably excellent institution, pretty much in the manner still preserved, proceeded to remark that the duties of managers & players, & of audiences, were reciprocal.

"The Manager should select moral & good pieces: the Auditory should applaud & encourage them. If any thing dull, or indecent, were brought forward, it should be driven off. So all false accent, action, &c. &c. in the performance, to be discountenanced: every thing proper countenanced."

"Taste not every where the same; nor even morality. Each nation requires some peculiar attention, on the part of the dramatist, who writes for it. Pernicious effects of deriving all our theatric exhibitions from other countries, as they relate to every different state of society, to follies & vices not so abundant here, & corrupt our taste & morals."

And here I shall transcribe some of the verses bestowed on this topic, with all their incorrectness.

As round the pole eternal winter reigns,
Eternal summer burns the tropic plains,
O'er arctic hills the hardy lichen spreads,
And spicy groves adorn the indian meads,
[Each various clime its various garb demands,
By this distinguish from all other lands;]
Nature & truth a different aspect wear,
So, by one law, but variously applied,
Peculiar tastes in different realms preside,
The statesman's study, the physician's care,
Call for new modes, new excellence desire,
And art appropriate, genial forms, require.

The two lines in brackets were only suffered as a connective—& the whole sentence is too much expanded & verbose.

As his who pours on flaming roofs the oil,
False is the author's, false the player's toil,
That, like Procrustes, with despotic rage,
Would frame one moral measure for the stage;
Each land, each race, each social state, demands
Peculiar models from the artist's hands.
 Pernicious custom that, from foreign shores,
On our devoted state its fury pours;
Thro' town & village, with contagion fierce,
Scatters the deadly venom of its curse;
Infects, in lisping infancy, our schools;
With vigourous manhood, in our councils rules;
Sways faltering age, its weak, domestic slave;
And swells the empty pageant of the grave;
Dress, motion, food, subjected to its throne,
And makes the shame of every land our own.
 Why, with blind passion, Europe's scenes explore,
And waft her mimic follies to our shore!
Baneful to us the servile zeal that brings
No tragic forms but warrior-chiefs & kings;
That spreads with tyrant pomp our rising stage;
Themes of a barbarous, or a slavish, age:
Baneful to us, that paints domestic life
One loathsome tissue of disgusting strife;
Of tame submission, of indifference blank,
And wasteful rage—(the fruits of noble rank);
Shews private virtue, public honor dead,
And deep corruption foster'd in their stead;
While pimps, cheats, peers, compose the motley crew,
And jails & brothels terminate the view.

"Our characters created or modified by surrounding circumstances. Foreign productions to be received with caution; native talents encouraged."

> Tis education forms the youthful mind,
> 'Just as the twig is bent the tree's inclin'd,'
> Scenes that we see, opinions that we hear,
> Make what we are,—or tender, or severe.
> Hence then, far hence, the products of the Muse,
> Shame of their sires! that love of vice infuse.
> With temperate praise, with prudent care, admit
> The dreaded offspring of exotic wit;
> Fear while you favour, doubt as you behold,
> Nor think the glittering figures wrought in gold.
> But to the germs of genius & of sense,
> That lie thick-strewn, a bounteous warmth disperse;
> With quickening heat your native soil pervade,
> And pierce, with kindly ray, the oblivious shade.
> Soon shall the teeming earth your fields adorn
> With flowers more beauteous than the opening morn;
> Soon shall the sickly groves their leaves renew,
> Their foliage deck'd with health's returning hue;
> *New groves* aspire, fresh flowers their buds expand,
> And fruits & fragrance bless the admiring land.

Here followed the lines in the Prologue—from 1. 33, 1. 50. stating a great example for patience, & perseverance. Then, instead of the lines which immediately succeed, from 1. 50, to 1. 59.—this sentiment was exprest —"that even feeble efforts of the american muse ought not to be absolutely discouraged. This might repress the genius & exertions of some who otherwise would acquire deserved eminence. That every thing is to be hoped from patronized (by the public) competition." Then succeeded the lines—from 1. 60 to the end—with occasional variations. These lines are omitted in what relates to Shakespere, between 1. 92, & 1. 93.

> His powerful wand the unwilling shades compel,
> And call up demons from the abyss of hell;
> Thro' the wide air his mystic summons fly,
> And charm the viewless tenants of the sky;
> His winning accents reach the heavenly bowers,
> And draw to earth the rapt celestial power.

So much for my Prologue—which few will attend to, fewer understand, & still fewer be benefitted by. Henceforth let the Muses repose themselves, on Pindus, or by the streams of Castaly, safe from my intrusion, till the fever of sonnetteering once more tingles in my veins.

Sunday, Jany. 7.—As I went late to bed, so I rose late. I had hardly time to swallow a hasty breakfast, before I was called to see a patient; & I have made four medical visits, & attended to one patient in my chamber this day. The remainder of the time principally devoted to reading Rousseau's Confessions. Yet I found time, from this fascinating employment, to write the succeeding letter to Dr. Morse, which I purpose to transcribe & send tomorrow. At Geo: M. Woolsey's, & at Mr. Catlin's, in the eveng., half of which has been spent at home.

Both Mrs. & Mr. H. Johnson, were burnt, sadly, last evening, in attempting to extinguish Mrs. J's gown, which accidentally took fire. This new misfortune, has affected my spirits, as well as Wm.'s & the rest; & made my time, away from home, unusually heavy & unpleasant.

Monday, Jany. 8.—Two medical visits. Errands. Visit from Dr. Miller. He informed me that Dr. Mease was in town. I called at his lodgings—but did not see him. Continued J. J. Rousseau. At S. Johnson's—to witness some Deed—which cost me half the afternoon. This is a duty we owe each other—& I am satisfied. H. & his wife are better. At Dr. Seaman's, & went with him to a consultation. Two medical visits. Drank tea at home. At the theater—saw "All in the Wrong"[65]—a lively Comedy—& not 100 dolls. in the House. Saw part of "Rosina" too. Williamson sings very well: Tyler never better: & little Miss E. Westby—prettily—& looked sweetly. A pleasing countenance, her growth & apparent timidity, & the character she had to perform, moved me almost to tears. These sensations—which long commerce with men have made sufficiently rare, are still very delicious. I wish I could feel them oftener. Came home: transcribed my letter to Dr. Morse, with only a few verbal deviations—& continued Rousseau.

Tuesday, 9.—Five medical visits, in the course of the day: two of them consultations. A visit from Dr. Mease. His pomposity has "grown with his growth, & strengthened with his strength." He stayed some time—& I made a few calls, with him. Corrected a proof of the Repository. Drank tea at Mr. Paiba's. Spent a part of the evening at Hodgkinson's: the rest at home. Wrote the letters to Brown, Dewees, & Chauncey. Continued Rousseau this day.

Wednesday, 10.—Four medical visits in the course of this day. Read the newspapers. Sketched the outline [of] a long report to the Manumission Society. Visit from Dunlap: from Miller: from Mr. Sharples & Dr. Haworth. Dined & spent the afternoon at Dr. Seaman's, in company with Dr. Mease. Our conversation did not amount to much. Spent the evening at Riley's—where I saw "Guillotina" for Jany. 1. 1798[66]—a very poor performance. Hopkins—& perhaps Nathl. Dwight, wrote it. I suspect Theodore of verses on Fayette. We shall see what Freneau can reply. Corrected a proof of the Medical Repository—& made some additions. Continued Rousseau.

To Jedidiah Morse

I feel myself much indebted to you for your friendly letter, by Mr. Johnson, & the numerous marks of kindness & attention which it displays; & I hasten to reply [to] it, in such manner as my present engagements will permit.

---

[65] Arthur Murphy, *All in the Wrong* (1761).

[66] "Guillotina" for January 1, 1798, was a collection of satiric New Year's verses attributed with reasonable certainty to Lemuel Hopkins, addressed to "The Readers of the Connecticut Courant," a broadside printed by Hudson and Goodwin (Hartford, 1798). Most reference books do not record the fact that there were a number of "Guillotinas" by Hopkins: two others in 1796, one in 1797, and one in 1799. See Evans, *Short Title Catalogue*.

In the first place, with respect to the Communications you were so obliging to make us for the Repository. When your letter arrived, we had just sent to press the "Medical News," for the third No. It was too late to have inserted any original & formal essay, in this No., had there been time to compose it. The information in the pages sent us, we deemed not only of the highest importance, *generally*, but *particularly* so at this time, as you will see from this No. the Canine Madness threatens us with extensive evil—as it prevails in Connecticut, on one side, & New Jersey, on the other. To have waited till next May, before a regular Essay could have been published in our Repository, would have been, perhaps, to sacrifice a fair prospect of doing good, to a very pitiful consideration—that of polishing a few phrases. These considerations determined us to insert the Papers as they were recd.—& in the full conviction that, (as it was impossible to receive any timely direction from you,) you would deem our conduct proper, when you were made acquainted with its motives. In regard to Dr. Brickell's request—it appeared of the less consequence, as his name had already been published with his directions; & beside, physicians are justly scrupulous, in such cases, of trifling to anonymous assertions. I hope you will not be displeased or dissatisfied with what we have done.

The want of a private & safe conveyance to Boston, will alone prevent me from sending on a further number of copies immediately. For three weeks, or more, I have been constantly, but ineffectually, in search of such an opportunity, by land or water. This has retarded till this time my letters to Dr. Eustis & Mr. Quincy, with some copies for them. Should you meet with those gentlemen, have the goodness to assure them of my respect; & that nothing but unavoidable difficulties have delayed the proofs of my attention to their requests.

I thank you, sir, for the intimation respecting the addition to the title on the Covers. You will find, however, that our prefaces, or advertisements, to each No. are regularly dated: The first July 26th—the second Nov. 7th. 1797.

We shall receive your promised Communication with great pleasure, & seize the earliest occasion of laying it before the public.

The volume of Dr. Lettsome's is not in this City. Should it be perfectly convenient to transmit it to me—I will be careful that it is properly used, & seasonably returned, & will cause such notice to be taken of it, as it shall appear to deserve.

Permit me to assure you, that your disinterested exertions in behalf of our infant publication, have made a deep impression on the minds of it's Editors; & that my associates heartily unite with me in the expressions of esteem & respect with which

      I am yours very
        Sincerely

Jany. 7. 1798.
Pine St. No. 45. N. York.   E. H. Smith.

To Charles B. Brown

Your letter, on many accounts, gave me uncommon pleasure. So long delayed, I began seriously to apprehend that you had put in execution your wild project of devoting yourself to the care of the sick, & that my simple question had been directed, not to the living but, to the dead. Your reply, kind tho' late, dissipated every melancholy incertitude; & was the harbinger of tidings equally new, unexpected, & joyful.

I rejoice at the proofs you have at length attained to & exhibited of perseverance, industry, & success. Henceforth, I dare to augur, timidly, I confess, better things of you. Send to us your various works. We shall receive them as from a friend; & speak of them neither as parasites, nor as men consumed by pride & envy. I assure you that nothing shall prevent me from declaring my sincere opinion concerning whatever you may write, & request my sentiments upon. But the copiousness or brevity of my decision may be determined by a thousand circumstances—none of which I can certainly foresee.

In return for your intelligence, receive a few words relative to myself. Few they must be: for the same crowd of petty concerns which have prevented me, till now, from answering your letter, have still sufficient importance to contract my present reply.

You despise Sonnets—Yet I have composed several since you were here which are not despicable. Otherwise the Muses have quietly reposed from my solicitations, till very lately, when I have summoned them to my assistance in the production of a Prologue for the opening of our New Theater—which may probably take place in about three weeks. This Prologue is not to be compared with Samuel Johnson's; nor it it as good as I should have made it, had not our Manager been afraid of promising too much, & receiving too little encouragement in doing as he ought to do; but, with all its mutilations, I dare expect that when you see it you will think it tolerable.

Medicine engrosses all my attention. Have you seen the Medical Repository? You will find it at Poulson's. I could wish you to look it over, & give me your opinion as to its literary character. In particular, I am anxious to learn your judgement on my Acct. of the Athenian Pestilence.

I have sent your letter to Dunlap. He will answer it. But it is very doubtful, or rather it is very improbable, that he will think to inform you that his "Andre"—is nearly finished; & that he has the courage to determine on bringing it upon the Stage this present Winter. I shall inform you of its success.

Hear you any thing lately, from Joseph? He wrote me a few lines, a long time ago—promising me a letter, in due form. Hitherto I have vainly expected it. What he wrote did not admit of an answer. Beside, my medical correspondence is very extensive & laborious.

You have not written to Roulet. I saw him to-day. He & his are well.

Johnson sends his love to you. Mine to all who kindly remember me.

Jany. 9. 1798.   E. H. Smith.

To William Dewees

I thank you for your obliging letter, by Dr. Miller, & still more for your friendly exertions in behalf of the Medical Repository. The first is a favor done to me, personally; the last, I am willing to believe, to science & mankind at large. Assure yourself that I shall appreciate them both, as highly as they deserve.

I am gratified to learn, by Dr. Mease, who is now here, that "The Medical Academy of Phila." is nearly organized; & that you are almost ready to give the world the maiden proof of the sincerity of your intentions, & success of your labours. You judged rightly when you thought that in this you had my good wishes. Future occasions shall not find me deficient in good exertions, in its favour. Our publications will mutually aid each other; &, if successful, i.e. if they obtain as wide circulation, will do more for Medicine, in ten years, than all that has hitherto been effected, since our establishment on this side of the Atlantic. Curiosity will be excited. Men can not bear to be ignorant of that with which others seem to be well acquainted. Those who read our publications, must read other things.

I congratulate you on your success as teacher of Midwifery; & I hope that the example may spread. Competition, generous competition, creates talents. The world were a stagnant pool without it, where the seeds of science & virtue must inevitably perish.

This letter is an evidence of the readiness with which I accept your proposition relative to a correspondence. To make it useful, I shall hope that it may be liberal in the interchange of professional intelligence, literary & practical.

Yours &c.

Jany. 9. 1798.   E. H. Smith.

To Charles Chauncey Jr.

Your very acceptable present demanded an earlier acknowlegement; & this it would certainly have recd. but for an accident which prevented me from writing while there was any hope of remedying it.

Immediately on the receit of your Oration I gave it a hasty perusal. The hurry I was then in determined me to postpone writing to you, till I should have read it attentively—as it well deserved to be. When I looked for my Copy, on the return of leisure, it was missing: & hitherto, I have ineffectually sought for it every where. Some of my friends must have taken it away, & will doubtless return it; but, in the meantime, were I to continue silent, you might justly charge me with neglect of the most obvious requisitions of politeness. I hasten therefore to express my sentiments, briefly, on your performance.

I will not give you so poor a proof of my sincerity as to pronounce your Oration faultless. Some incorrectness of style, & some errors of opinion, I think are observable in it. But, sir, it does you credit, in every respect: Credit, for the handsome manner in which it is composed, increasing in propriety to the conclusion—which much surpasses, in writing, the first part: Credit, for the frankness & courage with which you have advocated a most important moral truth, under the thunder of calvinistic orthodoxy, & amidst the fearful outcries against democracy, & modern philosophy. It was unquestionably *prudent* to discuss the topic of religion in the manner you have done—& *right* if you believed what you have advanced—but in nothing is the progress of improvement more discernible, in nothing is the superiority of the moderns more incontestible—& of the present century in particular, than in the metaphysical & moral systems which they have constructed. Here, where you have admitted your party to be weak, is it most powerful, is it omnipotent. Nor will you, long, hesitate to think so. Following the course of your own doctrine, it must lead you to this inestimable boundary. Your future progress is plain, & full of delight, if you have constancy, courage, fortitude.

Accept my thanks & my esteem, & make them acceptable to your father.

Jany. 9th, 1789.   E. H. Smith.

Thursday, Jany. 11.—Four medical visits, in the course of the day; and as they are to patients residing in very opposite parts of the Town, they occupy much time. Visit from Dr. Mease, & some calls with him. Visits from Dr. Miller, Dunlap, & Webster. At my printer's. Corrected proof sheets. Wrote a few lines to Mrs. Lovegrove. Transcribed the letters to Brown, Dewees, & Chauncey. Visits to H. Johnson, & to S. Johnson—dividing the first part of the evening at their houses. The latter part, at home. Finished Rousseau—the second part of his Confessions, with a volume of letters—3 vols. 12mo. edit Dubl. small print—pp.—about 800.

Friday, 12.—Three medical visits. Errands. Visit from Mr. Webster. We called on Dr. Miller, & all went to see Dr. Mease. We met him; & returned to Miller's, where we spent an hour or two, in very earnest conversation. Another medical visit, to Woolsey's—where I learned that Dr. Dwight was in town. Called on him, at Rogers's—& spent an hour with him. He is well & left his family so. Principal part of the evening at the Theater—where I saw "Wives as they were &c." Hodgkinson's *Sir William Dorrillon,* Mrs. Hodgkinson's *Lady Priory*, Mrs. Johnson's, *Miss Dorrillon,* & Chalmers's *Bronzoly*, were all excellent. Resumed & continued Kirwan on Phlogiston &c. I have been dreadfully afflicted with a cold, since yesterday afternoon.

Heard, circuituously, from Lichfield, & from Aurora, to-day: all well.

Saturday, 13.—Four medical visits—two of them calls. Went with Dunlap to see the New Theater—

which is in great forwardness. The old Theater closes to-night—forever. Visited Miss Morton, for the first time, since her return from Boston. Recd. a letter from El. Smith Junr. Finished Kirwan & his answerers—Edit. Lond. 8vo. pp. 817—close print. Corrected proofs. Club night—my turn—Present, Dunlap, Johnson, Kent, Smith, Dr. Miller, Mr. Sharples, & Dr. Mease, visitors. I read my Prologue in the beginning of the evening. Saw Dr. Dwight a few minutes, P. M.

To Elnathan Smith Jr.

With what joy do I receive the unexpected news of the re-establishment of your health! There is a sensation, or a state of mind, in consequence of intelligence like this, which resemble that which succeeds, or accompanies, the return of health & vigour after disease. We find new delights in our present security, from comparisons with our recent sufferings & apprehensions. And not from comparison merely, but actually from all the new actions which influence every fibre of the body, & every flexure of the mind.

This is one of the worst places in the world to send to for books; & I have no doubt but that those you desire me to look for, will be for sale in New-Haven several months before they reach New York. We have been attempting, for some time, to force our booksellers into the practice of importing new books; & this autumn, when, at last, we had persuaded one of them to enter into the measure, with some spirit, the French have captured the ship, & carried all our literature to feed the pasty-ovens of the demons of St. Domingo. Whether either of the books you write for, were of the number, I am uncertain. They are not now in Town. Perhaps, if they are reprinted in Ireland, we may receive them in the Spring. In that case, if you are not previously provided, I will give you early notice.

I thank you for your kind intentions—in respect to the Communications & Minerals; & hope that you will not fail of the performance. Indeed, we rely as much on private gentlemen, as on physicians, for the patronage of our work; &, in process of time, hope to make it as interesting to them. Our subscribers increase: & we have almost as many who are not, as who are physicians. By this time, I suppose that you have looked over some parts of the Work. I shall expect your opinion.

I have not had time to write to either of the Wellses—at present am immersed in a stupifying Cold: So that you must present my compliments, instead of a letter.

Give yourself no trouble concerning the Operas. Dispose of them at your leisure, & as you please.

I shall consider you as a subscriber for Brown's Dialogue—& will send it to you when it is published. The Copies are half a dollar each. You may get me as many subscribers as you please.

I sympathize, without partaking, in your connubial pleasures. My respect to Mrs. Smith.

Jany. 14. '98.   E. H. Smith.

Sunday, 14.—Continued the Monthly Magazine. Wrote & transcribed the preceding letter. A medical visit. Visit to S. Johnson's. Visit to Mr. Sharples—where I found Wm. We drank tea there, & returned to Seth's, & spent the evening.

Monday, 15.—My Catarrh still very troublesome. Unfit for study. Continued the Monthly Magazine. Visits from Mr. Roulet, Mr. Webster, Dr. Miller, Mr. Dunlap, Mr. Wortman, & Mr. Gahn. Dined at Dr. [blur] Miller's, with Dr. Mease &c. A medical visit. After dinner, Miller, Mease, & myself rode out to Webster's, where we spent the evening.

Tuesday, 16.—Three medical visits in the course of the day. Visit from Dr. Mease. Accompanied him on a visit to Mr. Stark Robertson; & to the Hospital. Visit from Dunlap. Dined at Kent's, in company with Dr. Dwight, W. W. Woolsey & others, & spent chief of the afternoon. The evening at the Manumission Society. Continued the Monthly Magazine. Composed a Report to the Manumission Society. Dunlap has finished his André. Recd. a letter from Dr. Buel, yesterday.

Wednesday, 17.—Two medical visits. Visit to Dr. Miller. Visit from Mr. Dunlap. Drew off, for collection, several accounts. At my printer's. Errands. Corrected a proof sheet. Sketched the plan of my Oration before the Manumission Society. Continued the Monthly Magazine. Part of the evening at Riley's: Part at Mr. Rogers's, with Dr. Dwight & others: part at home. Recd. a letter from Dr. Kollock.

Thursday, 18.—Two medical visits. A number of calls & errands. Visit to Dr. Miller. Spent the evening at Mr. Radclift's, with Dr. Dwight, Mr. Woolsey, Mr. Kent, &c. Wrote a few paragraphs on my Oration. Composed, & transcribed with many corrections, the letter to Dr. Beddoes. Continued the Monthly Magazine.

Friday, 19.—Two medical visits. Principal part of the forenoon at Dr. Miller's, engaged with him in some experiments on the respiration of the vapour of Ether.[67] Visit from Dunlap. Dined, & spent much of the afternoon at his house, with Dr. Dwight & others. Drank tea at H. Johnson's. Ineffectual calls on Miss Mason, on Johnsons, Comedians, at Hodgkinson's. Principal part of the evening at home. Recd. a letter from Mr. Tracy. Wrote a few lines, yesterday, to my father. Corrected proof-sheets of the Botanic Garden & the Repository. Continued the Monthly Magazine. Read the article Rheumatism in Darwin. Some further progress in my Oration.

Saturday, 20.—Dr. Mease breakfasted with us this morning. I saw him afterwards at Miller's—& he has left town. Two medical visits, in the course of the day. At Miller's. Saw Dr. Dwight there. At our printer's. Corrected proof-sheets. Recd. a letter from Mr. Backus

---

[67] Ether had been familiar to scientists for many years and something about its properties as an anaesthetic were known; nevertheless, it would be almost fifty years from this date before Dr. Horace Wells, a dentist in Hartford, had a tooth extracted painlessly while under the influence of this gas.

of Bethlem, Connect. Visit from Dunlap. Various calls & errands. Finished looking over the 3rd vol. of the Monthly Magazine. Read the Newspapers. Club night—G. M. Woolsey's turn—present—Dunlap, Johnson, Smith, & G. M. Woolsey. Our evening was somewhat interrupted by an alarm of fire. Dunlap informs us that we are likely to have Cooper on our Stage.

Sunday, Jany. 21.—Continued the 21st No. of the Monthly Magazine. Two medical visits. Visit to Dr. Kingsley—who is still exceedingly unwell, & I fear dangerously so. William & I took a walk of four or five miles. We dined & spent the afternoon, at Seth Johnson's; drank tea at Horace; visited in the evening at Riley's; but spent the principal part of it at Wm. W. Woolsey's—where we found Dr. Dwight. Came home, & corrected a proof of the Repository.

Monday, 22.—Three medical visits. Corrected two proofs. Read several articles in the Annals of Medicine. Visit to Dr. Miller. Wrote letters to Mr. Tracy & Dr. Kollock. A number of calls & errands. Visit from Mr. Gahn, who introduced to me a very agreable & sensible & well-informed Italian Gentleman—whose name I did not distinctly learn. He sat here an hour. Visit from Dunlap. S. Johnson & wife, Wm, & Fanny & myself spent the entire evening at Mr. Sharples's.

Tuesday, 23.—Finished all that I had to do with the Monthly Magazine. Two medical visits—one of which being at Woolsey's, I saw Dr. Dwight there a short time. Numerous calls & errands. Wrote a short letter to Mr. Backus of Bethlem. Made out a Catalogue of publications, in the United States, on Yellow Fever, for Mr. Scandella[68]—the Italian gentleman who was here yesterday. Wrote a few lines to Dr. Beddoes. Corrected a proof sheet of the Botanic Garden. Evening wholly at Dunlap's—with Mr. Cooper, the Comedian—who gave me some anecdotes of Godwin & Holcroft. I forgot to mention that I spent two hours, in the afternoon, with Dr. Dingley.

Wednesday, 24.—A visit, of more than two hours, from Mr. Scandella. We conversed on medicine, meteorology, & the politics of this country—& on Italy. Corrected proofs of the Medical Repository. Continued my Oration. Visit to Dr. Miller. Drank tea at Mr. Kent's. Spent the evening at Seth Johnson's. Col. & Mrs. Walker there. Miss Kirkland a short time. She is a *very* pretty girl.

To Thomas Beddoes

In the absence of Dr. Mitchill, who is now with the Legislature at Albany, I take the liberty of addressing a few lines to you, with the two first Nos. of the Medical Repository, & such part of the third No. as is already printed off. You would doubtless have recd. the two former, at an earlier period, but for the numerous engagements which occupied our Associate, previous to his departure from New York. Nor was it till since he left us that I discovered, from our register, that he had been so long neglectful of this part of his duty: the more incumbent on him to have performed, from the many similar obligations which, thro' him, you have conferred on us all, & on science in America.

From what you will observe, in our publication, you will be able to form a pretty correct opinion of the general state of medical science in the United States. You will not wonder at the small portion of Chemical & Natural History papers, which you see admitted into this Miscellany, when you are informed that these departments of knowlege have been, hitherto, very little cultivated; & that we are fearful of proceeding faster than we shall be able to interest our readers. The Practise of Physic, however, is on a tolerably respectable footing; & tho' we can not boast of many men universally learned in the physical sciences, yet, probably, we have fewer absolute quacks, than in any country of equal population. Boerhaave, Cullen, & Brown, Sydenham, Pringle, Huxham, & other practical writers, are generally read; & Zoonomia is slowly pervading the country. Indeed a spirit [of] observation & inquiry seems, now, to be lighting up, in every part of the Continent. And as this is in great measure to be attributed to the prevalence of pestilential fevers, in our principal towns, since the year 1790, it is not surprizing that the attention of our physicians should be more strongly directed to their history & progress, than to other subjects. This, which will, in some degree, impede a general cultivation of the science of medicine, will be ultimately serviceable to it; & the rigorous examination to which all the questions relative to Contagion are now subjected, authorizes us to believe that the subject will be completely elucidated. On this topic, Mr. Webster, a literary man, tho' not a physician, has considerably distinguished himself. His publications have been mostly confined to a paper of which he is the proprietor; but he is now employed in reducing his materials into the form of a regular treatise, which we shall have the pleasure of transmitting to you when published.

Many trials have been made here, with the Nitric Acid; with various, but generally with good, success. But our physicians are more ready to make trials, than willing to report their consequences in writing. It will be sometime, therefore, before we shall be able to add much new & interesting matter, relative to this remedy, to what has already been published elsewhere.

I am with respect & esteem
Yours &c.

Jany. 18. 1798.
Pine St. 45.   E. H. Smith.

[Omitted here, one manuscript page: "Zoonomia—conti. V."]

Thursday, 25.—Took up Darwin anew: read & analyzed the preceeding section, & read some part of the 14th. Visit from Dr. Seaman. Medical visit. Mr. Allen

---

[68] Joseph B. Scandella was a physician whose interest in these pages lies in the fact that it was while tending him that Smith succumbed to yellow fever.

arrived from Phila. We went to see Woolsey & Dunlap. We saw Dr. Dwight at Woolsey's Store, dined with [him] at his house, & drank tea with [him] at Mr. Rogers's—where we spent part of the evening with him—Mr. Tutor Huntington, Dunlap &c. I went with Allen to his lodgings. He leaves town in the morning. Visit to Dr. Miller's—where the remainder of the evg. was spent. Wrote a letter to Dr. Saltonstall of New London, Connect.

Friday, Jany. 26.—Medical visit. Continued Zoonomia, & the analysis—in which I made less progress than in reading. Visit from S. Johnson. Called on Mr. Scandella—vainly. Visit to Dr. Dwight. Some writing for the Medical Repository. Visit from Dr. S. Osborn—from Mr. Sharples: To our printer's: to Dr. Miller's—where I spent part of the evening—part with Miss Mason. Corrected two proofs of the Repository, one of the Botanic Garden.

Saturday, 27.—This day has been remarkably tempestuous with wind, snow, & hail; which still continue. I have kept house constantly. Completed the rough sketch of my Oration. A little writing for the Repository. Wrote the two succeeding pages: & have again finished the Section on Instinct, which I began yesterday—having read near fifty pages of it to day. The storm has prevented our Club.

Sunday, 28.—Read Walker's inquiry concerning Sterility—8vo. pp. 22—& Logan on Rotation of Crops—pp. 41[69]—8vo.—& wrote a short article by way of review for each. Visit at G. M. Woolsey's: at H. Johnson's. Wm. & I dined & spent part of the afternoon at Seth's: visited at Riley's—drank tea at Dunlap's—& went with him to see the New Theater lighted. Thence we all three went to W. W. Woolsey's—where we saw Dr. Dwight—who soon went away—(he leaves town tomorrow) & Mr. Huntington. Some question having arisen on the subject of promises, Wm. & I read the Chapter, in Godwin, on that subject, after our return home.

Monday, 29.—Read Townsend on Pot & Pearl Ashes—8vo. pp. 48—& a short pamphlet of Hosack's on Suspended Respiration,[70] & a former controversial Letter of Dr. Bayley's to Dr. John Bard. Visits from Dunlap, from Dr. Miller, & from Mr. Scandella. Various errands. Corrected proofs of the Repository. Cut my left hand very badly. Drank tea at Dr. Miller's. Went to the New Theater—which opened, for the first time, with my occasional Address, Mr. Milns's "Bustle, or The New House,"[71] & "As you Like it" & "The Purse."

---

[69] Walker, *An Inquiry into the Causes of Sterility* (Philadelphia, 1797); George Logan, *Rotation of Crops*, possibly a part of his publication entitled *Fourteen Agricultural Experiments* (Philadelphia, 1797), this particular pamphlet otherwise not found.

[70] *Pot Ash and Pearl Ash*, not found; David Hosack, M.D., *An Inquiry into the Causes of Suspended Animation from Drowning* (New York, 1792).

[71] Milne, New York writer previously cited, wrote *Bustle, or The New House* especially for the opening on the evening of January 29, 1798.

The crowd was immense—so that I could hear very little—& could not get into the body of the House. I came away about 8 o'clock—& called at Miller's—who dressed my wound. Instead of the last line of the Address—read—

"Pride of the young, & idol of the wise."

[Omitted here, two manuscript pages: "Zoonomia—contd. VI."]

Tuesday, Jany. 30.—Over-slept myself. Visit from Mr. Scandella, who left New York for Phila. Dr. Miller here all the forenoon. We read over Dr. Buel's Account of the Sheffield Fever & Dysentery,[72] together. I wrote a letter to Dr. Mitchill. Corrected the last proof of No. 3. of the Repository—& procured the Copy-right Certificate. Medical visit. Visit from Mr. Roulet. Medical visit, & spent part of the evening, at S. Johnson's. Spent part of the evening at Kent's. Read Zoonomia—Sect. on "Catenation of Motions."

Wednesday, 31.—A visit from Dunlap. At his desire, I wrote some account of "The New Theater," & its opening, for the "Commercial Advertiser" of this evening.[73] Read the News-papers—with the long Congressional Debates. Wrote a letter to William Buel, & another to Isaac Beers. Performed, also, various pieces of writing, for the Medical Repository. At our printer's. Corrected a proof-sheet of the "Botanic Garden." Various errands &c. A visit to Dr. Miller. I saw there, & read some part of, Whitaker's Review of Gibbon. Drank tea at Dunlap's. We went together to the Theater. The Prelude again;[74] The School for Scandal; & Lock & Key. I saw only a small part of the Prelude, & a part of the Play. The House was by no means full. I enjoy plays very little. My taste is either very much blunted, or very much refined. When I came home, I found letters from Dr. Mitchill, Thomas Mumford & Mary: The first copious—the two last, scanty. Read Darwin's Section on Sleep.

I have now come to the conclusion of the first month of the new year; &, notwithstanding many resolutions of industry with which it was commenced, find less done than for several preceding months. At least, such appears to be the fact, on a rapid & mental retrospection. Certain I am that all that has been done, might have been accomplished easily in one week.

Industry of January 1798

Reading

Zoonomia—P. 11. pp. 123—4to.—27 a second time.
Annals of Medicine—pp. 100.

---

[72] Dr. Buel's Account of the Sheffield Fever was perhaps intended for *The Medical Repository*. It does not appear to have been printed elsewhere.

[73] The account Smith wrote for *The Advertiser* of this date was a splendid piece of writing. It appeared unsigned. Odell, *Annals of the New York Stage* **2**: p. 7, quotes from it and calls it "the best, descriptively, with which I am familiar."

[74] *The Prelude* may be Smith's verses for the opening; if not, not found.

Kirwan &c—on Phlogiston &c. (the remainder— = to) pp. 152—8vo.
Rousseau's Confessions—P. 11. (translation.) 3 vols. 12mo. pp. 800.
Citizen Fauchet's pamphlet on French & American affairs—8vo. pp. 31.
Logan on Rotation of Crops—8vo. pp. 41.
Townsend on Pot & Pearl Ashes—8vo. pp. 48.
Walker's Inaugural Essay, on Sterility.—pp. 29—8vo.
Hosack on Suspended Animation—pamphlet.
Bayley's letter to Jno. Bard—pamphlet.
Monthly Magazine—about half of vol. III—& some loose Nos.

Writing

Composition

Letters, preserved in this volume . . . . pp.	11.
Do. not preserved	15.
Prologue (for the New Theater) &c. . . .	9.
Zoonomia.	3.
Review of Walker & Logan.	2.
Report to the Manumission Socy. . . .	4.
Sketch of an Oration before the Many. Socy.	36.

Transcription

Of Letters . . . . pp.	11.
Of Prologue.	5.
Of Report &c.	4.

Beside correction of proof-sheets—various writings for the Repository—occasional Reading—&c. &c. &c.

MEMOIRS. 1798. FEBRUARY.

Thursday, 1.—Read & abridged Darwin's chapter on Instinct. Read that on Reverie. It has occurred to me—why do I go thro' this drudgery? What purpose will it serve? Could I not read the work in the time I am writing the abstract of it? should I not profit as much by the reading, as by the writing? I fear that I shall never connectedly remember this work. I find no difficulty in comprehending it, as I read: but I can not distinctly remember it. What I want is, to be able, after having studied it, to draw out a concise & complete analysis, from recollection. And this I shall never be able to do. I am doubtful whether to continue or omit the writing.

Made out the preceding table of Industry. Read the news-papers. Visit from a patient. Drank tea at G. M. Woolsey's. Vain calls at Miss Morton's, Dr. Hosack's, Boyd's, & Riley's. Spent part of the evening at Mr. Duryee's—(the husband of Nancy Mumford) & saw there D, Wm. & Benjn. Mumford.[75] Remainder of the evening at home.

Friday, 2.—All the forenoon, & some part of the afternoon, at our printer's—busied in making up & directing packages, & writing letters respecting the Medical Repository. The rest of the afternoon, or great part of it, busy in arranging the accounts. Visit to Dr. Miller. Recd. a letter from Mr. Tracy; another from Dr. N. Dwight of Hartford, inclosing his essay on Sick-Head-Ach, which I read; another from Dr. Mitchill, with Treasurer Bancker's Report on the Finances of the State—which I read. One for Dunlap came with it, from Mitchill, also, containing the Report of the Commissioners of the State Prison—which I read. Eveng. Wm. & I spent with Mr. Kent. Mrs. K. gone to Poughkeepsie. He will be made judge of the Supreme Court, & will remove into the country. This is one of the most untoward circumstances which could have befallen our little Society here; & as such we all feel it. It may be well for him, however. It will, certainly be well for the State. Came home, & read Stock's Inaugural Dissertation on the effects of Cold on the Human Body —8vo. pp. 43—& wrote a short criticism on it.

Saturday, Feb. 3.—Read the news-papers. Much of the forenoon & afternoon attending to the accounts &c. of the Repository. Wrote a few lines to Drs. Dwight, Field, & Wheaton. Two medical visits. Spent the evening at W. W. Woolsey's. Recd. a letter from Alsop. Wrote a letter to Mr. Tracy. The New Theater was opened on Monday night—when the House was crowded—& the receits, notwithstanding much disorder & cheating, exceeded 1200 dollars: on Wednesday night they were about 500; on Friday, about 250—the expences of each night are about 400. Such is the sad statement which Dunlap gave me at Woolsey's, this evening. All prospects of gain, therefore, are at an end, for him —& if he saves himself he does well.

Sunday, 4.—Read two of Dr. Aikin's letters to his son. Two medical visits. Wrote a letter to Dr. Mitchill. Wm. & I walked. Called at H. Johnson's. We dined & spent the afternoon at Seth's. We drank tea, & spent part of the evening, at Mr. Sharples's: the remainder at Dunlap's.

Monday, 5.—Two medical visits—morning. Calls & errands. At Dr. Miller's. Took thence the vol. of Medical Commentaries for 1793—for the purpose of reading a paper of Chisholm's on the Grenada Fever of 1790: which having read I wrote a few sentences of addition to my Essay on the origin of the Grenada Fever of 1793. Having the book with me, I was induced to read one article, after another, till I have read the greater part of the vol. Miller called here on the evening. We made several unsuccessful attempts to see some ladies of our acquaintance. A medical visit. The remainder of the evening at home.

[Omitted here, five manuscript pages: "Zoonomia—Contd. VII."]

Tuesday, Feby. 6.—Three medical visits. Finished Med. Comment. 1793. pp. 500—of which I read all except a few pages. Errands. Wrote a letter to Richard Alsop. Continued Zoonomia. Visit to Riley's. Principal

---

[75] Benjamin Mumford (1772-1843; Yale 1790), a New York insurance broker, cousin to Thomas Mumford, Smith's brother-in-law.

part of the evening at Mr. Stark Robertson's. Wrote a few lines to C. B. Brown, Jos. Bringhurst Jr. & Dr. Barton—as introductory to Mr. Sharples, who goes to Phila. to-morrow: & a few lines to Mr. Sharples. He sent home a copy of my original portrait. It is not quite so good a resemblance as the original. I intend it for my parents.[76]

Wednesday, 7.—Read the Newspapers—town & country. Two medical visits in the course of the day. Errands. The greater part of the day occupied in writing &c. for the Repository: i.e. in preparing a form, to last for the whole year, for the Hospital Returns—rendered necessary by the carelessness & delays of the Apothecary there. Called, vainly, on Miss Morton, & on Dr. Hosack. Spent considerable part of the evening at Mr. Radclift's. Wrote a letter, of some length, to my father. Corrected a proof-sheet of the Botanic Garden—Notes.

Thursday, 8.—Read a number of newspapers. Medical visit. Some progress in Zoonomia. Visit to Miller. At the Hospital, on business of the Repository. Visit from Dunlap. We went together to see Stewart's picture of Washington—exhibited by Baker.[77] It is truly admirable. Dined, spent the afternoon, & the first of the evening, at William Leffingwell's. There were there G. M. Woolsey & wife, her father & mother, sister, sister & brother Coit, &c. &c. Medical visit. Read, again, Cooper's Inaugural Dissertation on the Datura Stramonium; & wrote a criticism on it, for the Repository. Recd. a letter from Mr. Tracy. My Prologue was published today—correctly I hope—for I have not yet seen the paper in which it is.

Friday, 9th.—Medical visit. At our printer's. Read over a long file of London papers. A visit from Dr. Miller. Conversation &c. relative to the business of the Repository. Recd. a letter from William Buel. Drank tea, & spent much of the evening, at Dunlap's. Brought thence the Monthly Review for Oct. '97—of which I have read the greater part. *Art. I.* Sir G. Staunton's Acct. of the Embassy to China. This is a long & entertaining article—in which, however, the reviewer sinks into the humble narrator: The extracts are well written, interesting, & selected with judgement. *Art. III.* Illustrations of prophecy. The Extract, at the close, concerning the Millenium has some merit; & would equally become a philosopher & a pietist. *Art. V.* The Minister &c. translated from Schiller, by Lewis. This is the tragedy, before published in english, under the title of "Cabal & Love." This translation, from the specimen here given, appears to have merit: the first was detestable. *Art. VI.* Mitford's History of Greece, vol. 3. The quotations are favorable specimens of the author's manner & spirit. In general he is said to be the apologist of Despotism. The Note concerning forms of Government, would incline one to a contrary belief. At least, there is nothing exceedingly objectionable in this Note —except that it may fairly be objected that as forms affect substance, they are not wholly inconsequential. The remarks of the Critic may be acceded to. In general, they are such as I should make. *Art. VIII.* Seward's Supplement to his Anecdotes. A valuable work for occasional reference & amusement. *Art. IX.* Townson's travels in Hungary. This is, likewise, an interesting article, & increases my desire to see a work which promises much instruction, as well as entertainment. *Art. XII.* Wakefield's Letter to Wilberforce. Tho' much force may be allowed, as well as pertinency, to the remarks of the reviewer, still I can not find great fault with Mr. Wakefield, in this instance. The extracts are masterly, in respect of style; & written in a spirit so bold & free, that I very much desire to look over the whole pamphlet. *Art. XIV.* Noble's Memoirs of the House of Medici. Of the justness of the criticisms I am not qualified to speak, tho' they are advanced with the confidence of justice. The extracts entertain *me*; tho' they are inferior to those from Mr. Roscoe's Work. As this contains some account of the whole dynasty, it may deserve reading, tho' not so well executed. *Art. 35, 36, & 37.* Dunlap's Afterpiece & Opera, & my Opera—all briefly noticed—& with as much commendation as was to be expected. *Art. 61.* Il Passatempo Italico. The Anecdote, relative to Petrarca & the old School master, is very pleasing. *Art. 71.* Mr. Miller's Manumission Oration. It deserved praise, but not so much as is here conferred upon it.

Saturday, 10.—Feby.—At my printer's, on business. Several errands, which took much time. Read the papers. Finished the Oct. '97—No. of the Monthly Review, & wrote the preceding notes. Re-read my Notes concerning Syracuse, & commenced the methodical arrangement. Club night—Johnson's turn—Present, Dunlap, Johnson, Smith, W. W. Woolsey—& Miller visitor. Separated at eleven—after a very social evening.

Sunday, 11.—Ablutions &c. as usual. These commonly occupy some considerable portion of every Sunday forenoon. Composed, from materials furnished me by him, a note to Buel's Essay on the Sheffield Diseases of 1796, 7. Wrote a letter to Buel. Wm. & I dined & spent the afternoon at Seth's. We drank tea & spent the evening at Kent's. Messrs. Boyd, Radclift, & Riggs were there—& the time was very socially & pleasantly

---

[76] Smith mentions one copy of his portrait which he intended for his parents. Actually, there were two copies. In the *Commercial Advertiser* for December 27, 1799, over a year after Smith's death, Sharples advertised that he would have for sale sets of copies, one of which sets included Dr. Elihue [*sic*] Smith. It is not clear whether this was one of his "polygraphic" prints. See G. Raddin, Jr., *The New York of Hocquet Caritat*, p. 30. In Knox, *The Sharples*, etc., p. 97, we read that the original and true copies were owned by Mr. Walter H. Crittendon, Mrs. W. Moylan Lansdale, and the New-York Historical Society. Probably the original is the portrait in the Historical Society. Later one of the copies became the property of Miss Frances G. Colt of Pittsfield, Massachusetts, and, after her death, went to Yale University.

[77] The "gallery" was the New City Tavern on Broadway. In addition to the Stuart (which Smith always spelled Stewart), the exhibit included ten other paintings. See Raddin, *The New York of Hocquet Caritat*, p. 29.

spent. Came home, corrected a proof-sheet of the Botanic Garden, & hastily sketched out, & not much to my mind, one of my Sonnets on Truth.

Monday, 12.—Continued the arrangement of my Notes on the Syracusan pestilence. A visit from Mr. Stark Robertson. Recd. Letters from Dr. Morse, & from Dr. Holyoke; also a letter from Dr. Oliver to Dr. Mitchill. Dr. Morse writes encouragingly concerning the Repository. Dr. Holyoke transmits two papers, to be inserted in it. Dr. Oliver sends, also, a third paper by Dr. Holyoke. All this is promising. Wrote short letters to Mr. Pickering, Mr. Scandella, & Mr. Poulson—Phila.—transmitting copies of No. 3. of the Reposy. At our printer's, where I corrected the first half sheet of No. 4. now printing. Visit from Dr. Dingley. Medical visit. Drank tea with Dr. Miller—with whom I read over the three papers of Dr. Holyoke, which I had previously read, by myself. An hour at the Theater. Reynold's contemptible comedy of "Fortune's Fool."[78] Came home, & wrote a letter of some length to Dr. Morse—inclosing also a long letter to a bookseller in Boston, now written. Wrote, likewise, a letter to Dr. Holyoke, & a letter to Mr. Tracy.

Tuesday, 13.—Medical visit. Visit from Mr. Tisdale. Called on Dr. Miller, & went with him to the Hospital, for the purpose of seeing a patient there with trismus, but who we found dead when we arrived. Wrote a lengthy letter to Nathaniel Dwight—principally in relation to his essay on Sick Head-Ach; which, for this purpose, I re-read. Recd. a letter from Mr. Tracy. Much of the afternoon spent in writing for the Manumission Society. Mr. Allen suddenly entered, on his return to Congress from Connecticut. He brought me letters from my sisters Abby & Fanny. Dunlap & I went to Mr. Hobson's—where Mrs. Dunlap was—agreable to a previous appointment, at Dunlap's, at whose house I was, a short time, this morning. I am desirous of cultivating Mrs. Hobson's acquaintance. After tea, I went to see Mr. Allen, at his lodgings. A medical visit. Continued the reading of Mr. Monroe's "View &c."[79] which I commenced this morning. Corrected proof-sheets of the Botanic Garden, & of the Repository.

Wednesday, Feby. 14.—Read the Newspapers—a laborious morning's employment. Great part of the day devoted to writing for the Manumission Society. A visit, in the forenoon, from Mr. Meigs, professor of Mathematics & Natural Philosophy at New Haven. He thinks of removing here—to assume the editorial charge of the Daily Advertiser. He communicated to me the following facts—

1. He was informed, by a Capt. from Salem (Mass.) employed in the fishery, that the fish, on the banks of Newfoundland, taken in the season of 1792, "were unusually lean, poor, & apparently sickly."

2. The late Dr. Stiles was exceedingly fond of Oysters, an accurate judge of them, & seldom past a day without eating them. He told Mr. Meigs that the oysters of New Haven had the Yellow fever (this was his expression) in 1794, (when it was in that town) being unusually poor & worthless.

3. Mr. Isaac Jones informed Mr. Meigs that, in the same year, his Cabbages never grew after transplantation—but, contrary to the usual fact, & when they had been treated as usual, sickened & perished.

Mr. Meigs recommends, as a Medical Correspondent, in the Island of Bermuda, the Hon. Francis Forbes M. D. & advises me to inquire of Dr. Forbes relative to an epidemic, observed there 12 or 15 years since, called the Great fever. I shall also inquire concerning there fever in 1795 or 1796. Dr. Forbes is a member of the council; about 55; & learned & ingenious, & communicative.

Two visits from patients. A visit to Riley's—where I spent part of the evening. Miss Alsop shewed me two versions of Songs from Metastasio,[80] by Mr. Alsop. Part of the evening at H. Johnson's. Came home—continued the reading of Mr. Munroe's "View &c." & corrected a proof-sheet of the Botanic Garden.

To Fanny Smith

And for once, my dear sister, I consent to pass your procrastination without violent censure. It is difficult, however, to discover any particular advantages in it. You take occasion, in consequence of an event which your letter communicates, to neglect, almost altogether, the business of replication to what I had previously written you. If, instead of this procrastination, you had answered me seasonably, I do not see but that you might have, just as well, communicated the intelligence which you comment on, now, with so much pleasure. There is never any thing lost by performing one's duty. And when it is proper for any act to be executed by us, within a given time, to execute it within that time becomes a part of our duty. All considerations on the possible advantages which may accrue from delay, & all felicitations on those which are supposed to have arisen, are so many pleas & plaisterings of the fiend Indolence.

I am pleased with the information given me by Abby, relative to your course & practice of reading. I wish that you may not hurry over what you read too much; as is apt to happen, in this mode of study. It is not how many pages you *read*, but how many you *comprehend & remember*, that is important. And, what is of still more consequence is, that you apply all this reading, by sedulous reflection, to moral, political & literary use. Not merely that you remember what others have done; but that you draw, from the history of their conduct, instruction on the conduct of your own life. I send a new Sonnet.

Feb. 15. '98.   E. H. Smith.

---

[78] Frederick Reynolds (1796).

[79] James Monroe, *A View of the Conduct of the Executive* (Philadelphia, 1797).

[80] Peter Metastasio (true name, Trapasse), eighteenth-century Italian poet, author of tragedies, elegies, and operas.

To Abigail Smith Jr.

I rejoice, my dear sister, in that increase of your happiness, which is marked by the conclusion of your last letter. Having already communicated with you, very freely, on this subject, generally, I have nothing new to add, but that I hope the event may be as permanently promotive of your welfare, as I am convinced it ought to be of any worthy man's, connecting himself with you. The interest which I take in this gentleman, being wholly founded on that which I feel for you, & on the representations you have made to me of his character, it is impossible that I should express any sentiment concerning him, from my own knowlege. He has never given me opportunity to judge of him. You know, however, that I am disposed to regard him with an eye of favour.

The information you give me, relative to the state of your intimacy with the Tracys, afflicts, but does not surprize me. In the ordinary course of human intercourse, persons become more & more engrossed with their own affairs, & take less & less interest in those of others, where their own are not blended, & especially if any way supposed contradictory to their own. The friendships of youth are apt to melt away, & to be succeeded by the more unimpassioned civilities of neighbours & acquaintance. And this you must be prepared for. It inspires a salutary lesson; & ought to teach us to learn to rely on ourselves, to multiply our own resources, & to be able to find in our own reflections, from our own observation, & by our own acts, independent happiness. I do not mean unsocial enjoyment: for this is impossible: But enjoyment arising out of our own benevolence towards others, & not from any necessity of favours from them. I know that hearts warm like ours my sister, are peculiarly exposed to be wounded by the dereliction of those we thought our friends. But the wound were deeper, were the fault our own. In the present case, I feel my compassion very strongly excited towards this family: for the lady, especially, must be unhappy. She has loved us; & she must have become jealous that we do not love her, or she could not betray any diminution of regard for us. Now this is the more unfortunate, as we love her, as we have always done; while she suffers the double torment of suspicion & alienation. For if she can not confide in us—who is there, in Lichfield, in whom she can confide? But, perhaps, this is only a temporary coolness, & will soon disappear. In either case, whether it is, or is not, say nothing of it—not even to your friends. We cherish no resentment. We feel only affection & compassion. Let not our compassion, by much speaking of it, operate like resentment. Be uniform, & prudent.

I approve of your reading meetings. Lose no time for improvement. Apply yourself, with redoubled energy, to the acquisition of all useful knowlege—before your opportunities are abridged, as they necessarily will be, by the superintendence of a family.

Feb: 15. 1798.   E. H. Smith.

To Mary S. Mumford

What I wrote you, on the subject of nursing, was composed under a belief that you were encumbered with a child beside your own, and had relation wholly to that supposition. I have since learnt, that the unfortunate orphan, who was temporarily committed to you, has been otherwise disposed of. My remarks, therefore, cease to be applicable to your situation. It was from suckling two children, at the same time, not from devoting yourself to the entire charge of your own, that I had some apprehensions. In general, where the mother has health, but little is to be feared from this circumstance, if this attention be not too long continued; & much is to be dreaded from its neglect. The signal for omitting altogether, or exceedingly diminishing this species of maternal care, is the appearance of teeth. When the child is able to divide solid food, it is time to supply him with food of this kind; & this in proportion to his ability to masticate & digest it.

I am well satisfied that my instructions for the cure of those complaints which are connected with Worms in children, met the approbation of Dr. Delanoe. If this gentleman is in the practice of physic, or in the habit of observation, it would gratify me, & may be no disservice to him, to receive from him occasional or methodical information respecting every occurrence & circumstance which concerns the health of his neighborhood, & the surrounding country. He probably knows that I am concerned in the publication of a periodical work, extensively connected with medicine & natural history. To him it might be of some value; communications from him, on any topics which fall within this general plan, we should estimate as important, & readily attend to. And this, if you think proper, you may inform him of.

In respect to the Books which you have—I am in no want of them. Such as are particularly useful to you, keep: the others may be sent, as opportunity presents, to Lichfield. I am particularly gratified by your remarks on "Political Justice." It deserves your frequent perusal. I wish you to be possessed, not only of all its fundamental doctrines, but of all the reasons, by & which they are supported, & of all the variations of which they are susceptible in their application to different states of society.

Connected with this subject, and as an article of literary information, which will give you pleasure, I may impart to you the knowlege of a little work, by our friend Charles B. Brown; for which I am now collecting subscriptions, & which I design to publish in the course of the spring. It is intituled "Alcuin; a Dialogue." In this dialogue, which is written with great spirit & elegance, he recognizes the intellectual quality of the sexes, & endeavours to determine what pursuits are best adapted to women, under the present, & perhaps the future state of human society. He inculcates a suppression of all desires for mingling in the active occupations of politics & war; & would rather that they should cultivate science in retirement, correct opinion by their writings, & improve men by their example. What further opinions he designs to maintain, I do not yet know; not having seen the whole of his performance. I think, however, that it will be worthy your perusal; & recommend it to Thomas to authorize me to subscribe for it. The subscription is 50 Cents.

Feb. 15. 1798.　　　　　　　　　　　　E. H. Smith.

To Thomas Mumford

I received your letter of a few lines from Albany, together with the books, & the inclosure, in due season. The last was sent to Lichfield soon after; and, having since heard from there, I have the pleasure to inform you that all our friends are well.

When Dr. Mitchill left this place, for Albany, he took with him a few lines for you—some books—& if I do not misremember, some letters from Lichfield. As neither he has mentioned them, in his letters to me, nor you in yours, I am apprehensive lest they should have miscarried, or been lost. He was to forward them, by some opportunity, to you. That they had not been recd. when my sister wrote, I infer from her silence. As you doubtless saw Dr. Mitchill, I hope, if the books had not been previously forwarded, that you took them of him, yourself. Of this, however, I wish to be informed; & will thank you to mention, when you write next.

Your friends, here, are all well, I believe. I have seen many of them, within a few days—& know nothing to the contrary. Your sister seems to be comfortably, & even pleasantly settled. Her husband appears as good-natured as herself: so that I think they are likely to jog along over the rough road of life without much jolting.

Johnson & I still remain together; & are likely to try it another year, at least. Perhaps, another & another; for I see no present probability of a change. Love to the children.

Feb: 15. 1798.　　　　　　　　　　　　E. H. Smith.

Thursday, 15.—Mr. Meigs breakfasted with us, & spent an hour afterwards. Wrote the preceding letters, of this date. At our printer's. Visit from Dunlap. Medical visit. Continued Monroe's "View." Dined at Mr. Stark Robertson's—at 4 P. M. & stayed till nine. Mrs. Sharples there—Genl. Gates & Mr. Garnet,[81] Dr. Dickson of Dublin, &c. Medical visit. Continued Monroe.

Friday, 16.—Medical visit. Continued Monroe's "View &c." Wrote a few introductory & additional remarks to my Examination of Chisholm: so that I have only to ascertain whether one fact be correctly stated, & alter or preserve it, & my piece is ready for the press. I obtained, from Mr. Garnet, to-day, both editions of Coleridge's Poems, with Lloyd's & Lamb's Poem's, Southey's & Castle's. They are in small duodecimo, & loosely printed. I have read both editions of Coleridge, Lloyd, Lamb, Castle, & a part of Southey: in all 720 pages. A visit from Mr. Roulet, in the forenoon, of some length. At Mr. Kent's, a short time, in the evening: a longer time at G. M. Woolsey's.

Saturday, 17.—Read the Newspapers. Medical visit. At the printer's. Visit to Charles Adams. Visit from Dr. Miller. Medical visit. Visit to Mr. Kent. Finished Southey's Poems—additional pages 146. Continued, & made considerable progress in Monroe's "View &c." Drank tea, & spent the evening, at W. W. Woolsey's. Club night—& his—present, Dunlap, Johnson, Smith, W. W. Woolsey—& Dr. Miller visitor.

Sunday, 18.—Wrote a short letter to Mr. Tracy. Medical visit. Commenced & wrote fifty lines (exclusive of erasures) of an Epistle, in verse, to Dr. Darwin—which, should I finish it agreably to my mind, I design to prefix to the american edition of the Botanic Garden. Medical visit. Drank tea at W. W. Woolsey's. Visit to Mrs. Sharples—where I spent part of the evening: the rest at S. Johnson's. Continued Monroe's "View &c."

Monday, Feby. 19.—Medical visit. At our printer's. At Dr. Miller's. Called to see Dr. Dickson—in vain. Errands. Finished Mr. Monroe's "View of the conduct of the Executive of the United States" 8vo. pp. 473—very close print. The introductory narrative bespeaks more art & method than appears to belong to the author of the official papers. From the whole I conclude that Mr. Washington was as much to blame as Mr. Monroe. Knowing, as the first did, the political sentiments & feelings of the last, the appointment should never have been made. Mr. Monroe's misconduct seems to have arisen from two sources, principally: 1st incapacity; 2nd an entire admiration & love of France, which blinded him to many of her failings, & permitted him to be frequently imposed on, which made him rely on her justice, & fear to offend her. Hence his insensibility to the true dignity of his own country, & his frequent derelictions of its interests—which may be well enough admitted, & not imply any want of honesty in this man. It certainly implies want of sagacity in the Executive. At the same time, Mr. Monroe may have acted dishonestly. It is possible that all the means of forming a right judgement of his conduct are not furnished us, in his book. Wrote a letter to Alsop. Visit from Mr. Tisdale. Medical visit. Drank tea at Riley's. Dr. Miller & I called to see Miss Templeton—she from home. Spent the evening with Miss Morton. Wrote 52 lines on my Epistle to Darwin. Read a paper of Fourcroy's, in the *Annales de Chimie*.

Tuesday, 20.—Medical visit. At Dunlap's, where I looked over the Article "Paper" in the Scotch Encyclopedia—& afterwards, at home, that of Printing—& finished the first outline of my Epistle to Darwin; the principal part tolerably correct—or at least as much so, as I am likely to make it. Other parts must be amended, & all transcribed. Transcribed my letter to Fanny, & also, for her, Sonnet Second. Re-read many of Cole-

---

[81] Garnet was probably a visitor in the city. His name does not appear in the New York directories of the time.

ridge's & of Southey's Poems. The day excessive stormy, & the walking almost impracticable.

Wednesday, 21.—Read the papers. At our printer's on business. Put into his hands "Alcuin," for printing, & paid him towards it, twenty three dollars & fifty cents. A medical visit. Re-read a number of Coleridge's & Southey's Poems. At Dr. Miller's part of the afternoon. Commenced, & made some progress in the transcription & correction of my Epistle to Dr. Darwin. William & I drank tea, & spent the evening, at Mr. Kent's. Mr. Dexter, of Charlestown, (Mass.) formerly a member of Congress,[82] was there. An agreable & sensible man. Recd. short letters from Mr. Tracy & Dr. Buel. Wrote a short reply to the former. Read the article Letter-boundary, in the Scotch Encyclopedia—& wrote the lines on this subject in my Epistle, as they now stand. Corrected a proof-sheet of the Notes to the Botanic Garden.

Thursday, 22.—Completed the correction & transcription of my Epistle to Darwin, & wrote a few words of preface for the american edition of the Botanic Garden. Two medical visits, to two opposite parts of the town. Visit from Dr. Miller. Wrote a letter to Buel. Recd. letters from Mr. Tracy, & from Capt. Frye—communicating meteorological observations—made on the Western lakes. Transcribed the letter to my sister Abby. Re-read a number of Southey's Poems. Medical visit. Drank tea at W. W. Woolsey's. Spent the evening at Dunlap's.

Friday, 23.—Medical visit. Visit to Dr. Dickson. Visit from Dr. Hosack, who left with me a Paper for the Repository. Visit from Mr. Miller: from Mr. Roulet. Medical visit. Visit & teaed at Dr. Seaman's. Evening at Home. Continued my Notes on Syracusan Plagues. Read some of Coleridge & of Southey's Poems. Wrote short letters to C. B. Brown & Capt. Frye. Transcribed the letters to Thomas & Mary. Corrected a proof-sheet of the american Edition of the Botanic Garden. The printers have made a few alterations in my Advertisement—for the worse.

Saturday, Feby. 24.—Read the papers. Medical visit. Visit from Dr. Miller—medical conversation, & on business of the Repository. Wrote the letter to Dr. Forbes of Bermuda. Commenced & made some progress in the transcription & correction of the Syracusan Plagues, for the Press—comparing anew, & noting all the authorities. Johnson sat down with me—& we had a conversation. Read some of Coleridge's & Southey's Poems. Visit from Dr. Osborn of Govr's Island—who drank tea with us. Club night—my turn—Present, Dunlap, Johnson, Kent, Smith, W. W. Woolsey, & Miller visitor. Separated at eleven o'clock. I read them—poems of Coleridge & Southey. Corrected a proof-sheet of notes to the Botanic Garden.

Sunday, 25.—Read several of Coleridge's & Southey's Poems. Continued the transcription & correction of my Syracusan Plagues, as before. Wm. & I dined & spent the afternoon & part of the evening, at S. Johnson's—(Miss Morton was there)—the rest of the evening at H. Johnson's.

Monday, 26.—Continued the transcription & correction of the Syracusan essay. What makes this so tedious is, the necessity of consulting authorities for every sentence, & stating the fact precisely as presented by them. Read, & reduced into some form, a long paper, on the Yellow Fever which appeared in Jamaica in 1793, 4, & 5, by a Dr. Walker. At our printer's, on business. Calls & errands. At Dingley's—he out. At Miller's, where I drank tea. At Kent's, where I spent part of the evening. From there, I went to the Theater, to see "Two Strings to your Bow"[83]—for the first time. Hodgkinson is excellent in *Lazarillo*. We shall certainly lose much, in losing him—& he goes to Boston in the spring. Came home, & corrected a proof of the prolegomena to the Botanic Garden—including the latter part of my Epistle to Darwin.

To Francis Forbes

The respect and esteem with which my friend Mr. Meigs, late of Bermuda, had spoken of you to me, and his kind assurances that you would receive this address with complacency, encourage me to write to you. My letter will be accompanied by three Numbers of a periodical work in which I am engaged, & which I must beg you to do me the favor to accept, as a token of the respect of myself & my Associates. These pamphlets will more fully apprize you of my situation & character, & will in some measure explain the more immediate purpose of this address.

It is the wish of the Conductors of the Repository to establish a correspondence with men of the first reputation for professional & scientific improvements in America & Europe: nor do we expect greater advantages from a correspondence with any other quarter of the world, than from the american Islands. It will immediately strike you, sir, that the more extensive this correspondence is, the more beneficial it will be to every person concerned in it. From this motive, as well as such others as will naturally suggest themselves to your mind, we venture to hope that you will view our solicitation as not improper, & will readily consent to second our wishes. In this hope, permit me to mention a few topics, connected with the place of your immediate residence.

I was lately informed that an Epidemic Fever prevailed in Bermuda, with considerable mortality, in the summer of 1796—I think it was. Of its origin, symptoms, & cure, I received no account. Mr. Meigs, also, lately mentioned to me that a disease, known in Bermuda by the name of the *"Great Fever"*—proved very mortal there, about 12 or 15 years ago.

---

[82] Samuel Dexter (1761-1816) Harvard 1871, a lawyer, U.S. House 1793-1795; U.S. Senate 1799-1800; secretary of war under President Adams 1800; secretary of treasury, January to May, 1801; minister to Spain, etc. "Charleston" was probably Charlestown, Massachusetts.

[83] Robert Jephson, *Two Strings to Your Bow* (1791).

Relative to these two Epidemics every species of instruction would be desirable to us, & esteemed as valuable. Should it suit with your convenience, & accord with your sense of the probable benefits of our work, you might greatly oblige us, & doubtless the medical world in general, by a succinct or minute history (as should best suit your own views of the subject) of these Diseases. The importance of noticing the local peculiarities of the Bermudas, will not escape you, in the present state of medical discussion & debate respecting the origin of pestilential diseases.

But, sir, tho' I have taken the liberty to refer specially to two subjects, it is by no means with any idea of controlling your own judgement, but solely from my own ignorance of other local topics. On the contrary, whatever information you may think proper to communicate, will be received by us with pleasure; & for our own part, we shall be proud to make you any similar return, which you may desire, & our situation permit.

With respect & esteem.
Yours &c.
Feb. 24. '98.   E. H. Smith.

Tuesday, 27.—Continued Zoonomia—which has lain by a long time; I made, however, no great progress in it. Some time at the Hospital, where two operations were performed. Dr. Dickson was there. Recd. a letter from Dr. Charles Coffin of New Bury Port, containing an account of the Fever of 1796, in that town. Dr. Miller here much of the afternoon. Mr. Gahn here—& Mr. Dunlap, Miller & I drank tea, and spent part of the evening, at Miss Templeton's. Miss Mason & Miss Nicholson were there. I spent the remainder of the evening at Dunlap's. W. W. Woolsey was there part of the time. Cooper, the Tragedian, all the time. He related to us a number of anecdotes relative to Godwin, Holcroft &c. Came home & corrected a proof of Botanic Garden.

Wednesday, 28.—Learnt, on rising, that my servant was sick at his wife's. Went there: Again, just before dinner; & again just before tea. Several errands in the morning—& visits from Mr. Roulet, & from Dr. Dickson. Continued Zoonomia. Corrected a proof of the Botanic Garden. Visit from Dunlap. Teaed at W. W. Woolsey's—where Dunlap & wife & Mrs. Hobson—who, with Woolsey & his wife, went to the play. I called on & went with Mrs. Kent & Miss Rogers. The Play "Hamlet," the afterpiece "The Adopted Child". *Cooper*, who has now joined our company, was *Hamlet* & *Michael*; & was in both excellent. His Hamlet, perhaps, excelled by that of no person living. Accompanied Mrs. Hobson home.

Industry of February 1798

Reading

Zoonomia, P. I. 4to. pp. 96.
Med. Comment. of Edinb. 1793—8vo. pp. 500.
Monroe's View of the Conduct of the Executive of U. S. 8vo. close print—pp. 473.
Coleridge, Southey, Lloyds, Lamb & Cottle's Poems—12mo. pp. 878.
De Non, Swinburne, Rollin &c. equal pp. 200 8vo.
Stock's Inaug. Dissert. on the effects of Cold &c.—pp. 43—8vo.
Cooper's Do. . . . . Stramonium—pp. 58, 8vo.
Aikin's Letters to his Son—pp. 20. 8vo.
Annales de Chimie—pp. 10. 8vo.
Monthly Review Enld. for Oct. 1797.
Articles Paper—Letter—boundary &c. &c. in the Scotch Encyclopedia—pp. 20.
File of London Papers.
Reports &c. of the N. Y. Legislature.
Mss. Communications for Med: Reposy.—pp. 30.

Writing

Composition

Notes from Zoonomia . . . . pp. 5.
Review of Stock's Essay . . . . . . pp. 2.
Review of Cooper's Do. . . . . pp. 3.
Syracusan Notes, arrangement . . . . pp. 22.
Epistle to Darwin . . . . pp. 5.
Analysis of Walker on Yellow Fever . . pp. 6.
Letters untranscribed . . . . pp. 50.
    Do. transcribed . . . . pp. 8.

Transcription

Letters, transcribed . . . . pp. 8.
Epistle to Darwin . . . . pp. 5.
Syracusan Notes . . . . pp. 15.

Beside the Blank Hospital Return, Correcting the Press, Newspaper Reading—Consultation of Authors, &c. &c. &c.

MEMOIRS. 1798. MARCH.

Thursday, 1.—Continued Zoonomia, at intervals thro' the day. Visits from Mr. Webster—(who has just returned from Boston)—from Mr. Dunlap, S. Johnson, & Miller: much conversation with the first & the last. Four medical visits. Errands. Recd. letters from Mr. Scandella, & Mr. Backus of Bethlem. Spent a part of the evening at Riley's. Wrote a short criticism—as such things are called—on the theatrical exhibitions of last night. Corrected a proof of the Botanic Garden—Notes. Writing on Accts. &c.

Friday, 2.—Continued Zoonomia. Three medical visits. Visit from Mr. Roulet, who brought me a file of London Papers; part of which I have looked over. Dined & spent the afternoon at Mr. Post's, in company with a number of physicians. Evening at the Theater —where I saw "King John"[84]—Cooper admirable as *John*, & Hodgkinson as *Falconbridge*—the whole play

---
[84] Shakespeare.

very well. Rest of the evening, on a medical visit, & at home. Recd. a letter from Wm. Buel.

Saturday, 3.—Medical visit. Read the papers, & finished my London file. Called on Dr. Miller, & we went together to see Mr. Maclean, the Chemical Professor from Princeton. He was absent—but we learnt that a Ship sailed tomorrow for London—& went to our printer's for copies of the Repository to send. I wrote a short letter to Dr. Thornton, & one to S. M. Hopkins. Dined & spent part of the afternoon at W. W. Woolsey's. Errands &c. afterwards. Recd. a letter from Dr. Wheaton. Club night—& Mr. Kent's—Present—Dunlap, Johnson, Kent, Smith, W. W. Woolsey. Boyd, Miller, & Radcliff visitors.

Corrected a proof of the Repository.

Sunday, March 4.—Medical visit. Wrote letters to Buel, Wheaton, & Mr. Backus. At one, went over to Governor's Island, in company with Dr. & Miss Osborn, Capt. Frye, & Mr. Swan, the Paymaster to Western Army—& dined & spent the afternoon. Mr. Swan related a number of facts, in addition to those contained in his letter to Capt. Frye, relative to the country on Lake Huron &c. Came back at evening. Called at G. M. Woolsey's—they out. Visit to H. Johnson's, & to S. Johnson's.

Monday, 5.—Continued Zoonomia. Errands. Visit from Mr. Webster. Read "The Westminster Election for 1796"—8vo. pp. 56.[85] Recd. a letter from Mr. Tracy, to which I replied, at some length. Calls. Visit at Riley's. Walked out & spent the evening at Mr. Roulet's. Returning, stopped in at the Theater—& saw part of the "Doctor & Apothecary"[86]—a miserable thing. Corrected a proof of Notes to the Botanic Garden.

Tuesday, 6.—Soon after I arose, I was seized with imperfect or double vision, soon succeeded, or rather followed by a disagreable pain in my head, & shortly after some inclination to nausea. The affection of the sight went off in about two hours. The head-ach in about six—tho' something of this, & of the stomach feelings recurred at intervals, slightly, thro' the day. This is more like my old Head-Ach than any thing I have experienced these three years; & I know not what to attribute it to, unless it should be (as I suspect) occasioned by eating a very small piece of cold ham, at Mr. Roulet's last evening—which was slightly tainted with Garlic. Continued Zoonomia. Visit from Dr. Miller. Read Dr. Joseph Browne's, of West Chester, Essay on the Yellow Fever—8vo. pp. 31.[87] A poor thing. Wrote a letter to Dr. Mitchill, & added a [few] lines to my letter to Dr. Wheaton. Visit to Miller. Called on Dr. Bayley, G. M. Woolsey, & Dr. Hosack; all out. Visit to Mrs. Dunlap. Corrected a proof of the Repository.

Wednesday, 7.—Medical visit. Read the Newspapers. Continued the transcription & correction of my Syracusan Notes. In the course of this last arrangement of them, I have discovered several errors into which I had fallen—& some in common with Mr. Rollin & Mr. Webster, in respect to a passage of Livy. The correction in this place will be of importance to the doctrine I maintain relative to the origin of the plague. Visit from Mr. Webster. Drank tea, & spent part of the evening at Mr. Kent's—the remainder at Mr. Rogers's. Recd. a few lines from Mr. Tracy. Corrected a proof of the Repository.

Thursday, 8.—Completed, for the press, my Syracusan Essay. At least I shall make no alterations in it, unless the inspection of Diodorus Siculus may furnish me with some additional facts. At present I have no prospect of gaining a sight of his work. It remains to add a few words of introduction—at the time when the Paper is called for. This will not be under six months. Corrected a proof of the Repository, & of the Botanic Garden—Notes—the end of Part I. Calls. Drank tea, & spent part of the evening, at S. Johnson's; part of it at Mr. Green's; & the rest at home. Continued Zoonomia.

Friday, 9.—Commenced and made some progress in the transcription & correction of my Oration. This is slow work, as I write slowly when I take pains to write, & correct at the same time. Corrected a proof of the Repository. At the printer's. Medical visit. Visit to Major Swan—who is to write me some account of the Climate of the Ohio &c. Visit to Dr. Miller. Continued Zoonomia. Drank tea at Dunlap's, & went with Mrs. D. to the Theater—to see "Romeo & Juliet." No important difference in the cast, except Cooper's *Romeo*, which was manly & pleasing.

Saturday, March 10.—Continued the transcription &c. of my Oration. Various errands & calls, which occupied much time—among others on Mr. Owens. Wm. & I walked out of town. A visit from a Mr. Chace, a friend of Michael Cunningham—whom, however, he has not lately seen. I must write to him, by the next Packet. Club night—at G. M. Woolsey's—Present—Johnson, Smith, the Woolseys—& Mr. Howland visitor. Read a number of pages in Clarissa Harlowe,[88] a volume of which I incidentally took up. Corrected a proof of the Botanic Garden. Recd. a letter from Mr. Tracy.

Sunday, 11.—Read further in Clarissa. Wrote a letter to Mr. Cunningham. Continued my Oration. Dined & spent the afternoon at Mr. Garnet's. Drank tea & spent the evening, at S. Johnson's. Saw there Mr. Bullfinch,[89]

---

[85] Not found.

[86] James Cobb, *The Doctor and the Apothecary* (1788).

[87] Joseph Browne, *Practical Treatise on the Plague* (London, 1720). Probable.

[88] Samuel Richardson, *Clarissa Harlowe* (1747-1748).

[89] Charles Bulfinch (1763-1844; Harvard 1781) architect, public official, of a wealthy, cultivated Boston family. The State House in Hartford, Connecticut, was begun from his plans in 1792, at that time one of the most ambitious projects in New England; also his is the Massachusetts State House on Beacon Hill completed in 1800, the most impressive building in the United States at the time, before the completion of the Capitol

the Architect, of Boston. Came home, & have read a pp. 100 or more in Clarissa. The British Packet arrived. H. Johnson has recd. a letter from Lovegrove—& such a letter—! Mrs. L. arrived safely, & early. They are contemptible & detestible.[90]

Monday, 12.—Finished my Oration. A visit from Mr. Johnson—Commedian. Made a few additions to my letters to Mumford & Mary, & gave them to Saml. Jones Jr. to carry to Albany, Wednesday. Corrected the first proof of "Alcuin." Visit to Dr. Miller. Went with Dunlap to our printer's, on business; & then to Woolsey's—where I drank tea, & spent part of the evening; &, after several fruitless calls elsewhere, another part of it at Mrs. Morton's. Miss Morton was there—& also Mr. Sitgreaves,[91] M. Congress.[92] Came home, & corrected a proof of the Botanic Garden—read Tom Paine's pitiful letter to the French—& p. 100 of Clarissa.

Tuesday, 13.—Drew off some accounts. Corrected a proof of "Alcuin." Transcribed, corrected, & with some additions, my paper on an Asthma of Infants. Visit to Miller. Johnson called, & we three walked out of town, & in, & round the Battery; in all five miles. Continued "Clarissa," with wonderful delight. Johnson & I drank tea, & spent the forepart of the evening, with Mrs. Sharples. I passed the remainder at Mr. Kent's. Corrected a proof of the Botanic Garden.

Wednesday, 14.—Read the Papers. Continued Zoonomia. Corrected a proof of the Repository. Visit from Webster—and from Dunlap. Called, ineffectually, on Dr. Haworth—who has returned from Phila. &c. Errands. Continued Clarissa. Read Dunlap's tragedy of André. Visit from Dunlap. Called at Riley's—all out. Drank tea, & spent part of the evening at Dunlap's. Called at Mr. Leffingwell's—all out. Part of the evening at G. Mumford's. Mr. & Mrs. Duryee there. At home. Corrected proof of the Botanic Garden. Continued Clarissa. Recd. a letter from Saml. M. Hopkins—dated Paris Decr. 27.

Thursday, 15.—Medical visit. Call from Dunlap. Visit from Mr. Roulet. Visit from Dr. Miller—who has recd. (address to the Editors of the Medl. Reposy.) a letter from Dr. Currie of Phila.—retorting upon Dr. Seaman of this place, for what he wrote of Currie, in the third No. of the Repository. It is a poor thing. Yet we must insert a part of it. But this shall be the last of personal disputes—in our Work. Recd. letters from my father—from Dr. Hall of Middletown—a monkey[93]—& from Dr. Dewees of Phila.—this last containing an interesting communication. Drank tea at Mrs. Miller's; & spent the evening at Dr. Hosack's—chiefly with Mrs. Hosack. The rest of the day devoted to the reading of "Clarissa Harlowe"—the 8th vol. of which I finished. I have, now, within a few days, read the greater part of the four last volumes of this admirable work. Parts of the preceeding volumes I have heretofore read.

Friday, March 16.—Visit from Dunlap—with a proof sheet of his André—which we corrected. Wrote the letter to Hopkins. Medical visit. Visit from Dr. Miller. Called on Mr. Gahn. Wrote letters to Dr. Dewees, Dr. Hall, Mr. Tracy, & C. B. Brown. Recd. letters from Mr. Tracy, & Mr. Rice of Baltimore. Walked out of town with Johnson. Corrected one Act of MS. of "André." Visit to Miller—where Seaman came. I drank tea there. Thence, went to the Theater. Saw two Acts of "Cymbeline."[94] Hodgkinson pretty well in *Leonatus*—Cooper's *Iachimo* excellent. Spent an hour & a half at Saml. Boyd's. Corrected a proof of the Botanic Garden. Continued, thro' the day, & this evening, Zoonomia.

Saturday, 17.—Read the Papers. In the course of the day, continued Zoonomia & finished the Section on "Generation." Wrote letters to my father—to Dr. Bird, & to Dr. Coffin. Transcribed the two last. Transcribed also great part of that to Hopkins. Visit from Dunlap. Corrected the 4th Act of his "André." Visit from Dr. Miller. Two medical visits—at some distance. Principal part of the day & evening at home. Corrected proof sheet of the Botanical Garden. No Club—to oblige some who wished to see Cooper's *Hamlet*.

Sunday, 18.—Lotions & Lavations. Medical visit. Finished the transcription of my letter to Hopkins. Read over, aloud, my Oration, with the double design of trying the power of my voice, & impressing it on my memory. I think I shall be able to read it, sufficiently loud, & without too great fatigue, to my Auditory. Johnson & I called to see Jno. Morton—& at Riley's. Dined, & spent the afternoon, at H. Johnson's. Medical visit. Wm. & I spent the evening at Dunlap's. Wrote a letter to James Rice—Baltimore.

Samuel M. Hopkins

Two days ago I recd. your letter from Paris of Decr. 27. This is the third time that I have personally heard from you; & I presume only the third time that you have written to me—unless you have written since this date. My answer to your first letter from London, you recd. To your second, I replied the beginning of last Novr. This reply was directed to you at London; & was accompanied by two copies of Mr. Kent's Dissertation, & a copy of the 1st & 2nd No. of the Medical Repository. About three weeks since I sent you, with a few lines, the 3rd No. of the Repository. You will see from this, that I have not been neglectful of you: neither do I design to be so. I suppose that you will return to London, before sailing for America. Perhaps you are already there. In this case you have my letters.

---

in Washington. Bulfinch was for many years one of the leading architects as well as one of the leading public figures in Boston.

[90] How much of his relationship with the Lovegroves Smith left out of his "Diary" is strongly underlined by this startling comment.

[91] George Sitgreaves, a New York teacher.

[92] M. Congress, apparently a Frenchman and probably a visitor; not in New York directories of the time.

[93] By no means the first gentleman of substance and considerable reputation that Smith "shot down." Glossed earlier.

[94] Shakespeare.

And tho', taking advantage of your information, I might excuse myself from writing at this time, under the pretext of the expectation of your speedy return, yet, so much do I wish to do you justice, that I write now, in the hope, tho' not with the certainty, that this will reach you, before you leave Europe. I shall confine my letter, principally to answering the suggestions contained in yours. And first, in respect to the state of Chemistry in our Country.

There is neither room, nor occasion, for me to engage in this science, as a Professor. Dr. Mitchill delivers a very excellent & extensive Course of Chemistry, in our College, annually; &, to shew you how far your notions of the inexpensiveness of such a course have been anticipated, performs several hundred—perhaps all the necessary, experiments, at an expence not exceeding fifty dollars, with an apparatus very moderate indeed. But he has few auditors: for the other parts of the Institution does not flourish. There is another Course of Chemical Lectures delivered at Harvard College. Not very good—I believe. At Princeton, they have a very ingenious Professor—who is faithful—& likely to become eminent. At Phila. more than sixty students attend a very complete Course of Chemistry, in the University. A Chemical Society is also formed there, which is devoted to Experiments, both of verification & research, & is gradually collecting an extensive apparatus. In the meantime, we have many chemical discussions going on. Dr. Priestley has made two publications. Mr. Adet & Mr. McLean (the Princeton Professor) answered his first. His last is chiefly a reply to Mr. Maclean—who is preparing an experimental answer. Dr. Mitchill has broached a number of new doctrines in Chemistry & Pathology, which he is still supporting with great ingenuity & extent of research; & which, whatever may be their foundation in truth, have attracted notice, & even advocates, in Europe. In Germany, more particularly, several of his Tracts have been translated—& one or more professors have published, and publicly taught his doctrine. Beside these, young gentlemen, graduating in Physic, frequently publish Inaugural Essays on Chemical subjects: so that the knowlege of, & relish for, chemistry is spreading thro' the country, as fast as can be expected. It is further designed, as soon as the funds will admit of it, to establish a Chemical Professorship at Yale College—which Institution, under the direction of Dr. Dwight, improves rapidly.

In respect to Mineralogy—there are four very respectable collections in this State—& three in this town—but chiefly of foreign minerals. At Phila. & Princeton, & New Haven, they are commencing: & at Cambridge, they have, with not more than XX exceptions, specimens of all the mineral substances known in Europe: presented chiefly by Dr. Lettsom of London, & the French Government. I am commencing an American collection—& hope, in the course of the ensuing year to have a number of very valuable specimens. Correspondencies are also beginning—& all these things will grow into shape, as fast as circumstances will permit. You will see, by our Repository, what Dr. Mitchill is doing, for this State; & Dr. Barton's intended publications will add still more to our mineralogical fund. Every year will increase it.

Several Cabinets for Models of mechanical Inventions exist in our Country. Our Agricultural Society has begun one. I remember one in Phila. in '90, '91—which contained several hundred models. I presume it continues. But the scientific consideration of Agricultural subjects is making rapid strides in the country. None of the matters you refer to have escaped attention. You will see by the Review & the Medical News, in our Repository, how many publications are made or making. Our 4th No. will contain some account of two publications on the subject of Rotation of Crops.

Medical discussion is carried to a great extent here. You would be astonished at the number & respectability of the pieces inserted in our newspapers—every summer & autumn, since 1793. Pamphlets & volumes are not rare.

The Yellow Fever has given birth to more than twenty publications, beside what you will find in the Repository, & beside what have been made in the newspapers; and others are now preparing: one from Dr. Rush, & one from Mr. Webster.

You will wonder where all this lay hid, when you were in America. But, (beside that some of these things have come to light, since you left us,)—your attention to them has been just excited. Had you inquired before you went—you would have found that we were not altogether idle.

If this reaches you in season, & it has not been previously noticed, I wish you to leave the Nos. of the Repository with the Proprietor of the Monthly Review. At any rate, dispose of them in Europe. If it has been noticed—can you not transmit them to Paris? It is uncertain whether our communication will reach there.

In my letter of Nov. I gave you a long list of recent American publications—or of things soon to appear. I may add, now, that most of them have appeared. Judge Minot of Boston, has published the 1st vol. of his Continuation of Hutchinson's History[95]—which is well spoken of; & Dr. Rush a vol. of Essays. Our friend Mr. Dunlap has a Tragedy in the press—& our friend C. B. Brown, a Dialogue on the model of the Ancients. These will be ready for you, when you arrive.

For domestic news—Judge Hobart is Senator from this State—& Mr. Kent judge—in consequence. Johnson, you know, was one of the Judges of a court constituted since your departure.[1] He is in the way of promotion, & is greatly respected. If you ask why he

---

[95] George Richards Minot, *Continuation of the History of the Province of Massachusetts Bay* 1 (Boston, 1798).

[1] Apparently William Johnson, Smith's housemate, is meant here. None of the usual sources mention anything about such an election.

has not written to you—would he not retort the inquiry?

In Connecticut—Gov. Wolcott & Mr. Adams are both dead. The next May will doubtless make Mr. Reeve & Mr. Ingersoll judges.

In my letter of Nov. so often referred to—I proposed several inquiries, relative to Gt. Britain, conformable to your wishes. When you are safe out of France, & dare hazard opinions concerning the politics of that country—I wish you to consider those inquiries as extended to that Despotism—mis-named Republic.

For us—all the North—& most of the Middle—is firm for independence. The epithets french or british, makes no difference in the public disposition towards foreign tyranny. The South is, as usual, divided. But the political differences shew greater in Congress than among the people at large. In this State, all will go well.

We are all in health, & tolerable spirits—& shall welcome you home, like the Prodigal Son. For Heaven's sake, make haste to quit that aceldama called Europe.

March 16. 1798.   E. H. Smith.

To Charles Coffin—NewBuryPort

I feel myself much obliged by your satisfactory answer to the inquiries which I took the liberty of addressing to you. At the same time, my Associates beg me to present you with their acknowlegements for your Communication: nor have we a doubt but that the public will testify a similar sense of its importance, when it is submitted to their inspection—which it will be in the course of two months.

I should have replied to your letter before this time, but that, beside the want of any direct conveyance, even to Boston, I have been very much engaged ever since its receit. In the hope that these are not the last letters which will pass betwixt us, I venture to inquire of you, whether any thing of Canine Madness has been observed in the vicinity of Newbury Port?—& if there has, in what degree? This disease is so general, now, in many parts of our country, that I can not but hope that some new lights may be gained as to its cause & cure. The least information, from any quarter, may contribute to this end. Be pleased, likewise, to communicate any information which you may have relative to diseases among domestic animals—if any occur in your neighborhood.

We have had a Catarrhal Disease very general in our City—but principally affecting children. Few young children have escaped it. In some cases, it has arisen to Croup, Pneumonia Notha, & Vera; & some deaths, I am informed, have happened in consequence. Yet pneumonic affections have not been remarkably frequent among adults.

If it be true, as many believe, and as there is some colour of reason for the belief, that the quantity of warmth is about the same, in every year; that long & cold winters produce very sultry summers; that from this great difference between the temperature of the seasons, men are more disposed to become sickly, in the sickly seasons; and that catarrhal epidemics are the forerunners of febrile or malignant epidemics; we have something to apprehend from the coming summer & autumn. These, however, may be mere conjectures. Still, they have so much weight as to excite attention.

In respect to subscriptions for the Repository, as direct communication with Newbury Port is very infrequent, I suppose that it will be easiest for such subscribers as may be found there, to receive their copies at Boston. In this case, I may inform you that a number of Copies are there for sale; I believe at Thomas & Andrews's. But, if any other arrangement is preferred by you, we shall attend to it, as soon as you shall please to indicate it.

I am, with much esteem & respect,

Yours &c.

March 17. 1798.
New York, Pine St. 45.   E. H. Smith.

To Seth Bird—Lichfield

In a letter which I received lately, from the Revd. Mr. Backus of Bethlem, an account is given of two remarkable Epidemics, which occurred in that town—the first, in 1750, the second, in 1760. Mr. Backus confines himself to general information respecting them, derived principally from the memoranda of his predecessor Dr. Bellamy; and refers me to you, for a more particular history of the disease, at each time, its symptoms & method of cure.

Considering the great attention which has of late been given to Epidemics; the havoc they have already made, & still threaten to make, in our country; and the importance of obtaining correct knowlege of them, as far as possible; I am emboldened to hope that you will not altogether decline the task of furnishing me with such facts as your memory, or perhaps your notes, preserve of those diseases, in which you had such extensive experience. In this hope, my Associates in the Medical Repository unite with me; & we all concur in testifying our respect & esteem, with which I

remain Yours &c.

March 17. '98.
Pine St. 45.   E. H. Smith.

Monday, 19.—Three medical visits. Visit from Dunlap. Visit to Dr. Miller. Calls. Drank tea & spent the evening at home. Finished Zoonomia Vol. I. Read pp. 32 in "Clarissa" Vol. I. Transcribed such part of Major Swan's Journal, as I deemed proper for the Repository.

Tuesday, 20.—Four medical visits, in the course of the day & evening, at a mile distance. Corrected a proof "Botanic Garden" & of "André." Dunlap here. At our printer's. Errands. Visit to Dr. Haworth—who lent me Currie on Bilious Fevers, & Paschalis on the Phila. fever of 1797.[2] Read some part of the first, & pp. XC of

---

[2] Felix O. Pascalis, *An Account of the Contagious Epidemic Yellow Fever* (Philadelphia, 1798).

the last. Read also some letters in "Clarissa." Errands. Drank tea at Dunlap's. Principal part of the evening at the Manumission Society. Just as I returned from a visit to my patient, which I made afterwards, I found Mr. Kent at my door. Went home with him, & spent an hour.

Wednesday, 21.—Medical visit. Finished Dr. Paschalis book—pp. 180, 8vo. A very insufficient performance. Read the Papers. Errands. Medical visit. Visit to Dr. Tillary.[3] Commenced, & made some progress, in Currie's book on Remitting Fever. Medical visit. Continued Currie.

My patient is very low—and I think will not survive this night. His disease Yellow Fever—which appears to be sporadic. I have tried the effects of Mercury, with a view to Salivation—very little to my satisfaction. My mind, as well as body are much harassed; which heightens the oppressiveness of this easterly weather. This day has been very rainy: & it still rains.

Thursday, 22.—Medical visit. Continued Currie's book. Visit from Dunlap, & corrected a proof of André. Medical visit. Errands. Medical visit. Drank tea at W. W. Woolsey's. Spent the evening at G. M. Woolsey's. In the course of the day & evening, read thro' the first vol. of Dr. Moore's novel—intituled "Edward."[4] Edit. Dubl. pp. 331. Corrected proof of Bot-Garden.

Friday, March 23.—We had a fire in town, last evening, which did some mischief. My patient, as I had expected, died this morning. He died of a fever—& salivated. This has suggested many reflections, which may be useful in future. I think I have discovered the source of some errors in general practice. Timothy Pierce left me, for Lichfield to-day. He has been here six months—during which time he has been very assiduous—& I think, will prove an ornament to his profession. He is more distinguished for patient, correct, & profound, than for ready & various apprehension. He thinks better, than he seizes quickly, & will develope, better than generalize. He discriminates better than combines; & will improve practice, rather than exact systems. Continued Currie's Book. Continued "Edward" thro' the day. Medical visit. Errands. Visit from Dr. Miller. Tiresome visit from another person. Attended the funeral of Capt. Almy. Drank tea with Benjn. Mumford. Saw a part of "Zorinski"[5]—at the Theater. Recd. a letter from Dr. Kollock.

Saturday, 24.—Read the Papers. Continued Currie. Finished "Edward"—vol. II. pp. near 400. Corrected a proof sheet of André. Medical visit at my room, by a gentleman who brought me a letter from Dr. Wheaton. Visit from Dunlap. He returned, bringing with him "The Minister," Lewis translation of Schiller's "Cabale und Liebe," we read two acts. Drew up a medical opinion. Medical visit. At our printer's. Visit to Dr. Miller. Went to Dunlap's. The day had been terribly stormy. The night continued so. It was Club night—but no one came. We finished "The Minister"—a most wonderful play. When I came home, found letters from Dr. Wheaton & Mr. Tracy. Corrected another proof of André at Dunlap's. The Minister 8vo. pp. 220. Wrote to Dr. Wheaton.

Sunday, 25.—Continued "Clarissa." Dunlap here. Corrected the fifth act of André. William & I walked. We called at G. M. Woolsey's. Dined & spent the afternoon at S. Johnson's. Horace & wife, & Mr. Bullfinch of Boston, there. We called at Miss Morton's. She was out. I visited Mr. & Mrs. Johnson—Comedians—& afterwards Hodgkinson. At Hodgkinson's came Cooper & Williamson. A long talk about the probable situation & conduct of this Country in case of a war with France, & of its means of defence—which I favored for the purpose of seeing the depth of Cooper's reflections—& to enjoy his earnestness.

I made no remarks on "Edward" yesterday: my mind had been so much occupied by "The Minister." A few words will now suffice. This Author possesses no remarkable powers, either for displaying original character, or for inventing a deeply interesting fable. Nor does he exhibit a great diversity of character, or characters in new situations, or very forcible delineations of character—nor does he lead the reader into the profundity of moral research. But, few men hit off more happily the manners, sentiments, foibles, & history (if I may say so) of genteel society—or rather of fashionable society: including all those who, from rank, talents, power, & fortune, are placed in it—or are ordinarily connected with such persons. And this [is] very evident in "Edward."

Monday, 26.—Mr. Bullfinch and I walked out to the new State Prison, and examined every part of it. Thence we crossed to Corlaer's Hook, & came home. This took up the forenoon. When I came home, I found letters from Mitchill, Dwight (Nathl.) & S. Field. The first inclosed a variety of papers. Wrote to Dr. Wheaton. At the printer's. Visit from Miller: from Dunlap—corrected a proof of "André."

Drank tea at Kent's. Called at Leffingwell's—nobody at home. Great part of the evening at Mr. Minturn's. The last of it at W. W. Woolsey's.

Tuesday, March 27.—I awoke with my old Nervous Head-ach (as it is called) which has continued, in some degree, all day, but most severe in the forenoon. About noon my eyes were very much affected with dazzling, motes &c. & became red, painful, & watry—so that I was obliged to give up business, & go out. Transcribed & corrected the minutes of the last meeting of the Manumission Society. Wrote letters to N. Dwight, Dr. Field, Dr. Osborn of N. Carolina & Mr. Tracy. Visit from Dunlap, & from Webster. Walked on the Battery for an hour. Recd. a letter from C. B. Brown informing me of his intended marriage, that his first novel is

---

[3] James Tillary, physician, 86 Broadway.

[4] Dr. John Moore, *Edward* (1796). Moore was a Scotsman, physician, author of novels, and a book of travel. To be distinguished from the Doctor Moore mentioned elsewhere in the "Diary" who was an American from German Flats.

[5] Thomas Morton (1795).

complete,⁶ & that he writes "The Man at Home" in the Phila. Weekly Magazine.⁷ This magazine I sought[?] & purchased, at least such Nos. as have come to hand—& read his pieces & several others. Errands. Visited Miller. Walked out to Mr. Webster's—where I drank tea. Found Mr. Kent & Boyd there. We returned together. Webster removes to New Haven Saturday next. I called at S. Johnson's. They were at Horace's— whither I went, & saw also Mr. Bullfinch. Thence I called on Miss Morton, & saw her a minute. Thence I called at Leffingwell's. They were out. Thence at Mr. Duryee's—where I spent an hour. Came home, & found a letter from Mitchill—it inclosed his Address to the Agricultural Society, Priestley's reply to his letter, & a paper on Stramonium by Dr. King of Connect.—all of which I read—& have since corrected a proof of the Botanic Garden.

Wednesday, 28.—Read the papers. Recd. letters from William Buel, and from Dr. Pascalis, addrest to the Editors of the Repository—complaining of the review of his Dissertations. Visited Miller, on the business of these late Communications. Attended a consultation at the Hospital. Read the pamphlet by the College of Physicians of Phila.—containing their proceedings relative to Yellow Fever. Visit from Dunlap. Wrote letters to Mitchill, Mr. Scandella, Dr. Pascalis, Dr. King, & C. B. Brown. Drank tea at Dunlap's, & went with his family to see "Douglas,"⁸ & "The Children in the Wood."⁹ Both the pieces were well played. No alteration of any importance has been made in the Cast of the Afterpiece. The tragedy was generally well done. Hodgkinson's *Old Norval* & Cooper's *Young Norval*, were excellent.

Thursday, 29.—Transcribed my letter to Dr. Forbes of Bermuda, & wrote a letter to Buel. Wrote a short notice of the Pamphlets of the Phila. College of Physicians—& two articles to form part of the review of Yates & Maclean's publication. Visit from Miller, & from Dr. Winthrop Saltonstall, & from others on business. Read parts of the Weekly Magazine of Phila. Dressed, & spent the night, till three in the morning, at Mr. Rogers—where we had a private ball & supper. This was the first time that I have danced in New York —& I have only once before danced any where since my removal hither. The party was of a convenient size, & the time very pleasantly spent.

Friday, 30.—It took me some time this morning to put things in order again. The early forenoon was dull, by eleven it had cleared off very pleasant. I walked. Visited the Millers. The Dr. & I walked. I came home, & read a new pamphlet, by Dr. Barton, which he sent me this day—his Collections towards an American Materia Medica—pp. 50. Walked on the Battery. At our printer's. Read the various Reports, Bills &c. sent me a few days since by Mitchill. Looked over, & wrote a short Review of Bordley's pamphlet on Rotations of Crops &c. Recd. C. B. Brown's proposals for his Novel —"Sky-Walk."¹⁰ Calls & errands. Drank tea at Kent's. Evening at the Theater. Saw Dunlap's "André." The House was full—the audience good-humored—but the piece most wretchedly played. Cooper miserably deficient.

Saturday, March 31.—Last evening corrected a proof sheet of the Botanic Garden. This work now draws to a close. It will be finished in about a fortnight. Read the News-papers. Continued Dr. Currie's book on Remitting Fever. Recd. a letter from Mr. Tracy, inclosing Mr. Harper's Speech, in reply to Mr. Gallatin. This is Harper's best speech—& is able. In many parts it is correctly reasoned—in others not so. Errands. Visit from B. W. Rogers—& from Dunlap. After dinner, called on Dunlap, & we on Johnson—& we walked out of town some miles. Returning, & near home, I met Dr. Haworth—who engaged me in conversation, & detained me in the street, near two hours. Club night. Met here in Johnson's turn. Present—Dunlap, Johnson, Kent, Miller, Smith, & W. W. Woolsey. Various, but lively, conversation. This is the last evening that Kent spends with us, previous to his removal.

To Benjamin S. Barton

I received your note, inclosing your Collections &c. yesterday; and tho' the time has been short, I have read the whole once, & some parts twice, with great pleasure. It is the commencement of what I hope in your hands will eventually grow into an extensive & much-wanted work: a Work to the furtherance & completion of which I shall earnestly contribute whatever chance or study may throw in my way.

When I first opened the cover, (not having heard that you had any thing of this kind in the press,) I fully expected to have found in it your promised memoir on Goitre, which I am anxious to see. Pray, when may we expect to have it published? Or do you first publish your strictures on Darwin? The mention of his name reminds me to inform you that we are publishing a new edition of his poem here. It will be correct, I think, & handsome; & at a price somewhat lower than the Dublin

---

⁶ *Sky-Walk,* one chapter appeared in *The Weekly Magazine* for March 24, 1798. See Warfel, *Charles Brockden Brown,* pp. 88 ff.

⁷ Portions of the novel appeared in regular weekly installments for a total of thirteen weeks starting with the issue of February 3. The story is based on his first-hand acquaintance with yellow fever and is set in Philadelphia. David L. Clark, *Charles Brockden Brown* (Duke Univ. Press, 1952), p. 161.

⁸ John Home, *Douglas* (1756).

⁹ Thomas Morton, *Children in the Wood* (1793).

¹⁰ The "lost" novel *Sky Walk* was announced in a kind of advertisement by "Speratus" (presumably Brown himself) in the *Weekly Magazine* for March 17, 1798. The following issue of the magazine contained a 1,700-word excerpt. Although it is clear that Smith read the work and that William Dunlap also read it, it was never completely set in type, never printed (owing to the author's death) and eventually lost as a complete body of work. However, according to Brown's biographers, sections of *Sky Walk* appear in other efforts of his. See Clark, *Charles Brockden Brown,* pp. 158-160.

Edition. I say I think it will be correct—for as the edition is, in fact, mine, I have taken some pains to have it so. It is in a single volume octavo, & well adapted for general use.

Our winter has gone off with little shew of literary & scientific exertion. Excepting our own, no medical publication has appeared but a small pamphlet, by Dr. Browne of West Chester, on the Yellow Fever—a new Theory—but not likely to advance our knowlege of the Disease in any one particular.

Mitchill has been all winter, & still continues, at Albany. I inclose for you the remainder of the first part of his Mineralogical Paper—which is as far as we have gone with it. The press of other matter, consisting of communications from various quarters, renders it impossible to say when the remainder of this Memoir will be printed.

I am with much esteem,

Yours &c.

March 31.—98— E. H. Smith.

Industry of March 1798

Reading

Zoonomia—4to. pp. 352.
Clarissa Harlowe—above—pp. 1500—close print, large 12mo. edit. Lond.
Edward—by Dr. Moore—edit. Dublin—large 12mo.—pp. above—700.
The Minister—from Schiller, by G. M. Lewis—edit. Lond. 8vo. pp. 220—large print.
The Weekly Magazine—Phila.—large 8vo.—pp. 100.
Pascalis on Yellow Fever of 1797—8vo. pp. 180.
Currie on Bilious fever oc. 8vo. close print, pp. 241.
Barton's Collections for Amer. Mat. Med.—8vo. pp. 50.
J. B. Bordley on Rotation of Crops &c.—pp. 76—8vo.
Mr. Harper's Reply to Mr. Gallatin—about pp. 50—close 8vo.
Proceedings of the Phila. Coll. of Phys.—relative to Yellow Fever—8vo.—pp—
Westminster Election for 1797—8vo. pp. 56.
Browne on Yellow Fever—8vo. pp. 31.
Tom Paine to the French on Sept. 4th. '97.—about pp. 20.
Reports &c. to N. Y. Legislature—pp. 50 8vo.
Dunlap's "André"—in M. S. about 60 pp. 8vo.
MSS. Mitchill's Agricultural Address, Communications to Med: Repos: &c.—pp. 60.
File of London Papers.

Writing

Composition

Letters—untranscribed . . . . pp. 62.
Do. — transcribed . . . . pp. 9.
On the Asthma of Infants . . . . . . pp. 6.
A Medical Opinion . . . . . . pp. 4.
Review of J. B. Bordley's Pamphlet . . . pp. 1.
Do. of Coll. Phys. Phila. Do. . . . . . 1.
Dramatic Critiques . . . . pp. 4.

Transcription

Letters – – – – – – – – – – – . pp. 9.
Syracusan Notes . . . . 7.
Oration . . . . 25.
Swan's Journal . . . . 7.
Manumission Minutes . . . . 8.

MEMOIRS. 1798. APRIL.

Sunday, 1.—Wrote and transcribed, with some addition, the letter to Dr. Barton. Visit from Dr. Haworth. We walked on the Battery, & met there Mr. Robertson, Dr. Miller, Johnson, & W. W. Woolsey. Visit to G. M. Woolsey's. Dined & spent the afternoon at H. Johnson's. Seth & his family, & some other persons, were there. Drank tea with Dr. Miller. We called on Miss Templeton. She was out. I spent the evening with Miss Morton. Corrected proof-sheets of the Repository, & of the Botanic Garden.

Monday, 2.—Finished Dr. Currie's book, of which I have not conceived the highest ideas. A visit from Dr. Morse of Charlestown (Mass.). He brings me the comfortable news that the Repository is well thought of in that part of the country, & will succeed there. He brought me a Communication from himself, which I have since read, & think valuable. He brought me also the 1st vol. of Dr. Lettsom's "Hints designed to promote Beneficial, Temperance & Medical Science"—pp. 273—8vo.[11] loose print—which I have also read thro. Visits from Dunlap & Miller. At the Hospital, where I commenced my Tour of duty. Called at Miller's on my return. Medical visit. Spent the evening at home—in conversation with Johnson & Osborn—& in reading various parts of C. B. Brown's Letters to me, suggested by conversation respecting him, & his new projects.

Tuesday, 3.—The storm has continued all day—& now, late in the evening, rages with increasing violence. Arranged my House, dinner & Cash Accts. Composed the Tables of Industry for February & March. Visit from Mr. Lent, late apothecary to the Hospital. At the Hospital. Continued Clarissa—vol. 1st. Johnson brought in & read Stearn's "A Ladies' Philosophy of Love"[12]—a miserable poem. We spent the eveng. together—& read poetry, conversed &c.

Wednesday, April 4.—Continued "Clarissa." Read the Papers—composed some Notes towards a brief acct. of American Poets, to be sent to Dr. Aikin[13] in London. Recd. the Weekly Magazine of Phila. four Nos. & was much surprized to find that Brown has

---

[11] John Coakley Lettsom, *Hints Designed to Promote Beneficence, Temperance, and Medical Science.* Curious situation in which all reference to the first edition seems to have been lost. Two dates given in standard references and library catalogs (5 v., London, 1799-1802); 3 vols., (1801).

[12] Charles Stearns, chiefly known for *Dramatic Dialogues For the Use of Schools* (Leominster, Mass., 1798).

[13] For these brief biographies which Smith skillfully composed with great speed, see hereafter. Aikin was editor of the English *Monthly Magazine.*

begun the publication of "Alcuin" in it. I immediately wrote him a letter, injoining his silence till the Dialogue should be published here. Visit from Dr. Miller, & from Dr. Morse. Dined, & spent the afternoon & evening at W. W. Woolsey's. Kent, Dunlap, M. Rogers, & G. M. Woolsey were there. Read the greater part of the four Nos. received this day of the Magazine.

Thursday, 5.—Finished the Weekly Magazine. Wrote a short account of Dr. Dwight & Mr. Trumbull, designed for the Monthly Magazine, London. Visit to Dr. Miller. At the Hospital. At our printer's, on business. Dined & spent the afternoon at S. Boyd's. Evening, partly at Mrs. Sharples's; partly at the Theater. Corrected a proof sheet of the Botanic Garden.

Friday, 6.—Finished "Clarissa" Vol. I. Wrote some sketches of American biography for the Monthly Magazine. Visit to Dr. Haworth. At our printer's. Visit to Dr. Saltonstall, who sails tomorrow for Bombay. Walked on the Battery. Visit from Dr. Miller. Wrote a letter to Mr. Tracy. Johnson & I walked out of town. Took tea at Riley's. Spent the evening at Dunlap's—Mr. [?], Hodgkinson, Cooper &c. there. Corrected a proof of the Repository & of the Botanic Garden.

Saturday, 7.—Read the papers. Nearly finished an account of Col. Humphreys for the Monthly Magazine. Visit from Dunlap. Medical visit. At the Hospital. Called, vainly, on Mr. Robertson. Visit to Miller's. Brought thence the Analytical Review for Novr. & Decr.—a very partial performance, on the whole—both of which Nos. I have read. Corrected a proof of the Repository. Recd. two letters from Mr. Tracy, & a long letter from Dr. Mease. Medical visit. Drank tea at Dunlap's, & went with Mrs. Dunlap to see "André" —for the third night. It was pretty well performed, & recd.—the house indifferent. Stayed to see Mde. Gardie make her first appearance for this year. Joseph Osborn left us today, for Connecticut: so that our family is now reduced to its original size. Mr. Kent & his family also removed to Poughkeepsie, this day. I attended them on board of the vessel. This is the heaviest stroke which our Society, has lately met with. Webster's & family's removal to New Haven, which took place last week on friday, is also a loss.

Sunday, 8.—A call from Mr. Robertson, to invite me to dine with him. Three medical visits. Visit to Dr. Miller. He was absent—& I had some conversation with the brother. Read aloud my Oration, by myself. Dunlap went for Phila. to-day. Dined & spent the afternoon at Mr. Robertson's. Dr. Haworth, Mr. & Mrs. Sharples &c. were there. Dr. Haworth & I came away together —& had much conversation on the way. Medical visit. Visit to H. Johnson. Visit to Dr. Miller. Corrected a proof of the Botanic Garden.

Monday, 9.—Wrote a long letter to Dr. Mease. Medical visit. At our printer's. Visit from a patient. Errands. Visit from Mr. Sharples. Walked on the Battery. Read Dunlap's tragedy—"André"—with the Appendix. I think better of the piece on this last reading. Visit from Dr. Miller. Finished my account of Col. Humphreys, for the Monthly Magazine. Wrote a short letter to Dr. Currie of Liverpool, England, to accompany a copy of the Medical Repository. Medical visit. Johnson & I walked out of town. We returned, & drank tea at Seth Johnson's. Thence I went to see Miss Mason— with whom I spent the evening. Came home, & corrected a proof-sheet of the Repository. Recd. a letter from C. B. Brown.

Tuesday, April 10.—Medical visit. At our printer's. Wrote a letter of some length to C. B. Brown. Recd. a letter from Dr. Thornton of London. By this I find that he has sent out to me a number of publications— by some Ship unknown. I have never heard of them. On inquiry, they are not in the Public Stores. As my first letter was sent by Capt. Drury of the Ship fame,[14] I suspect that the return was in her—& as she is lost, that my books are gone to the bottom with her. At the Hospital. Recd. a letter from Mr. Tracy, inclosing the Dispatches from our Envoys to Paris. I have read them. The Envoys are true men; our Government is pure; the french are corrupt to the very dregs. Errands, which occupied much time. Mitchill returned to-day. Visited him. Read at his room a Communication from Dr. DeWitt of Albany; relative to the Datura Stramonium. Medical visit. Spent the evening at Mr. Radclift's. Corrected a proof of the Botanic Garden. Wrote a letter to Mr. Tracy.

Wednesday, 11.—Read the papers. Medical visit. At our printers'. Called on Capt. Drury, master of the late Ship Fane—& suspect, by his acct. that my parcel from Dr. Thornton of London must have been lost, in that Ship, when it foundered. This is the more unfortunate, as Mitchill's Books &c. from Germany are also lost. Dr. Miller called on me. Sometime after I called on him, & his brother, the clergyman, & we went to the Presbyterian Church in Wall St. where, notwithstanding the violent storm of wind & rain, more than 300 gentlemen, and some ladies were assembled—to whom I delivered my Oration. Afterwards Miller & I called on Dr. Haworth. Of him, I got Porcupine's Democratic Judge— which I have read—pp. 102—& also Dr. Davidge's (of Baltimore) Treatise on the Yellow Fever[15]—of which I have read a part. Corrected the last proof of the Botanic Garden. Thus, I have this day got off, from my hands, two tasks—this work & the Manumission Oration. We drank tea at home—after which, Johnson & I spent two hours at Mr. Leffingwell's. When I came home, I found a note from Dr. Haworth. This obliged me to call on Miller. He was from home. Soon after he came to my house. We conversed an hour. He has recd. a letter from Dobson of Phila. with a bill of exchange for our due on the Repository—& information that he has

---

[14] Smith spelled the name as "fane," "Fane," and "Fame." Not identified. Another ship, *Fame* (U.S.N.) was captured by the British in 1813. Still another *Fame* (R.N. 74 guns) played a part in the American Revolution.

[15] John Beale Davidge, *a Treatise on the Autumnal Endemial Epidemick of Tropical Climates vulgarly called the Yellow Fever, etc.* (Baltimore, 1798).

sold all his copies, & will take twenty-five more. This is well. Corrected a proof of the Repository.

Thursday, 12.—Continued Davidge's Pamphlet. Medical visit. Transcribed, in part, with corrections, my acct. of Mr. Barlow, for the Monthly Magazine. Corrected a proof of the Repository. At the Hospital. Medical visit. Walked with Johnson on the Battery. Read the 9th No. of the Weekly Magazine. Dined & spent the afternoon, at the Miller's. Mitchill, Mr. Sharples &c.—there. Looked over some late London Papers, & the Gentleman's Magazine for Jany. there. Heard Mitchill read his Reviews of Priestley's P. II., of Woodhouse, & of Browne. Medical visit. Visit to Mrs. Dunlap. Remainder of the evening at W. W. Woolsey's. Recd. a line or two from Mr. Tracy, covering the Instructions to our Envoys to France—which I have read. Recd. also a few lines from Dr. Mease of Phila. covering the principal part of his Review of Dr. Currie's Book—which I have also read—with no great approbation.

Friday, 13.—Two medical visits. At our printer's. Corrected two proofs of the Repository. Finished my acct. of Mr. Barlow, & of Dr. Hopkins, with some account of the Anarchiad, for the Monthly Magazine. Errands. Walked, with Johnson, on the Battery. At G. M. Woolsey's. Two medical visits. The evening at the Theater. Mr. Burk's Tragedy of "Joan D'Arc"[16] played for the first time. A thin House—parts of the play applauded—but others hissed—on the whole it was *damned*—Still, it was much better than his "Bunker Hill"—& indeed was not fairly treated. Some of the scenes are good, & appeared to be not badly written. The afterpiece was Royal Tyler's—"Good Spec" &c.[17] —which has some merit. Recd. the remainder of Mease's Review—& read it.

Saturday, April 14.—Read the papers. Two medical visits. Wrote the following letter to Dr. Aikin—of London. At Miller's. We went to the Hospital. Visited Mitchill, & read or looked over at his room a variety of pamphlets lately recd. by him from Edinburgh. Brought away with me the "British Critic" for Jany. last. This is the Porcupine of British Journals, as the Analytical Review is the Bache.[18] In neither of them can confidence be reposed. I thought, yesterday, that I had recd. the whole of Mease's Review—when, lo! to-day a number of sheets more came tumbling in upon me. I can not, even now, flatter myself that this is the last of it. Two medical visits. Errands. Spent the eveng. Club night—at W. W. Woolsey's. Himself, with Johnson & myself made the whole Club. Corrected a proof of the Repository, & one of "Alcuin."

Sunday, 15.—Lotion & lavation. Two medical visits. Johnson & I walked out of town. Visited at Mr. Sharples's. Visited at G. M. Woolsey's. Dined & spent the afternoon at H. Johnson's. Medical visit. Called at C. Adams's. Went with Dr. Miller to see Miss Templeton, with whom we spent an hour & an half. The remainder of the evening at Dr. Hosack's. Brought from Miller's the Analytical Review for Jany. & have looked over a few articles.

Monday, 16.—Finished the Analytical Review for Jany. This is the best executed & most interesting No. of that Journal that I have ever seen; & I regret that I had not time to make some memoranda of its contents. Visit from Mitchill. Medical visit. Revised a proof of Alcuin at the printer's. Visit to Miller. At the Hospital. Wrote to Mr. Tracy. Some writing for the Med: Reposy. Recommenced Zoonomia P. II. Recd. a letter from Dr. Barton, inclosing a letter from Dr. Archer of Maryland—which I transcribed for the Reposy. Visit to Mr. Mason, the English Botanist,[19] & to Dr. Haworth—for whom I wrote several introductory letters to the Eastward. Eveng. at Mrs. Dunlap's.

To John Aikin

The *general* motives for this address are the respect which I entertain; in common with many of my friends & countrymen, for your private character, & for your various professional, moral, & literary labours; my *particular* motive arises out of the situation which I understand you are in, as Editor of a very respectable periodical publication—I mean the Monthly Magazine. It is a fact, which has been much lamented by the worthiest & most sensible men in the United States, that the information respecting our affairs, manners, opinions, & institutions, in the possession of the conductors of the ablest literary works in Gt. Britain, is so imperfect, partial, & erroneous. I will not pretend to assign the causes for this fact; they are numerous, & would lead me too far from my present purpose; but it is an undeniable truth that America is seldom spoken of in the best literary journals of Europe, without the commission on the part of the speaker, of some palpable absurdity. This may surprise you—but I speak from a long & intimate knowlege of this country—a knowlege which few who are not natives, & not every native, can attain it. That this is true, is certainly much to be regretted. For, among other evils which it occasions this singular misfortune is to be reckoned—That, as we are in the habit of receiving the greater part of every kind of information from Europe, & as the periodical publications referred to have an extensive circulation in our country, the misrepresentations respecting many things relative to the United States are received as truth, by our young people, & being uncontradicted, form a part of their belief, & influence their conduct when arrived to maturity. This mischief has operated very unfor-

---

[16] John Daly Burk (1775-1808), *Female Patriotism, or the Death of Joan D'Arc* (New York, 1798). Burk was an Irishman who wrote the play in America.

[17] The "*Good Spec,* etc." was sometimes called "*The Georgia Spec.*" "Spec" for "land speculation."

[18] Porcupine, a Federalist pamphleteer; Bache, a Republican writer and printer.

[19] No positive identification. Mr. Mason, or Masson, may be, but probably was not, Francis Masson, born in Aberdeen in 1741, who died in Montreal in 1805. He was or he also was, a botanist.

tunately in many instances, tho' it is slowly yielding as the intercommunication between the several parts of the Union is extended & perfected. Hitherto, those among us who have been satisfied of these facts, have been content with silently dissenting from foreign errors, or with a limited or verbal exposure of them. They have laughed at the ridiculous fictions of pretended philosophers & historians, & smiled at the credulity of those who put faith in their absurdities. But these fictions & absurdities have sometimes produced serious evils; & it is time that they should be overthrown where they arise, & extirpated as soon as they spring up. In the United States, such is the rapidity with which faithful intelligence is beginning to diffuse itself, that there is reason to believe the mischief, so far as it concerns ourselves, simply, may be destroyed ere many years have passed. The contentions of political parties have presented the principal obstacle to this event. They are now about to cease. But, it will, undoubtedly, be hastened by conveying faithful intelligence to Europe; while, to Europeans, this would open a fund of curious information & unlock a source of interesting research, which to them has hitherto been but partially disclosed.

There exists in this city, a small association of men, who are connected by mutual esteem, & habits of unrestricted communication. They are of different professions & occupations; of various religious or moral opinions; &, tho' they coincide in the great outlines of political faith, they estimate very variously many of the political transactions of the men who have, from time to time directed the councils of the nation. This diversity of sentiment, however, as it has never affected their friendship, has made them more active in investigation; & tho' they may have formed different judgements concerning facts, has led them to a general concurrence in the facts themselves. Natives of America, & of remote parts of the Union, they are in habits of constant communication with the several States, & are well informed of the state of letters, science, & opinions in these States, with some few exceptions.

The present is an important period to America. This country may soon present an interesting spectacle to Europe. It is for you to judge how far the correspondence of such a knot of men may be of consequence to your Work, or of value to your curiosity. It will be less important probably in the way of direct personal communication, than as a means of readily furnishing you with the publications made in the United States; with such occasional remarks as may enable you to estimate them properly. In this point of view, they will with pleasure contribute to your Work; nor will they withhold, altogether, that species of information which no books can furnish.

This being a mere letter of introduction to a Correspondence in embrio, & which may never be pursued, is only accompanied by a few small publications, some of which may, in part, apprize you of the characters of a few of the individuals referred to above. I have also ventured to inclose to you some account of the Poets of the United States. These articles are hastily drawn up; & amid incessant literary & professional occupation. You will, of course, dispose of them as you please: but should this species of information be acceptable to you, it can easily be extended so as to comprehend the whole circle of poetical, as well as literary, adventures in the United States. Papers of this kind are easily written— & should they be lost, can at any time be restored. This is not equally true of various other kinds of Papers— which was a motive not to be disregarded in the outset of a correspondence, whose fate is yet to be determined.

I am, with great respect & esteem, Yours &c.

April 14. 1798.
Pine St. 45. N. York.   E. H. Smith.

Tuesday, 17.—It snowed yesterday afternoon. In the evening the snow continued, & about one & a half inch remained, beside that which melted in the falling. The mercury fell below 25° of faht. at the College. This day & evening have been cold, tho' clear.

Medical visit. At our printer's. Continued Zoonomia P. II. Visit from Mr. Sharples & Dr. Haworth—with several other transient calls. At the Hospital. Called at Mitchill's—he out. Transcribed, with verbal corrections, Dr. Dewees's Case of Midwifery, from his letters, for the Repository: & made some progress in Nl. Dwight's Dissertation on Sick Head-Ach, of which I am forming an abstract, also for the Repository. Recd. a letter from Mr. Scandella. Called at Dunlap's, & found him returned. Charles had written by him, but he has lost the letter—a careless fellow! Looked over the No. 10 of Weekly Magazine, which he brought home with him. Medical visit. Met Mr. Cooper—Tragedian—& he came home with, & spent a short time with me. Rejoined Dunlap & his family at Mr. Rogers's—where we spent the evening. Went home with them, & supped. Came home, & read the Introduction & four first Chapters of C. B. Brown's Novel—"Sky-Walk"—the Ms. of which Dunlap brought me, as also the IIIrd & IVth parts of "Alcuin." This "Sky-Walk," is an extraordinary thing. The basis of it is *Somnambulism.*—Corrected two proofs of the Repository, & one of "Alcuin."

Wednesday, 18.—Read the papers. Medical visit. At our printer's. Visit from Dr. Miller, who read me such part of his Review of Yeats & Maclean as he has finished. Visit from Dunlap, & from Dr. Morse, who brought me a letter from Dr. Barton. Medical visit. Visit to Riley's. Part of the evening at the theater—to hear the music & see the shew of the "Siege of Belgrade." The rest of the day has been devoted to the eager perusal of "Sky Walk"—which I have not yet finished—tho I have read upon it this day, at least ten hours.

Thursday, 19.—Medical visit. Visit from Miller, who read me the continuation of his Review. We went together to call on Dr. Morse, but did not find him at home. At the Hospital. Corrected the last of the two first parts of "Alcuin," now publishing by me. Here is another task concluded. Corrected, also, two proofs of the Repository. Called at Miller's—we went to the printer's, & thence walked on the Battery. Medical visit. Johnson & I drank tea at home. Just as the cloth was removed, Mr. Radclift entered. He stayed till ten—& we passed a very sociable evening. In the morning I had finished "Sky-Walk." It had inexpressibly interested me. My whole spirit was affected by it. But my perusal had been too rapid, the interest too violent, too many other ideas had passed thro' my mind, to allow me to judge properly of it.

On these occasions we first feel—examination follows—the last thing is to judge. Johnson had two chapters. After Radclift's departure he took up the book, & read aloud the third & fourth. I followed him, & read to the tenth. The peculiar merits of the work were more obvious to me now, than before; for a double reason. My perusal was less passionate, & I had opportunity to mark the effects it produced on my friend. He has retired to his bed in a throb & tumult of curiosity, interest, & admiration. I have also read the third & fourth parts of "Alcuin" to-day. They merit my applause—but I must hesitate on the expediency of the publication. I must determine this doubt—by a reference to the decision of a woman, one or more, unaccustomed to such speculations & ignorant of the author—but who has good-sense & candour. Her advice shall be conclusive—at least for the present. I have also looked over the Weekly Magazine No. 10. This day has, therefore, been industriously spent.

Friday, April 20.—I received a letter from William Buel. Medical visit. At our printer's. Met Miller there, who accompanied me home, & read "Alcuin" P. III. & IV. I wrote letters to Dr. Mease, Dr. Barton, Dr. Buel, and Ch. B. Brown. I finished the Abstract of Nathl. Dwight's Dissertation on Sick Head-Ach, which I commenced a few days ago. I received a letter from Mr. Tracy. Johnson came in. I was tired of writing. He took up "Sky-Walk," & read aloud to me. Every sentence increases my admiration of this performance. Why are there any obstacles to its immediate publication? Why so little liberal curiosity in our country? Why such sordid doubts among our booksellers? Why have not I the property, as I have the wish, to incur myself the expence of publication? Medical visit. At the Theater. Saw "The Will,"[20] a whimsical Comedy—& Mr. Milns's "Flash in the Pan"—first time—& I hope the last.

Saturday, 21.—Read the papers. Medical visit. Revised a proof of the Repository. Called vainly on Mr. Mason the Botanist. Errands. Wrote introductory letters, for Mr. Post, to Drs. Senter, Wheaton, Eustis, N. Dwight; Osborn, & Dwight of New Haven. Called in vain on Mitchill. At the Hospital as usual. Read several chapters in "Sky-Walk." Letter from Dr. Barton—brought by a Capt. Hendricks,[21] the Sachem of the Stockbridge Indians—a respectable man. Visit from Mr. Roulet. Dunlap, Johnson & I walked. We drank tea at Dunlap's. Medical visit. Club night, & my turn. Present, Dunlap, Johnson, Smith, W. W. Woolsey—& Mr. Radcliff visitor. I read five full chapters of "Sky-Walk"—& the conversation was principally on the approaching elections. Revised a proof of the Repository.

Sunday, 22.—Lavation, as usual. Medical visit. Listened an hour to Johnson, reading "Sky-Walk." Obtained the "Annals of Medicine for 1797," & after a hurried survey of its contents, betook myself to the task of extracting & abridging the more material articles of intelligence which it contains. I was busied on this till dinner. Then I called on Dr. Miller, & gave over to his hands the volume, & the labour. Capt. Hendricks called on me early in the morning. I am pleased with this man's countenance & conduct. Dined, with all the Johnson's, at Seth's—where, also, we spent most of the afternoon. Wm. & I then walked out of town, & returning visited Roulet—& drank tea at Mr. Sharples's. Medical visit. Called at G. Mumford's: nobody at home. At Mr. Duryee's—the same. At Riley's—in vain. At Dunlap's—where I read aloud a number of Chapters of "Sky-Walk"—& whence I have just returned.

Monday, April 23.—Medical visit. At the printer's. Visit to Miller, & brought away with me "The Annals of Medicine"—of which I have hastily read the greater part. Visit from Miller—on business of the Repository. Transcribed, abridged &c. a number of articles from the Annals of Medicine. Recd. letters from Dr. Croswell & Dr. Wheaton. Was surprised by a visit from my friend Theodore Dwight. Woolsey came in with him—& they spent some hours with us. At our printer's—& corrected a proof of the Repository. Medical visit. Drank tea, & spent the evening at W. W. Woolsey's—Mr. Dwight, Radcliff, Johnson, & I there. At the Hospital—at noon. Very changeable weather. We have had rain & sunshine—very cold & very warm weather, several times. It is now clear & cold.

Tuesday, 24.—Medical visit. At the printer's—& corrected a proof of the Repository. Medical visit. Voted at the Poll. Called on Miller. At the Hospital. Visited Mr. Mason the Botanist. Called on Dingley. Performed some writing for the Repository. Corrected another proof. A visit from Miller. Recd. a letter from C. B.

---

[20] Frederick Reynolds, *The Will* (1796 or 1797); William Miln, *Flash in the Pan* (April 20, 1798), played only once.

[21] Captain Hendrick, not Hendricks, was a decendant, either son or more likely a grandson, of the original Hendrick (1680-1755). Captain Hendrick became Sachem, chief or one of the chiefs, of the Stockbridge Indians in 1771. He continued as chief while they were in Oneida, New York, and until they prepared to move to Green Bay in 1829. The original Hendrick was a Mohawk or at least was married to a Mohawk woman. He was an important figure in the Councils of the Six Nations and a consultant to Sir William Johnson, Superintendent of Indian Affairs. He was killed at the battle of Fort George, New York, September 8, 1755. See the *National Cyclopedia;* Electa Jones, *Stockbridge Past and Present* (Springfield, Massachusetts, 1854) pp. 14, 28, 92-96, 99, 103, 119-122.

Brown. It inclosed one for Miss Susan Potts—who is his Mistress—& who came to town yesterday. I delivered it, & have seen her. Without being beautiful—she is very interesting. Our talk was on common topics, as there was a third person present, but it evinced good sense. Found out Theodore. We drank tea at Riley's. Medical visit. At a meeting of young gentlemen, to which I was invited, to unite in the formation of a literary club. But few attended—nothing was done—& I shall not do any thing further. This mark of politeness is a sufficient return for theirs. Spent the evening at Dunlap's. Theodore & W. W. Woolsey there. Wrote a few lines to Mr. Tracy. Corrected another proof of the Repository.

Wednesday, 25.—Read the papers. Made up the article Medical News for our fourth No. of the Repository. Visit from Dr. Dingley. Two medical visits. At our printer's. Corrected two proofs of the Repository. Visit from Mitchill. After dinner, Miller & I went to the College, & spent some time, in reading over the Med: News of this No. & in other business of the Repository. Miller & I called at Riley's, to see Theodore Dwight—but he was gone. Read some part of "Sky-Walk." Drank tea, & spent some part of the evening with Miss Potts. There were others present—& ordinary beings—so that my opportunities for conversation with her were circumscribed. All that I see is in her favour. Knowing me to be possest of her secret—she entered into conversation in relation to C. B. Brown, without affectation. This pleased me. The rest of the evening at the Theater. "Macbeth"—Hodgkinson—*Macduff* Cooper: both well: the last quite well.

Thursday, 26.—Wrote a letter to Dr. Wheaton, & one to Mr. Scandella. Visit from Theodore Dwight. Went with him to Riley's. Thence to the Hospital as usual. Medical visit. At our printer's. Read the 3. & 4. parts of "Alcuin" a second time, with more approbation. Transcribed my letter to Dr. Aikin. Recd. letters from my father, from Dr. Wheaton, & from Dr. Belknap, informing me of my election as Honorary Member of the Massachusetts Historical Society. Visit from a patient. Errands. Drank tea, with Theodore & Johnson, at W. W. Woolsey's. Thence we went to the "Society for free Debate"—where we were entertained by the ridiculousness of some, & the good sense of others. The question was on the propriety of Embargoing or Arming—& the large majority—at least 4/5ths for the last, evinced the change of the public mind. I was much pleased with a Boy that I saw there—but know not who he was. Came home, & after my friends went away, corrected a proof of the Repository.

Friday, April 27.—Writing for the Repository. Read the 11th No. of the Weekly Magazine. Errands. At the printer's. Corrected a proof of the Repository. Medical visit. "Alcuin" this day published.[22] Visited Miss Potts. Called on Dr. Rodgers—on Dr. Miller, & on Mr. Garnet: He absent—saw Mrs. G.—they are moving. Found Theodore at Woolsey's Store. We went to Riley's. We dined, with Dunlap & Johnson, at W. W. Woolsey's—& spent much of the afternoon. Thence walked on the Battery. Recd. a letter from Dr. Senter of Newport. Evening at the Theater—saw Mr. Fawcett's (Commedian) New play of "The Lad of Spirit"[23]—now first played. As good as the common run of comedies; but a poor thing. Corrected a proof of the Repository.

Saturday, 28.—Read the papers. Wrote the following letter to Dr. Thornton of London—& made minutes for another letter to him on the subject of Contagion. At our printer's. Visit from Dwight—& from Dunlap. Errands. Visit to Miller. At the Hospital. Dined at Riley's with Johnson & Dwight. W. W. Woolsey & Dunlap came there—& we visited the State Prison. Wrote a few lines to Dr. Dwight (N. H.) to N. Dwight & Cogswell. Medical visit. Club night—G. M. Woolsey's turn—present—Dunlap, Johnson, Miller, Smith, G. M. Woolsey. Corrected a proof of the Repository.

Sunday, 29.—Lotions & Lavations. Several interruptions from visitants—& a visit from Dunlap. Medical visit. At the Hospital. Visit at Dunlap's. Called on Miss Potts, but did not see her. Theodore called in my absence—& has sailed for Connecticut. Wrote a letter of some length to Dr. Senter—containing my opinion on his case, & a method of cure. Dined & spent the afternoon at H. Johnson's. All the Johnsons there—& Mr. & Mrs. Winthrop & Miss Stuyvesant. A walk, with H., S., & W. on the Battery. Wm. & I called at Miss Morton's—she out. A walk on the Battery.—Called at Hodgkinson's. Benefits commence to-morrow. Came home & made out the Contents, advertisement &c. for the fourth of Volume first of the Repository—& did some other writing.

To R. J. Thornton

I had the pleasure of receiving your letter of the 20th of Jany. by the Packet, a few weeks ago; and should have replied to it immediately but that I thought it most advisable to wait the departure of Dr. Haworth, who has travelled in our country, & is soon to return to London. He will probably be the bearer of this letter.

To my great mortification and regret, the Books which you inform me you had sent out, have never arrived; nor can I learn any tidings of them. Indeed, as your letter contains no particular description of them, or information how or by whom they were sent, it is difficult to inquire concerning them to effect. I conclude, however, as my original letter was sent by the Ship Fame, & as this was one of the first American vessels

---

[22] Warfel, in his *Life of Brown* (p. 81), states that Smith paid for the printing or publication of *Alcuin*. In his "Diary" entry for February 21, 1798, Smith writes of paying twenty-three dollars and fifty cents "towards" it. Since it was not much more than a large pamphlet this may have been a substantial part of the cost.

[23] John Fawcett, *The Lad of Spirit* (1798; first time in New York). Possible confusion; advertised in New York as by R. Fawcett; an actor there; John apparently never left Covent Garden.

that sailed from London after its receit, that the Books were sent by her. If so they are irretrievably lost. This Ship foundered—& it was with the greatest difficulty that the people escaped, without saving any part of a cargo of near 90,000 dollars value. All small packages, of course, of which no account is taken, went to the bottom, & are lost without its being known to whom they belonged. This is the more unfortunate, as all our Booksellers' importations have been captured, & carried into the West Indies.

In respect to the interchange of Books, I cheerfully accede to your proposal; & shall wholly rely on your judgement. Nor will there be any difficulty in disposing of such as may not be immediately necessary to me. From this, however, you must allow me to except all expensive Works in Natural History. Our profession is too poor, & public curiosity too low, to make works of this kind saleable in the United States. Half the benefits that might flow from our public Institutions are denied us by reason of this poverty. The people are all comfortably rich; but that exorbitant wealth, accumulated in a few hands, which, at the impulse of vanity or superstition, or charity, erects great establishments, endows colleges, & portions Hospitals, scarcely exists among us; & Legislative Bounty is still restricted to more obvious calls upon it, & to the daily & urgent necessities of a new Country. Hence, our Hospitals are still deficient in that apparatus which is so necessary to furnish the physician with proper arms for the combat with disease. With very good dispositions towards them, & with every wish to institute experiments, the want of a Pneumatic Apparatus has hitherto prevented any proper trials of many of the new Remedies in America. We are, now, in hope of overcoming this obstacle. In other respects, there is considerable facility in undertaking Experiments; tho' here, as well as with you, opposition is always made. Yet, it is not so obstinate, & has not so many weapons at its command. But, tho' this be true, very little has been done among us, in respect to the Antisyphilitic remedies which have excited so much attention in Britain. For the last six months our Hospital has been under the care of gentlemen, two of whom were indisposed to trials, & two others not sufficiently attentive & persevering in them. Many, however, were made; but few were satisfactory, in the event. For a time every thing was promising; & on the report of the prescriber I wrote favorably to Dr. Beddoes. But, whether something was neglected, or whether the Physician was too easily discouraged, the remedies were changed, or mixed with others, & all activity was at an end. In one fact, however, all seemed to agree—that the effects of Mercury were greatly aided & hastened by the use of Nitric Acid. My course of attendance commenced with this month. At this season of the year we have few patients. I have commenced experiments; & they will be continued for the next three months. The result will be made public.

With this letter, I shall send you such of our publications as deserve your notice. Many are made, but few have any but comparative value. Perhaps some of them you may already possess—but, as you observe, it is best to err on the safe side; & what I send may be disposed of, probably, without difficulty.

In respect to the subject of Contagious fevers, I am inclined to believe that very great errors have been committed. At present great & warm discussions are going on amongst us relative to it. And it is our expectation to handle every topic connected with Contagion, in the course of the Repository. I think that the material points may be fixed. But I will not anticipate at this time. Should my leisure permit, I mean to trace the outline of my own creed to you, before this letter is sent off. One advantage, at least, may arise from it. It may lead to observations among you—& throw some additional light upon the subject, in consequence.

I feel myself much flattered & honoured, by your readiness in accepting my offer to Correspondence, & by the kindness which you have manifested in the conduct of it. The services which I can render you are comparatively small—but I shall do all in my power to make myself useful to you, & to bestow some value on the communications I may make you from time to time.

My Colleagues present their sincere respects.

April 28. '98.   E. H. Smith.

Monday, April 30.—Medical visit. At our printer's. Corrected a proof of the Repository. Visit to Dr. Miller. A visit from Dr. Mitchill. A short letter from C. B. Brown. He will not visit us. A visit to Miss Potts. A letter from Dr. Kollock. Medical visit. Corrected a proof of the Repository. Visit to Dunlap, at whose house I drank tea & spent part of the evening: The remainder at Mr. Boyd's. Corrected the last proof of the 1st Vol. of the Repository. Medical visit. Read the Monthly Review Enlarged for Novr. & Decr. 1797—& some articles in the Appendix. Month. Rev. Enl. vol. XXIV—Novr. *Art. I.* Sir Geo: Staunton's Acct. of the Embassy to China. This, like the preceeding articles relative to this work, is exceedingly interesting. The extract respecting the Chinese language &c. p. 242. is inestimable—& the general view of China by the Reviewer is valuable & instructive, & well deserves a place in our periodical Works. *Art. III.* Boville's Memoirs of the French Revolution. This article leads to an expectation of much information to be relied on from the Work reviewed. The Critics seem approaching to Moderantism in their political principles. They are not ready, in so great a degree as formerly, to applaud France in every thing. *Art. VI.* Fragments: in the manner of Sterne. The extract is in Sterne's best manner, & worthy of a better man; & excites a wish to see the whole. *Art. VII.* The Poems of Catullus. Of the original I am incompetent to form an opinion. There is great elegance in three of the little poems Rev: p. 276. *Art. VIII.* Lumisden's Remarks on the Antiquities of Rome. This is a curious article. Many of the extracts are pleasing. The Work is desirable as one of occasional reference. *Art. IX.* Pages' Secret Histy. of the F. Revolution. The extract Bailly's Address forms the chief value of the article. The acct. of his death is almost literally copied from Riouffe—which I am surprized to see pass unnoticed. *Art. XI.* Maton's Obs. on the West: Counties (of Engd.) This is a valuable work. *Art. XII.* Philos: Trans: P. I. '97. We must fall on some plan for regularly obtaining this work. The present publication is much to be desired. *Art. XIV.* Count's Rumford's Essays, No. 7. This Essay displays wonderful genius, & is worthy the most attentive study. To compare Franklin with this man, is to compare a butterfly to a honey-bee. *Art. XVI.* Kentish's Essay on Burns—suggests some novel & promising remedies. Month: Rev: Eng. Vol. XXIV. Decr. *Art. II.* Biog. Anecdotes of the founders of the French Republic. The hand of a man resolved at all events to justify or extenuate every thing that has been done in france is too evident in this work —a great part of which has been published in the Month. Mag. This article relative to Pichegru I have reason to believe materially incorrect in some particulars. *Art. IV.* D'Israeli's Miscellanies. The character of the author is hit off with admirable happiness & correctness. The extracts are all pleasing & deserve the encomiums passed on them. *Art. V.* Graham's Description of Vermont. *Puff.* It is wonderful that Williams's Work has never reached them. *Art. XIII.* Wakefield's Edition of Pope's Homer. This is a pleasing article. Wakefield is certainly [a] powerful critic—tho' he is sometimes redundant in epithet—as in the Extract before us: "frivolous puerility & wild licentiousness." Cowper's merits are well explained. I think the censure on his verse somewhat overcharged. *Art. XIV.* Gisborne's Tales of Wessex; a Poem. The Reviewers are correct—the extract merits their eulogium—yet this kind of poetry is essentially deficient—it does not touch the heart—& can not last. *Art. XVI.* Webster of the Effects of Slavery. A just tribute to this excellent Essay of my countryman. Here are, also, marks of returning moderantism. The proposition at the end, is that of Judge Benson & Mr. Hamilton. Various & unanswerable objections may be made to it. It would counteract itself. No mode is good, but that which will ameliorate the mental as well as personal condition of the Blacks. *Art. 33.* Elegaic Sonnets &c. by Charlotte Smith. Those quoted are of her best.

Industry of April 1798

Reading

Annals of Medicine for 1797—8vo. large.
Lettsom's Hints &c.—8vo. pp. 273—large print.
Davidge on Yellow Fever of Baltimore—8vo. pp. 65.
Clarissa Harlowe—Vol. I.
André &c. by Dunlap.
Monthly Review Enld. for Nov. & Dec. 1797.
Analytical Do.   Novr. Decr. & Jany. 1798.
British Critic, for Jany. '98.
Gentleman's Magazine, for Jany. '98.
Weekly Magazine,—XI first Nos.
Dispatches & Instructions from American Envoys at Paris.
Ms.
Sky-Walk—2 vols.
Alcuin III. & IV. Parts.
Mease on Currie pp. 40.

Writing

Composition
  Notes of American Poets—pp. 30.
  Letters, mostly uncopied. 50.

Transcription
  Principally the above Notes & letters ...... pp. 60.
I dismissed from the press, during this period, "The Botanic Garden," "Alcuin P. I. & II," & "Med: Reposy." No. 4 of Vol. I. Beside proof-sheets to be corrected almost every day—&c. &c. &c.

MEMOIRS. 1798. MAY.

Tuesday, 1.—Two medical visits. At our printer's. Errands. At Dr. Miller's; & at Mitchill's. At the Hospital. Returning in company with Miller; stopped in at his house, & saw Dr. Ramsay (of Charleston S. C.'s) very flattering letter, relative to the Repository. The 4th No. published to-day. Visit from Miller & Mitchill. Went with them to the printer's. Wrote there a short letter to Mr. Rice our Bookseller at Baltimore. Medical visit. Errands. Drank tea at Riley's. Call at Seth Johnson's: at Dunlap's, & went with them to see Miss Potts, with whom we spent part of the evening. Recd. letters from Mr. Tracy & from C. B. Brown—(the letter lost by Dunlap.) Two hours writing for the Repository, on accts. &c. Wrote a letter to Dr. Kollock. Finished the Appendix to the Month. Rev. Enld. vol. XXIV—but must defer notices for the present.

Wednesday, 2.—Read the papers. Medical visit. Wrote letters to Drs. Wheaton, Field, & Dwight, to E. Larkin, on business of the Repository. The forenoon at the Commencement of Columbia College. The afternoon principally devoted to writing for the Repository, & to making up packages of it for various persons & places. Wrote to Dr. Chisholm. Medical visit. I had called on Miss Potts in the morning, & she consented to accompany me to the Theater. After drinking tea with the Dunlap's, we called on her, & went together. The play was "The West Indian"[24]—& for Mrs. Johnson's Benefit. It was well performed, & gave us pleasure. This, as it has happened, was the first time of my having seen this piece performed.

Thursday, May 3.—Medical visit. Much of the forenoon employed in making up packages of the Reposy. & seeing to their sending off. Medical visit. At the Hos-

---

[24] Richard Cumberland, *The West Indian* (1771).

pital. Medical visit. Dined, with a large company, & spent the afternoon, at Mr. Leffingwell's. Called on Miss Potts, & accompanied her to Dunlap's. After tea—medical visit. Returned to Dunlap's—waited on Miss P. home—& spent an hour with her. Called on Dr. Miller. Read some part of the Weekly Magazine No. 12 which I recd. to-day. A visit from Dr. Haworth, morng.—who returned from the Eastward. He sails tomorrow for London. Transcribed my letter to Dr. Thornton.

Friday, 4.—Medical visit. Errands. At our printer's. Miller came there, & we called on Dr. Haworth. Came home & posted books for the Repository. Visit from Mitchill & Miller. They came with the expectation of meeting Haworth here, whose last visit it was to be. After they were gone, he came. I walked a square or two with him, & we parted. I suppose that he has sailed in the Packet for Falmouth, this evening. Posting the Books of the Repository & my own. Visit of some length, from Roulet. Two medical visits. Made up packages, at the printer's, of the Repository, for distant subscribers. At Dunlap's. Evening at S. Johnson's.

Monthly Review Enlarged, vol. XXIV, Appendix—*Art. I.* Gretry's Musical Memoirs—a pleasing article. What a petulant fellow was this same Jean Jacques! *Art. II.* Von Humboldt's Experiments on Irritated Fibres. This is a very important work; & I have an eager desire to examine it at large. I see nothing, however, that wars against the Zoonomia. Is it possible that some of the stories told of the Metallic Points may have accidentally been true, by this influence? *Art. VII.* Hist. of F. Revolut. &c. This work, apparently, deserves to be consulted by him who would form conclusive opinions concerning this wonderful event. *Art. VIII.* Chemical Annals—vols. 21. 22. This is a hasty sketch of the contents of these volumes. Many of the articles I have seen at length, in Nicholson's Journal. The vols. are very valuable. *Art. IX.* Meiner's Biographies. Few articles more interesting. The biographic notices are good. Some remarks of the reviewer at the close, go deep into a most consequential inquiry. It is difficult to decide either way. *Art. XI.* Schlichtegroll's Necrology—well deserves translation. *Art. XII.* Letters of the Wandering Jew—the letter extracted has merits; & no doubt the work is well executed. *Art. XIII.* Tiedman's spirit of speculative philosophy vol. VI. A curious & instructive article. Yet I do not feel that despair which the critic seems to feel. Men may be wise & good without religion. Ridiculous to infer the character of principles from their mistaken application! *Art. XIV.* Count Alfieri's tragedies. Would that I read Italian! The dedication to Washington is handsome. *Art. XV.* Barrere (a villain) on the scheme of Government. I just mark this to note—that Godwin's plan is mistated—& that in the natural progress of things, a duely organized Government would result in what is here a "peaceful anarchy." *Art. XVI, XVII, XVIII, & XIX*—All relative to Catherine II. of Russia —& all worthy of being read. Bad as were many parts of her character, she had many great qualities; &, on the whole, was, perhaps, as good a prince as the castle she governed could bear. *Art. XX.* Sprengel's Manual of Pathology. This smacks of Brown & Darwin. *Art. XXI.* Manual of the Theophilanthropists—the monkeys! *Art. XXIII.* Rivarol's Preliminary Discourse &c. This short article deserves repeated perusal. *Art. XXIV.* Delormel's Scheme of universal language, & *Art. XV.* Pasigraphy—&c.—both require more leisure than I possess to judge properly of them. They must, therefore, lie by for the present.

Saturday, May 5.—Read the papers. My friend Allen has made a spirited speech, & much to his credit. Three medical visits. At the printer's—where I wrote a few lines to El. Smith jr. Visit to Mitchill. At the Hospital. Read the Month. Rev. Enld. for Jany. 1798. Read a part of Lent's Dissertation on Pestilential Vapours &c. Visit to Miss Potts. Two medical visits. Club night—Miller's turn—& for the first time. Present, Dunlap, Johnson, Miller & Smith—S. Miller & Mitchill visitors.

Month. Rev. Enld. vol. XXIV Append. *Art. XXVI.* La Fontaine's Histories of Families. The Critic's part of this article serves only as a connecting link to the Extracts—which are uncommonly pleasing. The idea of Hennig's education is just. It ought to be more devellopped. It is impossible to do more than conjecture what would be the effect of an education, conducted on the plan of assembling, from the earliest infancy, all the implements & means of instruction around a child, that wealth, genius, & knowlege might conceive & procure: so that science should be inhaled, imperceptibly, & as it were with the ambient air. *Art. XXVII & VIII.* Tischbein & Böttiger on Grecian Paintings. This title announces a work of elegant curiosity, from any satisfactory knowlege of whose subject, we, in this country, are inevitably debarred.

Sunday, 6th.—Lotions & Lavations. Three medical visits. Visit from Dr. Miller. Medical visit. Mr. Stark Robertson, Dunlap, Miller, Johnson, & myself, dined & spent the afternoon at Mr. Sharples's. Two medical visits. Met Miss Potts in the street, & walked some ways with her. Called at Mr. Morton's. Finished Lent's Dissertation—8vo. pp. 54—loose print. A poor thing.

Month. Rev. Enld. Jany. '98. *Art. II.* Malone's Edit. of Sir J. Reynold's Works. The exhibition of the character of this celebrated painter is very pleasing. Is it true that Burke wrote his Discourses? *Art. III.* Ld. Monboddo's Ancient Metaphysics *Vol. V.* This is a strange writer. There is much shrewdness, however, in some of his remarks on money—but he has lost sight of the great principle in the wilderness of particulars. *Art. VI.* Knight on the Culture of the Apple & Pear. These remarks & conjectures deserve attention. Mr. Forsythe's experiments seem to go far towards their confutation. *Art. VII.* Rollo on Diabetes Mellitus. The subject of the work here reviewed has recd. in it the most important practical elucidations. Perhaps, however, that it is rather in an impaired, than too vigorous, action of the stomach that the disease originates. Every part of this work, seems to demand special attention. *Art. VIII.* Trans. of Socy. for Arts &c. vol. 15. This is a work which we ought to possess. The present vol. does not appear to contain much information particularly valuable to the physician. *Art. X.* Currie's Medical Reports. This is a work of high value. Nevertheless the view here given of it does not incline me to assent to all the author's positions & reasonings. But, then, no satisfactory opinion can be deduced from this article. *Art. XIII.* Beddoes' Introductory Lecture. This is ingenious, & the Extract worthy of the author. *Art. XIV, XV, XVI.* Three publications of the late Mr. Burke. There is much good sense in the remarks of the critic on all these papers. Of the Extracts, they are witty, able, & eloquent, & full of inermixture of truth & error. How admirable was the style of this writer for an orator! What pity that he had not been enlightened by a just philosophy! to the very verge of which he alternately reaches & recedes.

Monday, 7th.—A visit from Mr. Mason the Botanist. Medical visit. Called on Miss Potts. Miller & I went to Mitchill's, who commenced his course of Mineralogical Instructions to us this day. Our first Conversation took up near three hours. Saw Miss [Potts] sail off in the Amboy Boat, for Bordentown. Recd. a letter from C. B. Brown. My answer to him will contain my sentiments of this young lady. Read the principal part of the Monthly Magazine for October. Medical visit. At the printer's—to send off some copies of the Repository to Phila. Medical visit. Drank tea at Boyd's; & then went to the Theater with him & Radclift. Cooper's Benefit—"The Mountaineers." I do not like the part of Octavian, but Cooper made me cry heartily. "The Old Maid." Mrs. Brett, & Hodgkinson's Capt. Cape, excellent. A very full & federal house. The new Songs vociferously applauded.

Tuesday, May 8.—Two medical visits. Visit from Miller. We went to Mitchill's—where we had our second conversation [on] Mineralogy. This lasted till twelve—when we repaired to the Hospital. This took up the usual time. Two medical visits. Recd. a letter from Dr. King of Suffield Connect. Visit from Dunlap. Two medical visits. Call at Mr. Rogers's. Visit to Mr. Woolsey's. Finished the October, & the November numbers of the Monthly Magazine.

Wednesday, 9.—Two medical visits. Called at Miller's. Fast day—our Mineralogical meeting was deferred. Johnson, Dunlap, & I walked out of town. Dined & spent the afternoon at Dunlap's. Three medical visits. Part of the evening visiting Mr. & Mrs. Johnson—Commedians. Read the greater part of the Decr. No. of the "Monthly Magazine."

Thursday, 10.—Read the papers. Finished the Decr. No. of the Monthly Magazine. Wrote to Mr. Kent, a few lines. At our printer's. Two medical visits. Miller & I had our third Mineralogical Conversation with Mitchill. Three medical visits. Wrote a short letter to Dr. King of Suffield, Connect. & a lengthy one to Ch. B. Brown. Visit from Mitchill. Various calls & errands. Two medical visits. Read part of the Weekly Magazine 13. Miller & I spent the evening with Miss Templeton.

Friday, 11.—Finished the Weekly Magazine No. 13. Two medical visits. Miller & I spent the morning with Mitchill—on Mineralogy—Medical visit. Wrote letters to Dr. Currie of Liverpool (Engd.), Dr. Belknap of Boston, & Mr. Tracy. Business for my father. Visit to Miller. At our printer's on business. Two medical visits. Wm. & I spent the evening at Riley's.

Saturday, 12.—Two medical visits. Miller & I at Mitchill's. At the Hospital. Two medical visits. Read the Memorial of our Envoys to the french minister of foreign affairs—contained in the President's last Message to Congress—a pamphlet of 82 pp. 8vo. Walked with Johnson on the Battery. Two medical visits. Evening, Club night, at Dunlap's. Present, Dunlap, Johnson, Smith, W. W. Woolsey—Mitchill visitor. The last had recd. a letter from Dr. Davidson of Martinique—which I have read since I came home.

Sunday, 13.—Lotions & Lavations. Two medical visits. Johnson & I walked out of town. Dined & spent the principal part of the afternoon at H. Johnson's: the rest of the afternoon at Seth's. Miss Morton was there. Wm & I drank tea at Mr. Sharples's. We passed a part of the evening at Mr. Miller's. I called on Mr. Mason—he out. Went to Dunlap's—who read to me & his wife—Holcroft's new & very excellent comedy of "Knave, or not?"[25]

Monday, 14.—Johnson, Miller & I spent the principal part of the forenoon at Mitchill's—on Mineralogy. Dunlap here. The second time, he left M. G. Lewis's Play "The Castle Spectre"[26]—a singular performance, but not without considerable merit. I read it. Three medical visits. Errands &c. Read the first & half of the second volume of "The Nun"—by Diderot[27]—translation. Calls at Mrs. Miller's—Mr. Stansbury's—Spent the evening partly at G. M. Woolsey's—& partly at home.

Tuesday, 15.—Finished "The Nun"—vol. 2. 12mo. total pp. 507. Johnson & I went to Mitchill's as usual, but after waiting an hour Miller did not come—& we adjourned. Medical visit. Recd. a letter from Mr. Tracy. Contd. an Index of the Repository Vol. I. Recd. a letter from Dr. Senter, by his son. Called on Mr. Senter. We went to the Hospital together—where I prescribed, & shewed him the House. Afterwards we visited Dr. Miller—Mitchill & I walked out to Petersfield, where we spent the afternoon with Dr. Dickson. Medical visit, after my return. Spent the evening at the Manumission Society.

Wednesday, 16.—Read the papers. Recd. a letter from Dr. Buel. Johnson, Miller & I had a Mineralogical Lecture with Mitchill. I saw at Mitchill's Dr. Trotter's

---

[25] (London, 1798).
[26] (London, 1797).
[27] Denis Diderot (1796).

"Medicina Nautica"[28]—which contains some further facts tending to disprove the faithfulness of Dr. Chisholm's account of the Origin of the Grenada fever of 1793-4. Procured "James the Fatalist," by Diderot, & read some part of it. A visit to Mr. Trott the painter, at whose room I saw some very fine prints. At our printer's, into whose hands I put the copy of my "Manumission Oration." Mitchill & I dined & spent the afternoon at Dr. Dickson's. Part of the evening at Dunlap's—the rest at home reading James the Fatalist.

Thursday, May 17.—Miller, Johnson & I at Mitchill's —on Mineralogy. Medical visit. At the Hospital. Medical visit. Recd. a letter from Mr. Kent. Continued James the Fatalist. Visit from Miller. Wrote letters to Brown, Bringhurst, & Mr. Tracy. At the printer's. Medical visit. Visit to Mr. Stansbury's—his eldest son, from Alexandria (Virga.)—Samuel—is here. Drank tea there. At Miller's a short time. Visit to Mr. (Stark) Robertson. Visit to Hodgkinson.

Friday, 18.—This morning Johnson & I went over to Newark in the Stage—so far accompanying Dr. Miller, Mr. Sharples, Miss H. Cooper & Miss Giles, who sat off for Philadelphia. We went on business. This business consisted my proving, by Oath, before a Judge, the authenticity of a certain power of attorney, to which I had, unluckily, been witness.[29] This was soon done—& we walked & yawned for a small part of the rest of the day. The stupidity of no occupation was relieved for a while, by the company & conversation of Mr. McWhorter, a sensible lawyer of the place. We reached home at evening—& after tea, lavations, &c. &c. spent the evening at Riley's. Corrected the first proof of my Oration—& continued "James the Fatalist."

Saturday, 19.—Completed the hurried reading of "James the Fatalist & his Master"—3 vol. 12mo. loose print, in all pp. 816. Read the papers. Visit from Mr. Masson, the Botanist. Wrote letters to my sister Mary, & to Mr. Kent. Recd. a letter from Mr. Scandella. Waited on Mr. Mason to Dr. Mitchill's—where I partly looked over a Review, in french, published at Geneva, of Saltonstall's Dissertation, or rather of Mitchill's Doctrine. At the Hospital, as usual. Continued the Index to the Repository. Visit from Mitchill. At our printer's. Errands. Medical visit. Recd. a letter from my father. Errands. Most of the evening at home —it being Club night—& Johnson's turn. Nobody came. Dunlap & Miller are out of town. Have read about 160 pages of Trotter's Medicina Nautica.

Sunday, 20.—Continued the "Medicina Nautica." Finished the Index to the Repository—& performed some writing on the Accounts of that Publication. Called at Dunlap's. Medical visit. Walked with Johnson on the Battery. Visited at G. M. Woolsey's. Dined & spent the afternoon at S. Johnson's. Mrs. Sharples was there; & John Alsop of Middletown. Wm. & I drank tea at Dunlap's—who returned to-day from Amboy. Spent the evening at John Wells's—who is now our nearest neighbour.

Monday, 21.—Medical visit. Business for my father. Errands. Made out a List of Subscribers for the Repository. Visit from Dr. Mitchill. We called at Mr. Masson's—who was absent. Dr. Hosack being unwell, I prescribed at the Hospital in his stead. Called at his house—& saw Mrs. H. Brought up the Minutes of the Manumission Society to the present day. Recd. letters from Abby & Fanny. Visit from Dunlap. Medical visit. Errands. Visit to Mr. Radclift. Called at Miss Millar's. They have not heard from Miss Potts since her departure. A fire summoned me away. For a time it threatened very extensive mischief. Continued thro' the day, & this evening, the "Medicina Nautica."

Tuesday, 22.—The greater part of this day occupied in making purchases of Wines, medicines &c. &c. for my father. Visit from Dunlap. Continued "Medicina Nautica." Prescribed at the Hospital as usual. Recd. a letter from C. B. Brown, & answered it at some length. Wrote also to my sisters Abby & Fanny—and a short letter to Mrs. Tracy—the object of which is to know whether she will receive me on the terms of former friendship: an inquiry necessary, alas! from her silence —but on which I have long painfully ruminated. Corrected a proof of my Oration. Drank tea at Dunlap's. Mitchill & Mr. Miller were there. Called on Miss Morton—who was absent at the Concert. Visited Miss Mason. She was alone, & we had a sociable & pleasant hour. Walked on the Battery, the night remarkably fine.

Wednesday, May 23.—Read the papers. Continued at intervals, thro' the day, & have nearly finished, "Medicina Nautica." Attended to, & have gone far toward completing, my father's business. Wrote to him. Visit from Mr. Paiba: from Dunlap. At our printer's. Corrected two proofs of my Discourse. Drank tea at L. Coit's. Called, vainly, at Miss Morton's. Spent the rest of the evening at Miss Templeton's—very pleasantly. Miss Nicholson there at first.

Thursday, 24.—Occupied some portion of both parts of the day with my father's business. Read the 15th No. of the Weekly Magazine. Errands. Visit from Mr. Roulet. Corrected two proofs of my Oration. Visit to Mitchill. Prescribed, as usual, at the Hospital. Read Dr. Darwin's Essay on Boarding-Schools[30]—12mo. pp. 188—loose print, american edition. This book contains some good remarks—but is of no high value. Visit from Dr. Sl. Osborn. Two medical calls. Visit at Riley's. Evening at the Manumission Society.

Friday, 25.—A visit from one of my old Lichfield acquaintance. A long visit from Mr. Webster—his book

---

[28] Thomas Trotter, M.D., *Medicina Nautica, or an Essay on the Diseases of Seamen* 1 (1797); 2 (1799); 3 (1803). Trotter was physician to His Majesty's Fleet and wrote numerous books on scurvy, etc.

[29] For some reason Smith chooses to be secretive about this matter and nowhere makes it plain.

[30] Erasmus Darwin, *A Plan for the Conduct of Female Education in Boarding Schools, Private Families and Public Seminaries* (Philadelphia, 1798).

on Epidemics will not be out under four or five months. Medical visit to Mr. Leffingwell's—where I looked over several new Reviews & Magazines—among others the Monthly Magazine for Jany. 1798—which a number of interesting articles—literary & scientific—in particular relative to the Nitric Acid. Corrected the last proofs of my Oration: the printing will be finished tomorrow. At our printer's. Spent the evening with Miss Morton. Webster was there at first, & Johnson the latter part of the evening. During the rest of the day I have been employed in reading Lewis's Novel "The Monk"—Edit. Lond. vols. 3. 12mo.—pp. 834—This singular performance (which I had been deterred from reading by a supposition that it was altogether as voluptuous as it is in parts, but concerning which I have been lately better informed) with many faults; has great merit, & augers very favorably of the author's future performances.

Saturday, 26.—Much of this day occupied in reading over Currie's book on Bilious fever—Mease's Review of it—& in framing something like a Criticism out of this immense mass of heterogeneous matter. This task I have not yet completed. Wrote a short letter to Ch. B. Brown. Prescribed at the Hospital as usual. Did some business for my father. Made two medical visits. A long visit from Mitchill in the afternoon. Johnson & I walked out of town. We called at Mr. Sharples's, on our way out, to pay our respects to the lady—& at Dunlap's, on our return. He & his were absent. Spent the evening at home—partly in conversation with Johnson, & partly in looking over my last year's journal. Read the Papers, as usual.

Sunday, 27.—A considerable part of the forenoon occupied in preparations for, & in, a medical consultation. At the Hospital. Medical visit. Dined & spent most of the afternoon at H. Johnson's. Visit, with Wm. to Riley's. Drank tea at Woolsey's. Medical visit. Spent the evening at Woolsey's. Radclift & Johnson & Miss Alsop were there.

Monday, 28.—A long visit from Dunlap, that occupied my time till near ten. A medical visit & consultation. Wrote a few lines to Dr. Dwight. Finished the Review of Currie's Work on fever. Wrote a short account of Dr. Lettsom's "Hints" Vol. I. Wrote a few lines to Buel. Drew off a lengthy account. Visit from Dunlap. Calls. Visit to Mr. Miller. Medical visit. At our printer's. Drank tea, & spent the evening at home. Visit from Dr. Seaman. Read the Monthly Magazine for February 1798—the whole—& some articles in the Monthly Review of the same month.

Tuesday, 29.—Medical visit. Finished the Monthly Review for February 1798—the Monthly Magazine for Jany. '98—& the principal part of the Supplement to the fourth vol. of that work. Visit from Mitchill. At the Hospital, as usual. Visit from Dunlap. Corrected a proof of the Medical Repository. Spent the evening, with Johnson, at Dunlap's.

The February No. of the Monthly Review, tho' not one of the most important of this celebrated Journal, contains many pleasing articles—of which I shall, as usual, take some notice. *Art. I.* Dallaway's Account of Constantinople. The whole of this article is agreable, & the Extracts lead to a belief that much valuable information may be derived from the Work—which appears to be well executed. *Art. II.* Hatsell's Precedents Vol. 4. This work forms a curious & useful part of political history; & the biographical selections deserve to be read & remembered. *Art. IV.* Malone's Edit. of Sir Joshua Reynolds's Works. The critic's part of this article is nothing. The numerous Extracts can not be perused by the lover of the Fine Arts but with lively interest & elegant satisfaction. The style both of thinking & writing, is so correct & flowing, that I am disposed wholly to discredit Mr. McCormick's assertion that Burke wrote the Discourses of the President of the Royal Society. *Art. VII.* Okely's Pyrology. The extracts are curious. They amount to but little—& the concluding Notice of the author, shews how prone men are to relapse into absurdity from a despair of discovering the exact truth, or from the influence of a superstitious faith, the effect of early education, & most operating when least attended to. *Art. VIII.* Biographical, Literary, & Political Anecdotes. This work merits a reading. I have before noticed, from another Journal, the information it contains relative to the author of Junius' Letters. Perhaps we shall, at last, discover *whose name the cloud conceals. Art. XII.* Hutton's Mathematical Dictionary. This work which will, probably, never be of use to me from its Mathematical information, promises to administer to my gratification by its biographical notices. *Art. XIII.* Munoz's History of the New World Vol. I. This article does not raise very high expectations of the value of this publication. It seems impossible, however, that some important additions to our stock of knowlege respecting South America should not be made by the entire Work. *Art. 20.* Wieland's Select Fairy Tales. The mention is brief —but sufficient to excite curiosity. *Art. 39, & 40.* Harper's Observations & Monroe's View. The notice of the first is candid—by this account of the second it is evident that they do not understand the state of our Parties. *Art. 41. 2. 3.* Chamberlaine's Imitations of the Designs of Hans Holbein, Leonardo da Vinci, & the Carraci—magnificent but beyond the reach of american purses.

Wednesday, May 30.—Read the papers. Finished the Supplementary No. to the IVth Vol. of the Monthly Magazine. Two medical visits. Much of the forenoon, & some part of the afternoon, occupied in the business of the Manumission Society, & of my father. Johnson & I settled our Account for the last year. Read Dr. Linn's & Mr. Miller's fast Day Sermon's. Conversation with Johnson—& reading of one of Hume's Dialogues.[31] We planned out, with more precision than heretofore, a

---

[31] The reference is vague; possibly David Hume, *Dialogues Concerning Natural Religion* (Edinburgh and London, 1779).

weekly publication, somewhat on the scheme of the Weekly Magazine of Phila. We contemplate a Monthly Review—in a year or two—& perhaps an Annual Register. Wrote the preceding Notices of the contents of the Feby. No. of the M. R. E. for 1798. Made up the Minutes of the Manumission Society, for the last meeting.

Thursday, 31.—Read the papers. Medical visit. Wrote a few lines to Dr. Miller, now in Phila. At our printer's, & conversed with them on our project for a Weekly Magazine. Errands. At Mitchill's: he absent. At the Hospital earlier & later than common—having myself superintended some medical administrations there. Corrected a proof of the Repository. Wrote notes, inclosing copies of my Oration, to Mr. Wolcott, Goodrich, Allen, Tracy, Hosmer & Dana. Learnt that Dr. Osborn of N. Carolina was in town—called on him. He & his brother of the Army came here. Both spent some time—& the former all the afternoon. Wm. & I drank tea at H. Johnson's. We then walked out to Roulet's—where we spent most of the evening. Called to see Mrs. Sharples—who was from home. Made a visit at Riley's.

Industry of May 1798

Reading

Trotter's "Medicina Nautica"—8vo. about 500 pp.
Lent's Inaugural Essay on Pestilential Acids.
Memorial of our Envoys at Paris—8vo. pp. 72.
Darwin on Boarding-Schools—12mo. pp. 188—Phila.
Linn's & Miller's fast Sermons—about pp. 45 each 8vo.
James the fatalist, 12mo. 3 vols. pp. 816. Diderot ⎫
The Nun, 12mo. 2 vols. pp. 507. do. ⎬ Novels.
The Monk, 12 Mo. 3 vols. pp. 834. Lewis ⎭
Holcroft's "Knave or Not?"—comedy.
Lewis's "Castle Spectre"—play.
Monthly Review Enld. for February '98 & Append. to vol. XXIV.
Monthly Magazine, for Oct. Nov. Dec. Jany. Feby. & Sept to Vol. IV.
Weekly Magazine—4 Nos.

Writing

Composition
   Letters, uncopied . . . . pp. 50.
   Reviews, Index &c. . . . . 10.

Transcription
   Principally Papers sent for the
   Repository in Letters &c. with   pp. 20.
   corrections, & articles of News.

Add to this Miscellaneous Professional reading; Mineralogy; writing for the Repository; for Manumission Socy. &c. &c. Published my Discourse this Month.

MEMOIRS. 1798. JUNE.

Friday, 1.—Began to re-read & to review Dr. Davidge's Essay on Yellow Fever. Wrote a few lines to Mr. Quincy of Boston. Read the Weekly Magazine No. 14. 16. & 17. Corrected two proofs of the Repository. Dr. Seaman came here—& I accompanied him to see some of his patients, who he leaves under my care, during his journey to Phila.—whither he goes as a member of the Convention. A long visit to one of my patients. Errands. Visit from Mr. Gahn—who has just returned from his Southern tour. Visit from Dunlap. Medical visit. At Dunlap's. At Riley's—whence I went, with the family, to the Theater—where we saw Lewis's "Castle Spectre." The House was very full; the piece very well played; & remarkably well received.

Saturday, 2.—Read the papers. Three medical visits—all of which being at some distance, & some requiring much attention, occupied a large portion of the forenoon. Visit from Boyd. Visit to Mr. Miller—& to Dr. Mitchill. At the Hospital. Medical visit. Visit from Mitchill—we made a call together. Visit from Mr. Cooper, Comedian. Corrected a proof of the Repository. Visit from Dr. Osborn. He & Johnson & I walked on the Battery. There I encountered Mr. Senter of Newport, who has just returned from Phila. We drank tea at home—& went into the Warm Bath in the evening. Corrected a proof of the Repository—& also a paper for that publication. Recd. a letter from Mr. Rice, bookseller, Baltimore.

Sunday, 3.—All the forenoon busied in attending to Dr. Seaman's patients & my own—except that I visited Dunlap, & heard him read the two first acts of his new comedy "Rule a Husband, & have a Husband."[32] Dined, & spent part of the afternoon at H. Johnson's. Found Dr. Osborn here when I returned. Read to him & Wm. "Knave or Not?" Medical visit. Part of the evening at Catlin's. Read "False Impressions."[33] Poor thing.

Monday, June 4.—Mr. Senter breakfasted & spent some time with me. Four medical visits. Calls & errands. A medical visit. At our printer's. Visit from Dr. Osborn, & went with him on some business. Read Reynolds's "Cheap Living"—a poor Comedy: Arnold's "Shipwreck"[34]—a so so afterpiece—& Franklin "Wandering Jew," & "Trip to the Nore"—trifling things. Went with Mr. Senter & Dr. Osborn out to the State Prison. Medical visit. Corrected a proof of the Repository. Recd. letters from Mr. Allen, Congress—& Dr. Kollock. Read a part of Dr. Waterhouse's Discourse before the Middlesex (Mass.) Medical Association. Evening partly at home—the Osborns here; & partly at Mr. Radcliff's.

Tuesday, 5.—Three medical visits. Finished Waterhouse's Discourse—but think very lightly of it—both in

---

[32] Dunlap finished this comedy November 30, 1798 (Dunlap, *Diary* 1: p. 354); he does not mention it again in his *Diary*. Coad (*Dunlap*) does not discuss the play or list it as one of Dunlap's works.
[33] Richard Cumberland, *False Impressions* (1797).
[34] Frederick Reynolds, *Cheap Living* (1797). James Arnold, *The Shipwreck* (London, 1796); there are three other plays of this name: by Coleman, Jr., Richard Cumberland, and *The Shipwreck, or Neptune's Favor*, anonymous (1799).

respect of matter & manner. Errands—partly for my father, partly for myself. Posting the books of the Repository. At the Hospital, longer than usual—as I had some particular business there. Came home, & went with Dr. Osborn & Mr. Senter to see Dr. Post's Anatomical Museum—where we spent near two hours. Long visit from Mitchill, who brought with him, & read, three reviews—& to whom I read my review of Currie. Further labour with the Accounts of the Repository. I am getting all my little matters arranged that I may visit Connecticut. Visit from Dunlap—who read me his letter to Hodgkinson, & the impudent reply. Two medical visits. Johnson & I drank tea at G. M. Woolsey's—then walked on the Battery—where we were joined by Mr. Gahn, & by H. & Mrs. Johnson. We all went into Columbia Garden[35]—& on our return, Johnson & I spent the remainder of the evening at Mr. Morton's.

Wednesday, 6.—Read the Papers as usual. A visit from Mr. Deming of Lichfield, who brought me a letter from my father, & one from Mrs. Tracy. By this last I am reinstated in all her friendship—& its different, & even distant, dates bespeak the steadiness of her esteem. I am sorry to find her converted, by the French Revolution, to Christianity. Yet such is the fact. And it is probably the fact also of many others. I shall not attempt to unsettle her faith. In her situation some sentiment beyond what reason ordinarily inspires, some intellectual opium or incitant, may be necessary, or rather unavoidable. Let her continue to use it. She will still be one of the most excellent of women. Visit from Dunlap. Recd. Ebenr. G. Marsh's (of Wethersfield) *Phi Beta Kappa* Oration. This, considering his youth, & his having just emerged from College, is a very honourable proof of his industry & proficiency. Four medical visits. Errands for my father & self. Business at our printer's. Wrote to Dr. Kollock. Visit from Dr. Osborn. We dined & spent the afternoon at Dr. Post's. Mr. Senter, & several N. York physicians were there. Two medical visits. Calls. Drank tea & spent part of the evening at Mr. Miller's—the rest at Mrs. Templeton's. Miss T. has read half of Lavoisier. Executed further writing on the Accts. of the Repository.

Thursday, 7.—How small a part of my time is usefully employed—so numerous are my interruptions. Three medical visits. Dunlap writing here much of the forenoon. Call from J. Osborn. Made some little progress in my review of Davidge. At the Hospital, longer than usual. Recd. a letter from my sister Mary. She progresses as fast in philosophy as Mrs. Tracy in religion. Why am I so separated from this excellent sister? Continued my review of Davidge—amid much confusion of intellect—till, dissatisfied with what I had done, I threw it aside, & resolved to begin anew. To compose my thoughts, I looked over the contents of Stauton's Embassy & Hearne's Journal,[36] & read a few pages in Hugh Trevor, all of which I have this day got. I had just resumed my task, when Mitchill came in, & spent an hour. I made little further progress. Corrected a proof of the Repository. Drank tea at S. Johnson's. Wm. & I walked on the Battery. We visited at Riley's. Corrected a proof of the Repository. Continued Hugh Trevor, which I have once more commenced.

Friday, May 8.—Continued my review of Davidge, more to my mind. Four medical visits. Calls. At the Hospital, on account of a particular patient. At the meeting of citizens in my Ward for the appointment of a Committee, with Committees from the other Wards, &c. to fix on measures for the defence of the City. Learnt that Dr. Miller had returned. A considerable part of the afternoon with him, at his house. Mitchill there also. Account of the Journey, forth & back; of the Convention; Medical affairs; &c. &c.—Medical visit. Visit at Woolsey's—& to Mr. Senter. At intervals thro' the day & evening, read Hugh Trevor. Recd. short letters from Mr. Tracy, & from Mr. Wolcott—Secy. of the Treasy.

Saturday, 9.—Read the papers. Finished Hugh Trevor Vol. II. Continued my review of Davidge, considerably to my mind. A visit from Dunlap. A visit from Roulet. Three medical visits. At the Hospital. Continued Hugh Trevor. Medical visit. Long visit from Miller. At our printer's. Various errands. Medical visit. Johnson & I walked on the Battery, & went home with Miss Morton, & spent some time there. We went into the Bath—& afterwards called at H. Johnson's. I recd. a few lines from C. B. Brown—& continued Hugh Trevor.

Sunday, 10.—Continued & nearly finished Hugh Trevor. Wrote a letter to my Father. Three medical visits, each of which occupied much time. Johnson & I walked on the Battery. A visit to Dr. Seaman who returned yesterday. We dined & spent a part of the afternoon at H. Johnson's. Visit to Mr. Sharples. A visit to Mr. Deming of Lichfield, at his lodgings. Visit to Dunlap. Found Dr. Osborn of N. Ca. here, when I came home.

Monday, 11.—Medical visit. At Miller's. Read the publication of the Acad: of Medicine of Phila. on Yellow Fever 1797, in opposition to the Coll. of Phys. of Phila.—which is conclusive. Read also Saml. Harrison Smith's pamphlet on Education[37]—about pp. 90—8vo. a very moderate performance. Much, of both parts of the day occupied in errands for my father, for the Repository, & in writing for this last. A medical consultation at the Hospital. Some errands on my own business.

---

[35] Columbia Garden was near the junction of State and Pearl Streets. See I.N.P. Stokes, *Iconography of Manhattan Island* **3**: p. 977; **6**: p. 623.

[36] Sir George Staunton, *An Authentic Account of an Embassy from the King of Great Britain to the Emperor of China* ... (London, 1797); Samuel Hearne, *Journey from the Prince of Wales's Fort in Hudson's Bay to the Northern Ocean; undertaken by order of the Hudson's Bay Company for the Discovery of Copper Mines, a North-West Passage, etc. in the years 1769, '70, '71, '72* (London, 1795).

[37] *Remarks on Education* (Philadelphia, 1798).

Medical visit. A visit from Mitchill. Drank tea & spent part of the evening, at Mr. Rogers's—some further part of the evening at G. Mumford's. Read the Poetry, & the Histy. of English Literature, in the New Annual Register for 1796. Corrected a proof-sheet of the Repository.

Thursday, 12.—Finished the perusal & review of Dr. Davidge's pamphlet. Visit from Dunlap. Medical visit. At our printer's, & corrected a proof of the Repository. Errands. Visit to Mitchill. At the Hospital—& detained there longer than usual. Dined, & spent part of the afternoon at G. M. Woolsey's, in company with Genl. Gordon,[33] Mr. Rogers, W. W. Woolsey, Dunlap, & Johnson. Wrote a letter to Mr. Tracy. Medical visit. Called on Mitchill, & we went to see Miss Bayard of Brunswick, at her brother's, Dr. Bayard—where we drank tea. Miss Templeton was there—& Mr. W. Bleecker,[39] & Dr. Tucker,[40] formerly member of Congress from So. Ca. Came home & posted books for the Repository.

Wednesday, 13.—Read the papers. Medical visits. Visits of business, to collect money &c. At Miller's—& we went to call on Dr. Leigh of Virginia. He was not at home. Began, & made some progress in the transcription of Mitchill's review of Barton's Collections—with corrections & additions. A visit from Dr. Osborn & Dr. Leigh. Read Disborough's Inaugural Essay on Cholera Infantum—8vo. pp. 32. Dined at W. W. Woolsey's, with nearly the same company as yesterday. Visit from the Osborn's. Read the Monthly Review for March 1798—which, except Polwhelle's Devonshire & Howard's Thoughts on the Globe, contains very little matter of interest. Walked with Mr. Radclift, at whose house, after a visit to Mr. Duryee's, I past some time.

Thursday, June 14.—Two medical visits. Finished the Review of Barton's Collections. Visit to Miller. We went to see Mitchill. He was absent. We went to the Hospital. Read Mr. Cooke's Inaugural Essay on Tetanus—8vo. pp. about 40. Read Mr. Prioleau's on the Nitric & Oxygenated Muriatic Acids—8vo. pp. about 70. Book-posting for the Repository. Recd. short letters from Mr. Tracy & Nathl. Dwight. Two medical visits. Spent the evening at Riley's—where were Mr. & Mrs. Pomeroy, from Cambridge, Mass. W. W. Woolsey & wife &c. Wrote letters to Mr. Tracy, & to C. B. Brown & to Mr. Scandella.

Friday, 15.—Three medical visits. Errands for my father, self, & the Repository. At Miller's. Visit from Mitchill & Miller; & from Dunlap. Medical visit. Finished the writing for the Repository. Miller assisted me in adjusting one of the accts. At our printer's. Visit to Mr. Gahn, who will, probably have sailed for Europe before my return from the country. Three medical visits. Drank tea at Dunlap's. Visit to Miss Mason. Visit to S. Johnson's. Called, with Wm. at Riley's—all out. We walked on the Battery. Medical visit. Wrote letters to Dr. Kollock, Revd. Dr. Morse, & to my sister Mary.

Saturday, 16.—Read the papers. Three medical visits —the last in company with Dr. Seaman, on whom I had previously called, & who is to supply my place during my absence. Corrected a proof-sheet of the Repository. Visit from Dunlap: from Mr. Gahn, who is going to Phila. & will probably have gone for Europe before my return. Visit from Saml. M. Hopkins—who has just returned from France. He has been in Europe 22 months—is in good health, & has come back, as he went, an American; improved, but not corrupted. Called on Miller. Went to the Hospital. Mitchill was there. I prescribed, & left my patients under his care. Put up my things. Medical visit. Called on Woolsey. Came aboard the packet for N. Haven: had some difficulty in getting out—wind high—& directly a-head. Several passengers—nothing very remarkable.

Sunday, 17.—Notwithstanding the direct contrariety of the wind, we contrived to beat into New Haven, & landed about eight P. M. I was not sick in the least—& qualmish but for a moment. This was fortunate—& unusually so: for I am generally nauseated, tho' seldom sick. Called at Mr. Webster's, & saw them all, a few minutes. Secured my lodgings, for the night—& a place in the stage, for the morrow. A short visit to Dr. Dwight —at whose house I found Mr. Rogers from N. York— & some other gentleman. Webster had given me Humphrey Marshall's "Aliens."[41] I read this wretched pamphlet—supped & slept.

Monday, 18.—Rose before sunrise—& sat off in the stage, for Lichfield. Road bad. Breakfasted at Derby. A fine, picturesque, but small, view up the river, from the bank just before Wheeler's tavern. Dined, seasonably, at Woodbury, & here got rid of all my company. Southbury pleasant; & Woodbury. The Sugar-Maple-trees, on each side the street, very ornamental. They are one of our most beautiful trees; & on every acct. desirable. At Bethlem I saw Mr. & Mrs. Backus a few minutes. They look well & happy. He gave me a copy of his Election Sermon. Arrived at Lichfield between 5 & 6 P. M.[42] This is the first time that I have been here, in the summer season, since my residence in N. York—& the place never looked pleasanter. I found

---

[38] General Gordon: not identified.

[39] Mr. Bleeker was a prominent and probably wealthy New Yorker said to have been a member of the Friendly Club after Smith's death.

[40] Thomas Tudor Tucker, M.D. (1745-1828), studied medicine at the University of Edinburgh, a surgeon in the Revolution, U.S. House 1787-1788, 1789-1793, appointed U.S. Treasurer by Jefferson 1801-death 1828.

[41] Humphrey Marshall, "The Aliens: a Patriotic Poem" (Philadelphia, 1798).

[42] There is something very like advanced hysteria in this tremendous flurry of visiting which Smith carried on between June 18 and July 6. He called on and visited with at least one hundred fifty people and many more than that if one were to count the families of those he visited. It would be overdramatic to suggest that he had some forewarning of his imminent death and was therefore saying farewell to all of his friends, but certainly some force was working on him to raise his last trip home to Litchfield to a point of such social frenzy.

my sisters well—& my parents better than I expected. I spent the evening at home. Danl. W. Lewis was here a short time. He thrives & grows fat.

Tuesday, June 19.—Visited at Lewis's. He was gone. Betsey was at home—& looks better than usual. They have moved since I was here; & things look more comfortable about them. A long visit, of nearly the whole forenoon, at Mrs. Tracy's. This was the renovation of ancient pleasures, augmented by the presence, & intelligent conversation of her daughters, who are now old enough to contribute to the delights of confidential intercourse. The two youngest, of the three first, have grown very much: Susan the most. She is less disfigured by the Small-Pox than I expected—but, still, her countenance is considerably altered. They have a pleasing view of our Lakes from their window, which I never noticed so much before. And I saw one of our marsh-plants, or rather flower, of an uncommon form & beauty. I did not dissect, & can not, therefore, determine its place in the System, or its scientific name. The popular name is, "Jack-in-his-pulpit." After dinner, a visit to Frederic Wolcott, who is confined with Rheumatism. A visit to Parmele's. His wife has two fine children. Here I saw the medical veteran—*Bird*. He is surrendered to drink, in great measure—but we had an hour of instructive conversation. A visit to Collier. Sally Pierce drank tea with us. I spent part of the evening at Mr. Lord's. The Carbonate of Soda, which he took a year ago, by my direction, relieved all his complaints, & he continued free of them for a long time. Undue exertions of exercise &c. have brought them on in a degree. I advise the repetition of the remedy. His disease is, probably, a thickening of the bladder, from inflammation, occasionally returning—accompanied with some chemical change in the quality of the urine, & with some schircosity near the neck of the bladder. The remainder of the evening at home.

Wednesday, 20.—I wrote the preceeding notes, since my departure from New York, this morning; as also a letter to William Johnson. Visited Mr. Champion—Mrs. Brace—& Dr. Sheldon—at all of whose houses I spent some time. In the afternoon, Dr. Sheldon was here. Abby & I made a visit to Capt. Catlin's. All look healthy. Then we ascended the summit of the hill behind the house where Mr. Stanton used to live—whence we enjoyed the fine prospect of the lakes, & the pleasing view of our little town. When we returned, we visit Miss Pierce, & Miss Sally Pierce. We drank tea, with the rest of our family, at Mrs. Tracy's; & spent the evening. Capt. Bull & his wife, from Chestnut Hill were there—(he looks unwell) & Dr. Bull from Hartford—Mr. Gould & Mr. Day, the young gentleman who is to deliver the 4th of July Oration at Hartford, this year. He seems clever—& nothing more. When I came home I found Daniel W. Lewis & Dr. Sheldon here. They sat some time. This day, also, I saw my cousins Abby Morris & Hannah Hubbard. The first has grown very much: the last I have not seen since she was a child of four or five—she is now 14—and appears to be an amiable, intelligent girl.

Thursday, 21. June.—It rains. A call on D. W. Lewis. He is out. A call on Mr. Reeve, & he is from home. A visit to Dr. & Mrs. Catlin. A visit to Collier, with whom I find Lewis. A call on Mrs. Tracy. A visit at Col. Tallmadge's. At home some time in the afternoon. A visit from Gould. A visit to Lewis—Betsey unwell. A visit to Wolcott. Drank tea with Mr. Reeve. Gould lives there. Mr. Reeve sociable. His new wife a fat, ruddy, woman—neither very homely, nor handsome—nor remarkably stupid, nor intelligent. Came home, & found here Dr. Sheldon, Lewis, & the two Pierces—Timothy & James: the first of whom returned this day from his journey. He looks well, & really appears graceful & polite, by the side of his brother.

Friday, 22.—Visit from Dr. Sheldon. We went to see a patient of his; & as this was at Majr. Seymour's, I made my visit there. Afterwards I called at Lewis's. He was absent, & Betsey unwell. Visited at Skinner's. Called at Mr. Deming's, but he was absent. In the afternoon, read many of Mary's & Idea's letters from Aurora, to Abby. A visit from Mr. Chase, the Southfarms Clergyman. A visit to Mrs. Tracy, to whom I read Mrs. Paxon's "Contrast," "Charity"—& the three first *letters* between "Henry & Mary D."[43]—much to her gratification. Drank tea & spent the evening with the Pierces. Lewis & his wife were there. Polly Pierce has improved very much. She converses well—& her face is intelligent, & even handsome. Fanny went with me: Elijah came afterwards—& Hannah Hubbard was present. I like this little cousin very much, notwithstanding her forward mother. Sally Pierce has now a School of thirty young misses, from this town, & the neighbouring parts of this State & of Massachusetts. Polly assists her. The reputation of her school is established.

Saturday, 23.—A visit from Timy. Pierce—and from Dr. Sheldon. Pierce & I make a tour thro' woods, fields & meadows, looking at birds, flowers & trees, & plucking strawberries. Our principal search was after the flower mentioned in my Note of Tuesday last. We did not find it wild—probably as the time of flowering is past, & we did not know the plant. At length, we discovered a single flower in the garden of one who had had taste enough to remove & cultivate it. He permitted us to bear it off—& when I reached home, I busied myself in a plan of it, in various views. It is *Gynandria-Digynia*; and, if I am not much mistaken, a *Cypripedium*. In the afternoon, a long visit to Dr. Sheldon. Called at Sally Pierce's. A visit from Mr. Morris of the Sh. Farms. We went to Mr. Lord's. We drank tea at my father's. Called on Mr. Deming—& at D. W. Lewis's. Evening at home, reading the newspapers from New York. Recd. letters from Wm. Johnson, Mr. Tracy & Dr. Mease.

---

[43] Frances Paxton.

Sunday, 24.—The forenoon occupied in writing to Wm. Johnson, Mr. Tracy, Dr. Mitchill, Dr. Mease, & Dr. Buel. Afternoon at meeting. Drank tea, with Elijah, at Mr. Lord's. Calls at Mr. Adams's, Parmele's, Smith's &c. Evening at home. Lewis & his wife—the Pierces &c. here.

Monday, 25.—A solitary journey, on horse-back, from Lichfield to Hartford. I find few improvements on this road. The most obvious change, and one certainly to be regretted, is the destruction of wood. Birds were very plenty; yet not so plenty as formerly, when the road was more invested with woods. Between Bristol and Farmington I met Dr. James Wells of Berlin: well—& to be at home by the time I shall reach that place. At Farmington I saw the Smiths &c.—well; & the Lewises—well. Abby Lewis has improved in appearance. She recd. me with great cordiality. I saw also, for the first time, Joshua Saltonstall, the brother of Dudley—a young man whose appearance is prepossessing, & whose countenance indicates good sense, good humour, & sensibility. He is out of health. I saw Timy. Pitkin. At Farmington, likewise, I found Dr. Hopkins of Hartford—on a journey from home, & spent a few minutes with him—disappointed in not seeing him at his own house. I reached Hartford at sun-set. The evening was spent at Theodore Dwight's. He, his wife, & three children, are all well. Nathaniel Dwight, who was married last evening, was here with his wife—Ezekl. Williams & his wife—all well. N. Dwight goes to Northampton tomorrow. He accepts his appointment, as Surgeon's Mate, in the new Corps of Artillerists, & will, probably, soon leave Hd. This is a further & twofold disappointment: I want more conversation with him, now, concerning the Repository—& he will of course relinquish the care of it in that quarter. Slept at Bull's Tavern.

Tuesday, June 26.—Rose early, & looked around me. The Main Street of this town has altered less than I expected. Several good houses have been erected, the path is levelled, & the State House is handsome—the handsomer, I think, for the first story's being of stone—Called on Dr. Bull—& at Wm. Moseley's. Breakfasted with Dwight. After breakfast, we called at Capt. Chenevard's, to see Cogswell & the family. They look here much as usual. Dwight left me with Cogswell, who is the same to-day, & forever I believe. Our first call was at Dr. Hopkins's—not to see him, who is out of town, but his wife & daughter. This is a lovely girl. We next had a pleasant visit at Dr. Fish's. This gentleman recd. me with evident marks of pleasure. We made a short call at J. Chenevard's, principally to see his wife. She is a plain housewife now—& a stranger would wonder what had become of the beauties which were so much the theme of discourse & the occasion of rivalship, in Miss Julia Seymour. Next we visited at E. Morgan's. Here, also, it was the lady that I wished to see. Mrs. Morgan is the same as Sally Webb. We met with like expressions of kindness on either part; & saluted as we were wont, when we called each other brother & sister, of which she affectionately rememberd me, who had not forgotten it. She seems happily situated. A visit at Ezekl. Williams's, in whose office I wrote a hasty letter to Dr. Miller, terminated this forenoon's work. Cogswell dined with me at Theodore's, where also we found Saml. W. Pomeroy, who has just arrived from New York—leaving at Middletown—his wife, Miss Alsop, & J. Alsop, who had so far accompanied him. After dinner he returned to Middletown, Cogswell attended to his business, & Theodore & I sat off. Our first visit was to William Brown. He looks well. I did not see his wife—which I regret. He was to have spent the evening at Dwight's—but disappointed us. From Brown's, we called on Mr. Trumbull—(McFingal). He looks thin & pale—but is somewhat better than he has been. He was polite & sociable—sure marks that this attention on my part, was not displeasing to him. Returning from Trumbull's, we overtook Mrs. Thomas Chester—formerly Hetty Bull—& who once considerably influenced my conduct. I had planned a visit; but this accidental meeting spared me the trouble. She is little altered—& was sufficiently affable. Dwight went home. I sat off, alone, to make some further calls. I visited, for fifteen minutes, Mr. Strong. His daughter Nancy has grown to a woman. He is the same. I called at Amos Bull's. Lucy is at Middletown. He is unchanged. I visited Mrs. Asa Hopkins. She has three or four children. I had previously seen him in the morning. This has proved a happy match—for which I rejoice the more, as I was principally instrumental in effecting it. It was at Elisha Lewis's, that I had seen Hopkins, in company with Cogswell, & in the morning—a circumstance which I had forgot to mention; & another neglect was not to remark that I called at Hudson & Goodwin's, & made a conditional arrangement with them, relative to the Repository. From Hopkins's, I went to Col. Wadsworth's. Here Cogswell rejoined me. While there, Mr. Wadsworth, & Mr. & Mrs. Terry, returned from Lebanon. We drank tea there. The evening was spent at Dwight's. I slept at Bull's.

Wednesday, June 27.—Breakfasted at Dwight's. We went into the State-House. The view from the front gallery is pleasant: I admire neither the arrangement, nor ornaments, of the rooms. The Senate Chamber is least exceptionable. I made a visit to Mr. Terry. Cogswell joined me there. They were sociable. The *Carolina Chatterer* has appeared among them for the last three years—to the great destruction of fruits, & especially of *Peas.* Hence the people, here, who did not know the bird, have called it the "Pea-bird." The sealing-wax on the wing-quills, is curious. We called at Mr. Wadsworth's—but he was absent. This street is very pleasant, & much improved since I was here. Mr. Wadsworth's house is remarkably elegant. Cogswell & I called a few minutes on Kingsley. He is better—but far from being well. We went to see Emily Stillman. She is well. Morton is now here. We saw him, now, & before. These visits over—I mounted my horse, took leave of Theodore, & with Cogswell in company, pranced to Wethersfield. Our attention was attracted, on the way, by large numbers of the Pond Lily (Nymphœa), in some pools on the road, & by a still greater collection of another smooth-leaved water-flower. It is a blue—& grows in spikes. There was some difficulty in examining it on horseback; & I could not certainly determine whether it was *dian*—or *trian-dria, monogynia*. It is quite beautiful; & I must find it out. We called at Daniel & at Josiah Buck's—but saw only the ladies. They are well. Catharine M. Richards was at the first. She is much improved, and resembles Ben. Mumford remarkably. We found John Williams the same as ever—& dined with him. After dinner, we called to see my classmate, Dr. Moseley, who has moved into Wethersfield since I left it: but he was not at home. Cogswell returned to Hartford—& Williams also went over, with a small party, previously made up. I visited at Frederic Butler's. This family is much altered since I was here. The situation most to be lamented is by the death of Mrs. B's mother. The family is no longer interesting. I next called at Mr. Mitchill's—& saw him, Walter, & the twins—one of whom has grown a fine girl. The Judge was sociable & communicative, as usual. Hence to Josh. Webb's. He is in Jail. I saw his wife, & most of her children; a very pretty daughter of John Webb's, who is here. Mrs. Webb is a remarkably fine woman. She is much the same—except less cheerful than when I lived here—no doubt from the circumstances of the family. I had a longer visit at Stephen Chester's. I drank tea there. These people are also the same—except that Mrs. C. has grown too very fat—&, what I was still more sorry to see, did not look so nice as formerly. As I was retiring, Miss Chester entered, with her Grandmother Mrs. Huntington—from Norwich, the old lady who had been cured by me of dangerous fever in 1792. She was overjoyed to see me—& was loud in her grateful recollections of my services. When I went back to Williams's, I found Col. & Mrs. Belden there, & he just returned from Hartford. We soon left them—& made a visit to Col. Chester's. Mrs. C. was a-bed, with a 12th or 13th child. He is as formerly: but has three daughter's grown up since I was here. Hannah, the third, is an elegant girl. Several young misses were visiting here—& among others, Miss Hannah Mitchill—She is now a woman. We came home, & sat up some time to converse.

Thursday, 28.—After breakfast, Williams & I made a visit to Col. Belden's. On our way, we met & had some talk with Dr. Olcott. From Belden's, we called at Capt. Williams's, afterwards at the Sheriff's, who entertained me with a long story of a law-suit, and then at Mr. Marsh's. His daughter Polly is well-looking, promising girl. We called at Mrs. Riley's, & then at Mrs. Deming's. At this last place I saw Jennet Riley who is the finest looking girl I have seen here—tho' I left her a fat, chubby-faced, short child. I also made a short call at Capt. Tryon's. All this visiting being completed, I mounted my nag, took leave of Williams, & rode to Middletown to dinner. After a hasty repast at the tavern, went to Alsop's. He from home; but returned in about an hour. Mrs. Alsop well, as she used to be. His children all grown; & all queer. It is impossible to foresee what they will be. Alsop has been much busied with politics the winter & spring past. I read some of his pieces, in verse & prose. His prose is handsome. He translates Italian—& has been collecting his poetical scraps. They are not yet all transcribed. He has collected a few mineral specimens for me. He is also busy in collecting & preparing american birds, & has got one case of twenty. He has given away numbers to the Miss Russells, who are forming a collection to send to England. His small selection are beautiful, & well preserved. We visited at his mother's—& found there Mr. & Mrs. Pomeroy, Miss & Miss [sic] F. Alsop, & Mrs. Meigs their cousin, beside John, & the old ladies. At evening, I went out to my Uncle's—two & half miles from town. I found them pretty well, with the addition of three children since I was here last. My grandmother is near 91, & much weakened in body & mind.

Friday, June 29.—My grandmother recognized me perfectly by sun-light. She was unwilling to have me depart; & gave me all ghostly counsel, with many repetitions. Standing at my uncle's door, I noticed an excellence in the symphony with which a Boblincon preluded his song, altogether new & unrivalled. I find very little of this in the bird in general, & in many individuals nothing. I rode into town. I had just shifted my riding clothes, & dressed myself for my visits, when the Alsops besought me to join a party, for spending the day on a mountain at some distance. I went in a Coachee with Miss R. Alsop, Mrs. Pomeroy, & Mr. Pomeroy. Alsop rode my horse. We were several carriages & horsemen. The ride was pleasant, south west, nine miles, to the foot of the mountain. The principal divisions of the party had reached, ascended, & sheltered themselves on it, just as we arrived, & a most powerful thunderstorm came up. We sat dry & merry in the carriages, till it disappeared; and then, partly on horseback, & partly on foot, ascended the mountain—where we found a pleasant company, a magnificent prospect, music, & an excellent cold collation. The party, excepting servants, consisted of 14 ladies & 12 gentlemen, in all twenty-six—composed by—Mr. Russell, (formerly of Birmingham) his son & two daughters; Mrs. Sheridan, their aunt, from Maryland, & her two pretty daughters, Miss Russells & son Mr. Russell, by a former husband; Mr. Watkinson, the father, his two sons, his son-in-law, & his three eldest unmarried daughters, all pleasing; Capt. Mrs. & Miss Van [blur]; Mr., Mrs., Miss F. & Mr. J. Alsop; Mrs. Meigs, & Mr. & Miss Pomeroy, & myself. Never was a finer day, after the storm went over—& we stayed till five in the afternoon. They call this mountain, the Bassick, or Beesic mountain. The ancient Indian name of Middletown, according to Trumbull, was Mettabeesick—whence probably the name of this hill—which lies nearly between Durham & Wallingford—& commands a very beautiful & extensive prospect on the east & west—by a small change of position, of a few feet. The ascent on the east side is steep—& the precipice on the west, about 200 feet. On the east, the view extends to Mount Tom. near Northampton—to Brandford or Guilford on the South. On the West, you see beyond Southington, with great distinctness, northerly; & to the south, New Haven harbour & the Sound (in a very clear day Long Island) are fully visible. Water & stupendous mountains are wanting to the completeness of prospect which, without them, is unusually beautiful. Our ride home was pleasant. We had been very sociable—& the flute of the young men, & the voices of the young ladies united themselves, much to our delight, under the shades on the summit. I had scarcely alighted, when Dr. Osborn came to see me. I accompanied him to his house, where I made a short visit, & saw Joseph Osborn. Visit to my Uncle Elijah Hubbard's—in whose house I had not been, before, for ten or twelve years. I did not see his wife. She doubtless, did not wish to see me. Visit to Mrs. Alsop's. Here I saw Lucy Bull. Returned to Mr. Alsop's—where I slept.

Saturday, June 30.—My first visit was to Dr. Osborn. With him I had a long & sociable conversation—or rather I heard him talk freely. His discourse related principally to the state of medicine in Connecticut—which it is true, promises very little, suddenly. Called at Nehemiah Hubbard's. Sally is as pretty as ever. Visit to Dr. Hall. He subscribed for the Repository. Call on M. T. Russell. Call at Mr. Latimer's. His wife the same as when Miss Riley of Wethersfield. Visit & farewell at Mrs. Alsop's. Saw there, this morning, Mrs. Josh. Alsop—(Lucy Whittlesey) & went with Richard to her house; where I saw two fine views of Naples, & two of Vesuvie. Alsop & I called on Mr. Miller, & looked over his nascent collection of Minerals. Mr. Miller will be glad to promote our N. York mineralogical scheme. At Mr. Whittlesey's—& saw the ladies. Met Miss Bull there. Dined at Alsop's. My last visit was to Mr. Johnson's—& saw Mr. & Mrs. Johnson—& had previously seen Henry, in the morning. My ride to Berlin was, considering the heat of the day, very agreable; & I was regaled with the chant of birds & variety of beautiful prospects, at every stage of my progress.

Memoranda of receits &c.

Recd. of Dr. Cogswell 0..50 cents for "Barton's Collections." I am to send him Zoonomia & The Botanic Garden.
Recd. of W. B. Hall—2..50, for "Medical Repository Vol. I."—to be sent him.
Recd. of El. Smith jr. 1..50, for two of "Alcuin," & one of "André"; & 1 dol. for two of "Alcuin" P. 3 & 3. He subscribes for "Sky-Walk," & "Weekly Magazine." Dr. Todd subscribes for "Alcuin" & "Sky-Walk." I shall send him "Webster's Collections." Timy. Pitkin subscribes for "Alcuin."
To get a pound of opium for Saml. Smith of Farmington.
To subscribe for, or procure, for John Williams of Wethersfield—"The New Annual Register," "The Monthly Review," "The Monthly Magazine," "The Weekly Magazine," "The Botanic Garden," "Staunton's Embassy," "Alcuin," &c. pc.
Recd. of my father 2..50—for Aaron Coleman of Kent, a subscriber for the Repository.
To get for Mr. Miller of Middletown—six ʒ IV glass-stopper vials, two oil flasks, one small glass funnel, one glass rod, four glass syphons.
Mr. Reeve put, by mistake, 3 bushels of Gypsum on ¾ acre of exhausted land, clover only blow—naturally good—soil thin—small flat stones: clover above knees got off at the lowest estimation, two ton of hay—second year, very bad for hay, one ton & an half, real fruitfulness not diminished. Third year fed it—& more pasturage than from 4. acres of our common excellent pasture.
June 22nd gave my Note to Reuben Smith of Lichfield, for £48..5..9 Connet. Cury. or $160..94 cents.
Expences to Lichfield —7..76.
To Hartfd. &c. and back 2..86½.
4th July . . . . . 1..—
To New York . . . . 7..45.
                                    ―――
                                    19 –7½

Industry of June 1798

Dr. Waterhouse's Discourse before the Middlesex (Mass.) Medl: Associat.
Proofs of the Origin of Yellow Fever in 1797, by Acad: of Med: of Phila.
Disborough's Inaug: Es. on Cholera Infantum—8vo. pp. 32.
Cooke's .. do. .... on Tetanus... pp. 40—8vo.
Prideau's—on Nitric & Oxy-Muriatic Acids—pp. 70—8vo.
Saml. H. Smith's Prize-Essay on Education—pp. 90—8vo.
English History & Poetry of New Annual Register for 1796.
Holcroft's "Hugh Trevor"—4 vols. 12mo. edit. Dublin.
E. G. Marsh's Φ B K Oration.
Monthly Review for March.
Cumberland's "False Impressions."
Reynold's "Cheap Living."
"Shipwreck."—Franklin's "Wandering Jew" & "Trip to the Nore."[44]

Writing

Composition
  Review of Davidge . . . .—pp. 10.
  Letters, uncopied . . . . — 30.
Transcription
  Articles for Repository &c. . . . . . 10.

---

[44] Andrew Franklin, *The Wandering Jew* (London, 1797); also *Trip to the Nore* (London, 1797).

Deduct, a fortnight, employed in journeying: add the correction of Proof sheets, & adjustments of Accounts; beside current reading, study, & re-reading.

MEMOIRS. 1798. JULY.

Sunday, 1.—As I entered Berlin last evening, I met James Wells. He accompanied me to Elnathan Smith's, and spent the evening. I found Elnathan somewhat thin, and not in the most robust health, but pretty well. His wife a tall woman, & rather handsome—but not much improved. His child pretty. Miss Wright, who makes a part of his family, was unwell; & his brother Joseph not very well. We went to bed late. This morning we were alarmed by finding Joseph missing—tho the doors were locked, & most of his clothes remained in his room. Inquiry was made in all directions; & to shorten a story which I have not time to be minute upon, he returned at noon. It seems that he rose in sleep, put on only over-alls & surtout, & walked to his father's—which is 4½ miles distant. He had escaped thro' the chamber window from his brother's; he entered by the same passage at his father's, and went to bed, without waking. He rouzed, this forenoon, by some of the family entering his chamber—of whom he inquired what brought them to his brother's. Their reply, & the evidence of his own senses, soon apprized him of what had happened; but he could not persuade them of his somnambulism, till the messenger after him arrived from Elnathan's, with his letter. Poor Joseph returned; but his feet were sadly blistered—& he much fatigued. This will do for C. B. Brown. James Wells spent the day with us. Miss Wright was better. There is something interesting in the appearance, history, & character of this young lady. Sylvester Wells spent the afternoon with us. The two Welles related me some curious facts relative to Canine Madness. They have made a cure in one instance. I went with them to see a Boy, in whose brachea a thimble had been lodged near six years. I saw the thimble. The boy is now in health. The particulars I expect to receive, more fully, & for publication. I expect also the matters relative to Rabies Canina, &c. &c. from the Wellses. Elnathan's situation is very pleasant; & he has surrounded it with fruit-trees & flowering shrubs; & is making constant improvements in it. At five I sat off for Farmington. The day was sultry, but the agreableness of the country, & the musicalness of the birds, made the ride pleasant. I arrived at sunset, & went directly to Saml. Smith's. After a little visit, I went up to Mr. Lewis's. Here, beside the family, I saw Mr. Pitkin, Mr. Wadsworth (a brother of Decius), Joshua Saltonstall, & Dr. Todd. I spent the evening. I regret that I did not see Todd's wife; but I had no time to go to his house. He grows fat: admires "Alcuin"; & says that the "Repository" has roused his ambition. He has obtained 7 or 8 subscribers. He accompanied me to my temporary home. He promises a bundle of communications this autumn.

Monday, July 2.—The night was so hot that I could lie no longer than four in the morning. I took leave of the family, after breakfast, and was on horseback just as the clock struck six. I reached my father's at early dinner. I had previously made a short stop at Capt. Bull's. I found that Abby had been more unwell during my absence. Dr. Sheldon had done, & was doing something for her—she is better—but far from well. Visits from Dr. Sheldon, Mr. Wolcott, Mr. Gould, & my cousins Abby Morris & Hannah Hubbard. Evening divided between Danl. Lewis & Mrs. Tracy. At evening Dr. Buel arrived from Sheffield; but, after a few minutes conversation, went over to his mother's. I found when I came home, letters from William Johnson & Dr. Mitchill—to which I wrote answers, & put into the Mail.

Tuesday, 3.—Read some in "Robison's Conspiracy."[45] Buel came. Dr. Sheldon & others were here. We conversed. Visits to Collier—to Mrs. Tracy with whom we drank tea—& to Dr. Sheldon with whom we spent the evening. Buel lodged with us. We had a violent gust of wind here; followed by a short, but brisk rain. This renovated the atmosphere—& made the weather agreably cool. Preparations are now on foot for the celebration of the twenty-third anniversary of the Independence of the United States.

Wednesday, 4.—This morning, very early, Buel left us, to return. I devoted the morning to bringing up my Journal; & nearly conducted it to the conclusion of friday last—when Mr. Morris entered. I drest, & we joined the citizens, who had begun to assemble at Mr. Baldwin's. We had many gentlemen from Goshen. At a little after eleven the procession formed. The Independent Uniform Company, with a band of music went first, followed by the men in the order of age, & concluding by the Magistrates, Clergy, & the Orator of the day. We entered the Meeting-House, where the ladies &c. were assembled, in reverse order. The exercises opened with Music—Mr. Hooker of Goshen prayed—Mr. Gould delivered as a handsome Oration, & the whole was concluded with prayer & singing. We returned to Baldwin's, in the same order as we came. Here upwards of an hundred sat down, in the yard, to a clever dinner—patriotic toasts were drank—it was resolved to print the Oration, & a Collection was made for the purpose. Mean time the military paraded. They went thro' their firings, marchings &c. better than any corps I have seen in New York; & concluded by an unanimous Vote to offer their services to the President of the United States. This was done in a very handsome manner. They were shouldered—the Capt. desired those who were in the affirmative to order—& the order was consentaneous, & universal. The evening concluded without the least riot or disorder. Among others who

---

[45] John Robinson (1739-1805), *The Proofs of a Conspiracy against all the Religions and Governments of Europe, carried on in the Secret Meetings of Freemasons, Illumaniti and Reading Societies* (Edinburgh, 1797).

were present was Saml. M. Hopkins, who had come up from New York since I left it. He drank tea with me—as did Dr. Sheldon, Gould &c.—& his sister Susan spent the night here. Saml. & I were at Lewis's in the evening—where were the Miss Pierce's—Lucretia Collins &c. In fine, I saw many of my acquaintance this day, that [I] had not seen before, as well as others whom I had seen.

Thursday, July 5.—I have continued my Journal up to this Date to-day. I have pursued the reading of Robison's Conspiracy, till I have read nearly thro' his second chapter. Recd. letters from Dr. Miller, & from Johnson inclosing one from Dr. Dewees, & one from Dr. Buel—the last Buel mentioned his having sent to me—when he was here. These are the letters which Hopkins told me he had brought. Visit from Mr. Lord —& from various other friends & acquaintances. Hopkins & his sister went to Goshen. Visit at Aaron Smith's. Evening at Dr. Sheldon's. Dr. Hopkins of Hartford & his family there. I leave Lichfield in the morning, with many anxieties on acct. of my sister Abby, who is seriously unwell.

Friday, 6.—I took leave of my friends very early this morning—leaving Abby no better—& went, in the Stage, to New Haven. Nothing worthy of note occurred during the day. We reached N. Haven about six. I visited Dr. Dwight, Mr. Chauncey, & Mr. Webster. All well. The last is collecting materials for a Statistical Account of the State of Connecticut. I went on board the Packet at nine P. M.

Saturday, 7.—This morning we had completed near half our course. Notwithstanding, our winds were so light, & afterwards so contrary, that we did not reach New York till 7 P. M. This, however, was a short passage. The passengers few, vulgar, & noisy. I spent the evening alone, reading the newspapers. Johnson came in about ten—& we conversed till twelve. C. B. Brown has been in town some days. All are well.

Sunday, 8.—C. B. Brown breakfasted with us. He looks as usual. His health is pretty well restored. Visit from Dunlap. Visit to Dr. Seaman. Calls. Return home. Walk with Charles and William on the Battery. We all dined & spent the afternoon at H. Johnson's. Visit to, & walk with, Miller. He shewed me a short letter from Dr. Rush. His 5th vol. of Obs: and Inq. is soon to be published—and he wishes to be on good terms with the Critics—whose labours he, at last, discovers have attracted some attention. Evening at Dunlap's. Johnson & Brown there—and Mitchill.

Monday, 9.—C. B. Brown breakfasted with us. Miller called on me, and we went in search of Dr. Caldwell of Phila.—and after a tedious round of inquiry, learnt that he had gone home. Called at B. Minturn's, and found that his father has removed to Long-Island, & that I have a trip, by water to make every other day, of three miles, during the remainder of the summer. Called at Woolsey's: heard there that Mr. & Mrs. Wolcott of Phila. were at Mr. Watson's. Went thither, & found them. She quite unwell. They are on their way to Lichfield. He very sociable. Came home with me, & sat an hour. Dunlap here. At Swords's. Mitchill there. Read the papers in the 1st No. of Vol. II. of the Repository which I had not previously seen. Our printers have recd. near an hundred dollars on acct. of the Repository, since I have been gone. Writing for the Repository on the Books. Went, with several of the Minturns, to their father's place. We did not get back till after eight in the evening. Met Charles at the door, & we went, with Wm., to Seth Johnson's, where we terminated the evening. They all are well. Miss Morton was there. This day my father writes to me: I shall receive his letter on Thursday: O! that it may bring good tidings of my sister's health.

Tuesday, 10.—C. B. Brown breakfasted here. Read a number of news-papers at the "Spectator" Office. At the Hospital—where Mitchill transferred the patients to me—& I recd. some new ones. Errands. A medical visit. Visit from Mr. Roulet, from Dunlap—& Brown here. After dinner read pp. 84 in Brown's "Wieland." Medical visit, which engaged two hours. Visit at Gahn & Mumford's. Charles & I looked over and I read to him, many parts of my Journal. Medical visit. At Woolsey's—with Mr. & Mrs. Dunlap, Charles, & Johnson. Medical visit.

Wednesday, July 11.—Five medical visits in the course of the day, which has been excessively rainy. C. B. Brown has spent the day with us. He shewed me letters from his brother &c. relative to the unjustifiable means which have been employed to separate him & Miss P. A visit from Dunlap, who has been prevented by the rain from sailing, with his family, to Amboy. Finished Brown's "Wieland"—as far as he has carried it. This is a surprizing work—& no way inferior to "Sky-Walk." Continued the reading of my Journal to him. A visit from Mitchill—who brought me a letter from Dr. Wilkins of Baltimore. Yesterday I recd. a letter from Mr. Tracy. Mitchill is near concluding an arrangements for a Mineralogical Society. Johnson with us much of the day—& we indulged in conversation. Corrected two proofs of the Repository. At our printer's. We three walked on the Battery—& concluded the evening at Riley's. On our return, we read the Story which furnished the hint for a part of "Wieland."[46]

Thursday, 12.—If Dunlap went not last evening, he must have sailed to-day. As for Charles, he has taken up his abode with us. Read, yesterday, Revd. S. Griswold's (of New Milford, Connect.) pamphlet in vindication of himself: to-day Mr. Strong of Hartford's fast Sermon, Dr. Rockwell's Oration, & near half of Mr. Backus's Election Sermon. Two medical visits. At the

---

[46] The episode of Wieland's murder of his wife, five children, and a young girl is based on an account in the New York *Weekly Magazine*, July 20, 1796, "Of James Yates' Murder of His Whole Family in Tomhanick, New York in December, 1791." Warfel, *Charles Brockden Brown*, p. 104. For other direct and indirect sources see pp. 104-110.

Hospital. Visit to Mitchill, who read me part of a paper he is composing on Perspiration &c. Visit to Mr. Tisdale. Calls. Wrote letters to Mr. Tracy, Dr. Dewees, & my father. From the last, contrary to my expectations, I have recd. none. Visit medical. Visited Mr. Minturn on Long-Island, which, by unnecessary but unavoidable detention, occupied near four hours. Was relanded at Corlaer's Hook—whence I walked into town. Two medical visits. Several calls. Remainder of the evening at home—variously occupied but to no note-worthy purpose.

Friday, 13.—Finished Mr. Backus's Election Sermon, and read his funeral Sermon for Gov. Wolcott. Two medical visits. Visit to Mr. Miller. At our printer's. Numerous errands. Wrote letters to Dr. Dwight of Hartford, to Dr. Todd of Farmington, & to El. Smith Jr. of Berlin. Visit from Dr. Mitchill. Corrected two proof-sheets of the Repository. Visit from Mr. Roulet. Visit from Sam M. Hopkins, who brought me a letter from my sister Fanny. From this letter I fear that Abby is very little better, if at all. Brown, Johnson, & I walked out [of] town. We concluded the evening at home.

Saturday, 14.—Medical visit. Read the Papers. Medical visit. At the Hospital. Medical visit. Assisted Dr. Seaman &c. in an Operation. Medical visit. Read some part of Dr. Dwight's "Two Sermons." Two medical visits. Walked with Brown & Johnson to Corlaer's Hook. Thence I went over to Long Island. Was out in a storm on my return—& saw the most beautiful Rainbow that I ever saw. Two medical visits—the last at G. M. Woolsey's, whither came Wm. & his wife—who go to Connecticut tomorrow.

Sunday, 15.—Lotions & Lavations. Two medical visits. Calls on Dr. Post & Dr. Miller, ineffectually. Read some part of Dr. Dwight's Two Sermons. Brown, Johnson & I visited at Riley's, & walked on the Battery. We dined and spent the afternoon at Horace Johnson's. Thence we went to Roulet's—& from his house came back to Seth Johnson's. I left them there, & made a professional visit—which closed the day.

Monday, July 16.—Medical visit. Visit from Dr. Miller—who shewed me a letter from Dr. Mease, in which he speaks of sending us a review of a part of Dr. Rush's 5th vol. of Med: Obs. & Inq. I fear we shall have some trouble from this species of interference on the part of this man. We went to Mitchill's, resumed our Mineralogy, to which we devoted an hour, & spent the greater part of another hour on the business of the Repository. A visit to Mr. Gahn. Wrote a letter to Col. Humphreys, at Madrid, to send by Mr. Gahn, with a copy of the Repository &c. to put into the hands of some Physician or Naturalist in Spain, who may make us a similar return. Visit from Gahn. Read Triplett's Inaugural Dissertation on Apoplexy—pp. 32 8vo.—& Archer's on Croup, 8vo. pp. 46. Visit from Dr. Miller, & we went to our printer's. Thence I visited Hopkins, & procured of him a copy of Swediaur's new Work (in french) on Syphilis.[47] He came with me home—& drank tea with us; at which time we had a short call from Mr. Radclift. Then Hopkins, Brown, Johnson & I went to the College, on the business of constituting a Mineralogical Society.[48] The other Members are to be the two Millers, & Mitchill (who were also there)—Dunlap, who is out of town; Solomon Simpson, a Jew Merchant, & Geo. J. Warner, a Watch-Maker; which two last were not there. After waiting some time, we proceeded to converse & agree on the general plan, & Mitchill, Simpson & Smith were appointed a Committee to draw up Rules or a Constitution. We conversed scientifically & profitably. After I came home I read what Charles had this day written on his "Wieland"—& we conversed, & I read to him parts of my Journal.

Tuesday, 17.—Read Claiborne's Inaugural Essay on Scurvy, 8vo. pp. 43. A medical visit. Calls. At the Hospital, as usual. Went on with Mineralogy, with Mitchill & Miller. Wrote a lengthy letter to Dr. Senter of Newport, on Mr. Minturn's Case. Errands. Recd. six additional numbers of the Weekly Magazine, of all of which I read some part. Corrected two proofs of the Repository. Visit from Dr. Miller. Visit from Dunlap, who came up from Amboy last evening, & who drank tea with us. Recd. Dr. Morse, with his fast Sermon. Evening at Manumission Society.

Wednesday, 18.—Read the papers. Medical visit, where I saw Mr. Coit, one of the Connecticut Representatives. Errands & calls. At the College, & attending Mineralogy till twelve. Compiled the Domestic News for the Repository No. 5. Recd. letters from Mr. Tracy, & from Dr. Buel: Went with Dr. Post to Long-Island, to see Mr. Minturn. It was near six when we got back. Visit from Dr. Miller. Visit to Mr. Radclift—made several calls—the rest of the evening at S. Johnson's: Mr. Cragie of Cambridge, near Boston, here. Continued thro' the day the Weekly Magazine.

Thursday, 19.—Visit to Dr. Seaman. Medical visit. At the Hospital as usual. Mineralogy—after which Mitchill, Miller, & I, went to our printer's, on business. Corrected a proof-sheet of the Repository. Continued the Weekly Magazine. Visit from Mr. Allen—on his way from Phila. to Connect. Recd. a letter from my father—my sister is much better. I begin to believe that she will get well: This lightens my heart a little—Visit to Dr. Post; & we went to see two women, with Bronchocele, in the Alms-House. Visit to Dr. Miller. Called on Mr. Allen, with whom I saw Mr. Rutledge, the M. C. from So. Carolina. Allen & I visited Hopkins—Mr. Watson came there, & we went to his house. I found

---

[47] J. Swediaur, M.D., *Traité Complète sur les Symptoms les Effets, la Nature et le Traitement des Maladies Syphilitiques* (Paris, 1801). This is, of course, the text but the earliest edition found is too late.

[48] The Mineralogical Society is simply another example, if example were needed, of the indomitable vitality and breadth of interest of Doctors Mitchell and Miller as well as Smith.

Mr. Hosmer there—who with Allen & Hopkins, came to my house—& spent some time—& Dunlap also. I met Mr. Dana in the street. The evening at the College; where we met again, & agreed to the Constitution of the Mineralogical Society—& did some business.

Friday, July 20.—Wrote short letters to my father & to Mr. Backus. Mr. Allen breakfasted with us. We went to see Mr. & Mrs. Goodrich. I met Mr. Dana—& we all met at the Wharf, where the persons now named, & Mr. Hosmer—collected to sail for Connecticut. Recd. a letter from Mr. Tracy—inclosing Genl. Washington's Letter to Mr. Adams. At Mitchill's, with Miller; but the former was detained at the Hospital, & we had no lecture. Miller & I came home & settled the foreign News for the Repository No. 5. I finished the perusal of the Monthly Magazine for March 1798, which I commenced yesterday. It contains much interesting matter, as usual. Recd. a short letter from Mr. Scandella, & replied to it. Visit from Dr. Seaman, from Dr. Mitchill; & from Mr. Dunlap. Two medical visits in the morning, this afternoon Seaman & I went over to Mr. Minturn's on Long-Island. It was near eight when we got back. Called at Mrs. Templeton's. Miss T. is sick with Mumps. Saw Miss Eliza a few minutes. Remainder of the evening at Mr. Boyd's. Came home, & did some writing for the Repository, & some for the Mineralogical Society.

Saturday, 21.—Read the papers. At the Hospital as usual. Mineralogy with Mitchill & Miller. Visit from Mr. Sharples. Dunlap has gone to Amboy, & comes up Tuesday. At our printer's. Corrected two proofs of the Repository. Long visit from Dr. Mitchill. Read much in the Monthly Review & Monthly Magazine for April. Read Mr. Webster's 4th of July Oration. Visit from Dr. S. Osborn. Errands. Visit to Saml. M. Hopkins. Johnson & Fanny, Brown & myself, drank tea at Sharples's. Brown went home. We called at Riley's, & visited Miss Morton. Thence to S. Johnson's—where with H. Johnson & Mr. Cragie, we supped. Wrote a few lines to Mr. A. Miller, of Middletown. Dr. Miller & I mutually agreed, on my proposition, to qualify ourselves, in the course of the next two years—he for Theory & Practice, I for Mat. Med: & Botany.

Sunday, 22.—L. L.—Called on Miller, & he accompanied me to the Hospital, where I had two new patients to prescribe for. When I returned to his house, I looked over two cases of Bronchelous tumours the treatment of which had been much like that which I had proposed (in my own mind, on chemical principles, & without knowlege of these cases) for Mr. Minturn, but which circumstances rendered it impossible to pursue. Finished the Monthly Magazine & Monthly Review for April. Fanny Johnson went to Middletown to-day—& Mr. Tracy sailed in the same vessel, without my having seen him. Wm., Charles, Mr. Craigie & I dined & spent the afternoon at H. Johnson's. Charles & I walked on the Battery. I afterwards visited Catlin—& then took a fresh walk on the Battery, in the most beautiful evening. On the way Brown & I visited Hopkins & went with him to the Battery the first time. Finished the Weekly Magazine as far as recd.—i.e. finishing the XXIIIrd No.

Monday, 23.—Read Mr. Wells's Oration, & Dr. Morse's Sermon. Visit from a Mr. Stephens, who brought me a few lines from Dr. Barton. Mineralogy with Mitchill & Miller. At the Hospital. Arranged the foreign news for the Repository, & was at our printer's. The Swords' commenced the printing of Charles's "Wieland," this day. Isaac Riley is either agent for the purchaser, Caritat, or in part purchaser as well as Agent.[49] Brown has delivered the greater part of the Work, has recd. 50 dollars, & is to receive the rest, when he delivers the remaining sheets. Medical visit. Visit to Mr. Post. Read Horsfield Inaugural Dissertation on the Rhus Vernin, R. radians, & R. glabrum: 8vo. pp. 88. Recd. two letters from Joseph Bringhurst, & wrote at some length, in reply. Medical visit at G. M. Woolsey's, where I drank tea. Called on Miss Mason, but did not see her: at Mr. Robertson's—but he was out: Walked on the Battery. When I came home, found Mr. Cragie & S. Johnson here. After they went away, conversed an hour with Johnson & Brown.

Tuesday, July 24.—Medical visit. At the Hospital, & longer than usual. Mineralogy, till 12 o'clock. Visited Mr. Sharples's Exhibition. Commenced the reading of Dr. Rollo's publication on Diabetes.[50] Visit to my patient on Long-Island. It was six P. M. when I returned. At our printer's, and corrected a proof sheet of the Repository. Charles & I drank tea at G. M. Woolsey's. We walked on the Battery. I visited at Moses Rogers's. Continued Rollo, & have advanced pp. 172.

Memo.—Kalmia latifolia—(on the authority of my Uncle Micah Hubbard of Middletown, Connec.) poisons Sheep. The symptoms seldom occur very soon. Sometimes not till after several days. They are sickness at stomach; debility, with staggering; a choaking; & frothing at the mouth. He always cures it, & in no great time, by strong *Ley*. From one to 1 ½ & two pints, given at intervals. It has no sensible operation. A stranger, who sat by, says it is better cured by Rum.

Memo.—Boblincons first observed (1798) at Berlin, on May 7th by El. Smith Jr. Strawberries then in full bloom.

---

[49] For details of the publication of *Wieland*, see previously mentioned biographies of Brown by Clark and Warfel. Isaac Riley, Alsop's brother-in-law, was a wild man where investments were concerned and was frequently in financial straits involving huge amounts of money. It is strange to see him as here, concerning himself with anything so slight as a publication of *Wieland*. His associate and sometime partner, Hocquet Caritat, was a somewhat unusual proprietor of a private library, probably the only one who had his own privateer. See Raddin, *The New York of Hocquet Caritat*.

[50] Dr. John Rollo, *An Account of two Cases of Diabetes Mellitus, with Remarks as They Arise During the Progress of the Cure, etc.* (London, 1792).

These notes were not inserted in their proper place.

Wednesday, 25.—Dunlap has returned & breakfasted with us. Read the Papers. Visit from a patient. Visit from Hopkins. Visit from Miller. We went to our printer's. We went, for a short time, to the Hospital. We attended Mineralogy, with Mitchill. Continued Rollo on Diabetes. Recd. letters from Thomas & Mary. A short visit from John Mumford, who has lately returned, in good health, from Europe. Wrote to Dr. Wilkins of Baltimore. Dunlap drank tea with us. We four walked. D. left us. We continued on the Battery till after nine. Finished what Brown has written of "Wieland." Corrected a proof of the Repository & one of Wieland. I forgot—a long visit from Mitchill soon after dinner. Last, Wm, Charles & I had a long conversation, chiefly on a suitable catastrophe to his Tale; & we concluded the evening by reading the article of the Monthly Review which contains the analysis of Wieland's *Oberon*.

Thursday, 26.—Dunlap breakfasted with us. At the Hospital. Mineralogy as usual. Call on Mr. Day of Onondaga, ineffectually. At the printer's on business. Wrote a few lines to Dr. Buel. Visit from Mr. Tisdale, the Engraver & Painter. Wrote to Thomas & Mary. Visit from Dr. Miller. Visit to Mr. Stuart, the Asst. Atty. Genl. for the Western District. Calls & errands. Wrote a long letter to Buel, to elucidate our account, which has become nearly inexplicable: this gave me great trouble. Drank tea at home. Mr. Boyd came in soon after, & spent the evening. I met Genl. Bloomfield, in the street, from New Jersey, & he was to have visited me this evening, but he has not been here. Corrected two proof-sheets of the Repository. Finished the 1st vol. of Dr. Rollo's Work, & have read pp. 40 of the second vol. I expected a letter from Lichfield, by this day's Mail. As none has come, I presume my friends will write by Mr. Wolcott.

Friday, July 27.—Breakfasted at Mr. Boyd's, in company with Genl. Bloomfield. Afterwards, accompanied him to the Millers'. Visit from a patient. At the Hospital. Mineralogy as usual. Read the 24th No. of the "Weekly Magazine." Continued Rollo's Work. Drank tea at Miller's. Corrected a proof of "Wieland." Spent the evening at H. Johnson's. The President of the United States came in town today, from Phila. A false acct. that he would cross the ferry in the morning, occasioned the parade of the military at an early hour. He did not cross till five P. M. but the various information, &c. kept the parade up all day, & the citizens in hourly expectation. So that I, with others, lost much time in consequence. The parade was handsome, & must have pleased him.

Saturday, 28.—I suppose that Dunlap has returned to Amboy. Read the papers. Went into the North River early this morning. At the Hospital. Mineralogy. Calls & errands. At our printer's. Corrected a proof of the Repository. Finished Rollo's Work, which I have read with the intensest pleasure. Visit from Dr. Miller. After tea we all walked on the Battery—thence we visited Mr. Sharples. This day has been & the night is excessive hot.

Sunday, 29.—At the Hospital two hours. One of my fever patients will recover, the other will die. Looked over a great number of books of Cases &c. in search of Papers relative to Bronchocele, but to no purpose. Resumed the reading of Robison's Conspiracy &c. which I commenced in Connecticut, & made considerable progress towards the end. Corrected a proof of the Repository. Finished my letter to Buel. Wm, Charles & I dined at Seth Johnson's, & spent the afternoon. Mr. Cragie still there. We attended the funeral of Melancton Smith,[51] who died this morning of Yellow Fever. We met Dr. Miller at the funeral, & he came home with Charles & me. After sitting a while, we visited Miss Templeton—where we spent the evening. Afterwards we walked in the Mall.

Monday, 30.—Medical visit. At the Hospital. The patient died at 3 A. M. On opening the head, three or four ounces of water were found in the cavities of the Brain. Mineralogy as usual. Recd. a letter from Nathl. Dwight: also a few lines from Maclure & Co. by which I learn that Mr. Scandella has sailed. Read Theodore Dwight's Oration, at Hartford, on the 4th of July last. Finished Robison's Proofs of a Conspiracy &c. Visit to Dr. Seaman & to see a patient of his with tetanus. Visit from Dr. Mitchill. Visit to Woolsey's, who has just returned from New England, to see him, & Mr. Wolcott, who is at his house. Mrs. Wolcott is better; & my sister Abby, well. Visit from Mr. Woolsey & from Mr. Webster, in town from New Haven. We went to see Mr. Wolcott at Mr. Watson's, but he had returned to Woolsey's. Corrected a proof of "Wieland." Some writing for the Repository. A medical visit.

Tuesday, 31.—Medical visit. Went with Dr. Seaman to see his patient with Tetanus. At the Hospital. Mineralogy as usual. At Mr. Swords's—on professional & Repository business. Recd. a letter from Dr. Croswell. Visits from Mr. Cragie & Mr. Webster. The last left with me, for my perusal, the first part of his Essay on Epidemics. Errands. Visited Mr. Minturn, on Long Island. On my return called to see Seaman's man with Tetanus. Called afterwards at Seaman's. Medical visit. Drank tea & spent the evening at Miss Templeton's. Miss Mason & Nicholson, & Mrs. Bache of Phila., Dr. Miller & C. B. Brown &c. were there. Accompanied Miss N. home, & on the way stopt with her at Mr. Sand's—where I saw Miss Cooper. Two medical visits. Corrected a proof of the Repository. Read Dr. De Ros-

---

[51] Melancton Smith (1724-1798) was an elderly merchant and politician when Smith knew him. He had been a member of the Provincial Congress, a delegate to the Continental Congress, a member of the State Convention to ratify the State Constitution, a member of the State Assembly in 1791, and a circuit judge after 1792. With William Pitt Smith he was made a sachem of Tammany Hall in 1791. These two Smiths may have been related to each other but they were not related, at least immediately, to Elihu Smith.

set's acct. of the Wilmington fever of 1796.[52] Read Smucker on the Sabadilla—&c.

Industry for July 1798
Reading

Rollo on Diabetes Mellitus—2 vols. 8vo.
Horsfield's Inaug. Ess. on three sp. of Rhus. 8vo. pp. 88.
Claiborne's on Scurvy—pp. 43.—8vo.
Archer's on Croup———46.—do.
Tripplett on Apoplexy———32. . do.
Robinson's Proofs of a Conspiracy &c. 8vo. pp. 400.
Rockwell's, Webster's, Wells's, & Dwight's, 4th of July Orations.
Backus's Election Sermon, & Sermon at funeral of Gov. Wolcott.
Strong's fast Sermon.
Morse's fast Sermon.
Stanley Griswold's Defence &c.
Monthly Magazine for March & April.
. . . Review for April.
Weekly Magazine—7 Nos.
Ms.
   Wieland.
   Webster on Epidemics—1. & 2. Sect.

Writing

Composition
   Principally uncopied Letters—pp. 40.

Transcription
   Chiefly of News &c. for the Medical Repository.—10.
Deduct, a week of journeying: add Mineralogy, Proofs, Accts. &c. &c.

MEMOIRS. 1798. AUGUST.

Wednesday, 1.—Read the papers. Went with Dr. Seaman to see his patient, who is worse. I picked up, at Seaman's, some medical pamphlets, & have the introductory Letter, in Beddoes' account of Mayow.[53] A visit from a patient. Medical visit. Visit from Miller. Mineralogy as usual. A visit to Miss Mason. Visit to Miller's. Mr. Miller unwell. Corrected the last proof for Repository No. 1 Vol. II. at our printer's. Writing for the Repository. At Seaman's. Two medical visits. Long visit from Mr. Webster & Dr. Mitchill. Called at Miss Templeton's. She was absent—but I afterwards met her in the street, & walked some distance with her. A visit to Mr. Kent—he is well—& his family. A visit to G. Mumford's—to Mr. Duryee's—to Miss Morton. Read Mr. Quincy's Oration—4th July. Writing for the Mineralogical Society. Adjusted my accounts, as far as their disordered state will permit.

Thursday, 2.—Recd. letters from Mr. Tracy, Mr. Allen, & from my father, and wrote answers. At the Hospital. Mineralogy. Read Dr. Priestley's long letter to Mitchill. Visit from S. M. Hopkins. Corrected a proof of "Wieland." Visit to Mr. Miller—as he is unwell. Further progress in Mayow—or Beddoes' Pamphlet. Medical visit. At the Printer's. Med. Repos. No. 1. Vol. II. out, & the copies for Phila. sent. Visit to Miss Templeton, for the purpose of explaining to her more fully the doctrine of Chemical Affinity—than she had comprehended it from the perusal of Lavoisier. Afterwards conversation in indifferent subjects, tea &c: Visit to the Millers. Charles there. Conversation till nine. Medical visit. Visit at Mr. Leffingwell's, where Mr. Webster stays. Came home, & read two hours in his Ms. on Epidemics.

Friday, August 3.—Medical visit. Visit from a patient: from Hopkins: from Mr. Webster—who has gone to New Haven to-day. At the College—& mineralogy as usual. At Miller's. Recd. a letter from Dr. Dewees. Medical visit. Recd. an Anonymous letter from Savannah, intimating that Dr. Brickel was an impertinent pretender, & that we must admit his communications with some caution. Visit to my patient on Long-Island. Writing for the Mineralogical Society. Johnson, Brown, Dr. Miller & I, drank tea & spent the evening, with Miss Mason. Walked on the Battery. Medical visit. Continued now, & thro' the day, Holmes's Life of Dr. Stiles.

Saturday, 4.—Read the papers. Medical visit. At the Hospital. After prescribing, was detained there more than an hour, in expectation of a meeting of the physicians, which had been regularly warned. But none took place. While there looked over De Haen's Works. But by this detention I lost my Mineralogy. Notwithstanding I was at Mitchill's, & we all concurred in some business of the Repository. Visit to Mr. Miller who is better. Visit from a patient. Two medical visits. Continued Stiles's Life. Medical visit. At our printer's great part of the afternoon, preparing packages of the Repository to be sent away. Dr. Miller drank tea with us. Medical visit. Dr. M. spent much of the evening here. After which we called to see Mr. Kent; who was out. I returned, & wrote short letters, on business of the Repository, to Hudson & Godwin, Ebenr. Larkin, J. Rice, & to Drs. Field, Dwight, & Croswell. Continued Dr. Stiles' Life.

Sunday, 5.—Visit from a patient. Three medical visits. Finished Holmes's "Life of President Stiles." This is rather the history of the Christian than of the Scholar. An history of Dr. Stiles, properly written, would be the history, very nearly, of American literature for the last 50 years. Read Brown's conclusion to his "Wieland." We visited Mr. Radclift, & saw Mr. Kent. We dined & spent the afternoon at H. Johnson's. Mr. Cragie was there. Visit to Riley's. Two medical visits.

---

[52] Not found; probably never printed.
[53] Thomas Beddoes, "A Letter Respecting Citizen Fourcroy's Account of the Discoveries of Mayow," *Jour. Natural Philosophy, Chemistry, and the Arts,* ed. William Nicholson, **3**: p. 108. Probably *Chemical Experiments and Opinions extracted from a Work published in the last Century* (1790). Mayow was a doctor who wrote in Latin in the seventeenth century.

Mr. Kent, Mr. Watson, & Mr. Hopkins spent the evening with us. After this we walked on the Battery.

Monday, 6.—Two medical visits. Recd. a letter from Dr. Senter. At our printer's. At Dr. Miller's. At the Hospital—where the physicians met, & concluded on a permanent arrangement of the periods of attendance. Mineralogy as usual. We have now concluded XI Classes of Walker's arrangement.[54] Finished Beddoes' Acct. of Mayow's discoveries. Read the 1st part of Dr. Thornton's "Medical Extracts"—& Beddoes' Letter to Dr. Darwin. Drew off some accounts for Collection. Corrected a proof-sheet of "Wieland." Long visit from Dunlap, who unexpectedly came in this afternoon. Three medical visits. Drank tea at home. Walked out to Mr. Robertson's. He & his lady absent. Called at H. Johnson's. William & I bathed; & the uncommon beauty & brilliancy of the water induced us to search all the books for the explanation of this phenomenon, with very little satisfaction. Phosphorescency is the most plausible solution—yet how?

Tuesday, August 7.—Three medical visits. At the Hospital as usual. Mineralogy. At the Printer's. Visit from a patient. Wrote letters to Dr. Wheaton, Dr. Kollock, Freneau & Paine, & to a quondam gardener of Mrs. Lovegrove, from whom I recd. a letter inquiring after her. Posting books for the Repository. Three medical visits. At Dr. Miller's—his brother better. Dunlap, who breakfasted with us, went home to-day. Evening, at the College, in the Monthly Meeting of the Mineralogical Society.

Wednesday, 8.—Read the papers. Two medical visits. Visit to Hopkins. Mineralogy. On the business of the Repository, some time, at the printer's. Wrote letters to John Williams, to Cogswell, from whom I recd. a lengthy one, & a few lines to Mumford. Read the Editor's, Translator's, & Author's prefaces to Magellan's edition of Cronstedt's Mineralogy.[55] The day exceeding hot—so as to impede exertion. Medical visit. Read Brown's "Carwin,"[56] as far as he has written it, & corrected a proof of his "Wieland." We walked on the Battery, called at G. M. Woolsey's, & finished the evening at Moses Rogers's.

Thursday, 9.—Two medical visits. Recd. a letter from my father, with Mr. Smith's, Gould's, & Day's Orations on the 4th of July. I have read the first & the last. At the Hospital. Mineralogy. Errands. Read the 25, & 26th Nos. of the Weekly Magazine. Recd. a letter from Mr. Miller of Middletown. Medical visit. Dr. Miller, Brown, Miss Mason, & I drank tea & spent the evening, with Miss Nicholson. Mr. Gallatin there. He says little, & walks much by himself. We all went home with Miss Mason. Then Miss M. Miller, Brown & I called at Miss Templeton's, & with her & Mr. Ay. Bleecker proceeded to the Battery—where we walked & talked. I have looked over Mr. Day's Oration since.

Friday, 10.—Medical visit. Dr. Mitchill having gone out of town, by his desire, I waited on the Surgeon of the Topaz Sloop of War & Mr. J. Murray the younger, at breakfast, in his apartments; & afterwards accompanied them to the Hospital, where I prescribed for Mitchill. This occupied me somewhat longer than usual. Called on Miller. Three medical visits. Read Mr. Gould's Oration. Medical visit. Recd. a letter from Dr. Buel. Wrote the following letter to Dr. Darwin. A number of errands. Medical visit. Evening at Sharples's. Medical visit. Bathed in the Hudson. Transcribed six pages of close-written letter-paper, from Coleridge & Southey's Poems, for Alsop, & wrote a short letter to him.

Saturday, 11.—Read the papers. Two medical visits. Call on Mrs. Riley, who this day sailed for Connecticut. At the Hospital. A visit to Mr. Robertson of an hour & half, at whose house I met Mr. Arthur Noble. Visit from a patient. Calls. Visited my patient on Long-Island, which occupied the principal part of the afternoon. Two medical visits. Much of the evening at Miss Templeton's. I saw Miss Morton at Seth Johnson's—& Dr. Miller at Miss T's.

Sunday, 12.—Visit from a patient. Four medical visits. Transcribed my letter to Dr. Darwin, with some slight corrections. Brown & I dined at H. Johnson's, where we spent part of the afternoon. A further portion of it was spent at S. Johnson's—who had a return of his Ague to-day. From this Charles & I went to Mr. Roulet's, where we made a visit of an hour or two. Thence we crossed to W. W. Woolsey's at whose house the evening was concluded.

Monday, August 13.—Two medical visits. At the Hospital, & longer than usual. Wrote a letter to Dr. Sevediaur, at Paris. Visit to Hopkins. Wrote to Dr. Rush, to Dr. Senter, to Dr. Buel, & to Mr. Stanley, to the last relative to some minerals promised me. Calls. Medical visit. Visit from two patients. Medical visit & drank tea at Seth Johnson's—Brown with me. We walked. I called, & spent some time, at Genl. Hughes's, in hopes of seeing Mr. Kent—in vain. Brown & I took a long walk on the Battery. A medical visit. Corrected a proof of "Wieland."

Tuesday, 14.—There commenced, a little before six, & continued, till a little before nine, the most violent thunder storm that I ever knew. I have known much harder thunder & sharper lightning, but never saw so long-continued & violent a rain. The lightning struck the mast of a small vessel, in the North-River. Three

---

[54] John Walker, D.D., professor of natural history at University of Edinburgh, *Classes Fossilium, sive Characteres natureles et chymici Classium et Ordinum in Systemate Minerali, cum Nomienibus Genericis adscriptis* (Edinburgh, 1787).

[55] *An Essay towards a System of Mineralogy by Alexander Fordrie Cronstadt* (only edition found; second edition London, 1788). This translation by G. H. Magellan was not the first into English. Variant on the translator's name: Axel Frederick Crondstedt.

[56] *Carwin, The Biloquist* was intended as a preliminary volume to *Wieland*. The novel was left unfinished; such pages as survived were first printed in *The Literary Magazine and American Register* between 1803 an 1805. Warfel, *Charles Brockden Brown*, p. 112.

medical visits. At the Hospital. Found Dr. Miller here when I returned. Afterwards Mr. Sharples came in. Both stayed more than an hour. Recd. a letter from Dr. Mease. Wrote to Dr. Dewees. Several interruptions & a visit from a patient. Medical visit. Visit from Dr. Hart, of Farmington, Connec.—who brought me an introductory letter from Cogswell. Wrote, in his behalf, to Mr. Secy. Wolcott. He drank tea with us. Two medical visits. Visit from Mr. Kent. A principal part of the evening at H. Johnson's. Saw there Mr. Hill (the Swedenborgian) & his wife. Mr. Cragie was there. Medical visit. Wrote to Dr. Nooth, of Quebec, in behalf of Mr. Stephens. Was at Miller's in the eveng.

To Dr. Darwin

The occasion of the present address will I hope justify the liberty which is assumed by a stranger in making it. It would seem that, to a mind anxious for the welfare & desirous of the esteem of mankind, no tidings could be more acceptable than those which assured it of the extension of that welfare & the acquisition of this esteem among a large & respectable portion of the human race. And he who communicates this information may, at least, expect indulgence, tho' he perform the office uninvited & unexpected.

The determination of the proprietors of the American Edition of the "Botanic Garden," to undertake the publication of this Work, revived in me the desire of superintending an Edition which had been excited by the first perusal of it, at my friend & former instructor, Dr. Dwight's, in the autumn of 1789. The wishes of the publishers coinciding with my own devolved the execution of this duty upon me. This was the more agreable, as they were ready to make all suitable exertions to give it to the world in a dress worthy of the American press. In this I believe they will be thought to have succeeded. In respect to the more material character of the Edition, tho' I dare not venture to assert it to be unexceptionably correct, yet I trust no great number of gross errors will be discoverable in it. Of the prefatory Epistle, if it excite not the disgust of him to whom it is addressed, its author will be contented. The power to aid the circulation of a work which some local respect may confer, is all that is offered in extenuation of the attempt.

One of the Notes to this Epistle may require explanation to any but an American. The genius of Mr. Alsop may not have received any portion of transatlantic applause. A little volume, intituled "American Poems," which accompanies this letter, will enable you, sir, to judge with what propriety he has been commended by his friend. And some lesser publications, likewise forwarded, will convey some further idea of the state of polite literature in this part of the United States.

You have doubtless learnt, sir, that the "Zoonomia," has been republished in America. But you may not have been informed that there is every probability that a second edition will speedily be called for. In this case, superintendence of the impression will fall to the lot of one or all of the conductors of the periodical medical Work which is now sent to you. From this publication you will gain a knowlege of the ability of these persons to edit your work; &, should you desire it, will learn to whom any additional articles may be directed. Should the edition be undertaken, it will be commenced in the ensuing Winter, & be printed conformably to the Botanic Garden.

This letter, & the small package of books which accompany it, will be sent to the care of Mr. Johnson, London. Should they arrive safely, no circumstance could be more gratifying than to be apprized of it, by your own hand; nor could any greater pleasure be readily afforded me than to learn that my efforts were thought worthy your approbation, & that you would not be displeased to receive from me such further evidences of the cultivation of letters & science as my native country may from time to time produce.

Aug. 10. '98.   E. H. Smith.

Wednesday, 15.—The rain recommenced towards morning, without thunder & lightning, & continued nearly as long as yesterday, with great, but not with equal severity. Three medical visits. Read the Papers. Mineralogy. Visit from Mr. Roulet. Visit from a patient. Medical visit. Made out & transcribed my Tables of Industry for the four last months. Visit from Mitchill. At Caritat's. Drank tea at Radcliff's. We walked on the Battery; met Kent & Hopkins; & all returned to Radcliff's, where we stayed till nine. Read some pages in Cronstedt's Mineralogy.

Thursday, 16.—Two medical visits. At the Hospital. Mineralogy. Visit from a patient. Read the Analytical Review for April. Arranged the Minutes of the last meeting of the Mineralogical Society. Some writing for the Manumission Society. Medical visit. Mr. Boyd drank tea & spent most of the evening, with us. Charles & I walked an hour.

Friday, August 17.—Visit to Miller. Mineralogy. Finished writing for the Manumission Socy. Posted my books, which had long been neglected. Read the European Magazine for April last. Visit from a patient. Johnson & I walked on the Battery. We met Mr. Kent there. He came home, drank tea, & spent the evening, with us. I read him Dunlap's Song, Brown's Oration, & part of "Alcuin," P. III. & IV.

Saturday, 18.—Read the papers as usual. Visit from a patient. At the Hospital longer than usual. Longer at Mineralogy. Visit to Miller. Read a letter from Dr. Barker of Portland (Maine) to Dr. Mitchill, in favour of the administration of Alkalies in fever. Calls. Commenced & made some progress in Swediaur on the Venerial Disease—in french his new work. Visit to Long-Island—& detained near two hours by the rain. Visit to Seth Johnson's. Went into the Bath. Medical visit.

Sunday, 19.—Wrote letters to Dr. Mease, Mr. W. P. Beers, & Dr. Jas. Wells. Johnson, Brown & I walked.

We dined & spent the afternoon, principally, at Seth Johnson's. Brown & I went to the Millers'—where we passed the remainder of the afternoon, & drank tea. Brown went to visit Miss N. & Dr. Miller, Mr. Roe & I walked on the Battery & Mall—till near ten. When I came home, I found a letter from Alsop. We three had an hour of conversation.

H. & S. Johnson & Co. stopt payment on Monday last: some notes having been previously left unpaid at the Bank the Saturday before. This stoppage was unexpected to themselves, & without preparation. That is—they had expected to stop at some time—but the particular time was unexpected. They have adopted the most prudent & honourable resolutions, & will as soon as possible reduce their mode of living to great simplicity.

Monday, 20.—At our printer's. Medical visit. Mineralogy. Visit from Mr. Webster, who came to town yesterday. Medical visit. Errands. Visit to Mr. Webster. Visit from a patient. Transcribed a long poem of Coleridge's, for Alsop. Medical visit. Called at Mr. Morton's: all out. Spent the principal part of the evening at Miss Mason's. Miss Nicholson was there—& Brown, & Dr. Miller. B. went home with Miss N. Miller & I walked in the Mall &c.—after an hour, B. joined us. It was near eleven when we came home.

Tuesday, 21.—Two medical visits. At the Hospital. Mineralogy. Read the 29th No. of the "Weekly Magazine." Visit to my patient on Long-Island, which took up most of the afternoon. Visit from Webster, who drank tea with us. Afterwards Brown, Johnson & I walked on the Battery & bathed.

Wednesday, 22.—Read the papers. Mineralogy. Read the 27th No. of the Weekly Magazine. Continued Swediaur's New Work. Medical visits. Visit from Mitchill. Recd. a letter from Dr. Rush. Visit to Miller. Call, in vain, at G. M. Woolsey's—visit to S. Johnson's. Principal part of the evening at Miss Morton's. Met Johnson there. We walked on the Mall, & continued there the longer, having met Brown there. Wrote a letter of some length to Alsop last night. Was at the Hospital this afternoon.

Thursday, 23.—Continued Swediaur. At the Hospital. Mineralogy. After our lecture was thro', Miller & I walked out to Corlaer's-Hook, where we made a handsome collection of specimens of Granite rocks &c.—shewing the various intermixture of Quartz, Red & white feld-spar, Mica, Schorl, & Garnet. We found several of the Geodes, bits of Shistus &c. After dinner —errands—principally for my father, from whom I recd. a letter, & replied by a few lines. At Woolsey's Store—where I read a number of Phila. & N.York, Newspapers. At the Hospital—where I commenced the arrangement of my Notes relative to the use of Nitrous Acid in Syphilis. Drank tea at Mrs. Miller's. Met Dr. Miller there. We visited Miss Nicholson; & concluded the eveng. by a hour's walk in the Mall.

Friday, August 24.—Medical visit. Visit from a patient. At the College, with Miller, as usual; but Mitchill was detained at the Hospital till it was too late to attend to Mineralogy. While waiting for him we looked over many specimens, & a volume of Roger Bacon's Works.[57] When Mitchill came he read us his review of Thos. P. Smith's Oration—& we attended to some other business of the Repository. We were summoned to some new patients in the Hospital—whither we repaired—I taking the occasion also of calling on one of my patients. We came back to Miller's, where I stayed a little time. After dinner, wrote to my father, at moderate length. I can not write to D. W. Lewis—I can say nothing to assuage his or his wife's affliction. Medical visit. Two hours at the Hospital: where I attended to some patients, & went on with my Syphilitic Collection. Calls & errands. Visit to H. Johnson's. The remainder of the evening at home. Read Brown's additions to Wieland, & the rest of his "Carwin." Continued Swediaur.

Saturday, 25.—Visit from Dr. S. Osborn of the Army, who accompanied me to the Hospital; & thence, after prescribing, to the College, where we attended to Mineralogy as usual. Visit from a patient. Read the papers. Looked over some pretty well written papers in the "Philanthrope."[58] At the Hospital, where I attended to some patients & continued my Siphilitic Collection. Medical visit. Calls & errands. After tea, spent an hour at Mrs. Templeton's. Miss Nicholson was there. Medical visits. We all went into the Bath. The sickness increases in town.

Sunday, 26.—Medical visit. At the Hospital the greater part of the forenoon, prescribing & taking notes. Medical visit. We dined, spent the afternoon, & part of the evening, at Seth Johnson's. At tea, entered Miss Morton, Mr. Cragie, & H. Johnson & his wife. Wm., Charles & I walked on the Battery. I returned, for a time, to S. Johnson's, one of his family being sick.

Monday, 27.—Since I wrote the next preceding memorandum, I have been subjected to more than ordinary fatigue: hitherto with no bad effect. I did not enter my bed till after eleven. The heat & the musquitoes kept me painfully awake till some time after twelve. Scarcely had I fallen into imperfect slumber, when I was arouzed, obliged to rise, mount a horse, ride to Corlaer's Hook, & thence cross to Long-Island a mile above. It was half past four when I got home. I arose again a little after seven. Medical visit. A call for the same purpose. Went over to Long Island. It was near two when I returned. Medical visit. Another. At the Hospital. Visit to Dr. Miller. Medical visit. Calls. Medical visit. Went over to Long Island. Nine o'clock at night, when I was landed at the Hook. Thence I walked in the rain. Medical visit. Looked over some part of Dr. Rush's 5th vol. of Obs: & Inq.[59] which I have just recd. Recd. a letter from Dr. Buel.

---

[57] English philosopher and Franciscan monk (1214?-1294?).
[58] *The Philanthrope: After the Manner of a Periodical Paper* (London, 1797).
[59] *Medical Inquiries and Observations* . . . 5 (Philadelphia, 1798).

Tuesday, 28.—Medical visit. At the Hospital. Medical visits. Went over to Long-Island. Medical visit. At Dr. Miller's. Medical visit. At our printer's. Visit to Dr. Scandella—who has been obliged, from the leakiness of the ship in which he embarked, to return. He is well. Medical visit. Woolsey returned to-day. He is well; but leaves town with his family tomorrow. Visit to Dr. Rodgers. Medical visit.

Wednesday, 29.—Rose early & went over to Long Island, to see my patient there—where I breakfasted, & returned about nine. One, two, three medical visits. Visit to Dr. Scandella, who came home with & set some time at my room. We had an interesting conversation. Visit to Dr. Miller. Wrote letters to Dr. Senter & Dr. Todd, & a short one to Mr. J. Smith of Farmington, & a few lines to Alsop. Medical visit. Visit to Miller. We went to Mitchill's—intending to go on with Mineralogy—but other things prevented. He recd. & read to us, letters from Dr. Priestley, & Mr. Patterson of Edinburgh. Two medical visits. Went over to Long-Island. Four medical visits after my return.

Thursday, August 30.—Visit from Dr. Perkins, the Metallic-point Man. Medical visit. At the Hospital. Two medical visits. Went over to Long-Island; & returned to dinner. Previously, a visit from Dr. Scandella. Two medical visits. Dr. Miller & I went to Mitchill's, where we had a Mineralogical Lecture once more. All three visited Mr. Scandella. Miller accompanied me to see a patient. Dr. Scandella drank tea & spent the evening with us. Two medical visits.

Friday, 31.—I was scarcely asleep, when I was summoned to the house of my Long-Island patient, to a new sick-man. It was after five this morning, when I returned. I gained only three hours sleep. Dr. Scandella breakfasted & spent an hour with us. Three medical visits. Went to Long-Island. Medical visit. Miller & I attended Mineralogy with Mitchill, & finished Walker's Arrangement. Went to Long Island; & as I could get no horse—walked out & in. Two medical visits.

MEMOIRS. 1798. SEPTEMBER.

Saturday, 1.—Read the papers. Medical visits. Visit from Dr. Scandella, who accompanied me to the Hospital; afterwards to the College. Medical visit. Went over to Long-Island. I was very much affected by the sun, in my ride to the Ferry, & have felt unwell ever since. Medical visits. At Dr. Miller's. We went to visit Dr. Scandella. He was not at home. Afterwards he came here, & we went to Dr. Miller's, where we drank tea, & spent part of the evening. Then Dr. S. accompanied me home & stayed for the remainder with me. Recd. letters from Wm. P. Beers & M. F. Cogswell.

Sunday, 2.—Two medical visits. Dr. Scandella came to see me, & accompanied me to my Long-Island patients. The day & the ride & sail were pleasant, & I felt better. I dined, & spent most of the afternoon at S. Johnson's—in company with Wm & Brown. Read No. 30. of the Weekly Magazine. Wrote a letter to Cogswell. Visited Dr. Scandella—after sitting some time we walked, & our walk terminating at my house, he spent the evening here. I was much fatigued by this short walk, & find myself no better than last evening. I even fear that if this indisposition continues, I shall be seized with fever in a few days. The sudden change to a very cool & even cold temperature, enhances my debility. The single effect of a laxative pill a little relieves me.

Monday, 3.—An uncommon day for me. I have been so weak, & otherwise so unwell, that I have kept house all day, & been on the bed the greater part of it. Dr. Scandella visited me in the morning. He has gone to Phila. in search of his baggage. Mitchill, Miller & others, have been here.

Tuesday, Septr. 4.—This day is my birth-day. I am now twenty-seven. Still poor & solitary. I am better to-day. I sat up all the forenoon. I even read the pages of Brown's continuation to his "Carwin," of his new-begun "Stephen Calvert"—added a page to Brown & Johnson's joint letter, in reply to one recd. from Dunlap, (addrest to me,) yesterday; & wrote a short letter to W. W. Woolsey. Miller was here in the forenoon & others. I slept or lay most of the afternoon; & just at sun-set, made a consultation visit. Mitchill & Miller spent the evening. I am still feeble, but hope to get abroad to-morrow.

Wednesday, 5.—Medical visit. Went, with Miller, to Long-Island. This occupied all the forenoon. Medical visit. Lay down, but could not sleep. Droned away the afternoon, scorched with fever. Read the Papers. Medical visit. Evening at home. Looked over, cursorily, several articles in the New Annual Register for 1790. A little stronger, but quite unwell.

Thursday, 6.—Passed a restless & perturbid night, tormented with musquitoes & incongruous dreams. Felt too unwell to visit the Hospital, but at eleven make a consulting visit near by, & another towards eveng. The rest of the day & evening kept snug at home. Recd. letters from my father & Abby; & replied to the former. Looked over a bundle of old London papers. Miller & Mitchill here part of the afternoon & of the evening. Somewhat better.

Friday, 7.—Medical visit. Learnt that Joseph Miller of Delaware was dead, & visited the Millers. The Dr. on L. Island. Crawled on to S. Johnson's. Came home, stronger, but weak. Visit from Roulet. Dr. Cooper, now, as well Dr. Sayre of Phila. & Watters the Proprietor of the Weekly Magazine, are dead. Looked at Papers, tumbled over New Annual Register &c.—but with little relief. Medical visit. Visit to Miller. Saw the Dr. ———. Rest of the evening at home. Commenced printing No. 2. of Vol. II. of Med. Repos. Perpetual tears, & perpetual drizzling from the nose to-day: in other respects better.

Saturday, 8.—At the Hospital, for the first time this week. Medical visit. Read the papers. At the printer's. At the Millers'. Visit from Mitchill. Spent the evening at Mrs. Templeton's, with Brown & Johnson. Gained some strength; in other respects as yesterday.

Sunday, 9.—A Long visit from Dr. Miller. Walked on the Battery &c. with Johnson. We three dined at S. Johnson's, & spent part of the afternoon. Called at Mitchill's: he absent. Rest of the afternoon at the Millers'. While there looked over several articles in the Analytical Review for June. The evening at H. Johnson's. Mr. Cragie there, & Wm. & Charles.

Monday, 10.—Wrote letters to W. P. Beers, A. Smith Jr., Dr. Buel, & Dr. Rush. Errand to a printing office, where I read a mass of papers. At our printer's. Visit from Mitchill. Visit to Millers'—where I finished the Analytical Review for June. Medical visit. Visit to Mitchill. Medical visit. Visit & part of the evening, at Mrs. Templeton's. Miss T. absent. Remainder of the evening at Catlin's. Read some pages in Staunton's Embassy. Medical visit. Our fever increases.

Tuesday, 11.—Medical visit. At the Hospital. Four medical visits. Read on in Brown's "Stephen Calvert."[60] Looked over "Spallanzani's Travels."[61] Read a few pages in "Staunton's Embassy." Learnt that Dr. Scandella had returned, & that he is unwell. Went to him, & removed him to my house. Three medical visits. Evening principally at home. Scandella quite sick. Medical visit.

Wednesday, 12.—Scandella had a wretched night, & I, of course, was more than once obliged to rise. He has been sick all day, & is still quite so. Much of my time, to-day, has been devoted to him. Two medical consultation visits, in the morning. Two medical visits. Miller here. We visited some sick together. Miller here again at tea. Again we made some visits together. Mitchill here. Medical visit. Miller here. In the intervals, which have been very short, read the papers, & a few pages in "Staunton's Embassy."

Thursday, 13.—Called up in the night, & watchful with Scandella, who was very ill. Medical visit with Miller. Medical visit. At the Hospital. Seven medical visits in the day & eveng. Mitchill & Miller, here, & Mr. McClure the friend of Scandella, who, on the whole, after exciting the greatest fears, seems a little better. Recd. a letter from Dr. Rush, & replied to it; & wrote briefly to my father & to El. Smith Jr. Our sickness increases, & the desertion of the city.

Friday, Sept. 14.—All day & evening devoted, partly in company with Miller & others, in attention to my patients, & to Scandella. This evening, Miller & I were a little while at Hosack's, who has been unwell. Brown's "Wieland" was published to-day. Scandella is much better, to all appearance.

Saturday, 15.—This day, like yesterday, has been divided between my patients, & Scandella—except that I have also visited the Hospital. It has been a day of great fatigue of body, & still greater distress of mind. In one house, where I had six patients, two have been removed to Bellevue, & one has died. The situation of two others is principally dangerous from these events, but it is extremely distressful. But poor Scandella has excited all my apprehension & sympathies. I fear that he can not recover. The history of this most accomplished, & most unfortunate man is calculated to awaken the deepest interest & foster the profoundest regrets. Mitchill, Miller more particularly, & Maclure, have all been here—& the latter now continues with Scandella.[62]

---

[60] According to Warfel, *Charles Brockden Brown*, p. 115, *Calvert, Or The Lost Brothers* was intended as the first volume of "an uncompleted pantology." Entitled *Memoirs of Stephen Calvert*; it was published in Brown's *Monthly Magazine and American Review*, June, 1799, to June, 1800.

[61] Abbé Lazzaro Spallanzani, *A Translation [from the Italian] of his Travels in the Two Sicilies and some Parts of the Apennines* (London, 1798).

[62] Within twenty-four hours after this entry, Smith was terribly ill and Scandella was dying. Johnson had his friend removed to the home of his brother, Horace. There Mitchell and Miller worked tirelessly over him, using every remedy known. At Smith's own request they tried his favorite remedy, "salivation"; it was useless. Shortly after noon on September 19, Smith was dead. He is buried in the cemetery of the Presbyterian Church on Wall Street of which Samuel Miller was Pastor. After the funeral Johnson and Brown, still deeply shocked, left the city to stay for a time with William Dunlap in Perth Amboy. On September 28 Dunlap wrote: "Evening J[ohnson]: has letters from Tracey [*sic*] & others at Litchfield partly commissioned by Smiths [*sic*] parents to return thanks & make enquiries. Tracey in a postscript to Horace Johnson says 'Did Smith die a Diest [*sic*]? if you require, the answer shall be kept secret.' It appears that Mr & Mrs S. are anxious on this subject: Johnson is now happy that he can say nothing in answer, for our beloved friend was seized so violently that he was in a stupor until death, scarcely speaking & then but when roused from his sleep to answer some question which done he slept again." See copies of unpublished letters from William Johnson to Reuben Smith, dated September 17, 1798, informing him of his son's illness and the care that was being given him, and from Samuel Miller to Reuben Smith September 20, 1798, regarding Smith's death. "Colt Papers," Yale Medical Library. For a detailed discussion of Smith's last days see Dunlap, *Life of Brown* **2**: pp. 5 ff; Dunlap, *Diary* **1**: pp. 340, 341, 343, 345.

APPENDIX

Genealogy

Smith made notes for the following "Brief Notices . . ." in August, 1794. In the summer of 1797 he completed the study and finished copying it in his "Diary" on July 31. For the most part, the "Brief Notices . . ." agree with information to be found in genealogies of the Smith family; where there is a divergence it is usually in the number of children ascribed to a particular marriage. Occasionally the disparity seems to result from unrecorded deaths of infants or the fact that a later brother or sister was given the name of the deceased child.

BRIEF NOTICES
CONCERNING MY PATERNAL ANCESTORS

I. The first person of the family from which I am descended, of whom I have any account, is *Christopher Smith*.[1] He removed from Tower-Hill in London, to Providence, Rhode-Island. The precise date of his removal I have not been able to determine, but from circumstances conjecture it must have been as early as 1680. Nor am I informed what was his occupation. It is traditionary in the family that he was a man of unblemished character, & of exemplary piety. At the time of his leaving England, he had four children. Three were born to him in America. Six were sons. Of these sons, three settled in, or near, Providence. I am ignorant of their names; nor have I learnt what became of the daughter. A fourth son, Thomas, fixed his residence at Hartford; a fifth, Simon, at Haddam; & the sixth, William, at Farmington, ten miles west of Hartford all in Connecticut.

II. *William Smith* of Farmington, the son of Christopher, a man also of an excellent character, had five sons.[2] Of these—

III. *Samuel Smith*, settled in Farmington.[3] This respectable man, who maintained the reputation of his family for integrity and amiable manners, was a Weaver. I have but slender memorials of his life. "The noiseless tenor of his way," supplies but few materials for the biographer. The following circumstances of his death are extracted from a letter from my father, dated May 31. 1794.

"For some time before his death, he was unable to get any sleep at all, but by lying on his back, with his arms extended; some person sitting on each side his bed, & pulling his arms. I have been told that he was opened, after his death, in order to discover the cause of the very singular symptoms, and it was found that one lobe of his lungs was entirely shrunk & dried up, & the other very much contracted."

Samuel Smith had six sons and five daughters.[4]

1. *William*. He lived in Farmington; died young; &, I believe, without issue.

2. *Samuel*: Died at the age of nineteen; & without issue.

3. *Thomas*: resided in Farmington, and died there a few years since, at the age of eighty-nine. I well remember this amiable & venerable man. He was remarkably pious & cheerful, fond of the society of the young, & retained the vigour of his mind to his last hour. In consequence of a fall, by which he was much hurt, he was confined to his bed, for the last three years of his life. I recollect visiting him in company with one of my sisters, at this time. A mild vein of pleasantry had not then forsaken him. He conversed with us, familiarly, on grave & gay subjects. "I remember your Litchfield," said he "when there was but a single wigwam erected. My father had a right of Land there; & as the proprietors were about settling it, & it was necessary to keep a little fort there, to protect the settlers from the bears & Indians, my father offered to relinquish his right to the son who would go up to Litchfield, & take his turn in defending it. Litchfield is but little more than twenty miles from Farmington, you know, but at that time we thought as much of going to Litchfield, as people do now of moving to Genesee or Niagara. As I was the oldest, I agreed to go up & take care of the land. The township was called Bantam then. That was the indian name. Well—I stayed at Bantam a few weeks—but I soon became sick of my undertaking. There were no girls, & no cyder, & I relinquished my land. All my brothers made the same trial; & with the same event." Thomas Smith was the father of a numerous family: many of whom are yet living.

4. *John*.—removed to Goshen (Connec.). I have a slight recollection of this man. He sustained a respectable character; was noted for his facetiousness; left several children; & died aged eighty-four.

5. *James*.—

6. *Stephen*—also removed to Goshen; where he died lately, at the age of eighty-seven. I saw him but a year or two before his death. He was a Farmer, like his brothers; & of a cheerful & amiable temper. He left a numerous family.

7. *Sarah*—married a Mr. Stanley of Goshen. I know not that I ever saw this woman.

8. *Ruth*—died an infant.

9. *Martha*—married a Mr. Stanley of Goshen; the brother, I believe, of her sister's husband. She died in the 94th year of her age.

10. *Ruth*—married a Mr. Root of Southington, then a

---

[1] A Christopher Smith (?-1676) lived in Providence in 1655. He was a freeman, a landholder, and had a wife named Alice; see John O. Austin, *The Genealogical Dictionary of Rhode Island; Comprising Three Generations of Settlers who Came Before 1690* (Albany, New York, 1887). p. 376. The names of Christopher's children do not correspond with those given by Smith. In view of this fact, and the closeness of the dates for William Smith (said by E. H. Smith to be Christopher's son), it might be suggested that Christopher and William were brothers.

[2] William did not go directly to Farmington but first lived in both Wethersfield and Middletown. According to a generally well-regarded reference, he had four sons and four daughters. See Herman R. Timlow, *Ecclesiastical and Other Sketches of Southington, Connecticut* (Hartford, Connecticut, 1875), Part II: p. ccxxxiv.

[3] (1664-1724/5), *ibid*.

[4] Samuel married Ruth, daughter of Thomas and Sarah (Hart) Porter by whom he had eleven children. Timlow (*ibid.*) lists only ten, but Smith adds Elizabeth, who died in infancy.

parish of Farmington, & died when thirty-five, with issue I believe, but am uncertain.

11. *Elizabeth*—died an infant.

IV. *James Smith*—the fifth son of Samuel, settled at Southington. When a boy, he was apprenticed to the joiner & carpenter's trade. He learnt weaving of his father. Afterward, he exercised both trades; but was, when I first knew him, as people of all professions & trades usually are, in N. England, a Farmer. He married Ruth Judd, of Waterbury, & had issue Samuel, Keziah, Azubah, Reuben, & Ruth; the last of whom died a child; the others survive.[5] Mrs. Smith died a few years before her husband, whose death happened on the ninth of December 1787, from Dropsy of the breast. He was eighty three the 20th of the preceding October.

The part of Southington in which my grandfather lived, exhibited a few years since the reality of those exquisite pictures of simple manners & honest lives, of moderate wishes & temperate pleasures, that the poets have delighted to paint. The whole township consists of a beautiful & fertile valley, divided into small farms, devoted to grass, grazing, wheat, & maize; well-wooded; intersected & bathed by numerous streams; & bounded on the east & west by mountains of considerable height; forming part of the vast chain, terminating at the river St. Lawrence. The House and little Farm of my grandfather are at the foot of the West-Mountain. The care of one of his grandsons has made many improvements here, but I love to recollect the original simplicity which appeared in every part of the scene, in my days of childhood. I love to remember that tho' you entered by a door with a thumb-latch, which nevertheless was without a lock—every inner door had only a bobbin; that the coarse, but white floors, might be played on, with more security from dirt, than the costly carpets from Turkey that ornament our drawingrooms; that the wide chimneys permitted us to huddle into comfortable seats within the jamb; while our kind maiden aunt kept us busily employed on nuts, the bounteous harvest of some venerable trees that yet remain, the ornaments of the neighboring field. It was a dim light that entered thro' the lattice windows, now so rarely seen, but I loved it better than that which blazes thro' those which reach from the ceiling to the floor; for then our grandfather, seated in his arm chair, took his grandchildren on his knees & blessed them. A lofty & wide-spreading oak, before the door, towered above the surrounding fruit trees; and a stately chestnut over shadowed the orchard behind the house, on the edge of which it grew. There was a clear stream that rippled over the pebbles, at the foot of the garden, & lost itself in the meadow below. The sun which blazed on the top of the eastern mountain, lluminating the whole valley, sunk beyond the west mountain at an early hour, pouring a flood of day on the opposite hills, but spreading a long & exquisite twilight over the intermediate vale. I have seen sublimer & more extensive prospects than that with which you were presented from the west mountain, but none more beautiful: more that spoke so directly to the heart—"here is the abode of peace, & industry & content."

---

[5] Timlow (*ibid.*) lists the children of James as: Keziah, Samuel, Azuba, Ruth (died in infancy), Reuben, Ruth. Smith mentions only one Ruth, the one who died in infancy. Either Timlow is in error or, more probably, both Ruths died when very young. Smith was a visitor at his grandfather's home and it is impossible that Ruth could have been alive and not known to him.

If the scene around was so pleasing, he who lived in the midst of it was no less so. Were I called to select from the whole number of men I have known, one truly polite, I know not where I could more properly fix my choice than on my grandfather. That superficial polish which is only caught among the fashionable & the gay, he had not; his was the politeness of the soul, which gave ease to all his deportment, & shone forth in well-directed & incessant endeavours to accommodate & make others happy. Never was there a man of a more amiable disposition, of a more serene & resigned temper, of a more affectionate & generous, humane & sensible heart; of a more lively & sincere piety. Of a sound mind (not wholly uninformed by reading, chiefly moral & devotional) & stored with the treasures of faithful if not spacious reflection; of manners which attracted, without imposing, respect; never was he treated with contumely, or beheld without esteem, without vanity, & without pride, his superiority wounded the self-regard of none. The poor found in him a father; his neighbors their best friend, & the ablest & most faithful composer of all their little strifes. from his decisions never was there known appeal. He has been dead ten years; I frequently pass thro' the village where he lived; his memory is cherished, & no one mentions his name but with some testimony of respect.

The person of James Smith, tho' small, was active & vigorous. At the age of seventy-nine, he performed a full day's work, at Reaping—an exercise of which he was fond. —His wife was a worthy woman; & his children inherited his virtues.

1. *Samuel*—the eldest child of James Smith, resides in Southington. He was bred a Carpenter: but chiefly attends to his farm. He is the father of three sons & five daughters, all whom are living.

2. *Keziah*—has been twice married: first, to a Mr. Root, by whom she had two sons & a daughter; afterwards to a Mr. Hawley, by whom she had one son, who died while a child. She is now a widow. Her three oldest children are living, are married, & are parents. One of them, Josiah Root, a physician & surgeon, I may have occasion to mention hereafter.

3. *Azubah Smith*—was never married. This amiable woman, from whom much of the preceding information is derived, unites to the most exquisite sensibility, a magnanimity worthy of a Roman matron. I forbear to be particular, at present, in the hope of more minute information concerning her history hereafter. She now resides, with her sister Keziah, in a part of what was once their father's house.

V. *Reuben Smith*, youngest surviving child of James, was born July 12th. 1737—O. S. My knowlege of the particulars of his early life is very inconsiderable. The little which I have, in any perfectness, is here recorded. It is necessary to preserve the connection with what follows; & may be enlarged as time & occasion furnish new materials.

Till the age of fifteen, my father was employed on the farm of my grandfather. The severity of the winter in New England allows no great opportunity for farmers to labour; and especially very little occasion to employ their children. The winters, of course, are devoted to instruction; which those who are too young to labour receive throughout the year, but those whose age is sufficient to make their exertions serviceable can have leisure to obtain only during the winter. After the first years of childhood, therefore, till he was fifteen, my father acquired at the ordinary schools, the knowledge of reading & writing his native language, & was taught the first or ground rules of Arithmetic. At fifteen he was sent, seven miles distant, to the clergyman of a neighboring town (Waterbury) to be instructed in the rudiments of the Latin & Greek tongues; & to obtain so much knowledge of the authors who have written in them, as should enable him to gain admission into Yale College. With this Clergyman, Mr. Leavenworth, he remained till the September after he was sixteen; when he went to New Haven, was examined, & admitted as a freshman in Yale College. He passed thro' the classical studies usually pursued there with credit, & took the degree of Bachelor of Arts in September 1757. Three years after, the degree of Master of Arts.

The orignal intention of my grandfather was that his son should engage in the Ministry. But this proving disagreable to my father, he turned his attention toward Medicine. As his parents were not wealthy, he was necessitated to seek support from his own exertions. The business of teacher to a country-school is honourable throughout New England; & the most distinguished Statesmen & Men of Letters, Divines, Physicians, Lawyers & Soldiers which that part of the United States has produced, have laid the foundation of their future fortune & future eminence, within the walls of a parish school. It will be sufficient to mention the names of John Adams, Oliver Ellsworth, John Trumbull, Timothy Dwight, Joel Barlow, Nathaniel Greene, & Lemuel Hopkins. More, were it necessary, might easily be adduced. My father, therefore, could have no reasonable objection against an employment, that, in some parts of the Union & in Europe perhaps, would have effectually obstructed his progress to fortune & respect. In the situation of Schoolmaster he acquired a maintenance for the first year, at least, after leaving College, if not longer. Here he commenced the study of Medicine, which, after relinquishing the business of instruction, he pursued under the direction of a physician of more reputation than skill or learning. Medical erudition, indeed, was at that time at a very low point. Some common book of anatomy, & the Institutes of Boerhaave, were almost the only works of any value then generally in the hands of practitioners; & my father was able to obtain a few other works, not without great trouble, & after long intervals. I well remember the lively expressions of pleasure which he used in relating to me the delight he received from the first reading of Boerhaave's Chemistry, & the works of Sydenham. Afterwards he obtained Huxham, Pringle, & the writers of that class; & as he was assiduous in his observation of the cases which came under the care of his instructor, as he was indefatigable in his search after books, & as he read every thing he could find, relative to his profession, he probably, entered on the practice better prepared than was common at that period. Sometime in the year 1760 he commenced the practice of physic & surgery, & opened an apothecary's shop, in Litchfield, Connecticut.

Litchfield a town-ship of six miles square, divided into several parishes, & now containing about 3,000 inhabitants, at that time was mostly uncultivated and unsettled. The town, properly so called, consisted of eight or ten houses; tho' now the number is near an hundred. My father had for a near neighbor Mr. Sheldon, a Judge of the Court of Common Pleas, & one of the Senate of the State. Between the youngest daughter of this gentleman, Miss Mary Sheldon, & my father, a mutual attachment soon sprung up. She has been described to me as tall, well-shaped, genteel & easy in her manners, fair & with blue eyes, & more accomplished than women usually are. In particular, she had cultivated her mind by reading. Add to this, she was a woman of sensibility & piety—distinguishing characteristics of my father— & which, doubtless, had no small share in determining his choice. The courtship had proceeded so far, I am informed, that they were under mutual engagements at the time of her death; which was in the autumn of 1763. She left him a testimony of her esteem in a small collection of books, to which his children are indebted, perhaps, for the first rudiments of a relish for works of taste & fancy.

After the melancholly loss of his mistress, I know little of my father, more than that he continued the exercise of his profession, with increasing reputation, till, in October 1770, he married Abigail Hubbard of Middletown, Connecticut, the dear & intimate friend of Miss Sheldon. At this time my father had realized some part of the profits of his business; owned a house, that he had just built; & had for an apprentice my cousin Josiah Root.

When young, at the age of twenty, my father might have been called a handsome man. About five feet & ten inches in height, well-formed, fair, & of a ruddy complexion & fine teeth, with light chestnut hair; that, according to the fashion of the times, fell loosely to the bottom of his waist, he added to these natural advantages a graceful address, and a delicacy & propriety of language, diversified by a light & pleasant vein of humor, not often to be met with. He sang, too, both agreeably & justly; & the modulation of his voice, which possessed both sensibility & compass, have filled me with transport, many many years after age had considerably impaired its powers. The life of a country practitioner of medicine, especially in the commencement of its settlement, when the people are dispersed over a large tract of land, & the roads are imperfectly formed, & where the conveniences of life, & accomodations for for the sick, are with difficulty provided, is extremely severe. To a man of my father's temper, whose mind was so deeply engaged for the welfare of his patients that his anxiety for them often banished both appetite & repose, it was doubly distressing. At thirty he was bald; and the powers of his voice were somewhat lessened: still he might have been deemed a fine looking man.

My mother was of a good height & figure; a dark-complexioned woman, with fine colour; with large, mild black eyes, & black hair; & all her features regular & handsome. The continual attacks of disease, united to a constitution naturally frail, have not yet, in her 59th year, wholly obliterated her former freshness.

To these two persons, whose worth I rather feel, than am able precisely to describe, am I indebted for my existence.

Dear authors of my being! you in whom I have ever found the tenderest & most unshaken friends; whose care hath never been withheld; whose bounty hath been flowed; & the consolations of whose love have never been refused me; with what language shall I express the affectionate respect which animates my soul, when I recollect your virtues & your exertions for my welfare. Ah! that I were more worthy of this virtue! more deserving of these exertions! That in this vernal season of my youth, and while the infirmities of age are fast gathering upon you, instead of drawing support from your hands, I were able to confer that comfort, and that repose, which your years & labours merit, & which would be the consummation of my wishes, the anxious desire of all my life, the completion of my grateful vows!

# # #

ABIGAIL (HUBBARD) SMITH

Smith failed to record his mother's ancestry in the "Diary" although her family had come to America even earlier than the Smiths. George Hubbard, the immigrant ancestor, was born in England in 1601. He came overland with the first settlers from the Massachusetts Bay Colony and established himself in Hartford, Connecticut, before 1639. He was married in 1640 to Elizabeth, daughter of Richard and Elizabeth Watts, and was assigned a house lot and land on the east side of the Connecticut River. Of this union there were eight children. In March, 1650/51, with about fifteen other families, the Hubbards moved to Middletown (at that time called Mattabesit). Hubbard was a licensed Indian agent and trader as early as 1650 despite the fact that in 1649 he had been fined ten pounds for exchanging a gun with an Indian. In 1654 he was admitted a freeman. He lived on what is now Main Street, owned much land on both sides of the river, and was first sexton of the first meeting house.[6]

Joseph Hubbard, son of George, was born in Hartford on December 10, 1643, and died in Middletown on December 26, 1686. Apparently less given to extremes than his father, he is remembered only for the fact that he assisted him as sexton by beating the drum as a call to meeting and as a warning against Indians. He was married on December 29, 1670, to Mary Potter, and by her he had six children.[7]

Robert Hubbard, second son of Joseph, was born in Middletown in 1673 and died there in 1740. In March, 1703, he was married to Abigail Adkins Ward, daughter of Josiah and Elizabeth (Adkins) Ward, of Middletown. Of this union there were four children.[8]

Robert Hubbard, fourth child and only son of Robert, was born in Middletown on July 30, 1712, and died on January 29, 1779. At the age of eighteen he settled in East Long Hill and, on October 9, 1735, he married Elizabeth Sill, the daughter of Joseph and Phebe (Lord) Sill, of Lyme, Connecticut. Abigail Hubbard, Elihu Smith's mother, the third of the six children of this marriage, was born on January 5, 1739.[9] Elihu's childhood memories of his grandfather were vivid and no less pleasant than those of his paternal grandparent. We know that he frequently attended his mother on her semi-annual visits home and, on at least one occasion, he had been left with his grandparents for some time. Robert Smith, by occupation a shoemaker, also owned a large farm and, despite the humble nature of his work, was apparently a man of considerable importance in the community.

J.E.C.

---

[6] *New England Families, Genealogical and Memorial,* ed. William R. Cutter (New York, 1913) **1**: p. 108. Another reference gives his date of birth as 1601. See *American Ancestry* (Albany, New York, 1890) **5**: p. 135.

[7] Edward W. Day, *One Thousand Years of Hubbard History, 866-1895* (New York, 1895), p. 275. *American Ancestry* **5**: p. 135, gives Mary Porter as Mary Foster.

[8] Day, *One Thousand Years of Hubbard History,* p. 277. *American Ancestry* **5**: p. 135 gives Elizabeth Adkins as Abigail Atkins.

[9] Day, *One Thousand Years of Hubbard History,* p. 278.

INDEX

Significant incidents, names and titles of books, periodicals and plays are indexed here except for authors and titles of occasional inaugural essays. Summarized tables of contents of magazines are omitted unless they contribute otherwise unavailable information. When names of Smith's friends appear on almost every page, or many times on a page, first and last mention are given, supplemented by specific reference to any incidents of importance. For the convenience of professional readers Smith's letters, names of actors, and of doctors mentioned in passing appear under group headings.

Abby, 68. *See* Abigail Smith, Jr.
Aberdom, Alexandar, 275
Abolition Convention, 116, 118
Abolition of Slavery: bill for, 130
Abolition Society, 118
Abolition Society of New Jersey, 98
Absorbent System, The (Cruikshank), 160
Accidence: A Short Introduction to the Latin Tongue (Cheever), 27
Account of the Management of the Poor in Hamburg Since the Year 1788 (Voght), 274, 279
Account of the Russian Discoveries, etc. (Coxe), 222
Actors and actresses: Barrett, 345; Mrs. Barrett, 345; Bernard, 358, 366, 371, 384; Blisset, 384; Mrs. Brett, 131, 132, 135, 142, 273, 444; Miss Broadhurst, 140; Byrne, 316; Mrs. Byrne, 316; Chalmers, 410, 418; Cleveland, 136, 140; Mrs. Cleveland, 132, 136, 140; Collins, 286; Crosby, 266, 315, 348, 349, 351, 357, 367, 371, 413, 414, 420, 428, 429, 430, 433, 434, 436, 438, 440, 444, 447; Downie, 345; Fennel, 357, 371; Francis, 349; Mde. Gardie, 436; Mrs. Grauper, 345; Hallam (separate entry); Mrs. Hallam (separate entry); Harding, 384; Mrs. Harding, 384; Harwood, 349, 367, 384; Hodgkinson (separate entry); Mrs. Hodgkinson (separate entry); Jefferson, 131, 135, 140, 280; Mrs. Jefferson, 280; Johnson (separate entry); Mrs. Johnson (separate entry); Jones, 345; Marshall, 366; Mrs. Marshall, 366, 371; Martin, 240, 266, 273; Mrs. Melmoth, 240, 266, 414; Mrs. Merry (separate entry); Molton, 349; Moreton, 348, 351, 357, 366, 371, 414; Mrs. Oldmixon, 315, 357, 358, 366; Mrs. Pownal, 371; Prigmore, 316; Mrs. Seymour, 229; Simpson, 402; Mrs. Simpson, 404; Stockwell, 309, 318; Tyler, 131, 132, 135, 140, 142, 240, 266, 371, 416; Mrs. Tyler, 131, 140; Warner, 349; Warren, 366; Miss Westby, 416; Mrs. Whitlock, 354; Williamson, 345, 411, 416, 433; Mrs. Williamson, 344, 357
Adams, Andrew (Litchfield), 21, 432, 451
Adams, Andrew, Jr., 25, 29, 35
Adams, Charles, 43; member of the Friendly Club, 45, 46; 52, 54, 57, 72, 73, 74, 92, 106, 124, 137, 138, 153, 182, 200, 206, 208, 212, 228, 242, 247, 260, 268, 269, 298, 305, 321, 331, 333, 357, 365, 373, 383, 400, 404, 426, 437
Adams, Mrs. Charles, 72, 74

Adams, Elijah (Litchfield), 25, 407
Adams, Eunice (Litchfield), 18
Adams, George, 183, 184, 185
Adams, John, President, 16, 250, 262, 268, 390, 467
Adams, John, (son of president), 269
Adams, Mary (Litchfield), 18, 26
Adams, Thomas (son of president), 269
Adet, Pierre, 278, 292, 317, 367, 431
Addison, Joseph, 23, 24, 371
"Address of the President of the United States," 271
"Address to His Constituents" (Harper, S. Carolina), 138
Adopted Child, The (Birch), 229, 351, 428
Aeneid, 33
Aeschines (Eschines), 292
Africa, Cash (servant), 89, 105, 124, 132
Africa, Mrs. Cash, 124, 132, 134
African School, 95, 135, 152, 153, 155, 158, 159, 161-162, 180, 184, 197, 200, 213, 226, 231, 270, 280, 289, 290, 305, 317, 318, 356
Age of Reason (Paine), 156
Agreable Surprise (O'Keefe), 137, 410
Aikin, John, Dr., 116, 283, 406, 422, 437, 440
Albert, Rev. M., 334
Alcuin, a Dialogue (C. B. Brown), 342, 349, 364, 372, 380, 401, 405, 425, 430, 435, 437, 438, 439, 440, 454, 461
Algerine Captive, etc. (Tyler), 357, 409
Aliens, The (Marshall), 449
All for Love (Dryden), 315
All in the Wrong (Murphy), 416
All the World's a Stage (Jackman), 289
Allen, John, 87-459, *passim*
Almy, Capt., 433
Alsop, Miss, 317-451, *passim*
Alsop, F., Miss, 452
Alsop, Joseph, 365, 451, 452
Alsop, Mrs. Joshua (Lucy Whittlesey), 453
Alsop, Richard, 10-463, *passim*
Alsop, Mrs. Richard, 347, 365, 370, 376, 406, 452, 453
Ambrosia, or The Monk (Lewis), 336
America (ship), 219
American Biography (Belknap), 389
American Gazeteer (Morse), 389
American Geography, etc. (Morse), 16, 103, 319, 325, 327, 329, 331
American Magazine, The, 4
American Mercury, 11
American Museum, or Universal Magazine, The, 9
American Poems, Selected and Original, Vol. I, 10, 11, 14, 15, 66, 108, 121

Ames, Fisher, 162
Amorous Tale of the Chaste Loves of Peter the Long, The (Holcroft), 273
Anarchiad, The, 10, 163, 437
Anarchasis, 161 ff.
Anacreon (tr. Fawkes), 325
Anacreontic Society, 15
Analytical Review, 461, 464
Anatomy of Melancholy (Burton), 54
Anderson, George, 399
Anderson, Robert, 327
Andre (Dunlap), 417, 419, 430, 432, 433, 436
Anna St. Ives (Holcroft), 44, 325, 331, 351
Annals de Chemie (Fourcroy), 426
Annals of Medicine (Duncan), 331, 336, 420, 439
Answer to Dr. Priestley (McLean), 318
Apollonius Rhodius' Argonautica (tr. Fawkes), 328
Appeal to Impartial Posterity (Roland), 117, 158, 177, 178
Archers, The (Dunlap), 130, 134, 138, 157. Also: *William Tell*
Arctic Zoology (Pennant), 356
Aristides, 68
Armstrong, John, 28
Arnold, James, 447
Arrangement, etc. (Walker), 463
Aspinwall, Mr., 374
As You Like It, 159-160, 421
Athenian-Horanian (club), 15
Atkinson, Mr., 277, 280
Atmore, Miss, 119
Auger, A., 211
Aurora, The (paper), 6

B., Mr. *See* Mr. Bacon
B., Mrs. *See* Mrs. William Buel
Babcock, Mr., 122
Bachaumont, Mons., 181
Bache, Benjamin Franklin, 6, 162, 278
Bache, Mrs. B. F., 458
Backus, Rev. Mr., 419, 420, 428, 429, 432, 449, 457
Backus, Mrs., 449
Bacon, Asa, 85
Bacon, Ezekiel (Stockbridge), 228, 231, 282, 344, 397
Bacon, Mrs. (mother of Ezekiel), 397
Bacon, John (Eng. sculptor), 291
Bacon, Polly, Miss (Sheffield), 284
Bacon, Roger, 462
Bage, Robert, 243, 290, 388
Bailey, Marcia E., 3, 8, 10, 12
Baillie, Matthew, 161, 165

469

Baker, Gardiner, 97, 423
Baker's Observatory, 358
Baldwin, Mr., 363, 454
Baldwin, Ashbel, 21, 23
Baldwin, Nathaniel, 23, 25
Baldwin, Phineas, 88
Bancker, Mr., 422
Bank of North America, 271
Bard, Dr. (John or Samuel), 12
Bard, Samuel, Dr., 297
Barham Downs (Bage), 388, 391
Bark (quinine), 33, 59-60
Barlow, Joel, 10, 23, 73, 131, 136, 251, 263, 436, 437, 467
Barry, Commodore, 388
Barthelmy, Jean, 161, 238
Barton, Benjamin Smith, Dr., 8, 212, 287, 305, 309, 316, 319, 320, 321, 332, 334, 338, 361, 383, 386, 395, 397, 399, 401, 410, 423, 431, 434, 435, 437, 438, 439, 457
Barton's collections, 449
Basier, Mr., 320
Bauman, Mr., 73
Bay, Dr. (England), 332, 394, 410
Bayard, Miss, 392, 449
Bayley, Richard, Dr., 399, 429
Bayley, T. B., 401
Beach, Elnathan, Dr., 268, 391
Beacon Hill (Mrs. Sarah W. Morton: Boston), 386, 389, 391
Beckley, John, 316
Beddoes, Thomas, Dr., 108-460, *passim*
Beers, Abel, 376
Beers, Isaac (New Haven), 82-421, *passim*
Beers, William Pitt (Albany), 3-464, *passim*
Beers, Mrs. William P., 313
Belden, Col., 452
Belden, Mrs., 452
Belknap, Jeremy, Dr., 357, 389, 440, 444
Bell, Benjamin, 180, 327
Belles Lettres Club, 15
Belles Lettres Club Subscription, 220
Belle's Stratagem, The (Cowley), 10, 402
Belloc, William, 97
Benjamin, DeLucena, 35
Berquin, Mons., 90
Berry & Rogers (auction), 404
Bickerstaffe, Isaac, 156, 225, 280, 286, 344
Biddle, Miss, 119
Bilious Fevers (Currie), 432, 446
Bion (tr. Fawkes), 325
Birch, Samuel, 229, 351, 428
Bird, John, 29, 31, 33, 133, 136, 151, 245
Bird, Seth, Dr., 5, 430, 432, 450
"Birtha" (pseudonym), 8
Bisset, Rev. Mr., 63, 392
Blacklock, Thomas, 281
Blair, Hugh, 116, 141
Bleecker, W., 449, 460
Bloodgood & Hitchcock (grocers), 220
Blood-letting, a defense by Rush, 201
Bloomfield, Joseph, Atty. Gen., 315, 458
Boaden (Boeden), James, 64, 401
Boerhaave, Hermann, 467
Bomare, Valmont de, 328
Bonner, James, 135
Bon Ton (Garrick), 154
Bordley, Mr., 317
Borne, Samuel, 307

Botanic Garden, The (Darwin), 236-421, *passim*
Boulanger, Mons., 63, 309
Bournville Castle (Linn), 134
Bowles, William Lisle, 9
Bowne, Samuel, 180, 305
Boyd, William, 43-461, *passim*
Boyd, Mrs., 370
Brace, Mr., 86
Brace, Mrs., 450
Bradley, Abraham, Capt., 21, 29, 33, 343, 396
Bradley, Mrs. Abraham, 48
Bradley & Huggins (merchants, New Haven), 91
Brède, Baron de la, 199
Brewer, Mr., 69, 305
Briggs, Mr., 183, 215, 216-217
Briggs, Mrs. (Miss Norton), 199
Bringhurst, Joseph, Jr., 8-423, *passim*
British Critic, 437, 442
Broadhurst, Mrs., 131
Brooke, Frances, 231
Brooke, Henry, 24, 96, 176
Brooke, Mrs., 366
Broome, Mr.: calls on Alsop to protest his satire, 66
Broome, John, 64, 318
Broome, W. T., 106, 134
Broomes, The, 309
Brothers in Unity, 3
Brown, Mr. (Boston), 388
Brown, Dr. (Fort Stanwix), 245, 246, 268
Brown, Dr. (House of Rep.), 244-245
Brown, Mrs. (Amboy), 198
Brown, Armit, 118, 315
Brown, Charles Brockden, 8, 11, 14, 15, 16, 48, 56, 57, 59, 60, 74, 80, 81, 88, 93, 101, 102, 114, 117, 118, 119, 146-147, 163, 167, 168, 170, 184, 188, 189, 190, 197, 203, 208, 212, 213, 214, 219; gives language lessons to Roulet, 221; 222, 223, 225, 226, 228, 229, 231; reads from new, incomplete romance, 233; 237, 238; on truth, 239; 240, 242, 243, 244, 245, 255, 256, 258, 266, 267, 268, 269, 270, 271; criticism by Smith, 272; 273, 274, 275, 278, 279, 280, 281, 282, 286, 287, 288, 289, 290, 293, 294, 296, 297, 298, 300, 302, 309, 314, 315, 316, 321, 322, 325, 332, 333, 334, 336, 342, 349, 352, 364, 388, 395, 406, 413, 416, 417, 418, 423, 425, 427, 430, 433, 434, 435, 436, 438, 439, 440, 441, 442, 444, 445, 446, 448, 449, 454, 455, 456, 457, 458, 459, 460, 461, 462, 463
Brown, James, 118, 281
Brown, William, 451
Browne, Dr. Joseph, 429
Brown's dialogue, 419. See *Alcuin*
Brown's Elements (Beddoes, ed.), 108
Brownson (or Brunson), Mr., 26
Buck, Daniel, 452
Buck, Josiah, 452
Buel, Polly, 88
Buel, Sally, 88
Buel, William, Dr., 85-464, *passim*
Buel, Mrs. William, 284, 371, 396, 409
Büerger, Mr., 316. See Gottfried A. Bürger
Buffon, Georges, Compte de, 355, 392
Bull, Capt., 88, 450, 454

Bull, Miss, 19, 23, 25, 280, 453
Bull, Mr., 22, 23
Bull, Mrs., 88, 450
Bull, Amos, 451
Bull, Lucy, 274, 278, 459
Bull, Serena, 86
Bull, Susan. See Mrs. Uriah Tracy
Bullfinch, Charles, 429-430, 433, 434
Bunce, George & Co. (store), 98
Bunker Hill, 307-308, 357, 437
Buonaparte, Napoleon, 278
Bürger, Gottfried A., 228, 294, 316, 350, 404
Burgoyne, John, 133, 284
Burk, John Daly, 307, 437
Burke, Edmund, 300, 314
Burney, Frances, 87
Burr, Aaron, Col., 106, 134, 177, 310, 390, 406
Burt, Mr., 282
Burton, Richard, 54
Bustle, or The New House (Miln), 421
Butler, Miss, 316
Butler, Frederic, 452

Cabal and Love (Schiller), 94
Cadmus: or a Treatise on the Elements of Written Language (Thornton), 301
Caesar, Julius, 141, 242
Caldwell, Dr., 187, 455
Caleb Williams (Godwin), 53, 85, 181, 237, 243, 296, 307, 372
Calliopean Society, 15
Calvin, 83
Camilla (Mde. D'Arblay), 287, 288, 289, 294, 298, 302, 344
Cammel (Smith's servant), 332
Campbell, Mr., 355
Camper, Petrus (Pieter), 47
Camus, Armand G., 181
Candide (Voltaire), 159
Carey, Mathew, 162
Caritat, Hocquet, 457, 461
Carlisle, Mr., 335
Carr, Mr. (musician), 133
Carrier, Mons., 198
Carrington, Samuel, 388
"Carwin" (Brown), 464
"Case of Rabies Canina" (A. Johnson), 331
Case of the Soapboilers and Tallow Chandlers (Mitchill), 317-318
Castle, Mr., 426
Castle of Otranto, The (Walpole), 91, 92, 121, 336
Castle Spectre, The (Lewis), 444, 447
Catechism of Health for Use in Schools (Faust), 95, 306
Catechism of the Assembly of Divines at Westminster, 20
Catherine and Petruchio (Garrick), 244
Cathill, the crazy tailor, 64
Catlin, Capt., 450
Catlin, Aaron (Litchfield), 59, 140
Catlin, Almira (Litchfield), 87
Catlin, Lynde, Dr. (Litchfield), 85, 89, 450
Catlin, Mrs. Lynde (Litchfield), 85, 334, 450
Catlin, Lynde (son of Dr. Catlin), 3-464, *passim*
Cecilia (Burney), 87

INDEX

Celestina (Mrs. Smith), 62
Centlivre, Susanna, 223, 344
Chace, Mr., 429
Champion, Rev. Judah, 9, 28, 30-31, 32, 33, 34, 260, 450
Chapter of Accidents, A (S. Lee), 298, 318
"Character of Mahomet" (Gibbon), 143
Chardin, Sir John, 302
Charles, 88, 198, 199. See Charles Brockden Brown
Charles Tomson (Dunlap), 101
Charms of Fancy (Alsop), 62
Chase, Rev. Mr., 88, 450
Chatterton, Thomas: his inspired poetry, 91
Chatwell, Capt., 362
Chaucer, 327
Chauncey, Charles, Judge (New Haven), 83, 84, 90, 136, 416, 418, 455
Chauncey, Mrs. Charles, 136
Chauncey, Chas., Jr., 317, 364, 388
Cheap Living (Reynolds), 447
Cheasapeck (ship), 395
Cheever, Ezekiel, 27
Chemistry (Boerhaave), 467
Chenevard, Capt., 451
Chenevard, J., 451
Chenevard, Mrs. J. (Julia Seymour), 451
Chester, Col., 452
Chester, Miss, 452
Chester, Mrs., 452
Chester, Hannah, 452
Chester, Stephen, 452
Chester, Mrs. Stephen, 452
Chester, Mrs. Thomas (Hetty Bull), 451
Child labor: England vs. U. S., 64
Children of the Wood (Morton), 434
Chisholm, Dr. Colin, 384, 386, 399, 400, 401, 426, 442, 445
Christianity Unveiled (Boulanger, tr. William M. Johnson), 63, 367
Christie, Mr., 95
Church of Rome, 83
Cibber, Colley, 131
Cicero, 31, 33, 79, 141, 367
Cidevant Sec. of State (Randolph), 112
Circus, The (theater), 348
Clandestine Marriage (Garrick and Colman the elder), 142
Clap, Thomas (president of Yale), 2
Clarissa Harlowe (Richardson), 429, 430, 432, 433, 435, 436
Clark, Thaddeus, 95
Clarke, Rev. Sir William, 274
Classes Fossilium, etc. (Walker), 460
Clutterbuck, Mr., 142
Coates, Samuel, 8, 119, 329, 333
Coates, Mrs. Samuel, 119
Cobb, James, 147, 429
Coe, Mrs., 302
Coffin, Charles, Dr., 272, 328, 428, 430, 432
Cogswell, James, Dr., 13
Cogswell, Mason Fitch, Dr., 3-463, passim
Coit, Joshua (distinction between Coits not clear), 301, 332, 456
Coit, L., 308, 317, 328, 373, 374, 376, 423, 445
Coit, Mrs. (may be wife of either Joshua or L.), 314, 317, 374, 376
Coleman. See Colman

Coleridge, Samuel Taylor, 199, 229, 296, 426-427, 460, 462
Collection of Medical, Botanical, & Chemical Essays, A: proposed prose work, 54
College of the Leeks, 240
College of Philadelphia, 6
College of Physicians, 68, 69
Collier, Thomas, 11-12, 66, 85, 87, 88, 89, 92, 121, 133, 134, 139, 140, 141, 282, 450, 454
Collins, Mrs. Daniel (Eliz. Lewis), 21
Collins, Lucretia, 300, 455
Collins, Nancy, 231
Colloquies (Corderius), 28, 33
Colman, George, Jr., 131, 132, 142, 151, 229, 231, 233, 236, 241, 286, 444
Colman, George, Sr., 142, 384
Colt, Mrs., 97
Columbia College, 95
Columbia Garden, 447
Columbia Magazine, The, 8
Columbiad, The, 406
Comet, The (Miln or Milne), 287, 289, 293
Commercial Advertiser (paper), 421
Committee of Health, The, Reports of, 53, 162
Complete Edition of the Poets of Great Britain, A (Anderson), 327
Complete History of Connecticut (B. Trumbull), 389
Condorcet, Marquis de, 44, 48, 49, 53, 55, 59, 60, 63, 64, 66, 67, 97, 130, 131, 146, 242, 283, 306
Confessions (Rousseau), 414, 416, 418
Congress, Mons., 430
Connecticut (ship), 57
Connecticut Agricultural Society, 83
Connecticut Bible Society, 10
Connecticut Courant, 143
Connecticut Historical Society, 11
Connecticut State Medical Society, 10, 12
Connecticut Wits, The (Howard), 9, 11
Considerations on Lord Grenville's and Mr. Pitt's Bills, etc., By a Lover of Order, 158
Considerations on the Medical Use of Factitious Airs, etc. (Beddoes), 125, 331
Considerations on Phlogiston (Priestley), 317, 366, 394
Considérations sur les causes de la grandeur et de la décadence des Romains (Baron de la Brède), 199-200
Constant, Benjamin, 243, 244
Continuation of the History of the Province of Massachusetts Bay (Minot), 431
Contrast, Charity (Mrs. Paxon), 450
Controversy Between Kirwan and the French Academicians, on Phlogiston, The (Nicholson), 409
Coolidge (a crazyman of Boston), 73
Cooper, Miss H., 458
Cope, Thomas Pym, 8
Cornillon, Vicompte de, 270, 271
Cosway, Richard, 386
Cotton, Mrs., 176
Count Fathom (Smollett), 95-96
Country Girl, The (Garrick), 366
Cowles, Elias: case of, 102, 165
Cowles, Mrs., 87

Cowley, Hannah, 10, 242, 402
Cowper, William: receives manuscripts from Conn. Wits, 15; 54, 83
Coxe, Mr. (author), 222
Coxe, Mrs., 315
Cozine, Mr., 140
Cragie, Josiah (Cambridge), 317, 456, 457, 458, 459, 461, 462, 464
Critic, The (Sheridan), 158, 290
Critical Review, The, 336
Cronstedt, Alexander, 460, 461
Cross, John C., 401, 421
Croswell, Thomas O'Hara, Dr., 9, 40-42, 100, 268, 301, 302, 395, 396, 407, 409, 411, 439, 458, 459
Croswell, Mrs. Thomas (Ruth Pierce), 21, 42, 407
Cruikshank, William C., Dr., 160, 161, 162, 165
Cullen, William, 162, 388
Cumberland, Richard, 134, 135, 136, 203, 256, 298, 303, 442, 447
Cunningham, Michael, 366, 429
Cure for the Heart Ach, A (Morton), 411
Curiosities of Literature, 66, 67, 71, 73, 76
Currie, James, Dr. (England), 435, 436, 437, 444
Currie, Dr. (Philadelphia): refs. tentative; Smith sometimes does not distinguish between the two Curries, 60, 383, 384, 385, 388, 405, 430, 432, 433, 446, 447
Cymbeline, 314, 430

D., 43. See William Dunlap
Dagget, Naphtali (Yale pres.), 2. See Daggett, 311
Daily Advertiser, The, 44-424, passim
Dana, Mr., 278, 279, 280, 302, 317, 332, 333, 391, 447, 457
D'Arblay, Madame (Frances Burney), 287
Darwin, Erasmus, 74, 309, 332, 341, 342, 346, 356, 371, 404, 419, 426, 434, 445, 460
Davenport, James, 151, 305, 343, 389, 414
Davidge, John Beale, 436, 447, 448, 449
Davidson, H. Carter, 8
Day, Mr. (Hartford), 450
Day, Mr. (Onondaga), 309, 323, 458
Day, Thomas (author), 110
Days of Yore (Cumberland), 203, 211
De Fieux, Charles, 33
Dead and Alive (O'Keefe), 315
Deckar, Thomas (Dekker), 169, 366
Decline and Fall of the English System of Finance (Paine), 187-188
De la force Gouvernement actual de la France et de la nécessité de s'y rallier (Constant), 243, 244, 268
Defoe, Daniel, 54
Delai Lama, 240
Della Crusca, 327
Della Cruscan correspondence (Merry and Cowley), 8
Deming, Mr., 228, 373, 401, 402, 447, 448, 450, 452
Demosthenes, 292
Dennie, Joseph, Jr., 223, 298, 299, 300, 313, 326, 331, 332, 334, 335, 336, 349, 357, 364
Denning, Miss, 208, 319
Denon, Vivant (De Non), 369, 385

De Pauw, Mr., 238, 241, 399
"Descent of Frea" (Sayers), 136
Deserted Daughter (Holcroft), 128, 135, 137, 140, 229
Desmoulins, Camille, 93
Des Prisons de Philadelphia (Liancourt), 317
Devin du Village (Rousseau), 134
Dewees, Dr., 379, 383, 384, 401, 411, 416, 418, 430, 438, 455, 456, 459, 461
Dexter, Samuel, 427
Dialogues Concerning Natural Religion (Hume), 446
Dialogues of the Dead (Lyttleton), 21
Diary, The (paper), 411
Dibdin, Charles, 138, 140, 245, 303, 411
Dickson, Dr., 352, 426, 427, 429, 445
Dict.: d'hist. Nat. (Valmont de Bomare), 328, 329
Dictionnaire des portraits historiques anecdotes, etc. (Lacombe), 81
Dictionary of Engravers (Strutt), 406
Diderot, Denis, 444, 445
Dingley, Amasa, Dr., 48-440, *passim*
Discourse to the Asiatic Society (Sir John Shore), 102
Dispreau, Mons., 65
D'Israeli, 67, 69, 72, 75
Dissertation on Oxygene (Mitchill), 317-318
Dissertation on Septon (Saltonstall), 354
Dissertation on Slavery (Tucker), 317
Dissertation on the Yellow Fever of 1795 (Hosack), 318
Dissertation physique sur les différences réelles que présentent les traits du visage chez les hommes . . . (Camper), 47
Dissertations and Miscellaneous Pieces Relating to the History and Antiquities of Asia (Jones), 239, 272, 319
Dobson, Mr. (printer), 346, 400, 405, 436
Dobson's store, 335
Doctor and Apothecary (Cobb), 429
Doctor of Medicine: eighteenth-century requirements for degree, 7-8
Doctors mentioned in passing: Archer, 437; Bailey, 383; Barker, 268, 461; Bartlett, 408; Bayard, 449; Baynton, 332; Bellamy, 86, 432; Bollman, 124, 147; Borrows, 409; Bowen, 406; Brickel (also Brickell), 417, 459; Browne, 435; William Bud, 266; Bull, 450, 451; Bullfinch, 214; Burns, 103; Buxton, 404; Carrington, 267; Cooper, 463; Coxe, 391; Darling, 90; Davidson, 308, 309; DeRosset, 458-459; DeWitt, 436; Delanoe, 425; Dwight (New Hamp.), 440, 442; Farrington, 239; Bernard C. Faust, 95, 306; Ferriar, 215; George Fordyce, 270; Fowler, 161, 168; Gaubert, 303; Gimbernat, 270; Benjamin Gooch, 267; Hale, 147; Hall, 267, 430, 453; William Hammersley, 387; Hart, 461; Hawes, 72, 73; Henry, 399; Hitchcock, 333; Benjamin Hoadley, 404; William Hodgson, 388; Holliday, 223; Holyoke, 328, 424; Hulbert, 268; Huxley, 48; Jackson, 197, 315; Jill, 284; J. B. Jones, 383; King, 434, 444; Kirkpatrick, 245, 268; Kuhn, 404; Lamb, 67, 176; Ebenezer Larkin, 442, 459; Leigh, 449; Logan, 317; McClure (Maclure), 464; Maret, 334; Richard Mead, 305; Miller (of N.Y., not Edward), 11, 13; Muhlenberg, 239; Munson, 302; Elijah Munson, 268, 309; Eneas Munson, 268; Samuel Nicoll, 130, 137; Nooth, 461; North, 193; Elisha North, 278; Norton, 268; Olcott, 452; Oliver, 424; Orton, 267; Osborn (of N. Carolina), 448; Parke, 376, 379; Pike, 391; Pleasants, 318; Joshua Porter, 278; Potter, 272; Richard Price, 251, 263; Proudfit, 411; Ramsay, 218, 442; Rice, 430; Richter, 161; Ricketson, 385; Robert, 356; Rockwell, 267, 402; J. R. B. Rogers, 12; John Rollo, 457; Ross, 410; Patrick Russell, 305; Ebenezer Sage, 268, 367; Sayre (Philadelphia), 463; Scott, 331, 332; Sevediaur, 460; John Sinclair, 287; Smith, 361-362; Wm. Pitt Smith, 132; Spooner, 408; Stevens, 381; Sylvester, 267; William Thornton, 301; James Tillary, 384, 433; Eli Todd, 47; Torquid, 54; Tredwell, 371; Trotter, 444; Thomas Tucker, 449; Valentin, 343; Walker (Jamaica), 427; Warren, 331; Waterhouse, 408, 447; Williamson, 56; Wolcott, 27; Young, 185; Zeiss, 368; Zimmerman, 236
Doddridge, Philip, 24
Don Silvio de Rosalva (Wieland, tr. anon.), 281, 286
Double Disguise (O'Keefe), 298
Douglas (Home), 434
Downman, Mr., 306
Drummond, A. (bookseller), 220
Drury, Capt., 436
Dryden, 141
Dryden, John, 315
Duby, Rev. Mr., 334
Duchesne, Mr., 331
Duer, Mr., 347
Dumarsais, César, 135, 136, 138, 146, 155, 156, 157, 158, 160
Dumourier, Mons., 125
Dunlap, John, 280
Dunlap, Margaret, 280
Dunlap, William, 12-464, *passim;* member of Manumission Society, 13; *Life of Brown,* 15; member of Friendly Club, 45, 46; attempt to dramatize *Herman of Unna,* 64; *The Archers,* 130, 157, 267; *Fountainville Abbey,* 134; taking notes for his *History of the American Theatre,* 135; writes *William Tell,* 146; shows Smith a new comedy based on *Jerome Pointu,* 169; takes charge of Hartford Theater, 184; *Mysterious Monk,* 236, 238; *Ribbemont,* 240; reads *Tell Truth and Shame the Devil* to Friendly Club, 245; reads *Fall of Robespierre* to Club, 381; *Sterne's Maria,* 286; trouble with the Hallams, 290 ff.; his plays idolized, 347; delivers to Smith early chapters of Brown's lost novel, "Skywalk," 438; *Rule a Husband and Have a Husband,* 447
Dunlap, Mrs. William, 90, 115
Dunn, Mr. (Irish M. P.), 401, 405
Dupaty, Mr., 270
Duportail, Louis, Major Gen., 28
Dupuis, Charles F., 244
Durham, Miss, 316
Duryee, Mr., 422, 430, 434, 439, 449, 459
Duryee, Mrs. (Nancy Mumford), 411
Dwarf, 401, 404
Dwight, Miss, 308
Dwight, Nathaniel, Dr., 122, 270, 278, 302, 307, 312, 320, 350, 357, 374, 392, 393, 397, 398, 399, 409, 410, 411, 416, 422, 424, 433, 438, 439, 440, 449, 451, 456, 458, 459
Dwight, P., Miss, 318
Dwight, Sally, 133
Dwight, Theodore, 8-452, *passim*
Dwight, Mrs. Theodore, 278, 313
Dwight, Timothy (Yale pres.), 3, 4, 7, 9, 10, 16, 24, 58, 73, 83, 122, 125, 127, 128, 130, 133, 200, 248, 259, 263, 290, 331, 341, 342, 418, 419, 420, 421, 431, 439, 446, 449, 455, 456, 461, 467
Dwight, Mrs. Timothy, 282

Eagle (paper), 299
Earl of Essex (Jones), 133
Ebeling, Prof. (Hamburg), 154, 219
Echo With Other Poems, The, 11
Eclogues (Virgil), 31, 33
Eddy, Miss, 316, 318, 320
Eddy, Mr., 340
Eddy, Thomas, 14, 135, 301, 307
Eddy, William, 8
Edgar and Emmeline (Hawkesworth), 157
Edmonds, Mr., 389
Edward (Moore), 335, 433
Edwards, Brian, 229
Edwards, Jonathan, 239, 250, 251, 262, 279
Edwards, Timothy (Stockbridge), 279
Edwin and Angelina (Smith), 8, 67, 72, 73, 103, 129, 131, 133, 134, 141, 142, 151, 246, 269, 270, 272, 273, 280, 286, 287, 289, 290, 293, 294, 296, 298, 299, 302, 305, 307, 309, 312, 313, 318, 323, 358, 396, 407, 419
Electricity (Adams), 184, 185
Elegaic Sonnets (C. Smith), 91
"Elegy on the late Right Honorable William Pitt," 136
Elements of Criticism (Henry Home, Lord Kames), 141
Elements of Morality (Salzmann, tr. Wollstonecraft), 80
Elements of Natural History and Chemistry (Fourcroy, tr. anon.), 187
Elements of the Philosophy of the Human Mind (Stewart), 141
Eliot, Eliza, 103
"Ella" (Elihu Hubbard Smith), 5, 8, 9
Ellen, Alexander, 106, 111
Ellsworth, Oliver, 119, 301, 305, 448, 467
Embassy (Staunton), 464
Embree, Lawrence, 91
Emilius (Rousseau), 110
Emma Courtney (Hays), 341, 348, 349, 364, 372
English Review for 1796, 228, 241
Engravings of the Pictures etc. in the Florentine Gallery (Lacombe), 63

INDEX

Enquirer, The (Godwin), 305, 345, 346, 348, 349, 371
En resa til Norra Amerika, 152, 153. *See A Journey to North America, etc.* (tr. Forster)
Entertaining Dialogues (Erasmus), 29
Entertaining Stories (Newbery, pub.), 24
Equisse d'un Tableau Historique des Progrès de l'esprit humain (Condorcet), 43
Eremenian Society, 15
Essai sur les Préjugés (Dumarsais), 136, 146, 156
Essay on Colonization (Wadstrom), 384, 385
Essay on Electricity, etc. (Adams), 183
Essay on the Malignant Pestilential Fever, etc. (Chisholm), 384, 385
Essay on Man (Pope), 24
"Essay on the Public Merit of Mr. Pitt" (Beddoes), 208
Essays (Kite), 177
Essays (Benjamin Thompson, Count Rumford), 274, 278, 279, 280
Essays on Demonstrative Evidence (Beddoes, ed.), 129, 130
Ether, 419
Euphrasia (Dunlap), 96
European Magazine, The, 461
Eustis, William, Dr., 272, 328, 401, 404, 405, 407, 417, 439
Eutropius, 31, 33
Evans, John, 49
Evelina (Burney), 87
Evidences of Christianity (Paley), 309
Experiments and Observations on Electricity (Nicholson), 183
Experiments on Generation (Spallanzani), 96

Factor (ship), 237
Fair Penitent, The (Rowe), 351
Fall of Robespierre, The (Dunlap), 281
False Impressions (Cumberland), 447
Fame (ship), 436, 440
Fangeres, Mrs., 300
Farmer's Weekly Museum (paper), 298, 299
Farquhar, George, 136
Fasciculus, 293
Fashionable Lover, The (Cumberland), 303
Father. *See* Reuben Smith
Fauchet, Joseph, Baron, 52, 53, 114, 413
Fawcett, John, 440
Fawcett, Joseph, 269, 283
Federal Republican meeting, 153
Federal St. Theater, 344
Fellows, John: proposes that Smith become partner in *The Pocket Magazine,* 289, 302
Fellow's Book Store, 154, 272, 278, 286, 289, 294, 298
Fenno, John, 6, 8, 119, 315
Ferdinand Count Fathom (Smollett), 220
Fessendon, Thomas Green, 222, 299
Field, Dr. Simeon, 267, 302, 362, 392, 397, 422, 433, 442, 459
Fielding, Henry, 96, 220, 318, 351
Fire, 95, 200, 270, 272, **329**
First Love (Cumberland), 136

First Study of Nature (St. Pierre), 223
Fish, Dr., 12, 267, 312, 451
Flash in the Pan (Miln), 439
Flint, R., 142
Florizel and Perdita (Garrick), 152, 273
Fontenelle, Bernard, 240
Fool of Quality, The (Brooke), 24, 176
Foot, Rev. Mr., 36
Forbes, The Honorable Francis, M.D., 424, 427, 434
Ford, Mr., 300
Fortunate Country Maid (Charles de Fieux), 33
Fortunate Prisoners, The (Fangeres), 300, 304
Fortune's Fool (Reynolds), 424
Fountainville Abbey (Dunlap), 134
Fourcroy, Antoine, 187-426, *passim*
Fowler, W., 139
Franklin, Andrew, 447
Franklin, Benjamin, 267
Franklin, Walter, 118
French Revolution, 16
Freneau, Philip, 416, 460
Friendly Club, The, 10-445, *passim*
Frisbie, Anne, 23, 25
Frisbie, Mary, 25
Frye, Capt., 427, 429
Fugitive Prince, The (St. John Wyllys), 308

Gahn, Mr., 43-456, *passim*
Galerie de Florence, etc. (Lacombe), 62
Gallatin, Albert, 162, 293, 310, 460
Gallery of Portraits of the National Assembly, The, 82
Gamester, The (Moore & Garrick), 10, 348
Garat, D. J., 321
Garenne, M. de la, 65
Garnet, Mr., 411, 426, 429, 440
Garnet, Mrs., 411, 440
Garnett, Mr., 404, 411
Garrick, David, 142, 152, 154, 244, 273, 303, 348, 354, 358, 366, 384
Gaseous Oxyd of Azote (Dr. Mitchill), 75
Gates, Horatio, Gen., 21, 363, 405, 411, 426
Gates, Mrs. Horatio, 405, 411
Gazette of the United States, The, 6, 8
Genêt, Edmond Charles, 52
Gentleman's Magazine, The, 336, 437
Georgia land purchase, 137
Ghost Seer (Schiller), 92, 125, 133, 134, 228, 331
Gibbon, Edward, 143, 237, 238, 242
Gibbon's Geographical Collections, 371
Giles, Miss, 445
Gillespy, Dr., 388, 406
Godwin, William, 46, 53, 69, 85, 87, 96, 123, 143, 146, 237, 242, 249, 250, 251, 261, 262, 263, 269, 296, 305, 309, 334, 336, 343, 356, 364, 371, 372, 382, 389, 420, 421, 428
Godwin, Mrs. William (Mary Wollstonecraft), 386
Goethe, Johann W., 63, 92, 404
Goetz, Mr. (Goetze, Götz), 341, 361, 362, 365, 366, 373
Gold, Thomas R., 3, 87, 245
Goldsmith, Oliver, 254, 269, 392

Goodrich, Chauncey, 95, 118, 119, 131, 173, 269, 300
Goodrich, Mrs. Chauncey, 118, 119, 131, 173, 300, 457
Goodrich, Elizur, 35, 447, 457
Good Spec (Tyler), 437
Gorani, Joseph, 138, 139, 140, 141, 142, 143
Gordon, Gen., 218, 449
"Gospel of St. John," 32
Gould, James (Litchfield), 277, 283, 450, 454, 455
Gould, Susan, 454
Gower, 327
Gozi, Prof., 351
Gracie, Archibald, 355
Graham, J., 411
Granada fever (Chisholm), 386, 387, 388, 392, 422, 445
Grecian Antiquities (Potter), 241
Grecian Daughter, The (Murphy), 338
Greek Testament, 31
Green, Mr., 386, 429
Green, Matthew, 325
Greene, Nathanael, Gen., 467
Greene, Mrs. Nathanael, 90
Greene, "Master" (son of general), 90
Greenfield Hill (Dwight's Academy): description of, 4
Greenwich Street Theater, 349, 351, 358, 366, 367, 371, 384
Griffiths, Dr. Samuel F., 8, 118, 119, 270, 314, 315, 318, 320, 401
Griswold, Roger, 245, 332
Griswold, S., Rev. Mr., 455
Guillemard, Mr., 356
Guillemard, Mrs., 354
Guillotina (Hopkins), 416
Gustavus Vasa (Brooke), 96

H., Mr., 271. *See* Alexander Hamilton
H., Mr., 357. *See* Hopkinson
Hai Ebn Yohdhan (tr. Ockley), 294, 298
Hair Powder: a Plaintive Epistle to Mr. Pitt, etc. ("Peter Pindar," John Wolcott), 50
Hallam, Lewis, 131, 135, 142, 266, 280, 290, 303, 320
Hallam, Mrs. Lewis, 142, 290, 320
Haller, Mr., 322
Halsey, Mr., 86
Hamilton, Alexander, 13, 16, 65, 111, 139, 271, 310, 365
Hamlet, 209, 410, 428
Hankey, The, 384, 385
Harper, Robert G., 52, 138, 359, 434
Harpy Caleno, 92
Harrington, James, 371
Harrison (auditor of U.S.), 316
Hart, Abijah, 93, 102
Hartford Courant, 11
Hartford Wits (Connecticut Wits), 10 ff.
"Hasty Pudding" (Barlow), 73, 131, 136
Haunted Tower (Cobb), 147
Havens, Mr., 368
Hawkesworth, John, 157
Haworth, Dr., 394, 410, 411, 416, 430, 432, 434, 435, 436, 437, 438, 440, 443
Haygarth, John, Dr., 309, 314
Hayley, William, 90
Haymarket Theater, 344

Hays, Mary, 348, 349, 364
Health Committee, 59, 61, 64, 69
Hedges, Phineas, Dr., 334, 391, 392
Heiress, The (Burgoyne), 133, 284
Heller, Baron, 273, 274
Hemophilia, cured with common salt, 14
Henderson, John, 92
Hendrick, Capt., 439
Henriade (Voltaire), 116
Henrietta (ship), 153
"Henry" (pseudonym), 8
Herald (paper), 13, 98, 281, 285, 287, 289, 293, 344, 364, 410
Herman of Unna ("Kramer", Cramer, Naubert), 56, 181
Hermit of Warkworth (Percy), 405
Hermsprong (Bage), 243, 268, 269, 290, 301, 304, 391
Herodotus (Belloc), 97, 98, 107, 112, 125, 128
Hessiod (tr. Cooke), 325
Hewson, Dr., 161, 170, 174
Hicks, Dr., 331, 332, 371, 413
Higginson, Mr., 272
Hill, Mr., 461
Hillhouse, James, 82, 269
Hinsdale, Bissell, 87
Hints Designed to Promote Beneficial Temperance, etc. (Lettsom), 435
Hints on Education (H. Home), 110
Hippocrates, 321, 325
Hipsipile (Metastasio, tr. Hoole), 289
Historical View of the American United States (Winterbotham), 319
Histoire de la Médecine (Le Clerc), 321
History of the American Theatre (Dunlap), 15
History of Hobart, The (Torquid), 54
History of the Philadelphia Fever (Rush), 156
History of the Rebellion (Clarendon), 158
"History of the Sleepless Man of Madrid" (Gooch), 267
History of the Three Judges of King Charles I (Stiles), 83, 103
History of Thucydidies, 268
History of Yellow Fever, A (Hosack), 341
Hitchcock, Reuben, 3, 14, 36-39
Hitchcock, Roger, 85, 89, 137
Hitchcock, Valentine, 36
Hoare, Prince, 131, 172, 242, 269, 298, 316, 349, 421
Hobart, Judge John Sloss, 12, 431
Hobson, Mr., 424
Hobson, Mrs., 199, 326, 424
Hodgkinson, John, 14-447 *passim*; reads his plagiarism, *The Man of Fortitude*, to Smith, 302
Hodgkinson, Mrs. John, 170, 269, 272, 410
Hodgkinson's Narrative, 307. See *Narrative*, etc., 304
Hofner, Mr., 332
Hogarth Illustrated (Ireland), 135
Holcroft, Thomas, 44, 69, 69-70, 96, 128, 135, 137, 140, 143, 146, 175, 182, 203, 211, 223, 225, 273, 280, 294, 305, 311, 325, 331, 342, 349, 351, 356, 364, 385, 420, 428, 444, 447
Holliday, John, 214

Holmes, Mr. (possibly Uriel, Litchfield), 86, 282
Holmes, Abiel, 389, 459
Holmes, Uriel (Litchfield), 89
Home, Mr., 298
Home, Sir Everard, 221
Home, Henry, Lord Kames, 141
Home, John, 434
Honest Farmer, The (Berquin), 90
Honest Whore (Deckar or Dekker), 169, 366
Hook, Nathaniel, 226
Hooker, Mr., 284
Hooker, Rev. Mr., 454
Hoole, John, 289
Hope, Prof., 237
Hopkins, Dr. (of Paris), 245, 268
Hopkins, Asa (apothecary), 71, 451
Hopkins, Lemuel, Dr., 10, 12, 13, 200, 245, 267, 409, 416, 437, 451, 455, 467
Hopkins, Samuel M., 119, 127, 130, 131, 140, 141, 151, 152, 154, 156, 157, 158, 161, 163, 165, 186, 189, 200, 286, 291, 297, 312, 383, 388, 391, 395, 403, 416, 429, 430, 449, 455, 456, 457, 458, 459, 460, 461
Hopkinson, Francis, 357
Horace, 33, 141, 260
Hosack, David, Dr., 95, 247, 317, 318, 331, 341, 342, 356, 361, 376, 379, 383, 385, 406, 413, 422, 423, 427, 429, 430, 437, 445, 464
Hosack, Mrs., 430
Hosmer, Dr., 317, 333, 342, 347, 447, 457
Howard, John, 321
Howard, Leon, 11
Howland, Abby, Miss, 280, 297, 373
Howland, Mr., 429
Howlet, Mr., 287
Hubbard, Abigail, 467
Hubbard, Elijah, 85, 134, 236, 453
Hubbard, George, 468
Hubbard, Mrs. George (Watts), 468
Hubbard, Hannah, 450, 454
Hubbard, Joseph, 468
Hubbard, Micah, 16, 19, 457
Hubbard, Nemiah, 453
Hubbard, Phebe, 19
Hubbard, Robert, 19, 468
Hubbard, Mrs. Robert (Ward), 468
Hubbard, Mrs. Robert (Sill), 468
Hubbard, Robert, Jr., 468
Hubbard, Sally, 453
Hudson and Goodwin, 310, 312, 451, 459
Hudson, John, 66
Hughes, Gen., 460
Hugh Trevor (Holcroft), 182, 356, 385, 448
Humane Society, 15, 140, 169
Humane Society Trustees, 168
Hume, David, 92, 163, 299, 446
Humphreys, Col. David, 3, 8, 10, 436, 456
Hunter, John, 298, 300, 303, 407
Huntington, Daniel, 282, 421
Huntington, Mrs. Daniel, 452
Hutchinson, Mr. (Tory), 268
Huxham, 467
Hypocrites, 337

Incantation to Lok (Sayers), 108
"Incantatory Song," in *Scandinavia* (Alsop), 108

Inchbald, Elizabeth, 142, 238, 240, 241, 245, 269, 288, 404
Inconstant, The (Farquhar), 136
Infancy (Downman), 306
Information Society, 15
Ingersoll, Judge, 389, 432
Ingersoll, Mr. (New Haven), 83, 84
Inkle and Yarico (Colman, Jr.), 131
Inquiries and Observations, Vol. IV (Rush), 212, 223
Inquiry into the Nature, Cause, and Cure of the Angina Suffocation, etc. (Bard), 297
Inoculation ("small pox"), 32
Institutes (Quintillian), 69
Institutes of Boerhaeve, 467
Introduction to Making Latin (Clark), 31, 33
Iphigenia in Tauris (Goethe), 63, 92, 404
Ireland, John, 135
Irish Widow, (Garrick), 384
Iron Chest, The (Colman, Jr.), 233, 236, 241
Isaac, 347. See Isaac Beers
Isaacs, Benjamin, 193, 225
Isabella (Garrick), 354
Italian, The (Mrs. Radcliffe), 401
Italian Monk, The (Boaden), 401

Jackman, Isaac, 289
Jackson, Mrs., 316
Jackson, David, 8
James the Fatalist and His Master (Diderot), 445
Jay, Gov. John, 13; treaty abused, 68; 173, 271, 292, 310, 390, 395
Jealous Wife, The (Colman), 384
Jefferson, Thomas, 390: "jacobinical almost to lunacy"
Jephson, Robert, 427
Jerome Pointu (Robineau), 169
Joan D'Arc (Burk), 437
Jocelin, Mrs., 140
Jockey Club (Pigott), 281, 287
John, John, 187, 364
Johnson, Miss, 68, 319
Johnson, Mr. (London), 461
Johnson, Mr. (actor), 131, 135, 140, 142, 289, 294, 299, 319, 399, 413, 419, 430, 433, 444
Johnson, Mr. & Mrs. (Middletown), 453
Johnson, Mrs. (actress), 130, 131, 132, 135, 140, 142, 266, 278, 280, 289, 299, 309, 314, 319, 326, 345, 371, 399, 404, 418, 433, 444
Johnson, Mrs. (Stratford), 308
Johnson, Alexander, 331
Johnson, F., 298
Johnson, Fanny, 75, 457
Johnson, Henry, 453
Johnson, Horace W., xii-464, *passim*
Johnson, Mrs. Horace W., 462
Johnson, H. & S. & Co.: bankrupt, 462
Johnson, John, 147, 157, 180, 413
Johnson, Nathan (servant), 333
Johnson, Robert, 7
Johnson, Samuel, 75, 327, 417
Johnson, Seth, xii-464, *passim*
Johnson, W. M. (poet and doctor), 63, 64, 65, 70, 367, 401
Johnson, William (lawyer, Smith's roommate), 3-464, *passim*; member of

INDEX 475

Friendly Club, 45; tr. Riouffe with Smith, 152; helps revise constitution of Manumission Soc., 167-168; tr. Lucretius with Smith, 245; *Morse vs. Winterbotham*, 319, 325, 327, 328, 329, 331
John St. Theater, 354, 357, 401, 402
Join or Die (Halsey), 86
Jones, Mr. (Ireland), 405
Jones, Mr., 177
Jones, Mrs., 348
Jones, Hannah, Miss, 27
Jones, Henry, 133
Jones, Isaac, 424
Jones, Samuel, 67, 313, 430
Jones, Samuel, Jr., 60, 306
Jones, Sir William, 102, 238, 269, 330
Joseph. *See* Joseph Bringhurst
Journal (Gibbon), 240
"Journal" (Reuben Hitchcock), 208
Journal of the Paris Lyceum of Arts, 244
Journey to North America, A (Kalm, tr. J. Forester), 153, 154, 155
Julie (Rousseau), 182
"Julius of Tarentum," (Leisewitz, tr. Alsop), 298, 309

K., E. A., Miss, 14, 219, 228
Kalm, Peter, 152, 153
Kames, Lord, 110. *See* Henry Home
Kellgren (poet), 329
Kent, James, 3-461, *passim*; opinion of Smith, 14; member of Friendly Club, 45, 46; lectures, 102, 126, 133; moves to Albany, 279; a judge through influence of Senator Hobart, 431; moves to Poughkeepsie, 436
Kent, Mrs. James, 45, 48, 371
Kent, Moss (Oswego), 392
Kettle, Mr., 284
King, Apollos, 7
King John, 428
Kingsley, Dr., 404, 405, 411, 420, 451
Kirkland, Miss, 420
Kirwan and his Answers, 411, 413, 418
Kissam, Mr. Benjamin, 392
Kissam, Mrs. Benjamin, 392
Kissam, Richard S., Dr., 186, 207, 278, 279, 319, 321, 331, 332, 333, 392
Kite, Charles, 176
Knave or Not (Holcroft), 444, 447
Knox, Henry, Gen., 28
Knox, Vicesimus, 91
Kollack, Lemuel, Dr., 200, 233, 239, 270, 290, 300, 399, 400, 419, 420, 433, 441, 442, 447, 448, 449, 460
Kosciusko, Tadeusz, 362, 363, 365
Kramer, Prof., 57

L., Mr., 44, 98. *See* Charles Lovegrove
L., Mrs., 44, 298. *See* Mrs. Charles Lovegrove
Lacombe, Mons., 63
Lacombe, DeP., 81
Lad of Spirit, The (Fawcett), 440
Ladies' Philosophy of Love, A (Stearns), 435
Lafayette, 28, 124
Laffert, Mr., 142, 184, 302, 315
Lagarenne, Mr., 319
Lagarrenne, Charles, 82
Lailson's Amphitheater (The Circus), 315
Lamb, Charles, 426

Lamb, John, Gen., 67
Lambelle, Princess de, 11
Lansings, John, Judge, 12
Latimer, Mr., 453
Latimer, Mrs., 453
Lavoisier, Antoine Laurent, 221, 448, 459
Law, Samuel, 100, 108, 356
Law of Nature: or Catechism of Reason (Volney), 180
Lawrence, John, Jr. ("first typographer"), 201
Lawrence, Nathaniel (atty. gen., N.Y.): impeached before Manumission Society, 139
Lay Preacher, The (Dennie), 223
Learned, Amasa, 269
Leavenworth, Rev. Mr., 466
Lebon, Mons., 198, 200
LeBrun, Mr., 304
LeClerc, Daniel, 321, 325
Lectures on Education (Rev. David Williams), 281, 286, 303, 304
Lectures on Rhetoric (Blair), 116, 141
Ledyard, Miss, 269
Lee, Charles (U.S. atty. gen.), 284, 313, 315
Lee, Sophia, 298, 318
Leffingwell, William, 3, 321, 325, 328, 384, 392, 423, 430, 433, 434, 436, 443, 446, 459
Leffingwell, Mrs. William, 83
Leib, John, 315
Leib, Michael, Dr., 65, 75, 81, 118, 137, 187, 189, 270, 315, 316, 401
Leisewitz, Johann, 298
L'Elan and le Renne (Buffon; tr. Goldsmith), 392
Lempriere, William, 280
Lenora (Büerger: tr. Spencer 316; 350; tr. Stanley, 404)
Lent, Mr., 435
Les Ruines, etc. (Volney), 48
Lesser Hartford Wit, Dr. Elihu Hubbard Smith, 1771-1798, A (Bailey), 3
"Letter to Chevr. de Grugo" (Pickering), 366
"Letter to George Washington" (Paine), 278
Letters (Sullivan), 298
Letters from a Father to His Son, etc. (J. Aikin), 116, 282-283, 286, 422
Letters from France (Helen M. Williams), 92, 95, 99, 197, 247
Letters from Smith to: John Aikin, 437-438; John Allen, 101-102, 126-127, 149-151, 328; Richard Alsop, 346-347, 370, 406; Benjamin Smith Barton, 321-322, 397-398, 403, 434-435; Thomas Beddoes, 420; William Pitt Beers, 3, 13; Seth Bird, 432; Joseph Bringhurst, Jr., 93-94, 132, 166, 345; Charles Brockden Brown, 93, 114, 163-164, 170-171, 186-187, 311-312, 325, 332, 336, 349, 364, 417; William Buel, 94-95, 108, 135, 138, 167, 200-201, 236-237, 335, 346, 370, 381, 396; Charles Chauncey, Jr., 418; Charles Chauncey, Sr., 136; Charles Coffin, 432; Mason Fitch Cogswell, 6, 350-351, 375-376; Thomas O'Hara Croswell, 407; Erasmus Darwin, 461; Joseph Dennie, Jr., 299-300, 326-327, 335-336, 357; William Dunlap, 337; Nathaniel Dwight, 397, 410-411; Theodore Dwight, 121-122, 166, 174-175, 209-210, 247-252, 256-266, 349-350; William Eustis, 405; Samuel M. Hopkins, 291-293, 388, 430; William Johnson, 118; Lemuel Kollock, 301, 400; D. W. Lewis, 127-128; Mrs. Lovegrove, 179-180, 287-288; Jedidiah Morse, 417; Mary (Smith) Mumford, 96, 137-138, 181-182, 193-194, 225-226, 226-227, 275-276, 305-306, 322-323, 425-426; Thomas Mumford, 117, 129, 137-138, 177-178, 324, 344, 426; Dr. Muret, 354; Sally Pierce, 120-121, 231, 277, 308, 324; Evelyn Pierpont, 120, 201; Josiah Quincy, 407-408; Benjamin Rush, 189, 214-218, 386, 387, 400, 402-403, Abigail Smith, Jr., 115-116, 140-141, 221-222, 234-235, 276-277, 306, 307, 344-345, 397, 425; Elnathan Smith, Jr., 167, 305, 393, 419; Fanny Smith, 125, 128, 137-138, 202, 225, 274-275, 307, 368-369, 402, 424; Reuben Smith, 98, 117, 120, 139, 343, 371-372, 396, 402; Samuel Smith, 140, 194; Idea Strong, 188-189, 232-233, 306, 323, 381-382; Joseph Strong, 290-291, 334-335, 348, 363-364, 380-381, 408-409; Nathaniel Terry, 107-108, R. J. Thornton, 353-354, 394, 440-441, Uriah Tracy, 112, 129, 155, 162, 303-304, 310-311, 328-329, 336-337, 395; Mrs. Uriah Tracy, 103-105, 122-124, 124-125, 210-211, 294-296, 352-353; Levi Wheaton, 406; Henry Wilkins, 332-333; Helen M. Williams, 211; John Williams, 114-115, 148-149, 202-203, 309-310, 354-355; Oliver Wolcott, Jr., 111-112, 131, 136
Letters from Sweden, Norway and Denmark (Mary Wollstonecraft), 208
Letters on Emigration by a Gentleman Lately Returned from America, 229
Letters on Iceland (Uno vonTroil), 280, 286, 297
Letters to Mr. Volney (Priestley), 305
Letter to the Prince of Wales, A (Pitt), 53
Lettsome, Dr. John Coakley, 72, 73, 346, 417, 431, 435, 446
Leucippus, 292
Lever, Sir Ashton, 355
Levy, Mr., 429
Levy, Mrs., 316, 318, 331
Lewis, Miss, 84
Lewis, Mr. (Berlin), 454
Lewis, Mr. (Farmington), 84
Lewis, Abby, 133, 451
Lewis, Daniel, W., 3, 84, 85, 86, 87, 88, 89, 119, 120, 127, 133, 134, 282, 283, 291, 296, 306, 318, 321, 450, 454, 462
Lewis, Mrs. Daniel (Bessey), 85, 89, 128, 450
Lewis, Elisha, 451
Lewis, Ezekiel, 203, 246
Lewis, Matthew (Monk), 336, 370, 433, 444, 446, 447
Liancourt, Francois duc de la, 317, 356
Liberty-Pole, 20
Life of Adam Smith (Stewart), 177
Life of Benvenuto Cellini, 274
Life of Ezra Stiles (Holmes), 389, 459
Life of John Hunter (Home), 221, 298
Life of Pericles (Plutarch), 243, 268

Lincoln, Benjamin, Maj. Gen., 282
Linn, The Misses, 226
Linn, Rev. Dr., 138
Linn, John Blair, 134
Linnaeus, Carolus, 222
Linonian Society, 3
Litchfield Monitor, 5
Literary Magazine, The, 336
Little Pickle (Williamson), 357
Lives (Plutarch; tr. Langhorne), 366, 367
Lives of the Poets (Johnson), 327
Livingston, Robert R., Chancellor, 390, 395
Livy, 365, 366
Lloyd, Mr., 90
Lloyd, Robert, 426
Lock and Key (Hoare), 298, 316, 421
Locke, John, 2, 226, 250, 251, 262
L'Onanisme (Tissot), 45
London Med. Soc. Memoirs, 177
London World, The, 8
Lord, Mr. (Litchfield, probably Lynde Lord, Jr.), 71, 85, 133, 139, 282, 450, 451, 455
Lord, Mrs. (Litchfield), 89, 309
Lord, Lynde (Sheriff), 87
Lord, Thomas, 3
Lorrain, Claude, 133
Louisa (painting by Palmer), 92
Louvet de Couvray, Jean Baptiste, 146
Lovegrove, Charles, 44-237, *passim*
Lovegrove, Mrs. Charles, 44, 46, 56, 59, 64, 66, 74, 80, 87, 88, 90, 95, 98, 102, 103, 105, 108, 115, 117, 118, 120, 121, 138, 158, 172, 179, 180, 197, 199, 201, 212, 237, 243, 244, 246, 255, 270, 272, 274, 278, 280, 286, 287, 288, 296, 297, 298, 300, 302, 308, 309, 317, 318, 319, 321, 325, 328, 329, 330, 331, 333, 334, 336, 340, 341, 342, 343, 346, 348, 350, 351, 354, 355, 356, 361, 386, 391, 392, 394, 395, 401, 405, 418, 430
Lovegrove, Charles (baby), 179
Lt., Mr., 170. *See* Laffert
Lucretius, 245, 268, 320
Luther, 84
Lycidas, 12
Lycopolites, C., 327
Lyric Poems (Watts), 24, 71
Lyttleton, George, first Baron, 21

M., Mr., 358. *See* Capt. Robert Merry
Macbeth, 440
McClenchan, Blair, 316
McClure, Mr., 464
McLane, Mr., 316
McLane, Mrs., 314
Maclean, Mr., 429
McLean, Charles, 401
McLean, John, Prof., 318, 372, 373, 431
Maclean and Yates. *See* Yates and Maclean
Maclure & Company, 458
Macneill, Hector, 393
McWhorter, Mr., 445
Maddison (James Madison), 310
Madoc, Prince, 49
Mahomet the Imposter (Miller), 132, 264
Maid of the Haystack: painting (Palmer), 66, 92
Maid of the Mill (Bickerstaffe), 155

Man as He Is. See Hermsprong, or Man as He Is (R. Bage), 269, 306, 391
Man as He is Not (R. Bage), 269, 306
Man at Home (C.B. Brown), 434
Man of Fortitude, or The Knight's Adventure (Hodgkinson), 302, 304, 321
Man of Ten Thousand, The (Holcroft), 203, 211, 280, 289, 290
Manumission Society, 13-14, 15, 91, 92, 93, 95, 112, 117, 130, 132, 134, 136, 137, 138, 139, 159, 162, 163, 167, 168, 175, 182, 204, 229, 237, 266, 280, 300, 302, 308-309, 313, 314, 317, 322, 333, 393, 394, 416, 419, 424, 432, 433, 436, 444, 445, 446, 447, 456, 461
Marcellus, 365, 366, 367
Marchena, J., 200
Marsh, Ebenezer G., 355, 448, 452
Marsh, Olive, 20
Marsh, Polly, 452
Marsh, Samuel, 33, 35
Marsh, Truman, 33, 35
Marshall, Humphrey, 449
Mary, 20, 48. *See* Mrs. Thomas (Mary Smith) Mumford
Masdevall, Jose, 367
Mason, 122. *See* Mason Fitch Cogswell
Mason, Miss, 391-462, *passim*
Mason, Mr. (botanist), 437, 439, 444
Mason, Mr., 228, 245, 270, 271, 336, 444
Mason, Jeremiah, 2, 3, 162-163, 207, 242, 244, 268, 269, 273, 278, 279, 281, 298, 331, 332, 333, 348
Mason, John, 299
Massachusetts Magazine, 83
Masson, Mr., 445
Mease, Dr., 334, 416, 418, 419, 436, 437, 439, 450, 451, 456, 461
Medical Abstracts, 342
Medical Academy of Philadelphia, 418
Medical and Surgical Observations (Richter), 169
Medical Commentaries, 422
Medical Comments (Edinburgh), 334
Medical Essays (Kite), 176
Medical Essays (Lyson), 325
Medicina Nautica (Trotter), 444-445
Medical Repository, The, 4-463, *passim;* "Address to Physicians of U.S.," 245; agreement to proceed, 245; now published, 343
Medical Society, Hartford County, 10
Medical Society, New Haven, 10
Medical Works, Vol. IV (Rush), 236
Meerman, Gerado, 201
Meigs, Josiah, 23, 35, 83, 84, 90, 424, 426, 427, 452
Meigs, Mrs. Josiah, 84, 452
Meillan (publisher), 181
Melancthon, 84
Memoir Concerning the Fascinating Faculty Which Has Been Ascribed to the Rattle Snake, etc. (Barton), 212, 297, 327
Mémoires secrets et critiques des Cours, etc. (Gorani), 138
Memoir of the Revolution; or, Account of My Conduct (Garat, tr. R. Heron), 321
Memoirs and Anecdotes of Philip Thicknesse, 286
Memoirs and Miscellaneous Works (Gibbon), 238, 240

Memoirs, Autobiography and Correspondence of Jeremiah Mason, 3
Memoirs d'un Détenu, etc. (Riouffe), 132, 146, 147, 151, 152
Memoirs of Dumourier Written by Himself (tr. J. Fenwick), 125
Memoirs of His Own Life (Tate Wilkinson), 57
Memoirs of the London Medical Society, 172
Memoirs of Planates, 190
Memoirs on Contagion (Mitchell), 54
Merchant of Venice, 367, 372
Mercury (paper), 11
Merry, Robert, Capt., 8, 309, 327, 355, 358, 364
Merry, Mrs. Robert, 44, 309, 315, 348, 351, 355, 357, 358, 364, 365, 367, 371
Metallic points, 463
Metastasia (P.A.D.B. Trapassi), 289
Micromegas, etc. (Voltaire), 161
Midnight Hour (Inchbald), 42, 240
Mifflin, Gov., 413
Military Academy: projected, 271
Millar, M., Miss, 445
Millar, Mrs. Craig, 162
Miller, Allen (Middletown), 316, 453, 457
Miller, Edward, Dr., 200-464, *passim;* agrees to collaborate with Smith and Dr. Mitchill on *Medical Repository,* 245; discussion of agreement, 245 ff.; joins Friendly Club, 443
Miller, James, 132
Miller, Joseph (Delaware), 348, 463
Miller, Joshua, 346, 358
Miller, M., Miss, 393-462, *passim*
Miller, Rev. Samuel, xlix-459, *passim*
Miller, Mrs. Samuel, 58-462, *passim*
Miller, William, 3
Millers, the, 458, 463
Miln, Mr., 293, 401, 421, 439
Milns, William, 287, 289
Milton, 289, 327
Mineralogical Society, 456, 457, 459, 460, 461
Mineralogy (Cronstedt), 460, 461, 463
Minerva (paper), 44, 109, 244, 280, 286, 326, 361
Minister, The (Schiller's *Cabale und Liebe,* tr. Lewis), 370, 433
Minot, George, Judge, 431
Minturn, [B.], 433, 455, 456, 457, 458
Minturn, [J.?], 404, 406
Minturn, William, 388
Mirabaud, M., 388
Miranda, Francisco Antonio Gabriel, Gen., 91
Miscellaneous Works (Gibbon), 241
Miser, The (Shadwell or Fielding from Moliere), 350
Mitchell, Capt., 176, 186
Mitchell, Judge (Litchfield), 86, 87
Mitchell, Judge (Wethersfield), 85, 452
Mitchell, Mr. (Wethersfield), 452
Mitchill Donald G., 175
Mitchill, Hannah, 452
Mitchill, R., 154
Mitchill, Samuel Latham, Dr., 12, 15, 54, 71, 95; 129-460, *passim;* visits Smith, 156; praised in Smith's letter to Rush,

216, 217; writes preface to Amer. ed. of *Zoonomia*, 225; agrees to collaborate with Smith and Miller on *Medical Repository*, 245, 246; works on *Repository*, 327 ff.; begins mineralogical course for Smith and others, 444
Mitchill, Walter, 452
Modern Antiquities (O'Keefe), 279
Mohammedan Quakers, 294
"Moina" (Sayers), 136
Moniteur, ou Gazette Nationale, 222, 299, 323, 325, 326, 356
Monk, The (Lewis), 370, 446
Monroe, James, 424, 426
Monson, Sr., Dr., 176
Monson, Jr., Dr., 176
Monthly Magazine, 223
Monthly Review, 142, *passim*
Moore, Edward, Dr., 10, 245, 268, 342, 348, 433
Moore, James, Dr., 433
Moore (Thomas More), 371
Morbid Anatomy (Baille), 163, 165, 379
More, Miss Hanna, 66
Morgan, E., 451
Morgan, Mrs. E. (Sally Webb), 451
Morning Chronicle, 299, 386
Morris, Abby, 450, 454
Morris, James, 18, 19, 52, 53, 87-88, 109, 114, 282, 303, 321, 450, 454
Morris, John, 321
Morse, Jedidiah, D.D., 103, 319, 327, 329, 331, 354, 355, 357, 389, 392, 405, 408, 413, 416, 417, 424, 435, 436, 438, 449, 456
Morton, Miss (Boston), 391
Morton, S., Miss, 63-462, *passim*
Morton, Mr., 317-462, *passim*
Morton, Mrs. (New York), 91-462, *passim*
Morton, Jacob, 348
Morton, John, 44, 159, 289, 298, 301, 348, 367, 430
Morton, Richard, 115
Morton, Sarah Wentworth, Mrs., 12, 389
Morton, Thomas, 242, 305, 316, 411, 433, 434
Moschus (tr. Fawkes), 325
Moseley, Benjamin, Dr., 331, 333, 452
Moseley, Jonathan Ogden, 162, 238
Moseley, William, 451
Mountaineers, The (G. Colman, Jr.), 142, 151, 231, 286, 444
Much Ado About Nothing, 172, 280
Mulligan, Betsy, 91
Mulligan, John, 66, 91, 138, 142, 163, 178, 190, 193, 201, 225, 332
Mulligan (son of John), 75, 294
Mumford, Benjamin, 306, 433, 452
Mumford, G., 459
Mumford, John, 48, 56, 59, 458
Mumford, Nancy, 290, 318
Mumford, Thomas, 3-460, *passim*; yellow fever, 54-63
Mumford Mrs. Thomas (Mary Smith), 3-426, *passim*
Mumford, William (son of Thomas), 178
Muret, Dr., 351, 354, 355, 400
Murphy, Arthur, 229, 338, 416, 444
Murray, John, 175, 181
Murray, John, Jr., 256, 307, 460
Musaeus (tr. Fawkes), 325
My Grandmother (Hoare), 172

Mysteries of Udolpho (Mrs. Radcliffe), 181, 182, 226
Mysterious Monk, The, 240, 244, 302. See Ribbemont, etc.

Narrative of His Connection With the Old American Company, etc. (Hodgkinson), 304
Nath., 312, 350. See Nathaniel Dwight
National Bank, 271
National University, 271
Natural History, General and Particular (Buffon, tr. Smellie), 392
Nature and Art (Inchbald), 238, 241, 288, 306
Navy: project, 271
Nemochivitch, Mr., 365, 366
"Nestor," 5
New Annual Register, 271-463, *passim*
Newbery (publisher), 24
New Haven College (Yale), 40
New Method of Operating for the Femoral Hernia (Gimbernat), 270
New Nomenclature (John), 87
New Testament, 262
New Theater, 364, 418, 421; opening night, 422, 424
Newton, Isaac, 262
"New View of the Origins etc. of the Indians" (Barton), 334
New York Magazine, 317-414, *passim*
Nicholson, Miss, 330-331, 336, 462
Nicholson, William, 183, 392, 394, 460
Nicholson's Journal, 349, 350, 351, 356, 393, 394, 400, 401
Night Thoughts and Satires (Young), 24
Noble, Arthur, 460
Norton, Mr., 120
No Song No Supper (Hoare), 242, 316
Nugent, Thomas, 274
Nun, The (Diderot), 444

Observations and Recollections, etc. (Hester L. Piozzi), 280
Observations on Accidental Fires, etc., 297
Observations on Certain Documents, etc. (Hamilton), 365
Observations on the Nature and Cure of Calculus, etc. (Beddoes), 128
Observations on the Small Pox, etc. (Aberdom), 275
Ockley, Simon, 294
O'Keefe, John, 137, 223, 298, 315, 347, 401, 410
Old American Company, The, 13
Old Maid, The (Murphy), 229, 444
Old Theater, 344, 419
Oliver, Mr. (Tory), 268
On the Blood (Hewson), 170, 298
On the Blood, etc. (J. Hunter), 298, 300, 303
On the Egyptians and Chinese (DePauw), 399
On the Finances of the United States (Gallatin), 293
On the Liver (Saunders), 169, 172
"On the Nature of True Virtue" (Edwards), 279
On the Pulmonary System (Davidson), 308

"On Soap and Candle Manufacturing" (Mitchill), 370
On the Spartons (DePauw), 334
Oracle (paper), 247
"Oration" (C.B. Brown), 461
"Oration Against Vares" (Cicero), 367
Orations (Cicero), 141
Origine de tous les Cultes, 244, 246
Origines Typographicae (Meerman), 201
Osborn, Joseph, 368, 436, 448, 453
Osborn, Samuel, Dr., 200, 267, 302, 318, 328, 329, 333, 341, 373, 379, 392, 401, 404, 421, 427, 429, 433, 435, 439, 445, 447, 448, 449, 453, 457, 462
Osborn, Mrs. Samuel, 429
Othello, 266, 371
Otis, James, 268
Otway, Thomas, 24, 348, 357
Ouabi (Morton), 12
Owen, Mr., 301, 356, 367
Owens, Mr., 193, 362, 363, 365, 367, 371, 399, 402, 409

P., Miss, 455. See Miss Susan Potts
Paiba, Mr., 384, 388, 389, 392, 416, 445
Paine, Thomas, 156, 187, 278, 309, 430, 460
Pains of Memory (Merry), 309
Paley, William, 309
Palmer, Mr., 92, 199
Paradise Lost, 24
Parker, Miss, 280, 286
Parker, Mr., 198
Parmlee, Mr., 87, 450, 451
Parmlee, Lucy (Lewis), 85, 96
Parsons, Mr., 388
Parsons, Rev. Mr., 406
Paschalis, Felix O., Dr., 432, 433, 434
Paterson, Judge, 370
Patterson, Mr. (Edinburgh), 463
Paul and Virginie (opera, tr. H.M. Williams), 26, 246, 405
Paxon, Mr., 315, 316
Paxon, Mrs., 315, 316
Paxon, Timothy, 118, 119, 164
Paxton, Frances, 450
Pelisier, 270
Penn, William, 268
Pennant, Thomas, 348, 355, 356
Pennsylvania Hospital, 8
Percy, Thomas, 405
Peregrine Pickle (Smollett), 88
Perfectibility of man, 251
Periam, Mr., 86
Pericles, 292
Perkins, Elisha, Dr., 245, 388, 391, 413, 463
Pestalozzi, Johann, 4
Peter Pindar (John Wolcott), 50, 333, 334
Peters, Mr., 317
Petrarch, 44, 78
Pfister, Alexander, 106
Pfister and Macomber, 106
Pharmacopoiea (for pharmacopoeia), 272
Phelps, Judge, 177
Phelps, Oliver, Col., 62
Phelps, Mr., 193
Philadelphia Fever of 1795 (Rush), 184
Philadelphia Fever of 1797 (Paschalis), 432
Philadelphia Weekly Magazine, 434

Philanthrope: After the Manner of a Periodical Paper, 462
Philenia, 327
Philips, Calvin, 394
Phillips and Clark (druggists), 98, 117, 120, 220, 343, 396, 402
Philological Club, 15
Philological Society, 15
Philosophical Dictionary, etc., 116
Philos. Trans. Abrid., 392
Pichegrue, Mr., 386
Pickering, Timothy, 292, 293, 318, 390, 424
Pickering's Letter to Pinckney, 286
Pierce, Miss (sister of Sally), 450
Pierce, The Misses, 133, 455
Pierce, Mr., 392
Pierce, James, 450
Pierce, Polly, 86, 450
Pierce, Ruth, 21, 42. See Mrs. Thomas Croswell
Pierce, Sarah, 21-450, *passim*
Pierce, Timothy, 284, 347-348, 363, 371, 433, 450
Pierpont, Evelyn, 120, 124, 133, 186, 190, 201, 298
Pierpont, Mrs. Evelyn (Rhoda), 120, 298
Pierpont, Sophy, 88, 89, 90, 120, 121, 134, 151, 197, 199, 201, 212, 288
Pigott, Charles, 281
Pinckney, Mr., 310
Pindariana ("Peter Pindar," John Wolcott), 333, 334
Piozzi, Hester Lynch, 280, 287
Pitkin, Timothy, 96, 98, 451, 454
Pitt, William, 53, 141, 292
Plague of Athens (Thucidydes), 184
Plan for the Conduct of Female Education in Boarding Schools, etc. (Darwin), 445
Plan for Speedily Increasing the Number of Bee Hives in Scotland (Bonner), 135
Platt, Mr., 396
Plutarch (tr. Langhorne), 366
Pocket Magazine, The, 289
Poetry of the World, 405, 412
Political Justice (Godwin), 85-425, *passim*
Pollock, Mrs. H., 287, 308, 314
Polybius, 369
Pomeroy, Miss, 452
Pomeroy, B., 357
Pomeroy, Samuel W., 449, 451, 452
Pomeroy, Mrs. Samuel W., 449, 452
Poor House, 61
Poor Soldier (O'Keefe), 223
Poor Vulcan (Dibdin), 140
Pope, Alexander, 24, 282, 327
Porcupine, Peter (pseudonym), 303, 315
Porcupine's Democratic Judge, 436
Porcupine's Political Censor, 303, 304
Post, Dr. (Mr. Post, Professor Post: a bonesetter), 165-457, *passim*
Post's Anatomical Museum, 447
Potter, John, Archbishop of Canterbury, 238, 241
Potts, Susan, Miss, 439, 440, 441, 442, 443, 444, 445, 455
Poulson, Zachariah, 316, 401, 424
Poussin, Gaspard, 133
Prelude, The, 421

Priestley, Joseph, Dr., 302, 305, 317, 366, 394, 410, 431, 434, 437, 459, 463
Prisoner, The (prob. Rose), 163
Prize, The (Hoare), 269, 349
Provok'd Husband, The (Cibber), 131
Provost, J. B., 53
Puns, 70-71
Purse, The (Cross), 401, 421
Pye, Henry, 269, 358

Quaker, The (Dibdin), 138, 303, 413
Quakers of Philadelphia, 118
Quelques Chapitres, etc. (Riouffe), 180
Quelques Reflections, fugitives, etc. (Marchena), 211
Quince, Mr., 83
Quincy, Josiah, 317, 318, 319, 405, 407, 409, 417, 447
Quincy, Mrs. Josiah, 408

R., Mde., 287. See Mrs. John Roulet
Rabaut, de Sainte-Etienne, 177
Racine, 65
Radcliff, Mr., 266, 318, 439, 447, 461
Radcliff, Mrs., 182, 401
Radcliffe, Mr., 328, 333
Radcliffe, Ann, 226
Radclift, Mr., 379, 419, 423, 429, 436, 439, 444, 445, 446, 449, 456, 459
Radclift, John, Dr., 395 (incorrect sp. Radcliffe or Ratcliffe)
Radclift's traveling pupils, 395
Randolph, Edmund, 53, 73, 82, 83, 85, 112, 116
Rape of Helen (Coluthus Lycopalites, tr. Mr. C—), 327
Ray, Mr., 92
Rees, Dr., 405. See also Rev. Morgan J. Rhys
Reeve, Tapping, 24, 40, 85, 89, 141, 202, 282, 311, 370, 372, 389, 432, 450
Remarks on Education (S.H. Smith), 448
Remitting Fever (Currie), 434
Remsen, Henry, 271
"Reply to Priestley" (Adet), 317
Report of Camus etc. to the Council of Five Hundred, 181, 182
Report of Cases Adjudged (Root), 389
Report of the Committee on the Gov. Blount Affair, 409
Report of the Directors of the Sierra Leone Company, 122, 124
"Report on Rheumatism" (Fowler), 168
Researches Concerning the Greeks (De-Pauw), 241
Revenge, The (Young), 293, 357
Reynolds, Mr. (associate of Hamilton), 365
Reynolds, Frederick, 163, 424, 439, 447
Rhys, Rev. Morgan J., 48, 49, 404, 408, 409. See also Rees.
Ribbemont, or the Feudal Baron (Dunlap), 240. See first title, *Mysterious Monk*
Rice, Mr., 333
Rice, James, 401, 430, 442, 447, 459
Richards, Catherine M., 452
Richards, Samuel, 87
Richardson, Samuel, 22, 96, 432
Rickert's Circus, 338

Riggs, Mr., 272, 423
Riley, Mrs. (Wethersfield), 452
Riley, Mrs. C., 180
Riley, Isaac, 46-459, *passim*
Riley, Mrs. Isaac, 115-460, *passim*
Riley, Jennet (Wethersfield), 452
Riley, John (Philadelphia), 6, 315
Riley, Mrs. P., 318
Riot in the theater, 242, 303
Riouffe, Mr., 132, 180, 198
Rivington's Book Store, 60
Road to Ruin (Holcroft), 222, 223, 225, 349
Robert, Mrs., 356
Robertson, M. (tailor), 220
Robertson, Stark, Dr. (formerly Dr. Stark), 278, 405, 411, 419, 423, 424, 435, 436, 443, 445, 457, 460
Robertson, Mrs., 411, 460
Robespierre, 197, 239
Robineau, A.B., 169
Robinson, Mr., 78
Robinson, Mrs., 316
Robinson, Mrs. (Atmore), 315
Robinson's Conspiracy, 454, 455, 458
Rodgers, Dr., 128, 189, 281, 298, 332, 347, 373, 383, 384, 386, 388, 409, 410, 440, 463
Roe, Mr., 392, 395, 399, 462
Rogers and Woolsey (hardware) 220
Rogers, Miss (New York), 308-428, *passim*
Rogers, Mr. (Litchfield), 71
Rogers, Mr. (probably B.W. Rogers, New York), 45-449, *passim*
Rogers, Mrs., 54, 239, 308, 309, 326, 376
Rogers, Rev. Mr., 119
Rogers, David, Dr. (Greenfield), 4, 268
Rogers, Moses, 97-460, *passim*
Rogers, Susan (Greenfield), 48
Rogers, William, D.D., 8
Roland, Marie-Jeanne, 93, 117, 156, 158, 305
Rollin, Charles, 367
Rollins, Mr., 429
Romance of the Forest (Radcliffe), 226
Roman History (Rollin), 367
Romeo and Juliet, 271, 358, 429
Romp, The (Bickerstaffe), 286, 338, 348, 371
Root, Judge, 389
Root, Josiah, Dr., 89, 133, 140, 268, 343
Roscoe, Mr., 314
Rose, Rev. John, 163
Rosevelt, Mr. (New York), 90
Rosina (Mrs. Brooke), 231, 294, 296, 298, 366, 416
Rossier, Mons., 302, 322, 351
Rossier, Mrs. M., 351
Roulet, John Sigismund (Joseph is same man), 44-463, *passim*
Roulet, Mrs. John, 169
Rousseau, J.J., 44, 110, 160, 171, 414, 416
Rowe, Elizabeth, Mrs., 24
Rowe, Nicholas, 24, 143, 351, 357
Rowland, Miss, 287
Rozier, J.A. Bernard, 177
Rule a Husband and Have a Husband (Dunlap), 447
Ruling Passion, The (R. Paine), 389
Rush, Miss, 308
Rush, Benjamin, Dr., 6-7, 9, 14, 58, 63, 67,

INDEX

69, 108, 118, 119, 197, 201, 212, 213, 214, 223, 225, 236, 255, 268, 270, 314, 315, 316, 352, 355, 379, 381, 384, 386, 390, 391, 396, 399, 400, 401, 402, 410, 413, 431, 455, 456, 460, 462, 464
Russell, Miss, 452
Russell, Mr., 452
Russell, M.T., 452
Russell, Patrick, Dr., 305
Rutgers, Col., 75
Rutgers, Mr., 286
Rutheford, Mr., 405
Rutledge, Mr., 456

St. Mery, Moreau, 316
St. Pierre, Bernardin, 143, 196, 246
Sallust, 14
Saltonstall, Dudley, 291
Saltonstall, Joshua, 451, 454
Saltonstall, Winthrop, Dr., 421, 434, 436
Sand (or Sands), Mr., 89, 458
Sandford, Mr., 186
Sandiminian, 86
Sanford and Merton (Day), 110
Saturn, disease from, 142
Saunders, Dr., 161, 169, 172
Sayers, Frank, Dr., 108, 134, 136, 138
Scandella, Joseph B., Dr., 420, 421, 424, 428, 434, 438, 440, 445, 449, 457, 458, 463, 464
Scarlatina Anginosa (Thaddeus Clark), 95
Schaubert, Mr., 356
Schiller, Johann, 92, 94, 336, 370, 433
School for Arrogance (Holcroft), 294
School for Scandal (Sheridan), 138, 421
Scotch Encyclopedia, 399, 426
Scotland's Skaith, etc. (H. Macneill), 393
Seaman, Dr., 317-459, *passim*
Seba, Mr., 317
Seba, Mrs., 308, 317
Sebor, Jacob, 82
Secret Journal of a Self Observer (Lavater, tr. P. Will), 399
Secret Tribunal, The (Boaden), 64
Sedgwick, Miss, 297
Seduction (Holcroft), 223
Sedwick, Mr., 302
Seldon, John, 379
Selfish Quakers of New York, 118
Senter, Dr., 328-463, *passim*
Serenus Samonicus (Dr. Hopkins), 245
Sermons Delivered at the Old Jewry Meeting (Fawcett), 269, 283
Sewall, Mr. (Tory), 268
Seymour, Mr., 40
Seymour, Major, 450
Seymour, Moses, Jr., 371
Seymour's Shop, 124
Shadwell, Thomas, 351
Shakespere, 266, 321, 357, 371, 416
Sharples, James (Sharpless), 326-461, *passim*
Sharples, Mrs. James, 373, 394, 404, 405, 426, 436, 447
She Stoops to Conquer (Goldsmith), 269
Sheldon, Judge, 18, 467
Sheldon, Charlotte, 52, 85, 87
Sheldon, Daniel (boy), 5, 85
Sheldon, Daniel, Dr., 5, 40, 85, 86, 88, 89, 133, 189, 214, 266, 282, 302, 396, 450, 454, 455
Sheldon, Mary, 18, 467
Sheldon, R., Miss, 89
Sheridan, Richard B., 138, 158, 421
Sheridan, Mrs., 452
Shipwreck (Arnold), 447
Shore, Sir John, 102
Short Account of Putrid Billious Fever, etc. (Holliday), 214
Short Dissertation, A, etc. (Mead & Russell), 305
Siculus, Diodorus, 429
Sidney, Sir Philip. *See* Sydney, 371
Siege of Belgrade (Cobb), 279, 438
Siege of Calais (Colman, Jr.), 132
Signor Falconi's Exhibition, 395
Sill, Joseph, 468
Sill, Mrs. Joseph (Lord), 468
Silverstorpe, Mr., 244
Simple Story, A (Inchbald), 288, 289, 298
Simpson, Solomon, 456
Sitgreaves, George, 430
Sketch of a Plan to Exterminate the Casual Small-Pox, etc. (Haygarth), 309, 314
Sketch of the Present State etc. (Fauchet), 413
Sketch of the Revolution (Rabaut), 177
Skinner, Richard, 86, 282, 450
"Sky Walk" (Brown), 434, 439, 455
Smellie, William, 392
Smith, Miss (New York), 142, 153
Smith, Dr. (pres. of Nassau Hall), 314, 321
Smith, Mr. (Berlin), 233
Smith, Mrs. (New York; daughter of John Adams), 383
Smith, Aaron, 92, 333, 455
Smith, Abigail, Jr., 18-463, *passim*
Smith, Adam, 141, 299
Smith, Azubah, 17, 465
Smith, Mrs. Benjamin, 62
Smith, Calvin, 140
Smith, Charlotte, 9, 91, 96
Smith, Christopher, 465
Smith, Elizabeth, 465
Smith, Elnathan, Jr., 48-464, *passim*
Smith, Fanny, 26-424, *passim*
Smith, Frances (of Princeton), 314, 316
Smith, James (son of Samuel), 465
Smith, James (son of Stephen), 465
Smith, James R., 132
Smith, John (Farmington), 463
Smith, John (son of Samuel), 465
Smith, John C. (Sharon), 88
Smith, Joseph, 454
Smith, Keziah (daughter of James), 465
Smith, Martha, 465
Smith, Mary. *See* Mrs. Thomas Mumford, 426
Smith, Melancton, 458
Smith, Nathaniel, 107, 269
Smith, Reuben, Dr., 4-467, *passim*
Smith, Mrs. Reuben (Abigail Hubbard), 84-468, *passim*
Smith, Reuben (New York; "my kinsman"), 57
Smith, Robert, 468
Smith, Ruth (died in infancy), 465
Smith, Samuel, 84, 138, 140, 142, 188, 194, 317, 448, 454, 465
Smith, Samuel, Jr., 465
Smith, Mrs. Samuel (Porter), 465
Smith, Sarah, 465
Smith, Simon, 465
Smith, Stephen, 465
Smith, Thomas, 465
Smith, William, 465
Smollett, Tobias, 88, 95, 96, 220
Society for Free Debate, 440
Socrates, 68
"Solilioquy of Cato" (Addison), 23
Sollee, Mr., 344
"Songs from Metastasio" (Alsop), 424
Sophy. *See* Sophy Pierpont
Southern, Thomas, 357
Southey, Robert, 426, 427, 460
Spallanzani, Abbe Lazzaro, 96, 464
Spectator, The, 70, 396, 410, 455
Speculations (Reynolds), 163
Spencer, Ambrose, 244
"Spleen" (Green), 325
Spoiled Child, The (Hoare or Bickerstaffe), 131. *See also Spoil'd Child,* 225, 287; *Spoilt Child,* 344
Stagecoach, new line, 84
Stanley, Mr. (translator), 404
Stanley, Rufus, 300, 401, 460
Stansbury, Mr., 333, 384, 399, 444, 445
Stansbury, Mary, 298
Stansbury, Samuel (a son), 445
Stanton, Mr., 450
Stark, Dr., 278, 426. *See* Dr. Stark Robertson
Starno (Sayers), 134
State of Prisons in England and Wales, The, etc. (Howard), 321
Statistical Account of Scotland (Sir John Sinclair), 136
Staunton, Sir George, 443
Stearns, Rev. Charles, 389, 435
Stephen Calvert (Brown), 464
Stephens, Mr., 457, 461
Sterne's Maria (Dunlop), 286
Stevens, Mr., 330
Stewart (asst. atty. gen. at Onondaga), 342, 356, 364, 383. *Also spelled* Stuart, 302, 458
Stewart's picture of Washington, 423. *Ref. is to* Gilbert Stuart
Stewart, Dugald, 141, 177
Stewart, "Traveller" (John), 154
Stiles, Ezra, (pres. of Yale), 2, 3, 36, 83, 84, 103, 424, 459
Stiles, Mrs., 84
Stockton, Miss, 308
Stillman, Emily, 226, 266, 297, 451
"Stoic" (Hume), 163
Stone, Miss Hannah, 20, 21
Storace, Mr., 279
"Stowwood" (Alsop), 103
Strictures on Elementa Medicinae of Brown (Hedges), 391
Strong, Ashbel, 32
Strong, Idea, 5-382, *passim*
Strong, Jedidiah, 5, 33, 87
Strong, Mrs. Jedidiah (Susannah Wyllys), 5
Strong, Joseph, Dr., 3-451, *passim*

Strong, Nancy, 451
Strutt, Mr., 406
Stuart, "Traveller," 156. *See* Stewart
Stuyvesant, Miss, 96, 319, 440
Stuyvesant, Mr., 340
Stymets, Mr., 64
Such Things Are (Inchbald), 245
Sullivan, Richard J., 61, 269, 294, 296, 371
Sulpicia, 328
Sultan, The (Bickerstaffe), 280
Suspicious Husband, The (Hoadley), 404
Swan, Major, 429, 432
Swedenborg, 102
Swediaur, J., Dr., 456, 462, 463
Swift, Mr., 18
Swift, Zephaniah, 23, 389
Swinburn, Henry, 365
Swinburne's Travels, etc. (De Non), 385
Swords (printer), 286-458, *passim*
Swords's magazine, 412
Sydenham, Thomas, Dr., 48, 115, 191, 467
Sydney (Sir Philip Sidney), 371
Syphilis (Bell), 182
Systems of Laws of Connecticut (Z. Swift), 389
System of Nature, The (Mirabaud, tr. Hodgson), 388

T., Mr., 85, 270, 288, 294, 353. *See* Uriah Tracy
T., Mrs., 277. *See* Mrs. Uriah Tracy
Table Talk (Seldon), 379
Talmadge, Col., 89, 136, 139, 158, 165, 168, 367, 371, 450
Talmadge, Mrs., 89, 165
Taylor, Miss, 334
Taylor, Mr., 89
Telemachus (pseudonym), 390
Tell Truth and Shame the Devil (Dunlap), 280, 281
Temple, Sir John, 71, 354
Templeton, Miss, 392-464, *passim*
Templeton, Mrs., 464
Terry, Nathaniel, 103, 105, 107, 112, 451
Terry, Mrs. Nathaniel, 451
Teshoo Lama, 240, 252, 264
"The Task" (Cowper), 54, 83
Theater riot, 157, 244
Themistocles, 292
Theocritus (tr. Fawkes), 326, 327
Theodore, 28, 307, 308. *See* Theodore Dwight
Theory of Moral Sentiments, The (Smith), 141
Theory of Tides (St. Pierre), 143
Thickness, Philip, 280, 286
Thomas, 127. *See* Thomas Mumford
Thomas & Andrews (store), 432
Thompson, Mr., 316
Thompson, Benjamin, Count Rumford, 274
Thomson, Peter, 119
Thornton, Robert J., Dr. (London), 351, 353, 394, 429, 436, 440, 443, 460
Three Judges, The, etc., 89
Thucydides (tr. Smith), 213-366, *passim*
Tibellus, 322
Tiberius, 141
Tiffin, T., 220
Tigon (ship), 70
Timothy, 407. *See* Timothy Pierce

Tinsdale, Mr., 356
Tisdale, Mr. 395-458, *passim*
Tissot, 97
Tod, (Todd), George, 309, 314, 391, 392
Todd and Smith, 277
Todd, Dr., 84, 267, 454, 456, 463
Todd, Mr., 87, 282
Todd, Jas., 316
Tohi, 252, 264
Tom Thumb (Fielding), 318
Tontine, The, 128, 334
Tooke, John Horne, 225
Topaz (sloop of war), 460
Tour from Gibralter to Tangiers, etc., A (Lempriere), 280
Tour in Wales, A (Thomas Pennant), 274
Tours through Various Parts of Britain & France (Arthur Young), 136
Tracy, Caroline, 87
Tracy, Julia, 88
Tracy, N., 105
Tracy, Sally, 52, 84, 277, 282
Tracy, Susan, 344, 450
Tracy, Uriah, 3-459, *passim*
Tracy, Mrs. Uriah (Susan Bull), 14-454, *passim*
Tragedie Grècque, De la (Auger), 211
Tragedy of Jane Shore, The (Rowe), 24, 143
Traité Complète sur les Symptoms les Effets la Nature et le Traitement des Maladies Syphilitiques (J. Swediaur), 456, 461, 462
Traité Elémentaire de Chimie (Lavoisier), 221
Trans. of Amer. Acad. of A. & S., 367
Trans. of the Philos. Soc., 316
Trans. of the Royal Irish Academy, 355
Traveller in the East through Arabia, etc., (Anderson), 399
Travels (Bachaumont), 181
Travels (Chardin), 302, 304
Travels (De Non), 369, 371, 372, 373
Travels (Piozzi), 287
Travels (Spallanzani), 464
Travels (Volney), 152, 300
Travels Before the Flood, etc., (anon.), 274
Travels in the Two Sicilies (Swinburne), 365
Travels of Cyrus (Ramsay, tr. N. Hook), 226
Treatise on the Autumnal Endemial Epidemick, etc. (Davidge), 436, 437
Treatise on the Fevers of Jamaica, etc. (Jackson), 197
Treatise on the Gonorrhoea Virulenta, etc. (Bell), 180
Treatise on Tropical Diseases, etc. (Moseley), 333
Trip to the Nore (Franklin), 447
Triumph of Temper (Hayley), 90
Tropical Diseases (Moseley), 331
Trott, Mr. (painter), 357, 366, 367, 386, 445
Trumbull, Benjamin, 389
Trumbull, John (painter), 9
Trumbull, John (writer), 3, 10, 11, 24, 121-122, 436, 451, 452, 467
Trumbull, Jonathan, 173

Tryon, Capt., 452
Tschink, Cajetan, 228
Tucker, Capt., 401
Tucker, St. George, 317
Tudor, Edward, 7
Turell, Mr., 198
Turgot, A.R., 251, 263
Turnbull, Robert J., 316
Turner, Judge, 49, 315
"Two Letters etc. on a Peace with the Regicide Directory, etc." (Burke), 300, 304
Two Strings to Your Bow (Jephson), 427
Tyler, Royal, 357, 389, 409, 436

Union, The (club), 15
Union Society, The (club), 15
University of Pennsylvania, 7
Upson, Mrs., 90
Uranian Society (club), 15
Urbino, Rafaelle d', 406
Usong (Baron Haller, tr. anon.), 273, 274

Van Swisten, 309
Varick, Richard, 12
Venice Preserved (Otway), 24, 348, 414
Vicar of Wakefield, The (Goldsmith), 254
Victim of Magical Delusion, The (Tschink, tr. P. Will), 228
View of the Conduct of the Executive (Monroe), 424, 426
View of Nature (Sullivan), 61, 289, 290, 294, 296, 297, 304
View of the Science of Life (Yates and Maclean), 401, 426
Vindication of the Rights of Women (Wollstonecraft), 85
Virgil, 29, 141
Vishnou, 252, 264
Visit to the Philadelphia Prison (Turnbull), 316
Voght, Mr., 274
Volney, Constantin, F., 48, 119, 152, 302, 305, 315
Voltaire, 65, 116, 159, 160, 161
Von Troil, Uno, Dr., 280, 286
Voyage de Bachaumont et la Chapelle, 182
Voyage en Sicile, (De Non), 369. *See* Travels
Voyages du Jeune Anacharsis, etc. (Barthelmy), 161, 241

W., Miss, 110. *See* Mrs. William (Wollstonecraft) Godwin
Wadstrom, C.B., 384, 385
Wadsworth, Col., 70, 71, 451
Wadsworth, Mr. (brother of Decius), 451, 454
Wadsworth, Daniel, 348
Wadsworth, Decius, 3, 71, 100, 101, 103, 175, 176, 189, 192, 222, 223, 225, 233, 279, 383
Wadsworth, Jeremiah, 162
Wakefield, Gilbert, 327
Walker, Col., 420
Walker, John, Dr., 275, 460, 463
Walker, Mrs., 420
Walpole, Horace, 91, 121, 336
Wandering Jew (Franklin), 447

INDEX

Ward, Col., 106
Warner, George J., 456
Warton, Thomas, 269, 327, 358
Washington, George, 28, 144, 278, 288, 297, 365-366, 390, 426
Waterman, The (Dibdin), 245, 411
Watkinson, Mr., 452
Watson, James, 92, 95, 130, 155, 157, 172, 192, 200, 244, 269, 293, 302, 305, 318, 328, 333, 342, 383, 386, 455, 456, 458, 460
Watson, Mrs. James, 172, 383
Watters, Mr., 463
Watts, Isaac, 18, 22, 71, 94
Way to Get Married, The (Morton), 242, 305, 316
Webb, Mr. (apothecary), 69
Webb, Joshua, 69, 452
Webb, Mrs. Joshua, 452
Webster, Julia, 367
Webster, Noah, 3, 13, 15, 16, 23, 26, 47, 53, 57, 82, 91, 92, 100, 103, 117, 124, 127, 131, 135, 142, 147, 156, 161, 167, 176, 180, 184, 185, 186, 194, 201, 215, 219, 220, 236, 244, 278, 287, 294, 317, 318, 319, 321, 328, 334, 337, 342, 344, 361, 365, 366, 367, 383, 384, 385, 386, 388, 391, 396, 401, 405, 406, 409, 410, 413, 418, 419, 420, 428, 429, 430, 431, 433, 434, 436, 445, 446, 449, 455, 457, 458, 459, 462
Webster, Mrs. Noah, 47, 82, 124
Webster's Book Store, 313
Weekly Magazine, The, 435-463, *passim*
Wells, The, 419
Wells, Miss, 85
Wells, Mr., 19
Wells, J., 138
Wells, James, Dr., 7, 267, 270, 271, 272, 277, 451, 454, 461
Wells, John, 54, 69, 137, 207, 220
Wells, Sylvester, Dr., 270, 398, 454
Wells & Todd (store), 398
Welsh Indians, 49
Wentworth, Michael, Col. (New Hampshire), 61
Wertmüller, Adolf, 119, 206, 207, 223, 225
West Indian, The (Cumberland), 442
Wetmore, Ichabod, 3
Wetmore, Prosper; member of Friendly Club, 45, 46; 107, 116, 176, 286
Wheaton, Levi, Dr., 329-460, *passim*
Wheel of Fortune, The (Cumberland), 134, 135, 256, 298
Which is the Man (Cowley), 242
Whitehead, William, 269, 358
Whiting, Mr., 396
Whittlesey, H., Miss, 309, 318
Whittlesey, M.B., 279, 379, 453
Wieland (Brown), 455-460, *passim*
Wieland, Christopher M., 281, 286
Wiggins, Mr., 371
Wignell, Mr., 315, 338, 348
Wilcocks, Alexander, 8
Wilcocks, William, 52
Wilkins, Dr., 258, 321, 332, 333, 455, 458
Wilkinson, Miss, 297
Wilkinson, Mrs., 297
Wilkinson, Tate, 56, 58
Will, Rev. Peter, 399
Will, P., 228
Will, The (Reynolds), 439
William Tell (Dunlap), 130, 146. See *The Archers*
Williams, Capt., 452
Williams, Sheriff, 452
Williams, Rev. David, 281, 303, 309
Williams, Ezekiel, 238, 451
Williams, Helen M., 92, 93, 95, 99, 197, 247, 405
Williams, John, 9-460, *passim*
Winterbotham, William, 319, 327
Winthrop, Benjamin, 65, 440
Winthrop, Mrs. Benjamin, 440
Wirkham, Miss, 96
Wistar, Miss, 316
Wistar, Casper, Dr., 8, 118, 119, 315, 316
Wives as they Were (Inchbald), 404, 418
Wms., J., 128. See John Williams
Wolcott, Frederic, 29, 85, 91, 92, 95, 98, 105, 107, 111, 450
Wolcott, Oliver (Conn. gov.), 282, 343, 389, 432
Wolcott, Oliver, Jr., (sec. of treasury), 3, 6, 21, 31, 33, 86, 105, 106, 111, 114, 118, 119, 131, 136, 140, 154, 155-156, 282, 288, 293, 314, 315, 316, 333, 386, 447, 448, 450, 454, 455, 458, 461
Wolcott, Mrs. Oliver, Jr., 106, 131, 333, 386, 455, 458
Wollstonecraft, Mary, 80, 85, 109, 110, 208, 323, 382. See Mrs. William Godwin
Wonder, The (Centlivre), 223, 344
Wood, Silas, 319
Wood, T., 220
Woodhouse, Dr., 176, 177, 270, 316, 401, 414
Woolsey, George Muirson; 12-462, *passim*; member of Friendly Club, 45, 46
Woolsey, William W., 13-463, *passim*; member of Manumission Soc., 13; member of Friendly Club, 45, 46
Woolsey, Mrs. William W., 82, *passim*
Wonderful Narrative of Two Families, etc. (Telemachus), 390
Wortman, Tunis, 266, 273, 286, 289, 298, 327, 394, 419
Wright, Miss, 454
Wyllys, St. John, 307
Wynkoop, Mr., 388

Yale College: description of in 1782, 2; riots, 3-4; commencement and entrance examinations, 34-35; 259, 261
Yarico and Inkle, 229. See *Inkle and Yarico*
Yates, William, 401
Yates, Mrs. William, 317
Yates & Maclean, 401, 402, 404, 408, 434, 438
Yearsley, Mrs., 66
Yellow fever, 11, 48, 54-63, 58, 75-76, 81, 135
Yellow Fever of 1793 (Rush), 58
Young Chemist's Pocket Companion (Woodhouse), 414
Young, Edward, 24
Young Quaker, The (O'Keefe), 401
Youth's Instructor, The, 24

"Zephyrs, The," 404
Zoonomia (Darwin), 201-461, *passim*; preface to Amer. ed., Dr. Mitchill, 241
Zorinski (Morton), 433
Zwingle, Hildreich (or Ulrich), 84